POPULATION
IN
HISTORY

POPULATION
IN
HISTORY

Essays in Historical Demography

edited by

D. V. GLASS

and

D. E. C. EVERSLEY

LONDON EDWARD ARNOLD (PUBLISHERS) LTD

Printed in Great Britain by
Robert Cunningham and Sons Ltd, Alva

PREFACE

SINCE the 1950's, historians have been showing an increasing concern with the population factor in economic and social change. Demographers, on their side, have been paying more attention to history. And practitioners from the two fields have begun to work together, using their combined approaches in an attempt to assess and account for the population growth experienced by the West since the seventeenth century.

There is, of course, a long record of interest in the history of population. But the interest now being displayed is likely to be both more persistent and far more fruitful in its consequences. New studies have been initiated in many countries. And because the studies are more informed and systematic than many of those of earlier periods, they are already provoking the further spread of research. A much more positive part is now also being played by national and international associations of historians and demographers. It is not unlikely that, within the next fifteen or twenty years, the main outlines of population change in the seventeenth and eighteenth centuries will be firmly established for much of Europe.

Because the research is new, its results have tended to appear in specialist journals or monographs. Yet at this point of transition from the older to the newer studies, it seemed to us especially important to provide a more easily accessible publication. Equally, we thought it appropriate to include some of the earlier studies, both because of their intrinsic interest and because they provided the background and part of the stimulus to the later work. It is these considerations which explain both the origin and the contents of the present volume. Of the 27 contributions, 7 are unabridged reprints of earlier papers, and we are indebted to the authors for permission to include those papers in our volume. For the remaining contributions we are still more indebted, for they are either entirely new papers or represent substantial revisions of work published elsewhere.

D.V.G.
D.E.C.E.

ACKNOWLEDGEMENTS

Acknowledgements are due to the following journals for permission to reprint articles: *Population* for Chapters 3 and 20; *Population Studies* for Chapters 12, 14 and 16; *The Economic History Review* for Chapters 11, 13 and 17; *Economic History* for Chapter 10; *The Canadian Journal of Economics and Political Science* for Chapter 4; *Bull. Hist. Med.* for Chapter 5; *The Journal of Economic History* for Chapter 7; *Ann. Acad. Scient. Fenn.* for Chapter 23.

We are greatly indebted to Mrs Phyllis Scutt for her help in the proof reading of the volume.

CONTENTS

Part I

GENERAL

vii

PART III

EUROPE AND THE UNITED STATES

PART I
GENERAL

I

INTRODUCTION

D. V. GLASS

THE beginnings of a persistent interest in the history of population ante-date the founding of population studies. Demography, as a field of inquiry, originated in 1662 with the publication of John Graunt's *Observations*, though it was not until the middle of the nineteenth century that the discipline received its technical name. But interest in comparing past and present population sizes and characteristics was already visible in the period of debate which formed part of the background of the scientific revolution. There were, of course, earlier examples of such interest. Indeed, it might be argued that even the Augustan legislation, with its concern to prevent the decay of the senatorial classes, implied some comparison with their assumed state (and re-placement rate) in earlier periods. But it was the focus upon the question of historical decay—in England, exemplified most sharply in the conflict between Geoffrey Goodman and George Hakewill—which gave rise to the long con-troversy on population growth.[1] In its initial form, the controversy was theo-logical and philosophical, swinging between those who argued that the world was running down, that both nature and man had shown an historical descent into decay; and those who believed in a beneficent providence and in the possi-bility and reality of progress. In this form, though more explicitly directed to the history of population growth, the thesis of decline continued to show itself in the writings of Vossius and Montesquieu, of Whiston and Cumberland.[2] Robert Wallace, whose contribution to the controversy provoked the classic, sceptical reply of David Hume, argued for the superiority of the ancient world and later found a formula—which influenced Malthus—to demonstrate that, even if utopian perfection could ultimately be reached, it could not be sus-tained.[3] Along with these generalities, however, more limited hypotheses ap-peared, and of a kind more susceptible to empirical tests. Thus Richard Price contended that the population of England had been falling since the Glorious Revolution.[4] In so arguing, he not only called upon what appeared to be objective evidence, but also instigated the first serious attempts to assess the history of English population growth—the inquiries of William Wales, John Howlett and F. M. Eden, as well as Chalmers' survey.[5] From that point on-

[1] R. F. Jones, *Ancients and Moderns*, St. Louis, 1936, ch. 2.
[2] D. V. Glass, 'The population controversy in eighteenth century England', *Population Studies*, July 1952.
[3] R. Wallace, *A dissertation on the numbers of mankind in ancient and modern times*, Edinburgh, 1753; *Various prospects of mankind, nature, and providence*, London, 1761.
[4] R. Price, 'Essay containing an account of the progress from the Revolution, and the present state of population in England and Wales', in W. Morgan, *The doctrine of annuities and assurances on lives and survivorships*, London, 1779.
[5] W. Wales, *An inquiry into the present state of population in England and Wales*, London, 1781; J. Howlett, *An examination of Dr. Price's essay*, Maidstone, 1781; F. M. Eden, *An estimate of the number of inhabitants in Great Britain and Ireland*, London, 1800; G. Chalmers, *An estimate of the comparative strength of Great Britain*, London, 1786.

wards, in England, a line can be traced to Rickman and the early censuses, with their questions on marriages, baptisms and burials recorded in the parish registers; to Finlaison's and Farr's estimates of eighteenth-century population; and to Gonner, Brownlee and Griffith, all drawing upon Rickman's data though the two latter authors used them in different ways.[6] And the continuity can still be traced, for though Price's main contention was shown to be unsound, the basic questions relating to the population of England and Wales in the eighteenth century—how far and why it increased—have not yet been given definitive answers.

There were, of course, other strands of interest, too. Concern with the possible future led writers like Graunt, Petty and King to speculate on the rate of growth in the past—to try out various rates of doubling and to consider the speed with which the losses of plague were made good. The belief of many seventeenth-century virtuosi that the closer study of nature would reveal the workings of providence was applied to man and the line from Arbuthnot led, via Caspar Neumann and Derham, to Süssmilch, who collected historical data as a means of examining the constancy of certain vital phenomena—especially the sex ratio at birth—or in order to dispel superstitions—such as the belief in climacteric years.[7] Much of the resultant work was inevitably not demographic in any modern, professional sense. But the basic statistics collected are often worth re-examination. And there were some outstanding studies—on the technical side in the work of the mathematicians who contributed to the development of mortality analysis and provided base lines for the use of later demographers[8]; or in the form of new empirical investigations, such as those of Struyck[9]; or occasionally in the form of a direct historical inquiry, such as that of Muret.[10] In general, however, the serious study of demographic history had to wait until around and after the middle of the nineteenth century. The spread of periodic censuses helped to stimulate the production of gazetteers and repertories whose compilers endeavoured to bring together historical series of population data. Historians themselves began to examine and publish early population records—such as Konrad Hegel's work on the 1449 Nürnberg census and Karl Bücher's study of medieval Frankfurt.[11] Historically-minded statisticians and physicians attempted to use parish registers and similar sources to investigate mortality trends—Edouard Mallet in Switzerland and W. A. Guy in England are examples.[12] A mild form of chauvinism began to inspire the production of local studies, especially in France and Germany.[13] By the early

[6] See ch. 9 of the present volume.
[7] The belief in constancy sometimes went so far as to lead to the assumption that death rates calculated for one country might have universal validity.
[8] Beginning indeed with Halley and continuing with Deparcieux, De Moivre, Euler, Bernoulli and the many subsequent contributors.
[9] See J. A. Vollgraff (trans.), *Les œuvres de Nicolas Struyck*, Amsterdam, 1912. Struyck is, in my view, one of the most rewarding of eighteenth-century demographers.
[10] J. L. Muret, *Mémoire sur l'état de la population dans le canton de Vaud*, Yverdon, 1766.
[11] K. Hegel, *Chroniken der deutschen Städte*, II, Leipzig, 1864; K. Bücher, *Die Bevölkerung von Frankfurt am Main im 14. und 15. Jahrhundert*, I, Tübingen, 1886.
[12] E. Mallet, *Recherches historiques et statistiques sur la population de Genève*, Paris, 1837; W. A. Guy, 'Two hundred and fifty years of smallpox in London', *J.R.S.S.*, Sept. 1882.
[13] There were innumerable small, local studies; larger compilations were far less frequent. An example of the latter is the series of volumes produced in Germany under the editorship of F. J. Neumann, *Beiträge zur Geschichte der Bevölkerung in Deutschland*, 7 vols., Tübingen, 1883-1903.

twentieth century, the study of demographic history could show significant publications in several fields. They included analyses of earlier records, of which the work of des Cilleuls is an instance; studies of countries, such as Levasseur's work on France or, though very different in character, Sundbärg's compilation of Swedish data from the mid-eighteenth century onwards; reviews of earlier pioneer work, such as Graetzer's inquiry into the sources of Halley's famous life table and Westergaard's general survey of the history of mortality; and specialist contributions from the side of medicine, one of the most notable being Creighton's monumental history of epidemics in Britain.[14]

In spite of such encouraging developments, further progress until the 1940's was disappointing. There were, as in the earlier period, very useful contributions and some confluence of a number of formerly separate streams of research. Thus Willcox and Carr-Saunders reviewed and revised the earlier estimates of world population growth since the mid-seventeenth century.[15] Efforts were made to gather together the historical statistics of international migration.[16] Specific groups of migrants were given closer attention, the result in some cases being to throw new light on the social and economic context of population movements; the publications of Mathorez on foreigners in France during the Old Régime and of M. L. Hansen on emigration from Europe to the United States are noteworthy in this connection.[17] Local monographs were still in evidence and there were some rather more comprehensive approaches to the analysis of particular demographic questions, such as the impact of epidemics or the nature of population growth in England during the Industrial Revolution.[18] But looking at the field as a whole, the efforts were relatively unsystematic and much of the research was not very satisfactory from a technical point of view. The nature and limitations of the source materials were not always fully considered, and the techniques of demographic analysis used were often imperfect. Thus there were still many gaps in our knowledge of the history of population prior to the middle of the nineteenth century—indeed, more gaps than well-attested assessments. It is not surprising that controversy flourished.

Since the 1940's, there have been considerable changes in the extent and nature of research into the demographic history of the West. In large part, this is a reflection of a growing interest in population questions generally, stimulated in the 1930's by the apparent threat of population decline in the West and since World War II by the high and rising rates of population growth in underdeveloped societies. Research centres were established and larger numbers of

[14] P. E. Levasseur, *La population française*, Vol. 1, Paris, 1889; for A. des Cilleuls, see P. E. Vincent, 'French demography in the eighteenth century', *Population Studies*, June, 1947; G. Sundbärg, *Bevölkerungsstatistik Schwedens, 1750-1900*, Stockholm, 1907; J. Graetzer, *Edmund Halley und Caspar Neumann*, Breslau, 1883; H. Westergaard, *Die Lehre von der Mortalität und Morbilität*, 2nd edn., Jena, 1901. C. Creighton, *History of epidemics in Britain*, 2 vols., Cambridge, 1891 and 1894 (reprinted with introductions by D. E. C. Eversley and E. A. Underwood, London, 1965).

[15] W. F. Willcox, 'Increase in the population of the earth and of the continents since 1650', in W. F. Willcox, ed., *International migrations*, Vol. II, New York, 1931; A. M. Carr-Saunders, *World population; past growth and present trends*, Oxford, 1936.

[16] W. F. Willcox (ed.), *op. cit.*

[17] J. Mathorez, *Les étrangers en France sous l'ancien régime*, 2 vols., Paris, 1919 and 1921; M. L. Hansen, *The atlantic migration, 1607-1860*, Cambridge (Mass.), 1940. On emigration from Germany, see the much earlier, valuable symposium, E. von Philippovich, ed., *Auswanderung und Auswanderungspolitik in Deutschland*, Leipzig, 1892.

[18] References to the writings on population growth in eighteenth-century England are given in ch. 9 of the present volume.

professional demographers were trained. Some of the newer demographic techniques—such as cohort analysis, evolved in the analysis of replacement rates of Western countries; and derivatives of Lotka's stable population theory, found necessary to handle the imperfect data of countries in Asia, Africa and Latin America—were found to be very suitable for dealing with historical data.[19] Demographers themselves came to show more interest in population history. In France, for example, Louis Henry's interest arose from a need to estimate the levels of fertility in populations in which birth control was not practised to any sizeable degree. Data for present-day high fertility societies are generally rather poor, and the pre-nineteenth-century data for some Western societies (or for selected groups in them) appeared to offer a more reliable alternative. Hence the beginnings of the research on the Genevan bourgeoisie and, later, the initiation of a large-scale investigation based upon samples of the French parish registers.[20] In turn, the French example has helped to stimulate similar work—or at least new historical studies—elsewhere. Other demographers became interested in population changes in pre-industrial and early-industrial eras as part of their concern for the problems of transition in present-day developing societies. The theory of demographic transition does not, in its present form, provide an adequate framework for the study of contemporary societies. It could hardly do so, since it is rather mechanistic and, in addition, is beset by too many apparent deviations as well as by major gaps in essential information.[21] Historians, too, reacted, showing a much greater interest in the reciprocal relationship of industrialization and demographic change. This very interest has served to show how serious are the gaps in our data on mortality, marriage and fertility, as well as on sheer numerical growth. Controversial writing has by no means disappeared as a result, but there is now more in the way of careful examination of source materials, the discovery of hitherto unknown collections of historical data,[22] and a closer collaboration with demographers on the kinds of techniques which might best be applied in the construction of estimates and the analysis of trends. Reinforcement of interest has also come from the marked expansion of the history of medicine as a special field of academic inquiry. On the whole there has been relatively little collaboration between exponents of that discipline and demographers— the work of McKeown and his colleagues, though contributing to the history of medicine, is not formally part of it, having arisen in a quite different way.[23]

[19] J. Bourgeois-Pichat, 'Utilisation de la notion de population stable pour mesurer la mortalité et la fécondité des populations des pays sous-developpés, *Bulletin de l'Institut International de Statistique*, Tome 36, 2ᵉ *Livraison*, Stockholm, 1958; A. J. Coale, 'The effects of changes in mortality and fertility on age composition', *Milbank Memorial Fund Quarterly*, Jan. 1956; N. H. Carrier, 'A note on the estimation of mortality and other population characteristics given deaths by age', *Population Studies*, Nov. 1958.

[20] L. Henry, *Anciennes familles genevoises*, Paris, 1956; E. Gautier and L. Henry, *La Population de Crulai; paroisse normande*, Paris, 1958.

[21] I have tried to deal with some of these defects of 'transition theory' in a paper given at a conference on 'Research issues in public health and population changes', Graduate School of Public Health, University of Pittsburgh, 1964 (to be published in 1965).

[22] For example, during a recent visit to Prague I was told of the discovery of an important collection of 'census' data for seventeenth-century Bohemia. It is clear, too, that much valuable material has been found in Poland and is being analysed. See (A. Josefowicz), *Report on current demographic research in Poland*, Warsaw, 1961 (typescript).

[23] See ch. 12 in the present volume, and also T. McKeown and R. G. Record, 'Reasons for the decline of mortality in England and Wales during the nineteenth century', *Population Studies*, Nov. 1962.

But historians of medicine have recently made their own contributions—for instance, Miller's monograph on the adoption of inoculation and Shryock's studies of the development of medicine—which should certainly be taken into account by demographers.[24]

The advancement of research during the past twenty years—and especially during the past ten—will help to provide the bases for a quite new understanding of the history of population. This is all the more so in that there is now a much wider discussion of the needs and problems of the subject, a more systematic attack on major unanswered questions, and an extension of inquiry to include the Netherlands, Czechoslovakia, Poland and Hungary, not formerly well-represented in this field. But just because the developments are recent, the present volume represents a transition between the older and the newer approach and coverage. Its time span is limited, being focussed almost entirely upon the period of industrialization. Apart from some of the more general papers in Part I, the contributions are drawn very largely from Western Europe and the most recent types of research are represented mainly by the group of studies on France. One paper deriving from the earlier tradition is included—that by T. H. Marshall—because, at the time it was written, it gave a succinct account of the state of the controversy on population growth in England during the Industrial Revolution and because the paper leads on, through the articles of Habakkuk to that of McKeown and Brown, and to some of the newer work now being carried out in Britain. The relevance of the various studies to the appreciation of the interrelationship of demographic and economic variables is discussed in detail by Eversley in the next chapter. In what follows here, I shall be concerned mainly with general questions of demographic and affiliated investigations rather than with the specific contents of the individual papers in this volume.

There are, to begin with, general questions of approach, of the kinds of hypotheses formulated, and of the nature of the arguments used to support those hypotheses. The role of hypotheses has, of course, been discussed at great length by professional methodologists and was recently put before a larger public by P. B. Medawar in his radio talk on 'Is the scientific paper a fraud?'.[25] Few would argue that the mass collection of data—the field work equivalent would be the questionnaire which contains everything including the 'kitchen sink'—is likely to be profitable unless there are some guiding purposes in the collection. But that does not provide a case for hypotheses created in vacuo, nor does it sanctify the testing of hypotheses by using excessively imperfect data and without further scrutiny, or the appeal to support by analogy. These are the truisms of research methodology. And when Graunt undertook his pioneer study, he honoured most of these requirements. His hypotheses—or 'conceits, opinions and conjecture', as he called them—were formulated in the course of scrutinizing a few Bills of Mortality and subsequently tested on a very much larger collection. He considered the types and possible magnitude of errors in the source material and went so far as to conduct a direct inquiry in order to assess the reliability of the reported deaths from syphilis. And in

[24] For Miller, see subsequent reference. Much of Shryock's work is closely relevant. But see in particular, R. H. Shryock, *Medicine and society in America 1660-1860*, New York, 1960.
[25] Reprinted in D. Edge, ed., *Experiment*, London, 1964.

general he tried to distinguish between what he regarded as a reasonably well-established conclusion and a conjecture.[26] His successors have not always been so careful and this is the case particularly of those engaged in historical study. Of course, the range of interests of those involved in such study has been very wide and in earlier times some of the defects were the not-too-surprising result of assuming that certain demographic indices were constant in time and space, an assumption derived in part from the 'universalism' of Derham and Süssmilch. Thus Rickman saw no harm in estimating total populations from baptisms by assuming a constant ratio throughout the eighteenth century and equal to that which he calculated for 1801, and he appeared to believe that having once ascertained the age-structure of a population through a census, it was not necessary to repeat the effort.[27] But similar assumptions continued to be used until quite recently, and not only for whole countries but also for small areas in which deviations from the national age-structure might have been very considerable.[28] Even if the resultant population estimates are not wildly wrong—and for some purposes it may clearly be more useful to have an estimate subject to a 15 or 20 per cent error than no estimate at all—the method itself prevents any further possibility of examining the course of fertility (or mortality, if burials have been used as the basis). Again, it may be necessary—perhaps unavoidable—to accept this limitation, but it should at least be recognized. Rather more surprising is the relative attention given in some studies to the establishment of estimates of population increase (and its components) on the one hand and to the search for plausible explanations of that estimated increase on the other. An example of this is the work of Talbot Griffith, referred to by Professor Habakkuk as 'notable'[29]—and it no doubt is so in the sense that it was the first large-scale attempt to tackle the question. But the 'establishment' of the course of birth and death rates in England and Wales in the period 1700-1840 occupies only a small fraction of the work, makes no attempt to check the reliability of Rickman's statistics of baptisms and burials ('reliability' in the minimal sense that the collection was an accurate compilation from the parish registers) and applies very crude 'correction factors' to convert baptisms and burials into births and deaths. By far the largest portion of the work is devoted to the search for explanations of the course of vital events which can scarcely be viewed as firmly ascertained. And one section of the explanation—improvements in medicine as a cause of the falling death rate—has subsequently been heavily criticized by McKeown and Brown, who have argued that medical therapy contributed little if anything and have concluded that improvements in levels of living are a more likely cause.[30] Similar criticism has been levelled against Connell's argument that the relatively high rate of population growth in Ireland was to some extent the result of a fall in the age at, and an increase

[26] For assessments of the work of Graunt see my paper in *Proceedings of the Royal Society*, Series B, December 1963; and I. Sutherland, 'John Graunt: a tercentenary tribute', *J.R.S.S.*, Series A, 1963, Part IV.

[27] The disagreement between Rickman and Joshua Milne on this matter is discussed in D. V. Glass, 'Some aspects of the development of demography', *Journal of the Royal Society of Arts*, Vol. CIV, pp. 854-866, 1956.

[28] See, for example, the references in L. Munby, *Hertfordshire population statistics 1563-1801* (Bedford) 1964, p. 17.

[29] See ch. 11 in the present volume, p. 269.

[30] See ch. 12 in the present volume.

in the amount of, marriage.[31] And it is certainly the case that, as shown by the 1851 census, the proportions never-married in the age-group 45-54 years were not sensibly different from those in England and Wales.[32] As a final example of the problem of establishment and interpretation, we may cite an earlier paper by Krause—who is represented in the present volume by a comprehensive survey of the uses and defects of English parish register materials[33]—in which he doubts whether mortality fell in England in the later eighteenth century. He also argues by analogy, to the effect that 'if Sweden had a life expectation at birth of 36 years in 1751-1800, a figure of about 40 seems plausible for eighteenth century England'.[34] But mortality in Sweden was not constant during the period 1751-1800; for males, for example, expectation of life at birth varied from a low of 29·1 in 1771-5 to a high of almost 38 years in 1791-5.[35] And in pre-industrial societies these variations were probably of no less significance than the long term average. Further, the level which Krause believes may have obtained in England for the general population is not far short of that attained by dukes' sons born in the period 1730-79. Hollingsworth's more recent study of the complete peerage indicates that it was not until the cohort born in 1750-74, with its experience running through the period of inoculation, that the expectation of life at birth rose above 40 years. It was 44·5 years for the males in that cohort, compared with 38·6 years for the males born in 1725-49. If levels of living were an important factor in mortality trends, can it be assumed that the levels of the population at large were not very different from those of the peerage? And finally, Hollingsworth's data show a consistent rise in the expectation of life at birth among all cohorts born after the mid-seventeenth century. The low point was reached by the cohort born in 1650-74, spanning the last major outbreak of bubonic plague in England; and this also appears to have been the turning point, so far as the trend of mortality is concerned.[36] Is it likely that the population at large would have been entirely excluded from those more favourable circumstances which helped to bring down mortality—especially if they are primarily associated with levels of living? At the very least, a much closer scrutiny of economic and social conditions would be required before accepting Krause's contention. But what is still

[31] M. Drake, 'Marriage and population growth in Ireland, 1750-1845', *Economic History Review*, Vol. XVI, No. 2, 1963.

[32] For males, 11·6 per cent in Ireland, 11·5 per cent in England and Wales; for females, 11·4 and 12·2 per cent respectively.

[33] See ch. 15 in the present volume.

[34] J. T. Krause, 'English population movements between 1700 and 1850', I.P.U., *International Population Conference*, New York, 1961, Vol. 1, London, 1963. Krause also thinks that fertility fell after 1821 and that it had risen earlier. But assuming a stationary expectation of life at birth of 40 years and a total fertility rate of around 5 live births per woman, this would yield a rate of natural increase of around 1·6 per cent per year. A population growing at that rate would double itself in about 44 years. If such a rate had applied through the eighteenth century, then taking the population of England and Wales in 1821—12 millions—as a starting point, the population in 1701 would not have been much larger than 2 millions. There must have been a change in growth rates at some point or points of time; we still have to identify these points. As for the question of fertility or mortality change as an explanation, see the later discussion.

[35] Calculations based on Sundbärg's data.

[36] The reasons for the disappearance of the plague are still far from clear. L. F. Hirst (*The conquest of plague*, Oxford, 1953) thought it could be explained by the change of rat and rat-flea species during the eighteenth century. But R. Pollitzer (*Plague*, Geneva, 1954) argues that this replacement of *R. rattus* by *R. norvegicus* took place after the decline of plague in the West (though the last main outbreak in France—in Marseilles—was in 1720). He explains the change in terms of a 'natural decline' in the plague itself, rather than in response to outside factors.

more important is to establish the basic historical 'facts of life' before attempting
to formulate explanatory hypotheses, as well as to ensure that the hypotheses
are fully tested or, if this cannot be done from the available materials, are
explicitly stated to be no more than not unreasonable speculations.

In establishing the basic 'facts of life' the work of demographers and historians must inevitably be conditioned by the nature of the historical materials
available for their particular countries. But generally speaking, for some time
to come, at least, the absolute size of total populations is likely to be especially
difficult to establish with any precision. This does not mean that, for many
purposes, fairly reasonable orders of magnitude cannot be estimated. On the
contrary, there are already useable estimates for various countries—Sweden is,
of course, a special case, with its continuous series of population and vital
statistics since the mid-eighteenth century—and much more could be done
to test and improve the estimates. Vincent's comments on his own attempts to
'refine' early French estimates are instructive in that respect,[37] though historians
are well aware of the need to compare different versions of seventeenth- and
eighteenth-century lists used as a basis for population totals and to draw upon
as many sources as possible in trying to arrive at a final figure. Searches should
obviously be made for other enumerations, tax lists, communicant returns and
the like; it is most improbable that all the relevant materials still in existence
are catalogued and known, and even during the past few years many additional
basic documents have been rediscovered.[38] The work involved is, of course,
very substantial and such work may well seem unrewarding, since we cannot
foresee how far fruitful results are likely to emerge. But there is no easy alternative—not, at least, if we are to advance beyond conjecture.

For some countries historians may be fortunate in locating large series of
enumerations, of the kind available for Italy and utilized by Beloch. For others,
however, this is much less likely and it may be necessary to arrive at estimates
by working backwards from the earliest national censuses. If there are reasonable collections of parish register data, such a method may be fruitful. But a
good many difficulties are likely to be encountered, and they may be illustrated from the case of England, though some of the difficulties here are peculiar
to our own circumstances.

There are already several sets of estimates of the population of England and
Wales in the eighteenth century, and most of them have been derived in one

[37] P. E. Vincent, *op. cit.*
[38] Taking only the case of England, recent correspondence with archivists has shown that there
are certainly more returns produced under the 1694 Act (returns of the kind used by Gregory King)
than I was able to locate several years ago. A thorough search for such returns would be an essential
part of any comprehensive study of the population of England at the end of the seventeenth century.
Similarly, the inquiries organised at Cambridge by Peter Laslett have produced a very considerable
number of pre-1801 local censuses giving details of individuals enumerated, including ages. One
noteworthy rediscovery is that of the Ealing (London) census of 1599, found in 1931, specifying age,
sex and occupation (marital status can be inferred, but not very reliably). See K. J. Allison, *An
Elizabethan 'census' of Ealing*, Ealing Local History Society, 1962. Another 'discovery' is that reported
in answer to my own inquiries—an extremely detailed enumeration of Corfe Castle parish (Dorset)
in 1795 (*ca*), giving a wide range of information—on age, sex, marital condition, household structure,
occupation and 'probable weekly earnings'. The results of the enumeration are given in J. Hutchins,
History and antiquities of the county of Dorset, 3 vols., 2nd edn., London, 1796, Vol. 1. Hutchins was
rector of Holy Trinity, Wareham and perhaps he himself carried out the enumeration. (He recommended that similar surveys should be undertaken for other parishes.) An enumeration of this scope
might well be used as the basis of a local demographic-social study.

way or another from Rickman's compilation of parish register data. But the returns supplied to Rickman no longer exist and we do not know how accurately those returns were transcribed from the registers, to what extent dissenters were included, or even whether the interpolations used by Rickman to fill gaps in the returns were acceptable approximations. Hence any further serious attempt to investigate population growth during the eighteenth century on the basis of parish register material must break away from Rickman's series and begin with a new compilation (no doubt on a sample basis) of accurate year-by-year transcriptions and an equivalent analysis of the records of dissenting groups. But this would represent only the initial step.[39] To work backwards from the first periodic censuses of England and Wales requires a much closer assessment than has so far been undertaken of the changing completeness of ecclesiastical registration; a study of the reliability—in respect both of completeness and of the accuracy of the age data recorded in 1821, 1841 and 1851 —of the early nineteenth-century censuses; and new attempts to estimate the volume of net migration from England and Wales in the eighteenth and first half of the nineteenth centuries.[40] It is most unlikely that 'the truth' will be found by research conducted under any of these headings. Yet so little systematic work has been done that any serious research would almost certainly produce considerably better estimates than we now have, and at the same time provide a clearer idea of the margin of indeterminacy which still remained.[41] In addition, the new estimates might be checked against assessments based on other data—for example, if sufficient returns can be found, on compilations of the statistics collected under the 1694 Act, from which in part Gregory King's calculations originated.

How far this kind of approach can be followed for other European countries depends, of course, on their background of ecclesiastical registration. And even when it is practicable, the method cannot at the same time supply direct and unequivocal indicators of the components of population change—of the contributions of marriage, fertility and mortality. Crude marriage, birth and death rates can be computed. But these convey too restricted a meaning and in any case are influenced by changes in the age, sex and marital composition of the population. The study of marriage levels and patterns, of family size and birth spacing, and of the probabilities of death at various ages—more meaningful and more capable of being linked to complementary inquiries into relevant social, economic and medical influences on demographic change—is more satisfactorily achieved through cohort or generation analysis. And such analysis requires the 'reconstitution' of cohorts from parish register (or equivalent) data,

[39] Such transcriptions of parish register data, if they can be pushed back sufficiently far in time, might also help us to examine the amplitude of annual and other periodic fluctuations in deaths, to which Helleiner refers in his discussion of pre-industrial Europe (see ch. 4 of the present volume). It should, however, be remembered that it is in respect of the heaviest epidemics that the fluctuations are likely to be most understated by the records.

[40] 'Working backwards' referred to here does not mean applying assumed ratios, constant or otherwise, of population to marriages, baptisms or burials, but the use of a 'balancing equation' of the kind employed by Griffith, though the 'corrections' applied would be arrived at differently.

[41] A very full and effective discussion of the use of demographic techniques in correcting census data and in deriving birth-rates and fertility-rates from the corrected data will be found in A. J. Coale and M. Zelnik, *New estimates of fertility and population in the United States*, Princeton, N.J., 1963.

along the lines on which Louis Henry and his colleagues have pioneered.[42] The contribution of Henry to the present volume gives an indication of the high quality of the research and of its power in providing a new groundwork for studying the demography of eighteenth-century France. The technique requires the linking together of successive vital events occurring to an individual from birth to death (including his marriage and the birth of his children). In France such work has been possible because of the greater detail recorded in registration, the wider range of combinations of given names and surnames, and the relative immobility of the population. Whether these circumstances can be matched in many other countries can only be determined by pilot studies, of which not many so far have been completed or are in progress. In so far as the technique is applicable and is then applied to appropriate samples of parishes in various countries, far more solidly-based information on marriage, fertility and mortality will be obtained, as well as a considerable body of material on internal migration.[43] 'Reconstitution' is, however, a slow process and it demands a degree of co-ordination in research which, so far, has not been shown to any great extent outside of France. Moreover, the technique is not in general likely to throw much light on one important question, namely that of differences between social strata within countries.[44] Supplementary materials and techniques would be needed there, and they would in any case have to be used in countries for which a comprehensive 'reconstitution' is not practicable.

Several types of data may be available, the most extensive and reliable relating to well-defined sub-groups in the population. The ruling families are probably the most fully documented and their records have been analysed by Peller in his study of the Continental families[45] and by Hollingsworth in his studies of the British ducal families and of the complete British peerage.[46] The records of these groups are by no means perfect, especially for the earliest periods, and some of the resultant statistics would certainly need close scrutiny.[47] But it is unlikely that any other materials would be as reliable over so long a span of time, and it is the time-span in particular which is of value to demographers and historians. A search for similar materials in other countries is therefore worth pursuing. There are other groups which, for shorter periods of time, may be as well—or almost as well—documented. The bourgeoisie of Geneva, for example, gave Henry the opportunity for his first detailed study

[42] It appears from the report by Josefowicz, referred to earlier, that 'reconstitution' of this kind —or at least the construction of 'family cards'—has also been undertaken in Poland recently. For example, it is reported that such cards have been prepared from the material in the registers of 6 parishes in Poznan—1,600 cards covering 11,000 individuals over 3 or 4 generations. But I have seen no results. Earlier examples of this type of approach, used by Morrell and Roller are referred to by Hajnal in ch. 6 of the present volume.

[43] The information on internal migration would be obtained as a by-product, for in order to maximize the completeness of 'reconstitution' for a given parish, it would be necessary to search for missing individuals and their vital events in a fairly wide ring of surrounding parishes. A reasonable idea of the volume, direction and distance of migration might thereby be gained.

[44] Unless all the records give reliable and fairly detailed information on occupations. But regional and urban-rural differences could be ascertained.

[45] S. Peller, ch. 5 in the present volume.

[46] T. H. Hollingsworth, ch. 14 in the present volume and also *The demography of the British peerage*, supplement to *Population Studies*, Nov. 1964.

[47] In particular, the rather high expectations of life at birth for the earliest cohorts of the peerage; but also the fluctuations in completed fertility between the seventeenth and mid-eighteenth centuries.

of changing fertility.[48] In England the Quakers and the gentry offer similar possibilities and there are likely to be comparable groups in other countries. Each group would, of course, be somewhat of a special case. Yet the data would be worth studying in their own right, as displaying the behaviour of a stratum whose position and role in society can be investigated, while the examination of several such groups within and between societies might justify at least some limited generalizations. This might be especially so if the analyses were pressed forward into and through the nineteenth century, during which period comparisons between the selected groups and the general population would be feasible. And on particular aspects of demographic change, a still wider range of data relating to specific groups might repay study. On mortality, for example, there are the data on annuitants, members of tontines and of Friendly Societies in England and Wales and in some other European societies, as well as on the populations covered by life assurance organizations.[49] Such materials need to be treated with considerable caution, and the varying nature and degree of selection scrutinized.[50] But with these restrictions they might yield supporting information, especially as regards changes in adult mortality. Indeed, a rather wide variety of sources might be employed in examining adult mortality, any well-defined continuing group (such as clergy, doctors or members of parliament) for which the dates of birth and death of its members have been ascertained, being amenable to the calculation of age-specific death rates. Selection by social class or other relevant characteristic would, of course, have to be recognized; it would in fact be part of the interest. But mere survival to the beginning of adulthood would be a form of selection applying to the adult population in general.

Some of the sources and approaches suggested require primarily historians'

[48] There is a great deal of other valuable material available for Switzerland. For a very helpful discussion of Swiss demographic history, see Part I of W. Bickel, *Bevölkerungsgeschichte und Bevölkerungspolitik der Schweiz*, Zürich, 1947.

[49] There may, for example, be a good deal of annuitant material in the Netherlands. Some of it was reported and examined by eighteenth-century Dutch demographers—for example, by Struyck (*op. cit.*). The earliest material of that kind I have seen was collected by J. Hudde and relates to annuities entered into during the period 1586-90 (see Société Générale Néerlandaise d'Assurance, *Mémoires; pour servir à l'histoire des assurances sur la vie et des rentes viagères aux Pays-Bas*, Amsterdam, 1898). Rates calculated from the data show wide fluctuations. But taking the entrants at age 1 year and assuming an infant mortality of 250 per 1,000 (equivalent to Peller's data for the seventeenth century), expectation of life at birth would be around 35 years. If the infant mortality rate were 350 per 1,000, the expectation of life at birth would be only just above 30 years. It is of interest to compare this with calculations based on data collected by Struyck (*op. cit.*, p. 237), who analysed the parish register material for Broek-in-Waterland from the mid-seventeenth century onward, giving the numbers of births and the numbers of children dying by and between specified ages. I have taken as the basis the statistics for 1657-1706 (Struyck noted that mortality was higher in the period 1707-28), but have also used the data for 1657-1738 for partitioning the first year of life, since these specify deaths in the first 4 days, deaths under 1 week and deaths under 1 month of age. Calculating a life table up to age 6 (infant mortality appears to be 386 per 1,000 for males and 291 per 1,000 for females), I have spliced this to the life table for Madras males, 1872-81, which suggests a closely similar run of survivorships (census of India, *Actuarial reports for the census 1881, 1891, 1901, 1911, 1921, 1931 and 1951*, New Delhi, 1960, p. 40). The resultant expectation of life at birth (for males and females together) is around 24 years. In a later work, Struyck (*op. cit.*, pp. 369-70) gives more elaborate data for the same parish for the period 1654-1732—a period of higher mortality—distinguishing deaths by months during the first year of life and then by single years up to the age of 9 inclusive. For this longer period, infant mortality appeared to be around 415 per 1,000 for males and 333 for females and life tables (calculated in the way indicated above) yield an expectation of life at birth of about 23 years.

[50] Selection would be by social class and probably also to some extent of healthy lives. But this latter selection would be less significant at the adult ages.

skills for their manipulation, while others demand relatively advanced techniques of formal demography. Collaboration between demographers and historians would be especially desirable in the latter case. Recent developments in demographic analysis would be of value in setting the boundaries of likely reality and in providing alternative estimates which might serve to check results derived from parish registers or similar archives. Under the first heading, for example, are the results which can be derived from the work on stable population and quasi-stable population theory. The original studies of Lotka showed that, given persistent, specified rates of fertility and mortality, a population would develop a fixed age-composition, and fixed crude birth rates and death rates,[51] and Lotka's work has now been extended to populations with fertility and mortality changing at specified rates.[52] It has also been shown that the age composition of a population is far more heavily influenced by changes in fertility than in mortality.[53] In their simpler form, some of these findings have been used in demonstrating the relationships between levels of fertility and mortality, natural increase and age-structure. What is, for example, brought out sharply is that, even with a total fertility of about 5 live births per woman surviving throughout the child-bearing period (a figure somewhat higher than that found for Britain in the mid-nineteenth century),[54] no long term population increase would be achieved until the expectation of life at birth had risen above some 24 years. Similarly, with total fertility at about the level of mid-nineteenth century Britain (around 4·8), a persistent growth by natural increase of 0·5 per cent per year would require an expectation of life at birth of almost 30 years.[55] Computations of this kind offer some check on the interpretation of apparent population trends. Equally, some check may be obtained by reference to estimates of age structure. Thus if Gregory King's estimate of the age composition of the population of England and Wales were accurate (and it is obviously not) and if we could assume that the levels of fertility and mortality had been stationary for some fifty or sixty years (an assumption which is not realistic), it might be inferred that with a fertility equal to mid-nineteenth-century levels, the expectation of life at birth would lie between 30 and 40 years. If fertility had been slightly higher, the expectation of life at birth would be lower, nearer to the 30 years level.[56]

These are oversimplified calculations. But they could be brought closer to reality with the aid of the data collected since the 1940's and still more so with the new materials which are likely to be forthcoming during the next ten years— materials on age at marriage, birth-spacing and total fertility, and on the age-patterns of death rates associated with levels of mortality calculated from

[51] The work of A. J. Lotka is best seen in his *Théorie analytique des associations biologiques*, 2 vols., Paris, 1934 and 1939.

[52] Lotka's work has been amplified by A. Lopez, *Problems in stable age distribution theory*, Princeton, N.J., 1961. See also Coale and Zelnik, *op. cit.*

[53] U.N., *The aging of populations and its economic and social implications*, New York, 1956.

[54] A total fertility rate is obtained by summing the rates of fertility observed at each year of age (or in each five-year age group) during the child-bearing period, i.e. between 15 and 50 years. A gross reproduction rate is then obtained by taking only the female live-births and purports to show the number of female live-births borne by a woman living through the child-bearing period.

[55] These estimates were derived from the tables on pp. 26-27 of U.N., *The aging of populations*, cited previously.

[56] Fertility could be higher, with a given rate of marital fertility at each age, if age at marriage were lower and/or if a larger proportion of women married.

seventeenth- and eighteenth-century data.[57] More sophisticated computations would then be possible, providing sets of boundaries within which the inter-action and resultants of demographic variables were likely to have operated. More could also be done to demonstrate how specified changes in marriage propensity, total fertility and expectation of life affect the crude birth and death rates observed in the transition from one set of specifications to another. This has been a question of considerable importance in interpreting recent demo-graphic trends in the West, and it is likely to be equally relevant to the study of population change during industrialization.[58] For example, population projections for England and Wales computed some years ago—before the new kinds of research had been initiated—showed that various combinations of assumptions regarding fertility and mortality would produce a good fit to Gregory King's estimate for 1696 at one end and to the results of the early periodic censuses in the nineteenth century at the other.[59] One such projection assumed a constant general fertility rate (live births per 1,000 women aged 15-49 years) at the level of 1841-50. The base line of mortality was that of 1841-5 (assumed to apply from 1801 onwards) and this was raised by some 70 per cent for 1721-41; by just under 60 per cent for 1696-1721; and by slightly less than 30 per cent for 1776-1801. The crude birth rate showed relatively small variations, with the highest point around 37·5 per 1,000 in the early eighteenth century and thereafter fluctuating around a mildly falling trend line, reaching 34·0 per 1,000 in the 1820's and 1830's. The crude death rate rose to a peak of 33·5 in the late 1730's, falling gradually to just under 21 per 1,000 by the beginning of the nineteenth century and then appearing to stabilize at 21·0 in the 1830's. There were other combinations which fitted the end points but with somewhat different intermediate histories. All the projec-tions were crude and are not worth citing save as an illustration of what might now be done on a more satisfactory basis and—with the help of electronic computers—with more varied and more detailed sets of assumptions.[60]

The implication of this discussion is clearly that at present our knowledge of how far and why Western populations grew during the seventeenth and

[57] The calculations, which are derived from the U.N. volume, are over-simplified in three ways. (1) The life tables are based on modern experience. Though this is wide-ranging, including underdeveloped societies with very high mortality, it does not follow that their age-patterns of mortality would be the same as those of pre-industrial European societies with similar expectations of life at birth. (2) A fixed pattern of fertility is assumed, giving a mean age of mothers at the birth of their children of around 27·5 years. (3) Age-specific fertility rates without regard to marital status, were used, and fertility was assumed to be independent of mortality. But if marital fertility were to remain constant and mortality to fall, thus increasing the probability of marriages surviving intact, age-specific fertility rates would rise.

[58] The question of the relation between changes in the total fertility of generations or cohorts and annual variations in the crude birth rate (or other short-period indices) has been very pertinent to the study of recent trends in the birth rate in Europe and the U.S.A. See, for example, J. Hajnal, 'The analysis of birth statistics in the light of the recent international recovery of the birth rate', *Population Studies*, Sept. 1947. On the relevance of this question to the study of changes during the early nineteenth century, see two papers by N. B. Ryder, 'The influence of declining mortality on Swedish reproductivity', in Milbank Memorial Fund, *Current research in human fertility*, New York, 1955; and 'Problems of trend determination during a transition in fertility', *Milbank Memorial Fund Quarterly*, Jan. 1956.

[59] These calculations were undertaken in 1950, partly as a sequel to work on Gregory King.

[60] The more actual data can be fed into the assumptions, the more realistic they are likely to be. At the same time independent estimates can provide some form of check. For example, the resultant ratios of births to baptisms and deaths to burials might be compared with independent estimates of the changing completeness of ecclesiastical registration.

eighteenth century is highly imperfect. And this is made equally clear by the various contributors to the present volume. So far as basic data are concerned, only Sweden has a good and continuous run going back to the mid-eighteenth century. But even for Sweden there is much less light on the first half of that century, while we are still not entirely clear about the precise demographic processes (let alone their explanation) during the period from 1750 to the early nineteenth century. It should be emphasized that this is entirely understandable and that the analysis of recent demographic developments in the West, in spite of the availability of a very much wider range of reasonably reliable statistics, has been far from easy. This being so, it is not to be expected that the various contributions to the present volume should give firm answers to the broadest questions. What instead these contributions present—and especially the more recent studies—is a survey of the kinds of elements which, with further work, may later result in a much fuller picture of the changes which have occurred from the seventeenth century onwards. As for the incomplete picture which emerges at present, this is discussed in some detail by Eversley in the next chapter and there is no need here to do more than add a few supplementary considerations.

First, what evidence there is tends to give support to Helleiner's view that, prior to the seventeenth and perhaps even prior to the eighteenth century, population growth in Western Europe proceeded by fits and starts, increase being cut back from time to time by epidemics and famine both in peacetime and as associated with war.[61] Yet the trend line of expectation of life at birth could not have been much below 25 years—at least from the sixteenth century onwards. With a figure of only 20 years, for example, total fertility would have needed to be rather above 6 to secure significant positive growth and so high an average is not very likely in large societies in which what Hajnal has termed the 'European marriage pattern' had already spread. Where the marriage pattern was more 'underdeveloped' in character—with considerably earlier ages at marriage on the part of women and more nearly universal marriage— growth would have been achieved with higher mortality and, in addition, a low age at marriage would mean a shorter generation and thus a higher annual rate of increase for a given net reproduction rate above 1·0.[62]

Again, there is evidence to indicate, as Helleiner suggests, that during the eighteenth century—and especially in the second half—the periodic erosion of growth by epidemic or harvest failure became less marked. Though diseases replaced each other to some extent, nothing replaced the plague. For various reasons, which probably differed in different countries, the barrier between life and death appears to have become more solid. Yet if that were all, and if the plateau of life expectation had not been lifted somewhat, then it might seem either that the data for Sweden in the second half of the eighteenth century

---

[61] See ch. 4 of the present volume.

[62] I am not using the term 'net reproduction rate' in the conventional sense (that is, as based upon the fertility and mortality measured in a specified year or other short period) but only as a concept. In that sense, a rate of 1·0 means only that a newborn girl, exposed to specified conditions of fertility and mortality, would be replaced by exactly one girl in the next generation. A net rate of 1·3 would imply a 30 per cent increase between one generation and the next and if the generation (approximately the mean age at which mothers bear their children) were short, the annual rate of increase would be correspondingly higher.

show a curiously high level (save for one period, 1771-5, they all show expectations of life at birth well above 30 years and for half the quinquennial periods
above 35 years)[63] or else that the periodic cuts in earlier periods were very
substantial indeed. Yet the influenza pandemic in India at the end of World
War I, hitting a no doubt undernourished population and killing some 20
million people, did not altogether eliminate population increase between 1911
and 1921.[64] Further exploration is certainly required. At the same time it is
difficult to talk of an unchanged 'plateau' without considering how frequent
and powerful was the periodic erosion. The very removal of that erosion
would result in an increase in the mean expectation of life, and the violent
fluctuations were characteristic of a lower mean expectation.

What actually happened during the eighteenth century, we do not yet
know. But such evidence as there is at present would lean much more heavily
towards lower mortality as an explanation of population growth than towards
changes in marriage or fertility. So far as marriage is concerned, Hajnal's
contribution strongly suggests that, for Western Europe, the basic change in
marriage patterns occurred long before the eighteenth century and in a direction
away from that which would tend to favour either higher marital fertility or at
least higher crude birth rates. There are some divergent cases, as shown in
Henry's data on the *ducs et pairs* in France and on the Genevan bourgeoisie.
But these were associated with a fall in fertility, not a rise. And both Peller's and
Hollingsworth's data, also relating to special groups, show a fairly consistent
rise in the mean age at first marriage of men and women (though in Peller's
material the proportions marrying appear to have been higher for the eighteenth
than for the seventeenth century cohorts). For more 'typical' populations there
are at present no long series of data. But what there are for France do not
suggest a low age at first marriage or any great change in that age. Similarly,
the proportions never-married in the older age groups as reported in the 1851
census of England and Wales do not imply an unusually high marriage propensity among people born at the end of the eighteenth or in the early nineteenth century.[65] There were no doubt differences between countries, regions
and social classes, and there were variations over time which correlated with the
harvests and other economic indicators. But so far as our present knowledge is
concerned, only two major changes in marriage habits are visible—one occurring long before the eighteenth century and the other—involving a partial
return to the much earlier pattern—since the 1930's.

On fertility the information we possess is highly incomplete and not entirely consistent. One point is clear, namely that even in régimes in which there
is little deliberate control of conception and in which age at marriage is not
changing significantly, it does not follow that the number of live-births to a
marriage in which both partners survive to the end of the child-bearing period
is necessarily constant or extremely large. As to the first, ability to conceive

[63] The calculations are based on Sundbärg's data and derived from 'current' life tables—i.e.
from the age-specific death rates of the particular quinquennium specified.

[64] The male expectation of life at birth was around 22·6 years in 1901-11 and 19·4 in 1911-12.
See K. Davis, *The population of India and Pakistan*, Princeton, N.J., 1951, pp. 63 and 237.

[65] The 1795 Corfe Castle parish enumeration shows relatively low proportions ever-married
among the women: 15-19, none; 20-24, 25 per cent; 45-49, 85 per cent. These are all slightly lower
than for England and Wales 1881 and, at the younger ages, lower than for England and Wales in 1931.

may be related to nutrition or health (gonorrhoea may, for example, be an
impeding factor); foetal wastage may change[66]; and the probability of conception may be reduced by prolonged breast-feeding or by social or religious
taboos on intercourse such as are found today in India. The second point is
illustrated by Henry's work on Crulai, by the earliest cohorts of Peller's ruling
families, and by the levels of fertility shown by marriages in Britain and Norway
in the 1870's—some 6 live-births per marriage of completed fertility would be
a not unrealistic average, taking the distribution of ages at marriage into
account.[67] On the other hand, the total fertility rates for Sweden in the period
before any downward trend became visible would suggest a slightly lower
level. Unfortunately, there is as yet very little in the way of 'typical' data for
other populations, while for earlier periods we have only the analyses of special
groups, namely the nobility. Moreover, of the three such groups covered, two
show a fall in fertility during the eighteenth century, while the third—Hollingsworth's two studies—suggests a fall beginning with the late sixteenth-century
cohorts, and an upward swing beginning with the 1725-49 cohort. The results
certainly need further investigation, not least in that at their peak they exhibit
a somewhat low fertility. At the moment we can do no more than raise a
question. If the fertility exhibited in the eighteenth century was at, or slightly
below, the level compatible with largely uncontrolled family size, what kinds
of factors would have been likely to result in still lower levels in the seventeenth
century (other than changes in marriage, discussed earlier)? Until more cases
have been collected and studied we must reserve judgment.

For mortality, the data are considerably more consistent. The two larger
special groups—the European ruling families and the British peerage—show
an increased expectation of life at birth for the eighteenth-century cohorts.
Hollingsworth's calculations, which give the results for 25 year birth cohorts,
show an unmistakeable and persistent climb from the low point to which the
group born in 1650-74 had fallen. For women, for example, the increase was
from 32·7 years for that group to 49 years for the generation born in the last
quarter of the eighteenth century, the rise continuing thereafter without interruption. Comparison with national data for England and Wales is possible for
the generation of the 1840's; for the population as a whole, the girls born in
1840-1 had a life expectation at birth of 43·1 years, almost 6 years less than the

[66] As an example of early data on foetal wastage, see the statistics collected by Finlaison from the
registers kept by Dr Granville of 'poor married women delivered in their homes' in London—presumably in 1825 and earlier years. There were 876 women, with a total of 4,621 pregnancies, of
which 831—nearly 18 per cent—ended in miscarriages or still-births (176 still-births). *Report from the
Select Committee on life annuities*, B.P.P., 1829, III, pp. 134-5. Struyck (*op. cit.*, p. 238) gives some data
on still-births for a much earlier period. For the parish of Broek-in-Waterland, 1654-1738, there
were 1,882 births, of which 75 were still-births—that is, about 4 per cent of all births, about the same
as the rate based on Finlaison's material. There is little doubt that a fair amount of further information
on foetal wastage could be found, though its reliability would have to be assessed.

[67] Much higher levels are recorded for some small societies—e.g. the present-day Hutterites
and the French Canadians of the seventeenth century—as well as for the U.S.A. in the first half of
the nineteenth century. Age at marriage and proportions married are clearly important factors here.
Thus among the Hutterites in 1950, only 0·6 per cent of the men aged 45 and over and 1·3 per cent
of the women had not been married. Marriage does not take place at a very early age, but (for women)
is heavily concentrated in the 20-29 year age group, so that in the 30-34 year group only 14 per cent
were unmarried. (J. W. Eaton and A. J. Mayer, *Man's capacity to reproduce*, Glencoe, Illinois (1954).)
Very high fertility was also characteristic of some groups of rural, Catholic, French Canadians (in
the lower educational categories) in 1950.

select group of girls born some 50 years earlier.[68] The fall in mortality among the peers is thus evident. But almost equally evident is the probability that the population as a whole also experienced a considerable fall in its death rates. For given their different economic circumstances, it is hardly likely that the general population would have shown right back to the generations born at the end of the seventeenth century the relatively light mortality which was not achieved by the peerage until after the generation of 1725-49. As yet, however, there is little factual material available for groups below the peerage in economic and social status. Finlaison's attempts to produce comparative tables of mortality from tontine and annuitant data cannot be accepted without closer scrutiny; it is unlikely that the nature and degree of selection was constant as between schemes, while the death rates at the young ages are most unrealistic.[69] William Morgan's calculations for the whole life assurances of the Equitable are more satisfactory. The general policy of the company was pretty consistent over the period covered (1768-1826), and for an adult assured population which was composed almost entirely of males the mortality rates show declines around 50 per cent between 1768-87 and 1815-26, the main fall occurring by the end of the eighteenth century.[70] So far as other countries are concerned, Henry interprets the data for France as strongly suggesting a lower mortality in the second than in the first half of the eighteenth century, while both the relative rate of population growth and the run of the death rates point in the same direction for Sweden. It does not follow that, even in Western Europe, mortality fell at the same rate in different countries, but this question, like that of the initial levels from which the decline began, will have to await further inquiry.

So, too, will the related question of how the decline was brought about. In general the interpretation of the change in mortality in England has swung away from that put forward by Griffith, of improvements in medicine and medical care. And McKeown and Brown were undoubtedly correct in emphasizing how little progress 'medical science' had actually made by the end of the eighteenth century and how the use of the new hospitals, had that been extensive, would more probably have resulted in higher rather than lower death rates. But in considering their alternative explanation, namely a rise in the levels of living, both what they reject and what they propose as explanations would repay a more ample treatment.

In their discussion of medicine, for example, McKeown and Brown discount the suggestion that inoculation against smallpox would have had a sizeable effect on total mortality. They may well be right and it is in any case extremely

[68] Hollingsworth, *The demography of the British Peerage*, pp. 56-68.
[69] The data given in the *Report from the Select Committee*, B.P.P., 1829, III, at pp. 125 and 126. There was obviously very high selection at the younger ages—the run of the expectations of life at those ages is extremely unrealistic as compared with any subsequent general experience. At the adult ages—say at age 20—the comparison shows an increase in expectation of life between the older and the more recent data.
[71] There appears to have been a pause in the fall during the first part of the nineteenth century —as may well have been the case for the general population of England and Wales. For the peerage, too, some of the age-specific mortality rates appear to have been higher for the 1775-99 cohort than for that of 1750-74, but this may be partly the result of chance variations. Morgan's data are presented and discussed in W. P. Elderton and M. E. Ogborn, 'The mortality of adult males since the middle of the 18th century as shown by the experience of life assurance companies', *J.R.S.S.*, 1943, Vol. CVI, Part I.

doubtful whether at present we could reasonably assess the effect of that technique. It would depend upon many factors. The contribution of the disease to
total mortality, for example; depending in turn upon the type of smallpox,
variations in its virulence, and the immunity acquired by the population exposed to, and surviving through, epidemics. The age incidence of the infection
is also important, and especially in relation to the prevailing overall death rates.
If smallpox deaths fell primarily on the 0-9 year age group, as in Carlisle at the
end of the eighteenth century, and if the expectation of life at birth were around
35 years, the possible contribution of smallpox to total mortality would be
limited. It might account for 10 per cent but not as much as 15 per cent. Hence,
too, the effect of a reduction in smallpox mortality would be limited. At the
10 per cent level, a reduction by half would raise the expectation of life at birth
to only about 36 years. With a lower initial life expectancy, both the contribution of smallpox and effect of its reduction would be greater. At 25 years
expectation, 20 per cent of all deaths might be contributed by smallpox; in
which case a reduction in that cause of death by half would raise the expectation
of life to around 28 years.[71] If there were any similarity between these hypothetical examples and eighteenth-century reality, it is the former which would
more nearly resemble the conditions of the British peerage and the latter those
of the mass of the population. The contemporary evidence suggests, however,
that it was the upper groups who adopted inoculation more widely. In neither
example would the reduction in overall mortality be very large. And at least
in some of the large towns, smallpox continued to be a significant cause of
death until the very end of the eighteenth century.[72]

Yet quite apart from its effect on mortality, the adoption of inoculation is of
importance as indicating an emphatic and major development in private and
public concern for health. Particularly well-sponsored on its introduction in
England in the 1720's, the new preventive treatment soon became attractive
to the aristocracy. Later, with the reappearance of major epidemics in London,
it was blessed by the clergy and by the Royal College of Physicians, public
inoculation centres were established, and professional inoculators, like the
Suttons, claimed to have dealt with very large numbers of cases.[73] Such a

[71] For these calculations, which are based on U.N. model life tables, I am indebted to my col-
league, Norman Carrier.
[72] In London, according to Guy, between 1790 and 1799 it accounted for from 3 per cent to
over 18 per cent of deaths from all causes recorded in the Bills of Mortality, being above 7 per cent
in 7 of the 10 years (W. A. Guy, 'Two hundred and fifty years of smallpox in London', J.R.S.S.,
Sept. 1882, p. 433). In Glasgow, according to Watt, smallpox accounted for over 18 per cent of all
deaths reported between 1789 and 1800 (R. Watt, Treatise on the history, nature, and treatment of
chincough, Glasgow and London, 1813, Appendix). Even in Carlisle, where considerable efforts were
made to spread inoculation, the proportion of all deaths attributed to smallpox was above 10 per
cent in the period 1781-3 and 1785-7 (from John Heysham's Bills for the individual years, kindly
loaned to me by the Librarian, Carlisle Public Library. The set of Bills is unfortunately incomplete
and the relevant details are not given in the summary in Lonsdale's biography of Heysham).
[73] See G. Miller, The adoption of inoculation for smallpox in England and France, Philadelphia, 1957
and C. W. Dixon, Smallpox, London, 1962, ch. 11. A much more comprehensive study of the
spread of inoculation in Britain (and in some other countries) has been undertaken by Mr P. E.
Razzell (not yet published at the time of writing), who cites a wide range of contemporary statistics
of inoculations. But it is difficult to accept some of the claims—e.g. the claim made by the Reverend
Robert Houlton that Sutton and his assistants had inoculated 20,000 patients is clearly somewhat
propagandistic (see J. Moore, The History of the smallpox, London, 1815, ch. 10—though Moore was
a friend of Jenner and hostile to inoculation). For Carlisle, too, the claims made by Heysham do not
appear to tally with the numbers he himself reports as having been inoculated at the city dispensary.

growth in the concern for health was also shown in the sales of manuals of domestic medicine, intended not only—in some cases not primarily—for the practitioner but also for the clergy and for other local 'influentials' who might be asked for advice on sickness or health. One manual, Buchan's *Domestic Medicine*, first published in 1769, sold over a hundred thousand copies, and there were other, similar publications, both in Britain and abroad.[74] The advice given in these books on personal cleanliness and on infant and child care was by no means unhelpful. How far the advice was accepted and applied is a different question, though perhaps not completely impervious to study. But the very substantial market for the books suggests both a more rational interest in medicine by practitioners, and a stronger interest in personal health by a larger fraction of the public than in earlier times. These changes equally suggest as one component in their explanation a wider margin of free play in the economy, with less pressure from poverty.

There is room for more thorough study of these and other specific elements and aspects of levels of living—of tuberculosis as an indicator and of eighteenth-century poor law as a contributor, for example.[75] Far more, too, needs to be known, and can be discovered, about attitudes and behaviour in various fields relevant to population change, including abortion, contraception and in-fanticide.[76] Not all the research needs to be massive. Not all, in fact, needs to be focussed on the 'grand question' of exactly how and why populations grew in the eighteenth century. For we are just as ill-informed on many significant aspects of nineteenth-century population—on internal migration in relation to marriage and employment[77]; on the change in the city's status as a 'consumer of men'; on the employment of married women; on household structure; on the repercussions of the sale of birth control pamphlets; on the degree of in-volvement of women in campaigns for raising their legal and economic status. And there is far less justification for this ignorance, having regard to the great wealth of materials available, including the census schedules with their range of untabulated information. Demographers can certainly help, but there are few of them and their competence is relevant to only part of the field. The main burden of the work will have to fall upon historians and sociologists.

[74] See J. H. F. Brotherston, *Observations on the early public health movement in Scotland*, London, 1952, pp. 19-22.

[75] For a discussion of tuberculosis, see T. McKeown and R. G. Record, 'Reasons for the decline of mortality in England and Wales during the nineteenth century', *Population Studies*, Nov. 1962.

[76] Far too little work has been done on these questions. The only extensive background study is that for France—H. Bergues *et al*, *La prévention des naissances dans la famille*, Paris, 1960. Develop-ments in England are fairly well documented from the 1850's onwards (though much more could be done), but much more poorly for the first half of the century and scarcely at all for earlier periods. Some references to sources of information and publications on Continental experience are given in K. F. Helleiner, 'New light on the history of urban populations', *Journal of Economic History*, March 1958. N. E. Himes, *Medical history of contraception*, reprint, New York, 1963, is still the classic study of the early development of techniques, but scarcely deals with the practice of birth control save for the most modern periods.

[77] Koellmann's contribution to the present volume is an example of the usefulness of work of this kind undertaken for one urban community. Similar studies are being undertaken in England.

APPENDIX

In the preceding text there were several references to the changing expectation of life at birth of 'select' groups in comparison with the mortality of national populations. The data for the 'select' groups were based on 'generation' life tables—that is, life tables reflecting the actual mortality experience of a generation born in a specified period and followed through successive ages. National data, on the other hand, are usually presented in the form of 'current' life tables, calculated by splicing together the experience of a whole range of generations whose age-specific death rates are observed simultaneously in a specified year or other period. But only when mortality is stationary will both types of life table give the same results. Each type is useful for different purposes, and it would be of value to have more generation tables than are now available. Some have been constructed, however, and have been drawn upon in the following table, which compares the results based upon special groups with those derived from national population vital statistics. There are great gaps in the table—gaps which present and future studies will help to fill. Nevertheless, the table gives some indication of the kind of change in the level of mortality which may have taken place in many western countries. The significance of changes of this magnitude is probably shown more sharply in terms of survivorship than of expectation of life at birth. Thus, with an expectation of life at birth of 20 years, less than 50 per cent of a cohort of live-born babies would reach their fifth birthday, and less than 40 per cent their twentieth birthday. With life expectancy at 40 years, the corresponding proportions would be around 72 and 66 per cent. Today, expectation of life at birth is at, or approaching, 70 years in many developed societies. At such a level, 95 or 96 per cent of a cohort of live-born babies would attain their fifth birthday and 94 or 95 per cent their twentieth birthday.

Expectation of life at birth (years) based on generation life tables. Period of birth

	1650	1700	1750	1800	1850	1870
I. Upper groups						
Peller Ruling Families	1600–99: M. 28 F. 34		1700–99: M. 36 F. 37	1800–49: M. 46 F. 48		
Hollingsworth Peerage	1650–74: M. 30 F. 33	1675–99: M. 33 F. 34 — 1700–24: M. 34 F. 36	1725–49: M. 39 F. 37 — 1750–74: M. 45 F. 46	1775–99: M. 47 F. 49 — 1800–24: M. 49 F. 52	1825–49: M. 52 F. 58	1850–74: M. 55 F. 63
Henry Bourgeoisie	1600–49: M. 30 F. 35	1650–99: M. 32 F. 39	1700–49: M. 40 F. 46	1750–99: M. 46 F. 50	1800–50: M. 52 F. 53	1850–99: M. 59 F. 67
II. Local populations						
Crulai		(1654–1732: MF. 23)				
Broek-in-Waterland (Struyck)			1675–1775: MF. 30			
III. National tables						
Sweden			1750: M. 33·5 F. 36·7	1780: M. 34·1 F. 41·8 — 1800: M. 37·2 F. 40·8 — 1820: M. 41·4 F. 45·3	1840: M. 44·3 F. 47·9	1860: M. 46·6 F. 49·5
France				1820: M. 39·4 F. 41·0	1840: M. 38·2 F. 41·3	1860: M. 40·4 F. 42·7
England and Wales					1840: M. 39·5 F. 42·7	1860: M. 42·8 F. 46·5
Netherlands					1840: M. 38·0 F. 39·9	1860: M. 40·1 F. 42·9

Sources: S. Peller: see ch. 5 in the present volume.
T. H. Hollingsworth, *The demography of the British peerage*, Supplement to *Population Studies*, Nov. 1964.
L. Henry, *Anciennes familles genevoises*, Paris, 1956.
E. Gautier and L. Henry, *La population de Crulai*, Paris, 1958.
N. Struyck: *Les œuvres de Nicolas Struyck* (trans. J. A. Vollgraf), Amsterdam, 1912.
National tables: (P. Delaporte), *Évolution de la mortalité en Europe depuis l'origine des statistiques de l'état civil*, Paris, 1941.
Note: For a number of localities in France, life tables have been constructed for the first few years of life and give an indication of levels and change in mortality. The results are summarized below.

Survivors at specified ages (years) of 1,000 live births (MF)

Age (Yrs.)	Auneuil, 1656-1735	Beauvais St. Laurent-des-Eaux, 1700-1750	Ile-de-France 1740-1802	Sotteville-lès-Rouen 1760-1790	Region around Paris 1740-49	1750-1789	Broek-in-Waterland 1654-1732 M.	F.
0	1,000	1,000	1,000	1,000	1,000	1,000	1,000	1,000
1	712	674	788	756	722	770	585	667
5	567	450	646	611	556	628	493	594
10	529	399	613	572	508	(585)	474	563
20	489	366	—	—	—	—	—	—

Sources: Beauvais: P. Goubert, *Beauvais et le Beauvaisis de 1600 à 1730*, Paris, 1960, pp. 39-40. (See also the supplementary volume of graphs, nos. 45 and 46 for Auneuil and Mouy suggest a rise in survivorship to age 20 in the late eighteenth century.)
Ile-de-France: J. Ganiage, *Trois villages de l'Ile-de-France au XVIIIe siècle*, Paris, 1963, p. 106.
Sotteville-lès-Rouen: P. Girard, Aperçus de la démographie de Sotteville-lès-Rouen vers la fin du XVIIIe siècle, *Population*, July-Sept., 1959, p. 498.
Region around Paris: L. Henry and C. Lévy, Quelques données sur la région autour de Paris au XVIIIe siècle, *Population*, April-June, 1962, p. 310.

2

POPULATION, ECONOMY AND SOCIETY

D. E. C. EVERSLEY

I. *The new economic history*

THE object of this second introductory chapter is to show the relationship of the work on historical demography contained in this volume to some of the principal questions which concern the modern economic and social historian. If we take Chevalier's paper as the starting point of the wave of research which gave rise to the present collection, we find that the historian's interest in the role of population has been steadily increasing during the last few years. If we add the studies published since the choice of contributions to this volume was made, and the still unpublished ones to which many of our contributors refer, we notice that the greater part of the body of knowledge now accumulated originated in the last ten years. As has been stated at the beginning of the first introduction, we must regard the present state of research as marking the beginning of a new field of knowledge, and much of what is presented here as altogether provisional. But this wave of interest needs explaining in terms of the general development of historical research.

Until fairly recently, historians of industry and trade described economic change largely in terms of three main lines of development: technical innovation, the institutional framework, and economic policy. The Industrial Revolution, in these categories, appears as a succession of machines and engines, the story of particular firms, and the transition from mercantilism to *laissez-faire*. The greatest of the historians of that period were well aware of the significance of the mentality of the entrepreneur as an agent of change, and most of them provided descriptions of the workers, their industrial relations and their living standards. But apart from a sideways glance at the Malthusian dilemma, the individual, either as an agent of change, or in the mass, as producer and consumer, played little part in the account of industrial, commercial or agrarian revolutions.

In recent years, the application of economic analysis has begun to throw some doubts on the accepted versions. A number of questions were asked which the orthodox accounts could not answer, or, if they appeared to supply explanations, quantitative studies showed these to be wrong. Population began to be seen as an integral part of the fabric of change. At a transitional point references to the constant 'interaction' between population and economy hinted that the causal chain might be complex. The difficulties which stood in the way of any exact definition of this system of interaction lay partly in the lack of precise data, partly in the fact that available evidence both on population and economic growth tended to be in the form of national or very large regional aggregates. Yet in the nature of the economy, the links between people and industry would tend to be at a local or more narrowly regional level, and the actual process by which population grows or declines is measured in terms of the life and death of the individual. National movements are the aggregates derived from these individual movements, but because they are averages of local experience, they may tend to hide the nature of the mechanism of change. A national stationary population may conceal a wide range of growth and decline rates, and overall growth may be composed of quite different local phenomena—one place may show merely very moderate natural increases due to the disappearance of a certain disease, whereas others may be multiplying due to a combination of controlled mortality and rapidly increasing nuptiality and fertility.

Research into the process of population change is therefore based upon an investigation into the lives of individuals. This is in accord with tendencies in other fields of historical work. In entrepreneurial history, case studies are supplanting generalizations about innovation and investment. The sterility of general debates concerning the standard of living of industrializing populations is compelling historians to work out examples of wage, price and consumption structures in particular local contexts.

The individual firm or manor, the family or the bank, are used to test the validity of the general hypothesis, and the accumulation of life experiences constantly modifies previous assumptions. Man as a producer determines the availability of labour—numbers, education, expectation of life, and household composition need to be investigated to answer questions about wage levels, costs, and the rate of replacement of variable by fixed capital. Conversely, man as a consumer determines the size and structure of the market—this in turn involves questions of the elasticity of food supplies and other determinants of real wages, collective organization and bargaining power, as well as tastes, fashions, traditions and the effect on purchasing power of privately or publicly organized transfers of income. To put this matter in another way, one may group the explanations for fluctuating birth, death and marriage rates, and for migration, in terms of a series of economic phenomena. Roughly speaking, marriage habits are controlled by economic organization and social structure, and are sensitive to changing employment opportunities. Fertility within marriage varies, involuntarily, with the health of the parents, and voluntarily, with their standard of living—in some cases directly, in others inversely. Mortality depends, to a large extent, on nutrition and on environmental factors which are closely associated with the economic system and the real wages it produces. Migration is the result of political and religious pressures in earlier times, but, in the nineteenth century, bears a much closer relationship to the relative strengths of different regional, national and continental economies.

It is thus not surprising that some writers claim that population may well be treated as the central theme in economic history[1] in the established sense. In recent years, a new kind of social history has begun to make its appearance, which concerns itself less with the domestic manners of the middle classes or their sports and pastimes, but tries to trace the development of social structure and popular culture. In this field, almost by definition, demographic history

[1] Habakkuk, p. 146.

occupies an equally central position. But if we allow the subject such a significant place in historiography, it also follows that the presentation of data on population changes cannot be undertaken in isolation. Historical demography in the modern sense involves the juxtaposition of information of related materials in a variety of fields amenable to quantitative analysis. (We are not excluding the possibility of using descriptive material—but it has serious limitations in a discipline in which rigorous statistical methods alone seem to yield results.[2]) The provision of reliable series of figures, and their subsequent analysis, in the field of prices and wages, harvests, production figures, metereological information and of a chronology of war, famines and epidemics, are all indispensable counterparts to vital statistics. This new approach to economic history is closely linked with the principal tasks now confronting the historians both of highly developed societies and of those still in the process of development: to analyse and explain the process of economic growth. It is a truism to say that growth is organic—that it cannot be explained in terms of a single chain of physical events, but has to be set in the whole context of the environment in which it takes place. The process of industrialization is perhaps the most complex. It can no longer be described in terms of technological change and factory organization, since it involves changes in the mode of life of almost the entire population—it gives rise to a new social structure of incomes, status groups and family relationships. It is closely connected with a new educational system, and seldom leaves religious organization untouched. Alongside the growth of industrial production, we need to describe changes in agriculture and food supplies, in communications, in financial and commercial institutions, and in the system of government. In short, industrial change in historical perspective is to be written in terms of the history of a whole people. For this reason, the historian addresses questions to the demographer which go far beyond a simple curiosity about numbers. At each point of development he wants to know: How many were there, and where did they live? How were their households organized? At what age did they marry, how many children did they have, what was their expectation of life? What was the proportion of children and of old people, and how many mothers worked? How frequently did they move, and over what distance? How easily did they change their occupations, what was the degree of social mobility? How far do these measurements differ between town and country, between industrial and food-producing villages, between different occupations and social classes, between people of various religious persuasions and degrees of education? He will want to know something about the standard of living of these people at various times and in different places, what food they consumed, and how much of it, and how much they could buy of manufactured goods. What were their principal diseases, the causes of death and, perhaps even more important, disability? What was the length of their effective working life? What connection can be traced between new building materials, textiles, chemicals and hardwares on one hand, and, on the other, public health, and expectation of life? What contribution did medical and scientific advances (some of them related to industrial technology), make to health and survival?

[2] Glass, p. 239, n.

If we examine these topics in detail we find that only too often, in the absence of quantitative information, they are dealt with by presenting mere collections of impressions from literary sources, supported by statistical evidence consisting of isolated and sometimes irrelevant single occurrences of quantities or prices. (The disputes regarding the standard of living of the working population in the period of the Industrial Revolution are a good case in point.) Another famous controversy concerns the effect of the enclosure movement on rural population—a subject debated in the days of Bishop Latimer in the first great period of enclosures, and a constant topic for pamphleteers, statesmen and economists from Arthur Young to Sir Edward Gonner or more recent writers like Tate. Yet the only answer can come from an actual examination of the population size and structure of parishes at various stages of common field and enclosed farming over a number of generations.

Even such questions as that concerning the date of the beginning of the Industrial Revolution, or the 'take-off' into self-sustained development, may at least in part be answered by measuring the rates of change in occupational structure and the emergence of population growth centres, rather than in aggregate production or trade figures.

Although many historians will agree that all these data would be desirable in order to lend body to their general observations, they would probably say that since the material is not available, there is no point in making the demand. Yet as the contributions to this volume show, a great deal has been learnt in half a generation of work on surviving documents, and the findings of the demographers have just begun to affect the writing of industrial and social history. It is clear, however, that the bulk of the material lies untouched. Without doubt, the parish registers of most European countries provide the largest single body of material. But there is a wealth of other evidence in censuses and lists of various kinds. Where, as in England, even comparatively humble folk made wills and had the inventories of their estates recorded, we can learn a great deal about their social class and income, their standard of physical comfort and their system of family relationships. Apart from this wealth of documents, there is also archaeological evidence to be uncovered, especially in the case of towns and villages now abandoned, which have attracted the attentions of a new kind of archaeologist in several countries. The analysis of the cultivated area together with evidence about crop yields may supply answers to questions about nutrition. A scrutiny of names in the parish and other records may yield information about internal migration, as may anthropological investigations. In Sweden, very detailed work has been done on skeletons from extensive medieval burial grounds, and much may be deduced from pictorial representations, surviving garments and furniture, as well as present-day populations, and their linguistic and physical characteristics.

II. *The regional framework of research*

At the outset, we underline the self-imposed limitations of this volume of essays by saying that we are not here dealing with the evolution of population in history as a whole, but mostly with the relationship between population and economic change in the last 300 years. For many countries, this means explaining the 'new surge of people'[3] which makes its appearance in every country here surveyed at some time in the eighteenth century, gathers momentum in some areas in the nineteenth but slackens in France, and finally slows down at various points of time round about 1900. This movement is common to the most advanced industrialized areas and some rather backward agricultural countries. It shows no unambiguous pattern of causes and effects. We need to explain why it occurred, but perhaps equally why it was comparatively moderate in most areas. English growth rates may appear high, but they are low compared with American examples and we need to ask ourselves not only why growth took place but why, in the absence of visible obstacles, it was no faster.[4] It is clear at the outset that 'industrialization' as such is no answer. Finland's population doubled between 1750 and 1800, and if one takes 1721 and 1800 as the limits, its rate of growth was even larger than that observed in England at the time. Yet nothing like an industrial revolution occurred.

Terms such as 'Finland' or 'England' have little meaning except as political entities until the recent periods of fast long-distance communications, and even then the differences of soil, climate and natural resources in various parts of these politically identifiable countries are such as to suggest that we should search for a regional framework. We are familiar, in our own day, with the difficulties of defining what a region is, for instance for town and country planning purposes, even given modern statistical apparatus. The regional studies in this volume illustrate these difficulties, but at the same time we must remember that the sparser settlement of population in Western Europe during most of the period under review meant that there existed more clearly definable and to some extent isolated regions with their own distinctive patterns of economic and social structure. Mountains, rivers, and areas of low soil fertility created regions within which at any rate a very large proportion of movements of population could be traced in a pattern of complementarity, though they might have foreign trade, as it were, with other regions. The task of defining such regions in terms of their functions falls on the historical geographers, and it is to them that we owe some striking parallels between the characteristics of regions in different countries. Such comparisons arise, typically, between areas on opposite shores of sea spaces, as for instance between Normandy and Exeter.[5] But parallelism is merely an aid to identification. What is necessary is a rigorous set of definitions of what constitutes a region. One obvious division is according to basic soil-types and the associated economic activity, and we have an example of this in the Flemish study.[6] Equally the pattern of communications may determine fairly clearly what is meant by an economic region, with the associated determinants of natural obstacles. We find good examples in valley economies (e.g. Chambers' 'Vale of Trent', though this has by no means formidable barriers against the outside world). It would be a mistake, however, to confine regional definitions to such simple geomorphological criteria. In a recent study of the Austrasian coalfield, E. A. Wrigley has described the similarities and dissimilarities of a general economic region spanning a number

[3] Chambers, p. 324. [4] Potter, p. 631.
[5] Mauvret p. 578. [6] Deprez, p. 608f.

of political and religious divisions in northwestern Europe.[7] It is clear from this study that the underlying coal measures and their accessibility do not by themselves determine the speed or pattern of population and economic development. The system of ownership and administration, governmental policies and religious attitudes, all play their part in shaping the societies involved. We may therefore have to define regions in these administrative or social terms, or even in an old developed country like England, in terms of a previous economy. Thus one could group the villages named by Glass[8] by such considerations as the time of their enclosure, or even the method of enclosure, by reference to their dependence on the woollen industry, or by the customs of the moorland district. It is not so important that in each case similar criteria should be employed to determine the regional framework, but that the choices should be logical in terms of the actual situation encountered and that they should, empirically, bring into relief the factors involved in the changes to be described.

III. *The problem of periodization*

The second major problem of choice which faces us concerns the periods of investigation. We commonly use the term 'century' as if it had some normative meaning but this is clearly not the case. In some sense we are victims of our own national prejudices when we speak, quite loosely, of eighteenth-century England or seventeenth-century Holland. Again, notable reigns are sometimes used in this way, as in the phrases 'The France of Louis XIV', or 'The Victorian Era'. Economy and society can scarcely be measured in such terms. If we think of the 'Reign of Elizabeth' as connoting a time of economic expansion, we do not mean this to be due to some special virtue attached to the life of a particular sovereign. Though centuries tend to be internationally recognized for the purposes of periodization, reigns are not. The question is: what measure of time should be substituted? We are all familiar with terms such as 'feudal', 'manorial', or the 'mercantilist' or 'high capitalist' eras, the Age of Enlightenment, or of *Laissez-Faire*. These terms are, for chronological purposes, as imprecise as the concepts behind them. Similarly, though we can clearly describe a pre-industrial society, thanks to hindsight, it is hard to distinguish it from a non-industrial one.

These difficulties, which in a sense are peculiar to the kind of historian who deliberately ignores political events most of the time, can only be overcome by the same type of empiricism which we have had to employ in the case of our regional divisions. That is to say, we have to ask ourselves the purpose of our chronological divisions. For mere convenience of counting, years provide the basic unit, just as the parish does geographically. But the year has no meaning by itself. If we add the records of years in a series, we come, sooner or later, to natural limits backward in the shape of the failure of records to survive, and forward either to our own day or, more usually, to a natural break dictated by the discontinuity of records when parochial registration or partial or fiscal census-taking gives way to modern civil registration and statistically sophisti-

---

[7] E. A. Wrigley, *Industrial Growth and Population Change*, Cambridge, 1961.
[8] Glass, p. 177.

cated censuses. Even with these natural limits we may obtain, as in Scandinavia, apparently continuous records of strictly comparable material over a period of 200 years or more. Within such long periods, the selection and periodization then depends very largely on an *ex post facto* study of clearly discernible trends. Thus, for France, we divide the 'eighteenth' from the 'nineteenth' century not so much or solely by the Revolution and the wars which followed it, but by the break in the development of the population growth rates. The break which seems to have occurred in England in about 1740, and which can also be observed elsewhere, is the result of a large number of factors none of which respond to the attempt to define them in terms of decades, reigns, trade cycles or wars. If we call this period the 'upswing accompanying increasing industrialization', we create a category which may be used in other countries without prejudging the causal issue. Similarly many of our contributors draw attention to the phenomena of the declining fertility observed in advanced stages of industrialization (Potter, Bourgeois-Pichat, Koellmann, Cipolla), and thus create a clear case for a type of periodization, without, however, compelling us to adopt any one period of world history for this purpose. It is of course broadly true that similar stages of evolution occur at any rate within the European area studied here, in the course of the same half-century, and there is therefore a point of some significance in the suggestion[9] that future research should concentrate on a number of short periods (comprising the life-experience of about two generations each) which appear to exhibit similar phenomena in several countries. These key periods, though primarily chosen for the state of economic activity, will no doubt exhibit social structures appropriate to the state of economic organization, and may thus be defined in their demographic characteristics with direct reference to the total environment. If we find, as Marx stated, that each economic system has its own 'laws' of population movement, this can only be so because economic changes must have provoked changes in the state of law (relating to property and agricultural tenure in particular) and in the social structure (class mobility, patterns of marriage, income distribution) which can directly affect the movement of births, marriages and deaths.

In addition to this periodization in economic terms, there is however a case for the study of different societies at the same moment of time in the strict sense. A bad winter (such as 1709-10), a war of continental proportions, and especially the great epidemics such as the last important European plagues and, in the nineteenth century, the Cholera, require a series of comparative local or regional studies in depth within quite short spans of time. Such moments may sometimes be crucial as they may, by accident or precisely because of their effects on demographic structure or the economy, also emerge as turning points in long-term economic movements.

In some works, decennial or quinquennial periods begin with the year zero (1700-9, 1710-19, 1700-4, 1705-9, etc.), elsewhere and perhaps more usually with the first complete year of the decade or century proper (1701-10, 1711-20 and so on). The definitions of years themselves leave much to be desired. Apart from the complication of the Gregorian calendar and the consequent

[9] Deprez, p. 629.

shifts in what constitutes the beginning of a new year, we find that the division of events into calendar years is often unsatisfactory and other notions are used such as the harvest year (which runs from the appearance of the first new crop on the market to the gathering of the next harvest). But since the harvest takes place in different countries at different times, and since inclement seasons sometimes prolong the period of dearth before new supplies are available, the harvest year may in itself give rise to severe difficulties, being fixed neither in its actual length, nor its turn, so that if a notional beginning is adopted, it may do violence to the very facts the device is supposed to highlight. There is clearly a strong need for a new set of conventions on the time measurements and divisions employed in this field.

IV. *Some problems of measurement*

One of the special difficulties in the field of historical demography lies in the fact that so many of the series we investigate exhibit a cyclical character. This is in part a built-in, statistical phenomenon, in part it is due to certain biological facts connected with food supplies and living room, partly it is due to psychological reactions to over- and underpopulation, and partly it is so because the economy to which population is linked also undergoes a process of cyclical change. We are familiar with the trade cycle which has its visible origins in the eighteenth century[10] and becomes a dominant factor in the nineteenth. Sometimes this is connected with harvest cycles which may themselves be dependent on the cyclical behaviour of climatic determinants.[11] Both in demographic and in economic development, we encounter long cycles and shorter cycles. These concepts are related to types of causes. Fundamental changes in economic opportunity could produce changes in marriage patterns which would work themselves out in a wave-like movement (of diminishing intensity) over a period of several generations.[12] Something of this kind may be observed in England in periods grouped roughly around the years 1730, 1760, and 1790.[13] The propagation of the wave depends, of course, on births associated with a marriage peak, on the survival of this 'bulge' generation to nubile age, and on conditions prevailing when this age is reached. By definition, the minimum period between the crests of these wave movements is the generation interval of 25-30 years, under European conditions.

Both biologically and economically, it is likely that a 'well-stocked generation'[14] should be succeeded by a less numerous one, but there is no certainty of this and it is not possible to construct 'laws' to explain the length and intensity of these movements however frequently we may observe them in practice. The original impetus (assuming that we can trace such a point) may be closely connected with a clearly definable stage of an economic cycle, e.g. in capital investment. If a peak of fresh investment produces an increase in employment and a rise in real incomes it is likely to effect nuptiality and fertility. We know that such surges tend to be followed by troughs for a

[10] T. S. Ashton, *Economic Fluctuations in England 1700-1800*, Oxford, 1959.
[11] Cf. G. Haberler, *Prosperity and Depression*, 1946, ch. 7, p. 151, Theories of periodic harvest variation.
[12] Marshall, p. 259.   [13] Eversley, p. 405-6.   [14] Goubert, p. 471.

number of reasons. These cycles of investment are medium rather than long —of the order of 7 or 15 years rather than 30 or 50 and in any case there is no reason why their periodicity should coincide with the population cycle. It is clear that if an upswing in economic activity coincides with the recurrence of a marriage cycle, the effects on population growth would be quite different from those which would result from the advent of an investment boom in the trough of the population cycle.

Similar considerations apply to short cyclical movements. If we term those periods 'long' in which all the variables in the economic or demographic situation may be changed, we apply the epithet 'short' to those in which most of the facts in the situation are necessarily fixed (e.g. potential labour force or capital equipment), and where the variations in mortality or output are due to transient phenomena subject to immediate change. Such short cycles in demographic behaviour may be due to crises of the kind associated with violent epidemics and disastrous winters, with wars and revolutions.[15] The description of the disturbance created by such periods of crisis is of the greatest importance for the understanding of population behaviour. Unfortunately, the contemporary interest in the events of calamitous epochs was not sufficiently scientific to record the vital statistics of years preceding and following the catastrophe[16] and it is often difficult to reconstruct what happened.

These short-term demographic cycles have their counterparts in economic activity, and as with long cycles, they may or may not be interlinked. Thus, a harvest failure will produce increased mortality (directly, or through reduced resistance to epidemics), possibly lowered effective fertility, and postponement of marriages. But it may also, through a reduction of purchasing power, produce an industrial crisis, and therefore set in motion a reversal of medium-term trends in employment and investment. Conversely, a good harvest could produce its greatest influence on nuptiality indirectly through increases in agricultural profits, increased purchasing power, and export trade.

That populations tend, 'other things being equal', to grow at a very rapid rate, at least for a short time, after having been decimated by war, disease or famine, has been observed since Suessmilch and Malthus. Leaving aside the strong possibility that the number of casualties was probably exaggerated in many cases, we are still astonished at the speed with which former levels of population are regained. This could be due to temporary lowering of the age of marriage, a higher proportion of people marrying, or to increased fertility within marriage. Now the extent of this response to a previous decimation will depend on a number of factors. Psychologically, postponement of marriage or births (in so far as this was voluntary) can play a role.[17] Biologically, the weeding-out of weak elements may mean an increase in effective birth rates in the reduced population. Economically, the death of male adults may produce vacancies in agricultural holdings or industrial establishments, and a general labour shortage may raise real wages rates. Similarly, a very bad harvest may be followed by a series of good crops, and these, offered to a reduced population, will lead to low grain prices and increased real wages, with effects both on nuptiality and increased fertility.

[15] Jutikkala, p. 557.   [16] Meuvret, p. 509.   [17] Habakkuk, p. 272.

V. *Defects in source material*

One great obstacle to the more precise methods of investigating the populations of the past lies in the scarcity and unreliability of the source material. The difficulties are clearly threefold: where the records are in some way complete, as in the case of limited aristocracies or small village communities, they may not tell us much that is generally useful. Secondly, current registration methods and census returns may be both general and continuous, but lack essential information required, for instance, for full reconstitution. Ages at marriage are not given in most parish records and we can only calculate them if we know where the bride and bridegroom were born, but since this is not stated in the marriage record, and since even in the seventeenth century population was highly mobile, a large number of births are lost from view. Thirdly, in all areas, even continuous and full records are subject to imperfections due to careless incumbents, losses in war, religious dissensions and schisms and civil disturbances. There are a number of examples in this volume of quotations from nation-wide or partial census inquiries, some of them relating to the seventeenth century, which are not accompanied by any estimate of reliability or indeed information as to how the census was taken, for what purpose, and what questions it asked. The word is often lightly applied to rather casual inquiries on the part of ecclesiastical or civil authorities which did not aim to discover the total size or detailed composition of the population, but merely those who were available for military service, the communicants, or the taxable part of the community. Even if some general demographic aim was involved, the methods of execution might vary a good deal.[18] We find, both in the Low Countries and in Scandinavia and in certain parts of Germany, repeated attempts to count those eligible to take Holy Communion as a prelude to stricter enforcement of church-going, as a means of assessing the needs of local churches and schools, or of gauging the extent of non-conformity. Since it is quite usual to attempt to derive the total population from, for instance, the figures for male communicants or those over 18, there is clearly scope for some standardization of the conversion factors employed.

The same consideration applies even more strongly to a type of census encountered at one time or another in many parts of Europe—the hearth tax. Although the conditions of this tax differed, as to liability, exemptions, the level of impost, and administration, we have it as a common feature that the surviving lists give a clue to the number of households in each locality, and most writers have assumed that each entry corresponds to a family. Leaving aside the question of whether this is always true, we then find that the number of households is converted into total populations. The conversion factors range from as low as four to as high as seven or eight persons per set of hearths. Sometimes, very considerable evidence as to the actual composition of households at specific moments of time exists,[19] but in other examples the basis of conversion is meagre. The chief criticism of the method is that in almost every case we have an enumeration of households over a long period of years (that in England is exceptional in extending over less than a generation), whereas

---

[18] Potter, p. 646-7.   [19] Glass, p. 167ff.

the sample of households tends to be taken at a specific moment of time. This means that the argument is in danger of assuming a circular form. If we are trying to guess at the size and composition of the total population at two dates, and if between these dates the population grew through decreased mortality and increased marital fertility, this might not show at all in the number of hearths—each household might be larger. This is in fact unlikely, since some of the survivors would still be in, or create, separate households, but since the supply of houses might be highly inelastic in the short run or even over a period of half a century (owing to shortage of materials, or urban regulation), the increase in population might well be masked.

Poll-tax and militia lists were likely to be incomplete simply because of the strong incentive to evade listing, and communicant lists will depend for their completeness on the state of the authority of the church—if they were compiled to enforce attendance, or at a time of weakening sentiment for the official religion, they might well be least complete precisely at a time when great population changes took place, on the assumption that economic growth or decline, wars or rebellion tend to affect both the numbers of people and their religious affiliations. The end of the parish registers as a useful source of demographic information in England connected with the rise of non-conformity and urbanization, coincides with the start of the greatest period of economic growth and, probably, of fastest population growth, and this collapse is followed by the taking of the first census and an increasing demand for less inadequate registration.

There is a wealth of still untapped census-type information in Europe (especially in the former German states), and if this is to be made accessible, rules for exploitation will need to be drawn up. It is not enough to quote a writer of 1820 for his opinion that half the population is always under 20, and half above that age, as a basis for converting an estimate of adult population in 1760 into total population, if during the intervening 60 years there is a presumption that mortality or fertility has changed, especially if the figures thus calculated are to serve as a basis for computing birth and death rates. Yet this has been done. Clearly, a town like Liverpool which in the 1830's had an expectation of life at birth of 26 years cannot have conformed to this pattern.

The existence of isolated sets of reports, or defective registration series, brings us to the question of methods to allow for imperfections, corrections to make deficient series comparable, and the extent of information which may be derived from poor records. We find, for instance, that compilers of statistics from parish registers are faced with a whole year, or series of years, in a sizeable village where no marriages were recorded, and there is a temptation to assume that there was a failure to enter events, and to interpolate accordingly. Yet in years of disaster—harvest failure, epidemics, large-scale migration—it is quite possible that no marriages took place—at least the detailed accounts from some of the large French parishes suggest a reduction in such years, which could easily, in a smaller parish, bring us near the zero level. We must take into account the fact that such catastrophic factors would be likely to be felt still more strongly in a small place and that an accidental imbalance of the sexes in a given age-group allied to temporarily increased immobility, might easily produce the result in question.

The arbitrary character of some of the corrections employed should not, however, deter us from attempting to make use of fragmentary material. We may receive the impression, under the influence of the statistically completely satisfactory reconstitutions perfected in France, that nothing less is worth undertaking. But this is not so. If it were, we should have to give up any notion of ever investigating the highly mobile types of community which we find in seventeenth- and eighteenth-century England, in America, in parts of Scandinavia, the Low Countries, and capital city and port regions everywhere. It takes no more than a 5 per cent annual 'turnover' of population to open the possibility of an entire set of families 'disappearing' within a generation (though in actual practice it is far more likely that some of the population would have a large amount of stability and others a greater than average mobility). Under such circumstances, the chances of reconstituting the life and death experience of cohorts would be slim unless we were able to cover a whole area or region. Nevertheless, registers for such communities can, and do, show very striking fluctuations in the number of events recorded, and even where no ages attach to births or marriages or deaths, we may gain useful information from them in conjunction with economic records. We need to realize that in the primitive demographic régimes with which we are dealing so often in the pre-statistical period, the effects of outside influences on population tend to be of such a magnitude as to transcend mere deficiencies in registration, or peculiarities of age structure.

In a number of industrializing countries, we are faced with the possibility that urbanization led to under-registration especially of births (baptisms). If, in such cases, we observe an apparent rise in fertility despite the tendency to omit registration, the presumption of a secular change becomes all the stronger. In this case we are dealing with a change in long-term trends of two kinds: those of registration, and those of real events. Registration changes in two different styles: either by administrative action, or by custom. Where central legislation or efficient ecclesiastical jurisdiction enforces record-keeping, the change tends to be abrupt and to produce no comparable series, so that long term population trends have to be viewed in discrete compartments (as in England before and after 1837). Where registration changes as a matter of habit (usually in the direction of greater laxity), it is possible for the process to extend over similar periods as economic changes, or even longer epochs. Such a change may somewhat alter the angles of our population trend lines or curves for vital events, but would hardly falsify the general direction, or mask a break of a substantial nature, such as that occurring in Ireland after 1846, or in French fertility after 1780. Moreover, whilst changes in age and sex structure may mask the changes in trend in the short run, they cannot do so over a period of a generation. A very high birth-rate in a quinquennium may be due to the existence of a 'bulge' of marriageable persons at its beginning, but this will be compensated by a corresponding short-fall of marriages and subsequent births in the next quinquennium, so that over 25 years average fertility will not be distorted. Therefore even if we know nothing about age structure, and a given population produces different birth-rates in two generations, we are entitled to assume that social and economic conditions were different in the two periods. Long-term imbalances of sexes are of course possible where there is prolonged warfare or emigration, but the latter cause of unbalance is in itself a reflection of economic changes, so that we cannot speak of a reduction of fertility being due to a 'purely' statistical phenomenon—there will be a direct and an indirect link with economic conditions. Only where large-scale male immigration due to favourable conditions causes an apparent fall in the crude birth-rate would we have a divergence of movement.

VI. *The ecology of population change*

We now turn from the question of organization of research and the source material to the systematic analysis of the factors of population change in their relation to economic environment. This analysis may be carried out in various ways: by type of event or change (war, crisis, epidemic, change in real incomes); by type of environment or social structure; or by group characteristics (which may themselves be partially determined by the two other types of factors). In this way we may establish certain categories of responses and interaction mechanisms. For instance, we may produce an analysis of actual 'unemployment': increased mortality, postponed marriages, reduced marital fertility through increased practice of birth control and abortions, and then the reverse effect of falling demand, in the well-known accelerating movement towards the bottom of the cyclical trough. Alternatively, we may analyse population in a primitive agricultural society in the tropics, or under feudalism, showing its responses to the stimuli appropriate to the type of society whether they are climatic, political, or customary. Lastly, we may choose religious or other minority groups, like the English dissenters, as the universe to be investigated. We take into account, in this case, the totality of the conditions of life in which they find themselves. We see, for instance,[20] how their records reflect their social and political conditions; we become aware of their economic peculiarities[21] which are at once a cause of their cohesion and the result of their isolation. If Quakers lived longer than others in their social class, it may have been because they shunned towns with their corporate restrictions, because they were abstemious, because the practice of medicine was one of the few professions open to them, and because the persecution which they had suffered caused them to institute an efficient system for the relief of suffering amongst themselves. Good health, abstinence, honesty and an adequate system of education helped non-conformists to advance in industry and trade and may in turn have caused them to increase their numbers relative to other groups. Jews, again disadvantaged in social and economic matters, forced to reside in an unhealthy urban environment, may yet, thanks to their medical skill, hygienic regulations and family structure show favourable demographic experience, and their marriage customs in turn may have helped the growth of their wealth and influence.

What is true of such clearly identifiable religious minorities is probably also

[20] Glass, p. 236.   [21] Krause, p. 382.

true of less precisely definable sub-groups, such as skilled workers, agricultural labourers or fishermen.[22] In a sense, it does not matter very much which of these approaches to the study of interaction we adopt. The main requirement is that the demographer and the economic historian should describe the *context* of the process of interaction in as complete a manner as possible, so as to facilitate the comparison of groups, areas and epochs.

For any given group of human beings, the circumstances which we call 'economic' are clearly the most important. In this context, climate, soil morphology, flora and fauna, and natural resources of all kinds may be subsumed under the economic heading since all these factors affect the possibilities of economic activity, usually by way of outer limits to the chances of development in a given state of technology. Changes in economic organization or opportunity impress themselves on the demographic pattern through two sets of mechanisms: voluntary and involuntary. The latter mainly affect mortality, but may also cause variations in fertility. We may term these the main constituents of the original Malthusian system: they perform the adjustment of population to available subsistence. The voluntary mechanisms are those which increase or decrease nuptiality according to the prospects of gaining a livelihood (again in the Malthusian system), or adjust the level of births (in the neo-Malthusian manner). Migration also comes under this heading of voluntary reactions. In general it is probably true to say that the involuntary changes are by far the most important in the earlier periods investigated in this volume—the typical phenomenon here is the famine with its associated epidemics and the recovery from this setback in the next period of comparative prosperity. In the later period, the voluntary adjustment typified by birth control or postponed marriage, is more noticeable.

Conversely, we describe the effects of changes in population on the economic system. Here we understand the term in a narrower sense—that is to say, changes in the numbers or composition of the population have no effect on most of the basic determinants of the economic situation, only the immediate level or characteristics of activity. In this connection, man is seen alternatively as the producer, determining the possibility of industrial or agrarian production and exerting pressure on the provision of labour-saving capital equipment, or else as the consumer, able to determine the profitability of production for the market according to his ability to purchase food or consumer goods. When we begin to consider the interrelatedness of food supplies and their effect on survival and procreation on one hand and the inability of a starving population to spend money on consumer goods on the other, we realize that we are here faced with one of the fundamental relationships between population and economy. A parallel network may be traced when we consider the efficiency of agricultural production, the ability of the rural sector both to supply food to urban populations and to release surplus agricultural labour in the process, and the supply of capital originating from the profits of commercial food-growing. In such a network we may observe most of the vicissitudes of the nascent industrial states, and into these we may also fit most

[22] Cf. M. Drake, unpubl. Ph.D. thesis, Cambridge, 1964, on regional patterns of marriage in Norway.

of the changes in demographic data in the eighteenth and nineteenth century.

Although some writers would claim that all environmental determinants of social structure and change are economic (in so far as they are not purely physical), it will be convenient to distinguish some other categories which may have to be considered. There is for example, a political framework which obtrudes itself just as soon as we consider the counting of population from the institutional point of view. Given the purposes of census-taking (starting with Herod), we know that governments were seldom interested in the numbers of the people for purely scientific reasons.[23] This both affects the reliability of the census, and concentrates our attention on the pro- and anti-natalist policies of history. It may be doubted how effective they were, in many cases, but there can hardly be much dispute about them in modern times, as in France or Japan, to cite one example of each policy. The encouragement of procreation in cameralist times, or the repression of marriage in the German states influenced by Malthusian thinking,[24] are both sufficiently detailed in their intention and regulations to require consideration at least at the marginal level, whether they affected the actions of men and women directly, or merely influenced the climate of opinion sufficiently to tip the scales of voluntary decisions one way or another.

The laws relating to the holding and transmission of property,[25] the rules of partible inheritance and primogeniture, such as those which virtually postponed the marriage of a son until the death of a tenant or owner father, often in intention akin to the forced settlement of empty lands and frontier areas, fall into the same political framework, as do the rules relating to the privileges of urban corporations which admittedly were in existence originally to ensure economic prosperity but came to be the instrument of small oligarchies seeking to preserve their power at all costs, even that of their well-being. The creation or upholding of rights for privileged minorities of all kinds, the hierarchical systems of civil or ecclesiastical aristocracies, rules restricting the freedom of the individual to move, change his work or to marry—all these have their effects on population. At the same time population changes tend to affect these parts of the political framework. Rapid growth, or failure to grow, migration and urbanization, are parts of the shifts of political power, even before the days of wide franchises, and help to bring old rules and conventions into desuetude, or persuade governments to frame new codes. So, too, the rules and customs of religious faiths are intimately connected both with population changes and economic activity. Although few would now agree that the Catholic church encouraged fertility and throttled enterprise, or that Protestantism encouraged limitation of fertility but promoted thrift and new ventures, prevailing religious attitudes clearly had their effects on marginal decisions.

No one would question the truism that life and death are subject to the rules which biology applies to all living matter. Yet surprisingly enough most historians and many demographers seem to ignore the possibilities of genetic variation, in contrast to some professional geneticists who would like to explain

---

[23] Connell, p. 424.   [24] D. V. Glass, ed., *Introduction to Malthus*, 1953, p. 39 ff.
[25] Habakkuk, p. 275.

the growth of population, changes in mortality and fertility, as well as qualitative changes, very largely in terms of a process of selection. Some feel they
can explain social change itself by these means. We need not go to such lengths.
Nor need we give any further thought to the possibility that changes of the
magnitudes that some European populations experienced between 1750 and
1850, often in the space of a single generation, in the direction of decreasing
mortality and increased fertility, or, at a later state, in the direction of decreasing
fertility, could possibly be the result of genetic change. The experiments which
may be made with species which breed in a matter of days or weeks are unlikely to have much application to the human population with a generation
interval of 25 years. Galton's heiresses may demonstrate a clear connection
between an important economic phenomenon and hereditary peculiarities,
but similar processes are unlikely to have accounted for the size of mid-Victorian
English families or the comparative sterility of their French contemporaries.
Yet we know that miners tended to have large families, and that industrialization meant an increase in the proportion of miners in the population.[26] Growth
in the Ruhr area caused an influx of people from eastern parts of Germany
with altogether different patterns of life[27] and whilst we may postulate that
many of these were determined by mere social conventions or their previous
environment, we cannot altogether reject the possibility that different parts of
the population of Europe had inherently differing fertility and it is more than
likely that resistance to disease varied greatly on the basis of inherited characteristics as much as on a short-term nutritional basis. This possibility is strongest
where a population is undergoing fundamental changes in its circumstances of
life. We know of groups of people, especially in the developing countries, who,
with few exceptions, suffer from certain deficiency diseases. On the other hand
advanced nations are almost totally free from such afflictions. As a population
makes the transition from chronic want to general sufficiency, there will always
be some people at the margin of health and disease, and in this situation genetic
variations may be of great importance. In other words, when environmental
changes are occurring, the scope for genetic selection affecting growth rates
is much greater than normally, and inherited characteristics can influence the
situation much more rapidly than otherwise. The act of marriage in itself may
be taken, in the context of Western European history in the last 300 years, to
have been too deliberate and late in life to come into the category of biologically
conditioned events, and variations in the age of puberty, if they occurred and
were influenced by selection, will not have affected fertility. On the other hand
sterility or high fecundity, or anatomical characteristics favourable or unfavourable to successful child-birth, might well be inherited and encouraged or dis-
couraged by variations in the system of intermarriage. More generally, if
certain closed populations suffered from hereditary defects which were per-
petuated by inbreeding, then the general health of their offspring might well
have been improved substantially by intermarriage with healthier strains from
outside the closed system in a period of increased mobility. (Conversely it is
just conceivable that some dominant strain of an adverse characteristic might
spread through intermarriage into a larger population.) Immunity from some

[26] Habakkuk, p. 153.   [27] Koellmann, p. 601 ff.

diseases or resistance to them may certainly be a matter of inheritance. The mention of these possibilities is not to claim that they would influence the course of population change more strongly than observed habits resulting from agreed social conventions—such as conception as a condition of marriage, or prolonged lactation—but equally we cannot ignore them as factors in the 'surge' of population with which we began.

VII. *Marriage and population growth*

(i) *Age and frequency of marriage*

Of the three short-term regulators of population, marriage is the most sensitive to economic change, birth the second, and death the least. Marriage as a calculated act which takes into account present assets and future prospects was known in Greek and Roman times. Dowries and contracts regulated nuptiality not only amongst the rich but even in peasant societies. Marriage for love is held by some authorities to be an Anglo-Saxon invention of the nineteenth century, and the penniless, homeless match between young people, as a widespread phenomenon, is probably the product of full employment and social security in very recent times.

There are two possible ways in which marriage as such may regulate the rate of population growth: through the age at which it takes place, and through the extent of lifelong celibacy. The first of these factors is the subject of much dispute as to its effectiveness, and the extent of the second, where it has been proved, is so small as to cast doubts on its significance. We have evidence for France in the eighteenth century that the average number of marriages per woman was in fact 1·004, indicating that this maximum was very nearly reached since remarriages more than outweigh the numbers of those remaining spinsters.[28] Of these, 0·9 were first marriages, so that we have a large number of widows remarrying, and about 10 per cent remaining single. From the point of view of total fertility, one would assume that these figures could scarcely be bettered. Of those remaining single, some would bear illegitimate children and others might by physiologically or psychologically incapable of taking part in the reproductive process. We have little comparable evidence from other countries for the eighteenth century, but modern works suggest that the number of women who reach the end of the period of child-bearing unmarried did not change much over a long period of time and that an unbalance of sexes through war casualties is the main cause of the existence of large numbers of unmarried women.[29] There remains the possibility that there existed, in the seventeenth and early eighteenth century, a different pattern where spinsterhood was more common, and that the increases in population in the eighteenth century owe something to a rise in nuptiality.[29a] There would be a number of grounds for this assumption. First, as Hajnal shows, marriage at least in western Europe took place at what one must call, in view of the expectation of life at that time, an advanced age, showing that there was a

[28] Bourgeois-Pichat, p. 484; Henry, p. 453-4, see also Henry, *La Population de Crulai*, 1958, p. 74.
[29] United Nations, Population Studies No. 17, *Determinants and Consequences of Population Trends*, 1953, p. 73.
[29a] But see figures for Corfe Castle, ch. 1, p. 15 above, and discussion there.

great degree of deliberation about the act. This late marriage, given the differential mortality which affected adult males,[30] must have progressively reduced the chances of marriage in the late twenties. Secondly, as Ashton has shown,[31] the pattern of society before the age of industrialization militated against wide choices of spouses. He stressed the lack of social mobility implicit in hierarchical urban social structures, and it is likely that similar obstacles to marriages between persons of different degrees of rank or wealth existed in rural communities. Obstacles to mobility in the spatial sense must have been equally important. It is true that as far as England is concerned, the records show that even in the seventeenth century, despite Settlement and Poor Laws and the state of the roads, a large part of the population was mobile and marriages between partners at any rate within a 15 mile radius were frequent. But studies in other countries have proved that this state of affairs was by no means normal for Europe before the middle of the nineteenth century. In particular German work on *Heiratskreise* or marriage circles[32] shows the very limited area within which marriages were contracted even in the nineteenth century, and the acute obstacles to contact presented by rivers, moderate hill ranges, and forests. Given these hindrances, and the small size of the majority of settlements until very recently, the chances of finding marriage partners must have been lower than they are now. In a village of the Crulai type, with about 40 births annually early in the eighteenth century, and infant and child mortality at the prevailing level, the total number of those reaching marriageable age each year was not above 25, on the average, and with such small numbers it was unlikely that there would be an equal number of men and women, so that even if no social, economic or religious obstacles existed, it must have been very difficult to attain a total of 90 per cent of marriages for girls of the eligible age groups, without the chance of marrying outside the village. In fact, at Crulai it was found that early in the eighteenth century 30 per cent of the men and 55 per cent of the women came from outside the village. We should need to pursue such inquiries much further before investing this factor with a quantitative significance, but it cannot be ruled out.[33]

We are on very different ground when we come to the analysis of age at marriage. We know that the number of children per married couple is to some extent a function of the age at which the partners married, and more especially the age of the mother. Women bear children more frequently, in all societies, in the early twenties than in the late twenties, and so on, until child-birth becomes something of a rarity above the age of 40. Since the age at marriage is not an independent variable, we cannot say for certain how much it must be reduced to produce an extra child per union.

We now have to consider the evidence for any lowering in the age of marriage and the influence of economic conditions in this connection. Conventions in practice in this respect need not necessarily be connected with changes in economic circumstances, but may be merely a reflection of the expectation of life,[34] because in some societies, the man's marriage had to await

[30] Peller, p. 96.
[31] T. S. Ashton, *Economic History of England: The Eighteenth Century*, 1955, p. 5.
[32] E.g. by Professor I. Schwidetzky and Dr Schade in Mainz.
[33] Chambers, p. 329.   [34] Hajnal, p. 121.

succession to a paternal holding. This practice is well attested,[35] but it is also made clear by several authors that there were many exceptions to the rule, and that men married in their father's lifetime either because they could obtain paid employment, or because the father gave them a share or even possession of the land, sometimes in return for a life-rent.[36] The pure case of Leyzin must have been a great rarity.[37] In any case, here we are dealing with the husband's age, and the customs would not affect the wife except inasmuch, in general, we may infer that the younger the bridegroom, the younger the bride, since in most societies here studied brides were younger than grooms, though not by any constant margin, which may therefore simply have shrunk if the groom's age was reduced through changes in landholding.[38]

It is clear that as far as the European countries studied here are concerned, the average age at marriage does not appear to have changed significantly over the centuries. There have been fluctuations, and there are distinct differences in social groups, and various areas, but there is nothing like a general fall in the age recorded of the order required to produce the extra fertility postulated. Only in America do we meet clear evidence[39] that people generally married in their early twenties, and it is significant that European observers agreed that this was 'early'. But one would be reluctant to attribute American rates of increase to this sole cause. One would far rather say that there existed a number of circumstances favourable to marriage, birth, and survival (availability of land, mobility, and absence of trade restrictions), of which marriage at 21 or 22 is only one manifestation. The same statement is probably true of those areas and epochs in European history in which we may observe some slight temporary fall in marriage ages, as in some parts of Flanders. Higher birth-rates seem to accompany lower marriage ages, but we need not therefore assume that age was the cause. The converse is also true. In some areas, marriage ages rose for a time above the normal long-term average, and live births fell. But the fall may have been due to other causes—for instance, poor nutrition may have caused fewer conceptions or more miscarriages, or some form of birth control may have been practised. Some societies show consistently higher ages at marriage than the European average, and yet produce the same fertility, as was the case in Norway.[40]

It almost looks as if we are faced with something like a pattern of fertility appropriate for each society in its stage of social and economic development, and as if this pattern were produced by individual families having a wide range of fertility. It is this individual pattern which is obviously connected with the age at marriage, as for instance Henry clearly shows.[41] The younger they marry, the larger their families. Unfortunately, we do not know who these people were who married young. In Ireland, Connell thought the poorest peasants married youngest (and this opinion was widespread until recently). But M. Drake has thrown some doubts on this. These facts lead us at any rate

[35] Hajnal, p. 124, see also M. Drake's thesis, above.
[36] M. Drake, ibid.
[37] Malthus, Essay on Population, Everyman Edition, I, 203.
[38] M. Drake, 'Marriage and Population Growth in Ireland', Ec. Hist. Rev., NS XVI, No. 2, 1963, p. 307.
[39] Potter, p. 663.   [40] Drake, Ec. Hist. Rev., loc. cit., 309.   [41] Henry, p. 449-50.

to one supposition about the age at marriage and its connection with population growth. We must not be misled by the fact that it was so stable for given types of population and certain regions, for it is entirely possible that there was a shift into those groups, and into those regions, which had the more fertile pattern. None of the studies here presented could investigate this possibility. Presumably the emigrants from Europe to America underwent such a transition, but the same may have happened inside western European countries. That these regional differences at any one point of time were significant cannot be doubted.[42] Unfortunately in many cases we do not have the regional variations[43] at different periods to verify this hypothesis. Nevertheless, comparisons like those between Ireland and Norway, or Flanders and France, do leave the question open.[44]

One special aspect of marriage deserves mention as it is potentially more important for population growth. One must always distinguish between first and subsequent marriages. Unfortunately not all the studies in this volume make this distinction. Second and subsequent marriages amounted in some cases to 15 per cent and more of all marriages, and could therefore affect the average age seriously.[45] Remarriage is primarily a function of mortality—the more men and women die at an early age, the more widows and widowers remarry. Its extent also depends on the sex ratio of the affected age groups, and on the degree of nuptiality at first marriage age. Clearly the kind of figures we have for proportions of women ever-married are consistent with the *polygamia successiva* of Suessmilch's vocabulary.[46] The question is: what effect could a reduction in this practice have on the rate of population growth? The answer to this depends to some extent on the cause of female mortality and the age at which it had some significance. This may be partly a question of maternal mortality in childbed. We know little, at present, about the importance of this cause. If we look at Peller's figures[47] we are struck by the fact that total puerperal mortality was never above 113 (per 1,000 related births), and that for most of the age groups at risk male mortality was higher than female. But here we must recall that the men in question (of noble families) faced more occupational risks than the rest of the population, and that care in childbed was perhaps a little better in these families than in those of cottagers and labourers. The figures quoted by McKeown and Brown for the middle of the nineteenth century certainly do not suggest that maternal mortality was high in domiciliary confinements, but this information must be seen against the background of the authors' view that in this respect there had been great improvements during the eighteenth century, especially in the environmental conditions of childbirth.

If the position changes so that a higher proportion of all marriages are first marriages (because fewer women die in marriage), we may have the same total nuptiality, and the same proportion of women dying ever-married, but a higher rate of growth, because more marriages are contracted when both partners are young.

[42] Goubert, p. 468.   [43] Cipolla, p. 586-7.   [44] Deprez, p. 616.
[45] Drake, 'An Elementary Exercise in Parish Register Demography', *Ec. Hist. Rev.*, NS XIV, 1962, p. 443.
[46] Bourgeois-Pichat, p. 484; Peller, p. 89 (87·7 per cent ever-married women 1780-1879).
[47] Peller, p. 96.

Where there was equally great mortality amongst males, the point will not arise, since the limitation of effective union would come from both sides, but similarly the chances of remarriage for both widows and widowers would be high without resort to the pool of spinster or bachelors. In fact, it is worth noting the statistics presented in Hollingsworth's Table 24. We see from this that males achieved their modern chances of surviving the reproductive period as early as the middle of the eighteenth century, whereas women were still in the process of improving theirs. Though Hollingsworth, like Peller, deals with the aristocracy, his figures underline the importance of the possibility of reducing second marriages. He believes that this alone is not enough to account for the rise in reproductive rates, but he clearly shows that it has some relevance. He also says that frequent remarriage would reduce the significance of early death. This is so for his chosen sub-population, or if there is equal mortality—it clearly cannot be true of the population as a whole, or where mortality between the sexes is not equal.

(ii) *Marriage and economy*

So far we have treated marriage largely as a question of age structure and mortality, and in terms of the opportunities offered in a social or geographical sense. We have done so because the question of age and frequency of marriage seems central to the general problem of economic opportunities for marriage, which we must now describe briefly. This problem is a recurrent theme with most of our contributors. We encounter two principal sets of views: that the marriage rate increases with economic opportunity, and that it decreases with increased prosperity. These are, in their nature, short-term statistical observations, and they do not necessarily contradict each other. At the moment of favourable prospect, not only will couples marry who would have done so in any case, but also some who may have postponed marriage in a previous period due to high prices, low employment, or disturbed conditions, as well as some of those who might not otherwise have married till later. There is an element, therefore, of postponed and anticipated events in the short-term total. But over a decade or a generation, the rate must reflect a change in conditions. Specifically, we assume that if during the decade 1730-49 90 per cent of those reaching the age of 30 were married, compared with only 80 per cent in the previous period, then there was some improvement in economic outlook. Unfortunately, nuptiality statistics are rarely given in this form. In the other case described in most industrialized societies sometime after 1870, and very strikingly for Western Europe and North America in the 1920's and -30's, marriage is postponed by those sections of the population who have reached a certain standard of comfort, or who have formed certain minimum expectations of what life should offer them, to a limited extent when the economy is strong, and more strikingly, when there is a depression or when price levels operate against them.[48]

As far as the period before 1850 is concerned, (except possibly for France), the positive correlation between marriage and economic activity and opportunity is clearly the most important. The standards of what was considered

[48] J. A. Banks, *Prosperity and Parenthood*, 1954; *Determinants and Consequences*, ch. V.

adequate wealth or income for marriage vary greatly, as Malthus himself repeatedly showed, at different times and in various countries. The general assumption was that the lower the customary standard, the earlier and more general marriage would be, and hence the greater the tendency of the population to increase. This form of argument, however, fails to convince either in its Malthusian or in more modern form. If the standard of life is so low and hopes for the future no higher, the additional children which might be produced as a result of such a system will have so low an expectation of life as to make this type of marriage convention ineffective as a factor in increasing population, by itself. If, of course, the expectation of the marrying parties is in fact wrong, and if standards are rising, then the chances of survival will be greater. But the falsification of the original expectation will then make it impossible to impute the increase of population to low levels of living. We have already shown that such early, and quite heedless, marriages were not found to any large extent in western Europe, though undoubtedly national averages of 25 for the age at first marriage are not incompatible with some people marrying before they reach the age of 20. That the general level of prosperity of the European population has increased since 1750 will scarcely be questioned, yet the fact is that the age at marriage in the last 200 years has varied so little though it has fluctuated, and that today it again bears a strong resemblance to the pattern shown by our French, Belgian and Scandinavian contributors.

Every study so far made shows that the number of marriages shows more violent fluctuations than those for births or deaths. It is a fair assumption that during the years when there were few marriages the average age at marriage was also high, and *vice versa*. Clearly the speed with which population grows is affected by the number of years within each period of accounting in which marriages were frequent and early, and those which showed the opposite tendency. This would work out to a large extent through more successful conceptions and lower infant mortality, rather than through many additional births per marriage. The parallelism of marriages and births is general, and although we observe constantly that mortality also rises after an increase in births so long as infant mortality is a large factor in total mortality, the chances of successful procreation would be greatly increased during a period of good weather, good harvests, low prices, and high real wages. Such periods are fairly rare, but when they do occur as they seem to have done in most countries, they do give rise to a 'bulge' generation which may lay the foundation for long term increases, especially if its own emergence into adult life coincides with another period of prosperity.

Conversely, death and disaster arrest marriages, prevent or postpone them —wars, harvest failures, slumps. Some of the deferred marriages will never take place, because the circumstances of their postponement usually increase the possibility that one or other of the potential partners will die. But one of the most widely documented phenomena of demographic history is the recovery from such perils—the spate of marriages which follows the crisis.[49] The period of the hiatus will bear all the marks of a period of recession—falling

[49] Habakkuk, p. 272.

production followed by reduced demand and still further depression, failure to invest and destruction of capital assets. By contrast, the period of recovery —the apparently inevitable seven fat years which follow the seven lean ones— will see an upswing of activity, postpone marriages, building and investment, and reduced age specific mortality (whether or not one accepts the theory that the years of disaster weeded out the weaker sections of the community).

Those are the general trends. What of the specific mechanisms involved? The simplest are those which are directly associated with agricultural holdings or industrial or craft workplaces. We have already shown that these mechanisms are unlikely to have operated in such a crude fashion. Prudential checks of the Malthusian kind may have existed in some ideal peasant societies, but we have no proof of this.[50] Nor, on the other hand, is it true that the destruction of such societies removes all restraint.[51] In an urban environment, we can discern a similar rigid theoretical pattern equally unlikely to have worked so in practice. Apprenticeship regulations[52] and the prohibition of exercising a trade except under the control of gilds and corporations were supposed to be powerful bars to marriage and economic progress alike, and it is one of the commonplaces of economic history that initiative was exercised mostly outside the corporate towns. When or where the old system broke down, an urban proletariat was created, at least in some cases, and this may have led to a lowering of the age at marriage and the shedding of all prudential restraint. This transition, for instance, was supposed to have taken place in the North of England between 1750 and 1830. But it is equally possible to interpret the same movement as the response of a far from proletarian population to increased employment opportunities which occurred, in the absence of apprenticeship, at an early age and which provided maximum earnings for men (and often their wives) in the early twenties. When times were good, one might say the prosperity theory of marriage could be called in aid; at times of depression, the theory of misery. The fact is that so far we do not know what accounts for the fluctuations of marriages in detail, especially in societies undergoing industrial and agrarian revolutions. It is in more primitive communities where harvests and good prices play such a large role that we be fairly certain what caused the ups and down of the marriage curve.

To sum up this part of our discussion. Marriage is held to be, as a voluntary and controlled action, the most important factor in population growth so far as it can be related to economic development. Yet it can be shown that the general age at marriage in Europe did not change much in the last 250 years and that large changes would be required to ensure an increase in marital fertility. Nor did the proportion of people who married change significantly, but it is probable that fewer remarriages meant that fewer women spent a considerable part of their fertile period in a single state. This may have had some effect on fertility.

As for the economic reasons for contracting or postponing marriage, these

[50] Jutikkala, p. 556 ff.
[51] Chambers, p. 308 (quoting M. Dobb).
[52] Note that the vast amount of information contained in the manuscript *Index of Apprentices* (based on English indentures mainly of the eighteenth century, one copy in Birm. Univ. library) has never been exploited systematically.

seem easier to trace in societies relatively dependent on the state of the harvest or sensitive to natural disasters and other crises. Industrial revolution and agrarian re-organization may have facilitated marriage in some cases, but they also created fresh reasons against early marriage. Perhaps the most that can be said about these changes is that development was less subject to violent changes than had formerly been the case, and that the eighteenth century may have seen a comparative lengthening of the favourable periods compared with the adverse years, and that the children of those favoured generations carried total population upwards in a wave-like movement.

VIII. *Fertility of marriage*

We turn from the analysis of marriage to the problems of fertility, in so far as they have not already been described as an integral part of the determinants of nuptiality. We know very little, even now, about the limits of reproductive capacity. The fertility of women in the most productive age group, 20-24, varies widely, with some producing as many as 500 children per annum for every 1,000 women in the group, and others much less. The gross reproduction rates which were normal in France before 1800 mean that each woman produced more than 5 live births on the average.[53] Yet clearly in individual cases the range is large, for some women produce 20 children and more and others remain sterile. We do not even know whether fertility was ever completely uncontrolled. Writers like Himes have suggested that birth control has always been practised. In the countryside, everyone was supposed to know one old woman who could prescribe a herbal infusion to promote a miscarriage, or to interfere more actively to produce an abortion. We now distinguish between neo-natal deaths in premature babies, still-births and deliberate infanticide. It is doubtful whether past ages did so—still-births are rarely recorded in the registers. Many illegitimate births must have been concealed and figure neither in fertility nor in mortality statistics. All this makes it extremely difficult to discuss 'normal' fertility and therefore to produce deviations from it.

We have two main types of variation to explain: that between different regions at the same time, and fluctuations in the same place over the centuries. Leaving aside a consideration of the method of calculation, Deprez found in Flanders, in the eighteenth century, rates between 3·0 and 5·27 live-births per marriage,[54] but the ranges were consistently narrower early in the century (4·2-4·3) than at the end (3·3-5·27). Different parts of Flanders, however, show quite different rates. In Scandinavia, Utterstroem drew attention to the divergent rates for the colonizing regions of Finland and some of the older settled areas.[55]

Let us recall the possible causes of differences in the fertility of marriages, leaving aside, for the moment, illegitimacy, abortion and birth control. The first determinant is clearly the length of effective marital union. Some of the possible reasons for changes in this variable have already been discussed in the last section. It can be shown that even small reductions in general mortality may do a great deal to prolong marital unions provided that those spared are

---

[53] Bourgeois-Pichat, p. 482; Henry, p. 447-8.
[54] Deprez, p. 620.   [55] Utterström, p. 528.

in the most fertile age groups. On this point our information is still scanty, but infant mortality was not greatly reduced during most of our period, and the proportion of old people did not change appreciably. The main beneficiaries were, in fact, the married age groups. If marriages of women in the main took place between 23 and 25, and the age at the last confinement was what it was observed to be in France and Flanders,[56] that is scarcely ever much over 40, then the length of potential child-bearing life was between 16 and 18 years. Any curtailment of this period at either end clearly reduces the potential fertility of the marriage, more so at the lower end than the upper end. Another cause of reduction would be prolonged separation of husband and wife, such as we encounter during war periods and with migratory labour.

Given then, a large number of marriages which lasted 16-18 years during the fertile period, we should also observe a large number of families with 16 or 18 children. In fact these are a great rarity. What then causes the birth intervals to be as long as they are? Where we have information, it appears that the interval between marriage and the first intramaritally conceived birth is usually between 15 and 18 months, and thereafter births take place at intervals from 23–26 months or even more. One frequently heard explanation is that there is a basis of truth in the widespread supposition that conception is unlikely as long as lactation proceeds, and that this primitive form of birth control was widely practised, consciously or unconsciously.[57] But even if we accept this possibility, we find that observed fertility in marriages of 16 years' duration is still less than the 7 or 8 children we should expect. We are therefore forced to conclude either that a large proportion of pregnancies ended negatively, or that some form of birth control was resorted to. In fact both explanations are probable. Even under modern conditions, gynaecologists estimate that one in four or five conceptions fails to produce a live-birth. The proportion was probably higher in the past. This is easily seen in the pronounced dip in the births curve following any crisis like harvest failure or epidemics, especially of the diseases involving the digestive system and others which leave the victim exhausted and in a state of muscular lassitude. The delayed action of such events on births has been statistically demonstrated in modern times.[58] In other words, the fall in live births which so often accompanies or immediately follows a sharp rise in deaths is the principal cause of the failure to bear a child every year or every second year. We may assume that in part this phenomenon is due to death or severe illness or subsequent debility of the father, in part to illness of the mother, or her subsequent inability to keep the foetus alive, or increased danger of miscarriage in a state of general weakness, or even greater willingness to abort, to abstain from intercourse, or practice birth control.

Therefore the same factors which control mortality and produce a more

[56] Deprez, p. 616.
[57] Jutikkala, p. 563. The work of C. Tietze has shown that there is a considerable basis of fact in this view.
    Research now being undertaken by the present writer on the basis of detailed material relating to the Irish Quakers in the seventeenth and eighteenth century shows that the birth interval was above two years when the previous child survived, and somewhat lower when it did not. In the highly probable absence of any birth-control practice in this group, it seems that lactation may be the cause.
[58] H. and F. Hotelling, 'Causes of birth rate fluctuations', *J. Am. Stat. Ass.*, XXVI, 1931, 135-49.

regular marriage rate will also produce greater fertility within marriage unless, and this is an important reservation, the consequent increase in potentially successful conceptions leads at once to the adoption of stricter measures of birth control or an increase in abortions. Again both these are likely, for even when the old régime of frequent crises of famine and epidemics had been superseded by a new one where mortality was much smaller and fluctuated less wildly, even when lactation was shortened (as for instance in industrial societies where mothers went out to work), the marital fertility rate did not rise to anything like the maximum we might expect—indeed it barely exceeded 5 per family even in mid-victorian England. If, from the early eighteenth century onwards, 5 births per marriage had been standard practice in Western Europe, and there had been virtually one marriage per woman (i.e. first and subsequent marriages together), the rate of increase would have been much faster than it was, even allowing for infant mortality of the order experienced at the time. Observed marital fertility is almost everywhere considerably less than this maximum, and the rate of growth correspondingly slower.

From 1730 onwards Chambers[59] calculated consistently higher fertility in industrial villages than in agricultural areas, though even there the highest figure is 4·8. Deprez found these high levels of fertility mainly in areas of poor soil and widespread industrialization, whereas some of the richest agrarian areas shared with the city of Ghent fertility rates between 3 and 4 for most of the eighteenth century. In a rural area of Worcestershire on the fringes of the industrial Midlands, fertility rates did not rise much above 4 per marriage during the same period. On the other hand, Sogner, using the identical methods to those of Chambers and Eversley[60] in seventeen highly industrialized parishes in Shropshire, found marital fertility rates between 4·7 and nearly 6, and averaging 5·4, between 1711 and 1760. Industrializing areas may have high marriage/baptism ratios simply because married couples immigrated and had their children after their arrival.

We have few other divisions of births statistics apart from those into agricultural and industrial regions. The poorer peripheral parishes of Ghent have a fertility pattern similar to rural industrial or poor agricultural areas, the wealthier central parishes have fewer children per marriage, like the rich agricultural areas. This differential fertility closely accords with the uninstructed opinions expressed by economists a long time ago, whether they were Malthusians or Marxists: that industrialization, poverty, early marriage and large families go together. Conversely, the settled peasant with his jealously guarded holding is revealed as being less fertile, but the very rich as represented by the aristocracies whose living standards cannot be impaired by children, have still higher fertility than the urban proletariat. The Crulai peasants, on the other hand, seem during the period under review to be still producing large families (down to 1742) but after that fertility falls first slowly and then rapidly after the revolution.[61] The Geneva bourgeoisie[62] displayed fertility rates well

[59] Chambers, p. 333.
[60] S. Sogner, 'Aspects of the Demographic Situation in Seventeen Parishes in Shropshire, 1711–1760', *Population Studies*, XVII, pt. 2, 1963, p. 137.
[61] L. Henry, *Crulai*, p. 106.   [62] *Op. cit.*, p. 106.

below those of either the peasants or the industrial workers, and this accords well with the theory of restrictive oligarchies.

No clear conclusions can be drawn from this evidence by itself. As has been stated, the observed high rates of fertility amongst certain industrial populations could not have led to fast growth had they in fact been as miserable as some historians would suggest they were before they embarked on rearing their families, or afterwards, as the Malthusians would assert, because increased mortality would have led to the effects described by McKeown and Brown. Here we arrive at one of the central problems of economic history in general, not only of demographic evolution. There is a school of thought which does not believe that industrialization can in fact have depressed living standards to subsistence level, or below this level, for a substantial part of the population, for if this had been the case, the broad basis of consumer demand would have been eroded. Since most industrialized areas did in fact sell the greater part of their output in their own region or at any rate in their national economy, rather than for export, and since the typical products of the new industries were goods destined for the ordinary consumer rather than the luxury market, it is impossible to postulate that the economic upheavals of the eighteenth and nineteenth century meant proletarianization *tout court*. Nobody would deny the misery of dispossessed peasants, or of the handloom-weavers of Lancashire or Silesia—but these must have been, if the economic fabric was to hold together and to expand, a minority—substantial no doubt, at times, and in places, and deserving the publicity they obtained. But we cannot think of the mass of the population as a starving mob. Revolution was successful only in the agrarian countries; the industrial workers failed to revolt, however much they were urged to do so. This theme is still the subject of dispute, but for our purpose it would be safer to say that we think that industrialization, early marriage and large families may be found together, leaving out the poverty or the proletarian mentality, because neither of these are necessary or even useful parts of the argument.

If we accept this possibility, we have at any rate one set of explanations for the high rates of growth of Western European populations. As employment shifts in favour of those groups and areas which display high fertility, the rate of growth accelerates. More miners, more landless labourers, fewer apprentices, craftsmen and yeomen—so runs the sequence. Unfortunately we cannot assign an important role to this set of causes. First of all, as we have shown, earlier or more frequent marriage is not easy to prove, and secondly it would not have made a great deal of difference. Secondly infant mortality is still high round 1800, and in some cases rising, and most severe in large families.

But much more significantly; population increases even at high rates (i.e. at over 1 per cent per annum cumulatively) were not confined to industrializing countries, nor to colonizing areas. Norway and Ireland[63] exhibit very similar growth rates to those of England and Belgium. This does not prove, by itself, that higher fertility cannot have had the effects claimed for it, or that it was inoperative in some countries; it simply means that we must not rely on it as a sole cause, and that we shall have to consider the decline in mortality

[63] M. Drake, *Thesis*.

in greater detail later. In America[64] we observe the declining fertility of industrializing areas compared with the agricultural districts in the process of being opened up—this may constitute yet another type of case where the relative opportunities of a rich agrarian economy and the comparatively less favourable circumstances of the industrial areas lead to a reversal of roles. But both types of area still grow faster than their European counterparts. In other words, population change is only intelligible in terms of a total social and economic situation, and the nature of the change cannot be ascertained by crude rates or national totals.

If marriage frequency, mortality, and the number of children per marriage remain the same, population may still grow simply if marriage takes place slightly earlier, because there will be an overlap between the last generation and the next. (The effect of reducing the age at marriage from 30 to 25, all other factors remaining equal, would be to increase the population by one-sixth.) Moreover, if the population had not in fact been stationary, but there had been natural increase, the growth rate would obviously be greater if there were four generations in a century rather than three. If we add, as a third factor, the prolongation of life at adult ages, the rate of overlap becomes greater still, and one finally arrives at the acute shortage of household spaces experienced in modern communities when, so far from parents vacating houses in time for their children to marry, one cannot even be sure now that a system of succession to grandparents' estates is operating. It must be understood that for the generation interval to be shortened, and the overlap to be increased, again involves assumptions about the availability of employment and subsistence, especially in an industrial country, though the same phenomenon can be observed in Ireland, according to Connell, where potato culture, rather than industrial employment, makes the process possible.

The succession of generations comes to our notice most forcibly when we are confronted by peaks of fertility, or bulges, such as many of our contributors have noticed after the great disasters of the eighteenth century.[65] If recovery from a crisis often takes place in circumstances exceptionally favourable to population (good harvests, low prices, high wages due to labour shortage, widening of employment opportunities due to investment), we may expect not only a rise in the marriage and birth rate but also a better chance of survival for the newly born. Certainly such generations stand out quite clearly on the demographic map, not only by contrast with the preceding 'deficient' generation, but often with the succeeding 'normal' one—partly because of the possibility that marriages took place which were additional to normal maxima, partly because survival chances were better for children whose mothers had acquired some sort of immunity, partly perhaps because of the general atmosphere of confidence suspended, for the time being, any contraceptive practices.

The difficulty arises when this enlarged generation enters the next two crucial stages—when it starts looking for employment, and when the time comes for it to be married. In modern terms, we know this of the bulge generation of 1946 which entered the labour market to a great extent in 1962-4, with consequent difficulties for the less well qualified children, and which will set

[64] Potter, p. 678.   [65] Goubert, p. 471 f; Jutikkala, p. 557-8; Utterström, p. 547.

up an unprecedented additional demand for houseroom when it marries from 1967-72 and begins to produce children of its own. So too in Sweden the larger generation which was born in 1721-35 reached marriageable age in the fifties and sixties, fortunately at a time when there were many good harvests and generally favourable economic conditions. In fact a second 'bulge-generation' was born then but this one was less fortunate in reaching maturity in the eighties when conditions were in many respects adverse. In England, such a generation was born in the 1730's, a time of exceptionally low food prices and high real wages. It reached marriageable age in the late fifties, a time of war but greatly increased economic activity and again, except for one or two years, low food prices, and its impact on the marriage- and birth-rates of the time is clearly visible in most registers. The wave next reached a peak in the late 1780's, again a time of increasing trade and production and the quartern loaf at 6½d in London,[66] lower than the average of the seventies and much lower than the hungry nineties. That this coincidence between natural population waves and economic activity contributed to rapid population growth in England cannot now be doubted, whatever may have happened elsewhere. The registers in England after 1780 are no longer useful for statistical investigations[67] and in any case the hard outlines of the wave becomes very blurred after the first repetition, since the normal range of marriage ages and birth dates is clearly doubled at each successive stage, but the influence must have been there all the same.

Illegitimate births do not play a very large role in those parts of Europe which we have been studying. They are very low in France, and rarely exceed 5 per cent of all births in England until the end of the eighteenth century when they appear to increase sharply, as indeed they do in a number of other countries for reasons which may be connected with the war and revolution. Despite the absence or difficulty of contraception, fewer illegitimate children were apparently born in the eighteenth century than in recent times, *pro rata*, despite technical progress and enlightenment. Some of the more exact anthropological accounts of rural customs especially in the nineteenth century suggest that 5 per cent is a spurious figure. Deprez found up to 25 per cent pre-nuptial conceptions in his Flemish parishes, at Crulai they were negligible. Yet in nineteenth-century Germany rates of 25 per cent and more of illegitimate children are encountered. Clearly there were sharp cultural and religious differences. But unless we credit our ancestors with moral behaviour vastly superior to our own, we must assume that there is some falsification of the record—quite apart from the possibility of widespread abortion, there must have been infanticide, and certainly failure to baptize, or registration of babies under the wrong parents' name. But if one accepts that possibility, even if it is only up to the 10 per cent of all births observed in England at the end of the century, there is clearly some scope for an effect on total fertility, expressed either in crude birth-rates or even in fertility calculations where no distinction has been made between legitimate and illegitimate children. If wars and revolution increased the rate, we may here have one of the reasons why even widespread military service and other upheavals failed to depress the fertility of

[66] T. S. Ashton, *Economic Fluctuations*, p. 181.   [67] Krause, *passim*.

the population unduly in so many cases. But we have to admit that we have not enough facts on which to make definitive judgments, and we must leave open at least the possibility that a change in moral standards may have had a substantial effect in some areas and at some periods.

IX. *Mortality*

The traditional explanation of the rapid growth of population which began in the eighteenth century has always been that mortality decreased. As far as England is concerned, the classical account was that of Talbot Griffith, and this found its way into all text-books. In other countries, similar explanations were almost universally adopted. Only socialist writers, unable to believe that industrialization could be accompanied by a drastic fall in mortality, put forward the view that the demand for labour had led to early marriages and large families. In recent years, this idea has gained increasing support even from non-socialist writers, partly because doubts were thrown on the traditional accounts of why mortality fell, partly because there seemed to be statistical evidence for the other thesis. In preceding sections, we have tried to examine this evidence, and to show that it is capable of bearing only limited weight. We return, therefore, to a review of the evidence on mortality in its relation to economic changes.

The main characteristic of primitive demographic régimes is the frequency of sharp peaks in total mortality. These are often of an order of magnitude which rules out any possibility of statistical accident. Given the fact that populations grew mostly at very low rates before the eighteenth century—usually at annual compound rates of less than 0·3 per cent over long periods—it is sometimes assumed that the process was an irregular one, gains extending over years or even decades being wiped out again in a short time. The most notorious of these disasters was the Black Death in the fourteenth century, but periods like the Thirty Years' War in central Europe, the plagues of the seventeenth century,[68] and the wars of the turn of eighteenth century probably had similar consequences at least in some areas. Recent research has however thrown some doubt onto many of the exaggerated assumptions concerning these periods. Moreover, these disasters would need to kill 20 per cent of the population or more[69] to affect the issue significantly, for at a time of generally short expectation of life they only accelerated the deaths of adults at least by a few years. They are then followed by periods of comparatively low mortality, and the overall effect may be quite marginal. It depends to some extent on the age-incidence of the particular type of death—if, like smallpox, it affects children under five and if there is already high infant mortality, an increase of less than 25 per cent in total mortality may mean a doubling of child deaths and therefore severe long-term reductions of population growth rates. On the other hand a bad winter which might kill off a great many people over 55 would not affect growth rates at all. Next to the extraordinary periods of mortality, we can distinguish in our records recurrent peaks not connected with recorded catastrophes, but associated with the cyclical occurrence of the

[68] Cipolla, p. 573-4.   [69] Utterström, p. 541.

ordinary hazards of the times—the ever-present smallpox, typhus and dysentery outbreaks, as well as other epidemic diseases not clearly identified, the recurrent dearths not amounting to full-scale famine and the increased mortality from minor diseases and pandemics like tuberculosis at such periods of less than adequate nutrition. These periods are often difficult to analyse in the light of what has been said about the possibility that an increased number of deaths may be due to some built-in factor of population structure, but on the other hand the causes can often be identified by breaking down annual figures into seasonal totals.[70] A quinquennial mortality figure may be high for reasons connected only with the birth-rate at that time, or a generation earlier, but the concentration of deaths into a few months which shows clearly as a deviation from the seasonal trend figure needs a separate explanation. Unfortunately very few series of seasonal analyses are so far available for our period.

It is difficult to reconcile the conflicting accounts we possess so as to make general statements concerning the evolution of mortality from the seventeenth century onwards. The studies of the aristocracy show a definite increase in the expectation of life, but this is a special group both as to its occupational risks and its access to good medical care and its independence from the hazards of food supplies. Marshall was still able to state categorically[71] that the Industrial Revolution saw a significant fall in the death-rate. Bourgeois-Pichat would agree for France, and it seems to be equally true for Sweden.[72] But L. Henry could not find any general improvement in the second half of the eighteenth century, though it was better then than it had been previously. Infant mortality shows even less significant improvements over the whole of the century. Deprez, using slightly different methods, observed quite considerable improvements in adult expectation of life during the eighteenth century. Migration is apt to mask facts. An unhealthy and declining region from which people emigrate may have a larger surplus of births over deaths than one of immigration. The highest death-rates today are found in salubrious resorts to which the aged retire.

X. *Mortality: famine and epidemics*

We must now briefly classify the causes of death in relation to their dependence on economic factors and the associated social structure, as well as assessing to what degree changes in environment, man-made and natural, can have influenced the observed falls in adult mortality rates. The simplest models of the relationship between life and economy is of course the Malthusian, in its many variations. In the short run, means of subsistence are not augmentable, or any attempt to increase them is subject to diminishing returns, so that any growth in population at a rate greater than can be supplied by the existing agricultural system and other industries and services catering for basic needs, is bound to result in undernourishment or famine, sickness and death, crime, violence and war. In this sense, population and subsistence are always in balance —at any one time, the amount available is just enough to keep everyone alive,

[70] Utterström, p. 542-3.   [71] Marshall, p. 247-8.
[72] Bourgeois-Pichat, p. 485.

by definition. But many of those alive may be moribund, and death-rates will be high until a state of affairs is reached where the amount of available subsistence will keep the population at a standard of living compatible with survival, work, and successful procreation.

Medical care has no place in this simple model. If men are prevented from dying from one disease because a cure is found, they will die of something else if there is not enough food and shelter to keep them fit. We may, if we like, eliminate from this model also the more tendentious parts of the Malthusian system—crime, violence, vice, and war are not always connected with poverty, individual or national. Having done this, we are still left with the bare bones of Malthusianism—but by now they have become platitudinous. It is not worth saying that men cannot live without food. The Malthusian system only becomes a part of population science when it begins to be predictive, or tries to be so: when it asserts that population will rise when subsistence becomes more plentiful, and fall when it becomes short, and assign quantitative precision to this link. The system breaks down when we can show that, in fact, subsistence is only one of several variables to be considered in relation to the numbers of the people. This is what most of the contributions to this volume in fact to. We do not exclude the subsistence factor—we could not do so in view of the number of recorded famines, and epidemics accompanying them, or of the rapid increase of colonists in fertile areas. But we have to be cautious about the kind of view that is implicit, for instance, in Heckscher's account of the population of Sweden.[73] The moment we can show that there is only a limited correlation between mortality and food shortage, or, on the other hand, the birth-rate and an increase in the means of subsistence, we find ourselves either outside Malthus' school altogether, or, have to seek in his qualifications and footnotes some explanation for phenomena not consistent with the simple propositions which became familiar under his name.

Before we consider the two main subjects which occupy us in these pages, food and epidemics, it is worth noting that on one cause of death at any rate there need be little disagreement—war. Admittedly contemporary accounts have to be deflated before they can be used,[74] but any normal pattern of mortality and fertility will be affected by deaths in battle, and even more so, by the effect on civilian population of arson, pillage, the more rapid spread of infections, and the surplus or deficiency of potential fathers.[75] The extent of the damage of course depends on local circumstances, but it is worth noting that war casualties are to some extent a category of their own, with a distinct pattern of consequences and of recovery. We have seen the results of excess mortality of aristocratic males in prematurely disrupted unions,[76] and the same may have been true of the ordinary population. The end of the war tends to cause a surge in marriages and births when the survivors return, when crops are sown again on land which may have remained fallow, and when subsistence may be relatively plentiful compared with a decimated population.[77] Fortunately for the historical demographer, wars, unlike epidemics, are generally

[73] Utterström, p. 541.   [74] Goubert, p. 457-8.
[75] Hajnal, p. 117 (Zürich); Utterström, p. 536-7 (Northern War); Jutikkala, p. 557.
[76] Peller, p. 94-5; Hollingsworth, p. 369.
[77] Jutikkala, p. 555, Table I; Utterström, p. 537.

recorded in the annals, but surprisingly enough we still publish population tables without indicating the war years and their local effects.

When we come to consider food shortage as a cause of death, we are immediately faced with the opinion, held by many medical authorities, that hunger is a comparatively rarely ascertainable direct cause. We find, in the registers, many references to deaths from starvation, but this is sometimes attributable to ignorance, except in the case of quite specific diseases such as scurvy which are due to deficiencies rather than starvation. Even in countries of high mortality in our own time, hunger as such does not kill—rather, it weakens the body and makes it prey to disease. Hunger does not prevent conception, but it prejudices the chances of the foetus. The shortage of normal sources of food leads to the eating of rotten or diseased meat or vegetables, to children having resort to poisonous berries, to adulteration of flour with noxious substances. But all this does not amount to much by way of mortality, in itself. Nevertheless, we have to look to famine periods as turning points in demographic history. This is not solely due to increased death rates, from whatever cause, but to an interlinked effect on births, marriages and deaths.[78] This shows up sharply in the well-known years of disaster, though when famines cease to be important factors for reasons still to be discussed, their absence is noticeable only by implication and reference to earlier cycles.[79]

The exact connection between undernourishment and epidemics is still a matter of dispute. Clearly, there are some diseases which attack men almost regardless of their general physical condition, and where the proportion of those affected dying hardly seems to vary with their social class. These were the dreaded universal killers, of which plague and smallpox are the most notorious. Others are more selective in their incidence, even though those infected stood little chance of survival—the cholera is a case in point. But many other epidemics as well as endemic diseases are not only more likely to affect those who are poor and weak, but are also rarely fatal in those with well-nourished constitutions. Many of the diseases affecting the lungs and bowels come into this category. But the links between food and sickness are not confined to the field of resistance to infection. When food was short in the countryside, vagrants might invade the towns in search of work, and there was a persistent belief that rats, finding barns empty, went the same way. When, on the other hand, epidemics raged in the rural areas, towns might close their gates to traffic, and thus aggravate food shortages. This also happened when quarantines were imposed, as they were, for instance, in England as late as the cholera epidemic of 1831-2. It is only by remembering such institutional reasons for increased mortality that we can explain the full association between dearth and death such as that recorded by Meuvret[80] and the large differences between different areas all subject to the same sort of harvest failure, e.g. in 1693-4.[81]

One added complication lies in the fact that the same conditions which reduce food supplies may also directly lower resistance and cause increased mortality. A severe winter, a wet summer, and autumn floods might take their

[78] Henry, p. 442.
[79] Meuvret, *passim*, note discussion of years like 1693-4, 1709-10, and 1740-1, in all contributions.
[80] Meuvret, p. 517-8.
[81] *Ibid.*

toll even if food reserves prevented famine.[82] Even when it became more
common to transport food from one region to another, floods, ice or drought
could cause a breakdown of communications, at least until the days of the
railways. The Swedish measurement of the severity of a winter (by the date
of the break-up of the ice on Lake Mälaren) comprises the effect of a multiplicity
of factors on human chances of survival.[83] On the other hand, an interruption
of communications might prevent the spread of epidemics, and very cold
weather is also unfavourable to the growth and spread of some types of organ-
isms. Warm, moist climates, on the other hand may be favourable to harvests
and at the same time promote disease. In other words, we must see the connection between climate, food supplies and mortality as part of a total situation,
and not in isolation.

Leaving aside the question of environmental factors and disease, what
emerges from the history of epidemics so far that can throw light on the growth
in European population? Roughly speaking a reduction in mortality may be
due to a number of factors:

(1) medical or surgical therapy aimed at the cause of disease
(2) preventive therapy (inoculation, vaccination, as well as non-specific means
    of increasing resistance)
(3) spontaneous increase in immunity due to previous exposure to disease, or
    to changes in diet, working conditions, or habitat
(4) changes in the virulence of certain diseases, including the possibility of
    total disappearance due in some cases to the elimination of a carrier (rats).

All these factors have been noted in these pages, and it will be seen that
they are connected with economic phenomena to a varying degree. Medical
science may advance in a vacuum, but the application of the results of research
to the general population will depend on the standard of living, and on the
distribution of real income. Hospitals were, by all accounts, less than effective
in the days before antisepsis or the bacteriological discoveries of the mid-
nineteenth century, but after this period there was still an intermediate era
when practice was improving, but hospital care denied to the largest part of
the population. Effective preventive measures again depend on the political,
social and communications framework. Immunity is, as we have noted, partly
a factor of nutrition and exposure to danger in certain occupations and areas
of settlement. A virus will lose none of its virulence because the standard of
living rises, but rats may be excluded from towns by improvements in food
supplies, sanitation, and building standards.

The possibilities of a medical contribution to a reduction in mortality have
been discussed in the first chapter of this book and form the subject of McKeown
and Brown's essay. Clearly a great deal of work needs to be done in this field,
not only by fresh research in bacteriology and the history of therapy, but also
by relating medical practice and hospital work to the circumstances of the
population affected. Drugs, surgery, nutrition and the outward conditions of
life must be taken into account, not only in themselves, but in their effects on

---

[82] Jutikkala, p. 559—he calls the origins of the 1737 epidemic biological rather than economic.
[83] Utterström, p. 542.

each other, to produce a reasoned explanation of the observed fall in mortality, of a kind which we do not yet possess.

To sum up the position on mortality. We have seen that no one cause may be adduced for the reduction of infant or adult mortality. Everyone is agreed that the expectation of life was greater at the beginning of the modern statistical era than it had been in the seventeenth century. Yet we cannot pinpoint the improvement by time, area or cause. Every mortality curve we have seen has its ups and downs, though the trend is downward. If people lived longer, it must have been partly because they were cleaner, partly because some effective medical practice was known, partly because famines were no longer severe, but mostly because the great killer epidemics failed to return, for reasons which might not be connected with human actions at all. Other diseases supervened, the measles followed smallpox, and cholera established a reign of terror of its own, but nothing compared with the great plagues of earlier centuries occurred again. A growing and more mobile population, increasing urbanization and industrialization—these were the observed tendencies. Yet they did not lead to the increase in mortality which one might have expected. If they did not, it must have been due to some changes in economic organization, some connected with industrial advance, and others effective also in an agrarian setting. These we must now examine.

XI. *Population, industry and agriculture*

For western Europe, the period from the end of the seventeenth century to the present time is one of industrialization—first intermittent, then accelerating in one country after another in the stage known as the Industrial Revolution, and finally almost universal but not yet complete. It has to be understood that this process affected all parts of the half-continent, whether or not they came to possess their own industries. Increasingly, even the agrarian countries came to be geared to the industrial and trading world economy, as suppliers of food and raw materials as well as consumers. Of the countries described in this volume, England underwent the process of industrialization at a rapid rate after 1750, Belgium after 1820, France and Germany after 1850, America about the same time, and Sweden and northern Italy at the end of the nineteenth century. But Ireland, the rest of Scandinavia, southern Italy as well as countries not treated here, like Spain and Portugal, Switzerland and Austria, were increasingly involved in the process—they furnished grain, meat, timber, wool and wine, from them labour migrated to the new manufacturing areas, and they purchased the new products with the proceeds of their raw material exports. This is a much over-simplified picture, but it will serve as a model, not only internationally, but also to describe what happened as between Lancashire and rural Wales, between the Meuse valley and western Flanders, or between the Ruhr and Pomerania. National frontiers and protective barriers diminished the interchange, but the free trade world of Adam Smith was less of a future hope and more of a reality than one sometimes imagines even when he wrote, and was built up into a system by the middle of the following century.

It is true that even in England, by the year 1830, only a comparatively small minority of the population—probably less than 20 per cent—was directly or indirectly employed in, or dependent on, manufacturing industry. If only for this reason, we would not ascribe population growth to industrialization, even if it had not demonstrably begun long before Watt's first steam engine turned, or the same movement had not made itself felt a long way even from the indirect demands of the industrialized sector. Nevertheless, we are bound to take notice of the fact that, except in France, what had been very slow growth rates before 1780, of the order of 0·3 per cent p.a. and less, turned into accelerated growth by 1820 almost everywhere, and reached peaks of 1·5 per cent p.a. and above, before the curve turned downward again in the age of emigration and birth control. Even if we cannot with any assurance link the beginnings of the accelerated growth in the eighteenth century with economic development, it seems certain that the new rhythms observable after 1780 are closely connected with the rising standard of living of a large part of the population of Europe. There had been earlier periods of population growth followed by decimation or stagnation, and the novelty about the movement after 1740 is that it forms the first part of an accelerating growth pattern. In some countries, indeed, this movement is already discernible after 1675, but almost everywhere there were renewed disasters, ca. 1695, ca. 1710, ca. 1730, and 1740, so that the net gain over two generations was not yet in any way observable as the start of a new long-term movement.

How then do we trace the links between economy and population? Population may be seen in a dual role—man as the producer, and man as the consumer. The most important constituent factor in the total picture is the effective demand for labour at a greater rate than can easily be met by the growth of population. This may be a matter of time, place or skill, and would hardly ever have been universal. Therefore we can best formulate this factor by saying that a given population will grow under the best possible conditions if all the manpower it produces will, when it comes of working age, be in demand for its skill at a constant or rising real wage. Under any other circumstances, increasing population will be associated with a lowered standard of living. (We leave aside the question whether an increase in food supplies not associated with a demand for labour might keep up living standards since this is not a known case before the days of international economic aid.) Ideally, the demand for labour comes from both the agrarian and the industrial sector and is associated with both more extensive production and the adoption of more rational techniques, but this is not always the case. The demand for labour may, as far as any one economy is concerned, be merely for products grown or manufactured by existing techniques for an external market: exports create income which in turn stimulate production for the home market. This process tends to be inflationary, and long term price rises accompany the process in most of our areas, though inequalities of distribution ensure that inflation does not go very far until fairly recent times. At a much later stage, we meet the other extreme: technological advance with reduced demand for labour at any rate in some sectors, which means an increasing standard of living for those who participate in the new form of production and a reduction for those whom it deprives of work (e.g. Britain in the 1880's). But this is in the long run, and for the population as a whole, a hypothetical case, whatever the short run frictions of enclosure, power loom weaving, or steam shipping. Most of our actual cases consist of a mixture of mere production extension, and technological intensification, in various proportions and at varying speeds. Ireland after 1846 forms a special case which is not to be discussed within this framework.

The process thus described in general terms leads, as Adam Smith observed rather than demanded, to a local, national and international division of labour, and is associated everywhere with improved communications, an increased measure of local and national government regulation, and the emergence of new professional skills and services, especially in the field of health and education. This is the framework of economic growth, and at the same time the background to the mechanisms by which population was preserved from recurrent extermination.[84] It is also, of course, the framework for exploitation, industrial diseases, slums, restrictions on individual liberty, sometimes civil war and terrorism, colonial campaigns and global wars. The question we face is simply: which of the two aspects is the more important? This used to be something which the historian answered according to his fundamental social and political convictions. But from the point of view of the historical demographer, there can be only one answer: the equilibrium growth of population and economy (i.e. one which has a long-term accelerating trend and does not return to its point of origin after intermediate disturbances), is only possible if the life-saving and life-giving forces have greater weight than those which maim and destroy. This has nothing to do with any discussion as to whether our labouring ancestors enjoyed life under industrial capitalism or not, or indeed whether they were fairly treated, but our hypothesis is only a sort of anti-Malthusian tautology. If we look at our English experience,[85] or even that of Flanders[86] we observe that there is a steady growth rate in industrial regions as opposed to the apparently much faster rate of proletarianized rural agricultural or domestic industrial regions such as Ireland or *Le Vieuxbourg* which were later saved by emigration. This growth rate may again be defined in purely functional terms: if, at any one time, the supply of labour is too large in relation to the local demand for the skills offered, then the population will tend to suffer a reduction of its living standards and consequently growth will tend to be arrested by increased mortality and reduced fertility; if on the other hand the supply of labour is too small in relation to demand, this may inhibit economic growth and consequently living standards will again be affected adversely. It is only when the respective growth rates are such that neither subsistence nor investment are out of step with population movement, that any real progress can be made. This of course is a well-known part of the more theoretical models of economic development with which we have become familiar[87] but it turns out, in practice, that this is what actually happened. If we look at the shape of the index curves for England in the eighteenth and nineteenth century we find that the rate of population increase, agrarian and industrial production,

[84] Chambers, p. 335.   [85] Chambers, p. 308 ff.   [86] Deprez, p. 612 f.
[87] For a list of such models and a discussion of their significance in this context, see Eversley, 'Population and Economic Growth in England before the "Take-off"', First International Conference of Economic History, Stockholm, 1960, *Contributions and Communications*, pp. 460-1.
This essay also contains a systematic account of the factors of change.

and investment are never out of step seriously for long, at least until 1870, and that the trade cycle observable in embryonic form in the eighteenth century and more markedly after 1790 is no more than an oscillation around a trend which rises parallel to population.

We cannot, however, be content simply with the statement that logically regarded this must have been the case, but try to underline the general case with reference to specific mechanisms. In the first place we have to assert again that without a sufficiency of food there would have been no increase at all. In an industrializing society (however slow the process may be), agriculture has to perform a triple function: (1) it must feed the urban population sufficiently well to enable it to perform its arduous work and to propagate itself, (2) it must lower the price of food in relation to incomes sufficiently to liberate incomes for the purchase of industrial commodities, (3) it must improve its technical efficiency to the point where increasing amounts of labour can be released to enter the industrial production process. If food is insufficient, resistance to epidemics is weakened. Malnutrition may prevent conceptions and certainly reduces the number of successful conceptions.[88] Dearth prevents marriages and plenty encourages them.[89]

As far as England is concerned, we need have little doubt that the necessary improvements in agricultural organization took place and that all three requirements were met: before 1870, when serious food imports first took place, the agricultural industry supplied six times as many people as it had done 150 years before, it fed them substantially better (both as to quantity and variety) than it had done, and expenditure on basic foodstuffs had sunk from something like 75 per cent of total income to under 50 per cent even for the lowest groups of regular wage earners. It had done so although it employed, by 1870, less than 20 per cent of the total labour force (and this was to fall still further in the following years), and probably, in actual numbers, fewer men than it had done 150 years before. This was done by a variety of biological and mechanical improvements which greatly increased yields and the certainty of a harvest, and made it possible to cultivate previously barren ground. Although this applies particularly to England, it is also true, to a lesser extent, of all European countries and strikingly so of parts of the north western continent.[90] Countries which did not industrialize shared in this process because they began to act as granaries for areas not self-sufficient in food. The United States are a special case of a country where agriculture both met the stated lists of industrial requirements and also became a major supplier of food to older but equally industrializing countries—and of course it was there that mechanization first reached its modern level.

The effects of this movement may be seen in food price series (despite the difficulties these present especially before the nineteenth century). The violent annual and decadal fluctuations familiar from the middle ages gradually subside. The French Wars of 1793-1815 see a last major crisis of food prices, by that time weathered through improved communications not wholly destroyed

[88] Meuvret, p. 520.
[89] Eversley, p. 406.
[90] Slicher van Bath, *Agrarian History of Western Europe*, 1963, and 'Yield Ratios, 1810-1820', in *Afdeling Agrarische Geschiedenis Bijdragen*, 10, Wageningen, 1963.

by the Continental System. After 1825, food prices only fluctuated within fairly narrow ranges with the exception of single years of extreme shortage like 1846. Although these comparisons are somewhat difficult, it would generally be true to say that food was little dearer in 1850 than it had been 100 years earlier, in money terms—that is, very much cheaper in real terms, and after 1870 imports made prices fall further. This process means that the harvest cycle as a basis for fluctuations in nuptiality, fertility and mortality no longer applies for England in the nineteenth century. Once again, this is not a sudden change, and we can show that in the eighteenth century, as food supplies improve, the relationship between prices and vital rates becomes steadily more tenuous. More extensive cultivation should have increased the danger of bad harvests through the operation of the law of diminishing returns,[91] but in fact the advance in technical knowledge more than outweighed this risk.

Of all the agencies at work in the process of improving food supplies, the most important was the change in the pattern of communications, allied with the emergence of a national food market. If the food producers invested capital to increase production, it was not as a long-term speculation, but in response to clearly defined market stimuli: higher prices or the possibility of selling more without depressing prices induced them to rationalize field systems and tenancies, improve buildings and drainage, experiment with new crops and livestock. Such a response was dependent on communications. In England, river, coastal and canal navigations played the most important role in this process. The same appears to be true of the Rhine/Ruhr district, the Belgian coalfields, and the American heavy industrial areas, all of these starting the process of urban concentration before the days of the railways which finally solved the food problem and gave fresh impetus both to industrialization and agricultural change.[92] In Sweden the process of reducing mortality in bad harvest periods has been related to the reduction in isolation and the disappearance of local subsistence economies.[93] In general, the part played by the network of communications in determining the direction and magnitude of population movements still remains to be investigated, but some local studies suggest that industrial location factors have been stressed too much, leaving out the possibility of greater rates of natural increase owing to the greater facilities for the supply of food stuffs.[94] The process of interaction between industrialization, population growth, agricultural change and improvement in communications can be seen to advantage in eighteenth-century England. The new movements have no set starting date, nor do they progress at the same speed. But roughly speaking, agricultural change can be measured by the acceleration of the enclosure movement, population growth by the beginning of a permanent excess of births over deaths, and the passing of the last famine/epidemic cycle of catastrophic proportions. Canals make their appearance for all practical purposes in 1760, and the start of the 'change in the rate of change' of industrial production which is called the Industrial Revolution may be placed at any time between 1750 and 1780. These of course are national averages, and not meaningful in many local contexts. But the sequence must have been something like

[91] Habakkuk, p. 282-3.   [92] Habakkuk, ibid.
[93] Utterström, p. 542.   [94] Henry, p. 455.

this: increased dependent industrial or urbanized population with steady purchasing power, or an increase in purchasing power of the same population;
rise in food prices; lowering of transport charges; increased agricultural production; lowering of food prices; increasing purchasing power for industrial
goods and service; growth of urban or industrial population ... and so on,
without specifying where this 'cycle' has a point of origin, if indeed there was
one. But without some such model, it is not possible to explain the equilibrium
growth of population, food and production which was observed in practice,
subject to interruptions in years of stress and decline. The basic correctness of
this interpretation is attested by the fact that at any rate in the first phase of
population growth, from 1740-80, food prices rose very little, though England
was still an exporter of grain, on balance, and that after 1815, when the corn
laws still kept out most food imports in so far as the lack of overseas communications did not prevent them in any case, the vastly increased British
population was still fed by the agrarian system at prices which were, on average
only 25-30 per cent higher than they had been from 1760-90,[95] at a time when
money wages were probably about 50 per cent above the pre-war rates.[96]
These relationships can only have been maintained if agricultural output and
transport matched, or more than matched, the rise in population. We say 'more
than matched', for by 1840, when the railways began to make the next large
contribution to the process, a very large proportion of the British working
class was already a habitual consumer of industrial products on a large scale.
Exports dominated the scene in some branches, like cotton, but for the economy
as a whole, they accounted for only 10 per cent of the national product.[97]

The details of this process remain to be examined, but the general picture
is clear enough. For the industrial or urban population, assured food supplies
and steadier prices are a basis for marriage and an improved chance of survival
for them and their children. For the rural population, the assured urban market
plays much the same role. One may put different interpretations on these
phenomena; some historians for instance would say that agrarian reorganization
created a greater landless proletariat and that this was the reason for increased
rates of population growth in the countryside as well as the augmented supply
of labour for towns.[98] But it is not really important from our point of view
whether more extensive and intensive agrarian production, or the growth of a
rural proletariat, provides a better foundation for rapid population growth,
and in fact both views may be in part correct; the common aspect cannot be
doubted, i.e. that the increased market for agricultural produce made it possible
to support a larger rural population, and that an improvement in techniques
then released further increases in this rural population for urban work, however
disagreeable this process was in practice.

We do, however, notice that the improvement in long-term food supplies,
as demonstrated by the absence of severe famines, was not confined to countries
like England or Denmark where there took place widespread reorganization
of tenure and production methods, nor can we attribute very much to the

[95] Griffith, *Population Problems of the Age of Malthus*, Cambridge, 1926, p. 178.
[96] P. Deane and W. Cole, *British Economic Growth, 1688-1959*, Cambridge, 1962, p. 23.
[97] *Ibid.*, 310.
[98] Utterström, p. 529 and Chambers *passim*.

improvement of communications in central European areas, for instance, where they were still notoriously bad in the first quarter of the nineteenth century, and which were remote from water links with food producing areas. To explain this improvement we must have recourse to metereological observations. Weather is a 'random factor'[99] so far as our network of relationships between economy and population is concerned; it is truly a parameter to be taken into account when measuring the variables subject to a measure of human control. No other factor quite comes into this category unless it is a spontaneous variation in the virulence of micro-organisms unconnected with their habitat. But while it is random, it may yet be significant. We have already noted the favourable prices of food in England after 1730 and down to the wars at the end of the century. The absence of catastrophic harvests is also commented on elsewhere.[100] At present we lack any unified presentation of weather data for Europe in the seventeenth and eighteenth century in relation to food prices, but we do have yield tables which show clearly the improvements in average returns to seed. From the tables published by Slicher van Bath[101] we can see that in the eighteenth and early nineteenth century the proportion of 'normal' harvests greatly increased in a number of areas, and it is made clear[102] that each increase in yields is associated with a period of more rapid population growth. The author states his belief that much of this is due to improved techniques, but points out the significance of the weather in producing exceptionally good harvests. The possible role of such harvests has already been described. Very low food prices could of course ruin farmers, and farmers were inclined to complain loudly, so that the beneficial effects on population growth and industrial production tend to be overlooked, especially in the Malthusian era. Ample food could scarcely fail to have beneficial effects on marriage, fertility and mortality, whatever the long-term possibilities of a negative effect on marriage and fertility of a rising standard of living. We leave aside the question whether increased consumption of wheat germ which contains Vitamin E increased the number of successful conceptions or increased the sexual potency of males—both effects have been claimed by medical authorities.

XII. *The labour force and the domestic consumer*

We have already characterized population as fulfilling a dual role, as producers and consumers, both of them essential to economic growth. In each case there is, theoretically, an optimum in relation to the productive capacity of industry and agriculture at any one time. Too few producers hamper expansion, too many may depress wages and thus fail to give the right stimulus to investment in labour-saving inventions. Too few consumers depress the domestic market, too many raise prices and tend to live at subsistence level or below, and thus again frustrate the expansion of production.

It is against this background that we see the conflicting views of the significance of industrial development for the rise in population. It was for long

[99] Habakkuk, p. 156 f.   [100] Jutikkala, p. 561.
[101] Slicher van Bath, *AAG Bijdragen*, 9, 1963, p. 121 ff.
[102] *AAG Bijdragen*, 10.

usual to assume that the demand for labour created population, through the influences on marriage and fertility which have already been discussed and found to be of doubtful efficacy. The relationship is much more complex than this. Perhaps the simplest point to make is that even in industrial societies employing child labour extensively, it takes 10-15 years from the supposed original stimulus to produce a significant addition to the labour force. If, as has been postulated, high wages and assured prospects lead to increased marriages and additional children, the bottlenecks created by labour shortages would restrict production or demand long before additional workers arrive—unless of course it were by migration. If we include in the factors leading to population increase the attraction of Irish and Scottish workers, for instance, into England in the first half of the nineteenth century, we can certainly accept that increased activity creates an associated rise in population. But we have to beware of the strong possibility that the initial impetus may lead to an excessive inflow of labour which in time also competes with the additional children born (if there were such) during the boom period, and the cyclical depression may thus be aggravated.

From the entrepreneur's point of view, the availability of labour is certainly an incentive, provided he is already sure of his market, to enlarge the scale of his operations, especially where labour-intensive operations are involved. This would be true, for instance, in some of the early textile industries, in potteries, and mining. To that extent a growing population, provided it furnishes the right type of labour in the right place, can and does add to the prospects of increasing industrialization and possibly to the chances of an enhanced standard of living in the long run, through the rise in real wages. But it must be clearly understood that the borderline between sufficient and excessive labour forces is thin, and that the basis of purchasing power may be quickly eroded by a surplus of people seeking work.[103] Conversely, a 'plethora of labour was a brake upon technical innovation'[104]; that is to say, the greatest advances in mechanization and therefore ultimately in cost reduction were forced on entrepreneurs by a distinct shortage of labour—and for this the North American continent and the experience of European countries in war-time provides the best examples. Neither labour availability nor labour shortage should be seen as primary determinants of the rate of economic progress, but they do play their part at the margin of decision making. It is not particularly logical to say as Marshall does,[105] that the Industrial Revolution called into being no more people than it required and could sustain. In one sense this is a truism, like the parallel anti-Malthusian assertions concerning population and subsistence, since at any one time most of the people were employed and most had enough to eat. But the generalization is not particularly useful, since at local and regional level there are acute labour shortages as well as unemployed surpluses, and there are groups of contented and well-fed artisans as well as starving handloom weavers. Nevertheless, Marshall's expression conveys the fundamental truth that the process of growth is in equilibrium only when production, population and food supplies keep in step with each other. That they be so adjusted is not a law of nature, for the disequilibria of earlier centuries, of later crises, and of the

[103] Chambers, p. 308 ff.   [104] Chambers, p. 324.   [105] Marshall, p. 251.

great majority of countries where growth was hardly measurable, clearly show the altogether exceptional set of circumstances prevailing in Britain and later in other western European industrial countries, and in the United States. This is seen by contrast, for instance, with the Scandinavian countries where questions of industrial growth do not arise, and where population growth is ultimately controlled by the ability of the agricultural sector alone to supply the needs of human beings. This was Malthus' view, it was accepted by Heckscher, and even the critics of Heckscher and Malthus cannot controvert the long-term connection, at any rate as a limiting factor.[106]

Very similar considerations apply to the analysis of population as a consumer force. There can be, in theory, only one equilibrium rate of growth of purchasing power, at any rate in a closed economy. This is rather clumsy to express in words rather than symbols, but it may be defined as a rate which will ensure that since no products are sold abroad, they are taken up by home markets. This rate can be achieved if the factors of production are remunerated at a level leaving them a margin of purchasing power consistent with the quantity of goods offered for sale. If the rate of remuneration is less, there will be over-production. If it is too high (because of severe labour shortage, caused, for instance, by previous high mortality amongst skilled workers), the resultant price level may shrink the number of potential domestic market consumers. Growth is only possible, in other words, if there is an increase in the number of consumers with the same real wages, more extensive production, or there is a growth of real wages for existing producer/consumers (through technological change), or a combination of both. At any rate it is not possible to conceive, as we have previously stated, of a long-term equilibrium growth rate associated with widespread proletarianization. The growth of consumption, of course, does not mean an equal distribution of purchasing power within the community. In fact, it was the very sharp inequality of incomes in pre-industrial societies which prevented the rise of a mass market. The rich bought little that was manufactured. Their consumption pattern depended largely on imported goods or on things made by craftsmen, artists, or those in their personal service. The process of industrialization enriched many, but again it was hardly amongst the manufacturers or merchants of the new era that the bulk of the cottons, the coarse woollens, the common pottery wares were sold. Some of these products went to those in the service of wealthy, but more went to the middle classes, the artisans and skilled workers. Each country had its own proletariat, rural and urban, but whilst we cannot say how large a proportion of the population at any one time lived at or near the margin of subsistence, it must be clear that the number and proportion of consumers rose during industrialization. At the end of the nineteenth century, when the population of Britain had risen to over 30 million people, when 75 per cent of them lived in towns, and when the economy had been shaken by a series of crises, social investigators found that something like a third of them were poor in the special sense in which the word was defined—i.e. they had not enough regular income to keep themselves in health or decency even if their pattern of expenditure was sensible. But even this poor third consumed industrial products—boots, candles,

[106] Jutikkala, p. 561-3, on Utterström and Heckscher.

domestic ironmongery, or buttons. And even if we leave these out of account, we still see, in 1900, 20 million people in moderate comfort, of which 15 million were not to be considered consumers 150 years earlier, either because they did not exist, or because their earning power was devoted mainly to food-stuffs, whether they were themselves the producers of food, or, even more vulnerably, had to buy them.[107] This insistence on the importance of the con-sumer does not in any way contradict the evidence we have that particular sections of the population were, in a very real sense, proletarianized. The economic progress of a nation did not manifest itself in every region or occu-pational group. For peasants deprived of their land, or handloom weavers of their livelihood, there was no question of an improvement of their situation. Their incomes, in kind or in money, fell, their living standards were reduced. But we need not assume that because such depressed groups and areas existed, that the growth of population was adversely affected by their poverty—indeed the rapid increase in the families of the poorest people noted by Adam Smith, Malthus and their successors, is a tribute to the ability of an essentially growing economy to keep alive even those whose incomes were falling. Mr Dobb has argued[108] that a fall in the death rate due to improvements in health accelerated the proletarianizing process. This is true, in the sense that it increased the danger of local excess supplies of labour. But of course if this process had gone very far, the death rate would have risen again, and the usual Malthusian 'auditing with a red pencil' would have restored the balance. But since this did not happen, and since the alleged excessive progeny of the very poor was kept alive, we are led to the obvious conclusion that poverty is less fatal in a rich and growing society than in a poor or stationary environment. This may be so even if the poor society existed, as in Ireland, merely on the outer fringes of a rich one, and it is certainly the case if it merely forms a pocket in a wealthier tract.[109]

It thus turns out that the long arguments about the role of population in economic growth have an air of unreality about them. There can be no general rule as to whether population produced industrialization, or industrialization called forth extra population.[110] Neither process can stand by itself. To say that it is a continuous process of interaction is merely to hedge. The fact is that every region and every industry produces a different pattern. The history of the last 150 years has shown us that a country may first experience a rapid rise in fertility as prosperity increases; in the next stage the standard of living may reduce fertility to danger point, and at a later stage still the affluent society may choose to take out some of its prosperity in more babies rather than leisure or consumer durables. In some places we may obtain a sharp positive correlation between economic prosperity and the birth-rate but more usually the picture will be blurred.[111] Therefore the rate of population growth can-not exactly correspond to the rate of economic growth. There is a better correlation with mortality in industrializing countries, but elsewhere, as we have seen, mortality may fall without drastic improvements in real wages. In England, early in the nineteenth century, the death rate probably rose owing to increasing

[107] Goubert, p. 473.   [108] Chambers, p. 308.
[109] Deprez, p. 628 (*Le Vieuxbourg*).   [110] Habakkuk, p. 270-1.   [111] Cipolla, p. 583-5

concentration in insanitary towns despite continuing industrial expansion, though this was a transitory phase, and in the second half of the century mortality fell as real wages rose. On the whole it is not conceivable to have a falling mortality rate side by side with a stationary or even falling standard of living. Everything that prolongs life food, shelter, clothing, leisure, recreation, environment, public services, transfer incomes (such as medical, educational or relief services)—costs money, and means real incomes being applied for the benefit of those whose mortality is to be reduced. If this does not take place, then the most vulgar of Malthusian models must operate. This is the dilemma now facing the world, and it must have been present in our society 200 years ago. We cannot now have any doubt of the long-term outcome of the race between growth and subsistence, mortality and living standards.

XIII. *Conclusion*

The evidence presented in this volume is obviously not sufficient to enable us to make definite judgments about the nature of the growth of population in Europe and North America since the seventeenth century, or to explain unambiguously the links between population and economy. Our contributors have provided a vast range of possible connections between changes in nuptiality, fertility and mortality on one hand and the agricultural and industrial patterns of their regions on the other.

But they have also provided much evidence of the existence of movements in vital rates not visibly corresponding to economic patterns. Apart from the autonomous variables of climate, we find that diseases do not always run their courses according to prevailing living standards or employment opportunities. Harvests and sickness fluctuate, but not always together. Marriage and fertility respond to changes in the levels of real wages, but the relationship is sometimes direct and sometimes inverse. In other words, social conventions, traditions and prejudices, political necessities and religious scruples supervene to blur the simple outline. The pattern may be highly complex, and allow no simple or unitary explanations. Each facet of the situation may have its own set of data and causal links.

At this stage of investigation, the gaps in our knowledge are fairly clear to the observer. The economic historian, faced with the need to throw light on the process of growth and change in an industrializing society, has certain quite specific requests to make of the historical demographer to assist in the task of clarification. The first set of these is concerned mainly with statistical method, and necessarily outside the scope of this volume. There is much need for standardization—of measurements, of division into periods of account, and especially of presentation in intelligible series and a proper framework of relevant data. As regards the actual measurement of change, there is now widespread agreement as to the inherent superiority of the Henry/Fleury method, but ways and means will have to be found to achieve similar coherence even where the data make it difficult or impossible to reconstitute large numbers of families. Equally important is the requirement that population statistics should not be collected or presented out of their historical and physical context. The demographer is inclined to believe that the historian will, in any case, know the background to population change. But this is not always so. If the trained statistician is unable to supply the complementary information, analysis and presentation may become a matter of team work, so that data concerning climate, harvests, epidemics, employment, wages and prices are not merely collected but are at once correlated with the vital statistics series.

Apart from these methodological considerations, the economic historian is also inclined to ask that the demographer should turn his attention to specific periods and regions which are of special interest in the present state of work in the field of economic development. Industrialization takes place in different countries in its various phases from the seventeenth century to the present time, and its demographic implications have not yet been studied everywhere. There is at present an understandable preoccupation with the seventeenth and eighteenth centuries, since these pre-statistical periods offer in some ways the most exciting challenge of unanswered questions. But it needs to be pointed out that even for the middle of the nineteenth century, and often later, i.e. periods when reasonably adequate censal and civil registration material is available, the study of the growth of the labour force, of urbanization, of the causes and courses of declining mortality and fertility, are all still in their infancy. Only where depopulation threatened have there been intensive studies of the fall in the birth-rate and its causes, especially in France. But even for England we are still largely ignorant, for instance, about the composition of the growth pattern of the industrial labour force after 1815, the period of intensive urbanization and concentration into steam-powered manufacture. It is true that we possess successive census reports and can tell, in rough terms, where the population grew and where it declined,[112] but very little work has been done to describe in meaningful detail the changing area and occupational structure of the big cities, their growth by natural increases and migration respectively, the composition of households and the regional variations in female and juvenile labour in their relationship with expectation of life and family size. The census schedules from the beginnings to 1861, now open to public inspection, still await analysis,[113] as do the greatly improved civil registers after 1837. Even the parochial registers from 1812-37, despite all their deficiencies,[114] because they are kept in printed forms, are still capable of yielding useful results especially in those areas which were still dominated by the Anglican parochial organization. Similar rich mines of material still exist in other countries. Where, as in many German states, an active local bureaucracy, perhaps influenced by cameralist considerations, made repeated inquiries into the numbers and conditions of the people, large scale continuous records often survive from the middle of the eighteenth century and await detailed analysis.[115] In Scandinavia, a great mass of local census-type lists and registers containing records of education, communicants, migrants as well as the more usual

[112] For types of analysis, see A. Redford, *Labour Migration in England 1800-1850*, ed. W. Chaloner, 1964; J. Saville, *Rural Depopulation in England and Wales, 1851-1951*, 1958.
[113] Work on the census schedules of York, 1841-61 is now being carried out by Mr W. A. Armstrong of Nottingham University, to find answers to the questions raised here.
[114] Krause, *passim*.
[115] Some results published by K. Blaschke, of Dresden cf. 'Zur Bevölkerungsgeschichte Sachsens vor der industriellen Revolution', *Beitr. z.d. Wirtschafts- und Sozialgeschichte*, Berlin, 1962.

baptisms, burials and marriages are only now beginning to be used to the full extent possible in some areas.

There are large possibilities, then, for regional studies of population in its economic and social context, from the beginnings of record keeping in the sixteenth century until recent times. If such regional studies follow a similar pattern and yield comparable data, they may be built up into national and eventually international series in the same way as investigations into population movements, trade, production and public health are now collected and published by United Nations agencies. From such series we may one day be able to build up a more comprehensive picture of our past evolution as working populations.[116]

[116] For an attempt to produce a methodology of work in this field, and standard statistical practice, both for aggregative analysis and for re-constitution, and static (census) material, see: Eversley, Laslett and Wrigley, (ed. Wrigley), *Introduction to Historical Demography in England since 1500*, to be published in 1965.

3

TOWARDS A HISTORY OF POPULATION
LOUIS CHEVALIER

From: *Population*, 1946, 245-56
Translated by Peter Jimack

Editor's Note: Professor Chevalier's essay is here reprinted as it first appeared. It marked the beginning of the renewed interest in the field of historical demography at the end of the war. As appears from the work that followed, his pessimism regarding the availability of primary sources for the sort of history he had in mind was not altogether justified, but his view of the importance of parish registers turned out to be correct.

The essay contains the emphasis on the local nature of historical demographic studies, and though it deals mostly with France, draws attention in general to the inter-action between changes in political, economic and social structure on one hand, and population movements on the other.

Demographic history as an instrument of history and of demography

RESEARCH in demography, like studies in economics or politics, is very much inclined to use history as a kind of charming and somewhat antiquated preamble to more serious, and, materially, more profitable considerations. In France more than in any other country this preliminary evocation of the past is insisted on, as a customary, but more or less meaningless ritual. There are few technical programmes, few administrative texts which do not begin with some historical considerations, invoking the aid of great predecessors. There is not a political or economic congress which does not invite to the inaugural session, but to no other, the historian or the sociologist. Thus the distant shades of Sully, Richelieu, Colbert, often indistinct in outline, float round the doorways to our modern laboratories, only to disappear as quickly as the scholar who called them forth. Amid the preoccupations of today, concerned with swift and precise solutions, history is simply one of those obligatory gestures of politeness which an old country owes to its past and to itself, and the historian, in the words of Richelieu, is intended chiefly to 'embellish the top of the basket'.

Let us admit though that generally he is resigned to this role of prestige value and uselessness, when, in fact, he is not the first to recognize, if not the prestige value, at least the uselessness. He has an acute awareness of the differences between periods, far more so than of their similarities. It is never without some uneasiness that he hears those dangerous analogies, those parallels between policies, so readily indulged in by those who make a practice of using history to support their actions. The historian of foreign immigration into France does not believe that the immigration policy during the *Ancien Régime* can throw any light at all on a present-day policy of immigration; he does not even think that one can speak of an *Ancien Régime* immigration policy. The specialist in economic history will refuse to quote the investment plans of the provincial administrators of the eighteenth century or of M. Thiers in connexion with present-day investment plans. In any case he will be most unwilling to draw those chronologically and technically sound conclusions required of him by impatient administrators. Historical research is vast and slow, whereas decisions have to be immediate. Nor does he believe that his documentation is sufficiently exact and sufficiently continuous to permit valid conclusions and to allow programmes to be defined. He often, in fact, retains this idea that history can be of no use in guiding history.

And yet, if these too occasional and too formal contacts between history and current policies usually serve merely to underline the differences and mutual misunderstandings, there are vast common fields to be exploited by lasting and continuous research, for the greatest benefit to both forms of activity.

Albert Sorel, who was both an historian and a man of action, has already emphasized how much the historian has to gain by taking a share in the responsibilities of his country, and how much the politician has to gain by day-to-day working at some common task together with the specialist on the past. It is true of the fields of politics and economics. It is even more true in the field of demography. Discipline both in history and in demography can only gain by this joint research. Over and above the mere narrative, in the customary political, economic and social terms, to which history is generally confined, the technique of demography will enable history to comprehend those basic human phenomena, about which it requires qualitative, but also quantitative information.

For a long time, history was solely political and administrative. It has become more and more economic and social. Only by appropriating demography will it finally understand the why and the how of the past. Having concerned itself with knowing how, in different periods, men thought and acted, having concerned itself with knowing how they lived materially, history cannot avoid seeking the ultimate explanation which birth and death alone can provide. In this way, history can find the programme it needs for its future research, as well as the verification of its past researches, and even the means of testing the validity of their results. The exploitation of political and administrative archives is by now very advanced; for many periods, it can now give rise only to fresh interpretations, minor corrections, and individual *tours de force* on the part of subtle and inspired researchers. Economic history, although still possessing less well explored sources of documentation, and particularly fairly new regional sources, will, it seems, quickly bring about that state of complete exploration of the sources which political history has more or less reached. One must also bear in mind the almost total destruction of archives by the public administrations of Paris and the 'départements' since the turn of the century; it will be impossible to trace an exact history of agriculture, industry and commerce in France since 1900, because, apart from a few 'miraculously' surviving files, whole categories of documents have been destroyed. On the other hand, thanks to censuses and local registers of births, marriages and deaths, demographic history presents vast fields which are both unexplored and relatively well protected, as well as possibilities of entirely new research.

The benefit to demography will not be less. Through history, it will be able to escape the calculations of statistics, often excessively abstract, and that exactness which is so often very far from exact. Statistics on their own are valid only when they can be based on sufficiently large numbers, covering considerable periods of time and wide geographical and administrative areas; the exact history of a 'département', of a 'canton', and even of a parish, of their political life, of their economic and social structure at different periods, may enable statistical investigation to become more defined and more thorough, in fact, to some extent to eliminate chance. The humps and depressions in the pyramid of ages of one canton, compared with the pyramid of ages of another, can be explained by local structure and local evolutions which history can identify. In short, history can make statistics a far keener and more effective instrument.

Nineteenth-century history and the explanation of contemporary demographic phenomena

If we try to define the role of history in the study of demographic problems, we see however that the demographic history of the nineteenth and twentieth centuries must be distinguished from the history of earlier periods. The aims and methods are different in the two cases, as are the ways in which history can contribute to the explanation of contemporary demographic questions.

The role of history in the study of current demographic problems results first of all from the fact that most of these problems appear basically in an historical form. This is perhaps true of many countries, but it is especially true of France, where the influence of the past, or of traditional ways of thought and behaviour, as some would say, is particularly strong—whether or not we think this a good thing. It is impossible to understand the quantitative and qualitative appearance of the present population of France, as well as the geographical distribution of this population, unless one begins by reconstituting in its entirety, and by recognizing without ambiguity, the evolution which has brought about the present situation, or rather which is continued in it. Cut off from the past which both explains and produces it, this situation could contain no valid solution and could permit no sure policy. The history of France is without those relatively recent economic and social crises which, for other nations, mark the beginning of new phases, vastly different phases, from the political, economic and demographic points of view, which one can, without exaggeration, count as the starting point of a period that is truly contemporary and easier to study.

It is a well-known fact that from the economic and social points of view, the Revolution of 1789 was not accompanied by that upheaval which characterized it in the political field. If one studies even regions close to Paris, such as Brie or Beauce, one will find that, although the châteaux have sometimes changed hands, the system of land use has remained the same and social groupings have changed only slightly. And, most important of all, the economic evolution of the nineteenth century, industrialization, and the expansion of urban centres have been so slow and so steady that it would be quite artificial to distinguish phases in them, and even more so to see in this development any economic or demographic revolution.

On this point, France is quite different from England, where the economic revolution in the middle of the eighteenth century produced changes far more important than did the thunder of our Revolutionary assemblies. It is different too from Germany, whose economic, political and demographic evolution assumes after 1870 such a new shape that the demographic study of Germany in the twentieth century can perfectly well begin from the industrialization at the end of the nineteenth century, taking that as a safe starting point, the beginning of a new period. Dutheil's book on the population of Germany brings out well the transformation stemming from this development of industry. Compared with the Germany of 1848, it is economically a new Germany: but it is also a Germany made demographically unrecognizable by the pattern and social structure of the birth rate, and by the fact that the accent on working-class fertility in the Germany of William II gave the country itself an almost completely new social structure.

The history of France has none of these breaks and new beginnings. The transitions in it are imperceptible. Present-day demographic knowledge tries in vain to find in the recent past some safe basis for study, some acceptable limit, marking sufficiently clearly the beginning of a phase which could be considered as contemporary.

In fact, the present state of the French population seems to belong to an evolution which can be said to date back to the first quarter of the nineteenth century, and which has been described by M. Landry as the 'Demographic Revolution'. As the work of M. Labrousse has shown, up to the middle of the eighteenth century France had a high birth rate, but also a high death rate, due to the poor harvests, the famines, and the absence of means of communication; during the course of the eighteenth century, the birth rate remained high, but, as a result of the improvement in communications and those roads admired by Arthur Young, the death rate went down. During the years following the wars of the Revolution and Empire, the birth rate declined, and, in some years, fell below the death rate.

This demographic period, to which we still seem to belong, must be considered as a whole. It is an historical unit, at the heart of which must be sought and confronted the developments which still exert their influence.

Modern demographers are thus concerned with the same problems as the demographers and economists who were the first to recognize that phenomenon which, about 1856, Hippolyte Passy, Legoyt and Léonce de Lavergne described as hard to believe; faced with this problem, they could only confess their ignorance. And we have to repeat this confession of ignorance. For, after the brief misgivings produced by the first results of the census of 1856, and until very recent times, enlightened opinion turned away from a situation it could not understand. The *Journal des Economistes* provides most significant reading in this respect; after a certain number of articles devoted to this new aspect of French demography, gradually, and until well into the twentieth century, we see far more interest shown in more specifically economic and social subjects. Men were resigned to not understanding.

The situation has become worse, but the main elements do not seem very different, and it is now the historian's turn to tackle the problem which the economists of the Second Empire had already formulated, but which, being too close to the phenomenon and possessing too little statistical information, they were not able to solve: how does the general evolution of France since the beginning of the nineteenth century prepare and explain the demographic situation of today?

Let us merely indicate here the different aspects of this general evolution and the hypotheses of men such as Léonce de Lavergne or Hippolyte Passy, which we must now be in a far better position than they to test.

It is above all a matter of social and economic evolution. Is it possible to detect the influence on the standard of living of the population and on the birth rate, of the system of property and land-development on the one hand, and on the other hand of the economic variations inherent in this framework? In particular, is it possible to assess the influence of the system of inheritance? About 1860, Leplay and Legoyt adopted opposite positions over this question, which has been asked by Montalembert about 1840, and on which some information can already be found in Arthur Young's *Travels in France*. From the industrial point of view, one must consider the influence on fertility of the localization of industries and of its developments, both in the industrial sector itself, and also in the artisan and peasant sectors in which industry has developed.

And then, starting from these developments in peasant and industrial society, one ought to describe the pattern and the volume of those internal migrations, about which the only available information is lacking in precision, and which, nevertheless, explain the human configuration not only of our towns, but also of our rural areas. It is by no means sure that the usual description of the drift to the towns, its causes, the paths it followed, and its efforts, is an accurate one. It is probable that this movement assumed various forms in different periods and different regions, and it is these various forms which must be described if one intends to construct a demographic and economic policy which is no longer improvised, but the result of reflection and to some extent of experience.

This historical evolution cannot be confined to the economic and the social. The influence of strictly political events, if one can in fact isolate the political from the economic, can be easily measured by the generally recognized effect of wars and even of revolutions on fertility. This effect of revolutions, or merely of disturbances and insecurity in internal politics, seems to have been greater immediately after the long period of political stability under the *Ancien Régime* than it is today. Tocqueville saw in the political instability which followed the French Revolution, and which he said would long continue, the cause of the lasting social and demographic disturbances in France. The fall of the monarchy brought about a great political and social upheaval, the scale of which can be measured by means of local history; traces of it can still be found at the end of the Second Empire. And the social and demographic repercussions of revolutions like those of 1830 or 1848 have been incomparably greater than their political consequences; their extent cannot fail to surprise one.

It is no less surprising that fertility, which had considerably diminished from 1815 to 1848, increased again up to about 1861, a period of political stability, and only began to fall again in 1865; this is, indeed, one of the more curious problems of the demographic evolution of nineteenth-century France.

Finally, these economic, social and political evolutions were accompanied by a moral evolution, an evolution in moral standards and behaviour, which some contemporary demographers, following the example of the Academy of Moral and Political Science during the Second Empire, are very inclined to see as the essential cause of the demographic evolution of France in the nineteenth and twentieth centuries. This influence is at once easier and more difficult to define. The conflict between religious feelings and what Renan called 'material interests', and the improvements in education, both in quantity and in quality, might perhaps contribute important elements to this study. Let it be said at once that, although much has been written on the subject in vague terms, there has been very little precise and clearly localized research. Yet it is perhaps this type of research which can provide the surest solution to the problem.

Furthermore, the importance of these factors differs from region to region, and it is within the framework of varied geographical units that one must attempt to compare these developments, which it would be artificial to study in isolation and in the far too large framework of the whole of French territory. Demographic history must be regional, and even local. We need to compare different or similar evolutions taking place in carefully selected natural environments. It is only in such restricted, intimate areas that it will be possible to collect together all the necessary documents, only in these units that we shall be able to assign economic, social, political and religious influences to their true place and determine the relationships between them. Through these influences, perhaps, we shall even discover, for some regions, an ethnic determinism which has a sounder base and more lasting validity. M. André Siegfried's work, *La tableau politique de la France de l'Ouest*, offers for this kind of study both a method and an example to be followed.

It would be interesting to compare the similar demographic evolution of two regions which are far apart but offer a number of resemblances in physical or moral structure, which would bring out more clearly other, completely dissimilar elements. I have in mind a comparison between the demographic evolution of Brittany and of the Basque country in the nineteenth and twentieth centuries: the same high level of fertility, the same social composition, the same influence of the area, the same strong religious feeling, but different economies, and above all, different ethnic backgrounds; a demographic study would have to determine the precise influence of these various elements. It would, however, be still more useful to attempt comparisons between geographically closer units, thus eliminating the unknowns which result from the two regions belonging to such different civilizations. I have myself tried to study the evolution of the population in three cantons of Vendée, taken from the three districts of Plaine, Bocage and Marais, in terms of land-distribution and the social and religious structure of these regions.

Seen in this way, history no longer appears as the more or less reliable purveyor of examples to follow or avoid; it becomes identified with the present, large fields of which it at once appropriates, refusing to be dissociated from it. Investigation in the present and historical research are really one and the same thing, throwing light upon each other. The exploration of local registers of births, marriages and deaths, or of the archives of 'départements', cannot recognize any vague chronological limits, marking the transition from the present day to the dusty realm of the past.

Needless to say, the collaboration of many investigators is required for the successful completion of this study. It must be based on monographs on communes and cantons, drawn from the exploration of local archives and particularly from registers of births, marriages and deaths. The *Institut national d'études démographiques* contributes to these researches a memorandum specifying the composition of such documents and uniform and useful methods of analysing their contents. Only profitable collaboration between the Universities and the *Institut* will enable these investigations to develop to the desired extent.

The usefulness of the demographic history of an earlier period

But history can also contribute in other ways to the solution of demographic problems.

We are no longer concerned with the continuous evolution of France during the nineteenth and twentieth centuries and the present-day 'Demographic Revolution', in which current problems are linked without a break to a relatively recent past. We are concerned now with the history of an earlier period, in which questions are no longer exactly the same, and are even completely different, a period in which, above all, incomplete, or more frequently, non-existent statistics prevent one from tracing any genuine evolutions. I refer to that vast field which is most generally the subject of historical research, and which extends from the first utilizable documents to the end of the eighteenth century and the first continuous statistics.

In what way can history, thus defined, throw any light on contemporary demographic studies?

The documents themselves are an ill-assorted collection and there have been few studies based on them. M. Landry, in his *Révolution démographique*, has reviewed the principal documents concerning Greek and Roman antiquity. We have also J. Beloch's work, *Die Bevölkerung der griechisch-römischen Welt*, published in 1886, and the studies by Otto Seeck and Fahlbeck, together with the more recent work by Rostovtzeff. For the Middle Ages, the *Polyptique* of Irminon, Abbot of Saint-Germain-des-Prés, and the register of parishes and households in 1323 provide valuable information about the population of France at the beginning of the ninth and fourteenth centuries respectively; F. Lot's studies on the early Middle Ages contain a certain amount of information about population, starting from the end of the Roman era.

For more recent times, the information available becomes more plentiful and more precise. In 1579, certain procedures for the registration of vital statistics had been introduced in France; and, far earlier than in other countries, life-insurance had begun to appear. The administrators' accounts for thirty-two provinces, submitted to the King between 1698 and 1700, were made use of by Vauban, Saugrain (1720) and Boulainvilliers (1727). In 1766, Messance published his *Recherches sur la population des généralités d'Auvergne, de Lyon, de Rouen et de quelques autres provinces et villes du Royaume*, and in 1778 appeared Moheau's *Recherches et considérations sur la population de la France*. Antoine Deparcieux (1703-68), in an attempt to work out some reliable guiding principles for life insurance, published in 1746 his *Essai sur la probabilité de durée de la vie humaine*, based mainly on the study of five religious communities.

All this documentation is no doubt fragmentary, and yet, as M. Landry points out, 'with fragmentary facts, one can not only produce an impression, one can also create a theory'. It has thus been possible to define certain major demographic rhythms, which contain large areas of obscurity, admittedly, but also, as a result of more thorough, or merely more fortunate, local studies, moments of absolute clarity. Let us confine ourselves here to indicating the principal stages in this evolution. The population of ancient Greece seems to have begun to decline in the third or the second century B.C., and a host of literary and epigraphic documents enable us to point to some of the reasons. Depopulation in the Roman Empire begins to be apparent well before the second century A.D., and it is not impossible to discover the principal factors in this trend. As for the fate of the Western Empire during the early Middle Ages, the studies of F. Lot have emphasized certain essential and sometimes unexpected aspects. Thus it was internal troubles far more than barbarian invasions which brought about the downfall of the Empire: 'Germania, with only a small population, was incapable of ethnically engulfing the Mediterranean world . . . the means at its disposal were absurdly small. . . . At the most critical period, Julian had to fight against only 30,000 Alemanni.' From the tenth century onwards, the population of the Western Empire, rid of the Saracens, the Norsemen and the Magyars, began to increase; many people were compelled to leave their family tenures. This demographic development is revealed in the departure of Norman adventurers to Italy, and, following William the Conqueror, to England; the first Crusade and extensive cultivation of new land afford further evidence of this rise in population, which was to continue until the end of the thirteenth century. Lot estimates that at the end of the reign of St. Louis the rural population of France was as high as 15 millions. The fourteenth and fifteenth centuries, on the other hand, a period of political, economic and social crisis, show a reversal in the trend: the relatively dense rural population of Capetian France underwent a decline, which statistics only rarely enable us to compute, but which is emphasized by a wide variety of texts.

The researches of contemporary historians and specialists in human geography on the economic and social evolution of France from the sixteenth century to the end of the eighteenth century would give exact information about this demographic evolution, which requires a considerable mass of documents and which can only be the by-product of extensive social and economic studies. Thus the most reliable conclusions in demographic history come from M. Coornaert's research in economic history, or M. Dion's research in human geography, while the economic investigations of M. Levebvre or M. Labrousse throw some important light on the demographic evolution of eighteenth-century France. In the same way, the most reliable conclusions about the history of the English population are derived from the work of

G. N. Clark or Trevelyan, whose social history of the English people is particularly illuminating concerning the evolution of the population.

The exacting statistician will not perhaps feel entirely at home with these complex studies, which differ from his in the documents used, in the interpretation of sources, and in the nature of the conclusions drawn. But he would be wrong to scorn them and to underestimate the importance of this work towards the creation of a contemporary demographic policy. 'We know today that our civilizations are mortal', wrote Valéry. It is this relationship in life and in death that such studies in history, even ancient history, enable us to bring out, a community of fate emerging from the diversity of periods.

4

THE VITAL REVOLUTION RECONSIDERED[1]

K. F. HELLEINER

From: *Canadian Journal of Economics and Political Science*,
Vol. XXIII, No. 1, 1957

Reprinted with minor revisions by the author

THE historian's understanding of past situations benefits greatly from the fact that he, unlike any contemporary observer, knows a good deal about the subsequent development. It is only in retrospect, if at all, that germinal forces, unnoticed or underestimated at the time, can be seen in their true significance. However, hindsight also has its dangers. Reading history backwards we are easily misled into postulating specific 'antecedents' and 'early phases' of phenomena which seem to require a long period of gestation; and we are almost inclined to distrust our records if they fail to confirm our expectations.

It is well to be on guard against this temptation when trying to appraise the general character of the closing years of the seventeenth, and the early decades of the eighteenth century. Certainly, as far as the demographic situation of this period is concerned, there was little if anything to herald the impending changes. Man was still very much at the mercy of the elements. As late as the 1690's a succession of poor and indifferent harvests created severe subsistence crises in almost all countries of Europe. So far from growing, the population declined here and there, as dearth and starvation stalked through the lands from Castile to Finland, and from the Scottish Highlands to the foothills of the Alps. In 1698, after a serious crop failure, certain regional death rates in Sweden are known to have risen to 9 and 16 per cent respectively.[2] (The present death rate in Canada is 9 per mille!) In one Finnish province, Tavastland, no less than one-third of the inhabitants must be assumed to have perished during the famine of 1696-7.[3] Many parts of France had suffered comparable losses a few years earlier, in 1693-4.[4] An enumeration held in the Duchy of Brabant in 1709 failed to reveal any gain in numbers over those ascertained in

---

[1] This paper was presented at the annual meeting of the Canadian Political Science Association in Montreal, 6 June 1956. Its main substance will be incorporated, in slightly extended form, in the author's contribution to the forthcoming fourth volume of the *Cambridge Economic History*.

[2] Eino Jutikkala, 'The Great Finnish Famine in 1696-97', *Scandinavian Economic History Review*, III, no. 1, 1955, p. 56. See below, pp. 549-69.   [3] *Ibid.*, 51 ff.

[4] There exists ample information of a local or regional nature on the impact of the French famine of 1693-4. The following recent studies may be mentioned: Jean Meuvret, 'Les Crises de subsistance et la démographie de la France d'Ancien Régime', *Population*, I, 1946, 643-50; Pierre Goubert, 'En Beauvaisis: problèmes démographiques du XVIIe siècle', *Annales: économies, sociétés, civilisations*, VII, 1952, 453-68, and his 'Une Richesse historique en cours d'exploitation: les registres paroissiaux', *ibid.*, IX, 1954, 83-93. See below, pp. 457-473 and 507-522.

1693.[5] The Kurmark, in 1728, counted slightly fewer inhabitants than forty years earlier.[6] In the British Isles, a period of acute distress which lasted from 1693 to 1699 was long afterwards remembered as the 'seven ill years'.[7] Though they may not have caused a diminution, they must certainly have checked the growth of population, if not in England, at any rate in Scotland.

Nor was this the last visitation of the kind. The excessively cold and long winter of 1708-9, followed as it was by widespread crop failures, again caused intense misery and high mortality among the poorer classes, especially in France, where this season was long remembered as 'le grand Hiver'.[8] In England, the scarcity did not reach famine proportions,[9] but the price of grain rose very high,[10] and the London Bills of Mortality record an unusual incidence of fatal cases of 'fever'.[11]

Meanwhile Europe had once again entered upon a phase of universal belligerency. While the campaigns of the War of the Spanish succession (1701-14) were fought in the west, the nations of the north-east were engaged in an even longer and fiercer conflict, the Great Northern War (1699-1721). Historians have tended to minimize the *direct* demographic effects of warfare; and in general this view of things is probably correct. However, the Great Northern War appears to have been an uncommonly sanguinary affair. This may be inferred from Finnish population data from the middle of the eighteenth century, which reveal a highly abnormal sex distribution in all the older age groups. At that time, there was an excess of females over males in the groups born between 1676 and 1695, ranging from 21 to as high as 68 per cent.[12] The conclusion to be drawn is that a significant proportion of the men who were of military age during the period of hostilities perished in the war. The effect of such losses on the reproductive power of the nations involved need no emphasis.

Nevertheless, the number of military casualties, if it could be ascertained, would undoubtedly be dwarfed by the heavy losses inflicted upon the civilian population by wartime epidemics. While the theatres of operations in the west experienced the usual flare-up of typhus, northeastern Europe was once again invaded by plague.[13] Though virtually extinct in the west, plague was still endemic in the eastern parts of the European continent. As early as 1708 the infection appears to have spread through Poland into Silesia; and in the next few years, undoubtedly in connexion with military movements, but probably fomented also by the food crisis of 1709-10, the disease invaded

---

[5] A. Cosemans, *De bevolking van Brabant in de XVIIe en XVIIIe eeuw* (Brussels, 1939), 57, 222. See also Deprez's article, Part III.

[6] Karl Theodor von Inama-Sternegg and Rudolf Häpke, 'Die Bevölkerung des Mittelalters und der neueren Zeit bis Ende des 18. Jahrhunderts in Europa', in *Handwörterbuch der Staatswissenschaften* (4th ed., Jena, 1924), II, 672.

[7] Charles Creighton, *A History of Epidemics in Britain* (Cambridge, 1891, 1894), II, 47 ff.

[8] Arthur M. de Boislisle, *Le Grand Hiver et la disette de 1709* (Paris, 1903).

[9] J. D. Chambers, *The Vale of Trent 1670-1800*, 26. (See Part II, below, p. 327-34.)

[10] James E. Thorold Rogers, *A History of Agriculture and Prices in England* (Oxford, 1866-1902), VIII, Part 1, 7 ff.

[11] Creighton, *A History of Epidemics in Britain*, II, 54 ff.

[12] Eino Jutikkala, 'Die Bevölkerung Finnlands in den Jahren 1721-49', in *Annales Academiae Scientiarum Fennicae*, B LV, no. 4 (Helsinki, 1945), 21. See below, pp. 549-69.

[13] Georg Sticker, *Abhandlungen aus der Seuchengeschichte und Seuchenlehre*, I, part 1, *Die Geschichte der Pest* (Giessen, 1908), 214 ff.

Brandenburg-Prussia, the Baltic countries, and Scandinavia. In the city of Danzig and its suburbs, 32,600 persons—between one-third and one-half of the population—are reported to have died of plague during the epidemic of 1709; Copenhagen is said to have lost about a third of its inhabitants in 1710-11. Other cities of north-eastern Europe such as Königsberg, Riga, Stockholm, Uppsala, and Helsinki also suffered grievously. Nor was it only the urban centres that were afflicted. As Süssmilch's figures for East Prussia and Lithuania indicate,[14] mortality was very heavy throughout the Baltic littoral in 1709 and 1710. In East Prussia nearly 11,000 vacant farms are said to have been counted after the plague.[15] Progressing relentlessly toward the west, the infection reached north-western Germany in 1712, and Austria, Bohemia, and Bavaria in 1713. However, by this time, the epidemic, while still murderous in some places, seems to have exhausted its powers of diffusion. Before it was able to penetrate into Italy and the west of Europe the plague ceased abruptly.

To people in western Europe it must have seemed as if their countries had acquired some sort of immunity against plague: after all, the last pestilential visitations of western Europe had occurred a generation or two before. Moreover, events in the following years, though very upsetting at first, could not but confirm men in their optimism. I am referring to the last great outbreak of plague in western Europe, the visitation of Provence.[16]

In May 1720 a ship coming from a plague-infested port in Syria brought the deadly disease to Marseilles. There followed a furious outbreak, killing about 40,000 of the city's 90,000 inhabitants. Within a few weeks after its first appearance the epidemic was sweeping through Provence; and though in some places the losses were relatively light, in others, especially in the more populous towns and cities, the death toll was appalling. Aix-en-Provence, Martigues, and Saint-Rémy lost about one-third, Toulon, Auriol, and Berre about one-half, and Arles and La Valette about three-fourths of their inhabitants.

The news of this catastrophe caused grave anxiety throughout Europe. Authorities everywhere hastily decreed quarantine and other precautionary measures—the Pope had six of Rome's sixteen gates walled up so as to facilitate the inspection of incoming freight and travellers. In England—such is the tangled skein of historical causation—the scare produced an unexpected boom in the textile trades, as people stopped buying French manufactures and transferred their demand to English goods.[17] However, the fears proved unfounded. Inexplicably, the plague failed to spread beyond the borders of Provence and a few adjoining districts of Languedoc; and by August 1721 it was all over.

I

The sequence of crises which, often reinforcing one another, had afflicted most nations of Europe during the 1690's and the early years of the eighteenth century was followed by a period which appears considerably more auspicious by comparison. The two decades from 1715 to 1735, with one or two excep-

[14] They are quoted by Thomas Robert Malthus in the (Second) *Essay on Population*, Book II, chap. xii.   [15] Erich Keyser, *Bevölkerungsgeschichte Deutschlands* (2nd ed., Leipzig, 1941), 386.
[16] Sticker, *Die Geschichte der Pest*, 222 ff.
[17] M. Dorothy George, *England in Transition* (Penguin Books, 1953), 54.

tions, were marked by abundant harvests. Endemic diseases, such as typhoid, continued to exact a heavy toll of life, especially in the big cities; but there were no more epidemics of plague, except that limited outbreak in Provence. Fighting was tapering off: the Spanish succession was settled by treaty in 1714, and Austria's conflict with Turkey ended in 1718. The Northern War was in its last phase, and terminated in 1721. The stage was set for demographic recovery and advance.

At this point in his narrative the historian of population, for the first time, finds himself in a position to support his conclusions with tolerably reliable figures arranged in time series; though in the beginning it is only for a very limited territory—Finland and ten counties of Sweden—that this kind of information becomes available.[18] In both these countries the death rate remained remarkably constant and very low for a period of about fifteen years following the end of the Northern War, the average being 21·2 per mille for Sweden[19] and 20·8 per mille for Finland in 1721-35. A recent student of Swedish population sums up the state of affairs in these words: 'For no subsequent period during the rest of the century did the death rate remain at so low a level and in spite of wide fluctuations in the death rate in later years it was very rare for the rate to fall again to the low level of 1721-35, and in no year did it fall below that earlier level. Not until the 1830's in Sweden and the 1870's in Finland did the death rate fall to a comparably low figure.'[20]

To some small extent this uncommonly low death rate can be explained by viewing it as a function of the birth rate. Since infant mortality formed a very important component of total mortality in the eighteenth century, a low birth rate would tend to reduce the death rate. As a matter of fact, in consequence of the highly unfavourable age and sex distribution referred to above, the Swedish and Finnish birth rates were relatively low in this period. However, since the death rate was substantially lower still, the population of the two countries was growing rapidly. In Finland, the average annual increase in the twenties and early thirties of the eighteenth century was almost 16 per thousand, only a little lower than the rate of natural increase in Canada in recent years. In the ten Swedish counties for which information is available, natural growth, if considerably slower than in Finland, was also quite impressive.

However, the time had not yet arrived when European societies would be capable of weathering adversity well enough to produce an excess of births over deaths year after year, and decade after decade. In Sweden, for instance, natural increase turned negative momentarily as late as 1809-10. To be sure, the secular demographic trend was rising in all the Scandinavian countries after 1720. Subsistence crises and epidemics in the period under review were

[18] See Eli F. Heckscher, 'Swedish Population Trends before the Industrial Revolution', *Economic History Review*, Second Series, II, no. 3, 1950, 266-7; H. Gille, 'The Demographic History of the Northern European Countries in the Eighteenth Century', *Population Studies*, III, no. 1, 1949, 3–65; Gustav Utterström, 'Some Population Problems in Pre-Industrial Sweden', *Scandinavian Economic History Review*, II, no. 2, 1954, 103-65. See also the studies by Eino Jutikkala cited above in notes 2 and 12 and Part III, below, pp. 549-69.

[19] This figure, which is based on slightly defective contemporary compilations from the church registers, would have to be raised to 23·9 per mille if the corrections suggested by a regional investigation were to be applied to the whole Kingdom. See Bertil Boëthius, 'New Light on Eighteenth Century Sweden', *Scandinavian Economic History Review*, II, 1953, 151, n. 2.

[20] Gille, 'Demographic History', 50.

very much milder, to all appearances, than those of the seventeenth century. Yet the gravest of them, for instance those of 1737-43 and 1771-3, were still sufficiently powerful to slow down population growth, and even reverse it temporarily. In no case, however, were the losses caused by hunger and disease crippling. Finland by 1745 had already overcome the demographic effects of the bad years after 1736. The net losses suffered by Sweden and Norway in the early seventies did not amount to more than 2·3 and 3·5 per cent of their respective populations, and were also made good within three or four years.

Demographic developments in eighteenth-century Scandinavia were in many respects typical of what was happening elsewhere in Europe at that time. Though the rates of growth varied widely from country to country, the population was on the increase everywhere from about 1720 onwards. The statistical evidence for this statement cannot be given here. Suffice it to say that the figures at our disposal—there are plenty of them—are of unequal value, and even the best of them should not be pressed very hard. Yet even if they be used for no purpose other than that of demonstrating the universal character of the demographic upswing in the eighteenth century, their heuristic value remains very great indeed: for it is only by taking cognizance of the universality of this phenomenon that we can hope to understand its causal mechanism. It is to this very problem of causation that the remainder of this paper will be devoted.

II

Surveying the course of demographic history over the last five hundred years in the various countries of Europe, one becomes dimly aware of some rough synchronism. In certain periods, seemingly unrelated or at any rate not closely related events appear to form congruent patterns of adversity which are found to have produced a downward trend of population over wide areas. At other times, conditions seem to have been sufficiently favourable to permit an increase of people almost everywhere. As far as *short-run oscillations* are concerned, this synchronism is perhaps not surprising. It may be explained on the ground that epidemics, and even wars, have a tendency to spread, and that climatic disturbances are often extensive enough to cause simultaneous crop failures in many countries. However, the parallelism of *secular trends* is not so easily accounted for. Even such a relatively recent phenomenon as the universal demographic upswing in eighteenth-century Europe still awaits an adequate explanation.

Some of the theories advanced by students of the earlier phases of the Vital Revolution certainly are not convincing.[21] The vaunted advances in medical knowledge and skill to which the reduction of mortality in this period has been partly attributed can hardly have exercised much influence on life expectancy in, let us say, Finland or Spain, or even in the rural districts and city slums of western Europe. It is safe to say that the great majority of the people received no medical attention at all, and those who did might have been better off without the radical purgings and bleedings administered even by the more enlightened practitioners of the art of healing. As a contemporary, Jacques

---

[21] See G. Talbot Griffith, *Population Problems of the Age of Malthus* (Cambridge, 1926).

Casanova, remarked in his *Memoirs*, 'More people perish at the hands of doctors than are cured by them.'[22] Though there had been some progress in medical theory, eighteenth-century therapy was not much different from that inflicted upon Molière's *Malade imaginaire* a hundred years earlier.

It is not always realized how little medical men could do to cure any of the major ills that flesh is heir to before the coming of antiseptic surgery and the discoveries of salvarsan, insulin, and the antibiotics. Even though a few drugs of potential efficacy (such as mercury, digitalis, ipecacuanha root, and cinchona bark) were already known in the eighteenth century, they were by no means always used correctly. In any case, not many of these newer remedies can be regarded as life-saving; and it is almost certain that their use cannot have had any appreciable effect on the national death rate.[23]

As to preventive medicine, the profession was equally helpless. To be sure, inoculation, a crude method of immunization against smallpox, had been introduced to western Europe early in the eighteenth century; but its practice remained limited, and its value was, moreover, doubtful. For the treatment was risky; and while it may have helped individuals to overcome the dreadful disease more easily than if they had caught an infection at random, the inoculated person did go through an attack of real smallpox, and was therefore a source of danger to his family and attendants. The discovery of vaccination came too late to have any effect on mortality in the eighteenth century: Edward Jenner's famous essay on cowpox appeared only in 1798.

Nor did eighteenth-century medicine have any effective means of protecting people against such infections as puerperal fever or typhus. That being the case, it seems doubtful whether the establishment of new hospitals in the period under review can properly be listed among the factors which contributed to the decline in mortality. What beneficent effects such institutions may have had were almost certainly more than counterbalanced by the dissemination among their inmates of those dangerous germs. For some time to come the hospitals' reputation of being gateways to death was not undeserved.

Another development which is usually mentioned among the factors held responsible for the fall of the death rate in eighteenth-century Europe—advances in sanitation—also requires reconsideration. That there were some improvements in public water supply and sewerage should not be denied. However, what progress there was affected only urban populations, and may, moreover, have been offset, at any rate in Britain, by the growth of appallingly unsanitary slums in the new industrial centres. Yet even if it be granted that, on balance, sanitation was improving, the effects on total mortality should not be overrated. Cleaner water and proper sewers, while they must have been instrumental in reducing the incidence of such diseases as typhoid and dysentery, could not prevent the spread of such equally potent killers as typhus, smallpox, diphtheria, or tuberculosis. Some of these could have been checked by a higher degree of

---

[22] Madeleine Boyd, ed., *The Memoirs of Jacques Casanova* (Modern Library ed., New York, 1929), 7.
[23] Thomas McKeown and R. G. Brown, 'Medical Evidence Related to English Population Changes in the Eighteenth Century', *Population Studies*, IX, 1955, 119-41, esp. 123 ff. This author was gratified to see views which he had developed independently receive confirmation in this study. See below, pp. 285-307.

personal cleanliness, better housing, and adequate nutrition. But have we any evidence of such improvements on a *general* scale? Other facts, such as the gradual draining of the fens in East Anglia, which may have been responsible for the disappearance of 'ague' from England, or the drastic drop, after 1751, in the amount of spirits consumed by the English, must indeed have had wholesome effects on *regional* morbidity and mortality; but any such local reductions of the death rate cannot of course, be held accountable for the universal growth of population in eighteenth-century Europe. It is this larger phenomenon which requires an explanation.

Most students of the history of population seem to agree that a significant reduction in mortality was the primary cause of the demographic upswing; and, though the statistical evidence is inconclusive, we see no reason why this proposition should be challenged. Indeed, it can be shown that, when mortality is high (as it still was in the eighteenth century), a decline in the death rate is inherently a more powerful causative factor of population growth than a rise in the birth rate.

We should argue, however, that it was the peaks rather than the plateau of mortality that were lowered. In other words, it was not so much a reduction of mortality in 'normal' years that produced the secular downward trend of the death rate, but an unmistakable abatement of the 'great crises'. The disappearance of plague above all, but also a very sensible mitigation of subsistence crises seem to have been chiefly responsible for the increase in life expectancy.

Not that dearth and epidemics had become a thing of the past: for instance, the late thirties and early forties, afflicted as they were by pandemics of influenza and typhus as well as by widespread crop failures (in 1740-1), were times of acute distress in most countries of Europe; and so were the early seventies of the eighteenth century. However, while death rates greatly increased in such periods, and momentarily exceeded the birth rates, mortality no longer assumed *catastrophic* proportions. Even death rates of 69 and 112 per mille, such as were recorded in Norway and the Swedish province of Värmland in 1742, are still a far cry from those experienced by some regions of Europe in times of adversity half a century earlier. As M. Goubert put it, 'Après 1741, un monde démographique semble défunt: les mortalités s'attenuent jusqu'à disparaître.'[24] (The fact that subsistence crises, unlike those of previous centuries, could no longer raise the spectre of plague had of course a great deal to do with this attenuation.)

Since famines and epidemics are known to have been particularly hard on the very young, it is safe to conclude that the general abatement of crises must have had disproportionately beneficial effects on infant mortality; and the fact that a higher percentage of the population survived to the reproductive age could not fail to exercise a favourable influence on the birth rate. One further corollary should be noted. As I hope to show in my forthcoming contribution to the *Cambridge Economic History*, severe crises invariably caused not only a jump in the death rate, but also a drastic drop in the number of conceptions and live births. It follows that the substantial mitigation of crises which becomes

[24] 'En Beauvaisis', 466.

obvious in the course of the eighteenth century must also have tended some-what to raise the secular level of the birth rate.

III

Having sketched the demographic history of eighteenth-century Europe, the historian can hardly avoid asking himself whether it is proper to call these developments a 'Vital Revolution'. The opinion, still widely held, that before the eighteenth century, Europe's population, though subject to violent short-run fluctuations, remained stationary over long periods, or was growing only imperceptibly, is, I believe, no longer tenable. There is sufficient evidence to indicate that those oscillations were superimposed on clearly recognizable 'long waves'. At least two periods of secular increase can be tolerably well identified in the demographic history of medieval and early modern Europe, the first extending from about the middle of the eleventh to the end of the thirteenth, the second from the middle of the fifteenth to the end of the sixteenth century. What the exact rates of growth during those earlier phases of expansion were it is impossible to ascertain, but their order of magnitude can be estimated with some confidence; and there can be no doubt that it was comparable to that observed in the early phases of the Vital Revolution. *In this sense the demographic development of the eighteenth century was not unique.* What was unprecedented about it was the fact that the secular upward movement started from a higher level, and that it was able to maintain, and for some time even increase, its momentum. Population growth in the eighteenth and nineteenth centuries, unlike that of previous epochs, was not terminated and reversed by catastrophe. When increase did slow down eventually, it did so owing to the personal decisions of millions of human beings, not to Acts of God such as the Black Death of the fourteenth century.

However, it would be vainglorious for European man to claim that the partial victory over the forces of death, which enabled the Vital Revolution to run its course, was altogether of his own making. To insist on the co-operation of strictly exogenous factors is not to belittle man's proud achievements in the fields of agricultural and industrial production, transportation, and marketing. Without these advances and equally impressive accomplishments in the theory and practice of hygiene and therapy, demographic growth would have been arrested very soon by the inexorable operation of Malthusian forces. However, when all is said, an obscure ecological revolution among rodents—the disappearance of the black rat[25]—which we believe to have been largely responsible for the cessation of plague in Europe should also be given its due, not merely in the sense that it helped to eliminate the greatest single agent of mortality, but in the sense that perhaps only a society freed from the fear as well as from the material and spiritual consequences of sudden death was able to achieve that high rate of intellectual and technical progress without which population growth could never have been sustained. The historian can only subscribe to the wistful words of Albert Camus: 'Personne ne sera jamais libre tant qu'il y aura des fléaux.'

[25] See L. Fabian Hirst, *The Conquest of Plague: A Study of the Evolution of Epidemiology* (Oxford, 1953), 123 ff.; and Sticker, *Die Geschichte der Pest*, 207 f.

5

BIRTHS AND DEATHS AMONG EUROPE'S RULING FAMILIES SINCE 1500[1]

SIGISMUND PELLER

Editor's Note: The earlier publications by Dr Peller of which this paper is a revision are listed at the foot of the page. See also Dr Hollingsworth's study of the British Ducal families, Part II, p. 354.

UP to the late seventeenth century, there was little interest in demography. In assessing some belatedly discovered data of earlier centuries, one must not expect results similar to G. Villani's discovery of the sex ratio at birth (at baptism), or J. Graunt's and E. Halley's achievements. Dealing with a *terra ignota* these men drew original, and to some extent still valid, conclusions from quite inadequate sources, and pointed the way for future research. But the present use of data deriving from the distant past has to reckon with gross incompleteness and errors, and has its justification only if the data are by chance substantially complete and correct, and demographically representative either of their period as a whole or of their specific social group.

No amount of labour, no application of more or less arbitrary ratios and statistical techniques, can transform the 'Domesday Collection', the lists of landholders, poll tax returns, or court inquiries regarding available heirs[2] into data suitable for demographic analysis. Even official demographic data of the eighteenth century show at times a staggering lack of reliability and of respect for truth—in spite of the already awakened interest in demography as attested by the familiar names of the pioneers[3] who help us to gain insight into the problems of their time.

For the analysis of demographic trends since the early years of the modern era, a unique source is found in the genealogical records of the high aristocracy (Peller, 8,500 members of the ruling families; T. H. Hollingsworth,[4] 1,900 members of English Ducal families). For the Middle Ages and even for the sixteenth century this source is also often unreliable; for many members of these families, especially the females, there are no data on birth, on the age at death, or on the age at marriage. For some who 'died young', sex is not recorded—indicating miscarriages or stillbirths. Most probably even in the late sixteenth century the Family Bibles failed to list some babies who had died at the threshold of life.

---

[1] This contribution is based upon the material discussed in the author's papers, 'Studies in mortality since the Renaissance', *Bull. Hist. Med.*, XIII, 1943; XVI, 1944; and XXI, 1947. The material has, however, been retabulated and additional data included.

[2] See J. C. Russell, *Human Biology*, 1937, 9:528; *British Medieval Population*, 1948.

[3] Bland, Clarke, Kundmann, Süssmilch, Wargentin, B. Rush, Struyck, Gohl, Heberden, Short, Milne, Tetens, D. Bernoulli and Duvillard.

[4] T. H. Hollingsworth, *Population Studies*, 1957, II: 4-26; see below, p. 354.

Genealogies of the European ruling families were worked out in part by Westergaard and by Prinzing.[5] My own report is based *chiefly* on Isenburg's[6] genealogical tables. In transforming them into demographic material, one of my main purposes was to disentangle socio-economic factors from the achievements of medicine and hygiene.

Marriage and birth

Of 2,888 male members of the European ruling families, born since 1500[7] and surviving their 14th birthday, 1,615 married within their own status group a total of 2,048 times; 1,219 married once, and 396, or almost a quarter, more than once. At their first marriage, men were older, on the average, than women. The age at first marriage of men was 25·9 years (sixteenth century), 27·5, 27·3, 28·4 (in 1800-49) and 29·95 years (1850-99), and that of their brides was 20·2,[8] 22·7, 21·7, 22·2 and 22·5 years. Generally there was an increasing tendency to eliminate great disparities in the ages of bride and groom, to delay the marriages of men up to age 25 and to reduce the proportion of brides of less than 20 years of age.

As compared with the first hundred years, during the eighteenth and nineteenth centuries the younger age groups showed declining percentages becoming married (males at 15, 20 and 25 years of age; females at 15 and 20), while in the older age groups the percentages rose, implying a diminishing proportion of elderly bachelors and spinsters. In the century of long wars and of the devastation of the continent, males and females were less likely to marry below the age of 30 than in the sixteenth or eighteenth centuries.

The number of remarriages per 100 men was 36, 23, 13 for the generations born in 1500-1699, 1700-1849 and 1850-1920 respectively. The fall in the remarriage rate is accounted for by the diminished mortality of young first wives and by the decline in the incidence of childlessness among them. During the sixteenth century, 23 per cent of the first marriages were childless; in the following centuries the corresponding figures were 18, 20, 16 per cent and in 1900-20 14 per cent. Taking the whole span of time covered (i.e. 436 years), 18·4 per cent of men's first marriages were childless. If remarriages are included, the percentage falls. Of the total of 2,048 marriages in which the 1,615 men were involved, 249 or 12·2 per cent remained childless, while the fertile marriages yielded 8,506 births (including stillbirths), resulting in an average of 5·27 children per male ever married, and of 5·92 per father.

In addition to the socially endogamous marriages, 145 men chose their wives from the ranks of commoners or of the lower nobility, or from the 'natural' (illegitimate) daughters of men of the ruling class. Of these men, 110 married once only and 35 more than once, again a remarriage rate of about 25 per cent.

[5] H. Westergaard, *Die Lehre von der Morbidität und Mortalität*. Fischer, Jena, 1901. Fr. Prinzing, *Hdb. d. mediz. Statistik*, Fischer, Jena, 1930-31.
[6] Wm. H. Isenburg, *Stammtafeln zur Geschichte der Europäischen Staaten*, Stargardt, Berlin, 1936-37.
[7] The terminal date varies with the particular analysis.
[8] These ages may differ somewhat from the 'true' averages, for the year of birth is unknown for substantial proportions of the women of royal rank—some 20 per cent in the sixteenth century and some 11 per cent in the seventeenth century.

Of the total of 1,760[9] first marriages, 407 second and 98 later marriages, 8·2, 14·0 and 15·3 per cent respectively were socially 'mixed' marriages. Up to the year 1749, 'mixed' unions amounted to 4·7 per cent[10] of all marriages, thereafter to 11·2 per cent.[11] For marriages contracted after 1800, the proportion rose to 16·6 per cent.

TABLE I

Percentages of men and women who were, or had been, married by specified ages

age in years	males born				females born			
	1480– 1579	1580– 1679	1680– 1779	1780– 1879	1480– 1579	1580– 1679	1680– 1779	1780– 1879
15	0·7	0·1	0·5	—	5·6	2·1	2·4	0·5
20	8·9	7·3	9·9	1·7	37·9	23·5	33·5	24·4
25	32·2	26·5	30·6	22·9	57·8	47·9	60·0	60·8
30	48·5	47·5	49·3	52·0	66·2	61·6	72·6	74·0
40	67·7	70·4	69·2	75·2	71·4	71·0	82·9	83·2
50	70·3	75·7	79·6	82·6	75·9	75·1	86·8	87·7

In contrast to the men, only a small proportion of women married more than once.[12] Of the marriageable females, 1,964 married (once or more) within their class, and 404 or 20·6 per cent remained childless.

The high percentage of childless women is accounted for by (a) a smaller percentage of remarriages, (b) by the shorter average duration of married life per married woman, (c) by the too advanced age of some brides,[13] and occasionally (d) by the age disproportion in the contrary direction.

The highest level of fertility in the ruling families was reached in 1600–49 (Table 1a, col. A–C). The first suggestion of a decline in fertility appeared 1650–99.[14] The decline became more rapid in 1700–49.

Men who became fathers of twins (col. C) were the most prolific subgroup, but this subgroup also showed a sharper decline in fertility. Men who married once only (col. D) began to display a fall in the number of births in 1700–49, a half-century later than the rest.

It seems very likely that, from very early times, efforts were made to keep family size within certain limits. This was done (a) by keeping a large, though in the course of time, diminishing sector of marriageable men out of the marriage market (41 per cent of the men remained bachelors in the first two centuries, 37 per cent in the eighteenth, and 31 per cent in the nineteenth century); (b) by an increasing number of mésalliances; (c) by raising the age at the first marriage from 25·9 to 30 years for bridegrooms, and from 20·2 (?) to 22·5 years for brides; (d) by a reduction in the incidence of remarriages; (e) by birth control among the married, manifesting itself from 1650–99. Some of the developments may have been stimulated by the fall in child mortality,

---

[9] 1,615 + 145.

[10] 45 out of 965.

[11] 89 out of 795.

[12] Thus, e.g., in the sixteenth century there were only 20 such women: 19 remarried once, and 1 twice, while of the men 91 remarried once, and 19 at least twice.

[13] e.g. a woman aged 50 years was married to a man 26 years her junior.

[14] A further indication of the beginnings of declining fertility is given by the distribution of fathers by the numbers of their children. Taking the groups of 1–5, 6–10 and 11 and more births, the percentages for 1600–49 are 47·6, 36·6 and 15·7; while for 1650–99, they are 55·8, 32·2 and 12·0. The proportions of childlessness are 14·0 and 14·3 per cent for the two periods.

TABLE 1a

Number of children in marriages of equal social standing

Date of parents' marriage	A Average of all (a) marriages Births per married man	A father	C average number of births per father of twins(b)	D average number of births per father in first marriages which were only marriages	E followed by other marriages
1500–49	5·8	6·55	8·75	5·6	4·5
1550–99	6·0	7·0	11·6	6·1	6·3
1600–49	6·2	7·2	12·5	6·0	4·6
1650–99	5·9	6·9	10·8	6·1	4·4
1700–49	5·0	6·0	9·9	5·7	3·1
1750–99	4·6	5·6	9·3	4·9	4·4
1800–49	4·65	5·2	7·0	4·7	4·1
1850–99	4·0	4·5	4·3	4·5	4·0
1900–20	3·1	3·5	{ (4·5) (c)	3·4	2·9
1921–5	2·5	2·9		2·9	(1·0)

(a) *all* between members of the ruling families; excluding mixed marriages.
(b) all fathers who in one or more of their marriages produced twins.
(c) only two fathers in total.

others by changes in the cultural pattern. Purely dynastic considerations gave way increasingly to individual aims.

Mortality: the perinatal period[15]

Of 1,000 children born in the sixteenth and seventeenth centuries, 100 died perinatally; the ratio fell gradually, reaching a level of only 8 per 1,000 in the first thirty-six years of the present century (Table 2). Among the ruling families, perinatal mortality had already fallen to only 23 per 1,000 in 1850–99, while in the general population, even in 1900–35, a perinatal death rate of 100 per 1,000 was not unusual. Now the rates are much lower, but nowhere has an overall average of 23 per 1,000 been achieved, let alone one of 8 per 1,000. In England, in 1930, 1940, 1950 and 1962 perinatal mortality amounted to 62, 58, 37·5 and 31 per 1,000, respectively. Even in the most modern American hospitals with an almost complete eradication of maternal mortality, perinatal mortality is over 23 per 1,000 births.[16]

[15] Perinatal mortality covers foetal deaths (from the 29th week on) and those which occur not later than 7 days after birth. Biopathogenetically these two components are a unit.* In 1936† I introduced the concept 'birth-death', and replaced it in 1944‡ with the term perinatal mortality (P.M.).

Up to the middle of the 1930's medical efforts did not affect the perinatal period, while mortality of the 2nd to 4th postnatal weeks yielded to them. This difference was for decades obscured by improper delineation of the neonatal period.

* S. Peller, 'Die Säuglingssterblichkeit', *Wiener Klin. Wochenschrift*, 1923, Nos. 45, 47; 1924, Nos. 4, 5.

† S. Peller, *Der Geburtstod*. Deuticke, Vienna and Leipzig, 1936; 'Growth, Heredity and Environment, *Growth*, 1940, Vol. 4, pp. 277-89.

‡ S. Peller, 'Studies on Mortality since the Renaissance', part D, *Bull. of History of Med.*, 1944, Vol. 16, pp. 362-81.

[16] In Memorial Hospital, Long Beach, Cal., with only *one* maternal death among 32,465 deliveries, P.M. amounted to 31·1 per thousand (foetal component being 13·6 and the neonatal 17·5). The data published by St. G. Pillsbury (*J.A.M.A.* 1960, 174:2151) were supplemented by private communication.

TABLE 2

Perinatal mortality (per 1,000 births) in ruling families

Date of parents' marriage	A all born	B stillborn per 1,000 births	C born alive	D neonatal deaths per 1,000 live births	E perinatal (a) mortality per 1,000 births	F infant mortality beyond the first week, per 1,000 live births
1500-99	1,903	11·7(?)	1,882	89	100	104
1600-99	2,716	32	2,628	75	105	171
1700-99	1,862	29·5 (b)	1,807	47	75	106
1800-99	1,611	20	1,579	23	42	45
1900-35	414	3	413	5	8	3

(a) Calculated per 1,000 of all born (stillbirths and children born alive).
(b) In my table 2 on p. 449 (*Bull. Hist. Med.*, 1943) 3·6 per cent was incorrectly given, instead of 2·95 per cent.

It is a matter of obstetrical skill to prevent perinatal deaths from anatomical disproportions, toxaemia, placenta previa, blood incompatibility, multiple births, unfavourable position, severe injuries to the central nervous system, asphyxia, infections, maternal diabetes and similar conditions. These pathological conditions were certainly not handled more skilfully during the second half of the nineteenth century in the castles of the nobility than they are now in general hospitals. Hence the improved handling of pathology was less significant for the changes in perinatal mortality than was, and is, the reduction in the non-medical complex responsible for prematurity.[17]

In a large fraction of perinatal mortality among premature births the cause of death evades us, and too often the interpretation of post-mortems is faulty. To gain some understanding of the remarkable decline of perinatal mortality in the ruling families, I shall refer to studies on the role of rest-homes (maternity homes) for pregnant women.

In the 1920's, in Vienna, babies born out of wedlock had a perinatal mortality of 102, or 43 or 32 per 1,000, respectively, and legitimate children of the economically low strata had one of 88, 30 or only 16 (!) per 1,000, depending on whether their mothers had been sheltered in the *pre*delivery maternity division of the General Hospital for 0-7, 8-28, or 29-56 days.[18] Similarly, illegitimate Jewish children in New York City, 1939-48, had a perinatal mortality rate of 40, 32, or 26 per 1,000,[19] depending on the length of mother's stay in the shelter during pregnancy. Recently these findings gained support from Pakter *et al.*,[20] according to whom, in New York City, the *neonatal* mortality of white illegitimate children (excluding foetal deaths) in 1957-59 varied between 31 and 13 per 1,000, depending on whether the mothers were not or were sheltered during pregnancy. The sheltered group had a considerably

[17] S. Peller, *Klin. Wochenschr.*, 1930, 9:844; *Zbl. Gyn.*, 1931, No. 5. According to G. W. Corner and G. W. Anderson, postmortems in the Johns Hopkins since 1937 left unexplained about ¼ of all deaths of babies heavier than 1,000 g at birth. In about ¼ of the deaths there was no discernible pathology in the babies or their mothers.
[18] S. Peller, *Wien. Klin. Wochenschr.*, 1923-1924 *l.c.*; *Klin. Wochenschr.* (Berlin), 1930, 9:844.
[19] S. Peller, *et al.*, *N.Y. State Jour. of Med.*, 1950, 50:1837.
[20] J. Pakter, H. Jacobziner, H. J. Rosner and Fr. Greenstein, *Am. Jour. Publ. Health*, 1961, Vol. 51, p. 846.

lower proportion of premature babies. The maternity home for pregnant women proved of higher significance for the level of mortality than ethnic origin, race, marital or economic status.

Over the period as a whole the perinatal mortality of twins has improved more than that of singletons; first 390 per 1,000 of the twins died, then 250 per 1,000 and since 1800 only 100 per 1,000[21] (Table 3). To assess the significance of

TABLE 3

Perinatal Mortality per 1,000 Births

Period of birth	singletons		twins	
	total number of cases	no. of deaths per 1,000	total number of cases	no. of deaths per 1,000
(a) Ruling Families				
1500–1699	4,511	96	108	389
1700–99	1,826	72 } 53	36	250 } 182
1800–1935	1,995	35	30	100
1500–1935	8,332	76±3	174	310±35
(1) Families with 〕 perinatal mortality			66 (a)	485±61
(2) Families without ∫ in singletons			98 (a)	224±42
(b) Vienna *Allgemeines Krankenhaus* (all 3 divisions)				
1915–21	43,468	131±2		
1912–23			1,606	292±11

(a) 10 twins in families without singletons were not included.

the rate of 100 it should be compared with that in the general population around the time of the First World War. Of all twins delivered 1912–1923 in the Vienna General Hospital, 292 per 1,000 died perinatally, with limits as high as 481 per 1,000—if the mother entered the hospital only 0–7 days before delivery—and as low as 105 per 1,000 if she had been sheltered for the last 8 to 56 days. These tremendous differences are not accounted for by unequal obstetrics, by differences in pathology of the mother or baby, or by genetic factors. The only important differential was the length of the period of better nutrition, physical rest and—at least for unmarried mothers—restored emotional equilibrium.

Infant mortality

Of all the children born alive in the sixteenth and seventeenth centuries, 193 per 1,000 and 246 per 1,000, respectively, died during the first year (see Table 2, col. D and F). This increase of mortality in a century of long wars, pestilences and famines is surprisingly high when compared with the changes observed in the population of Central Europe during the First World War. After 1700, infant mortality improved rapidly; the rate was 153 per 1,000 in

[21] Among the ruling families, those with perinatal deaths among their singletons had, in the 436 year period, a twin P.M. of 485±61 per 1,000 as compared with 224±42 per 1,000 for twins in those families whose singleton siblings showed no perinatal deaths. In the first two centuries, of those born alive, 659 per 1,000 of the singletons survived childhood and 354 per 1,000 of the twins. After 1700, the survival rates of the twins increased to 710 per 1,000 and almost reached those of singletons, namely 770 per 1,000.

the eighteenth century, but 96 and 41 per 1,000 in the first and second halves of the nineteenth century. In 1900-35, of all born alive only 8 per 1,000 died, 5 per 1,000 in the neonatal period and 3 during the whole remaining 11¾ months! So far no country or city has been able to compete with the last three low rates.

The difference between the rates for the ruling families and for the general population—taking Vienna in 1752-5 as the yardstick—was larger during the post-neonatal period of infancy than in the neo- or peri-natal period. Thus, the rates for the post-neonatal period were 106[22] as compared with 331[23] per 1,000, while for the neonatal period they were 47 as compared with 75, and for the whole perinatal period 77 as against 166 per 1,000. Since that time post-neonatal infant mortality has proved more amenable to reduction than perinatal mortality.

In the ruling families, twin infants also had a high mortality during the post-neonatal period, namely 175 ± 34 per 1,000,[24] as compared with $118 \cdot 6 \pm 3 \cdot 6$ per 1,000 for singletons.[25]

Children aged 1–14 years

In the course of the 436 years mortality improved inversely with age. Infants profited most. In the first 200 years almost *twice* as many infants (0–11 months) died as children in all the fourteen following years together. In the general population a similar relation still persisted in the eighteenth century (see Vienna in mid-century) while in the ruling families of that century the relation had already become reversed: infant mortality had dropped considerably, and mortality at age 1-14 had increased from around 160 to 200 per 1,000. The deterioration was more marked at 4-9 than before or after that age. After 1800, children aged 1-14 years also shared in the improvement. Thus, mortality fell to around 140 per 1,000 in the first half of the century, 60 per 1,000 in the second, and in the years 1900-20 to 29 per 1,000, or about equal to the mortality level of 1-14 year old white American children in the 1930's.

Out of a theoretically possible fifteen childhood years, a live-born child lived an average of 11·3, 10·2, 10·4 years[26] in the first three centuries, respectively. Later the conditions improved rapidly. The children of 1800-49 lived 12·4 years, those of 1850-99 13·7 years, and those of 1900-20 14·5 out of the possible 15 years. Through the whole period surveyed, boys lived 11·1,[27] and girls 11·5[28] out of the possible fifteen years of childhood. In the earlier centuries the sex-conditioned differences were more substantial. The lowest point of childhood survival, 628 per 1,000, occurred in the seventeenth century. From the next century on, the probability of survival gradually improved, reaching a peak with 964 per 1,000 for the combined groups of singletons and twins

---

[22] In the *Bull. Hist. of Med.*, 1943, Table 4, p. 452, the figure was printed incorrectly: 14·6 per cent. Table 3, the absolute numbers and Table 6 disclose the error and indicate the correction to 10·6 per cent.

[23] S. Peller, *Zeitschr. f. Hyg. u. Infektionskr.*, 1920, 90:227, for data on Vienna in 1752-5.

[24] 21 out of 120 twins.

[25] 909 out of 7,660 singletons.

[26] Sixteenth, seventeenth and eighteenth century respectively.

[27] 10·9, 9·9, 10·65, 12·3, 13·5 and 14·3 years.

[28] 11·7, 10·5, 11·0, 12·5, 13·86 and 14·75 years.

(Table 4). This figure equals that of white American children, as shown by the Life Table for 1949-51.[29]

TABLE 4

Of 1,000 born alive

| To parents who married | number surviving the | | |
	first year of life	fifth year of life	fifteenth year of life
1500–99	807	745	712
1600–99	754	661	628
1700–99	847	723	664
1800–49	904	833	789
1850–99	960	923	888
1900+...	992 (b)	983 (c)	964 (d)
USA whites, Life Table 1900-02 (a)	878	821	794
USA whites, Life Table 1929-31 (a)	944	925	910
USA whites, Life Table 1949-51 (a)	973	968	962

(a) *Vital Statistics, Special Reports* 1954, vol. 41, pp. 14, 28, col. lx.   (b) Born up to 1935.
(c) Born up to 1930.   (d) Born up to 1920.

In the pre-bacteriological era, the survival rates for the ruling families were far ahead of those of the general population. For instance, in 1752-5, of 1,000 Viennese born alive, 590, 413 and 359 per 1,000 survived the first, fifth and fifteenth year of life respectively,[30] as compared with 847, 723 and 664 per 1,000 for the children of the ruling families of that century. A century and a half later, with improving sanitation and the application of bacterioserological achievements to the urban population, with better nutrition, more widely spread school attendance and with life in the school hygienically superior to playing in narrow streets and in overcrowded homes, the health status of the children of the general population improved rapidly. The gap in survival between them and the most privileged group, still wide around 1900, was closed within the following fifty years.

Taking the period as a whole, more boys died than girls. The disproportion was higher among stillbirths (1·55:1) than in infancy (1·18:1) or in later childhood (1·23:1).

Adolescence and early maturity

At 14, the mortality curve begins to climb. As a rule, male rates have been ahead of female rates but in later centuries the male death rates were more sharply cut than those of females and thus, in the nineteenth century, the sex differences were almost obliterated (Table 5).

For the group as a whole, a considerable fraction of the men who died between 15 and 49 years of age succumbed to violence. Of those who died at the ages of 15-19, 20-24, ... , 35-39 and 40-49 years, the proportions (per 1,000) dying from violence are: 67, 161, *176*, 134, 77 and 46. For bachelors, the corresponding proportions are still higher: 70, 174, *203*, 168, 109 and 62 per 1,000. It was the 20-34 year old bachelor who bore the brunt of political feuds.

[29] During the course of the four centuries the average lower and upper limits of childhood survival were for boys 607 and 934 per 1,000, and for girls 653 and 979 per 1,000.

[30] The data are based on the unpublished lists of births and deaths, preserved in the Archives of the City Hall; see (a) my quoted paper of 1920, and (b) 'Mortality, Past and Future', in *Population Studies*, 1948, 1:405-56.

TABLE 5

Of 1,000 who were born alive

	1500–99	1600–99	1700–99	1800–85
	(a) died before age 50			
males	719	737	587	392
females	561	644	568	380
	(b) lived up to age 50 an average of . . . years per person			
males	27·3	24·6	29·2	38·1
females	32·95	28·6	30·4	38·9
	(c) had an average total life expectation at birth in years			
males	32·2 (a)	28·1	36·1	45·8 (b)
females	35·9 (a)	33·7	37·35	48·0 (b)

(a) excluding those who died at unknown ages (3 males and 97 females).
(b) only those born 1800–49.

Up to the age of 44, but not beyond, the bachelors had also higher mortality rates from non-violent causes, as compared with married men (Table 6). How unequal the risk of dying a violent death was, may be demonstrated for the 15–29 year old; of 441 bachelors $15·0 \pm 1·7$ per cent were killed; of 132 childless married men $2·3 \pm 1·3$ per cent; and of 930 fathers only $0·3 \pm 0·2$ per cent.

TABLE 6

Number of deaths per 1,000 person-years of men born

	1480–1679 (a)		1680–1879 (a)	
	who at the age of . . . were			
	bachelors	married men	bachelors	married men
20–24	23·2	15·0	17·4	8·3
25–29	26·3	14·7	19·8	9·9
30–34	27·5	16·8	19·4	10·0
35–39	27·5	22·3	15·7	8·6
40–44	25·2	26·3	15·1	11·9
45–49	32·5	37·8	13·4	18·5

(a) These values are averages of the means for each of the centuries.

It is a moot question whether the higher losses of bachelors were the result of their being sent on dangerous missions and placed at endangered places in wars or due to a temperament which led them to do both, to dislike the yoke of marriage and to like adventure. In the light of this historical experience, it is interesting to note the present policy of selecting and training preferably married men and fathers for the dangerous task of astronauts. The policy is based on the consideration that in situations of comparable danger family-men are more likely to survive than bachelors.

For *childless* married men, the age-specific death rates per 1,000 person-years were higher than for bachelors and correspondingly higher than for fathers. The healthier bachelors married and became fathers if neither they nor their wives were sterile, or if they did not die prematurely as a result of war or pestilence.

In spite of the additional risks associated with reproductive activity in earlier centuries, age-specific mortality rates were lower for married women than for spinsters, especially at 15-34 years of age. The differences were larger than those between bachelors and married men, and bear witness to the bad health status of the group of women who did not marry.

In the course of time, improvement of mortality of the 15-34 year old males and females lagged behind that of the 35-49 year old. This resulted in a more gentle slope of the mortality curve for men while for women the curve became almost parallel to the base line (Table 7).

TABLE 7

Total age-specific mortality rates per 1,000

	Men born			Women born		
	1480-1679	*1680-1779*	*1780-1879*	*1480-1679*	*1680-1779*	*1780-1879*
15-19	64	43	29·5	43	39	42
20-24	102·5	92·5	47	55	59	42
25-29	104	67	44·5	79·5	67	44
30-34	95	74	61·5	86·5	71	51
35-39	100	81·5	24	94·5	67	42
40-44	105	82	41	116·5	70	38
45-49	158	104	62	136·5	77	42

Young women continued to succumb to mortality from puerperal causes; not until 1850-99 was there a slight improvement. Deaths per 1,000 deliveries amounted to 19·4 in the first two centuries, 20·2 in the eighteenth century, 18·8 during the first half and 14·7 during the second half of the nineteenth century. High as these losses appear to us now, having regard to present-day maternal mortality rates as low as 0·4 per 1,000, they were much smaller than the losses which obtained in the contemporary general population.

Looking at the situation in terms of the fertile women only, the number of deaths in the puerperal state per 1,000 women amounted to 113 during the first two centuries. The rate fell to 89·4 for 1800-49 and to 58·8 per 1,000 in 1850-99. Because of the decline in family size after 1650-99, the reduction of maternal mortality per 1,000 fertile women was much larger than that per 1,000 deliveries (Table 8).

TABLE 8

Average maternal mortality per 1,000 fertile women who were married in

	1500-1699	*1700-99*	*1800-49*	*1850-99*
20-24	31·0	55·4	34·0	26·1
25-29	34·5	25·6	24·7	17·5
30-34	24·5	13·2	12·5	17·2
35-39	27·4	17·5	13·3	11·8
40-44	17·7	—	—	—
45-49	3·0	3·9	—	—

Late maturity

In the course of time, prolongation of life changed the age pyramid, stabilized family life and reduced the frequency of remarriages and the proportion

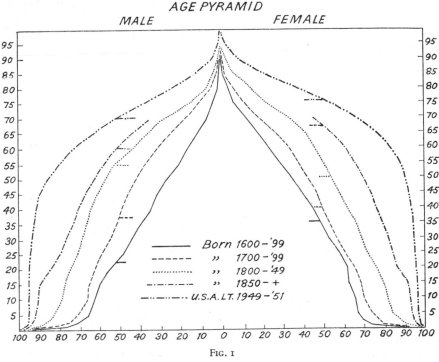

Fig. 1

Changes in Age structure 1600-1951

of orphans. Stepmothers came to play a much smaller part in the family. (See *age pyramid*.)

In 1500-1699 of a thousand reaching the age of 50, over 240 had already been remarried and 140 would remarry subsequently. After 1700, of men reaching the age of 50 only 110 per 1,000 had been remarried. In the eighteenth century 130 per 1,000 of men aged 50 would subsequently remarry, and in 1800-1920 only 90.

Of men aged 50 years and born 1500-99, 1600-99, 1700-99 and 1800-49, respectively, deaths before 70 years of age amounted to 768, 752, 600 and 538 per 1,000. The increased survivorship, slight in the century of the Thirty Years' War, gained momentum afterwards. In 1800-49, over one-third of those 50 year old men who, in the sixteenth century, would have died before age 70, survived. This considerable progress is overshadowed by further developments affecting not simply the privileged group but the population as a whole. During the first half of the twentieth century, the chances of death between the ages of 50 and 70 years were very greatly reduced for men in the general population, and at a rate much steeper than had occurred during comparable stretches of time in past centuries. Thus, according to the USA Life Tables for white men 1900-02 and 1949-51, the proportions of those who died were 465 and 396 per 1,000, respectively. Similar improvement occurred in the survival rate of women (Table 9).

In the four successive centuries, men of the European ruling families who reached 50 years of age lived within the age span 50-69 an average of 11·2,

TABLE 9

Survival to age 70

	males alive at 0	males alive at 50	females alive at 0	females alive at 50
	the numbers alive at age 70 were:			
(a) Ruling Families, born				
1500–99	6·9	23·2	10·2	27·6
1600–99	6·3	23·9	12·6	34·0
1700–99	16·8	40·6	19·2	44·4
1800–49	25·5	44·8	34·3	62·0
(b) USA whites, Life Table population				
1900–2	30·6	53·5	35·2	57·7
1949–51	51·7	60·4	67·5	74·5

12·9, 13·9 and 15·2 years, respectively, and the corresponding values for women
were 12·5, 13·0, 14·5 and 15·2 years.

Old age

Table 10 provides information on the changes in average life expectancy
at the age points 0, 15, 50 and 70. In the ruling families the future life span, or
the 'mean after-life-time' of persons at 70, increased from 4·9 to 7·4 years for
males, and from 6·8 to 10·4 for females. According to the US Life Table the
corresponding values for 1900–02 were 9·0 (male) and 9·6 (female) years, and
for 1949–51 10·1 and 11·7 years. The 70 year old people of the US Life Table
population of 1900–02 were coeval by birth with the group of members of the
ruling families born around 1830, while those of the Life Table 1949–51 were
born one half-century later. Thus, within a half-century 70 year old American
whites gained around 1 to 2 years in life expectancy, that is, well above the
gain the ruling families achieved in equal stretches of time during the past
centuries.

TABLE 10

Average future life span (e_x) in years

	Males at the age of 0	15	50	70	females at the age of 0	15	50	70
(a) Ruling Families born								
1500–99	32·1	30·9	14·0	4·9	36·0	35·1	14·6	6·8
1600–99	28·1	30·2	14·9	6·5	33·7	36·2	15·5	7·2
1700–99	36·1	39·5	17·5	6·9	38·2	39·9	17·9	7·7
1800–49	45·9	43·2	18·7	7·4	48·1	44·6	22·0	10·4
(b) USA whites, Life Table Populations (a) Table								
1900–2	48·2	46·2	20·8	9·0	51·0	47·8	21·9	9·6
1949–51	66·3	54·2	22·8	10·1	72·0	59·4	26·8	11·7

(a) Life Tables for 1949–51 US Dept. of Health, Education and Welfare *Vital Statistics, Special
Reports*, 1954–9, Vol. 41, No. 1–5.

In about three centuries, starting with members of the ruling families born 1500-99, and ending with the US Life Tables for 1949-51, the future life span of a person at 70 just about doubled. The gain *in years* (approximately 5·5 years) was about half of that at age 50 (approximately 10·5 years), and about a quarter of that at 15 (23·8 years).

At the ages of 0, 15, 50 and 70 years, the life expectation of members of the ruling families born in the sixteenth century surpassed that of ancient Rome, as suggested by Ulpian, by only about 4, 3, 2·5 and 1 years, respectively. During the subsequent two and a half or three centuries, the same group of persons (born 1800-49) added to their life expectancy approximately 13, 11, 6 and 3 years. The progress achieved since 1500-99 in persons 70 to 90 years of age is shown in Table 11. In these high age groups, women were more numerous than men, and the numbers of married and widowed persons exceeded those of bachelors and spinsters.

TABLE 11

Survival to higher ages

the following numbers were alive at age	Of 100 persons born alive in									
	1500-99		1600-99		1700-99		1800-49		1850-64	
	M	F	M	F	M	F	M	F	M	F
70 years	6·9	9·0	6·3	12·0	16·3	19·2	25·5	34·3	35·0	45·6
80 years	0·6	2·0	1·2	3·9	5·0	6·8	7·2	15·7	?	?
85 years	0·1	0·6	0·3	1·1	1·7	1·9	3·4	6·5	?	?
90 years	—	0·1	—	0·5	0·4	0·5	0·5	2·2	?	?

Summary

1. During the past four centuries, among the ruling families of Europe, the probability of first marriage has increased and so, too, has the age at first marriage. Remarriages have become less frequent, while the contrary has been true of mésalliances.

2. Fertility began to decline around 1650-99, some two centuries earlier than in the general population. At the same time, the incidence of childlessness has fallen.

3. Mortality began to fall in all age groups long before the development of modern medicine. The fall in infant mortality is especially striking. Perinatal mortality also showed a marked reduction, the result of a complex of social factors.

4. The average duration of life of those born between 1500 and 1849 increased by around 13½ years for men and 12 years for women. Among adults, both total mortality and deaths from violence have been related to marital status and to childlessness.

5. Changes in maternal mortality were slow and had to await relevant developments in medicine.

6. Though mortality fell systematically among the ruling families after the

seventeenth century, the rate of decline was slow in comparison with that shown by the general population during recent decades.

7. Save for epidemics and infectious diseases, little is known about causes of death prior to the nineteenth century. In earlier centuries, tuberculosis threatened children and young adults far more than adults over 50 years of age. Smallpox, frequent among children, was a rare disease for young adults and more or less absent among persons over 40. The diseases to which older adults succumbed were mostly so ill-defined that the reports are of little use in tracing the changes over time.

8. The main changes in cause-mortality for older adults can probably be better inferred by projecting backwards from the data for the present. Thus taking the quarter-century between 1931-3 and 1957-8, in which mortality was very substantially reduced in England and Wales, the numbers of deaths registered for the great killers of our time, cardiovascular-renal diseases and cancer (group (a) in Table 12), increased while the importance of all other causes (including tuberculosis, diabetes, anaemia, etc.) diminished considerably.

TABLE 12

England and Wales, annual mortality per 1,000 persons by sex and age

	1931–33	1957–59		1931–33	1957–59
			Age 50–54		
	Men			Women	
(a) cardiovascular and cancer	3·9	6·7		3·9	4·0
(b) all other causes	9·4	2·9		5·7	1·45
	13·3	9·6		9·6	5·45
			Age 55–64		
	Men			Women	
(a) cardiovascular and cancer	9·6	15·55		7·95	8·3
(b) all other causes	14·1	6·45		9·4	2·7
	23·7	22·0		17·35	11·0
			Age 65+ ...		
	Men			Women	
(a) cardiovascular and cancer	44·35	58·15		40·4	45·3
(b) all other causes	41·5	24·2		33·2	13·9
	85·85	82·35		73·6	59·2

9. In the more distant past, it is likely that the group (a) diseases played an even smaller role than in England in 1931-3. In addition, since in earlier centuries the population contained a substantially smaller proportion of older persons, the group (a) diseases may well have made relatively little impression on the minds of contemporary physicians. But it is these diseases, and the development of new prophylactic and therapeutic methods for dealing with them, which will determine the possibility of further increases in life expectancy in developed societies in the future.

6

EUROPEAN MARRIAGE PATTERNS
IN PERSPECTIVE

J. HAJNAL

The uniqueness of the European pattern

THE marriage pattern of most of Europe as it existed for at least two centuries up to 1940 was, so far as we can tell, unique or almost unique in the world. There is no known example of a population of non-European civilization which has had a similar pattern.

The distinctive marks of the 'European pattern' are (1) a high age at marriage and (2) a high proportion of people who never marry at all. The 'European' pattern pervaded the whole of Europe except for the eastern and south-eastern portion.

Let us consider data for 1900.[1] The European pattern extended over all of Europe[2] to the west of a line running roughly from Leningrad (as it is now called) to Trieste. The European pattern may be seen in Table 2 below. On the other hand, the countries east of our imaginary line are shown in Table 3. Several of the Slav countries in Table 3 displayed quite a different marriage

TABLE 1

Selected European countries in 1900: percentages single at selected ages
(Single population as per cent of total population in age group)

Country	Men			Women		
	20–24	25–29	45–49	20–24	25–29	45–49
'European pattern':						
Belgium	85	50	16	71	41	17
Sweden	92	61	13	80	52	19
'Eastern European pattern':						
Bulgaria	58	23	3	24	3	1
Serbia	50	18	3	16	2	1

Note: Figures relate to territories as of 1900. For source see Table 2.

[1] 1900 is a convenient date for several reasons. By this time there are data in suitable form for substantially the whole of Europe, the political frontiers are more convenient for the present purpose than they became after the 1914-18 War, post-war data are influenced by the casualties of the war which created an abnormal surplus of women, etc.

[2] It was most inconvenient not to have a term for the area where the European pattern obtained and I have felt free (when there is no possibility of misunderstanding) to use 'Europe' to denote this area. It is awkward to exclude Eastern Europe from Europe and it might be thought more accurate to use terms like 'Western Europe', and 'Western European pattern'. However, since these concepts had to be referred to so frequently, brevity was a great advantage. Europe in our restricted sense is in fact the area dealt with in many a history of Europe.

pattern from the European one. Let us call theirs the Eastern European pattern.

The volume of data in Tables 2 and 3 is hard to digest and, as a beginning, it is better to select a few countries for comparison. We may (Table 1) contrast say Belgium with Bulgaria, or Sweden with Serbia. (Alliteration is as good a principle of selection as any other.)

Table 1, like the succeeding tables, shows the proportion of the population who are still single in certain age groups. The numbers remaining single at 45-49 may be taken to indicate the numbers who never marry at all. In the European pattern (Belgium, Sweden) a substantial proportion remain single throughout life, in the Eastern European countries almost none. The proportions single at 20-24 and 25-29 are indications of the age at marriage. Here also the contrast is clear. For example, by age 20-24 some three-quarters of women are still single in the European pattern, while in Eastern Europe three-quarters are married in this age group.

TABLE 2

Europe (except Eastern Europe) around 1900: percentages single at selected ages
(Single population as per cent of total population in age group)

Country	Men			Women		
	20-24	25-29	45-49	20-24	25-29	45-49
Austria	93	51	11	66	38	13
Belgium	85	50	16	71	41	17
Denmark	88	50	9	75	42	13
Finland	84	51	14	68	40	15
France	90	48	11	58	30	12
Germany	91	48	9	71	34	10
Great Britain	83	47	12	73	42	15
Holland	89	53	13	79	44	14
Iceland	92	66	19	81	56	29
Ireland	96	78	20	86	59	17
Italy	86	46	11	60	30	11
Norway	86	54	11	77	48	18
Portugal	84	48	13	69	41	20
Spain	81 (a)	34 (b)	6 (c)	55 (a)	26 (b)	10 (c)
Sweden	92	61	13	80	52	19
Switzerland	91	58	16	78	45	17

Notes: Political boundaries as of 1900.

Data based on censuses taken in 1900 and 1901 except for Ireland (1891) and Italy (1911). (By these variations in date it was possible to achieve consistency in the age groups used except for Spain.) Age groups for Spain: (a) 21-25 (b) 26-30 (c) 46-50.

Source: Institut International de Statistique, *Annuaire International de Statistique*, Vol. I, 'Etat de la Population (Europe)', La Haye, 1916.

The reader may satisfy himself by the study of Tables 2 and 3 that this contrast is not due to an arbitrary selection of countries. Table 2 shows all[3] the countries sharing the European pattern arranged in alphabetical order. Any of them would have done equally well for purposes of illustration. There are many differences between the marriage patterns of various western European countries, but there is a distinct cleavage between any of them and the Eastern European pattern of Bosnia, Bulgaria, Romania, Russia or Serbia (Table 3).

[3] Some small areas (Luxemburg, Faroe Islands etc.) have been omitted.

The cleavage is especially marked for women. For example fewer than 5 per cent of women remained single around their 50th birthday in Eastern Europe, whereas in Table 2 the figure is nowhere below 10 per cent and often above 15 per cent. In the European pattern unmarried life for an adult woman was accepted as a normal (if perhaps exceptional) alternative to marriage. In Eastern Europe this alternative scarcely existed.

TABLE 3

Eastern Europe around 1900: percentages single at selected ages
(Single population as per cent of total population in age group)

Country	Date of census	Men			Women		
		20-24	25-29	45-49	20-24	25-29	45-49
Greece	1907	82	47	9	44	13	4
Hungary	1900	81	31	5	36	15	4
Romania	1899	67	21	5	20	8	3
Bosnia	1910	63 (a)	31 (b)	6 (c)	23 (a)	6 (b)	2 (c)
Bulgaria	1900	58	23	3	24	3	1
U.S.S.R.[4]	1926	51	18	3	28	9	4
Serbia	1900	50	18	3	16	2	1

Notes: Age groups: (a) 21-24, (b) 25-30, (c) 41-50.
Source: Same as Table 2, except U.S.S.R. figures taken from United Nations, *Demographic Yearbook, 1949-50*, Table 6.

There are, of course, intermediate possibilities between the European pattern of Table 2 and the Eastern European situation—for example, in Hungary and Greece.[5] (The countries in Table 3 have been arranged in descending order of the figures in the first column.) The populations included within the boundaries of a sovereign state are not necessarily homogeneous. It would be a worthwhile study to trace the variations on the fringes of the area where the European pattern prevails. Significant departures from the European pattern may probably be found not only as one proceeds eastward but on the southern edge of Europe as well. Parts of southern Italy or Spain are more like Greece than like Belgium or Sweden.

How far would a more recent date than 1900 have yielded a different picture? Any date up to about 1940 would have left unchanged the basic contrast between the general European pattern and Eastern Europe. Indeed most of the figures for individual countries would have been substantially the same,[6] except for Eastern Europe where the revision of frontiers after the 1914-18 War altered drastically the composition of the territories for which statistics are available. Also in some areas 'modernization' may have brought about some shift away from the traditional and towards the European pattern.

[4] For European Russia in 1897, the percentages single were as follows:

	Men	Women
20-29	42	23
40-49	4	5

[5] Intermediate patterns have also been characteristic of the United States.

[6] The major exception is France where there was a considerable reduction in the percentages single among women over the first three decades of this century. Indeed the reduction was already proceeding in the latter half of the nineteenth century. France, in this respect as in the reduction of the birth rate, seems to have anticipated at a leisurely pace changes which elsewhere in Europe were to take place much later. See Bourgeois-Pichat, below, Pt. III, p. 489.

In the last two decades much of Europe has experienced something like a revolution in marriage habits. People marry more and earlier than in former days. The percentages remaining single, especially among women under 30, are now far lower than in the earlier 'European pattern' illustrated in Table 2 and the numbers remaining unmarried throughout life are being greatly reduced and may in several countries fall below 5 per cent in the near future. The 'European pattern' seems to be disappearing.

Non-European civilizations are like Eastern Europe, or more so. Percentages single are very low by European standards, at least for women; in the age group 20-24 there are often fewer than 20 per cent single. (For men the contrast with Europe is less clear.) Very few women remain single throughout life (not infrequently 2 per cent or less) and for a man to remain a bachelor is not much more common. Figures for many of the larger countries in Africa and Asia are reproduced in Table 4. The countries are listed roughly in order from west to east.

TABLE 4

Africa and Asia: percentages single at selected ages
(Single population as per cent of total population in age group)

Country	Date of census	Men			Women		
		20-24	25-29	45-49	20-24	25-29	45-49
Morocco (Moslems)	1952	59	28	2	8	3	2
Algeria (Moslems)	1948	68	37	5	23	10	2
Tunisia (indigenous population)	1946	73	46	6	29	13	4
Egypt	1947	69	35	2	20	6	1
Mozambique	1950	54	23	4	17	7	3
Mauritius	1952	72	33	5	24	12	5
Turkey	1935	49	24	3	18	6	3
India (inc. Pakistan)	1931	35	14	4	5	2	1
Ceylon	1946	80	43	8	29	12	3
Thailand	1947	61	24	4	30	11	3
Malaya (Malays)	1947	54	17	2	7	2	1
Formosa	1930	52	19	4	15	4	0
Korea	1930	33	10	1	2	1	0
Japan	1920	71	26	2	31	9	2

Note: All figures relate to territories as of the dates stated.
Sources: Morocco, Algeria, Tunisia, Mauritius—United Nations, *Demographic Yearbook 1955*, Table 12.
    Mozambique—Portugal, Provincia de Moçambique, Repartiçao Tecnica de Estatistica. *Recenseamento geral da população em 1950*. Vol. III, 'População nao civilizado' (Lourenço Marques, Table 2 1955) pp. 12-13.
    Other countries—J. Hajnal, 'The Marriage Boom', *Population Index*, Vol. 19, No. 2 (1953).

There are considerable difficulties about comparing figures such as those in Table 4 with European data. In the first place the family as an institution has different characteristics in different cultures and it is not possible to define 'marriage' in a unique way for statistical purposes in all countries. Clearly the term 'married' has a different meaning in a country such as India where child marriage is traditional from that which it has in a European setting. For the purposes of this paper marriage means roughly entry into a union which is regarded as appropriate for the bearing and rearing of children in the society in question. Such a definition will be meaningful in very many societies.

For many areas the available data on marital status unfortunately may not represent anything even remotely corresponding to the definition just sketched. For India it would clearly be preferable to have data where only those were classified as married who had completed the second marriage ceremony ('gauna' ceremony) after which consummation takes place. Even after that it seems customary in some areas for the girl to return to her parents' home for months or even more than a year so that she only joins her husband permanently some time later. In Indian data people are counted as married who, for our purposes, should not be so classified. The opposite difficulty occurs in many cases. Sometimes official statistics count as married only persons who have been declared married by the civil or ecclesiastical authorities, whereas the people themselves take little notice of the requirements of these authorities. In some societies there are several accepted forms of marital union, only some of which are classified as marriages in the census. The precise scope of census classifications even as intended by those in charge of planning the census is often unclear; unimaginative imitations of European classifications have often been used in societies where these were inapplicable. How the definitions were applied as the enumeration was carried out is even more dubious.

In many instances (e.g. Ceylon and Japan) the proportions of persons single if the true facts were known would undoubtedly be even lower than those given in Table 4. Marital status data for Latin American countries and the Caribbean area have been largely useless because so many people who, on our type of definition, ought to be counted as married have been treated in the statistics as unmarried.[7] More accurate and meaningful data than are yielded by the official censuses are sometimes available in special studies (e.g. the Trinidad survey described by Braithwaite and Roberts). Information on the numbers of women who have borne children may also be used in several countries to show that the marriage pattern cannot be of the European type.[8]

A further difficulty is that figures on age distribution are known to be highly inaccurate in many countries. What is worse, information on age and marital status may not be independent, i.e. there may be a tendency for census

[7] There is a recent review of the available information by Mortara. (Details of works mentioned may be found in the list of references at the end of this article.)

[8] A collection of data of this kind may be found in United Nations, *Demographic Yearbook 1955*, Table 17. The accuracy and meaningfulness of marital status data for European countries is, of course, not always above suspicion. For example, if consensual unions were taken into account the percentages single would be lower than those given in Tables 1 and 2. For nineteenth-century Sweden a relatively high illegitimacy rate and references in the literature to consensual unions ('Stockholm marriages') suggest that the effect might be substantial. Fertility data may be cited to show that correction for this effect would still leave a wide gap between the European figures and others. For European countries the fertility data should relate to a period before the widespread use of fertility limitation. The following comparison of age specific rates based on all births, legitimate and illegitimate, shows clearly the differences between Sweden and Bulgaria in the proportions of women living in unions of all kinds at ages under 30. (At higher ages differences in the percentage of widows have to be taken into account in interpreting such data.)

Fertility rates per 1,000 women (of all marital conditions)

Age group	15-19	20-24	25-29
Sweden 1871-5	9	106	207
Bulgaria 1901-5	24	289	312

(Data from Kuczynski, *The measurement of population growth*, p. 123.)

enumerators to put down a woman as being above a certain age if she is married, but to treat her as younger if she is unmarried.

The fact that most of the figures in Table 4 are for recent dates must also be remembered. For our present purpose the proper contrast would be provided by figures which described non-European countries as they were before their social structure began to be modified by changes derived from Europe. If we had statistics going further back in time (e.g. for nineteenth-century Japan) the contrast with Europe might well be greater in several cases than Table 4 suggests.

No survey of the information for small pre-literate societies appears to exist. However, it would seem that in the large majority of these, marriage, for women at any rate, is early and universal.

When all the qualifications about the data have been made, there can be no doubt that our original generalization remains. The European marriage pattern is unique for all large populations for which data exist or reasonable surmises can be made (e.g. it may be surmised that those Chinese populations for which we have no data are similar to those for which figures exist). Europeans have married very much later than others and far more of them have remained un-married throughout life. In non-European civilizations there are scarcely any single women over 25. It is not, of course, intended to suggest that non-European civilizations do not show wide variations in the pattern of their marriage rates. But all the varieties that exist are separated by a distinct gap from the European pattern.

The eighteenth century

The reason why four Women out of six do not bear children every year is that they cannot marry because of the discouragements and difficulties in their way.

RICHARD CANTILLON: Essai sur la nature du
commerce en général (1755).

If the European marriage pattern is unique, it is natural to ask, 'when did it arise?' Curiously enough, this question seems scarcely to have been asked, let alone adequately answered. The suggestion has occasionally been made that late marriage is characteristic of urban-industrial societies while agricultural countries have early marriage. The suggestion is certainly unfounded. Eigh-teenth-century Scandinavia can hardly be described as urban or industrialized.

The question about the origins of the specifically European marriage pattern ought to be answered by historians well versed in Europe's economic and social history back into the Middle Ages, as well as experienced in handling such statistical material as can be reconstructed for periods earlier than the eighteenth century. A demographer accustomed only to deal with modern data cannot go very far.

What follows is really only a survey of the most easily accessible territory. There may well be much more material, even of a statistical nature, in places where a demographer would not be able to look for it.

The first step is to see how far back into the past the specifically European pattern can be traced. The type of data used in Tables 1-4 unfortunately does not go very far. Censuses with cross-tabulations of age and marital status do not go back even in Europe before about the middle of the nineteenth century except for some Scandinavian materials. For Norway and Denmark we can go back to the end of the eighteenth century, and for Sweden the cross-classification of age and marital status has been reconstructed back to 1750. (For the Scandinavian data, and nineteenth-century data for other parts of Europe, see Hajnal (Pop. Index, 1953).) There is also some information from marriage registration. Marriage in Scandinavia in the eighteenth century may well have occurred earlier and there may have been fewer remaining single throughout life than in the nineteenth century, but there can be no question that marriage habits conformed to the European pattern and not to the pattern common to the rest of the world.

Nor indeed would one expect anything else. Historians on the whole appear to have taken it for granted that marriage patterns in Scandinavia and indeed throughout Europe in the eighteenth century were of the same general type as later. The changes in the marriage habits which have been looked for have been changes in the opposite direction, namely towards more and earlier marriage as a possible explanation for the spurt in population growth.

Much more information could probably be extracted from the early censuses or enumerations. When the European pattern prevails this fact will usually be clear from any data on the distribution of the population by marital status, even without cross-classification by age, since the gap between the marital status distribution characteristic of Europe and those of other civilizations is substantial. Of course, if no cross-tabulation of marital by age is available, it will not be possible to deduce whether the proportion remaining single throughout life is high or whether it is only late marriage which is responsible for a high percentage of unmarried persons.

Unfortunately most of the published information before 1800 on distributions of populations by marital status relates to cities. Cities, however, are far from being closed populations. The distribution of their populations by marital status is influenced not only by their marriage habits but also by migration. European cities in particular have frequently shown signs of this by having a surplus of unmarried persons and especially women (in former days many of these were servants). This phenomenon occurs throughout the centuries back to the Middle Ages. The right inference to draw from a high proportion of single women in a city is often not so much that urban life discourages marriages but that cities provide opportunities for single women to earn a living and single women, therefore, go to live there.

However, some information is available from a number of counts covering rural populations in the eighteenth century. A review of this material has been placed in an Appendix to this paper. All of it, as far as it goes, suggests the general conclusion that the European pattern originated before the eighteenth century.

For studying marriage in the eighteenth century, we are not confined to data on the distribution of the population by marital status. The distribution of marriages by age, and the mean age at marriage calculated from it, provide perhaps the most natural approach. We may begin with the series for Venice published by Beltrami.[9] These figures are mean ages at marriage for all marriages without distinction between first and later marriages.

	Men	Women
1701-5	29·9	28·8
1720-4	31·0	29·8
1740-4	31·4	29·3
1760-4	31·6	28·1
1780-4	31·7	28·0

To interpret figures on mean age at marriage[10] we must inquire what mean ages should be regarded as characteristic of the European pattern, and what levels would indicate a non-European pattern. There is little direct information on the distribution of marriages by age for countries where the marriage pattern is non-European. Such countries in many cases have no system of marriage registration at all or else the registration system covers only an inadequate portion of the marital unions, as explained earlier. Even where the registration system covers the bulk of marriages, statistics of age are often unreliable since many people do not know their ages. However, information on the age at *first* marriage[11] may be obtained by indirect calculation from the proportions of single persons in successive age groups. Calculations of this sort suggest that a non-European pattern implies that the mean age for marriages of single women is below 21. According to the European pattern the mean age for the marriages of single women must be above 23, and has in general been above 24.

It is much more difficult to specify limits for the overall mean age of marriage of women, i.e. if the marriages of widows and divorced women are included. (In European populations in the eighteenth century and earlier, there are for all practical purposes no marriages of divorced persons.)

If we assume that the mean age at first marriage is at most 21·0 years and make rather extreme assumptions about the proportion of marriages which are remarriages and about the mean age of the bride at such marriages[12] it

[9] See Beltrami, p. 181. The original distributions (by single years of age) are given in the Appendix, Table 12. The marriage rates on p. 183 of Beltrami's book for the age group 14-59 go back right up to 1601. They are a good deal higher in the seventeenth century than in the eighteenth and this suggests that more people married and married earlier in the seventeenth century than in the eighteenth. Beltrami's book contains much additional information which would lend itself to further analysis (e.g. indirect standardization of marriage rates for age, or analysis of the accuracy of age statements).

[10] The crude mean age at marriage (i.e. the average of the ages at which marriages are contracted in a given year or years) can be a very misleading index when calculated for a year or a few years in periods of rapidly changing marriage habits such as much of Europe has experienced in the last three decades. The mean ages at marriage cited in this paper are almost all based on data for substantial stretches of time. Moreover, our interest is not in the study of small changes. The difference between the European and non-European marriage patterns is a wide one. For our purposes, doubts about crude mean ages at marriage can safely be set aside.

[11] The mean age at *first* marriage for men is the mean age at marriage of all men who are single before marriage including those whose brides are widowed or divorced. Similarly the mean age at *first* marriage of women refers to all marriages of single women, including those who marry widowers or divorced men. A method of computing mean ages at first marriage from proportions single is explained in Hajnal, 'Age at marriage and proportions marrying' (1953), Appendix III.

[12] The two factors (the proportion of remarriages and the mean age at remarriage) are not independent. A lower age at first marriage for women, a greater age difference between bride and bridegroom and higher mortality are all factors which make it possible for widow marriages to constitute a higher percentage of marriages in non-European societies than in nineteenth-century Europe; but these same factors lower the average age at which widows remarry by comparison with European standards. Divorce also increases the proportion of remarriages, but divorced women

seems likely that the overall mean age at marriage in non-European societies could hardly exceed 25 years. The subject needs investigation.

Probably the overall average age at marriage of women would in fact almost always be below 24 and indeed usually below 23 years in societies exhibiting a 'non-European' marriage pattern. As an actual example, the following data for Serbia may be quoted.

	Mean age at marriage of single women	Mean age at marriage (all women)
1886-95	20·0	21·7
1896-1905	19·7	21·3

In societies with a European pattern the overall mean age at marriage of women is sometimes as low as 24·5 (Italy 1911-14), but usually a good deal higher.

Going back to the eighteenth-century Venetian data, we can now say that they are clearly of European type. The number of marriages in which the age of the spouses was not given is remarkably low for eighteenth-century Venice. However, in parish registers of that period, statements of age are generally not given or are too incomplete to be of much use. There are, therefore, very few studies making use of age statements at marriage registration. According to one study[13] the age of the participants was stated in the records of 63 of 83 marriages celebrated in 1664-9 and 1693-5 in the village of Someren in the Netherlands. The average age of the bridegroom was 27 years 4 months, that of the bride 26 years 8 months.

Another Dutch study (by van Nierop) takes us back another century. It is based on the registers (civil, not ecclesiastical) of the city of Amsterdam and covers 11,597 marriages contracted in 1578-1601. In 9,247 marriages the bridegroom was a bachelor and 8,052 of them stated their ages, though only 4,664 did so without adding some indication that the information was approximate. There were no bridegrooms under 18. The percentage distribution of the stated ages (including approximate ones) was not unlike the distribution of the ages of bachelor bridegrooms in England and Wales in 1891-95:

	Amsterdam 1578-1601	England and Wales 1891-5
18-19	2	2
20-24	51	47
25-29	34	34
30 and over	13	17
	100	100

remarry at a younger average age than widows. Within recorded European experience the proportion of marriages in which the bride was a widow has apparently not exceeded 20 per cent and has usually been below 15 per cent. 40 seems a high average age for widows marrying (40 was the mean age of widows marrying in England and Wales at the beginning of the century). If we take 20 per cent for the proportion of remarriages and 40 for the average age at remarriage we obtain an overall mean age at marriage of 24·8, since

$$21 \times 0·8 + 40 \times 0·2 = 24·8$$

Approximately the same figure is reached if we increase the proportion of remarriages to 25 per cent, but assume that the average age of the bride at such marriages is only 36 years, or assume that the proportion of remarriages is 30 per cent, but the average age at remarriage 34 years, etc.

[13] I have not seen the original paper by Sassen. The details quoted are from Mols (Vol. III, p. 137). Mols' monumental work provided an invaluable guide to the sources for the preparation of the present paper.

Unfortunately van Nierop made no analysis of information about the brides; she felt the bridegrooms were more interesting.

In general, however, in marriage registers of the eighteenth century and earlier, statements of age are not given or are too inaccurate to be of much use. This difficulty can be overcome by the laborious procedure of matching each marriage certificate with the baptismal certificates of the spouses so that their ages can be determined directly from their date of birth. The earliest study in which statistics on age at marriage were obtained by this method may well have been that published by Roller[14] in 1907. It relates to the small town of Durlach in Bavaria (Germany). The mean ages at *first* marriage were as follows:

	Men	Women
1701-20	28·7	26·5
1721-50	27·4	25·4
1751-80	27·6	25·6
1781-1800	26·6	25·1

For comparison it may be added that the average age at first marriage in the whole of Bavaria in 1896-7 was 27·4 for men and 24·9 for women. There is thus no substantial change from the eighteenth century.

In the pioneer study by Morrell (1935) of the registers of two English parishes (North Elmham in Norfolk and Wedmore in Somerset) ages at marriage were obtained by the matching of marriage and baptismal records. This study is also remarkable in going back to the sixteenth century. The overall mean ages at marriage (including remarriages) were as follows:

	North Elmham 1561-1606	Wedmore 1634-45
Men	27·6	27·9
Women	24·5	24·6

The numbers of marriages upon which the averages are based is not given, but it seems likely from other information that this number exceeded 150 in each parish. It is not clear whether it was possible to establish the age of the spouses for all the marriages taking place in the stated periods.

In recent years the technique of matching records has been applied in a number of studies. Such work can be greatly assisted by modern data processing equipment and is likely to be undertaken on an increasing scale, so that, in a few years, much more information on the age at marriage in the seventeenth and eighteenth centuries should be available. The series given in Table 5 relates to an Italian village and covers a period of $2\frac{1}{2}$ centuries. It is the product of an extensive study whose focus is on human genetics. The project is under the direction of L. L. Cavalli-Sforza who has very kindly made available the data reproduced in Table 5. It will be seen that the mean ages at marriage fluctuate (partly on account of small numbers), but no trend appears.

The matching of parish records was also the technique employed in the well-known study of the French village of Crulai in Normandy published by Gautier and Henry in 1958. No change appears within the period covered,

[14] I have not myself seen Roller's study. The figures on age at marriage are taken from Mombert, *Bevölkerungslehre*, p. 118. Mols (Vol. II, p. 268, note 3) suggests that they were obtained by the matching of marriage and baptismal records.

TABLE 5

Marriages in village of Riana (Parma diocese), Italy

Year	No. of marriages	Average age of bridegroom ± S.E.	Average age of bride ± S.E.
1650–99	30	33·2± 1·4	25·4± 1·2
1700–49	29	34·3± 1·8	30·4± 1·5
1750–99	10	32·2± 2·8	29·1± 2·1
1800–49	12	33·8± 2·6	30·2± 2·2
1850–99	49	32·8± 1·1	27·8± 1·0

Notes: Restricted to marriages where both bride and bridegroom are born in the village.
The table refers to all marriages (including remarriages).
S.E. means standard error.

namely 1674–1742. The mean age at *first* marriage was 26·6 years for men and 25·1 years for women.[15] For another French parish at a somewhat later period (1760–90) Girard obtained mean ages at first marriage of 27·4 for men and 26·2 for women. These figures compare with 28·3 and 24·1 respectively for the whole of France in 1851–5. We may also refer to a figure of 24·75 years for the mean age at first marriage for women in Paris in the eighteenth century. Bourgeois-Pichat (1951)[16] states that it is based on 'recherches directes dans registres de l'état à Paris'.

Some very interesting information on the average age at marriage in seventeenth- and eighteenth-century England is given in J. D. Chambers' monograph on *The Vale of Trent* (1957).[17] The basic data are not parish registers but 'allegations' of marriage for Gloucestershire and 'certificates' of marriage for Nottinghamshire. Only those who wanted a quick or quiet wedding, without the formalities of the usual procedure, are included and the poorer classes are under-represented. We are not told what percentage of all marriages is covered and the accuracy of age statements is not discussed. Presumably re-marriages are included, not only first marriages. Chambers uses medians not means. Occupational groups are distinguished. This study gives by far the earliest significant information on differences between the marriage habits of social groups.[18] The Gloucestershire data go back to 1637. The median ages at marriage show no trends over time. They could come very well from nine-teenth-century or twentieth-century European data.

Some further mean ages at *first* marriage may be added from an unpublished

[15] The figures are based on 272 marriages of bachelors and 216 marriages of spinsters respectively. These are marriages where the date of birth of the spouses, and hence their age, could be established. For the marriages of persons where the baptismal certificate was not found (presumably in almost all cases these persons were not born in the village) approximate ages at marriage were computed as far as possible from the ages at death. The means calculated from these approximate ages are somewhat higher than those given above.

[16] He quotes a publication entitled *Recherches Statistiques sur la ville de Paris et le département de la Seine*, Paris, Imprimerie Royale, 1829. Bourgeois-Pichat's article also contains an indirect calculation broadly confirming this figure of 25 years as the mean age at the first marriage of women for eighteenth-century France. See below, Part III, p. 484.

[17] See below, Part II, p. 327.

[18] Unfortunately the next earliest study, relating to Bari in Italy in 1750, was not published in adequate detail (see De Meo 1934).

paper by Paul Deprez.[19] These are based on genealogies of Flemish rural
families and subject to possible selection bias, perhaps in favour of the inclusion
of those who left more offspring. Such a tendency would presumably lead to
underestimating the age at marriage. No information is available on the repre-
sentativeness of the genealogies in regard to the social composition of the
population. Here are the mean ages at first marriage of persons born in the
periods stated:

	1680-99	1700-19	1720-39	1740-59	1760-79
Male	25·3	25·9	26·4	26·7	24·1
Female	23·9	24·2	25·1	25·1	23·1

Another type of data sometimes available for the eighteenth century is the
classification of deaths by age and marital status. One way of using this information is to compute the percentage of deaths of women dying over say
50 years of age. This gives an estimate of the percentage permanently remaining
unmarried. In the study of the French village of Crulai, which has already been
mentioned, there were in the period 1750-1800 224 burials of women over 50.
198 were of married or widowed women, 4 were single and in 22 cases the
marital status cannot be determined. The percentage of single women among
women dying over 50 may thus have been as low as 2 or as high as 11·6 (according to whether we assume that all or none of the 22 were single). More likely
the truth lies somewhere in between.[20] In any case the percentage seems to have
been low by nineteenth- or twentieth-century standards even for France (which
had the lowest proportion in Europe of women remaining single throughout
life). Apart from the possibility of accidental variations, it is necessary to keep
in mind the effects of migration. Some women from Crulai may have become
nuns and died in a convent away from the parish. Other single women may
have emigrated to a city, for example as servants. The distribution by marital
status and age of deaths in 1715-44 in the parish of Saint-Sulpice in Paris was
published by Deparcieux (1746). Of the women dying over 50, 15 per cent
were single and of the men no fewer than 20 per cent; Deparcieux remarks that
there were many servants in the district.

For Pomerania the distribution of the deaths of persons over 25 by marital
status is recorded by Süssmilch[21] for the nine years 1748-56. There were in all
over 40,000 deaths of persons over 25. 10 per cent of the female deaths and
13 per cent of the male deaths were of single persons. Since the lower age limit
here is 25, so that some of the deaths took place at ages when marriage is not
yet too rare, these percentages are rather low by later European standards.
However, they are far too high (especially in the case of women) for any non-
European population.

To sum up, the European pattern in age at marriage can be traced back in
many countries to the first half of the eighteenth century or even earlier. There

[19] Delivered at a conference in Nottingham, 14 December 1960. For a later account by Deprez
using these data, see below, Part III, p. 608.
[20] Similar results to those of Crulai on the women dying single were obtained from another
parish for the end of the eighteenth century by Girard.
[21] Vol. I; Appendix, Table 12.

is no record anywhere[22] of a non-European early age at marriage. (There is some suggestion in the data that fewer people remained single throughout life in the eighteenth century than after 1850.)

The aristocracy

> The unmarried Ladies and Gentlemen in this City, of moderate Fortunes, which are the great Bulk, are unable to support the Expence of a Family with any Magnificence . . . they, therefore, acquiesce in Celibacy; Each Sex compensating itself, as it can, by other Diversions.
>
> CORBYN MORRIS: Observations on the Past Growth and
> Present State of the City of London. (1751)

Before the latter half of the seventeenth century, there is almost no statistical evidence on marriage, at least so far as unselected data (i.e. covering all inhabitants of an area) are concerned.

A continuous record going back earlier is available for selected upper class groups, and above all the aristocracy. Table 6 gives data from a study of the British peerage by Hollingsworth (1957).[23] The figures relate to the legitimate children of kings, queens, dukes and duchesses. In genealogical records of this type it is possible to trace the vital events (marriage, birth of children, death) occurring throughout an individual's life. It is most useful to analyse the data by 'cohorts', i.e. to consider individuals born in successive periods, and study their marriages (as against the more customary method of studying the marriages occurring in successive periods). It is thus possible to consider the numbers remaining single of the survivors at successive ages. Two ages have been selected for Table 6.

The story told by Table 6 is a remarkably clear one. The first two lines represent a marriage pattern quite different from the later 'European' one, but

TABLE 6

British peerage study

Period of birth	Men Per cent still single at		Women Per cent still single at	
	20	50	20	50
1330–1479	70	9	42	7
1480–1679	79	14	45	6
1680–1729	93	23	75	17
1730–79	97	21	76	14
1780–1829	100	22	89	12
1830–79	100	20	80	22

Source: Hollingsworth (1957) p. 14. The numbers on which percentages and average ages at marriage were based are not given. At birth there seem to have been between 120 and 200 of each sex in each cohort, but of course the number of marriages was smaller, especially in the early cohorts.

[22] It has been suggested by Connell (1950) that early marriage was characteristic of eighteenth-century Ireland. A special Irish marriage pattern developed in the decades after the famine, with very late marriage and high percentages remaining unmarried. Connell's theory that there had been a shift towards earlier marriage in the decades before the famine is unsupported by any statistical evidence worth considering. Even before the famine the age at marriage in Ireland was, however, probably similar to that in other North-West European countries as shown by the percentages single recorded at the census of 1841. (See Hajnal, 'The Marriage boom' (1953), p. 95, Note 6.) For Connell's view, see below, Part III, p. 423.
[23] See below, Part II, p. 354.

something like that found, for example, in Bulgaria, at least so far as age at marriage is concerned. The population remaining permanently single is higher than in non-Western societies. From the third line of the table onwards the picture is a typically 'European' one.

The mean ages at first marriage show the same drastic change[24] as we pass from the Middle Ages to the eighteenth century.

Period of birth	1330–1479	1480–1679	1680–1729	1730–79	1780–1829	1830–79
Men	22·4	24·3	28·6	28·6	30·5	30·0
Women	17·1	19·5	22·2	24·0	24·7	24·2

We turn now to the records of what should, perhaps, be termed a republican aristocracy, the ruling families of Geneva. Their demographic characteristics have been studied in a monograph by Henry (1956). The figures for the earliest groups (especially among women) seem to show traces of a former 'non-European' marriage pattern. As Table 7 shows, the change from an earlier to a 'European' pattern may have occurred at roughly the same time as among the members of the British peerage; but too precise a comparison should not be attempted.

TABLE 7

Ruling families of Geneva

Period of birth	Per cent single of those who die over 50		Mean age at first marriage	
	Men	Women	Men	Women
1550–99	9	2	27·2	21·4
1600–49	15	7	29·1	24·6
1650–99	15	25	32·6	25·7
1700–49	29	29	31·6	26·3
1750–99	19	31	31·5	24·0
1800–49	22	25	29·4	22·7
1850–99	15	17	29·2	24·7

Source: Henry (1956) pp. 52 and 55.

Notes: The computation of the percentage dying single is complicated by the fact that some persons are lost from observation while young (e.g. owing to emigration). This difficulty is far greater for the men than for women and Henry calculated two series of estimates by making allowance for this factor in two ways. The figures given above for men are the averages of the two series. The mean ages at marriage given for women include not only the daughters of the 'ruling families' covered by the study, but also the brides (if single) of the men in the ruling families.

Sampling fluctuations need to be kept in mind: The estimated numbers of women dying over 50 in successive cohorts were: 60, 91, 177, 133, 89, 52, 96. The standard errors of the mean ages at marriage vary between 1·0 and 1·7 for the men, between 0·8 and 1·2 for the women. In earlier cohorts the number of marriages of spinsters occurring at ages over 35 and indeed over 50 appears very high.

Peller in his study of the European aristocracies[25] analysed his material in a manner less suitable for our present purpose. His data suggest that in the continental European aristocracies a 'non-European' pattern persisted far longer than in the British peerage. The families studied by Peller retained a position of

[24] This change in marriage pattern is also observed in a recent article by Stone, a sociological study of marriage in the English nobility. I only got to know of Stone's article after this paper was completed.

[25] See above, p. 87.

substantial feudal privileges and a distinct manner of life far longer than their British counterparts. The very highest layers of the French aristocracy, the 'Ducs et Pairs', also preserved a pattern of very early marriage, distinct from the customs of the majority of the French population, right into the eighteenth century, as recently shown by Henry and Levy. Indeed the comparison with British conditions was noted by at least one contemporary observer, the son and heir of the Duc de la Rochefoucauld who visited England in 1784 at the age of 18. His charmingly romantic view of marriage in England deserves quotation:

> 'Husband and wife are always together and share the same society. It is most uncommon to see one without the other. . . . They always look perfectly harmonious; the wife especially looks so contented that it always gives me pleasure. . . . I am not sure whether having to live constantly with one's wife makes it necessary to marry at a much later age, but I am inclined to think so. In England, to have a wife whom you don't care for must make life a misery. An Englishman, therefore, makes a greater effort to get to know his bride before marriage; she has the same desire and I believe that this is why marriage before the age of twenty-five or twenty-eight is rare. Perhaps another reason for this is because it is usual to set up house immediately after marriage. The young couple never stay with their parents. . . . English husbands have an advantage over us of which they sometimes avail themselves, namely divorce.'[26]

The analysis of the genealogies of some families in Württemberg (Germany) presented by Rümelin (1926) can also be included in this section. The occupations recorded show that the families involved belonged largely to the more prosperous urban sections of society (the agricultural population is hardly represented). The selection effects which may bias genealogical data collected on account of the interest of descendants (for example, selection in favour of families which have numerous offspring) were mentioned above.

The precise nature of the records is not described in Rümelin's paper and

TABLE 8

Age at first marriage according to genealogical records of a family in Württemberg (Germany)

Century	Men		Women	
	No. of cases	Mean age at marriage	No. of cases	Mean age at marriage
16th	51	25·3	34	21·4
17th	134	26·3	68	20·8
18th	116	28·9	90	24·0
19th	91	31·1	94	25·3

Source: Rümelin (1926), Tables 3a and 12a ('Family L').

There is no explanation why there are so many more cases for computing the male ages than for the female ages.

[26] François de la Rochefoucauld, *Mélanges sur l'Angleterre*. The quotation is from an extract translated in Francesca M. Wilson, *Strange Island*, London (Longmans, Green and Co.), 1955, p. 124.

there is no discussion of completeness or accuracy. Data from the one group of records which includes material on women's age at marriage going back to the sixteenth century are summarized in Table 8. The men in this genealogy were largely salaried professionals, in particular civil servants and clergymen.

There are hints in Table 8 of a non-European marriage pattern in the earlier centuries. No weight can be attached to this fact, but if original records of the type used by Rümelin are still in existence[27] they might be promising material for an analysis on modern lines.

It is, of course, entirely possible that, before the modern era, the aristocracy and the upper classes generally married much earlier than the bulk of the population. (In the nineteenth century, the aristocracy, at least in England and Scandinavia, married later and less frequently than the population as a whole.) We now consider the scanty data available for unselected populations in the Middle Ages.

The Middle Ages

Good Sirs, since I was twelve, some years ago,
(Thanks be to God that I am still alive)
Of husbands at the church-door I've had five.

CHAUCER: Wife of Bath's prologue
(Modern version by W. van Wyck)

A few urban administrative documents (mainly taxation lists) which permit a marital status classification of the adult population are available even for the fourteenth and fifteenth centuries. The marital status classification must be made on the basis of indications in the original records which were intended for other purposes (e.g. taxation) and the indications of marital status are therefore more or less incomplete (e.g. in the case of servants or adult children living in their parents' home). Moreover, the age distinction between children and adults may have been unclearly specified when the lists were compiled and, in any case, must have been of dubious accuracy.

For the reasons mentioned earlier, data of this kind for cities would be difficult to interpret on account of the effects of migration, even if the records were fully complete and accurate, and it was known exactly how they had been compiled.

As an illustration, Table 9 summarizes what is perhaps the most promising series of this kind. It relates to Zürich in Switzerland which has for many centuries been one of the most important commercial centres of Europe. In the seventeenth century lists of all the inhabitants were periodically drawn up by the clergymen. Some of these were analysed in the last century by Daczynska. More recently medieval taxation lists which contain indications of marital status have been studied by Schnyder. The tax levied in 1357 was a property tax only, but in 1467 there was a head tax as well as a property tax. The head tax applied to all persons aged 15 and over, so that in theory the figures for 1467 refer to a clearly defined age category. The data for 1637 are for the population aged 16 and over.

The general picture in Table 9 is very roughly constant through the cen-

[27] See Mols, Vol. I, pp. 37-38.

TABLE 9

Adult population of Zürich (Switzerland) by marital status

Year		1357	1467	1637
Men				
Number		1,612	1,187	2,185
Per cent	Single	} 40	37	49
	Widowed		2	1
	Married	60	61	50
Women				
Number		1,962	1,649	2,974
Per cent	Single	46	49	48
	Widowed	5	7	15
	Married	49	44	37

Source: Schnyder (1926), pp. 56 and 71.
Daczynska (1889), pp. 387 and 389.

turies. The proportions single among women are high; but there is every reason to suspect a high rate of migration into the city which was a tiny enclave in an overwhelmingly rural population. (The age distribution in 1637 gives clear indication of immigration from the teens onwards.) The great excess of women over men suggests that the balance of immigration was particularly great for women. Large numbers who are single are thus no proof of abstention from marriage. The very small numbers of widowers and even widows in the Middle Ages (though not in the seventeenth century) are surprising in view of the very high urban mortality of the time. If correctly recorded they imply very high rates of remarriage. But very high rates of remarriage for the widowed with very large numbers remaining single make an odd combination. Could it be that the distinction between a widowed and a single person was not always recorded? The number of married persons is in analyses of records of this type deduced from the number of couples listed together; the distinction between the widowed and the single depends upon the recording of a fact which is not usually relevant to the administrative purposes of the listing, but which may emerge, for example, owing to the presence of children.

The data for isolated medieval cities are thus of little value for our purpose.[28] Similar difficulties apply with even greater force to various fragments of data available for the early Middle Ages, at least in the form in which they are available so far in published work. A survey of these materials has been made by J. C. Russell (1958), who draws various conclusions from them which seem to me to be largely unwarranted.

The most solid body of evidence concerning marriage frequency in the Middle Ages is provided by the English poll tax records of 1377, analysed by Russell in his earlier book *British Medieval Population* (1948). The special tax of one 'groat' was levied in theory on all adults over 14 (except for the clergy

[28] Perhaps, in some cases, some revealing method of analysis may yet be discovered, though this would certainly necessitate going back to the original records. The wider inferences to be drawn if there were good information about marriage in cities would have to be carefully weighed. Late marriage in some of the large centres in the fifteenth century might be an indication not of general late marriage in the period, but of the beginnings of new marriage habits which then spread throughout Europe.

who were separately taxed, and open beggars) and many of the tax lists have been preserved. It is possible to identify married couples in some of them. (There seems to have been no uniform pattern for drawing up the lists of persons who paid.) Russell analysed such lists for a number of villages and towns. His main results are summarized in Table 10. In addition he has assembled data from parts of London boroughs and other places amounting in all to a few thousand further persons. The proportions married are similar to those in Table 10.

TABLE 10

Percentages married among those aged 14 or more from the English Poll Tax Returns of 1377 (villages and towns of varying size)

Size of place (range in total no. of inhabitants) (a)	Names of towns	Total persons taxed	Per cent of taxed persons married	
			Men	Women
1–25		118	82	86
26–50		660	68	75
51–100		1,560	74	74
101–200		1,830	71	71
201–400		1,811	66	67
759	Dartmouth	506	68 (b)	68 (b)
1,017	Carlisle	678	59	56
2,325	Kingston-on-Hull (c)	1,550	60	58
4,365	Colchester (c)	2,910	62	61

Source: J. C. Russell (*British Medieval Population*, Tables 7.1–7.7).
Notes: (a) The total number of inhabitants is obtained by Russell by applying a constant factor of 1·5 to the number taxed, to allow for excluded classes, omissions and children under 14.
(b) For Dartmouth only a common percentage for both sexes can be calculated because there are 104 servants of unstated sex (assumed to be unmarried).
(c) The total populations of Kingston and Colchester were calculated from 1,557 and 2,955 persons taxed, but in some cases sex and marital status could not be established; the percentages married are based on 1,550 and 2,910 persons.

The interpretation of these data is not subject to the difficulties arising out of small numbers or the distortions due to migration. So far as coverage of towns and villages of varying size is concerned, we seem to have here better data than any available for any country before the era of the modern census.

As has already been mentioned, the clerical population are omitted from the tax returns summarized in Table 10. In an earlier paper Russell (1944) made estimates of the clergy using Domesday, records of the special poll taxes levied on the clergy and other sources. In total the number of male clergy appears to have amounted to under 5 per cent of the population aged 14 or over.

There were some 2,000 nuns in a total of some 700,000 women over 14. Contrary to popular belief, the number of women taking the veil was very small; indeed nuns appear to have come mainly from the upper classes.[29] The percentages married among men would thus have been a few per cent lower than those suggested by Table 10 if the clerical population were taken into account. For women inclusion of nuns would make no appreciable difference.

[29] See also Eileen Power, *Medieval English Nunneries*.

The percentages of married persons in Table 10 are much higher than could be expected on 'European' standards. It must be remembered that the widowed are included with the unmarried and that the vast bulk of the population was in the villages. Suppose we assume that the data are unbiased by marital status, i.e. that the chance that a non-clerical person of over 14 be included in the tax lists was the same for persons of all marital conditions. Then the percentage of married among women over 14 in the population from which the poll tax samples of Table 10 are drawn could not have been under 67 per cent and was probably somewhere near 70 per cent. The per cent married among those over 15 must have been over 70 per cent (though knowledge of age at this period would hardly have been very precise). On the European pattern, the percentage of women over 15 who were married in a country as a whole was below 55 and usually below 50 in the nineteenth century.[30]

The percentage of women married according to the poll tax records is thus of quite the wrong order of magnitude for a population of European pattern. On the other hand it is very definitely of the right size if the marriage pattern was non-European. For example, in censuses taken in 1900 the following percentages married (among women aged 15 and over) were recorded:

Bulgaria   69
Rumania   65
Serbia   69

Unfortunately there seems no way of knowing whether the chance that a non-clerical person be included in the tax lists varied with marital status. On general grounds it is possible, and perhaps probable, that the paupers who were not subject to tax and those who were omitted though they ought to have been taxed were largely unmarried. Among those near the lower age limit the unmarried could perhaps more easily escape taxation by claiming to be too young. It was perhaps sometimes possible to conceal the presence of unmarried relatives, while the head of the family and his wife could hardly be missed. Russell believes that the total number of paupers and untaxed is only of the order of 5 per cent. If half of them were women (in fact one is tempted to assume that fewer than half were women) then the true percentage married would still have been very definitely 'non-European' even if all those omitted were unmarried. Only if the number of omissions was very large with a heavy preponderance of the unmarried among those omitted could the populations covered by the poll tax records of 1377 have had a European marriage pattern.

If, on the other hand, the proportions of Table 10 are within a few percentage points of the truth one is tempted to conclude that the marriage pattern of at least some parts of medieval England in the fourteenth century was not at all like that of the eighteenth-century Europe, but much more like that of non-European civilizations.

Further work on the poll tax records is needed before much confidence could be placed in such an interpretation. Is there anything abnormal in those

[30] These generalizations are based on data from censuses of 1850–1910 collected in *Annuaire International de Statistique* (1916), Vol. I, 'État de la population (Europe)', Table D.2.

The percentage of women married in the population aged 14 and over is some 3 per cent below the percentage married in the population aged 15 and over.

few tax lists where married couples can be distinguished? Did the villages covered by these lists have any special character? The poll tax records are by far the most important data so far available on marriage patterns in the Middle Ages. Russell's pioneer work on them needs to be extended with more detailed studies based on the original documents.

Another type of evidence, the 'inquisitions post mortem', i.e. legal documents involved in establishing claims to inheritance, has been used by Russell, and cited by others, to support the contention that women married relatively 'late' in the Middle Ages at least in the social class covered by these documents. It is possible to classify the inquisitions by age and by the marital status of the heiress; and one can then attempt to determine the age at which one half of the heiresses are married. Statistically, this procedure is closely analogous to the methods in the biological assay of, for example, insecticides. Groups of insects are exposed to treatment with an insecticide at various dosages. The dosage in biological assay corresponds to age in the inquisitions. With increasing dosage an increasing percentage of insects die, just as with increasing age an increasing percentage of heiresses are married. The problem is, in the one case, to determine what dosage is sufficient to kill just 50 per cent of the insects, and in the other, at what age just 50 per cent of the heiresses are married. The statistical problems of such data are tricky; and it might be interesting to attempt an analysis of the inquisitions by the techniques of biological assay. Casual inspection suggests that the numbers Russell has been able to collect are far too small to support his conclusion, that in the reign of Edward I some 50 per cent of heiresses were still unmarried at 24. Apart from the question of numbers, there are several other uncertainties in the interpretation of the inquisitions (the accuracy of the determination of marital status is suspect, etc.). In any case, we now have the peerage materials assembled by Hollingsworth (see Table 6) and the inquisitions seem to fit in broadly with the pattern revealed, on much more solid evidence, by the peerage data.

We return below to some indirect evidence relating to marriage in the Middle Ages. That some change in marriage habits took place between the fourteenth century and the eighteenth seems scarcely in doubt. In the Middle Ages the betrothal of children and the marriage of very young adolescents were apparently widespread throughout the population (not only among the nobility). These practices had almost entirely disappeared by the eighteenth century. It does not seem possible that the populations of medieval Europe had the fully developed European marriage pattern; they must either have had a marriage pattern clearly classifiable as non-European, or else some mixture of the two types with a wider variation of age at first marriage than is found later.

The ancient world

As soon as they are fourteen, women are called 'ladies' by men.
When they see that their only resource is to be marriageable, they
begin to doll up and put all their hopes in that.
EPICTETUS: The Manual (2nd century)

Surprisingly, there is some statistical evidence on marriage in the Greco-Roman world. One source of information is provided by the inscriptions on tombstones. These often state the age at death; in the case of a married person dying the number of years he or she had been married is also sometimes stated. By subtracting the duration of marriage from the age at death one can compute the age at marriage. Harkness in 1896 collected 171 inscriptions for women and 191 for men from which age at marriage could be calculated. The only more recent attempt to assemble such data seems to be that of McDonell (1913) who covered a far smaller number. With the enormous increase in the number of published inscriptions since that time, a far greater collection could now be obtained (see Russell (1958)).

TABLE II

Distribution of women's ages at marriage derived from tombstones

	Roman Inscriptions		Norway 1841-50 per cent	Crulai (France) 1674-1742 per cent
Age	No. of Inscriptions	Per cent		
10-14	67	39	—	—
15-19	60	35	8	17
20-24	26	15	33	40
25-30	7	4	30	27
30-34	8	5	14	9
Over 35	3	2	15	7
Total	171	100	100	100

Sources: Harkness (1896), Gautier and Henry (1958), p. 83 and Norway, Statistiske Centralbureau, *Oversikt over de vigtigste resultater av de statistiske tabeller vedkommende folkemaengdens bevaegelse, 1866-1885.* Norges Officielle Statistik, Tredie Raekke, No. 106, Kristiania 1890, p. 143.

Table 11 summarizes Harkness' data for women. The sharp distinction which separates the distributions derived from the inscriptions from the two 'European' distributions added for comparison is evident at a glance.[31] The distributions derived from tombstones is certainly biased. The distributions of ages at death derived from inscriptions clearly do not represent the distribution of deaths in Roman times. For example, the deaths of young women are very probably over-represented (see Durand (1960) and Henry (1957 and 1959)). A further bias is almost certainly introduced in the selection of the very small subgroup of all tombstones from which the age at marriage can be calculated. Probably the bias is in favour of those who married young; one reason may be that the duration of marriage is most likely to be recorded by the surviving spouse if the marriage has lasted a long time. (On the other hand married persons who die before their spouses are likely to be old relative to their spouses.) When data of this type are published in the future, a cross-tabulation of age at death by duration of marriage should be published and not only the distribution of the computed ages at marriage.

Whatever the bias, the conclusion to be drawn from Table 11 for our present argument cannot be in doubt. No conceivable bias in selection could produce from eighteenth- or nineteenth-century European marriage data the

[31] The distribution for Crulai is for *first* marriages only. If remarriage were included the percentages for the higher age groups would be raised considerably.

distributions yielded by the inscriptions. The population whose deaths the tombstones record had a marriage pattern of 'non-European' type.

The same conclusion emerges from an entirely different type of data, the 'censuses' of Roman Egypt. These were enumerations made for levying taxes. Declarations were required listing all the members of each household. Some two hundred of these declarations are preserved and a full study of them has recently been published by Hombert and Préaux. The declarations give information on relationship between members of each household and also data on age. Something about age at marriage of women can be deduced by subtracting the age of the oldest child present from the age of the mother. The figure so obtained will, in general, be higher than the true age at marriage and sometimes much higher (e.g. when the first child had died or left home). Nevertheless Hombert and Préaux found (pp. 160-1) that of 155 women known to be married, at least 51 had married before 20. This shows marriage at a much younger age than in the 'European' pattern.

According to the data from Roman Egypt, husbands were usually considerably older than their wives. This suggests that men may have married fairly late in life. That men married late and indeed often deliberately abstained from marriage permanently both in Greece and later in Rome, has been inferred from literary evidence (notably Polybius) and from the Roman legislation designed to stimulate marriage. It has been disputed whether these trends extended beyond the upper classes. Some fragments of statistical evidence were assembled by Landry (1936).

Non-statistical evidence

I have no faith in anything short of actual measurement and the Rule of Three.

CHARLES DARWIN: Letter to W. D. Fox (1855)

Was there, as the scanty statistical evidence suggests, a fundamental change in marriage habits over much of Europe between 1400 and 1650? If so, where did the process begin and by what steps did it spread? What social or economic changes caused the new pattern of marriage to emerge? So much is known about the period, and indeed about the Middle Ages, that there ought to be plenty of materials for answering such questions—or so it would seem to one who is not a historian. If the characteristically late 'European' age at marriage should turn out to go back before the Middle Ages, the prospects for discovering its origins are, of course, less promising. It is probably too late now to determine whether Tacitus' statement[32] about the late age at sexual maturity among the

---

[32] The relevant passage (*Germania*, section 20) reads as follows (in the Loeb edition): 'sera juvenum venus, eoque inexhausta pubertas. nec virgines festinantur; eadem juventa, similis proceritas: pares validaeque miscentur. . . .' It is tempting for one who has to rely on a dictionary and Latin learnt long ago to translate: 'The love life of young men begins late; and so their strength in young manhood is not drained away. Nor are the girls rushed (into marriage?). Their life in youth is the same, their stature is similar. They are mated when equal (in age?) and strong. . . .' The phrases supplied in brackets, which are crucial, are suggested by Lewis and Short's Latin Dictionary under 'festino' and 'par' (in the former case with particular reference to this passage). This is clearly the meaning accepted by those, like Westermarck, who view the passage as evidence for late marriage among the Germans. However, it is possible, and very much in accord with the general tenor of his remarks, that Tacitus did not intend to say anything about age at puberty or at marriage, but was merely praising the Germans for their modesty before marriage (in contrast with the Romans). The translator of the Loeb edition seems to take the passage in this sense.

Germans had any basis in fact or even exactly what he meant. It is hard to see how he could have had any sound information on such a topic.[33]

The proposition that arguments about statistical matters from literary evidence are risky can be illustrated from discussions of the age at marriage. Thus Russell has pointed, in support of his view that people married late in the Middle Ages, to the doctrine that a man should have a living before he marries. But such doctrines can be found in the literature of other civilizations. There is, for example, a statement in the Talmud that 'a man should first build a house, then plant a vineyard and after that marry'.[34] Yet it can hardly be doubted that the Jews of Talmudic times married young.

One difficulty with literary evidence is, of course, the vagueness of terms like 'late marriage'. In many societies with a distinctly non-European marriage pattern women marry late by Indian standards, but very early by European ones.

If they were looked for, promising lines of evidence which are not directly statistical might well turn up. An interesting possibility is suggested by the work of Backman (1948). He briefly reviewed the references, mainly in legal literature, to the age of puberty, and concluded that the average age at menarche had been constant since classical times at around 14 years, but that about 1500 a process of retardation set in throughout Europe. It is possible that changing opinion concerning the age at puberty and changing definitions of legal majority after 1500 reflected physiological changes. However, it seems at least as likely also that we have here the accompaniment in legal thought of the social changes related to later marriage. On either interpretation the type of material reviewed by Backman may well yield evidence that a change in age at marriage occurred some time around the sixteenth century.

Clearly changes in the laws relating to marriage (including the minimum legal age) are of interest in this connexion. A related matter is the controversy about the nature of marriage at the Reformation. Could the controversy have been in one aspect an attempt to adapt theology to social change? Some of the themes (the voluntary agreement of the spouses, parental consent) might clearly arise at a time of change towards later marriage. It is striking that the properly organized registration of marriages spread during the sixteenth century over almost exactly the area where the European marriage pattern is later known to have prevailed.[35]

The interpretation of statistics in the matter of marriage has sometimes been distorted by general historical preconceptions. An interesting example is provided by Inman (*Domesday and Feudal Statistics*, p. 120) who studied the 1379 poll-tax data for one small area (the 'wapentake' of Claro in Yorkshire). He found that the percentage married was much higher than in nineteenth-century England. He concluded that the data must be at fault and the unmarried must have been especially prone to escape taxation. (He had other reasons for suspecting significant omissions from the tax lists.)

Preconceptions drawn from the modern world have also influenced Homans'

---

[33] His statement on sexual behaviour among Jews (*Histories*, V, 5) does not strengthen one's confidence in the soundness of his information on such matters.

[34] Babylonian Talmud, Tractate Sotah 44a (quoted in A. Cohen, *Everyman's Talmud* (London, Dent 1932), p. 171).   [35] See Mols, Vol. I, pp. 76-84.

work on *English Villages in the Thirteenth Century* which seems to be by far the
most thorough study of marriage in a medieval rural population. Because the
rule was observed that a man could marry only after he acquired land, Homans
infers that the age at marriage was high. 'If a man had to wait until his father
died or gave up his holding, he would be likely to marry rather late in life'
(p. 158). Under conditions of high mortality such as existed in the Middle Ages,
the conclusion does not follow. Over half the children in thirteenth-century
England may have lost their father before they reached their 17th birthday.
If they all married on their 17th birthday and the remainder immediately after
their father's death, there is no reason to think that the average age of all men
at first marriage would have been above 24.[36] In fact, of course, as Homans
documents in detail many were married during their father's life-time when
the father turned over the land to them. Other aspects of Homans' argument
for a high age at marriage are vulnerable on similar grounds; for example the
analogy of modern Ireland[37] is misleading among other reasons because of its
far lower death rates. When Homans wrote little was known in detail about the
mortality of pre-industrial Europe, or other underdeveloped societies. The
frequency with which in former days men's lives were disrupted by the death
of a relative is very hard to grasp for those living in modern Western societies.[38]

Bücher's little monograph on the position of women in the Middle Ages
—originally a lecture delivered in 1882—was expressly based on the belief that
the problems of women, and in particular of single women, in his own day
were similar to those of medieval times. All his evidence relates to a few cities
where indeed there was a substantial surplus of women. These cases are atypical
not only because all towns were atypical in an overwhelmingly rural population,
but because Bücher's data refer only to some of the largest commercial centres
of extensive regions (Nuremberg, Frankfurt, Basle). There is reason to believe
that the population of such centres was heavily recruited by immigration and
that the female surplus then (as in more modern times) was larger in these cities
than in smaller towns. Bücher ignores migration; he believes that the female
surplus he found was due to excess male mortality which he attributes mainly
to wars and debauchery.

Eileen Power's essay on women in the volume on *The Legacy of the Middle
Ages* (1926) draws on Bücher. It is impossible to say whether without his work
she would have made her categorical statement that 'it must not be imagined
that marriage was the lot of every woman and that the Middle Ages were not
as familiar as our own day with the independent spinster'. She does, however,
hint at additional evidence not derived from Bücher, and, moreover, evidence

[36] These guesses are broadly in agreement with the calculations given by Fourastié (1959) in an article contrasting a typical life-cycle under conditions of high mortality with those of present-day Europe.
[37] It is a mistake to treat modern Ireland as a stable and closed society. So far as marriage is concerned, its unique pattern of very late marriage and frequent celibacy for those who remain in Ireland was developed only in the latter part of the nineteenth century. This pattern is accompanied by a very high rate of emigration. The natural inference is that many of those who want to marry early emigrate and marry abroad (hardly a possibility in medieval England).
[38] The striking calculations of Jean Fourastié (1959) referred to above showing for example how rarely parents must have lived to see the marriage of their own children or how frequently men lost their wives should encourage others to construct models of this sort, so that eventually a firmly based body of results may be available. Facts on these matters should sink deeply into the consciousness of anyone concerned with the study of the Middle Ages.

relating to the rural population: 'A glance at any manorial "extent" will show women villeins and cotters living upon their little holdings and rendering the same services as men; some of these are widows, but many of them are obviously unmarried.' However, she does not present her material in detail; she seems to expect the reader to feel that a high proportion of spinsters is not an unlikely state of affairs.

The interpretation of the history of European marriage should be informed by an awareness of the almost universal prevalence of other marriage patterns, and, preferably, by some knowledge of how they function. For example, Professor Ashton (*English Economic History*, p. 9) has argued that marriage rates must have increased in the early eighteenth century because improved communication made it possible for people who would otherwise have been prevented from marrying to find partners. But most human societies throughout history have achieved nearly universal marriage at young ages with far worse conditions of transport between human settlements than those of seventeenth-century England. If the mechanisms for performing this feat no longer existed in the seventeenth century, when did they break down? Was the eighteenth century, with a pattern of late marriage, preceded by a different pattern of even later marriage in the seventeenth century[39]—a pattern which departs even more radically from the norm of other societies? If such a remarkable situation existed in the seventeenth century, how did it originate? The hypothesis formulated by Professor Ashton is conceivable, but it is not rendered plausible by his type of *a priori* argument.

The age-sex composition of the population

When the baby is born, if it is a boy, let it live; if it is a girl, expose it (to die).

From a letter dated 1 B.C. written by Hilarion to Alis (presumably his wife)†

Though there is an enormous volume of literature on marriage and the family, little of it has started from the statistical end. Answers to some of the simpler questions raised by a statistical approach seem not to be available.

How has it been possible, in most societies, to arrange for every woman to marry? There are several questions here; one question would be answered by a comparative study of the various mechanisms by which marriage partners were found. The vast majority of human beings have always lived in small communities, such as villages of a few hundred people between which movement was difficult and often hazardous. The number of potential marriage partners must have been small and often diminished by rules (e.g. those of caste) or conventions (e.g. of class) restricting the circle of those whom it is proper to marry. How was it possible to find a partner for every girl?

The mechanisms by which this can be achieved must operate in very

† *Selections from the Greek papyri*, edited by George Milligan (Cambridge 1927), p. 33.
[39] R. H. Tawney (*The Agrarian Problem in the Sixteenth Century*, pp. 104-6) made a suggestion which tends in the opposite direction. He thought that there may have been a trend to late marriage between 1377 and 1500, while in the sixteenth and seventeenth century there may have been a movement towards earlier marriage. There was an increase in numbers of the landless proletariat who had no incentive to postpone marriage.

different ways in different societies. For our purposes, the most relevant question is, what is done in difficult cases where no suitable match for a girl seems available? Comparative studies of the various devices by which this need is met would be of great interest. (The professional marriage brokers of Eastern European Jewish communities are an example, see Katz, (1959)). No doubt a relevant factor which distinguishes modern Western populations from the majority of societies is the conviction that marriage should be decided upon only after the future spouses have got to know each other well. This may render the finding of a marriage partner very difficult since people often have opportunities to become acquainted only with a few young persons of the opposite sex. If, by contrast, it is possible to arrange a marriage between people who have never met, the circle of potential spouses is greatly widened. It becomes feasible to undertake lengthy journeys to trace a suitable partner, as when Abraham sent his servant to travel to a distant country to find a wife for his son (see Genesis, Chapter 24).

The restrictions (e.g. of caste), which limit the number of potential spouses for a given person in the village where he lives, operate also to designate the people among whom a partner may be sought elsewhere. These restrictions, therefore, do not have the effect of keeping women unmarried; such restrictions do mean, however, that a network of kinship relationships is maintained across larger areas than would be necessary if all those living in one place could intermarry. They thus have an important effect both on the social organization and genetic structure of human populations.

A particular puzzle raised by those societies where almost 100 per cent of women marry, is the fate of girls who are seriously handicapped by physical or mental disease or deformity. Though the line between slight defects and those which seriously affect a person's chances of marriage is hard to draw, there are in modern Western societies probably one or two per cent in this condition (blind, deaf, spastic, epileptic, mentally defective, etc.). In other times and places, the scars left by malnutrition, disease and ignorant treatment must have added to their numbers. On the other hand, many of those who were born with handicaps or acquired them when young probably died before reaching marriageable age. How were partners found for the rest? The answer again, must vary widely. In polygamous societies such women can become secondary wives. Elsewhere they may constitute the bulk of those who never marry. No one seems to have discussed the problem.

We have so far discussed the methods by which spouses may be found for particular people. How can the overall account be balanced, if there are surplus women? In Europe, it has been customary to think of a 'female surplus' and the resulting spinsters as a normal condition occasionally aggravated by war. Wars have not been unknown in other societies.[40] How did they find enough men to have every woman married? A tempting answer to this question is 'poly-

---

[40] An interesting study might, perhaps, be made of the way in which societies which take the universal marriage of women for granted deal with a grave shortage of men due to war losses. In ancient Athens, after the disastrous Sicilian expedition in 413 B.C., a law was passed permitting double marriage. Among those who availed themselves of it was Socrates who took a second wife, a destitute widow, in addition to the notorious Xanthippe. (See Alfred Zimmern, *The Greek Commonwealth*, fifth edition, Oxford, Clarendon Press 1931, p. 340.)

gamy'. But it is probably not an important factor in many societies which permit the practice; for it is often on too small a scale.

The ratio of the total number of men to the total number of women in the population, though frequently mentioned in this context, is not very relevant. Nor is the ratio of adult men to adult women. For example in England at the present time, there is an excess of over $1\frac{1}{2}$ million women over 15 compared with the number of men over 15. Yet so far as availability for marriage is concerned, there is a shortage of women. The 'surplus women' are mainly widows over 60.

The first point to consider then is the ratio of male to female population at the prime marriageable ages. It is probable that in eighteenth-century Europe this ratio was much less favourable to women's chances of marriage than in many non-Western populations. There is, of course, always an excess of boys at birth, some 105 male births for every 100 female births. Male mortality is heavier than female mortality and in eighteenth-century Europe the excess of males dying was probably sufficient, not only to produce equality of the sexes by the marriageable ages, but to create a female surplus. In the Scandinavian countries there was a considerable female surplus. By contrast, in non-Western countries there seems not infrequently to be a shortage of women. A famous example is India. One theory (put forward, for example, by Coale and Hoover) is that women have been underenumerated at censuses to a greater degree than men.

Other commentators on the figures (e.g. Jain, 1954, p. 26) have, however, taken the view that the excess of men is genuine and can be explained by supposing that preferential treatment given to boys causes the death rate of boys to be lower than that of girls. There have been similarly divergent interpretations of the excess of men observed in several Chinese populations. However, the excess of men in the population and the excess of female mortality is found also in the data for Formosa at the beginning of the twentieth century and these data appear to have been of good quality.[41] Moreover, a good deal of data on death rates in underdeveloped countries has become available in recent decades and two world-wide comparative surveys of mortality (by Stolnitz and by the United Nations Secretariat) have shown that where mortality is high, an excess of female mortality in childhood and at young adult ages is not infrequently found.[42]

We may, therefore, accept it as probable that in many non-Western populations there has been an excess of female mortality and a shortage of women at marriageable ages. There are traces of the same tendencies in the data for Southern and Eastern Europe for the nineteenth century and beyond. The impression of a considerable surplus of women in the population and a higher male mortality seems to derive mainly from the statistics of Northern and Western Europe. In the Middle Ages and earlier a shortage of women, or at most a slight excess, was perhaps typical all over Europe. Laplace found that parents in the eighteenth century abandoned girls more often than boys to

[41] See papers by Taeuber and Taeuber (1959) and Taeuber (1961).
[42] This phenomenon is separate from the question of high maternal mortality. The effects of the latter have been widely exaggerated.

the Foundling Hospital in Paris. The preference for boys may well have been at work on a larger scale in earlier times.

The ratio of men to women at marriageable ages does not, by itself, determine the numbers of men and women who can be married in the course of their lives. For single women need not marry single men; they can marry widowers. If many marriages are dissolved by death while the surviving spouse is young, and if widowers remarry far more frequently than widows, it is possible for every woman to get married at least once in her life even in a population where the number of men falls far short of the number of women. In this respect the remarriage of widowers works like polygamy. The point is not new, but often overlooked. Two hundred years ago, Süssmilch (Vol. II, p. 281) called the tendency to remarriage 'polygamia successiva'. For him the issue was theological. The view that the excess of male mortality neatly cancelled the excess of boys born and resulted in an equality of the sexes by around age 20 had been an important doctrine of 'physicotheology'. It illustrated not only that everything in nature was harmoniously co-ordinated in accordance with a Divine plan, but also showed that the Christian principle of monogamy was in accordance with the intentions of the Creator and superior to the heathen practice of polygamy. Süssmilch discovered, however, that in the data available to him from several parts of Europe, the deaths of males under 20 exceeded those of females under 20 by a greater margin than the excess of boys among births, i.e. that by age 20 there were more women than men living. In this dilemma 'polygamia successiva' came to the rescue. Süssmilch could argue that there was nevertheless harmony in the Divine plan which included provision for monogamy, since the tendency for widowers to marry spinsters compensated for the surplus of women.

The degree of successive polygamy is variable and makes it possible to combine different sex compositions of the population with universal marriage. In eighteenth-century Europe, there were probably often between 5 and 10 per cent more women marrying for the first time than men. (See Table 12.) The degree of successive polygamy can be rapidly varied in response to changing circumstances. The history of Formosa described by Barclay provides a striking

TABLE 12

Effect of remarriage in compensating for imbalance in numbers of men and women

Country and date	Per cent first marriages among marriages of		Excess of women marrying (per 100 marriages)
	Men	Women	
Pomerania (Germany): 1748–54	79	84	+5
Sweden: 1750–1800	81	87	+6
France (Crulai): 1674–1742	81	91	+10
Formosa: 1906	72	64	−8
1910	75	69	−4
1920	78	75	−3
1935	89	89	0
1943	90	92	+2

Sources: Süssmilch, Vol. I, p. 183; Gille, p. 29; Gautier and Henry, p. 83; Barclay, p. 225.

example of the magnitude of this effect. At the beginning of the century the number of men aged 10–49 was about 20 per cent greater than the number of women in the same age group. This shortage of women was in part compensated for by female successive polygamy, i.e. remarriage was more frequent among women than men. As the sex ratio in the population became normalized and the proportion of remarriages was reduced owing to a decline in widowhood and divorce, the situation came to resemble European conditions more closely.

The relationship between the numbers of each sex and their chances of marriage is also affected by the difference between the ages of brides and bridegrooms at marriage. The point is most easily understood by a consideration of some hypothetical simplified examples. We first make three assumptions. (i) All brides are married at 20 to grooms aged 25. (ii) Men marry in any case, but the proportion of women who marry is determined by the availability of men. (iii) The number of births is roughly constant from year to year. Under these conditions the proportion of women married will be reduced by the fact that the available number of men is diminished by death between 20 and 25. Suppose that the system were to be changed and girls aged 20 were to be married to men aged 20 (everything else remaining the same). Under these circumstances, the proportion of girls marrying is higher, because the men who die between 20 and 25 are now available for marriage. If on the other hand men married at 30 (while women continue to marry at 20) the supply of bridegrooms would be further reduced, compared with our initial assumption, by deaths between 25 and 30.

It is thus seen that changes in the *difference* between the ages at marriage of men and of women may compensate for variation in the balance between the numbers of each sex. The effect of differences in marriage age is even greater if we suppose that assumption (iii) above (namely that births are constant from year to year) does not hold. Suppose that the population is increasing, i.e. the number of births is increasing from year to year. If women aged 20 marry men aged 25 they marry men born five years before their own date of birth. But five years earlier fewer births were occurring. A large difference between the ages at marriage of men and women in a population of high mortality with an increasing number of births tends greatly to reduce women's chances of marriage.[43]

[43] A remarkable feature of European marriage data is that there is often a relatively small excess (only 2 or 3 years) of the mean ages of men at first marriage over those of women. This is surprising because, other things being equal, a great excess reduces the chances of women at marriage. Yet it is in Europe that the percentage of women remaining single has been highest. The solution of the paradox is that among non-Europeans the great excess of the male over the female age at marriage is counterbalanced by other factors, notably a greater degree of polygamy (successive or simultaneous). In fact a high frequency of (simultaneous) polygamy is possible usually only in a society where young men remain unmarried for a comparatively long period and then marry wives much younger than themselves. In such a system where almost all the women over 16, but only somewhat older men, are married, a high percentage of married men can have two or more wives. (It is not necessary to suppose that men have been decimated by war, etc.) This fairly simple point has usually been overlooked in discussions of the relation between polygamy and the sex ratio. It was apparently first explained by Sonnabend in his demographic study of the Bantu (on pp. 171-3). He claimed that the Zulu 'have a clearer idea (although a purely intuitive one) of the relationship between the ages at marriage of the two sexes and the frequency of polygamy than certain European authors'. Indeed, by varying the relationship between the ages at marriage of the sexes, the rates of first marriage and remarriage etc. one could construct imaginary marriage patterns which are very strange to Western ideas, but in which most or all women are married and hence adequate repro-

From the beginning of the eighteenth century onwards a number of forces probably combined over much of north-western Europe to reduce the availability of men for marriage when compared with the number of women. The decline in death rates reduced the number of widowers and hence the scope for successive polygamy. For example, in Sweden by 1901-10, only 10 per cent of all marriages were contracted by widowers, as against 19 per cent in 1750-1800. This type of decline from about 20 to about 10 per cent is probably typical of much of Europe. The decline in death rates indirectly reduced women's chances of marriage by increasing the rate of population growth. The effect of this was explained in the previous paragraph. Thirdly, emigration in the nineteenth century was a predominantly male affair. Finally in many countries there was a decline in the marriage rates of men, as well as those of women, in the latter half of the nineteenth century, a decline which has sometimes been regarded as an initial response to the feeling that population growth needed to be restrained, as part of the same set of changes which brought about the spread of birth control. (France and Ireland have exceptional marriage histories and some of this paragraph does not apply to them.)

As a result of these developments, the proportion of women never marrying rose to levels probably unprecedented in much of north-western Europe by the end of the nineteenth century. The effect was temporarily reinforced by the First World War. However, since 1920 the situation has been completely transformed and the 'surplus of marriageable women' which had come to be regarded as a permanent condition has given place to a shortage of women.

Conclusion

The main theme of this paper is not new. It is one of the main topics of Malthus' *Essay* and indeed implicit in its very structure (especially in the revised version of the second edition). Malthus devoted Book I of his *Essay* to 'the checks to population in the less civilized parts of the world and in past times', and Book II to 'the different states of modern Europe'. In Europe he traces again and again the workings of the 'preventive checks of moral restraint' which implies 'principally delay of the marriage union' and he contrasts the condition of Europe with that of the peoples described in Book I.

Was Malthus right in thinking that late marriage in Europe resulted in lower birth rates, and hence lower death rates, than obtained among non-European populations? Whatever the nature of the causal connexion, his notions about the levels of birth and death rates gain some support from modern research. European birth rates, so far as we can tell, were rarely over 38 before the spread of birth control; in underdeveloped countries, they are almost always over 40 and often over 45. So far as mortality is concerned, the contrast is less clear cut, but there seems no record in European experience

duction would be possible. For example, one might work out systems in which old men marry young women and young men old women. Something of this sort seems to have been practised among the Tiwi of North Australia, according to a fascinating recent study by Hart and Pilling. Among the Tiwi, these authors maintain, every woman is married (or betrothed) from birth till death. She is betrothed at birth to a man old enough to purchase her; he will thus be at least 40 years old by the time she is old enough to cohabit with him. But young men can marry old women; one possibility, they say, is for A to obtain B's mother to be his wife by giving his (i.e. A's) mother to be B's wife.

since the eighteenth century of conditions such as those in India or Formosa in the initial decades of the twentieth century.

The way in which a non-European marriage pattern goes with non-European birth and death rates may be illustrated by a recent study by Csoscán of the parish registers for three Hungarian villages in the eighteenth century. This population is not in 'Europe' as defined for this paper. The distribution of marriages by age of bride in 1770-1800 was quite definitely 'non-European', as the following figures show:

Age group	Per cent distribution[44] of	
	Bridegrooms	Brides
Under 20	11	52
20-24	48	25
25-29	14	9
30-39	15	9
40 and over	12	5
Total	100	100

In the same period (1770-1800) the crude birth rate in these Hungarian villages was 52 per 1,000 and the death rate was 43 per 1,000. This may be compared, for example, with the following figures for the French village of Crulai given in the study by Gautier and Henry:

Period	Birth rate	Death rate
1675-1749	36	31
1750-89	31	28

The marriage data for Crulai which have been mentioned several times are, of course, quite clearly 'European'. The eighteenth-century Hungarian villages are thus non-European in all three respects (age at marriage, birth rate, death rate) in contrast with the European levels of Crulai's vital rates, as well as its marriage pattern.

There was a widespread conviction among eighteenth-century authors that European conditions were fundamentally different not only in marriage, birth and death rates, but above all in standards of living, from those obtaining elsewhere in the world. Europeans, a large proportion of them, not just the rich, had better housing, better clothing, a greater variety of food, more furniture and utensils, than people elsewhere. This uniqueness of Europe, so evident to contemporaries, has been largely ignored in recent discussions of economic development; all that is pre-industrial, including eighteenth-century Europe, is often lumped together in generalizations about 'agricultural' or 'peasant' or 'underdeveloped' societies.

Presumably the uniqueness of Europe in standards of living and in death rates did not extend back beyond the seventeenth century (except in limited regions). But if European death rates were as high as in other parts of the world, could birth rates have been lower? And if the European birth rate before the seventeenth century was as high as elsewhere, does this not imply that European women must have married young as in other populations of high fertility?

[44] These percentages are based on 440 cases for men and 442 for women. The number of marriages in which the age was not recorded was, surprisingly for this period, very small. The figures are from page 106 of Csoscán's paper. Remarriages are included and they form a high proportion of the total.

These large and vague questions need to be broken up and investigated by careful calculations on the interrelationships between marriage, birth and death rates. Even the relation between marriage patterns and crude birth rates is not nearly as obvious as is often supposed and it is not independent of mortality.

An inquiry into the origins of the European marriage pattern will inevitably take one into fundamental issues of economic and social history. This is so not only because of the connexions just discussed between marriages and births and deaths. There are other links. A marriage almost by definition requires the establishment of an economic basis for the life of the couple and their children. The arrangements current in a society for achieving this must fit in with the marriage pattern: they will shape it and will be in turn influenced by it. Unmarried men and women must be attached to households in some way, or form independent households. The structure and size of households and the rate of formation of new households and disappearance of old ones, therefore, depend on the marriage pattern. In societies where the household is the principal unit of economic production as well as consumption, all this means that the marriage pattern is tied in very intimately with the performance of the economy as a whole. The emotional content of marriage, the relation between the couple and other relatives, the methods of choosing or allocating marriage partners— all this and many other things cannot be the same in a society where a bride is usually a girl of 16 and one in which she is typically a woman of 24. These things are perhaps obvious, but they have not been much explored, at least not in histories which trace the emergence of modern Europe. A full explanation of the background of European marriage patterns would probably lead into such topics as the rise of capitalism and the protestant ethic.

The economic system influences the marriage pattern through the arrangements by which the economic basis for the support of a couple and their children is established. It is equally true that the marriage pattern influences the economic system. The traditional argument, that late marriage retarded population growth, has already been mentioned but other possible effects need to be explored. In the European pattern a person would usually have some years of adult life before marriage; for women especially this period would be much larger than outside Europe. It is a period of maximum productive capacity without responsibility for children; a period during which saving would be easy. These savings (e.g. by means of the accumulation of household goods in preparation of marriage) might add substantially to the demand for goods other than the food etc. required for immediate survival. In this respect delayed marriage may be similar to income inequality in stimulating the diversion of resources to ends other than those of minimum subsistence; but when later marriage is the norm the total volume of demand generated might be much larger than that which can be caused by a small class of wealthy families in a population at subsistence level.[45] Could this effect, which was uniquely European, help to explain how the ground-work was laid for the uniquely European 'take-off' into modern economic growth?

[45] The mere presence in the labour force of a large number of adult women not involved in child-bearing or -rearing must have been a considerable advantage to the eighteenth-century European economies.

If late marriage brings about wealth, wealth may equally cause late marriage. It was suggested in the eighteenth century (for example by Cantillon) that people married late because they insisted on a certain standard of living (a standard varying with the social position of the individual) as a prerequisite of marriage. More simply, men marry late because they cannot 'afford' to marry young; they have to wait until they have a livelihood, a farmer till he acquires land, an apprentice till he finishes his apprenticeship and so on.

It is tempting to see in this feature a key to the uniqueness of the European marriage pattern. In Europe it has been necessary for a man to defer marriage until he could establish an independent livelihood adequate to support a family; in other societies the young couple could be incorporated in a larger economic unit, such as a joint family.[46] This, presumably, is more easily achieved and does not require such a long postponement of marriage. This line of argument seems especially convincing if the larger economic unit is such that extra labour is often felt to be an economic asset. A system of large estates with large households as in Eastern Europe might thus be conducive to a non-European marriage pattern, while small holdings occupied by a single family and passed on to a single heir would result in a European pattern. If this reasoning has substance, the uniqueness of the European marriage pattern must be ascribed to the European 'stem-family'.[47] (The term 'stem-family' was coined by Le Play in describing the type of family organization in which land descends to a single heir, the other sons going elsewhere.) This explanation calls attention to a force which may have helped to bring about the European marriage pattern, if it did not exist in the Middle Ages. If men had to wait till land became available, presumably a delay in the death of the holders of land resulting from declining death rates would tend to raise the age at marriage. Whether there was, in fact, a decline in mortality over the relevant period is a dubious point (the decline in question must have occurred before the eighteenth century); but this is certainly a hypothesis that merits study.

The connexion between the death of the holder of land and its availability for the founding of a new family is, however, rather an indirect one. Under the mortality conditions of the Middle Ages fathers often died while their children were very young; interim arrangements had to be made till the son was old enough to take over. Even if the father survived to old age, it does not

[46] The young Duc de la Rochefoucauld whose remarks on his visit to England were quoted earlier (p. 115), makes a similar point: 'Perhaps another reason for this (i.e. late marriage in England) is because it is usual to set up house immediately after marriage. The young couple never stay with their parents and they must be sensible enough to avoid extravagance both in their conduct and in their expenditure.'

[47] The extent to which generalizations can justifiably be made about the family system in parts of Europe at particular times (let alone about the whole of Europe or all non-European societies) is totally beyond my competence. There have been large estates and joint families in some regions of Western Europe in the Middle Ages and beyond. Presumably it would be possible to have a system in which each couple is in principle an independent economic unit, but in which early marriage is made possible by arrangements to provide for the couple until they achieve complete independence. The study by Katz (1959) mentions such arrangements among Jews in Eastern Europe. Arrangements of a related kind in medieval England which are described by Homans are referred to below. Joint families can perhaps be regarded as fulfilling the function of such transitional arrangements. In countries where in theory joint families prevail the average size of household is not large. Households consisting of several nuclear families may not remain long in this condition, but this arrangement makes it possible for young couples to be part of a larger unit at the beginning of marriage for some years.

follow that a young family could not be set up on the holding until he died. Homans in his book on thirteenth-century England describes many instances where a father made over the land to his son while he lived, thus permitting the latter to get married. He also mentions instances where a father, while he lived, turned over his holding to be shared between two sons, where a man transferred his holding to someone other than his son, etc. To understand the effect on the frequency of marriage and age of marriage of a rule that a man must acquire land before marrying we should have to know the frequency of the various arrangements by which land was passed on. The rate at which land became available for the founding of new families may have been controlled not so much by death as by social arrangements. It is not at all clear *a priori* how a rule that a man must have a livelihood before marrying would operate to produce just such a postponement as is in fact observed. Even if we understood how the age at marriage of men was determined at a given period it would still need to be explained how women's age at marriage was effected. The uniqueness of the European pattern lies primarily in the high age at marriage of women (often with a relatively small difference between the age of husband and wife), rather than in a high age at marriage for men.

There is no space for further speculation on the causes or consequences of the European marriage pattern. The primary concern of this account has been the mere existence of the pattern. This aspect should be kept distinct from the search for explanations. It has been shown (1) that the distinctively European pattern can be traced back with fair confidence as far as the seventeenth century in the general population; (2) that its origins lie somewhere about the sixteenth century in several of the special upper class groups available for study and in none of these groups was the pattern European before the sixteenth century; (3) the little fragmentary evidence which exists for the Middle Ages suggests a non-European pattern, as do scraps of information for the ancient world.

Some at least of the data presented have probably been mis-interpreted. In dealing with sources of a type of which one has no experience coming from remote periods of whose historical background one is ignorant, one is very likely to make mistakes. In an effort to survey so great a variety of materials, some of them could only be looked at superficially. Even if individual pieces of information have been soundly interpreted, there remains the problem how far generalizations can properly be based on isolated demographic facts. This is a basic problem of much of historical demography. We wish to draw conclusions about the demography of large groups. The terms in which questions are posed (like the distinction between European and non-European marriage patterns) are based on modern statistics for whole countries; but the historical data often relate to small groups such as one village. To what extent are conclusions from such data to larger units justified? How far are statistics of particular groups likely to deviate from those of larger populations of which they form a part (aside from sample fluctuations)? Are data likely to be systematically misleading because they do not relate to a closed population? (This last defect is discussed once or twice in the present paper, particularly with reference to cities.)

In spite of these and other difficulties, there seem to be good prospects of obtaining substantial further information on the origins and spread of the European marriage pattern. The distinction between European and non-European patterns is substantial so that no very refined measuring instrument is required for its detection. There is probably a good deal of material for the seventeenth and even the sixteenth century. The parish registers offer a large mine of information waiting to be exploited. If it were indeed to prove the case that in the Middle Ages the marriage pattern of Europe was entirely 'non-European', traces of the transition should be visible in some of the early parish register materials. Even for the Middle Ages there seems hope that various types of records (for example manorial extents[48]) if carefully handled may yield useful information. If the recent rate of output of studies in historical statistics is maintained, and if those who engage in such work keep their eyes open for information on marriage, the mystery of the origins of European marriage patterns may be cleared up.

APPENDIX

The evidence from data on marital status in the eighteenth century

In the Scandinavian countries, the regular modern series of censuses began in the eighteenth century. The percentages single are easily accessible (see Gille (1949) and Hajnal (1953)) and have been described in the text. They clearly show a 'European' pattern as far as age at marriage is concerned.

For other parts of Europe the results of a number of isolated enumerations giving some information on the composition of the population by marital status have been preserved from the eighteenth century. We do not, in most cases, have the full cross-classification of age and marital status which was utilized in the preparation of Tables 1-4. Usually we have only the distribution by marital status of the whole adult population, without further subdivisions by age. An additional deficiency in some cases is the inclusion of widowed persons with the single population; this means that the effects of widowhood and remarriage are to some extent confounded with the frequency of first marriage. We first discuss data of this kind.

In Denmark some enumerations were undertaken in the seventeenth century for tax purposes. Mackeprang found the original lists from 1645 for the island of Moen (except for one parish) and published an analysis of them in 1907. In a total population of 4,014 in 5 rural parishes 39 per cent of men and 41 per cent of women over 15 were unmarried (i.e. single or widowed). These percentages seem intermediate between 'European' and 'non-European' levels. Mackeprang compared his figures with the data collected for the same area at the censuses of 1769 and 1901. The percentages for the population over 15 (both sexes combined) were as follows in the 5 rural parishes.

	Married	Unmarried
1645	60	40
1769	65	35
1901	55	45

The figure for 1769 seems 'non-European', in so far as one can tell without separation of the single from the widowed. This figure may be misleading. The census of 1769 was very defective; the clergy who conducted the enumeration were required only to draw

---

[48] The recent study by Hallam (*Economic History Review*, Vol. X), which came to my attention after this paper was written, suggests that promising material may be awaiting analysis.

up summary tables, not lists naming each individual. The total distribution of the Danish population by marital status according to the 1769 census does not seem to be available. In 1781 the percentage married among those 15 and over was 53 for the whole of Denmark; in 1901 it was the same. Did rural Moen in 1769 differ very much more considerably in respect of the percentage married from the national average than in 1901?

In the Austrian census of 1754, the single and widowed were also grouped together. Some cross-classification by age is, however, available. This census covered a population of over 6½ millions and thus seems before the nineteenth century by far the largest enumeration for which marital status data are preserved. The returns of the census were long believed lost, but were rediscovered by Peller (1920). If his figures are trustworthy, there were no married persons under 20 in most provinces. For the age group 20-39 the proportion of non-married persons (i.e. single and widowed taken together) strongly suggests the European pattern (represented here by Great Britain):

Per cent single or widowed in age group 20-39

	Men	Women
Austria 1754	41	38
Great Britain 1851	48	45
Bulgaria 1900	28	11

A detailed study of Peller's data, comparing them with later materials for the same areas, could be useful. Is it credible that in most of Austria not one woman under 20 was married? Or perhaps the ascertainment of age was not completely independent of marital status? In the present context the mere fact that it was possible for contemporaries to compile data showing no one under 20 as married is highly significant.

The enumerations carried out in various parts of the Austrian Empire towards the end of the eighteenth century might yield valuable information on marital status, e.g. the Hungarian enumerations of 1784 (see the volume edited by Kovasics). Very interesting analyses relating to a part of Belgium (now known as East Flanders) are contained in Faipoult's *Mémoire Statistique* of 1804-5, a modern edition of which has recently been published by Paul Deprez.[49] Faipoult was a French administrator, but the statistical materials for 1789 which he quotes were presumably collected under the Austrian administration. He was specifically interested in the age at marriage. If his figures are to be believed, there were in 1789 only 7,132 married persons under 30. This number is only 8 per cent of the population aged 20-29. He concludes: 'Donc on se marie rarement, dans ce pays, audessous de 30 ans' (p. 25). His statistical work gives a general impression of competence, but the figure quoted seems suspicious not only on general grounds, but because there seems to be a discrepancy between the marital status data from which it is derived and those for 1801 which he gives elsewhere (pp. 37-46).

We now turn to data where the single have been separately classified. In most cases the only division by age is a distinction between children and adults (say those aged 15 or over). If over 30 per cent of women 15 or over are single one may be certain that the population had a marriage pattern of the European type. This is a very cautious criterion; in Eastern Europe and in non-European countries well under 20 per cent of women aged 15 or over are single.

Unfortunately, many of the enumerations which supply marital status data for the eighteenth century and earlier relate to cities. The composition by marital status of urban populations is often much influenced by migration; European cities in earlier times, as now, often contained many unmarried people, not because city dwellers refrained from marriage, but because unmarried people migrated to the cities.

The evidence from the enumeration of urban populations is thus difficult to interpret. Nevertheless the urban material should be considered. A large volume of data has been

[49] See below, Part III, p. 608.

assembled in the survey by Mols. The eighteenth-century data on the whole suggest a pattern of late marriage and substantial numbers remaining unmarried through life.

One set of data published since Mols wrote should be added both because it is a detailed cross-classification by age and marital status and because it takes us back as far as 1700. Aleati gives the following figures from an enumeration of three parishes of the city of Pavia in Italy in 1700. The total population of these parishes was 2,168, representing some 13 per cent of the total population of the city.

	Men				Women		
Age group	20–24	25–29	40–59		20–24	25–29	40–59
Per cent single	78	52	15		41	27	11
Total population in age group	81	106	205		111	119	202

The distribution makes an unmistakably 'European' impression. Over 10 per cent of each sex remain single at the end of the marriageable period.

The only other detailed tabulation by age and marital status for a city at so early a date is that derived from an enumeration of Lichfield in 1695 by Gregory King. The figures have been published from King's manuscripts by Glass (1946 and 1950). They cover 2,861 persons. The percentages single among those over 40 are very low, but high under 40. (Did elderly spinsters claim to be under 40?) The fact that there is only one married woman under 20 would be sufficient by itself to show that these figures could not possibly have been the result of an enumeration in any non-European city.

Gregory King also made calculations giving for the whole of England in 1695 the numbers of bachelors and spinsters as also of husbands, wives, children, servants and sojourners. His London estimates, which he states separately, are fairly close to the Lichfield data and were presumably derived from them.[50] We do not know how much statistical basis he had for his estimates relating to the 'villages and hamlets' which contained the bulk of the population. King's work embodying these calculations was not published till 1802,[51] but the figures were given in an essay which Charles Davenant published in 1699. The estimates of marital status appeared plausible to contemporaries competent to judge, for they were applied in the eighteenth century to their own countries by continental writers on statistics. Unfortunately it is not entirely clear how King's estimates on sex, age and marital status fit together and they may not be altogether consistent. The proportion of single persons in the population at ages under 25 seems comfortably within the European range, but the proportion single among older people seems rather on the low side.

The earliest enumeration of a complete territory, urban and rural, which provides marital status data is the census of Iceland taken in 1703. The original records were preserved in their entirety in the Danish National Archives and rediscovered in 1914. Detailed tabulations were published by the Icelandic Statistical Office in 1960.[52] The proportions recorded as married are staggeringly low even for a European population and (if unmarried really means celibate) seem scarcely compatible with the permanent maintenance of the population in the face of the death rates of that time. For example, only 34 per cent of the men and 39 per cent of the women aged 30–34 are recorded as married. These data call for further investigation. They are quite unlike any data recorded at other times in Iceland or indeed anywhere else, except by obvious misclassification of the married. The age structure of the Icelandic census of 1703 suggests a rapidly declining population with a low birth rate.

[50] See Glass (1950) for a discussion of the way in which King used his Lichfield materials on age distribution. See below, Part II, p. 183 ff.

[51] The marital status data appear on pages 415–6 of the 1802 edition of Chalmers' *Estimate of the comparative strength of Great Britain*.

[52] For earlier and more easily accessible figures from the 1703 census see Gille (1949).

The Icelandic Statistical Office (according to the English summary of their Icelandic text) surmise that the number of married people is somewhat understated, because the marital status may not have been given for married people who had separated and passed into the classes of servants and paupers. Presumably the economic distress which was the reason why the census was ordered may have caused a large number of temporary separations. The data collected were apparently not really intended to provide classification by marital status in the modern sense; the aim was perhaps rather to get economic information, i.e. about the nature of the dependence on the head of the household. The tabulations published by the Iceland Statistical Office throw some light on the matter. Over 97 per cent of the women classed as married are the wives of heads of households. This certainly suggests that when a married woman was not the head's wife, her relationship to him (e.g. as a servant) would be recorded and not the fact that she was married. The vast majority of servants and paupers are classified as single. The very small numbers of widows among the older female servants and paupers seem particularly strange. Was the failure (from our modern point of view) to record marital status confined to servants and paupers and in these categories to persons who lived apart from their spouses? Among relatives of the head marital status might be implied by such descriptions as 'daughter-in-law'. But only two sons-in-law and nine daughters-in-law were reported. There were some 2,500 households with a male head over 50; did only 9 of them have a married son living with them? In view of the circumstances it seems likely that this census was distorted by substantial errors and vagueness of definition (especially when the results are tabulated in modern form). However, since the original records are preserved, there is a unique opportunity to discover something of the processes of the enumeration (and also to study in quite unusual depth the social conditions of a past age).

Apparently the only rural population (apart from Iceland) for which a full cross tabulation of marital status and age (in 5 year groups) is available in the eighteenth century is the Dutch village of Warder. The astronomer and statistician Struyck reports[53] that at his request Pieter Bakker, schoolmaster and precentor of the village, very carefully enumerated the whole population between 20 March and 17 April 1742. A condensed version of the data is reproduced in Table 13.

TABLE 13

Population of Warder (Netherlands), 1742, by age and marital status

Age	Single	Men Married	Widowers	Single	Women Married	Widows	Servants from elsewhere
Under 20	69	0	0	90	0	0	6
20–24	9	4	0	7	7	0	0
25–29	3	6	0	2	12	1	0
30–39	1	23	0	0	19	2	0
40–59	1	29	6	1	25	8	1
60 and over	0	4	8	0	3	7	0
Total	83	66	14	100	66	18	7

The almost entire absence of single people over 30 is non-European. The proportions single between 20 and 30 are low for the European pattern, but look high enough to be quite outside any well authenticated non-European experience. However, the numbers are far too small for any real conclusion.

[53] *Nader Ontdekkingen*, p. 13.

Struyck organized the enumeration of many other communities, but apparently not in the same detail. He gives for 45 villages and towns comprising a total population of 29,562 persons a classification by marital status of those over 10.[54] Here, as in the case of Warder, 'domestics' are treated as a separate category—a practice not uncommon in data for the eighteenth century and earlier.

In Struyck's figures for Dutch villages and towns the domestics form about 7 per cent of those over 10 for each sex. Presumably most of them were under 20 and single, as in Warder. Most contemporary and modern authors agree that servants were almost all unmarried. Including servants with the single population we obtain the following percentages, which are definitely 'European'. As will be seen, the Dutch figures show slightly fewer persons single than in Sweden in 1750.

	Men		*Women*	
	Dutch Villages 1742	Sweden 1750	Dutch Villages 1742	Sweden 1750
Single	40·5	44·8	39·2	42·3
Married	50·8	51·8	48·7	44·3
Widowed	8·7	3·3	12·1	13·4
Total	100·0	99·9	100·0	100·0

The assumption that the servants were almost all single is perhaps not entirely indubitable. Moheau (1778) in analysing French data omitted servants altogether in computing the distribution of the population by marital status. He did this because he thought that the distribution of domestics by marital status is 'presumably of the same order as that of the rest of the population'.[55] In the French materials there is several times as high a population of servants as in the Dutch data and one may suppose that an appreciable number were married, though Moheau's procedure, which implies that no higher fraction of servants was unmarried than in the general population, seems to go far beyond any reasonable assumption. Presumably there were differences between countries and regions in the number and type of servants employed and the manner of their treatment.[56] If we treat Struyck's figures in the fashion of Moheau and exclude the servants, we can compute the percentage single in the remaining population. This gives 36·3 for men and 34·4 for women, figures which seem intermediate between European and non-European levels (they relate to the population over 10 years of age). These results are, however, undoubtedly further from the truth than those given by the earlier calculation.

Data somewhat similar to Struyck's are reported by Messance (1766) from enumerations of small towns and villages in the 'géneralités' of Auvergne, Lyons and Rouen in France. The enumerations (people were 'comptés tête par tête') took place in 1756 (Auvergne), 1759 (Lyons) and 1762-3 (Rouen). The populations enumerated amounted to some 19,000, 20,000 and 61,000 respectively, mainly in small parishes. Messance himself believed the proportions found in the enumerations to be representative of the total populations of their respective regions. He gives for persons aged 15 and over of each sex the numbers of single, married and widowed (lumped together) and domestics.

The percentages single calculated on the two assumptions mentioned work out as follows:

[54] *Nader Ontdekkingen*, p. 87; the figures are also given by Süssmilch (Vol. II, p. 270).
[55] See p. 55 of the reprint of Moheau's *Recherches*, edited by Gonnard. It is convenient to refer to Moheau as the author of the work published in his name.
[56] See Chambers, *The Vale of Trent*, p. 51. See below, Part II, p. 327 f. Mackeprang in his study of the island of Moen in 1645 gives an interesting analysis of the distribution of servants by age and social origin. The servants were all young. He shows that a high proportion of the youth of Moen must have spent some time in service before marriage.

		Treating domestics as single	Excluding domestics
Auvergne	Men	41	32
	Women	38	31
Lyons	Men	39	30
	Women	39	28
Rouen	Men	40	32
	Women	39	33

These percentages are high and clearly European. For Sweden in 1750 the corresponding figures are 36 for men and 35 for women. Additional data similar to those given by Messance, but in less detail, are quoted by Moheau (1778), who also reproduces Messance's figures, without acknowledgement.[57]

Finally mention should be made of the estimates for Vaud in Switzerland, published by Muret in 1766 and quoted in Malthus's *Essay* (in the second and later editions). Among the 76,000 adults in Vaud, there are supposed to be 38,000 unmarried persons of whom probably 9,000 were widows or widowers. This leaves a comfortably European margin for the single. Malthus also quotes some similar figures for Berne. I have not consulted the originals from which one could presumably discover on what enumerations these estimates are based.

This examination of the eighteenth-century materials on the composition of the population by marital status has been superficial, but it is quite clear that, so far as these data go, there is no real trace of anything but a European pattern.

REFERENCES[58]

Editor's Note: Those marked † will be found wholly or partly reprinted in the volume.

ALEATI, Giuseppe. *La populazione di Pavia durante il dominio spagnolo.* Università degli studi di Pavia. Instituto di Statistica. Publicazione N.1, Milan 1957.

ASHTON, T. S. *An Economic History of England; The eighteenth century.* London 1955.

BACKMAN, Gaston. 'Die beschleunigte Entwicklung der Jugend.' *Acta Anatomica* (Basel), Vol. 4 (1947-8), pp. 421-80.

BARCLAY, George W. *Colonial Development and Population in Taiwan.* Princeton, New Jersey 1954.

BELTRAMI, Daniele. *Storia della populazione di Venezia dalla fine del secolo XVI alla caduta della reppublica.* Padova 1954.

BICKEL, Wilhelm. *Bevölkerungsgeschichte und Bevölkerungspolitik der Schweiz seit dem Ausgang des Mittelalters.* Zürich 1947.

† BOURGEOIS-PICHAT, Jean. 'Évolution de la population française depuis le dix-huitième siècle.' *Population,* Vol. 6 (1951), pp. 635-62.

BRAITHWAITE, L. and ROBERTS, G. W. 'A gross mating table for a West Indian population.' *Population Studies,* Vol. 14, No. 3 (1961), pp. 198-217.

BÜCHER, Karl. *Die Frauenfrage im Mittelalter.* 2nd edition. Tübingen 1910.

BUOMBERGER, Ferdinand. 'Bevölkerungs- und Vermögensstatistik in der Stadt und Landschaft Freiburg (im Uechtland) um die Mitte des 15. Jahrhunderts.' *Zeitschrift für Schweizerische Statistik,* Vol. 36 (1900), pp. 205-54.

[57] For a discussion of Moheau's material see a note signed L.H. (Louis Henry) in *Population* (1954), Vol. 9, No. 3, pp. 542-5.
[58] A few works which are not cited have been included.

† CHAMBERS, J. D. *The Vale of Trent 1670-1800. Economic History Review* Supplements, No. 3, 1957.

COALE, Ansley and HOOVER, Edgar Malone. *Population growth and economic development in low-income countries: a case study of India's prospects.* Princeton 1958.

CONNELL, K. H. *The population of Ireland 1750-1845.* Oxford, Clarendon Press 1950.

CSOSCÁN, Jenő. 'Három Pest megyei falu népesedése a XVIII század második felében' (Demographic changes in three villages in the county of Pest in the second half of the 18th century). *Történelmi Statisztikai Közlemények* (Publications of Historical Statistics), Vol. 3, No. 1-2 (Budapest, 1959), pp. 58-107. (Hungarian, with summaries in English, Russian, etc.)

DASZYNSKA, Sophie. 'Zürichs Bevölkerung im XVII Jahrhundert.' *Zeitschrift für Schwetzerische Statistik*, Vol. 25 (1889), pp. 369-415.

DAVENANT, Charles. *An essay upon the probable methods of making the people gainers in the balance of trade.* London 1699.

DE MEO, G. 'Alcune carattestiche demografiche di Bari nel 1753.' *Rivista italiana di statistica, economia e finanza*, Vol. VI (1934), pp. 342-50.

DEPARCIEUX, Antoine. *Essai sur les probabilités de la durée de la vie humaine.* Paris 1746.

DIEPGEN, L. 'Statistisches über Fürstenehen 1500-1900.' *Archiv für Hygiene*, Vol. 120 (1938), pp. 193-4.

DURAND, J. D. 'Mortality estimates from Roman tombstone inscriptions.' *American Journal of Sociology*, Vol. 64, No. 4 (1960), pp. 365-73.

FAIPOULT de Maisoncelle, Guillaume Charles. *Mémoire Statistique du département de l'Escaut.* Paris, Imprimerie Nationale An XIII [1805]. Reprint, with introduction by Paul Deprez, published by Maatschappij voor Geschiedenis en Oudheidkunde te Gent, Verhandelingen X, Gent 1960.

FOURASTIÉ, Jean. 'De la vie traditionelle à la vie tertiaire.' *Population*, Vol. 14, No. 3 (1959), pp. 417-32.

GAUTIER, Étienne and HENRY, Louis. *La Population de Crulai, Paroisse Normande.* Institut National d'Études Démographiques, Travaux et Documents, Cahier No. 33. Paris 1958.

GILLE, H. 'The demographic history of the Northern European countries in the eighteenth century.' *Population Studies*, Vol. 3, No. 1 (1949), pp. 3-65.

GIRARD, Pierre. 'Aperçus de la démographie de Sotteville-lès-Rouen vers la fin du XVIIIe siècle.' *Population*, Vol. 14, No. 3 (1959), pp. 485-508.

† GLASS, D. V. 'Gregory King and the population of England and Wales at the end of the seventeenth century.' *Eugenics Review*, Vol. 38, No. 1 (1946), pp. 170-83.

† GLASS, D. V. 'Gregory King's estimate of the population of England and Wales, 1695.' *Population Studies*, Vol. 3, No. 4 (1950), pp. 338-74.

HAJNAL, J. 'The marriage boom.' *Population Index*, Vol. 19, No. 2 (1953), pp. 80-101.

HAJNAL, J. 'Age at marriage and proportions marrying.' *Population Studies*, Vol. 7, No. 2 (1953), pp. 111-36.

HALLAM, H. E. 'Some thirteenth century censuses.' *The Economic History Review*, Second Series, Vol. X, No. 3 (1958), pp. 340-61.

HARKNESS, Albert Granger. 'Age at marriage and at death in the Roman Empire.' *Transactions of the American Philological Association*, Vol. 37 (1896), pp. 35-72.

HART, C. W. M. and PILLING, Arnold R. *The Tiwi of North Australia.* New York 1960.

HENRY, Louis. *Anciennes Familles Genevoises.* Institut National d'Études Démographiques, Cahier No. 26. Paris 1956.

HENRY, Louis. 'La mortalité d'après les inscriptions funéraires.' *Population*, Vol. 12, No. 1 (1957), pp. 149-52.

HENRY, Louis. 'L'âge au décès d'après les inscriptions funéraires.' *Population*, Vol. 14, No. 2 (1959), pp. 327-8.

HENRY, Louis and LEVY, Claude. 'Ducs et pairs sous l'ancien régime.' *Population*, Vol. 15, No. 5 (1960).

† HOLLINGSWORTH, T. H. 'A demographic study of the British Ducal families.' *Population Studies*, Vol. XI, No. 1 (1957), pp. 4-26.

HOMANS, George Caspar. *English Villagers of the Thirteenth Century*. Cambridge (Mass.) 1942.

HOMBERT, Marcel and PRÉAUX, Claire. *Recherches sur le recensement dans l'Égypte romaine*. Papyrologica Lugduno-Batava, Vol. V. Leyden 1952.

ICELAND, Statistical Bureau. *Manntalid 1703* (Population Census 1703), Hagskyrslur Islands (Statistics of Iceland), II, 21. (In Icelandic, with English and Esperanto summary and English table headings.) Reykjavik 1960.

INMAN, A. H. *Domesday and feudal statistics*. London 1900.

JAIN, S. P. *Life Tables—1951 Census*. Census of India, Paper No. 2. New Delhi 1959.

KATZ, Jacob. 'Family, kinship and marriage among Ashkenazim in the sixteenth to eighteenth centuries.' *The Jewish Journal of Sociology*, Vol. 1, No. 1 (1959), pp. 3-22.

KING, Gregory. *Natural and political observations and conclusions upon the state and condition of England 1696*, published in George CHALMERS, *An estimate of the comparative strength of Great Britain and of the losses of her trade from every war since the revolution*. New edition. London 1802.

KOVASICS, József (editor). *A történeti statisztika forrásai* (Sources of historical statistics). In Hungarian with English and Russian summaries. Published by the Hungarian Central Statistical Office. Budapest 1957.

KUCZYNSKI, Robert R. *The measurement of population growth*. London 1935.

LANDRY, Adolphe. 'Quelques aperçus concernant la dépopulation dans l'antiquité gréco-romaine.' *Revue Historique*, Vol. 61 (1936), pp. 1-33.

LAPLACE, Pierre Simon de. *A philosphical essay on probabilities*. Trsl. by F. W. Truscott and F. L. Emory, New York 1951.

MACDONELL, W. R. 'On the expectation of life in Ancient Rome.' *Biometrika*, Vol. 9 (1913), pp. 366-80.

MACKEPRANG, E. P. 'Et Brudstykke af en Folketelling fra 1645' (A fragment of a census of 1645). *Nationaløkonomisk Tidskrift*, Series III, Vol. 15, No. 3 (1907), pp. 248-70.

MESSANCE. *Recherches sur la population des généralités d'Auvergne, de Lyon, de Rouen et de quelques provinces et villes du Royaume*. Paris 1766.

MOHEAU. *Recherches et considérations sur la population de la France, 1778*. Modern edition by René Gonnard, Paris 1912.

MOLS, Roger. *Introduction à la démographie historique des villes d'Europe du XIVe siècle au XVIIIe siècle*. 3 Vols. Louvain 1954-6.

MOMBERT, Paul. *Bevölkerungslehre*. Grundrisse zum Studium der Nationalökonomie, Band 15. Jena 1929.

MORRELL, C. C. 'Tudor Marriages and Infantile Mortality.' *Journ. State Medicine*, Vol. 43 (1935), pp. 173-81.

MORTARA, Giorgio. *Le unioni conjugali libere nell'America Latina*. Università di Roma, Istituto di Demografia. Roma 1961.

MURET, J. S. *Mémoires sur l'état de la population dans le pays de Vaud*. Yverdon 1766.

VAN NIEROP, Leonie. 'De bruidegoms van Amsterdam.' *Tijdschrift voor Geschiedenis*, Vol. 48 (1933), pp. 337-57; Vol. 49 (1934), pp. 136-60 and 329-44; Vol. 52 (1937), pp. 144-63 and 251-64.

PELLER, Sigismund. 'Zur Kenntnis der städtischen Mortalität im 18. Jahrhundert.' *Zeitschrift für Hygiene und Infektionskrankheiten*, Vol. 90 (1920), pp. 227-62.

† PELLER, Sigismund. 'Studies on mortality since the Renaissance.' *Bulletin of the History of Medicine*, Vol. 13 (1943), pp. 439-61; Vol. 16 (1944), pp. 362-81; Vol. 21 (1947), pp. 51-101.

PIRENNE, H. 'Les dénombrements de la population à Ypres au XIVᵉ siècle.' *Vierteljahresschrift für Sozial- und Wirtschaftsgeschichte*, Vol. 1 (1903), pp. 1-32.

POWER, Eileen. 'The position of women' in *The Legacy of the Middle Ages* edited by C. G. Crump and E. F. Jacob. Oxford 1926.

POWER, Eileen. *Medieval English nunneries, c. 1275-1535.* Cambridge 1922.

ROLLER, O. K. *Die Einwohnerzahl der Stadt Durlach im 18. Jahrhundert in ihren wirtschaftlichen und kulturgeschichtlichen Verhältnissen dargestellt aus ihren Stammtafeln.* Karlsruhe 1907.

RÜMELIN, Eduard. 'Heiratsalter und Fruchtbarkeit der Ehen und ihre Entwicklung seit 1500.' *Württemb. Jahrb. für Stat. und Landeskunde*, 1923-24, pp. 11-31 (published in 1926).

RUSSELL, Josiah Cox. 'The clerical population of medieval England.' *Traditio* (New York), Vol. II, pp. 177-212 (1944).

RUSSELL, Josiah Cox. *British Medieval Population.* Albuquerque, N. Mex. 1948.

RUSSELL, Josiah Cox. 'Late Ancient and Medieval Population.' *Transactions of the American Philosophical Society*, Vol. 48, Part 3, 1958.

SCHNYDER, Werner. *Die Bevölkerung der Stadt und Landschaft Zürich vom 14. bis 17. Jahrhundert.* Schweizer Studien zur Geschichtswissenschaft, Vol. 14, Fasc. 1. Zürich 1926.

SONNABEND, Enrico H. *Il fattore demografico nel' organizzazione soziale dei Bantu.* Rome 1935.

STOLNITZ, George J. 'A century of international mortality trends', Part II. *Population Studies*, Vol. 10, No. 1 (1956), pp. 17-42.

STONE, Lawrence. 'Marriage among the English nobility in the 16th and 17th centuries.' *Comparative Studies in Society and History*, Vol. 3, No. 2 (1961), pp. 182-215.

STRUYCK, N. *Nadere ontdeckingen noopens den staat van 't menschelijk geslagt.* Amsterdam 1753.

SÜSSMILCH, Johann Peter. *Die göttliche Ordnung in den Veränderungen des menschlichen Geschlechts.* 3 Vols. 4th edition. Berlin 1775.

TAEUBER, Irene B. 'Population growth in a Chinese microcosm: Taiwan.' *Population Index*, Vol. 27, No. 2 (1961), pp. 101-26.

TAEUBER, Irene B. and TAEUBER, Karl E. 'The fertility of the Chinese in North East China' in *International Population Conference Vienna 1959.* Union Internationale pour l'Étude Scientifique de la Population. Vienna 1959. Pp. 348-54.

TAWNEY, R. H. *The agrarian problem in the sixteenth century.* London 1912.

UNITED NATIONS, Department of Social Affairs, Population Branch. *Age and Sex Patterns of Mortality.* Model life tables for under-developed countries. Population Studies No. 22. New York 1955.

WESTERMARCK, Edward. *The history of human marriage.* Vol. I. Fifth edition. London 1925.

PART II

GREAT BRITAIN

7

THE ECONOMIC HISTORY OF
MODERN BRITAIN

H. J. HABAKKUK

From: *Journal of Economic History*, 1958, pp. 486-501

Editor's Note: This article is reprinted without the author's revision as an introduction to the problems discussed in this section to show their relevance to the development of the British Isles in general. It also contains bibliographical references to earlier work in this field which is not elsewhere reprinted or mentioned in this volume.

THERE is now a rough consensus of opinion among English economic historians about the broad chronology of English population history. According to this chronology there were three main phases of rapid growth. The first occurred in the twelfth and thirteenth centuries, and was brought to an end by a marked fall in population in the fourteenth century. The second phase occupied most of the sixteenth century and the early seventeenth, after which there was some slowing down in the later seventeenth century and possibly an absolute check in the 1720's and 1730's. And finally there was the sustained cumulative increase that started in the later eighteenth century.

This periodization has come to occupy an important part in the interpretation of the main developments in English economic history. Thus some recent accounts of medieval economic development ascribe to population change a leading role in the rise of prices and internal colonization in the thirteenth century, and in the fall in prices and the contraction of the cultivated area in the later Middle Ages.[1]

Population movements do not occupy so central a place in explanation of the sixteenth and seventeenth centuries, but population pressure is one of the traditional explanations for the overseas migrations, and many ingredients of a demographic interpretation have been advanced in recent work. Phelps Brown has shown how pressure of population in the sixteenth century simultaneously depressed money wages and caused agricultural prices to rise relatively to prices of industrial goods, and how the check to population growth in the seventeenth century had the reverse effects.[2] And F. J. Fisher suggests that one reason 'why the middle and later years of the seventeenth century present a somewhat brighter picture (than the late sixteenth and early seventeenth) may be that population growth was temporarily checked by emigration and bubonic plague, to be resumed only when agricultural, industrial and commercial

[1] M. M. Postan, 'Some Economic Evidence of Declining Population in the Later Middle Ages', *Economic History Review*, 2nd ser., II (1950), 236.

[2] E. H. Phelps Brown and Sheila V. Hopkins, 'Wage-rates and Prices: Evidence for Population Pressure in the Sixteenth Century', *Economica*, n.s., XXIV (1957), 289-306.

expansion were more fully in their stride'.[3] Some historians would be prepared
to argue that the sixteenth-century price rise itself, in so far as it was not due to
debasement and government expenditure, was the result of population pressure.
Coleman has reconsidered mercantilist attitudes to such problems as labour in
the light of hypotheses about demographic history.[4]

In interpretations of the period of classic Industrial Revolution, population
growth has always played an important part. It figures largely in explanations
of rising prices, at least in the period before the suspension of cash payments
and the heavy government expenditure of the Napoleonic Wars; it is one of
the traditional explanations for the agrarian changes of the later eighteenth
century; and many writers interpret the social discontents of the early nineteenth
century as a fulfilment of part at least of the Malthusian prophecies. But some
recent work has integrated population change much more closely into the
economic history of the period. Mingay and Chambers have ascribed to population change more direct responsibility for the check to agricultural investment in the 1730's and 1740's and for its revival in the 1750's.[5] Chambers has
also argued that the industrial proletariat of the early nineteenth century was
principally the result not of expropriation and the enclosure movement but of
natural increase, and largely the natural increase of a proletariat that existed
before the Industrial Revolution. Population pressure is assigned a central role
in Brinley Thomas' interpretation of the Atlantic economy of the nineteenth
century: 'The cycle in the rate of natural increase (of European population)
played a part in determining the timing of the major waves of oversea emigration from Europe.'[6]

For those who care for the overmastering pattern, the elements are evidently
there for a heroically simplified version of English history before the nineteenth
century in which the long-term movements in prices, in income distribution,
in investment, in real wages, and in migration are dominated by changes in
the growth of population. Rising population: rising prices, rising agricultural
profits, low real incomes for the mass of the population, unfavourable terms
of trade for industry—with variations depending on changes in social institutions, this might stand for a description of the thirteenth century, the sixteenth
century and the early seventeenth, and the period 1750-1815. Falling or stationary population with depressed agricultural profits but higher mass incomes
might be said to be characteristic of the intervening periods.

I

There are dangers as well as fascinations in an explanatory influence of such
power, the more so since, before the nineteenth century, our knowledge of
population movements is partly inferred from economic evidence—that is,

[3] F. J. Fisher, 'The Sixteenth and Seventeenth Centuries: The Dark Ages in English Economic
History', *ibid.*, p. 16.
[4] D. C. Coleman, 'Labour in the English Economy of the Seventeenth Century', *Ec. Hist. Rev.*,
2nd ser., VIII (1956), 284-7.
[5] G. E. Mingay, 'The Agricultural Depression, 1730-1750', *ibid.*, pp. 335-6; J. D. Chambers,
'Enclosure and Labour Supply in the Industrial Revolution', *ibid.*, V (1953), 319-43. See below,
p. 308.
[6] Brinley Thomas, *Migration and Economic Growth* (Cambridge, Cambridge University Press
1954), p. 157.

from the behaviour of wages, prices, and rents—which the population movements are then invoked to account for. There is therefore no rigorous control
on the natural temptation to turn 'population growth' on and off as the occasion requires and to treat it sometimes as independent of economic change and
sometimes as a response to economic change. For economic historians this is
the real issue of demographic history: not whether the birth rate or the death
rate had most influence in population changes (though this is the mould in
which controversy tends to set) but the extent to which particular population
changes were the *result* of economic developments, or sprang from forces
which were, from an economic point of view, fortuitous. In many ways the
most interesting work on this problem has been done by medievalists but, for
obvious reasons, I shall confine this paper principally to the eighteenth and
early nineteenth centuries, and for the other periods satisfy myself with in-
cautious asides.

The statistics available for this period are, by modern standards, extremely
imprecise. The medievalists have never been under any illusion about the
fragility of their data. But until not long ago it was believed that as the result
of the work of Brownlee and Griffith, we had for the eighteenth century
estimates of total population and of birth and death rates that were sufficiently
reliable for the historians' purpose.[7] One of the results of later work has been to
convince most historians that, heroically ingenious as these calculations were,
the results are useless for explanatory purposes. There are many and complicated reasons for this, but the principal reason is quite simple. These estimates
depend on the baptisms and burials entered in the parish registers; but an
allowance has to be made for births and deaths that were not registered. The
estimates for birth and death rates are highly sensitive to the allowance that the
particular estimator thinks fit to make, and the evidence on this point is so
scanty that we do not know within a very wide margin what the right allowance would be. Even accurate birth and death rates are a very imperfect guide
to the real facts of population change; an apparent rise in the birth rate, for
example, may be due to the fact that because people are living longer fewer
marriages are broken by death. But for the eighteenth century the estimated
rates themselves are suspect as to absolute level, and conceivably, on occasion,
even misrepresent the direction of change.[8]

One result of the paucity of statistics is that we cannot test explanatory
hypotheses and weed out from among the many that are plausible those that
fit the facts. Worse still, it is often not clear what precisely it is that has to be
explained. How rapidly, for example, did population grow during these expansion periods? In the early decades of the nineteenth century population
increased at a rate of about 1·5 per cent per annum. That is something that does
really call for an explanation. But how rapidly was English population increas-

[7] J. Brownlee, 'The History of the Birth and Death Rates in England and Wales Taken as a
Whole, from 1750 to the Present Time', *Public Health*, XXIX (1915-16), 228-38; 'The Health of
London in the Eighteenth Century', *Proceedings of the Royal Medical Society*, XVIII (1925), Section
of Epidemology and State Medicine, 73-85; G. Talbot Griffith, *Population Problems of the Age of
Malthus* (Cambridge, Cambridge University Press 1926), ch. i and ii; 'Rickman's Second Series of
Eighteenth-Century Population Figures', *Journal of the Royal Statistical Society*, XCII (1929), 256-63.
[8] The statistics are extensively discussed by J. T. Krause, 'Changes in English Fertility and
Mortality', *Ec. Hist. Rev.*, 2nd ser., XI (1958), 57-70. See below, p. 379.

ing in the later decades of the eighteenth century? It is quite in the cards that
the pace was no greater than in previous periods of growth and on the Continent
at the same period. For at the end of the seventeenth century the population
was probably about 5,200,000 and by the first census of 1801 it was only
9,168,000.

The rate of increase may have been no more than 0·5 per cent.[9] The attempts
to arrive at population statistics for England as a whole for the seventeenth
and eighteenth centuries have produced results that are very slight in relation
both to the effort that has gone into their making and to the demands historians
wish to make upon them, and further manipulation of the aggregate statistics
is unlikely to yield much of value. The main hope of further information lies
in detailed studies of specific areas and of genealogical populations. Studies of
the first sort have been initiated by Chambers and Eversley.[10] The former has
analysed the statistics of baptisms, burials, and marriages of a large number of
Nottinghamshire parishes. The latter has made an intensive study of twelve
Worcestershire parishes. There is an important study of the second sort by
Hollingsworth, who has examined the demographic data relating to 1,908
individuals who were the legitimate offspring of British kings, queens, dukes,
or duchesses, and who were born between 1330 and the end of 1954.[11]

Another decade or so of work on these lines and we shall be able to generalize
with confidence about the nature of population change in this period, but in
the present situation perhaps the simplest way to assess the significance of
contributions to the subject and its present possibilities is to consider, in a
simplified Malthusian-type version, one way in which changes in population
growth might result directly from economic changes.[12]

Before the intervention of modern medicine and methods of birth control
there was, according to this version, a mechanism for keeping population in
line with resources, at a given standard of living. This standard was conventionally determined and so itself liable to change (Malthus argued that the
low grain prices of the 1730's and 1740's accustomed people to higher living
standards which they attempted to protect by not marrying earlier), but it was
not liable to rapid change and was not in itself an important variable. The first
part of the mechanism was the age and extent of marriage. If resources were
plentiful in relation to population, marriages were earlier, there were fewer
never-married adults, and population growth was rapid; the converse, if and
when resources were scarce. But where the changes in the age at marriage and
in nuptiality were inadequate and population increased faster than resources

[9] The figure for the later seventeenth century is the revision by D. V. Glass of Gregory King's
estimate in 'Gregory King's Estimate of the Population of England and Wales, 1695', *Population
Studies*, III (1949-50), 338. See also, by the same author, 'Gregory King and the Population of England
and Wales at the end of the Seventeenth Century', *Eugenics Review*, XXXVII (1945-6), 170-83. See
below, p. 159.

[10] J. D. Chambers, *The Vale of Trent, 1670-1800* (*Ec. Hist. Rev.*, Supplement 3; London 1957).
D. E. C. Eversley, 'A Survey of Population in an Area of Worcestershire from 1660-1850', *Population
Studies*, X (1956-7), 230-53. See below, p. 327; 394.

[11] T. H. Hollingsworth, 'A Demographic Study of the British Ducal Families', *ibid.*, XI (1957),
1-26. See below, p. 354.

[12] There have been many studies of Malthus in recent years, thus G. F. McCleary, *The Malthusian
Population Theory* (London, Faber and Faber 1953); D. V. Glass, ed., *Introduction to Malthus* (London,
Watts 1953); A. T. Peacock, 'The Theory of Population and Modern Economic Analysis', *Population
Studies*, VI (1952-3), 114-22, VII (1953-4), 227-34.

warranted, the balance was preserved by an increase in the death rate. Thus it has been suggested that the high mortality of the early fourteenth century may have been a penalty for the population growth of the preceding century, and that the harvest failures and outbreaks of plague in the seventeenth century were perhaps a penalty for the growth of the sixteenth. The argument for supposing that nature did 'audit with a red pencil' is a general one: that during a period of rapid growth much of the additional population had recourse to soils with low yields and, moreover, yields that were difficult to sustain permanently; so that the population after a period of rapid growth was likely to contain an unusually large number of people living near the physical margin of subsistence and cultivating land that was more subject than most to failures of yield. In these conditions harvest deficiencies were both more likely to occur, and more likely to cause heavy mortality by famine-stimulated disease. Plague and harvest failure might of course occur purely fortuitously, but the most serious visitations—those that had permanent effects—were Malthusian visitations. And independent outbreaks of disease would find a less resistant population. Conversely, an increase in resources, due, for example, to an increase in agricultural output, had a favourable effect on mortality; famines and the outbreak of disease that accompanied them were less likely to occur.

II

How far, on the present evidence, did the population changes take this form? Consider marriage first. It is clear that in the very long run marriage was used as a regulator of population. As Russell's study shows,[13] from early in European history marriage has been linked to the setting up of a household, and changes that made it easier to set up a household encouraged marriages. Of course the link with means of subsistence was loose. A change in inheritance laws, for example, might make marriage easier without contributing to any increase of resources. An extension of peasant proprietorship or an increase in consumption standards might make people more reluctant to marry, despite an increase in resources. But the general tendency was to prevent too wide a divergence between population and resources. In any region the rate of growth in a normal year, that is, one free from war, famine, and epidemic, was set by age at marriage and nuptiality, and where contemporaneous societies differed widely in their population growth it was predominantly because of differences on this point. Where resources were abundant, population, even in early times, could expand very rapidly. A recent study by J. B. Harley has shown how much greater was the increase in a thinly settled area than in one well populated to start with.[14]

But the fact that marriage habits were influenced by the abundance of resources does not prove that marriage was sufficiently sensitive to regulate the rate of population growth over periods as short as, say, a century. Granted that age at marriage and nuptiality *tended* to vary with economic opportunity, could they have varied enough to have contributed substantially to the observed

[13] J. C. Russell, *British Medieval Population* (Albuquerque, N. Mex., University of New Mexico Press 1948).
[14] J. B. Harley, 'Population Trends and Agricultural Developments from the Warwickshire Hundred Rolls of 1279', *Ec. Hist. Rev.*, 2nd ser., XI (1958), 8-18.

changes in population growth? Did population grow more rapidly in the periods of rapid growth because the excess of births over deaths became greater in a normal year, or simply because there were more normal years free from war, famine, and plague?

In a paper which, though thirty years old, is still very relevant to present discussions, T. H. Marshall shed some light on this problem. Though he accepted that at the end of the eighteenth century there had been 'an unprecedented fall in the death rate, caused for the most part by non-economic forces', he concluded that in 'seeking an explanation of the rapid increase in population, we must pay as much attention to the forces which kept the birth rate up as to those which pulled the death rate down'. He argued that the birth rate in the late eighteenth and the early nineteenth centuries was sustained at an undesirably high level by the demand for child labour in the factories and by the element of children's allowance in the Speenhamland system, which encouraged marriage.[15] More recently K. H. Connell has ascribed the increase in the population of Ireland in the late eighteenth century to a fall in the age at marriage, and I attempted to argue that the same was true of England.[16] A most forceful and pertinent criticism of this view has been made by two medical historians, T. McKeown and R. G. Brown.[17] They argue, principally on Irish data for the later nineteenth century, that (1) only a considerable change in age at marriage of women would have significantly altered the number of births, and (2) that changes in age at marriage are likely in fact to have been slight. Moreover, the effect of any increase in births would be further reduced by a rise in infant mortality, since large families have a higher proportion of infant deaths. And on general grounds, where both birth and death rates are high, an acceleration of population growth is more likely to result from a fall in the latter than from a rise in the former.

There has been very little systematic study of the effect on births of age at marriage in pre-birth-control societies. The Irish data presented by McKeown and Brown suggest that 'an advance in mean age of wives at marriage of about 5 years would be needed to reduce the mean number of live births by 1' (that is, per marriage). This calculation does not, of course, show the full effect of a fall in age at marriage since no account is taken of (1) the fact that more women would live to marry and (2) the close succession of the generations. These no doubt are minor considerations, but even an increase of one child per family would, on reasonable assumptions, be sufficient to produce a not imperceptible increase in the rate of population growth. Moreover, besides age at marriage one must take account of nuptiality. It has been pointed out that it is the age at marriage of the women that is important demographically rather than that of the men; but in so far as a fall in the age of marriage of men is *not* accompanied

[15] T. H. Marshall, 'The Population Problem During the Industrial Revolution', *Economic History* (Supplement to the *Economic Journal*), I (1926-9) (reprinted in E. M. Carus-Wilson, ed., *Essays in Economic History* (London, Arnold 1954)), 434, 445, 452. See below, p. 247.

[16] K. H. Connell, *The Population of Ireland, 1750-1845* (Oxford 1950); 'Land and Population in Ireland', *Ec. Hist. Rev.*, 2nd ser., II (1950), 278-89 (see below, p. 423); 'Some Unsettled Problems in English and Irish Population History, 1750-1845', *Irish Historical Studies*, VII (1951), 225-34; H. J. Habakkuk, 'English Population in the Eighteenth Century', *Ec. Hist. Rev.*, 2nd ser., VI (1953), 117-33. See below, p. 269.

[17] T. McKeown and R. G. Brown, 'Medical Evidence Related to the English Population Changes in the Eighteenth Century', *Population Studies*, IX (1955), 119-41. See below, p. 285.

by an equivalent fall in the age of marriage of women, it must produce an increase in the number of ever-married women. The most detailed calculation on the effect of marriage known to me is in an unpublished thesis by Goran Ohlin, who suggests that at least in conditions not too dissimilar from those in eighteenth-century Sweden, even fairly slight shifts in age or frequency of marriage would significantly affect long-run rates of growth—possibly by 3 or 4 points per 1,000.[18] We obviously need to find out much more about age at marriage and nuptiality, but I am not convinced that we must at this stage reject the possibility that a fall of two or three years in the age at marriage, plus some increase in nuptiality, *could* have caused an acceleration of the rate of growth of the sort we observe in the later eighteenth century.

The much more doubtful question is whether there were in fact changes in age at marriage of this order of magnitude. There is a reasonable amount of evidence that the average age of marriage in England before the Industrial Revolution was quite high; the median age at marriage of a large group of yeomen in the period 1637-80 was 27-28 and of their wives 24-25.[19] People in the later eighteenth century *could*, therefore, have married earlier than their forebears. But did they? A fall in average age at marriage might take place in two ways: as a result of earlier marriages within existing social groups, and/or as a result of an increase in the size of those groups where marriages at all times tended to be early. As an example of the first, there is some contemporary suggestion that agricultural labourers tended to marry earlier where the practice of boarding them in the farmhouse was discontinued; board wages became less common during the Napoleonic Wars because the labourers, being less plentiful than before, could make better terms; and there was no revival of the practice after the wars, partly because the farmer liked having the house to himself, partly because day labourers could be more easily subsidized from the rates.[20] But within any given social group marriage habits might be expected to be stable, and it is likely that a large part of any change in age at marriage was the result of shifts in the relative importance of groups with different marriage habits. That there were significant differences in age at marriage in different social groups is strongly suggested by the differences in fertility. That these were considerable in the early nineteenth century, Krause has recently shown in his calculations of fertility ratios; the ratio of children 0-4 to women of childbearing age in the censuses of 1821 and 1841 was substantially higher in some counties than in others.[21] It has been shown that of the couples married in the decade 1861-71, textile workers had a marital fertility 6 per cent below the general average and miners one of 13 per cent above.[22] It is improbable that such differences were a secondary product of (1) differences in age composition,

[18] Per Goran Ohlin, 'The Positive and Preventive Check: A Study of the Rate of Growth of Pre-Industrial Populations' (unpublished doctoral thesis, Harvard University), ch. iii.
[19] Brian Frith, ed., *Gloucestershire Marriage Allegations, 1637-1680* (Bristol and Gloucestershire Arch. Soc. 1954). See the review of this work by J. D. Chambers in the *Ec. Hist. Rev.*, 2nd ser., IX (1956), 145. See below, p. 331.
[20] A. Redford, *Labour Migration in England* (Manchester, Manchester University Press 1926), pp. 63 ff.
[21] Krause, 'English Fertility', pp. 67-69.
[22] D. V. Glass, 'Changes in Fertility in England and Wales, 1851-1931', in L. Hogben, ed., *Political Arithmetic; Symposium on Population Studies* (London, Allen and Unwin 1937), pp. 173-94.

(2) differences in adult mortality (that is, differences in the number of marriages broken by death before the end of the childbearing period), or (3) differences of control of births within marriage. The main causes must be differences in age at marriage and in nuptiality.

Ideally, one would like to be able to compare the age at marriage of different groups over time, but though information is not yet available for this period, there seems nothing improbable in supposing that, on balance, the groups which as a result of economic changes were becoming larger had also a relatively lower age at marriage, and that the shifts were great enough to produce changes in the average marriage age of real significance for population growth.

Whatever the initial causes of the rapid population increase, one secondary influence was, as T. H. Marshall argued, the failure of births to fall as soon as one would have expected under the pressure of population. The number of children per marriage does not apparently begin to decline until the women born in the 1850's, and initially the decline was small; as has been shown from an examination of the 1911 census data, there was little change in fertility between couples married in the period 1851-61 and those married in 1861-71. The marked fall came with the women married in the decade 1871-81, who had on an average 9 per cent fewer children than those of the preceding decade. There is some evidence that the fall, when it came, was associated with a deferment of marriage; the age at marriage rose slowly between 1871 and 1900 from 24·30 to 25·14 (for spinsters), and Lorimer has suggested that the forces making for fewer births found expression first in postponement or avoidance of marriage, and only later in increased emphasis on methods of controlling fertility within marriage.[23] But in the decades before the 1870's there appears to have been little control over population exerted by way of marriage. This may have been because of social inertia and the fixity of marriage habits. Alternatively, it may be, as Lorimer argues, that the age at marriage responded only to economic pressure or to inducement within a certain institutional framework or above certain levels of income; the change of the early nineteenth century had disrupted the old institutional supports and it was not until the 1860's and 1870's that rising standards of living provided a setting in which large groups of people were prepared once again to calculate about marriage. Or in part the explanation may be, as T. H. Marshall suggested, that in the early part of the century there were specific economic forces maintaining the level of marriage.

III

We must now consider the second part of the mechanism—the variations in death. There is no doubt that variations in death were a major influence upon the rate of population growth. It is evident that the spectacular fall in population in the fourteenth century and the more modest check in the later seventeenth and early eighteenth centuries were due to an increase in deaths. What part a fall in deaths played in the increase in population between 1760 and 1850 is a more debatable question. The standard opinion, based upon the work of G. T. Griffith and M. C. Buer, used to be that the fall in deaths was

[23] F. Lorimer, *Culture and Human Fertility* (UNESCO 1954), pp. 209-11.

the principal cause.[24] I suggested some years ago that the estimates of Griffith and Brownlee did not afford reliable evidence of a fall in death rates after 1780, and recently Krause has examined these estimates in detail and provided evidence for concluding that there was a very marked increase in the deficiencies of registration between the 1780's and the 1820's. Everyone who has worked on the population statistics of this period has, of course, recognized the difficulty and the necessity of devising appropriate multipliers. Krause's contribution on this point is to have assembled sufficient facts to suggest that omissions of registration increased so rapidly in the 1780's that it would not be implausible to ascribe all or almost all the apparent fall in the death rate to this cause. Nevertheless, though little reliance can be placed on the rates, two conclusions about mortality may be ventured. The first is that mortality was lower in the second half of the eighteenth century than in the first. In Hollingsworth's data on British ducal families, the cohort born between 1730 and 1779 had a very much higher expectation of life than those born between 1680 and 1729. The second is that the expectation of life at birth in the 1840's and 1850's was higher than in the 1770's and 1780's. The expectation of life at birth in English Life Table III, which covers the period 1838-54, was 39·9 years. While it is not inconceivable that the expectation in England in the later eighteenth century was roughly as high as this—Milne calculated on the basis of the data collected by John Heysham for Carlisle in the period 1779-87 that the expectation of life at birth was 38·72 years—it is extremely unlikely that this was so. In Sweden in the later eighteenth century the expectation of life at birth was about 35 years, and one would expect the English rate to be lower not higher, since a higher proportion of Englishmen lived in towns. I think we must accept the probability, therefore, that some time between the 1780's and the 1840's and 1850's there was an improvement in the expectation of life, a more substantial improvement possibly than that between the 1850's and 1880's, since the expectation of life by the 1880's had risen to only 45 years.[25] Such an improvement should, I think, surprise us, but the alternative to being surprised is to rewrite the demographic history of earlier centuries.

The question that needs to be decided is how far the fall in mortality reflects developments that were fortuitous from an economic point of view, and how far they were the result of economic changes and, in particular, of an increase of resources.

It was long thought that improvements in medical knowledge and facilities were the main cause, but a cause that for present purposes we should rank as external. But McKeown and Brown have shown that so far as the eighteenth century is concerned, medicine can have had little to do with it. Instead, they suggest that the explanation must be an improvement in economic and social environment, and a consequent relaxation of the Malthusian positive checks. This was substantially the view of the early-nineteenth-century demographer

[24] Griffith, *Population Problems in the Age of Malthus*; M. C. Buer, *Health, Wealth and Population in the Early Days of the Industrial Revolution* (London, Routledge 1926).

[25] In 1953 I suggested that the fall in the death rate in the 1780's—or such fall as might remain after the imperfections of the statistics had been taken account of—might simply be due to a change in age composition because of an earlier rise in birth rates. This was an ill-considered suggestion since age at death varies so widely that only the effect of implausibly great changes in age composition would be perceptible.

Rickman, who, writing in 1816, ascribed the decline in mortality since 1780, which he believed himself to have established, to food and cleanliness. The standard of living during the Industrial Revolution is itself the subject of a large and controversial literature, to which Ashton and Hobsbawm have recently contributed from different points of view.[26] Ashton has distinguished between the large class raised well above the level of mere subsistence who were able to share in the benefits of economic progress and, on the other hand, the masses of unskilled or poorly skilled whose incomes were almost wholly absorbed in necessities. How large the minority was we do not know, but in view of the relatively slight increase in expectation of life in the later decades, it is difficult to believe that the improvements in the standard of living can have had important demographic consequences. Such developments as improvements in internal transport and marketing may have alleviated the demographic consequences of local shortages, but other economic developments, particularly the increase in urbanization, would lead one to expect higher mortality.

While medical historians have been thrusting the problem back at the economic historian, some economic historians have been tempted to find an explanation of variations in death rates in the varying behaviour of diseases. Recent work has been damaging to the Malthusian view of the death rate on two points. There is no evidence that the frequency and severity of deficient harvests in the eighteenth century were determined by population pressure. The effect on total mortality of a bad harvest was no doubt determined by the general standard of living, and so probably was the particular incidence of mortality between different groups. But the harvest failures themselves reflected ascertainable vagaries of the climate, not the density of population in relation to resources. Of even greater importance is the fact that deficient harvests were not the main agents of mortality. In the region examined by Chambers they were overshadowed by outbreaks of disease which were not associated with dearth. There is some evidence that over the country as a whole severe dearth did cause higher mortality.[27] And the mortality of London, like that of all great cities in the eighteenth century, was very sensitive to harvest deficiency.[28] But the coincidence between high mortality and dearth in the general statistics is not a great deal higher than one might expect from the fact that seasons of both were common. In Nottinghamshire the famine of 1708-10 had 'no specific demographic effect', while the long period of good harvests between 1729 and 1740 saw a succession of epidemics and years of high mortality. There was a devastating outbreak of smallpox in the later 1720's and a series of influenza epidemics, generally accompanied by increased activity among the endemic diseases.[29] These epidemics were not an exclusively English pheno-

[26] T. S. Ashton, 'The Standard of Life of the Workers in England, 1790-1830', in F. A. Hayek, ed., *Capitalism and the Historians* (Chicago, University of Chicago Press 1954), pp. 127-59. E. J. Hobsbawm, 'The British Standard of Living, 1790-1850', *Ec. Hist. Rev.*, 2nd ser., X (1957), 46-68.

[27] William Farr, 'The Influence of Scarcities and of the High Price of Wheat on the Mortality of the People of England', *Journal of the Statistical Society*, IX (1846), 158-74.

[28] D. M. George, 'The Increase of Population in the Eighteenth Century as Illustrated by London', *Economic Journal*, XXII (1908), 325.

[29] The study of a single region cannot of course provide conclusive proof that pure epidemics were more damaging than dearths, simply because the geographical incidence of the former was

menon but were general throughout northern Europe. They cannot have been a Malthusian punishment inflicted on an overexpanded population, since the 1720's and 1730's were, in general, years of abundant harvests. Utterström has investigated these epidemics in Sweden, and probably his explanation of the high mortality of these years and the low mortality of the decades immediately following applies also to England, and the variations in the severity of disease were due primarily to climatic changes.[30] Not only did harvest failures reflect weather, not population pressure; weather could and usually did affect mortality directly without the mediation of a poor harvest—indeed, the weather that was good for the carriers of disease might also be good for the crops.

In a notable article Helleiner has argued, of the later eighteenth century and of Europe generally, that 'it was not so much a reduction of mortality in "normal" years that produced the secular downward trend of the death rate, but an unmistakable abatement of the "great crises"'. The disappearance of plague above all, but also a very sensible mitigation of subsistence crises, seems to have been chiefly responsible for the increase in life expectancy.[31] Considering only England, it is doubtful whether such preponderant importance should be attached to the plague as compared, say, to influenza, and smallpox; indeed, whether such preponderant importance is to be attached to epidemics as compared to fluctuations in the severity of the endemic diseases. And, so far as one can judge from their effect on prices, the dearths of the late eighteenth century, for example those of 1795 and 1800, seem to have been as severe as those of the late seventeenth or early eighteenth. If their effect on mortality was slighter—as was the case—it was perhaps principally because the diseases that dearth tended to provoke were less vigorous. And for the reasons for this, I think we must look to the historians of climate and disease.

It also seems to me that any further improvement in mortality that had been achieved by the middle of the century is more likely to be due to changes in the virulence and character of diseases than to environmental changes. The probability is that it was an improvement in infant mortality, since there is no evidence of an improvement in adult expectation of life. Vaccination clearly reduced the infant death rate. Writing in 1812, the actuary Joshua Milne considered that 'that increase (that is, in the excess of births over deaths as a ratio of total population) has been accelerated within the last ten years, principally by the practice of vaccination'. On the other hand, it has been argued that the effect of vaccination was in part counterbalanced by an increase in the severity of other diseases, for example, measles in later childhood.

IV

Did the Industrial Revolution create its own labour force? Or did the vagaries of disease and the weather produce an additional population that either stimulated an Industrial Revolution or had the luck to coincide with one

more random and localized than that of the latter. See Milne, *A Treatise on the Valuation of Annuities* (London 1812), II, 461.

[30] G. Utterström, 'Some Population Problems in Pre-Industrial Sweden', *Scandinavian Economic History Review*, II (1954), 103–65; 'Climatic Fluctuations and Population Problems in Early Modern History', *ibid.*, III (1955), 3–47. See below, Part III, p. 523.

[31] Karl F. Helleiner, 'The Vital Revolution Reconsidered', *The Canadian Journal of Economic and Political Science*, XXIII (1957), 7. See above, p. 85.

independently generated? To say that population and economic change were both cause and effect of the other would be to evade the problem, which is to get some idea of proportions, and though we are not yet in a position to assess these, it would be surprising if they were fifty-fifty. Initially the increase in the second half of the eighteenth century must have been due simply to the absence of the exceptional causes of high mortality in the early part of the century, though it may have been reinforced by changes in the balance between peasant and landless labourer among the rural population. It was this phase of growth mainly that stimulated the rise in agricultural prices and the increase in agricultural investment, particularly enclosures, which is evident from the 1750's onward. It is true that the abruptness with which enclosures appear to increase about this decade is partly due to a change in the legal form—from chancery proceeding to private act—but the major part of the increase was certainly genuine. One of the main desiderata of English agrarian history is an attempt to estimate the order of magnitude of the capital cost of enclosures, but in relation to the relevant contemporary magnitudes it must have been considerable. One can think of several plausible ways in which an increase in investment and income in so important a sector of the economy might have stimulated industrial investment, and one of the questions that needs to be further investigated is how the growth of home agricultural incomes compared as a stimulus with the increase of incomes in England's overseas market. The other problem which, on this reading of the situation, needs to be explained is why the output of English agriculture was so much more 'responsive' in the eighteenth century than in the sixteenth. On this we may expect light from the large-scale history of agriculture that is being written under H. P. R. Finberg's editorship.

So far as the early decades of the nineteenth century are concerned—the period when population growth in England unambiguously diverged from that of Continental Europe—substantial weight has, I think, to be attached to the effect of the industrial changes in explaining the persistence of high levels of fertility. How far these changes offered positive opportunities for early marriage and how far they simply weakened the older restraints on marriage —these are questions which can be answered only when the evidence of the parish registers has been more systematically analysed.

8

TWO PAPERS ON GREGORY KING

D. V. GLASS

Editor's Note: The earlier papers are here reprinted with some dated and signed additions by the author.

Introductory Note

THIS volume is not the place in which to attempt any comprehensive account of the life of Gregory King, nor, in any case, are the presently available materials adequate for that purpose. Some brief notes are, however, necessary as a prelude to the two subsequent papers, for little has been published on King himself, as distinct from surveys of his work, since George Chalmers included an outline biography[1]—largely based upon King's own autobiography—in one of the editions of his book.

King's early life is reasonably well documented in his own account—no doubt not completely objective in its contents. He was born in Lichfield (Staffordshire) in 1648, the son of a man who was apparently a competent mathematician, but who earned his livelihood by surveying, making sundials, teaching writing and book-keeping and occasionally designing gardens. It was not a very substantial income that he gained—less, according to his son, than his talents should have provided, had he not been 'addicted to company-keeping and to that vice which to make it a vertue they call good fellowship'.

Gregory King did not under-value his own childhood abilities. His education began when he was 2; at 3 he could read the Psalter and at 4 the Bible. After a serious illness he entered school at the age of $5\frac{1}{2}$ and was learning Latin and Hebrew in his 7th to 8th years and Greek when he was 10. During the next two years, while still at school, he did some teaching on his own account. School appeared to become less full-time when he was 13, for he then occasionally undertook surveying for his father. In any case, he left at the age of 14 to become clerk to Sir William Dugdale, then Norroy King of Arms—a position found for him by a Lichfield friend, Dr Hunter. Gregory King spent 5 years with Dugdale, attending him on his visitations, and learning French and heraldry. When this work came to an end, in 1667, he took service with Lord Hatton, who was compiling a series of arms of the nobility, and stayed with him until 1669. Then followed a short period back in Lichfield, spent in what

[1] G. Chalmers, *An Estimate of the Comparative Strength of Great Britain*, London 1804, Appendix (separately paginated): 'Notices of the Life of Gregory King'. The appendix was later republished separately. King's autobiographical sketch (the MS. of which is in the Bodleian, Rawlinson MSS. C.514) was published in full in J. Dallaway, *Inquiries into the Origin and Progress of the Science of Heraldry*, Gloucester 1793. Unless otherwise specified, the quotations in this note are from Dallaway's reprint, Appendix, pp. xv *et seq*.

appear to be various odd jobs, until he obtained employment with the Dowager Lady Gerard, remaining with her until 1672. At that time he seems to have chosen to try his fortune in London, and it was on the metropolis that his subsequent career focused.

Arriving in London, he called on Wenceslas Hollar, the engraver, who sent him to John Ogilby, the surveyor and cartographer. It was in association with the latter that King worked for five years. He etched plates for various books; engaged in cartography, including the preparation of a map of London on the scale of 100 feet to the inch, and a map of Westminster on the like scale. Later he surveyed Soho Fields, 'whose streets and square were all projected by him, and most of the first articles for building thereof'. During these years he became a friend of Thomas Lee, Chester Herald, and did some work for him and for Francis Sandford, Lancaster Herald. It was at Lee's suggestion that King was appointed Rouge Dragon in 1677. But this was a part-time occupation, at least so far as income was concerned. King explained that during the first two years, 'his dividends in the office came but to £11 and the salaries not payd at all, (though a pursuivant's is but £20)'. So he continued with engraving and other work. Gradually, his association with the College of Arms brought him improvement in status—he became registrar to the College and then, in 1688, Lancaster Herald. He was involved in various heraldic visitations and later (from 1689 onwards) took part in the journeys associated with the investiture with the Order of the Garter of the Elector of Brandenburg, the Duke of Zell and the Elector of Saxony. Presumably his financial position improved. He had complained (in 1688) that he had never been able to save much money. Before his marriage he had been helping his family. After his first marriage—in 1674 he married Anne Powel, of a Gloucestershire family, with whom he had been lodging in Covent Garden—the pressure was no less, both as a result of such help and also because of a 'generous way of living, to which both his own and his wife's inclinations led them'. He had attempted to increase his income by buying the leases of some houses, but the net return was very low. At any rate, circumstances seem to have been somewhat better after 1688, for his auto-biography—which unfortunately ends in 1694—gives no further reference to financial problems.

But there were difficulties in his association with the College of Arms—a quarrel with the Earl Marshal and a question of the misuse of certain fees.[2] Perhaps it was these difficulties—no less than his lack of personal support in high places—that help to explain why he was passed over when the office of Clarenceux Herald became vacant. He had in 1704 drafted a letter to the Earl Marshal, which began: 'I hope an humble application to yor. Lo[p]. to set me right again *in yor favor* while it is in yor power, will not be reckond a Presump-tion in one who truly honours yor Lo[p] thô I have not been so happy as to par-take of those Favors which yor Lo[p] had to bestow.'[3] At any rate it was not he but Sir John Vanburgh, who received the appointment—an event which prompted King to write to Robert Harley of 'the disservice to the public, to

---

[2] According to biography by Thompson Cooper in *Dictionary of National Biography*, Vol. XXXI.
[3] Harleian MSS. 6839, fol. 39. He wanted a dispensation to acknowledge that the fees received by him at the installation of the Dukes of Bedford and Malborough were rightly his.

have the heads of a Society Ignorant in their Faculty, and Coadjutor himself to want a Coadjutor'.[4] Chalmers' own comment (and explanation) was that 'Vanburgh's wit, I fear, prevailed over King's arithmetick'.[5]

But King's failure to reach his desired heraldic pinnacle could not have been quite as disturbing as the cold facts would imply. The complaining tone of his autobiography must have derived from an especially dark hour. Certainly he had friends and was convivial—to the point of organizing an annual meeting of persons bearing the surname 'King'.[6] His journeys abroad must have given him some sense of importance and probably helped to put him in touch with Leibnitz, who subsequently referred to King's work on political arithmetic.[7] It is this latter work which, praised by both Davenant and Chalmers, accounts for King's distinction as a pioneer demographer and it is necessary to examine how it came to be undertaken.

Unfortunately we do not at present know exactly when or why Gregory King began the work which ultimately found its most succinct expression in his *Observations and Conclusions, Natural and Political, upon the State and Condition of England*. The autobiographical sketch stops short at 1694, at which point there is no indication of the subsequent work. The two main manuscript working-journals now extant are replete with computations and analyses, and clearly date from the period during which the *Observations* were being written. The background may well have been given in earlier journals, of which so far no trace has been found.[8] Some inferences can, however, be reasonably drawn

[4] King to Harley, 2 January 1710 (Harl. MSS. 7525, fols. 40–41; a copy of this is in Add. MSS. 4253, fols. 36–37). 'As to the Heralds in General, there being only the Two places of Garter and Clarenc^x of any tolerable profit, what a Discouragem^t must it be to Learning and Industry in Our Faculty to have those places always filled up wth Strangers when some of the Society have spent the Prime of their days and a Number of years in qualifying themselves for those Imploym^{ts} beside the Consequence to the Publick to have the heads of a Society Ignorant in their Faculty, and a Coadjutor himself to want a Coadjutor.'

In addition, Harl. MSS. 6821, fol. 208 consists of an unsigned and undated statement concerning the possible appointment to Garter King of Arms—a statement which must at least have been inspired by Gregory King, although the writing appears slightly different from his script. The statement reads: 'Touching Garter King of Arms and who is fitted for that Office. If Sr Henry St George Clarenceux King of Arms be nominated to be Garter King of Arms It is to be Observed—That by reason of his Age and Infirmity he is altogether unable to Execute this Office—Being near 80 years of Age, very Paralitick and very defective in his Sight Is not Intituled to it by Succession there being no Instance that Clarenceux King of Arms was ever yet made Garter—The two next Officers viz Norroy King of Arms & Richmond Herald are likewise very old & Infirm Mr. King Lancaster Herald is the next in Course & the best Qualified for that Office his Age a little above 50, has been a Member of the Corporation for 26 years, has bred up two of the present Heralds has managed the business of the Office of Garter for the 2. last Garter Kings for 20 years past, is at this time the Sworn Deputy Garter, had the Hon^r to Carry the Garter to the present Elect^r of Russia, the late Elect^r of Saxony and the present Elect^r of Hannov^r for which last Embassy there is still due to him 200$\pounds$.'

The document dates itself as of around 1699.

[5] Chalmers, *op. cit.*, pp. 25–26.

[6] In 1686. Harleian MSS. 6815, fol. 233. He also learned to play the violin and was grateful to John Ogilby for providing the violin teacher. See Dallaway, *op. cit.* When Ogilby died, he apparently owed King 'above £100'. Throughout his life, King apparently had difficulty in collecting fees which he considered were owed to him. An undated letter claimed that £200 was owed to him in connexion with his embassies to the King of Prussia, the Elector of Saxony and the Elector of Hanover. He also wrote to John Ellis, 1 October 1703, saying that he was '£200 the worse' for his journey to Hanover and asking for his claim to be allowed to go to the Treasury. (Harl. MSS. 6821 fol. 208; and Add. MSS. 28,891, fol. 96.)

[7] In connexion with one of his journeys, there is a letter (in Latin) from Gregory King to Leibnitz, dated Hagenburg, 2 September 1701, conveying greetings from Dr Gee. The letter is addressed to: 'Illustrissimo Domino Dño. Godefrido Leibnitio Serenissimo Principi Electori Brunswico Luneburgico . . .' etc.

[8] The L.C.C. Burns journal was originally labelled 'G.K. No. 51'.

from the manuscripts themselves and from what is known about King. First, it is abundantly clear that King was both methodical and fascinated by computations as such[9]; he was, so to speak, an intuitive statistician, and much more on the model of John Graunt than on that of Petty. Secondly, his interest in political arithmetic, though no doubt reflecting the intellectual climate of his period, must have been especially stimulated by the 1694 Act for levying taxes on burials, births and marriages, and annual dues upon bachelors and childless widowers, for this Act promised to provide, and on a national scale, the kinds of basic statistics for which Petty had clamoured a generation earlier. King must have worked at great speed for the Act did not come into force until 1695, yet he had already produced some analyses during that year and had sent them to Davenant in June 1696. Perhaps this speed was prompted by King's desire to find alternative employment to supplement or replace his appointment at the College of Arms—certainly one of his computations (on the population of Gloucester) was sent to the Board of Trade in September 1696 through the intermediary of George Stepney.[10] And King did later find additional employment. But all the indications in the manuscripts are of a genuine and wide interest in political arithmetic for its own sake and for the sake of its relevance to public policy. There is not the slightest suggestion of hasty calculations designed to produce a result primarily to serve King's personal advancement or tailored to suit the political needs of those in power. Indeed, one of King's criticisms of Petty was that he had started out with the intention of glorifying and magnifying England and London. In King's view, even if this were the ultimate and legitimate intention, it was still necessary for government to know the objective facts. Thus he wrote: 'Sr William Petty was lookt upon as the best Computer of his time, But in all his Computations of the Numbers of People in England and London, It is Evident he designed to Represent both ye one and ye other much greater than they truly were; And tho' Writing to the Publick might make it Excusable so to do, Yet least those Publick Acco^{ts} of His should be too much Relyed on by those who sit at ye Helm, to whom a true Account of the Kingdom is more necessary than to others I shall endeavour to give such an Account thereof as will bear the Touchstone of Truth.'[11]

It is clear that, by contrast, King regarded Graunt as a master. One of

[9] And not solely on political arithmetic. Thus the P.R.O. Bundle (T64/302) contains a paper, dated 21 April 1711, entitled: 'Computation of the No. of Great and Small Flowers to be wrought in Mrs. Kings fine Callico Gown begun by Mrs. Mince about 18° April 1711 or rath^r Tuesd. noon 17 Apr 1711.'

[10] And another on endowed hospitals and almshouses in 1697. See Chalmers, op. cit., pp. 23-24. The latter computation is in the B.M. Add. MSS. 34712 fol. 220. That King had in mind the possibility that his political arithmetic would qualify him for another appointment is strongly suggested by a draft letter, directed to Sir Stephen Fox—the wealthy Commissioner of the Treasury—but addressed to an undesignated 'My Lord' (dated 19 December 1695), in which he stressed the usefulness of his new computations in estimating the likely yield of any proposed tax and concluded: 'But if yor Hono^r will Comand me to give you such an Estimate as may be depended upon to be the Produce of any Project on foot for Raysing of money, I shall demonstrate to yor Lo^p That this poynt hath been well studyed by yor Lo^{ps} most Obed^t Humble Servt G.K.' (L.C.C. Burns journal, p. 241). George Stepney, referred to above, was a poet and diplomat. He acted as envoy to various European courts (especially in Germany) and was also a Commissioner of Trade and Plantations. It was in keeping with the period that King aimed at—and succeeded in—holding several appointments simultaneously.

[11] L.C.C. Burns journal, p. 49: 'Of England and London'.

King's manuscripts consists of a summary of the main points in the 'Epistle dedicatory' in Graunt's *Natural and Political Observations*.[12] Further, in the substantial working-journal in the Public Record Office, one page is devoted to a summary of Petty's calculations, but several pages (and in much more detail) to Graunt's analysis, the summary of Graunt's results often being compared with the results obtained by King himself.[13] King's correspondence, too, showed that he attempted to obtain from the Continent information which would help him to arrive at a more reliable comparison of England and other European countries. Thus when Stepney was sent as the King's Envoy to the Rhineland Princes, King wrote to him (in April 1696) explaining that he had originally intended to estimate the 'true number' of the people of England, but that his inquiry had led him much further. It was in connexion with these further developments that he wrote: 'Now because in these Disquisitions, as some things are more certain, so others are but Conjectural, I find it necessary to give you a general abstract that I may thereupon have yo[r] thoughts, and the opinion of such Virtuosi as you shall think fitt to discourse upon those matters w[ch] are less certain and positive.'[14]

Finally—and no less indicative of his intellectual integrity—though his communicated results were in substantial degree presented without explanation of the bases of calculations, he was fully prepared to explain how he had arrived at his estimates. One of the most valuable of King's manuscripts—the Kashnor copy of the *Observations*—displays just that kind of exchange which one might hope to find between a political arithmetician and an inquiring statesman, in this case Robert Harley. Most of Harley's queries concerned the detailed bases of various estimates, and King's replies are very full, acknowledging his guesses as well as referring to his more realistic calculations, taking issue with some earlier assessments[15] and freely rejecting Harley's proposed alternatives when they, too, appeared to be in error. The replies which illustrate King's approach in his estimates of the population of England and Wales are contained in the second of the papers reprinted in this volume. Something more of King's viewpoint and methodology may be seen from the two further replies given below.

[12] In P.R.O. Bundle T64/302, paper entitled: 'Positions in Graunt's Epistle. Ded. to my L[d] Roberts of Truro L. Pr. Seal'—no date, but after 1695.

[13] Also in T64/302. The journal is entitled: 'Computations of the Number of People &c.'. The references are: Petty, p. 1; Graunt, pp. 6, 7 and 13. Page 21 consists of an interesting (though incomplete) table which distributes marriages by age of bride and which proposed to obtain the age distribution for conceptions. [14] L.C.C. Burns journal, p. 171.

[15] Including a scepticism regarding some of the statements of Classical historians, which anticipated the point of view of David Hume in his Discourse, 'Of the Populousness of antient Nations' (see D. Hume, *Political Discourses*, 2nd edn., Edinburgh 1752). King wrote: 'There is nothing so fallacious as the Acco[t] of Numbers brought into the Field or Slain in Battle being either wonderfully enlarged or lessen'd as the Victor or Defeated think fit to recount. The Roman Forces here at their First Invasion, seem by their Writers to have been about 30,000, which considering the State of Navigation at that time & what a number of Transport Vessells are requisite for such a Force, I can scarce allow to be more than 20 or 25 M. in Caesar's Ingagements. Tis true He says the Britons incompast him, which (if it be no Flourish) does not necessarily imply above 50 or 60 M. Britains, And I take it that almost the whole Force of Britain was then gather'd together, Now in 400,000 Souls w[ch] I compute at Our Saviour's Birth, the Fighting men may be 100,000. And in Boadicea's time being near 70 years after, about 120,000. Out of which it is possible 50 or 60 M. men might be got together pro Aris et Focis. But I shall never Credit the Acco[t] That her Army was 230,000, as the Roman Writers are pleased to say It was, or that 80,000 were actually slain, and but 400 Romans, tho' the Women in those times frequently appearing in Arms might increase her Numbers a 5th or 6th part and raise them to about 70,000' (Kashnor MS., p. 9).

(a) King had stated that one of the reasons why marriages in London produced fewer children than marriages in the country seemed to be 'from the Unhealthfulness of the Coal-smoak'. Harley queried this 'cause', saying: 'Severall Observers assure me many places more offended than London wth Coal-smoak abound in Children wonderfully To instance in New Castle upon Tine particularly and especially the Outstreets.' King replied: 'As to the un-healthfulness of London arising from Coal-smoak I think that about four score or 100 years ago, when that Jewel came first to be in a more general use than formerly, It was complaind of as unhealthfull, and thereupon some re-straint laid upon the use of it by Law. Mr Grant makes the like Observation pag. 94. And Vouches New Castle for it's unhealthiness on the same Acco^t And it is notorious that many even Adult persons cannot endure the Coal smoak of London, but are forced to live in the neighbouring Villages, or at least at the Outside of the Town next the Fields. But this with some pains might be examined by Collecting in New Castle as I have done in London, the Proportion of married Couples to the number of Souls, and the number of yearly births, and comparing them with other great townes where they burn little or no Sea-Coal. And for the Operation of Coal smoak upon Children, by computing the number of Children alive under 5 or 6 years of age, in such places as afore-said, and comparing them with the number of Births. But since I find that London wants about 2000 births P. an to keep it from Decreasing notwith-standing it hath a greater number of married Couples in proportion than ye Country, I assign that of the Coalsmoak as one of the 5 Reasons only, for such Deficiency of Births, And that among other things the Coalsmoak in London does impede the fecundity of teeming Women, and either hinders Conception or increases Miscarriages, Abortives & Stilborn. But whatever effect it may have in those Cases I am clearly of Opinion It suffocates & destroys a Multitude of Infants, Tho' perhaps in New Castle it may not have the same Operation, where the Air is sharper, the Town not above a 50th part of London, nor nothing near so close built.'[16]

Whatever the factual basis, a methodology for the study of the influence of smoke pollution—nowadays a serious factor in bronchitis in England and Wales—is there in rudimentary form.

(b) In connexion with King's estimate of the 'Annual Income & Expence of the Nation, as it stood A° 1688', Harley raised several queries, and in answer to one of them King explained the basis of his computations on national ex-penditure on consumers' goods. His discussion of expenditure upon food is of particular interest. He wrote that Petty's estimate of per capita expenditure on food, housing and clothing at £6 13s. 4d. per year was certainly too low, 'unless he confines it to personal Necessaries only. . . . I then Consider'd the Principal Article, Dyet, according to the severall Degrees of Living; and I found the poorest Sort whose General Expence was but 3£p. head p. an, or 2^d per diem, spent 2 Thirds, or somewhat above 5 farthings, p. diem in Dyet. The middle Sort whose Gen.^{ll} Expence was 7£ p head, spent 4£ p an in Dyet And the better sort whose Gen^{ll} Expence was above 50£ p head p an, spent less than a Third in Dyet. I distributed my People into Classes. I proportion'd

[16] Kashnor, MS., p. 12.

their Food & Rayment & other Expences. I considered how this answer'd the General Product of the Land.' It is not too great an exaggeration to suggest that, in discussing the ratio of expenditure on food to total expenditure per head, King was anticipating, at least in outline, Engel's law, developed in the nineteenth century on the basis of family budget studies.

To return, however, to King's life and career. It is not entirely surprising that, having composed the *Observations, Natural and Political*, and having communicated them to Robert Harley and Davenant among others, he should come to be considered for a relevant official appointment. He became Secretary to the Commissioners for the Public Accounts, an office which he appears to have fulfilled satisfactorily. At least the Commissioners certified, in March 1704, that King had 'approved himself to be a Person of great Application, good Abilities and unquestionable Integrity in the Discharge of that Trust reposed in him . . .'.[17] Not, perhaps, too glowing a testimonial—the kind which might be written for a useful but not outstanding research assistant—though it may be explicable in terms of the English official habit of understatement. Later he applied—apparently without success—to Lord Godolphin for the post of Comptroller of the Prizes in the West of England.[18] But he held other official appointments—Commissioner to state King William's debts,[19] and Secretary to the Comptroller of the Army Accounts, the latter employment affording him a salary of £300 per year.[20] In all, he must have been reasonably happy and financially comfortable, at least in a modest way. His first wife had died and he had remarried in 1701 to Frances Graham—happily remarried, judging from the references to 'my dear wife' in the Will which he drew up in 1709.[21] He was moderately 'well-connected'—his brother Thomas was in the Excise Office in London; his brother-in-law, Thomas Savage, was married to the dowager Countess of Coventry; and his nephew, Lawrence Cromp, was York Herald. He still had friends in the College of Arms—Samuel Stebbing, Somerset Herald, was one of them, and John Hesket, Portcullis pursuivant, another.[22] He had a fairly extensive correspondence, both official and academic, on matters of political arithmetic,[23] and his writings had been acknowledged abroad by Leibnitz. 'Dans l'occasion', Leibnitz wrote to Samuel Stebbing in 1708, 'je vous prie Monsieur de faire mes complimens à Monsieur Van Bruck et aussi à Mons. King qui obligeroit le public s'il publioit ses calculs politiques.'[24]

---

[17] Harleian MSS., 6944, fol. 92. In the introduction to G. E. Barnett, *Two Tracts by Gregory King* (Baltimore 1936), Barnett suggests (pp. 5-6) that King was Secretary for two periods, 1705-6 and then again after 1708. Chalmers, *op. cit.*, says that he 'continued . . . to the hour of his death.' But there certainly appears to have been an interruption in that employment, for in his petition to Lord Godolphin, referred to below (Harl. MSS. 6944, fol. 94), King described himself as 'late Secry to the Commrs of Publick Accots' [18] Harleian MSS., 6944, fol. 94.
[19] Barnett, *op. cit.*, p. 6, citing Narcissus Luttrell.
[20] This is so recorded in John Chamberlayne, *Magnae Britanniae Notitia*, London 1710, p. 559.
[21] Prerogative of the Court of Canterbury, Barnes 171. Codicils were added later in 1709 and in 1712. The dates of King's marriages are given by Chalmers, *op. cit.*, pp. 14 and 26.
[22] The relatives and friends are referred to in King's will.
[23] As judged from the papers preserved in the Public Record Office. In addition, among the last of his correspondence which I have so far come across are two letters, addressed to John Chamberlayne, F.R.S., containing comments on Arbuthnot's paper (published in the *Philosophical Transactions*, 1710) on the constancy of the sex ratio at birth. King believed that the excess of males at birth was likely to be a universal characteristic, even though he had apparently found (and was unable to explain) the contrary excess in the births in Lichfield, Staffs. (. . . 'the only place I ever found the like in . . . '). See letters of 27 April 1711 and 3 May 1711 in Royal Society Archives, 12, K, 24 and 25. [24] Harleian MSS., 6944, fols. 116-17.

King died in 1712, leaving legacies to his relatives and friends.[25] No children survived him and there were few published works to keep his name alive.[26] It is to George Chalmers that we owe the rediscovery of some of his major manuscripts, writings which, in my view, establish King as second only to John Graunt among the pioneers in the emerging study of statistics.

APPENDIX

In the two subsequent papers, King's estimates of age structure are considered in relation only to Lichfield and to the Kingdom as a whole. Precisely what additional age statistics King used in arriving at his estimate for the Kingdom has not been ascertained. In the Kashnor MS., he stated—in a reply to Harley—that he had based his calculations on data relating to 'about 5000 People in severall places', whereas Lichfield itself had a population of about 3000. He also referred to a further collection of age statistics which he had gathered after writing his *Observations*, again without specifying the localities.[27] However, there are some age statistics—apart from those of Lichfield—in the various King manuscripts and it may be of interest to give them here in summary form, since

(a) Population in broad age groups (per cent distribution)

Age (years)	Buckfastleigh persons	Ringmore persons	Shustoke persons	Swepstone persons
under 15	34·3	24·2	33·7	31·7
15-59	59·6	56·4	57·6	55·9
60 and over	6·1	19·4	8·7	12·4
N.	M560 : F546	M82 : F104	M126 : F150	M64 : F82
Total	1106	186	276	146

(b) Age composition of Buckfastleigh population

Age (years)	Numbers		Total	Per cent distribution
	Males	Females		
0-4	60	70	130	11·8
5-9	54	52	106	9·6
10-14	80	63	143	12·9
15-19	51	38	89	8·0
20-24	50	50	100	9·0
25-59	230	241	471	42·6
60 and over	35	32	67	6·1
Total	560	546	1106	100·0

they were not reproduced in my two earlier papers. Two sets—Shustoke, Warwick; and Swepstone, Leicester—may have been included in his original calculations. The other two—Buckfastleigh and Rinmore, Devonshire—may have formed part of the later collection, for they derive from enumerations carried out in 1698.

The Shustoke and Swepstone data are the least satisfactory. They are given in groups

---

[25] His London leases apparently proved profitable in the end and he had property elsewhere and stock in the East India Company, according to his will. The will also indicates that he was a Governor of St. Bartholomew's Hospital.

[26] According to Chalmers, he had one son and two daughters, all of whom died before their father, *op. cit.*, p. 26.   [27] Kashnor MS., p. 8.

of ages, the age groups used differing between the two localities.[28] And it is not clear whether infants under 1 year of age were included, in spite of the fact that, in respect of Shustoke, King drew attention to the apparent deficiency in the number of children under 6 years of age. His marginal comment was: 'But note that of ye Children under 6 year old—there seems to be above 20 wanting of ye due Proportion. For ye yearly Births cannot be less than 9 or 10. or 1 in 28 or 30 of the Coexisting People. So that the Births in 5 years at 9 p.ann. should be 45 and if 10 of those 45 die in 5 years there should remain 35 whereas there are in this Assesm^t but 14. So that either they are omitted in ye Assesment or ye ages are mistaken or their has been some late mortality among ye young Children of 1.2. and 3 years old, as ye Small Pox or ye like.'[29] But he did not appear to use any correction factor. The Swepstone statistics show a similar deficit.[30]

For Rinmore and Buckfastleigh, the Harleian Collection contains manuscripts listing each individual by age and names.[31] Sex has to be inferred, and can be for almost all cases. Marital condition is indicated, but only directly for wives; they are listed immediately after their husbands. But it is far from clear whether some widows and widowers are included among the unmarried; very few are designated.

[28] The data had to be 'manipulated' to fit them into comparable, broad age groups.
[29] L.C.C. Burns journal, p. 95. Of the 276 people in Shustoke, 57 are classified as 'Alms People' and the remainder as 'Solvent People'. [30] L.C.C. Burns journal, p. 94.
[31] Rinmore: Harl. MSS., 6832, fol. 121—'Devonsh. Rinmore. A List of all men, women & Children in ye Pish taken Sep. 14th 1698.' Buckfastleigh: Harl. MSS. 6832, fols. 107-18—'Buckfastleigh 1698. A List of all the persons names, within the Pish of Buckfastleigh aforesaid, as ffolloweth.'

GREGORY KING AND THE POPULATION OF ENGLAND AND WALES AT THE END OF THE SEVENTEENTH CENTURY

From: *Eugenics Review*, Jan. 1946, 170-83

Gregory King, that 'curious computer', as Chalmers called him, affords one of the most intriguing puzzles in the history of British demography. He was described, on his monument in the Church of St. Benet, Paul's Wharf, London, as 'a skilful herald, a good Accomptant, Surveyor, and Mathematician, A curious penman, And well versed in Political Arithmetick. . . .'[1] In this last province, political arithmetic, he achieved marked contemporary recognition, being widely quoted by Davenant, who depended upon him for calculations in fields as diverse as population and coinage. Chalmers, who resuscitated his work and found both the manuscript of the *Natural and Politicall Observations* and Harley's comments upon it in the Harleian collection, referred to him in the most enthusiastic terms: 'He who surpassed Petty, as a political calculator, must be allowed to have been a master of moral arithmetick.'[2] This high regard persists to-day. Yet King's only publication in the field of political arithmetic was a broadsheet summarizing the rates and duties payable under the Act of 6 and 7 William and Mary, c. 6 (levying duties on marriages, births, burials, bachelors and childless widowers).[3] The *Natural and Politicall Observations*, upon which King's position now largely rests, though forming the basis of

[1] J. Dallaway, *Inquiries into the Origin and Progress of the Science of Heraldry in England*, Gloucester and London 1793, Appendix II, p. xlviii.
[2] G. Chalmers, *An Estimate of the Comparative Strength of Great Britain*, London 1804, Appendix, p. 27. The 1804 edition is referred to throughout this paper. [3] B.M., 816.n. 6/80.

much of Davenant's work—evidence that King was, as Chalmers says, 'of a very communicative disposition'—remained in manuscript until first published by Chalmers in 1802 as an appendix to his own book, and the only modern reprint is that edited by Barnett.[4]

Moreover, the *Natural and Politicall Observations* themselves, bold and even startling as they are in their approach to the question of estimating the size and structure of the population of England and Wales—with which the present paper is concerned—raise more questions than they answer. In fact they can only be said to answer any of the major questions with which King deals if not only the methods but also the basic statistics to which the method is applied are accepted. It is, however, difficult to do so, for King's work is peculiarly lacking in explicitness. The techniques are not explained, except in appearance. For example, King arrives at an estimate of the population of England and Wales by taking certain figures of the numbers of houses in the different divisions and multiplying them by a series of factors of persons per house. The origin of these factors is not, however, explained, except by stating that they are 'according to what we have observed from the said assessments of marriages, births, and burials in several parts of the Kingdom'.[5] Similarly, save for the material regarding the town of Lichfield (Staffordshire), which he says he collected (or at least that he collected the *Observations*[6]) his indications as to source material are vague. The number of houses in the Kingdom was that 'as charged, in the books of the hearth office, at Lady-Day, 1690'.[7] The remaining material is derived from the 'assessments (on) marriages, births and burials, parish registers, and other public accounts'.[8] In fact, for a large part of the field covered, we cannot check, from King's finished product, either the statistics or the methods used in arriving at specific results. As Jones and Judges suggest, 'If King is to be censured, it is for puzzling his readers by handing in a fair copy from which too many of the rough notes have been torn.'[9]

There is, however, some additional material which bears very closely upon the methods and validity of King's work. Some of this—dealing with the results for London—has been analysed and evaluated by Jones and Judges in the study referred to above. Other material consists of a bundle of King's manuscripts in the Public Record Office[10] and a bound manuscript volume now in the possession of the London County Council.[11] Still more material is to be

---

[4] G. E. Barnett, *Two Tracts by Gregory King*, Baltimore 1936, which also contains a facsimile of the title page of the *Observations*, and a valuable introduction, to which I am greatly indebted for source references.   [5] Chalmers, Appendix, p. 34.

[6] *Ibid.*, p. 45.   [7] *Ibid.*, p. 33.   [8] *Ibid.*, p. 33.

[9] P. E. Jones and A. V. Judges, 'London population in the late seventeenth century', *Economic History Review*, October 1935, pp. 45-63, at p. 56.

[10] This bundle is listed as T.64/302 in the *Lists of the Records of the Treasury*, etc., London, 1921, p. 51. But though so listed and also referred to by Barnett in his edition of King, it does not seem as if the papers have been used in considering the basis and value of King's population estimates. This conclusion is, I think, the more likely in that the bundle contains what appears to be a working journal on which King based his *Natural and Political Observations*. The bundle is noted in the *Lists* as '1695-1712. Papers of Gregory King', but the written description on the bundle itself is 'Mr. Gregory King. Exercises in politl. Arithmetic and various miscells. Papers.'

[11] This volume is evidently another, and very much larger, working-journal. A study of it and comparison with the material in the P.R.O. suggests that King was extremely methodical. Apparently, he made his initial computations on rough working sheets and then entered a relatively fair copy in the large journal, which contains about 300 pages, beginning with a list of the armorial bearings of various persons named 'King', and ending with an index to the contents. The contents themselves include, among other material, several drafts of what ultimately became the *Natural and*

found in the Harleian Collection of manuscripts in the British Museum.[12] As the latter manuscripts are not at present accessible, this paper must be regarded as of a preliminary character, to be supplemented when the British Museum documents become available. Nevertheless it is possible even now to throw light upon a number of questions, particularly those concerning King's factors of the numbers of persons per house, and the special analysis for the town of Lichfield, as well as in general upon King's material and methods. Before proceeding to deal with those questions, however, it is necessary to draw attention to the general background of population statistics during the period in which King produced his estimates.

Throughout the seventeenth and eighteenth centuries the State collected, or ordered the collection of, statistics which were and still are, to some extent, used for estimating population size and trend.[13] Apart, however, from the question of degree of incompleteness which applies to all the taxation returns used in such estimates, there is the further complication caused by the need to arrive at factors with which to transmute the crude statistics into population estimates. To use the hearth-tax figures, it is necessary to apply some average number of persons per hearth, and a similar device is required if the later statistics in respect of the window tax are used. Nor can the crude data of the Bills of Mortality or the parish registers be used—again, apart from the question of their incompleteness—unless the population bases are arrived at. The alternatives—to assume a stationary population, or constancy in the birth and death rates—beg the question which the analysis purports to illuminate. Different individuals attempted to construct such factors, with varying degrees of appropriateness, and the great population controversy of the eighteenth century raged in part around the factors used.

Yet at the end of the seventeenth century the State collected information which should have provided factors, population bases and vital statistics for the whole country and for a common period of time. This was under the Act

---

Politicall Observations, a collection of population data for various parts of England and Wales, extracted from the results of the 1695 enumeration (for which, see the subsequent discussion), and a detailed summary of the results of the Lichfield survey (referred to below). The volume itself belonged to Viscount Sydney and passed to the late John Burns, apparently in 1917. Burns himself looked through it several times and appears to have shown it to the late Professor Henry Higgs. Barnett himself also examined the volume and refers to a calculation on the influence of scarcity on the price of corn (*op. cit.*, p. 6). But no one, as far as I can tell, ever made use of the demographic material in the volume, though it contains a great deal of King's work on population. The volume now belongs to the London County Council, being one item in the collection purchased by Lord Southwood from the Burns' library and presented to the Council. I am greatly indebted to the Council for permission to make use of the volume. In this paper, the larger journal will be referred to as the Burns journal and the smaller as the P.R.O. journal.

[12] In addition to the manuscript copy of the *Observations* (No. 1898), and of Harley's comments (No. 6837), the Harleian collection contains other valuable material relating to King's work—e.g. (No. 6832), a list of the inhabitants of Buckfastleigh, with their ages; returns (perhaps under the 1694 Act) from Worcester, Stafford and Gloucester, and some miscellaneous correspondence of King; (No. 6839) 'Observations in the handwiting of Gregory King' (12 August 1695) on the population of Lichfield; and (No. 7022) the names of all the inhabitants of Lichfield. The latter document has been used by L. M. Marshall (*The Rural Population of Bedfordshire, 1671 to 1921*, Aspley Guise, 1934, p. 7) and inferred to be a return under the 1694 Act. But if, as seems likely, it is the basis of King's analysis of Lichfield and gives the ages of all persons, it is probably the result of a different survey, of the kind to which later reference is made. (As may be seen from the following paper, the Lichfield material was probably collected, but in greater detail, in connexion with the provisions of the 1694 Act. D.V.G. 1962.)

[13] I do not include, under this head, local censuses or partial enumerations, of which there were many, especially during the eighteenth century.

of 6 and 7 William and Mary c. 6, of 1694, and the subsequent amplifying Acts, which, for the purpose of providing revenue for carrying on the war against France, levied taxes upon burials, births and marriages, and annual dues upon bachelors over 25 years of age and upon childless widowers.[14] For the purpose of implementing the 1694 Act, which came into force as from 1 May 1695, certain statistical information was indispensable. It was necessary to know the size and structure of the population, in order to assess the numbers, at the initial point of time, liable to the various taxes and surtaxes; and it was also necessary to adapt the existing or devise new machinery for recording as quickly and accurately as possible the burials, marriages and births occurring throughout the country.

To collect the former category of statistics was the duty of the Assessors appointed by the Commissioners of the Act. These Assessors had to appear before the Commissioners on a chosen day (on or before 30 April 1695, presumably, since the Act came into force on 1 May) 'and bring in their certificates in writing of the names sirnames estates degrees titles and qualifications of all and every the persons dwelling or residing within the limits of those places with which they shall bee charged dividing them into several columns as they are in quality estate and qualification and the names of all other persons chargeable by this Act and the sums they are or ought [to pay respectively] upon burials, births or marriages and or their being unmarried according to the rules and directions of this Act without concealment love favour dread or malice upon pain of forfeiture of any sum not exceeding Five pounds to bee levied as by this Act is appointed' (Section XI). That is, a complete enumeration of the population was envisaged, distinguishing bachelors, widowers and persons of various ranks and professions, and this enumeration was to be brought up to date at the end of each year during the five years for which the Act was originally imposed (Section XVI).[15]

As regards the current vital statistics, persons in Holy Orders were to keep accurate accounts in their registers of marriages, and burials, and of all persons 'christened or borne', under penalty of £100 fine (Section XX). Moreover, the Act placed a considerable responsibility upon the parents for notification of birth, for it provided 'that the Parents of every Child which shall be borne att any time within the same terme of Five Years or one of them shall within Five days after such Birth give notice to the Collectors or one of them of the Parish or Place where such Child was borne and of the Christian Name of such Child and the day of its Birth And the said Collectors or one of them shall thereupon give a certificate in writing under his or their hands unto such

[14] The taxes are summarized in King's digest. For persons without specified property or other qualifications, they were 4s. for burial, 2s. for birth, 2s. 6d. for marriage, 1s. per year for bachelors and 1s. per year for childless widowers. Persons in receipt of alms were exempt, but in the case of burial, the parish had to pay the tax. In the case of the bachelor tax, 'Fellows, students and scholars in the universities' were also exempt. In addition to these basic rates, there were also sur-taxes varying with rank and place in the family. Thus in the case of a duke, the burial fee was an additional £50, but only an additional £25 for the younger son of a duke. The lowest rates of sur-tax were charged to persons 'of 50L. per Annum, or 600L. Personal Estate'

[15] At the end of each year, a copy of the assessments and collection for each division, parish or place, was to be made, 'with such alterations therein as shall be necessary by reason of the death change of quality or degree or removal of any person or persons or otherwise . . .' (Section XVI). Lodgers and servants were to be noted in the enumeration, for they were taxed at their place of residence (Section XXIV).

Parent testifying that such notice was given without fee and reward for the same.' The penalty for failure to comply was 40s., of which half was to go to the King and the rest to the informer. Provision was made for the notification of stillbirths (Section XXI), and to cover nonconformists, Catholics and Jews (Section LVII).[16] Finally, special provision was made for recording the vital statistics of the nobility and gentry. When one of them died, a certificate was to be delivered to the Receiver-General (and transmitted by him to the King's Heralds), recording 'the name sirname title quality office and employment (if any) of such deceased person with the age time of death place of burial marriages and issue and the ages of such issue together with the names sirnames titles and qualities of the parents of such deceased persons . . .'. The King's Heralds were then to 'number schedule and digest the same in alphabetical order in Books to bee provided for that purpose', and to 'file upp the Originals in the College of Arms for publick use . . .' (Section L).

In terms of the potential supply of population and vital statistics, this was clearly a remarkable Act. It provided for the first complete census (and no other was taken until 1801), registration of births within five days[17] (as compared with 42 days under our present system), and the creation of a special register of statistics on differential fertility.[18] Such provisions are even more remarkable in that this Act was originally intended to apply only for five years—it was subsequently extended for a further five years—and one is tempted to believe that the elaborate statistical system was envisaged for other than purely fiscal purposes. Gregory King was well aware of the statistical significance of the Act, and made use of some of the resultant data. It might even have been at his instigation that so elaborate a statistical system was provided for.[19]

Subsequent legislation, tightening up the provisions of the 1694 Act, suggests that the statistical system was by no means perfect. Under the original Act, for example, births were notifiable to the Collector, who presumably used the parish register as a partial check. But births could still escape registration because the parish register covered only those children who were christened

[16] The clause relating to stillbirths stated: 'And in case any Child shall be borne dead then one of the Parents thereof shall bring a Certificate under the hands of Two or more persons testifying the same unto the said Collectors or one of them. . . .'

[17] This was, in fact, civil registration; it would not necessarily mean that parochial registration was 'speeded-up' in the same degree. The 'speeding-up' of parochial registration was provided for in an amplifying Act.

[18] For the range of people covered (i.e. persons having £50 per year or £600 personal estate, or of higher status), the fertility and social information to be collected for this register was rather more comprehensive than that recorded, under the Population (Statistics) Act of 1938, at the death of married women. Cf. Registrar-General's Statistical Review of England and Wales, 1938, Tables, Part II, p. 108.

[19] The original proposal for levying taxes on marriages and burials appears to have come from Richard Frith. The P.R.O. bundle contains a printed broadsheet entitled A Probable Calculation of the Annual Income to be Raised by a Tax on Marriages, Burials, and Legacies, with a note in King's hand-writing on the back: 'Fryth's Project of ye Duty on Marriages Births and Burials.' The Calendar of Treasury Papers, 1556-7-1696, London 1868, p. 481, item 63, notes a petition from Richard Frith to the Treasury, 'showing that about six years before, he thought of raising money on burials, marriages and christenings, and imparted it to the Duke of Shrewsbury, who acquainted the King, and in this sessions it was accepted by the House of Commons; praying their bounty for his charge and pains'. The Treasury comment was: 'To be considered if there be any places to be disposed on this fond.' The P.R.O. bundle also contains copies of some of the marriage, birth and burial returns (for a few areas) and an analysis of the enumeration data for Sevenoaks and for a number of London parishes. The Burns journal contains a summary of such enumeration material as King was able to collect. This material will be referred to later.

by the Church of England. Hence, under 7 and 8 William III, c. 35, it was made obligatory upon parents as from 24 June 1696 to notify a birth within five days to the 'respective Rector Vicar Curate or Clerk of the Parish or Place' in which the birth occurred, whatever the religious faith of the parents and whether or not the child was to be christened. The parish register was by that means intended to become a complete record of births and not only of christenings. Similarly, some deaths escaped the burial tax because the deceased had died in parishes in which they were strangers, with no one in the parish liable for the tax. But as from 24 June 1696, such deaths were to be notified, within ten days after burial, by the 'Deans Parsons Vicars Curates and Their respective Substitutes', to the collectors of the parishes in which the persons had last lived.[20]

Even these additional safeguards did not overcome the defects, especially as regards the parish registers. The latter were never, as a whole, fully comprehensive, in spite of the fact that parsons and other appropriate ecclesiastical persons were to receive (from the parents) sixpence for the registration of each child not christened in their churches, and were liable to a fine of 40s. (presumably in addition to the £100 penalty provided for in the original Act) for failing to keep a 'true Register' of unchristened children.[21] The defects were, in fact, recognized and accepted by the Act of 4 and 5 Anne, c. 23, which stated that, where the duties under the 1694 Act had been 'really answered and paid or notified and brought in charge to the Collector', the parsons, vicars, curates or other persons who had 'neglected to keep a Register in Writing as aforesaid of all and every or any Person or Persons so married buried christened or born' should be 'indempnified against and discharged from' any penalties to which they were liable. This was done because 'several Parsons Vicars and Curates and other Ecclesiastical Persons not being sufficiently apprized of the full Import of the said Acts of Parliament have not exactly observed the Directions therein', and 'they and their Families remain therefore exposed to Ruin . . .' (Section X).[22] Yet, in spite of these acknowledged defects, the statistics collected

[20] See also 9 William III, c. 32, for further safeguards and penalties. The Act was extended until 1 August 1706, by 8 and 9 William III, c. 20. For references to contemporary discussion of the difficulties in enforcing the legislation, see Jones and Judges, *op. cit.*, p. 49.

[21] King was fully aware of the defects of the legislation. One of the items in the Burns journal (pp. 120 A/D) is a draft Bill to improve the system as a means of raising revenue. The proposal was that, from 1 May 1699, the duties 'payable upon Marriages Births and Burials occasionally happening shall be converted into certain Annual payments . . .'. In the *Observations*, too, King makes an allowance for underenumeration. The register of unchristened children was to be kept separately (7 and 8 William III, c. 35, Section IV).

[22] This phrase, 'full Import', also suggests that the Acts were designed for more than fiscal purposes, or at least more than immediate ones. Certainly it would be difficult to select a tax requiring more complex and elaborate machinery to levy it. R. E. Chester Waters, 'A Statutory List of the Inhabitants of Melbourne, Derbyshire, in 1695; printed from the original M.S. Assessment with a Commentary and Explanatory Notes', *Journal of the Derbyshire Archæological and Natural History Society*, Vol. VII, January 1885, pp. 1–30, says (though without citing his authorities) that the 1694 Act created distrust in all sections of the community, and that 'the tax was so unpopular that the local authorities took pains to destroy the machinery for levying it'. Certainly Davenant, who was a friend of King, was opposed to it. Contrasting the situation at home with the pronatalist policies of ancient Rome and seventeenth-century France, he said: 'But we in *England* have taken another Course, laying a Fine upon the Marriage-Bed, which seems small to those who only contemplate the Pomp and Wealth round about 'em, and in their View; but they who look into all the different Ranks of Men, are well satisfied that this Duty on Marriages and Births, is a very grievous Burthen upon the poorer Sort, whose Numbers compose the Strength and Wealth of any Nation' (*An Essay upon the Probable Methods of Making a People Gainers in the Ballance of Trade*, 2nd edn., London 1700, p. 22).

were more comprehensive than any provided previously and, indeed, than any subsequent statistics, prior to the establishment of the full mechanism of censuses and civil registration in the nineteenth century.

The legislation discussed above has long been known to genealogists and, in general, to writers on the history of parish registration. Few writers, however, appear to have appreciated the significance of the Acts as regards the provision of population statistics. R. E. Chester Waters drew attention to this. He wrote: '. . . the historian ought to have learned from the statute book that a thorough and complete enumeration of the inhabitants of every parish in England, with a full and precise statement of their several names, occupations and qualities, was made in 1695. . . . A copy of the assessment was returned into the Exchequer, and this return must obviously contain the precise information which the historian required.'[23] Since this comment in 1885, the only study seen by the present writer which makes use of the data collected in accordance with 6 and 7 William and Mary, c. 6, has been that by Jones and Judges, based on the City of London returns, a copy of which is among the Guildhall records. One difficulty, of course, is that so far the returns for the country as a whole —originally sent to the Exchequer, according to Waters—have not been ocated. Another is that even local copies of returns for specific areas do not seem to have turned up, except in the case of Melbourne, in Derbyshire.[24] Nor has it so far been possible to trace any of the special returns concerning the nobility. But in view of the importance of the returns as a possible contribution to the economic and social history of the country, it is clearly most desirable to encourage a search among central and local archives for the original data.

Whatever the ultimate fate of the returns, there is no doubt that they were, in fact, the 'assessment on marriages, births and burials' to which King referred, and which formed the basis of much of his work. The King manuscripts abound in references to the original assessments and in notes on the results for various parts of the country. This would seem to make the puzzle even more puzzling, for King used the statistics in a limited and very indirect way. Instead of deriving his estimate of the population of England and Wales from the sum of the individual parish and county assessments, he used those assessments only for the purpose of providing ratios of persons per house, obtaining his population by multiplying the ratios by the numbers of houses, as derived from the hearth tax returns. Taking the estimates in their final form, as given in the *Observations*, the following combined table (Table 1) may be drawn up, as covering the whole population save for certain transients omitted from the returns— soldiers, sailors, gipsies, pedlars, and so forth—estimated separately by King at 80,000 persons.[25] The table shows that King, having obtained his original ratios and thus his first population estimate, then found it necessary to allow

[23] *Op. cit.*, pp. 1-2. Occupations were stated in the Melbourne returns (except for widows and widowers).

[24] Waters implies that he had come across returns for other areas. He wrote (p. 5): 'It is, therefore, not to be wondered at if these lists of inhabitants were generally destroyed as soon as the Taxation Act expired, and the few which have been preserved are commonly found in the hands of laymen.' (Additional returns have now been discovered for Bilston, Staffs.; Bristol; Kent—Wingham Division and New Romney; Lincolnshire—Wapentake of Candleshoe; Lyme Regis, Dorset; Leicester City; Shrewsbury; Southampton; and Westminster. D.V.G., 1963.)

[25] Chalmers, *op. cit.*, Appendix, pp. 35-36.

TABLE 1

King's estimate of the population of England and Wales

Region	Inhabited Houses	Persons per House	Estimated Population	Persons Omitted %	Persons Omitted Numbers	Total No. of Persons	Derived Ratios of Persons per House
The 97 parishes within the walls	13,500	5·4	72,900 ⎫		7,290	80,190	'almost 6'
The 16 parishes without the walls	32,500	4·6	149,500 ⎪		14,950	164,450	'above 5'
The 15 out parishes in Middx. and Surrey	35,000	4·4	154,000 ⎬ 10	10	15,400	169,400	'above 4·8'
The 7 parishes in the city and liberty of Westminster	24,000	4·3	103,200 ⎪		10,320	113,520	'almost 4¾'
Total for London and the Bills of Mortality	105,000	4·57	479,600 ⎭		47,960	527,560	'above 5'
The other cities and market towns	195,000	4·3	838,500	2	16,500	855,000(a)	'almost 4·4'
The villages and hamlets	1,000,000	4·0	4,000,000	1	40,000	4,040,000	'4·4'
England and Wales	1,300,000		5,318,100		104,460	5,422,560	'above 4·17'

(a) Chalmers gives this figure as 835,000, clearly a typographical error.

for persons omitted from the assessments (other than transients) and thus ultimately arrived at a second set of ratios.

In their study of the London returns, Jones and Judges quite rightly express surprise at this method of successive approximation. Taking the 1695 returns for the City of London within the Walls (and making an estimate for the seventeen parishes the returns for which they were unable to trace), they arrived at a total population of 69,581. King's first estimate, based on a ratio of 5·4 persons per inhabited house, was 72,900. After allowing for omissions he chose the higher figure of 80,190, from which he calculated a final ratio of 'almost 6' persons per inhabited house. The latter ratio is, in fact, close to that found by Jones and Judges, namely 6·1 persons, the difference between the total populations arising from the larger number of inhabited houses taken by King (13,500 instead of the 11,469 found by Jones and Judges).[26] In other words, King finally arrived at a ratio which he could have calculated in the first place by using the assessment returns and without making any allowance for omissions.

The explanation put forward by Jones and Judges is an ingenious one. They suggest that King had made up his mind in advance to estimate the population on the basis of the numbers of houses recorded in the hearth tax returns and that, at the same time, he also had an estimate derived from the marriage, birth and burial assessments. Comparing these two results he may have found that the ratios of persons per inhabited house were 'too low for his previously formed estimate' and he thus increased the population by 10 per cent, with a corresponding rise in his ratios. 'The result is a higher population for London

[26] Jones and Judges, op. cit., pp. 53-55 and 58-62. The Jones and Judges figure for inhabited houses is also in part an estimate, since it includes an allowance for the seventeen missing parishes.

in the revised estimate than the factors available to King seem to justify', while at the same time the allowance of 10 per cent per persons omitted 'gave him the average size of "household" which we know that he could, and apparently did, extract straight out of the marriage-duty assessments . . .'.[27]

The error in this explanation is its assumption—and the authors had no basis for a contrary belief—that King had access to the complete returns, or at least access to those for London. But the P.R.O. manuscripts and the Burns journal make it clear that this was not the case. There is little doubt that King himself had hoped to make use of the full material for London, for the P.R.O. manuscripts contain a table entitled: 'An Extract of the Number of Houses and

TABLE 2

King's data for the London parishes, compared with those of Jones and Judges

No.	Parish	King's Data			Jones and Judges		
		No. of Houses	Total Population	Persons per House	No. of Houses	Total Population	Persons per House
2.	Allhallows, Bread St circa.	(85)	512	6·0	80	512	6·4
15.	St. Andrew, Wardrobe	108	505	4·7	106	505	4·8
16.	St. Anne, Aldersgate	145	852	5·88	145	852	5·9
22.	St. Benet, Gracechurch	65	396	6·0	65	396	6·1
23.	St. Benet, Paul's Wharf	124	562	4·5	120	557	4·6
25.	St. Botolph, Billingsgate	60	350	5·8	55	350	6·4
27.	St. Clement, Eastcheap	60	372	6·2	61	371	6·1
35.	St. Gregory by St. Paul's	282	1,661	5·9	275	1,666	6·1
41.	St. John Zachary	83	475	5·72	90	477	5·3
51.	St. Margaret, New Fish Street	73	461	$6\frac{1}{3}$	74	461	6·2
73.	St. Michael, Bassishaw	149	846	?	135	908	6·7
90.	St. Peter, Cornhill	186	1,111	6 feré	—	—	—
93.	St. Stephen, Coleman Street	429	2,713	$6\frac{1}{3}$	—	—	—
104.	St. Bride	1,241	5,145	4·15	1,229	5,165	4·2
106.	St. Dunstan in the West	437	2,671	6·1 feré	436	2,673	6·1
101.	St. Botolph, Aldersgate	1,241	4,966	4·0	618	3,358	5·4
107.	St. Giles, Cripplegate	1,842	8,528	$4·6\frac{1}{4}$	(1,852)	(8,514)	(4·6)
—	Trinity, Minories	131	538	4·1	—	—	—
—	St. Dunstan, Stepney	8,680	39,302	4·6	—	—	—
—	St. John, Hackney	535	2,896	5·4	—	—	—
—	St. John, Wapping	1,496	5,530	3·7	—	—	—
—	St. Katherine's Tower	743	1,614	2·18	—	—	—
—	St. Leonard, Shoreditch	1,585	6,629	4·18	—	—	—
—	St. Mary, Whitechapel	2,583	11,439	4·4	—	—	—
—	St. Paul, Shadwell	1,443	7,891	5·4	—	—	—

Note: The parish numbers are those given in Jones and Judges, pp. 58-62. The latter do not include in their study the outer parishes in Middlesex and Surrey. Jones and Judges refer to their statistics of houses as 'inhabited houses'.

[27] Jones and Judges, *op. cit.*, p. 55.

People from ye Assesmt. upon Marriages Births and Burials aᵒ. Dni. 1695', which lists all the London parishes and has against them a number of ruled columns headed: Houses, People, Quality, Bachelors, Widowers, Yearly Marriages, Yearly Births, Medium of 1683 and 1684 Yearly Burials, and Ratio of Mortality. It is clear that King intended to enter in these columns the statistics relating to every parish, and it is equally clear that he did not succeed in collecting the data except for a few of them. Table 2 gives the numbers of houses, population and size of household (King's own calculations) for those parishes, and gives the comparable statistics derived by Jones and Judges from the Guildhall records. Comparison shows a close approximation between the two sets of statistics, especially for total population, except in the cases of St. Michael Bassishaw, and, particularly, of St. Botolph, Aldersgate, there being no immediately apparent explanation for these two discrepancies. As far as can be seen from the available manuscripts, the data listed in Table 2 comprise all the London parishes for which King was able to obtain copies of, or access to, the original returns.

To arrive at a total population for London, he had thus of necessity to base his estimate on a series of ratios of persons per house. In fact he used different sets of ratios at different times and he was evidently much concerned with the question of which ratios would be nearest the truth. In most cases he gives no real statistical reason for using the particular set of ratios adopted at the time. But one of the calculations in the Burns journal suggests that, whatever subsequent alterations he may have made, he based himself originally on the information summarized in Table 2, for, taking the parishes listed, he arrives at the following results[28]:

	'Houses'	'People'	'People to a House'
The 7 parishes within the walls	670	3,652	5·4
The 5 parishes without the walls	4,892	21,848	4·47
The 7 Out Par. in Middx. (& Surr.)	17,065	75,301	4·413
	22,627	100,801	4·455

These ratios, derived from the statistics of nineteen of the twenty-five parishes listed in the P.R.O. manuscripts, are very similar to the first set of ratios given in Table 1 of the present paper. It would seem, therefore, that the initial set of ratios used by King for London were based upon a sample of the returns collected in 1695.[29]

For the rest of England and Wales, King's data appear to have been much more sparse. They are given in a series of summaries in the Burns journal (pp. 90-92), and the main overall results are reproduced in Table 3. The precise

---

[28] Burns journal, p. 58. King gives no explanation for his exclusion, from the above calculation, of data for St. Clement, Eastcheap; St. Gregory by St. Paul's; St. Margaret, New Fish Street; St. Michael Bassishaw; St. Peter, Cornhill; and St. Stephen, Coleman Street. He also refers to the number of houses recorded for St. Katharine's Tower, as being incorrect: 'it has not above 600 houses, They (the Assessors) having reckoned all ye Divided houses or those in which there is 2 or 3 Families for so many distinct houses, but those divided houses are generally but one or 2 in a Family being generally Pensioners.' The various calculations in the Burns journal appear to date from 1695-6 though it is clear that King must have made further entries as late as 1700 (see p. 92 of the journal).

[29] Although this initial set of ratios is quite straightforward, the various sets of secondary, derived, ratios are by no means easy to explain.

TABLE 3

King's data for various parts of England and Wales

Place	No. of Houses	Population	Persons per House
Lichfield City, Staffs	616	2,833	4·6
Lichfield Close, Staffs	39	205	5·2
	655	3,038	4·7
Sevenoaks, market town, Kent	206	891	4·3
Riverhead, Sevenoaks parish	80	371	4·6
The Weald of Sevenoaks	80	311	3·9
	366	1,573	4·3
Swepston parish, Leicester	40	145	3·6
Heather parish, Leicester	33	134	4·2
	73	279	3·9
Barnet, market town, Herts.	176	850	4·8
Fetherston Const., Staffs	14	65	4·6
Holy Cross ats. Abbey pish. in Shrewsbury (*circa* 230)	222	935	4·20
Atcham juxta Shrewsb. one of ye 6 Townships in Atcham parish and in Upton magna Allotment, Shropshire *circa*	25	127	5·0
Berwick Township in Atcham parish *circa*	10	55	5·5
Utkinton, Chilton, Crankill, Elmstree	33	161	4·9
	68	343	5·0
Hackney Parish by London in 10 Hamlets	535	2,896	5·4
Poplar and Blackwall, part of Stepney parish	575	2,255	3·9
Mile End, New Town in Stepney	313	1,600	5·1
Spitalfields New Town in Stepney	863	6,595	7·4
Wapping Stepney in Stepney parish	2,450	9,329	3·8
Stepney parish in all	8,680	39,302	4·6
Tower within, Extra-paroch., London	60	343	5·7
Tower extra, Extra-paroch., London	50	239	4·8
Norton Folgate Lib. in St. Faith's Parish	449	2,349	5·2
Old Artillery Ground in Tower Division, Extra-Paroch.	162	1,635	10·0
Stratford, Bow and Old Ford in Middx	178	772	4·4
The Whole Tower Hamlets	19,443	86,882	4·458
Shustoke Parish near Coleshill, Warwick	59	275	4·7
Coleshill Town and parish, Warwick	245	1,109	4·5
Eynsford Hundred in Norfolk, 30 villages whereof 2 are market towns, 1,437 houses or rather	1,500	5,880	4·1 or 3·9
Brookstreet Hamlet in S. Weald, Essex	37	164	4·5 feré
The Uplands in S. Weald, Essex	84	368	4·5 feré
Burntwood market town in S. Weald, Essex	139	638	4·6 feré
	260	1,170	4·5 just
Norwich City (A.D. 1696) (a)	(6,790)	28,546	4·226
Culliton, Devon	237	1,554	6·56
Kingsbridge, Devon	122	686	5·6
St. Stephen's, Exon. (cum Bedford)	69	443	6·42
Widworthy, Devon	96	255	2·66
St. Mary, Ye Moor (Exon)	255	1,820	7·14
St. Thomas Parish, Devon	309	1,705	5·52
Gloucester City	1,126	4,756	4·225

(a) King also gives a figure for Norwich in 1695 at 29,332 population.

Notes: (i) King's tables also give population data (without any numbers of houses) for Salisbury (total population 7,408, information apparently given in October 1700) and Buckfastleigh, Devon (total population 1,123).

(ii) The calculations of persons per house are those given by King himself.

way in which King made use of these results in his estimates of the population of cities, market towns, villages and hamlets is by no means clear. But the general scheme of calculation is shown—in a number of variations—at several points in both the P.R.O. and Burns journals. Three examples are given in Table 4. King might have been expected to derive the ratios of persons per house in the various categories given in the examples from the basic material of Table 3. But if he did this—and he must certainly have made some use of the returns in his calculations—the derivation is not a direct one, and the manuscripts seen so far do not explain what in fact he did.

TABLE 4

King's calculations of the population of England and Wales, excluding London

		Houses	Persons per House	Population
(a)	5 Cities of 4,000 houses each	20,000	4·4	88,000
	40 Towns of 500 houses each	20,000	4·3	86,000
	100 Towns of 300 houses each	30,000	4·2	126,000
	300 Towns of 200 houses each	60,000	4·16	249,600
	400 Towns of 150 houses each	60,000	4·125	247,500
	500 Towns of 100 houses each	50,000	4·08	204,000
	1,000 Vills of 60 houses each	60,000	4·04	242,400
	20,333 Vills of 45 houses each	915,000	3·993	3,653,600
		1,215,000		4,897,100
(b)	5 Cities of 4,000 houses each	20,000	4·6	92,000
	40 Cities and Towns of 500 houses each	20,000	4·4	88,000
	100 Towns of 300 houses each	30,000	4·2	126,000
	300 Towns of 200 houses each	60,000	4·12	247,200
	400 Towns of 150 houses each	60,000	4·06	243,600
	1,000 Villages of 100 houses each	100,000	4·04	404,000
	7,000 Villages and Hamlets of 80 houses	560,000	4	2,240,000
	10,000 Lesser Hamlets and houses of name	365,000	3·98	1,452,700
		1,215,000		4,893,500
(c)	5 Cities of 400 houses each	20,000	4·8	96,000
	20 Towns of 500 houses each	10,000	4·6	46,000
	100 Towns of 300 houses each	30,000	4·5	135,000
	300 Towns of 200 houses each	60,000	4·4	264,000
	400 Towns of 150 houses each	60,000	4·3	250,000
	500 Towns of 100 houses each	50,000	4·2	210,000
	1,000 Vills of 50 houses each	50,000	4·1	205,000
	919,000 Houses more	919,000	3·8	3,492,200
Add 215 Houses at		215	3·8	817
	259 Houses more at	259	3·8	984
		1,199,474		4,700,001

Sources: (a) Burns journal, p. 61; (b) Burns journal, p. 122; (c) P.R.O. journal, p. 30.
Note: All calculations (except additions) are as given by King.

The above discussion suggests the kind of problem with which King was faced in making his estimates. He was in the position, so far as the returns on marriages, births and burials were concerned, of an outside individual—outside the government service—at a time when statistics of the kind with which he wanted to deal were generally regarded as confidential. He almost certainly had to content himself with such material as he might obtain through in-

IN Parishes of about an Hundred Families, and
wherein the Regiftry of the Births, Burials,
and Marriages hath been well kept, Enquire,

1. The Number of the Inhabitants, Male and
Female.

2. Married and Unmarried, and their Trades.

3. Widdows and Widdowers.

4. The Age of each Perfon, Man, Woman, and
Child.

5. The Number of Families and Hearths.

As in the following Scheme, *Viz.*

Hearths.	Males.	Females.
3.	*John Smith*, Taylor, 45. 17. 15. 1.	His Wife 40. 16. 14. 4.
2.	*Richard Sims*, Carpenter, 52. 30. 22. 11.	His Wife 46. 24. 12. 2.
4.	*Robert Hughs*, Shoemaker, Widdower, 50. 16. 14. 2.	18. 6. 1.

And put the Births, Burials, and Marriages into the
following Scheme, for the 7 laft Years.

	Born.		Buryed.		Married.
Anno 1676.	Males	Females.	Males	Females.	
77.					
78.					
79.					
80.					
81.					
82.					

Defcribe the Soyl and Scituation of the Parifh, and the Reputed Number of Acres which it containeth.

FIGURE I

Schedule for a 'sample' census

fluential friends. He knew, at least in part, the limitations of the basic data[30] and of his own calculations derived therefrom, acknowledging that 'What ye true Number of ye People of England may be, is not only uncertain but very difficult to compute; by reason of the great neglects and omissions in all the Publick Registers and Assessments.'[31] He would nevertheless argue that the attempt was worth making. He had his own interests to serve and he was clearly desirous of obtaining a position in which his talents would be better used.[32] But at the same time he genuinely wished to improve the statistical basis used in estimating the probable revenue of projected taxes and he also felt that, especially in the grave circumstances of the time, it was essential that statesmen should be properly informed as to the total population and its composition. He was more than dubious as to the value of Petty's contribution in this field. He could still hope that, with all its defects, his own estimate would be nearer the truth than any previously constructed.

In addition to the official data of the assessments, King used private material which he must either have collected himself, or else possibly instigated friends and acquaintances to collect for him. The population returns for Salisbury, referred to in the note to Table 3, appear to be of this kind. But the private material also includes statistics of a much greater interest, namely those reporting the age structure of a number of areas in England and Wales. The Burns journal contains summaries of such information for three localities, Lichfield City (Staffs), Shustoke Parish (Warwick) and Swepston Parish (Leicester).[33] King does not explain how he obtained the statistics, but two supplementary documents may help to throw some light on this. The first is a printed sheet bound up in the same volume of *Tracts Relating to Customs, Excise and Taxes*, which contains King's only published work in the field of political arithmetic, the summary of duties and rates payable under the Act of 6 and 7 William and Mary, c. 6. The sheet in question is reproduced in the present paper and is clearly the schedule for a proposed or actual sample study, the sample consisting of parishes with 'about an Hundred Families and wherein the Registry of the Births, Burials, and Marriages hath been well kept . . .'.[34] For such parishes it was intended to collect full information on the age, sex, and marital condition of every inhabitant as well as the vital statistics for the years 1676 to 1682. There is no direct evidence to connect this schedule with King, but the schedule itself does at least show that plans for gathering the kind of statistics in which King was interested were in the air in King's period. The second document is in the P.R.O. bundle, and consists of a thirteen-page list and summary (the whole appearing to be in King's handwriting) entitled 'The Names of the People in

[30] He made various estimates of the extent of under-enumeration in the assessments, those in the *Observations*, being the most generous, namely 10 per cent in London, 2 per cent in the other cities, and 1 per cent in the villages and hamlets. Nevertheless, Robert Harley believed the allowances were insufficient and that, in particular, there was likely to be a greater degree of omission in the country than in London. (See Chalmers, *op. cit.*, p. 52.)

[31] Burns journal, p. 121.

[32] *Ibid.*, p. 241. In a draft of a letter to Sir Stephen Fox, dated 19 December 1695, he represents his ability to 'give you such an Estimate as may be depended upon to be the Produce of any Project on foot for Raysing of money'.

[33] Burns journal, pp. 93-95. The Buckfastleigh returns (Harleian MSS., No. 6832) seem to be of the same type, but it has not been possible to confirm this since the documents are not available at present. (The Buckfastleigh returns, like those for Lichfield, give the ages of the population. D.V.G. 1962.)   [34] The original sheet is in the British Museum, at 816 m.6/80.

Harefield near Uxbridge in Com. Middx. with their ages—Taken ye latter End of Oct. 1699.' This list goes through every dwelling in Harefield and itemizes the inhabitants in each. In the first two pages the age of almost every person is recorded, but subsequently the ages become sporadic and it seems evident that it must have been very difficult to ascertain them. However, the list shows King's interest in the subject and suggests a house by house enumeration.[35]

TABLE 5

The ages of the population of Lichfield city, 1695

	Bachelors	Spinsters	Husbands	Wives	Widowers	Widows	Total
Under 5	167	201	—	—	—	—	368
5 –	227	183	—	—	—	—	410
10 –	156	127	—	—	—	—	283
15 –	136	170	—	1	—	—	307
20 –	44	125	15	22	—	—	206
25 –	49	72	38	69	1	3	232
30 –	9	25	68	81	7	5	195
35 –	6	22	105	87	7	29	256
40 –	1	3	52	43	4	16	119
45 –	1	1	66	46	6	13	133
50 –	1	2	21	22	3	12	61
55 –	4	—	37	38	8	25	112
60 –	2	1	17	23	3	22	68
65 –	—	1	21	10	8	41	81
70 –	—	—	2	1	2	9	14
75 –	1	—	—	—	4	5	10
80 –	—	—	—	—	1	2	3
85 –	—	—	—	—	1	1	2
90 –	—	—	—	—	—	—	0
95 –	—	—	—	—	—	1	1
	804	933	442	443	55	184	2,861

Note: In the original list (which gives single years for the first 10 years of life) the age groups are described as 10 to 15 inclusive, 15 to 20 inclusive, etc. But there is no overlapping and the totals are correct, so it appears that exclusive groups are meant. The results have therefore been expressed in terms of the customary 5-year groups.

This information gives some support for the belief that the age statistics for Lichfield, Shustoke and Swepston were based on genuine enumerations. The Lichfield statistics are obviously those on which King constructed his special fertility analysis, and they are summarized in Table 5 and reproduced (in part) graphically in an accompanying population pyramid. The latter figure shows the marked concentration of ages in the second half of each ten-year age group. It also shows the marked underenumeration of male children. King himself comments on this and writes, in a marginal note: 'Now ye Births in Lichfd. in all ye 3 parishes being yearly at a medium 107. Whereof for these 2861 People (being Exclusive of ye Close of Lichfield and of some out Villages

[35] King found in Harefield, according to his summary, 109 inhabited and 8 empty houses, 122 families and 563 persons, and arrived at ratios of 5·16 persons per inhabited house and 4·61 persons per family. (It now seems clear that King collected these demographic data while carrying out a survey of the Newdigate estate in Harefield. The Middlesex County Record Office has a field notebook belonging to King, covering his survey work from 6 September 1695 to 9 July 1700, most of the work having been done after 7 September 1699. Page 96 of the notebook lists the names and ages of 49 inhabitants (GR 136, Mx. EM 11). I am indebted to Miss E. D. Mercer, County Archivist, for drawing my attention to this notebook. D.V.G. 1963.)

which parish to Lichfield but being without ye Liberties of ye City and County of Lichfd. are not included in this Assessment) The Yearly Births may be about 100 which in 5 years would be 500 whereof a Fifth part dying there should remain about 400; But whereas there is but 368, there seems to be 32 wanting, Either in ye Assesmt. itself, or by reason of ye mortality by ye Small Pox which hapned among ye young children a year or two ago, which appears more plainly by ye Number of Children of 1, 2 and 3 years old, Those of 1 and 2 years being fewer in Number then those of 3, whereas they should be more.'[36]

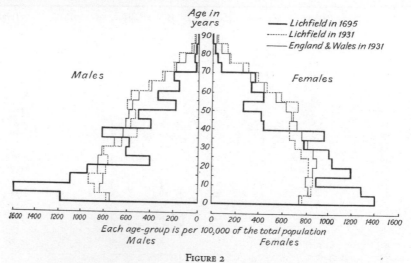

FIGURE 2

Age structure of Lichfield in 1695 and 1931 and of England and Wales in 1931

Leaving aside the question of underenumeration at the early ages, the population pyramid shows a situation similar to that in 1841, a period of high mortality and high fertility. It is interesting, therefore, to estimate the fertility of Lichfield in 1695. Assuming that King was right and that the annual average of births was about 100 (and this figure is more likely to understate than to overstate the facts), the number of births per 1,000 women aged 15 to 49 years would be about 120, as compared with 62 for Lichfield and 56·4 for England and Wales in 1931. Relating births to married women in the same age groups would yield a rate of almost 287 per 1,000 women for Lichfield in 1695, as compared with 106·7 for England and Wales in 1931 and 124 for Lichfield at the latter date. Marital fertility in 1931 was thus less than half of what it appears to have been in 1695. But, on the other hand, the 1695 rate appears to be very similar to that for England and Wales in the 1850's.[37]

The object of this paper has been to inquire into the methods and materials

[36] Note that King uses the term 'Assessment' for this table. It is possible that the additional information on ages was collected by the assessors in the course of their enumeration for the marriage-duty Act. If so, it was a type of information not required by the Act itself.

[37] For England and Wales in 1850-2 the number of live births per 1,000 married women aged 15-49 years was over 265. Correction for under-registration in the period would raise the figure still higher. The Lichfield data suggest fairly late marriage, but a high marriage probability. Half of the women aged 25-9 years were single, while this was so for only one out of sixty in the age group 45-9 years. (See discussion of this point in Hajnal, above, p. 137.)

used by Gregory King in his work on the population of England and Wales at the end of the seventeenth century. The relevance of the discussion for any new estimates of the population in 1695 must be left for later consideration. But so far as the first point is concerned, one fact is abundantly clear: King was a worthy successor to Graunt. Hampered by inability to use the full official data, he showed great imagination in his handling of what was available. Above all, his work demonstrates his awareness of the questions which need to be posed in studying population trends.[38] His approach and knowledge of his own limitations are perhaps best summed up in a motto which he intended to use in the introduction to an alternative version of the *Observations*: 'Pour bien savoir les Choses, il en faut savoir le détail: mais pource qu'il est presque infiny, nos Connoisances sont toujours superficielles et Imparfaites.'

[38] Some of these questions are posed by him in the P.R.O. journal, p. 8, namely: how many marriages annually; at what ages persons marry; how many widows and widowers; at what ages they become such; how many 2nd, 3rd, 4th, 5th, 6th and 7th marriages; how many barren marriages; how many teeming women; how many die in childbed; how many die in labour; how many marriages produce only one child, 2, 3, 4, 5, 6, 7, etc. Similar awareness is shown in the *Observations*, p. 46, where he notes that 'from a consideration of the male and female children in the said town, and the ages of their parents, at the time, when such children were respectively conceived, a scheme may be established, of the powers of generation . . .' and one of the draft tables in the P.R.O. journal, p. 21, was designed to do this by relating conceptions to married women at individual ages.

GREGORY KING'S ESTIMATE OF THE POPULATION OF ENGLAND AND WALES, 1695

From: *Population Studies*, Vol. II, 1950, 338–74

In an earlier paper, an attempt was made to review the demographic work of Gregory King.[1] His observations on the population of England and Wales at the end of the seventeenth century were examined against the background of certain manuscripts in the Public Record Office and in the library of the London County Council. Analysis of this material, and comparison of King's data for London with the statistics compiled by Jones and Judges from the City of London returns collected in accordance with the 1694 Act (levying taxes on marriages, births and burials, and on bachelors and childless widowers),[2] suggested the lines on which King had proceeded in his estimate of the population of England and Wales. He had taken a 'sample' of the returns made for London under the 1694 Act, and perhaps also a smaller number of returns for areas outside London, and had used these data to produce a ratio of persons per house.

[1] D. V. Glass, 'Gregory King and the population of England and Wales at the end of the seventeenth century', *Eugen. Rev.*, January 1946. See above.

[2] P. E. Jones and A. V. Judges, 'London population in the late seventeenth century', *Econ. Hist. Rev.*, October 1935. In connexion with the duties levied under the 1694 Act (originally passed for 5 years, but extended for a further 5), provision was made for the collection of detailed and comprehensive demographic statistics. A fuller discussion of the nature of these statistics is given in my earlier paper. Briefly, however, they were intended to consist of (1) a complete enumeration of the population, to be taken before 30 April 1695, and to be revised annually, and (2) a much improved system of registration of marriages, births and deaths, covering stillbirths and births to nonconformists, etc., and including especially detailed registration statistics for the nobility and gentry. There was, as might have been anticipated, a wide difference between what was prescribed and what was actually done. Nevertheless, it is likely that the demographic statistics actually collected were better than those for any subsequent period until the initiation of regular censuses and civil registration.

The returns for areas outside London had, in addition, apparently been used to suggest ratios for different types of agglomeration. The ratios were then applied to statistics of houses, obtained from the hearth-tax records, and some allowance was made for under-enumeration.

Since the previous paper appeared, additional material has become available. In the main this consists of King manuscripts in the Harleian collection, including the original enumeration lists for Lichfield,[3] Buckfastleigh[4] and Rinmore,[5] and those queries on King's estimates which Chalmers attributed to Robert Harley.[6] But a further and especially valuable manuscript has also appeared—a contemporary copy of King's *Natural and Politicall Observations*, with the addition of Harley's queries and, still more important, of King's answers to those queries.[7] This manuscript belongs to the Museum Book Store, and I am greatly indebted to Messrs L. and D. Kashnor for permission to make use of what is, to the best of my knowledge, hitherto unexplored material. With the aid of these additional manuscripts it is now possible to discuss, on a more secure basis, a number of problems concerning King's estimate of the population of England and Wales, and also of the age structure of that population.

To begin with, the Kashnor MS. helps to give a much fuller explanation of the foundation and possible defects of King's formula for estimating the total population of England and Wales, and particularly as regards the statistics of the total number of houses and the distribution of houses among urban communities of various sizes. The latter question has some immediate interest, for it is evident from the Burns journals[8] that King experimented with a variety of ratios of persons per house for those different urban groups, although in the final version of his estimate, he distinguished only between the segments of London, other cities and market towns and, for the rest, the villages and hamlets.

On the number of houses in England and Wales, King began with the total 'as charged in the Books of the Hearth-Office at Ladyday 1690', namely, 1,319,215.[9] This total was then adjusted to allow for an increase between the

---

[3] Harleian MSS. 7022, fols. 1-42. See also King's notes on this in MS. 6839, fol. 158.

[4] Harl. MSS. 6832, fols. 132-43. Buckfastleigh is in Devonshire.

[5] Harl. MSS. 6832, fol. 146. Rinmore (Ringmore) is in Devonshire.

[6] There are two sets of queries in different handwriting, though the contents are closely similar: Harl. MSS. 6837, fols. 128-33, and 7021, fols. 46-50. Chalmers attributes both sets to Harley, but quotes from the latter (G. Chalmers, *An Estimate of the Comparative Strength of Great Britain*, London 1786, p. 45).

[7] The manuscript, consisting of a book of thirty-seven numbered leaves, was originally in the possession of Reginald Marriott, of Parsons Green, Middlesex. The title-page reads: *Observations & Conclusions, Natural and Political, Upon the State and Condition of England &cᵈ by G. K. Esqʳ Lancaster Herald of Arms. Aᵒ Dnⁱ. 1696. With Notes, Observations, & Inquiries, Upon the same By R. H. Esqʳ Aᵒ Dnⁱ. 1697. And Mr. K's Further Observations In answer to Mr. H's Inquiries. Aᵒ 1697.* Each double page is ruled into four columns, with the following headings: (1) 'Mr. K's Observations &c.'; (2) 'Mr. H's Notes and Inquiries' (dated 26 April 1697); (3) 'Mr. K's further Observations, in answer to Mr. H's Inquiries' (dated, at the end of § 9 of the volume, 'ultᵒ May 1697. Gr. K-g'); and (4) 'Occasional Remarks upon the whole, By a Third hand'. The fourth column seems superfluous, for there are no 'occasional remarks'. The queries and comments do not go beyond § 9 of the *Observations*. The present paper deals only with the demographic material in the Kashnor MS., leaving without comment King's replies on the economic questions. I am indebted to Professor F. A. Hayek, who first told me of the existence of the Kashnor MS. (The manuscript has since been purchased by the Australian National Library, Canberra. D.V.G. 1962.)

[8] The King journal now in the L.C.C. Library, formerly in the possession of John Burns.

[9] In his *Observations* King did not specify the immediate provenance of this figure, but appeared to refer to it as one which could be taken for granted. That the figure was Davenant's is made clear by the acknowledgement in the Burns journal, p. 48, and there is no reason to doubt that it was taken

years 1690 and 1695, the figure for the latter year being taken at the round sum of 1,326,000. Since the allowance of an additional 6,000-7,000 houses was based in part upon an estimate of the excess of births over deaths in the nation during the period, and a translation of this excess back into houses by using a ratio of persons per house, not much reliance can be placed upon it. Harley raised a question on the relation between population growth and new construction. He noted: 'Experience shows us, In the Country there is no proportion between the Increase of People & of Houses. And in London it may be thought that the Humour of Building & other Reasons increase the Houses beyond the proportionable increase of the People.' King explained that his estimate did imply a smaller proportionate increase in the number of houses, in relation to population growth, in the country, but provided no justification for his particular allocation.[10] However, the increase in the number of houses between 1690 and 1695 is a relatively small matter.

Secondly, since King had based his population estimate on the number of inhabited houses, multiplied by a ratio of persons per house, he had further to adjust the hearth-tax statistics to allow for both divided and empty houses. He had stated in his *Observations* that the 'chimny-money' was charged on the tenant of the specific dwelling, so that 'The divided houses stand as so many distinct dwellings in the Acco^{ts} of the said Hearth-Office',[11] while empty houses, 'smith's shops', etc., were included in the hearth-tax account. In his replies to Harley, in the Kashnor MS., King admitted that his estimate of the number of 'divided houses, Smith's shops &c.' were 'by computaçon'—i.e. hypothetical. Empty houses were 'generally exprest in the Books of the Hearth Office, But the Assesments on Taxes shew them to be about 2 or $2\frac{1}{2}$ p. cent of the whole, but much greater in London'.[12] In the *Observations*, however, for the adjustment on account of both empty and divided houses, King had allowed a total of 'near 3. p. cent', or about 36,000, leaving a net total of 1,290,000 separate houses, and then rounded the figure to 1·3 millions. Even assuming King to be correct in his estimate of $2-2\frac{1}{2}$ per cent for empty houses, it would seem very unlikely that the remaining $\frac{1}{2}$ or 1 per cent would be adequate to cover divided houses. Jones and Judges have argued that, for multiple occupancy alone, the allowance would need to be above 3 per cent. They point out that, for London, tax returns for 1673 and 1678 show at least 107 families living in every 100 houses within the City walls, and at least 121 families per 100 houses in the wards without the walls. Although King probably suspected that there was more subdivision in London than elsewhere, yet it would seem, looking at his estimate of the population of the ninety-seven parishes within the walls, that even for the City of London he assumed too large a proportion of separate houses, for he gave a figure of 13,500 instead of the 11,469 inhabited houses found by Jones and Judges (this latter figure was,

from (C. Davenant), *An Essay upon Ways and Means of Supplying the War*, London 1695, table facing p. 76. To facilitate reference to the various points raised, the edition of the *Observations* cited throughout this paper is that of Barnett, reproduced from Harl. MSS. 1898 (G. E. Barnett, ed., *Two Tracts by Gregory King*, Baltimore 1936).

[10] Kashnor MS., p. 1.

[11] That is, the 1690 figures relate to occupiers or 'households', not to separate houses. This point was debated during the eighteenth-century population controversy.

[12] Kashnor MS., p. 2.

in part, estimated), and his resultant population for the City appears too high.[13]

The number of houses allotted by King to London also raises the third point, the distribution of the total number of houses between King's main regions. As Jones and Judges comment, 'There is just as much room for dispute about his method of apportionment among regions, whether it is the hearth-money local aggregates he employs, or those of the marriage duty, or whether again he fakes the sequence of his argument by coming upon an answer through a back door, to arrive later with a key to open it from the other side.'[14] It was clear, however, from the Burns journal that the marriage-duty statistics could not have been the basis, for the data available to King related only to a few areas. The Kashnor manuscript confirms that the hearth-tax records were the basis, for Harley also posed the question—'Are these estimated or numbred from the Hearth books? If estimated, By what Rule are the proportions made?'—and King gave the following reply:

Mr Adams did about 18 years ago, collect the number of Houses in the Cittys & great Townes as well as in the Villages from the Hearth Books; And I must here take notice That the General Housing of the Kingdom amounted upon his Totting them but to 1120,000, or thereabouts, The Increase since that time is not 40,000. And the new Discoveries for which there was particular Encouragements including all the Cottages & Paupers could not be by the year 1690? above 60, or 80,000 more, Whereby the Generall Acco! of the Kingdom will not rise to above 1220. or 1240.000 Houses. I was privy to the Acco! & this previous Knowledge with my own Observations from ye Assessm![s] on Marriages, Births & Buryalls return'd me from severall Cities & Market townes in the Kingdom, was a Foundation for me to compute the number of the houses in the Citties and Market Townes (Exclusive of the London Bills of Mortality) thus:

	Houses
4 Cittys of between 5. and 6000 houses each, one with another	22,000
10 other Citties or great Townes of 1800 each	18,000
30 other Citties and great Townes of 500 each	15,000
100 other great Townes of 300 each	30,000
250 other Townes of 200. each	50,000
400 other Townes of 150. each	60,000
794	195,000[15]

The 'Mr Adams' to whom King referred was undoubtedly John Adams, author of *Index Villaris, or an Alphabetical Table of All the Cities, Market Towns, Parishes, Villages, and Private Seats in England and Wales*, published in 1680 (London), and also, in a revised edition, in 1690. In the preface to the first edition, Adams explained: 'I have used all Possible Care, Industry and Pains, in comparing the *Villare Anglicum* of Sir Henry Spelman, and the printed Tables of Speed's Maps, with the Maps themselves, as well as those of Saxton and others, and regulating the whole by an Abstract taken from the Books of the Hearth Office, and other private accompts returned me from several Counties.' The implication is clear. One of the sources used was the hearth-tax statistics, Presumably Adams established from these his list of towns and other places,

---

[13] *Op. cit.*, pp. 53-55.   [14] *Op. cit.*, p. 53.   [15] Kashnor MS., p. 2.

and there is little reason to doubt that it was this original abstract or list to which King had access. Unfortunately, the *Index Villaris*, in its published form, gives no indication of the numbers of 'houses' or occupiers in the various places included. But a distinction is made, either by specific description or by typography, between the different types of community. Thus cities are named as such and printed in large italicized capitals. A second set of places is printed in large capitals and a third in small capitals, the remaining names in the list following the normal printing style, being in lower case with initial capitals. Taking the first three sets of names yield a total (excluding London and Westminster, and allowing for the double entry of one place, Church Stretton) of 788 separate places. Although these are not defined in the 1680 edition as representing all the cities and market towns in England and Wales, the point is in fact made clear in the 1690 edition, in a map which explicitly lists the names of 779 places (excluding London and Westminster) under the heading: 'An Alphabeticall Table of all the Cities and Market Towns in England and Wales.' There are changes between the two editions; some of the earlier names are omitted and a few new names are inserted. But over almost the whole range the list given in the 1690 map is identical with that constructed from the three sets of names in the 1680 edition. It requires no great stretching of probabilities to surmise that King may have added a few names to the list of 788 and thus have obtained his total of 794 places. It is thus reasonable to explain King's division of England and Wales between urban and rural as having been based on Adams's analysis of the hearth-tax statistics (though for an unspecified year), the term 'urban' covering all cities and market towns.

On the division of urban communities by numbers of houses, the Adams lists do not give much help, for they cannot be equated with King's categories. Adams accounted for twenty-five cities, but these were defined by having a cathedral or (in two cases, Bangor and Llandaff) being 'bishopricks'. Similarly, Adams's second set of names, comprising twenty-three places, is given without reference to population or other index of size. How exactly King computed the numbers of towns in his various categories is thus not known, and the results cannot be tested for reliability until a fresh analysis of hearth-tax statistics has been made. However, in his final computations, King did not use this detail, but simply the distinction between London (divided into major segments), the other cities and market towns, and the rest of England and Wales. And that broad distinction, even if not fully accurate, had at least a reasonable foundation. It was based on an analysis, apparently carried out around the year 1680, of the hearth-tax statistics, and adjusted for the estimated increase in the number of houses since that time.[16]

At the same time, the reference to the data collected by 'Mr Adams' also suggests that King's initial estimate, in the *Observations*, of the total number of households in England and Wales was too high and that, in fact, it should not

[16] That is, King used Davenant's figure as his total for 1690 and adjusted that to 1695, while using Adams's data to help in the regional allocation. An example of this allocation (though evidently not in its final form) is given in King's working journal (P.R.O. bundle), p. 10. King writes:
'Now as to yᵉ Houses in London and Bills of Mortality Dr. Davenant gives us London Westmʳ and Middx to make 111,215 Houses. Now Middx. I take to be but about the 8ᵗʰ part of a Comon County; in Acres, But yᵉ 3ᵈ part of a Comon County in Houses or 150ᵗʰ part of yᵉ whole. So that there being 1.130.000 Houses in yᵉ Kingdom, Middx (without London & Westmʳ) should answer to

have been above 1,240,000. King gave some further information on this in reply to Harley's comment—which will be referred to again later—on the general validity of the returns under the 1694 Act. In answering Harley, King admitted:

> Now that the inhabited houses of ye Kingd^m are not above 1240,000 or 1250,000 I am apt to believe from ye manner of Totting 'em from ye Hearth books, wch being Transcribed every half year, were to contain 20 lines in each pag. & the Transcriber who was paid by the Hundred, totted up the numb^r at ye end of each book, reckoning the names of the Places and Streets &c. as well as the names of persons into ye acco^t. So that generally one pag. wth another, did not contain at a Medium above 19 neat houses. And ye Author of Ways and Means seems to be of opinion upon discoursing this Article, that the true numb^r of inhabited houses, is not much above 1200,000.[17] And indeed upon comparing the Acco^t of

7,533 Houses. But allowing 533 for ye ground contained within the Bills of Mortality; Then there must be deducted for Middx but 7000 Houses. So that London & Westm^r should contain 104,000 Houses besides Southwark & that part of Surrey within ye Bills of Mortality.—

		a^o 1693		—	a^o 1693
Which are these Parishes	St. George Southw.	402	Lambeth		306
	St. Olave Southw.	741	Bermondsey		387
	St. Saviour Southw.	567	Newington		249
	St. Tho. Southw.	96	Rotherhith		152
		1806			1094

1806
1094

2900 ⎫
——— ⎬ which is a 7th pt. of ye whole or 15,000 houses.—But a^o 1690 not above an 8th
20959 ⎭ part of ye whole or 13,000 houses.

Now as I remember Mr. Adams took ye Houses in ye Bills of Mortality Circ. ann. 1680 to be 105,000 Since which time to ye year 1690 in Ten years the people have Encreased 64,000 and Consequently ye Houses have Encreased 11,000 at near 6 to a House, the building being better than ye Comon Rank, which makes Houses in London & Bills of Mortality a^o 1690 to be 116,000. Again If London & Westm^r and such part of ye Bills of Mortality as are within Middx (ye County of Middx excluded) do contain 104,000 houses, and ye parishes in Surrey 13,000, Then ye Bills of Mortality did contain 117.000 houses a^o 1690 And now in 1695 are Increased 5000 Houses more and contain 122.000 Houses, So that in a round number they may be computed at 120.000 Houses. at 5 to a House which makes 600.000 people.

King's final version gave 105,000 inhabited houses and, allowing for under-enumeration, 527,560 people.

[17] The reference to 'ye Author' is to (C. Davenant), *An Essay Upon Ways and Means of Supplying the War*, London 1695. The data referred to, given in the table facing p. 76, cover houses and hearths as shown in the hearth books of Lady Day 1690. Davenant's table was widely quoted by eighteenth-century writers. But neither in the book referred to above, nor in *An Essay upon the Probable Methods of Making a People Gainers in the Ballance of Trade*, London, 1699, did Davenant query the hearth-tax total. In fact, in the former book, he took 1·3 million houses or families (confusing the two) as the basis and multiplied by a ratio of 6 persons per house to get a total population of nearly 8 millions. It is clear, too, from the latter book, p. 24, that he did not fully understand King's work, for describing King's results he says: 'What he says concerning the Number of the People to be 5,500,000 is no positive Assertion, nor shall we pretend any where to determin in that Matter; what he lays down is by way of Hypothesis, That supposing the Inhabitants of *England* to have been, *Anno* 1300, Two Millions 860,000 Heads, by the orderly Series of Increase allow'd of by all Writers, they may probably be about *Anno* 1700 Five Millions 500,000 Heads; but if they were *An.* 1300 either less or more, the Case must proportionably alter; . . . .' But this was not King's own view. It is clear that he regarded the estimate of 5·5 millions as his basic fact, and the past and future rates of increase as fitting in with that fact but not determining it. See G. E. Barnett's edition of King, p. 25. King's reference in the Kashnor MS. to Davenant's opinion perhaps relates to a personal discussion with Davenant, prompted by Harley's queries.

Incidentally, the Burns journal appears to answer a question raised by Barnett, namely, when and how Davenant first saw King's estimates. Barnett points out (*op. cit.*, p. 5) that Davenant referred to

Rutlandshire, wch I took myself from the Hearth Books A^o 1678. with the Acco^t publisht by that Author, the Number will scarce reach above 1250,000. The Account is Thus.

		Houses	Chimnys
Rutlandshire	1678	3072	5805
	1690	3661	5998
	diff.	589	193

Now to make up ye numb^r of 589 houses, wch is the difference between that Authors Acco^t & mine in 12 years, I allow—

1. For Houses omitted or New Discoveries 1 in 12—   300
2. For Increase in that County for 12 years 1 in 400 yearly   89
3. For names of Places &c. reckon'd as houses 1 in 18   200
                                                                  ———
                                                                  589

So that ye Deductions for this last Article being 200 in 3661 or 1 in 18 the Deductions in 1319000 Houses in ye Kingdom in general will be ab^t 74000. And consequently the true numb^r of Houses A^o 1690 1245000 To wch adding 7000 for the increase of Houses between 1690 & 1695, makes the number of Houses A^o 1695 but 1252,000. But deducting further ab^t 27000 for Empty houses, vizt 8000 in Lond^n at 8 p. cent. & 19 or 20000 more for the rest of Engl^d wch is little above 2 p.cent in general, there remains for inhabited houses but about 1225000.—[18]

King thus concluded, on reconsidering the question, that the figure of 1,319,215 'houses', used as the starting-point of his population estimate, was too high, the exaggeration being the result of careless addition by the person transcribing the data from the hearth books. Certainly the reduction of this figure by one-eighteenth, to about 1·246 millions, would bring it more nearly in line with the other contemporary total, that of 1·176 millions reported by John Houghton, though the resemblance may be fortuitous.[19] But disregarding for the moment the possible increase in the number of houses between 1690 and 1695, King's revised estimate would, by his own account, still seem too high, for while making an allowance for empty houses, it allowed nothing for subdivision. As shown in an earlier citation, King himself claimed that, according to the assessments on taxes, empty houses constituted about 2 or 2½ per cent of all houses. In the absence of other evidence we must accept this for the moment,[20] though it would seem from a manuscript in the Public Record

King's work as early as 15 July 1696, in a manuscript entitled 'A memorial Concerning Creditt'. The Burns journal contains an earlier version of King's *Observations*, entitled 'Some Observations arising from the Knowledge of ye true Number in England, and such other Circumstances as have been Collected by Gr. King Esqr a^o 1695. Dtt. to Dr Dav. June 96' (Burns journal, p. 221). This was presumably the version originally seen by Davenant, though it is clear from internal evidence that he must also have seen the final version.

[18] Kashnor MS., p. 3.

[19] On Houghton's statistics see the Appendix to the present paper. It should be noted, however, that Houghton's statistics are described by Pepys as referring to 'names', that is, the number of names of occupiers. If that is true, they would also need to be reduced to give the number of inhabited houses.

[20] The proportion is lower than that shown in the 1801 census of England and Wales (*Population Abstract*, pp. 451 and 496), namely, about 3½ per cent. There is some contemporary evidence, for, as King said, the empty houses were stated in the hearth-tax rolls. Thus the 1664 roll for Surrey (C. A. F. Meekings, *Surrey Hearth Tax 1664*, Surrey Record Society, nos. XLI, XLII, London 1940,

Office that King subsequently tried to obtain direct evidence of the proportion of empty houses, as well as of the degree of subdivision.[21] It is evident, however, that at the time of writing the *Observations*, King had no data relating to subdivision, and we can only guess at the extent. Jones and Judges's ratios for London—107 families per 100 houses within the walls and 121 per 100 without—may be too high for the country as a whole. But even a ratio of 105 per 100 would bring down the number of houses, as distinct from households, to about 1·187 millions, and allowing 2 per cent for empty houses the revised total of inhabited houses would be about 1·16 millions. Assuming that King was correct in estimating the increase between 1690 and 1695, the result would still be only about 1·17 million inhabited houses, substantially below the figure used in the *Observations*.[22]

The Kashnor and other MSS. also give a certain amount of fresh information on another point of major importance—the validity of the basic population data collected under the 1694 Act and used by King to construct his series of ratios of persons per house. It has already been pointed out that the 1694 Act provided in some detail for the annual enumeration of the population of England and Wales, as well as for comprehensive vital registration. The detail involved, and the efforts made after 1694 to improve the administration of the statistical side of the Act, suggest, especially in relation to the possible financial yield of the tax, that the government may perhaps have been as much concerned with the collection of population statistics as with fiscal objectives. It is true that the 1694 Act and the subsequent related legislation do not refer to demographic statistics as an objective. But popular superstition alone—the

pp. lxxxix *et seq.*; for some areas the data of the returns have been used, where the roll material was not available) gives 351 empty houses out of a total of 17,292 (chargeable and non-chargeable occupiers, plus empty houses), or 2 per cent. (It should be noted that the data for Southwark are not included in Meeking's edition.) In fact, even if the statement of empty houses is complete, the percentage would be a little above 2, for the chargeable and non-chargeable names would need to be reduced to obtain inhabited houses. Similarly, the Suffolk tax records for 1674 (S. H. A. Hervey, *Suffolk in 1674 being the Hearth Tax Returns*, Suffolk Green Books, no. x., Vol. 13, 1905, p. xxix) show 665 empty houses out of a total of 29,125 (composed as for Surrey), or about 2·3 per cent. Thus King's figure of 2-2½ per cent does not seem unrealistic, though it would need to be checked by analysing far more hearth-tax records.

There is also the question of whether empty houses had already been excluded from Davenant's figures. But if they had been derived from the official transcript it is highly probable that they included empty houses. It is difficult to decide how far the 1801 census proportion is comparable with King's estimate. According to the *Population Abstract*, p. 496, of the houses returned as uninhabited, 'many are ruinous and uninhabitable; and in many Counties the Uninhabited Houses, are said to be mostly Houses now building, and consequently not yet habitable'. The only hearth-tax reference of which I am aware, that in the transcript of the 1674 Suffolk material, states that houses recently burned down or demolished were included in the empty houses.

[21] King manuscripts, P.R.O., T64/302, 'The Names of the People in Harfield near Uxbridge in Com. Middx. with their ages—Taken ye latter End of Oct. 1699'. King's summary of the returns lists 109 inhabited and 8 empty houses—almost 7 per cent of all houses being empty—and specifies 122 families living in the 109 inhabited houses, or 1·12 families per house. The 1801 census of England and Wales (*Population Abstract*, pp. 496-7) gives a ratio of 1·2 families per inhabited house. But the census report states that 'no great Reliance' can be placed upon the results, for 'in many Counties it has been variously understood, in others not replied to; in the latter Case the Number of Families has been presumed to be, that of Inhabited Houses'.

[22] It is not, of course, conclusive that King's second thoughts were more nearly correct than his first, and the discussion in the appendix raises a number of questions in this connexion. The lower figure found by Adams might be explained by a less complete return, or at least explained in part by this. On the other hand, Davenant's figures do show a very low ratio of hearths to occupiers, and this might be explained if the numbers of hearths, chargeable, non-chargeable and unoccupied, were obtained from the financial audit, with the number of occupiers being derived from the kind of incorrect summarizing process described by King.

fear of incurring divine wrath, a fear mentioned during the debate on the 1753 Population Bill—would explain this. Certainly the Act of Indemnity, 4 and 5 Anne, c. 23, passed to save the clergy from the financial penalties to which they were liable for inadequate discharge of the duties laid upon them by the legislation, was somewhat mysterious in its reference to the 'several Parsons Vicars and Curates and other Ecclesiastical Persons not being sufficiently apprized of the full Import of the said Acts of Parliament . . .'.[23] And this impression would appear to be supported by the views of an unidentified writer who contributed to the attack on the 1753 Population Bill.[24]

This does not, however, mean that the statistics were comprehensive or exact. And, indeed, the passing of an Act of Indemnity implies that the registration statistics at least were not complete. The reliability of the material was a point raised by Harley. He commented: 'It is to be doubted these Assessm^{ts} [on marriages, births, etc.] are no very good Foundation', and he added: 'In many Counties especially remote from London, Some from Superstition of numbring the People, Others from other Reasons, were less exact than in London.[25] King's reply falls into two parts. First,

> The Assesm^{ts} on Marriages Births & Buryalls are the best Foundation Wee yet have for adjusting the numb^r of Souls to each house. Tho' generally they are very imperfectly taken. For in many places They made no Assessments of Names, but only a Schedule of Rates: In other places the Batchelors & Widdowers only are taken notice of, In others many Servants & Children omitted, and sometimes whole Familys; In others the Houses & Families are not distinguisht one frõ another. However I find many of them very Regular, and for greater Certainty I made particuler Enquiries into the defects of some of ye best of 'em: and from their Concurrence in ye several Pticulers of married Couples, Widows & Widowers, Children Servants & Sojourners, I am morally certain that if ye numb^r of inhabited houses may be depended on, as I think it may, to be between 1240 & 1280m. The number of Souls actually in Engl^d at any one time is much about 5,400,000, vizt not less than 5,200M. nor more than 5,600M.

---

[23] Section x of the Act.
[24] *A letter to a Member of Parliament, on the Registering and Numbering the People of Great Britain*, London 1753, p. 7: 'As you know I am now very aged, I remember when the Numbering the People in King *William's* Time was attempted with the greatest Care imaginable. Mr. *Lock*, Sir *Isaac Newton*, and other great and curious Men were then alive. And to render the Thing effectual, it was thought that giving the Government a Poll-Tax would make the Matter be carefully executed. The Poll-Tax was pass'd; but those great Men found, that notwithstanding all the Endeavours of the Government, no Foundation could be laid upon the Numbers returned.' According to J. S. Burn, *The History of Parish Registers in England*, 2nd ed., London 1862, p. 111, n. 1, the inclusion in the 1694 Act of special provisions for registering the vital statistics of the nobility was inspired by a petition of the College of Arms, wishing to have the authority to register certificates of the marriages, births and deaths, etc., of the nobility and gentry. Burn says: 'The Ministry, however, at that time distressed for ways and means to raise the great demands they had for money to carry on an extensive war, instead of listening to the reasonableness of the matter, made it a *Money Bill* to supply the exigencies of state. . . .' It is known, however, that a proposal for raising money by such taxes was also put forward by Richard Frith (*Calendar of Treasury Papers, 1556-7 to 1696*, London 1868, p. 481, item 63). In any case the College of Arms, in reply to a personal inquiry, have stated that the special registers for the nobility and gentry do not seem ever to have been compiled.
[25] Kashnor MS., p. 3. In Harl. MSS. 7021, fol. 46, the following version of this query is given: 'Omissions in the Countrey probably are greater then in London, because numbring the people is more terrible in the countrey then in Lond^n The polls are instances, familys of 7 or 8 persons being not numbered at above 3 or 4 in some remote countys.'

Secondly,

As to the Country Assessm.ts. I am certain that where they were anything regular, they were more exact than those in London, For the Parishes in England having at a Medium but 130 houses to each parish, containing about 550 Souls, there is scarce an Assessor but knows every man, woman and child in the parish, which is much otherwise in London, where the Parishes have One with another 800 houses, and 4000 Souls, And where an Assessor shall scarce know 5 Families on each side of him. So that I am of opinion My Allowance for the Omissions in those Regular Assessments (for it was such only that I could make any use of) is very near the matter.[26]

There is, of course, no independent evidence of the accuracy of the more 'regular' assessments. Nevertheless, there are grounds for accepting King's view that they give a reasonable account of the population of the particular areas concerned. For some of the areas for which the original returns are available, the enumeration seems to have been carried out with substantial care and conscientiousness. This certainly appears to be the case for Bristol[27] and Melbourne (Derbyshire),[28] places to which King did not refer, while Jones and Judges are of the opinion that the London survey 'was, almost throughout the City, conducted with more diligence and with fuller results than was usual in the period', and indeed that it was 'carried out with greater thoroughness than the earliest modern census examinations.[29] The return for Harefield (Middlesex) may owe its apparent thoroughness to King's direct intervention, and this is almost certainly so for the Lichfield (Staffordshire) list, to which further reference will be made. It is also clear from correspondence concerning the Lichfield results that in this case King did pay considerable attention to the defects in the material and addressed many queries to the person responsible for the assessment.[30] There is no evidence that King addressed similar queries to the assessors of other areas than Lichfield. But the journals in the Public Record Office and in the L.C.C. library give abundant testimony to King's methodical nature and to his concern for detail. There is no reason to suppose that he did not at least consider and attempt to allow for the deficiencies of specific returns.[31] Further, the Lichfield, Harefield, Melbourne and Bristol material also show that these enumerations were undoubtedly carried out house by house, the name of each inhabitant being specified. The following excerpts from the

[26] Kashnor MS., p. 3.

[27] Miss E. Ralph, of the Bristol Archives Department, kindly allowed me to obtain photographs of these returns, which cover all the parishes of Bristol. Some of the returns were entered on sheets with headings specially printed (in Bristol) for the purpose. The population totals obtained by analysing these Bristol returns amount to 8,519 males and 10,625 females (19,403 persons in all, including 259 persons of unspecified sex). It is possible that some names have been missed in the parish of St. Thomas, since for this parish the ends of a number of pages are torn. But it is unlikely that the omissions are very substantial.

[28] See the details in R. E. Chester Waters, 'A statutory list of the inhabitants of Melbourne, Derbyshire, in 1695', J. Derbyshire Arch. Nat. Hist. Soc., January 1885, pp.1-30.

[29] Op. cit., p. 48.

[30] The letter—or, rather, an extract from it—to a Mr Lamb, who seems to have been responsible for the Lichfield enumeration, is in the Harl. MSS., no. 6839, fol. 158. It is discussed later.

[31] In the Burns journal, p. 58, King raises a query concerning the results for St. Katherine's Tower, London, arguing that the assessors returned the 'divided houses' (i.e. households) as 'so many distinct houses'.

returns for Harefield[32] and Bristol illustrate the range of variation in the detail given in the surveys. In the Harefield survey each house is shown separately and an attempt made to obtain the ages of the inhabitants. The Bristol returns, on the other hand, do not distinguish the houses or provide any information on ages. Nevertheless, the Bristol returns do name each inhabitant.

Finally, in the case of the City of London, for which only summary totals are given in the King manuscripts,[33] comparison between those totals and the statistics extracted by Jones and Judges from the detailed Guildhall records (for 1695) show, in almost all cases, a very close agreement, indicating that King must have used the original returns or else have obtained accurate copies. The general impression made by all this material is, therefore, that it was fairly solidly based. Clearly it could not have been perfect, but it is important to remember that even a modern census is, in some degree, inaccurate. King was no doubt right to make some allowance for under-enumeration, though the specific allowance chosen—10 per cent in London and the Bills of Mortality, 2 per cent in the other cities and towns, and 1 per cent in the villages and hamlets—was not explicitly justified and is not likely to have been based upon any empirical assessment of the omissions. In all, however, the basic data appear to be far more reliable than any other contemporary material, and may even be more accurate than some of the local enumerations undertaken for the 1801 census.[34]

(a) Harefield.

				Age
	1.	At the place, S.ᵗ R.ᵈ Newdigates .		
		Mat. Heyward Bayliff & Tenᵗ .		42
		Ann his wife		43
		⌠ Susan		20
		⎮ ———— a son dead would have been 18		
		⎮ Eliz		16½
ch.		⎨ Agnes		11 fere
		⎮ Tho.	9 8½	9
		⎮ Mat.	9 7	8 fere
		⌡ Anne		4
		⌠ Mary Weedon		26
ser.		⌡ Anne Lathom sojournᵗ gone . .		12½
		⌠ John Clark, Gardner . . .		39
ser.		⎨ John Birch Husb. man . . .		18
		⌡ Tho. Paie Husb. man . . .		21
	2.	John Hanyan Esq.ᵗ		55
		Susanna his wife		55
ch.		⌠ Henry, Bach		30
		⌡ Eliz.		22

---

[32] P.R.O. bundle. I should explain that in this case the ages are given only for a proportion of the population. But the details of household composition are given for all households, and the 'doubled-up' households are indicated. The Melbourne and Bristol returns do not give ages, but list each inhabitant by name. The Lichfield returns are as detailed as those for Harefield, and give the age of almost every individual.

[33] P.R.O. bundle.

[34] Certainly there were many complaints of the inaccuracy of the 1801 census. Thus John Heysham wrote, as regards the enumeration of the Carlisle population: 'The survey of 1801, I have reason to think, was made in a slovenly manner: 1811 is tolerably accurate . . .' (H. Lonsdale, The Life of John Heysham, M.D., 1870, p. 141). Malthus was also inclined to believe that the 1801 census understated the population, this view being based on an estimate of the probable population growth between 1801 and 1811 (Essay on the Principle of Population, 5th ed., London 1817, Vol. II, pp. 93 ff.).

ser.	{ Charles Henson	23
	{ Rob? Cholmley	20
	Anne Lee	22
	Dorothy Hill	20
	Eliz. Pierce	20

3.	Franc Ashby gent	40
	Judith his wife	37
	Judith Turner her moth? widow .	60
ch.	{ Sarah	6
	{ William	3½
	. . . . Nash . . . .
ser.	{ George Living . . . .
	{ Rowland Clark . . . .
ser.	{ Audry Nichols . . . .
	{ Sarah Osmund . . . .
	Jane Gladman M?ˢ Turners maid .

4.	Eliz. Baldwin wid. Alehouse .	61
	Sarah Eve or Eves grandch. . .	3
ser.	Eliz. Rice	19
	Tho. Robinson Sojourn? gone .	5

5.	Frances Bennet wid. of James .	60
	Frances her daur	27[35]

(b) *Bristol: St. Peter's Parish.*

John Brown and Elizabeth his wife.
Sarah Brown and Joseph Martin Servts.
George Arthur and Rachell his wife.
John Parnall and Mary James Servants.
Margarett Rennalls Widow.
John Green and Jonathan Wear child.
Susan Pegter & Thomas Bryant Servts.
Thomas Jenkins Bachor.
William Parnell and Mary his wife.
Robert William & Elizabeth children.
Joan Doane Servant.

Unfortunately, however sound the local enumerations carried out under the 1694 Act, the returns available to King covered only a few areas. For London the statistics were limited to seventeen of the 110 parishes of the City, and to a number of districts beyond the City limits, namely, Hackney, Shoreditch, Stepney, the Tower parishes, Stratford and Bow, and the Tower Hamlets. Outside London, according to the King manuscripts so far traced, the proportionate representation of urban and rural communities was even more limited. Of the larger towns, Norwich was the sole representative (the Bristol returns not being noted among King's references), while the smaller were confined to Gloucester, Lichfield, Sevenoaks (Kent), Barnet (Herts), Coleshill (Warwick), Burntwood (Essex), Culliton and Kingsbridge (Devon) and Buckfastleigh (Devon). The Burns journal also gives the population of Salisbury, but this appears to relate to the year 1700 and, if so, could not have been taken

[35] It is clear from the P.R.O. journal and other material in the P.R.O. bundle that the returns for Sevenoaks (Kent) and South Weald (Essex) were also derived from a house by house enumeration. This is also true for Buckfastleigh and Ringmore, and, according to Jones and Judges, for the City of London.

into account in King's *Observations*.[36] The rural districts are the least well represented in the available King manuscripts, though King's reply to Harley's comments on the reliability of the rural data might be interpreted—the inter-

TABLE I

Parish statistics used in King's London estimate

	Houses	People	People to a house	Yearly burials	Yearly (a) part buried
Allhallows Breadstreet	085	512	6·	21	24⅓
St. Andrew Wardrobe	108	505	4·7	53	9·6
St. Anne Aldersgate	145	852	5·88	41	21·0
St. Bennet Gracechurch	065	396	6·	11	36·
St. Botolph Billingsgate	060	350	5·8	11	32
St. John Zachary	083	475	5·72	14	34
St. Bennet Paulswharf	124	562	4·5	44	12·8
	670	3,652	5·4	195	18·74
St. Bridgets Parish (b)	1,241	5,145	4·15	345	15·
St. Botolph Aldersgate	1,241	4,966	4·	206	24·1
St. Dunstans West	0,437	2,671	6·1	253	10·6
St. Giles Cripplegate	1,842	8,528	4·6¼	1,439	5·92
Trinity Minories	0,131	0,538	4·1	024	22·4
	4,892	21,848	4·47	2,267	9·64
St. Dunstan Stepney	8,680	39,302	4·6	2,161	18·2
St. John at Hackney	0,535	2,896	5·4	085	34·
St. John Wapping	1,496	5,530	3·7	189	29·3
St. Katharines Tower	0,743	1,614	2·18	150	10·8
St. Leonard Shoreditch	1,585	6,629	4·18	500	13·26
St. Mary Whitechapell	2,583	11,439	4·4	1,090	10·5
St. Paul Shadwell	1,443	7,891	5·4	460	17·2
	17,065	75,301	4·413	4,635	15·13
The 7 parishes wth in the walls	0,670	3,652	5·4	195	18·74
The 5 parishes wth out ye walls	4,892	21,848	4·47	2,267	9·64
The 7 Out Par. in Middx (& Surr.)	17,065	75,301	4·413	4,635	15·13
	22,627	100,801	4·445	7,097	14·2

(a) These rates are, of course, 1 in 24⅓, 1 in 9·6, etc., not rates of 24·3 or 9·6 per 1000.

(b) St. Bride, according to the Jones and Judges tabulation.

Throughout the table the headings given are those used by King.

pretation would perhaps need to be generous—as implying a wider range of enumerations than has so far come to light.[37]

Moreover, the statistics collected by Jones and Judges show that, for the

[36] The Buckfastleigh return given in King's summary may also be later than 1696. The enumeration sheets in the Harl. MSS. are dated 1698, but it is possible that the summary total in the Burns journal refers to an earlier year.

[37] The main collection of places and populations is given in the Burns journal, pp. 90-92, and is summarized in my earlier paper on King's work. It should be emphasized that the Burns journal may be one of a number of such volumes (the Burns journal is labelled G.K. no. 51), but I have found no trace of the others.

City of London, the sample of parishes actually used by King was not a representative one. It understated the ratio of persons per house. Jones and Judges note that their figure of 6·1 persons per house for the ninety-seven parishes within the walls was about the same as King's revised figure of 'almost 6'.[38] But this latter figure included a 10 per cent inflation to account for persons omitted from the enumerations; King's uncorrected ratio was only 5·4. At the same time, the computations in the Burns journal leave little doubt that King did not use the data for all the parishes for which he had returns; he omitted six of the thirteen parishes within the walls. The data which King appears to have used in constructing his estimates are given in Table 1, and exclude the returns for St. Clement, Eastcheap; St. Gregory by St. Paul's; St. Margaret, New Fish Street; St. Michael Bassishaw, St. Peter, Cornhill; and St. Stephen, Coleman Street.[39] The returns for these latter parishes are shown in Table 2. Although King does not explain why those six parishes were excluded, the answer is obtained by comparing the Burns journal data with the parish returns contained in the P.R.O. bundle—King had not obtained burial statistics for those parishes, though why this was so is far from evident. Perhaps because he anticipated that his London returns would be incomplete, King apparently intended to arrive at an estimate of the population not only by applying ratios of persons per house to the hearth-tax statistics of 'houses', but also—probably as a check—by calculating a series of burial rates and by applying these to the numbers of burials recorded in the Bills of Mortality. The burial statistics reproduced in Table 1 are, according to the P.R.O. list, the annual averages for 1683 and 1684, suggesting either that King could not wait for the death registration statistics specified by the 1694 Act, or that he did not regard them as more satisfactory than the statistics already available.[40] In the Burns journal calculations, King took a total of 24,000 burials per year for the whole of London (including the parishes in Westminster, as well as those in Middlesex and Surrey) and obtained population estimates ranging from 503,000 to 528,000, depending upon the mortality rate used.[41]

But the use of the burial rate method introduced further problems, for King was not satisfied that the rates for the parishes listed in Table 1 were representative. He argued that St. Andrew Wardrobe, St. Bennet Paul's Wharf, St. Katherine Tower and St. Mary Whitechapel 'have fewest People to a house but do bury most'; that St. Botolph Aldersgate, Trinity Minories and St. John Wapping 'have fewest people to a house & bury fewest'; and that St. Dunstans

---

[38] Op. cit., p. 55.

[39] See Burns journal, pp. 58-62. The parish names, column headings and statistics are as stated by King.

[40] Probably both causes were relevant. The registration returns for 1695-6, the first year of operation, were no doubt particularly defective (cf. Jones and Judges, op. cit., p. 47). But the terms of the 1694 Act would tend to increase the omission of burials from the records, as compared with births, since the duties on the burials of members of families in receipt of relief were chargeable to the parish poor-law funds. This was not the case with births. On the other point, as most of King's calculations were done in 1696, he could not have waited for the less defective returns of 1696-7.

[41] This figure of about 24,000 burials included an allowance of 1,000 for omissions. In some of the calculations, the total of 23,000 was used, being apparently a rounded version of 22,530, the average for 1683 and 1684, as stated by King in the P.R.O. list of parishes. This is slightly higher than the figures given in (Heberden), A Collection of the Yearly Bills of Mortality, London 1759, for the years 1683 and 1684, namely, 20,587 and 23,202, with an average of just under 22,000. But these figures cover the periods from 19 December 1682 to 16 December 1684. Since deaths were rising in 1684, a calendar year basis (if by any chance King used this) would yield a slightly higher average.

T ABLE 2

*Statistics for parishes apparently excluded from King's estimate of
the population of the ninety-seven parishes*[42]

	Houses	People	(Persons per house)
St. Clement Eastcheap	60	0372	6·2
St. Gregories by Pauls	282	1661	5·9
St. Marg^t. New Fish Street	73	461	$6\frac{1}{3}$
St. Michael Bassishaw	149	846	$5\frac{2}{3}$
St. Peter Cornhill	186	1111	6 feré
St. Steven Colemanstreet	429	2713	$6\frac{1}{3}$

West and St. Giles Cripplegate had most people to a house and buried most.
He concluded:

> So that omitting those 9 parishes above mentioned as being anomalous,
> the other midling Parishes will stand thus

	People to a house	Rat. of Mort.
In y^e 97 par.	5·88	26·3
16 cir.	5	21
14 cir.	4·63	17·7[43]

Hence the burial rate for the ninety-seven parishes within the walls was to be
based upon the statistics for five parishes. This was, however, only the starting-
point for further calculations. With his propensity to modify and smooth
the statistics—and the manuscripts testify only too fully to that habit—King
then tried various amendments to the rates, and one table, noted as giving 'the
best proportions', specifies burial rates of 1 in 23·2, 1 in 21·$\frac{3}{4}$ and 1 in 21·5
instead of the rates given in the citation above.[44]

Perhaps it was because of the small number of 'satisfactory' parishes retained in calculating the burial rates, and the tenuous basis of the subsequent
modifications, that King did not use this method in his final estimate, as put
forward in the *Observations*, of the population of London or England and Wales.
Nevertheless, there is a marked similarity between his final ratios of persons
per house for London and the ratios given in Table 1 and in the subsequent
citation. This is brought out more clearly in Table 3 below, from which it
would seem very probable that the nineteen parishes in Table 1 formed the
basis of the uncorrected estimate, and almost as if the results for the still more
restricted number of parishes (ten in all) had suggested to King the 10 per cent
correction factor used in his final estimate. In fact the gyrations followed were
hardly necessary to provide a more or less acceptable ratio for the City within
the walls (the ninety-seven parishes). Had King based himself on the original
thirteen parishes within the walls, for which he had the statistics of houses and
persons, he would have obtained a ratio of 5·85 persons per house, almost the
same as that yielded by his subsequent manipulation. But comparison with the

[42] These are from the King MS. entitled 'An Extract of the Number of Houses and People from
ye Assem^t upon Marriages Births and Burials a^o Dni. 1695', P.R.O. bundle.
[43] Burns journal, p. 58.
[44] *Ibid.*, p. 61.

Jones and Judges results suggests that King's manipulation of the London material did at least tend in the right direction. His final estimates for the ninety-seven parishes within the walls and for the sixteen parishes without are remarkably close to the ratios obtained by Jones and Judges from their much more nearly complete set of returns.

TABLE 3

King's ratios of persons per house in London

	The Observations (a)		The Burns journal		Jones and Judges's (b) ratios
	Un-corrected	Allowing 10 per cent under-enumeration	From Table 1	From the later citation	
1. 97 parishes within the walls	5·4	'almost 6' [5·9]	5·4	5·88	6·1
2. 16 parishes without the walls	4·6	'above 5' [5·1]	4·47	5·	5·1 (c)
3. 15 out parishes (Middlesex and Surrey)	4·4	'above 4·8' [4·8]	4·413	4·63	—
4. 7 parishes in City and liberty of Westminster	4·3	'almost 4¾' [4·7]	—	—	—

(a) Barnett edition, pp. 17-18. The figures in square brackets are the rates calculated directly from King's data on houses and population.

(b) *Op. cit.*, pp. 61 and 62.

(c) In the case of Jones and Judges, the data refer only to thirteen parishes and precincts, and appear to cover about a third of the population embraced by King's final estimate. King's data are intended to cover, in addition, St. George, Southwark; St. Saviour, Southwark; St. Thomas, Southwark; and Trinity, Minories. *Cf.* King's list of Parishes in the P.R.O bundle.

On the ratio for Westminster, the Jones and Judges data can throw no light. At one point in the Burns journal,[45] King gives a figure of 4·8 persons per house, very close to his final estimate of 'almost 4¾'. At another point he offers a much lower figure, 4·2¼ persons per house,[46] close to his first uncorrected estimate of 4·3. But no justification is offered for either estimate in the manuscripts so far studied. It is unlikely, in view of King's general procedure in this field of estimation, that the two figures are simply unreasoned guesses. But certainly no factual basis has yet been established.

This is equally true of King's ratios for the rest of England and Wales. King divided the remaining territory into two categories, 'other cities and market towns', and 'villages and hamlets'. For the former, his uncorrected and corrected ratios were respectively, 4·3 and 'almost 4·4' persons per house, while for the latter the corresponding figures were 4·0 and 4·04.[47] But no direct justification for these factors has been found. Here, too, it may be that the factual basis and detailed computations and adjustments were contained in other manuscripts not yet traced or no longer in existence. This is not improbable, for even where the basic data are far from adequate or, as in some

---

[45] p. 59.   [46] p. 61.

[47] *Observations*, Barnett ed., pp. 17-18. In fact, the corrected figure for villages and hamlets is given as 4·4, and it appears as such in the Kashnor MS. and in the Chalmers edition. But this must have been due to a copyist's mistake. The Burns journal, p. 160, gives it as 4·04, which is what, arithmetically, it should be.

instances, quite hypothetical, King usually puts forward several sets of calculations. It is not in keeping with the material in the available working papers for there to be no reference at all to the procedures followed in trying to arrive at an acceptable result; King is often inexplicit, but he is not taciturn. At

TABLE 4

King's data on persons per house in town and country

	No. of houses	Population	Persons per house
Urban:			
Lichfield, Staffs	655	3,038	
Sevenoaks, Kent (*a*)	366	1,573	
Barnet, Herts	176	850	
Coleshill, town and parish, Warwick	245	1,109	
Burntwood, Essex (*b*)	260	1,170	
Norwich, Norfolk	(6790)	28,546	
Culliton, Devon	237	1,554	
Kingsbridge, Devon	122	686	
Gloucester, Glos	1,126	4,756	
St. Stephen's, Exon (cum Bedford) (*c*)	69	443	
St. Mary, Ye Moore, Exon (*c*)	255	1,820	
St. Thomas parish, Devon (*c*)	309	1,705	
Holy Cross ats Abbey parish in Shrewsbury (*d*)	222 (*e*)	935	
	10,832	48,185	4·45
Rural:			
Swepston and Heather parishes, Leics	73	279	
Fetherston Const., Staffs	14	65	
Atcham, etc., Salop	68	343	
Shustoke parish, Warwick	59	275	
Eynsford Hundred, Norfolk	(1500) (*f*)	5,880	
Widworthy, Devon	96	255	
	1,810	7,097	3·92

(*a*) Including Riverhead and the Weald.

(*b*) Including Brookstreet Hamlet and the Uplands.

(*c*) I am informed by Mr C. F. Meekings of the Public Record Office, that these parishes were part of urban Exeter.

(*d*) Mr Meekings pointed out that this parish was part of urban Shrewsbury.

(*e*) King also says 'circa 230 houses', but uses 222 in his own table.

(*f*) King gives the original figure of 1,437 houses, but adds 'rather 1,500', and uses the latter figure in his own table. The area is said to consist of 30 villages 'whereof 2 are market towns', but no details are given.

present, however, the only specific calculations for areas outside London, are those summarized in my previous paper, which also gave, by way of illustration, three of the apparently tentative schemes tried out by King in estimating the population of the rest of England and Wales.[48] There is no obvious link between the schemes and the statistics. The schemes follow, with some variation, the pattern shown in King's answer to Harley's query on the allocation of houses between London and the rest of the country. Though there are differences between the individual schemes, they have one important feature in common, the steady fall in the ratio of persons per house with a fall in size of

[48] Glass, *op. cit.*, pp. 178-9.

community. For example, in one scheme the ratio of persons per house is shown to fall consistently from 4·4 for cities with 4000 houses, to 3·993 for 'vills' of forty-five houses each. And this is also in keeping with the trend of the ratios for London, highest for the City, and falling towards the outer segments. The specific statistics cited by King do not, however, seem to show this consistent trend for the urban sub-groups. It is difficult to be definite about what trend is shown, for there is insufficient guidance as to exactly which boundaries King used for his 'other cities and market towns'—for example, whether the Weald of Sevenoaks was included in the town, or the Uplands in South Weald were included with Burntwood town (Essex). But as has already been noted, King did not use this detailed subdivision in his final estimates. Instead he adopted the broad distinction between other towns (other cities and market towns) and the country (the villages and hamlets). Taking King's statistics of places outside of London, given in my previous paper, and allocating those places to town and country in accordance with Adams's *Index Villaris*, Table 4 is obtained.

It will be seen that the crude average for the urban communities is 4·45 persons per house, while that for the rural areas is 3·92. Thus the averages derived from the data in Table 4 are in fact quite close to the ratios given by King in his *Observations*.

It is important to emphasize that there is no evidence in the King manuscripts to suggest that the statistics for the communities outside London were used in such a manner. The analysis given in Table 4 is hypothetical in that respect. Indeed, there is no direct evidence in the King documents so far studied that these particular statistics were used at all in constructing the ratios for the other cities and market towns and for the rest of the country. There is only a presumption, so to speak, that since this type of material was demonstrably used for the London ratios, similar statistics probably formed the basis of the other ratios. At the same time there is no direct appeal, as there is for London itself, to a larger collection of contemporary statistics to demonstrate the way in which, and the validity with which, they were used for arriving at ratios of persons per house. Such a direct comparison cannot be made until many more of the returns under the 1694 Act have been found and analysed.

Although the present inability to examine in detail King's ratios for the other cities, market towns and villages means a serious weakness in the analysis, it is nevertheless possible to discuss the ratios from a slightly different point of view and at least to consider whether those ratios are compatible with what can be established from external data. For example, it is possible to use the results of the 1801 census—the nearest in time to King's period—to see whether the kind of gradation applied by King can be substantiated from the data of the first of the periodic censuses. Further, data for subsequent censuses can also be used with the object of seeing if the kind of pattern found in 1801 was transitory, or continued to be a feature of population and housing distribution in England and Wales. Clearly, if the 1801 pattern, whatever it may be, continues to apply throughout the nineteenth century, in spite of the very substantial changes in the economy and in the geographic distribution of the population, there is at least a presumption that such a pattern constitutes a relatively stable attribute of English society.

A major difficulty in analysing this census material is the definition and selection of urban communities. In view of the impact of changes in population and socio-economic structure, it would not be appropriate to apply a single definition at all points of time. Until, therefore, a good deal more work has been done on the analysis of urban development and particularly on the significance of urban communities of various sizes in their historical context, there is something to be said for defining towns as places regarded as being such in the official statistics for the separate points of time studied. This raises various questions, but it does at least make it easier to obtain the relevant statistics. Thus in analysing the census returns for the nineteenth century, the definitions of London and of the other towns in England and Wales have been those found in the successive census reports. What this involves is shown in the notes to Table 5, which summarizes the analysis. In addition, it seemed of some interest to see what relationship would emerge if, in using the 1801 census returns, the urban community were defined as consisting of all the towns listed in the 1680 edition of Adams' *Index Villaris*. The results of applying this latter definition are also shown in the table.[49]

Except where the 1680 list of cities and market towns has been applied to the 1801 census returns, the table shows a fairly consistent pattern. In all the remaining columns (including that for the 427 towns identified in the 1801 census) the ratios are highest for London, lower for the remaining towns, and lower still for the rest of England and Wales. This pattern is evident in spite of the variations in the scope of the urban definition applied to the different censuses. The exception mentioned—in taking as urban, in 1801, all the cities and market towns listed by Adams—is not surprising, for many of the places included in Adams' gazetteer were not towns in 1801, though they might well have been urban communities in the England of his period. In sum, therefore, the pattern shown by the census statistics of nineteenth-century England, is by no means incompatible with the gradation of King's ratios. Whatever the basis of those ratios for the towns outside London, and for the rural areas, the trend shown is not inherently improbable, though the evidence now available cannot testify to its accuracy.

[49] The comparative ratios for the various segments of London are shown in the table below. In trying to make the contents of the segments in 1801 comparable with King's division, certain obvious errors of Rickman's allocation have been corrected. But it is unlikely that complete comparability has been achieved.

Ratios of persons per inhabited house, London

	King's final data		1801 Census data	
	No. of houses	Persons per house	No. of houses	Persons per house
97 parishes within	13,500	5·9	8,970	7·25
16 parishes without	32,500	5·1	21,934	7·17
Inns of Court (extra-parochial)*	—	—	1,230	1·55
15 out parishes	35,000	4·8	56,207	6·49
7 parishes in Westminster	24,000	4·7	18,231	8·68
Rest of London	—	—	14,657	8·04
	105,000	5·0	121,229	7·13

* King does not explain in which division the Inns of Court were included.

It will be seen that, in 1801, there is a fall in the ratios of persons per house from the inner city to the outer parishes. Westminster and the rest of London do not fit in with this scheme, but this might perhaps be due to the different nature of the new construction in those areas in the eighteenth century.

TABLE 5

Ratios of persons per inhabited house, England and Wales, 1801–1911

	1696 King's final estimate	1801 Towns included in Index Villaris	1801 Towns defined as such in census	1851	1871	1891	1911
London and the Bills of Mortality	5·0	7·13	7·13	7·72	7·79	7·73	7·89
Other cities and towns	4·4	5·43	5·60	5·48	5·33	5·21	4·91
Rest of England and Wales	4·04	5·54	5·47	5·07	4·91	4·76	4·51
England and Wales as a whole	4·17	5·63	5·63	5·47	5·33	5·32	5·05

Notes: (1) Of the 788 towns listed in the *Index*, 750 were identified in the 1801 census returns and are included in the calculation.

(2) 427 places are described as towns (including small market towns) in the 1801 census returns and are included in this calculation. If to Adams's list are added the other towns (92) described as such in 1801 but not included in the *Index*, the ratios become, 7·13, 5·47, 5·52 and 5·63. The Census does not indicate whether the boundaries of the communities designated as towns are coterminous with the truly urban areas.

(3) The towns (533 plus the London division) are taken from the list of 'Population and Inhabited Houses in the Cities, Boroughs and Principal Towns in England and Wales', 1851 *Census*, Population Tables 1, Vol. 1, pp. cciv, 2. Table XXIII, p. xlvi, of the *Report* refers to 580 towns (including London as one town), but not all of the 580 could be identified.

(4) The towns (260 plus the London division) are taken from the list of 'Houses and Population in the Cities and Boroughs having defined Municipal or Parliamentary limits', 1871 *Census*, *Preliminary Report*, Table VIII, p. 9. The population in this urban group amounted to 10·7 millions as compared with a total of 12·9 millions given (*Report*, p. xxi) as constituting the population in the 141 urban districts and 57 subdistricts. Not all of the districts could, however, be identified.

(5) The urban segments comprise the London division plus the 1010 urban sanitary districts (1891 *Census*, Vol. II, Table II, p. vi). The total urban population so defined was practically identical with the population specified as urban in the *Report*, Table IV, p. xxxiii.

(6) The urban segments comprise the Administrative County of London, plus the other areas defined as urban by the census.

Summarizing the discussion of King's estimate of the population of England and Wales in 1695, the following points may be made:

(1) The figure of 1·3 million 'houses' taken as the starting-point in the *Observations*, may well be too high. Indeed, this must be so if we can accept King's explanation, in the Kashnor manuscript, of the error made in counting the number of households recorded in the hearth-tax returns, though, in the absence of the original returns, the suggested allowance of 1 in 18 to compensate for that error cannot be tested. In any case, the proposed allowance was derived from the scrutiny of earlier returns and involved assumptions for which no basis was given. Further, in translating households into separate houses, King's original 3 per cent adjustment is most probably inadequate. In the Kashnor manuscript, King suggested with apparently some factual basis, an allowance of some 2 per cent for empty houses, and it would be necessary to add a further allowance—certainly above 1 per cent, if the data for London are any indication—for multiple occupancy. In all, it is likely that the number of separate inhabited houses was not above 1·17 or at most 1·2 millions.

(2) A study of some of the original returns suggests that the population enumerations used by King in constructing his ratios of persons per house,

while by no means perfect, were nevertheless reasonable in quality. But the 'sample' of returns used by King is not likely to have been representative and, indeed, this was definitely shown for the City of London within the walls, for which the original ratios of persons per house were too low. Nevertheless, by inspired adjustment, King arrived at final ratios, for the City within and without the walls, which are close to the ratios calculated by Jones and Judges from much more nearly complete returns. The question of under-enumeration still arises, however, and some allowance should no doubt be made on that account.[50]

(3) The account given in the Kashnor manuscript provides some factual basis for King's allocation of houses between London, the other cities and market towns, and the rest of England and Wales. It has not been possible to reconstruct in detail the process by which King arrived at differential ratios (of persons per house) for the areas outside London. But comparison with analogous ratios obtained from the 1801 census of England and Wales does not, at least, suggest that there is anything inherently improbable in the trend of King's ratios.

(4) On the basis of the above comments, a very crude attempt might be made to 'revise' King's estimate of the population of England and Wales by setting a lower limit, taking note of King's explanations in the Kashnor manuscript, as well as the data given by Jones and Judges. This would give a result of under 5 millions as compared with King's figure of 5·4 millions (excluding transients and vagrants omitted from the assessments, estimated by King at about 80,000 persons).[51] King's final figure of 5·5 millions for England and

---

[50] King's final ratios include an allowance for under-enumeration, but, even so, still only approximate to Jones and Judges's unadjusted results. An allowance for under-enumeration in the Jones and Judges returns would therefore still be called for.

[51] This 'revision' is based on the various adjustments discussed in the text, and is arrived at in the following way:

(1)	'Houses' (2)	Col. (2) $\times \frac{1\cdot326}{1\cdot300}$ (3)	Col. (3) $\times \frac{17}{18}$ (4)	Empty house factors (5)	Col. (4) adjusted by col. (5) (6)	Separate house factors (7)	Separate inhabited houses (8)	Persons per house ratios (9)	Total population (10)
London:									
97 p'shes within	13,500	13,800	13,000	× 0·92	12,000	× 100/107	11,200	6·1	68,300
16 p'shes without	32,500	33,200	31,400	× 0·92	28,900	× 100/121	23,900	5·1	121,900
15 out parishes	35,000	35,700	33,700	× 0·92	31,000	× 100/107	29,000	4·8	139,200
7 p'shes in West.r	24,000	24,500	23,100	× 0·92	21,300	× 100/107	19,000	4·7	93,500
Cities & market towns	195,000	198,900	187,800	−3,300	184,500	× 100/105	175,700	4·4	773,100
Villages & hamlets	1,000,000	1,020,000	963,300	−16,700	946,600	× 100/105	901,500	4·04	3,642,100

4,838,100

Column (2). King's 'corrected' figures for houses.
Column (3). King's figures brought back to hearth-tax figures of households, including King's allowance for new construction.
Column (4). King's estimate of error in counting numbers of households—the upper limit used in his Rutland example.
Column (5). King's estimate of empty houses—8 per cent in London, and about 20,000 in the rest of the country.
Column (7). Transformation of households into separate houses. For London the factors are those found by Jones and Judges. It has been assumed that the 'City within' factors apply to the out parishes and to Westminster (very probably an understatement) and that the ratio of 100/105 applies to the rest of the country (probably an understatement).
Column (9). The ratios for the 'City within' and the 'City without' are those found by Jones and Judges. The remaining ratios are King's.

It may perhaps be of some interest to note that the 'revised' estimate of the number of separate, inhabited houses in the 'City within' (col. (8), 11,200) is fairly near to the actual figure (consisting of the enumeration results for 81 parishes and an estimate—derived from the reported births and deaths—for the remaining 16 parishes) given by Jones and Judges, namely, 11,469. It is certainly much nearer than is the figure of 13,500 given by King.

Wales may perhaps represent the upper limit of probability, and a more acceptable figure (including an allowance for under-enumeration) might be some 250,000-350,000 below that limit. But in any case, such a revised estimate, at about 5·2 millions, would confirm rather than destroy the general plausibility of King's work.

(5) It should be emphasized, however, that the 'revision' is given by way of illustration and not as a considered alternative to King's results. To replace those results would require far more work. It would be necessary, for example, to trace the 1690 hearth-tax material—in so far as it exists—and to use that or earlier material to estimate more accurately the numbers and distribution (in agglomerations of various sizes) of households. To turn these into separate, inhabited houses would require the scrutiny of local tax returns of the kind referred to by Jones and Judges. Finally, to achieve more satisfactory ratios of persons per house for Westminster and the areas outside London would require a search for far more returns under the 1694 Act than have so far been made available. Those returns—and it is not unlikely that they still exist for a considerable number of areas—would be of considerable value in themselves as well as an indispensable aid in estimating the population of the kingdom. But for all such material assistance the demographer is in the hands of the historian, and especially of the local historian.

Apart from the question of the total population, the manuscripts now available also provide a more definite basis for another section of King's contributions to demography, that relating to the age-composition of the population of England and Wales. It will be remembered that the *Observations* give the numbers of males and females—shown separately—in a series of age groups.[52] These constitute the earliest age statistics for England and Wales as a whole, and there were no subsequent age statistics for the kingdom until the 1821 census was taken.[53] Inevitably, two main questions arise: first, what kind of material, and with what validity, did King use in constructing his estimate; and secondly, how did he use this material to produce a generalized picture of the age structure of the total population?

On the first point, it might well be imagined that King's age distribution, like Graunt's, was derived from a hypothetical life table. This would seem to be indicated by the fact that the section of the *Observations* containing the relevant statistics begins with the phrase 'That the Yearly Births of the Kingdome Being 190,000 Souls', and then proceeds to detail the age distribution. It is also true that King's journals, and especially the working journal in the P.R.O. collection, contain many calculations starting from assumed annual numbers of deaths or births and then computing the numbers of persons living at the several ages. Moreover, King had obviously read Graunt's volume with great care— the P.R.O. journal contains a digest of the contents—and at one point compares the survivors in Graunt's life table with those in an obviously similar table of his own.[54]

[52] *Observations*, Barnett ed., p. 23.
[53] The estimate given by John Graunt (*Natural and Political Observations*, reprinted with an introduction by W. F. Willcox, Baltimore, 1939, pp. 69-70) related only to London and was obtained by distributing an estimated population in the proportions of a hypothetical life table, using the l_x columns as if they were T_x columns.   [54] P.R.O. journal, p. 7.

But at the same time, it was noted earlier that the Burns journal contains statistics relating to the age composition of specific communities, namely, Lichfield city (1695), Shustoke parish (Shustoke, Warwick), and Swepstone parish (Swepstone, Leicester).[55] The nature of this material—even the concentration of ages around the 'tens'—made it apparent that the statistics were derived from actual enumerations, and this is confirmed by an examination of the detailed enumeration lists, in the Harleian collection, for Lichfield and also for Buckfastleigh (1698) and Rinmore (1698).[56] In what connexion these local enumerations were taken is still not quite clear. The entries on the Lichfield sheets leave no doubt that those particular statistics were collected as returns under the 1694 Act. The Act did not require ages (save for the purpose of identifying bachelors over 25 years of age), and it is therefore likely that the additional information was collected, at the special request of King, by the 'Mr Lamb' who appears to have been responsible for the enumeration. Since King was born and brought up in Lichfield, he probably had especially good connexions with that city. The enumeration lists for Rinmore and Buckfastleigh do not show any entries in respect of the 1694 Act. It may be that these particular surveys were also made by the assessors under the Act, perhaps as a particular favour to King, or alternatively that King persuaded some influential local resident to undertake a special enumeration. That a substantial correspondence may have occurred in connexion with these enumerations is suggested by a summary, to be found in the Harleian collection, of a letter sent by King to Mr Lamb, the person apparently responsible for the Lichfield survey.[57] Because of the relevance of this summary in showing King's grasp of the data and of their defects, it is reproduced in full below:

Her. Off. 12 Aug 1695.

Extract of my L[rr] to Mr. Lamb of Lichf[d]

I observed that in the Boys in Lichf[d] there were but 16 of a year old and yet 29 of 2 year old and 51 of 3 year old, whereas there should be most of 1 year and fewest of 3 year, vizt. about 40 of 1 year. 31 of 2 year & 25 of 3 year Supposing that in 2800 People living at one time the yearly Births should be about 80 vizt. 42 Males & 38 or 40 Females.

That there were but 33 of 4 year old after which they encreased in Number to 50 of 9 year old & about as many of 10 year old I desird ye reason of ye diff. betw. 1 year old & 3 year old being almost trible, whether 2 last years were unhealthy or ye 3d year past over fruitfull

The encrease from 4 to 10 I reckond from Schollars & Boarders out of the Country, for otherwise ye Numbers should decrease.

From 51 of 10 year old it fals to 27 of 11 year old & holds much about ye same Number to 15 year old, whence I guess the Boarders & Sojourners returnd in those years to ye Country again.

Of 16 year old there are 51 again whereas there was but 30 of 15 year old—and 32 of 17 year old, which I reckon to be Apprentices & Servts from ye Country.

---

[55] Glass, op. cit., pp. 180-1.
[56] I am indebted to Mr A. L. Reade, author of *Johnsonian Gleanings*, for permission to use his transcript of the Lichfield enumeration list.　　　　　[57] Harl. MSS. 6839, fol. 158.

From 16 years they decrease to 6 of 22 and but 2 of 23 years. So that London for Apprentices, Gentlemens Services and ye wars seems to drain them of Males those years for very few could be married before 23 year old. (note that this acco^t is all along of the Bachelors) I desired a Recourse to ye Parish Reg^{rs} for ye males & Females born each year for 5 or 6 years past, with the Burials of Males & Females in that time and ye yearly marriages.

I observed there are 1280 Males & 1560 Females, vizt. 280 Females more than males in these 3 Articles.

$$\left.\begin{matrix} 50\ \text{Widowers} \\ 190\ \text{Widows} \end{matrix}\right\}\text{diff. 140} \qquad \left.\begin{matrix} 580\ \text{sons} \\ 680\ \text{daurs} \end{matrix}\right\}\text{diff 100} \qquad \left.\begin{matrix} \text{Menservts}\ 100 \\ \text{Maids}\qquad 140 \end{matrix}\right\}\text{diff 40}$$

Which seemed to be occasioned by ye Women overliving the men: 2 more widows resort to great Towns for Conveniency of Living: 3dly Widowers oftener marry again Widows; 4 The Wars draw many Husbands away where they are slayn before their ordinary time.

As to the Surplus of Daurs., London, Gentl. Services, & ye Wars drains ye males.

As to Maid Servts All great Towns require more than Men Servts, ye Country otherwise.

Lastly I desired ye Ages of the Females & married Persons. And a copy of ye Assessmt. for the Close and out parts that parish to Lichfd. with ye circumference of ye County of the Citty.

This letter must ante-date the enumeration list in the Harleian collection as well as King's detailed analysis of the statistics, given in the Burns journal (p. 93), for in both the latter the numbers of people at various ages differ from those mentioned in the letter, while the ages of 'the Females & married Persons' had also been obtained. It is also clear that the 'copy of ye Assessmt. for the Close' was also subsequently provided by Mr Lamb, for King noted the main contents in the collection of population statistics given in the Burns journal (pp. 90-2), namely, 39 houses, 205 persons, 90 males, 115 females, etc. But the ages and marital condition (except that 27 married couples, 2 widowers and 10 widows are mentioned—which would be in accordance with the returns required under the 1694 Act) for the Close do not seem to have been collected, and the detailed age analysis of Lichfield contained in the Burns journal (p. 93) relates to Lichfield city. The general impression made by this material is that considerable trouble must have been taken in collecting the age statistics and further that, as a result of queries raised by King, it is possible that some of the more obvious errors in the original returns were corrected subsequently —that is, by re-interviewing part of the population.

That statistics of this kind were actually used by King in producing his estimate of the age structure of England and Wales is fully confirmed by his statements in the Kashnor manuscript. Harley had made several comments on King's table of 'the Severall Ages of the People',[58] of which the most important are the following: 'To the Age of 16 the males exceed the Females, & after the Females exceed ye Males'; 'Are adult Females more durable than Males? The Accidents from Childbearing is after 16 generally'; and 'In the

[58] *Observations*, p. 23. Harley's comments and King's replies are given in Kashnor MS., p. 8.

pag. before, Children are reckon'd at 45 P. Cent, 2,500,000, wch differs from this. By this Rule about half attain the age of 21 years. Some Calculate 42 P. Cent are alive to 21. & 58 P. Cent above 21. & half arrive to 24, 25 years.' King's reply is given below.

The Bills of Mortality & Parish Registers of the Kingdom in general, plainly shew that more Males are buried than Females. Consequently more Males are born than Females in general. And by most of the Acco^{ts} of Births or Christnings wch I have received from divers Parish Registers, the Male births exceed the Females; which Observation the London Bills of Mortality do also confirm, as well as the other Acco^{ts} of Christnings exhibited by Mr. Grant, But the due proportion of that Surplus of Male Births for the whole Kingdom is very difficult to establish, since some places do afford a Surplus of Female Births; However upon a serious consideration I have adventured to state it at 1 in 26 or 27 vizt 14 Males to 13 Female Births or thereabouts; accordingly in 190,000 annual Births, there should be 98,500 males, & 91,500 Females, vizt A Surplus of 7000 males which number is not much more than equal to the males carried off extraordinary by wars, the Sea, & the Plantations, in wch Articles the Females are very little concern'd.

On the other side the numbers of co-existing Males is less than the Females in general by 1 in 28. or rather 2 in 28, as I have since more carefully collected them from the Assessm^{ts} on Marriages Births & Buryalls. So that if more males be constantly born, and yet more Females be always co-existing. there is an age when the Males & Females are equal, wch by collecting the ages of ye Men Women & Children in several Places, I think I have very nearly adjusted, as well as the intermediate proportions in this page. with some small alterations since the first Stating thereof. Now tho' I do not find but that near as many males arrive to 75, or 80 years of Age as Females, Yet there is no question but that a much greater number of Females arrive to 60 & 65 years of Age than there does of Males; The Widows being near treble to the Widowers.

The Accident of dying in Childbed strictly speaking Grant states but at 1 in 200. So that it signifies little to the many occasions. wch expose the lives of the males, beyond that of the Females, even from 3 or 4 years old to the end of their days, wch We may estimate at ab^t 9 in 200.

In reckining Children at 45 P. Cent of the whole, It is to be understood of such Children, as being unmarried are found at home with their Parents and in the said Assessments, not of the children under any determinate age.

....

About one half of the People are under 20 years of age, and the other half above 20, vizt One half of the males are under 19, and One half of the Females under 21.

The Comon Computation (Grant. p. 94. S. 1.) used to be that one moiety of the co-existing people were under 16, and the other Moiety above 16 years old. The Computation you mention of One half arriving to 24, or 25 years is very different from that of 16 years; and both of them

208

can hardly be consistent with truth, if either of them be, since that of 16 must suppose an Extraord. quantity of very young Children & very few adult persons, and the other the quite contrary; But mine falling near the middle of these 2 Calculations, is more than a bare Computation, for it is a Collection of the Ages of about 5000 People in severall places, or else I should not have adventured to have differ'd so widely from Sr Wm Petty, who says that in Collecting the Ages of the People in 9 severall Parishes, they answer'd at a Medium to 16 years, whereas mine answers to 27 years & ½ vizt. Not less than 26 years, nor much above 29 at a medium. So that Sr Wm Petty's Acco.^t is certainly mistaken or misrepresented. And I am further confirm'd in this Proposition by a future Collection of the Ages of near 5000 persons more whose comon age is at a Medium about 28, wch being more than the Comon Age of the Kingdom in general depends upon particuler Reasons easie to be Assigned. I would gladly See the Calculation you mention in this Particuler.

This reply has been reproduced at length because of the general light it throws on King's approach to demography. But at the present point in the discussion the relevant passage is that explaining the estimated age structure of the kingdom as based upon the ages 'of about 5000 People in severall places', and there is no reason to doubt the statement. It is unfortunate that King did not specify the places. Lichfield must certainly have been one of them, and it is likely that Swepstone and Shustoke, the returns for which are given in the Burns journal, were also included. But that makes a total of only 3,282 persons.[59] Buckfastleigh (1,106 persons) and Rinmore (188 persons) may have formed part of what King termed his 'future Collection of the Ages of near 5000 persons more', but, since they were enumerated in 1698, could not have been used in the *Observations*.

Again, because King is inexplicit, even in his working journal, it is not possible to say at present exactly how he used the statistics for Lichfield and the other communities in constructing his generalized estimate for England and Wales. But the manipulation, in the Burns journal, of the Lichfield statistics does at least provide some indication of the way in which King smoothed the data to allow for errors in the age statements and for possible omissions in specific age groups.[60] The details of the Lichfield population, together with King's smoothing of the results, are presented in Table 6. The extreme right-hand columns of the table show the reallocation of persons between the various age groups, as well as the testing of this reallocation by the use of first and second differences. The reallocation between the age groups of 0-4 and 5-9 years[61] was undertaken to overcome the errors introduced by omissions, and in the right-hand margin of the original sheet (in the Burns journal), King commented on these omissions in the following terms:

Now ye Births in Lichf.^d in all ye 3 parishes being yearly at a medium 107. Whereof for these 2861 People, (being Exclusive of ye Close of Lich-

[59] The age data given in the Burns journal, pp. 93-95, consist of 2,861 persons for Lichfield, 276 for Shustoke and 145 for Swepstone.　　[60] Burns journal, p. 93.
[61] Although King's table refers to children as 'of 1 year old', etc., it seems clear that the meaning must be 'under 1 year', etc. In the text, the age groups are thus referred to accordingly.

In the City of Lichfield 1695–2861 People

	Bach.	Maid.	Husb.	Wives	Widrs	Widows	In all	A Medium of ages for the 2861 People in ye City of Lichf. (a)
Of 1 year old	17	31	00	00	00	00	48	
2	28	48	00	00	00	00	76	
3	52	51	00	00	00	00	103	
4	36	35	00	00	00	00	71	
5	34	36	00	00	00	00	70	
	167	201	00	00	00	00	368	400
6	41	49	00	00	00	00	90	
7	36	38	00	00	00	00	74	
8	42	31	00	00	00	00	73	
9	55	30	00	00	00	00	85	
10	53	35	00	00	00	00	88	
	227	183	00	00	00	00	410	350 (778)
10 to 15 Incl.	156	127	00	00	00	00	283	310
15 to 20 Incl.	136	170	15	01	00	00	307	277 (590)
20 to 25 Incl.	44	125	15	22	00	00	206	249
1 to 25 Incl.	730	806	15	23	00	00	1574	1586 — 438
25 to 30 Incl.	49	72	38	69	01	03	232	224
30 to 35 Incl.	09	25	68	81	07	05	195	201
35 to 40 Incl.	06	22	105	87	07	29	256	179 (451)
40 to 45 Incl.	01	03	52	43	04	16	119	158
45 to 50 Incl.	01	01	66	46	06	13	133	138 (252)
50 to 55 Incl.	01	02	21	22	03	12	61	117
55 to 60 Incl.	04	00	37	38	08	25	112	094 (173)
60 to 65 Incl.	02	01	17	23	03	22	68	070
65 to 70 Incl.	00	01	21	10	08	41	81	047 (149)
70 to 75 Incl.	00	00	02	01	02	09	14	026
75 to 80 Incl.	01	00	00	00	04	05	10	012 (24)
80 to 85 Incl.	00	00	00	00	01	02	03	005
85 to 90 Incl.	00	00	00	00	01	01	02	002·2 (5)
90 to 95 Incl.	00	00	00	00	00	00	00	000·7
95 to 100 Incl.	00	00	00	00	01	01	01	000·1 (1)
	74 / 730	127 / 806	427 / 15	420 / 23	55 / 00	184 / 00	1287 / 1574	2861 People (b)
	804	933	442	443	55	184	2861	

1737 (885, 239)

Top-right age medium groupings: 50 {, 40 {, 33 — 7, 28 — 5, 25 — 3, 10 {

(a) Smoothed age data.
(b) In fact the total is 2860.

	Males	Females	above 25	under 26
	804	933		
	442	443		
	55	184		
	1301	1560		

2861

field and of some out Villages which parish to Lichfield but being without
ye Liberties of ye Citty & County of Lichf. are not included in this Assesment) The yearly Births may be about 100. which in 5 years would be 500
whereof a fifth part dying there should remain about 400; But whereas
there is but 368, there seems to be 32 wanting, Either in ye Assesm! itself,
or by reason of ye mortality by ye small Pox which hapned among ye
young children a year or two ago, Which appears more plainly by ye
Number of ye Children of 1. 2. and 3 years old, Those of 1 and 2 years
being fewer in Number then those of 3. whereas they should be more.

But there is a further puzzle. Having commented on the omissions of
children (due either to under-enumeration or to excess mortality from smallpox), King then proceeded to construct a 'life table', shown below in Table 7.
The question is whether the smoothed age data shown in Table 6 derive from
the 'life table', or whether the main body of the 'life table' derives from the
smoothed age data. The question is a relevant one, for upon the answer must
depend our view as to the realistic or hypothetical character of King's smoothed
age statistics for Lichfield. In turn, as will be shown subsequently, this is bound
up with the generalized estimate for England and Wales as a whole. Examina-

TABLE 7

King's 'life table' for Lichfield

Year (1)	Yearly born (2)	Dye (3)	Deaths added (4)	Remains living (5)
1	100	10	10	90
2	100	7	17	83
3	100	5	22	78
4	100	3	25	75
5	100	1·5	26·5	73·5
	500	26·5	100·5	399·5
6	100	1·5	28	72
7	100	1	29	71
8	100	1	30	70
9	100	1	31	69
10	100	1	32	68
	500—	5·5	150	350
15	500	38	190	310
20	500	45	223	277
25	500	50	251	249
30	500	55	276	224
35	500	60	299	201
40	500	64	321	179
45	500	68	342	158
50	500	72	362	138
55	500	76·5	383	117
60	500	81	406	94
65	500	86	429	71
70	500	90·5	453	47
75	500	95	474	26
80	500	98	488	12
85	500	99	495	5
90	500	99·5	497	2·2
95	500	99·8	499	0·7
100	500	99·9	499·9	0·1

tion of Tables 6 and 7 suggests that it was the smoothed data which came first and the 'life table' afterwards. There are two reasons for this conclusion. First, the original sheet shows that King's calculations and adjustments were done on the columns in Table 6. Secondly, the only straightforward and consistent explanation of the quantities in the 'life table' requires that King began his 'life table' calculations with column (5) of Table 7. If that is postulated, the remaining columns derive immediately in the following way: column (4) is obtained by successive subtraction of column (5) from the assumed annual cohort of births (100 or 500, depending upon the size of the age group); and column (3) consists of the successive differences between the quantities in column (4) in the case of single-year age groups, while for 5-year groups the results in column (3) are obtained by taking one-fifth of the corresponding quantity in column (4) and (in most cases) rounding to the nearest whole number.[62] It would seem, therefore, that the smoothed age statistics given in Table 6 are the result of manipulation of the original census data, and not derived from a hypothetical life table.

Although the Burns journal shows in some detail the adjustment of the Lichfield data, no comparable indications are provided for the Shustoke and Swepstone material. There is thus no direct evidence of the way in which King blended together the age statistics for his '5000 People'. But it can be demonstrated that the adjusted Lichfield statistics do, in themselves, give a close approximation to King's final estimate for England and Wales.

To provide this demonstration, it is appropriate to alter the form of King's estimate, which is given as a series of cumulatives, perhaps under the influence of Graunt's life table. The figures as given in the *Observations* are reproduced in Table 8, and it was necessary to interpolate in order to obtain age groups comparable with the adjusted Lichfield returns. It was found that, when plotted on a semi-logarithmic graph, King's final estimate almost perfectly describes a straight line—in itself evidence of considerable smoothing—and the first differences of the logarithms were thus used for the purpose of interpolation and adjustment. The resultant percentage distributions are shown in Table 9,

TABLE 8

King's estimate of the age composition of England and Wales

	Persons	Males	Females
Under 1 year	170,000	90,000	80,000
Under 5 years	820,000	415,000	405,000
Under 10 years	1,520,000	764,000	756,000
Under 16 years	2,240,000	1,122,000	1,118,000
Above 16 years	3,260,000	1,578,000	1,682,000
Above 21 years	2,700,000	1,300,000	1,400,000
Above 25 years	2,400,000	1,150,000	1,250,000
Above 60 years	600,000	270,000	330,000
Total	5,500,000	2,700,000	2,800,000

[62] If column (4) had been derived from column (3), the number endings in column (4) would be quite different. For example, there would be no reason for the number against age 30 to be 276, or for that against age 25 to be 251. Instead the numbers would have been 275 and 250.

TABLE 9

Percentage age distributions (persons)

| Ages (years) | Lichfield Returns | | England and Wales (interpolated from King's estimate) |
	Unadjusted	King's smoothed data	
0 –	12·86	13·99	14·90
5 –	14·34	12·24	12·73
10 –	9·89	10·84	10·73
15 –	10·73	9·69	9·45
20 –	7·20	8·71	8·36
25 –	8·11	7·83	7·13
30 –	6·82	7·02	6·35
35 –	8·95	6·26	5·33
40 –	4·16	5·52	4·56
45 –	4·65	4·83	3·84
50 –	2·13	4·09	3·16
55 –	3·91	2·29	2·73
60 and over	6·25	5·69	10·73
	100·00	100·00	100·00

together with both the unadjusted and the smoothed data for Lichfield. The smoothed data for Lichfield show a strong resemblance to those in the estimate for England and Wales, especially in the younger half of the population pyramid, though the estimate for England and Wales has a greater emphasis on the youngest and oldest age groups. This, too, can be explained, at least in general terms. In the Burns journal, at the bottom of the page containing the Lichfield material, King uses his data on Lichfield, Shustoke and Swepstone to estimate the mean ages of the respective populations. From that he proceeds, by adjustment, to transform the results into mean ages for London, the other towns, and the rest of the country—that is, using Lichfield, Shustoke and Swepstone as his three indicators. Finally, these mean ages are used to provide the following broad age groupings:

Males and females	London	Towns	Country
Under 16	390	420	450
Between 16 and 60	510	480	440
Above 60	100	100	110
Total	1000	1000	1000

Thus the data at his disposal apparently suggested to King a larger proportion of the very young and the very old in the country as compared with London and the other towns. Lichfield being the basis of King's views on the age structure of London, the smoothed data were modified accordingly in producing the estimate for England and Wales.

The previous discussion has shown that King's estimate of the age composition of the kingdom was based to a major extent on a detailed enumeration undertaken in Lichfield, and adjusted to provide a more generalized picture. There is still the question of how far either the Lichfield or the adjusted structure is likely to have been representative of the country as a whole, and this question clearly cannot be answered in a direct way. But it is possible to appeal to some indirect evidence—to see how far, for the nearest points of time for which complete enumerations are available, Lichfield compares with England and Wales as a whole, and also to compare King's estimate with the earliest European census returns.

On the first point, the earliest English censuses giving age statistics are those of 1821 and 1841. In 1821 the question on age was not a compulsory one. But

TABLE 10

Percentage age distribution, Lichfield and England and Wales, 1821 and 1841

| | 1821 (a) | | | | 1841 (b) | | | |
| | Males | | Females | | Males | | Females | |
	Lichfield	England and Wales	Lichfield	England and Wales	Lichfield	England and Wales	Lichfield	England and Wales
0	13·53	15·38	11·41	14·40	13·56	13·41	11·16	12·99
5	12·20	13·48	10·79	12·69	11·59	12·19	11·09	11·68
10	12·66	11·72	9·92	10·58	10·58	11·27	10·16	10·45
15	9·52	9·89	10·23	9·96	8·74	10·00	9·83	9·88
20	} 14·64	14·67	18·68	16·75	8·33	9·26	9·34	10·15
25					7·39	7·82	7·78	8·25
30	} 11·26	11·53	13·06	12·07	6·45	7·23	7·32	7·39
35					5·16	5·57	5·08	5·52
40	} 10·01	9·36	9·88	9·31	6·16	5·58	6·31	5·55
45					4·55	4·01	4·34	3·99
50	} 7·81	6·64	6·71	6·55	4·42	3·93	4·18	4·02
55					2·90	2·43	3·06	2·48
60 and over	8·37	7·33	9·32	7·69	10·17	7·30	10·35	7·65
0–14	38·39	40·58	32·12	37·67	35·73	36·87	32·41	35·12
15–59	53·24	52·09	58·56	54·64	54·10	55·83	57·24	57·23
60 and over	8·37	7·33	9·32	7·69	10·17	7·30	10·35	7·65
	100·00	100·00	100·00	100·00	100·00	100·00	100·00	100·00

(a) In 1821 the enumeration of Lichfield covered the parishes of St. Chad, St. Mary and St. Michael, together with the Close (extra-parochial).

(b) In 1841 the enumeration of Lichfield covered the city and borough, namely, St. Mary Parish, St. Michael (part), St. Chad (part), the Close and the Friary, Pipehill township (part) and Freeford hamlet.

the ages were in fact stated for about 88 per cent of the population. Moreover, the vast bulk of the omissions related to whole parishes or other enumeration districts and not to special groups of persons—for example, the relatively aged —within the districts.[63] The returns may therefore be accepted as giving a fairly reasonable indication of the age composition of England and Wales, while for Lichfield the returns were complete. The problem does not arise at the 1841 census, by which time the question on age was compulsory.

The percentage age composition of Lichfield and England and Wales is given, for 1821 and 1841, in Table 10. It will be seen that at both points of time there was a strong resemblance between the part and the whole. Further, a

[63] See *1821 Census, Enumeration Abstract*, pp. v and xiv. Study of the returns for the individual counties shows that, for England and Wales as a whole, out of the 1,431,000 persons whose ages were not stated, only 34,000 were persons in districts giving otherwise complete age returns.

substantial part of what difference is apparent is in the direction in which King adjusted his Lichfield data when aiming at the generalized estimate. That is, England and Wales tended, in 1821 and 1841, to contain a larger proportion than did Lichfield of persons under 15 years of age, and it was in this direction that King adjusted the Lichfield data.[64] On the other hand, in 1821 and 1841 England and Wales showed a smaller proportion than Lichfield of persons aged 60 years and over, and King's adjustment here would seem to have been in the wrong direction. In general, however, seen in the light of the census returns of 1821 and 1841, it would appear that by taking Lichfield as a basis, King began with a collection of statistics which were probably not markedly untypical, and then adjusted them in a way which may have at least in part rendered them more acceptable as an indication of national structure.[65]

Finally, King's estimate for the kingdom may be compared with the age distribution obtained from the earliest large-scale censuses taken in various European states, including the distribution for England and Wales in 1821. The comparison is shown in Table 11, the data for Scandinavia and Iceland being taken from Gille's study.[66] Once again, in spite of the individual differences, there is a strong general resemblance between King's results and the age distributions for Scandinavia in the eighteenth century.[67] The resemblance is especially strong for Finland in 1751. Finland at that time was a country with a higher fertility than Sweden or Denmark, and was nearer in general age structure to England and Wales in 1821. And, indeed, King's estimate is very similar to the age structure of England and Wales in 1821. In general the main point of difference in King's figures is the apparent exaggeration of the proportion of older persons, and it was noted, in discussing his manipulation of the basic data, that he seemed to have gone astray in adjusting the age group of 60 years and over. Even in the case of Iceland the differences between King's estimate and the Iceland census returns of 1703 are smaller than the overall figures suggest. It is likely that the very severe winter of 1702–3, together with under-enumeration of young children, produced an abnormally low proportion of children under 10 years of age.[68] Taking only the age distribution of persons above 10 years of age, the differences between King's figures and those for the 1703 census are greatly reduced. Certainly the comparison does not suggest that King's estimate is very widely off the mark.

The discussion of King's estimate of the age structure of England and Wales in 1695 may now be summarized.

---

[64] Lichfield in 1821 and 1841 included the Close (the clerical area), excluded from King's age statistics.

[65] King's adjustment of the population aged 60 years and over is somewhat curious. As shown in Table 9, he first adjusted them downwards, as if believing that some exaggeration of age had occurred in the enumeration. But he then raised them very substantially—almost double—in proceeding to the generalized picture for the country as a whole.

[66] H. Gille, 'Demographic history of the northern European countries', *Population Studies*, June 1949.

[67] The resemblance to the Swedish results of the mid-eighteenth century was pointed out in H. Westergaard, *Contributions to the History of Statistics*, London 1932, pp. 42–43. Westergaard thought that King also gave too high a proportion of children. But the Finnish results also show a higher proportion than Sweden.

[68] *Cf.* T. Thorsteinsson, 'The first census taken in Iceland in 1703', a paper presented at the 1947 conference of the International Statistical Institute. See also Statistical Bureau of Iceland, *Mantalid 1703*, Reykjavik 1960 (English summary, pp. 27–31).

TABLE 11

Comparative age distributions (percentages)

Age (years)	England and Wales G. King 1695	Sweden 1750	Sweden 1800	Finland 1751	Finland 1800	Denmark 1787	Denmark 1800	Iceland 1703	Iceland 1800	England and Wales 1821	England and Wales 1841	(Omitting ages 0–9) Iceland 1703	(Omitting ages 0–9) England and Wales G. King
0 –	27·63	23·72	22·78	27·03	26·41	23·15	23·11	16·68	26·61	27·94	25·23	—	—
10 –	20·18	18·53	18·44	19·90	19·07	17·27	17·45	20·95	13·74	21·06	20·85	25·13	27·89
20 –	15·49	16·74	15·70	16·82	16·83	16·94	16·14	16·65	15·75	15·74	17·80	19·97	21·40
30 –	11·68	13·14	13·71	10·41	13·82	13·90	13·30	14·84	15·04	11·81	12·89	17·81	16·13
40 –	8·40	10·28	11·95	9·05	10·64	11·41	11·60	13·89	9·06	9·34	9·59	16·68	11·61
50 –	5·89	7·93	8·65	7·66	6·93	8·65	9·01	9·55	8·86	6·59	6·45	11·47	8·14
60 +	10·73	9·66	8·77	9·13	6·30	8·68	9·39	7·44	10·94	7·52	7·19	8·94	14·83
	100·00	100·00	100·00	100·00	100·00	100·00	100·00	100·00	100·00	100·00	100·00	100·00	100·00
0 –	38·36	33·19	32·36	37·17	36·25	(a)	(a)	26·88	(a)	39·08	36·11		
15 –	50·91	57·15	58·87	53·70	57·45			65·68		53·40	56·70		
60 +	10·73	9·66	8·77	9·13	6·30			7·44		7·52	7·19		

(a) Not possible for these countries, because of the 10-year groups in which the basic statistics are given.

(1) Although, like Graunt, King was greatly interested in the construction of 'life tables', the estimate of the age structure appearing in the *Observations* was based primarily on the results of actual enumerations covering some 5,000 persons in several communities. Exactly which communities were covered is not known, but it is obvious that Lichfield was the main constituent, and it is very probable that Shustoke and Swepstone were also taken into account.

(2) It would seem, judging by the original lists, that the Lichfield enumeration was carried out with reasonable care. King's letter to Lamb also shows that many of the obvious defects were noticed, and it appears possible that some may have been dealt with by further interviews with the people enumerated.

(3) King adjusted the Lichfield data to allow for omissions and misstatements of age. The adjustment must have been rather arbitrary, but does not seem unrealistic. The adjusted statistics were then further manipulated, presumably taking into account the returns for the other areas, to produce a generalized estimate for the kingdom. Here, in particular, the adjustments must have been arbitrary. But once again, having regard to the relationships shown by the census returns for 1821 and 1841, the adjustments may have been in the right direction as regards children, though the proportion of aged persons was no doubt exaggerated.

(4) Comparison of King's estimate with the census returns for Scandinavia in the eighteenth century and for England and Wales in 1821 shows a strong resemblance.

No doubt much research remains to be done before King's estimate can be accepted as a reliable picture of the age-structure of the population of England and Wales at the end of the seventeenth century, or before any revised estimate can be substituted. Perhaps the most important next step would be to initiate a search for further King manuscripts and particularly for the missing journals. Knowledge of exactly which areas were taken into account in King's work, and access to the returns for the additional 5,000 persons—to which he refers in the Kashnor manuscript—would greatly help the demographer. Even at present, however, having regard to the nature and limitations of the basic material with which he worked, it is evident that King's estimate was a remarkable effort, and it is likely that in general terms it is not far from the truth. Greenwood, using the images of archery in speaking of John Graunt's estimate of childhood mortality in seventeenth-century London, said that he 'used a bow with a frayed string and made no allowance for windage, but his arrow hit the target not far from the white'.[69] The study of the available manuscripts persuades me that King would be no less deserving of such a tribute.

APPENDIX

Note on the number of houses in England and Wales, 1690

Since there is some confusion in the historical literature regarding the statistics of 'houses' at the end of the seventeenth century, a more detailed note on the subject may be of interest.

In the first place, it should be emphasized that the total number of 'houses' (i.e.

---

[69] M. Greenwood, *Medical Statistics from Graunt to Farr*, Cambridge 1948, p. 32.

households) taken by King as his basis, namely 1,319,215, is not, as was considered by E. C. K. Gonner (*J. R. Statist. Soc.* February 1913, pp. 261-2), original to King. It has been shown in the earlier discussion that King obtained the figure from Davenant,[70] and probably directly from his book, *An Essay upon the Ways and Means of Supplying the War*. In his *Observations* King treated the figure as if it were well known and requiring no comment (save in respect of transforming households into separate houses, and making an allowance for empty houses), and it would seem that it was Harley's queries which provoked King to reconsider the reliability of the statistics.

John Houghton, who issued the other series of statistics of 'houses', published them at least twice—in *A Collection for the Improvement of Husbandry and Trade*, no. 26, 3 February 1692-3,[71] and in a separate broadsheet, produced by Houghton in London in 1693, entitled *An Account of the Acres & Houses, with the Proportional Tax, &c. of each County in England and Wales.*[72] Exactly how Houghton obtained these statistics, or to which date they refer, is not known. Gonner (*op. cit.*, p. 262) treated them as if they related to the year 1691, but there is no reason to believe that this is correct. In fact, since these statistics must have come from the hearth books, and are so described in the MS. copy in Pepys's library,[73] they must relate to some year earlier than 1690, for the hearth tax was abolished in 1689. This would apply equally to Davenant's statistics. Even though they are described as the 'Numbr of Houses in each County according to ye Hearth Books of Lady day 1690', it is more likely that the correct date was 1689.

At the time of the eighteenth-century population controversy, William Eden argued in favour of Houghton's statistics, as compared with Davenant's, on the ground that the former had been compiled by William Halley, the distinguished astronomer and creator of the first realistic life table.[74] There seems to be no justification for this belief. It was true that Halley helped Houghton, but, as Gonner pointed out,[75] the help related to the calculation of the acreage of the counties of England and Wales. Certainly Houghton published a letter from Halley on that subject,[76] but no letter referring to the numbers of 'houses'. It is much more likely that Houghton obtained access to the hearth-tax statistics and had a transcription made, as Davenant must also have done and as Adams had done earlier. It is clear that Davenant and Houghton did not work from the same transcript, for there are considerable differences between their results, as is shown in Table 12. For the vast majority of counties the numbers given by Houghton are lower than those given by Davenant, the exceptions being Devonshire, Dorset and Somerset. It is difficult to account for the excess in the case of the latter counties. On the other hand, the generally lower level of Houghton's figure might well fit in with King's account of the inflation in the transcript used by Davenant.[77]

There is no doubt that the statistics published by Davenant and Houghton need to be checked against and replaced by a fresh analysis of the hearth-tax material. But there are two difficulties. First, there are substantial variations in the scope of the hearth-tax returns, and in their availability. Although the tax—amounting to a shilling per half-year on each chargeable hearth—was levied from 1662 to 1689, the nature of the statistics sent to the Exchequer was not the same throughout the period. The Accounts of local

[70] See Burns journal, pp. 10 and 48.
[71] See the edition by R. Bradley, Vol. 1, London 1727, pp. 74-75.
[72] B.M. 105, f. 17 (36).
[73] 'Mr Houghton's computation of the number of villages and persons in each county of England and Wales, collected from the books of the Hearth-Office', J. R. Tanner, *Private Correspondence and Miscellaneous Papers of Samuel Pepys*, Vol. 1, London 1926, p. 44.
[74] William Eden, *Four Letters to the Earl of Carlisle*, 3rd ed., London 1780, Appendix, p. xxi.
[75] *Op. cit.*, p. 269, n. 16.
[76] *A Collection for the Improvement of Husbandry and Trade*, Friday, 20 January 1692/3, no. 24, Bradley ed., pp. 68-70.
[77] It may be, of course, that Houghton's figures relate to an earlier year than do Davenant's. But this still would not explain the excess numbers for the three counties.

areas of administration were not audited in the Exchequer except for the periods 1662 to Lady Day 1666 and Michaelmas 1669 to Lady Day 1674. For these periods the Exchequer received Assessments (giving a record of what ought to be collected) and Returns (listing what had and had not been collected), while copies of the Assessments were sent to the Sheriff or Quarter Sessions. It is for those periods, therefore, that such records (listing persons and hearths) have been preserved, the Exchequer records being in the P.R.O. and the other records in county archives or in private ownership. For the re-

TABLE 12

England and Wales. Number of 'houses' by counties,
according to Davenant and Houghton

Counties	Davenant	Houghton (a)
Bedfordshire	12,170	12,170
Berkshire	16,996	16,906
Buckinghamshire	18,688	18,390
Cambridgeshire and Ely	18,629	17,347
Cheshire and Chester	25,592	24,054
Cornwall	26,613	25,374
Cumberland	15,279	14,825
Derbyshire	24,944	21,155
Devonshire and Exon	56,202	56,310
Dorsetshire and Poole	17,859	21,944
Durham, Northumberland and Berwick	53,345	38,725
Essex	40,545	34,819
Gloucestershire and Gloucester	34,476	26,764
Herefordshire	16,744	15,006
Hertfordshire	17,488	16,569
Huntingdonshire	8,713	8,217
Kent	46,674	39,242
Lancashire	46,961	40,202
Leicestershire	20,448	18,702
Lincolnshire and Lincoln	45,019	40,590
Northamptonshire	26,904	24,808
Nottinghamshire	17,818	17,554
Norfolk and Norwich	56,579	47,180
Oxfordshire	19,627	19,007
Rutland	3,661	3,263
Shropshire	27,471	23,284
Staffordshire and Lichfield	26,278	23,747
Somerset and Bristol	45,900	49,808
Hampshire	28,557	26,851
Suffolk	47,537	34,422
Surrey and Southwark	40,610	34,218
Sussex	23,451	21,537
Warwickshire and Coventry	22,700	21,973
Worcestershire and Worcester	24,440	20,634
Wiltshire	27,418	27,093
Westmorland	6,691	6,501
Yorkshire, York and Hull	121,052	106,151
Wales	77,921	60,473
London, Middlesex and Westminster	111,215	100,136
Total	1,319,215	1,175,951

(a) From the broadsheet. The statistics differ from those reproduced in the Pepys correspondence (Tanner, *op. cit.*, p. 44) in one particular—Wales, for which the latter give a total of 49,055 instead of the 60,473 given above. In the Pepys correspondence the statistics are entitled 'names'.

mainder of the time during which the tax was in force, similar records were kept by the central and local hearth offices. But they have not generally survived—though some may still be found in private ownership—for they did not have to be sent to the Exchequer or to the Sheriff or Quarter Sessions.[78]

Secondly, because of the local interests of existing record societies, historians working on hearth-tax data have tended to concentrate upon the returns for particular counties, and even so relatively few returns have been analysed and published. It must be emphasized that the analysis of hearth-tax material is difficult and laborious, and it is in any case unlikely that any absolute set of statistics for the whole country could be obtained. But what could be done is to use the available records to build up a more consistent statistical account, and work in this direction should be encouraged.

One existing set of national statistics with which we may compare Davenant's and Houghton's tables is that relating to payments for the transcription of names, contained in the Tax Incidents Bills in the Treasury Money Books for the period 1684-9 and repeated in the Declared Accounts of the Commissioners (both in the Public Record Office). Mr C. A. F. Meekings, of the Public Record Office, whose special field is the hearth-tax records, has transcribed the Accounts and Bills and has generously supplied the relevant details.[79] Since the data of the Tax Incidents Bills are the more comprehensive (for the corresponding dates the amounts are the same as in the Declared Accounts), they are used here.

The first citation refers to Michaelmas 1684, and the Bills state that £138 9s. 3d. was paid for the transcription of 1,107,650 names, at the rate of 2s. 6d. per thousand. Subsequent entries are less specific, mentioning the total payment for transcription but not the number of names transcribed. Assuming the rate of payment to have remained unchanged, Table 13 may be constructed.

TABLE 13

Payments for transcription and inferred numbers of names

Books for collection at	Total sum paid			Inferred no. of names
	£	s.	d.	
1684 Michaelmas	138	9	3	1,107,650 (stated)
1685 Lady Day	147	4	0	1,177,600
Michaelmas	145	7	11¼	1,163,175
1686 Lady Day	151	10	6	1,212,200
Michaelmas	172	12	6	1,381,000
1687 Lady Day	168	17	6	1,351,000
Michaelmas	171	15	5	1,374,170
1688 Lady Day	175	3	1	1,401,230
Michaelmas	173	18	7½	1,391,450
1689 Lady Day	160	13	0	1,285,200

It will be seen that numbers of names stated or inferred in 1684-5 are not widely different from those given by Houghton. On the other hand, the inferred number for Lady Day 1689 is fairly near to Davenant's figure for '1690'. It is, to say the least, extremely unlikely that there was a genuine increase in the number of households, between

[78] A valuable account of the administrative and statistical aspects of the hearth tax is given in the introduction of C. A. F. Meekings, *Surrey Hearth Tax, 1664*, Surrey Record Society, nos. XLI, XLII, London 1940. See also L. M. Marshall, *The Rural Population of Bedfordshire, 1671-1921*, Publications of Bedfordshire Historical Record Society, Vol. XVI, Aspley Guise, 1934 and C. A. F. Meekings, *Dorset Hearth Tax Assessments, 1662-4 (Dorset Natural History and Archaeological Society (Mowlem Bequest))*, County Museum, Dorchester 1951.

[79] I am greatly indebted to Mr Meekings not only for this material, but for much other information relative to the hearth-tax statistics.

Michaelmas 1684 and Lady Day 1689, of almost 180,000, or a fall between Lady Day 1688 and Lady Day 1689 of over 100,000. At the same time we cannot be sure that the later figures are more nearly correct than the earlier, for, in the absence of a specific description, we do not know precisely what was included under the heading of transcription. Was it simply the names of the occupiers, plus the names of counties, hundreds, parishes and streets? If so, was Davenant's figure of 1,319,215 occupiers quite such an exaggeration as King, on second thoughts, concluded? If we accept King's upper estimate that the names should be reduced by 1 in 18 to obtain occupiers, and apply this correction to the inferred total for Michaelmas 1688, the reduced figure would be 1·314 millions, very close to Davenant's total. On the other hand, if King were right, should not the correction factor be applied to the inferred total for Lady Day 1689, 1,285,200, a smaller total than Davenant's, and thus yielding an even smaller net figure of occupiers than King envisaged in the Kashnor manuscript?

It is impossible to give a reasonably secure opinion on such questions without much more work on the available hearth-tax documents. What is required in the first place is the publication of the original data for all the years and areas for which the material exists. It would then be necessary to examine the internal consistency of the results—as between different areas and points of time. Some external check might also be obtained by comparing the results with the data obtained from other sources—for example, with the returns of the 1692 poll tax, and with any of the 1694 Act enumerations now available or which may be found.[80] But this kind of work is beyond the capacity of any one historian or demographer. It can only be done by the co-ordinated efforts of a number of workers from the two fields.[81]

[80] I understand that returns (under the 1694 Act) for a number of parishes in north-east Kent have now been found. This gives further support to the plea for a systematic search among record collections for whatever returns under that Act may still exist. The 1640 Protestation returns and the Compton 'census' data might also be used for comparison.

[81] (See also the comparison of King's statistics for Sevenoaks, Kent, with the Hearth-tax returns for that town—C. A. F. Meekings, *Dorset Hearth Tax Assessments, 1662-1664*, Dorchester 1951, p. xxxv.—D.V.G. 1962.)

9

POPULATION AND POPULATION MOVEMENTS IN ENGLAND AND WALES, 1700 TO 1850

D. V. GLASS

Editor's Note: This paper was originally prepared, at the end of 1945, for the Statistics Committee of the Royal Commission on Population. The paper was not published, though copies were circulated and are in a few libraries. Since 1945, new work on historical demography has been done in this country. I have not taken that work into account, for that would have meant writing at much greater length. In any case, the main object of the paper was to examine a number of well-known estimates of population growth in the eighteenth and early nineteenth centuries rather than to deal more comprehensively with the historical demography of England and Wales. I have omitted a section on Gregory King's estimates and have compressed the discussion of under-registration of births in the period 1831-70; both these subjects have been considered more fully in other published papers.[1]

THIS paper does not attempt to give the results of any fresh calculations of population movements in England and Wales before 1850. The purpose is rather to survey and evaluate the work already published in this field and to consider whether there are any profitable new lines of inquiry which might be undertaken. My conclusion is that, although much of the past work has considerable value, it has all been somewhat haphazard. A great deal of work remains to be done if we are really to understand the population history of England and Wales since, say, the middle of the seventeenth century and such work should yield results of considerable value. But in the main, the nature of the data is such that the only effective means of research is by collaboration. Unless it is possible to have a group of statisticians and historians working on the material, we cannot hope to get very much further in any reasonable length of time.

Leaving aside for the moment the controversialists of the eighteenth century —Price, Howlett, Wales, Forster, Brakenridge, Chalmers and F. M. and William Eden—the main attempts at demographic reconstruction are those of Rickman, Farr, Brownlee and Griffith.[2] Although their work has already been discussed by other writers, it is nevertheless appropriate, in the present general survey, to review the methods they used and the results they obtained, in order

[1] See pp. 159-220 above, and D. V. Glass, 'A note on the Under-Registration of Births in Britain in the Nineteenth Century' (*Population Studies*, Vol. V, 1951-2).

[2] I omit from this general discussion, E. C. K. Gonner's interesting study, 'The Population of England in the Eighteenth Century', *J.R.S.S.*, Vol. LXXVI, Part III (Feb. 1913), for although it summarizes previous material, it largely accepts the results of Rickman's second series of estimates. Similarly, I have omitted consideration of T. H. Marshall, 'The Population problem during the industrial revolution', *Economic Journal* (Economic History Series, No. 4), January 1929, since he largely adopts the calculations of Brownlee.

to ascertain whether any further work may profitably be done on the lines of overall, national, estimation.

Rickman made two estimates of the course of population in the eighteenth century. The first appeared in the *Observations on the Results of the Population Act, 41 Geo. III*,[3] while the second was published posthumously in the preface to the Enumeration Abstract of the 1841 Census. The first estimate was based on the returns obtained in reply to a question in the Schedule of the 1801 Census: 'What was the Number of Baptisms and Burials in your Parish, Township, or Place, in the several Years 1700, 1710, 1720, 1730, 1740, 1750, 1760, 1770, 1780 and each subsequent Year, to the 31st day of *December* 1800, distinguishing Males from Females?' Rickman knew that the material collected was not fully trustworthy. For one thing, the Parish Register Abstract is studded with references showing that, for many parishes, there were considerable gaps in the records.[4] This is scarcely surprising, since both contemporary and modern writers on the history of parish registers testify that it was by no means a rare occurrence for a register to find its way into private hands, its pages being used for kettle-holders and wrapping paper, and that on occasion preliminary entries were made on scraps of paper or in informal notebooks and never copied into the registers themselves, so that the facts of baptism and burial were never formally recorded. When there were gaps in the records, Rickman's method of dealing with the difficulty was simple. 'In Cases where the Returns are stated to be in some Years "defective", such Defects have been supplied, in every Instance, by an Average Number of Baptisms, Burials, and Marriages (or of either) taken from the Returns of the same Parish, in such of the Years specified in the respective Tables as are immediately preceding and subsequent to such Defect.'[5] The abstract of the registers is thus full of these 'adjustments'. But since, according to Barbara Hammond, the original returns were destroyed by Order of a Departmental Committee in 1904, it is no longer possible to go back to the original material and reclassify it.[6]

Rickman also realized that, even within themselves, the registers were very defective. Burials were not the statistical equivalent of deaths and—probably in a still greater degree—baptisms were not the equivalent of births. Nevertheless, his view was that 'in England and Wales the Registers of Baptisms and Burials were found to be in a state sufficiently correct for any general Purpose'.[7] One further possible source of error did not occur to him—that incorrect

[3] This is a 13-page report, dated London 1802, presumably published to be bound up with the main results of the 1801 Census, but often missing from the volumes. The report is signed 'J. R.'. The description of the questions asked on baptisms and burials is not quite correct as reported in the *Observations*.

[4] On the history of parish registers and registration, see in particular R. Bigland, *Observations on Marriages, Baptisms and Burials*, London 1764; J. S. Burn, *The History of Parish Registers in England*, 2nd edn., London 1862; R. E. C. Waters, *Parish Registers in England*, London 1882; A. M. Burke, *Key to the Ancient Parish Registers of England and Wales*, London 1908; J. C. Cox, *The Parish Registers of England*, London 1910; and *Report from the Select Committee on Parochial Registration*, 1833 (BPP. 1833, Vol. XIV). It is an interesting comment on the status of historical demography in England that the best histories of registration have been produced by genealogists interested in tracing pedigrees or in establishing acts of civil status. Even the Select Committee was primarily concerned with this latter problem, though it also took evidence from witnesses who were interested in vital statistics as such.

[5] 1801 Census, *Parish Registers*. Preface.

[6] B. Hammond, 'Urban death rates in the early nineteenth century', *Economic Journal* (Economic History Series, No. 3), January 1928.

[7] *Observations*, p. 5.

transcriptions from the registers were made by the parish priests or other officiating clergy. Yet this may have been important. The penmanship in some of the registers would certainly require a knowledge of paleography for transcription and Cox points out that many of the local clergy made a poor job of even reporting the dates covered by the registers in their possession.[8] Nor did Rickman believe that variations over time in the proportion of unregistered burials or baptisms would seriously affect his calculations. Of burials, he said 'though the Registry of Burials is certainly deficient, no cause can be assigned for believing that the Deficiency has been increasing in the last Twenty-one Years'; and of baptisms, 'nor is it known that any material Alteration in the Number of Dissenters, or in the other causes of Deficiency in the Register of Baptisms has taken place'.[9]

He finally based his calculations upon baptisms, because he found them less subject than burials to annual variations and because the marriage statistics were regarded as thoroughly inaccurate prior to 1754, when Hardwicke's Act was implemented. Taking the baptisms and using as his starting point the adjusted[10] 1801 figure of the population—9,168,000—he applied the 'Rule of Proportion', arguing 'Thus: if 255,426 Baptisms (the average Medium of the last five Years) were produced from a Population of 9,168,000, from what Population were 152,540 (the Baptisms of 1700) produced?'[11] The results of these calculations are given in Table 7. Since they depend for their validity upon the implicit assumption of a constant birth rate they beg some of the most important questions to answer which such estimates are made. In practice, estimates of population arrived at in that way may be fairly near the truth. But they cannot be used for indicating the course of birth rates in the eighteenth century.[12]

Rickman must have been aware of the theoretical objections to his method of estimation, for in his report on the 1831 census he proposed a new method —it may have been suggested by Finlaison—which seems to have been overlooked by Brownlee and Griffith. He assumed that, between 1821 and 1831,

[8] J. C. Cox, op. cit., ch. 13.

[9] Observations, pp. 6 and 8. Rickman's belief in the validity of the baptism statistics for his purpose derived in part from an erroneous interpretation of the ratios between baptisms and marriages over the period 1760-1800. He found that this ratio did not fluctuate by more than 5 per cent. He assumed that the marriage figures were correct and argued that the constant ratios meant a constant degree of omission in the baptisms. His argument as regards the baptism statistics for 1700, 1710 and 1720 was also unsound. He said that there had been a 'dearth' in 1709 and 1710 but that 'the nearly concurrent amounts of Registered Baptisms in 1700 and 1720, and the known cause of Diminution in 1710, must be allowed presumptive evidence of a probability, that the Deficiency caused by incorrectness was not greater then than it is at present'.

[10] This adjustment was only to allow for soldiers, sailors, etc. not enumerated in 1801. Although Rickman was aware that the 1801 census was defective—some parishes sent in no returns and the returns sent in were not perfect—he made no attempt to estimate the error involved or to correct the figure for his base year. Nor, with the exception of Finlaison—whose method of correction was not stated—has any subsequent statistician working on the eighteenth-century material, though everyone has acknowledged the defective nature of the first census. Malthus, who was in any case suspicious of Rickman's method and believed in working back on the basis of absolute births and deaths (after correcting the baptisms and burials), started from 1810 (really the 1811 census), and arrived at a figure of 9,287 millions for 1800 (really 1801). Essay on the Principles of Population, 5th edn., London 1817, Vol. 2, pp. 84-95.

[11] Observations, p. 9.

[12] Rickman's county estimates are, of course, subject to the same error. Rickman also found that his 1801 statement of baptisms and burials was incorrect because of some duplication and certain omissions. He gives a corrected statement in the 1811 Census report, but since he applies a constant correcting factor to his historical data, this has no effect upon his population estimates.

any emigration from Great Britain would have been counterbalanced by immigration from Ireland and that the increase in the population of England and Wales—amounting to 1,978,312 persons—could be accounted for entirely by natural increase. In the same period there were 2,462,907 registered burials. He added 94,890 for unregistered burials reported by the local clergy in making their returns to him, and a further 100,000 to allow for unnoted interments, making a total of 2,657,797. He then concluded (by what appears to be a slightly incorrect addition) that there must have been 4,636,672 births in the period, as compared with 3,753,493 baptisms, and that baptisms had to be increased by 24 per cent to make them equal to births. His view was that 'no better approximation to the Population of the Decennary Years of the first Half of the last Century can be obtained than by reliance on this proportion as applied to the Registered Baptisms and Burials of each Decennary Year'.[13] Following this statement, he gave a new estimate of the population growth of the eighteenth century, constructed not by himself but by Finlaison. Of this estimate, Rickman wrote, 'The best Statement which can be given of the progressive Population of England and Wales is here subjoined, on the authority of Mr Finlaison, of the National Debt Office, who is engaged in a sedulous investigation of the expectancy of human life, from infancy to old age, founded on the materials herein explained, after subjecting them to all the tests furnished by the present State of Physical and Statistical Knowledge.' No further explanation is given as regards this estimate, which is reproduced in Table 7. It may be noted, however, that the ratio of 1·24 between births and baptisms is almost precisely the same as that reached by Brownlee in his 1916 study.

The method which Rickman suggested in the report on the 1831 Census was not followed up by him in any way. Instead, he reverted to a variant of his earlier method of estimation, this time attempting to go much further back in his computations. In 1831 he had ascertained the conditions and extent of the registers in each parish and had found that not much less than half the parishes possessed registers going back to 1600, of which three-quarters began as early as 1570. On this basis an inquiry was made in 1836. The officiating clergy were asked to state the baptisms, burials and marriages for three-year periods, centred on each of the years 1570, 1600, 1630, 1670, 1700 and 1750, these particular years having been chosen by Rickman as being 'unexceptionable'. From the returns, he took those for parishes giving data for both 1570 and 1800 and calculated three sets of population estimates for each county. The method used was the same as for the 1801 estimates. For example, there were 394 baptismal entries for Bedfordshire for 1570 and the same parishes returned 772 baptisms for 1800. The population of Bedfordshire being 63,393 in 1801, it was estimated at (63,393) (394/772), or 32,353, in 1570. The same kind of cal-

---

[13] 1831 Census, *Enumeration Abstract*, Vol. I (London 1833), p. xlv. In his report (p. xlvii) Rickman also argued against taking censuses more frequently than once in ten years. He believed that there was much to be said for an 'established period'. Also, the expense would be substantial so far as the parishes and county rates were concerned. Hence, he concluded 'that any proposal for more frequent Enumerations will not be lightly entertained by the Legislature of the United Kingdom'. How right he was. It was not until the 1920 Census Act that provision was made for quinquennial censuses and so far that provision has not been used. (Further comments by Rickman on the omissions in parish registration are given in 'Concerning the defects and results of English parish registers . . .', *London Med. Gazette*, Vol. XVIII, 1836, pp. 436-43. See also the criticism of T. R. Edmonds in 'On the law of mortality in each county of England', *Lancet*, 1835-6, Vol. I, pp. 364-71. D.V.G. 1963.)

culations were also made on the basis of burials and marriages and the results were then averaged to give a final estimate. Rickman himself died before the 1841 census was taken, but his new estimates were published posthumously in the report on the 1841 census.[14] They are, of course, subject to the same kind of criticism as the first estimate—in fact, to an even greater extent, since they assume the constancy over an even longer period of marriage and death rates as well as of the birth rate. Moreover, there is no reason to believe that the parishes used in the calculation constituted a random sample.[15]

Like Rickman, Farr made two sets of calculations. Unfortunately, he was much less explicit than Rickman, and, in addition, his second calculation was incomplete, stopping short at an estimate of the births for each decade back to 1741-50. But, as in the case of all Farr's work, the approach to the problem is interesting in itself and the estimates are certainly worth consideration, particularly as they influenced Brownlee's subsequent work on the same question.

Farr's first estimate, which appeared in the report on the 1861 census,[16] is apparently a compound of two entirely different methods. Farr wanted to establish the population of England and Wales in the middle of the nineteenth, eighteenth and seventeenth centuries. For the seventeenth-century figure he took Rickman's 1841 data as a basis and made some unspecified deductions. He stated: 'By Mr Rickman's estimate the population of England and Wales was 5,600,517 in 1630; after various corrections we find the population for that year to be 5,466,572; and the population of 1670 to be 5,090,045[17]; we assume that the population of England and Wales was 5,466,572 in 1651.' No further explanation is given of the 'corrections' to Rickman's estimate. They seem, however, to be somewhat different from those used in establishing the population in 1751. For this, Farr recalculated the populations at each tenth year back from the first census, stopping short at 1701. His account of the method is as follows: 'A comparison of the excess of Baptisms over Burials in 1801-10 shows that the excess of Baptisms over Burials must be raised nearly *one third part* for the births of children who are not baptized to make it equal to the

[14] 1841 Census, *Enumeration Abstract*, London 1843, preface, pp. 34-37. The original computations —not apparently in Rickman's hand—are in Somerset House; *vide* G. T. Griffith, 'Rickman's second series of eighteenth-century population figures', *J.R.S.S.*, 1929, Part II. Griffith is right in taking Gonner to task for his statement that Rickman's second estimate was more soundly based than his first (a view shared by Sir Ernest Clarke; *cf. J.R.S.S.*, Feb. 1913, Part III, pp. 300-1). Gonner had either not read or not fully understood the census explanations of the methods used in making either of the estimates. But then, Gonner was not really aware of the technical problems involved in making historical estimates of population. Thus he said (*op. cit.*, p. 302): 'The only point on which he would like to suggest a correction was that an estimate ought to take into account the different ratio borne by these factors (i.e. burials, baptisms, marriages) to the population at different times. He thought, therefore, there ought to be certain allowances made.' But that, too, of course begs questions which the estimates are supposed to answer. It was Finlaison who persuaded Rickman to ask for the Parish Register returns for 3-year periods rather than for single years.

[15] In the historical tables given in the 1841 census report, a correction was made in the figures for 1570, giving a result slightly different from the average of the estimate based on baptisms, burials and marriages. This correction was made for two reasons: first, because no parish registers were available for 1570 for Monmouth or Northumberland. So an adjustment was made on the basis of the 1600 estimates. Secondly, too small a number of registers was available for Wales for 1570, so a comparable adjustment was made, based on the 1600 estimates. These adjustments still further reduce the validity of the estimates for the earliest periods.

[16] 1861 Census of England and Wales, Vol. III. *General Report* (B.P.P. 1863, Vol. LIII, part 1), p. 22. It is, of course, an assumption to say that these estimates were made by Farr, since no single authorship is stated in the Census reports. However, it seems most unlikely that anyone else in the G.R.O. would have done this work.

[17] This appears to be either a misprint for 1570, or a misprint for 6,090,045.

increase of population. Proceeding backwards in this manner from 1791 to 1741, the probable increase of population is obtained for every 10 years; and by referring back to the probably deficient registration of baptisms in the earlier period the series is carried back to 1701.' For the latter half of the eighteenth century, this implies that Farr assumed either, as Brownlee pointed out, that the proportionate omissions were the same for both baptisms and burials or that the omissions of both are always compensatory.[18] But there is good reason to believe—taking the evidence of contemporary observers and of modern analysis—that baptismal registration was the more deficient. As for the first half of the eighteenth century, Farr's method is obscure and no explanation is given of what is meant by 'referring back to the probably deficient registration of baptisms'. No one doubts that the registration was deficient. What is needed, however, is some check on the degree of deficiency and Farr's first estimates do not provide this.

To some extent, however, this gap is filled by Farr's calculations in the report on the 1871 census.[19] He was primarily interested in tracing the development of given generations of males and females. Thus, he said there were 1,864,198 males aged 10 to 20 years in 1851 and these became reduced to 1,689,180 aged 20 to 30 years in 1861. Knowing the deaths by age during the intervening period, it was thus possible to estimate what part was played by net emigration in this reduction. According to Farr, of the total reduction of 9·4 per cent in this particular group of males, 7·2 per cent was due to death and the balance to the excess of emigration over immigration. From this calculation Farr deduced that such 'rates can be employed as factors, and on the assumption that they remain for a time constant, or vary not enough to produce any marked perturbation, the ages unenumerated in 1831, in 1811, and even in 1801 and 1791 can be determined by their means with sufficient accuracy'. In estimating the ages for 1831, Farr appears to have moved forward from 1821 and back from 1841, taking some adjusted figure between the two results. 'Thus, from the 1,027,487 men living of the age of 30-40 in 1841, by means of the appropriate factor, the numbers of men of the age of 20-30 in 1831 were deduced; they were compared with the numbers of the same age deduced by another factor from 1,295,104 youths of 10-20 years of age enumerated in 1821. The number of the men of the age 20-30 in the Kingdom in 1831 was thus found to be 1,207,641; and the same method applied to the ten other decenniads of life gave a total of 6,968,155 males and 7,136,065 females of all ages, making the total population 14,104,220, or only 33,539 more than, and probably quite as near the truth as, the 14,070,681 enumerated.' By extending

[18] I am unable to check Farr's calculations in detail. To obtain his ratio of 'nearly one third part' involves taking burials and baptisms from mid-1801 to mid-1811. But the application of this ratio to earlier baptisms and burials does not give exactly the same results as those published by Farr, though the differences are small. Farr's own comment on his calculation was: 'The method which has been here employed of making the estimate appears, upon the whole, to be better than that of assuming any constant relation to subsist between the population and the marriages, births and deaths. The methods that have been made by others differ somewhat from these for the first forty years; but the excess of *Burials* over the *Baptisms* in the same parishes during the three years 1710, 1720, 1730, appears to show conclusively that the population decreased in that period' (*op. cit.*, p. 22, note to Table IVa).

[19] 1871 census of England and Wales, Vol. IV, *General Report* (B.P.P. 1873, LXXI, Part II), pp. xiii-xiv and 54-56.

the method, Farr pushed back his estimate of age structure to the end of the eighteenth century and in the same way deduced the numbers of births for each decade from 1741-50 onwards.[20] From these estimates of births it is possible to construct ratios between births and baptisms and also—as was done by Farr—to gain some idea of the completeness of registration of births after the introduction of civil registration but before the provision of a penalty for non-compliance with the Act. The data are set out in the following table.[21]

TABLE I

Ratio between estimated births and baptisms
(Births and baptisms in thousands)

Period	Farr's estimate of births (α) (a)	Baptisms (to 1840) (β) and Registered Births (b)	Ratio a/b
1741-50	1,707	1,801	0·948
1751-60	1,882	1,894	0·994
1761-70	2,079	2,032	1·023
1771-80	2,379	2,209	1·077
1781-90	2,641	2,397	1·102
1791-1800	2,988	2,618	1·141
1801-10	3,675	2,879	1·276
1811-20	4,425	3,255	1·359
1821-30	4,798	3,753	1·278
1831-40	5,289	3,966	1·334
1841-50	5,869	5,489	1·069
1851-60	6,665	6,472	1·030
1861-70	7,636	7,500	1·018

(a) 1871 Census of England and Wales, *General Report*, Table 61.

(β) The baptisms for each decade from 1741-50 to 1771-80 are taken from Farr's adjusted figures, given in the 1861 Census of England and Wales, *General Report*, p. 22. The figures are estimates, since the actual returns gave the baptisms for each *tenth* year up to 1780. The baptisms for 1781-1810 are Rickman's adjusted figures (adjusted to allow for duplications and omissions in the 1801 returns). The data for the decades from 1831-40 onwards are given by Farr in the 1871 Census, *General Report*, Table 60, and in the 1861 Census, *General Report*, p. 22.

According to his own account, Farr used constant factors in undertaking his calculation.[22] The assumption of constant mortality, the major factor used in the calculation, has two results. First, it begs the whole question as to the actual course of mortality and therefore, at least in part, defeats the purpose for which the estimates were made, for they cannot be used for the construction of death rates. Secondly, if mortality rates (especially infant mortality) were in

[20] The eighteenth-century extension did not cover all the age groups—in fact, even the 1801 calculation excluded the ages above 60 years.

[21] Farr did not compare baptisms with his estimates of births and the comparison between estimated and registered births is given only incidentally in the census report. It is unfortunate that Farr was not more specific in describing the methods he used, for it is now extremely difficult to check his calculations. Farr made two other comments on under-registration of births after the introduction of civil registration. In the *Thirty-Fifth Annual Report of the Registrar-General*, p. v, he estimated the annual deficiency at 65 per 1,000 in 1841-50; 29 per 1,000 in 1851-60; and 18 per 1,000 in 1861-70. This is comparable with the estimates (in fact, really the same) given in the 1871 Census, General Report, p. 55. But in the *Thirty-Ninth Annual Report of the Registrar-General*, p. v, he assumed that the birth rate during the period 1837-76 must have been about 36 per 1,000, and he thence deduced the omission of 1,441,603 births, or about 5 per cent for the period.

[22] Presumably he based himself on English Life Table No. 3, 1838-54. It is not, however, at all clear whether he assumed a constant migration factor on the lines suggested by his example for 1851-61, or, in fact, any migration factor at all.

fact higher in the first part of the period covered than in the second, then it is evident that this method of estimation would arrive at birth figures too low in comparison with the probable reality. The table above shows precisely this trend in the data. From 1801-10 backwards, each decade shows a lower ratio between estimated births and baptisms returned, until, in the two earliest decades, the recorded baptisms appear to be in excess of the births, a most unlikely conclusion. It may, of course, be true that, at the same time, the proportionate omissions in the recorded baptisms were increasing as the eighteenth century drew onwards. This is supported by what we know of the growth of Dissent. But in view of the improbable results for the decades 1741-50 and 1751-60, it is likely that a large part of the increase in the ratio is due to the unjustified assumption of the method of estimation.[23]

The methods used by Rickman and Farr were relatively simple. But Brownlee, though finally adopting simple correction factors, built up a complex system of checks and inferences,[24] and it is not very easy to distinguish between the methods used in arriving at factors and those used for testing their validity. However, the essence of his method of computation is to be found in sections (E) and (F) of his paper and the present comment will concentrate primarily upon those sections.

Taking the analysis in what seems to be the logical order, Brownlee began by comparing the baptisms with births and the burials with deaths for the three years during which two systems of registration most closely overlapped, namely 1838-40. For those years he found 1,458,664 births as compared with 1,109,617 baptisms, giving a ratio of 1·317 births per baptisms; and 1,041,373 deaths as compared with 883,912 burials, giving a comparable ratio of 1·178. Brownlee believed that these were minimum ratios, since it was highly probable, in the first few years of registration, that there was considerable underregistration of births and deaths. He then went on to consider a more direct way of estimating the ratio between births and baptisms, namely that used by Farr. His view was that the ratios derived from Farr's estimates fluctuated 'in a manner which can only be regarded as very improbable'. This was particularly so for the period 1800-1840, during which time the death rate varied considerably, a factor not allowed for by Farr. Brownlee's conclusion as to the probable variation in the death rate over the period 1800-1840 was based on an examination of the burial rates—that is, the numbers of registered burials per thousand

[23] I should add that in compiling English Life Table No. 3, the birth data for the period 1838-54 were adjusted to allow for under-registration. Farr's adjusted births were 9,718,886 for the 17 years from mid-1837 to mid-1853 (4,973,401 males and 4,745,485 females) compared with 9,284,210 actually registered. If this adjustment were incorrect, the Life Table must be incorrect and thus also the survival factors derived from it. (See W. Farr, English Life Table. Tables of Lifetimes, Annuities and Premiums, London, H.M.S.O. 1864, p. xxi.) However, the method does provide a clue to the mortality of the eighteenth as compared with the nineteenth century, for it suggests—in the absence of any substantial net excess of emigration—that eighteenth-century mortality was substantially higher than that in the period 1838-54. An additional estimate of the population, 1761-1801, is given in the Eighth Annual Report of the Registrar-General, 1848, p. xxvi, and is presumably also attributable to Farr. The basis is curious, being described as follows: 'The population increased 0·283 per cent faster than the marriages through the period 1801-1841; the rate of increase of marriages, in 1761-1801, was raised to that extent, and these taken to represent the increase of the population in the same period.' The resultant populations are (in millions): 1761, 5·802; 1771, 6·353; 1781, 7·144; 1791, 8·057; 1801, 9·149.

[24] John Brownlee, 'The History of the birth and death rates in England and Wales taken as a whole, from 1570 to the present time', Public Health, June 1916, pp. 211-22, and July 1916, pp. 228-38.

total population—for the first four decades of the nineteenth century. These
he found to be 19·9, 17·6, 18·8 and 19·5 respectively and he believed that the
differences between the rates 'can hardly be due to difference of registration,
but must represent some real condition'.

With these observations as a basis, Brownlee then embarked on the process
of correction of the raw data. He assumed that the ratio of 1·18 deaths per
burial—ascertained for the years 1838-40—would justifiably apply to the whole
of the decade 1831-40. Taking the intercensal increase of the population and
making no allowance for migration, he thus arrived at a corrected figure of
5,580,000 births in the decade, as compared with Farr's estimate of 5,289,000.
For the decade 1821-30, Farr's estimated births were accepted, as the death
rate (presumably Brownlee meant the burial rate) did not suggest the need for
any correction. Accepting this figure, and bearing in mind the population
increase shown by the censuses of 1821 and 1831, a corrected figure of deaths
was obtained for the decade, and this again proved to compare with registered
burials in the ratio of 1·18 to one. For the decade 1811-20, Brownlee based
himself on a scrutiny of Farr's estimate of the population aged 0-10 years in
1821, derived from the births of the decade of 1811-20. In view of the substantially lower burial rate in this decade (17·6 as compared with 18·8 for the
decade 1821-30), Farr's ratio was adjusted to the lower mortality as indicated
by the crude rate, and the estimated births reduced correspondingly to approximately 4,140,000. Again taking into account the intercensal growth of population, an adjusted figure of deaths for the decade was obtained and this was
found to bear substantially the same ratio to the registered burials as in the
previous decade. (It was, in fact, of the order of 1·2 to one.) It was therefore,
justifiable, in Brownlee's view, to assume a constant ratio of deaths to burials
and on this basis the births were calculated for the decade 1801-10 and found
to amount to substantially the same figure as that given by Farr. By using
what amounts to a system of continuous cross-reference, Brownlee thus built
up his births and deaths, and the rates based upon them, from 1801 to the
beginning of civil registration. For the decades from 1841 to 1870, he accepted
the official death statistics and made his own estimates of births (slightly different
from those of Farr) by comparing the populations aged 0-5 years, as derived
from the births and deaths, with those enumerated at the relevant censuses. In
this way, a continuous series was built up from 1801 to the point of time when
registration may be assumed to have become complete.

For the eighteenth century, the approach was rather different. The ratio of
deaths to burials was taken at a constant 1·2 and this provides the basis for
estimating the number of deaths in the decade 1791-1800. To estimate the births
in the same decade, two methods are employed. The first involves a scrutiny
of the ages recorded at the censuses of 1821 and 1841. Comparing the number
of females of the same ages (by ten year age groups) recorded at the two censuses, he found that the ratios between the respective numbers showed a
marked difference as the end of the eighteenth century was passed—that is,
'between those born 1781-90, with those born 1801-1810, and between those
born 1791-1800 with those born 1811-20 . . .'.[25] There was a much higher ratio

[25] As the censuses were for 1821 and 1841, the appropriate comparisons for the same age-groups

for the females born at the later date to those born at the earlier date than was typical for the comparisons as a whole, this ratio falling again as soon as comparison was made between the females born in 1801-10 and those born in 1821-30. Brownlee concluded that 'in the eighteenth century, from 1740 onwards, as the births went up, the deaths went down'. He found the ratios between the survivors of the births of 1751-60 and 1731-40; 1761-70 and 1741-50; and 1771-80 and 1751-60 of the order of 1·3, with a slight but consistent upward trend. For the survivors of the births of 1791-1800 compared with those of 1771-80, the ratio spurted to 1·357 and rose still more for the next two twenty-year comparisons, after which it fell back to a low level. As recorded baptisms were not rising proportionately during the period, Brownlee attributed the increase in the ratios to a continued fall in the death rate. He obtained a factor for correcting Farr's estimate of births for the decade 1791-1800 (given by Farr as 2,988,000, and deriving from the assumption of constant mortality) by dividing the average of the two high ratios into an average of the two lower ratios immediately preceding, and the first lower ratio immediately subsequent to them. He thus reached a figure of 3,326,000 births. He attempted

TABLE 2

Comparison between age groups enumerated at the 1821 and 1841 censuses (reproduced from Dr Brownlee's study, Public Health, 1916, p. 219)
(absolute figures in thousands)

Age Group	Males 1821	Males 1841	Ratios	Females 1821	Females 1841	Ratios	Periods of birth of compared populations	
0	1,682	1,991	1·183	1,665	2,006	1·205	1811-20	1831-40
10	1,261	1,653	1·311	1,261	1,654	1·311	1801-10	1821-30
20	856	1,327	1·550	1,030	1,497	1·452	1791-00	1811-20
30	673	994	1·479	742	1,050	1·415	1781-90	1801-10
40	546	745	1·363	572	776	1·357	1771-80	1791-00
50	388	494	1·274	402	528	1·314	1761-70	1781-90
60	262	328	1·251	284	368	1·298	1751-60	1771-80
70	130	158	1·220	142	184	1·296	1741-50	1761-70
80	33	41	1·227	41	53	1·285	1731-40	1751-60

to check this result by a rough computation of the death rate (estimated at about 27 per thousand for the decade 1791-1800) and an estimate of the rate of growth of the population during the period, which he found to be such as would involve a doubling of numbers in 50 years.[26] He had previously drawn up twenty sets of type-populations, based on five different life tables and four assumptions as to the rate of population growth. These assumptions ranged from a zero rate of increase to one involving a doubling in 50 years. For each type-population he had computed the implicit birth and death rates and the ratios between the sizes of various age groups. He found that the type-population based on the Manchester Life Table, 1881-90, and assuming a doubling in

could only be made at 20-year spans of time. The ratios consist of, for example, dividing the 1821 population aged 20-30 years (i.e. born 1791-1800) into the 1841 population aged 20-30 years (i.e. born 1811-1820). They are thus in the reverse order from that specified by Brownlee.

[26] Presumably using the theorem postulated at the beginning of his paper, for estimating birth and death rates without knowing the size of the population (on the assumption of constancy of the rates over the period considered).

50 years, corresponded most closely to the circumstances of 1791-1800 and from that population, with the help of the estimated (presumably Farr's estimate) number of persons aged under 10 years living in 1801, he derived a figure of 3,154,000 births for the decade. Adjusting himself to 'the habit of compromise, inherent in the English mind', which he later implied was responsible for one of Gonner's figures, he took the mean of his two results, namely 3,240,000 births, and thus obtained a population figure for 1791. By assuming the constancy of the 1·2 ratio between deaths and burials, he also obtained a ratio of 1·243 between births and baptisms. This was the last ratio he was able to check. He held it, and the ratio of deaths to burials, constant for the rest of the eighteenth century and projected his populations back to 1701.[27]

It need hardly be said that Dr Brownlee's methods of estimation are most ingenious. They represent a high form of statistical gymnastics applied in attempting to produce reasonable results from inadequate basic data. But in judging the validity of the results, the relevant criterion must clearly be not that of the degree of ingenuity applied, but of the acceptability of the implicit and explicit assumptions. To reach a conclusion as to the validity of those assumptions, it will be convenient to deal separately with the estimates for the nineteenth and eighteenth centuries.

Taking the decade 1831-40, it will be remembered that Brownlee began his estimate by calculating the ratios between deaths and burials and births and baptisms, based on the data for 1838-40.[28] A glance at the table below, which sets out the available national data for the period 1831-40, will show that the trend during the change-over from parochial to civil registration was a peculiar one. During the year in which the new system came into force, both baptisms

TABLE 3

Baptisms and births

Year	Births	Baptisms	Ratio of births to baptisms	Deaths	Burials	Ratio of deaths to burials
1831		389,122			278,619	
1832		387,971			298,161	
1833		400,043			290,508	
1834		405,875			283,097	
1835		405,067			281,545	
1836		405,137 (b)			281,685 (b)	
1837		462,893 (c)			336,994 (c)	
1838	463,787 (a)	377,114	1·230	342,760 (a)	292,650	1·171
1839	492,574	368,063	1·338	338,984	286,855	1·181
1840	502,303	364,440	1·378	359,687	304,407	1·181
1838-40	1,458,664	1,109,617	1·317	1,041,431	883,912	1·178

[27] This involved interpolation for the period prior to 1780, but I shall not deal with that question. The remainder of Brownlee's study consists mainly of an attempt to check his results, especially as regards the course of the death rate, and of a comparison between his estimated birth rates for the early eighteenth century and some rates derived from T. Short, *New Observations, Natural, Moral, Civil, Political and Medical, on City, Town, and Country Bills of Mortality*, London 1750.

[28] Registration under the Act of 6 and 7 Will. IV, c. 86, began 1 July 1837, but comparison with the parochial material is not possible before the whole year, 1838. The baptisms in Table 3 are from the 1841 Census, *Parish Register Abstract*, pp. viii, xi and xiv; the births and deaths from *Eighth Annual Report of the Registrar-General*, London 1848, p. v.

and burials increased by about 50,000 as compared with the previous year, that is, 1836. After 1837 they both slumped, burials to about the pre-civil registration level and baptisms to considerably below that level, and on a downward curve. Marshall's explanation of this sudden increase of baptisms in 1837 is that it was either a clerical error or could otherwise 'only be explained on the assumption that, in that year, 50,000 baby girls were carried to church on a wave of patriotism and christened "Victoria" '.[29] This explanation is amusing but scarcely realistic. The rise was exhibited in many parts of the country, and it was slightly higher for boys than for girls. It is far more likely that it was due to anticipation of the new system—possibly to fear that delay in baptism might result in the imposition of penalties, possibly also to church propaganda to the effect that registration would not be a substitute for baptism.[30] Similar factors would probably also apply to burials. In fact, judging from the statistics in the table above, it might seem that the increase in baptisms and burials between 1836 and 1837 was indicative of almost the whole gap between births and baptisms and between burials and deaths. Brownlee constructed his ratios on the average for 1838-40 believing—contrary to the views expressed in the *Abstract* of parish registers for the period 1831-40[31]—that parish registration did not fall off as a result of the introduction of the new system. So far as burials are concerned, Brownlee's belief seems to be supported by the statistics of 1838-40. But it does not appear to be true of the baptisms, and Brownlee's reasoning in favour of his own case is not really satisfactory. He set a lower limit[32] on the deaths for the decade by applying the death rates at each age for the decade 1841-50. In this way he estimated the total numbers of deaths in the decade 1831-40 and, by addition to the intercensal increase of population, obtained an approximate figure of 5,341,000 births for the decade. This gave him a ratio of 1·347 births per baptism for the decade 1831-40 and, as this is higher than the observed ratio for 1838-40, he concluded that parish registration had not become more defective after 1837. But this conclusion is not acceptable as statistical proof unless the number of births for the decade can be established with considerable accuracy, and that was obviously not done by Brownlee. For one thing, birth registration in 1838-40 was incomplete, so that the ratios of actual births to baptisms should be higher than Brownlee's estimates. Brownlee himself realized this—though he did not make use of the results for the decade 1831-40—as a result of subsequent computations concerning birth omissions for the decades 1841-50, 1851-60 and 1861-70.[33] Further,

[29] T. H. Marshall, *op. cit.*, p. 442.

[30] Among the contemporary material in the possession of the General Register Office are some pamphlets drawn up on these lines, e.g. one written in 1837 by the Deputy Registrar of the Diocese of Exeter, entitled *The Church Register not superseded by the New Register*, and another entitled *Registration is not Baptism*, which achieved its third edition in 1841.

[31] 1841 Census, *Parish Register Abstract (Abstract of the Answers and Returns made pursuant to Acts 3 and 4 Vic. c. 99, and 4 Vic. c. 7)*, P.P. 1845, XXV, p. vi.

[32] A lower limit, since he believed (on the basis of the burial rates) that the death rate was higher in 1831-40 than in 1841-50.

[33] Brownlee's estimate of this deficiency is too low for it is based upon a comparison of the calculated population 0-4 years of age, with the comparable enumerated population at each of the subsequent censuses. But we know from recent and current experience that our censuses understate the number of children under 1 year of age—perhaps because some parents do not regard a child as 'existing' until birth has been registered. Calculations based on births and deaths also suggest deficient enumeration of the age group 1 and under 2 years. Thus Brownlee slightly under-estimated the incompleteness of registration in the 1850's and 1860's.

Brownlee's computation assumes no net balance of emigration, and this may mean understating the births. As against Brownlee's view, finally, the statistics for 1838-40 show falling baptisms and rising births—in other words, a widening gap between births and baptisms.

Referring again to the table of baptisms and births, it would seem more justifiable to estimate the gap—at least as a first approximation—by comparing the figures of civil registration in 1838 with those of parochial registration in 1836 (i.e. ratio a/b), the last apparently undisturbed year of the old system. This would give 1·145 for births to baptisms and 1·217 for deaths to burials. Alternatively, as there appears to be a rising curve for births and, to a slighter extent, for deaths, it might be more appropriate to derive ratios by comparing the parish registration data in 1837 (when they spurted, almost to civil registration level) with those for 1836 (i.e. ratio c/b). This would give 1·143 for births to baptisms and 1·196 for deaths to burials. In both cases the ratio of deaths to burials is slightly higher than that used by Brownlee. On *a priori* grounds, it is likely that under the new system of registration, unregistered deaths were very few[34] and it may therefore be assumed—subject to further corroboration—that the ratio of deaths to burials at the point of transition from the old system to the new was of the order of 1·21, or slightly less.

If, for the moment, we assume that the numbers of registered deaths in 1838 and subsequent years are substantially correct, it is possible to make an approximate test of the completeness of birth registration in the decade 1831-40 by constructing populations from the births and deaths of 1838-41[35] and comparing the results with the data of the 1841 census.[36] Judging from the experience of the 1911 census the best age groups for use in testing under-registration of births are probably those of 3 – and 4 – years.[37] The latter age group cannot be used here, for civil registration had not been introduced when the births concerned took place. And for the age group 3 – some correction of the estimate is required, for the registered births from which it derives (mid-1837-mid-1838) numbered only 399,712. This is below the baptisms for the calendar year 1837 and below the registered births for the calendar year 1838, and it is clear that abnormally low registration took place. The registered births for mid-1837-mid-1838 have therefore been replaced by the means of the baptisms of 1837 and the births of 1838 and the corrected estimate then arrived at. The combined age groups 1 – and 2 – also offer some check when compared with the adjusted census population. The table suggests under-registration of births in 1837-38 in a marked degree. Bearing in mind the possible slight under-

---

[34] The Registrar-General was of this opinion. He wrote, in the *Second Annual Report*, 1840, p. 4, 'Assuming . . . that it is unnecessary to allow a greater correction than 2 per cent for omissions in the Registration of Deaths . . .'. The run of the death statistics for ages under 5 seems to corroborate this, though more stringent tests are really needed.

[35] The method adopted is that used by George King in his analysis of under-enumeration and mis-statements of age in the census of 1911. (See my article, 'A note on under-registration of births in Britain in the Nineteenth Century', *Population Studies*, July 1951.) The construction of the population as of the middle of 1841 is made simpler because, for the first four years of registration, the annual reports relate to mid-1837-mid-1838; mid-1838-mid-1839, etc.

[36] The census was taken in 6-7 June 1841, so that the results may be regarded as sufficiently close to mid-year figures. The census data, adjusted by Farr for unstated ages, are from the *Eighth Annual Report of the Registrar-General*, London 1848, p. lxxxi.

[37] Marked under-enumeration is evident at ages 0-, 1- and 2-, and there is also clearly some transference from 1- to 2-. It is possible to allow for these errors, based on subsequent experience.

TABLE 4

Enumerated and estimated persons in mid–1841 (males and females combined) and related births
(figures in thousands)

Ages in years	Calendar year of birth	Census popn.	Corrected (a) census popn.	Popn. estimated from births and deaths		Estimated Births (c)	Ratio of estimated to registered births (d)
				Uncorrected	Corrected (b)		
	mid-						
0–1	1840–41	429·2	527·4	451·7		} 1,129·9	1·12
1–2	1839–40	429·6	459·3	411·2			
2–3	1838–39	437·0		369·6		547·9	1·14
3–4	1837–38	409·9		277·8	341·4	531·8	1·15

(a) The 0–4 year population was multiplied by 1·05 to allow for under-enumeration, the addition being allocated to the ages 0–1 and 1–2 years.

(b) Using the mean of the baptisms and registered births as indicated in the text.

(c) Estimated births = (Census Population – Estimated Population) + Registered Births.

(d) No allowance made for under-registration of deaths. See text.

registration of deaths, too, it seems probable that a factor of about 1·16 or even higher is required to raise registered births to actual births for those years and perhaps slightly less for the years 1839-40. From the previous discussion we may fairly reasonably conclude that a factor of about 1·144 is required for the transition from parish registration, so that the combined factor for raising baptisms to actual births for the period 1831-37 is probably not less than 1·33. For raising burials to actual deaths for the same period would appear to be about 1·23, allowing for a 2 per cent omission of deaths during the initial years of civil registration. Errors in these estimated factors are more likely to be on the side of understating than of overstating the necessary ratios.[38]

The ratios arrived at for the period 1831-40 are very similar to those estimated by Brownlee, though the factors are slightly higher than his. But, in the absence of any further evidence, it would be unsafe to proceed backwards on Brownlee's lines, to the beginning of the nineteenth century. Brownlee, for example, assumes that Farr's estimate of births for 1821-30 is acceptable because the death rate suggested no need for correction. But this involves the assumption of a constant degree of omission in the burial register. It is not, therefore, surprising that, when Brownlee compared his estimate of deaths in the period with the statistics of burials, he found approximately the same ratio as for the subsequent decade. Yet contemporary evidence suggests that, between 1800 and 1840, increasing numbers of cheap burial grounds were provided in the larger towns, primarily for the poor, for which no records were kept. This would therefore suggest a lowering of the necessary ratio of deaths to burials in the earlier years of the century. The same criticism applies to Brownlee's calculations for the decade 1811-20 and to his consequent adoption of a constant

[38] For example, if there were a net excess of emigration during the period, the birth ratio arrived at would be too low, for a certain, though small, proportion of the emigration would consist of infants and young children. Thus, of the 256,940 emigrants leaving U.K. ports in 1870, at least 11,604 were infants under 1, and an additional 42,598 were children under 12 years of age. (*Thirty-Third Annual Report of the Registrar-General*, London 1872, p. lxxvi.)

ratio of 1·2 deaths per burial, and thus also to his estimates for 1801–10. The latter estimates contain a further possible source of error in that Brownlee accepted as correct the results of the 1801 census, which Rickman and other contemporaries believed to be defective.[39]

In producing his estimates for the first half of the nineteenth century, Brownlee at least had as a check the results of successive censuses, which provided the basic populations and placed some limit on the margin of error in the calculation of births and deaths. No such limiting factor was available to him for the eighteenth century and any systematic error in estimation would therefore tend to be cumulative. This should be borne in mind in weighing up the probable accuracy of his estimate for 1791–1800, for all his conclusions for the earlier part of the eighteenth century derive from the results for that decade alone. It was noted that, in dealing with this decade, Brownlee postulated the continuance of the ratio of 1·2 deaths per burial. Then he assumed that the increasing numbers of survivors found in passing from the middle to the end of the eighteenth century was in a large measure due to the fall of mortality in the same period, since there was not a proportionate increase in baptisms. It may be seen that, taking twenty-year spans comparable with those used by Brownlee, there was a considerable increase in the crude baptism figures. But allowing for this increase by dividing the ratios in the table below into those obtained by Brownlee in comparing the sizes of comparable age groups at the 1821 and 1841 censuses, and then correcting Farr's estimated births by the resultant quotient, a birth figure very similar to Brownlee's would be obtained. But the critical point in the estimate turns upon the implicit assumption that, between 1741–50 and 1791–1800, the deficiency of baptismal registration was

TABLE 5

Baptisms in compared decades
(in thousands)

Decade	Baptisms	Decade	Baptisms	Ratio of second to first decades
1741–50	1801	1761–70	2032	1·128
1751–60	1894	1771–80	2209	1·166
1761–70	2032	1781–90	2397	1·180
1771–80	2209	1791–1800	2618	1·185
1781–90	2397	1800–10	2879	1·201

constant. If the deficiency actually grew throughout the period then it may be possible to explain the whole, or almost the whole, of the increase in the numbers of the survivors as between the 1821 and 1841 censuses in terms of increasing births and without any recourse to a fall in mortality. If, on the other hand, there was a fall in the deficiency, then Brownlee's estimate of the decline in mortality is understated and the number of births in the decade 1791–1800 should be lower than his estimate. The statistics used by Brownlee offer no

[39] For example, Malthus (previously cited); William Day, *An Inquiry into Poor Laws and Surplus Labour*, 2nd edn., London 1833, p. 8 (Day said that 'the accuracy of the census of 1801 has been generally disputed'); John Heysham believed that the enumeration was defective as regards Carlisle, of the population of which he had an intimate knowledge (see his correspondence with Joshua Milne in H. Lonsdale, *The Life of John Heysham, M.D.*, London 1870, Appendix, esp. p. 166).

check upon either possibility. Nor, at present, are there other statistical checks to which recourse might be had. For the moment all that can be done is to point to two factors in the history of the eighteenth century which would seem to throw considerable doubt upon Brownlee's implicit assumption. First, it is generally agreed that Dissent grew markedly in the eighteenth century, especially in the latter half, and this would tend to reduce the completeness of parish registration to a greater degree as the decades passed by.[40] Secondly, the Act of 23 Geo. III, which came into force on 1 October 1783, levied a stamp duty of 3d. on the entry of every burial, marriage, christening or birth in the parish registers. This was extended in 1785 to the registers of Dissenters, at least partly in response to their own petition. Dissenters had imagined that, by this means, their own registers would be given the legal status of the normal parish registers. In fact this was found not to be the case and the Act was repealed in 1794, having apparently been disliked by many sections of the people. The point is, however, that during the period in question—which cuts into the decade used by Brownlee for evolving his eighteenth-century correction factors—there is good reason to suppose that the defectiveness of parish registration may have increased. In a mistaken belief concerning the legal status of their own non-parochial registers, Dissenters would increasingly abstain from using parish registers for providing acts of civil status. At the same time, the imposition of a tax—without any corresponding imposition of an injunction, under penalty, to make the entry—would tend to reduce the entries made on behalf of poorer persons.[41] On the other hand there was still in force at the beginning of the eighteenth century an Act which should, at least theoretically, have tended to make registration much more effective than at any subsequent time before the introduction of the civil system. This was the Act of 6 and 7 William and Mary c. 6, 1694, originally passed for five years but extended for five more

[40] As the author (W. Heberden) of *A Collection of the Yearly Bills of Mortality, from 1657 to 1758 inclusive*, London 1759, pointed out, the degree of deficiency would not be the same for baptisms and burials. He said, pp. 4-5, 'Some few indeed among the poorer sort, both of papists and dissenters, who live at a distance from their respective burial-grounds and cannot bear the expense of being carried thither, are buried according to the rites of the Church of England, and by that means have a place in the weekly bills. Some have been willing to think, that, though the bills are defective in the several articles of births and burials, yet they are defective in nearly the same degree; so that a proportion is still in some measure kept up. But the last observation destroys this supposed proportion; as the burials of some few papists, and of more dissenters, but the births of none in either persuasion, are registered there.' No doubt this conclusion is a little too sweeping. It is likely that, since entry in the baptismal register was the only legally acceptable evidence of descent, some couples paid for registration of their children even when they were members of a quite different faith. For example, this was occasionally done by Jews. Further, it is known that some entries were made for deaths of Jews, even when the interment took place in Jewish burial grounds. (See W. S. Samuel, 'Sources of Anglo-Jewish Genealogy', *Journal of the Society of Genealogists*, December 1932.) But it is probable that, in the main, the conclusion is correct.

[41] J. S. Burn, *op. cit.*, pp. 34-35, says that 'the poor refused to pay, and the clergyman was placed in the disagreeable situation of a tax-gatherer, with a remuneration for the trouble of collection, and often preferred paying the tax out of his own purse, to incurring the ill-will of his parishioners. In Scotland . . . it was the means in many parishes of the omission of Registration altogether.' There is no reason to suppose that a similar, though perhaps not quite so devastating an effect, did not take place in England. There would in any case be a tendency to omit registration of the very poor. For example, among the Heysham manuscripts (for access to which I am indebted to the Chief Librarian of Carlisle Public Library, Mr Thomas Gray, F.L.A.) there is a note from J. Parker, Curate of Wreay, in Cumberland, that 'There were several burials of Mendicants, belonging to the Parish of Heskett, while Heskett poor house was kept at Wreay; but as the Minister Clerk etc., of the Mother Church demanded 13½ pence for every burial without exception, I was for this and other reasons which were then thought more weighty, advised not to register them in our Book.' This kind of consideration must surely have been of more than local importance.

years by 8 and 9 William III c. 20. This legislation not only imposed taxes on births, marriages and burials, but also made it incumbent upon people to give the assessors full and speedy information whenever any of these events took place. The Acts applied equally to Dissenters, and the clergy were to keep exact accounts and registers of all marriages, burials and christenings (in the latter term the Act included 'christened or borne') under penalty of £100 fine. It is known that the legislation was not completely effective. Various supplementary Acts were passed to increase the efficiency of operation and, in the end, Parliament had to pass an Act of Indemnity (4 Anne c. 12, 1706), to protect the clergy from prospective ruin through failure to maintain full and accurate registers. But it is still probable, particularly in view of the effort devoted to enforcing the legislation, that registration from 1695 to 1705 was considerably more effective than at the end of the eighteenth century.

The above evidence suggests that Brownlee's calculations for the eighteenth century were wrongly based. Nor can appeal be made to the other check used by Brownlee—deriving births from type-populations. If those type-populations have a sound theoretical basis, they must be equivalent to 'stable' populations in the sense in which Lotka used the term. At the time Brownlee was writing, Lotka had not yet fully developed his analysis and its derivatives.[42] In any case, although there are now well-developed mathematical techniques for making more effective use of limited demographic data, these techniques involve assumptions of a kind which mean that certain important questions are bound to remain unanswered. Moreover, the basic data needed for proper use of these techniques were not available to Brownlee and are still not available.[43] If Brownlee's calculations for the decade 1791-1800 are not entirely beyond reproach, there is little reason to believe that the estimates for the remainder of the eighteenth century, for which the data are still more tenuous, are—save by accident—more reliable.[44] It is important to appreciate the great skill used by Brownlee in attempting to make bricks without straw. His estimates are more subtle than those of Rickman, Farr or Griffith. Yet in view of the manifold possibilities of error to which they are liable, they must be regarded as not proven.

By contrast with Brownlee's methods, the approach used by Griffith[45] is extremely simple. It is, in essence the method suggested, though not followed up, by Rickman in the report on the 1831 census, namely that of finding

---

[42] The essential part of this analysis is given in A. J. Lotka, *Théorie analytique des associations biologiques*, Part II, Paris 1939.

[43] ('Stable' and 'quasi-stable' population analysis is often used nowadays to give estimates of birth and death rates for less developed societies, for which reliable vital statistics are not available. But a growth rate must then be known or assumed, and/or a reasonable estimate of mortality levels or of the age-distribution of deaths. It is possible to fill many gaps by such techniques, but not every gap. As more data are collected for the eighteenth century the opportunities for applying these techniques will be increased. See also N. H. Carrier, 'A note on the estimation of mortality and other population characteristics given deaths by age', *Population Studies*, November 1958; J. Bourgeois-Pichat, 'Utilisation de la notion de population stable pour mesurer la mortalité et la fécondité des populations des pays sous-développés', *Bull. Inst. Intl. de Statist.*, Vol. 36, Divraison 2, Stockholm 1958; A. J. Coale, 'How the age distribution of a human population is determined', *Cold Spring Harbor Symposia on Quantitative Biology*, Vol. XXII, 1957. D.V.G. 1963.)

[44] It should be remembered that, for the period before 1780, the baptisms and burials are given only for every tenth year. Even if they were correct, they would scarcely be adequate as a basis for elaborate calculations.

[45] G. T. Griffith, *Population Problems of the age of Malthus*, Cambridge 1926, chs. 1 and 2.

correcting factors to raise baptisms to births and burials to deaths, and then of working back from 1801 by addition and subtraction. This, it is true, was also the object of Farr and Brownlee, but the processes by which they attempted to arrive at it were far more complex. What Griffith did was to take as his starting point the 'jump' in the vital rates produced by the change from the old system to the new. He found that by using a ratio of 1·15 for baptisms and 1·10 for burials, he disposed of the 'jump' and smoothed the trend from the baptisms and burial rates of 1825, 1830 and 1835, to the birth and death rates after the introduction of civil registration.[46] These factors are, in the light of earlier discussion in the present paper clearly too low and, of course, it may well be unjustified to assume a smooth curve between 1825 and 1841. Griffith assumes, in addition, that birth registration was complete by 1841. Further, Griffith shares with Brownlee the assumptions that the 1801 census results were correct and that there was no significant excess of emigration during any part of the eighteenth century. In general, Griffith tends to under-estimate both births and deaths in the period prior to 1850 and his birth and death rates are correspondingly too low. It is because of his low correction factors that his derived populations are consistently higher than those of Brownlee.

Looking back at the various national estimates which have been considered it seems probable that they are all in some measure defective, those of Farr, Brownlee and Griffith perhaps being the least unsatisfactory. Criticism of the individual estimates does not, of course, mean that they are useless. On the contrary, if the object is to guess at the approximate size (within, say, a margin of 10-15 per cent) of the population of England and Wales at the beginning, middle and end of the eighteenth century, it may well be that they are all sufficiently near the truth to be accepted. And in spite of the different processes and correcting factors used, all three estimates are quite close to each other. This is especially so of Brownlee's and Griffith's estimates. It is, in fact, clear that, within fairly wide limits, almost any reasonable approach produces comparable results.

But in studying the history of the population of a given country, the interest does not lie solely in broad figures of total size, a half-century apart.[47] What is interesting is far more the short period variation, the movement of birth and death rates, and, if possible, of more appropriate fertility and mortality rates. What, further, requires to be known—if it can be ascertained—is the territorial distribution of population at different points of time, the variations in the degree of urbanization, the occupational and social structure, social and other differences in fertility, and changes in marriage frequency and marriage habits. The two latter questions are, of course, essential to an understanding of the history of the family, which, so far as England and Wales is concerned, is largely an untold tale. In this broad field of demographic and kindred problems, the estimates discussed cannot afford very much help. We cannot be at all certain that the indicated trends in the birth and death rates are correct, quite

---

[46] It is not clear exactly how Griffith did his actual calculations. His discussion is given on pp. 15-16 of his book.

[47] Even the broad figures may be unsatisfactory. For example, taking the figures fifty years apart, Farr's estimate shows a negligible rise in the first half of the eighteenth century, while Brownlee and Griffith show significant rises. Which of them is right?

apart from the question of the actual levels of those rates and what they mean. And the levels themselves are of importance in conditioning our views as to the nature of demographic fluctuations. For example, if we were to accept the birth rate levels estimated by Griffith we should probably also have to accept and explain a more substantial rise in fertility between the 1830's and the 1870's than if we based ourselves on Brownlee's figures. Similarly, what we believe to be the birth rate level in the eighteenth century will condition our views as to the level and course of fertility in periods in which, as far as we are aware, birth control was not practised to any significant extent by married couples. Further, unless we can be reasonably sure of the level and course of vital rates we may be swayed by attractive general theories which have no real, factual foundation. For example, Brownlee himself believed in 'race physiology'. He thought that his estimates confirmed the view that fertility was high around 1600 and 1800 and low in the intervening period, especially around 1700. He saw the present period as just another epoch of low fertility and it is clear from his writings that he interpreted it in terms of a 'lower level of vitality', of 'natural causes', rather than as the result of conscious limitation.[48] To confirm or refute such theories, to give a deeper insight into the variations in reproductive habits over time, we need both more sure and more detailed material than that presented in any estimates so far compiled for this country. In making this statement there is no intention of minimizing the interest of the previous estimates. On the contrary, the writers concerned produced helpful results out of relatively thankless material. The questions to be considered are, however, whether the material can be manipulated in any more profitable way, and whether there is any additional material—not so far used—which might help to produce more detailed and significant results. From the estimates which have been discussed only two broad conclusions appear to emerge. First, mortality in the eighteenth century may have been higher, in the main, than in the first half of the nineteenth century, and the crude death rate was probably higher. Secondly, there is reason to believe that the crude birth rate was high at the end of the eighteenth century—perhaps higher than is suggested by Brownlee—and that a high rate was maintained during the first three quarters of the nineteenth century. Can these conclusions be given further precision and amplification?[49]

Earlier discussion showed that it would be possible to establish, with a reasonable approximation to the truth, the births and deaths for the decade 1831-40. Using the method noted, the births amount to about 5·450 millions,

[48] See, for example, his evidence before the National Birth-Rate Commission, *The Declining Birth-Rate*, London 1916, pp. 149-65. He did not deny that birth control played a part, but he felt that long-wave variations in vitality might be the basic cause. Similarly, he concluded his article in *Public Health* by stating that around 1600 and 1800 there were high birth rates in England and Wales; that around 1700 and again at present the birth rates were considerably lower; and that 'in my opinion a considerable part of this oscillation in the birth-rate is an expression of race physiology'. See also his article, 'Germinal vitality', *Proc. Royal Philos. Soc. Glasgow*, 1908.

[49] I wish to avoid the use of 'background material' for supporting hypotheses—that is, material of the kind displayed in abundance by M. C. Buer, *Health, Wealth and Population*, London 1926, and M. D. George, *London Life in the XVIIIth Century*, 2nd edn., London 1930. Such material may be used to explain or support a wide variety of apparent statistical trends and although it is of great value in helping us to understand why certain developments took place, it is safer not to have recourse to it until the statistics have been tested as rigorously as possible by *statistical* means. To paraphrase the late R. R. Kuczynski, it is easy to explain an event which did not really take place.

similar to Brownlee's figure of 5·505 millions. Application of this same technique may be used to correct the under-registration of births in subsequent decades, on the assumption that death registration was almost complete by 1841. The results are shown in the following table:

TABLE 6

Crude birth rates for England and Wales

Period	Official birth rate	Estimated birth rate	Brownlee's birth rate
1831–40	—	36·6	36·6
1841–50	32·6	35·1	33·9
1851–60	34·1	35·5	35·0
1861–70	35·2	35·9	36·3

They suggest the maintenance of a relatively stable birth rate during the period. No doubt part of the discrepancy between Brownlee's rates and the revised rates for the period 1841-70 is mythical, due to the inherent errors in both methods.

TABLE 7

Estimates of the Population of England and Wales, 1701 to 1801
(in millions)

	Rickman (a)	Rickman (b)	Malthus	Finlaison	Farr	Brownlee	Griffith
1700	5·475	6·045		5·135	6·122	5·826	5·835
10	5·240			5·066	6·252	5·981	6·013
20	5·565			5·345	6·253	6·001	6·048
30	5·796			5·688	6·183	5·947	6·008
40	6·064			5·830	6·153	5·926	6·013
1750	6·467	6·517		6·040	6·336	6·140	6·253
60	6·736			6·480	6·721	6·569	6·665
70	7·428			7·228	7·153	7·052	7·124
80	7·953		7·721	7·815	7·574	7·531	7·581
85	8·016		7·998	—	—	—	7·826
90	8·675		8·415	8·541	8·256	8·247	8·216
95	9·055		8·831	—	—	—	8·656
1801	9·168		9·287	9·187	9·193	9·156	9·168

Sources: Rickman's first estimate: *Observations on the Results of the Population Act*, 41 Geo. III, p. 9.
Rickman's second estimate: 1841 census, *Enumeration Abstract*, Preface, pp. 36–37.
Malthus: *Essay*, 5th edn., London 1817, Vol. 2, p. 95. The figures are really for 1781, 1786, 1791 etc. Malthus estimated omissions of a sixth in birth and a twelfth in death registration (i.e. in the parish registers) and also allowed for deaths of males abroad.
Finlaison: 1831 census, *Enumeration Abstract*, p. xlv. The populations are for mid-years, the last being actually for mid-1800.
Farr: 1861 census, Vol. 3. *General Report*, p. 22. The figures are for (mid-year) 1701, 1711, 1721, etc.
Brownlee: *Public Health*, 1916, p. 228. The figures are for 1701, 1711, 1721, etc.
Griffith: *Population Problems*, p. 18.

TABLE 8

Estimated birth and death rates
(per 1,000 total population)

Period	Brownlee (a) Birth Rate	Death Rate	Period (d)	Griffith (b) Birth Rate	Death Rate
1701–10	31·6	28·6 (e)	1700	31·1	26·0
1711–20	31·4	31·1	1710	27·5	26·7
1721–30	33·9	34·9	1720	30·5	29·7
1731–40	35·6	35·8	1730	32·0	33·4
1741–50	36·9	33·0	1740	33·3	31·7
1751–60	36·9	30·3	1750	34·1	28·2
1761–70	37·0	30·0	1760	33·3	26·7
1771–80	37·5	31·1	1770	34·0	27·9
1781–90	37·7	28·6	1780	34·4	28·8
1791–1800	37·3	26·9	1785–95	35·44	25·65
1801–10	37·5	23·9	1796–1806	34·23	23·14
1811–20	36·6	21·1	1806–17	33·84	19·98
1821–30	36·6	22·6	1816–26	33·39	20·33
1831–40	36·6	23·4	1826–36	32·36	21·65
1841–50	33·9	—(c)	1836–46	31·43	20·80
1851–60	35·0	—	1851–60	34·13	22·23
1861–70	36·3	—			

(a) *Op. cit.*, p. 232.
(b) *Population Problems* etc., pp. 28 and 36. The rates for 1851–60 are the official ones.
(c) Brownlee accepts the official deaths for 1841–50 and subsequent decades.
(d) For 1700 to 1780 the rates are for single years only. For 1785–95 to 1836–46 they are eleven-year averages.
(e) Brownlee thought that this rate was too low. It was based on the number of burials given in the 1811 census. Using Rickman's figures he arrived at a rate of 31·5 (*op. cit.*, p. 232).

To go back still further in the nineteenth century is more difficult and requires different manipulation of the data, or additional material, or both. One possible approach—perhaps the least liable to error—would be from the point of view of mortality. Recent studies[50] have shown that there is some tendency for each generation to carry its own levels of mortality with it. That is, if mortality is plotted by the calendar years of birth of the age groups concerned, there is a marked parallelism between the separate age-curves, especially for ages above 10 years, and curves fitted to data on this basis give a good approximation to the facts. This is not, of course, to argue in favour of extrapolation in any mechanical way, for that is always a dangerous venture. But for the decades immediately preceding 1841, when registration of deaths became reasonably effective, we have a number of checks which would help to limit the error involved in extrapolation. First, we can make a fairly good guess at the total number of deaths in the decade 1831–40. Secondly, as the estimate of births for the same decade was made independently of any assumptions regarding the net excess of emigration or immigration, it may be possible —coupled with the data from the reports of the Emigration Commissioners— to form a reasonable idea of the size and direction of that excess. Thirdly, we

[50] For example, V. P. A. Derrick, *J. Inst. Actuaries*, July 1927; W. O. Kermack, A. G. McKendrick, and P. L. McKinley, *Lancet*, 31 March 1934; *Id., J. of Hygiene*, December 1934; H. Cramer and H. Wold, *Skandinavisk Aktuarietidskrift*, 1935; M. Greenwood, *J.R.S.S.*, 1936; E. C. Rhodes, *J.R.S.S.*, 1941.

have the census of 1831 which provides a check in terms of total numbers and also, to some extent, as regards age-composition, since the census gives the numbers of males over and under 20 years of age.[51] Similarly, for the decade 1821-30 we have as a check the ages recorded at the 1821 census, given by 5-year age groups up to 20 years and by 10-year for subsequent ages.[52] There are also further possible sources of corroboration, among which the following may be mentioned. First, as regards the omission of deaths due to the establishment of cheap burial grounds, it is possible to apply a check for the years covering the transition from parish to civil registration. It is known, for example, that such burial grounds existed in London, Manchester, Newcastle-on-Tyne and other large towns.[53] Detailed histories exist for all these towns, as well as many local social surveys made during the period 1830-50.[54] It would be by no means impossible to obtain a reasonably accurate list of the burial grounds, and the dates of their establishment, in all the major towns and this should help to throw light upon the course of deficiencies in death registration. Secondly, many of the individual or local studies contain useful material on the trend and level of mortality. There is, for example, the work of Neison,[55] Ansell,[56] and Ratcliffe,[57] based largely upon insurance statistics. The work of Milne[58] on the Carlisle data provided by Heysham is well known. What is apparently not so well known is that all the basic data are available, including the original returns of the census which Heysham took, and that it is possible to construct quite accurate birth rates for the years 1779-96 and death rates for the years 1780-1813.[59] Equally valuable material exists for Glasgow, owing to the initiative of James Cleland, who took a special census of the city in 1819,[60]

[51] The age material should be used with some caution for the method adopted at the 1831 Census for returning ages was not beyond reproach. The Overseers were told, in their instructions, that in general about half the population should be aged 20 and upwards and that if their returns differed markedly from this proportion, some error had probably occurred and the answers to that question should be examined and, if necessary, corrected.

[52] The ages were given for almost 88 per cent of the population of England and Wales. The question was largely a voluntary one and the omissions were for whole parishes and not for unstated ages. The latter fact should lower the error involved in redistributing the population of unknown age though, of course, the general errors of age statements were almost certainly higher in 1821 than in later censuses. Some check is also offered by the fact that the ages of death were returned for registered burials during the years 1813-30. (Detailed, special instructions were given for answering that question.) At least, comparison with the estimated death rates might indicate whether or not the resultant proportionate omissions for the separate age groups appeared reasonable.

[53] 1831 census, Enumeration Abstract, p. xxxiv.

[54] I refer particularly to the surveys undertaken by the various provincial statistical societies founded in that period, e.g. by the societies founded in Manchester in 1833, in Birmingham in 1835, in Bristol and Glasgow in 1836, and in Leeds and Liverpool in 1838. Various studies were also reported to what is now the Royal Statistical Society and at the early meetings of the British Association. (Cf. for example, T. S. Ashton, Economic and Social Investigations in Manchester, 1833-1933, London 1934.)

[55] F. G. P. Neison, Contributions to Vital Statistics, London 1845.

[56] C. Ansell, Jun., On the Rate of Mortality at Early Periods of Life, etc., London 1874.

[57] H. Ratcliffe, Observations on the Rate of Mortality and Sickness etc., Manchester 1850.

[58] J. Milne, A Treatise on the Valuation of Annuities and Assurances on Lives and Survivorships, 2 vols., London 1815.

[59] The data include the printed bills of mortality for the various years (issued by Heysham and containing a wealth of information), the abridgement published in W. Hutchinson, The History and Antiquities of the City of Carlisle and its Vicinity, Carlisle 1796, and a collection of Heysham's manuscript material, including data gathered together by him for Wales and Howlett, two prominent figures in the eighteenth-century controversy with Price. (This material was made available to me by Mr Gray and I hope to publish some of it in the second part of my study of the eighteenth-century population controversy. D.V.G. 1963.)

[60] J. Cleland, Enumeration of the Inhabitants of the City of Glasgow, Glasgow 1820.

and was in charge of the 1831 enumeration of the town, as a result of which he published a very elaborate and useful report.[61] In connexion with both these censuses, he made special arrangements for collecting more reliable statistics of births and deaths, so that mortality and fertility rates might be derived from them. Material of this kind, too little known and rarely used, would contribute to our understanding of early nineteenth-century demography. Finally, on the question of the deficiency of baptismal registration, some help could be obtained by a more detailed knowledge of the history of Dissent—probably best obtained by studying the records of the religious groups concerned—and by a scrutiny of the Dissenters' (non-parochial) registers of births (or baptisms). Registers of the kind were kept by all the Dissenting groups. Over 3,000 such registers were authenticated and deposited in the General Register Office in accordance with the Act of 10 August 1840, and a further 265 after the passage of 21 Vic. c. 25, which extended the provisions of the earlier Act.[62] Some of these registers have been transcribed and are accessible at the Society of Genealogists. But far more remains to be done and it is a great pity that the work of transcription of parish and non-parochial registers has been left in private hands, dependent exclusively upon private interest and support. The registers form part of our national archives. As such, it should be the duty of the State to preserve them and to make them accessible in printed form, for research. Up to the present, the interest in these registers has been primarily genealogical. Yet, properly used, they contain a wealth of information on the demography of England and Wales, not only for the early nineteenth but also for the eighteenth and seventeenth centuries. One of the major sources of any comprehensive historical study of our population should be the registers.[63]

Summing up the previous discussion, there is no doubt that a considerable amount of material is available to help us push back, with greater certainty than is found in any existing study, a survey of fertility and mortality to the beginning of the nineteenth century. Similar work might perhaps also be done for the main regions of the country. An analysis of the progress of urbanization offers no insuperable difficulty and it might even be possible to produce suggestive studies of differential fertility for the early nineteenth century.[64]

For the eighteenth century the problem is very much more difficult as there are no checks provided by national censuses. Nevertheless a great deal can be done on certain aspects of the subject. In this connexion, we should remember that though 'political arithmetic' in England and Wales showed less originality

[61] J. Cleland, *Enumeration of the City of Glasgow*, Glasgow, Edinburgh (and London) 1832. See also J. J. Duncan, *Tables of the Probability and Expectation of Male and Female Life in Glasgow*, London and Edinburgh 1829, and W. Jones, *The Expectation of Life in the City of Glasgow*, Glasgow 1925. I am using Glasgow solely as an example of a large town showing early nineteenth-century conditions at, perhaps, their peak. For reasons of time and space I do not deal with the demographic history of Scotland as such in this paper.

[62] The first Act was passed as a result of the Royal Commission of 1836 and the second as a result of the Royal Commission of 1857. See J. S. Burn, *op. cit.*, pp. 242-3. It should be noted that the parish register returns made at the censuses of 1811, 1821, 1831 and 1841 included some unregistered baptisms and burials of which the clergy concerned had received information.

[63] (Any specific information obtainable on trends and levels in migration, mortality or fertility would make the application of stable population techniques more useful in assessing national levels and structure. D.V.G. 1963.)

[64] I have in mind, for example, the extension of my own study on differential fertility in London 1851-1931 (*Eugenics Review*, July 1938) back to 1821. Cleland's material suggests that a study might be made for Glasgow, going back as far as 1831.

in the eighteenth than in the seventeenth century, the later period made up for this deficiency to some extent by much greater industry. The participants in the great population controversy often made wrong assumptions and still more wrong deductions but they collected material which will bear fresh interpretation. They frequently refer to estimates of the population of various towns and parishes made at different points of time in the eighteenth century and it is, in fact, apparent from the local histories—especially those published at the end of the eighteenth and the beginning of the nineteenth century—that there were numerous local 'censuses' during the century.[65] Some of them are, of course, rather unreliable, based perhaps upon a guess at the number of houses or, if the number were correctly enumerated, upon an assumed multiplier of persons per household or per family.[66] But many of them seem to have been at least as well done, for the localities they dealt with, as the 1801 census. For Carlisle, for example, there was, in addition to Heysham's census of 1780, a census taken by the local constables (by order of the Court of Quarter Sessions) in 1787. The results of this census are available, as well as Heysham's corrections to allow for under-enumeration.[67] The 1787 census applied not only to Carlisle but to the whole of Cumberland and the results are given in William Hutchinson's *History of the County of Cumberland* (Carlisle 1794). A further census of Carlisle was taken in 1796.[68] Going backwards into the eighteenth century, a census of Carlisle was taken in 1763 by order of Bishop Littleton.[69] The material for Carlisle is no doubt exceptionally good. But many other cities had at least one and often two enumerations during the eighteenth century (and sometimes earlier) and this was also the case for a number of rural parishes. It might well be possible to assess the growth during the century of all the towns of any importance. County surveys also frequently contained local estimates of population, some of which were based on conscientious inquiries. Many of the volumes of reports to the Board of Agriculture gave such estimates, made in the last decade of the eighteenth century.

On birth and death rates little more could be done on the basis of the burial and baptism statistics collected by Rickman. It is possible that the additional inquiries suggested for the early nineteenth century, might help to throw light upon the extent of the omissions in parish registration. But no realistic work could be done unless it were possible to substitute, for Rickman's data, the full material of the parish and non-parochial registers. This is particularly the case for the period before 1780, for which Rickman's data are most inadequate. At the same time it would be essential to study afresh the material on emigration and immigration in order to arrive at the most reasonable estimates of the course and level of such movements.[70] Local research might, of course, be

[65] For examples of these local population estimates, see R. Price, *Observations on Reversionary Payments*, 5th edn., London 1792, Vol. 1, pp. 298-99; J. Howlett, *An Examination of Dr. Price's Essay*, Maidstone (1781), p. 149; W. Wales, *An Inquiry into the Present State of Population in England and Wales*, London 1781, p. 67.

[66] These multipliers are extremely difficult to check not only because of the paucity of appropriate comparative data but also because the concepts of family, household and dwelling have had such loose interpretation so far as statistical measurements are concerned.

[67] John Heysham, *Observations on the Bills of Mortality in Carlisle for the Year MDCCLXXXVIII*, Carlisle 1788.   [68] See Lonsdale, *op. cit.*, p. 56.

[69] See Heysham MSS. collection, Bibliotheca Jacksoniana, Carlisle.

[70] A study of the intake into North America would help greatly in this matter.

undertaken, into communities in which it is known that there were few Dis-senters. But this would be most profitable for areas for which there were several enumerations during the eighteenth century. In the absence of a complete transcription of registers, and this is very unlikely, the most profitable line of research would be in the detailed analysis of local registers. The object would not be to compile birth and death rates, but to gain some idea of mortality, marriage habits and marital fertility by following groups of children born in a given year or other period. A sufficiently large area would need to be studied in each case, because of the question of internal migration, and the study would necessarily assume that the date of baptism approximated sufficiently closely to the date of birth for the purposes of the analysis.[71] Records of hospitals, dispensaries and foundling or similar institutions would also yield interesting material, though it should be remembered that in such cases the population covered would represent a selected and not a random sample.[72]

The establishment of eighteenth-century levels and trends would, of course, be made easier and more secure if it were possible to collect reasonable statistics relating to the end of the seventeenth century. The question, however, is whether this can be done. To answer this, we must revert to the Act of 6 and 7 William III, c. 6 (1694). This Act was passed to raise money for carrying on the war against France by levying a tax on marriages, burials, births (or bap-tisms), and an annual tax on bachelors above the age of 25 years and on childless widowers.[73] From the demographer's point of view, this was a most remarkable Act, providing for census and vital statistics far in advance of any collected in the subsequent hundred years. The extent to which Gregory King drew upon 'samples' of the statistics has been discussed elsewhere.[74] So far, little in the way of additional returns have been located. Yet many copies of the returns were made and some may still be in existence; a systematic search of private and public archives should be sponsored, for additional returns would not only throw light upon the demographic and economic situation in the late seven-teenth century, but also help in interpreting other partial material now available.[75]

[71] In practice this may not be much more incorrect that our customary usage of assuming that the date of registration is equivalent to the data of birth. During the Cromwellian period, following the Act of 1653 which temporarily placed registration in civil hands, births were registered, not baptisms. However, registration reverted to the clergy at the Restoration and baptisms once again replaced births. See Burke, op. cit., p. 15, which also provides a very useful guide to extant registers. On copies of parish registers, see K. Blomfield and H. K. Percy-Smith, *National Index of Parish Register Copies*, London 1939.

[72] (Records of special groups would be even more interesting and might throw more light on general trends. See T. Hollingsworth's study of British ducal families included in the present volume. This study has since been extended to cover the whole of the British Peerage. Similar work might be undertaken on the Quaker records. D.V.G. 1963.)

[73] A table of rates was prepared by Gregory King and published in 1695. (See B.M. 816.m.6-80.) Tax was payable on burials, even in respect of persons who had been receiving alms, but in that case the parish was liable for the tax.

[74] (See my papers on Gregory King, included in the present volume, above, pp. 159-220. D.V.G. 1963.)

[75] For lack of space, I have refrained from discussing the various estimates and partial censuses of the sixteenth and eighteenth centuries. A few of them are referred to in M. Atsatt, *Population Estimates for England and Wales from the Eleventh to the Nineteenth Centuries*, n.d. (This is a photo-graphed typescript, available from Science Documentation Service, Washington, D.C. The study was prepared in connexion with some historical research undertaken by Professor F. J. Teggart.) More are noted by the anonymous author of *A Discourse of the Growth of England in Populousness and Trade since the Reformation*, London 1689, and by G. Chalmers, *An Estimate of the Comparative Strength of Great Britain*, London 1786. Still more are among the Harleian manuscripts, including summaries of the Armada musters (see No. 168, 280, 368, 412, 6839, 6848 and 7021 in the Catalogue).

At this point, the present study must be concluded. Although only a small part of the available material has been referred to, it is evident that, up to the present, research into the history of the population of England and Wales has been both cursory and rather haphazard. In fact, systematic inquiry into the questions involved has scarcely begun, and there is a wealth of material waiting to be used by scholars. It is difficult to know why it has not already been drawn upon to any appreciable extent. In part this may be due to the still customary view of history, which assumes constant progress and which cannot therefore imagine that useful demographic material might have been collected a hundred and fifty or two hundred years ago. In still larger part it is perhaps due to the very great labour involved in analysing the original records. Even to study a single early census—say, the religious census of 1676—entails much work, since the initial stage must be to check every county and every parish, to see which sections, if any, are missing. Such work is often beyond the scope of an individual. If it is to be done, it must be done by combined effort, by developing a research programme in which many individuals, perhaps from many universities, participate in an agreed way. Otherwise, the situation will remain much as at present. In that case important aspects and segments of history will continue to be lacking and historians will continue to use great subtlety in explaining developments which, were the demographic material analysed and at hand, might be capable of resolution in simpler and much more realistic terms.

10

THE POPULATION PROBLEM DURING THE INDUSTRIAL REVOLUTION: A NOTE ON THE PRESENT STATE OF THE CONTROVERSY

T. H. MARSHALL

From: *Economic History*, I, No. 4 (*Supplement to the Economic Journal*), 1929

Editor's Note: The word 'present' in the title refers to 1929. The article is here reprinted as it originally appeared, without revision by the author, partly as an introduction to the volume by G. Talbot Griffith, *Population Problems of the Age of Malthus*, which is here reviewed extensively. Professor Marshall's criticisms may be taken as the starting-point for many of the later revisions which are printed below.

THE problem of the English population a century ago has recently attracted several independent—too independent—investigators. It is naturally tempting to economic historians, since it offers them an opportunity for the exercise of the now popular quantitative method in a field in which they have not been seriously anticipated by the statisticians. They should remember, however, that they owe the privilege of priority chiefly to the absence of statistics, and that, consequently, the appeal from logic to mathematics is here particularly dangerous. Mr Griffith's book on *Population Problems of the Age of Malthus* made an immediate impression, as, indeed, it deserved to, but his estimates have been too readily accepted and his conclusions too hastily grasped as a cudgel with which to belabour a certain school of historians and theorists. Even when the facts have been ascertained, their interpretation is a matter of great delicacy. And the facts can, for the most part, only be guessed. In these circumstances the results of statistical research have no more title to respect—probably less—than the views of well-informed contemporaries and the reasoned expectations of the modern historian and economist.

One point, at least, is clear. However great may be the margin of error in Mr Griffith's calculations, it cannot wipe out the great dip in the death-rate curve during the Industrial Revolution. This can be accepted as fact. The statistical evidence is convincing, and it does not conflict with evidence of other kinds. There is a logical explanation in the advance in medical science, affecting in particular infant mortality, and there is corroboration from contemporary sources. All the investigations into local and particular death rates made at the time pointed that way,[1] and the belief that mortality was declining in England

---

[1] See M. C. Buer, *Health, Wealth and Population*, 270-1.

as a whole was shared, not only by Rickman and McCulloch,[2] but also by
Malthus himself. The second edition of the Essay, written shortly after the
first census, contains the following passage: 'It would appear, by the present
proportion of marriages, that the more rapid increase of population, supposed
to have taken place since the year 1780, has arisen more from the diminution
of deaths than the increase of the births.'[3] The point was reiterated in the Report
on the 1851 Census, and the main causes of the decline of mortality since the
seventeenth century were sketched.[4]

These facts should by now be well known. Mr Griffith admits that Malthus's
second thoughts differed little from his own theories, but he does not acquit
him on that account. Malthus has laid himself open to a new charge, that of
either missing or deliberately suppressing the logical implications of his knowledge. He should, it is suggested, have considered the falling death rate as proof
that the population was not too large. But he was looking to the future, and
in twenty years the death rate was rising again. If he still insisted that a check
was desirable, 'he might have been tempted to advocate measures which,
instead of checking the birth- and marriage-rates, should check the decline in
the death-rate. The obvious impossibility of advocating such measures is
probably one reason why it was not done.'[5] This is a cruel libel on a man whose
one object in desiring to reduce the birth rate was to keep down the death rate,
to substitute 'preventive' for 'positive' checks. He could not have been tempted
for a moment, and his reasons are perfectly obvious. It is a fallacy to suppose
that, in this matter, the nature of the cause is an index to the nature of the
remedy. It is perfectly logical to hold that population pressure induced by a
falling death rate should be alleviated by reducing the birth rate. In fact no
other course is possible. As Sir William Beveridge has neatly said, 'the idea that
mankind . . . can control death by art and leave birth to Nature is biologically
absurd'.[6]

It is, indeed, fatally easy to distort the picture. The obvious temptation is to
assert that the death rate was not only the variable, but also the determining,
factor in the increase of population, and that, to understand the causes of this
increase, we should study the deaths rather than the births. But, clearly, a
horizontal line on a graph may be as dynamic as a diagonal; the forces that
prevent a birth rate from falling may be as significant as those that make it
rise. This is elementary. The next stage along the road of error is travelled, I
think, under the influence of a sense of symmetry, which demands that the new
theory should be the exact reverse of the old. Tradition said that the increase of
population during the Industrial Revolution was accompanied by a high death
rate but a still higher birth rate. The truth is that the birth rate was low and the
death rate lower. We know why the death rate fell: we must look for the
forces which pulled the birth rate down, as Malthus looked for those that were
pushing it up. The most recent writers on the subject, J. S. Blackmore and F. C.

---

[2] See Griffith, 40-41.
[3] Second edn. (1803), 311.
[4] 'The first evident cause of the increase of the population is a diminution of their mortality',
I, ii, p. lii.
[5] Op. cit., 99.
[6] The Economic Journal (December 1923), 473.

Mellonie,[7] are so ingenious as to force symmetry one step further by selecting the same cause as Malthus, the Speenhamland Poor Law policy, and attributing to it opposite effects. Their article is in many ways remarkable. They very diffidently submit the, to them, new theory that the death rate was falling, in apparent ignorance, not only of the authorities cited above, but also of the recent writings of Dr Brownlee and Mr Griffith, and they show a touching faith in the sanctity of even the shadiest figures. Arguments, they say, are 'empty theorizing', unless supported by a study of 'objective facts'. But it is folly to suppose that any facts obtainable about the allowance system of those days could hold their own for a moment against the theories of modern economists, based, as they are, on far more accurate observations of human action. I shall return to their figures.[8]

Undoubtedly many contemporaries believed that the birth rate was rising, and grossly under-estimated, or even denied, the fall in the death rate. It has been proved that they were wrong. But the essence of what we may call the 'Malthusian' position was this. First, the population was increasing faster than was desirable. Secondly, the birth rate should be checked. Thirdly, the birth rate was being stimulated by certain economic forces which could be removed by proper political action, notably the Poor Laws and the demand for child labour. I wish to suggest that the best modern estimates of the births and deaths for England and Wales as a whole most certainly do not prove this view to have been false. Rather, they appear to confirm it, or, as I prefer to say, in view of the highly speculative nature of the statistics, they are consistent with it. The result is purely negative. It is only by a comparative study of local figures that there is any hope of proving the last, and most important, point of the three either true or false. That I have not attempted.[9]

We may approach the problem from various angles. We may speak of a law of population. If we do we shall be in good company. It is not necessary for this argument to believe that the law of growth is capable of exact expression nor to subscribe to the theory of Professor Raymond Pearl that all growth follows the logistic. We may say, for example, that population growth is determined by births and deaths, emigration and immigration, and that these are related to the socio-economic environment of the people in ways that can be analysed and, to some extent, foreseen. But we must go a step further to avoid confusion. More fundamental is the relation between the total population of a country and its socio-economic organization, the relation on which is based the theory of the optimum. The total is, of course, regulated by the ratio between births and deaths—if we ignore migration as irrelevant to our particular problem—but both the birth rate and the death rate vary independently under the influence of forces which do not affect the conditions which determine the

[7] 'Family Endowment and the Birth-Rate', *The Economic Journal*, Historical Supplement, no. 2, May 1927.

[8] In a second article, *The Economic Journal* (Supplement), January 1928, these authors have abandoned their theory. They find no evidence of a relation, positive or negative, between family allowances and the birth rate.

[9] For the difficulties involved in local estimates, see Barbara Hammond, 'Urban Death-Rates in the Early Nineteenth Century', *The Economic Journal* (Supplement), January 1928. As they arise largely from 'the bewildering tangle of English local divisions', they are greatly reduced when a national average is taken.

optimum. If population growth and economic progress are to keep step together, a balance must be maintained between births and deaths, but that
balance is bound to be frequently disturbed by the action of forces which have
nothing whatever to do with social and economic progress, measured by its
capacity to sustain population. If there is any truth in the conception of a law
of population, we should expect to find that, when the balance is disturbed in
this way, it tends to rediscover itself, probably at a new level. For example, a
victory of medicine over disease will lower the death rate and increase the pace
of population growth without providing sustenance, employment or the rudi-
ments of comfort for a single extra person. If no corresponding economic
progress takes place, we should, on this hypothesis, expect to see the birth and
death rate curves, which have diverged, converge again, though, very possibly,
without exactly recovering their previous relation; we should, at least, assume
a pressure or pull in favour of a *rapprochement*. A similar state of affairs may
arise if an economic revolution stimulates a rapid increase of population, and
the population gathers a momentum which carries it further than is required.
We have, then, a path sketched out for the population curve by the conditions
of economic progress, and oscillation about that path caused by the disturbance
and readjustment of the balance between births and deaths. This path is, of
course, not necessarily that of the optimum. This view is consistent with the
fact to which Mr Yule has drawn attention, that, although short-period percentage increases of population give an incoherent succession of ups and downs,
when long-period figures are taken, for fifty years in the case of England and
Wales, these oscillations disappear, and a smooth and clearly directed movement is revealed.[10] It is as though Nature were trying to hit the mark by a
system of trial and error, each error setting up a pull in the contrary direction.

A further symptom that should appear if there is a law, in this very general
sense, in operation, is an associated movement of birth and death rates. The law,
by prescribing limits within which the balance should fall, links the two
together. Mr Yule has examined this point also with some interesting results.
His first assertion is that, among nations of about the same state of economic
development, or, as supporters of a more precise law would say, at about the
same point in the cycle of growth, the higher the death rate the higher the birth
rate, and *vice versa*. This is sustained by a correlation of $+0.81$ between the
figures for 1901-10 for twenty-two western European States. This does not
merely mean that where the rate of growth is the same, the excess of births
over deaths must be the same also, except for a relatively small allowance to be
made for migration. That is axiomatic. Nor does it merely mean, though this
is important, that since western Europe became an economic unit, the rate of
population growth in the parts selected—and it should be noted that they do
not include France—has been of the same order of magnitude. Its significance
is this. It suggests that the more fundamental forces controlling the aggregate
population of an area, and therefore the rate of increase, are stronger than the
particular forces working directly on the births and deaths, and that over an
area of this kind, in normal times, variations in birth and death rates are greater

[10] 'The growth of population and the factors which control it', *Journal of the Royal Statistical
Society*, LXXXVIII, 12.

than variations in the rate of population growth. Consequently, when we find, as we do in England at the end of the eighteenth century, an unprecedented fall in the death rate, caused, for the most part, by non-economic forces, we should not expect the whole of this to be passed on, unmodified, into the rate of population growth. We should assume a pull set up, tending to drag the birth rate down, and if the birth rate did not fall, we should conclude that exceptionally strong forces were at work holding it up.

Mr Yule goes on to show the 'consilience between the movements of the birth-rate and the death-rate', illustrating it with two tables. The first covers fifteen countries between 1841-50 and 1871-80, the second nineteen countries between 1871-80 and 1901-10. The former is the more important for our purpose, as it deals with a period when deliberate control of births played about the same part as in the England of the Industrial Revolution. The correlation here is +0·70. In nine cases a falling death rate is associated with a rising birth rate. What is the interpretation? The table clearly covers a period when conditions in western Europe were favourable to a high rate of natural increase and a rising birth rate. In only two cases, Sweden and Belgium, did it fall. Of these, Sweden heads the list on the death rate side with the biggest fall recorded, namely, 2·3 points per 1,000. Belgium comes third. The correlation suggests, therefore, that the more the death rate fell, the less the birth rate rose, and that a falling death rate is a limiting check on a rising birth rate. We observe, too, that when the fall exceeded 2 per 1,000, the rise was negatived. As the fall in our case was, at the least, nearly 9 points we may say that this statistical evidence fits in with the view that, in such circumstances, a stationary, or slightly falling, birth rate must be taken as indicative of phenomenally high fertility. Mr Yule concludes with the important confession, which should be carefully weighed by students of the population problem of this period, that 'my neglect of the death-rate as a factor in the movements of the birth-rate in former papers was a serious mistake'.[11]

But, even if the birth rate was surprisingly high, it does not follow that it was undesirably high. The downward pull might have been counteracted by the rapidity of economic progress, and the truth may be that the Industrial Revolution called into being no more people than it required and could sustain, so that the balance between births and deaths was not upset by the doctors, but simply adjusted to the needs of the new situation. So neat a harmony between unrelated forces would be very startling. Nature does not, as a rule, imitate the ballet dancer, who springs accurately through the air and lands in perfect equilibrium. She is more likely, under the influence of a severe shock, to oscillate like a drunkard steering for a lamp-post. And there are special reasons for expecting this in our case. For even if it cannot be proved that the population ever became excessive, yet it can be urged that the peculiar character of its growth brought pressure to bear locally on those responsible for bearing and rearing the new generation, which might have been expected to depress the birth rate even if such a depression were not imperatively demanded by the economic circumstances. We know that the chief feature of the falling death rate was a rapid decline in infant mortality. It was a question of saving lives in

[11] *Loc. cit.*, 33.

the first few hours, days or weeks after birth. Imagine the effect on parents. It may be possible to bring ten children into the world, if you only have to rear five, and, while one is 'on the way', the last is in the grave, not in the nursery. But if the doctor preserves seven or eight of the ten, and other things remain equal, the burden may become intolerable. In so far, therefore, as there was, at this time, any conscious or unconscious control of the birth rate in the interests of economic welfare or physical comfort, the decline in infant mortality must have acted as a strong incentive to restriction. The point appears more substantial if it is treated nationally rather than individually. The economic historian is interested in the rate of increase of a population in relation to the social and economic conditions of its country. The birth rate is a factor in that rate of increase. With respect to its economic consequences—and they become, in turn, economic causes—a decline in infant mortality is almost exactly equivalent to an increase of births. It is true that new persons arrive without new confinements, but the economic significance of a confinement is small compared with that of the labour of suckling, nursing and rearing, the cost of feeding and clothing, the pressure on house-room, which follow. We might, in fact, speak of the number of children reaching the age of six months or one year as giving the 'net birth rate', which is more vital than the 'gross birth rate' to the population problem as it presents itself to the economic historian. In the early part of our period a stationary, or slightly declining, 'gross birth rate' implies a rising 'net birth rate'. It is, therefore, misleading to contrast a falling death rate with a rising birth rate as causes of population growth, without pointing out that death may come at any age, but birth usually occurs about the end of the ninth month. If the lives saved had been those of septuagenarians, the contrast would be real. Actually it is false.[12]

In the foregoing discussion I have avoided using the phrase 'over-population'. I did not want to queer the pitch. In the exact sense to which modern theory would confine it, it is of so little service to the discussion of actuality that even the most reputable writers on practical problems use it to denote something less tenuous and equally entitled to the name. Still nearer to the heart of life we find the frank misuse by the journalist, which defeats all clear thinking. Consequently, the word is, to any argument in which it appears—if I may be allowed to mix my metaphors—a loophole through which every critic can draw a red herring. In its exact sense it is a term of static economics denoting a state of affairs such that a reduction in the numbers of the occupants of the area under consideration, while all other circumstances, including the age distribution, remained the same, would be followed by an increase in returns per head. Writers on practical issues use it in a dynamic sense to indicate the presence within the area of more persons than can be supported without a fall in the standard of life, or, perhaps, without retarding the rise in the standard, within

[12] On this point compare M. Rubin and H. Westergaard, *Statistik der Ehen*, 109. They produce statistical evidence to show that infant mortality rises in proportion to the number of children in the family. This is partly due, they say, to the increased difficulty of caring for the children. They then add: 'Uebrigens wird man auch mit einigem Rechte behaupten können, dass nicht die vielen Kinder die aussergewöhnliche Sterblichkeit hervorrufen, sondern ungekehrt die grosse Sterblichkeit die vielen Kinder, insofern der Kinderverlust physiologisch und psykologisch die weitere Kindererzeugung ermöglicht und dazu anspornt.' If high infant mortality is an incentive to births, then low infant mortality must be a deterrent.

a reasonable time and assuming a normal adaptability of economic structure to changing conditions. This view is implicit in Sir William Beveridge's address on Population and Unemployment, where, arguing that unemployment in 1879 was not a sign of over-population, he remarks that anyone who 'had argued that the existing population of the United Kingdom was all that the country could support without lowering its standards would have been lamentably discredited at once'.[13] The country had received a shock, it had been disturbed by the emergence of new economic factors, but, by adapting itself to the changes, it swiftly recovered and resumed its progress, and this recovery required only a reasonable time—three or four years perhaps—and demanded, not a revolution, but simply the amount of vitality normal in a healthy economic society. That is the picture suggested.

I shall not try to prove that the England of, say, 1820 was over-populated in either of these senses. Conditions were in such a state of flux that an application of the first test is hardly possible. Miss Buer, in her recent essay on the Malthusian controversy,[14] leaves us in some doubt whether she intends to apply it or not. 'Strictly speaking,' she writes, 'over-population was impossible according to Malthus's theory. He, however, was not a clear thinker.' This certainly suggests the pure classical conception. But when she proceeds to argue that in fact England was not over-populated at this time, she permits herself the following sentence: 'From the point of view of food supply there seems little historical basis for the statement that England in 1815 was over-populated as compared with earlier periods,' which suggests no conception at all. Malthus's retort is a simple *tu quoque*. Her exact meaning, however, is unimportant, as she does not get within measurable distance of a proof. Two arguments are put forward. One is that food imports did not increase with the population, a point that only carries weight if it can be shown that the people continued to eat the same quantity of food per head. The history of Ireland shows that a country may export food while living on the brink of famine. The other is the familiar assertion that the distress is fully accounted for by the effects of war, based on a false analogy with 1918. Careless comparison of these two epochs has done much harm to the cause of historic truth. A subsidiary argument, derived from the age-constitution of the people, is interesting, and I shall revert to it later. Over-population in the second sense certainly did not exist, for it is demonstrable that, within a reasonable time, the country supported an even larger population at a definitely higher standard of life, and a sudden cessation of population growth at that moment might have shot economic progress dead in its tracks.

There are, however, peculiar features in the history of the early nineteenth century which suggest two things. First, that economic conditions created a force calculated to check the rate of population growth in the immediate future. Secondly, that this force was consequent on the pace and character of population growth in the immediate past. In other words, even if there were not over-population, there was population pressure, resulting from a failure of economic progress and the increase of numbers to keep step together. A pressure of this

[13] *The Economic Journal* (December 1923), 448.
[14] 'The Historical Setting of the Malthusian Controversy' in *London Essays in Economics*, see 138 and 141.

short-period dynamic kind, being not that of a moving body impinging on a stationary one, but of two moving bodies in frictional contact, will be remedied, not by an absolute reduction in the size of the population, but by an adjustment of the rate of growth. But before we can appreciate this we must have certain figures before us.

Take first the annual rate of increase of the total population, including army, navy and merchant seamen, as given in the Census Report for 1861. The figures are[15]:

TABLE I

1801–11	1·307
1811–21	1·533
1821–31	1·446
1831–41	1·326
1841–51	1·216
1851–61	1·141

The rate of increase, as is well known, reached its maximum in the second decade of the century. Although we expect some lag in the response of population growth to economic conditions, it is rather surprising to find the lag so great. The first years of this decade saw acute food shortage, amounting almost to famine, and we should have expected this to reduce the rate for the decade. But in this same period the death rate reached its minimum, a fact which the mere cessation of hostilities must have contributed to produce. The decline in the rate which begins after 1821 lasts till 1861. In the following decade the rate was 1·23. Here again there is a slight lag, since, without doubt, the period 1851–61 was more prosperous than the period 1841–51, though the change was gradual. But the correspondence between population growth and economic prosperity is clear, and can be traced on into the twentieth century.

The next point is to determine the share of the birth rate and death rate respectively in producing this response to the pressure of economic distress. The most recent, and best known, estimates of these rates are those in Mr Griffith's book, but they do not stand examination. On the birth rate side the problem is to discover by what factor to multiply recorded baptisms in order to arrive at the probable number of actual births, it being well known that a considerable proportion of births were not registered among the baptisms. Mr Griffith uses a constant factor of 1·15. He found that this, applied to the figures for 1825, 1830 and 1835, obliterated the jump which occurs when civil registration became effective, about 1841. This is all he tells us. The calculation is suspect from the first. Civil registration was far from effective in 1841. Farr estimated the number of births unregistered annually between 1841 and 1850 at over 38,000, and believed that, taking the period 1838–76 as a whole, 5 per cent of the births remained unrecorded.[16] Secondly, it is certain that the ratio of births to baptisms was not constant. Mr Griffith made the mistake of ignoring the work of Farr. The name does not even appear in his index. And yet his contribution to the subject is more important even than that of Rickman.

[15] *General Report*, I, 81.
[16] *Vital Statistics*, ed. N. A. Humphreys, 523 and 89.

Rickman spent infinite pains collecting and sorting the material, but Farr was its first fully competent interpreter.

In Table 61 in the Appendix to the General Report on the census of 1871 appears a calculation—presumably the work of Farr—of the births in each decade from 1741 to 1850. The purpose of the Table is to show the age constitution of the people, and the births seem to have been estimated by working down through the age groups from a recorded figure, using Farr's Life Table, 1838-54, with an allowance for migration based on the three censuses of 1841, 1851 and 1861. These factors are treated as constant. The results are checked by comparing the calculated and enumerated totals in the nineteenth century, and the biggest error is one of 35,000 in 1801. If we set beside these the registered baptisms and the resulting ratios we get:

TABLE 2

	Registered Baptisms (000)	Estimated Births (000)	Ratio
1781-90	2,397	2,641	1·102
1791-1800	2,618	2,988	1·142
1801-10	2,879	3,675	1·276
1811-20	3,255	4,425	1·359
1821-30	3,753	4,798	1·278
1831-40	3,966	5,289	1·334

The result differs profoundly from Mr Griffith's constant of 1·15. The fact that the latter almost agrees with Farr for the decade 1791-1800 will not inspire us with confidence, since Farr's figure is there certainly wrong. By not allowing for the rapid decline in infant mortality about the year 1800 he has seriously underestimated the births needed to sustain the later age groups at their known level. This decline in infant mortality is attested by contemporary evidence and confirmed by modern research. Its effect is seen in the age statistics of the Censuses for 1821 and 1841. As has been pointed out in an article by the late Dr Brownlee, to which I shall refer more fully in a moment, the high rate of increase of the age group 20-40 between these two dates as compared with that of other groups indicates that those born in the early nineteenth century had a much better chance of survival than those born at the end of the eighteenth. Further examination of the figures shows that the decline in infant mortality became effective about 1780, reached its climax about 1800 and expired during the first decade of the nineteenth century.[17]

It follows that Farr's estimate of births for 1780-1800 must be too low, but that he is probably approximately correct for the period 1800-40. Mr Griffith bases his whole calculation on an estimate of the ratio of births to baptisms in the years immediately before the introduction of civil registration. His estimate is 1·15, Farr's 1·334. The difference is vital, and Farr's method is, at this point, undoubtedly superior. Mr Griffith's whole scale must therefore be abandoned. If it is correct for earlier periods it can only be so by accident.

Farr's figures must be our starting-point, but they need correction. Fortu-

[17] 'The History of the Birth- and Death-Rates in England and Wales taken as a whole from 1570 to the present time', *Public Health* (June and July 1916), 219.

nately for historians they have been corrected by an eminent statistician. Brownlee's work on the history of the English birth and death rates deserves more attention than it has received.[18] His calculations are far too elaborate for summary and should be studied at first hand. He starts with the assumption that the known ratio of deaths to burials for 1838-40, namely, 1·18, can be taken as constant for the whole decade 1831-40.[19] From this, and the recorded increase of the population, he calculates the births. In working back he uses the burials to estimate the correction that should be made to allow for changing mortality, and he checks the births for 1811-20 by reference to their survivors, the 0-10 age group in the 1821 census. His correction for the high mortality of the eighteenth century is derived from the ratio between age groups in 1821 and 1841, on the lines indicated in the discussion of the fall in infant mortality. Having thus found a ratio of births to baptisms for 1791-1800, he treats it as a constant for the eighteenth century. This may give rather too high a ratio for the decade 1781-90, since at that time registration was deteriorating with the spread of Dissent. Further back I do not propose to go. Below are his ratios, with Farr's repeated for comparison.

TABLE 3

	Brownlee	Farr
1781-90	1·243	1·102
1791-1800	1·243	1·142
1801-10	1·276	1·276
1811-20	1·272	1·359
1821-30	1·278	1·278
1831-40	1·388	1·334

The resulting birth rates are:

TABLE 4

Birth rates per 1,000

1781-90	37·7
1791-1800	37·3
1801-10	37·5
1811-20	36·6
1821-30	36·6
1831-40	36·6
1841-50	33·9

The steady decline throughout the most active period of the Industrial Revolution disappears. Instead, we find the abnormally high rate of the late eighteenth century maintained into the first decade of the nineteenth. Even the slight drop shown from the maximum of 37·7 would be reduced if it is true, as suggested, that this figure is slightly too high. The decade 1811-20 shows a

---

[18] See also 'The Health of London in the Eighteenth Century', *Proceedings of the Royal Society of Medicine* (1925), XVIII, Epidemiology, 73.

[19] Mrs Hammond's criticism of Brownlee's calculation (*The Economic Journal*, Supplement (Jan. 1928), 426) is mistaken. It is true that registration was compulsory in the years 1838-40. That is why Brownlee accepts the figures in the *civil* registers as equalling the total deaths. It is by comparison with these figures that the 'leakage' in the *parish* registers can be measured, and the parish registers were not affected by the Registration Act.

fall of one point. This is not much for a period which saw the famines of 1811–12 and the bread riots of 1816–19. The rate then remains stable till 1831–40, after which there is a sharp drop. For the third time the country was threatened with famine, and now the birth rate seemed to have lost its buoyancy. Is it pure coincidence that this collapse followed close on the Factory Act of 1833 and the New Poor Law of 1834? It is quite possible; but there is a *prima facie* case for the 'Malthusians'.

Compare with these figures the statement of Miss Blackmore and Miss Mellonie, that 'the definite slump in the baptism rate comes between the years 1811 and 1821'.[20] The rates per 1,000 that they quote are 33·3 and 28·6. I have failed to discover how they arrive at these figures. Taking eleven-year averages about the census year, I get rates of 30·4 and 29·5. When, on the next page, they convert baptisms into births, the slump in the rate is equally surprising, from 38·1 to 34·1. However, the quality of our surprise changes when we observe that their estimate of the births for 1821 is well below the number of recorded baptisms. But have they not themselves written, 'the most deadly alternative hypothesis that can be brought up is the charge of absolute un-reliability of the figures'? We are disarmed.

It must be admitted that there are peculiar causes of uncertainty in the figures for the last two decades. The recorded baptisms in the late 1830's fall off with unnatural rapidity, except for a phenomenally high rate for 1837, which, if not a clerical error, can only be explained on the assumption that, in that year, 50,000 baby girls who normally would not have been baptised were carried to church on a wave of patriotism and christened 'Victoria'. Brownlee applied statistical tests which satisfied him that the baptism rate did not fall off as a result of the introduction of civil registration. The authors of the 1851 Census Report disagree. They reject the baptism figures for 1837–40 and substitute a computed average. If we take this figure and apply Farr's ratio to calculate the births in this decade, and take Farr's estimate of the deficiency in registration in the following decade, we get the following average birth rates:

1831–40	36·9
1841–50	34·8

On this basis the drop is reduced, but it is still about twice as big as the interval between the highest and lowest rates recorded from 1780 to 1840.

We now turn to the death rate. As there is no serious disagreement about the direction and extent of its movement, I take Brownlee's figures without question. They are based on a death-burial ratio of 1·2.

TABLE 5

Death rates per 1,000

1781–90	28·6
1791–1800	26·9
1801–10	23·9
1811–20	21·1
1821–30	22·6
1831–40	23·4

[20] *Loc. cit.*, 208.

There is a very marked rise in the last two decades. This, it appears, is the result chiefly of higher mortality in the early years of life. Of those born 1801-21, 75 per cent were alive at the date of the 1821 census. Of those born 1821-41, only 71 per cent were alive at the 1841 census. And yet the progress of medical science had not suddenly stopped. The effects of the discoveries and improved practices of the late eighteenth century should still have been spreading through the country. The death rate from smallpox, the principal non-economic scourge of infancy, was still declining. Porter gives a table of smallpox mortality which, though he does not say so, is presumably for London.[21] It only shows the decline of the share of smallpox in the general death rate, not the movement in smallpox mortality. Farr's summary for London is more useful. 'In 1771-80,' he writes, 'not less than 5 in 1,000 died annually of small-pox; in 1801-10 the mortality sank to 2; and in 1831-5 to 0·83.'[22] Nor can the rise be attributed to the devastations of a new and unconquerable disease. Epidemic cholera appeared first in 1831. The mortality is unknown, but it is suggested that in London the death rate from cholera in the period 1831-5 was no higher than it had been at the end of the seventeenth century.[23] Cholera had always taken its toll of life. The peril grew in the 1840's, and became a terrifying scourge in the seven years 1848-54, when, according to Farr, a quarter of a million people in the United Kingdom died of cholera and diarrhoea.[24] It is impossible to trace the movement in puerperal mortality. Lying-in hospitals usually include all deaths in childbed from whatever cause. General registers often include under this heading deaths consequent on childbirth only. Hospital records are not typical and vary amazingly. Mrs George quotes, from Willan, figures for the British Lying-in Hospital showing a fall from 1 death in 42 deliveries in 1749-58 to 1 in 914 in 1799-1800.[25] This is utterly misleading, as the rate for the five years 1799-1803 was 1 in 187·5.[26] In the Dublin Hospital the rate fell from 1 in 67 for 1761-70 to 1 in 113 for 1791-1800. It then rose again to 1 in 66 for 1811-20, and in the 1860's was about 1 in 32.[27] Farr, writing in 1871, was prepared to accept Le Fort's statement that the average for all institutions, not only in England, was 1 in 29.[28] But the Royal Maternity Charity could show a rate of 1 in 435 for the years 1875-7.[29] Outside the hospitals we have Willan's evidence that an eminent physician lost of his private patients, between 1786 and 1800, just over 1 in 100, including all deaths in childbed,[30] and Miss Buer quotes estimates for London in 1760 and 1781 of 1 in 60 and 1 in 66,[31] which are consistent with this if Willan's friend worked only among the rich. The official figures for England and Wales, 1847-54, are 1 in 189,[32] but Matthews Duncan, after careful research, put the general rate in 1870 at 1 in 120.[33] But Duncan was distinctly pessimistic. Certainly progress was made in the eighteenth century, and it seems probable that the rate of mortality was approximately halved between 1800 and 1870. Under this head forces are favourable to a fall in the general death rate.

[21] *Progress of the Nation* (1912), 9.   [22] *Vital Statistics*, 305.
[23] *Op. cit.*, 305.   [24] Farr, *op. cit.*, 352.   [25] *London Life*, 49.
[26] *Account of the British Lying-in Hospital*, 1808.
[27] J. M. Duncan, *On the Mortality of Childbed*, 93.
[28] *Op. cit.*, 274.   [29] *Ibid.*, 280.
[30] *Reports on the Diseases in London* (1801), 320.
[31] *Health, Wealth, etc.*, 147.   [32] Farr, 270.   [33] *Op. cit.*, 24.

Finally, we require the marriage rate. Below I give—(A) the number of persons married per 1,000 of the population, reckoned by taking twice the annual average of recorded marriages in each decade in proportion to the population on 1 January, the middle day of the decade.[34] For the eighteenth century I have used Brownlee's population estimates. (B) Mr Griffith's marriage-rate figures, based on eleven-year averages. Mr Griffith uses his own population estimates for the eighteenth century and Rickman's figures for the nineteenth, without allowing for the different time-intervals between the censuses. Hence the disagreement.

TABLE 6

Marriage rates per 1,000

	(A)	(B)
1761	17·2	16·70
1771	17·0	16·78
1781	17·5	17·20
1791	17·5	17·46
1801	17·3	17·30
1811	16·4	16·50
1821	16·2	16·16
1831	16·1	16·32
1841	15·6	15·78

It will be observed that here the fall from the high level of the eighteenth century—a more consistent high level in my figures than in Mr Griffith's—is steadier and more continuous than in the case of the birth rate. In my figures it is uninterrupted. But, in interpreting this fall, we must remember that there are several possible causes of a fall in the marriage rate which do not imply any discouragement of marriage. For instance, a steadily falling death rate will have this effect, by increasing the average duration of married life and reducing the number of second and third marriages.[35] We know that this cause was present until about 1820. Secondly, the fall may be a mechanical after-effect of a reduction of the average age at marriage. A marriage-rate rises by anticipation and falls by postponement. It therefore moves in waves. A gradual lowering of the marriage age may produce a long wave. The rate rises at first, but, in time, automatically relapses towards its former level. For, if every girl in the country were to get married at 20 instead of, say, 25, the marriage rate would only rise permanently in proportion to the loss by death between the two ages. It is quite possible that the hump, or wave, which has its peak about 1790, represents a change of this kind. As Mr Griffith has shown, the late eighteenth century saw a decline of apprenticeship and of the custom of living-in, both of which had made early marriage difficult for the poorer classes.[36] The Danish Census of 1787 gives clear testimony to the importance of the factor of economic

[34] The figures are in the Eighth Report of the Registrar-General, 30.
[35] *Cf. Sweden*, ed. J. Guinchard, i, 132: 'We must here point out the extraordinary decline in the numbers of re-marriages, a circumstance which, no doubt, stands in connection with the decline in mortality.'
[36] *Op. cit.*, chap. v.

and social independence in determining the marriage age. Of males between the ages of 20 and 30 the following percentages were married or widowed in various classes: journeymen and apprentices 8·2 per cent, domestic servants 4·1 per cent, handicraftsmen (i.e. small masters) 62·8 per cent, 'other independent' 51·4 per cent.[37] There is testimony to early marriages in the Reports on the Poor Laws.[38] This, however, is less significant. It probably expresses moral horror at juvenile weddings, whereas the fact of economic importance is that certain classes, previously obliged to postpone marriage till they were past 30, were becoming free to marry at the normal age. A fall due to this cause will not indicate that a smaller proportion of the population is marrying, and, as the Census Commissioners of 1851 said, 'the proportion of children to a marriage, and consequently the population, are regulated not so much or so immediately by the numbers of the people who marry as by the age at which marriage is contracted'.[39] Thirdly, the fall may be due to a declining proportion of women of marriageable age. This possibility must be examined.

We know that the population began to increase rapidly about 1780, and continued to do so, at an accelerating pace, till 1820, with a high birth rate and a falling death rate, particularly among infants. We should expect to find from 1791 to 1821 a rising percentage of children and a falling percentage of adults. This may prove to be the most potent cause of the steady fall in the marriage rate. If a marriage rate is to be taken as an index of the readiness or reluctance of the people to marry, it must be reckoned in relation only to those of marriageable age. Similarly, if the birth rate is to be taken as an index of the extent to which the population was utilizing its powers of reproduction, it must be reckoned in relation, not to the total population nor to the married women of child-bearing age, but to all women of child-bearing age. When this is done, the presumed change in the age-distribution will make the fall in the rate between 1790 and 1820 diminish, and possibly disappear, and the fall after 1820 increase. This same fact will affect the interpretation which should be put on the movements of the death rate.

The age-distribution is also, as Miss Buer has pointed out, relevant in another way. Excess in the unproductive ages throws an extra burden on active adults. A higher productivity per head is demanded of them if the standard of life is to be maintained for the whole population. Economic distress in such circumstances may be evidence, not of an excessive aggregate population, but of a relatively diminished working population. But Miss Buer does not attempt any statistical measurement of this factor.

Our starting-point is the age-figures in the Censuses for 1821 and 1841. In the former the return of age was voluntary, but the response was wide enough to allow a reasonably accurate estimate of the whole. These can be supplemented from the Tables in the 1871 Census General Report, already referred to as the source of Farr's ratio between baptisms and births. Table 58 gives the sex and age of the population from 1801 to 1871, Table 61 gives ages only, but goes back, for the younger groups, to 1761. As the calculation is based on

---

[37] M. Rubin, 'Population and the Birth-Rate', *Journal of the Royal Statistical Society*, LXIII, 602·
[38] Griffith, *op. cit.*, Appendix II.
[39] *1851 Census*, I, ii, p. xlvi.

survival in 1821 and after, the higher ages, 60-80 and over, cannot be estimated even for 1811, and the proportion of the population covered dwindles as the date recedes. The Report describes the eighteenth-century figures as 'less certain' than the nineteenth, and makes no strong claim of accuracy even for the latter. The reader is consoled by the comment that 'her past is of much less practical importance than her future population to England'.[40] Below I give the percentage of the population falling in the age group 20-60 at certain dates. The figure for 1801 is taken from the above estimate, and is probably slightly too high.[41]

TABLE 7

Age group 20-60

	per cent
1801	46·3
1821	44·0
1841	47·0
1861	47·6
1871	47·1

Obviously Miss Buer's theory has foundation. The composition of the 1821 population was abnormal. Had it been divided in the same proportions as that of 1871 there would have been about 361,000 more people alive between the ages of 20 and 60. But is it obvious that this would have been an advantage? It is probably true that a population deficient in adult members is more susceptible than the average to economic stress, but it must be remembered that this deficiency was due to an excess of the young, not of the aged, and that it coincided with a rise in the economic value of the child. The Industrial Revolution did not set children working for the first time, but it certainly did increase the productivity of child labour by linking it to the machine. We hear not only of parents overworked to support their children, but also of children working to support their parents. Secondly, one of the periods of most acute distress occurred round 1841, when the deficiency had been remedied. May it not have been due to the rapid arrival of those missing thousands to swell the ranks of the adult workers? This aspect of the phenomenon is probably even more significant than that to which Miss Buer draws attention. Here is a change rapid enough to cause a crisis, its effect magnified by concentration, while the other was weakened by diffusion; an 'earthquake wave of labour supply',[42] breaking into a labour market already invaded by women and children and weakened by many lean years of uncertain trade. Here are two forms of pressure, both derived directly from the rate at which the population had been growing, and both calculated to exert a check on that growth, the first by emphasizing the burdens of parenthood, the second by discouraging early marriage among the working class. The second was probably the stronger, and I suspect that it was an important cause of the rapid fall in the marriage rate and birth rate after 1830.

[40] *General Report*, p. xiv.
[41] My rough calculations below make it 45·9 per cent.
[42] Beveridge, *loc. cit.*, 466. Referring to the Edwardian age.

To measure the birth rate and marriage rate in proportion to those capable of marrying and giving birth, I have taken as standard the number of women aged 20-40. This fits in better with the available statistics than the more correct age group 15-50, and it gives a satisfactory index of change. To compare with the figures given in the 1871 census, I have made a rough calculation of the numbers in this group back to 1781, avoiding the assumption of constant mortality on which those estimates are based. The method by which I arrived at my guesses—for they are little more—is as follows:

Of the total female population living in 1801, 69·3 per cent survived in 1821. Of the total female population living in 1821, 73·5 per cent survived in 1841. If we assume the same ratio between the survival rates of age groups, we can calculate from the recorded number of women aged 40-60 in 1821 that the women aged 20-40 in 1801 numbered, to the nearest thousand, 1,389,000. A similar calculation for the two sexes together makes the whole 20-40 group number 2,705,000. These estimates are likely to be on the high side. The general survival rate is influenced by the death rate among infants, which was certainly higher in 1801 than in 1821. In the group survival rate this should not enter. It is true that within a few years from these starting-points the position was reversed, and infant mortality was higher in 1831 than in 1811, but by that time even the youngest members of the populations under consideration had left the most dangerous ages behind them. If, however, as is not unlikely, the death rate among the old followed a similar course, this would have a compensating effect.

In an attempt to correct this error, I made a second calculation on the basis of the death rate in the groups concerned, that is, between the ages of 20 and 60. Unfortunately the existing figures only allow a comparison between rates for the closing year of each period, based on an average of seven years about that point. We have, that is to say, burials by ages for 1818-24, and deaths by ages for 1838-44.[43] The returns were not complete, and we have to begin with a proportional distribution of the cases where age was not given. Then the burials must be converted into deaths. As it is certain that failure to register was most common in the case of infants, we cannot apply to adults the ratio found appropriate for all ages. The crude death rates for the seven-year periods round 1821 and 1841 were 21·8 and 21·7. If the deaths per 1,000 living under five varied in the same proportion, then the ratio for converting adult burials into deaths in 1821 works out at 1·034. The resulting death rate per 1,000 living aged 20-60 for 1821 is 11·9. The corresponding rate for 1841 is 12·25. If we use this mortality ratio in place of the survival ratio used previously, we arrive at a 20-40 age group in 1801 of 2,563,000. The same method applied to women only gives 1,316,000. These figures set the lower limit, as no ratio more favourable to the mortality of the earlier period is worth considering. As I think the second estimate is further below the mark than the first is above it, on the grounds that the fall in the death rate from 1801 to 1821 was not all in infant mortality, while the rise from 1821 to 1841 probably was, I have made my final guess by adding two-thirds of the differences to the lower figure. The result is:

43 *1831 Census*, I, p. xxxviii *et seq. Eighth Report of Registrar-General*, 187.

TABLE 8

Age group 20–40 in 1801

	My estimate (000)	Census estimate (000)
Women	1,364	1,371
Men	1,293	1,351
Total	2,657	2,722

The journey back another twenty years to 1780 is extremely hazardous. We can fill in the age group 40–60 in 1801 by the same method, using the ratio between survival rates just established for the 20–40 group by means of the above estimate. The result, in thousands, is 1,559. To find a ratio between the probable survival rates of the periods 1781–1801 and 1801–21 is difficult. I used the ratio between the general survival rates for the whole population as in the first estimate made of the 20–40 group in 1801. I adopted Brownlee's estimate of the 1781 population, namely, 7,531,000, and arrived at the population over 20 in 1801 by deducting from the recorded total an estimated 0–20 age group, the latter being derived from the 20–40 group in 1821 by the use of the same type of ratio. The resulting figure for the age group 20–40 in 1781 is 2,253,000. There is not enough evidence about age mortality to make correction of this figure possible, and I propose to take it as it stands, remembering that it is little more than a guess. I propose to reckon that 51 per cent of these were women.

TABLE 9

Age group 20–40

	My estimate			1871 Census Tables 58 and 61		
	(1)	(2)	(3)	(1)	(2)	(3)
1781	1,149	2,253	29·9	1,104	2,186	29·0
1791	1,242	2,427	29·4	1,219	2,414	29·3
1801	1,364	2,657	28·9	1,371	2,722	29·6
1811	1,541	2,990	28·6	1,561	3,063	29·2
1821	1,775	3,440	28·2	1,775	3,440	28·2
1831	2,157	4,187	29·8	2,136	4,181	29·7
1841	2,553	4,981	31·0	2,553	4,981	31·0

(1) Number of women in thousands.
(2) Number of both sexes in thousands.
(3) Percentage of the population contained in the age-group.
The Census Table does not distinguish the sexes for the eighteenth century. I have taken women as 50·5 per cent as a compromise between my 51 per cent and Farr's 50·36 per cent for 1801.

The percentages in 1821 and 1841 were 51·61 and 51·25. This fall reflects the lower infant mortality when the second group was born. On these grounds the eighteenth-century figure should be higher still, but against this we have the heavy losses through puerperal mortality in this age group.[44] It is probable that

[44] Price's age mortality estimates for the eighteenth century do not bear this out, but they are based on insufficient evidence. His Table for Chester, 1772–81, shows female mortality exceeding male only at ages 28–36. His Swedish Table, 1755–76, shows no female excess, but equality from

the percentage rose slightly from 1781 to 1821. My estimates for 1801 give 51·34. For Denmark in 1787 the percentage was 50·2, a remarkably low figure.[45] On these grounds I take 51. I have interpolated figures for 1791, 1811 and 1831 on the assumption that the same proportion of the twenty years' increment falls within the first decade in the case of the group as in the case of the whole population. The results are shown in Table 9.

The next Table shows the resulting birth rates and marriage rates in proportion to women aged 20-40, based on eleven-year averages about the census year and Brownlee's ratio of births to baptisms.

TABLE 10

	Marriages per cent Women 20-40		Births per cent Women 20-40	
	My estimate	1871 census	My estimate	1871 census
1781	5·73	5·95	24·8	25·8
1791	5·79	5·89	25·5	25·9
1801	5·82	5·79	25·2	25·0
1811	5·61	5·54	25·6	25·2
1821	5·57	5·57	25·4	25·4
1831	5·25	5·31	24·3	24·5
1841	4·93		22·0	
1851	5·27		21·6	
1861	5·35		22·1	
1871	5·44		23·1	

Although the difference between the two estimates is not great, it does affect the general character of the curves. My figures put the climax both of the birth rate and of the marriage rate rather later than the census figures. This makes the period 1791-1821 mark a definite peak in the birth curve rather than the first step in a fall by stages. The result depends very much on the highly speculative eighteenth-century figures. I feel convinced that Farr was wrong in putting the 20-40 age group in 1781 as low as 29 per cent of the total population, lower, that is, than at any other date except 1821. Between 1750 and 1780 the rate of population growth had been low and constant, showing a slight slackening in the last decade. The percentage increases by decades, on Brownlee's estimates, were 7, 7·4 and 6·8. The birth rate had risen by about 0·5 per 1,000. Brownlee's analysis of the London Bills of Mortality shows that infant mortality fell about 1750, but rose again slightly by 1770. The big fall came between 1761-70 and 1781-90. Death rates for the country as a whole seem to have followed a similar course, with a lag of nearly ten years. The increase caused by the first fall would, in part at least, have passed into the age group 20-40 by 1781, while the second increase would not yet have made itself felt.

At the same time the middle ages were gaining at the expense of the old. Between 1760 and 1800 the death rate in London for ages 10-50 fell considerably, the biggest fall being one of 15·6 per cent at age 20-30. But the death rate

30 to 35 (*Observations on Reversionary Payments*, 5th edn., II, Tables 40 and 42). In Farr's figures for England and Wales, 1838-54, female mortality exceeds male from the age of 10 to 35 (*op. cit.*, 183). The highest excess of female over male adult mortality in the eighteenth century is found among French nuns, as compared with monks (J. Milne, *Treatise on the Valuation of Annuities*, Table XVI).

[45] M. Rubin, 'Population and the Birth-Rate', *Journal of the Royal Statistical Society*, LXIII, 599.

among persons over 50 rose slightly, the biggest rise being one of 5·9 per cent at age 50-60.[46] It is reasonably certain, therefore, that the proportion of persons aged 20-40 must have been higher in 1781 than in 1801, probably higher than in 1831. I think my figure is, if anything, too low, and under-estimates the rise in the birth rate between 1781 and 1801.

The conclusions to be drawn from this study are mostly of the nature of hypotheses, amenable to a greater or less degree to the test of detailed research. They can be summarized as follows:

1. The crude birth rate during the whole period 1750-1830 was remarkably high as compared both with what went before and with what followed. Its climb to these heights is not altogether surprising, since it followed close on an age when the death rate was phenomenally high and the population stationary. The maintenance of this high rate, with only insignificant fluctuations, during the last forty years of this period is, however, very surprising, in view of three circumstances—the spectacular fall in the death rate which began about 1780, the decline in infant mortality, itself equivalent in its economic consequences to a rise in the birth rate, and the occurrence of a succession of acute economic crises. It follows that, if we are seeking an explanation of the rapid increase of population, we must pay as much attention to the forces which kept the birth rate up as to those which pulled the death rate down.

2. If the birth rate is reckoned in proportion to those capable of bearing children, its buoyancy is even more remarkable. It rose steeply till 1791 and maintained its level till 1821. Farr's estimates and my calculated figures (omitting the interpolations) agree in showing a slight rise during the first twenty years of the century. Not until about 1830 did the rate relapse to the level of 1780. The births on which these high rates are based stretch from 1786 to 1826. Within these limits fall at least three severe economic crises—those associated with Speenhamland, Luddism and Peterloo. For fully half the time the country was at war and was obliged to surrender her manhood for service at sea and on the Continent, a limitation on the national reproductive powers not allowed for in a rate based on the number of adult women.

And yet the rate in the middle of the war was 18·5 per cent higher than in 1851, and the rate for the miserable years of peace, 1816-26, was 10 per cent higher than that for 1871, the climax of the 'Golden Age'.

3. The marriage rate may have risen up to the end of the eighteenth century, but it fell in the nineteenth, and both estimates make it lower in 1821 than it had been in 1801. This suggests that either fertility rose or illegitimacy increased, probably both.[47] If it is true that the wave in the marriage curve which reaches its summit in 1801 represents a lowering of the average age at marriage, higher fertility would naturally follow. It would result immediately from the fact that young marriages are more fertile in their early years, and it would intensify with time, since young marriages have a longer child-bearing period.[48]

[46] J. Brownlee, 'The Health of London in the Eighteenth Century', Proceedings of the Royal Society of Medicine (1925), XVIII. Epidemiology, 73 f. Especially Table VI.

[47] No trustworthy figures for illegitimacy exist before 1842. Rickman's estimate for 1830, from which Mr Griffith deduces that 5 per cent of the births were illegitimate, is far too low (p. 125). The rate for 1851-60 was 6·5 per cent, and it had been falling (Farr, op. cit., 101).

[48] In 1911 the highest average number of children born per year in marriages of completed fertility occurred where the mother married at 17. Census, XIII, 354-5.

Mr Griffith's fertility curve,[49] which shows a steep rise from 1795 to 1815, would, on this hypothesis, exaggerate the movement, since it is based on the relation of births to marriages celebrated, and the decline in the number of the latter would not, in fact, indicate a decline in the number of married couples living. If this theory is accepted, and allowance is made for the effects of the falling death rate, there is no need to assume a real falling-off in marriage before 1820, still less a reduction in the number of mothers, married and unmarried.

4. The crude death rate, having reached its lowest point about 1811, began to rise a few years later, and continued to do so until the late 1830's. This rise coincided with a change in age-distribution favourable to a low death rate, namely, an increase in the proportion of those in healthy middle-life. It is therefore more serious than it appears. On a basis of seven-year averages, the death rates in 1821 and 1841 were 21·8 and 21·7. Had the 1841 population been constituted, as to age and sex, in the same proportions as the 1821 population, the death rate would have been 22·8, an increase of 5 per cent. It seems probable that this rise, most marked among infants and in the big towns,[50] was the result of economic causes, using the term broadly to cover deficiency of food-supply, housing and sanitation.

5. Somewhere between 1820 and 1830 began a definite decline both of the marriage rate and of the birth rate. By 1831 the birth rate, measured in proportion to women aged 20-40, got back for the first time to the level of 1781 (this is a guess); by 1841 it had slumped far below it (this is a fact). Now it is only fair to old theories to point out how this fall by stages, slow at first and then rapid, reflects the history of child labour and the Poor Law. In the 'twenties restrictions on the employment of children had begun, though feebly, and apprenticeship was giving place to contractual labour,[51] a system which does not relieve the parent so completely of the responsibility for the child. From 1815 to 1834 the Speenhamland system was still widely in force, but the rates of relief had been drastically reduced wherever possible. Justices began to protest against the 'rate in aid of wages', and in several cases it was pronounced illegal.[52] In the 1830's came an effective Factory Act and the new Poor Law.

6. This converging of the birth and death rates, with its consequent check on the rate of population growth, seems to be the result of economic pressure. Now observation has shown that the death rate is not quick to respond to the fluctuations of economic prosperity, whereas the marriage rate and birth rate are more sensitive. This is fully discussed, with the relevant statistics, by Mr Yule in two articles in the *Journal of the Royal Statistical Society*.[53] In the earlier article he shows the close correlation between the marriage rate and various indices of national prosperity, including foreign trade and employment. In the second article he examines the death rate as well, and draws certain general conclusions. 'It will be seen', he writes, 'that the death rate shows no tendency

[49] pp. 31 and 44.   [50] Griffith, 186.
[51] Redford, *Labour Migration in England*, 25-30.
[52] S. and B. Webb, *English Poor Law History*, i, 182-9.
[53] 'On the changes in the Marriage and Birth-Rates in England and Wales during the Past Half-Century' in LXIX. 'The Growth of Population and the Factors which control it' in LXXXVIII. See also R. H. Hooker, 'On the Correlation of the Marriage-Rate with Trade' in LXIV.

to vary inversely with trade and the marriage rate. On the contrary, over the period 1859-1908 the prosperous periods show, on the whole, a higher death-rate than the periods corresponding to the troughs of the depression.' He concludes that 'all the facts seem consonant with the view that, in recent historical times and in civilized States, it is the birth-rate that must be regarded as the regulating factor in population: no other view seems possible'.[54] This may not be as true of 1800 as of 1900, but it can hardly be the exact reverse of the truth. Certainly birth control was not widely practised, though some knowledge of it existed. Perhaps Francis Place exaggerated when, in 1822, he wrote that among the working people 'the means to prevent conception' (he corrected this to 'to destroy the fœtus') 'is already in use to a considerable extent'.[55] The heated interest shown in the subject in the early nineteenth century is no accident. It reflects both a desire to escape from the supposed pressure of population and a real conviction in some quarters that the use of undesirable methods by ignorant people constituted a serious danger to life and health. The main check, however, would probably come through the postponement of marriage. The fact that the birth rate did fall rapidly in the 1830's indicates that it was responsive to economic pressure. The previous rise in the death rate suggests that this pressure was present at least in 1815, probably sooner. This thought again leads us to ask why it was that the birth rate did not begin to fall earlier. Even if it suffered a check when the war began, it quickly recovered, and remained buoyant for another twenty years.

7. The economic pressure was in part a direct result of the rapidity of population growth. Urban concentration was a condition of this growth, and caused the high town mortality which drove up the national death rate. The particular phenomena which acted most strongly to lower the birth rate were, first, the burden of supporting the children saved by the declining infant mortality; secondly, the subsequent inrush of a wave of young adults into an already despondent labour market. These young people are unable to marry, and the birth rate sags. These are both by-products of the population curve.

Such are the presumptions created and the hypotheses suggested by the general statistics of the period. So far as the Malthusians are concerned, it is evident that, whether they were right or wrong in the details of their analysis, their anxiety was abundantly justified and they were absolutely right to regard the birth rate as the key to the situation. Things fell out as Malthus had feared. The preventive check was slow to act, and the positive check came into operation to arrest the pace of population growth. Malthus held that the failure of the preventive check was in part due to the evil influence of the Poor Law. Rickman thought that the Poor Laws were 'much less conducive to an Increase of Population than they are usually stated to be in Argument', but he believed that the manufacturing population was increasing rapidly, partly 'because in many Manufactures, Children are able to maintain themselves at an early age, and so entail little expense on their Parents, to the obvious encouragement of

---

[54] pp. 29 and 33.
[55] M. Stopes, *Contraception*, 273. *Cf.* Farr, in 1871, *op. cit.*, 32: 'The births, again, are under control to an extent which has not yet been duly appreciated, but is now rendered clear by the Census.'

marriage'.[56] On these views the general statistics cannot claim to pronounce judgement, but I hope I have shown that they can only be forced to give evidence against them under torture.

[56] *1821 Census*, p. xxx.

ENGLISH POPULATION IN THE EIGHTEENTH CENTURY [1]

H. J. HABAKKUK

From: *Economic History Review*, 2nd series, VI, 1953, 117–133

Editor's Note: This article is again reprinted without alterations. It may be said to have marked the revival, at least in England, of interest in the unsolved questions concerning population growth in the eighteenth century, and it influenced subsequent work by reviving the possibility that this growth might after all have been due to changes in fertility to a much greater extent than had previously been thought possible.

FEW generalizations are so well established in the books as that which ascribes the increase in the population of England and Wales in the second half of the eighteenth century to a fall in the death rate caused primarily by improvements in medicine, medical skill, and public health. Thus, for example, Dr Plumb writes:

> After 1740, however, there was a steady growth of the population due to a marked, if small, decline in the death rate. Almost certainly this was due to improved midwifery . . . and to the foundation of lying-in hospitals; the first kept the children alive, the second prevented them being exposed.[2]

Not unnaturally the view general among historians has been accepted by economists.

> It seems probable . . . that the more or less stable-sized populations which seem to have been the rule before 1750 were due to a combination of high birth-rate with high death rate. The principal development which upset this primitive equilibrium was a marked fall in the death rate, due (beyond all doubt) to the improvements in sanitation and medical skill which were beginning to be effective in the north of Europe by the middle of the eighteenth century. . . .[3]

So far as England is concerned, this conclusion rests principally on the notable work of Mr Talbot Griffith. The most substantial sections of his work, it should be noted, relate primarily to the period after 1780, and even for this period Mr Griffith's conclusions are more guarded than later generalizations based upon them; he allows more weight to movements in the birth rate and to non-medical influences on the death rate. But he too frames a general conclusion applying to the eighteenth century as a whole:

---

[1] I am greatly indebted to discussions with Mr Buckatzsch and Mr K. H. Connell.
[2] J. H. Plumb, *England in the Eighteenth Century* (1950), p. 78.
[3] J. R. Hicks, *The Social Framework* (Oxford, 1942), p. 43.

The birth rate rose from 1710 to 1790 but the rise was not as spectacular as the fall in the death rate from 1730 to 1810. The birth rate was contributing in an important way. . . . The really important factor, however, is the fall in the death rate.[4]

And, in his view, the fall in the death rate was due, not exclusively but at least to a very considerable extent, to improvements in medicine and public health.

This was not the view of eighteenth-century population growth which was held by some of the most observant contemporaries. In so far as they had a consistent theory of the subject, economic writers of the later eighteenth and early nineteenth centuries supposed that long-term changes in the size of the population were primarily the result of changes in the supply of or demand for labour. An increase in supply might arise from a fall in the cost of the labourers' customary standard of living; this would both induce earlier marriage and therefore more births, and also allow the survival of an increased number of the children born. An increase in demand for labour, by raising earnings and so increasing the labourers' command of their customary standard of living, would have a similar effect on both the age at marriage and the survival rate. Though the logic of this explanation allowed for factors influencing both supply and demand, most writers appear to have assumed, when they discussed the facts of their own day, that the most important influences operated on the side of demand. Adam Smith observed that, if the demand for labour were continually increasing, 'the reward of labour must necessarily encourage in such a manner the marriage and multiplication of labourers, as may enable them to supply that continually increasing demand by a continually increasing population'. 'What is essentially necessary', wrote Malthus, 'to a rapid increase of population is a great and continued demand for labour.' Nor was this belief confined to the systematic thinkers; 'Is it not evident', asked Arthur Young, 'that demand for hands, that is employment, must regulate the numbers of the people?'[5]

Which of these two explanations, or what particular blend of the two, we adopt is an important matter for our general interpretation of the Industrial Revolution in England. If the increase in population was primarily the result

[4] G. Talbot Griffith, *Population Problems of the Age of Malthus* (Cambridge 1926), p. 260. See also M. C. Buer, *Health, Wealth, and Population in the early days of the Industrial Revolution*, and J. H. Clapham, *An Economic History of Modern Britain* (2nd edn., Cambridge 1930), I, 54-56. T. H. Marshall, 'The Population Problem during the Industrial Revolution', *Econ. Hist., I* (Jan. 1929), 429-56, presents a significantly different view of the problem, and I am greatly indebted to his article. (See p. 247 above.) In addition, see E. F. Heckscher, 'Swedish Population trends before the Industrial Revolution', *Econ. Hist. Rev.*, 2nd. ser. II (1949), 266-77, and K. H. Connell, 'Some Unsettled Problems in English and Irish Population History, 1750-1845', *Irish Historical Studies*, VIII (Sept. 1951), 225-34. Eighteenth-century views are in process of being surveyed by D. V. Glass, 'The Population Controversy in Eighteenth-Century England, Part I; The Background', *Population Studies*, VI, 69-91.
[5] Adam Smith, *The Wealth of Nations*, ed. Cannan, I, 82. T. R. Malthus, *Principles of Political Economy* (2nd ed., 1836), p. 234. Arthur Young, *Political Arithmetic* (1774), p. 86; the whole of the section on population, pp. 61-86, contains pertinent observations on relations between population and demand. See also the same writer's *Political Arithmetic*, Part II (1779), pp. 55-58. My attention was drawn to this literature by J. J. Spengler's 'Malthus's Total Population Theory: a Restatement and Reappraisal', *Canadian J. of Econ.*, XI (1945), 83-110 and 234-64. The similar views of Benjamin Franklin are discussed by Spengler, 'Malthusianism in Eighteenth-Century America', *Amer. Econ. Rev XXV* (1935), 691-8. The same type of explanation was advanced by certain French writers: see Paul E. Vincent, 'French Demography in the Eighteenth Century', *Population Studies, I* (1947-8), 70-71.

ENGLISH POPULATION IN THE EIGHTEENTH CENTURY

of improvements in medicine and public health, it may, for purposes of analysis, be regarded as an external factor in economic development, and it is reasonable to consider whether the Industrial Revolution was a response to the challenge of increasing population. But if the population increase was primarily a consequence of an increased demand for labour, we must look elsewhere for the mainsprings of economic change in this period. It is now over a quarter of a century since Mr Griffith wrote, and although little fresh evidence has appeared on English population movements in the eighteenth century, work has been done on the population problems of other periods and societies, and it may therefore be worth-while at this stage to review his conclusion in the light of later acquisitions of knowledge. This article is a first attempt at such a review. It is not the work of a demographer presenting fresh evidence, or applying new techniques to the existing evidence, but an attempt by someone interested in the genesis of the great industrial and agrarian changes to examine, in the light of some of the existing evidence, the balance of probabilities on the population problem in the eighteenth century.

One preliminary point needs to be emphasized. The statistics at present available do not allow more than an assessment of probabilities. All the global estimates of eighteenth-century birth and death rates depend, in greater or less degree, on the information, collected in the 1801 census, about the number of baptisms and burials in each parish for 1700 and every tenth year to 1780, and then for every year to 1800. The calculations based upon this information, though sometimes employing great ingenuity, necessarily involve a large number of debatable assumptions, and the final estimates are subject to a wide margin of error. Only a detailed analysis of these assumptions could demonstrate this point fully, but the fragile nature of any conclusions should be evident from the mere fact that for most of the eighteenth century the baptism and burial figures relate to only every tenth year—years which sometimes were clearly exceptional from a demographic point of view.[6]

The evidence about population changes in pre-industrial societies suggests that there is a distinction to be drawn between the forces which determine the long-term changes in the size of the population, and those which determine short-term fluctuations. In section I we discuss short-term fluctuations.

I

One obvious feature of such societies was the marked fluctuation in death and birth rates. This is suggested by Mr Smith's study of the population of Barcelona between 1457 and 1590, by Professor Heckscher's work on Sweden's population in the eighteenth century; as well as by the population history of India in the nineteenth and twentieth centuries.[7] Of these fluctuations those in the death rate were much more violent than those in the birth rate. The reason for this is obvious. In the nature of things, the range of possible fluctuation is much greater for the death rate—from nobody dying in a year to everyone dy-

[6] Mr Joslin drew my attention to this point.
[7] R. C. Smith, 'Barcelona Bills of Mortality and Population, 1457-1590', *J. Pol. Econ.*, *XLIV* (1936); Heckscher, *op. cit.*, and H. Gille, 'The Demographic History of the Northern European Countries in the Eighteenth Century', *Population Studies*, III, no. 1 (June 1949), 1-65.

ing in a year—than for the birth rate. In the period with which we are concern-ed, fluctuations in the death rate were due primarily to harvest fluctuation and to the varying incidence of war and disease. The relative importance of these three factors is not now in question—on many occasions, it appears, it was less the deaths from war and famine which were significant than the scope which war and famine gave to the spread of disease—but all three tended to be violent in their effects. Fluctuations in the birth rate, on the other hand, arose from causes which in their nature operated more slowly. Such fluctuations might arise from: (a) changes in fecundity: though there is no reliable evidence, it is sometimes suggested that there were such changes, arising from the periodic in-cidence of disease, changes in diet or a widening of the field from which mar-riage partners were chosen; (b) changes in the age distribution of the class of married women of child-bearing age, variations, that is, in the proportion of married women in the particularly fecund age groups, arising from past changes in fertility or in death rates; (c) changes in the age distribution of the total population; (d) changes in the age of marriage. In all these cases physiological fact and the stability of social habits limited the speed and range of fluctuation.

The fluctuations in the death rate, besides being more violent, appear often to have been the effective cause of the fluctuations in the birth rate; or, more properly, the fluctuations in the birth rate were often the response of society to the periods of high mortality caused by war, famine and disease. Birth and death rates at any given time and place were obviously the result of a great variety of different influences; the effects of a period of high mortality were determined not only by the social structure of the region concerned, but by the causes and duration of the high mortality. But there is a sequence of reactions common to enough societies, and occasions, to be worth isolating.

We shall first consider the effect of a period of high mortality on *birth rates*. Stripped of the complications which accompanied it in any specific case, the central sequence of events appears to have been this. Disease, famine and war caused a sudden reduction in the population of the region affected, but where they did not permanently injure the long-term capacity of the region to support people, this reduction tended to stimulate the birth rate. This might happen in a number of ways. No doubt some of the ways which have been suggested look fanciful. It has been suggested, by Lavergne for example, that there is 'an ines-capable physiological law which ... ordains that the means of reproduction in-crease in proportion to the chances of destruction.[8] As against this it might be argued that the hardships suffered during bad harvests would tend to injure re-productive capacity. But at least for two effects of high mortality on birth rates there is reasonably good evidence. It is possible, first, that in certain circum-stances, high mortality caused marriage to be deferred; this appears to have hap-pened in Sweden during the very bad harvests of 1771 and 1772, and there are signs that it happened elsewhere. For this reason, the period after the years of high mortality saw an abnormally high marriage and birth rate. In the second place—and this is probably the effect of greatest importance—in the period after years of high mortality, people could afford to marry earlier; some sons of peasants inherited their father's holding earlier than would otherwise have been

[8] *Rural Economy* (1855), pp. 366-7. I owe this reference to Mr Connell.

the case, landless men found it easier to obtain holdings, and wage-earners gained from the higher wages caused by the scarcity of labour. Hence earlier marriages and more births.

A period of high mortality tended also to have an effect on *death rates* in the period that followed. In the first place disease and famine tended to weed out the weak and to leave a population that was tough and resistant. This was an immediate effect, and the fall in the death rate from this cause alone was often great as well as sudden. There was also a longer-term effect which may some-times have been important; as a result of the higher birth rate stimulated by the high mortality, the population some time after tended to contain an abnormally high proportion of young adults, i.e. of the people least likely to die. For both these reasons the death rate tended to be unusually low in the decades after a period of high mortality.

Thus, to sum up, the situation in the years immediately following a period of high mortality was a curious one. The total population was, of course, smaller than if there had been no period of high mortality, but the birth rate was ab-normally high, the death rate abnormally low, and the *rate* of population in-crease, therefore, unusually high. The existence of this chain of reactions is very clearly suggested by Professor Heckscher's analysis of the Swedish statistics, and it receives some support from Mr Yule's conclusion, based on a study of several European countries in the period before their major industrialization, that in most cases a falling death rate was associated with a rising birth rate.[9]

There might well be further, if less uniform, reactions. Population growth, once stimulated, might be so vigorous that it went beyond the level prevailing before the period of high mortality, beyond the capacity of the economy in the long run to support it at customary standards. For an acceleration of the rate of growth, once it started, was not easy to reverse; it tended to persist long after the circumstances which originally favoured it had ceased to exist. Earlier acces-sion to the paternal holding, for example, or higher wages enabled people to marry earlier and produce more children than they would otherwise have done. The disappearance of these favourable circumstances did not, however, provide an automatic adjustment. The additional children continued to exist and, in their turn, produced further children. Any rise in the age of marriage which might occur could not offset them. Nor did the lowering of living standards involved when population overshot the mark invariably apply a rapid check; Malthus's positive checks were often slow to appear, because people were fre-quently capable of reducing their customary living-standards substantially and for long periods. It was precisely in this situation, when a growing population was straining at resources and a large part of it living near the margin of sub-sistence, that a society was particularly vulnerable. In these circumstances har-vest failure or an attack of disease might cause a disproportionately great rise in the death rate and even complete social disaster. Such circumstances appear to account for the exceptionally severe effects of harvest deficiency on the Scan-dinavian death rates between 1736 and 1743. The great Indian famines of the nineteenth century appear usually to have followed periods when conditions

9 G. Udny Yule, 'The growth of population and the factors which control it', *J. Roy. Stat. Soc.*, LXXXVIII, 32; T. H. Marshall, *op. cit.*, p. 434. See above, p. 251.

were exceptionally favourable, and population growth, we may reasonably suppose, exceptionally rapid. In a similar way, what made the effects of the failure of the Irish potato harvest so far-reaching was that it occurred in a society where the population had been increasing rapidly. Quite apart therefore from the incidence of disease and the vagaries of climate, there appears to have been some tendency to a periodical occurrence of periods of high mortality.

The model we have just described is a highly simplified one. In any particular society the interaction of the various forces was enormously complicated by the peculiarities of structure of the particular society, the extent of peasant proprietorship, for example, and the nature of inheritance laws. But the evidence available does suggest that this is a characteristic pattern of population change in pre-industrial societies. In essence it represents, much as Malthus said, a series of oscillations around a trend, oscillations which have some tendency to offset each other.[10]

II

There is a contrast when we turn to consider what determines this trend, i.e. when we turn from short-term fluctuations to consider the long-term movement of population. In a number of pre-industrial societies for which we now have information, the most important influence on the long-term trend appears to have come from the side of the birth rate. To this agency are commonly attributed (a) changes which have taken place over long periods in the rate of population growth in a single country, and (b) the differences in rates of growth, as between various societies at the same period of time. This is not to suggest that in pre-industrial societies there were no significant differences of death rates in different periods and places. It is only to suggest that such differences as existed were probably slighter and less influential than those in the birth rate. Thus the relatively slow rate of population increase of France in the later eighteenth century can most plausibly be attributed, as it was by some writers of the time, to a low birth rate; there is no reason to suppose that the French death rate was unusually high.[11] The rapid natural increase of population in colonial America was fairly clearly due in the main to a high birth rate.[12] Mr Connell places the weight of his explanation of the rapid rise of Irish population upon factors influencing the birth rate.[13] Mr Aries suggests that the high density of the population of modern Brittany is due to the high birth rate of this region.[14] The figures given by Heckscher suggest that if Finland's population increased more rapidly than that of the other Scandinavian countries it was mainly because of her very much higher birth rate.[15]

[10] There is a good deal of evidence for the features of this pattern in chap. VII of Malthus's *Essay on Population* (1798). He remarked, e.g., on 'the rapidity with which even old states recover from the desolations of war, pestilence or the accidents of nature'. These countries 'are then for a little time placed a little in the situation of states with ample supplies of land' (pp. 109-10).

[11] For contemporary discussions see J. J. Spengler, *French Predecessors of Malthus* (Duke University 1942), esp. chap. III, and *France Faces Depopulation* (Duke University 1938) by the same author. See also Professor Chevalier's article, above, Part I, p. 70.

[12] See A. J. Lotka, 'The size of American Families in the Eighteenth Century', *J. American Stat. Assoc.*, XXII (1927), 169.   [13] K. H. Connell, *The Population of Ireland* (Oxford 1950), p. 240.

[14] Philippe Aries, *Histoire des populations françaises* (Paris 1948), pp. 19-54.

[15] Heckscher, *op. cit.*, p. 275.

In such societies, the most likely causes of differences in the birth rate were the age at and frequency of marriage, and probably of these two causes the former was the more important, though most of the argument that follows applies to both. 'The question of the age at marriage is at the heart of Irish population history.'[16] This is probably true of most other pre-industrial societies. In its turn, the age at marriage is greatly influenced by economic opportunity, both directly as it affects the age at which a man can afford to marry, and indirectly as it influences general social attitudes to marriage. The age of marriage is of course influenced by a wide variety of factors, but there is a good deal to be said for the view that, in the societies with which we are concerned, difference of economic opportunity was the most important cause of differences in the age of marriage. Thus it is probable that even before the provisions in the *Code Napoléon* relating to inheritance, French peasant proprietorship favoured late marriage; the peasant had an incentive to defer marriage until he succeeded to the family holding—possibly indeed he had some incentive to delay it even further in order to limit the number of sons and diminish the likelihood of subdivision of the family holding. In colonial America, by contrast, there was an abundance of land and an active demand for labour and therefore a positive incentive to marriage. According to Heckscher the high Finnish birth rate was due to the room for expansion afforded by the large amount of uncultivated land in Finland.[17] Mr Aries suggests that the relatively denser populations of the western and eastern fringes of Europe are due to the fact that these regions were originally the most sparsely settled.[18] The connexion of early marriage with economic opportunity—in this case the availability of holdings—has been demonstrated for Ireland by Mr Connell; these were more holdings partly because the spread of the potato, and the shift from pasture to arable facilitated subdivision, and partly because more land was brought into cultivation. It was easier therefore for sons to acquire holdings and marry early. A similar train of events seems to have followed the rise of kelp production in the Western Highlands of Scotland.[19]

The response of population to a given increase in the opportunities depended on a variety of circumstances. In a society where every one normally married as soon as physiologically possible there would be no scope for an increase of marriages when economic opportunities developed. The assumption we have made, and which is indeed crucial for the present argument, that, in the societies under discussion, there was such scope is one which clearly needs to be verified by detailed investigation of the age at marriage and the frequency of marriage. But it is not an improbable assumption, and has some contemporary warrant. 'The growth and increase of mankind', wrote Halley, 'is not so much stinted by anything in the nature of the species, as it is from the cautious difficulty most people make to adventure of the state of marriage, from the prospect of the trouble and charge of providing for a family.'[20] The attitude of labourers

---

[16] K. H. Connell, 'Land and Population in Ireland, 1780-1840', *Econ. Hist. Rev.*, 2nd ser., ii (1950), 280. See below, Part III, p. 425.
[17] Heckscher, *op. cit.*, p. 278.
[18] Aries, *op. cit.*, pp. 23-25.
[19] Malcolm Gray, 'The Kelp Industry in the Highlands and Islands', *Econ. Hist. Rev.*, 2nd ser., IV (1951), 204-5.
[20] E. Halley, 'Some further Considerations on the Breslau Bills of Mortality', *Proc. Roy. Soc.* (1693), no. 198, p. 654. See also R. Cantillon, *Essay on the Nature of Trade*, ed. H. Higgs (1931), p. 81.

towards their customary standard of living is also an important factor; where they chose to employ an increased command over resources, not to marry earlier but to improve their standards, the mechanism we have described would not of course operate. A great deal depends too on the size of the gap between the minimum subsistence level and the customary standards; the lower the standard of living at the start of the population increase, the more likely was it that the increase would be halted by Malthus's positive checks. Societies varied greatly in respect of such conditions, but, among those we have mentioned, an increase in economic opportunity appears in all cases to have stimulated some growth of population.

III

With this general picture in mind we can re-examine the thesis that the increase of population in eighteenth-century England was due to a fall in the death rate induced by medical and similar improvements. That there was a fall in the death rate towards the end of the century is not in question; indeed, as Mr Griffith pointed out, the fact was clear to contemporaries including Malthus himself.[21] It appears, too, on the figures at present available, that an important difference between the 1770's and the 1780's is that the death rate was rising in the former decade and falling in the latter. But it by no means follows from this that the fall in the death rate was the most important cause of the population increase. For what is in question is the nature of the fall of the death rate. Griffith takes the view that the fall is due to an increase in the expectation of life, particularly an increase in the expectation at birth. People were living longer, primarily because of improvements in medicine and public health. Professor T. H. Marshall, whose general emphasis differs significantly from that of Griffith, states categorically that 'the chief feature of the falling death rate was a rapid decline in infant mortality'.[22] Now it is essential to Griffith's argument that the fall in the death rate should represent an increase in the expectation of life, and furthermore an increase of a sort that would increase the number of potential parents in the population. It will not do if it is merely a question of people surviving to 70 who would previously have died at 60; this would produce some increase of population, but not a cumulative increase of the sort that has to be explained. The evidence, however, that there was an increase in the expectation of life in the eighteenth century is not systematically examined by Griffith, and it turns out to be rather fragile. And the alternative possibility is not considered that the fall in the death rate was due to a change in the age-composition of the population.

It is true that Rickman believed himself to have proved that 'Since 1780 life has been prolonged as 5 to 4'.[23] But such reliable evidence as there is for the eighteenth century relates only to the area covered by the Bills of Mortality for London. These were the basis for some ingenious calculations by Dr Brownlee, from which it appears that in the area covered by these Bills, 'a very remarkable fall in infant mortality took place'.

[21] See Malthus, *Essay on Population* (2nd edn., 1803), p. 311; Marshall, *op. cit.*, p. 430.
[22] Marshall, *op. cit.*, p. 435. See above, p. 251.   [23] Quoted by Griffith, *op. cit.*, p. 20.

From 1730 to the end of the century there is a steady decline in the number of the deaths of children under 2 years, the death rate at the end of the century being only 60 per cent of what it was in 1730-40.[24]

According to Brownlee, the infant mortality in London in the last decade of the eighteenth century was not very much higher than in the decade 1861-71. There are other calculations from the same source which confirm this conclusion.[25]

There are, however, three observations to be made about these statistics. In the first place, the figures relate only to the expectation of life of infants; at later ages Dr Brownlee found no improvement of any moment in the expectation of life in the eighteenth century. Secondly, they exaggerate the decline in infant mortality over the century as a whole. The deaths under the age of two in the decade 1731-40 were a peak; the period was at the height of the gin-drinking mania. Deaths under 2 were not recorded until this decade, but if with Brownlee one assumes that deaths from convulsions (for which figures are available from the beginning of the century) are a reliable index of infant mortality, the fall between the beginning and end of the century, though substantial, is much less dramatic. The third and most important limitation is that the figures relate only to the area covered by the Bills of Mortality, i.e. to the Greater London of that day. Can we presume, from the London evidence, a similar decline in infant mortality throughout the country as a whole? Brownlee's estimates of the crude death rates suggested to him that 'in the eighteenth century there is very little difference between the mortality in London and England as a whole'.[26] His own estimates, however, show a curious feature. In every decade between 1701 and 1770, except in the decade 1751-60, the London rate was higher than the English rate; but, in the decades 1771-80 and 1781-90, it was lower, and in the decade 1791-1800 the same. The estimates will not stand much strain, but may not this uncharacteristic behaviour of the London rate after 1770 be due to a decline in London infant mortality which was not shared by the country generally? It is not improbable. For, in view of nineteenth-century experience, it would be surprising if, in the eighteenth century, the infant mortality rate for the country as a whole had fallen *in advance* of the general death rate. Moreover we can conceive good reasons why the history of infant mortality in London should have been exceptional. Much of the fall in infant mortality from the peak of 1731-40 was probably a result of the decline in gin-drinking and may represent no more than a return to the level prevailing before gin-drinking became widespread. Gin-drinking was essentially a London vice, and there is no reason to expect in the rest of the country the sort of rise and fall that seems to have taken place in London. In so far as there was a genuine fall below the level prevailing before the gin decades, it appears to have been due to improvements that are unlikely to have had much influence outside London and some of the larger towns, to better arrangements for parish children after the 1767 Act, to the

[24] J. R. Brownlee, 'The Health of London in the Eighteenth Century', *Proc. Roy. Soc. Med.* (1925), XVIII, Epidemiology section, p. 76.
[25] M. D. George, 'Some causes of the increase of Population in the Eighteenth Century as illustrated by London', *Econ. J.*, XXXII (1922), 346-7; Thomas Bateman, *Reports on the Diseases of London* (1819), p. xi.   [26] Brownlee, *op. cit.*, p. 75.

extension of the lying-in hospitals, to improvements in draining and paving.

The London mortality figures are, therefore, an unreliable guide. The only evidence of a statistical kind relating to the country as a whole is derived from the data on ages given in the censuses for 1821 and 1841. Using this source, Brownlee was able to compare the survivors of the people born in the various decades of the eighteenth century. For every 1 male born between 1761-70 who survived in 1821, *1·274* males born in 1781-90 survived to 1841; but for every 1 male born in 1771-80 who survived to 1821, *1·363* males born 1791-1800 survived to 1841; and for every male born 1781-90 who survived to 1821, *1·479* males born 1801-10 survived to 1841.[27] The proportion in italics increases until the end of the century. The increase in this ratio of survivals Brownlee interpreted as evidence of a decline in the death rate, because the birth rates he had calculated did not provide an explanation. But the alternative explanation is still open to us that it was due to an increase in the birth rate, i.e. that more were surviving because more were being born. For it seems highly probable that the birth rates which Brownlee calculated under-estimate the births in the second half of the eighteenth century; he assumes that the deficiency in baptismal registration was constant, whereas the spread of non-conformity alone suggests that the deficiency must have increased over this period. The first argument for agnosticism about the explanation under discussion is therefore the unsatisfactory nature of the statistical evidence for an increase in the expectation of life in the later eighteenth century.

In the second place, the improvements in medical services, and in allied fields, which are adduced to explain the fall in the death rate, and which, in the absence of satisfactory statistical evidence, remain the main reasons given for supposing that there *was* an increase in the expectation of life, look curiously inadequate to sustain so large a conclusion. The checking of smallpox is of obvious significance, but, as Mr Griffith says, it belongs to the early nineteenth century rather than to the eighteenth; and the other advances in medical knowledge do not look as though they could have been of very general demographic importance. The new hospitals were few and confined to the towns. Improved sanitation was no doubt of greater effect since it diminished the importance of such diseases as typhus, but sanitary improvement was likewise an urban phenomenon, and the towns where improvements were made contained, after all, only a minority of the population. A general increase in the expectation of life cannot be inferred from such improvements, and if later statistical research proved that there had, in fact, been a significant increase in expectation of life in eighteenth-century England, we should have to look beyond such improvements for an adequate explanation. The view under discussion has sometimes been supported by reference to some more recent examples of population increase in which, by common consent, medical improvement has played a large part. But the parallel is not accurate, for there now exists a large corpus of medical knowledge and experience which, when a country starts to modernise itself, can be assimilated with sufficient speed to produce important demographic results. This was very far indeed from being the case in eighteenth-century England.

[27] Brownlee, *op. cit.*, Table v, p. 76.

Neither the statistical nor the medical arguments in favour of the view under discussion are, therefore, at all conclusive. Furthermore, there is an alternative explanation of the fall in the death rate, that it was the result of changes in the age composition of the population brought about by the rising birth rate of earlier decades, and the result also, perhaps, of the existence of a smaller proportion of vulnerable people in the population. On this reading of events, the fall in the death rate would be a fall of the type that often followed after a period of high mortality; it would register changes due to other causes, and not be itself a prime cause of cumulative population increase. It is impossible to say, on the statistical evidence available, how much truth there is in the alternative explanation, but it has a certain plausibility. The fluctuations of birth and death rates do suggest that the influences we have discussed earlier may in some degree have been present in eighteenth-century England, and though it would be foolish to place much confidence in the short-term movements revealed in such notoriously imperfect statistics, one could make out a case for the contention that the figures do betray some suggestion of the pre-industrial pattern of population growth. They show a marked rise in death rate from 1700 to 1730 and a second slighter rise—very slight on Brownlee's figures—between 1760 and 1780. Thus we have two periods of high mortality, the first commonly associated with an increase in gin-drinking but probably more reasonably attributed to bad harvests of the period, the second and slighter coinciding with a period of bad harvests. During both these periods there was a quickened rise in the birth rate which continued for a decade or two beyond, and after each of these two periods there was a fall in the death rate. There are perhaps signs here of a compensating movement of the sort we have analysed earlier; indeed, as Professor Marshall has suggested, the fall in the birth rate and the rise in the death rate in the 1830's may also have been in part the result of equilibrating forces. All this suggests that the fall in the death rate from 1730 to 1760 and the much greater fall from 1780 to 1810 may, in some degree, have been reactions to periods of high mortality.

IV

We turn now to consider the long-term changes. The most striking feature here is the rise of the birth rate which climbed to 1790, and remained thereafter for several decades at a very high level. Whatever changes later research introduces into our picture it is unlikely to overthrow the conclusion that the birth rate was higher in the second half of the eighteenth century than in the early decades. To what extent was it this factor which was responsible for breaking the pre-industrial pattern of population change in England, and for precipitating the marked and continuing increase of population in the second half of the century? It is of course true that a high birth rate, no less than a low death rate, may be the result of changing age-composition, the result of earlier increases in births and/or of the saving of infant or other life. In so far as the high birth rate of the later eighteenth century was due to a rise in the birth rate at some earlier period, it is still the birth rate that is the operative factor. The possibility that it was due to an earlier saving of life is more critical for our argument, and we shall consider it later; but the long period during which the birth rate was sustained at a high level, and the nature of contemporary comment, makes it likely that there were other circumstances than a favourable age-composition which favoured an increase in births. One such factor may have been a fall in the age at marriage.

According to contemporary theory there were two principal ways in which marriages, and so births, might be stimulated; the labourers' command over their customary necessities might increase, on the one hand because of a fall in the price of these necessities, and, on the other, because of an increase in earnings. Now there were in the eighteenth century considerable improvements in agricultural efficiency, and there is no logical difficulty about supposing that these stimulated a lowering in the age at marriage. But the supposition could be reconciled with the facts only by making some rather unplausible assumptions. So far as the cost of necessities is concerned, the long run of good harvests between 1730 and 1755 was probably of greater significance. The importance of this long period of cheap grain in the genesis of eighteenth-century industrial and population changes has never been adequately explored. Malthus took the view that the cheaper food of these years did not produce a proportionate increase of population but that 'their (the labourers') increased corn wages, instead of occasioning an increase of population exclusively, were so expended as to occasion a decided elevation in the standard of their comforts and convenience.'[28] If he was right, it may well be that the Industrial Revolution was stimulated by the increase in the demand for 'comforts and conveniences' released by this long period of low food prices. But the increased command over subsistence may also have favoured earlier marriages, and thus given an impetus to population increase.

Malthus himself, however, and most earlier writers who wrote in a similar vein, laid most stress, not on the decline in the cost of a subsistence diet, but on an increase in the earnings, or, more accurately, the resources of labourers. These resources were enhanced in the second half of the eighteenth century by an increase in the economic value of children in industrial employment, and by the system of family allowance involved in the Speenhamland arrangements.[29] It seems clear, however, that the stimulus Malthus had mainly in mind was an increased demand for labour. The greater demand for labour increased the earnings of the wage-earner and so enabled him to marry earlier. This point was crucial to Malthus's argument; the age at marriage was the mechanism linking demand for labour with population. 'Employment', Malthus argued, 'regulates the wages of labour on which the power of the lower classes of people to procure food depends; and according as the employment of the country is increasing, whether slowly or rapidly, these wages will be such as either to check or encourage early marriages, such as to enable a labourer to support only two or three or as many as five or six children.'[30]

---

[28] Malthus, *Principles*, pp. 228-9.
[29] Malthus, *Essay*, pp. 83-94. Malthus's views on this subject are apt to be misinterpreted. He did not argue that people had more children in order to profit from the earnings of children in factories, or enjoy larger poor-law benefits. His point was that the prospect of parish relief and the earning capacity of children at an early age reduced the force of the incentive to postpone marriage.
[30] Malthus, *Essay* (2nd edn.), p. 471.

Some eighteenth-century writers appear to have thought that industrialization itself, as distinguished from an increased demand for labour, would stimulate population growth. Population growth depended on an increase in the demand for labour and this, in turn, on an increase in the effective demand for goods. But the growth of effective demand might be checked by hoarding, and also by what seems to have been the possibility foremost in their minds, by a desire for leisure. 'The luxury of indolence tends always to swamp the luxury of goods.' These writers feared that people might avail themselves of any improvement in their powers of production to enjoy increased leisure rather than consume more goods. Should this happen, effective demand would not be sufficient to maintain production at the level warranted by existing resources and techniques. And where production was restrained, population growth was hindered. Signs of this attitude are to be found in Steuart,[31] and traces of it can be seen in Malthus. Industrialization would help to remove this check to population growth in two ways. It tended in the first place to create a succession of new tastes among consumers. The technical possibilities of increased production, and so of increased demand for labour, were therefore less likely to be frustrated by failure of effective demand. Secondly, industrialization tended to produce a distribution of income less in favour of the rich, whose demand was for goods with a small labour content, and more in favour of those whose demand was more for goods with a high labour content. Demand for goods with a high labour content had a more stimulating effect upon population.

There is therefore a case for supposing that the new industrial changes were stimulating population increase. There is also reason to suppose that the decay of older institutions of peasant proprietorship and the master craftsman may have had a similar effect. Professor Tawney suggested long ago that, by postponing the age of maximum earning power, these institutions tended to defer the age of marriage and so to curb population increase, and that the decay of these institutions may have had the reverse effect.[32] Labourers reached their maximum earnings earlier than peasants and, moreover, did not have the incentive to limit births in order to keep the family holding intact.[33]

It is one thing to indicate the ways in which the expansion of economic opportunities may conceivably have stimulated population increase. It is quite another thing to demonstrate that these were the most important stimuli, and to distribute responsibility between them. Some of the mechanisms which contemporaries believed to have been at work are unlikely ever to be fully verifiable, and may have to rest permanently on grounds of general plausibility. Others need a generation of collaborative work on parish registers and other local sources; it may be possible, for example, to find out whether marriage habits, particularly age at marriage, varied significantly according to period, region and social group. But this much can be said now. There is contemporary warrant for the view that the acceleration of population growth in the later eighteenth century was to a very large extent the result of a high birth rate, and that this in turn was the result of the economic developments of the period. On

[31] Sir James Steuart, *Works* (Dublin 1770), I, 38-40, 44, 47, 157, 193.
[32] R. H. Tawney, *The Agrarian Problem in the Sixteenth Century* (1912), p. 104, n. 3.
[33] There is a good discussion of the effects of economic conditions on age at marriage in Griffith, *op. cit.*, pp. 106-28.

the evidence so far published there is no positive reason for rejecting this view, and it does in fact accord better than the explanation which at present holds the field with what we know about the mechanism of population change in other comparable societies.

V

In this essay we have opposed to each other two explanations of population growth in the eighteenth century, one which attributes it to a fall in the death rate, induced by improvements in medicine and public health, the other which attributes it primarily to an increase in births induced by widening economic opportunity. But these do not, of course, exhaust the possibilities. Despite the unsatisfactory state of the statistical evidence, there may have been an increase in the expectation of life, particularly at the earlier ages, due—or due in the main—to causes other than improvements in medicine and sanitation. M. Goubert's study of the population of Auneuil shows that the expectation of life was higher in the later eighteenth century than in the second half of the seventeenth.[34] The high mortality of the later seventeenth century, he suggests, was due to the concentration of a number of very bad harvests, as a result of which, population increase, which had been rapid before the Fronde, was continually thrown back. In England, too, there were a number of very bad harvests in the later seventeenth and early eighteenth centuries. The period between 1730 and 1755, on the other hand, saw a long run of good harvests; only one harvest, that of 1739-40, was decidedly unfavourable.[35]

There is no doubt that such runs of bad and good harvests were of considerable demographic importance in England as in France. The difficulty is in knowing how far they were a natural, and how far a social phenomenon, how far the exclusive offspring of wind and weather, and how far the symptoms of population change initiated by other agents. What is the explanation of the occurrence of a run of bad harvests and a period of high mortality? Is it that, simply because of chance climatic variation, the harvest yields were exceptionally poor? Or that the yields were not in fact exceptionally poor, but that small deficiencies caused high death rates because population growth and falling living standards had already made the society vulnerable? Or is it that yields *were* exceptionally low, not however because of climatic variations, but because a growing population had been trying to extract from the soil more than was warranted by existing techniques? In a somewhat similar way, it is difficult to determine how far the existence of a run of good harvests with the absence of high death rates is merely the reflexion of the emergence of a more prudent balance between population and resources. To settle the point we need detailed studies of particular localities, but until these appear we may conjecture, on the basis of the contemporary descriptions of weather, that at least the long run of harvests in the 1730's and 1740's was primarily a natural phenomenon. We have already discussed the possible effect of these good years on marriages. Here the point is

---

[34] Pierre Goubert, 'En Beauvaisis: Problèmes démographiques du XVIIᵉ siècle', *Annales* (Oct.-Dec. 1952), p. 457. See below, Part III, p. 457.
[35] Thomas Tooke, *History of Prices* (1838), I, 59.

a different one—their effect on survival. The mere absence of the severe dearths which had been of major importance in checking population, would have resulted in a more rapid increase in the eighteenth century.

It is sometimes suggested that, quite apart from any such run of good harvests, there was in the course of the eighteenth century a long-term improvement in nutrition, and therefore greater resistance to disease. M. Goubert points out that the bad seasons of 1770 and 1788 in France did not cause such heavy deaths as did the bad seasons of the later seventeenth century.[36] And there is some suggestion that in England likewise the bad harvests of, for example, 1793-5 and 1798-1801 did not have so severe effects on the death rates as those of earlier periods. Is this a sign that the population of the later eighteenth century was better fed? An improvement in nutrition might have occurred in two ways. First, by an increase in labourer's earnings. Though many observers, Young and Malthus for example, wrote as if an increase in earnings had its main effect on marriage habits, it would be quite consistent with their views to suppose, as did Adam Smith, that the main result of 'the liberal reward of labour' was that it enabled labourers 'to provide better for their children, and consequently to bring up a greater number'.[37] An improvement in nutrition might also have occurred because of an increase in the quantity and nutritional content of food due to developments in agriculture. Improved nutrition, whatever its origin, is clearly a possibility that cannot be ruled out, but it is one which it is particularly difficult to assess. On occasion, the mere fact that there was an increase in total food output in the eighteenth century has been taken as sufficient proof of improved nutrition. But the relevant question is whether there was any increase in consumption per head, and this is still an open question. The wide regional variations of diet, no less than the scantiness of the evidence, makes any judgement dangerous, but the surviving examples of labourers' diets hardly suggest that any improvement in their diet can have been substantial. Even without any long-term improvements in nutrition, it would not of course be surprising if England in the later eighteenth century were less vulnerable to bad harvests, since improvements in marketing and transport must have had the effect of alleviating local deficiencies; the poor-law arrangements, too, whether or not they improved the general position of the poor, mitigated the effects of bad harvests, since it was then that poor-relief payments tended to be highest.

It is still open to us to believe that, for any of the reasons just discussed, the prospects of survival were better than in earlier periods, and that this was a major factor in the population increase of the period. But if we consider the one of these factors most likely, on the face of it, to have had wide demographic effects, i.e. the improvement in food production, it seems plausible to regard it, not as a positive source of population increase by its effect on survival, but as a development which allowed an increase to gather way which was primarily due to other causes. Its main demographic importance, that is, was to defer the operation of the Malthusian positive checks. Was it because, at earlier periods, agricultural output in England responded only sluggishly to the demands of increasing population that population growth was retarded? It might be argued that,

[36] Goubert, *op. cit.*, p. 468. See below, p. 457.
[37] Adam Smith, *op. cit.*, I, 81.

because of social impediments to enclosure and because of technical ignorance, population increase, in the sixteenth century for example, tended to raise prices rather than increase production, and thereby provoked the application of the positive checks. By the mid-eighteenth century, because of such developments as changes in the agrarian structure and the wider diffusion of technical knowledge, English agriculture was much more capable of responding to the demands of increasing population, and for this reason an increase of population, once started, tended to proceed much further.

We shall now attempt to sum up. Any stimulus to the rate of population growth in pre-industrial societies—an increase in the ratio of resources to population, for example, or a run of good harvests—tended to have a cumulative effect. Even where the food supply could not easily be increased, the movement so generated might persist a long time before it was halted by famine and disease; and where, as in eighteenth-century England, the supply of food was capable of considerable expansion, population might continue to increase for a considerable period. An appreciable part of the population increase in England in the eighteenth century may be due to the operation of such traditional stimuli in an unusually favourable agricultural environment; and if this is so the burden of explanation we must impose upon some new force is correspondingly diminished. But new forces there evidently were in the later part of the century. The question is whether they were the improvements in medicine and public health, or the increase in economic activity in the period. One purpose of this essay is to argue that we have been premature in our rejection of the traditional answer to this question, and to suggest, in the light of our knowledge of the mechanism of population change in pre-industrial Europe, that the acceleration of population growth was primarily the result of specifically economic changes, and in particular of an increase in the demand for labour. This still leaves open the mode of operation of this increased demand. Was its principal effect to lower the age at marriage, and in this way to increase births? Or to increase the ability of the labourers to feed their children? The second purpose of this essay is to reinstate, as a hypothesis, the view that the first effect was the more important, i.e. that the increased demand operated more via the birth rate than the death rate. Its final purpose is to urge that the causation of the eighteenth-century population increase is still an open question, and that the statistical evidence does not allow to choose with confidence between the explanations that are logically possible.

MEDICAL EVIDENCE RELATED TO ENGLISH POPULATION CHANGES IN THE EIGHTEENTH CENTURY

THOMAS McKEOWN and R. G. BROWN

From: *Population Studies*, Vol. IX, 1955, 119-41

Editor's Note: In this article (reprinted as first published), the discussion was opened out by the challenge of Professor Habakkuk's view (stated in the preceding contribution) that increased fertility might have influenced population growth. But in returning to the evidence for decreasing mortality, the paper provided the final rejection of the thesis stated by Talbot Griffith thirty years earlier.

IN a recent communication[1] Professor Habakkuk has raised doubts about the acceptability of the traditional view which attributes the increase in the population of England during the eighteenth century to a fall in the death rate. He is unable to accept Griffith's[2] suggestion that medical measures introduced during that century had a substantial effect on the death rate, and considers the statistical evidence that mortality declined unreliable. These conclusions led Habakkuk to re-examine the possibility that an increase in the birth rate was the more important cause of the rise in population, and he suggests that the acceleration of population growth in the late eighteenth century was to a very large extent the result of a high birth rate, and that in turn was the result of the economic developments.[3] His reason for preferring this interpretation is not merely that the traditional view is unacceptable; he is also impressed by evidence of the significance of the birth rate in the growth of population in certain pre-industrial societies (such as eighteenth-century France and colonial America), as well as by opinions expressed by eighteenth-century writers about the effect of economic conditions, in particular the demand for labour, on the birth rate.

These views are influenced by recent work on population problems. But in the period since Griffith's book was published there has also been a considerable advance in medical knowledge of matters which have a bearing on the interpretation of population trends. For example we are now able to assess more accurately the contribution of medical measures to reduction of the death rate during the eighteenth century. We can also express a more confident opinion about the probable effect of environmental change on the common causes of mortality. Finally, and perhaps most important in this context, we can form a

[1] H. J. Habakkuk, 'English Population in the Eighteenth Century', *Economic History Review*, Second Series, vol. VI, 1953, pp. 117-33.   See above, p. 269.

[2] G. T. Griffith, *Population Problems of the Age of Malthus*, Cambridge 1926.

[3] Habakkuk, *op. cit.*, p. 130.

judgement about the relative difficulty of (*a*) increasing the birth rate, and (*b*) reducing the death rate, in a period when both rates were undoubtedly high.

The discussion which follows is mainly concerned with a review of the medical evidence. This evidence supports the conclusion that specific medical measures introduced during the eighteenth century are unlikely to have contributed substantially to a reduction in the death rate, but seems to us to suggest that a decline in mortality is, nevertheless, a more plausible explanation of the increase in population than a rise in the birth rate. We begin by inquiring to what extent medical effort contributed to reduction of the death rate. The traditional interpretation of the rise in population has rested on Griffith's answer to this question.

1. *Effectiveness of medical measures during the eighteenth century*

At first sight a list of developments in medicine during the eighteenth century seems impressive. It includes expansion of hospital, dispensary and midwifery services; notable changes in medical education; advances in understanding of physiology and morbid anatomy; and introduction of the first example of effective protective therapy (inoculation against smallpox). It is scarcely surprising that Griffith, like most other writers, should have concluded that these changes contributed materially to the health of the people. This conclusion derives from failure to distinguish clearly between the interests of the doctor and the interests of the patient, a common error in the interpretation of medical history. From the point of view of a student or practitioner of medicine, increased knowledge of anatomy, physiology and morbid anatomy are naturally regarded as important professional advances, as indeed they are. But from the point of view of the patient, none of these changes has any practical significance until such time as they contribute to preservation of health or recovery from illness. It is because there is often a substantial interval of time between acquisition of new knowledge and the possibility of any demonstrable benefit to the patient, that we cannot accept changes in medical education and institutions as evidence of the immediate effectiveness of medical effort. To arrive at a reliable opinion we must look closely at the work of doctors during the eighteenth century, and inquire whether in the light of modern knowledge it seems likely to have contributed to the health of their patients.

(*a*) *Surgery*

There is little difficulty in coming to a conclusion about the value of eighteenth-century surgery. Before the introduction of anaesthesia, operations were almost restricted to the following: amputation, lithotomy, trephining of the skull, incision of abscess and operation for cataract. For a modern reader, the circumstances in which these procedures were carried out are almost unbelievable. The discovery of the anaesthetic properties of nitrous oxide in 1800, and a practical demonstration of the use of ether in 1846, greatly extended the scope of surgery. It did not increase its safety, and as recently as the last quarter of the nineteenth century results of the common operations were, by any standards, appalling. In 1874 the senior surgeon to University College Hospital reviewed thirty years' experience in surgery,[4] and concluded that 'skill in the perform-

---

[4] J. E. Ericksen, *On Hospitalism and the Causes of Death after Operations*, London 1874.

ances has far outstripped the success in the result'. He showed that mortality following all forms of amputation was between 35 and 50 per cent, and following certain forms it was as high as 90 per cent. These figures were based on the work of the most expert surgeons, working in the largest hospitals, and are probably no worse than would have been obtained elsewhere; indeed in continental hospitals at the same period mortality was even higher. Results of other types of operation were equally bad; it was not until the introduction of antiseptic procedures that surgery became relatively safe. Ericksen's observations were based upon the third quarter of the nineteenth century; there is certainly no reason to suppose that earlier results were better, and Singer is unquestionably correct in his judgement that 'surgery had an almost inappreciable effect on vital statistics, until the advent of Anaesthesia and Antiseptics'.[5] Indeed from the point of view of the surgeon this is a generous judgement.

(b) Midwifery

To assess the influence of midwifery on mortality we must consider two important changes in obstetric practice during the eighteenth century. These were the introduction on a substantial scale of institutional delivery, and a change in obstetric technique and management which possibly had its main impact on domiciliary practice.

Before 1749, when the first lying-in hospital was founded in London, institutional delivery was very uncommon. A considerable number of lying-in hospitals were established during the second half of the eighteenth century, and Griffith included them among 'notable improvements during the period'.[6] It is very easy to satisy oneself that when first introduced, and for many years after, the practice of institutional confinement had an adverse effect on mortality. We shall first examine statistics for the nineteenth century, which are more reliable and complete than those for the earlier period.

During the 13 years 1855 to 1867, there were 4·83 maternal deaths per thousand deliveries in England.[7] But results of institutional and domiciliary delivery were quite different. Lefort[8] estimated mortality in a large number of confinements in all parts of Europe as 34 and 4·7 per thousand deliveries for institutional and domiciliary deliveries respectively; contemporary English estimates[9] were consistent with these figures. There were substantial variations in the rates from one hospital to another, and the same hospital from year to year, but with few exceptions hospital death rates were many times greater than those for related home deliveries. Indeed the difference was so conspicuous that it was obvious to contemporary observers, and Ericksen noted that 'a woman has a better chance of recovery after delivery in the meanest, poorest hovel, than in the best-conducted general hospital, furnished with every appliance that can add to her comfort, and with the best skill that a metropolis can afford'.[10] There is of course no mystery about the reason for the high death rates; in most cases death was due to puerperal infection.

[5] C. Singer, A Short History of Medicine, Oxford 1928, p. 162.
[6] Griffith, op. cit., p. 238.   [7] 30th Annual Report of the Registrar General, 1867, p. 223.
[8] L. Lefort, Des Maternités, Paris 1866.
[9] F. Nightingale, Introductory Notes on Lying-in Hospitals, London 1871.
[10] Ericksen, op. cit., p. 43.

The figures quoted are from the mid-nineteenth century, and it may be asked whether results of institutional delivery at the earlier period were equally bad. There is reason to believe that they were worse. National statistics are not, of course, available, but from records of individual hospitals[11] it seems probable that results were slightly better in the nineteenth century than in the last quarter of the eighteenth. There can be no doubt that the effect of institutional confinement on maternal mortality was wholly bad, and indeed had the proportion of deliveries conducted in hospitals approached that in some modern communities, the results would very rapidly have been reflected in national statistics.

We must now inquire whether changes in obstetric technique and management contributed to a reduction of mortality. During the second half of the century delivery by forceps and other artificial means became more common, and the formidable instruments in earlier use had been modified to some extent. Data quoted by Simpson and others[12] show that even in hospital practice delivery by forceps was unusual (a few cases in every thousand deliveries), and results on the mortality of mother and child were extremely bad. For example, in a Dublin series the proportion of deaths after operative or artificial delivery was approximately 3 in 4 for children and 1 in 4 for mothers.[13] Even if artificial delivery were relatively more common in home confinements, as is unlikely,[14] and if results were much better than in hospital, as is quite possible, it seems inconceivable that the use of instruments had any substantial effect on results of obstetric practice.

A far more significant influence was a change in the conditions under which deliveries were conducted. This was not so much a change in obstetric technique as an improvement of hygiene in the labour room. White[15] for example recommended cleanliness and adequate ventilation, and claimed that by having regard to these essentials he had lost no patients because of puerperal infection. We do not know how widely such practices were followed in domiciliary obstetrics in the late eighteenth century, and it must be remembered that many years later it was by no means generally accepted, even by medical men, that the environment contributed to ill-health. Nevertheless there is reason to believe that maternal mortality fell during the eighteenth century,[16] and the simple hygienic measures practised by White and others are undoubtedly the most important contribution which doctors made to this improvement.

We have so far been examining the influence of midwifery on maternal mor-

---

[11] R. Bland, 'Some Calculations . . . from the Midwifery Reports of The Westminster General Dispensary', *Transactions of the Royal Society*, vol. LXXI, 1781, p. 355. J. Clarke, 'Observations on Some Causes of the Excess of the Mortality of Males above that of Females', *Transactions of the Royal Society*, vol. LXXVI, 1786, p. 349. R. Collins, *A Practical Treatise on Midwifery*, London 1835. H. Graham, *Eternal Eve*, London 1950, p. 369.

[12] Bland, *op. cit.*, p. 360. F. B. Hawkins, *Elements of Medical Statistics*, London, 1829, p. 123. J. Y. Simpson, *Obstetric Memoirs and Contributions*, vol. I, Edinburgh 1855, pp. 626, 855.

[13] Simpson, *op. cit.*, vol. I, p. 626.

[14] In respect of use of forceps Collins stated: 'Most physicians, in private practice, would require to use them but seldom; as, supposing an individual to attend 4,000 cases in the course of his life, which is a greater number than falls to the lot of most men, the forceps or lever would be necessary in little more than six cases' (*op. cit.*, p. 10).

[15] C. White, *A Treatise on the Management of Pregnant and Lying-in Women*, 1773. Cited by F. H. Garrison, *An introduction to the History of Medicine*, 3rd edn., Philadelphia 1924, p. 347.

[16] Estimates from the London Bills of Mortality suggest that maternal mortality was halved in the period 1700-1800. Merriman, *A synopsis of Difficult Parturition*, p. 343. Cited by Simpson, *op. cit.*, vol. II, p. 544.

tality. Today in most western countries maternal mortality is so low that the mortality of the foetus or newborn infant provides a more sensitive index of the effectiveness of an obstetric service. But in the eighteenth and nineteenth centuries high infant death rates were generally regarded as inevitable, and infant mortality rates were not given in national statistics until 1841, and stillbirth rates until 1927. Nevertheless, there seems no reason to doubt that the conclusions which emerge from consideration of maternal mortality would be confirmed if statistics on foetal and infant mortality were available. These conclusions are:

(*a*) That the introduction of institutional confinement had an adverse effect on mortality. Newborn infants are even more vulnerable than their mothers to infectious disease. It should be noted that the point is not that there was no improvement in mortality among children delivered in hospital during the second half of the eighteenth century,[17] but that mortality rates in hospital were consistently much higher than in domiciliary practice.

(*b*) That the only change in obstetric practice likely to have contributed to a reduction of maternal or infant mortality was an improvement in the hygiene of the labour room.

(*c*) *Medicines*

The number of drugs available for treatment of disease during the eighteenth century was very large. Fortunately, in the present context we are not required to assess the pharmacological properties of these remedies, but need only inquire whether there were improvements in therapy, either by introduction of new drugs or from more efficient use of existing ones, which are likely to have contributed to a reduction of mortality.

According to Singer[18] the only important drugs introduced between Hippocratic times and the beginning of the nineteenth century were laudanum, liver extract, mercury, cinchona, ipecacuanha and digitalis. Laudanum, liver extract (in the circumstances in which it was then used) and ipecacuanha cannot be regarded as life-saving remedies, and we need only consider more fully the claims of mercury, digitalis and cinchona.

The use of mercury in the treatment of syphilis was introduced during the late fifteenth century, largely abandoned during the sixteenth and seventeenth centuries, and re-introduced during the eighteenth. This drug is no longer used by itself, although until recently it was valued as a therapeutic agent in syphilis. But while mercury may have had some effect upon the course of the disease in individual cases, it is hard to believe that its influence can have been reflected in national mortality rates.

Even today, when used correctly, digitalis adds no more than a few years to the life-expectation of well chosen patients. The drug was included in the London Pharmacopeia of 1650,[19] but was certainly used incorrectly before 1785, when Withering published his *Account of the Foxglove*, and can have had very

[17] It is possible that there was some improvement in mortality rates in lying-in hospitals during the second half of the eighteenth century, although from present knowledge of the incidence of deaths from causes other than infection, the figures given by Heberden for mortality in the British Lying-in Hospital (in 1799-1800: 1 in 938 for mothers and 1 in 1118 for children) are frankly incredible. Cited by Griffith, *op. cit.*, p. 241.

[18] C. Singer, *British Medical Journal*, 1951, I, p. 569.

[19] F. A. Flückiger and D. Hanbury, *Pharmacographia*, London 1874, p. 422.

little value before the nineteenth century, when Bright distinguished between dropsy of cardiac and renal origin. It is inconceivable that digitalis made any substantial contribution to treatment of heart disease during the eighteenth century, much less that it had any effect on mortality trends.

Cinchona was known in England from about 1655 and was listed in the London Pharmacopeia in 1677.[20] It is undoubtedly effective in the treatment of malaria, and in some modern communities (for example in Cyprus) control of this disease has very rapidly influenced both the death rate and growth of population. During most of the eighteenth century cinchona was given in doses which were too small to be really effective,[21] until Lind demonstrated in 1786 that large doses were essential; it was also used indiscriminately, since malaria was not clearly identified from other fevers. Moreover, the number of deaths attributed to ague was insignificant in relation to the total death rate; according to Blane[22] there were 44 deaths in the Bills of Mortality 1728, and only 16 in 1730.[23]

We have been discussing drugs introduced during or shortly before the eighteenth century. Among the large number used in ancient medicine were a good many which are still included in modern pharmacopeias. A few of these older remedies were of some value, but perhaps the only one which might now be regarded as of life-saving character is iron. It was not greatly valued by Greek and Arabic physicians, but was widely used in the seventeenth and eighteenth centuries. Sydenham and other physicians employed it as a tonic, and gave it in a variety of conditions which appear to have included some iron deficiency anaemias. It is impossible to express a confident opinion about what this treatment achieved, but it can safely be asserted that it could have had no appreciable influence on the national death rate.

(d) Hospitals and dispensaries

Great significance has always been attached to the rapid growth of hospitals during the eighteenth century. In 1700 there were two hospitals in London (St. Bartholomew's and St. Thomas's), and only five in the whole of England; by 1800 there were at least 50 hospitals in England, and according to Griffith[24] accommodation available in London was nothing to be ashamed of even when judged by modern standards. But in assessing the contribution of hospitals to reduction of mortality we are less concerned with the number of beds than with the results of treatment of the patients who occupied them. On this matter the evidence is far from reassuring.

Griffith assumed that the growth of hospital accommodation was largely

---

[20] Flückiger and Hanbury, op. cit., p. 304.

[21] G. M. Findlay, Recent Advances in Chemotherapy, 3rd. edn., vol. II, London 1951, p. 271.

[22] G. Blane, 'Observations on the Comparative Prevalence, Mortality and Treatment of Different Diseases', Medico-Chirurgical Transactions, vol. IV, 1813, p. 94.

[23] Not all epidemiologists are agreed that endemic malaria ever existed in Great Britain. Professor Shrewsbury believes that the common ague was not malaria, on the grounds that (a) the clinical descriptions of individual cases of 'ague' recorded in medical and lay writings during the sixteenth and seventeenth centuries show that any febrile state, which was not accompanied by an identifiable eruption, was classed as 'ague'; (b) ague was common in districts where anopheline mosquitoes are relatively scarce today; (c) when, as at the end of war, malaria is introduced from abroad, no new cases are found after the first winter; (d) there is no evidence that the climate of Britain during the last thousand years has been more favourable for the overwintering of the malarial plasmodium than during the years immediately succeeding the last two world wars (personal communication).

[24] Griffith, op. cit., p. 219.

responsible for the steady drop in the death rate during the late nineteenth and early twentieth centuries, and concluded that hospitals must also have contributed materially to reduction of mortality in the eighteenth century. On present evidence it seems most unlikely that either the assumption or the conclusion based on it is correct. The decline of the death rate during the nineteenth century was almost wholly attributable to environmental change, and owed little to specific therapy, preventive or curative. (A reservation must be added in respect of vaccination against smallpox.) Perhaps the only useful contribution made by hospitals was the isolation of infectious patients, first in separate wards of general hospitals and later in fever hospitals (mainly after the passage of the 1875 Public Health Act). But during the eighteenth and early nineteenth centuries the importance of segregating infectious patients was not appreciated. It was believed that infectious and non-infectious cases could be mixed in the ratio of one to six, and as recently as 1854 persons infected with cholera were admitted to the general wards of St. Bartholomew's Hospital.[25]

Indeed, the chief indictment of hospital work at this period is not that it did no good, but that it positively did harm. Contemporary accounts of the unsatisfactory conditions in eighteenth-century hospitals are available in the writings of Percival, Howard and others,[26] and we have already referred to the very bad results of surgery and institutional midwifery. The common cause of death was infectious disease; any patient admitted to hospital faced the risk of contracting a mortal infection. This risk existed until the second half of the nineteenth century, when Florence Nightingale found civil hospitals 'just as bad or worse' than military hospitals, and introduced her *Notes on Hospitals* with the well-known observation that the first requirement in a hospital is 'that it should do the sick no harm'. This objective was certainly not realized during the eighteenth century; it was not until much later that hospital patients could be reasonably certain of dying from the disease with which they were admitted.

It is somewhat more difficult to assess the influence of the dispensary movement in the second half of the eighteenth century. The first London dispensary was founded in 1769, and sixteen more were added before 1800. Unquestionably they brought treatment within the reach of a greater number of poor people, but whether the treatment was of any value is another matter. We have already seen that few of the medicines available in the eighteenth century would now be judged to be of value. Moreover, their usefulness was restricted by inability to identify the conditions in which they should be given and by lack of knowledge of methods of administration. It is evident that the therapy administered from dispensaries was no better, even if no worse, than that available in hospitals and private practice.

Yet it is possible that dispensaries made a more important, if less specific, contribution to health. According to Lettsom[27] they had a substantial effect upon sanitary standards, by teaching the importance of cleanliness and ventilation. Their contribution is comparable to that of obstetricians who added nothing to

[25] W. M. Frazer, *A History of English Public Health, 1834-1939*, London, 1950, p. 152.

[26] For a description of the poor conditions in French hospitals see Tenon, *Mémoires sur les hôpitaux de Paris*, Paris 1788.

[27] J. C. Lettsom, *On the Improvement of Medicine in London on the Basis of Public Good*, 2nd edn., London 1775, p. 51.

the safety of the act of delivery, but justified their presence in the labour room by recommending improved standards of hygiene.

(e) Preventive therapy

The only disease upon which specific preventive therapy could conceivably have had a substantial effect during the eighteenth century was smallpox. Throughout the century about 10 per cent of the deaths recorded in the London Bills of Mortality were attributed to smallpox, and a marked reduction in its incidence would undoubtedly have been reflected in national mortality trends.

Vaccination was not introduced until the beginning of the nineteenth century, the procedure used earlier being inoculation with infected material obtained from patients with smallpox. This was practised on a modest scale between 1721 and 1728, rarely used during the next twelve years, and revived in 1740. Inoculation was an expensive as well as a dangerous practice, and after preliminary trials on convicts it was at first mainly restricted to the upper classes. But in the later years of the eighteenth century charitable funds made it possible for large numbers of persons of all classes to be inoculated.

In Creighton's opinion inoculation was not a success. He stated that 'the ordinary course of smallpox in Britain was little touched by inoculation'.[28] Not all historians of infectious disease agree with this view.[29] But in the present context it will suffice to note that in the London Bills of Mortality both (a) the number of deaths attributed to smallpox and (b) the proportion of all deaths attributed to smallpox, remained fairly constant throughout the eighteenth century.[30] These observations are of course consistent with a reduction in incidence if the population was increasing and the death rate from all causes decreasing. But with due regard for the unreliability of death registration, and for the unrepresentative character of the London Bills of Mortality, it is hard to believe that inoculation can have been responsible for a reduction in the incidence of smallpox large enough to have had a substantial effect on national mortality trends.

(f) Control of the environment

We have concluded that the therapeutic measures employed by doctors, whether in the field of preventive or curative medicine, could have had no appreciable effect on eighteenth-century mortality trends. Indeed it might safely be said that specific medical treatment had no useful effects at all, were it not for some doubt about the results of the use of mercury in syphilis, iron in anaemia, cinchona in malaria and inoculation against smallpox. But during the century doctors began to interest themselves in a far more significant if less spectacular field: they started to explore the association between environment and disease. The most important contributions are too well known to require detailed comment but the dates of publication are of interest: Mead's *Short Discourse concerning Pestilential Contagion, and the Methods to be used to Prevent it*, 1720;

---

[28] C. Creighton, *A History of Epidemics in Britain*, vol. II, Cambridge 1894, p. 516.

[29] Professor Shrewsbury, for example, believes that inoculation influenced smallpox mortality (personal communication).

[30] G. Blane, *A Statement of Facts Tending to Establish an Estimate of the True Value and Present State of Vaccination*, London 1820, p. 17.

Pringle's *Observations on the Diseases of the Army*, 1752; Lind's *Treatise on Scurvy*, 1753; Baker's *An Essay concerning the cause of the Endemial Colic of Devonshire*, 1767; Blane's *Observations on the Diseases of Seamen*, 1785.

Each of these works was important; collectively they represented an immense advance in understanding of the influence of the environment on disease, particularly infectious disease. It was not of course an understanding based on knowledge of the mechanism of infection; it was derived empirically by noting the association between sickness and bad living conditions. But some of the simple measures prescribed by Mead as early as 1720—better housing, cleanliness, ventilation, disinfection, control of nuisances—were those applied extensively during the nineteenth century, for whose effectiveness the science of bacteriology finally provided a rational explanation.

There is thus no doubt that early in the eighteenth century a few doctors were alive to the significance of the environment in relation to health. What interests us in the present context is whether their teaching made any immediate impact on hygienic practices. We propose to leave the question open at this point, and to return to it in Section 5. For the present we conclude that specific medical treatment had no effect on population trends during the eighteenth century, and any influence exerted by doctors resulted from their contribution to improved living conditions.

2. Relative influence of the birth rate and death rate on population according to the levels of the two rates

It would probably be generally agreed that no statistics are available which put the relative importance of the birth rate and death rate during the eighteenth century beyond dispute. In these circumstances interpretation of the existing evidence is inevitably influenced by the point of view from which it is approached. Griffith, for example, approached the matter with the conviction that medical effort had had a substantial effect on the death rate. Habakkuk, on the other hand, was not persuaded that medical measures were important, but was impressed by the apparent significance of the birth rate in certain pre-industrial societies. Before considering once again the uncertainties of the statistical evidence, it seems worth while to inquire in what circumstances an increase in the birth rate or a decrease in the death rate is the more likely primary cause of a rise in population.

At the outset we should recognize that the probable influence of the two rates is mainly determined by their levels. When both rates are high it is very much easier to increase the population by reducing the death rate than by increasing the birth rate; when the rates are low the reverse is true.

(a) When the birth rate and death rate are high

The relatively high death rates in some countries today, and in all countries in the recent past, are chiefly attributable to a high incidence of infectious diseases. The incidence of infection is largely determined by environmental conditions, and when it is high, even modest improvements in the environment are very rapidly reflected in a reduced death rate. This reduction mainly affects young children and infants: unless offset by a decline in fertility it results, first in an increase in population; second, in a temporary reduction in the birth rate (because the number of persons alive is increased, but not at once, proportionately, the number of births); and third, in a rise in the birth rate, as young people who have survived reach reproductive age.[31] Hence when the death rate is high, relatively small improvements in environmental conditions will be reflected immediately in an increase of population, and later in a rise in the birth rate.[32]

It is much more difficult to effect an increase in population by a primary increase in the birth rate, when that rate is already high. Natural fertility sets limits to the number of children born, and unless the rate of reproduction has previously been artificially restricted (for example, by contraception, or by changes in frequency or age of marriage) it cannot be much increased. That is to say when the birth rate is very high it can scarcely increase much except in consequence of a shift in the age distribution of the population (secondary to reduced mortality, as suggested above).

(b) When the birth rate and death rate are low

When both rates are low it is evidently easier to influence population by increasing the birth rate than by lowering mortality. The low birth rate is voluntarily restricted, and could be increased voluntarily, for example in response to improved economic conditions. But lack of medical knowledge sets limits to the extent to which mortality can be reduced, even among individuals in the most favourable environmental circumstances. For example, inspection of the common causes of infant deaths indicates that without new knowledge infant mortality is unlikely to be reduced much below about 15 (per 1,000 live births); nor can we yet add appreciably to expectation of life of persons in the older age groups.

Finally, we must consider the situation when the death rate is high and the birth rate is not. (For although no one is likely to question that mortality was high throughout the eighteenth century, it is evidently not generally accepted that the birth rate was also. Habakkuk's conclusion that economic conditions influenced the birth rate presupposes that it was restricted at certain periods.) Even in these circumstances there are reasons for believing that an increase in the rate would be unlikely to have much influence on population so long as mortality rates remain high. In the first place the deaths of a considerable proportion of children within a few years of birth substantially reduce the effect on population. Secondly, because mortality in infancy is sharply related to family size, the increasing birth rate would be still further compensated by an increase in mortality due to increasing family size. This is true of the relatively small

[31] These conclusions are consistent with Lorimer's projection of populations having initially high mortality and fertility rates. He examined a transition from Indian to Japanese levels of mortality, on the assumption that the birth rate at each age remained constant, while the death rate at each age declined to reach, at the end of 30 years, the level of the Japanese life table for 1926-30: there were large decreases in death rates over a wide range of ages, and especially in the ages of infancy and early childhood. The saving of lives at the early ages had a strong influence in accelerating the rate of population growth, and the proportion of children under 15 rose slightly. F. Lorimer, 'Dynamics of Age Structure in a Population with initially high Fertility and Mortality' in United Nations: *Population Bulletin* no. I, 1951, p. 31.

[32] This seems to us the most acceptable explanation of Yule's observation that in several European countries a falling death rate was associated with a rising birth rate. G. U. Yule, 'The Growth of Population and the Factors which Control It', *Journal of the Royal Statistical Society*, vol. LXXXVIII, 1925, p. 1.

families and low mortality rates of today.[33] The effect must have been much more marked in the eighteenth century when families were larger and mortality greater. The increase in mortality would be expected unless the change in the birth rate were mainly due to an increase in the number of one-child families. This would require a substantial increase in the proportion of women who marry, which we later suggest did not change much.[34]

To sum up. The relative difficulty of effecting an increase in population by reducing the death rate or increasing the birth rate is determined by the levels of the two rates. High mortality rates are mainly due to a high incidence of infectious disease, and are very sensitive to improvements in the environment. Reduction of mortality from infection has an immediate effect on population, and, since it mainly affects infants and young children, may also have a delayed effect from a secondary rise in the birth rate. So long as mortality remains high, an increase in the birth rate can have relatively little influence on population growth, first, because a high proportion of children die shortly after birth, and second, because the proportion who die increases as the birth rate increases. These considerations lead us to conclude that when mortality is high a reduction in mortality is inherently a more plausible explanation of population growth than is a rise in the birth rate.

3. The birth rate

We now examine the possibility that a rise in the birth rate was the primary cause of the increase in population during the second half of the eighteenth century. The birth rate in a given year is determined by (1) the proportion of the population which consists of women of childbearing age, and (2) the number of live children born during the year to women of childbearing age.

(1) The proportion of the female population[35] which consists of women of childbearing age may increase as a result of (a) an increase in the birth rate, or (b) a change (increase or decrease) in mortality rates which favours females in or below the reproductive age groups more than those in older age groups. It follows from what has been said above that because of high early mortality and the marked association between mortality rates and family size, an increase in the birth rate would need to be very substantial to have much influence on the age distribution of the female population when mortality from infection is high, unless accompanied by a reduction in mortality rates. If this is true a substantial increase in the proportion of females in reproductive age groups is unlikely to have occurred except as a secondary effect of a change in mortality.

[33] For example, in Birmingham in 1947, infant mortality was generally more than twice as great among fourth and later children than among first born, and about eight times as great in the case of children in the poorest environment. The higher death rates experienced by late born children were almost entirely due to infectious disease. J. R. Gibson and T. McKeown, 'Observations on All Births (23,970) in Birmingham, 1947, VII. The Effect of Changing Family Size on Infant Mortality, British Journal of Social Medicine, vol. VI, 1952, p. 183.

[34] The high level of fertility observed among women who married late during the nineteenth century makes it unlikely that changes in age at marriage would have much influence on the proportion of one-child families. England and Wales, Census 1911, Vol. 13. 'Fertility of Marriage, Part 2', Table XLIV, p. xcvii.

[35] Although the incidence of some causes of death, including some infectious diseases, is different in the two sexes, it seems to us permissible in this context to consider only changes in the age composition of the female population. That is to say we are assuming that the sex ratio of the total population did not change very much.

(2) If we ignore variations in the incidence of illegitimacy, the number of children born to women of childbearing age is determined by (a) the proportion of women who marry, (b) mean age of women at marriage, (c) reproductive capacity[36] of married women and (d) the extent of deliberate limitation of family size.

(a) It is recognized that there is an association between economic circumstances and marriage rates. Data for England and Wales examined by Glass show a high correlation ($r = 0.706 \pm 0.065$) between marriage rate and an index of real wages during the period 1856-1932.[37] But the correlation is mainly determined by changes in age at marriage, rather than by variation in the proportion of women who ultimately marry. This is suggested by the fact that between 1851 and 1911 the percentage of persons married varied between 19 per cent (1911) and 28 per cent (1871) for ages 20-24, but remained fairly constant at 86-88 per cent for ages 50-54.[38] From 1851, from which time data are fairly complete, a woman's chance of getting married before the age of 50 fluctuated between 82 per cent (in 1910-12) and 96 per cent (in 1940).[39] Since the proportion of women who can marry is considerably below 100 per cent (it is well below 96 per cent for any prolonged period)—because of the greater proportion of women than of men in the adult population—it is clear that at no time since 1851 has there been scope for a substantial increase. There is no evidence that frequency of marriage was substantially lower in the eighteenth century.[40] Data examined by Griffith[41] and Marshall[42] show no considerable increase in English marriage rates during the second half of the century; reliable statistics are not available.

(b) It seems to us that we should require very strong evidence before accepting the view that changes in age at marriage had a substantial influence on the mean number of children born to women of childbearing age during the eighteenth century. As suggested above the correlation between marriage rates and economic conditions is almost certainly attributable to variation in age at marriage, rather than to changes in the proportions who ultimately marry. But it does not follow that variation in age at marriage was substantial, for the high correlations are quite compatible with relatively small changes in mean age. For example in England and Wales for the years 1890-1907 and 1926-32, correlations between marriage rate and an index of real wages were 0.603 and 0.677 respectively; yet changes in mean age at marriage of women during the period 1896 to 1951 were trivial.[43]

---

[36] 'Reproductive capacity' is used in the sense in which it was employed by the Royal Commission on Population (1949), in preference to the more ambiguous terms: fertility and fecundity.

[37] D. V. Glass, 'Marriage Frequency and Economic Fluctuations in England and Wales, 1851 to 1934', in L. Hogben (ed.), *Political Arithmetic*, London 1938, p. 266.

[38] *Report* of the Royal Commission on Population, Table XIII, p. 22, London 1949.

[39] PEP. *Population Policy in Great Britain*, London 1948, p. 1.

[40] According to Swedish estimates, in 1750 only 74·6 per cent of women aged 45-49 were married. But the proportion of men married in 1750 at the same age was 91 per cent and the proportions of women aged 45-49 married in 1900 and 1940 were 71·2 per cent and 69·3 per cent respectively. This suggests that the relatively low proportion of women married in 1750 was determined by the low proportion of men in the adult population. H. Gille, 'The Demographic History of the Northern European Countries in the Eighteenth Century', *Population Studies*, vol. III, 1949-50, p. 27.

[41] Griffith, *op. cit.*, p. 34.

[42] T. H. Marshall, 'The Population Problem during the Industrial Revolution', *Economic Journal*, 1929, p. 444. See above, p. 259.

[43] Glass, *loc. cit. 74th Annual Report of the Registrar-General*, 1911, Table VII, p. xvii General Register Office, *Statistical Review, Tables, Part II, Civil, 1951*, Table 1, p. 71, London 1953.

Moreover there are reasons for believing that postponement of marriage would have less influence on the number of live births than is commonly supposed. In the first place there is no evidence that within fairly wide limits age of husband has any biological influence on reproductive capacity, and when they postpone marriage men frequently marry women younger than themselves. In England and Wales in 1911, when postponement is believed to have been common,[44] men at all ages over 21 married wives younger than themselves, and the difference in mean age increased as age at marriage increased: mean ages of wives of men aged 22 and 35-39 were 21·98 and 31·97 respectively.[45] In Ireland, where postponement of marriage is common, it is also more marked among men than among women: in 1936 proportions unmarried in the age group 35-39 were 48·4 per cent and 32·8 per cent for males and females respectively.[46] Secondly, in the absence of widespread birth control, a moderate increase in mean age at marriage does not have a very marked effect on fertility. For women married 30-35 years in rural Ireland in 1911, whose ages at marriage were under 20, 20-24, 25-29 and 30-34, mean numbers of live births were 8·81, 8·04, 6·79 and 5·57 respectively.[47] The impression that fertility drops sharply with increasing age derives from consideration of the general population of women, who marry relatively early. In these circumstances, mothers who have a first child late have smaller families than those who have a first child early, partly because the remaining reproductive period is shorter, and partly because the birth of a first child at a late age means that on the average they are less fertile. The comparison provides no reliable information about the number of children to be expected when women of normal fertility postpone reproduction. The best indication of the effect of postponement of childbirth among normal women is obtained by relating mean numbers of liveborn children to age at marriage (as above), or by examining the proportion of women who were childless according to age at marriage.[48]

In short, if we may accept the Irish data as a rough guide to the effect of postponement of marriage on the number of liveborn children in families whose size is not intentionally restricted, it appears that an advance in mean age of wives at marriage of about 5 years would be needed to reduce the mean number of live births by 1. Since 1896 mean age of women at marriage in England and Wales has varied by little more than a fraction of a year (range: 25·66-27·14).[49] Unless we are prepared to believe that changes in age at marriage in the eighteenth century were of quite a different order, it seems unlikely that they can have had a very marked influence on the mean number of live births per family.

(c) A third influence affecting the mean number of children born to women of childbearing age is reproductive capacity, and it has been suggested that it may have fluctuated during the eighteenth century as a result of disease, changes of diet and other environmental influences. This possibility cannot be excluded. But the effect of such influences on reproductive capacity—defined as the ability

[44] *Report* of the Royal Commission on Population, p. 22.
[45] From data in *74th Annual Report of the Registrar-General*, p. 132.
[46] Ireland. *Census of Population*, 1936, vol. v, Part I, p. 217.
[47] D. V. Glass and E. Grebenik, *The Trend and Pattern of Fertility in Great Britain*, Part I, p. 271, London 1954.   [48] *Ibid.*, p. 96.
[49] *74th Annual Report of the Registrar-General*, p. xvii. General Register Office, 1953, *op. cit.*, p. 71.

to conceive and give birth to living children—must have been small as compared with their effect on mortality in infancy. Post-natal mortality is incomparably more sensitive to change in the environment than is either the conception rate or pre-natal mortality.[50]

(d) The only methods of limiting family size which could conceivably have been effective during the eighteenth century were abstinence, abortion and *coitus interruptus*. Needless to say we have no worthwhile information about them. Abstinence was recommended by Malthus and others as the only acceptable means of avoiding pregnancy, but it is doubtful whether it has ever had much influence on population trends. It is agreed that abortion is now very common,[51] but the two effective methods—insertion of a foreign body into the cervix of the uterus, and interference by a professional abortionist—cannot have been either common or safe until recent times. Again, the probability of death of the child after birth must have made termination of unwanted pregnancies less urgent than it is today,[52] and it is believed that the incidence of abortion increased during the second half of the nineteenth century.[53] *Coitus interruptus* is among the oldest forms of contraception; it is less reliable than the alternative methods now available, and to be effective requires more self-control than is usually credited to the majority of people. Nevertheless the early fall in the French birth rate is usually attributed to withdrawal.[54] Kuczynski,[55] however, found little evidence of the practice of birth control in the English demographic literature of the century preceding the industrial revolution, and there is no reason to believe that it was common during the later years of the eighteenth century. Recent experience of countries such as Puerto Rico[56] and Japan[57] indicates that even when effective methods of contraception are readily available, an appreciable reduction in fertility cannot be rapidly effected.

This examination of possible causes of a change in the birth rate leads us to conclude that a substantial increase is unlikely to have occurred during the eighteenth century, except as a secondary result of a reduction of mortality. Moreover, the effect of an increase in the birth rate on population would be seriously reduced by post-natal mortality. Infant mortality (deaths in the first year of life) cannot have been less than 200 per 1,000 live births (the rate was 150 in 1900), and was probably considerably more. The extent of mortality in childhood is

[50] It is well recognized that of the four relevant rates—conception rate, abortion rate, stillbirth rate and infant mortality rate—the fourth has responded much more sharply than the other three to improvements in the environment since 1900. This difference must have been even more conspicuous during the eighteenth century, when mortality from infection was much higher. In Sweden the stillbirth rate has not altered to any appreciable extent since 1751: Gille reported stillbirth rates of 24·8 (per 1,000 total births) in 1751-60 and 27·9 in 1936-40, *op. cit.*, p. 32.

[51] The literature is reviewed in the 'Report of the Biological and Medical Committee on Reproductive Wastage', *Papers of the Royal Commission on Population*, vol. 4, London 1950.

[52] If the average risk of death of children was anything like so high as suggested by Garnett and others (cited by Griffith, *op. cit.* p. 242), the probability of death of an unwanted child must have been very high indeed.

[53] *Report* of the Royal Commission on Population, p. 33. United Nations, *The Determinants and Consequences of Population Trends*, 1953, p. 76.

[54] *Report* of the Royal Commission on Population, p. 37.

[55] R. R. Kuczynski, 'British Demographers' Opinions on Fertility 1600-1760', in L. Hogben (ed.), *Political Arithmetic*, London 1938, p. 283.

[56] J. L. Janer, World Population Conference, Rome 1954.

[57] T. Honda, World Population Conference, Rome, 1954. I. B. Täuber and E. G. Beal, 'The Dynamics of Population in Japan', in *Demographic Studies of Selected Areas of Rapid Growth*, New York 1944, Milbank Memorial Fund.

exhibited in a table prepared from data reported by Bland,[58] who gave numbers of previous live births and surviving children for 1,389 pregnant women attending the Westminster Dispensary between 1774 and 1781. However large the number of previous live births, the mean number of surviving children is in no case higher than 3·38.

Mortality according to parity (from data for the Westminster General Dispensary, 1774–81, reported by Bland, 1781)

Parity (number of previous children)	Number of women	Total number of children born	Total number of children living	Proportion of children surviving $\left(\frac{c}{b}\right)$	Mean number of children surviving $\left(\frac{c}{a}\right)$
	(a)	(b)	(c)		
1–2	553	807	430	0·53	0·78
3–4	377	1,300	592	0·46	1·57
5–6	227	1,224	502	0·41	2·21
7–8	130	966	364	0·38	2·80
9–10	55	517	177	0·34	3·22
11–24	47	605	159	0·26	3·38
Total	1,389	5,419	2,224	0·41	1·60

The data also exhibit an association between the proportion of surviving children and parity, and while this association is, of course, considerably influenced by the different periods at risk (children in nine-child families had a much longer period at risk than children in one-child families) mortality was evidently affected by family size. For example in families with 9–10 previous children 2 in 3 died within a few years of birth. It can scarcely be doubted that this death rate was much higher than the average for all children. If this is true, the influence of a rise in the birth rate on population would have been largely offset by a secondary rise in mortality (because children would mainly be added to existing families).

To sum up: Of the possible causes of an increase in the birth rate during the eighteenth century, the only one which seems to us to merit serious attention is a decrease in age at marriage. It is suggested that so long as mortality rates remained high a change in age at marriage is unlikely to have had a substantial influence on growth of population. This conclusion is based on the following considerations.

(a) Within wide limits, age of husband has no biological influence on fertility, and postponement of age of marriage is less marked in the case of women than of men.

(b) Unless eighteenth-century changes in age at marriage were very much more marked than those recorded in the nineteenth and twentieth centuries, their effect on the birth rate is unlikely to have been large.

(c) An increase in the birth rate would have been due chiefly to addition of children to existing families, rather than to an increase in the number of one-child families. Since mortality from infectious disease in infancy and childhood

[58] Bland, *op. cit.*, p. 366.

increases sharply with increasing family size, any increase in the birth rate would have been largely offset by an increase in post-natal mortality.

4. *The death rate*

We have already suggested reasons for believing that the primary cause of the rise in population was not an increase in the birth rate, and now inquire whether from a medical viewpoint it seems more reasonable to attribute it to a change in mortality rates. So far as we are aware the statement that mortality declined during the later years of the eighteenth century has not been seriously questioned: it was accepted by contemporary writers, and supported by statistical evidence examined by Rickman, Farr, Brownlee, Griffith and others. What has been questioned is the view that a decrease in mortality was the primary cause of the increase in population, rather than a secondary 'result of changes in the age composition of the population brought about by the rising birth rate of earlier decades.'[59]

Griffith's interpretation has been so widely accepted, that its rejection may be thought seriously to weaken the evidence for the significance of mortality. But medical effort is only one of the possible causes of a reduction of mortality, and the conclusion that it had no substantial influence merely leaves the relative importance of the birth rate and the death rate an open question.

There is little doubt about two important points concerning interpretation of mortality trends during the second half of the eighteenth century. Firstly, death rates were consistently much higher than modern rates for England and Wales. Mortality rates prepared by Brownlee and Griffith[60] for the third quarter of the century are all above 25 (per 1,000 population). Secondly, with due regard for the unreliability of medical diagnosis, there can be no doubt that the high mortality was chiefly attributable to infectious disease,[61] whose incidence was much greater in infancy and childhood than in adult life. Brownlee[62] estimated mortality in London during the first two years of life to be 300-400 (per 1,000 live births) and according to Edmonds,[63] 51·5 per cent of infants baptized in London in the period 1770-89 were dead before the age of 5. The association between mortality and age was shown by Bland[64] from information given by pregnant women attending the Westminster Dispensary between 1774 and 1781; he concluded that 5 of 12 children born were dead before the age of 2 and 7 of 10 before the age of 26. His estimate was based on the erroneous premise that mortality and frequency of births are unrelated to family size, but in spite of this error it is certain that mortality was highest shortly after birth. The same conclusion emerges from Brownlee's data.

We must now consider the central question: if we accept the view that medicine made no specific contribution, is it likely that the observed decline in mor-

---

[59] Habakkuk, *op. cit.*, p. 127. See above, p. 279.
[60] J. R. Brownlee, 'The History of the Birth and Death Rates in England and Wales taken as a Whole, from 1750 to the Present Time', *Public Health*, vol. XIX, 1916, pp. 211, 228. Griffith, *op. cit.* p. 35.
[61] Creighton, *op. cit., passim.* J. R. McCulloch, *Descriptive and Statistical Account of the British Empire*, London 1854, vol. II, p. 610.
[62] J. R. Brownlee, 'The Health of London in the 18th Century', *Proceedings of the Royal Society of Medicine*, vol. XVIII, 1925, p. 75.
[63] T. R. Edmonds, 'On the Mortality of Infants in England', *The Lancet*, 1835, I, p. 692.
[64] Bland, *op. cit.*, p. 369.

tality was anything more than a secondary phenomenon? To answer this question we must turn once again to evidence from the nineteenth century, when a decline in mortality was brought about by a reduction in the incidence of infectious disease, and was almost wholly independent of specific therapy. (The only medical procedure which can be accepted as having made a substantial contribution earlier than the twentieth century was vaccination, and its influence was limited to a single disease.) As stated previously, Griffith and others who considered this matter were completely mistaken in attaching great significance to growth of hospitals and other medical institutions.

It may be asked whether we are entitled to draw conclusions about what may have happened in the late eighteenth century from what we believe happened in the late nineteenth. Between 1775 and 1850 there had undoubtedly been a considerable reduction of mortality, and some change in the relative importance of different infectious diseases as causes of death. Nevertheless in respect of the two matters referred to above which affect the interpretation of mortality trends (the predominant position of the infectious diseases, and the very high death rates in infancy and early childhood) the position was virtually unchanged. We conclude that the decline in mortality in the second half of the eighteenth century could have been independent of a rise in the birth rate.

Because it is based on a nineteenth-century analogy, the last conclusion has been stated cautiously. But it gains considerable support from the fact that the alternative explanation which ascribes the fall in the death rate to a secondary effect of a rising birth rate is unacceptable. It is evident that a reduction in mortality which was most marked at early ages, would probably, though not certainly, be followed by a secondary rise in the birth rate. But as suggested previously, at a time when mortality from infection was high, a rising birth rate would inevitably be followed by a substantial increase in mortality, (a) because new births added to the population enter the most vulnerable age groups, and (b) because mortality in the vulnerable age groups would probably increase, since expansion of the population would mainly be due to an increase in size of existing families.

Moreover, unlike a rising birth rate, which we have suggested would have relatively little effect on population when mortality is high, a declining death rate would be very effective. Every death prevented makes an immediate addition to the population; the addition is most commonly in the younger age groups where expectation of life is longest once the hazards of the first few years are passed; and a rise in the birth rate is a probable secondary result of the decline in mortality.

Professor Habakkuk concluded that the birth rate was more important than the death rate, and that 'the most likely causes of differences in the birth rate were the age at and frequency of marriage'.[65] In coming to this conclusion he was influenced by views expressed by other writers about certain pre-industrial societies.

(i) The slow growth of population in France in the late eighteenth century, for example, was attributed to a low birth rate, largely on the grounds that 'there is no reason to suppose that the French death rate was unusually high'.

[65] Habakkuk, op. cit., p. 123. See above, p. 275.

It is generally believed that the French birth rate declined during the last years of the century,[66] but the statistics are certainly no more reliable than English data for the same period, and scarcely permit a confident assessment of the relative importance of the birth rate and death rate. For what they are worth, the mortality rates quoted by Spengler for the eighteenth century[67] are a little higher than the corresponding English rates.[68]

(ii) The rapid increase in population in colonial America was said to be due primarily to a high birth rate. But data provided by Lotka[69] do not justify this conclusion. He had no information about eighteenth century mortality rates, and merely estimated the average number of live births per married woman, according to certain assumptions about mortality. From a medical viewpoint it seems more probable that the rapid increase in population resulted from a relatively low incidence of infectious disease in a thinly populated country. The much publicized risk of death from violence in the new world was almost certainly less serious than the risk of death from infection in the old.

(iii) Attention was also directed to recent work on the acceleration of population growth in Ireland after 1780, which Connell attributes to economic improvements affecting age at and fertility of marriage.[70] But his only demographic data prior to the census of 1821 were estimates of population derived from hearth-money returns, and his argument is largely based on literary sources which do not consistently support it. It seems at least as likely that the agrarian improvements which he suggests occurred in the late eighteenth century, particularly the improvement in quality and quantity of the potato crop, were effective in reducing mortality in childhood.[71] Connell supports his views by reference to early nineteenth-century statistics, from which he infers higher fertility (a) of earlier marriages in Ireland than in England, and (b) in rural than in urban Ireland. It is true that age at marriage was a little lower in Ireland in 1830-40 than in England and Wales in 1847[72]; but the difference was considerable only at ages under 20 (when proportions married were 28·1 per cent and 11·3 per cent respectively) and was small at ages under 25 (66·5 per cent and 62·2 per cent respectively). At a period when mortality was high, in the absence of birth control, differences in age at marriage of this order could be expected to have little influence on fertility. Connell's conclusion that fertility was substantially affected is based on a comparison which can scarcely be accepted, between fertility of Irish marriages in 1831 with that of English marriages in 1901[73] when measures of birth control were widespread. There is in fact little difference between crude birth rates for Ireland in 1832-41[74] and for England

[66] The decline of the French birth rate during the nineteenth century was attributed to control of conception, probably mainly by withdrawal. No opinion was expressed about the reason for the decline in the late eighteenth century. United Nations, op. cit., 1953, p. 72.

[67] J. J. Spengler, France Faces Depopulation, Durham, North Carolina 1938, p. 41.

[68] Brownlee, 1916, loc. cit.

[69] A. J. Lotka, 'The Size of American Families in the 18th Century', Journal of American Statistical Association, vol. XXII, 1927, p. 154.

[70] K. H. Connell, The Population of Ireland 1750-1845, Oxford 1950. See also below, Part III, p. 423.

[71] The infant mortality rate in Ireland in 1840 (129, estimated from data given by Connell: pp. 193, 267) compares favourably with that for England and Wales in 1841-45 (148: General Register Office, Statistical Review, Tables, Part I, Medical, Table 3).

[72] Connell, op. cit., p. 39.   [73] Ibid., p. 31.

[74] Ibid., p. 261.

and Wales in the same period.[75] Connell's data[76] suggest that in the early nineteenth century birth rates were highest in rural areas where there had been the greatest increase in population. But urban-rural differences were more marked in mortality than in fertility. The number of births in 1840 (per 1,000 women aged 16-45) was 14 per cent higher in rural than in civic districts,[77] and the infant mortality rate in 1840 (derived from Connell's data)[78] was 36 per cent lower.

(iv) As another example of the influence of the birth rate on growth of population Habakkuk cites modern Brittany. It is true that Aries attributes the relatively dense population of Brittany to a high birth rate,[79] but this is probably due to the absence of birth control in a modern community which has retained to a considerable extent a primitive way of life, and the observation has little bearing on growth of population in the eighteenth century.

In short, none of the pre-industrial societies to which we have referred seems to us to provide clear evidence of the influence of the birth rate on population. Moreover, Swedish data, which are generally acknowledged to be the most reliable for any European country during the eighteenth century, suggest that the death rate was more important than the birth rate at the beginning of its industrial development. The population of Sweden increased by 28 per cent between 1761-1765 and 1806-1810, and by 54 per cent between 1811-15 and 1856-60.[80] For the two fifty-year periods respectively mean birth rates (per 1,000 population) were 32·60 and 32·58, and mean death rates 27·56 and 22·69.[81] Infant mortality (deaths in the first year of life per 1,000 live births) fell continuously from 216·1 in 1761-70 to 198·7 (1801-10), and from 183·4 (1811-20) to 146·0 (1851-60.)[82]

We may now summarize our reasons for preferring a decrease in the death rate to an increase in the birth rate as an explanation of the rise in population in the eighteenth century. We have regarded the view that both rates changed as being established, our task being to decide whether the one was more important than the other. Three observations are of first rate importance: according to modern standards mortality was excessively high; the death rates were mainly due to infectious disease; and the highest risks were experienced by infants and young children. The level of the birth rate seems to us to be less significant, although in general it was undoubtedly high.

Of the possible causes of an increase in the birth rate, it is suggested that only a change in age at marriage requires serious consideration. The effect of postponement of marriage on fertility is probably less marked than has been thought, because when men delay marriage they usually marry women younger than themselves (in this context age of husband has no independent significance), and the decline in fertility with increasing age of wife is smaller than is commonly supposed. It is suggested that a change in mean age of marriage during the eighteenth century is unlikely to have been great enough to have had a substantial effect on the birth rate. But perhaps more important, so long as

[75] Brownlee, 1916, loc. cit.   [76] Connell, op. cit., pp. 247, 261.
[77] Ibid., p. 36.   [78] Ibid., pp. 193, 267.
[79] P. Aries, Histoire des populations françaises, Paris 1948, p. 32.
[80] From data provided by R. R. Kuczynski, The Balance of Births and Deaths, New York 1928, p. 99.
[81] From data provided by A. Myrdal, Nation and Family, London 1945, p. 20.
[82] Myrdal, loc. cit.

mortality from infection remained high, a rise in the birth rate would have relatively little effect on population, because a high proportion of children die shortly after birth. The proportion dying would be greater than the prevailing mortality rates suggest, because the additional children would chiefly be added to existing families, and mortality increases sharply with increasing family size.

Under the conditions which we have described, the fall in the death rate could have been due to a reduction in the incidence of infectious disease, even in the absence of a specific medical contribution, as it was in the nineteenth century. It is hard to believe that it could have been secondary to a rising birth rate, since an increase in the birth rate would have been followed by an increase in mortality. Moreover, a primary reduction in mortality from infection would have a pronounced effect on population, both because the reduction is greatest in young age groups, where expectation of life is longest, and because a rise in the birth rate is a probable secondary result.

These conclusions seem to us to be supported by the most reliable statistics available for a country in the same phase of its development, those for Sweden, and to be not contradicted by statistics of various pre-industrial societies which have been thought to show the influence of the birth rate on population. We turn now to an examination of possible causes of a reduction in the incidence of infectious disease.

5. *Possible causes of a reduction of mortality*

We must now consider what is perhaps from a public viewpoint the most important question in medical history: To what do we owe the reduction of mortality from infectious disease? Having regard to its importance it is surprising that this question has had so little attention; Greenwood[83] is one of the few epidemiologists who have seriously considered it.

The possible causes of a reduction of mortality can be grouped under three headings: (*a*) specific preventive or curative therapy; (*b*) improvements in the environment; and (*c*) a change in the balance between the virulence of the infective organism and the resistance of the host.

The relative importance of these three groups of causes is not the same in different infectious diseases. For example, it is probable that the disappearance of cholera resulted from purification of water supplies; that the virtual elimination of smallpox owes much to vaccination; that the prolonged decline in mortality from tuberculosis is mainly attributable to a general improvement in living conditions; and that the change in scarlet fever from a serious killing disease to a relatively trivial complaint owes little or nothing to therapy or environmental change, and is almost certainly the result of a modification of the virulence of the streptococcus, or of man's resistance to it. In short, to provide a satisfactory answer to the question about the cause of a reduction of mortality, we should require separate and detailed consideration of each infectious disease. Tuberculosis[84] is one of the few diseases in which such an examination has been made.

[83] M. Greenwood, *Epidemics and Crowd-Diseases*, London 1935.
[84] V. H. Springett, 'An Interpretation of Statistical Trends in Tuberculosis', *The Lancet*, 1952, I, pp. 521, 575.

In these circumstances it may be asked whether any generalizations about the cause of the decline in mortality from infection are permissible. The conclusion which we regard as most important in the present context is a negative one: it is that the fall in the death rate during the eighteenth and nineteenth centuries was not the result of medical treatment, as Griffith and others have supposed. Only in the case of vaccination against smallpox is there any clear evidence that specific therapy had a substantial effect on the prevention or cure of disease earlier than the twentieth century. The decline in mortality from diseases other than smallpox was due to improvement in living conditions, and to changes in virulence and resistance upon which human effort had no influence.

About the relative importance of environment and of changes in virulence and resistance no firm opinion can be expressed. The relationship between an infective organism and its host is a constantly changing one, which reflects the interaction of nature and nurture in both, and in centuries earlier than the eighteenth there were undoubtedly periods of increase and decrease in the incidence of infection which were largely independent of changes in the environment. The question arises: Is it possible that the reduction of the incidence of infection during the eighteenth and nineteenth centuries was wholly the result of a natural change in infectivity and resistance?

Such a conclusion is plainly unacceptable. In earlier centuries although the birth rate was unrestricted, the excess of births over deaths was sufficient to permit only a slow increase in population. It seems most unlikely that the decline of mortality which resulted in a marked and consistent rise in population can be attributed to a modification in the character of the infectious diseases, and we conclude that it was mainly due to changes in the environment.

So far as the second half of the nineteenth century is concerned this conclusion presents no difficulty. By that time the influence of the environment on health was well recognized, and improvement in living conditions had been accepted as a major objective of public policy. Moreover later knowledge and experience has shown that measures introduced even before the discovery of bacteria were such as would have had a profound influence on the incidence of infection. But it is not equally certain that living conditions improved during the late eighteenth and early nineteenth centuries, and it may be asked whether the same interpretation can be accepted for this period.

Before considering this question we should attempt to clarify what is meant in this context by an improvement in living conditions. We refer to any change which would have reduced the risk of infection, or increased the survival rate among those infected: under the first are such measures as improvement in housing, water supply or refuse disposal; under the second influences affecting the general standard of health, of which by far the most important was probably nutrition.[85] Indeed at a time when infectious disease was widespread, almost any change in economic or social conditions which could be regarded as

[85] In this context Lack's conclusion about the reason for limitation of growth of wild animal populations is of interest. He noted that control of numbers probably comes through variations in the death rate, the critical mortality factors being food shortage, predation and disease. Any of these influences may be paramount; often they act together. In many species food supply appears to be the chief natural factor limiting numbers. D. Lack, *The Natural Regulation of Animal Numbers*, Oxford 1954.

an improvement would have some effect on the risk or fatality of infections.

Whether economic and social conditions did improve in the late eighteenth and early nineteenth centuries is a question for the economic historian, and not one to which there is as yet a clear answer. Let us note, however, that if we accept the view that the rise of population was not due to medical therapy, or to a change in the balance between immunity and infection, we must conclude that it resulted from an improvement in economic and social conditions. This is true whether we attribute more importance to the death rate or the birth rate; for in the later case the only conceivable explanation is a substantial decrease in mean age at marriage of women in consequence of the economic developments of the period.

These conclusions have some bearing on the direction of future inquiry. So long as medical measures were believed to have been effective, it was considered unnecessary to look further for a cause of a decline in mortality. The decision that medicine had no influence re-opens the question of the relative significance of birth and death rates. If the birth rate is thought to be more important, attention will be focused on such matters as changes in marriage rates and age at marriage. But if we accept the view that the rise in population was probably due to a fall in mortality, it will be more rewarding to consider in what respects the social and economic environment changed in the late eighteenth century. Did economic conditions improve? Were the improvements in diet which resulted from the good harvests of the first half of the eighteenth century maintained in the second half? Did the teaching of Mead, Clarke and others have a substantial influence on hygienic practice of the period? Were contemporary observers[86] correct in thinking that housing and clothing improved? If a positive answer can be given to any of these questions it would strengthen what we regard as already a strong case for believing that the rise in population in the last quarter of the eighteenth century was mainly due to a decline of mortality.

To sum up. Three possible causes of a reduction of mortality from infectious disease are considered: specific medical therapy; changes in the balance between the virulence of the infective organism and its host; and improvements in the environment. Reasons have been given previously for rejecting the first cause, and it is suggested that although there have undoubtedly been changes in the character of individual infections, it is unreasonable to attribute to this alone the progressive decline in mortality from infections as a whole, after many centuries in which mortality remained high. Improvements in the environment are therefore regarded as intrinsically the most acceptable explanation of the decline of mortality in the late eighteenth and nineteenth centuries.

It is well recognized that in the late nineteenth century living conditions improved in ways which quite certainly influenced the course of the infectious diseases. Although there is no equally good evidence that living conditions improved in the last quarter of the eighteenth century—in some respects they probably deteriorated—it is quite conceivable that there was a general advance

[86] Blane, (1813), *op. cit.*, *passim.* Hawkins, *op. cit.*, p. 231. W. C. Heberden, 'Some Observations on the Scurvy', *Medical Transactions of the College of Physicians*, vol. IV, 1813, p. 70. T. Percival, 'Observations on the State of Population in Manchester', *Transactions of the Royal Society*, vol. LXIV, 1774, p. 58; vol. LXV, 1775, p. 327. W. White, 'Observations on the Bills of Mortality at York', *Transactions of the Royal Society*, vol. LXXII, 1782, p. 42.

in the standard of living in consequence of the economic developments of the period. It is noted that whether we accept the birth rate or the death rate as the more important influence on the rise of the population, the conclusion that conditions improved in the late eighteenth century must follow rejection of the effectiveness of medical effort.

THREE ESSAYS ON THE POPULATION AND ECONOMY OF THE MIDLANDS

ENCLOSURE AND LABOUR SUPPLY IN THE INDUSTRIAL REVOLUTION[1]

J. D. CHAMBERS

From: *Economic History Review*, 2nd series, Vol. V, 1953, 319-43

Editor's Note: The first two of these reprints have been extensively edited and corrected by the author, partly to avoid overlap, partly to exclude matter not connected with the main subject of this volume. The third piece, of more recent date, has minor amendments. Together, the three essays form, at present, the only British example of an integrated regional study relating population growth to economic development.

UNTIL the advance, a generation ago, in the study of the demographic aspect of the Industrial Revolution, the function of enclosure in regard to labour supply was regarded as crucial. Its special importance in recruiting the industrial labour force was developed in a series of important studies as the result of which it came to be generally regarded as a basic postulate of the new large-scale economy.[2] More recent examination of the growth and movement of population has done something to modify this view, but the conventional picture of catastrophic change effected by enclosure continues to find adherents. Any alternative to it, says Mr Maurice Dobb, implies the assumption that 'the appearance of a reserve army of labour was a simple product of growing population which created more hands than could be fed from the then cultivated soil. If this were the true story, one might have reason to speak of a proletariat as a natural rather than an institutional creation and to treat accumulation of capital and the growth of a proletariat as autonomous and independent processes. But this idyllic picture fails to accord with the facts.'[3] This formulation of the problem invites discussion on several counts, but from the angle of the regional historian (from which it is viewed here) it generalizes a process which he sees in terms of its separate parts, i.e. as actual movements of popu-

---

[1] Based on a paper read to the Annual Conference of the Economic History Society, Easter 1952.

[2] For the most explicit statement of this view see Marx, *Capital* (Everyman, ed.), G. D. H. Cole, II, 793 and M. Dobb, *Studies in the Development of Capitalism* (1947), p. 223. 'The capitalist system pre-supposes the complete separation of the labourers from all property in the means by which they can realize their labour. . . . The expropriation of the agricultural producer, of the peasant, from the soil is the basis of the whole process.' See also H. Levy, *Large and Small Holdings* (1911), p. 38; 'The expropriated small farmer, degraded to the position of labourer . . . swelled the rural exodus being driven into the towns.'

[3] Dobb, *op. cit.*, p. 223. But see pp. 257, 272-3, where the increase of population is attributed to the fall of the death-rate owing to improvements in public health, and 'natural increase' is stated to 'have powerfully reinforced' the proletarianizing process. There remains, however, the question of the 'institutional' creation of the proletariat, by which is meant the forcible dislodging of the peasantry from the soil.

lation in particular places; and he is impelled by the force of his methodology to test the abstract formula of 'institutional creation' by fitting it to the local facts as he knows them. Such is the purpose of this article; but some clarification of the formula is necessary at the outset.

The question which is raised here is not the institutional origin of the proletariat, but whether enclosure is the relevant institution; not whether the growth of the proletariat can be treated in isolation from capital accumulation, but what form the relationship took. It centres on the emergence of what Professor Tawney has called 'a residual population' of propertyless free labour,[4] and the factors, in addition to enclosure and eviction, which accounted for its growth; and a brief résumé of the early stages of the problem is necessary to indicate the context of its later stages with which we are here concerned. It is relevant, for instance, to recall that as early as the thirteenth century, among the limiting conditions for the growth of a free labour force, were the localized customs of partible and impartible inheritance and the influence they exerted on the age of marriage. In the area of open-field or 'Champion' England, where, we are told, holdings usually descended undivided to one son, the rise of a free labour force from younger sons and daughters would have taken place more rapidly but for customary restraints upon their marriage.[5] These, it has been suggested,[6] would be relaxed when alternative means, e.g. the domestic woollen industry, were offered for rearing a family. Moreover, where partible inheritance prevailed, the multiplication of small peasant holdings is now seen[7] as one of the deciding factors in the rise of many important centres of domestic industry.

These sources of growth operated silently and perhaps we may say organically, i.e. they were not the direct or indirect product of compulsion; and for that reason there is a danger that they may be overlooked. For opposite reasons enclosure and eviction may be given too much importance: they operated, in Mr Dobb's phrase 'institutionally', i.e. compulsorily, as the result of the exercise of power, and stirred the social conscience to protest and the victims to riot and rebellion. But their effectiveness as a recruiting agent for the labour army remains a doubtful quantity, especially in the light of the knowledge we now have of the scale on which they worked. Sixty villages 'wiped out', fifty of them by

[4] R. H. Tawney, *The Agrarian Problem in the Sixteenth Century* (1912). 'A residual population, which cannot fit itself into the moving mechanism of industry without ceaseless friction and maladjustment', p. 104, and especially pp. 104-6, n. 3, and pp. 21-23, n. 2.

[5] G. C. Homans, *English Villagers of the Thirteenth Century* (1940), p. 137. A 'husband' held a substantial tenement and could therefore afford to be a husband and parent. For the rest 'no land, no marriage'. Mr Homans notes elsewhere that Norfolk and Suffolk were areas of partible inheritance and here 'there were large numbers of small and perhaps impoverished landholders and the two shires where the revolt of 1381 held most imperious sway'. Homans, 'Partible Inheritance of Villagers' Holdings', *Econ. Hist. Rev.*, VIII (1937), 48. In Kent 'a parcel of $1\frac{1}{2}$ acres would pass to co-heirs'. H. L. Gray, *English Field Systems* (1915), p. 292. See also J. C. Russell, *British Medieval Population* (Albuquerque 1948), pp. 31, 65-66.

[6] See J. Granat, *The Disappearance of the Peasantry in England* (Moscow 1908), where special importance is given to the part played by the heavy English soils which, the author thinks, necessitated the use of numerous cattle for the plough-team and thus provided a barrier to the subdivision of the holding. This in turn would produce a class of landless labourers long before the capitalist era from younger sons and daughters (*cf.* Homans on the heavy soils of 'Champion' England). Granat also thinks this accounts for the slow rate of population growth until the rise of the wool industry which attracted labour from the soil (see especially chapters II and V kindly translated for me by Mr J. Twardowski). See also summary by E. A. Kosminsky in *Econ. Hist. Rev.*, I (1928), 222.

[7] See 'Industries in the Countryside' by Joan Thirsk in *Essays in the Econ. and Social History of Tudor and Stuart England*. ed. F. J. Fisher (1961).

PIH L

enclosure between 1450-1600 in Leicestershire alone; the desertion of ninety-three sites in Warwickshire and 'other hundreds to be discovered'[8]; changes of this order must have made a sizeable contribution to the army of the landless; but it seems to have provided only a temporary alleviation of the labour shortage and did little to stimulate population growth.[9] 'The problem of population', says Professor Tawney, 'was the problem of under-population'; and contemporary writers were beginning to explore the possibilities of rewards for parents of large families and penalties for bachelors.[10]

The period immediately preceding the era of parliamentary enclosure with which we are primarily concerned here, seems to have followed a not dissimilar pattern; it was marked by the buying out of freeholds and leases for lives as a prelude to enclosure on such a scale as to give rise to the erroneous view that the yeomanry had already disappeared by 1750.[11] But rapid and ruthless as this process may have been, it failed to meet the labour needs of the time or to accelerate substantially the processes of proletarian reproduction. 'The fear of scarcity of labour', we are told, 'seems constantly in the minds of eighteenth-century employers'[12], and 'for a century following the Restoration', says Mr Dobb, 'the growth of capitalist industry must have been considerably handicapped by the comparative weakness of the labour army'[13]; but from the middle of the eighteenth century, 'the pace of dispossession quickens'[14]; and enclosure at last takes place on a scale sufficient to perform its allotted task of reducing the

[8] W. G. Hoskins, *Essays in Leicestershire History* (1950), p. 101; W. G. Hoskins, 'Leicestershire Farmer in the Seventeenth Century', *Agricultural History*, Jan. 1951, p. 16; M. W. Beresford, 'Lost Villages', *Geographical Journal*, June 1951. Mr Beresford's statement that 'each represents a landowner pursuing his advantages to the point of destroying a farming community' (*loc. cit.*, p. 129) is somewhat modified later when he suggests other 'non-institutional' factors which might have operated; and it would not be difficult to add to them, but the aggregate of the evicted must have been large.

[9] Mr Dobb notes that the surplus of labour thus produced was turned into a deficit in the next century owing partly, he thinks, to the slackening of enclosures. But the evidence for this in the seventeenth century is lacking. Dr Hoskins finds that in Leicestershire it was greatly accelerated ('Leicestershire Farmer . . .', *loc. cit.*, p. 17), though I think his figures are necessarily swollen by his inclusion of all enclosure by agreement in the pre-1730 period. There was certainly no slackening in Nottinghamshire; see my *Nottinghamshire in the Eighteenth Century* (1932), pp. 147, 187. The explanation for the shortage of labour may be associated with the recurrences of plague years followed by severe epidemics of fevers and smallpox. See p. 345-6 below.

[10] Tawney, *op. cit.*, p. 104, n. 3, quoting T. A. Starkey. Dialogue between Cardinal Pole and Thomas Lapret (1534-6).

[11] Marx, *op. cit.*, II, p. 800, quoting a letter of 1795, but see p. 312, n. 18, below.

[12] J. Lord, *Capitalism and Steam Power* (1923), p. 204.   [13] Dobb, *op. cit.*, p. 227.

[14] Mr Dobb's citation in this connexion of Lord Leicester's remark: 'I am like the ogre in the fairy tale and have eaten up all my neighbours' calls for comment. Marx says it was made when he contemplated 'the solitude' which he had created as a result of building his famous house at Holkham (*loc. cit.*, vol. II, p. 767; see also A. M. W. Stirling, *Coke of Norfolk and his Friends* (1912), p. 38). To cite this as an example of enclosure producing a 'solitude' is a particularly unfortunate choice. The builder of Holkham found his estate 'open and barren' when he succeeded to it in 1707. He reclaimed 400 acres from the sea and began planting trees as a wind-break; he grew turnips as early as 1723 and wheat, clover and lucerne by 1731 and probably before. See Naomi Riches, *Agrarian Revolution in Norfolk* (Chapel Hill 1937), p. 95, and J. E. T. Rogers, *History of Agriculture and Prices* (1902), VII, 636-704. As early as 1752 it was said that where these practices were followed 'there is three times as much work for labourers in plowing, hedging, threshing, which supports twice as many families'; quoted Riches, *op. cit.*, p. 77. See also C. W. James, *Chief Justice Coke and his family at Holkham* (1929), p. 265. His great-nephew continued these improvements. He is said to have increased the number of farms on his estate by twelve, and to have spent half a million on palatial farms and—for those days—model cottages, and even earned a rare encomium from Cobbett. See E. Rigby, *Holkham and its Agriculture* (1817), p. 52: Stirling, *op. cit.*; Cobbett, *Rural Rides* (ed. G. D. H. Cole), I, 47. The population of Holkham, which was said to be 200 in 1770, was returned as 550, 585, 810, 792, 683 between 1801-41. The decline from 1821 is a reflection of the post-war slump, especially disastrous in North Norfolk with its inferior soils. To apply the words 'ogre' and 'solitude' in this context would be a case of post-Coke propter-Coke thinking!

peasantry to a landless proletariat and removing the last prudential checks upon their increase.

At this point, the existence of census returns, enclosure awards and land tax duplicates makes possible the application of more exact tests to the claims which are made for enclosure in recruiting the labour force, and to this aspect of the discussion we may now turn.

The first effect of bringing the method of quantitative inquiry to bear on the problem seems to be to diminish the role assigned to enclosure. Professor Gonner, in his exhaustive study of census returns, could find no general connexion between enclosure and movement of population.[15] Professor Redford finds that the impact of agricultural change, at least during the war years, was more often to stimulate the growth of rural population than the reverse, and that side by side with the growth of urban communities, there was also a growth of entirely new agricultural communities as well as the reinforcement of those already existing.[16] Among the examples he gives we might refer especially to Lincolnshire, where the distressing lack of originality in rural nomenclature emphasizes the novelty of the new creations: East Ville, Midville, West Ville, Langrick Ville, to mention only four entirely new rural communities emerging as a result of an enclosure act of 1812. There was a parallel movement in Cheshire where the enclosure of Delamere Forest was the midwife of a new community. And the enclosures of Sherwood Forest, Charnwood, Enfield Chase, Bere Forest, Beeley Heath, Hampton Common, of wastes in Cumberland, Dorset, Derbyshire, Lancashire, Yorkshire, Northumberland, continued to stimulate the growth of population in rural areas almost up to the middle of the century.

But it may be objected that the peopling of the waste places is merely a variant in a rural setting of the movement of expropriated peasants from the old established rural centres under the expulsive force of enclosure. It is also possible that such a movement was masked by the growth of rural industries, and that the extruded peasantry were being transformed into a rural industrial proletariat as the first step to their recruitment in the army of urban labour.

An attempt has been made to examine this objection within a limited area of 119 villages in Nottinghamshire with results seen on Fig. 1. It shows that the population of the predominantly agricultural villages rose only less fast than that of the villages in which manufacturing or mining industry prevailed; and that of the agricultural villages, those that had been enclosed by act of parliament before 1800, rose faster than any.

Such evidence, however, leaves the larger question unanswered. The increase in population which is seen to be taking place in all types of villages, whether enclosed or not, may well be compatible with the reduction of the small-scale producer to the level of labourer and a stripping of the cottagers of

[15] E. C. K. Gonner, *Common Land and Inclosure* (1912), pp. 441 ff.
[16] A. Redford, *Labour Migration in England* (1926, p. 63): 'It appears', Professor Redford writes, 'that the agrarian changes of the early nineteenth century were part of an evolutionary process by which the rural population of each district was specializing in the kind of agriculture to which the district was physically and climatically suited. . . . During Cobbett's life-time no single county . . . reported a decreased population at *any* of the successive census returns. Cobbett countered this argument by flatly refusing to believe the census returns; but in this he was narrowly anticipating Dame Partington's opposition to the Atlantic Ocean' (p. 69). See also G. E. Fussell, 'English Countryside and Population', *Econ. Geography* (1936), p. 296.

their last remaining vestiges of independence. In regard to the section loosely called the yeomanry, that is (to adopt the working definition of Sir John Clapham) the farmer-owner with a holding sufficient to occupy his whole time, it would appear that he held his own or even made something of a recovery, at least during the war-time boom, and that the post-war decline was not catastrophic, as the Agricultural Reports of 1833 and 1836 show.[17]

In regard to the earlier period when it is suggested the yeomanry actually made something of a recovery, we need make no more than a passing reference to the many examples quoted by the Agricultural Reporters[18] to show that economic conditions were not always unfavourable to the independent owner-occupier and that there was a widespread tendency to buy on the rising market. Where the soil was favourable to the small freeholder, enclosure might permit him to develop a form of mixed husbandry, as in south Wiltshire, where 'there are so many parts of the land, that, when enclosed, may be applied to the purposes of a small farm, without the necessity of keeping a flock of sheep to manure it; viz. by keeping that part which will be necessary to remain in arable, on a turnip system . . . by laying the wet parts to grass . . . and by applying the sand lands on a garden system'.[19] An interesting confirmation of this opinion is provided by Rutland where great varieties of soil occurred at short distances so that nearly all the farms had suitable land for all kinds of husbandry 'thus producing everything useful in themselves', which helps to account for the continued survival of the small farm, e.g. of 20-50 acres after enclosure.[20] An example of a different kind of advantage enjoyed by the small farmer at this time comes from Knaresborough Forest where, after enclosure, the small proprietors, we are told, 'took the lead and brought their small shares into the completest state of cultivation', while the larger proprietors were handicapped through shortage of labour and extravagantly high wages demanded, so that many of the larger allotments had not even been fenced fifteen years later.[21]

Most of these examples refer to the small owner. The small tenant was in a far worse case and contemporary opinion leaves us in no doubt that this class generally suffered in numbers heavily from enclosure[22]; but the economic context of enclosure cannot be assumed always to have been fatal to the small man at this time; it varied in its incidence according to local circumstances. Enclosure marked only a phase—though an important one—in the ascendancy of the large farm with its lower comparative costs; it was not the signal for the extinction of the small farm as an economic unit everywhere.

[17] See J. H. Clapham, *Economic History of Modern Britain* (1926), I, 103-5.
[18] See A. H. Johnson, *Disappearance of the Small Landowner* (1909), ch. VIII; Ernle, *English Farming Past and Present*, pp. 292 ff.; Clapham, *Economic History of Modern Britain*, I, 99-104; W. Hasbach, *History of the English Agricultural Labourer* (1920), pp. 70-7; and H. C. Taylor, *Decline of Landowning Farming in England* (Wisconsin 1904) for valuable summaries of this evidence. For an interesting contemporary summary see Thomas Robertson, *General Report upon Size of Farms submitted to Board of Agriculture* (1796), county by county, including Scotland.
[19] T. Davies, *General View of Wiltshire* (1794), p. 139.
[20] R. Parkinson, *General View of Rutland* (1807), pp. 17 and 30.
[21] G. Rennie, etc., *General View of Yorkshire* (1794), p. 76.
[22] See, for example, 'Chalk Wiltshire', where the small farmer was eliminated through the destruction of the common sheep-fold system. In some enclosures the commissioners saved the small farmer by retaining the commons without which he was doomed, an example of institutional factors coming to his rescue. On the other hand 'Cheese Wiltshire' remained the stronghold of the small family farm. See Davis, *op. cit.*, p. 85, and chapter of the *Wiltshire V.C.H.*, Vol. IV, 1959, on 'Agriculture and Estate Management 1609-1793' by E. Kerridge.

If we turn to the statistical evidence, we find confirmation of this supposition. A number of localized inquiries may be cited which tend to show that the survival-value of the small man under the impact of enclosure should not be underestimated. In Professor Lavrovsky's exhaustive analysis[23] of eleven villages in Suffolk enclosed between 1797 and 1814 he finds that the peasantry, in the form of small owners and leaseholders, were very numerous before enclosure, and that the former were somewhat more numerous afterwards. Moreover, owners and tenants were so intertwined that it was difficult to distinguish between them,

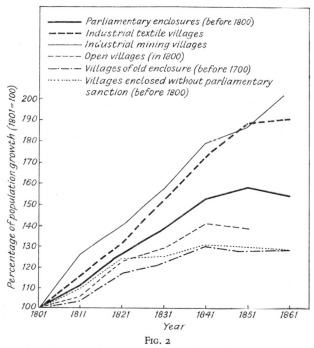

FIG. 2

Growth of Population in Nottinghamshire villages 1801-61.

as they frequently held land from each other besides occupying their own, and a surprisingly large number were absentee landowners. After enclosure, the copyholders as well as the freeholders received allotments in compensation for loss of common rights; common-right owners without land were compensated and so came into the category of landowners for the first time, thus increasing the numbers of the smallest owners, i.e. the cottagers with an average of rather less than an acre each and the small farmers with an average of just under 10

[23] V. M. Lavrovsky, 'Parliamentary Enclosures in the County of Suffolk (1797-1814)', *Econ. Hist. Rev.*, VII (1937), 193, 207-8. He points out that the penetration of capitalist elements into the English village did not always take place through the medium of capitalist farming. Sometimes a group of rich, well-to-do peasants arose from among the peasantry themselves, i.e. before enclosure. See also *Econ. Hist. Rev.*, XII (1942), 92, for review of his important book on *Parliamentary Enclosure of Common Fields in England* by Christopher Hill, where he confirms the view of students of the land tax returns that the late seventeenth and early eighteenth centuries, rather than the age of the French Revolutionary wars, was the most critical period for the peasantry and concludes that by the time enclosure took place there had been a growth of the largest peasant holdings (those over 50 acres) and the smallest (less than 25 acres), but the middle category had become relatively insignificant. 'And this had occurred in unenclosed parishes.' In old enclosed parishes the process had gone much further. E. Davies found that 'the occupying owners had almost ceased to exist in the old enclosed parishes' before 1780, *Econ. Hist. Rev.*, I (1927), 103.

acres each. But in size of properties the average amount held by the smallest owners remained unchanged while that of the handful of larger owners was substantially increased, the effect of enclosure thus being to accentuate the economic differentiation between large and small owners while adding to the numerical advantage of the latter. In a further study[24] of twenty enclosure awards in different parts of the country he finds there were few large farms but (except in four out of the twenty) a numerous peasantry. Moreover, the awards indicate, he says, 'an extraordinary development of peasant ownership' as a result of the sale and division of some of the large farms; and he refers especially to the village of Newbold in Leicestershire, where at the auction of land held by the Commissioners to defray expenses, nineteen small owners, who he thinks were new to the parish as their names were not found among those receiving allotments at the enclosure, acquired an average of three acres each. Whether the small tenants came off equally well is another matter. As Professor Lavrovsky says, they were more immediately affected 'as parliamentary enclosure signified the temporary suspension and annulment of leases, though it is true on a basis of some "compensation" to lessees'. There may have been consolidation and a reduction in numbers; 'doubtless, large farms might have been formed under favourable circumstances', to quote this scrupulously careful author again, but the fact that so many of the tenants were also small owners would serve as a brake upon any catastrophic fall into the category of landless labourers.

Nothing, however, is said of the lowest group of all, the cottage labourers with customary usage of the common; and nothing statistically can be said. Since they had no proprietary rights to defend they do not appear in the enclosure award or land-tax returns though they occasionally occur in estate accounts, as is the case of the Duke of Kingston's accounts of Gedling, Carlton and Stoke Bardolph where sixteen cottagers paid rent before enclosure but none afterwards[25]; these landless or semi-landless workers, together with the small tenants who disappeared through consolidation, represent the real victims of enclosure, and unless they are constantly kept in mind, they may also become the victims of the statistical method. It is of such—tenant cottagers and small tenant farmers—that Dr Hasbach can truthfully say: 'Enclosure was the last act in the drama of proletarianisation'; but it does not seem that this was necessarily true even of the smallest owner or copyholder who could substantiate a legal claim to the satisfaction of the enclosure commissioners; and in the light of recent research it would seem that the commissioners were not too difficult to satisfy. Indeed they stand in striking and pleasing contrast to the squires and rich yeomen of the fifteenth and sixteenth centuries who 'wiped out' the villages of the Midlands by the hundred, turning the dispossessed away 'tearfully' and 'into idleness'. Whatever may be said of the method of enclosure by act of parlia-

[24] V. M. Lavrovsky, 'Tithe Commutation as a Factor in the Gradual Decrease of Landownership by the English Peasantry', *Econ. Hist. Rev.*, IV (1933), 273.

[25] G. Mingay, *Landownership and Agrarian Trends in the Eighteenth Century*, pp. 445-6 (Ph.D. thesis, University of Nottingham). In Cotgrave the twenty-one cottages continued on the rent roll after enclosure as before, but with no provision for loss of the usage of the common. Enclosure Awards sometimes give examples of houses and tofts in occupation of tenants who would lose the use of the common by enclosure, e.g. forty-nine at East Keal, but there is no means of giving an over-all statistical picture of this 'stripping of the cottagers'. Arthur Young cites thirty-seven enclosures in twenty-five of which the poor lost pasturage for their cows: 'a mischief that might easily have been avoided'. See *Inquiry into the Propriety of Applying Wastes etc.* (1801), p. 19.

ment, it represents a milestone in the recognition of the *legal* rights of humble men.[26]

So much for the immediate effects of enclosure in these thirty-six examples examined by Professor Lavrovsky. What of the delayed effects—the fencing of allotments and paying the expenses of enclosure? Unfortunately, no answer can be given to this question for the villages under review, and in order to throw light on it the results of inquiries elsewhere must be explored. There is, for instance, the interesting study—the most extensive yet made—by Mr Swales of seventy Parliamentary enclosures in Lindsey in which he finds that the number of owners receiving allotments reached a total of 1,374 of whom 82 per cent were owners of less than 50 acres.[27] The burden of expenses was heavy on the small owners and he cites between seventy and eighty examples of sales in nine villages either before or after enclosure. There may have been more of which he has no knowledge, and there is evidence, in the case of the earliest examples, of substantial decline after enclosure; but the author has no doubt from the evidence of the land tax returns that this loss was more than made up afterwards by the influx of fresh purchasers during the period of high prices, especially in the Fen parishes.

Elsewhere, in Lincolnshire, the small owner, wherever economic conditions favoured him, was very strong, whether subject to enclosure or not; Arthur Young,[28] writing in 1799, notices 146 proprietors at Kirton enclosed six years before; 120 at Barton, enclosed at the same time; Laceby, apparently a village of old enclosure, 'where every man lives of his own'; in the Fens where half the area was in the hands of small freeholders. The Lincolnshire historian Canon Massingberd was certainly correct when he said, as early as 1910,[29] that small owners were numerous where the land lent itself to small-scale production, as in the overwhelmingly peasant villages of the Isle of Axholme, but were at a

[26] See W. H. Hosford, 'Some Lincolnshire Enclosure Documents', *Econ. Hist. Rev.*, 2nd ser., II (1949), 73, where it is shown that the Commissioners accepted verbal claims, although the official notice stated that claims must be made in writing. 'They appear to have been honest men—careful, conscientious and even considerate' (p. 78). See also T. H. Swales, 'Parliamentary Enclosures of Lindsey', *Lincolnshire Arch. Soc. Rep. and Papers* (1936), where examples are given of allotments of small men being more conveniently placed than those of large. Arthur Young in 1770 speaks of their 'ignorance, knaving and self interest . . . combined with despotic power' (*Northern Tour* (1770), I, 256), but in 1799 gives an example of a Commissioner of 28 years' standing who made it his invariable custom 'to begin to line out and allot for the smallest proprietors first . . .' *General View of Lincolnshire* (1799), p. 85). See also Davis, *General View of Wiltshire*, p. 85, for attempts by enclosure Commissioners to protect the small owners. 'Policy and humanity forbid that they should be injured even with their consent.' Gonner thinks the Commissioners were men of experience and integrity, *op. cit.*, pp. 94-95. For generally favourable verdict based on exhaustive study of Commissioners' Minute Books, etc., see M. W. Beresford, 'Commissioners of Enclosure', *Econ. Hist. Rev.*, XVI (1946), 130, and W. E. Tate: 'Oxfordshire Enclosure Commissioners 1737-1856', *J. Mod. Hist.*, XXIII (1951), 138. But of the poor *without* legal rights it remains true that 'by nineteen enclosure bills out of twenty they are injured, in some grossly injured' (Young, *op. cit.*, p. 42).

[27] Swales, *op. cit.* A point which has not been investigated is the proportion of absentee owners. It was usually high, and some of them would no doubt be among those who sold. The range in the size of holdings was as follows:

Over 100 acres	Between 50-100 acres	Between 20-50 acres	Between 10-20 acres	Between 5-10 acres	Between 2-5 acres	Between 1-2 acres	Under 1 acre
150	103	169	201	214	255	124	158
10·9%	7·5%	12·3%	14·6%	15·6%	18·6%	9%	11·5%

The total acreage was 81,502.

[28] Young, *op. cit.*, pp. 19-20.

[29] *Lincolnshire Notes and Queries*, XI, p. 31. Warp lands owed their fertility to the deposit of silt by regulated flood water—an expensive process.

disadvantage where the essential condition of success was large capital expenditure as in the warp lands alongside the Trent.

It will be noticed, however, that all these examples are drawn from the predominantly arable areas where corn growing continued to flourish after enclosure under the scarcity conditions of the Napoleonic wars, or where cash crops could be grown under specially favourable conditions as in the Fen parishes of Lincolnshire and in the Isle of Axholme. What of the pasture areas where corn growing gave way to grass and the age-old economy of the open village passed under the yoke of the grazier and fat-stock dealer?

Even William Marshall, who can usually see no ill in enclosure, was prepared to admit that in the Vale of Evesham corn growing and population had been severely reduced as a result of enclosure owing to the conversion of rich deep-soiled arable grounds to permanent pastures; there were other areas where these results were felt: the Vale of Berkeley, the country round Horncastle and—for special reasons—Downland Wiltshire. But it would be unwise to assume that the enclosure of rich arable always had the results commonly attributed to it even in the classic pasture county of Leicestershire, as the following inquiry into the twelve villages in the north-east of the county clearly proves. The area was chosen, in the first place, because it is singled out by Dr Slater[30] as an example of the evil effects of enclosure of rich arable for conversion to pasture, a process which was calculated, according to a well-known pamphlet quoted by Dr Slater, to reduce the population by fifteen families per thousand acres. Of the twelve parishes cited, enclosure awards exist for five and the land tax returns for all, so that a statistical picture can be drawn of what was happening.

The main impression from this localized inquiry is one of remarkable stability. Here was no spectacular growth of cottage property, as in so many of the Lincolnshire villages[31]; but neither was there any marked advance by the large owners. The pattern of property distribution of 1780 remained basically unaltered in 1830. The large owner—the Duke of Rutland—in 1780 paid in land-tax £290 out of £647 (45 per cent); in 1830 he paid £366 out of £665 (55 per cent). The remainder was divided among 250 small owners in 1780; in 1830 there were 305, of whom 128 were resident in 1780 and 157 in 1830. The small owners were getting smaller but there were more of them. The tenants showed a decline from 211 in 1780 to 198 in 1830 which indicates some degree of consolidation, perhaps a higher degree than the figures themselves suggest, since they would include a number of tenant tradesmen as well as tenant farmers. Of the villages which have enclosure awards only one shows any marked change in property distribution; this is Harby where forty-four owners received allotments at the enclosure in 1790 and fifty-eight paid land tax in 1830.

A question which calls for examination at this point is the nature of the evidence on which these figures are based. The land tax was a tax on land as measured by its annual value, taking into account the value of the buildings on it as well as the land. It was therefore levied on tradesmen, shopkeepers, innkeepers, canal proprietors, as well as landowners in the strict sense of the word.

---

[30] G. Slater, *English Peasantry and Enclosure of Common Field* (1907), p. 97.
[31] Davies, *op. cit.*, and my 'Enclosure and Small Landowners in Lindsey', *Econ. Hist. Rev.*, x (1940), 118.

But since the villages under review were essentially rural and boasted of their immunity from the incubus of poverty-stricken industrial workers, especially stockingers, the number of property units at any given time may be taken as a true reflection of the rural community, though not exclusively of property in land. Moreover, since many land-tax payers bought themselves out under the redemption act of 1798, the returns are actually an understatement of the number of property owners after that date.[32] The figures quoted for these villages show that the ownership of property, most of which was landed property, was almost as widely distributed in 1830 as in 1780 though the tenancies were more consolidated; but they hardly bear out Dr Slater's assumption that enclosure, even of the richest arable, necessarily resulted in wholesale consolidation of farms and depopulation.[33] He might have been more cautious if he had paid greater attention to the account given by the Reporter to the Board of Agriculture in 1809.

> The Duke (he writes) is a kind landlord, never oppresses and seldom removes a tenant. The advanced rent has been in part produced by the enclosure, but in part certainly by a change of time and circumstances; the land has been much improved by laying the richest part to grass, and by drainage, etc.; the occupations are mostly small, few individuals rent above £100 in an estate of £21,000 per annum. A numerous and able bodied peasantry is now supported; no stockingers or other manufacturers, and care taken that there shall be none; poor rates low, rents well paid. . . . The enclosure of this Vale has not at all, I believe, hitherto lessened the number of its inhabitants, as the farms are small and few changes of tenantry have taken place.

The writer anticipates that as old farm houses fall into decay and new ones are erected in their place, farms will be consolidated on principles of economy and let to the more active and diligent farmers, and the rejected occupier and his family will have to emigrate into towns or elsewhere for employment.[34] This melancholy result, however, seems to have been delayed for another forty years for the area in question shows a steady rise of population until the middle of the century when the rate of increase begins to slow down.[35]

If we go over the border into the neighbouring county of Rutland we find again that enclosure was by no means incompatible with the survival of the small farm. The Agricultural Reporter[36] himself refers to the great number of very

[32] Freeholders were known to be reluctant to get themselves put on the land tax lists. There were said to be 700 in Holland and 300 in Lindsey who had escaped notice in 1825, see Stapylton, 'A list of Freeholders of Lincoln 1825'. This would be a deficiency of between 8 and 9 per cent. (Kindly brought to my notice by Dr J. W. F. Hill.)
[33] The explanation seems to be that Dr Slater included these enclosures among the enclosures for pasture of the first half of the eighteenth century which may very well have had the effects he described. He notes (p. 97) that the enclosures took place between 1766 and 1792 and it would appear that he is transposing the effect from the earlier to the later period. The dividing line should probably be 1770-80 or even earlier. See Fussell, quoted below, p. 320, n. 42. A more intriguing example of confusion in the matter of periods is provided by his citing of Wistow and Foston (Slater, op. cit., p. 100). They are said, on the authority of Rev. John Howlett, quoting a correspondent, to have been enclosed and almost entirely depopulated. But both of them are classed as deserted villages of the period 1450-1600. See Hoskins, Essays in Leicestershire History, map opposite p. 72. L. A. Parker, 'Depopulation Returns for Leicestershire in 1607', Trans. Leics. Arch. Soc., XXIII, pt. II (1947). The Hearth Tax Returns of 1670 (kindly made available to me by Dr Thirsk) give eight householders in Foston and seven in Wistow. Perhaps these villages were in process of being repopulated, only to be re-depopulated within the century, or perhaps Howlett's correspondent was drawing on a folk-memory of 200 years earlier!   [34] W. Pitt, General View of Leicestershire (1807), p. 15.
[35] The relative increase for the first five census periods was 100, 111, 131, 147, 167 and 172, counting 1801 as 100.
[36] R. Parkinson, General View of Rutland, pp. 2 and 29. The decline of the small farmer in Rutland seems to have taken place later in the century. In 1886 there were still 743 farms under 50 acres out

small farms, and these were found equally—or even more frequently—in the villages where pasture predominated as in the mainly arable villages. Thus out of twenty-nine villages where pasture and meadow together were three times as extensive as arable, 27 per cent of the villages had farms of 20 acres or less compared to 18 per cent in the twenty-seven predominantly arable villages. It is also worth noting that out of twenty-eight villages enclosed between 1774 and 1801, eleven still had copyhold tenure when the Report was written in 1809. Many small farmers had withstood the shock of enclosure in Rutland because the basic condition of agrarian success, wide variety of soil in close proximity, enabled them to survive until the agricultural crisis of the 1880's.

A far more typical example of enclosure in the pasture area than any yet mentioned is that of Queniborough, enclosed in 1794. Here a large part of the arable had been converted to pasture, and the Reporter, a strong critic of enclosures, tells us[37] that productivity was no greater in any department, no more corn nor cattle, nor increased produce of butter or cheese or beef. The output of grain remained about the same on a smaller acreage owing to an increase in yield by about 50-100 per cent; the sheep were fewer in number but were fed on green fodder crops and sold fat instead of lean; and there were far fewer losses from disease to which they were liable on the open fields. Indeed, he quotes a local farmer to the effect that the losses had been so heavy that there was some doubt whether the occupiers could have gone on in the open fields; and when we hear, as we do again and again,[38] of flocks being halved or entirely swept away by sheep-rot on the undrained and disease-ridden commons, of the scourge of abortion among cattle on the commons, of the frequent outbreaks of cattle plague to which the Quarter Sessions Minute Books refer, we can well believe it. Our concern, however, is not with the mortality of sheep and cattle on the commons, but with that of peasants in the enclosed villages. In Queniborough there was no benevolent Duke of Rutland to temper the harsh winds to the shorn lamb; on the contrary there were two large owners who pressed their tenants hard by raising their rents from 12s. to 23s., greatly reduced the arable area and diminished the head of stock. Here we have all the circumstances that might be expected to result in a sharp decline of the small cultivator and to a reduction of population. But an examination of the enclosure award and the land tax returns does not confirm this expectation. For ten years before and after enclosure there is no sign of change either in numbers of tenants or of owners or in amounts of tax paid; the names of the allottees at the enclosure recur in the land tax returns and remain substantially the same until about 1810 when new owners and tenants come in, possibly as a result of an invasion of the villages by stockingers to which the Agricultural Reporter had referred in 1809;

of a total of 1,163. In 1914 there were 496 out of 907; in 1944 there were 254 out of 631. (Information kindly supplied by Mr Green, School of Agriculture, Sutton Bonington.)

[37] Pitt, op. cit., p. 71.

[38] Among many examples see Young, Oxfordshire (1809) (quoting a local farmer), 'I have known years when not a single sheep totally kept in open fields has escaped the rot. Some years within my memory rot has killed more sheep than the butchers have. Since enclosure has not lost one sheep from rot in nineteen years.' C. Vancouver, Cambridgeshire (1794), pp. 87 and 208—'owing to abortion among cows due to foulness of pasture twenty-three cows have lost ninety calves in five years'; and (p.107) 'half the sheep in Dry Drayton and 1,000 out of 1,400 in Croxton carried off last season from rot due to bad drainage'. See also T. Rudge, Gloucestershire (1807), p. 250; G. Rennie, etc., Yorkshire (1794), p. 32; W. T. Pomeroy, Worcestershire (Appendix 2) (1794).

and it may be that we must look to this source for the steady increase of population—25 per cent between 1801-51—which the census figures reveal. The number of farm tenancies seems to have declined somewhat, from twenty-four in 1790 (three years before enclosure) to twenty-one in 1810 and twenty in 1830 though there was an increase of very small tenancies which again may be due to stockinger influx.

But the case of Queniborough does not dispose of the problem of enclosure and depopulation in Leicestershire. The census returns show many cases of declining population during one or more of the census periods, an average in fact of between forty and fifty in each period. The responsibility of parliamentary enclosure for this result is, however, hard to establish, since most of the villages in question belong to the area of old enclosure, i.e. before 1700. Of the twenty-one villages enclosed by act of parliament after 1790, the census returns show some evidence of decline in ten, but all of them seem to belong to the area of stiff clay which was too heavy for mixed agriculture based on turnips. Like the Vale of Evesham, they seem to fall into the category of deep rich grazing grounds which lent themselves to permanent pasture. In villages such as these e.g. East and West Langton, Slawston, Bringhurst, Drayton, Great Eaton, enclosure was rounding off two centuries of adaptation to the special circumstances of the soil; but even here, where, as Dr Hoskins has shown,[39] the authentic voice of depopulation is unmistakably heard, the fall is far from catastrophic, the highest figure being 24 per cent decline in Slawston between 1801-11, the others oscillating between 4 and 17 per cent, though they show a slight over-all increase in the period 1801-51.

Perhaps we may inquire at this stage what were the factors that tended to keep the rural population on the soil and indeed to increase it even where the opposite results might have been expected.

One important factor contributing to the stability of the agrarian population during this period was the high level of employment which was maintained both in enclosed and open parishes where the improved agriculture was adopted. The explanation seems to be that new agricultural practices had developed in advance of the technical devices for dealing with them.[40] Thus the yield of corn per acre went up (e.g. at Queniborough from 50 to 100 per cent) after enclosure but the methods of ploughing, sowing, reaping and threshing were not substantially speeded up until the 1830's and 1840's. At the same time the spread of turnip cultivation and green fodder crops both in open and enclosed villages called for labour throughout the year in field, barn and stackyard; the maintenance of a milking herd or fat stock involved continuous field work throughout the year in pasture districts as well as in arable, except where the land was too stiff for mixed farming as in south-east Leicestershire; and the hedging and ditching of

[39] 'Leicestershire Crop Returns' in W. G. Hoskins's *Studies in Leicestershire Agrarian History* (ed.) (1949), p. 130-2.
[40] It is not always realized that the widespread use of drilling machinery was a feature of the nineteenth century, not the eighteenth. It was vehemently opposed by Arthur Young in 1770, and by Sir John Sinclair as late as 1817. Corn was dibbled when not sown broadcast. Wheat was dibbled in Norfolk as late as 1831, see Riches, *op. cit.*, p. 116. As Naomi Riches feelingly writes: 'When one considers that all the work of plowing, sowing, harvesting was done with little agricultural machinery, the complexity of labour organization on these (Norfolk) farms becomes intriguing. Imagine harvesting 800 acres of barley by hand', i.e. by scythe and sickle and hand-made straw bands.

the new enclosures found winter work for casual labour to a greater extent than the open villages. As for enclosure of forest, moor and fen, labour was attracted from far and wide. As a result of the enclosure of the Forest of Knaresborough we are told,

> the poor cottager and his family exchanged their indolence for active indus-
> try, and obtained extravagant wages; and hundreds were induced to offer
> their labour from distant quarter; labourers of every denomination, carpen-
> ters, joiners, smiths and masons, poured in, and met with constant employ-
> ment. And though before the allotments were set out, several riots had hap-
> pened; the scene was now quite changed; for with all the foreign assistance,
> labour kept extravagantly high. . . . In consequence the product is increased
> beyond conception, the rents more than trebled and population advanced
> in a very high degree.[41]

In regard to parishes mainly given over to pasture like Queniborough and other Leicestershire parishes, we should remember that much of it was in con-vertible leys, i.e. an arable form of grass farming. William Marshall speaks[42] of the grass farms of the old enclosures being subjected 'to an alternacy of grass and arable the land having lain six or seven years in a state of sward, it is broken up for oats', then wheat and barley and then a further six years under grass; and mentions the practice of growing wheat on a clover ley even in the open fields. Moreover, in ley farming on heavy land, grass may take the place of tur-nips, so that although in many parishes in Leicestershire turnips were not grown, this need not imply that the new farming was unknown there. Indeed, I am told there are still parishes in Leicestershire where convertible leys are preferred to turnips owing to the high cost of producing them on heavy soil.

In regard to the numerical increase of cottage owners revealed by the land tax returns at a time when the most cautious authorities—e.g. Sir John Clapham and Professor Gonner—are of opinion that they were stripped of their small properties, it should be remembered that in addition to the reasons already given —the recognition of the claims of the smallest owners, who may have thus come into the land tax returns for the first time; the sale of land in small lots to pay expenses; the influx of purchasers from outside—there was also the stimulation of rural trades and industries as a result of the greater productivity of farming, the rise of population and the increasing traffic on the roads. The Agricultural Reporter for Leicestershire, in accounting for the maintenance of rural popula-tion in the Vale of Belvoir in spite of enclosure, speaks of the mechanics, black-

[41] G. Rennie, etc., *General View of Yorkshire* (1794), p. 76. For other examples of energetic attack on moorland waste, see A. Young, *Northern Tour*, II, 263-75; *Eastern Tour*, I, 213-20. See also 'In-closure of Open Fields', a poem celebrating enclosure, translated from the Latin by Dorothy Halton, *Northamptonshire Past and Present* (1951), p. 35, and Lord Tennyson, *Northern Farmer* (Old Style), verse x.

[42] Marshall, *Rural Economy of Midland Counties*, I, 115, 187, 213, and Hoskins, *Agric. Hist.* (1951), *loc. cit.*, for seventeenth-century ley farming in Leicestershire. See also G. E. Fussell, 'Animal Hus-bandry in Eighteenth Century', *Agricultural History* (April 1937), p. 99: 'The topographers whose evidence is too scattered to cite in full (lead to the conclusion) that the effect of eighteenth century progress was not to lay the Midland counties to grass, but on the contrary to restrict the acreage devoted to grazing and make them primarily corn growing counties by the middle of the nineteenth century', and *Economic Geography* (July and October 1936), p. 296: 'It is doubtful whether any such drastic change from cornfield to grass was the consequence of enclosure in the second half of the eighteenth century.'

smiths, wheelwrights, tailors, weavers, who with the labourers and their families together may equal ten or twelve to every 100 acres. Moreover, the
£5,000,000 or £6,000,000 spent in poor relief would represent a redistribution
of rural incomes most of which, as the Hammonds do well to remind us, would
find its way into the pockets of rural tradesmen who had an interest in supplying
the pauperized labourers with the goods which they could have partly supplied,
before enclosure, for themselves. For all these reasons, there seems no doubt
that the cottage-owning population continued to grow in the newly enclosed
villages, though in character and personnel it may have been very different from
the cottagers of the pre-enclosure village.[43]

It will be seen, therefore, that the enclosure acts had the effect of further
reducing, but not of destroying, the remaining English peasantry. They came
at the end of a long period of attrition by consolidation and purchase and direct
eviction which practically eliminated the peasantry from the parishes of old enclosure; but in the open villages, although there had been differentiation among
the peasantry themselves, especially at the expense of the middle peasant, as well
as attempts at consolidation by the landlord, the small owners and tenants were
still remarkably strong. With the upward turn of rents in the 1750's (of which
accelerating enclosure was a symptom) there was further loss of tenants by consolidation and of owners by purchase; but when prices took their war-time leap
and the attack on the waste got under way, there were gains of both as well as
losses. What the net loss in farming units was it is not possible to calculate, but
it was catastrophic only in particular localities,[44] and where large areas of waste
were involved or where conditions were especially favourable to small-scale cultivation, there was considerable increase in numbers. Professor Clapham has
reminded us that the ratio of labouring families to farming families rose slowly
and that while it was 1·74 to 1 in Gregory King's time, it was still only 2½ to 1
in 1831. He concludes that 'the Census Figures are entirely destructive of the
view, that as a result of agrarian change and class legislation, an army of labourers toiled for a relatively small farming class; we have not a proletarian army
under officers'; . . . 'numerically the average agricultural unit must be compared,
not with the factory, but with handicraft workshops—master, journeyman or
two, prentice or two'.[45]

[43] This differentiation between the cottage-owning class and the proletarian labourer helps to
throw some light on the problem which puzzled the foreign traveller, Louis Simond, who wrote:
'I do not know where the common labourers live. . . . There is no appearance of poverty anywhere. . .
it is impossible to look round without the conviction that this country is upon the whole one of the
happiest, if not the happiest, in the world. Every cottage with roses and honeysuckle and vines' (sic).
Then he is told that the labourers live in some small town or village in the neighbourhood and walk
several miles to work. 'There are, it seems, obscure corners where the poor are swept out of the way.'
Simond, Journal of a Tour, 1810-11, quoted W. Smart, Economic Annals of the Nineteenth Century, I,
312. Besides the closed and open villages there were also the villages where model landlords were
trying to attach the labourers to the soil by cottage and cow-pasture schemes (see below, p. 322-3).

[44] The effect on the small tenant seems to have been disastrous whenever the soil was unsuitable
for mixed farming. See above, p. 312, n. 19. No attempt can yet be made to represent this statistically,
but its social effect has received classic expression in Dr and Mrs Hammond's Village Labourer, especially ch. VIII, 'The Isolation of the Poor'. The purpose of this article is not to question the existence of
this problem: on the contrary; but to suggest that its contribution to the industrial labour supply
calls for revision.

[45] J. H. Clapham, 'Growth of an Agrarian Proletariat 1688-1832', Camb. Hist. J., I, 92, and
Economic History of Modern Britain, I, 113. See also Concise Economic History, p. 115, where he says:
'To (Davenant) a typical cottager was obviously landless and possibly a claimant on the rates.' Dr
Hoskins reminds me that the Hearth Tax Returns of 1670 provide a statistical basis for a consideration

Moreover, in view of the great amount of enclosure for pasture in the first half of the eighteenth century a large proportion of the fall in the number of farming units had occurred before the great era of parliamentary enclosures opened; 'Sweet Auburn, loveliest village of the plain', the deserted village of Goldsmith's poetic imagination, was written in 1770, and had few if any authentic successors.[46] Since the rural population in general was unmistakably on the increase during this time, the contribution which the dispossessed made to the industrial labour force came, in the majority of cases, from the unabsorbed surplus, not from the main body.

But to say this—and much else that might be said in clarification of the statistical picture—is not to minimize the social consequences of the loss of the commons. The appropriation to their own exclusive use of practically the whole of the common waste by the legal owners meant that the curtain which separated the growing army of labourers from utter proletarianization was torn down. It was, no doubt, a thin and squalid curtain, for it will be remembered that Gregory King classed them all as actual or potential paupers who 'decreased the wealth of the country'; but it was real, and to deprive them of it without providing a substitute implied the exclusion of the labourers from the benefits which their intensified labour alone made possible.[47] The conscience of an age which had felt the impact of Wesley as well as of Rousseau could not remain unmoved by a form of injustice that aroused fear of consequences in the next world as well as this, and the ethical protest which it evoked had its champion if not its martyr.[48] Side by side with this emotional response, a characteristically empirical approach to the problem was being made by practical men—experts like Kent, Stone, Davies, Arbuthnot; landlords like the Earl of Winchilsea, Lord Carrington, Lord Egremont, and Lord Sheffield had schemes for endowing the labourers with cow-pastures and other forms of self-help. They converted such influential figures as Eden, Arthur Young, Sinclair, Wilberforce and even Pitt himself[49]; and the general Enclosure Act of 1801 referred to the possibility of

of the relative proportions of the social classes. The figures for Leicestershire give a total of 13,833 assessed to the Hearth Tax, of whom 4,249 were excused payment on grounds of poverty, i.e. 30·7 per cent of the whole. This implies that a great many labouring families in Leicestershire must have paid hearth tax or Gregory King's proportion of 1·7 to 1 does not apply to that county. Cf. however, Professor Tawney's figure for Gloucestershire in 1608 of two independent producers to one labourer. See 'An Occupational Census of the Seventeenth Century', *Econ. Hist. Rev.*, v (1934), 53. Rapid as the growth of the agricultural semi-proletariat may have been in the seventeenth century, it is difficult to believe that the proportion of labouring families to independent producers went up from 0·5 to 1·7 to 1 between 1608 and 1688. There is need for further research on a regional basis before final conclusions can be drawn.

[46] It may be noted that the twenty-nine villages in the Vale of the Wiltshire Avon which Cobbett found so shrunken had suffered a collapse of the carding and spinning industries. 'It is now wholly gone', says Cobbett, and the women and girls had to find work outside. *Rural Rides* (ed. Cole), II, 376.

[47] See Riches, *op. cit.*, p. 133, for speeding up on big Norfolk farms.

[48] Samuel Whitbread, who introduced the Minimum Wage Bill in 1795 and again in 1800, a 'large and comprehensive Poor Law Bill in 1807', and opposed the Peninsular War 'for his compassion for the miseries of the English poor. . . . He spent his life in hopeless battles and he died by his own hand of public despair.' Hammond, *The Village Labourer*, I, 136 (Guild Books 1948). See also Smart, *Economic Annals of the Nineteenth Century*, I, 137, 444.

[49] At any rate, he included in his Poor Law Bill of 1797 a clause permitting loans to be made by the parish for the purchase of a cow or other animal if it seemed likely that such a course would enable the recipient to maintain himself. But he bowed to the storm from ratepayers and magistrates and to 'the objection of those whose opinions he was bound to respect', of whom the most noteworthy was Bentham (Hammond, *op. cit.*, I, 147). For an excellent summary of the ideas of Lord Winchilsea and others see Hasbach, *op. cit.*, pp. 164-8 and Hammond, II, 154 ff., and D. C. Barnett, *Ideas of Social Welfare* 1780-1834 (London 1964).

grouping little allotments for those 'interested in commons and waste lands'.

In Rutland, almost entirely an enclosed county, cottagers frequently had sufficient land to enable them to keep one or two cows. 'This practice', we are told, 'does not prevail in all parishes' but was sufficiently general to account for the comparatively low poor rates. After citing numerous cases in Lincolnshire, Arthur Young refers especially to Sir John Sheffield's estate covering twenty miles of country where the cottagers paid a rent of 40s. a year for house, garden, a rood or a half acre of land and feeding for two cows and two or three pigs. Moreover, the landlords wisely kept the cottages in their own hands, knowing well that the farmers would use them to give a further twist to the screw which already pressed so hard upon the labourers. But in his enthusiasm for the growing 'cow-ocracy' of Lincolnshire, Arthur Young unwittingly let a portentous cat out of his rather hastily packed bag when he wrote that as a result, the 'population increases so that pigs and children fill every quarter; in the last twenty years the baptisms at Burton have exceeded the burials by 136. The women, however, are very lazy; they do nothing but bring children and eat cake'.[50] He was soon to be made to realize that he had confounded himself out of his own mouth. In a subsequent edition of the famous *Essay*, Malthus invoked against him, partly with the aid of his own evidence, the inexorable logic of the *Principle of Population*, and endeavoured to prove that the labourers' most ardent champions were in the long run their worst enemies.

Whether the influence of Malthus was decisive there is no means of knowing. He was swimming with the tide of interests—tradesmen, farmers and most landlords—but against the main current of sentiment if not of ideas. The volume and virulence of the opposition showed the strength of the 'philanthropic Jacobinism' which he challenged, and we are left wondering what might have happened if his basic humanitarianism had taken a Tory instead of a Utilitarian form. In the upshot, he helped to cement an alliance between vested interests and economic theory which was sufficient to kill the scheme for cow-pastures for labourers, and the opportunity to reverse the verdict of the enclosures was lost: the labourer was now separated in theory as well as in fact from all proprietary interest in the product of the soil which he tilled.

That this was a social calamity—brought into relief all the more by contrast with the contemporary land settlement in Denmark[51]—may be conceded without admitting the measure of responsibility it is usually given for the recruitment

[50] A. Young, *Lincolnshire* (1799), p. 462. He was obviously impressed by the Malthusian argument when he wrote: 'It might be prudent to consider the misery to which the progressive population might be subject when there was not a sufficient demand for them in towns and manufactures, as an evil which it was absolutely and physically impossible to prevent' (quoted Malthus, *Essay on Population* (edn. 1890), Appendix, p. 557). The dilemma with which Arthur Young and other agrarian reformers like Sir Thomas Bernard were faced should be considered before final judgement is passed on the statesmen and policies of the time.

[51] B. O. Binns, *The Consolidation of Fragmented Agricultural Holdings*; F.A.O.; Washington (1950), p. 41. The scheme was carried through under the inspiration of the Counts of Bernstorff and strengthened the proprietary rights of the peasants while giving them the benefits of consolidation, but it destroyed the village as a community. 'It was an attack from above' as Mr Dobb says, but it was undertaken in the interests of the peasants themselves who later put a memorial up to the man who had made it, see Binns, *op. cit.*, p. 42. In England the influence of Malthus was a powerful force against the attempted reconstruction by some landlords of the village after enclosure on the basis of allotments for labourers. See especially Hammond, *op. cit.*, ch. VIII and D. C. Barnett, *op. cit.* Humanitarianism in England was thus left to oscillate between the cheap-jack benevolence of Speenhamland and the pursuit of the net social product by Chadwick. See D. C. Barnett, *op. cit.*

of the reserve army of labour. As we have seen, the cottage-owning population seems actually to have increased after enclosure. Even the proletarianized labourers continued to remain on the soil in increasing numbers in most areas until the 1830's and in many parts to the 1840's, when improved farming machinery and railway transport caught up with the new farming practices. It was then that the real flight from the country-side began.

If agrarian change, as symbolized by enclosure, cannot be regarded as the chief recruiting agent of the industrial proletarian army, where did the new drafts come from which not only manned the expanding industries but the expanding agriculture also; and manned them in such strength that in some departments, the very plethora of labour was itself a brake upon technological innovation?

Economic historians are generally agreed that the fever of technical improvement in the early phases of the Industrial Revolution was partly occasioned by labour shortage even though enclosure was reported to be emptying the villages and bringing desolation to the country-side. What happened to transform the situation so that in the last quarter of the eighteenth century labour became available for an unprecedented expansion of industry and agriculture, for fighting a twenty years' war and for summoning up the grim spectre of the Malthusian population formula to the terror of statesmen who might otherwise have been prompted to remedial action? The only answer can be that at some unspecified time in the eighteenth century the movement of population had taken an upward turn in village and town alike and provided an entirely new supply of human material beside which the dislocations caused by enclosures were of secondary importance. The Isle of Axholme, an example unique in England, of a peasant community of the continental type, is a case in point.[52] There was no question here of the 'institutional' pressure of enclosure and the large farm. The inhabitants, small cultivators growing successive crops of corn, potatoes, hemp, flax, on their little farms of from four to fifty acres, with a few large ones of 200 or more, worked like negroes, says Arthur Young, and the smallest of them lived worse than the occupants of the poor house, but 'all is made amends for by *possessing* land'. An examination of the land tax returns shows that between 1783 and 1800 the numbers of freeholders rose from 829 to 1,326, an increase of 60 per cent; and between 1800 and 1829 to 1,444, a further increase of 9 per cent.[53] But while the property owners were increasing by 9 per cent, in the same period the population went up by 33 per cent (from 7,214 to 9,626). Thus in this classically peasant region, the population rose faster than the units of property; a proletariat was coming into being by the natural increase of the peasant population. Moreover, it will be seen, by comparing the growth of these villages with the non-peasant villages around, that they grew in numbers

[52] W. B. Stonehouse, *History of the Isle of Axholme* (1839), writes: ' . . . these small freeholders are generally very badly off (far worse off than the generality of labourers—p. 33). Further inheritances have become so incumbered with mortgages that the interest is a very high rent, and inconvenience necessarily attending the descent of land not entailed in the same family from the provision which has to be made, at different times, for the younger children. . . . The worst landlord must give way to the circumstances of his tenant; but a mortgagee is a perfect land shark, his heart is as hard as that of a political economist' (Preface, p. x). 'Had the Isle of Axholme continued in the sole property of one Lord Paramount, such as the present Duke of Northumberland, the Earl of Yarborough . . . what a different state would it now be in' (p. xiii).

[53] W. O. Massingberd, *Lincs. Notes and Queries*, XI, *loc. cit.*

side by side with the landlord villages until the 1840's and then they diverged, the landlord villages showing a steady decline, the peasant villages going on for another two generations until they, too, began to falter in the teeth of the blizzard which blew up for farmers of all kinds in the last quarter of the century. The difference of institutional structure seems to have made no difference to the contribution made to the reserve army of labour: it may, for all we know, have been proportionally the same: no more and no less, until the second half of the century when the non-peasant villages entered on their numerical decline.

If it be conceded, as I think it must, that the period 1780-1840 saw only a sporadic exodus (apart from the migration of the surplus) from the rural areas which have formed the subject of this paper, and side by side with it, an actual filling up of empty spaces and a steady rise in the great majority of established centres of rural population, we are tempted to ask, from what hidden springs

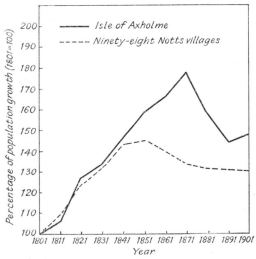

FIG. 2   Population Growth 1801-1901, Isle of Axholme and Nottinghamshire villages.

did this surge of rural population come, a surge that not only flowed over into what had formerly been empty and almost desert places—the 'black lings' of Tideswell and Castleton, the heights of Mam Tor, and a score of sparsely occupied forests and marshes, and yet had a surplus to spill over into the growing centres of industry in towns and industrialized villages? This phenomenon of rural fecundity is all the more remarkable since it follows a period marked by enclosure and the consolidation of farms on such a scale as to persuade many observers that the rural population was actually on the decline, being driven from their homes by the improving farmer and the rent-hungry landlord.

The remarkable paradox of visible population growth side by side with lamentations of rural desolation engaged the attention, among others, of John Howlett and Arthur Young. Both agreed that in so far as enclosure was associated with capital investment in improved agriculture, it was followed not by a decline but by a growth of population. Arthur Young elaborates on this theme again and again and expounds, with a wealth of illustrations, the theory that an expanding economy will call into being its own labour supply by providing incentives to early marriage. In his *Northern Tour*, written in 1770, he says 'the only complaint he met with was the high price of agricultural labour, the causes of which he attributes to turnpikes, navigations, drainages and enclosures: all these conspired to make hands scarce and to depress the farmer'. But he goes on:

> It is employment that creates population: marriages are early and numerous in proportion to the amount of employment. In a great Kingdom there must always be hands that are idle, backward in the age of work, unmarried for fear of having families, or industrious only to a certain degree. Now an increase of employment raises wages and high wages change the case of all these hands; the idle are converted to industry; the young come early to work; the unmarried are no longer fearful of families and the formerly industrious become so in a much greater degree. It is an absolute impossibility that in such circumstances the people should not increase. . . . Provide new employment and new hands will inevitably follow.

In more measured language, Adam Smith was writing in much the same strain and at the same time pointing out that 'the real recompense of labour' had risen which 'enabled them to provide for their children and consequently to bring up a greater number of them'. Twenty years later, Eden and Malthus related population growth to the greatly increased demand for labour 'combined with a greatly increased power of production, both in agriculture and manufactures'.[54]

Later historians have been inclined to look for the reason in the institutional factors of enclosures and poor law, which, they tell us, reduced the dispossessed peasantry to hopelessness and despair and removed the last remaining restraints upon 'unbridled impulse'.[55] The regional historian has no competence to discuss these views in their wider implications, but he may be able to set them within the context of the local economy in so far as the special tools of his trade enable him to re-create it. In addition to those already used in this article there are others, in particular, parish registers, a study of which in the region under review, points to a lessening of the impact of epidemics in the second half of the century as the initiating factor in the upward movement of population. This, it is suggested, together with the return of prosperity to agriculture after the long period of falling prices and rents, provided the conditions for a parallel movement of economic and demographic growth.[56]

Whether this conclusion will bear the test of wider inquiry remains to be seen, but the evidence is such as to cast doubt on the *a priori* assumption that the reserve army of labour for large-scale industry was an 'institutional creation' in the sense of being a response to the exercise of power by a ruling class; it may also be seen as the outcome of the complex of forces represented by an

[54] Young, *Northern Tour*, IV, 411 ff.; Adam Smith, *Wealth of Nations*, Book 1, ch. viii; F. M. Eden, *State of the Poor* (1797), 1, 407; Malthus, *op. cit.*, p. 243.

[55] See especially Hasbach, *op. cit.*, pp. 170, 361, 390, where impressive evidence is cited showing the part played in the increase of population by the large farm with its out-cottages and the spread of rural slums in the 'open' parishes. But he omits the very numerous examples of increase of population in response to the widening market for labour resulting from drainage of heavy soils and fens, etc. See also important discussion by T. Griffith, *Population Problems of the Age of Malthus* (1925), especially ch. VI.

[56] See J. D. Chambers, *The Vale of Trent 1670–1800, Economic History Review*, Supplements (3), pp. 44–46.

expanding economy which offered inducements as well as compulsions, e.g. to inventors to supplement the labour force and to parents to augment it, while making possible for their offspring a more favourable chance of survival than had ever before been known. A demographic change was thus set in motion which itself became a fact of history, and has to be taken into account if a balanced picture is to be drawn of the social stresses of the time[57]; and in a recognition of this lies the best hope of reconciling the apparent inconsistencies of the sociological and the economic approach with which this article began.

[57] See also, E. F. Heckscher, 'Swedish Population Trends before the Industrial Revolution', *Econ. Hist. Rev.*, 2nd ser., II (1950), 270: 'The progress in production was taken out first and foremost in the form of an increase of population, not in raising the standard of living . . . the lives of pre-revolutionary people were insecure and irregular; they felt helpless victims of the inexplicable and unpredictable freaks of nature.' Also W. Sombart, *Der Moderne Kapitalismus* (Leipzig 1928), III (i), 361: 'Der Kapitalismus ist es also letzten Endes selbst, der sich sein Proletariat herbeischafft, wenn auch nicht in der Weise, wie Marx es wollte.' And pp. 363, 373-7 for a valuable discussion of the evidence prior to the appearance of T. Griffith, *op. cit.*

ii

THE COURSE OF POPULATION CHANGE

From: *The Vale of Trent 1670-1800: A Regional Study of Economic Change* (Economic History Review Supplement No. 3, 1957)

The parish registers, or rather, as in the present case, the transcripts[1] made for the diocesan record, provide material for the study of population which has hitherto received little attention.[2] They are, in a very real sense, the short and simple annals of the poor, providing a continuous record of that ceaseless two-way traffic—of bodies into the churchyard and babies from the font—the favourable balance of which alone makes history of any kind possible. This implies that the record of the parish registers is a substantial reflexion of the actual births and deaths. In the case of the Midland parishes examined, this certainly appears to be the case, though there was no doubt a wider margin between births and baptisms than between deaths and burials, especially in parishes at great distances from the parish church. In the Marsh parishes in Lincolnshire, for instance, where the church may be five miles from the outlying farms, the failure to baptize the newly born in church was a much more common occurrence than to bury the dead in the churchyard, and this was reflected in the greater frequency with which burials outstripped baptisms.[3] No such parishes are included in this inquiry, and there is no reason to think that any large error arises from this source.

A more difficult question is presented by the nonconformist records. These are numerous and continuous for the baptisms of Nottingham, but there are

[1] Besides their greater accessibility and legibility, the bishop's transcripts often supply missing leaves or mutilated entries of the registers and provide information not otherwise recorded. The Nottinghamshire transcripts are kept in the Library at Southwell Minster and I would like to take this opportunity of expressing my thanks to the librarian, Mr Beaumont, for allowing me such free access to them.
[2] For a valuable summary of the purpose to which they may be put see E. J. Buckatzsch, 'The Constancy of Local Population and Migration in England before 1800', *Population Studies*, No. 5, 1951-2.
[3] I am indebted to Mr W. Hosford and the work of his adult classes at Algarkirk for this information.

no records of burials before 1785 except those of the Quakers,[4] and the records for the villages are too meagre to be worth taking into account. The inquiry therefore has been based upon the Anglican records except where otherwise stated; in any case, there is no reason to think that the parish registers excluded the majority of the nonconformist burials since the number of nonconformist burial grounds was small, and the registration both of births and marriages was regarded as of importance by members of all sects. The chief criticism of the registers as a trustworthy record is made in connexion with those of towns like Manchester and Sheffield at the end of the eighteenth century[5] where population was growing rapidly, but Nottingham was still a small though rapidly growing town, and there is no reason to think that registration by the parish authorities either rural or urban became noticeably less reliable during the period of this survey.

Whatever grounds there may be for criticisms of the records, there seems to be no doubt about the general pattern of the struggle between life and death as represented in numerical terms by the parish registers of the region under review. The present inquiry starts with a favourable balance of baptisms between 1674 and 1678 followed by a period of very heavy mortality everywhere beginning about 1678, reaching its climax in 1680, and continuing in some of the villages until 1696. We know that 1680 was a fatal year in many parts of the country, for Thomas Short marks it as one of the most unhealthy in the series,[6] and the medical evidence points to an epidemic of fevers 'some aguish, some typhus', with an outbreak of a malignant typhus in 1685-6 which spread from the poorer quarters of London to 'the Court end of the Town'. Its effects were felt most severely in the old plague-season of summer and autumn, and had 'slight relation to famine or scarcity, or to other obvious cause of domestic typhus'.[7] In Derbyshire it was known sarcastically as the 'New Delight'[8] owing to its unfamiliar symptoms, and it may perhaps be held partly accountable for the high mortality cycle from 1678 to 1689 in the villages near the Derbyshire border which form a large portion of the so-called industrialized villages.

In the subsequent period, the evidence of the registers suggests that population change ebbed and flowed in three long-term movements, of which the last, starting about 1750, represents an upswing of an entirely new order. The forces of demographic growth were now on the move, mainly as a result of the changing incidence of epidemic disease. The birth rate may also have risen, because of differential rates of marriage and fertility among the population of the industrial villages.

The registers thus provide evidence of an ebb and flow of births and deaths which, among other results, helped to regulate the expansion of the labour force. The main agency in the earlier periods had been the plague which, prior

[4] Chas. Deering, *History of Nottingham* (1751), gives burials for the Independents and Baptists but these are not to be found in the records at Somerset House. On the other hand, Deering gives no baptisms for the Presbyterians although their registers in the library at Low Pavement Chapel and in Somerset House provide an unbroken series. The Independents and the Baptists had their own burial grounds, but not the Presbyterians.
[5] See Barbara Hammond, *Economic History* (3), 1929.
[6] Thos. Short, *New Observations . . . on City, Town* and *Country Bills of Mortality* (1750), p. 87. Out of 137 parishes studied, 54 showed an excess of burials over baptisms.
[7] Chas. Creighton, *History of Epidemics* (1894), Vol. II, p. 21.
[8] Creighton, *op. cit.*, p. 329.

to its last appearance in the 1660's, had 'once in a generation made a clean sweep of a fifth or a fourth part of the inhabitants' in towns like London, Newcastle, and Chester 'including hardly any of the well-to-do; its broad effect was to cut off the margin of poverty as if by a periodical process of pruning'.[9] The subsequent period was marked by epidemics which may have served the same purpose with hardly less efficiency since they then fell more heavily on children than on adults. 'The incidence of infectious mortality had already (in 1661) begun to shift towards the age of childhood', says Dr Creighton. 'The plague was particularly fatal to adult lives; on the other hand, the mortality from infectious diseases in our own times falls in much the larger ratio upon infants and children. It looks as if this change, now so obvious, had begun before the end of the plague in Britain, having become more marked in the generation following its extinction'.[10]

At the same time, the social and institutional checks to the birth rate were only slowly relaxed. As Professor Ashton has shown, in an illuminating discussion,[11] there were social and geographical barriers to the area of choice of marriage partners which helped to keep both the age of marriage and the number of the unmarried high, but the improvement of transport facilities and the demand for labour by new enterprises did much to break them down to the advantage both in number and quality of the population. In nine Nottinghamshire parishes between 1670 and 1700 the proportion of extra-parochial marriages was 10·8 per cent (89 out of 819 marriages): between 1770 and 1800 it was 26 per cent (352 out of 1351 marriages).

How far these figures should be allowed to imply a high degree of immobility in the choice of marriage partners is doubtful, however. There was much movement of village population, and there is good reason to think that those in search of marriage partners were no exception to the rule, as the remarkable example of Fledborough proves. In this tiny parish where, between 1712 and 1730, only eleven marriages were solemnized, the grant of powers to marry by licence was interpreted by the incumbent to enable him to marry all comers,[12] and of the 490 couples who were married by him in the following twenty-four years, only fifteen were resident as to one or both partners, in the parish itself. Of the rest, the marriage partners of 284 were drawn from different parishes, sometimes at considerable distances from one another: Samuel King of Cotes (Leicestershire) and Jane Trotter of Lincoln, Joseph Hinde of Bolsover and Mary Westby of Gamston, Anthony Smith of Oulston (Yorks) and Catherine Bland of Kelham had travelled far to meet one another; and having met, decided to marry at Fledborough. Perhaps there was a magic in the incumbent's name: the Rev. William Sweetaple. The local Gretna Green over which he presided so successfully for nearly a quarter of a century at least shows that there was no lack of matrimonial mobility for those who really wanted it.

Perhaps the rise in the literacy of marriage partners may be accounted a

[9] Creighton, op. cit., p. 39.
[10] Op. cit., p. 18.
[11] T. S. Ashton, An Economic History of England, the Eighteenth Century (1955), pp. 6, 7.
[12] T. M. Blagg and G. P. Proctor, Nottinghamshire Marriage Registers, xx (1915). The editors think he became a surrogate about 1728 since it was then he began to marry by licence, but the non-parochial marriages were irregular 'being a violation of the marriage service and of canon 62' (p. 178).

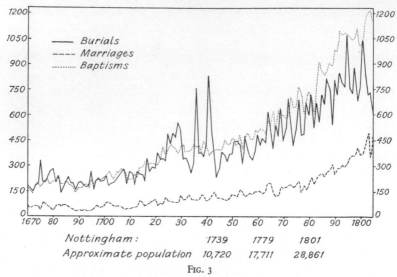

Nottingham: 1739   1779   1801
Approximate population   10,720   17,711   28,861

FIG. 3

Baptisms, marriages and burials: Nottingham, 1670–1805
(Including non-conformist registered baptisms and calculated burials)

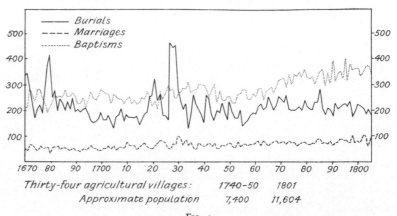

Thirty-four agricultural villages: 1740-50   1801
Approximate population   7,400   11,604

FIG. 4

Baptisms, marriages and burials: agricultural villages, 1670–1805

factor in the increase in the area of choice: the average proportion of bridegrooms in five Lincolnshire parishes who could sign their names in 1769-9 was
47·3 per cent; in 1810-19 it was 68·5 per cent. The corresponding proportion of
brides was 27·7 per cent and 54·2 per cent.[13]

Whatever may be said as to the factor of mobility, there seems no doubt that
conditions of employment frequently militated against a high marriage rate.
Menservants and maidservants—a large class—would usually have to remain
unmarried or leave their employment,[14] and agricultural labourers, on the av-

[13] I am indebted for the figures to Mr W. Hosford for kindly making available to me the work
of his adult classes in Kesteven. A further enquiry on a larger scale shows that the improvement in
literacy among bridegrooms was confined to the Fens, and gives the following less favourable results:
bridegrooms, a rise from 60 per cent to 66 per cent; brides from 33 per cent to 42·5 per cent.
[14] Hume, *Essays* (1907 edn.), I, 387: 'At present all masters discourage the marrying of their
male servants and admit not by any means the marriage of the female.' A. Young also noted this in
contrast with the practice in Ireland. See *Tour of Ireland* (1780), II, 198.

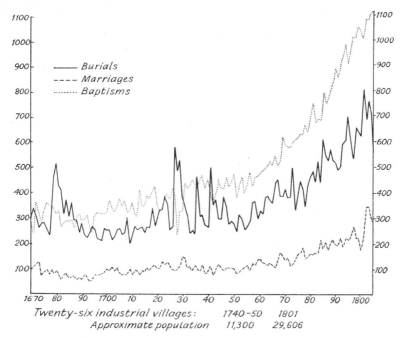

Twenty-six industrial villages: 1740-50   1801
Approximate population   11,300   29,606

FIG. 5

Baptisms, marriages and burials: industrial villages, 1670-1805

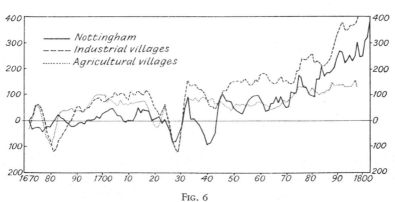

FIG. 6

Balance of baptisms over burials (five-yearly moving averages):
(1) Nottingham; (2) industrial villages; (3) agricultural villages

erage, may have married later than workers in industry because of the large proportion who lived in with their masters. There were also prudential checks connected with the inheritance of property which appear to be reflected in the records where the ages at marriage are given, e.g. in the marriage by licence without banns. The table below is an analysis of a number of groups from Gloucestershire and Nottinghamshire.[15]

[15] Brian Frith, *Gloucestershire Marriage Allegations, 1637-1680*, Records Section of Bristol and Gloucs. Arch. Soc. (1954), p. 213, and T. M. Blagg and E. A. Wadsworth, *Nottinghamshire Marriage Certificates* (1930), Vol. II. I am indebted to Mrs Sonia Coats for the extraction and presentation of this material and I would like to take this opportunity of expressing my thanks to her for this valuable assistance.

TABLE 1

Gloucestershire allegations of marriage

Date	Gentlemen				Yeomen				Husbandmen				Clothiers Cordwainers, tailors, broadcloth weavers			
	No. of husbands	Median age	No. of wives	Median age	No. of husbands	Median age	No. of wives	Median age	No. of husbands	Median age	No. of wives	Median age	No. of husbands	Median age	No. of wives	Median age
1637–8	20	26	15	22	44	28	40	25	53	30	49	25	22	24	15	22
1661–9	198	26	178	22	556	28	482	25	95	28	87	28	186	26	164	23
1670–80	126	25	110	22	790	27	670	24	42	24	30	26	123	26	100	23

TABLE 2

Nottinghamshire certificates of marriage

Date	Gentlemen				Tailors, clothiers weavers, cordwainers				Labourers			
	No. of husbands	Median age	No. of wives	Median age	No. of husbands	Median age	No. of wives	Median age	No. of husbands	Median age	No. of wives	Median age
1701–20	168	26	153	22	57	25	53	24	138	26	114	25
1721–40	118	28	112	24	133	25	116	24	89	27	85	25
1741–53	55	25	50	21	119	24	106	23	85	25	75	24

Date	Yeomen farmers				Husbandmen				Framework knitters			
1701–10	96	26	93	23	169	26	144	23	93	24	149	23
1711–20	45	27	45	24	318	27	291	23	133	24	103	22
1721–30	43	30	36	25	428	26	379	24	190	24	168	23
1731–40	143	26	130	24	267	26	205	24	124	23	119	23
1741–53	412	25	370	22	275	26	254	23	173	23	74	24

This type of evidence does less than justice to the unskilled, i.e. the non-apprenticed labourer; it deals only with those who wanted a quick or quiet wedding, and this, apparently, was a luxury which only a small proportion of labourers allowed themselves in Nottinghamshire and hardly any in Gloucestershire. Out of a total of 4,643 bridegrooms in the latter county comprising 180 different categories of employment only seven are described as labourers.[16] The parish registers cannot easily be consulted on this since they rarely give either the age of marriage or the occupation of either of the marriage partners until the last quarter of the century; and the only way to find it is by the prohibitively laborious process of tracing back references from the marriages to the

[16] Op. cit.

baptisms.[17] From the evidence of the allegations and the certificates it seems that the farmers—yeomanry and husbandmen—married between twenty-five and thirty; the gentlemen about twenty-six; the apprenticed workmen at about the same age except the framework knitters who married between twenty-three and twenty-four and chose slightly younger wives. The farmers' wives seem to be slightly older—between twenty-two and twenty-five—whereas the gentlemen and the apprenticed workmen chose wives about twenty-one to twenty-four. It would appear, therefore, that apprenticeship was less of a bar to the fertility of marriage (in so far as this is determined by the age of the wife) than the preparation required for taking over a farm.[18] Even the labourers, most of whom came from villages and would probably be farm labourers, married at a slightly higher age and chose slightly older wives. This would hardly be the case, however, in the later part of the century when farms were growing larger under the influence of enclosures and more farm workers were being housed in cottages instead of in the farm-houses. The proportion of small independent farmers who apparently married late also declined, and the propensity of the growing labouring class to marry would be encouraged, at least in 'open'[19] parishes, by the relaxed poor law. Most country parishes would have a surplus of labour to spill over into the growing industrialized centres and perhaps this, as much as the already existing tendency to marry early by the industrial population, would account for the differential birth rate which appears to have been present in the industrial villages from the middle of the century. This is seen in the following calculation where ten yearly averages of marriages are divided into ten yearly averages of baptisms five years later:

Baptisms per marriage

	1700–9	1710–19	1720–9	1730–9	1740–9
Agricultural villages	4·3	3·8	3·7	3·3	3·3
Industrial villages	3·7	4·4	3·5	3·9	4·4
	1750–9	1760–9	1770–9	1780–9	1790–9
Agricultural villages	3·4	3·7	3·6	3·7	3·7
Industrial villages	4·8	4·5	4·8	4·7	4·8

The dip in both series in 1720–39 may be connected with the heavy loss of children before baptism and the higher proportion of remarriages during the epidemic period, but the rapid recovery of the industrial villages and the consistently higher level maintained to the end of the century confirms the supposition of a differential birth rate as a factor in the growth of the industrial population. The increase in the industrial population was partly self-generated through its higher

[17] Something has been attempted along these lines with the aid of the indexes compiled for the Bedfordshire registers and the work is still going on.

[18] Professor T. H. Marshall has quoted figures from Denmark of 1787 showing the large proportion of married masters (62–68 per cent) (see above, p. 260). But my figures would not include apprentices since they were not normally allowed to marry, and as there was no shortage of jobs for skilled artisans at the time the figures were taken, it is not surprising that they married early. The conditions for Nottinghamshire journeymen would not be very different from that of small masters in this respect.

[19] i.e. parishes in which property was divided among numerous owners and restrictions on building by landlords were absent.

birth rate[20]; at the same time it was absorbing the surplus from the villages and assimilating the balance of births over deaths made wider by the lessening incidence of epidemics and by other factors making for a fall of the death rate.

[20] See also A. K. Cairncross, 'Internal Migration in Victorian England', *The Manchester School of Econ. and Social Studies*, Vol. XVII (1949), for a study of differential birth rates of industrial and rural districts between 1841 and 1901.

iii

POPULATION CHANGE IN A PROVINCIAL TOWN
NOTTINGHAM 1700-1800

From: *Studies in the Industrial Revolution*, Essays presented to T. S. Ashton, (ed. L. S. Pressnell), London 1960

Among the distinguishing characteristics of the new industrial society that was coming to birth in England in the eighteenth century was its capacity to support a vastly larger population than before, and, more significantly, to permit its continuous growth. There had been earlier occasions when population had taken a leap forward: there had never been a time when the direct checks to population growth had continuously receded until they virtually disappeared under the influence of successive triumphs of man over his environment. Above all, the age-old balance between town and country was being upset and the character of social life was on the eve of transformation through the growth of industrial towns and the problems of the quality of urban life to which it gave rise.

The economic processes involved in this break with the past have been studied with a success to which this book[1] is itself a tribute; but the process of change from small-scale to large-scale society, from provincial market town to populous industrial centre with only vestigial connexions with the surrounding countryside, has received less attention than it deserves.[2] One reason is that the mechanics of population growth during the period are still under discussion.[3]

[1] *Studies in the Industrial Revolution*, Essays presented to T. S. Ashton (ed. L. S. Pressnell, 1960).
[2] For the most detailed treatment of the demographic side of urban history at this time, see F. Beckwith, 'The Population of Leeds during the Industrial Revolution', *Thoresby Society*, xli, Miscellany, Vol. xii, pt. ii (1948), pt. iv (1953). For the general development of urban history, see the important bibliographical studies of S. G. Checkland, 'English Provincial Cities', *Econ. Hist. Rev.*, 2nd ser., vi (1953), 195-203, and W. H. Chaloner, 'Writings on British Urban History', *Vierteljahrschrift für Sozial- und Wirtschaftsgeschichte*, xlv, pt. i (1958), 76-87. In the former of these two studies, Professor Checkland also discusses problems of method in the writing of urban history, and suggests that 'it is time that the professional historian turned his attention to the nature of cities as determinants of national life rather than as end products' (*op. cit.*, p. 202).
[3] For a discussion of the two sides of the theoretical aspect of this question, see H. J. Habakkuk 'English Population in the Eighteenth Century', *Econ. Hist. Rev.*, 2nd ser., vi (1953), 117-33, see above, p. 269, and Professor Thomas McKeown and R. G. Brown, 'Medical Evidence related to English Population Changes in the Eighteenth Century', *Population Studies*, ix (1955-6), 119-41. See above, p. 285. Mr D. E. C. Eversley in his article 'A survey of Population in an Area of Worcestershire from 1660-1850 on the Basis of Parish Records', *Population Studies*, x (1956-7), 253-79, see below, p. 394, has provided data relating to population change in a rural area in the light of which these theoretical models can be considered. In this study of Nottingham I have followed Mr Eversley's lead and have attempted to present a series of births, marriages, deaths and child deaths for the period 1700-1801. The employment of uniform ratios throughout the century for converting baptisms into births, and burials into deaths, in which I have followed Mr Eversley, is open to obvious objections, but no satisfactory alternative ratios have been devised. For the most recent discussion of this problem,

How did the change from small-scale to large-scale community take pace? To what extent was it the consequence; to what extent the cause of concurrent economic growth; and what is the answer to the paradox of population check during the period of unprecedented food surpluses, and population advance during the period when surplus gave way to shortage amounting, in the last years of the period, to near famine?

One way of approaching these problems is to examine them where they can be seen at close quarters and in the greatest detail; and such conditions can best be found in villages which experienced enclosure of common and common field and in those provincial towns and industrialized villages which were caught up in the swift advance of industry and population in the second half of the eighteenth century. The story of enclosure of village commons continues to be told and retold and never fails to throw fresh light on the infinitely varied nature of agrarian change[4]; but the experience of the semi-agricultural provincial town which was transformed into a populous industrial centre was an even more radical breach with the past and provides, to a greater extent than the village, the essential characteristics of the general situation with even richer sources of information on which to draw.

The problem of enclosure was present here, too, but it was incidental, not central to the process of transition. The form which it took, however, varied from town to town, and might exercise an important influence on subsequent economic development and social conditions. This is pre-eminently exemplified in the history of Nottingham. The fields and meadows surrounding it were separately owned while those who exercised common rights over them were burgesses with a limited municipal as well as a parliamentary franchise, and so the question became an issue in local politics. In 1787, a plan was presented to the Nottingham Corporation by a committee of gentlemen for 'Improvements of the Town' to be financed from the revenues which would arise from enclosure of the fields and meadows over which the Corporation possessed manorial rights. The plan was rejected, and when an advocate of enclosure presented himself for election as senior councilman, he was decisively defeated by a majority of 600 out of a total poll of 1,051, 'the largest number of electors who ever exercised their privilege in one day for the appointment of a senior councilman'[5]; and the question was not raised again for twenty years.[6]

By this decision the town left itself no choice but to grow within its ancient manorial boundaries, and before the end of the century there were complaints that it was being overlaid with streets, courts, alleys, yards—'a resurrection of buildings generally without order, seated like clusters of mushrooms in a field cast up by chance'.[7] By turning its face against enclosure, it had condemned itself to a period of unparalleled overcrowding and squalor, and any

see J. T. Krause, 'Changes in English Fertility and Mortality, 1781-1850', *Econ. Hist. Rev.*, 2nd ser., xi, no. 1 (August 1958), 52-70.

[4] This is especially well brought out by the two most recent but contrasting studies, W. G. Hoskins, *The Midland Peasant* (1957), and Joan Thirsk, *English Peasant Farming* (1957).

[5] *Nottingham Borough Records* (hereafter *NBR*), vii, 223, and W. H. Wylie, *Old and New Nottingham* (1853), p. 331.

[6] *NBR*, viii, 48-49, October 1806; it was raised again in 1813 (*ibid.*, 172-3); in 1822 (*ibid.*, 293); and in 1833 (*ibid.*, 410).

[7] F. C. Laird, *Topographical Description of Nottinghamshire* (1810), p. 102.

advantage that later generations gained by the postponement of building on the common lands was bought at a heavy cost to those who had to suffer the immediate consequences. When at last enclosure came in 1845, a densely packed community of 53,000 people were contriving to live and multiply on a site which a century earlier had been occupied by slightly more than one-fifth of that number, and the economic growth of the town had been slowed down almost to the point of stagnation.[8] The study of enclosure in its urban as well as its rural setting has a contribution to make to the understanding of the processes of industrialization.[9]

One reason for the disparate share of attention received by the village and the town may be that the growth of the one has frequently been regarded as the counterpart and consequence of the decline of the other; the villages, it has been widely believed, were being emptied by enclosure to provide a labour force for the towns. This explanation fails to take into account the fact that, in the absence of technical changes which would effect economies in the use of labour, the numbers engaged in agriculture tended to rise rather than to fall, and except for those villages which were unsuitable for arable cultivation, enclosure appears to have had little effect on the movement of population.[10] The contribution of rural immigration to urban growth was of course enormous, but this was nothing new; the novelty lay in the fact that the towns no longer relied on the villages to keep them alive[11]; if Nottingham is any guide, they were able from the middle of the eighteenth century to expand with growing momentum through their own powers of natural increase; and though in actual volume the tide of immigration rose, the ratio of urban growth which came from this source substantially declined. That this upward improvement of urban population would have taken place without enclosure, few would now deny; whether it would have taken place without large-scale industrialization is a more difficult question. There is good reason for thinking that it was under way before the impact of the new mechanized industry was felt and in places where it was never felt at all. The rôle of industrialization seems to have been not to initiate population growth so much as to sustain it, to enable the expansive forces to retain their momentum and to prevent them from falling back, as they had so often done before, in face of the direct checks which had hitherto been generated when population growth outstripped the growth of productive forces.

The provincial town is a microcosm within which this unique alliance of industrial and demographic forces may be observed, and a brief report on one

[8] See Wylie, op. cit., and J. D. Chambers, Modern Nottingham in the Making (1940).

[9] See also the valuable study by Phyllis M. Giles, 'The Enclosure of Common Lands in Stockport', Transactions of the Lancashire and Cheshire Antiquarian Society (1950-1), p. 73. I am indebted for this reference to Dr J. D. Marshall. For the influence of urban landowners on the burst of enclosure activity in the late 1750's and 1760's, see H. G. Hunt, 'The Chronology of Parliamentary Enclosure in Leicestershire', Econ. Hist. Rev., 2nd ser., X (1957), 265-72. In regard to the enclosure of the Leicester open fields, which began in 1764, Dr W. G. Hoskins says that the houses generally had ample yards and often gardens, and there was 'nothing remotely resembling the horrors of Nottingham': The Making of the English Landscape (1955), p. 223.

[10] Even in Leicestershire, the classic county of enclosure for pasture, this appears to be true. See V.C.H. Leics., iii (1955), 148: 'Over much of Leicestershire inclosure had no apparent effect on population. . . . The parishes in which numbers did fall after inclosure were those on the heavy clays. . . . Depopulation following parliamentary inclosure . . . was thus merely the last episode in a long history of the adjustment of farming methods to soils and relief which were essentially unfavourable for arable cultivation.'

[11] See Ashton, Eighteenth Century, p. 8, for destructive effects of town life on population.

such town during the period of profound sociological change may not be out of place in a volume dedicated to one who has done so much to illuminate the economic context in which it took place.

In many ways, Nottingham in 1700 retained the classic characteristics of the village from which it had sprung. On three sides it had fields and meadows, an area of nearly 1,500 acres, mainly in the hands of private owners but subject to common rights by burgesses and by the inhabitants at large.[12] The fields—the Sand and Clay fields, an area of 654 acres—appear to have been in regular course of cultivation in the middle of the seventeenth century when 'some had to be annually sown with corn' or, according to another account, 'cultivated two years by the plough . . . and every third year enjoyed exclusively by the housekeeper burgesses', but before the opening of the eighteenth century, 'It was agreed that the proprietors should fence their respective lots, if they chose; that the land should be laid down for mowing and pasturage . . . and that two gaps in each fence should be made on or before the 12th August and which should continue open till the 12th November; during which time the production of the fields was to be the sole property of the burgess house-keepers.' Since many of the burgesses were said to be too poor to buy cattle, it was agreed that the non-burgesses should have the privilege of turning in three head of cattle each during the commonable time. As late as 1807 the non-burgesses were protected in this right as a result of legal action, with the proviso that the right should be enjoyed only by those who occupied toftsteads.

In addition there were the Meadows (283 acres), divided into East Croft and West Croft and commonable by the burgesses for various periods of the year. There was also a considerable area in the possession of the Corporation as lord of the manor consisting of the Forest (124 acres), Mapperley Hills common (54 acres) and the Coppice of the Hunger Hills which was open all the year round to the burgesses and inhabitants at large. Except on the east, where there was a narrow break in the green ring, the town was entirely surrounded by its ancient fields, meadows and waste; and so it remained until the enclosure acts of 1839-1845.

The approaches to the town were as medieval as the fields and meadows through which they made their way. From the south, the road from the bridge which spanned the Trent was carried over the Meadows partly by means of the Leen Bridge, consisting of twenty-two arches, the repair of which was determined by an inquisition in the reign of Henry VIII which derived its authority 'from time immemorial'. It carried its passengers to Bridge End from which point they made their way through swampy ground to Hollowstone, a narrow precipitous cart-track up the face of the rock to St. Mary's Hill, Stoney Street Broad Lane and the road to York. The western entrance was a deep cutting made by centuries of traffic over Lenton Sands, past the end of Butt Dyke—'where the townsmen used to exercise themselves, in shooting at a Mark with Bows and Arrows'—to Chapel Bar, 'the only Ancient Gate which had escaped the Injuries of Time, and was preserved entire until 1743'.[13] In that year it was

---

[12] See C. Deering, *Nottinghamia Vetus et Nova* (1751), p. 2, and J. Blackner, *History of Nottingham* (1815), p. 30.
[13] Deering, *op. cit.*, p. 3.

pulled down in the course of widening the road at the cost of Lord Middleton and with the aid of his colliers, presumably in order to enable his coal-carts to make the journey more easily. At the same time Hollowstone was widened and the gradient reduced 'so that two or more carriages may conveniently pass each other'; and it may be supposed the swamp at Bridge End was made good for wheeled traffic.

For more than half a century before this, however, the town had been growing in economic importance and still more in social significance. The economic advance was due to the expansion of the framework knitting industry which, from small beginnings in the seventeenth century, had developed rapidly in the early decades of the eighteenth century until, in 1750, it is said to have found employment for 1,200 frames working in wool and cotton, and for a considerable number of workers in the ancillary industries of needle-makers, sinker-makers, setters up of frames, etc. The growing social significance of the town sprang from its position as a local capital to which the aristocracy and gentry of the region gravitated on important social occasions. Some of them also lived in the town and left an unmistakable tribute to the graciousness of their age and way of life in the houses which have survived the flood of industrial building and the zeal of twentieth-century townplanners.

The social pre-eminence of the town dated from 1674 when the Duke of Newcastle began the building of his palladian mansion on the site of the old castle with its 64 acres of deer park. His successors intended to make gardens of it—'the finest in all that part of England', as Defoe says—but unfortunately it remained only a reported intention not an accomplished fact. But Nottingham now possessed a ducal seat and became a centre of attraction to the people of quality in the neighbourhood. They thronged to the races—'Eleven or twelve noblemen, an infinite throng of gentlemen from all the countries round, nay even out of Scotland itself,' and 'a train of coaches filled with the beauties from the north was not to be described'—a finer assembly than could be seen at Newmarket.[14] Eleven gentlemen including the Hon. Wm. Pierrepont, the Hon. Rothwell Willoughby, John Sherwin, Francis Thornhaugh, maintained coaches besides a considerable number who kept chaises or chariots, and several had handsome residences set about with beautiful formal gardens and orchards. Contemporaries spoke with admiration of Pierrepont House and Plumptree House and John Sherwin's house. The last had a close of grassland in Pilcher Gate and a large cherry orchard and the site was remembered, a century later, in the densely packed areas of Cherry Street, Cherry Place and Sherwin Court. Other streets that carried into the nineteenth century the fragrance of those days were Currant Street, Garden Street and Orchard Street. Those houses of the period that survived, Newdigate House (1675), Willoughby House (1730-40), People's Hall (1740), Lord Howe's House (1752) and perhaps especially Bromley House, built for George Smith the banker in 1732, reflect the ideas of comfort and elegance of early Georgian England. But from the point of view of the conditions that determined its growth the buildings which failed to survive are of greater importance.

These may be easily located with the aid of Deering's list of streets and the

14 D. Defoe, *Tour* (Everyman edn., 1928), ii, 148-9.

accompanying map by Badder and Peet.[15] By far the greatest concentration was on Back Side, later called Parliament Street, where there were 214 houses and 1,313 inhabitants out of a total population of 10,720. The map shows several solid blocks of property separated by extremely narrow passages, with only one thoroughfare (Sheep Lane, now Market Street) wide enough to admit the passage of a farm-cart. There can be no doubt that the density of population in this area was approaching a nineteenth-century standard and the term 'Rookeries' by which this and other congested places came to be known, would not have been inappropriate a century earlier.

The next largest concentration was Narrow Marsh, along the foot of the rock on which the old Anglo-Danish burgh had been built. Here there were 535 inhabitants, but their houses were more dispersed and they had tree-lined avenues and gardens down to the banks of the Leen. This was no doubt an advantage to the tanners who congregated there in the seventeenth century, but it rendered the houses liable to flooding. In 1736, we are told, the parlours were two feet under water. In normal times the Leen meandered vaguely over the meadows, leaving semi-stagnant loops and wholly stagnant pools and collecting on its way to the Trent the surface drainage from the upper part of the town. It was highly esteemed, however, by the inhabitants of Nottingham who admired it for its sylvan beauties and gratefully used its waters for industrial and domestic purposes.

Narrow Marsh and its continuation Broad Marsh were not the only areas liable to flooding. A similar problem existed in the neighbourhood of St. Peter's Church. This was the focal point of a number of busy thoroughfares—St. Peter's Gate, Pepper Street, Wheeler Gate, Hounds Gate, St. Peter's Lane—and it also received the water of the little brook or drain, the 'Rowell'[16] which ran down Wheeler Gate from the upper part of the town towards the Leen. The area was so boggy that it could only be crossed 'not without danger' by the aid of a plank and a handrail from St. Peter's Church side to Castle Gate, and from this point through Lister Gate and to the Leen was 'one continued Swamp'.[17] In 1706 the immediate neighbourhood of St. Peter's Church was raised and paved and the sheep market moved there. In 1729 it was to be swept and kept clean, and the standard of cleanliness was laid down precisely in the order of 1748. 'The Dirt to be taken away from Peter's Church Wall twice in the winter and once in the summer if necessary.'[18] Not a high achievement as a measure of public health, but an improvement on the laconic entry of 1706: 'Twenty loads of mucke betweene Sheepe Penes and ye Hen Crosse 12/–.'[19] In accounting for the remarkable improvement in public health which took place in the middle of the century, the crude measures taken by obscure town officials cannot be ignored.

The margin of swamp was thus slowly being pushed back, and the process was assisted by the arrangements for the disposal of 'Rammell'; it was to be carried into Trent Lanes, the Swan Pool, Sheep Skin Pool, the 'Holloway at the west end of Castle Gate and Hunsgate to fill up the same.'[20] But this thoughful–

[15] Map printed in Deering, op. cit., between p. 12 and p. 13.
[16] See NBR, ii, 445, and vii, xiv.
[17] Deering, op. cit., p. 17.   [18] Ibid., 32.
[19] NBR, vi, 221.   [20] Ibid., 28, 68, 91, 172.

ness on the part of the Corporation may have had its penalties as well as its advantages since the Leen which provided the main drainage for these areas was also the main water supply of the town. No misgivings seem to have been entertained, however, on this score. Deering, a doctor and leading scholar of the town, wrote as to the Leen: 'it lies at the foot of the Town, and tho' it is slower than the Trent, yet are not the Vapours thence arising capable of becoming hurtful, not only on Account of the Great height the town stands above it, likewise because of the Openness of the Ground below, which readily admits the Ventilation of the Wind to disperse all noxious Particles, and the few boggy Enclosures between the River and its backwater, are by the prudent Care of the Corporation raised and made good Land.'[21]

The presence of hurtful vapours was evidently a matter of some concern. The water supply, however, was felt to be above suspicion. The town had formerly been supplied from its numerous wells and by water-carts bringing a supply from the river, but in the last decade of the seventeenth century a company had been formed to supply the town with water from the Leen by means of 'an engine', one of the many joint-stock pumping enterprises undertaken at that time. 'The original sharers', writes Deering, 'as in all new Projects, met with many difficulties and found it very expensive for some Years, before they could rightly bring it to bear, but of late is brought to a competent Perfection, so that they are in condition of supplying any part of Nottingham; the East part of the Town has Water immediately from the Engine, whilst the West part receives it from a large reservoir made in Butt Dyke . . . besides this, least any time, there should be want of water on account of the River Leen being low, the Company rent of his Grace the Duke of Newcastle, a large Pond in the Park, lying close by the River, to which they have fixed Flood-Gates, serving in Time of Floods to let water in, and in Time of Scarcity, to furnish water enough to set the Engine to Work.'

The historian of 1740 could look back with pride on what had been accomplished 'during these forty years last past. It is plain', he says, 'that the Improvement of the Town, by mending Roads and raising and paving Streets as well as beautifying it with Sightly Buildings, was a Task left to later Generations . . . and no Stranger who has taken the Pains to consider the situation and present Buildings, the State of Trade and Manufacture, the plenty of Provisions brought to Market, the excellent Malt Liquor brew'd at Nottingham, but will gladly subscribe to what is said of them in the following lines:

> Fair Nottingham with brilliant Beauty graced,
> In ancient *Shirwood's* South West Angle placed
> Where Northern Hills her tender Neck protect,
> With dainty Flocks of golden Fleeces deckt. . . .

The geographical situation here delicately alluded to moved Deering to ecstasy: 'Were a Naturalist in Quest of an exquisite Spot to build a Town or City upon, could he meet with one that would better Answer his Wishes?' At that time the town consisted of about 2,000 houses containing between 10,000 and 11,000 people, arrayed along the southern face of a sandstone outcrop

---

[21] Deering, *op cit.*, p. 85.

stretching from Hollowstone along High Pavement, Back Side, Butt Dyke, to the Castle Rock; to the north, west and south of this sandstone crescent lay the open fields and meadows, the famous crocus meadows which in early spring spread a purple hem to the skirts of the old town. No town in England, it was said, had so fine approach as 'the most beautiful mile' which lay through the crocus meadows between Trent Bridge and Hollowstone; and from the last quarter of the seventeenth century when it was described by Thomas Baskerville as a 'paradise restored'[22] and by Celia Fiennes as one of the neatest-built towns she had seen, to the last quarter of the eighteenth century when the German tourist Moritz said it was the best he had seen outside London, and certainly the cleanest, there was a chorus of praise. It echoed somewhat sadly down the years to the beginning of the present century when in 1901 Ann Gilbert looked back with touching nostalgia to the time when the fields lay open and the streets laid out by the enclosure commissioners were no more than field paths bordered with blackberry brambles and the Meadows were a playground, the very mention of which called up idyllic memories. 'I cannot hope to give you an adequate idea of that fair expanse. Often in my dreams I find myself and companions wandering by its streamlets watching the fish in the clear water, or the dragon flies skimming along the surface, or gathering the flowers that grew along the banks. . . . But the most interesting and beautiful custom of all was the yearly visit in March to our crocus covered meadows, young and old turning out . . . to revel among them'.[23]

According to eighteenth-century standards, Nottingham was a clean and well-appointed town, it was also reputed by Deering to be a healthy one, owing to the fact that it stood on a well-drained sandstone site above the flood plains of the Trent and was free from the evil vapours and stinking fogs to which medical opinion attached so much importance. His criteria of healthfulness may not be ours; and, as will be shown later, he was more complacent than the facts warranted, even on his own showing. On another aspect of the well-being of the town, however, he is completely convincing; he leaves us in no doubt that it was well supplied as to quantity, quality and variety of food, and that the level of prices was such that the poorest members of the community could share both in the abundance and the variety.

There was ample room in the Market Place, one of the biggest in England, for the display of every kind of merchandise: corn, malt, oatmeal; stalls and booths for bakers, gardeners, milliners, pedlars, turners, braziers, tinners, chandlers, collar-makers along Long Row on the northern side; a horse market, formerly separated by a wall, on the southern side; a beast and swine market on the west, and at the east end there were the shambles for no fewer than sixty butchers, capable, says Deering, of supplying five times as much meat as the town required. There was also a poultry market round the Hen Cross, where

22 'Paradise restored, for here you find large streets, fair built houses, fine women, and many coaches rattling about, and their shops full of all merchantable riches. . . . It is divided into the upper and lower towns, for when you have a mind to leave the large and more spacious parts of this town . . . you must descend right many stairs ere you get to the bottom and here you find . . . another town full of shops and people, who have a convenience to cut in the rock warehouses, stables, and what rooms they please': 'Thomas Baskerville's Journeys in England, tem. Car. II', *Hist. MSS. Comm.*, 13th Rep., Appendix, pt. ii, Portland Papers, ii, 308–9.
23 Mrs A. Gilbert, *Recollections of Old Nottingham* (2nd edn., 1904), pp. 18, 28.

the country folk sold geese and turkeys and pigs on Saturdays, and a market at Week Day Cross for butter, poultry, fruit, fish on Wednesdays and Fridays, and still more butchers' shambles.

The town had a further advantage 'hardly to be matched by any other of the Kingdom, to wit: not only good Barley to turn into Malt and Ale (for which the Town is famed all over England) but the best, coolest and deepest Rock Cellars to stow their Liquor in'; and the inhabitants equipped themselves with 147 licensed houses, one to every eighty or so, in which to consume it.[24]

He divides the supplies of food available into 'immediate necessaries' and 'less necessaries', and in the former he includes carrots, turnips, parsnips, cabbages, savoys, potatoes as well as meat, bread, butter, cheese, eggs, beans and peas and, of course, beer, small ($1\frac{1}{2}$d. a gallon, middling 2d. a gallon) and strong ale (4d. a quart). The 'less necessaries' include all forms of poultry, rabbits, a long list of freshwater and sea fish, and also 'Broccoli till within six or seven Years was only to be met in Gentlemen's Gardens, but now are sold in the Market, cauliflowers, asparagus . . . Sugars, Spices and all sorts of Grocers Goods almost as cheap as in London', wine and cider 'as about London'. Tea, coffee, chocolate were also available and the use of the first had spread 'so that almost every Seamer, Sizer and Winder will have her Tea and will enjoy herself over it in a Morning, not forgetting their Snuff . . . and even a common Washerwoman thinks she has not had a proper Breakfast without tea and hot buttered white Bread'.

As to prices, he says that nothing was so cheap as to be contemptible, nor anything requisite to a comfortable way of living so dear but that 'middling People' may have a share, but the fact that tea was beginning to compete with beer among the poorest classes suggests that the standard even for them included something more than the bare necessities of life.

At the same time, all forms of meat could be bought at a low price, beef, veal, mutton and pork being sold at about $2\frac{1}{2}$d. per lb.; eggs were three or four a penny; fowls could be bought for 1s. 3d. a couple; a pig or Christmas goose cost less than half a crown and rabbits were 3d. each. William Felkin, writing of his grandfather at this time, states that during his apprenticeship he paid 5s. a week for his board and lodging and had 2s. 6d. for himself, and 'when he got out of his apprenticeship he could earn 12s. a week; thus he could save 5s. to 7s. a week'. Food, he says, was cheap, but clothing and furniture were dear.[25] Since employment opportunities were expanding, especially for skilled men, owing to the development of framework knitting and its dependent industries, and to the important discovery in 1730 that cotton yarn could be used in the frame, the conditions of life of the artisan class were probably as good as in any provincial town in England, and better, as far as Nottingham was concerned, than they were to be again for a hundred years.

In spite of those favourable circumstances, the town was scarcely able to maintain itself by its own powers of natural increase. The century started well

[24] The names and locations are given in *NBR*, vii, 552.
[25] I am indebted to Mr S. D. Chapman for this extract from the newly discovered memoir, 'Progenitors of the Felkin Family as ascertained by William Felkin III and summarised in a Memo. dated 1872', p. 53. William Felkin I was born in 1745 and died in 1838, so that the extract above would refer to the last phase of the cheap period, i.e., 1750-65.

with a balance of births over deaths in each of the first two decades but there followed a period of high death rates; between 1720-30 the death rate (i.e. based on church burials inflated by 1·10) never seems to have fallen below 40 per thousand and three times was over 50; in 1736 it was over 70 and in the year March 1741 to March 1742 it was nearly 80 and one in thirteen of the people died.[26] But in the five years centring on 1745 it fell to slightly under 30 and remained within three or four points of that figure for twenty years. As far as Nottingham is concerned, the age of massacre by epidemic was over; the age of continuous growth by natural increase had begun; and whereas between 1700 and 1740 there was an excess of deaths over births, between 1740 and 1780 about 40 per cent of the town's growth came by excess of births over deaths and somewhat over 40 per cent between 1780-1801.[27] From the fifth decade of the century, it can no longer be said that this town—whatever may be said of others—destroyed life almost as fast as the countryside replenished it.

It is not easy to associate this new demographic pattern with corresponding changes in the town's economy, and still less with an improvement of its food supply. It was a period of rising prices and it was marked, for the first time since 1701, by food riots sufficiently serious to have left some local record. In 1754 the quartern loaf was 4d.; in 1757 it was 10d.; and miners and their wives expressed their disapproval at the expense of unfortunate millers who were using efficient newfangled French equipment, and corn dealers who had adopted the enlightened practice of selling by sample. The episode gave rise to a remarkable pamphlet by an anonymous writer who showed that the results of the riots were the opposite to those intended, since selling by sample brought more, not less, grain to market, and the use of French grinding-stones and bolting mills had the effect of raising the efficiency of milling, not, as the miners believed, of adulterating the flour with gypsum and bones.[28] In 1762 the Corporation forwarded a petition to Parliament on the distresses of the people and in 1766 occurred the famous cheese riots when cheeses were rolled down Wheeler Gate and Peck Lane and flung about with such energy that the Mayor, who was struck with one as he was on the point of reading the Riot Act, had to be carried insensible into the Exchange.[29]

On the side of industrial expansion there were numerous innovations devised by the ingenious Nottingham mechanics beginning in 1756 with the tuck-press

[26] The 'unconverted' March to March burials for 1736 and 1741 were 747 and 818 respectively. The population according to Deering, corrected by Sir John Sutton, was 10,720 in 1739. The immigration was probably between 75 and 100 per annum. Cf. the worst known death rates of the nineteenth century: Byron Ward, 30·9 between 1840 and 1843. See my *Modern Nottingham in the Making* (1940), p. 12. The month of maximum burials, July 1736, coincided with the high point of the flood of that year, when the water rose three feet in the houses of Narrow Marsh. Other years of high floods and high mortality are February 1683; midsummer 1728; May 1787; February 1795.

[27] These figures have been obtained by calculating the difference between births and deaths (i.e., baptisms and burials inflated by 1·15 and 1·10 respectively), and working back from the figures of population given by local historians in 1739 and 1779, and forward from the Hearth Tax Return of 1674. This gives a different result from that obtained by using the Dissenters' registers. See J. D. Chambers, *The Vale of Trent* (1957), pp. 19-21. Owing to inconsistencies in the records of the Dissenters, the present method appears to be more satisfactory for comparative purposes until improved ratios have been devised.

[28] *Seasonable Considerations upon the Corn Trade, as it respects Landowner, the Tenant, the Miller and Baker, and the labouring parts of the population.* . . . By a true-born Englishman (Nottingham 1757). Not in the Nottingham Library or in the British Museum, but quoted extensively by T. Bailey, *Annals of Nottinghamshire* (1852-5), iii, 1231 ff.

[29] *Ibid.*

which enabled the stockinger to produce a variety of shades in a vertical line and so give the appearance of coloured ribs. In 1759, Jedediah Strutt established his Derby Rib workshop at Derby for the production of ribbed hose, and in 1763 it was adapted by a Nottingham workman to the making of eyelet holes, the first step towards the making of machine-made lace. In 1767 velvet was made on the stocking frame; in 1768 brocade, 'the most beautiful article ever wrought thereon. Here all the variegated colours of the rainbow were cast into captivating shades, all the tints of the full blown carnation were displayed in diversifying splendour; the twigs and branches of trees were represented in all their intertwining forms'[30]; in 1776 knotted work, 'the most beautiful and durable stockings ever made by human hands'; and the warp machine which 'united the stitch of the stocking frame with the warp of the loom' and made the cloth for the jackets worn by the sailors at Trafalgar and the earliest form of net for window curtains.

Brilliantly skilful and ingenious as the Nottingham mechanics were, they provided only a supporting chorus for the two principals of world-wide fame who had recently settled in their midst. In 1768 James Hargreaves and Richard Arkwright were both in Nottingham with their epoch-making innovations in the spinning of cotton. Besides Hargreaves's own mill in Mill Street, by 1777 Nottingham had its jenny mills containing the machines of Hargreaves's own make. One of these was described as having three carding engines worked by horses, about fifty 'Spinning wheels' of twenty-six spindles each, with slubbing wheels, doubling jacks and 'every necessary implement for finishing cotton yarn for hosiery'.[31] Arkwright's cotton mill in Hockley was a large establishment; on 3 September 1772 'upwards of three hundred persons employed in Mr Arkwright's mill built in Hockley walked in a procession through the town, with streamers flying, preceded by the head workman, who was clothed from head to foot in white cotton. After parading the streets, they marched to the Marshall-hills[32] to gather nuts, and on their return in the evening, were regaled with a plentiful supper.'[33] Mr Arkwright was already practising the gentle art of personnel management at which he later proved himself so adept.

These events cannot be said to have initiated but only to have reinforced and sustained the upward trend of population growth. It was already well under way before they took place and, in its early stages, has more claim to be regarded as a cause than an effect of industrial expansion. There is more reason to relate the change to non-economic causes, such as the greater immunity of a population that had been savagely thinned by successive attacks of disease during the previous twenty years, or perhaps to the reduced virulence of the organism which carried the infection. Contemporaries themselves had little light to throw on this subject. Deering, himself a doctor, was content to say that 'Once in five years a Distemperature in the Air, either brings with it some Epidemical Fever (tho' seldom very Mortal) or renders Small Pox more dangerous than at other

[30] Blackner, *History of Nottingham*, pp. 223-4.
[31] A. P. Wadsworth and J. de L. Mann, *The Cotton Trade and Industrial Lancashire* (1931), p. 494. Hargreaves's mill was a three-storey building 40 feet by 30 feet situated at the north end of a passage leading from Chapel Bar to Back Lane (now Wollaton Street); see Bailey, *Annals*, iv, 6.
[32] Between the Coppice and Carlton.
[33] John F. Sutton, *The Date Book of . . . Nottingham and its Neighbourhood, 1750-1850* (1852), p. 95 (3 September 1772).

Times, of this last, the year 1736 was a fatal Instance for from the latter end of May to the beginning of September, the Distemper swept away a great number of Souls (but mostly Children). . . .' Apart from this reference the subject excited no contemporary comment, and even the visitation of 1741-2, when one out of thirteen of the townspeople died, gave rise to nothing more than a collection of examples of those who had exceeded 'the ultimate Term of the Psalmist or even were outliving 93 the Age of St. John the Evangelist'.

The stolid indifference with which these epidemic years were met contrasts strongly with the activity amounting sometimes to panic to which the visitations of the plague had given rise a century before. On those occasions the borough authorities made arrangements to isolate the sick in huts built for the purpose, appointed 'visitors' and provided them with funds, presumably for the benefit of the victims; they also ordered the slaughter of cats and dogs, and the confinement of swine, advised against large gatherings at funerals and unnecessary visitings, and forbade the holding of Goose Fair.[34] In 1667 we are told that the plague made 'a cruel Desolation in the higher part of Nottingham, for very few died in the lower, especially in the street called Narrow Marsh, it was observed that the Infection had no Power, and that during the whole Time the Plague raged, not one who lived in that street died of it, which induced many of the richer sort of People to crowd thither and hire lodgings at any Price, the preservation of the People was attributed to the Effluvia of the Tanners Ouse (for there were 47 Tanners in that Place) besides which they caused a Smoak to be made by burning moist Tanners Knobs'.[35] That men should choose these dire alternatives is perhaps itself a sufficient tribute to the terror which the plague inspired.

The greater attention that was paid to plague was probably due to the fact that it is reputed to have been a disease of adults rather than of children and to that extent represented a greater threat to the family as a whole through the death of the bread-winner. Since the parish registers distinguished between the burials of children and adults by referring to the former as 'son of' or 'daughter of', and to adults as wife, widow, spinster or, in the case of a man, by name, it is possible to test this by comparing the proportions of the categories so distinguished at the two periods. Deering seems to have used this method when he states that out of 2,331 burials between 1732-9 (excepting the year 1736) there were 1,072 'infants'. Such a total would give a ratio of 46 per cent of child[36] burials for those years. A more satisfactory basis of comparison with the plague years would be 1736 when the ratio was 72·9 per cent. This is the highest of the century, but lesser peaks were reached in 1708 (56·1 per cent), 1717 (66·5 per cent),[37] 1725 (55·2 per cent), 1730 (62·1 per cent), 1739 (57·1 per cent). The

[34] NBR, v, 184 (20 June 1637); 247 (27 February 1645/6); 253 (August 1647).

[35] Deering, op. cit., pp. 82-83. See also L. F. Hirst, Conquest of Plague (1953), p. 44.

[36] Since a number of registers in the latter part of the century give the age at death, it becomes possible to define 'child' deaths more clearly. Mansfield, a growing framework knitting centre, had 51·8 per cent of its burials under 20 between 1779 and 1799; I am indebted to Mr Yewdall for the information that between 1779 and 1788 the proportion of burials at Leeds (township only) under 10 was 51·7 and between 0 and 20 was 57·1; six Bedfordshire parishes between 1780 and 1789 give a ratio of 48·9 per cent under 10 and 55·2 per cent under 20; Mr Eversley defines 'child' burials as 20 years or under: see 'A Survey of Population in an Area of Worcestershire', Pop. Studies, x (1956-7), 261. See below, p. 402.

[37] St. Mary's and St. Nicholas's only.

ratios of child deaths in the plague years 1637-8 are 35·3 per cent and 39 per cent; 1645-6, 38·8 per cent and 38·6 per cent; 1647-8, 48·5 per cent and 56·3 per cent. In 1649 it goes down to 34·9 per cent. (The figures of 1667 are useless as the distinction between adult and non-adult burials was largely ignored.)

An interesting confirmation of the view that plague was feared because of its differential impact upon adult lives is provided by the panic that suddenly arose and as suddenly subsided in 1781. The outbreak of that year evidently gave rise to the fear that plague had returned; on 26 June 'a thousand handbills on fine paper about the Plague reported' were printed at the cost of the Corporation, but within four days the report was contradicted.[38] Instead of plague the town was probably suffering from an attack of influenza.[39] It is interesting to note that though the death rate rose to over forty per thousand, the proportion of child deaths was only 38 per cent, the lowest of the century.

On the assumption of unbroken consistency in the differentiation of child deaths, a comparison of the two periods shows that the ratio of child deaths tended to rise in the last quarter of the seventeenth century.[40] The passing of the plague era brought relief, apparently, only to the adult death rate; and what is more surprising, this differentiation in favour of adult lives seems to have been more pronounced in the second half of the century than the first. Thus, between 1701 and 1750 the ratio of child deaths in five-year periods never fell below 46 per cent (1711-1715) nor rose above 56·2 per cent (1736-40). But in the second half of the century it never fell below 52·1 per cent (1781-5) and it rose in 1791-5, to 61·7 per cent. It would appear, therefore, that in so far as there was a fall of the death rate of the town population in the second half of the century, it did not operate to the special advantage of the lower age groups (except in so far as the particularly severe child epidemics such as occurred in 1708, 1717, 1725, 1730, 1736 and 1739 were somewhat less frequent) and that it implied the saving of adult lives to at least the same extent as of the lives of children.[41] In regard to the behaviour of the crude death rate, it will be seen from the table given at the end of this chapter that it fell from a very high level between 1725-40 to a low level between 1745-60; it returned to a level slightly below that of the first two decades of the century until the last quinquennium of the period, when it took a sharp turn downwards. It is not a question, therefore, of a steady decline under the influence of ameliorating factors of diet and environment, but rather of a sudden and temporary plunge downwards as a result of the absence of a factor which had made the preceding period one of exceptionally high mortality,

[38] NBR, vii, 128. Unfortunately none of these handbills has survived.
[39] See C. Creighton, History of Epidemics (1891), ii, 364. The attack of 1782 'affected ¾ to ⅘ of the adults everywhere, but the children not so much'.
[40] The large parish of St. Mary's gives the following percentages of 'child' deaths for the century (years of defective registration omitted):

1601-10	1611-20	1621-30	1631-4	1645-55
55·8	31·9	36·7	37·2	43·6

1658-65	1671-80	1681-90	1691-1700	
36	42	46·5	50·8	

In regard to the period 1601-10 there is evidence of plague in the town in 1603, 1604-5, 1609-10; NBR, iv, 267-99. It may also have been accompanied by smallpox, which was receiving widespread notice at the end of the sixteenth and beginning of the seventeenth century, including its first mention in literature in 1602: Creighton, op. cit., i, 463.
[41] See also Eversley, op. cit., 265, for an interesting discussion of this question in relation to the village populations studied. See below, p. 403-5.

followed by a return almost to the death rates of the pre-epidemic period. It has been suggested above that the fall from 1745 may have been due to the greater immunity enjoyed by the surviving population after the severe thinning process endured by the previous generation; but it is of equal significance that, though there was a return to the moderate death rates of the early decades of the century and a rise of the child death rates above them, there was no return, in spite of rising prices and increasing urban congestion, to the high plateau of 1725-40. The death rate stayed in the foothills until it took its descent into the valley at the end of the century.

It would not be true to say that in this period the town experienced an industrial revolution since the expansion consisted of the proliferation of the types of small units that already existed; only two steam factories were established in these years—a worsted mill in 1788 (burnt down in 1791 and not replaced) and a cotton mill in 1792; but the immense impetus given to the hand-frame industry by the innovations mentioned earlier and by the successive steps in the mastery of machine-made lace, together with the stimulus given to machine building and maintenance and to the housing industry, provided employment opportunities for a growing volume from outside as well as for the increasing supply of the native-born labour from within. Between 1779 and 1801 the population grew by 11,000 of which nearly 60 per cent were immigrants. In these circumstances a rise in the marriage and birth rates is to be expected, an expectation that, as the figures show, is more than amply realized.

The very high birth rates from 1770 must themselves be included among the factors accounting for the higher child death rate: there were more children in the community and they provided a relatively higher proportion of the deaths. The surprising thing is that the crude death rate remained steady and in the last period centring on 1801 took a turn downwards when conditions of life might have been expected to lead to the opposite trend. It was a period of acute social tension arising partly from industrial fluctuations—accentuated by the vagaries of fashion and technological change and the incidental casualties of fire and flood—but especially from the effects of food shortage and famine prices. In 1792 a mob of hungry men and women made a bonfire of the doors, shutters and implements of the butchers as a protest against the price of meat; in 1795 a subscription was raised to provide bread tickets for the relief of the poor suffering from 'deficiency of employment and the extraordinary rigour of the season'; it was the year of the six-week frost from 24 December to 9 February when the Trent was frozen over as low as Gainsborough, and the thaw which followed flooded the houses of Narrow Marsh to a depth of three feet and the Trent 'bearing down in its mighty stream horses and sheep, haystacks and trees . . . was amply sufficient to show the unprecedented extent of the calamity'. Conditions in the following year were if anything worse; wheat rose to 100s. a quarter; bakers' shops were looted by hungry mobs, and again in the following year. In 1800 prices were higher still, and 'bread was an article of great scarcity this year'; fierce food riots broke out in April and again in August; the Corporation opened a subscription to assist the poor but the most effective measures were taken by two local mill owners, Messrs Davison and Hawksley, who supplied 'an immense quantity of corn, considerably below the price they had given for it' to their own work-people and sent flour which had been ground by their own steam engine to be sold at a reduced price in Nottingham. In the same year a local surgeon, Mr Attenburrow, began to vaccinate free of charge, and a first step was taken to tame this 'disease of fearful malignity, committing extensive and frightful ravages.'[42] That the death rate should fall to the second-lowest figure of the century is a tribute to the efficacy of vaccination in stemming the rising tide of epidemic disease, and to the humane impulse of a single man.[43]

Environmental factors also contributed to this result. The new houses in which the working population lived may have been better and, at this time, even less crowded than those of their forebears half a century earlier, but they were innocent of the elementary decencies of life and lacked a regular water supply.

'The gathered filth within doors is scattered daily, in the dirty passages without . . . and many of these streets and lanes, if so they may be called, are without any sort of pavement, consequently without regulated water courses.'[44] Until 1830, when Thomas Hawksley inaugurated one of the greatest civic innovations of the age—filtered water under pressure supplied in standpipes for the use of the working population—the inhabitants had to buy their water in pails from water-carriers. The Leen, however, was no longer the main water supply. In the last quarter of the century, nine pumps had been erected by the Corporation, but the water was 'hard and curdling', so that many householders continued to use the Leen water for culinary purposes although it constituted the main sewer of the town.[45] During the same period a society was formed by the Quakers for relieving distress 'by the aid of medicines, by the distribution of apparel, by temporary loans', by arranging visits in time of sickness and lying-in. In September 1782 the General Hospital was opened and by 1814 it claimed to have treated 10,913 in-patients and 28,954 out-patients, of whom a total of 27,300 were said to have been 'cured'.[46] The cumulative effect of these changes cannot be measured but it should not be overlooked. The initiating impulse in the new pattern of population growth must, however, be looked for in the long series of substantial balances of births over deaths between 1743 and 1763, a change which took place independently of contemporary economic factors, and may, perhaps, be described as an example of the autonomous action of the death

[42] Sutton, op. cit., p. 233.

[43] On 25 March 1799 the doctors of the town, moved 'by the great mortality amongst the children of the poor from Smallpox', gave their consent to a plan for free inoculation at the General Hospital. This was a doubtful expedient owing to the difficulty of arranging the isolation of those affected. In the following year Mr John Attenburrow began free vaccinations in his surgery on Beast-market Hill. His example was followed by the other doctors and in 1805 a public subscription was opened to provide the services of a surgeon for this purpose and in 1813 the service was taken by St. Mary's Workhouse and in 1814 a 'fever house' was also established there. See F. H. Jacob, *A History of the General Hospital Nottingham* (1951), pp. 102-3.

[44] Laird, *Topographical Description of Nottinghamshire*, pp. 102-3.

[45] Blackner, op. cit., p. 26. For the work of Hawksley, see my *Modern Nottingham in the Making* (1940). For erection of new pumps see NBR, vii, 196 (in 1779); 193 (in 1782); 196 (three in 1793); 234 (in 1788); 251 (1790 and 1791); 284 (in 1793). In 1804 one of them had to be removed because 'the ordure had so far penetrated the rock . . . which rendered the water . . . at times . . . quite nauseous to the taste and altogether unfit for culinary purposes'. Blackner, op. cit., p. 26.

[46] See also Jacob, *A History of the General Hospital Nottingham*, pp. 54 ff., on methods and treatment. He notes that treatment had altered little by 1854, which suggests that Nottingham medical practice had reached a mid-nineteenth-century standard by the end of the eighteenth century.

rate. It followed a period when the death rate had behaved with almost equal independence of external circumstances but in the reverse direction. The epidemics between 1720-30 were no doubt reinforced by the weather and harvest conditions and again in 1741-2; but the demographic effects were disproportionately severe. In terms of subsistence none of these years was as critical as 1709-10 but all were overwhelmingly more critical in terms of mortality; and the crisis of 1736 was entirely a crisis of public health not of subsistence. During the period of low death rates which followed the fearful visitation of 1741-2 the child population was recruited as fast as but, it would appear, no faster than the adult population; whether there was an increased expectation of life is unknown; we can only say that the adult population—perhaps the group from fifteen to fifty-five—was being rapidly reinforced both by natural increase and by immigration, and the effect was reflected in the rising marriage rate and birth rate. Here was the new industrial army in full spate of self-recruitment; marrying and competing for jobs and houses; stimulating the local economy by their production and consumption; creating new markets for their products by their own inventive genius (all the inventions in the stocking industry were the work of ordinary mechanics, including those of Strutt in the first instance); hoping to make a fortune—which they never did—but determined to fight for the standards which they had enjoyed in good years when prices were low and reliable workmen in short supply; organizing the Framework Knitters' Union of the Midland Counties during the slump of the American war and rioting fiercely when they were denied parliamentary help in the attempt to regulate wages[47]; looting the bakers and terrorizing the butchers in times of famine; ducking the 'Jacobin democrats' in their midst with savage delight while the Corporation looked on in complacent apathy, and taking a condign revenge on the troops—with equal disregard of decency and fear of reprisals—when they carried out their duties of keeping order with excessive zeal[48]; but above all, marrying and begetting children and filling up the vacant spaces within the boundaries of the old town. From 1770-80 the emphasis shifted from the death rate to the birth rate; for the first time since the epidemic years it topped forty per thousand and reached a climax in 1790 of more than forty-six per thousand from which it fell in 1801 to forty-one—an explosion of population brought about by the changing age structure supported by—and supporting—an expanding industrial economy.

If 1770 marked the beginning of the explosive birth rate, it also marked the return of the higher death rates, especially of children. While the general death rate remained at about the level of the first twenty years of the century, the child death rate definitely rose above it. Factors making for the greater chances of life for children—cheaper and more suitable clothes, more plentiful supply

---

[47] I have described these riots in *Nottinghamshire in the Eighteenth Century* (1932), pp. 40-44.

[48] On the occasion of a dispute between the stockingers and a hosier in 1791 the Oxford Blues, after the Riot Act had been read, charged a meeting of the men with drawn swords and 'the Troopers ensured to themselves the hatred and contempt of the working men . . . the consequence of which they felt most severely during the winter for it was customary to see them with their faces as dark coloured as their coats. At length an order came for their removal; and, as they had to go down Hollowstone which was very narrow, the people planted themselves on the top of the rock, well provided with night soil in vessels from the privies . . . with which they plentifully supplied the Troopers as they passed below.' Sutton, *op. cit.*, p. 178.

of soap and domestic utensils, a more enlightened attitude to nursing and child care, better facilities for the provision of food supplies, a better water supply— were not equal to the pressure exerted by larger families and the increasingly severe struggle of a lowly paid labour force to meet the difficulties of rising prices and cyclical unemployment. In view of the severities of the time, it is remarkable that the rise was not higher; but it came within striking distance of the bad years from 1720-40. The general death rate, however, kept well below it, and since vaccination had so far made no impact on the ravages of small-pox, something must be allowed to the influence of environmental factors for the restraint upon the death rate. By 1800, thanks to the charitable impulse of a local doctor, vaccination was in full swing; and this more than anything else accounted for the fall of the death rate at the end of the period. The power of epidemic disease was now definitely tamed; the death rate might rise under the influence of overcrowding and falling health standards; but it could never again run amok; the town had broken through the demographic barrier that had formerly kept its population in check, and it was now launched on the uncharted path of continuous growth.

APPENDIX

1. The basis for the rates which follow consists of the baptisms, burials and marriages of the three parishes of St. Mary's, St. Peter's and St. Nicholas's taken from January to December and quinquennial population estimates calculated from the difference between births and deaths and counting back from the enumeration made of Deering in 1739 and Sutton in 1779 and forward from the Hearth Tax of 1674. The births and deaths have been arrived at by inflating baptisms by 1·15 and burials by 1·10. The use of these inflation ratios for the whole period is open to serious objection. For this reason the uninflated raw figures are also presented in five-yearly averages.

2. The marriages have been inflated by 1·10 (until 1754) after deducting those marriages in which both partners came from outside. These marriages are very numerous: between 1700 and 1754 (inclusive) they numbered 1,918 compared with 5,149 marriages in which at least one partner was a native. It may be presumed that some of the marriages from outside would be contracted by immigrants who would settle in the town after marriage and these, together with the unrecorded marriages of Quakers, Roman Catholics and others (e.g. in parishes outside the town) make some inflation necessary though the particular ratio chosen may be open to question.

3. The registration of child deaths between 1703 and 1719 (inclusive) in St. Peter's Parish was defective and a correction by inflating by 1·3 was made to bring them into line with the preceding and succeeding years. I am grateful to Mr C. W. J. Granger, M.A., for his advice on this and on other matters relating to the statistical aspect of this study.

	Population	Natural increase	Immigration	Birth rate per thou	General death rate per thou	Child death rate per thou	Marriage rate per thou
1700	7,000			35·55	33·13	17·91	10·81
		+102	98				
1705	7,200			34·31	31·93	16·37	9·56
		− 55	80				
1710	7,225			31·61	35·26	19·95	7·52
		− 49	824				
1715	8,000			35·33	34·35	19·41	10·07
		+157	843				
1720	9,000			35·29	37·23	17·91	10·36
		− 271	1,071				
1725	9,800			39·73	43·93	23·17	10·93
		− 614	814				
1730	10,000			36·25	44·40	22·68	11·48
		+333	267				
1735	10,600			39·06	40·06	23·83	11·17
		− 193	363				
1740	10,770			38·35	48·33	23·10	11·62
		− 350	500				
1745	10,920			38·75	31·17	15·17	11·68
		+343	787				
1750	12,050			37·96	34·27	17·45	10·50
		+187	613				
1755	12,850			38·46	32·00	16·64	10·83
		+444	506				
1760	13,800			36·22	31·25	15·93	10·10
		+ 38	482				
1765	14,320			38·63	36·32	17·10	11·49
		+323	597				
1770	15,340			40·32	38·54	21·44	11·06
		+400	770				
1775	16,510			43·03	34·27	18·67	12·22
		+557	883				
1780	17,950			40·67	35·64	17·45	10·72
		+687	1,393				
1785	20,030			42·92	35·85	20·13	12·30
		+952	1,818				
1790	22,800			46·29	33·94	19·11	12·51
		+1,239	1,311				
1795	25,350			45·38	35·16	21·76	12·01
		+1,739	1,772				
1801	28,861			41·07	30·79	17·25	13·42

			Child	
	Baptisms	*Burials*	*burials*	*Marriages*

Uninflated five-yearly averages of:

	Baptisms	Burials	Child burials	Marriages
1698–1702	216·4	210·8	114·0	68·8
1703–7	214·8	209·0	107·1	62·6
1708–12	198·6	231·6	131·0	49·4
1713–17	245·8	249·8	141·2	73·2
1718–22	276·2	304·6	146·6	84·8
1723–7	338·6	391·4	206·4	97·4
1728–32	315·2	403·6	206·2	104·4
1733–7	360·0	386·0	229·6	107·6
1738–42	359·2	473·2	226·2	113·8
1743–7	368·0	309·4	150·6	116·0
1748–52	397·8	375·4	191·2	115·0
1753–7	429·8	373·8	194·4	139·2
1758–62	434·6	392·0	199·8	139·4
1763–7	481·0	472·8	222·6	164·6
1768–72	537·8	537·4	299·0	169·6
1773–7	617·8	514·4	280·2	201·8
1778–82	634·8	581·6	284·8	192·4
1783–7	747·6	652·8	366·6	249·6
1788–92	917·8	703·4	396·2	285·2
1793–7	1,000·4	810·2	501·4	304·4
1798–1802	1,030·6	807·8	452·6	387·2

4. A comparison of the data provided by the register and the 'Abstract of the Answers', etc., published in connexion with the Census Returns of 1801 and 1811 shows some disturbing discrepancies. On nine occasions between 1760 and 1800 the totals of baptisms and burials given in the Abstract differ by 15 per cent to 33 per cent from those provided by the registers, whether taken from March to March or January to December, and for each year between 1807-10 the baptism totals of the Abstract compared with those of the registers are short by 425 (33·8 per cent), 499 (41·0 per cent), 467 (39·4 per cent), 590 (49·2 per cent) respectively. There are also discrepancies in the marriage record but not on this scale. The printed registers, edited by W. P. W. Phillimore, T. M. Blagg and J. Ward (1898-1902) have been used throughout. The case for a large-scale re-examination of the registers becomes more urgent in view of these difficulties regarding the printed Abstract.

5. The quinquennial totals of population and quotas for immigration are necessarily very speculative, and are in the nature of guesswork in the light of the only known facts, i.e. the entries in the registers and the enumeration of population in 1739 (10,720), 1779 (17,711) and 1801 (28,861). Any change in the ratios of inflation would, of course, alter these totals, and the rates associated with them. They are presented for what they are worth as a basis of comparison throughout the century.

6. The effect of the 'famine' of 1709-10 seems to be reflected in the marked fall of the marriage and birth rates rather than the death rate. It should be noted, however, that the fall in the number of marriages began in 1708, which was also the year of the highest mortality, much higher than 1709. The figures (uninflated) for this obscure period are as follows:

	1707	1708	1709	1710	1711	1712
Baptisms	241	221	193	188	177	214
Burials	241	287	200	217	265	189
Marriages	56	42	50	45	50	60

7. The fall in the general death rate in 1745 was proportionately greater than that of the child death rate and the rise in 1770 was entirely confined to the child death rate; but in 1780 there was a rise in the general death rate and a fall in the child death rate probably connected with the peculiar incidence of the influenza epidemic of 1780-1 on adults (see above, p. 346). Possibly this also helps to explain the fall in the marriage rate and birth rate at this time. The relatively low marriage rates of the period 1750-60 would probably be a reflection of the very high child mortality rates of 1725-40, though the effect would be largely neutralized by heavy immigration.

8. The lower general death rate between 1775-95 compared with that of 1765 and 1770 implies considerable saving of adult lives since the child death rate shows a substantial rise, but the fall in 1801 (1798-1803) is entirely confined to child deaths and is almost certainly due to the introduction of free vaccination in 1800.

14

A DEMOGRAPHIC STUDY OF THE BRITISH DUCAL FAMILIES

T. H. HOLLINGSWORTH

From: *Population Studies*, Vol. XI, No. 1, 1957, 4–26

Editor's Note: This article summarizes the first part of Mr Hollingsworth's work on the British peerage which has since been extended to cover the lesser ranks of the nobility. This has now been published as a special number of *Population Studies*, Vol. XVIII (1964), under the title: 'The Demography of the British Peerage'. The text has been extensively revised by the author.

Introduction

A TOTAL of 1,908 individuals were traced who were the legitimate offspring of British kings, queens, dukes or duchesses, and who were born between 1330 and the end of 1954. The former date was chosen because it was the birth-year of the first duke created (the Duke of Cornwall). These 1,908 individuals form the population under study. Demographic data about each individual were collected, coded and transferred to punched cards. The present paper presents the analysis of this information.

The amount of information available about such exalted people is very great, and since about 1700 seems to be almost as complete demographically as it is reasonable to desire. In 1676 Sir William Dugdale produced his *Baronage*, and in 1710 Arthur Collins his *Peerage*, and these works account for the great improvement in the completeness of peerage records at that time. Since 1780, the only information missing at all often relates to the birth dates of dukes' wives, and the families of dukes' daughters who married commoners. On the other hand, before 1500 it seems clear that quite large numbers of dukes' children are not mentioned at all.

Many studies using peerage records have been undertaken, particularly in the second half of the nineteenth century. The methods used were often fallacious and the results were sometimes very odd. A careful study of the complete peerage would be interesting from many points of view: historical, demographic, sociological and biological. The dukes and kings have been chosen because they form a group just large enough for some significant results to emerge, and because data relating to that group are more complete than for any other. The work of Peller[1] on European ruling families is the

---

[1] Peller, S., *Studies on Mortality since the Renaissance*: (A) 'General Mortality of Women', *Bull. Hist. Med.*, XIII, 1943 pp. 422–41; (B) 'Maternal Mortality', *ibid.*, pp. 441–7; (C) 'Infancy and Childhood', *ibid.*, pp. 447–61; (D) 'Twins and Singletons', *Bull. Hist. Med.*, XVI, 1944, pp. 362–81; (E)

only really comparable study, and our results have been compared with his.

It is extremely important that the data on which a study of this kind is based should be reliable. No conclusions can be drawn if much suspicion rests upon the accuracy of the raw material on births, marriages and deaths.

The major problem is posed by an entry stating that someone was, for example, 'born about 1500'. If we include such persons, we need to be very careful how we mix them with those whose dates are exact. I have taken this course, although other workers, almost without exception,[2] have simply omitted all persons for whom the information was imperfect. It is possible that these omitted persons may form a special class, different from the rest. Yet the assumption that omitting 20 or 30 per cent of the population will make no difference is usually tacitly made—and is therefore never properly discussed; at the outset it is not easy to guess in what way they will be different, but that is no reason for assuming that no difference exists. In general, we might expect that the group with imperfect records, which I have included and most of my predecessors have not, and whose size we do not know, will tend to contain people with uneventful lives, the obscure, the unmarried, the short-lived, the childless, and that it will be mainly drawn from the early part of the period investigated. Everything depends on the care with which we attempt to reconstruct these partially recorded lives.

System of Classification of Information

All dates, except those explicitly stated, were classified into four grades. There are thus really five grades in all, viz.

(i) 'Blank', or 'Z'—assumed correct.

(ii) 'A'—known to within an interval of one year, e.g. 'Died 1731' will often be rendered 'Died A 1 July 1731'. This is the *worst* kind of 'A', because the possible margin of error is a *whole* year. In fact, owing to the old style (pre-1752) calendar system, '1731' *might* mean as late as 24 March 1732. We should then have a margin of nearly 15 months. I have assumed, however, that all dates are in new style unless there is evidence to the contrary.

There are better 'A' dates than this. 'Born August 1771' for example, would be rendered 'born A 16 August 1771', but the month is now recorded. Baptismal and burial dates were adjusted by 19 and 6 days respectively to give 'A' dates of birth and death, the month for which I assumed was then correct.[3]

(iii) 'B'—known to within 5 years. For example, 'About 1620' would be 'B 1 July 1620', and '1670 or 1671' would be 'B 1 January 1671'. The possible range of dates is only two years in the latter instance: in the former, it is an indeterminate, but presumably small, number. Many other considerations may lead to 'B' dates, but the accuracy is never as good as one year, or it would be 'A'.

'Man's Reproductive Activity', *Bull. Hist. Med.*, xxi, 1947, pp. 51-65; (F) 'Men's Mortality', *ibid.*, pp. 66-101; 'Mortality, Past and Present', *Population Studies*, i, 1948, pp. 405-56. See Part I, p. 87, above.

[2] One exception was T. R. Edmonds, 'On the Duration of Life in the English Peerage', *The Lancet*, 10 February 1838, pp. 705-9.

[3] Sometimes the month so found might be one out (a baptism on 19 June becomes a birth on A 31 May) because the 19 and 6 day intervals were chosen without any real investigation of the problem, but they are presumably sensible.

(iv) 'C' dates are little more than guesses of a less wild kind than

(v) 'D' dates—a class which was introduced half way through when it was found that many 'C' dates were correct to within 10 or 15 years, but a few were based on practically no evidence at all. Women, in particular, sometimes married outside the circle of the aristocracy, and were not traced after their marriage. Thus 'married 1536' may be the last information we know of a daughter. If she was stated to have had issue, we know she must have lived a little longer at least, and perhaps her death would be 'D 1 July 1576'—a pure guess, liable to a 50-year range of possible error.

The division between C and D dates is thus arbitrary. For some purposes, where information in 5-year age groups was required, C and D dates or ages were not punched, but the Z, A and B grades were always punched. Sometimes a B age (say 29 years 11 months) would be put into a group (25-29 years in this case) which may easily have been in error, but no attempt was made to relate the certainty of the age to the actual 5-year groupings used.

I have been led to produce a more complete genealogical account of the immediate families of the British dukes than was in existence. This was not my main task, but I tried to perform it with great care. An extension to earls might take about three times as long, although the numbers would be about six times as large, since many of the books of reference need never be consulted, and the forms with slight modifications could be used as they stand.

Mortality

1. *Introduction*

We may divide the population into seven groups, by date of birth, viz. 1330-1479, 1480-1679, 1680-1729, 1730-79, 1780-1829, 1830-79, 1880-1954. The main considerations in deciding how to choose the groups were (*a*) to have roughly the same number in each group, (*b*) to have equal intervals of time as far as possible, (*c*) to have sufficient numbers for sampling errors to be small and (*d*) to have enough groups to show secular trends. This leaves some room for choice, particularly in the number of groups, but Peller's work[4] is similar to mine in some respects, and I have chosen groups which would correspond most closely with his, so that comparisons could be made. His groups were: 1480-1579, 1580-1679, 1680-1779, 1780-1829, 1830-79, 1880-1936. In my last cohort (born 1880-1954) some dukes' children do not contribute to a table (e.g. of mortality over the age of 20) and so the headings have been altered where this applies (to, for example, 1880-1934).

The simplest way of expressing mortality as a whole is the crude death rate. However, the base population is difficult to compute from genealogical data and no attempt has been made to calculate crude death rates. The cohort expectation of life, on the other hand, can be found quite easily. It is, in fact, the average age at death of all the people in the cohort. Its reciprocal, the death rate in the corresponding stationary population, may be used as an alternative index of mortality trends.

Before proceeding further, it may be well to emphasize the difference

[4] S. Peller, *loc. cit.*

between the cohort expectation of life and the expectation of life in a hypo-thetical stationary population whose mortality is defined to be the same at every age as that prevailing at some prescribed epoch. This latter expectation is used by insurance companies and it cannot be determined without careful manipula-tion of the death figures. Its great advantage is that it gives information about current mortality, whereas cohort expectations cannot be properly completed until the whole cohort has died. My 1830-79 birth group, nearly all of whom are dead, yields a reasonable life expectation, for example, but the post-1880 group can only be dealt with by making various assumptions—we can only guess their mortality after the age of 75.

Cohort life tables do, however, have the merit that they deal with actual people who really lived and died. Actuaries' life tables are artificial, in that they do not relate to actual persons.[5]

The expectation of life was not obtained by adding the ages at death of members of the cohort and dividing by their number. This would not yield sufficiently detailed information. Moreover, in the earlier cohorts most ages at death were not accurately known, and had to be dealt with carefully. Abridged life tables, giving the actual numbers surviving for successive quinquennia, were constructed. To estimate the years lived in the quinquennium, x to $x+5$, the formula $2\frac{1}{2}(l_x + l_{x+5})$ was used. This procedure is not quite ideal, but it is good enough, and reduced the anomalies which would arise if single years had been taken. The only exception to the rule had to be made for the first quinquennium of life. A study of various life tables, in particular those of Russell,[6] suggested $l_0 + 4l_5$ as a suitable formula. This assumes that children dying under 5 die at a mean age of 1 year.[7]

In the last two cohorts some people are still alive; the rule for finding the years lived by the population in each quinquennium was not altered, but the numbers surviving were found from the successive quinquennial mortality rates.

2. Corrections to the Data

It is highly likely that many children dying in infancy in the early groups will not have been enumerated. There will not, however, be many omissions at older ages, although the ages at death are not very accurately known for the first cohort of males and the first three cohorts of females.

It seems reasonable to assume, therefore, that the only errors of omission are of children who died before reaching the age of five and who tend to be ignored by published peerage records. After due thought, the following numbers were added to correct for this tendency:

Cohort born 1330-1479   25 boys   30 girls
Cohort born 1480-1679   0 boys   8 girls

Every figure in this article which includes these additional children has been

[5] See L. I. Dublin and M. Spiegelmann, 'Current versus Generation Life Tables', *Human Biology*, XIII, 1941, pp. 439-56.
[6] J. C. Russell, *British Medieval Population* (Albuquerque 1948), pp. 175-91.
[7] In modern times the mean age at death of this group will be less than 1 year, but since only a few die, the difference in the years lived by the population during the ages 0-4 becomes negligible whether an age of 1, $\frac{1}{2}$ or $\frac{1}{4}$ year is assumed.

marked with an asterisk. The main considerations used in finding the numbers were: the sex-ratio at birth, the ratio of child mortality rates between the sexes, and the child mortality rates in the third cohort. We have implicitly assumed that the proportions of children who died under the age of five, and who were in fact noticed in the peerages were:

Cohort born 1330–1479	Boys 44%	Girls 14%
Cohort born 1480–1679	Boys 100%	Girls 81%

The accuracy of the age at death is crucial to a study of mortality. The proportion of ages at death in each of the five classifications, Z, A, B, C and D are therefore given (per cent) in Table 1.

TABLE 1

Accuracy of age at death

	Males					Females				
Cohort born	Z	A	B	C	D	Z	A	B	C	D
1330–1479	22*	15*	26*	15*	22*	7*	18*	10*	16*	49*
1480–1679	36	27	20	14	3	24*	22*	17*	22*	15*
1680–1729	56	22	12	10	—	36	22	17	19	7
1730–79	83	10	6	2	—	76	12	7	3	1
1780–1829	94	3	2	1	—	96	2	1	1	—
1830–79	100	—	—	—	—	99	1	—	—	—
1880–1954	100	—	—	—	—	99	—	1	—	—

Group D includes the additional children added as a correction for incompleteness.

Table 1 may be used as a guide to the relative value of the estimates of expectation of life quoted.

3. Results

(i) General Mortality

TABLE 2

Expectation of life at birth (all deaths)

	Expectation of life at birth (in years)		Corresponding death rate per 1,000 living		
Cohort born	Males	Females	Males	Females	Both Sexes
1330–1479	24·0*	32·9*	41·7*	30·4*	35·2*
1480–1679	27·0	33·1*	37·1	30·2*	33·4*
1680–1729	33·0	33·6	30·3	29·7	30·0
1730–79	44·8	48·2	22·3	20·8	21·5
1780–1829	47·8	55·4	20·9	18·0	19·5
1830–79	49·8	61·5	20·1	16·3	18·2
1880–1954	54·6	70·1	18·3	14·3	16·2

Except in the third and fourth cohorts, the excess expectation of life for females shown in Table 2 is surprisingly large. An obvious explanation is the high incidence of deaths from violence, both in the early years, when civil wars and executions for treason were fairly frequent, and in the later years when a large number of young men were killed in world wars. It is therefore instructive to remove all violent deaths from the calculations, and assume that the later mortality of such people would have been the same as for the rest of the population.

104 men and 9 women suffered deaths from violence: amongst the men who died over the age of 15 the proportion of violent deaths to all deaths is shown in Table 3.

TABLE 3

Violent deaths

Cohort born	1330–1479	1480–1679	1680–1729	1730–79	1780–1829	1830–79	1880–1939
Violent deaths (%)	46	19	10	4	5	8	48

The figure for the last cohort in Table 3 is particularly high because most of the members are still alive and will presumably die peaceful deaths.

The revised expectations of life, omitting all violent deaths, are given in Table 4.

TABLE 4

Expectation of life at birth (non-violent deaths only)

Cohort born	1330–1479	1480–1679	1680–1729	1730–79	1780–1829	1830–79	1880–1954
Males	31·0*	30·1	34·7	45·8	49·5	51·5	62·5
Females	33·0*	33·9*	33·7	48·2	55·4	61·7	70·2

Table 4 shows that violent deaths would account for the difference between males and females in the early groups, but since 1780 the discrepancy is still rather large.

The other features of Table 4 are the relative stability of the figures in the first three cohorts, the great increase taking place about 1730, and the steady increase since that time. In the last cohort, the numbers become small when violent deaths are omitted and the increase over the previous cohort's expectation should be treated with caution.

The most remarkable variation is the increase in the expectation of life at birth shown between 1680–1729 and 1730–79. Deaths from violence were very few at that time and it makes little difference whether or not they are included when considering the change that had occurred. For male babies, the increase in expectation of life at birth was 11·8 years or 36 per cent, for female babies 14·6 years or 43 per cent.

(ii) *Child Mortality*. Deaths under the age of 5 have already been mentioned in connexion with adjustments for under-enumeration. The proportions of all children born who died before their fifth birthdays are shown (per cent) in Table 5.

TABLE 5

Children dying under 5 years

Cohort born	1330–1479	1480–1679	1680–1729	1730–79	1780–1829	1830–79	1880–1954
Males	36*	34	27	20	18	14	6
Females	29*	29*	28	15	9	6	5

It will be seen that the reduction in child mortality began early in the eighteenth century and has continued ever since. In contrast, there was very little decrease in child mortality in the general population of England and Wales from the time registration of births and deaths began in 1838 until 1901.[8]

The great difference shown in Table 5 between the sexes for the cohorts born 1780–1879 is peculiar. In the general population the ratio of female to male child mortality fell with falling mortality rates, but not by nearly as much as it did in the cohorts born from 1680 to 1879. The numbers are so small, however, that it is just possible that the very low ratios are caused by chance.

(iii) *Mortality over the Age of 5 years.* The expectations of life at the age of 5 years are important, as distinguishing between the effect of child mortality and other mortality. They are given in Table 6.

TABLE 6

Expectation of life at age 5 years (all deaths)

Cohort born	1330–1479	1480–1679	1680–1729	1730–79	1780–1829	1830–79	1880–1949
Males	31·9	35·8	40·0	50·7	53·1	52·9	52·9
Females	40·9	41·0	41·5	51·4	56·1	60·1	68·6

Deaths from violence account for a great deal of the difference between the expectations of life of the two sexes. If they are omitted, we have Table 7.

TABLE 7

Expectation of life at age 5 years (non-violent deaths only)

Cohort born	1330–1479	1480–1679	1680–1729	1730–79	1780–1829	1830–79	1880–1949
Males	42·8	40·3	42·4	51·9	55·1	54·9	61·2
Females	41·0	42·1	41·6	51·4	56·1	60·3	69·2

The difference between the two sexes in Table 7 is small until the cohort born between 1830 and 1879 is reached, most of whom died in the present century. The difference of 5·4 years compares with 4·9 years at the same age in the 1952 life table[9] for England and Wales. The last cohort shows a widening of the gap between the sexes to 8·0 years, a very large amount, but liable to

[8] The 1838–54 life table shows 26 per cent dying under 5, the 1891–1900 life table 23 per cent.
[9] *United Nations Demographic Yearbook*, 1954.

considerable error since the number of non-violent deaths is relatively small.

The change in expectation of life at age 5 between the third and fourth cohorts is as marked as the change in expectation of life at birth. A great decline in adult mortality must have been taking place during the second half of the eighteenth century. The further increase in expectation of life after the fourth cohort is relatively small until the last cohort is reached. Although the number of deaths on which the last expectations of life are based is small, the increase is probably real, reflecting improvement in public health, particularly since 1919.

The variations in expectation of life and probability of survival at higher ages are what we should expect. Exclusion of violent deaths considerably reduces the difference between male and female mortality. The actual expectations of life are given in Tables 8 and 9.

TABLE 8

Expectations of life at adult ages (all deaths)

Cohort born	1330–1479	1480–1679	1680–1729	1730–79	1780–1829	1830–79	1880–1934 (etc.)
Males							
Age 20	21·7	26·3	30·0	39·9	42·7	39·8	39·8
Age 40	13·1	18·3	22·4	25·7	27·0	27·2	29·4
Age 60	10·0	9·2	13·2	12·7	13·3	13·4	14·7
Females							
Age 20	31·1	29·1	35·4	44·2	44·8	46·2	54·3
Age 40	19·2	18·3	24·9	29·9	32·8	31·5	37·4
Age 60	8·2	10·3	12·3	16·1	17·6	16·6	21·2

TABLE 9

Expectation of life at adult ages (non-violent deaths only)

Cohort born	1330–1479	1480–1679	1680–1729	1730–79	1780–1829	1830–79	1880–1934 (etc.)
Males							
Age 20	31·5	30·5	32·8	41·3	44·1	41·9	49·4
Age 40	18·7	19·9	23·0	26·0	27·4	28·0	31·8
Age 60	12·3	9·2	13·3	12·7	13·3	13·4	18·1
Females							
Age 20	31·1	29·6	35·5	44·2	44·8	46·4	54·9
Age 40	19·3	18·5	25·1	29·9	32·8	31·8	37·4
Age 60	8·4	10·3	12·6	16·1	17·6	16·6	21·2

After the age of 40, the difference in expectation of life between the cohorts born 1680-1729 and 1730-79 is slightly less than between those born 1480-1679 and 1680-1729. The centre of the period of rapidly falling mortality was thus about 1755.

To complete the results, tables of survivors are given (Tables 10 and 11).

TABLE 10

Survivors per 100 born (all deaths)

Cohort born	1330–1479	1480–1679	1680–1729	1730–79	1780–1829	1830–79	1880–1954 (etc.)
Males							
Age 0	100	100	100	100	100	100	100
Age 5	64*	65	73	80	82	86	94
Age 20	54*	54	63	73	74	82	90
Age 40	28*	33	41	61	66	66	68
Age 60	8*	15	23	42	47	49	50
Median Age	23*	22	29	53	58	58	60
Females							
Age 0	100	100	100	100	100	100	100
Age 5	71*	71*	72	85	91	94	95
Age 20	61*	65*	59	72	84	92	94
Age 40	43*	44*	43	62	69	80	87
Age 60	19*	17*	29	48	56	63	77
Median Age	36*	36*	32	55	64	68	78

TABLE 11

Survivors per 100 born (non-violent deaths only)

Cohort born	1330–1479	1480–1679	1680–1729	1730–79	1780–1829	1830–79	1880–1954 (etc.)
Males							
Age 0	100	100	100	100	100	100	100
Age 5	64*	66	73	80	82	86	94
Age 20	58*	56	63	73	76	82	90
Age 40	44*	40	45	63	69	69	84
Age 60	19*	21	26	44	50	53	62
Median Age	30*	26	32	56	60	61	72
Females							
Age 0	100	100	100	100	100	100	100
Age 5	71*	71*	72	85	91	94	95
Age 20	61*	67*	59	72	84	92	94
Age 40	43*	45*	43	62	69	80	88
Age 60	19*	18*	29	48	56	64	78
Median Age	36*	37*	32	55	64	69	79

[10] *Loc. cit.*, Papers C and F. See pp. 90–99 above.

(iv) *Comparison with Peller's Results.*[10] Peller's rates for 1480–1579 and 1580–1679 have been averaged to give a comparable figure. The data related to the ruling families of Europe. Tables 12 and 13 compare expectations of life.

TABLE 12

Expectation of life at age 15

Cohort born	British ducal families		European ruling families	
	Males	Females	Males	Females
1480–1679	27·7	33·2	31·2	35·9
1680–1779	37·8	41·6	36·8	39·7
1780–1879	45·0	49·6	43·7	45·6

TABLE 13

Expectation of life at age 50

| Cohort born | British ducal families | | European ruling families | |
	Males	Females	Males	Females
1480–1679	15·0 (a)	13·7	13·4	14·8
1680–1779	19·3	21·5	16·5	17·8
1780–1879	20·5	24·2	18·7	21·0

(a) based on only 34 men

The British ducal families have had an advantage over the European ruling families for the last two centuries. Previously the position seems to be reversed.

Tables 14, 15 and 16 compare survival rates at three periods of life.

For child mortality, Peller does not distinguish between boys and girls; and the data are tabulated by date of the parents' marriage. The best comparison we can make is therefore with the mortality under 16 of the children of dukes' sons.

TABLE 14

Child mortality

| | British ducal families | European ruling families | |
Father born	% children dying under 16	Parents married	% children dying under 15
1480–1679	31·1	1500–1699	34·1
1680–1779	21·1	1700–1799	32·3
1780–1829	15·9	1800–1849	21·3
1830–1879	7·7	1850–1899	9·0
1880–1934	5·3	1900–1930	3·6

The mortality is decidedly lower in Britain than on the Continent, except in the last group, where the number of deaths involved is very small (8 out of 151), so that the rate is liable to considerable random error. If only about 90 per cent of dukes' children born between 1480–1679 and dying under the age of 5 were noticed in the peerages, however, as we have assumed, then the figure of 31·1 per cent of dukes' sons' children in that group is likely to be too low by at least one-tenth. The British and European mortalities would then be almost the same.

TABLE 15

Mortality between 15 and 50 years (% dying)

| Cohort born | British ducal families | | European ruling families | |
	Males	Females	Males	Females
1480–1679	62·9	54·5	57·0	45·9
1680–1779	44·7	37·5	43·4	37·3
1780–1879	29·2	23·4	27·3	26·5

Male mortality has always been rather higher among British dukes' sons, but dukes' daughters' mortality has fallen more rapidly than that of the women of the ruling families of Europe, and is now the lower of the two.

TABLE 16

Mortality between 50 and 70 years

| Cohort born | British ducal families | | European ruling families | |
	Males	Females	Males	Females
1480–1679	67·6	80·0	77·4	69·9
1680–1779	52·1	43·1	65·9	56·3
1780–1879	48·3	33·7	56·1	45·7

The treatment is the same as in Table 15, but the numbers, especially in the first period, are rather small.

The general conclusion we can draw from Tables 12 to 16 is that mortality among the British aristocracy may have been higher for those born before 1680, but it has since been lower than among the European princes.

Nuptiality

1. *Age at Marriage*

The age at marriage of the dukes' children has varied considerably over the years, but is presumably typical of the age at marriage of the aristocracy in general. The method of analysing nuptiality most suitable to study such changes is to consider the depletion of the number of bachelors and spinsters through marriage. Thus in the 1330–1479 female cohort, there were 51 spinsters at the age of 15, and during the next five years 17 of them married and 2 died, leaving 32 spinsters at the age of 20. The number 'at risk' was 51 – (half the number dying) = 50, and so the probability of marriage was 0·34. The probability of continued spinsterhood was accordingly 0·66.

TABLE 17

Nuptiality

Cohort born	1330–1479	1480–1679	1680–1729	1730–79	1780–1829	1830–79	1880–1939
Males							
Age 15	91	95	99	100	100	100	100
Age 20	70	79	93	97	100	100	100
Age 25	50	49	73	63	80	77	73
Age 30	35	32	57	40	52	44	42
Age 35	14	23	38	34	37	28	30
Age 40	9	19	30	30	26	24	21
Age 45	9	17	24	21	24	22	7
Age 50	9	14	23	21	22	20	5
Eventually	9	7	17	14	16	12	5
Females							
Age 15	64	89	97	100	100	100	100
Age 20	42	45	75	76	89	80	93
Age 25	15	19	37	44	46	53	47
Age 30	12	16	22	26	24	35	22
Age 35	7	11	18	20	20	25	12
Age 40	7	6	17	17	15	25	10
Eventually	7	6	17	14	12	22	7

The product of these last probabilities for each age group up to 15 was 0·64, and so 0·64 × 0·66 = 0·42 is the probability that a girl, living up to the age of 20, would remain single.

The proportions (per cent) of those still single at five-year intervals are shown in Table 17.

There is an obvious decline in frequency of marriage of men under 20 and women under 15, but beyond that, marriage by the age of 25 (or 35) has become steadily less common for dukes' daughters until the last cohort, which reflects twentieth-century conditions. The men show a correspondingly high proportion of bachelors at the age of 35 in the three cohorts born between 1680 and 1829.

TABLE 18

Mean age at marriage

Cohort born	1330–1479	1480–1679	1680–1729	1730–79	1780–1829	1830–79	1880–1939
Males	22·4	24·3	28·6	28·6	30·5	30·0	30·0
Females	17·1	19·5	22·2	24·0	24·7	24·2	24·9

The general increase shown in Table 18 is to be expected, but the women show no decrease in the last cohort.

2. Marriages of Completed Fertility

We define a marriage as being of completed fertility if at its conclusion the wife had reached the age of 45. A very few marriages in which the wife was over 45 at the time of the marriage are thus included in the completed group. There are about 3 per cent of marriages for which our information is so poor that we cannot even guess whether fertility was complete or not. They are allotted in proportion to the two definite groups in order to produce comprehensive results.

TABLE 19

Proportion of marriages in which fertility was complete (per cent)

Cohort born	1330–1479	1480–1679	1680–1729	1730–79	1780–1829	1830–79	1880–1939
Dukes' sons' marriages	15	27	35	60	74	71	44
Dukes' daughters' marriages	24	34	39	58	71	70	44

In the last cohort many marriages are still in existence, although their fertility is as yet incomplete. The difference between the cohorts born 1680–1729 and 1730–79 is remarkable, particularly since men married rather younger in the fourth cohort than in the third.

There is some tendency for the marriages of completed fertility to be those which were contracted when the wife was older than the mean for the cohort.

TABLE 20

Mean age at marriage

Cohort born	Dukes' sons		Dukes' daughters	
	Fertility completed	Fertility not completed	Fertility completed	Fertility not completed
1330–1479	23·2	22·3	20·6	16·0
1480–1679	24·2	24·3	21·7	18·4
1680–1729	31·2	27·3	23·0	21·7
1730–79	28·8	28·2	25·2	22·2
1780–1829	30·1	31·4	25·5	22·9
1830–79	30·7	28·2	24·8	22·9
1880–1939	28·6	28·4	26·1	24·0

The ages of 20 per cent of the wives of dukes' sons are not known, the two worst cohorts being born 1680–1729 (30 per cent) and 1880–1934 (36 per cent). However, using only those whose ages were known, their mean ages at marriage are shown in Table 21.

TABLE 21

Mean age at marriage of wives of dukes' sons

Husband's cohort born	Fertility completed	Fertility not completed	All marriages
1330–1479	26·0	16·2	17·9
1480–1679	22·9	17·7	19·3
1680–1729	26·4	20·1	22·4
1730–79	24·2	21·8	23·4
1780–1829	25·1	22·5	24·5
1830–79	25·3	22·0	24·3
1880–1934	25·8	22·9	24·4

The figures for all marriages agree very closely with those for dukes' daughters, which is satisfactory. The constancy, to within 3½ years, of the mean age at marriage when the fertility of that marriage proved to be complete, is largely accidental; the figure for the first cohort might well have been 20·0 or thereabouts.

Fertility

1. Reliability of the Data

Only legitimate live births were considered, the data for illegitimate births being too incomplete and not so important demographically. It should be remembered, however, that all rates of reproduction and fertility will appear smaller than they really were, because illegitimate births would contribute a small amount (perhaps 10 per cent) to the total fertility of the population. Although reproduction and fertility rates are usually calculated in terms of births per woman, they have also been expressed as births per man, both because there will be greater completeness in the basic information, and because sociologically the population consists of great families governed by male descent, giving the sons a special importance.

In 11 instances, a daughter married and simply 'left issue'. These can be used to estimate the incompleteness of the birth numbers. I have kept such cases separate from those where she 'left with other issue, a son John', for example. This is not a very useful distinction, but it may be used when estimating the proportion of childless marriages. Study of the apparent proportions dying young and of the families known to be incompletely enumerated suggests that in the first cohort, perhaps 25 per cent more births should have been found; in the second about 7 per cent more; in the third 4 per cent more; and in the fourth 2 per cent more. No rates have been corrected to allow for such additional births.

2. *Generation Reproduction Rates*

A simple measure of the fertility of each cohort would be the total number of children born to it, divided by the original number of individuals.

For example, the 100 males in the first cohort had 154 children, and the 91 females (their sisters) had 216 children. Thus 370 children were produced by 191 parents. The ratio, 1·94, is a possible measure of fertility. However, only one parent of each of the 370 children is included in the total of 191, so that a clearer idea of fertility is found by halving the ratio. This halved ratio can be called the generation reproduction rate, and it has the property of being unity when the population is exactly reproducing itself. For the cohort born 1330–1479, the generation reproduction rate is 0·97. The figures are affected by under-enumeration, but this reproduction rate is probably fairly accurate. In the section on mortality, as a correction for under-enumeration, the number of persons in the cohort was increased to 246, and the 370 births recorded should presumably be increased by 25 per cent to 462. In the second cohort the effect of under-enumeration of the base population is negligible.

The corresponding results for the other cohorts are given in Table 22.

TABLE 22

Generation reproduction rates

1330–1479	0·97
1480–1679	1·04
1680–1729	0·80
1730–79	1·51
1780–1829	1·52
1830–79	1·16
1880–1939	0·98[11]

These figures give a general view of the rates of increase or decrease among the aristocracy. The population was apparently stable until 1700 or so, when it began to decrease. It is thought by historians that in the second half of the sixteenth century there was a rapid increase in the general population: as there were very few dukes at that time, only a small proportion of the 1480–1679 cohort were born in 1530–79, the relevant period. Thus any possible high fertility among the aristocracy at that time cannot appear in our figures.

[11] The figure is approximate, those born 1880–1929 being taken as the base, and all the births to members of the cohort being included. Thus the eventual figure is somewhat reduced by those people over 25 who may have further children, but somewhat exaggerated by those under 25 who have already had any. The probable effect is to underestimate fertility.

After a time of failing to reproduce, a great change took place during the middle of the eighteenth century, and the average rate of generation increase was over 1·5[12] for a century. The consequence of this high rate of increase between about 1760 and 1860 would be to multiply the numbers of the aristocrats by about 4·3 during the hundred years. The general population also increased, but not perhaps quite so rapidly. In the later nineteenth century, the rate of increase declined, and at present the aristocracy is probably decreasing slightly.

This superficial treatment gives us the general picture. The period when the great increase was beginning, around 1760, will be especially interesting, since the rise appears to have been much more rapid than the subsequent fall a hundred years later.

In a more thorough analysis a host of factors affecting fertility suggest themselves, not all of which can be considered with such a small body of data. The difference between the reproductivity of the two sexes, mortality, age at marriage, and social position (in this group, well-defined), should certainly be considered.

If the sex ratio among children born to a cohort is assumed to be 105, which is roughly in accordance with general observation, we can produce male and female generation reproduction rates separately. The actual numbers of children by sex are known, but assuming a sex ratio of 105 will tend to give a fairer picture, as it removes some of the chance tendencies towards one sex or the other. The generation reproduction rates are shown in Table 23.

TABLE 23

Generation reproduction rates by sexes

Cohort born	Male	Female	Combined (as above)
1330–1479	0·79	1·16	0·97
1480–1679	0·95	1·14	1·04
1680–1729	0·76	0·83	0·80
1730–79	1·53	1·48	1·51
1780–1829	1·31	1·75	1·52
1830–79	0·96	1·35	1·16
1880–1939	0·84	1·12	0·98

The difference is remarkable. Dukes' sons must have had fewer children than dukes' daughters, since incompleteness in the data will tend to occur in the daughters' families rather than in the sons', the daughters sometimes marrying obscure men, while the sons' families, being in the line of succession, would be kept under observation. Sons also remained unmarried more frequently than daughters.

The peak was reached earlier for males than females: we may guess that the cohort born around 1770 for males, and that around 1800 for females, had the highest reproductivity. It is clear, moreover, that we cannot safely take the two sexes together, especially for the period 1730–1829.

[12] N. H. Carrier has shown that a female rate of 1·416 was found among the general population, born 1838–43. 'An Examination of Generation Fertility in England and Wales', *Population Studies*, IX, 1955, pp. 3–23.

Mortality may be the key to understanding the changes in the generation reproduction rate before the nineteenth century, when birth control began to be important. Griffith[13] had this opinion with respect to the general population. Habakkuk[14] suggested that during the eighteenth century a considerable increase in fertility may also have occurred. For the aristocracy as defined by our population of dukes' children, we may hope to decide what was the cause of the great rise in the reproduction rate, so that in theory the population would be doubled in about 45 years, after a long period of comparative stability.

We have already seen that mortality fell sharply between the 1680-1729 and 1730-79 cohorts. Did it, however, fall enough almost to double the generation reproduction rate?

I have calculated the proportions surviving the age-periods 20-54 for males, and 15-49 for females, for each cohort. Because these ages correspond roughly to the reproductive age group, we should be able to judge how much mortality affected fertility. The percentages who reached the end of each age-period of those who were alive at the beginning of it are shown in Table 24.

TABLE 24

Survival through the reproductive ages

Cohort born	Males (20-54)	Females (15-49)
1330-1479	18	50
1480-1679	34	45
1680-1729	45	57
1730-79	66	69
1780-1829	72	75
1830-79	64	78
1880-1939 etc.	66	87

The low reproductivity of males in the early periods was clearly affected by heavy mortality.

The rise between the third and fourth cohorts is less than 50 per cent for males and less than 25 per cent for females. This is hardly sufficient to account for rises of 100 per cent and 80 per cent in the reproduction rate, although the reproductive performance of each sex is affected by the chance that the spouse will die, thus terminating the marriage, as well as by the chance of the individual's own death. Frequent remarriage would tend to eliminate this effect.

Mortality before the reproductive period must also be taken into consideration. A sharp fall in childhood mortality would help to raise the generation reproduction rate, since a higher proportion would reach marriageable age.

The percentages of males surviving the first 20 years of life, and of females surviving the first 15 years are shown in Table 25

The figures marked with a dagger seem affected by incompleteness, and again the big improvement in mortality took place between the third and fourth cohorts.

[13] G. T. Griffith, *Population Problems of the Age of Malthus*, Cambridge 1926.
[14] H. J. Habakkuk, 'English Population in the Eighteenth Century', *Econ. Hist. Rev.*, 2nd Ser., VI, 1953, pp. 117-33. See above, p. 269.

TABLE 25

Survival up to the reproductive age

Cohort born	Males	Females
1330–1479	67†	88†
1480–1679	54	71†
1680–1729	63	63
1730–79	73	79
1780–1829	74	86
1830–79	82	94
1880–1954	90	94

3. Family Size

The fertility of each cohort may be divided into that which arose from marriages of completed fertility, and that which arose from marriages of incomplete fertility. The mean family sizes for the different groups are shown in Table 26.

TABLE 26

Mean family size

Cohort born	Dukes' sons		Dukes' daughters	
	Fertility completed	Fertility not completed	Fertility completed	Fertility not completed
1330–1479	3·7	1·8	4·6	1·5
1480–1679	5·9	2·7	4·6	2·8
1680–1729	4·3	2·7	4·5	3·1
1730–79	5·6	2·7	5·4	3·7
1780–1829	4·3	3·9	5·6	3·7
1830–79	3·0	2·2	4·0	3·4
1880–1939	2·4	2·2	2·9	2·2

The marriages for which completeness was not known are omitted, since the sizes of such families are almost certainly understated.

When the first marriage was not of completed fertility, it was sometimes followed by a second marriage from which there were children. The total fertility (of all marriages) of the dukes' daughters whose first marriages were not of completed fertility is considerably higher than that first-marriage fertility. Table 27 shows the ultimate size of these daughters' families.

TABLE 27

Mean ultimate family size (fertility not completed with first marriage)

Cohort born	1330–1479	1480–1679	1680–1729	1730–79	1780–1829	1830–79	1880–1939
Family size	2·8	3·5	3·3	4·5	3·8	3·7	2·6

The dukes' daughters born 1330–1679 and 1730–79 are affected most.

4. Childlessness

Where the first marriage was of completed fertility, the proportions child-less are as in Table 28.

TABLE 28

Childless marriages (marriages of completed fertility)

Cohort born	1330–1729	1730–1829	1830–1934
Males	16%	20%	20%
Females	17%	18%	13%

These rates seem rather high. The social system may be partly responsible for these large proportions of childless marriages amongst the aristocracy.

Now, if we take *all* marriages, first and subsequent, fertility completed or not, the proportions of people who never had offspring are those of Table 29.

TABLE 29

Childless marriages (all marriages)

Cohort born	1330–1729	1730–1829	1830–1939
Males	27%	19%	17%
Females	23%	19%	12%

For persons born since 1730, these rates, which allow for remarriage, are remarkably similar to those for the first marriages which were of completed fertility. Apparently after about 1760, the absence of children in a first marriage was quite often made good if the spouse died before the fertile period was completed.

5. Conclusions

The mean family size for females whose first marriage lasted to the end of the fertile period suggests strongly that there was a real rise in fertility in the fourth and fifth cohorts. The rise was from about 4·6 to about 5·5 children, and occurred quite suddenly amongst the group born round about 1730, the dividing date between the third and fourth cohorts. The later fall was even more abrupt, and began amongst the group born about 1830. Thus 1760 and 1860 are the rough limits of the period of high fertility.

Those whose first marriage was not of completed fertility show a high average family size at the same period.

The dukes' sons do not show quite such a clear pattern, but apparently the cohort born 1730–79 had a considerably higher level of fertility than the cohort born 1680–1729. The first marriages of completed fertility do not show a similarly high fertility in the cohort born 1780–1829, but those marriages for which fertility was not completed nevertheless show a remarkable fertility. The only feature which does not conform to the pattern of fertility established for their sisters is the high fertility of dukes' sons in the cohort born 1480–1679. The period is so long that it may well contain fluctuations in fertility, and historical evidence would suggest a high level of fertility for people born about 1530–79.

6. Age-Specific Fertility

We may also study the age-specific fertility of first marriages. The punched cards contain the data required where they were known to within five years. The remainder, which is a relatively small number except in the two earliest cohorts, has been distributed among the groups, for trying to estimate the actual dates (C and D) from the original forms would be tedious. There is a danger of placing all the births at the most likely age, and it would lend more respectability to the figures than they deserve.

Using Tait's law,[15] we may fit a regression line to the age-specific fertility rates of each female cohort. We thus obtain some idea of the range within which the actual fertility of the cohort should be. The total fertility between the ages of 20 and 49 is shown in Table 30, which takes no account of possible under-enumeration of births.

TABLE 30

Female fertility, 20-49, births per married woman

Cohort born	Regression estimate	95% confidence range	Direct calculation
1680–1729	5·12	4·80 to 5·44	4·98
1730–79	7·00	5·84 to 8·16	7·29
1780–1829	7·84	7·49 to 8·19	7·91
1830–79	5·87	5·12 to 6·62	5·67
1880–1939	4·82	3·81 to 5·83	4·81

The effect of the regression technique is to reduce the two highest estimates, and raise the three lowest ones.

Tait's law, using single years of age, sterility at age 50 and $k = 1·5$ per cent per year, gives a value of 6·975 for Edinburgh and Glasgow women in 1855 aged 20-49. At that date the fertility of dukes' daughters was falling rapidly from 7·84 to 5·87; it may well have been close to that of ordinary women of 1855.

The only two pairs of consecutive cohorts where pooling of the data would be statistically tenable are the second and third and the fourth and fifth. 1680-1729, 1730-1829, and 1830-1939 are thus possibly natural periods in the demographic history of the highest social class.

It would be agreeable if we could show that the fertility of women born before 1830 had always been at the same high level, averaging about 7½ children per woman who married at 20 and neither died nor lost her husband until she was past 50. When we remember that other evidence[16] suggests that about one-eighth of marriages in this social class are naturally sterile, this represents a very high level of fertility among the remainder.

Lorimer et al.[17] found that about 8 births per woman was the highest average fertility ever observed in practice among a large number of people. Under-

---

[15] J. Matthews Duncan, *Fecundity, Fertility, Sterility and Allied Topics* (Edinburgh 1866), p. 213. Also P. G. Tait, 'Note on Formulæ representing the Fecundity and Fertility of Women', *Trans. Roy. Soc. Edin.*, XXIV, 1866, pp. 481-90.

[16] e.g. T. B. Sprague, 'On the Probability that a Marriage entered into by a Man of any Age will be fruitful', *Proc. Roy. Soc. Edin.*, XIV, 1887, pp. 327-46.

[17] F. Lorimer (ed.), *Culture and Human Fertility*, UNESCO 1954.

enumeration of births, and marriage before 20 place the 1730-1829 dukes' daughters in just this class. Is there any evidence that the 1680-1729 cohort should be placed so high? Now 5 out of the 87 women in the cohort who married, or about 6 per cent, left 'issue', number not stated. Of the remaining 82, 17 proved sterile. The 65 fertile women had, at least, 307 children by all marriages, or 4·72 per woman. Thus the remaining 5 may be allowed 23·6 children between them: say 22 by their first marriages (I have not checked whether any of them married twice). This would only raise the number of children by first marriages from 293 to 315, or by about 7½ per cent. The consequent rise in the estimate of total fertility (20-49) is from 5·12 to 5·51. Moreover, the same argument would raise the fertility of the 1730-79 cohort by about 3 per cent (7·00 to 7·24 children per woman). The 1730-1829 cohorts now appear more uniform than ever, and almost as markedly different from the 1680-1729 cohort as before.

TABLE 31

Age-specific fertility rates

Males Ages Cohort born	20-4	25-9	30-4	35-9	40-4	45-9	50-4	Total 20-54
1680-1729	1·94	1·68	1·56	1·31	0·88	0·47	0·30	8·14
1730-79	1·84	2·03	1·91	1·32	0·98	0·40	0·08	8·52
1780-1829	1·81	1·99	1·65	1·32	0·70	0·34	0·08	7·89
1830-79	1·94	1·71	1·02	0·73	0·45	0·14	0·09	6·08
1880-1934	1·83	1·18	1·07	0·54	0·37	0·16	0·04	5·19

Females Ages Cohort born	15-19	20-4	25-9	30-4	35-9	40-4	45-9	Total 15-49
1680-1729 (a)	1·99	1·70	1·44	1·01	0·65	0·18	0·00	6·97
1730-79 (a)	1·84	2·13	2·09	1·64	1·04	0·36	0·03	9·13
1780-1829	2·63	2·58	2·15	1·52	1·10	0·54	0·02	10·54
1830-79	2·31	2·09	1·66	1·16	0·51	0·23	0·02	7·98
1880-1939	0·00	1·97	1·32	0·76	0·58	0·18	0·00	4·81

(a) The rates for the female cohorts born 1680-1729 and 1730-1779 should probably be about 7·5% and 3·3% higher respectively, to allow for families described as 'issue', number not stated.

The second possible explanation of the difference is the kind of husband married. Peers have large families, and there are complete records of their number; commoners seem to have smaller families, and records are poor. However, the average number of children born to dukes' daughters marrying peers rose from 4·1 (1680-1729) to 6·3 (1730-79). This will be partly explicable by falling mortality and earlier marriage, but the smaller increase from 3·4 to 4·5 observed for the total number of marriages, was, as we have seen, too large to be explained in such ways. The proportion of daughters who married peers remained constant at 52 per cent over the two cohorts.

A third possible explanation of the rise would be the omission of large numbers of children who 'died young' born to the first cohort. Interpreting 'died young' as died under 16, the apparent proportions dying young were successively 28·7 per cent and 16·3 per cent. The fall in apparent mortality was thus very great; the fall in real mortality can hardly have been any greater.

We conclude that the higher fertility of dukes' daughters born after 1730 compared with those born before 1730 was real, and it remained at a high level for a century before it began to fall.

Further Topics

Four minor demographic aspects of the population are discussed briefly:

(1) *The Marriages of Eldest Sons and their Brothers.* We know whether a duke's son was the eldest or not. Since the whole life of the eldest son was a preparation for the time when he would inherit, eldest sons should be treated as a distinct class. The problem immediately arises of what to do when the actual first born son died in infancy, and his next brother became the heir. In the eighteenth century, a large proportion—about 30 per cent—of eldest sons never grew to maturity, and so some younger sons were virtually eldest sons. I therefore made the following rule: when the eldest son died under 16, the next living brother at the time of his death is counted as a 'virtual' eldest son. It is possible for several brothers to be successively 'eldest' in this way. This procedure is not ideal, but it removes most of the anomalies.

Eldest sons married younger than the other sons. The marriage of a duke's eldest son was the occasion on which the estate was settled on him, and the fathers may have encouraged their eldest son to marry early. The younger sons, on the other hand, had no great fortune, and would tend to delay marriage, or not marry at all.[18] This is borne out by the present study.

We may construct a table of the proportion surviving who were still bachelors at five-year intervals of age, in the same manner as we earlier did (Table 17) for dukes' sons and daughters.

TABLE 32

Nuptiality of dukes' sons

Age	Born 1330–1679		Born 1680–1829		Born 1830–1954	
	Eldest	Younger	Eldest	Younger	Eldest	Younger
0	100	100	100	100	100	100
5	99	98	100	100	100	100
10	96	98	100	100	100	100
15	88	97	100	100	100	100
20	64	81	96	97	100	100
25	39	56	55	83	63	83
30	19	42	29	63	33	49
35	4	28	18	47	14	37
40	4	21	14	37	14	29
45	4	19	10	31	8	22
50	4	17	10	29	6	20
Eventually	4	9	8	20	3	14

It is obvious that eldest sons marry younger than do their brothers and are much less likely to remain bachelors. Over the six centuries, eldest sons have married progressively later, but their younger brothers, since about 1855, show a tendency to be married rather sooner than formerly.

[18] A. Goodwin (ed.), *The European Nobility in the Eighteenth Century* (London 1953), chap. 1, by H. J. Habakkuk.

The ratio of younger sons to eldest sons at the age of 15 has been almost constant:

Born 1330-1679	177 per 100 eldest sons
„ 1680-1829	170 „ 100 „ „
„ 1830-1939	154 „ 100 „ „

The reproductivity of the younger sons is considerably reduced by their tendency to marry late or remain single.

(2) *Heiress Marriages.* It has been suggested[19] that marriages with bourgeois heiresses are detrimental to fertility in peerage families. We may classify wives into three categories: peerage families, commoners and foreigners. (The last group is very mixed—German princesses and American heiresses, for example.)

TABLE 33

Family size of dukes' sons

1st wife's origin	Born 1330-1679			Born 1680-1829			Born 1830-1934		
	No.	Children	Av.	No.	Children	Av.	No.	Children	Av.
Peerage	72	202	2·8	121	562	4·6	62	203	3·3
Commoner	29	77	2·7	97	314	3·2	67	135	2·0
Foreign	19	57	3·0	20	66	3·3	26	59	2·3
Total	120	336	2·8	238	942	4·0	155	397	2·6

In the two latter periods, the advantage of the wives from peerage families is unmistakable. The proportion of marriages with daughters and grand-daughters of peers has fallen from 60 per cent to 40 per cent, however. This has contributed to the decline in fertility, but each class shows reduced fertility in the third period compared with the second. The first period is liable to various errors of omission of births, but all three classes seem equally fertile. There is no difference between the wives of eldest and younger sons in this respect, except that eldest sons, marrying earlier, always had rather larger families.

The same kind of analysis for the daughter cohorts, in which we must remember that a few births from non-peerage marriages are missing, yields a similar pattern.

TABLE 34

Family size of dukes' daughters

1st husband's origin	Born 1330-1679			Born 1680-1829			Born 1830-1839		
	No.	Children	Av.	No.	Children	Av.	No.	Children	Av.
Peerage	109	351	3·2	159	850	5·3	81	318	3·9
Commoner	35	70	2·0	81	215	2·7	69	173	2·5
Foreign	17	33	1·9	19	64	3·4	22	73	3·3
Total	161	454	2·8	259	1129	4·4	172	564	3·3

The omissions cannot account for the great difference in average family size between peerage marriages and commoner marriages. The age at marriage,

---

[19] F. Galton, *Hereditary Genius* (London 1869), pp. 130-40. Also, for example, W. Wagner-Manslau, 'Human Fertility', *Eugenics Rev.*, XXIV, 1932, pp. 195-210 and 297-304.

being perhaps lower for marriages with peers, may explain some of the difference.

(3) *Actual Family Size.* Here we consider all the marriages of an individual. Childlessness has declined, but there have also been fewer large families in the modern period. No attempt was made to allow for differing durations of married life. Falling mortality since 1680 will therefore exaggerate any real decline in the incidence of large families. However, the changing proportions of small and of large families have an intrinsic interest.

Eldest sons had more children than did their brothers, but not because they were less frequently childless. A remarkable fact is that the sons, and even the eldest sons, appear to have been more inclined to have no children than the daughters. The percentages of dukes' sons ever married having families of stated size are shown in Table 35.

TABLE 35
Family size distribution of dukes' sons

Family size	Born 1330–1679		Born 1680–1829		Born 1830–1934	
	Eldest	Younger	Eldest	Younger	Eldest	Younger
None	26	31	23	20	17	18
1–4	30	40	25	44	51	69
5–9	26	22	38	26	30	13
10 and over	18	7	14	10	2	0
Total	100	100	100	100	100	100

TABLE 36
Family size distribution for all dukes' children

Family size	Born 1330–1679		Born 1680–1829		Born 1830–1939	
	Sons	Daughters	Sons	Daughters	Sons	Daughters
None	29	22	21	19	17	12
1–4	36	49	36	37	62	60
5–9	23	21	31	30	20	25
10 and over	12	8	12	14	1	3
Total	100	100	100	100	100	100

Proportions of over 20 per cent of married people dying childless seem high. Under-enumeration of births is not an important cause of this high rate, since although Peller[20] found only 15 per cent of married men childless among the ruling families of Europe, who had a fairly similar marriage system, and a similar desire for children, it is hard to believe that after 1700 the family of many eldest sons of dukes would not be fully chronicled, yet 23 per cent of the eldest sons born 1680–1729 married without apparent issue.

The lateness of some marriages and early termination of marriages would be quite a common reason for childlessness. (See section on marriages of completed fertility.)

[20] S. Peller, 'Man's Reproductive Activity', *Bull. Hist. Med.*, xxi, 1947, pp. 51–65.

(4) *Sex ratio*. It has often been remarked that the first child has a tendency to be male.[21] We can see how far it is true of the present cohorts (first marriage children only), since simple χ^2 tests of association can be made.

TABLE 37

Sex of dukes' grandchildren

| | Male cohorts | | | Female cohorts | | |
	Male	Female	Total	Male	Female	Total
1st child	209	172	381	247	202	449
Other children	659	637	1296	869	829	1798
Total	868	809	1677	1116	1031	2247
		χ^2 1·89			χ^2 2·09	

Grouping the two cohorts together would not be valid, since there were a number of marriages between the sons and daughters of dukes, so that the two tables are not independent. All we can say is that the observed first child sex-ratio is about 122 males per 100 females, and the observed other children sex-ratio is about 104, but even with such large numbers, the difference is not statistically significant.

Summary

The available records of the ducal families of the British Isles have been studied in order to determine fertility and mortality among the highest social class.

The expectation of life was considerably higher for females than males, but a large part of the difference could be explained by deaths from violence. Mortality fell rather abruptly about the middle of the eighteenth century, and perhaps again in the twentieth century. At other times mortality has fallen gradually.

The mortality of the aristocracy was similar in Britain and the Continent. The differences are rather in favour of Britain, especially for children and old people.

The mean age at marriage rose from 22 to 29 for men, and from 17 to 24 for women, between the fourteenth and the eighteenth centuries. Thereafter it has scarcely varied. Eldest sons have always married at younger ages than did their brothers.

Between about 1760 and 1860, the rate of fertility was remarkably high. To a large extent, falling mortality accounts for the sudden rise in fertility in the mid-eighteenth century, but it does not explain all the increase. After 1860 or so, fertility fell, as in the general population, and at present ducal families are probably just failing to reproduce themselves.

In every period, roughly one in six of all marriages of completed fertility were childless. The decline in fertility was thus brought about by a reduction in the proportion of large families.

[21] For example, R. C. Punnett, 'On Nutrition and Sex Determination in Man', *Proc. Camb. Phil. Soc.*, xii, 1903, pp. 262–76.

Especially since 1700, marriages into another peerage family produced more children than did other marriages. There is no evidence that the first child was significantly more often male than were subsequent children.

ACKNOWLEDGEMENTS

My thanks are due to Professor D. V. Glass for suggesting the subject of this work and subsequent advice; to Professor A. L. Banks for his kind help and encouragement throughout; to the East Anglian Regional Hospital Board for punching my cards; and to the staff of the Department of Human Ecology of the University of Cambridge for their constant assistance.

15

THE CHANGING ADEQUACY OF ENGLISH REGISTRATION, 1690-1837[1]

J. T. KRAUSE

Editor's Note: Apart from this work on the statistical basis of work in historical demo-graphy, Professor Krause has done several years' work on British population movements which remains substantially unpublished at the time of closing this collection. The article printed here is intended to serve as a background to those other contributions which rely on parochial registers for their main source material.

AFTER 1929 it seemed that the major problems of English population history in the period 1700-1850 had been solved.[2] According to this view, infant mortality started to fall after about 1750, fell sharply around 1800, and started to climb again after 1821, although never again regaining the levels of the early eighteenth century. The changes in infant mortality were marked enough to affect crude mortality rates strongly at a time when birth rates were apparently constant, so that changing infant mortality seemingly determined changes in rates of increase.

However, in the last decade this classical view has been challenged in several ways. Some investigators have suggested that fertility was the major variable over the period 1690-1850[3]; others, although believing that mortality was the important variable, have stressed the decline of adult, rather than infant, mortality.[4] While the new research is so far suggestive, rather than definitive, some points of agreement are emerging.[5] First, mortality fell between the

[1] I wish to thank the Rockefeller Foundation whose grants for the years 1959-61 made possible the research on which this essay is based.

[2] The main works were: J. Brownlee, 'The History of the Birth- and Death-Rates in England and Wales taken as a Whole from 1570 to the Present Time', *Public Health*, XXIX (1916), 211-22 and 228-38; T. H. Marshall, 'The Population of England and Wales from the Industrial Revolution to the World War', *Economic History Review*, V (1935), 65-78; T. H. Marshall, 'The Population Problem during the Industrial Revolution', *Economic History*, I (1929), 429-56 (see above, p. 247). G. T. Griffith, *Population Problems of the Age of Malthus* (Cambridge 1926).

[3] H. J. Habakkuk, 'English Population in the Eighteenth Century', *Econ. Hist. Rev.*, 2nd ser., VI (1953), 117-33 (see above, p. 269), and J. T. Krause, 'Changes in English Fertility and Mortality, 1781-1850', *Econ. Hist. Rev.*, 2nd ser., XI (1958), 52-70.

[4] D. Eversley, 'A Survey of Population in an Area of Worcestershire, 1660-1850', *Population Studies*, X (1957), 253-79 (see below, p. 394). J. D. Chambers, 'Population Change in a Provincial Town, Nottingham 1700-1800', in L. S. Pressnell (ed.), *Studies in the Industrial Revolution* (London 1960), 97-124 (see above, p. 334).
    For a survey and evaluation of other work which has been done or is being done on English population history see D. Eversley, 'Population in England in the Eighteenth Century: An Appraisal of Current Research', to appear in the collected papers of the Conference of the International Population Union, New York 1961. Also, I might note the valuable article of D. V. Glass, 'A Note on the Under-Registration of Births in Britain in the Nineteenth Century', *Pop. Stud.*, V (1951-2), 70-88 which, although dealing with the period after 1840, has implications for the earlier period.

[5] The estimates in this paragraph are based on Krause, *Changes in English Fertility and Mortality*, and J. T. Krause, 'English Population Movements between 1700 and 1850', to appear in the collected papers of the Conference of the International Population Union, New York 1961. This description has been used by J. D. Chambers, *The Workshop of the World* (London 1961), 173-5. Also, Eversley's

1810's and the 1840's instead of rising as in the classical view. Secondly, the crude birth rate of the 1810's was at least 40 per 1,000, and thus was higher than that of the 1840's, another difference from the classical view which stressed virtually constant birth rates. These new estimates are based on an analysis of the age distribution of 1821 and the population total of 1811 and thus provide a rough measure of the adequacy of parish registration in the 1810's. They imply that the rates of omission of births and deaths for the 1810's were much higher than those on which the classical view has been based and that those rates were not constant from decade to decade, as assumed in the classical view.

Certainly, work remains to be done on the early nineteenth century, but most research will concentrate on earlier periods and will in large part be based on parish registers. While it is generally agreed that parish registers were better demographic sources in the eighteenth century than they were in the 1810's, the timing of the deterioration and the factors which were responsible are not well understood. Indeed, no satisfactory study of the parish registers as demographic sources exists. Numerous works by genealogists touch upon some aspects of the problems, but ignore too many others.[6] The present essay is an attempt to summarize my findings on the changing adequacy of registration between the years 1690 and 1837.[7] The reader will not be given any neat series of decadal rates of omission for the period because the data are too incomplete and their interpretation involves little explored aspects of religious, political, and social history. The impressionistic methods of the historian, rather than the quantitative methods of the statistician, must be relied upon.

This analysis of registration will be most important for studies of parish registers, but it will also be relevant to the interpretation of the national statistics for the period 1780-1837.[8] Many previous investigators have been fascinated by the fact that the number of burials in the 1780's was virtually the same as that of the decade 1801-10 (a situation somewhat similar to that found in many parish registers), although the population had presumably increased considerably during the time. The apparently obvious conclusion is that the death rate had fallen considerably.

English parish registers have a number of quirks which differentiate them from the continental registers to an important degree, quirks which need some exploration before the main analysis can get under way. While an ecclesiastical system of registration functioned with relative efficiency in Sweden and many other countries, the number of Dissenters from Anglicanism posed problems. Here, one must remember that many Dissenting clergymen had occupied Anglican churches during the Commonwealth and that Anglican doctrine, as established during the time of Elizabeth, was a compromise which was designed

---

statement in *Population in England* that 40 per cent of the deaths were omitted in the 1810's implies acceptance of the above description.

The classical estimates are to be found in Brownlee, *The History*, 232, and Griffith, *Population Problems*, 27-35.

[6] J. C. Cox, *The Parish Registers of England* (London 1910). W. Bradbrook, *The Parish Register* (London 1910). R. E. C. Waters, *Parish Registers in England* (London 1882). J. S. Burn, *The History of Parish Registers in England*, 2nd ed. (London 1862). A. M. Burke, *Key to the Ancient Parish Registers of England and Wales* (London 1908). This list is not exhaustive, but contains the main works on the subject.

[7] I shall treat the subject in a detailed way in my book on English population history.

[8] The data to be found in the various parish register abstracts of the years 1801-41.

to accommodate many different shades of belief. Thus, many Anglicans might be greatly affected by dissenting ideas.

As a result of the number of Dissenters and the prevalence of dissenting ideas, certain ambiguities in T. Cromwell's order which established parochial registration in 1538 possessed much potential importance.[9] Firstly, the order called for the recording of all christenings.[10] But what exactly was a christening? Was it a private baptism, i.e. one performed at the home of the infant by a clergyman or a layman when the infant was presumed to be too sick to go to church? Or was it the public baptism performed in the church? Any layman could validly baptize so long as the ceremony involved the sprinkling of water and an invocation to the Trinity, but some clergymen preferred to delay registration until the infant had been baptized publicly in church. Thus, some privately baptized infants who died before public baptism were not entered in baptismal registers. Parenthetically, I might note that parents were expected to provide a feast for the relatives and friends at the time of the public baptism, a feast which was often relatively costly.

Secondly, burial registration had its difficulties. Cromwell's order called for the recording of burials, but the term 'burial' meant different things to different people. To some it meant only burials at which the Anglican service was read; yet the clergy were forbidden to read those services for suicides, executed criminals, excommunicants, and most important, those who died unbaptized. Thus in parishes in which baptism was postponed significantly, important members of burials might have gone unrecorded. However, some clergymen took literally the definition of the term 'burial' and recorded all burials, even stillbirths.[11]

I should also mention that neither Cromwell's order nor any subsequent legislation, with the exception of Lord Hardwicke's marriage act of 1753 (26 Geo. II c. 33) and the Parish Register Act of 1812 (52 Geo. III c. 146), provided any set forms of entry. The result was that some registers provided very little information, sometimes being mere lists of persons baptized, married, and buried without any other information. At best, the highest level attained by most parishes was the naming of both parents in the case of baptisms and burials of children. Considering the prevalence of certain surnames in each locality and the relative paucity of christian names, the registers did not provide good genealogical evidence, which was often needed in cases which involved inheritance or proof of age. Much of the criticism of parish registers over the centuries was directed at the insufficient detail, a failure which does not affect

[9] The text of Cromwell's order is in the Public Record Office, *State Papers*, 6/3 (1), and has been published by Cox, *The Parish Registers*, 2-3.

[10] The following discussion is based on B. L. Manning, *The Protestant Dissenting Deputies* (Cambridge 1952), 296-8; W. A. Fearon and J. F. Williams, *The Parish Registers and Parochial Documents in the Archdeaconry of Winchester* (Winchester and London 1909), 20-21; and an examination of a large number of registers. For example, in the parish of Selattyn (Salop) burials of chrisom children in the second half of the seventeenth century are recorded, but there is no record of a baptism in the particular family. Hence, the ceremony must have been private, and such baptisms must not have been recorded. I shall not give the usual bibliographical references to parish registers because the information can easily be found under the name of the parish in both the catalogue of the British Museum and of the Library of Congress.

[11] One can observe this difference in numerous parishes even before the various acts for burial in woollen (to be discussed shortly) were passed. Parishes such as Stoke-upon-Trent (Staffs.) did not record stillbirths while others such as Wylye (Wilts.) did so.

the registers as sources of the numbers of baptisms, burials, and marriages.[12]

In examining the data for the 1690's and the early eighteenth century, it seems that the system probably functioned well as a demographic source. For one thing, the distribution of churches and clergymen coincided rather closely with that of the population, and there were sufficient churches and clergymen to provide religious services adequately. Altogether, there were about 550 persons per church, and somewhat more per clergyman (pluralism, the holding of more than one benefice, was unusual but not unknown).[13] Inasmuch as non-residence was relatively uncommon and as the congregations were relatively small, two important factors in causing negligent registration in the early nineteenth century were not very significant.

Moreover, the Dissenters probably affected registration only slightly. While they probably made up about 10 per cent of the population about 1700, they did not cause corresponding amounts of omission.[14] The Dissenters were often people of substance, people for whom the legal status of the registers had its attraction. These people had to worry about the transmission of property to their heirs, about the necessity of obtaining apprenticeships or preferred positions in the army or navy for their sons. Then, leaving aside the Baptists who will be treated separately, the Dissenters of the time did not object to the sacraments as such, but mainly objected to the type of church government. Hence, Dissenters were often baptized in the Anglican church or had the fact of birth or baptism by a Dissenting minister registered parochially.[15]

However, the Baptists do pose a problem, not nationally because they were too few, but in some counties.[16] They not only objected to infant baptism, but had little incentive to record their births in the registers because they were drawn mainly from the lower classes. Inasmuch as Baptists were not baptized until the age of 15 or later, those who died before that age were not entitled to an Anglican funeral ceremony. Hence, even though they were buried in the churchyard, the registers did not necessarily record the fact.

However, two laws, or sets of laws, affected both Anglicans and Dissenters and were very important for the registration process. Firstly, a law of 1666, which was amended in 1678 and 1680, provided that all corpses had to be buried in nothing but pure woollen cloth, an affidavit to this effect had to be obtained and recorded by the parish priest.[17] Further, the churchwardens had to keep a list of the affidavits and present those lists periodically to petty or quarter

---

[12] See Pub. Rec. Off., *State Papers Domestic*, Wm. III, 1698, 441–4, and R. Bigland, *Observations on Marriages, Baptisms and Burials* (London 1764).

[13] The estimate is based on a total population of six millions, an estimate which will be discussed in my book. On the growth of pluralism and non-residence see *Black Book, The Extraordinary, of Church, State, Law and Representation* (London 1831), 35.

[14] Much of this paragraph is based on E. D. Bebb, *Nonconformity and Social and Economic Life 1660–1800* (London 1935), *passim*.

[15] For example, see the parish registers of Lesburn (Northumberland), Tarrant-Hinton (Dorset), Ottery St. Mary (Devon), Betley (Staffs.), Rushton (Northants.), Toft (Cambs.), Penrith (Cumb.), and Gawsworth (Chester). Many others could be cited especially for the period 1695-1705.

[16] A. C. Underwood, *A History of the British Baptists* (London 1947), *passim*; the excellent series of Bedfordshire parish registers which have been edited by F. G. Emmison provides abundant evidence of the effects of the Baptists on registration.

[17] 18 and 19 Chas. II c. 4; 30 Chas. II c. 3; and 32 Chas. II c. 1. According to Waters, *Parish Registers*, 20, it became customary for the parish clerk to call out at the grave, 'Who makes affidavit?' The churchwarden's accounts at Ash-next-Sandwich (Kent) contain lists of the burials of each year, and many other churchwardens must have done the same.

sessions. In most parishes the parish register was used to record the affidavits so that the parish registers tended to be a register of all burials, not merely a register of Anglican funeral services.

Secondly, a tax was placed on births, deaths, and marriages for the years 1695-1705, and a series of acts provided for stringent enforcement.[18] Parish priests were made virtual civil registrars, and their records were supposed to have been kept in great detail. Undoubtedly, registration of births improved significantly in these years. It is commonplace knowledge that the births or baptisms of Dissenters were more often included in the registers for this period than for any other. The major contemporary criticism of the registers was that the clergy did not keep the registers in the required detail, a criticism which has nothing to do with the counting of entries.[19]

However, the registers were not perfect in the early eighteenth century. In some cases affidavits on burial in woollen were listed, not in the register, but in a separate volume; hence, some burials of those who had died without baptism went unlisted in the registers. Also, the lists of those who were born or died without Anglican services between 1695 and 1705 were not necessarily kept in the registers. Moreover, one should not jump to the conclusion that the rudimentary administrative system was capable of enforcing 100 per cent compliance with the law.

But it is not wise to make too much of these exceptions. Of course, exact measurement is impossible, but I should hazard the guess that omissions of births were much greater than those of deaths in the early eighteenth century. Where Griffith assumed that the percentage of omitted baptisms was only 50 per cent greater than that of deaths and Brownlee thought the differential even less, I suggest that it was much higher, perhaps double.[20] As a guess, 10 per cent of the births and 5 per cent of the deaths were omitted by the Anglican registers of the time, estimates which may well be too high, almost certainly so for the period 1695-1705. Marriage registration was probably highly accurate, although there must have been some negligence.

Throughout most of the eighteenth century the system functioned reasonably well, although probably never attaining the efficiency of the period 1695-1705. An important contributory factor was the decline of Dissent throughout much of the century. A recent student of Dissent approvingly noted an estimate of decline of roughly a third in the number of Dissenters between 1714 and 1760.[21] Nor did the number of Dissenters apparently begin to

[18] The acts were: 5 and 6 Wm. and Mary c. 21; 6 and 7 Wm. and Mary c. 35; 8 and 9 Wm. and Mary c. 20; and 9 Wm. III, c. 32. (*Editor's note:* for details of the effect of this act, see Glass above, p. 170 ff.)

[19] The indemnity act of Anne's reign (4 and 5 Anne c. 23) has often been used to argue that there were numerous omissions from the registers, but a reading of the act shows that it did not cover those whose negligence resulted in a loss of revenue for the crown and that it forgave those guilty of insufficiently detailed registers.

[20] Additional evidence for a considerable differential between omissions and of births and of deaths is given in P. E. Jones and A. V. Judges, 'London Population in the late Seventeenth Century', *Econ. Hist. Rev.*, VI (1935), 45-63, 51. In London it is evident that the most Dissenters' births were not recorded in the parish registers.

[21] M. B. Whittaker, *The Revival of Dissent, 1800-35* (unpublished thesis for the M. Litt. degree at Cambridge in 1959), 43. The numerical decline of Dissent cannot be doubted, although there is no agreement on its exact extent; see Bebb, *Nonconformity and Social and Economic Life*, 45; Underwood, *History of the British Baptists*, 116-48; H. S. Skeats and C. S. Miall, *History of the Free Churches in England* (London 1891), 266.

increase significantly until the 1790's, a development which I shall discuss shortly.

Another factor which tended to produce adequate registration was the *relative* harmony which existed between the Dissenters and Anglican clergymen until the outbreak of the French Revolution.[22] Throughout most of the period, both groups were strongly affected by deism with its emphasis on rationalism and its distrust of enthusiasm. Some Anglican clergymen even encouraged Dissenting ministers to preach in their neighbourhoods, and many parish registers contain entries of the ceremonies of Dissenters. Of course, many Dissenters still found the parish registers useful because of their legal status; however, it is crucial to note that the Anglican clergy did at least allow the recording of Dissenters' births, baptisms, or burials, a condition which was not often true of the early nineteenth century.

Burial registration probably remained relatively adequate because non-Anglican burial grounds, outside of London, were unimportant until the 1780's, and probably increased very slowly until about 1800. Even Manchester, which had grown so rapidly during the eighteenth century, had less than 5 per cent of its recorded burials taking place on non-Anglican grounds in the 1770's, as compared with a minimal estimate of 30 per cent in the 1810's.[23] Carlisle, a city of relatively rapid growth, had an insignificant number of burials in non-Anglican grounds in the 1780's. And, much evidence shows that non-Anglican grounds did not become important until the early nineteenth century.

While accuracy of registration of marriages has always been assumed, probably a relatively valid assumption, some slight improvement was probably made by Lord Hardwicke's Act of 1753 (26 Geo. II c. 53). While the act was primarily intended to prevent the marriages of eloping heiresses, the fact that a standardized register was provided which had to be signed by both parties undoubtedly led to a reduction of negligence.

However, some factors tended to lessen the effectiveness of registration. Even before the improvements of the 1780's, the North country's population had grown more rapidly than the South's. Considering that the Anglican church had done little to adjust itself to the changing distribution of population, there were obviously potential difficulties. And as Dissent declined, its social base changed significantly as many wealthy Dissenters went over to Anglicanism; the poorer Dissenters had relatively little incentive to seek the legal recognition afforded by the parish registers.[24] Then, the act for burial in woollen had been increasingly ignored after about 1750 and almost totally so by 1780. Thus, the registers became primarily lists of Anglican funeral services, rather than of burials as such. This failure took place when baptism was probably being postponed increasingly, with presumably an increase in the number of infants who died without baptisms. Many Bedfordshire registers after about 1765 show an increasing postponement of baptism until the saint's day of the

[22] C. J. Abbey, *The English Church and its Bishops*, 2 vols. (London 1887), II, 85–86. C. Smyth, *Simeon and Church Order* (Cambridge 1940), 178–9 and 266–7.
[23] T. Percival, 'On the State of Population in Manchester, and Other Adjacent Places', *Philosophical, Medical, and Experimental Essays*, 4 vols. (London 1776), III, 1–84, 4. The figure for the 1810's is calculated from the data given in Pub. Rec. Off., H.O. 71.
[24] Bebb, *Nonconformity and Social and Economic Life*, 57.

particular parish, the day of the annual 'feast'.[25] While the influence of these factors in the years before 1795 should not be exaggerated, they undoubtedy had some effect, not so much among the Dissenters who were not very numerous, but among the Anglicans.

It will be noted that I have not mentioned the tax on entries in parish registers for the years 1783-94 (23 Geo. III, c. 67). The fact that this tax was extended to Dissenters' registers in 1786 (25 Geo. III, c. 75) has been used to argue that so many Anglicans were being baptized and buried by Dissenters that Parliament acted to prevent this evasion. However, the fact of the matter is that the Dissenters lobbied for the extension of the tax to their registers in the hope that their registers would thereby gain legal equality to the Anglican.[26] They got the tax, but not the equality. Actually, it does not seem that this tax affected registration significantly perhaps because poverty could be used as an excuse for non-payment, certainly many registers show a suspicious number of paupers.[27]

Although exact measurement of leakages from parish registers is impossible for the 1780's, informed guesswork should not be disdained. Even though the number of Dissenters had fallen since the early 1700's, the leakage from the baptismal registers must have increased because of the decreased tendency of some Dissenters to have their births or baptisms recorded in Anglican registers and because many Anglicans were postponing the baptisms of their children, the important factor here. Relatively speaking, leakage from the burial registers probably increased more than did that from baptismal ones because of the virtual lapsing of the making of affidavits for burial in woollen, the probable growth of the burials of the unbaptized, and of course some areas were affected by the opening of non-Anglican burial grounds. For the 1780's perhaps something like Griffith's rates are close to the truth, a birth-baptism ratio of 1·15 and a death-burial ratio of 1·10. These estimates, a 50 per cent increase of the rate of omission for baptisms and a doubling of the estimated leakage of burials, show a worsening of registration since 1700, but that it was still relatively adequate.

However, the system virtually collapsed between the 1790's and 1820, and statistics for both town and country became utterly misleading. Certainly by 1821 the maladjustment between church facilities and people had become serious because of accelerated population growth, internal migration, and the failure of the Anglican church to expand. There were roughly 1,200 persons per church, and given the fact that most pews were rented, sometimes at high prices, obviously there were few places for the poor.[28] Regional differences in church facilities were exceptionally marked. Whereas some counties, such as Rutland, had less than 500 persons per church, others, such as Lancashire and Middlesex, had such high ratios that it was obviously impossible for many to attend the Established Church; in Lancashire there were 3,665 persons per church and in Middlesex 9,490.

[25] See the introduction to the register of Blunham (Beds.). The staff at the Bedford County Record Office have noted that this phenomenon occurred in many other parishes of the county.
[26] Manning, *The Protestant Dissenting Deputies*, 259-60.
[27] Note the comment in the register of Whittlesey St. Mary, Cambridge which is cited in Cox, *The Parish Registers*, 21-22.
[28] A convenient summary of data on persons per church is found in *The Black Book*, 87.

Especially in rapidly growing towns, the shortage of burial facilities was acute because of the limited size of the churchyards and lack of money to extend the grounds. As a result, the cost of burial in many urban grounds was raised, or in some cases the churchyard was closed altogether. Poor parishioners had a choice of three possibilities: to pay the higher prices, to be buried in another parish (in which rates would also be high because the rates for non-parishioners were generally twice as high as for parishioners), or to be buried in a cheap non-Anglican ground, the number of which grew so rapidly in the early nineteenth century. While the changed balance between church facilities and population was most obviously an urban phenomenon, many rural areas, especially mining areas, had the same sort of changes, although to a lesser degree.[29]

Affecting the rural areas in an important degree, the decline of the religious zeal of the clergy and the growth of non-residence brought many of the effects produced by the changed distribution of the population.[30] Although there had been a growing tendency in the eighteenth century for the upper classes to put their younger sons into the clergy, the sharp rises in agricultural prices in the second half of the century, especially after 1794, and the consequent increased value of the tithes accelerated this tendency. And not having been content with the increased tithes, this more aristocratic clergy increased the extent of pluralism and non-residence. Even the act of 1803 which some thought would restrict pluralism and non-residence had no such effect: indeed, it probably aggravated the problems. While many non-residents hired curates, assistants to provide religious services, the curates themselves were often pluralists and non-residents. The obvious results were that the number of religious services was reduced, that clergymen were simply not available for emergencies, and that supervision of the maintenance of registers was lax.

Considering the growing imbalance between churches and population and the increase of pluralism and non-residence, it is not surprising that Dissent grew rapidly after 1795, that religious indifference became marked, and that many Anglicans became increasingly negligent in obtaining sacraments. Unfortunately, such statistics as we possess on the number of Dissenters are highly unreliable, consisting as they do of a conflicting mass of unsubstantiated claims and counter-claims. There are, however, figures on the decadal numbers of licences which were granted for the founding of new Dissenting congregations (see Table 1). It is most important to realize the biases of the figures because they make this not unimpressive explosion of Dissent seem even more remarkable than the figures suggest. Firstly, the last three decades of the eighteenth century witnessed such ferment among the Dissenters, and many of the applications for new licences resulted from secessions from old congregations in which there was no corresponding increase in the number of individual Dissenters. Secondly, and most important, the Methodists were forced to obtain such

[29] M. Cook (ed.), *The Diocese of Exeter in 1821*, 2 vols. (Torquay 1958-60), I, *passim*. Vol I. deals with Cornwall whose parochial organization was not well situated to provide religious services for much of the population.

[30] The following paragraph is based on: *The Black Book*, 35; A. T. Hart, *The Eighteenth Century Country Parson* (Shrewsbury 1955), *passim*; G. F. A. Best, *Church and State in English Politics 1800-33* (unpublished doctoral dissertation, Cambridge 1955), 165-6. Cook, *The Diocese of Exeter, passim*.

licences beginning in 1783, *but* the Methodists did not cut themselves off from Anglican sacraments during Wesley's lifetime.[31] Only in 1795 did Methodists begin to separate themselves entirely from the Anglicans. Thirdly, some Dissenters simply did not bother to apply for licences in the 1810's. Hence, the congregational statistics undoubtedly understate the growth between 1780 and 1820 of religious congregations which had broken off contact with the Anglican church. Not surprisingly, by 1812 Dissenting chapels outnumbered Anglican churches in parishes with more than 1,000 inhabitants.[32] Nor should it be imagined that the urban areas were the only ones affected. Rural counties, such as Cornwall and Norfolk, showed the greatest increases in the number of applications for licences, and the predominantly rural East Midlands and East Anglia were the areas in which Baptist expansion was most marked.[33] Of course, numbers of congregations are not infallible guides to the number of people, but it would be quite surprising if the percentage of Dissenters had not at least tripled between the 1780's and the 1810's, after all the number of applications for permanent places of worship had increased more than fifteen-fold.

TABLE I

Decadal number of permanent and temporary places licensed
for the performance of non-Anglican worship (a)

Decade	Houses, dwelling houses, rooms or otherwise as temporary buildings	Chapels, buildings, meeting houses or permanent buildings	Total number of places certified in each decadal period
1771–80	1,107	175	1,282
1781–90	1,266	332	1,598
1791–1800	3,479	915	4,394
1801–10	3,975	1,485	5,460
1811–20	7,497	2,644	10,141

(a) The data have been compiled from *Returns Relating to Dissenters' Places of Worship*, Parl. Papers, 1852-3, LXXVIII, 164. The returns omit five counties in the 1780's and nine in the 1770's but I have filled the gaps by assuming that the missing data of those decades bore the same relation to those of the other counties as in the 1790's.

However, the numerical increase of Dissent was not the only variable. New sects or sects which had not been important in most of the eighteenth century came to the fore, mainly the various kinds of Methodists and the Baptists. Gaining the bulk of their recruits from the lower classes, they had little incentive to seek the legal benefits of parochial registration. Moreover, there was a widespread illusion among Dissenters, not ended until about 1823, that their registers had legal parity with the Anglican because of the tax which had been placed on their registers in 1786.[34] Moreover, the new Dissenters objected to the Anglican church in a more fundamental way than the old Dissent had done. No longer was the emphasis on church government, but upon the emotional salvation experience of the adult. The most obvious example of the new anti-sacramentalism was of course furnished by the Baptists who grew so rapidly after 1795 especially in the mainly rural regions of the East Midlands and East

---

[31] L. F. Church, *More About the Early Methodist People* (London 1949), 264-8.
[32] Skeats and Miall, *Free Churches*, 454.
[33] Krause, *Changes in English Fertility and Mortality*, 55.
[34] Manning, *The Protestant Dissenting Deputies*, 259-60.

Anglia.[35] Not only did Baptists actively object to infant baptism, but they also denounced the practice of burial in consecrated ground. Baptists were very active in opening burial grounds, but certainly many Baptists were buried in Anglican churchyards without any mention being made in the parish register because the funeral service had not been read. Although John Wesley defended the practice of infant baptism in debate against the Baptists, the Methodists evidently postponed infant baptism to a significant degree, as I shall show shortly.

But even had the Dissenters been most anxious to have their births or baptisms registered parochially, many Anglican clergymen would not have done so.[36] Especially after 1793, the belief that Dissenters were indistinguishable from French Revolutionaries became widespread among the clergy, the squirearchy, and other groups. Among other pressures brought to bear, Anglican clergymen, either in ignorance of canon law or desirous of harassing Dissenters, denied the validity of non-Anglican baptisms and refused to read the funeral service for persons so baptized. In some cases, the clergy went so far as to forbid the burials in the churchyard.

Of course, all persons who did not attend the Anglican church were not Dissenters. While there were certainly many who were indifferent to religion, any estimate of their number is out of the question. A recent study of Sheffield shows that neither Anglicans nor Dissenters provided religious facilities for the mass of the city's population, a point which has often been made of other urban areas in the early nineteenth century.[37] Again, this was not purely an urban phenomenon by any means. T. S. Ashton long ago pointed out that mining areas were virtually without any kind of religious facilities, and there is of course the long-known example of Cheddar (Somerset) whose houses were all visited by Hannah More who found that only one contained a Bible, and that was used to prop up a flower pot.[38]

Nor were those who remained in the Anglican fold unaffected by the conditions of the early nineteenth century. The early evangelicals, active in the second half of the eighteenth century, had strongly emphasized the conversion experience, and some of their successors of the early nineteenth century even seceded from the Established Church over the issue of infant baptism.[39] Many Anglicans undoubtedly attended the services of Dissenters and were affected to some extent by the ideas that they heard there. One result was a considerable strengthening of the tendency to postpone baptism, but I should also note that a few clergymen in 1811 stressed poverty as an important factor in causing the postponement of baptism.[40] Poverty was undoubtedly an important factor in many areas south and east of the line between the Severn and the Wash. The numerous bad harvests between 1795 and 1821 meant that many did not have

[35] Underwood, *History of the British Baptists*, 147-200. Also, the comments of the clergy in 1811 show the great headway made in these counties by the Baptists, see British Museum, Add. MSS. 6896.
[36] L. F. Church, *More about the Early Methodist People*, 82; Whittaker, *The Revival of Dissent*, 78-83; Best, *Church and State*, 185-93; Skeats and Miall, *Free Churches*, 402 and 451; Manning, *The Protestant Dissenting Deputies*, 290. B.M., Add. MSS., 6896, fols. 16, 44, 93, and many others.
[37] E. R. Wickham, *Church and People in an Industrial City* (London 1957), 47-48, 74-75, and 90.
[38] T. S. Ashton, 'The Coal Miners of the Eighteenth Century', *Econ. Hist.*, I (1928), 307-24, 327; and Skeats and Miall, *Free Churches*, 385-6.
[39] Smyth, *Simeon*, 178-9, 254, and 266-7; Skeats and Miall, *Free Churches*, 445.
[40] B.M., Add. MSS. 6896, fols. 125 and 168.

the means to give the customary party and had to postpone the public baptism until they could afford it. Postponement of public baptism need not have been so important if private baptisms had been given and duly recorded; however, the comments of the clergy in 1811 show that many clergymen were extremely reluctant to give private baptisms and that where they were given, they were generally not recorded. The comments also show that these clerical attitudes toward private baptism were relatively new, and were a response to the great increase in the number of requests for private baptism.

Another factor which operated on Anglicans, Dissenters, and the religiously indifferent alike in regard to burials was the burial of many outside Anglican grounds. For one thing, at least 12,400 Englishmen died abroad annually during the wars, not so much from enemy actions as from disease.[41] Other factors were the growth of hospitals, workhouses, and sometimes barracks, many of which had chaplains who baptized infants and buried people in the place's burial ground.[42] Inasmuch as these places were often extra-parochial, their ceremonies were not listed in the parish registers, nor were figures obtained from them for the national statistics of the 1810's. Obviously, the hospitals and workhouses tended to collect the people who were most likely to die and thus affected the statistics of some areas to a perceptible degree.

Far more important than these factors, however, were the burials which took place in non-Anglican burial grounds in England and Wales. Outside London, such grounds had been virtually irrelevant during the eighteenth century, but grew very rapidly after the turn of the century. The returns which the clergy submitted in 1831 covered the period 1813-30 and thus provide invaluable light on the 1810's (the returns for 1821 have not survived).[43] These returns note the existence of at least 1,100 non-Anglican grounds, many of which had not kept any records prior to 1823 and 450 of the 1,100 did not keep any during the 1820's either. Moreover, the figure of 1,100 is certainly far too low. Even the incomplete collection of non-Anglican burial registers at the General Register Office contains at least 198 registers which the clergy did not mention in 1831.[44] And a number of the 1831 returns state that the Dissenters buried in neighbouring parishes, but one generally finds no mention of these grounds in the returns from those parishes or in the collection at the General Register Office. Given this situation and the fact that the clergy was under no compulsion to collect the data on non-Anglican grounds, I suspect that the true number of non-Anglican grounds was not under 2,500.

While most of these grounds were probably small and catered for relatively small rural groups, unless they were on the outskirts of large cities, the largest such grounds were undoubtedly located in the cities. Of course, London had some of the largest. About 7,000 burials took place in these grounds by 1794 and the number increased about 1800, but fully 73 per cent of the *known* burials

[41] Krause, *Changes in English Fertility and Mortality*, 57.

[42] B.M., Add. MSS. 6896 fols. 20, 60, 85-89, 122-3, 139, and elsewhere. The Parish Register Act provided for the inclusion of these entries in the parish registers, but the act was not complied with to any significant extent until the 1820's.

[43] These returns are found in Pub. Rec. Off., H.O. 71.

[44] *Report of the Commissioners appointed to Inquire into the State, Custody, and Authenticity of Registers*, Parl. Papers, 1838, XXVIII, 8-13; *Report of the Commissioners appointed to Inquire into the State, Custody, and Authenticity of Certain Non-Parochial Registers*, Parl. Papers, 1857-8, XXIII, 5.

in Manchester took place in such grounds by 1830.[45] The clerical returns of 1831 show that a total of 88,929 known burials took place in non-Anglican grounds during the 1810's, but the figure is certainly too low because records were often not kept and because the clergy did not obtain them from many grounds which did keep them.[46]

Some might think that John Rickman, in collecting the national totals of baptisms and burials, would have been aware of these leakages and have taken steps to counteract them. But such was not the case. Rickman's methods of collecting the data were rather unsystematic. The national statistics up to 1801 included the totals from Bunhill Fields, probably the largest non-Anglican ground at the time, but such totals were omitted between 1801 and 1820. This omission is more than enough to account for the decline in the number of burials between the 1790's and the first decade of the nineteenth century,[47] a decline which has impressed a number of observers. Only a small part of the known burials in non-Anglican grounds, less than 1,300 out of 88,929, was included in the totals of the 1810's. That Rickman did not use the 1831 returns to warn the public of the known omissions of the statistics of the 1810's seems astonishing, but he never seemed to have been too anxious to stress the weakness of his data.

Ranking with the non-Anglican grounds as a cause of leakage from the parish registers in the early nineteenth century were the burials of the un-baptized. One can rarely measure the phenomenon directly, but when it is possible such measurements are impressive. The parish register shows that fully a quarter of Kempston's (Beds.) burials in the churchyard during the years 1801-12 were of unbaptized persons, mainly children. The corresponding percentage for Cardington (Beds.) was 17 per cent. Cardington also had a non-Anglican ground for which we have no records. While these two rural parishes in which Baptists were numerous were probably not typical of the country, they probably were typical of other Baptist areas. Fortunately, for Kempston it is possible to calculate the time between birth and baptism for some periods: in the 1740's the median time between birth and baptism was 13 days, and 7 per cent of the baptisms occurred on the day of birth; by 1801-12 the median had risen to 87 days, and none took place less than 10 days after birth. Presumably, the vast majority of these baptisms were of children whose parents were Anglicans, but who were affected by Baptist ideas or by poverty.

[45] The estimate for London in 1794 is based on data given in Parish Register Abstract of 1811, Parl. Papers, 1812, XI, 714, and B. Holmes, The London Burial Grounds (London 1896), 191-2, discusses the increase about 1800. The figures for Manchester were obtained from Pub. Rec. Off., H.O. 71, bundle 41.

[46] The clerical returns of 1831 can be used to calculate the number of burials in non-Anglican grounds which were included in the returns for the 1810's and 1820's (points on which the Parish Register Abstracts of 1821 and 1831 give little information) because the 1831 returns were concerned with two subjects. Firstly, the numbers of baptisms, burials, and marriages for each year 1821-30 were to be entered on the inner fly-leaf. Secondly, most of the rest of the booklet was to be used to put down the numbers of burials by age for each year 1813-30. These pages also included a section in which the clergy were requested (not ordered) to enter the annual numbers of burials in non-Anglican grounds. In compiling the official statistics of the 1820's, Rickman used the first of the above materials which sometimes did and sometimes did not include the totals from the non-Anglican grounds. Also, he gave no inkling of the number of burials which had taken place in such grounds in the 1810's. However, using these returns, one can calculate the numbers of such inclusions in the 1810's and 1820's.

[47] Krause, Changes in English Fertility and Mortality, 55-59.

Many other parishes also show a considerable increase of the time between birth and baptism. Especially marked in many parishes of the East Midlands and East Anglia about 1800 was a dramatic increase in the numbers of children of the same family being baptized at the same time.

That burial of the unbaptized was a serious problem for much of England is shown by a variety of data. While the clergy's comments of 1811 often noted its importance,[48] some statistics furnish the best evidence. First, it is possible to calculate infant burial rates for the country and for each county in the period 1813-30.[49] The national rate was 122 per 1,000 baptisms, a rate that does not look too improbable until one realizes that the great omission of births inflates the rate. Some county rates are even less reassuring: Cornwall, 63; Cardigan, 83; Westmorland, 87; Pembroke, 87; and ten other counties were under 100. If one assumes that the percentage of omitted births in 1813-30 was the same as shown by the official figures of 1839-40,[50] the figures (infant burials per 1,000 estimated births) become even more unbelievable: Cornwall, 45; Monmouth, 59; West Riding, 70; and 30 English counties had a rate under 100 (the 1839-40 data are not available for single Welsh counties). Given the known incompleteness of the 1839-40 data, these low rates are fantastic, unless one assumes that the infant burial data are extremely defective. That Cornwall, a Methodist stronghold, should lead the list so definitely is strong evidence that many Methodists did not practise early infant baptism.

TABLE 2

Infant burial rates in selected parishes
(per 1,000 recorded baptisms) (a)

Parish	Date	Rate	Parish	Date	Rate
Tarrant-Hinton (Dorset)	1800-12	60	Plymtree (Devon)	1813-17	16
Halberton (Devon)	1813-20	72		1818-22	55
Kelsale (Suffolk) (b)	1801-12	95	Lapford (Devon)	1813-22	79
Wylye (Wilts.) (b)	1813-20	71	Selattyn (Salop)	1801-12	71
Camborne (Cornwall)	1813-30	50	Crosthwaite-cum-Lyth (Westmorland)	1805-12	52

(a) Computed from printed parish registers which do not have the same data for the same periods.

(b) Private baptisms were recorded in Kelsale and Wylye.

Obviously absurd infant burial rates can also be gathered directly from the registers, as shown in Table 2. Considering that many births were undoubtedly omitted in these parishes, the rates are higher than they otherwise would have been, rates which are simply not found for most of the eighteenth century. Something, presumably postponement of baptism, had clearly affected infant burial registration in the early nineteenth century. Also, in some parishes one finds an utterly unlikely pattern of infant mortality. In Wylye (Wilts.) between 1813 and 1820 not a single infant died under two months of age, and in Camborne between 1813 and 1830 the fourth month was the period of apparently

[48] See B.M., Add. MSS. 6896, fols. 15-16, 52-53, 95, 108, 140-2, and many others.
[49] *Parish Register Abstract, 1831*, Parl. Papers, 1833, XXXVIII.
[50] *Parish Register Abstract, 1841*, Parl. Papers, 1845, XXV, xix.

highest infant mortality, both rather improbable. Again, Methodist strongholds are strongly represented in the list of parishes (the Devonian parishes and Camborne), and the registers of these parishes show a marked difference from those of Baptist areas: whole families are rarely baptized at the same time, and thus a superficial examination of the registers does not suggest that registration was so defective.

Thus parochial registration had become very inefficient by the 1810's. In an earlier article I suggested that a birth-baptism ratio of 1·41 and a death-burial ratio of between 1·45 and 1·48 could validly be applied to the national data of the 1810's, and I believe that the foregoing analysis shows the plausibility of these estimates.[51] While some have expressed surprise that omissions of burials should exceed those of baptisms, this condition, unusual though it was, is easily understandable. Anglicans made up the majority of the population and most were eventually baptized as were some of the Dissenters and some of the religiously indifferent. On the other hand, many of the Anglicans and others were buried abroad, in extra-parochial grounds, and in non-Anglican grounds. Some evidence suggests that a majority of those buried in non-Anglican grounds were in fact Anglicans, who presumably had been baptized in most cases.[52]

Another aspect of deteriorating registration should be noted, an aspect which concerns only local data. Lord Hardwicke's Act had partially broken down: large numbers of couples did not marry in their own parishes, but went elsewhere, usually to large cities such as Birmingham, Exeter, London, Oxford, or Plymouth, where they lied about their parish of normal residence.[53] Not only were local marriage totals affected by this practice, but ratios between baptisms and marriages were also, of course.

Obviously, one does not have to explore the causes of the improving registration after 1821 in great detail because the fact that mortality fell after 1821 while burial rates were rising strongly suggests improved registration. A study of the clerical returns of 1831 shows that nearly 126,000 burials in non-Anglican grounds were included in the official totals of the 1820's, enough to account for the rise in the burial rate for that decade. Moreover, the official totals of the 1830's contained over 156,000 such burials, although singularly little warning of this fact was given to the readers of the *Parish Register Abstract, 1841*.[54] Thus, it is not difficult to account for the rising burial rates of the national statistics.

Moreover, Anglican registers improved as demographic sources after 1821, although they did not attain the adequacy that they had had during most of the eighteenth century.[55] Not only did much church-building and extension of churchyards take place after 1819, but pluralism and non-residence began to decline, significantly so in the 1830's. The awakening of the Anglican church

[51] Krause, *Changes in Fertility and Mortality*, 69-70.
[52] *A Supplementary Report on the Results of a Special Inquiry into the Practice of Interment in Towns*, Parl. Papers, 1843, XII, 48. *Surplice Fees and Parish Register Fees*, Parl. Papers, 1834, XLIII, 39-59.
[53] B.M., Add. MSS. 6896, fols. 32, 42, 56, 144, 153-4, and many others.
[54] *Parish Register Abstract, 1841*, 95.
[55] All the standard church histories contain data on the subject, but the best works are: W. L. Mathieson, *English Church Reform 1815-40* (London 1923); and A. Blomfield, *Life of Bishop Blomfield*. 2 vols. (London 1864).

to its responsibilities in the new society was accompanied by an increased zeal on the part of the clergy and improved relations with Dissenters. Strong efforts were made to curb the neglect and postponement of baptism, and as a result of the Parish Register Act of 1812 (which in many respects became effective only in the 1820's) private baptisms were recorded more regularly than had been the case in the first two decades of the century. One can follow the decline of the time between birth and baptism in the registers of parishes such as Kempston and Blunham (both in Beds.); also, it is obvious that private baptism was increasingly given to infants on the verge of death in Camborne (Cornwall). Moreover, after 1823 Dissenters could no longer be under the illusion that their registers were the legal equals of the Anglican. While T. H. Marshall once intended to dismiss the marked increase in the number of baptisms in 1837 as a possible clerical error, I agree with D. V. Glass's judgement that the increase resulted from the reaction of the clergy to the introduction of civil registration.[56]

Hence, it seems that parochial registration was relatively accurate in the early eighteenth century, became somewhat less so in the 1780's, virtually collapsed between roughly 1795 and 1820, and then improved somewhat between 1821 and 1837. So poor a demographic source had parochial registration become even in the countryside that it seems doubtful that any significant gains in research can come from the study of parish registers of the early nineteenth century. And although the registers of the eighteenth century were relatively reliable demographic sources, one cannot assume that this conclusion is applicable to any individual register or set of registers of that time. In working on any local area, one must draw upon a wide variety of religious sources: the Compton 'census' of 1676, episcopal visitations, the Evans manuscript in Dr Williams's Library (which provides data on the number of Dissenters in many localities in the early eighteenth century), and various national and local histories of religion.[57] Particular attention has to be devoted to the Baptists. If they were important in the area which is being investigated, then there is a strong possibility that the parish registers omitted many births and deaths, although the acts for burial in woollen helped to keep down the leakage of the latter. Unless studies of parish registers are based on a relatively thorough investigation of the factors which affected registration in the particular area, the results are apt to be misleading.

[56] Marshall, *The Population Problem*, 442, and D. V. Glass, *Population and Population Movements in England and Wales 1690 to 1850* (a memorandum produced for the Royal Commission on Population—October 1945, but never published), 19. (*Editor's note:* This Memorandum is now printed above, pp. 221-46. The reference cited is at p. 232.)

[57] G. L. Turner (ed.), *Original Records of Early Nonconformity under Persecution and Indulgence*, 2 vols. (London 1911). An example of a relatively good county history is T. Timpson, *Church History of Kent* (London 1859).

16

A SURVEY OF POPULATION IN AN AREA OF WORCESTERSHIRE FROM 1660 TO 1850 ON THE BASIS OF PARISH REGISTERS

D. E. C. EVERSLEY

From: *Population Studies*, Vol. X, 1957, 253-79

Editor's Note: Apart from minor corrections, a few signed and dated notes have been added to the original version. The author does not now believe that the mortality of 1725-30 was chiefly due to an epidemic of smallpox, and references to this have been qualified or omitted.

THE object of this study was to test the practicability of using parish registers to gain additional knowledge about population movements in the eighteenth century. Widespread dissatisfaction exists among historians and demographers concerning the factual basis of the conventional hypotheses. It has, therefore, been suggested in various quarters that a fresh assessment is necessary.[1] In France, a large-scale inquiry along the same lines has been initiated.[2] In England new studies of parish registers are already in progress in some districts.[3] It is, however, clearly recognized by some students of the subject that a mere counting of entries of baptisms, burials and marriages is not sufficient to produce useful evidence. John Rickman based his estimates for the eighteenth century on the number of entries for every tenth year, at any rate up to 1780. Quite apart from their general inadequacy, it has been shown that the selection of years was probably not at all representative.[4]

As a first step toward fuller analysis of the material a survey was carried out in north Worcestershire by members of the Seminar in Population History and Theory in the University of Birmingham in the spring of 1956.[5] The report here presented should be taken as a guide to possible methods in further exploration, rather than as a considered statement of the causes of population increase. The original survey included more extended investigations into particular phenomena, such as the effects of the smallpox epidemic of 1725-30. These have been omitted or summarized very briefly in so far as they illuminate the method.

[1] *Cf.* H. J. Habakkuk, 'English Population in the Eighteenth Century', *Econ. Hist. Rev.*, 2nd ser., vol. VI, 1953-4, no. 2, p. 119. (See above, p. 269.)

[2] M. Fleury and L. Henry, *Des registres paroissiaux à l'histoire de la population. Manuel de dépouillement et d'exploitation de l'état civil ancien.* Paris 1956.

[3] See chapter by J. D. Chambers, above, p. 308.

[4] Habakkuk, *ibid.*

[5] I should here like to acknowledge the help given by student members of the Seminar, as well as by some volunteers, and our research assistant, Miss Janet Blackman. Thanks are also due to the parochial clergy who allowed us free and prolonged access to their registers.

1. *Choice of parishes*

It was decided at the outset that in order to avoid distortions, it would be necessary to carry out the survey in a single continuous area, preferably around a known centre of importance. If that is not done, local accident may destroy the value of the figures obtained. Even at a time of limited mobility, couples married and bore children in two or three different parishes during their life-time.[6] By taking an area, a good deal of this sort of temporary migration, and a substantial part of permanent migration, is absorbed in the total figures. At the periphery, of course, there is wastage; but the larger the area the better the chance of forming an undistorted picture.

Bromsgrove was chosen as the centre, both because it is convenient to Birmingham and because it is in the centre of an area which has become evenly divided into industrial and agricultural parishes, at least so far as acreage is concerned. During the period investigated (1660-1850) Bromsgrove itself, Tardebigge (which included Redditch), Stoke Prior, Belbroughton, and later Cofton Hackett came to be centres of an industrial population. By 1821, these parishes accounted for more than half the total population of the chosen area.

A rough circle of about five miles radius from Bromsgrove was then drawn and the whole or part of the following parishes were found to be within this area: Alvechurch, Belbroughton, Bromsgrove, Chaddesley Corbett, Clent, Cofton Hackett, Elmley Lovett, Elmbridge, Hampton Lovett, Hanbury, Dodderhill, Rushock, Stoke Prior, Tardebigge and Upton Warren.

This choice of parishes turned out to have been bad in several respects. First of all, Dodderhill is so closely integrated with Droitwich that its statistics are meaningless by themselves, even when seen in the aggregate with 14 other parishes. Cofton Hackett, though close to Bromsgrove, within the ancient manor, and on the south side of the Lickey watershed, proved to be closely connected with King's Norton (i.e. the Birmingham area). Clent seemed to be orientated more towards South Staffordshire (to which county the parish in fact formerly belonged). However, it would probably be difficult to find any area in Britain which does not suffer from some such defect, especially if one wishes to include an industrial region. Tardebigge had to be excluded since the incomplete records of the chapel at Bentley invalidated the main series of registers.

2. *The registers*

A list of available registers was printed by John Rickman in the 1831 census report. This already showed that many registers did not start until the second half of the seventeenth century, and even after that period there were some gaps.[7] At Bromsgrove, the entire marriage register from 1754-73 is missing.

---

[6] T. Nash, *Collections for the History of Worcestershire*, 1781, says (vol. II, p. 302), 'Chaddesley was the usual place of the burial of the dead for (the people of Rushock)—but that being a long mile distant, the inhabitants obtained leave to bury here'. I do not know to what period he refers. The registers show no deficiency, but then they only begin in 1686.

[7] On the history of parish registers in general, and their local peculiarities, see the works of R. Bigland, J. S. Burn, R. E. C. Waters, A. M. Burke and J. C. Cox, as well as the *Report from the Select Committee on Parochial Registration*, 1833. The evidence relating to existing statistics is summarized in D. V. Glass: *Population and Population Movements in England and Wales. 1690-1850*, see above, pp. 221-46.

Close investigation revealed various minor gaps. The only method of filling these gaps is to use the bishop's transcripts, which are now deposited in the County Record Office at Worcester. These are, however, still in the process of being sorted, and although in fact available to the public, are rather a time-consuming method of closing these *lacunæ* (they are arranged by years, not by parishes). Any full-scale investigation would, of course, need to use them.[8]

The quality of the records varies considerably. No register was reliably kept for every one of the years 1660-1850. Most showed at least three or four years in which no entries were made, or where the number of entries was a very small fraction of the usual. This could never be due to a lack of vital events. All registers were wholly or partially deficient during the Commonwealth period, with the possible exception of Alvechurch, which reveals no obvious flaw. But it was necessary to exclude the period 1640-60 from our calculations, and the number of parishes with a good 25-year run before that time turned out to be so small that no practical conclusions could be drawn. Before 1754 no form of entry was prescribed; from that date marriages, and from 1813 baptisms and burials as well, had to be entered on printed forms; but this was not always done at once, and where it was done, not all the required information was furnished. Origin and status of marrying parties, and age or occupation of a deceased person, were most often missing. The usual practice before the days of forms was to give full names to male adults or widows, full name and 'wife of . . .' to women whose husbands were alive, both parents' names at baptisms, and at least one parent's name at child burials.

There is much additional information in many registers. In years of exceptional sickness, the prevailing epidemic is often indicated. Towards the end of the eighteenth century, those who were buried 'on the parish' are often marked as paupers. Where a coroner's inquest was held the cause of death was sometimes entered, thus throwing light on contemporary conditions.

Illegitimate children appear under a variety of guises—'bace', 'spurious', 'supposed child of' and so on. Abandoned children, and nameless offspring of 'strangers', 'sojourners', and 'travelling women' abound. Soldiers are frequent, especially at Bromsgrove during the wars after 1790, either as marrying parties, or blamed for illegitimate children.

3. *The defects of the registers and the methods of allowing for them*[9]

Apart from the physical effects already mentioned, we are also faced with incompleteness arising from absolute failure to register by carelessness; the effects of nonconformity and of migration.

Obvious physical defects can be easily remedied by interpolation. Where figures were inserted, it was always done on the assumption that there was no change in the long-term trend for the parish concerned, even if the averages for the other parishes showed such a change. In no case could any error in this procedure have made more than a minute difference to the result, with the one exception of marriages at Bromsgrove, which are missing from 1754-74. An

[8] (These transcripts are now sorted and easily available. D.E.C.E., 1963.)
[9] See also Krause's article, p. 379 above.

error of more than 15 per cent in the estimate of marriages for Bromsgrove in a ten-year period could be enough to smooth out the very slight dip in the marriage rate for 1770—it could not affect the long-term horizontal aspect of the curve.

If baptism took place, only error or laziness would lead to failure to record. But there are many instances of private baptisms, especially in wealthy households or where children were very ill: this should have been followed by public reception into the congregation and an entry to that effect; but very likely it was often omitted.

Unmarried mothers probably often concealed births; but judging by the chances of survival of those illegitimate children who did receive baptism, no great difference to the population could result. Burials cannot often have been omitted, except in the case of Quakers, who had their own burial ground at Droitwich. Marriage records are likely to be much more complete, too, than baptisms; even after civil marriage was permitted, and there were in the country as a whole many nonconformist places of worship licensed for marriages, the Registrar General records for Worcestershire only a handful of marriages outside the established church.

This last observation also leads us to believe that nonconformity in the eighteenth century cannot have led to very many omissions. From the account of nonconformity in Worcestershire in the *Victoria County History*, it appears that there was much evidence of Quakers and Baptists at the end of the eighteenth century. But both ecclesiastical censuses and accounts from other sources have few mentions of conventicles or congregations outside Droitwich and Bromsgrove. Even the latter place did not have substantial congregations of nonconformists until the 1830's. Chapels in the district mostly begin after 1830.

Even where there were nonconformists, the registers show that they made use of the church's sacraments. When the Quakers buried their dead at Droitwich, the certificate of burial in woollen was still issued in the church and registered there. There are a few entries of burials of Catholics in the parishes near Droitwich. Two of the incumbents in the district informed us that Methodists regularly attend church services, for want of public transport to their own nearest chapel. It is impossible to estimate what ought to be allowed for nonconformity—that it is very little I have no doubt.

Nevertheless, all these factors mean that some correction rate must be used, and that this rate must be greater for baptisms than for burials. Talbot Griffith used the figure of 15 per cent for baptisms, and 10 per cent for burials, uniformly throughout this period. This method has been sharply criticized by Professor Marshall,[10] referring to the work of Brownlee and Farr. Although I share his dissatisfaction, I was unable to discover a local correction factor more accurate than that of Griffith. I have set out, in the Appendix, an examination of the effect of the application of Brownlee's methods to our figures here. The main conclusion for the eighteenth century is that it makes little difference what one

[10] T. H. Marshall, 'The Population Problem during the Industrial Revolution', *Economic History*, *Supplement to the Economic Journal*, 1929, reprinted in E. Carus-Wilson (ed.), *Essays in Economic History*, 1954, pp. 306 ff. (see above, p. 254), and J. D. Chambers, above, p. 334.)

does, as long as one inflates baptisms a little more than burials. After 1820 the story is very different; but this period was of less interest to us. I also inflated marriages by 10 per cent, although I was far less convinced that this was necessary; not to correct them would mean no change in the behaviour of marriage or fertility rates: the former would be slightly lower, the latter slightly higher. If one assumed that the registration of marriages was worse before 1754 than after, the drop in the marriage rate would be even greater.

Migration had its greatest effect towards the end of the period. Birmingham was then growing rapidly, and, of course, a substantial proportion of this increase came from immigrants from the area studied. It is therefore obvious that whatever figure we adopt for our base population in 1665, the 'natural increase' which we would derive by adding baptisms and deducting burials from that date to the census of 1831 would be larger than the actual increase shown.

Immigration into the area undoubtedly also occurred, as is shown by the constant occurrence of new names, especially Welsh ones, the distant origins of the bridegrooms in many cases after 1754 and other external evidence.[11]

4. The use of rates and the attempt to calculate base populations

Rickman's method of estimating his base population was to assume that the same relationship between the total population and baptisms and burials existed throughout the period he investigated. This was unwarrantable—had the rates in fact remained at their 1730 level, the population would not have grown.

One way of calculating the population is to count backwards from the census. This works quite well on the national scale, but in local studies one soon comes up against the fact of migration. The figure arrived at by deducting baptisms and adding in burials is almost certainly too small. Thus, if the 1821 census gave a figure of 1,000, and there were 500 baptisms and 300 burials in the preceding 20 years, this would suggest there were only 800 people living in the parish in 1801. In fact it is quite likely that there were 900, and that the census would have shown 1,100, had not 100 emigrated (even omitting the variations caused by the deaths, marriages and consequent baptisms of those that migrated). The result will be that in any village where emigration was substantial the counting back process will lead to a zero population in fairly recent times. Where, on the other hand, there was immigration, the population figures for the base period will be much too large.

Since we cannot say how much emigration there was, we have to use other means of correcting the figures. The best known method of establishing the population at the end of the seventeenth century is that used by Gregory King—

[11] On the disappearance of old names and the arrival of new ones, as proof of great geographical mobility, see E. J. Buckatzsch, 'The Constancy of Local Populations and Migration in England before 1800', *Population Studies*, vol. v, p. 62, 1951. Although we did not investigate this point, my impression is that there is greater constancy of names in the north Worcestershire area, especially in the western half. On the other hand, when the census reports began to show places of birth of inhabitants, substantial immigration could be proved. In 1841, more than 20,000 inhabitants of the Halfshire Hundred were born outside the county of Worcester, compared with 72,000 born inside it. But for our 12 parishes, the proportion of 'foreigners' was smaller: 2,732 out of a total population of 19,600. Clent had the most (being closely associated with Staffordshire), industrial Stoke Prior had nearly a quarter of immigrants, but Elmbridge had only 24 out of 360.

finding out the number of inhabited houses from the hearth-tax returns and multiplying this figure by a constant.[12]

For any *one* individual parish the result of working back is highly unlikely to give a figure for 1660 which in any way ties up with the result of the hearth-tax calculation.[13] In most cases working back gives a population either much too large, or much too small.

(a) Hearth-tax returns

The method used here attaches a great deal of importance in one sense, to the accuracy of the hearth-tax returns. In view of the known lack of reliability of some of these documents, this may seem rash. The best way of looking at their employment is this: in 1660 the population of the twelve parishes cannot have been zero, and it is highly unlikely to have been more than half that of 1811 (which would make it 7,500). The hearth-tax returns should be useful in fixing an approximate starting point between those two extremes. Even if they provide estimates which are as much as 20 per cent out, the result will not affect the relative changes in rates, only their absolute size. As it happens, using the assumptions stated below, the total population of the 12 parishes in 1811, as calculated from the registers, was within a fraction of 1 per cent of the census figure.

The Worcestershire hearth-tax returns in the Public Record Office have the particular disadvantage that they are without the exemptions normally kept together with the assessments.[14] Where, in neighbouring counties, the complete records exist, the proportions vary greatly.[15] Besides this defect, the figures for Worcestershire vary quite considerably as between the assessments of 1662, 1665, 1671, and 1672.[16] It is highly unlikely that the number of houses in each parish was substantially different at these dates. But the number of assessments varied, as in the case of Upton Warren, from 16 houses (1672), to 40 (1662). There is no consistent pattern—each assessment showed maximum figures for at least one parish. We have here worked on the basis of the largest available figure for 1662-72, on the assumption that houses could hardly have been invented, though it was easy to omit them.

To convert the figures thus derived into persons, I have assumed an average of $4\frac{1}{2}$ persons per house (i.e. per set of hearths separately assessed). King's multiplier of 4·04 for the rural areas of England was obviously too small, since we did not have the exemptions. On the other hand most of the exemptions would be one-hearth houses occupied in many cases by pauper couples or widows. A multiplier of 5 would have been too large, however; the census of

---

[12] For a full discussion of this method and its possible errors, see D. V. Glass, 'Gregory King and the Population of England and Wales at the end of the Seventeenth Century', *Eugenics Review*, no. 37, January 1946, pp. 17 ff., also 'Gregory King's Estimate of the Population of England and Wales, 1695', *Population Studies*, vol. III, 1950, pp. 338 ff., and the works on the hearth tax quoted in the later article (see above, pp. 159-220).

[13] But it does so in some cases, e.g. Chaddesley Corbett.

[14] Except in the case of Belbroughton, Chaddesley Corbett and Clent, where partial exemption lists are extant.

[15] Mr P. Styles informs me that in Warwickshire there are two assessments for every exemption. But in Staffordshire the proportion of exemptions was smaller, and also in the printed Shropshire assessment so far as we examined them. It seems difficult to make a general rule. See Styles in M. Walker (ed.), *Warwick County Records*: Hearth Tax Returns, Vol. I, 1957.

[16] P.R.O., Exchequer Records, E.179/201. Various bundles.

1801 showed 2,532 houses with 13,945 inhabitants, i.e., more than 5 persons per house, and about the same proportion at succeeding census dates to 1831. But this was after a period of population growth and increasing marital fertility, so that we could hardly assume so great a state of overcrowding in 1660. As pointed out above, even if this figure of 4·5 is a little too large or a little too small, the effect on rates will be very small indeed, especially in the later eighteenth century.

(b) Other estimates of the size of parishes

Nash, in his *Collections*, printed the number of houses as given in two episcopal surveys, that of Bishop Sandys in 1563 and that of Bishop North in 1776-7. As the earlier original[17] contains figures for each of the parishes here investigated, they have been used as they stand. For 1777, two parishes are missing, Elmbridge and Belbroughton, and the figures inserted in the table have been interpolated on the assumption that for both these parishes the population of 1777 was as much below the total for 1811 as the aggregate of the remaining parishes. Both surveys measure houses. For 1563 the conversion factor used was 4½ (as for 1665). For the later period, five was nearer the state of affairs revealed in the census. These calculations naturally serve only as a check on the plausibility of the estimates from the other sources—since many counties have them, they appear to be a useful guide.

5. The population of twelve parishes

The following table shows the results achieved by beginning with the hearth tax estimates, adding corrected baptisms, and deducting corrected burials. The 1801 census has been ignored, as being probably less reliable than that of 1811. It will be seen that the overestimate from the registers gets worse after 1811—undoubtedly due to the increasing rate of migration into Birmingham and the Black Country. (Birmingham grew from 73,600 in 1801 to 85,750 in 1811—a rate not greatly exceeding that of our 12 parishes, and fully accounted for by underregistration in 1801, natural increase and a very small amount of immigration.) According to the 1831 census report, Birmingham had extremely low death rates in the first decade of the century, probably due to its age structure rather than its sanitation. From 1811 to 1821, Birmingham increased to 106,722 or by about 25 per cent, in the face of rising death rates,[18] and from 1821 to 1831 it grew to nearly 147,000 or by nearly 40 per cent. It is clear that migration will vitiate Worcestershire figures more at the end.

The close agreement of the final population of the area in 1810 with the census figures in the following year appears to be largely due to the happy accident that the net immigration into Bromsgrove just about matches the net emigration from the surrounding parishes. Yet this is exactly what we would expect from the general picture of the changes of population during the period of industrialization. It is in fact only in terms of such short-distance migration that the figures for each parish can be explained. It is highly unlikely that the

---

[17] Brit. Museum, Harl. MSS. no. 595, fol. 210.
[18] (The assumption of rising death rates in urban areas during this period is now disputed. But even if they were constant, the drain in Worcestershire would still be heavy. D.E.C.E. 1963.)

TABLE I

Population of twelve parishes, 1563–1831

Parish	1563	1665	1776-7	1810 Est.	1811 Census	Difference Emig.	Difference Immig.	1830 Est.	1831 Census	Difference Emig.	Difference Immig.
Alvechurch	459	472	1,000	1,892	1,344	548		2,215	1,548	667	
Belbroughton	306	540	939	2,135	1,318	817		2,444	1,489	955	
Bromsgrove	1,364	2,052	5,050	3,945	6,932		2,987	5,629	8,612		2,983
Chaddesley Corbett	522	580	1,170	1,455	1,222	233		1,761	1,404	357	
Clent	207	288	750	1,353	737	616		1,597	922	675	
Elmbridge	125	176	230	567	322	245		693	334	359	
Elmley Lovett	216	366	320	663	381	282		816	432	384	
Hampton Lovett	108	135	190	207	192	15		198	143	55	
Hanbury	383	522	900	964	1,018		54	1,139	1,073	66	
Rushock	77	104	90	369	185	184		451	177	274	
Stoke Prior	261	414	550	1,417	796	621		1,786	1,100	686	
Upton Warren	141	180	300	-42	402		444	91	474		383
Totals	4,169	5,829	11,489	14,929	14,849	3,561	3,485	18,820	17,708	4,478	3,366

| | | | | | Net emigration 76 | | | | Net emigration 1,112 | |

(Figures in italics interpolated)   For sources, see text

general health of the population of the twelve parishes was substantially different over the years. Yet they show widely different patterns of excess of baptisms over burials. These differences cannot be explained by location, size or occupational structure; so if they are real at all they must be due to migration. The greater the excess, the greater the emigration; where there is least surplus, immigration must account for growth. As already pointed out, the habit of burying, marrying or baptizing in neighbouring churches may also help to explain the facts.[19]

There is a possibility that certain villages were less touched by, say, fever epidemics than others. Thus, we find that Clent was less severely visited by the great mortality of 1725-30, being the only one of our 12 parishes to show a slight excess of baptisms over burials during that quinquennium. But such differences can hardly account for the long-term discrepancy. Over the first 50 years of the eighteenth century, although the 12 parishes did not exhibit uniform patterns of increase, the differences are much less great than in the later period, when we assume migration to have been greater.

From 1700 to 1750, seven of the parishes were either stationary or exhibited growth or decline of the order of less than 10 per cent. Stoke Prior grew by about 20 per cent and Alvechurch, Belbroughton and Clent each grew by between 30 per cent and 40 per cent.

If we compare the 1811 census position with that of 1831, we find that the loss by emigration has considerably increased by the later date. Bromsgrove appears to have ceased to attract fresh population from the surrounding villages; but this is no doubt an illusion since there must have been much movement from Bromsgrove into Birmingham, apparently balanced by continued immigration. The other villages exhibit much the same pattern; except that the four smallest ones show a much greater loss by emigration than formerly. This was the beginning of a long-term trend.[20]

6. Population growth by stages

Table 2 shows the increase of population since 1665, for the 12 parishes taken together. In each case the year in the first column is the middle year of a ten-year period, the totals apply to that period and the rates are calculated as averages for those ten years on the estimated population of the middle year. In the case of the first period, the 1665 population is that estimated from the hearth tax returns. The rates for years from 1670-1700 have not been separately calculated, but the net difference between baptisms and burials to 1699 has been used to get the population figure for 1700.

The baptism, burial and marriage rates are all crude rates calculated from the original entries corrected as previously (marriages were also increased by 10 per cent). The child mortality figures were derived from all entries marked 'son' or 'daughter of', as previously explained, up to 1812; after that date they are based on actual ages entered in registers.[21]

---

[19] Thus, we know that when the church at Upton Warren was being rebuilt, marriages were performed in Bromsgrove though burials could still take place in Upton churchyard. If baptisms also took place at Bromsgrove, as seems likely, part of the curious figures for Upton is explained.

[20] See J. Saville, *Rural Depopulation in England and Wales*, London 1957, for a generalized statement of this phenomenon.   [21] Child: 20 years or under. Infant: under 2 years.

The fertility rates were calculated by dividing successive 20-year totals of baptisms by the marriages contracted in the 20-year period half overlapping it. Thus baptisms 1705-24 divided by marriages 1685-1714, give a fertility of 3·62 recorded against '1710', i.e. the period 1705-14.[22]

In the case of the last four sets of figures, either estimated or census figures alone could be used, but we have inserted both figures in order to show that even if the base population estimate were substantially wrong in earlier years the general behaviour of the *rates* could scarcely be affected.

The totals given for the 12 parishes are very slightly different from the figure for the sum of the parishes in Table 1—this is due to a difference of about one in each parish when rounding off the inflated figures.

(a) The crude rates

The pattern of baptism rates is a good deal less clear than emerges from Talbot Griffith's figures for England as a whole. There is no doubt about an initial rise from the low figure of 1665 to the very high one of 1700[23]—the intermediate figure for 1670-4 for instance was 38·2. From this peak there is a temporary fall down to 1725. Then there is a sharp recovery after the great period of mortality to a peak at 1746; then a steady long-term drop down to 1820, interrupted only by a short boom round about 1780. The last figure, for 1831, is definitely up again. These changes are difficult to relate to the marriage and fertility rates. Certainly the marriage-rate peak of 1730 coincides with the beginning of a baptism peak, and a 20-year rise in fertility. This suggests that many of the marriages following the period of heavy mortality were in fact *additional* marriages which would not have taken place but for the vacancies created by the epidemics. But from 1750 to 1800 the marriage rate was virtually fixed—it varied only from 9·16 to 9·81 per 1,000. Fertility suffered, on the whole, a long-term fall from 1750 to 1790 and then rose continuously for 30 years.

(b) Interpretation: 1750-90

What then is the correct interpretation for the period 1750-90, forty years during which the population increased by one-third? It was not a period of noticeably lower death rates—both general and child death rates fell only fractionally over the whole period and in fact increased somewhat round about 1770. We can understand the increase by one-third in the period 1790-1820 much more easily, since during that period death rates fell sharply and fertility rates rose. The answer lies partly in the simple difference between baptisms and burials: each year there was a surplus of survivors. But the most significant feature of the period is probably the failure of the marriage rate to fall at a time of rapidly growing population.

It is perhaps best to put the problem this way. During the period 1750-90,

[22] No defence is offered for this proceeding. Had time allowed, we should have calculated annual moving averages. It is, however, unlikely that the long-term result would have been very different.

[23] There is also a strong possibility that the exceptionally high figures for the period round 1700 were due to the greater effectiveness of registration under the acts from 1694 onwards, which imposed taxes on births, marriages and burials and prescribed penalties for failure to register (see Glass, 'Population and Population Movements in England and Wales, 1690-1850', above, p. 170 ff).

burial rates fell slightly, with an intermediate rise at 1770. This fall seems to have been due mostly to changes in child mortality. At any rate a small part of the total increase in population may be attributed to these changes in mortality—in 1759 the annual increase of population due to differences between baptisms and burials was about 1·16 per cent. In 1790, this same difference accounted for an increase of less than 0·7 per cent. In other words, the fall in the baptism rate narrowed the gap more than the fall in mortality rates opened it. This is what we would expect,[24] since, other things being equal, each year the same number of baptisms would have to be related to a larger population. 'Other things' in this case, are of course the reproductive habits of the existing population.

TABLE 2

Crude rates for twelve parishes

		Totals (10 years)			Rates (per thousand)				Fertility (Baptisms per marriage)
Year	Population	Bapt.	Burials	Marr.	Bapt.	Burials	Child burials	Marr.	
1563	4,169								
1665	5,828	1,979	1,620	401	33·96	27·80	—	6·88	
1700	7,167	3,405	2,343	852	47·51	32·69	—	11·89	
1710	8,441	3,021	2,473	851	35·79	29·30	10·03	10·08	3·62
1720	8,789	3,142	2,812	910	35·75	31·99	10·77	10·35	3·60
1730	7,803	3,200	4,029	1,060	41·01	51·63	17·43	13·58	3·29
1740	8,468	3,726	2,919	717	44·00	34·47	14·55	8·47	3·84
1750	9,018	3,548	2,518	826	39·34	27·92	11·30	9·16	4·45
1760	9,785	3,323	2,636	960	33·96	26·94	9·92	9·81	3·92
1770	10,519	3,786	3,022	973	35·99	28·73	11·27	9·25	4·22
1776-7	11,489								
1780	11,719	4,370	3,172	1,115	37·29	27·07	10·35	9·51	4·10
1790	12,504	4,188	3,317	1,185	33·49	26·53	9·59	9·48	3·73
1800	13,609	4,393	3,258	1,074	33·28	23·94	9·30	7·89	4·09
1801 (Census)	13,495				32·55	24·14	9·38	7·96	
1810	14,916	4,844	3,144	1,190	32·48	21·08	8·11	7·98	4·25
1811 (Census)	14,849				32·62	21·17	8·15	8·01	
1820	16,500	4,786	3,487	1,043	29·01	21·13	7·31	6·32	4·88
1821 (Census)	16,181				29·58	21·55	7·45	6·45	
1830	18,833	6,108	3,704	1,256	32·43	19·67	7·90	6·67	
1831 (Census)	17,708				34·49	20·91	8·40	7·09	

Professor Marshall, following Brownlee, did not admit the fall in the baptism rate at all, at least until after 1840. By using a greater inflating factor for baptisms throughout the period when the rate falls in our table, he produces a uniform plateau of births virtually from 1780 to 1840. This stability, as opposed merely to a fall at a lesser rate than the growth of population produced, would mean an even more phenomenal increase in fertility. This in turn could only be due to a much greater expectation of life, or much earlier marriage. To bring baptisms of the period 1815-25 to the same *rate* as that obtaining in 1780, would mean an average product of each marriage of more than six

[24] See T. H. Marshall, *op. cit.*, and G. Udny Yule's article quoted there ('The Growth of Population and the Factors which control it', *Jour. Roy. Statist. Soc.*, Vol. lxxxviii).

children—that is, probably an increase of 50 per cent in the effective childbearing capacity of each mother. Of this one would want more independent evidence.

Whether the baptism rate did in fact fall as much as one would expect from the fall in the burial rate we cannot say, since we know nothing of the general age structure of the population. But this much is clear: the marriage rate should have fallen at approximately the same pace as the baptism rate, allowing for the fact that there was a slight decrease in child mortality, and therefore more infants survived to be married. In fact, the marriage rate does not fall at all. What is the result of this phenomenon? The baptism rate fell by about 13·2 per cent between 1750 and 1790. Had the marriage rate dropped by, say, 10 per cent during the same period, the result would have been a baptism rate of only about 30, instead of 33½ in 1790, assuming the same changes in fertility, etc., through the period. We must then assume that a good deal of the increase in population is due to changes in marriage habits—without these, the increase would have been much less.

At this point we must, of course, ask ourselves whether the steadiness of marriage rates and the decline in fertility may not in some way be connected, and point to the same source of error: the registers. For if marriages had in fact been more seriously under-registered before 1750 than afterwards, and a consequent upward correction of the marriage figures before 1750 been necessary, we should find that there would be a drop in the marriage rate after 1750, but the drop in fertility would disappear; fertility would be lower for 1750 than it now appears. One would immediately think of Hardwicke's Marriage Act, and assume that registration of marriages improved after 1754—since our periods of reference are 1745-54 and 1755-64. This theory would effectively dispose of any changes in fertility between 1750 and 1760.

It will be easily seen that even if this new correction were applied, it would do nothing to dispose of the difficulty of the behaviour in rates after 1750. Assuming that the marriage figure for 1760 were more nearly free from error than the earlier ones, subsequent marriage rates should still have fallen as did the baptism rate. The fall does not, in fact, set in till after 1805. Nevertheless, it may be worth while making some such correction, for if we do, a secondary set of explanations for our figures follows. Between 1760 and 1780, there is a noticeable rise in the baptism rate, as well as a slight rise in fertility. Now if we assume that the steadiness of marriage from 1750 to 1760 is in fact due to a statistical error, the significance of the same behaviour from 1760 onwards is thereby enhanced. For during that time we could clearly say that there was a change in marriage habits, and although fertility did not change much, the baptism rate did increase. This upward movement of baptisms is, as we would expect, initially reflected in a rise in child mortality and a similar movement in general mortality. After 1770, however, we have the combination of a still rising baptism rate, falling burial rates and child burial rates, combined with a steady marriage rate, but falling long-term fertility rates. [25]

The decade 1770-80 is thus pinpointed as one of great significance. The increase in population between the two dates is 11·4 per cent which is higher

[25] It should be remembered that the latter would anticipate to some extent the baptism rate of the next decade.

than any previous increase except the phenomenal 17·7 per cent between 1700 and 1710 (perhaps a less reliable period), and higher than any subsequent one until after 1810.

Referring back to the original summaries from parish registers, we find in fact that the peak of the baptisms occurs in the period 1775-9, when the rate was approximately 38. The peak of marriages occurs in the same quinquennium —the rate was then over 10 per 1,000. What explanations can we find for this development? There is a well-known periodicity about marriage rates which is connected with related fluctuations in the birth rate. Now we know already that following the epidemics of 1725-9 there was a great surge of marriages, followed by a similar surge of baptisms.[26] In the ordinary way this earlier surge (with a peak of baptisms in the period 1735-40) should have been followed by a related peak of marriages about 25 years later, i.e. 1760-5. A close analysis of the figures for the decade 1755-64 does in fact show that such a peak occurred then, although it is hidden, as in the later period, by the deceptive horizontal aspect of the marriage rate curve. The marriage rate for 1760-4, calculated on the 1760 population, is 9·94, the highest since the period 1730-4, and very similar to that in the period 1775-9. Undoubtedly, part of the rising baptism rate 1760-80 is due to these extra marriages of 1760-4, in themselves an echo of the epidemics 30 years earlier. It is quite clear from this that the second peak of marriages (or should we say the second failure of the marriage rate to fall) in 1775-9 cannot possibly be related to the earlier period: for those who then married belonged to an apparently deficient generation, that born between 1750 and 1755. The baptism rate for that quinquennium is only 33·44—part of a continuous fall from 1745-60. One therefore comes to the conclusion that the marriage rate for 1775-9 must represent a reaction to favourable conditions for marriage during that period. What these conditions were, we have not yet ascertained: but it is here that we should seek for 'causes' of population increase in the dynamic sense.[27]

(c) Some other observations from Table 2

It is noticeable that the period of relatively stationary fertility of marriages (1760-90) is also a period with no significant change in the burial rate. As soon as burial rates begin to fall more quickly again after 1790, fertility rates begin to rise. During this period, most of the fall in the burial rate was obviously due to a greater expectation of life of adults: between 1790 and 1820 total burial rates dropped from 26·53 to 21·55, but child burial rates fell only from 9·59 to 7·45—that is to say, of five lives saved out of every 1,000, compared with the earlier period, two were children's lives. This appears to be one explanation of rising fertility: the expectation of life of parents was increased, the length of childbearing life was extended. But this would in itself probably not be enough to increase the number of children quite so much: one would suppose that earlier marriage also had something to do with the increase in fertility. For this our figures provide no evidence. But we know in general of the increase

[26] See below, p. 408, for details of these movements.
[27] (One factor in the structure in 1775-9 was the abundance of cheap food: wheat prices fell sharply. Exports dropped, but production and home sales rose, as did total employment. These conditions seem favourable enough to account for the rise. D.E.C.E. 1963.)

in those occupations where early marriage was possible: many workers in the district were engaged on the building of the Birmingham and Worcester Canal (completed 1815) and in the Bromsgrove nail industry. It is also possible that enclosure, virtually completed during that period, increased the number of agricultural labourers as opposed to small tenants. Certainly the registers after 1812, which give occupations, show an appalling preponderance of the description 'labourer' over every other calling. There are very few 'farmers' amongst the parents of children.[28] This development is also reflected in the growth of the number of separate houses: if our calculations are correct, there were about 1,300 houses in 1665, and the census of 1801 shows only 2,532: 30 years later there were 3,543. These houses may be taken in two ways: as the response to an urgent demand created by an increase of population, or as one of the factors facilitating earlier marriage. To put the matter cautiously, we can say that the more elastic the supply of houses in a given economy, the fewer the obstacles to marriage. It is certainly striking that in those 30 years there was an addition of 40 per cent to the supply of houses, when in the previous 140 years their number had probably not quite doubled. Unfortunately, we cannot check on the number at intermediate periods, since the window tax returns refer only to a minority of houses.

It may be objected that if these additional incentives to early marriage existed the marriage rate should not show such a downward tendency as it does after 1790. But it has to be clearly understood that earlier marriage does not mean, in itself, a greater total nuptiality. It merely means an anticipation of the normal age of marriage, with an increase in totals in the years when this movement begins, and a drop when stabilization is again introduced. The only net additions to marriages are those of persons who would otherwise have died between the former mean age of marriage and the new, lower age—in the absence of life tables we cannot say what that proportion was. In any case, it would not seriously affect the rate.

Thus the marriage rate drops. Even assuming that the proportion of those of marriageable age who stay single shows a further drop on the period 1775-9, the much reduced mortality of the population leads to such an increase in the total that rates are bound to fall.

It is all the more surprising then, to find the baptism rate taking another upward movement in the last decade under investigation. This can hardly be attributed to any improvement in registration—if anything, in this last decade registration generally deteriorated owing to an increase in nonconformity and the building up of many new chapels. Nor can it be assumed that there was any startling change in the age composition of the population—emigration presumably affected most strongly the young and marriageable age groups. In 1841, Worcestershire's age structure was almost exactly the same as that of England as a whole, the only notable deficiency being in the age group 15-40. These were the children born in 1801-25, and those were precisely the emigrants of 1820-30 who helped to swell Birmingham's population.[29] But amongst the under 15's Worcestershire had a slight lead over the rest of England (37·42 per

[28] See also occupational analyses in census reports.
[29] The figures are: Worcestershire 15-40, 38·69 per cent, England 40·12 per cent.

cent as against 37·01 per cent). The fertility of marriage had been higher than that for the country as a whole, and thus we can only be confirmed in the view that a great deal of emigration of young people took place. Possible reasons for this higher fertility have already been discussed. It would have been most interesting to pursue the enquiry from the registers further into the period 1831-41, to watch the trend of the rates, but there is much evidence that the degree of deficiency increased alarmingly in that decade, obviously owing to the advent of civil registration (see Appendix).

7. The mortality of 1725-30[30]

The most startling feature of the whole eighteenth century is the pattern of the period 1725-30, the only time when burials exceeded baptisms.

TABLE 3

		Baptism rate		Burial rate		Child burials	Marriage rate
1705-14		35·79		29·30			10·08
1720-4		37·20		35·06			10·35 (a)
1725-9	1725-34	38·24	41·00	65·92	51·63	17·43	12·80
1730-4		43·76		37·34			14·34
1735-44		44·00		34·47			8·46

(a) 1715-24.

(In the original survey, Table 3 was followed by a detailed examination of the incidence of the epidemic in a number of parishes. The severity of the outbreak varied, but not according to any recognizable pattern. A conservative estimate of the net loss of population at Hanbury is 164 out of the 716 alive in 1715.)

What do the rates in Table 3 mean? First, as regards baptisms, we notice that the rate was already rising slightly before the epidemics broke out. The figure for 1725-9 does not constitute a further rise, but merely results from the fact that baptisms are calculated on a smaller population. On the basis of the 1725 population, the rate would have been little over 33. In other words, at the height of the epidemics baptisms declined, due no doubt to a high incidence of the disease amongst young women, or miscarriages in cases where the victim did not die. But as soon as the epidemics had passed there was a real increase in the propensity to marry, and consequently a rush of baptisms. Even calculated on the 1735 population, the baptism rate was over 42. Thus we must see the response to the devastation in a rush to fill vacant places.[31] The ratio of children dying to total deaths was constant so that we have to reckon two-thirds of all the extra deaths occurring as being adult deaths.

The normal wastage (taken from the pre-1715 death rate) would be 10 adult

[30] (There are a number of references to deaths from smallpox in the registers during this period, and in two of the villages this was clearly the major cause of mortality. But since this article was written, the same degree of mortality, or even greater havoc, has been observed in hundreds of parish registers examined, and in only very few cases is there clear evidence that smallpox is to blame. Contemporary accounts, however, underline what is apparent from the weather records and the course of food prices: that it was a time of wet summers, hard winters, food shortages, and fevers consequent on these. All age groups were affected though in some districts there was an observable tendency for male adult deaths to rise disproportionately. D.E.C.E. 1963.)

[31] The natural tendency for this to happen was already explained by J. P. Süssmilch in the middle of the eighteenth century. Malthus used and misused Süssmilch's evidence. (See K. Smith, The Malthusian Controversy, 1951, p. 268-71.)

males per 1,000 of the population per annum. If we assume that male adults constituted 25 per cent of the population (as they did in the census period), this wastage may be reckoned as an annual turnover of 4 per cent of all tenancies and jobs. At the height of the epidemic, however, this wastage would be 22 adult males per 1,000 of the population, or 8·8 per cent. This, then, would create an extra four or five vacancies per 1,000, and the increase in the marriage rate from 10·08 to 14·34 quite adequately fits in with this assumption.

How would these marriages be contracted? In part they would represent opportunities to marry for people who would not otherwise have found it economically possible to do so. In part they would be remarriages of widows and widowers. It is difficult to know whether one is to regard these as basically insignificant in the demographic pattern or not. If most of the marriages were between a widow and a widower, they might be seen as the continuation of one union out of two. But where widows or widowers married bachelors or spinsters, they should normally mean a net addition to the potential fertility of the population.[32] In this respect the marriage of a widower to a spinster is more important; we have to take it that this creates a new complete life capable of bearing children. Where the widow remarries she has to be regarded as possibly using the unexhausted part of her reserve of fertility. In the absence of precise figures I am inclined to look on these remarriages as being somewhat below fresh marriages in demographic significance, but by no means negligible. But for the great part they would be marriages of people who otherwise might have waited a little longer. How much weight to give to each of these factors may be gauged with some plausibility from the subsequent drop of the marriage rate, in the period 1735-44, to 8·46. One might guess that of the extra four marriages per 1,000 contracted, immediately after the epidemics, two were 'extra' marriages, or remarriages and two were 'anticipated' marriages.

That there were in the true sense more marriages in the long run, and not only marriages representing a mortgage on future years, may be inferred from the baptism rate of the period 1735-44, i.e. the time when the greater number of births from the post-epidemic marriages took place. Had marriages over the whole period 1725-39 been stable, in the sense of the years 1730-4 balancing out the postponed or anticipated marriages of the years before and after, the baptism rate should have shown an equal averaging out.

The extra marriages and their product may be roughly estimated as follows: We assume the period 1725-44 to have been the 'disturbed' period of the epidemics and their after-effects. We find that the average marriage rate for this period was 11·04, and the average baptism rate 42·50. If we take the average of marriages in the 'undisturbed' periods before and after (1715-24 and 1745-54) we find that they are 9·62 per 1,000, and the baptism rate similarly computed 37·75. Thus we find that the disturbed period produces an extra 1·43 marriages with an extra 4·75 baptisms.

It is in some such terms that we must see the astonishing recovery of the population after 1730. Admittedly, it took more than 25 years to recover the position of 1720. But the population of 1750 must have been younger than the

[32] Reference to later registers, where civil status is given, suggests that very few marriages took place between two bereaved people.

earlier one, and the double effect of this different age composition and factors making for a greater expectation of life, may be seen as an important constituent part of the increase in population after 1740.

The existence of a secondary peak (i.e. failure to fall) in the marriage rate around 1765, and an associated rise in the baptism rate, has already been noted. It may also be surmised that part of the failure of the burial rate to fall as much after 1780 as it had done after 1770, may be due to the fact that this was the period when the 'bulge' generation of 1730-40 reached its expected life span. The consequences of the epidemic of 1725-30 may thus be seen to extend over a considerable space of time.

8. Some other demographic information derived from the registers

(a) Child mortality and infant mortality

As was pointed out earlier, there were great difficulties in finding precise evidence about children and infants. In the larger parishes the attempt to check back over the baptisms of two years for each child burial was frustrated by the time factor. Even for the medium sized parishes the task would often take half an hour for each year of burial entries. Nevertheless, the attempt was made for nine parishes, and the results are set out below, for the periods when even moderate reliability may be placed on them. A certain amount of interpolation has been used, but no results are printed where more than one period of five years in 25 was without precise figures.

TABLE 4

Period and number of parishes for which calculated	Child burials (as % of baptisms)			Infant burials (as % of baptisms)		
	All	Largest	Smallest	All	Largest	Smallest
1675-99 (6 parishes)	28·5	42·0	15·9	12·3	17·6	10·0
1700-25 (7 parishes)	26·5	42·3	22·3	11·4	20·0	8·0
1725-49 (6 parishes)	35·7	73·4	26·6	11·5	20·7	7·4
1750-74 (5 parishes)	24·7	34·4	19·6	9·2	14·5	5·3
1775-99 (6 parishes)	24·7	26·6	11·4	7·1	9·9	4·1
1800-24 (9 parishes)	20·0	28·7	11·9	7·5	8·7	4·8
1825-49 (8 parishes)	26·7	35·8	18·6	13·8	17·2	7·3

The figures quoted represent in each case child or infant burials as a percentage of baptisms during the same 25-year period. In this case no correction was applied on the assumption that at least the same correction rate as that generally used for baptisms, i.e. 15 per cent, would have had to be used for child burials: not only did these go unnoticed more often than adult burials, but in some cases the name of the child was written into the register without the name of the parents, and was thus not counted.

The figures quoted here present a somewhat different picture from that obtained by looking at child mortality in Table 2. In the main table, we took child burials as a rate on the total population, but in this one they are related to baptisms in the same period. The long-term improvement now looks even less good than it did before. Here we have the burials related to 'the population at risk', i.e. the new-born children.

It has to be stated at once that all these figures are subject to much larger errors owing to careless entries than the others. Our impression was that clergymen became less punctilious about details in the later part of the eighteenth century than they had been a century earlier. This is probably the true explanation of the apparent deterioration after 1800, when, gradually, the more accurate printed registers were brought into use. It is also possible, of course, that child mortality really did increase quite considerably, mainly during the cholera period, which has had a strong effect on the last 25-year period.[33]

There is a further source of error arising from the way in which the figures were calculated. Before 1812, the instructions to the register-searchers were to look back for the baptism of each child buried in the entries for the year in which burial took place, and the previous year.

Although this method would find all infants under one year,[34] it obviously might omit some between one year and two years from date of baptism, depending on the time of year when burial took place. It was not possible to be more accurate than this because the date of burial was often not entered, or the entries were not chronological, and in any case the children were often many weeks old at baptism.

Nevertheless, after 1812 we included all children less than two years old, so that some increase in numbers was inevitable. Had the method of enumeration represented a serious fault, there should have been an immediate jump after 1812. But this is not the case. 1815-19 was a period of very high general mortality, so all burial figures rise, but 1820-5 exhibits the same pattern of infant mortality as the years before the new register.

The period 1725-49 is, as we would expect, brought into high relief by the mortality described above. But it is astonishing to see that infant mortality did not rise *pari passu* with child mortality. There is a possibility that small children acquired immunity from mothers who had already recovered.

The general picture which emerges from this partial survey of child mortality is that there was some apparent improvement in the eighteenth century, but that at the time of greatest population increase, between 1810 and 1830, improvements in child and infant mortality can hardly have made any contribution to the increase, and in fact a real deterioration probably set in.

How far this is to be described as an accident of registration, and how far it is a genuine development, it is not possible to say. Famine took many child lives, and so perhaps did the hazards of industrial life. At Stoke Prior, in the 1830's, where there was a child burial percentage of more than 23, we find that in some years four or five children (out of a total average child burials of 10) were recorded as having drowned in the Birmingham and Worcester Canal, along which workmen's cottages were being built.

There is a further argument against the supposition that the saving of child lives made a substantial contribution to the increase in population. If we did assume that in 1800-24 four extra new-born children survived to marriageable age, compared with 1750-74, we should expect the marriage rate to go down

---

[33] That, at some period, child mortality figures rose again after an initial improvement, is agreed by Marshall and others. (But mortality from cholera in 1831-2 was insignificant in the area. D.E.C.E. 1963.)

[34] Except where parents migrated in the interval.

less sharply than it did after 1790. These four children could, after all, provide two extra marriages per 1,000. But the decline in marriages went on. Perhaps more survivors simply meant more bachelors or spinsters. I am more inclined to the view that the figures for 1825-49 represent the correct long-term incidence of child mortality, and that some of the apparent improvement in the second half of the eighteenth century is due to faulty registration of child burials. The registers at Alvechurch and Chaddesley Corbett, which appear to be amongst the best kept as well as having been very conscientiously worked over, show little improvement of child mortality over the whole period. On the other hand there can be no doubt as to the low infant mortality figures for these two parishes for the period 1775-1824. Clearly the evidence is, so far, inconclusive.

(b) The origin of marriage partners

One of the objects of this inquiry was to find out whether there was any change in the patterns of marriage. I had believed (from evidence collected in Somerset) that one of the outstanding features of the demographic pattern of the eighteenth century was the increase in mobility, geographical and social.[35] Since many clergymen before 1754 recorded the places of origin of the bride and bridegroom, especially where banns were called, and after that date the forms provided for this information to be stated, I thought it might be possible to say with tolerable accuracy whether there had been such an increase. Once again the records, however, are imperfect, and in many parishes the necessary information was omitted, even after 1754, for some years. But fortunately such lapses became infrequent after 1800 and virtually unknown after 1837, and this enables us to state quite clearly that marriages between partners of different parishes were actually more frequent in the eighteenth than in the early nineteenth century. Where we have a full statement of places of residence of bride and bridegroom, as at Chaddesley Corbett, the position is beyond doubt. From 1700 to 1725 out of 457 marriages, 364 were between partners one or both of whom lived outside this fairly large parish. While this was exceptional, we can say that in no subsequent period was the percentage less than 20, and there was no noticeable increase up to 1850. Similar high percentages are found at Clent and other places during that century. There does not seem to be any pattern in this: one would have expected that the smaller the parish, the greater the need for 'mixed' marriages, owing to the impossibility of finding a partner in a place of 200 souls. But this is not so in every case. At Rushock indeed, 70 out of 91 marriages between 1700 and 1749 were 'mixed' in this sense; but only 20 out of 39 in the first half of the nineteenth century.

It is when we get to the figures for the period after 1800 that we have the highest percentages of 'home' marriages in the large parishes. At Bromsgrove, from 1800 to 1824, all but 102 out of 1,010 marriages were marked as being between a man of 'this parish' and a woman of 'dto'.

It would, of course, have been much easier for a man to have found a wife at home in a parish of 7,000-8,000 people: but not so much easier than it had been, say, early in the eighteenth century when Bromsgrove had between 3,000

---

[35] See T. S. Ashton, *An Economic History of England: the Eighteenth Century*, 1955, p. 5, and Chambers, above, p. 329.

and 4,000 souls; but one-third married outside the parish. It is possible that the reason for this strange change is again purely statistical. We know that the settlement laws operated less strictly as the eighteenth century progressed: could it have been that in earlier times the place of origin was always the place where one or the other partner had their settlement, even if they were by that time living in the parish where they married, and that by 1800 it had become customary to describe their abode at the time of the banns or the granting of the licence?

The answer is not really important, for we know that people migrated freely in the early nineteenth century, and now we know with equal certainty that they moved early in the eighteenth and even earlier. In the tiny village of Elmbridge, on the outskirts of Droitwich, 17 out of 22 marriages in the period 1675-99 were 'mixed'. Mobility did not begin with the industrial age.

Nothing has so far been said about the distance of marriage. It was not possible, within the time available, to draw charts of concentric circles from each parish to measure distances. We recorded marriages as mixed even if the other parish was only two miles away. But it was by no means true in any of the ten registers examined for this point that more than half of the 'mixed' marriages were with partners from the nearest neighbouring parish. In the case of Chaddesley Corbett there was a very high proportion of places at a considerable distance beyond the neighbouring large places, Kidderminster and Bromsgrove.

Whatever inferences might be drawn from a detailed study of the marriages from the geographical point of view, the conclusion must stand that greater freedom of movement cannot have contributed to increase of population by providing more scope for marriage.

(c) Miscellaneous information

Attempts to make records of illegitimacy and of the remarriage of widowers also largely failed owing to insufficient precision of entries. An entry of the baptism of a base-born child is definite evidence, an entry with the mother's name alone is not. Certain periods stand out clearly, however, in the ten parishes where records in this respect are fairly consistent, as having produced unusually large numbers of illegitimate children. There was a marked increase after 1789, figures were fairly high throughout the war. But the peak period was 1815-19, when these ten parishes showed 73 illegitimate children, compared with only 50 in the following five years. Whether this was due to the fortuitous advent of local Don Juans during or after the war, or to great difficulties put in the way of marriage by the times, one cannot say. Some would undoubtedly adduce these figures as proof of the immorality engendered by out-relief.[36]

The widowers were equally disappointing. We had hoped to find out whether remarriages of widowers became fewer owing to improvements in maternal health. Had fewer mothers died in childbed, fewer husbands would have had to remarry. But again the evidence is not good enough. 33 out of 190 marriages at Stoke Prior between 1825 and 1849 were with widowers—the proportion could hardly have been higher in earlier periods. At Hanbury, on the other hand, 14 per cent of marriages were with widowers from 1750-74,

[36] Cf. e.g., the 1832 Poor Law Report.

about 12 per cent in 1775-90, and 8 per cent in 1800-24, and a quite negligible proportion in the last 25 years.

In certain individual years, following very high general mortality the number of widowers marrying increased—but so did the widows, which would be expected. No analysis was made to find out whether years of exceptionally heavy female mortality were followed by many widowers marrying, or whether the frequency of such years decreased.

Besides the demographic material here evaluated the registers contained a large amount of general historical material. Often the entries throw light on the changes in population—but the marginalia which brighten the pages are evidence of the intelligence or otherwise of the vicar, rather than of long-term changes. It is usually possible to detect the period of economic change through entries of occupation of husband or father—for convenience of identification before 1812 and as a matter of law thereafter. In all the parishes we can date the advent of the canal and the railway with fair accuracy, especially as both were, in the early days, responsible for many deaths.

Towards the end of the eighteenth century, many incumbents marked paupers as such.[36a] Where this was done (as at Dodderhill, one of the registers not incorporated in our tables), it is possible to form an estimate of the proportion of the population dependent on poor relief, which in this case was well over half.

9. Conclusion

The main demographic evaluation of this very limited material has already been set out. The increase in population in the twelve parishes after 1740 appears to have been due to a combination of a long-term fall in the death rate and a greater opportunity for marriage, both together producing a long-term rise in fertility. The effects of the great epidemics of 1725-9, though depopulating at the time, may in the long run have contributed to the increase.

We can say, however, that this is not a full evaluation of the material in these registers. By using child and infant mortality, we have already been able to progress beyond Rickman. The main need now is for a full analysis on the basis of a card index. To provide useful evidence every entry in registers (including any nonconformist ones available) must be transferred to a card, and these cards re-sorted into families. Owing to imperfections, migration, and losses at the margin even of a large area under investigation, many of these family cards would not be complete. But if the scale of operations were sufficiently large, sufficient whole histories of families should emerge from such a procedure to enable us to do what the present investigation failed to do, to construct life tables for different localities and occupations, to see clearly the pattern of marriage and re-marriage, the size of completed families and so on.

Such an investigation, we conclude from the present survey, need not be prohibitive in cost. All the evidence points to the most startling changes having taken place between 1740 and the beginning of civil registration. Over this period, registers are both more complete and more legible than in earlier periods.

[36a] For the legislation under which this was done, see Krause, above, p. 385.

Nevertheless it would be a pity, if funds were available, not to make a contrasting study also of the demographic pattern in a relatively static population before 1740.

The completion of this research would do more than answer a vexed problem. The social and economic structure of the country before 1801 would be illuminated in much the same way as was done by the nineteenth century census reports. To obtain accurate statistics for north Worcestershire in the eighteenth century is to further the study of the effect of enclosures and the growth of neighbouring Birmingham.

APPENDIX

Dr Brownlee's Method[37]

When Professor Marshall attacked Mr Talbot Griffith in 1929 for adopting a uniform factor for the correction of baptisms before 1840, he took him to task for not studying the work of William Farr and Dr Brownlee.[38]

It seems necessary therefore to defend the continued employment of a procedure which has been discredited. It is not put forward as an excuse that the results appear to be plausible. The main reason for having to reject Brownlee's methods is that while it is possible to use them for the country as a whole, they cannot be applied to a single area. I have already concluded that no final settlement of the vital questions is possible without more elaborate investigations of the registers with the help of card indexes.

Farr and Brownlee used various methods to estimate the probable conversion factors of baptisms and burials into births and deaths. The essence of the procedure is to find out for any given period what birth rate would have been necessary to produce a given population increase, given known mortality. Most observers have concluded that the registration of burials was more trustworthy than that of baptisms. Brownlee started from a conversion factor 1·18 for the period 1838-40, for burials, and assumed that this was applicable to the entire decade, and in fact that a constant ratio of 1·20 would serve as far back as it was desirable to make calculations.

For baptisms, the correction factor was 1·317, but Brownlee concluded that this was not enough for the earlier 1830's, when in fact a ratio of 1·347 would be needed to explain changes. Going further back, he obtains a figure of 1·243 to correct baptisms right back into the eighteenth century.

Let us first check how far these corrections are applicable to Worcestershire. The editors of the 1841 census had warned against taking the drop in baptisms in the country after 1837 too seriously: they claimed that many clergymen had drawn their attention to the new habit of taking civil registration as a substitute for church ceremonies, especially baptism.[39] Hence it would be thought that a comparison for those three years

[37] A fuller discussion of Brownlee's method came to my knowledge after the completion of this Appendix. It is to be found in Professor Glass's unpublished study previously mentioned, *Population and Population Movements in England and Wales, 1690–1850*, pp. 6 ff. (see p. 228 ff above). Although the methods used by Professor Glass are at a much higher level of sophistication than mine, some of his conclusions are very similar to those presented here: first, that Brownlee, for all his expertise, overestimates the necessary correction to baptisms in the 1830s; second, that after criticizing Farr's constant corrections for earlier periods, he falls into the same trap himself, on quite unwarrantable assumptions; and thirdly, that in the end it does not seem to matter very much which method of conjecture one adopts since the results are not so dissimilar. On the other hand, even the agreed results are so much the product of speculation, that only a much larger concerted effort can hope to break the deadlock. (*Op. cit.*, Conclusion, p. 246.)

[38] T. H. Marshall, *op. cit.*, above, p. 254 f. Brownlee's paper appeared in *Public Health*, June-July 1916, pp. 211 ff. Farr's work (though anonymous, bearing the marks of his method), in the *General Reports to the Census* of 1861 (Vol. III, p. 22) and of 1871 (Vol. IV, pp. xiii-xiv and 54-56).

[39] *Census*, 1841, Vol. IV, *Parish Register Abstracts*, p. vi.

between baptisms and the (as yet imperfect) civil registration would be inappropriate. Brownlee rejected this, and kept to his correction factor for the *whole* decade and thought that underregistration was even worse before civil registration. He knew the intercensal increase, 1831-41, and the number of deaths which occurred, assuming his constant mortality correction. Thus he derived the number of births which would be needed to bring about the known increase. Now we cannot do this for Worcestershire, since the intercensal increase is obviously less than the natural increase, owing to emigration.

But there are some other ways of checking the plausibility of the parish registers.

The following table gives the recorded figures for England and Wales, Worcestershire, and three registration districts relevant to our survey. (King's Norton is out of the area, but they are here used together, since the Registrar General's early reports do not separate the three districts.) This shows clearly that there was a fall, after 1837, mainly in baptisms but also slightly in burials, down to 1839, but not in marriages. Now Brownlee and most others accept the marriage figures to be very nearly correct (though they cannot test them before 1838). If we do so, we find that there is, after 1837, a sudden sharp drop in the fertility of marriages. This is highly improbable.

TABLE 5

	England and Wales			Worcestershire			Droitwich, Bromsgrove and King's Norton Registration District		
	Marr.	*Bapt.*	*Burials*	*Marr.*	*Bapt.*	*Burials*	*Marr.*	*Bapt.*	*Burials*
1831	112,094	389,122	278,619	2,485	8,996	6,433	610	1,509	1,220
1832	116,604	387,971	298,161	2,795	8,927	7,375	696	1,576	1,267
1833	120,127	400,043	290,508	2,938	9,220	5,735	706	1,639	1,044
1834	121,884	405,875	283,097	3,011	9,507	6,311	735	1,579	1,087
1835	119,598	405,067	281,545	3,086	9,761	5,989	775	1,614	1,095
1836	120,849	405,137	336,994	3,046	9,902	6,667	805	1,665	1,214
1837	112,727	462,893	292,650	2,690	10,763	7,823	732	1,794	1,304
1838	113,123	377,114	286,855	2,828	9,638	6,124	691	1,589	1,022
1839	116,677	368,063	304,407	2,920	9,359	5,962	724	1,541	1,036
1840	115,548	364,440		2,887	9,023	6,492	834	1,496	1,178

Source: Census, 1841, Vol. IV, Parish Register Abstracts, p. vi.

If, in Worcestershire, we divide the baptisms of each year after 1836 by the marriages five years earlier, as a rough test, we get the following ratios:

TABLE 6

$\dfrac{1836 \text{ baptisms}}{1831 \text{ marriages}}$	3·98 children per marriage	
$\dfrac{1837}{1832}$ "	3·85 "	"
$\dfrac{1838}{1833}$ "	3·28 "	"
$\dfrac{1839}{1834}$ "	3·11 "	"
$\dfrac{1840}{1835}$ "	2·92 "	"

Such a drop did not previously occur, and, in the absence of contraceptives, is highly improbable. One therefore concludes that baptisms were much more heavily under-registered after 1837 than before. Since the same drop cannot be observed for the country as a whole, it seems likely that Brownlee was right to some extent: but here too there is a reduction. For the three registration districts, fertility appears to be lower throughout, but the drop is similar. It is likely that the figures for these areas are vitiated after 1831 (a period outside our survey) since the drift of young people to Birmingham was very strong by this time: so that many who married there would not stay to have their children. Nevertheless there is no evidence that this migration took place at an increasing rate in the late thirties.

If we assume the number of marriages in Worcestershire in 1834 and 1835 to have been correct, and apply to them the average fertility of the marriages of 1831 and 1832, we obtain the following results:

TABLE 7

	Baptisms recorded	Baptisms calculated from earlier fertility	Registered births
1839	9,359	11,788	11,593
1840	9,023	12,080	11,835

Brownlee and Farr relied a great deal on life tables to find out what ought to have been the number of baptisms in certain periods. Farr projected his 1838-54 life table too far back: he did not allow for fluctuations in infant mortality. Brownlee, with much more elaborate methods, tried to allow for this. Nevertheless, since accurate life tables for the population as a whole are not obtainable further back than 1821, all these calculations are of little use to us for the eighteenth century. If we do not know what ought to have been the mortality, we cannot check on baptisms. To illustrate the difficulties of using life tables, I have here tried to estimate the plausibility of the recorded baptism figures by finding out how many deaths there ought to have been in 1841, as against those which actually took place. The life table used in the first table is that for Surrey in 1841, from the fifth report of the Registrar General, 1843, pp. 16 ff. Surrey's mortality pattern, as given in the parish register abstract of the 1831 census, did not differ greatly from that of Worcester.[40]

TABLE 8

	Worcestershire (less Dudley) 1841			Droitwich, Bromsgrove and King's Norton 1841		
	Baptisms	Expected deaths	Actual deaths	Baptisms	Expected deaths	Actual deaths
1831-6 (mid-year/ mid-year)	30,791	231	250	7,607	57	56
1836-7 ,,	7,406	92	95	1,730	21	15
1837-8 ,,	7,264	105	139	1,692	24	19
1838-9 ,,	6,881	151	191	1,565	34	43
1839-40 ,,	6,684	247	408	1,519	56	69

The conclusion is again the same: that unless there was a great change in the pattern of expectation of life, the differences in the death experience of the age groups can only be explained in terms of a much more serious underestimate of baptisms after 1838 than before.

[40] The figures there were based on recorded burials, 1813-20.

While it is comparatively easy to use a life table for such a short period of time, longer periods present much greater difficulties. We see from the table below that for Worcestershire as a whole, the Surrey life table appears to be too favourable in 1841 —that is to say, there are more deaths than Surrey experience led us to believe. This is shown in the following table. We have here taken the total number of baptisms in Worcestershire (including the very unhealthy district of Dudley), in the period 1831-6, and applied to it different life tables, and compared the result with the enumerated number of survivors in the 5-10 age group in the census of 1841.

TABLE 9

Baptisms 1831-6 (mid-year):	42,254	
Survivors estimated from Surrey 1841 table	33,465	
Metropolis 1841	30,238	
Liverpool 1841	23,099	
Worcestershire 1831	27,304	Actual survivors: 28,386

(From *Census*, 1831, Vol. III, p. 375)

It will be seen that the experience of Worcestershire in 1813-30 was more relevant to the situation there in 1831-41, than the more contemporary evidence from Surrey, London or Liverpool.

But taking the calculation further back brings much greater difficulties. If we try to test the baptisms of 1801-10, against the survivors aged 30-40 in 1841 by the same useful 1831 life table, we find a very bad underestimate: the life table would have given us 21,724 in that group by 1841, in fact there were 29,437—and that without allowing for emigration! The use of a more favourable table (Surrey 1841) gives us 32,376. Quite obviously, then, there were more survivors in the early years of the century from those then born, than the experience of 1813-30 suggests. This we already knew!

If we attempt to use some of Brownlee's figures for the country as a whole, in Worcestershire, the following results appear.[41]

TABLE 10

	Population			Baptism rates		Burial rates	
	By Brownlee's correction	Census	Own est.	Brownlee	Own	Brownlee	Own
1770			10,519		35·99		31·27
1780	11,922		11,719	39·61	37·29	29·02	27·07
1790	12,737		12,504	35·54	33·49	28·50	26·53
1800	13,909	13,495 (1801)	13,609	36·12	32·55	26·33	24·14
1810	15,547	14,849 (1811)	14,916	35·95	32·62	23·09	21·17
1820	18,547	16,181 (1821)	16,500	32·87	29·58	23·51	21·55
1830	21,003	17,708	18,833	41·63	34·49	22·82	20·91

I have not attempted to go back further than 1770 with the correction by Brownlee's rate. First of all, it is just as arbitrary as Griffith's; secondly it would make no difference to the behaviour of the rates. As Brownlee himself pointed out in his article, there are many different combinations of corrections which give the same eventual result. Up to 1800, the matter is apparently of little consequence. After this, Brownlee's population

[41] Burials corrected by 1·20, baptisms by 1·243 in the earliest period, rising to 1·38 in the last.

naturally rises much faster, given both the greater correction for baptisms and the greater surplus of them. Even so there are no great differences in the behaviour of the rates even after 1800, until we get to the question of the baptism rate of the period round 1830. There is every indication that it went up: but that it rose as drastically as Brownlee's correction suggests, I cannot believe. For one thing, since infant mortality was still as high as we know it to have been, there ought to have been a further rise in the burial rate. This was not the case. On the other hand, if there was as much net emigration as the first column suggests, it is possible to think of the lower burial rate as simply the consequence of so many people born in the county dying elsewhere. This cannot be ruled out.

In conclusion, one would say that for the period after 1800, Farr's and Brownlee's work is obviously still of the greatest importance. The more defective the registers become, and the more information is available from the census reports, the more scope is there for complex statistical measurements, especially for the country as a whole. But as we go back into the eighteenth century, we shall not have knowledge until we re-analyse the registers: from that we shall calculate new life tables, and with their help finally overcome the imperfections of registers in some parishes.

PART III

EUROPE AND THE UNITED STATES

17

LAND AND POPULATION IN IRELAND
1780-1845
K. H. CONNELL

Editor's Note: This paper was originally published in *The Economic History Review*, 2nd series, Vol. II, 1950, and is here reprinted with minor amendments by the author. The argument is elaborated and more fully documented in his *Population of Ireland, 1750-1845* (Oxford 1950).

THE initial and often insurmountable problem in any attempt to explain the growth of population in a period before appropriate and reliable census material is available is to measure the rate of increase. In Ireland the first of the decennial censuses was taken in 1821; because of the inexperience of the enumerators and the reluctance of the people to allow themselves to be counted, its figures for the total population may fall short of the truth. Ten years later, when some of the enumerators were paid by results, the error may be in over-statement. There is little doubt, nevertheless, that the first three censuses give a tolerably accurate picture of the growth of population. Our difficulties begin when we try to find figures as satisfactory for the previous seventy years. That we must be sceptical of the contemporary estimates is shown by a glance at those tabulated below; we can scarcely credit a rate of increase of over 50 per cent between 1781 and 1791, nor one of some 70 per cent in the thirty years before the first census.

The Population of Ireland, 1725-1841*

	Traditional estimates based on returns of hearth-money collectors	Revised estimates
1725	2,317,374	3,042,000
1754	2,372,634	3,191,000
1767	2,544,276	3,480,000
1777	2,690,556	3,740,000
1781	2,500,000–2,750,000	4,048,000
1791	3,850,000–4,206,612	4,753,000
Census figures:		
1821	6,802,000	
1831	7,767,000	
1841	8,175,000	

* The sources of the traditional estimates, and an explanation of the processes of their revision, will be found in Connell, *Population of Ireland, 1750-1845* (Oxford 1950), pp. 1-26.

These eighteenth-century estimates were mostly based on returns made by the hearth-money collectors of the number of houses in the country, together with other estimates of the average number of residents in a house. When we consider the obstacles which beset the collectors and the temptations to which they were subject, we can understand why many houses were omitted from their records. They were working, often in wild country, among a people anxious to escape their notice. Their acquisitiveness as well as their laziness added to the deficiency of their returns: when they pocketed the tax themselves they did not record the houses that paid it. The traditional estimates, then, have to be revised, and there is no doubt that the revision must be upward. The figures in the second column of the table have been derived from the hearth-money returns, modified by internal evidence of error, by other contemporary material and by data drawn from the early censuses. That the revised figures have any precise accuracy is, of course, out of the question. Nonetheless we can be fairly confident that the doubling of the population which they show in the sixty years before the Famine reflects at least as great a rate of natural increase. The four million Irish in 1781 were the progenitors not only of the eight million of 1841 but of another million and three-quarters who had travelled to Britain or North America.

Our problem now is to account for the extraordinarily rapid rate of natural increase which seems to have begun by the 1780's. Unfortunately no national statistics earlier than those of the 1830's give us any help in determining the relative contributions of falling mortality and rising fertility. We are dependent up to then, and not altogether satisfactorily, upon the literary sources for evidence of developments which encouraged longer life or higher fertility.

Logically there are several forms which an increase in fertility might have taken, but which we may dismiss as of little influence, or of an influence which we are unable to estimate, but which was probably slight. Few contemporaries considered the problem of fecundity—whether, that is, there were more births because less sterility. When the matter was discussed it was usually in the terms of Townsend's reference to co. Cork. 'Children', he said, 'abundantly follow [marriage], for barrenness is almost unknown among the lower classes.'[1] But there is no evidence, nor is it probable, that a low level of sterility was a recent development. Similarly, it is unlikely that illegitimacy rose after the 1770's. Many witnesses, some of them severely critical of the habits of the Irish, pointed to the small number of illegitimate births in the Irish countryside. Perhaps the most impressive testimony came from Colonel Colby, who in the 1830's was directing the Ordnance Survey. He said that he was employing in Ireland some eight hundred Englishmen, chiefly soldiers, 'who had almost all married there in consequence of the chastity of the Irish women'.[2] Several factors helped to lower the level of illegitimacy: the influence of the priests, in the confessional and elsewhere, tended both to reduce the number of illegitimate conceptions and to transform those which did take place into legitimate births; to the unkind critic the Anglo-Irish waifs of the English ports were some measure of the moral restraint of the Irish countryside. But what seems of greatest influence

[1] H. Townsend, *Statistical Survey of the County of Cork* (Dublin 1810), p. 89.
[2] Quoted by Frederick Page (author of *Ireland and its Economy*, 1830) in evidence before the Select Committee on the State of the Poor in Ireland, Parl. Papers, 1830, VII, 829.

was the tendency of early and general marriage to lessen the inclination towards extra-marital relationships.

Any increase in fertility, we may deduce, must have been in marital fertility. Here again we can dismiss, as of little consequence, two possible causes of rising marital fertility. In the seventeenth and eighteenth centuries only a trivial proportion of the population seems to have remained unmarried. The teaching of the Church was to encourage marriage; the economic and social structure of the countryside gave little inducement to remain single. Arthur Young, after his tour of Ireland in the 1770's, believed marriage to be much more general in Ireland than in England; he hardly ever met an unmarried farmer or cottar and nearly all domestic servants were married.[3] It is unlikely, then, that a greater incidence of marriage led to higher fertility—except, of course, that the increase of population earlier in the century may have meant that after 1780 an abnormally large number of women were of ages at which marriage was customary.

In the second place, it is almost certain that fertility did not rise because there was less deliberate restriction of births. No evidence has come to light that the Irish, in the period under review, or earlier, tried to limit fertility. This absence of evidence is some indication that the practice did not exist. So many critics eagerly berated the Irish for their failings, that lack of condemnation for what contemporary opinion regarded as sinful seems to exculpate them from having practised it. Nor can we believe that the eighteenth-century Irish would have welcomed small families, had they been able to achieve them. Children were no impediment in a struggle to clamber up the social scale; social ambition was ill-developed, and a large family was less a drain upon resources than the promise of comfort and material well-being in years to come. It is improbable, moreover, that fathers and mothers had any idea that by limiting the number of their children each might be given a better chance in the world; their world certainly made such ideas implausible.

We seem now to be driven logically to conclude that if fertility increased it must have been by earlier marriage—that women spent more of their child-bearing years in the state of marriage, and therefore, in the absence of contraception, bore more children. The age at marriage is at the heart of Irish population history before the Famine as well as in the twentieth century (when Ireland, unlike her neighbours, achieves smaller families by Malthusian, rather than neo-Malthusian, methods). There is little doubt that in the late eighteenth and early nineteenth centuries the Irish married while unusually young. In co. Kildare, early in the new century, 'an unmarried man at twenty-five, or a woman at twenty, is rarely to be met with in the country parts'.[4] In Sligo, a few years later, women were said to marry between the ages of fifteen and twenty.[5] In the Dingle district of Kerry, unusually early ages were quoted, 'fourteen and thirteen, are common ages for the marriage of girls; fifteen is not considered at all an early age for marriage; and there are even instances of their having been contracted at so early an age as twelve'.[6]

[3] A. Young, *A Tour in Ireland* . . . (2nd ed. 1780), II, 198.
[4] T. J. Rawson, *Statistical Survey of the County of Kildare* (Dublin 1807), p. 23.
[5] W. S. Mason, *Statistical Account of Parochial Survey of Ireland* (Dublin 1816), II, 360.
[6] H. D. Inglis, *Ireland in 1834* (1835), I. 247.

Any movement towards earlier marriage must clearly have been the result of two sets of causes, one which made people want to marry while very young and a second which allowed them to do so. Before we can fruitfully discuss the first we must know something about the institution of marriage in the contemporary countryside. In the present century, in much of Ireland, many a peasant marriage has been 'arranged' by the fathers of bridegroom and bride. Such an institution has a long pedigree; its salient features were observed in the seventeenth century as well as in the decades before the Famine. Must we, then, in seeking the causes of youthful marriage, look for influences to which middle-aged or senile patriarchs were sensitive, rather than influences which moved their children? It seems that we do not. Observers in our period who refer to features of the 'match' usually do so to criticize the popular disrespect for so prudent an institution. They lament the usurpation of the father's authority by his children. There did not exist, moreover, an environment favourable to the arranged marriage. It is an institution adapted to a community whose numbers expand slowly, if at all. Typically, as in Ireland today, it allows one boy and one girl to succeed their father and mother; the boy takes over his father's land, the girl marries the heir to a neighbouring farm. The son delays his marriage and accepts his father's choice of a bride in return for the property which allows him to settle in his own district. The arranged wedding, then, presupposes either small families, or the dispersal of brothers and sisters. But before the Famine (at least until the 1830's) large families and restricted opportunities for emigration meant that more children than two had to be provided for near home. Fathers, doubtless, were aware of this, and they certainly divided their land among their children, not in their own old age, but when their children wished to marry. And even if a father were stubborn, or if his land were too small for further subdivision, his children's marriage was not necessarily postponed. A neighbour might be more obliging; and, if not, there was endless mountain and bog on which the tiny holding conventionally necessary for marriage might be enclosed.

In the century before the Famine, we may conclude, the timing of marriage was usually determined by the free choice of the persons married. Why did they choose to marry while unusually young? Fundamentally, no doubt, the explanation is biological, not historical. But, even so, we must ask why economic and social restraints to marriage operative in most other societies were felt so little in Ireland. Several factors combine to solve this problem. An incidental point, often stressed in contemporary comment (though perhaps of more interest than influence), was that the priests, hard-pressed for money and aware that their Church esteemed fruitful marriage, encouraged people to marry because of the fees and gifts which they received at weddings and christenings and which made up so large a proportion of their income. Croly, still himself a Catholic priest, lamented that by the 1830's the clergy, formerly content with a standard of living little different from that of the peasantry, had come to ape the country squire, to keep sporting dogs, to sit at public dinners with peers of the land and members of parliament. The new standard of living required an enlarged income which, he argued, was most readily found in wedding-dues.[7]

7 D. O. Croly, *Essay . . . on ecclesiastical Finance* (Cork 1834), pp. 28-33.

Secondly, the value of children was said to create a climate favourable to youthful marriage. The peasants' 'happiness and ease', according to Young, 'were generally relative to the number of their children'.[8] Their recklessness, in the third place, their willingness to marry however bleak the future, tended in the same direction. But undoubtedly of greatest importance were the wretchedness and hopelessness of living standards. Innumerable writers would have agreed with Dr Doyle, the Catholic Bishop of Kildare: 'poverty and population', he said, 'act reciprocally upon each other, like cause and effect; remove the one, or lessen it, and you will thereby check the other'.[9] A Catholic curate from Mayo told a Royal Commission that 'small holders are induced to marry by feeling that their condition cannot be made worse, or, rather, they know they can lose nothing, and they promise themselves some pleasure in the society of a wife'.[10] Many of his fellow-witnesses pointed to the fact that people who were rather better off than their neighbours were slower to marry; the comfortable farmer's son, it was said, waited for a wife with a 'fortune'.

Living conditions were not only bad but, by and large, without hope of improvement; whatever his industry and thrift, the Irish peasant had little chance of bettering his lot. The journeyman had the inducement to defer marriage until he set up on his own; the wage-earner until he drew his maximum income or had put by some savings. But there was no prospect that the Irishman would be better off at thirty than at eighteen. Why, then, should he delay his marriage?

We cannot here describe living conditions, but that they were wretched and hopeless is incontrovertible. On the eve of the Famine the Devon Commission thought that the sufferings of the labouring classes were 'greater . . . than the people of any other country in Europe have to sustain'.[11] That the peasant could see little prospect of his condition improving arose largely from the fact that rent was no residual payment for the special quality of certain land; by and large it was a payment which the spirit and structure of Irish landlordism pushed virtually to the point where it appropriated the entire fruits of the soil, save the peasant's subsistence. Often, indeed, rent was so swollen that subsistence was precarious; and continuously the principal food was the potato, the crop that allowed a maximum area of each holding to be used to earn the rent. In such a rural economy it is no wonder that the outlook was bleak. To improve a holding, to increase its yield, was merely to ask for a higher rent. Like his proverbial laziness, the Irishman's improvident marriage was part of his adaptation to his environment, part of his resentment of his exploitation.

Why were the Irish landlords, in the main, so exclusively mercenary in their attitude towards their property? Fundamentally, doubtless, the explanation goes back to the origin of their property in confiscation; the grantees felt insecure, and the traditions they established stemmed from their anxiety to get quick returns while the title was theirs. Many of them, moreover, were already endowed with land in England. This they may well have administered with

---

[8] A. Young, op. cit., II, 198.
[9] J. K. L. (i.e. James, Kildare and Leighlin), Letters on the State of Ireland (Dublin 1825), p. 112.
[10] Poor Law Inquiry (Ireland). App. F, Parl. papers, 1836, XXXIII, 43.
[11] Report of Royal Commission . . . [on] the Law and Practice in respect to the Occupation of Land in Ireland, Parl. papers, 1845, XIX, 12.

feeling for the duties as well as the rights of property. Their longstanding ties with their English tenants and their living among them impelled them to look to their Irish property when additional income was wanted. The Irish they were willing to regard as a barbarous people amongst whom it was foolhardy to live; that they were a people alien in national loyalty, in religion, custom and language made them more unequivocally vassals to be exploited, not dependants to be protected and taught. Their loyalty to England, in a mercantilist period, gave the landlords further excuse for drawing tribute from the economy of her colony.

So much for the spirit of Irish landholding; its mechanism of exploitation, we must dismiss as summarily. Absentee owners told their agents to 'send money, not arrears or expenses'. Agents, anxious to make a distasteful job personally worthwhile, rack-rented and imposed arbitrary fines and degrading personal service. The series of middlemen commonly intervening between ultimate owner and peasant meant that the exploitation, more competitive, was more certain and extreme. The practice of letting farms by auction in a country where land was almost the only resource encouraged tenants to outbid one another in the tribute they offered to acquire the right to potato-land. Finally, as rents rose in the new century, landlords became more and more reluctant to give reasonable leases; either the length of tenure was shortened or, more often, no agreement was drawn up which might legally restrain a landlord from evicting a peasant if another offered a higher rent. Beyond Ulster the question of compensating tenants for unexhausted improvements seldom arose.

An analysis such as this of why people wanted to marry early and why they were aware of so few inducements to defer marriage is important to our problem of explaining the acceleration in the rate of population increase, but it is of passive importance. What was changing by the 1780's was not people's attitude towards early marriage, but the opportunity of gratifying a long-standing desire to marry young. Degraded living conditions were no novelty at the end of the eighteenth century. Indeed, it is probable that a stimulus to economic activity (given initially by the national parliament and continued by the French wars) brought, for thirty years, rather better conditions. This same stimulus to economic activity, reinforced by other developments, had consequences of the greatest importance to our problem. However anxious people were to marry young, in the economy of rural Ireland marriage had to be deferred until a settlement could be acquired—until the couple intending to marry could find the holding on which their cabin might be put up and on which their potatoes might be grown. The real key to our problem is that by the 1780's and for another half-century there were settlements almost for all who wanted them; at however youthful an age a man wanted to marry he encountered little difficulty in finding a scrap of land on which he might rear a family. Settlements became so abundantly available for two reasons, because of the acute subdivision of holdings and because of widespread reclamation of waste land.

First, let us look at subdivision. Fortunately, we have statistics which allow us to measure the extremes to which it had proceeded by 1841 In that year, leaving out of account the considerable number of holdings of less than one acre, 45 per cent of all holdings were reported as less than five acres. It is significant that Connaught, the province whose population seems to have risen fastest, was not only (according to figures of the 1830's) the province where women married earliest, but also the province where parcellation of the land was most acute; there, 64 per cent of holdings above one acre were under five acres.[12]

How can we explain this movement towards tiny holdings? Its vigour until the 1820's must be attributed to the fact that by then, for forty years, landlords and tenants, in strange harmony, had been anxious to foster it. The landlords saw in smaller holdings the prospect of higher rents; to the peasants, with larger families, they were the only way of providing for their children. But this is only a partial explanation; we want to know not only why the rural population wanted smaller holdings, but why it could have them—why, by the 1780's more than before, a tiny scrap of land promised a family its living and the landlord more rent.

There are two principal strands in the explanation of this problem: first, the widespread dependence of the people on the potato; second, a swing, begun by the 1780's, towards arable farming. The conquest by the potato of the Irishman's board and fields is a major theme in Irish social and economic development. The potato was introduced to the country probably in or around 1588; within little more than a century and a half it was the staple food in practically every part of the countryside. Several reasons help to explain so complete a change in food-habits and cropping: natural conditions were well suited to the potato; the rigidity of a three-field system did not hinder its dissemination; in disturbed times it had the recommendation of remaining safe underground because marauders, who might burn or steal corn, or drive away cattle, were little tempted by so bulky a foodstuff. But probably of greater importance was the landlords' zeal to maximize rents, with its corollary, the dependence of the people on the crop which would sustain them with the greatest economy of land. There are wide variations in contemporary accounts of the relative productivity of a given area of land (in terms of the number of people it would support) when producing grain or potatoes; probably about three times as many people could be fed when wheat-land was planted with potatoes. The important point in our present context is that the generalization of the potato physically allowed the fragmentation of holdings; where one family had formerly got its living the potato allowed two more families to settle—more, indeed, than two because the potato succeeded a dietary in which milk and milk products bulked larger than any kind of corn. In fact, at the time of its introduction, the potato did not lead to such subdivision; the landlords were interested in it as a means of increasing not population, but rent. Nonetheless its potentiality as a divider of land and as a stimulus to the growth of population was felt by the 1780's when, in a new environment, the increase in arable farming made rising population a condition of the maximization of rents.

That in the first three-quarters of the eighteenth century pastoral farming was the more thriving, the colonizing element in Irish agriculture was the result

---

[12] Parl. papers, 1848, XLIX, 13; *Census of Ireland, 1841*, Parl. papers, 1843, XXIV, 460 ff.

partly of natural conditions, but, much more, of Ireland's colonial status. Her native economic writers were good mercantilists, but they erred, in the eyes of their English fellows, by an arrogant wish to apply to their country the part of mercantilist thought which pertained to the mother-country, not that which taught a colony to make its economy tributary to that of its parent-nation. The Irish mercantilists pleaded for laws, like England's, subsidizing the export of grain and penalizing its import. But such legislation could hardly be expected while English landlords valued their Irish market and feared Irish competition. By the 1780's, however, a new situation had arisen. Such was the growth of England's population that even in a good year, she could not count on producing all the foodstuffs she required. This new situation was soon followed in Ireland by Foster's Corn Law of 1784, an outstanding example of legislative encouragement moulding economic development. Before long the French wars created a food-scare in England and led, in 1806, to her throwing open her ports to Irish corn; the price of grain in Ireland shot up.[13] Landlords quickly realized that their policy of drawing ever greater rents now implied a policy of extending arable farming. But, in the circumstances of Ireland, an increase of arable farming needed a reduction of the size of holdings because there was no class of men with the capital or the skill to manage large tillage farms. The swing towards arable, moreover, required an increase in the labour force; the landlords now became interested in stimulating the growth of population.

Each peasant's holding could be regarded as divided into two segments, one producing the peasant family's subsistence, the other producing the rent crops. By the 1780's dependence on the potato had reduced the subsistence segment to a tiny area; the swing towards arable farming, because of the greater productivity of cornland than pasture, was likewise reducing the rent-producing area. Greatly reduced holdings became physically possible; the landlords wanted them because they were a prerequisite of advanced rents. For this reason the peasants, long needing them to provide for their children, were now able to have them. Subdivision of holdings allowed the earlier marriage which led to the necessary increase in the labour force.

In the extent and motivation of reclamation there is a field of inquiry very relevant to population history. Every new holding marked out in mountain or bog made possible the creation of a new family. Both statistical and literary evidence make it clear that there was substantial reclamation, at least during the French wars and in the dozen or so years before the Famine.[14] The state, for all the advice of government committees and private investigators, played no significant part in works of drainage and clearance until the time of the Famine.

---

[13] Oats, for instance, advanced from 8s. 11d. a barrel in the 1780's to 18s. 5d. by 1815. *Report from the Committee . . . to consider the Corn Trade between Great Britain and Ireland*, 1802; *Reps. Cttees. of H. of C. 1774-1802* (1803), IX, p. 169; Parl. papers, 1821, XX, 102-3. The earlier price is for the years 1786-90 and relates to the whole of Ireland, the later is the average price on the Dublin Market from 1811 to 1815.

[14] If the figures of the Ordnance Survey are to be trusted, in Donegal there was an increase of 8 per cent in the cultivated area between the early 1830's and the early 1840's (Parl. papers, 1849, XLIX, 430-1). Elsewhere the progress of reclamation may have been less rapid but (with the possible exception of Leinster) it seems everywhere to have been a movement of great significance. In Leinster, In 1841 there was proportionately less than half as much waste as in any other province (*Census of Ireland, 1851*, Parl. papers, 1856, XXXI, xi). See K. H. Connell, 'The Colonization of Waste Land in ireland, 1780-1845', *Economic History Review*, 2nd series, iii, 1950, pp. 44-71.

The landlords, with outstanding exceptions, were hardly more active. The main agent of reclamation was the peasant himself. In spite of the immense discouragement of tenurial relationships which increased rent in proportion—or more than in proportion—to the increase in the value of his holding, he steadily added an acre or two a year to his cultivated area; or his sons established themselves on land hitherto unused. The peasant and his children were driven to such arduous and unrewarding work by the two forces which give their distinctive character to many of the institutions of the Irish countryside—the pressure of population and the landlords' demand for ever-increasing rents.

So much for the economic and social forces which tended to increase fertility. We must turn now to those tending to lower mortality. Commonly, the rise in the population of England during the industrial revolution is attributed largely to a fall in the death rate; this, in turn, is regarded primarily as the result of greater cleanliness, of advances in the theory and practice of medicine and of improvements in water-supply and drainage. The theory should be treated with caution, if only because these life-preserving improvements impinged only slightly on the rural majority of the population, and, when reading the literature of urbanization, we are driven to regard their effects even in the towns as minimal.[15] But England did, at least, have a large number of towns in which such developments, if their existence can be credited, could have been felt. Ireland had not, and therefore any such theory seems inapplicable to her conditions. Like England, she opened new hospitals and dispensaries. Yet, by 1851, in the whole country beyond Dublin there were fewer than 2,000 infirmary beds.[16] As practically all of these were available in the towns they made no great contribution towards lowering rural mortality. That fever-deaths diminished because of greater cleanliness is also out of the question. That a seventy-year 'gap in the famines', and therefore in famine-fever, began in the 1740's is broadly true. But this hardly accounts for an acceleration in the rate of population-increase beginning some forty years later. Soon after the end of the French wars, famine and fever became widespread—in the 1830's nearly one death in ten was attributed to fever[17]—and yet there appears to have been no diminution in the rate of natural increase.[18] If, in these years, a changing incidence of fever contributed to the growth of population, the causal link was not a lowering of mortality; it may well have been that as more tenants died of fever, more settlements were vacated and there was some easing of the difficulty, commonly reported in the 1830's, of finding the holding that would permit a marriage. In the control of smallpox there may be a more positive contribution, even though the spread of vaccination was more restrained in Ireland than elsewhere by prejudice, the difficulties of terrain and the small number of country doctors and resident gentry. Still, by the 1830's, smallpox in Ireland was second only to fever as a cause of mortality; of every

15 *Editor's note.* These were the author's views in 1950. The reader is referred to the papers in the first two sections of this volume for more recent views. See, especially, McKeown and Brown above, pp. 285 ff.
16 *Census of Ireland 1851, Report on the Status of Disease,* Parl. papers, 1854, LVIII, 100-3.
17 *Census of Ireland, 1841, op. cit.* Table of Deaths, facing p. 183.
18 It is true that the censuses show a greater rate of increase for the 1820's than for the 1830's. But the Commissioners of the 1841 Census were confident that this was the result of increasing emigration not of a dwindling excess of births over deaths (*Census of Ireland, 1841, op. cit.* p. viii).

thousand deaths in this decade it accounted for forty-nine, while in England in the 1840's the comparable figure was twenty-two.[19]

In the influence of nutrition there is a possible cause of low mortality. The Irish, we have seen, were driven to their extreme dependence upon the potato largely because it was the crop that would sustain them with the greatest economy of land. A diet, in which boiled potatoes were normally the only solid food and some form of milk the only liquid, can have given little pleasure to the palate. But such a diet, when harvest and appetite allowed it to be consumed to the full, was almost completely adequate. One of the most striking of the many paradoxes in the Irish economy in our period is that a people whose wretchedness was said seldom to be exceeded seem, nevertheless, to have enjoyed over many years a diet which the biochemist could hardly rate as other than excellent; he might, indeed, have difficulty in finding another community in which so large a class was continuously so well fed. There is abundant, and apparently trustworthy, information on the quantity of potatoes normally consumed by the Irishman in a day. It comes, amongst other sources, from Arthur Young, from The Times' "commissioner", from Charles Edward Trevelyan writing in the Edinburgh Review and, in great detail, for nearly every barony in the country, from the 1836 Report of the Poor Inquiry Commission.[20] It leaves us no alternative but to accept an amount of between ten and twelve pounds as a conservative estimate of an adult man's daily consumption of potatoes.[21] There are other, though sparser, data suggesting that, at least until the 1820's, milk was fairly abundantly available. On the assumption that the typical Irishman had ten pounds of potatoes a day, together with one pint of milk, he had a daily intake of over 3,800 calories; this exceeded by 800 calories the amount recommended by the Combined Food Board for an adult man engaged in moderate activity.[22] Of protein he had 64 of the recommended 70 gm., and, with a single exception, he had an abundance, often a superabundance, of the listed minerals and vitamins.[23] A biochemically excellent diet undoubtedly tended to lengthen life and to diminish sterility. But it is improbable that such developments can go far to explain the steepening of the rate of population increase in the 1780's. There was no sudden change in food-habits; dependence upon the potato came gradually, and it was probably nearly as generally the Irishman's staple in 1750 as in 1780. The influence of the potato was fundamental, but in this context it probably was felt more through allowing the survival of additional people born rather than by prolonging the lives of the number of people who would have existed had there been no increase in fertility.

[19] Report . . . by the Small-Pox and Vaccination Committee, 1853, Parl. papers, 1852-3. CI, 171; Census of Ireland, 1841, op. cit. Table of Deaths, p. 182.

[20] Young, 1780, op. cit. II, 119-20; T. C. Foster, Letters on the Condition of the People of Ireland (1846), p. 75; 'The Irish Crisis', Edinburgh Review (1848), LXXXVII, 234; Poor Law Inquiry (Ireland), App. H, Parl. papers, 1836, XXXIV, pt. ii, passim.

[21] The eating of so large a quantity of food depended, it should be repeated, on a plentiful harvest. With the exception of the disastrous years 1800 and 1801 there seems to have been no major deficiency in the potato crop between 1741 and 1816. But from 1816 until the Famine there probably were nearly as many years of deficient yields as of abundance; in these latter years the demographer must frequently reckon with the effects of malnutrition upon mortality and fertility.

[22] Combined Food Board, Food Consumption Levels (1944), p. 30.

[23] The exception was vitamin G, of which the yield of the diet we are considering was 11 per cent deficient.

On the argument of this paper, the Malthusian theory, freed of its mathe-matical strait-jacketing, had a precise relevance to Irish conditions—with the qualification that what limited the growth of population was not the overall supply of foodstuffs, but the supply from that area of land which the landlords' demand for rent left for the people's subsistence. By the 1780's changed market-ing conditions made a grain-growing tenantry a more profitable proposition to the landlords than the pasture farmers who then occupied so much of their land. To acquire a tilling tenantry smaller holdings were necessary; their provision led almost inescapably to an increase in numbers. It swept away the old restraints to marriage. The peasant's children could, and did, marry as soon as they pleased and the earlier a girl married, the more children she was likely to bear. That so many of her children survived to create the rapid growth of population was largely the result of the nutritional excellence of their diet. By the 1820's the landlords realized the incompatibility of endless parcellation and the maximization of rents. They saw that subdivision was accompanied by such rapid multiplication of the people that the subsistence segment of the peasant's land threatened the rent-producing segment. The landlords strove to halt the process, but, for once, the peasantry had the whiphand. Arson and murder, the boycott and cattle-maiming were some of their weapons in usually successful attempts to prevent the landlords from 'clearing and con-solidating'. In spite of the mounting stream of emigration they knew that they must continue to break up their land if they were to provide for their children. Subdivision, early marriage and high fertility persisted until the mid 1840's, when, after recurring deficiencies in the yield of the potato, its national and almost complete failure brought a classic demonstration of Malthus's 'positive check' and in five years cost Ireland a fifth of her people.

18

THE POPULATION OF FRANCE IN THE EIGHTEENTH CENTURY

LOUIS HENRY

Translated by Peter Jimack

T HE eighteenth century is, at least for France, of special demographic interest. According to contemporary evidence, it was in fact towards the end of the *Ancien Régime* that birth-control began to spread among the mainly rural mass of the population: therefore this period marked the beginning, imperceptible at first, of the decline in the French birth rate, which occurred so much earlier than in other European countries.

This fact alone makes the eighteenth century in France a turning point, a period of transition from an old world, which in some respects had no doubt remained unchanged for centuries, a world in which men and women left it to nature to decide the number of children they would have, and in which fertility was reduced only by the relative lateness of marriages (lateness, that is, compared with other civilizations rather than with present-day practice, since Western Europe is still characterized by a later marriage age, at least for women, than most other parts of the world).

The eighteenth century is in other respects also a period of transition: in its early years occurred the last great famine, in 1709-10, and then, although only in Marseilles and part of Provence, the last plague epidemic. On the other hand, it is generally accepted that the death rate went down in the eighteenth century, and that there was consequently a considerable increase in the population well before 1800.

It is true that this century did not witness the beginnings of industrialization, as in England; so it is not in France a century of transition in the economic field; but it does mark a turning point, to an exceptional extent, in the field of ideas, and, through the Revolution, in the political field.

For all these reasons, the study of the population of France in the eighteenth century is rich in promise. If it is taken as far back as the beginning of the century, or even to the end of the seventeenth century, this study can add precise information to our admittedly rather scant knowledge of traditional demographic conditions, conditions which have held good with only a few variations for hundreds, if not for thousands of years in the Western world, and, with other variations, in a great number of agrarian-type civilizations. If the study is extended to the whole of the country, we shall be able to verify generally accepted hypotheses concerning the decline in mortality and the increase in the population; if we carry it further in depth, it may enable us to identify the very beginnings of the practice of birth-control, throwing light on the various stages involved in this major change in social behaviour. Finally, there arise other problems, as we shall see, and these can only be solved after a thorough study of eighteenth-century demography.

Problems

The first of the problems posed by the eighteenth century concerns the evolution of the population. The few data available suggest that, from the beginning to the end of the century, there was a noticeable increase in the population. The uncertainty of the data, however, leaves the matter open to debate, at least regarding the real extent of the increase; in addition, the precise way in which this increase occurred remains to be determined: whether for instance it was continuous, or interrupted by a temporary decline, spread out over the whole century, or concentrated in a far more limited period.

If we accept that there was a marked increase, whenever precisely it may have occurred, another problem arises. As France was not industrialized in the eighteenth century, the additional population could not be absorbed by new types of activity; it could only stay where it was, in the country, where excess births were no doubt most numerous, or move to the towns, and add to the urban population either more artisans, or more servants, or a mass of people with little or nothing worth-while to do, ready and waiting for adventures. The choice of an answer to this question is certainly of considerable significance for political history.

We must also ask whether all classes of society shared equally in this expansion of the population, or whether on the contrary some increased only slightly in numbers, while others grew rapidly. If the demographic expansion of the middle and lower middle classes was faster than that of the rural population, which is an hypothesis that cannot be ruled out, this could certainly have been a source of trouble, particularly when one takes into account the general rise in the standard of education and the fermentation of ideas which, in France, characterized the eighteenth century.

The second problem of eighteenth-century demography is posed by the decline in mortality; this is not peculiar to France, since the same problem has arisen for Great Britain. The question we have to answer is this: how can mortality have declined in the eighteenth century while medical progress was only very slight?

A third problem concerns legitimate fertility in the absence of birth-control, that is fertility as it most likely was in the great mass of the population before the last quarter of the eighteenth century. Impressed by extreme cases, some authors have had no hesitation in writing that, in the absence of birth-control, a married woman of an age to bear children would have one child a year. Curiously enough, a similar opinion is found in advanced circles of countries only now being developed. Of course, people who propose such figures have no notion of what they represent in terms of birth rate and, consequently, of mortality, over thousands of years during which the number of men living on the earth has increased only very slowly. A more precise understanding of 'natural' fertility is thus more or less essential if we are to arrive at any sort of exact knowledge of the demographic history of mankind.

Many authors of the second half of the eighteenth century described celibacy, both ecclesiastical and secular, as a deep-rooted malady characteristic of the period, and this opinion has been adopted by some twentieth century authors. In 1919, Mathorez wrote: 'The number of unmarried persons increased in the eighteenth century, . . . secular celibacy was just as great a danger (as ecclesiastical celibacy) to the growth of the French population.'[1]

More recently, G. Duplessis has restated Mathorez's thesis; in addition, he stresses the frequency of remarriage, believing he has thus removed the contradiction between the large number of marriages noted at the end of the *Ancien Régime* and the supposed prevalence of celibacy[2]: 'Under the *Ancien Régime* there must have been more unmarried adults than today, in spite of a nuptiality comparable to ours, *because it was often the same people getting married*' (*op. cit.* p. 19, author's italics).

As a further point, he quotes (p. 16) Michelet, who gives the example of his own family, in which the sisters let themselves become the mere servants of their brothers, and never left their village.

Morals and birth-control in marriage create another problem, the last of those I intend to mention here. In the opinion of authors of the time, morals were very lax at the end of the *Ancien Régime*. The prevalence of secular celibacy, already mentioned, was for them one aspect of this moral looseness; another was the 'art of cheating nature', which, about this time, is said to have passed from the upper classes to the rural masses. Since such opinions were based for the most part on very little data, we must ask ourselves the following questions: 'Were morals as lax as the authors of the time maintain?'—or, in another form, 'were morals the same in the mainly rural mass of the population as in the aristocracy, especially of Paris and Versailles, with which the authors were particularly familiar?' And finally, 'Did birth-control spread among the rural population before the Revolution, and if so, how?'

Sources available

We find these in two forms: either as evaluations, published or unpublished, and worked out to varying degrees, or as source material.

Sources of the first type are, all things considered, far from numerous. They consist mainly of population figures and mortality tables. They include nothing about fertility, in spite of the interest shown in this subject by authors of the second half of the eighteenth century; admittedly, many of these authors are far more concerned with theories than with knowledge.

Sources of the second kind, on the other hand, are extremely plentiful, at least as far as population changes are concerned. This is to a great extent due to the very early organization of the registration of births, marriages and deaths, in a form very similar to the present-day system. Confined to the main outlines, the picture is as follows:

As early as the fifteenth century, some bishops instructed parish priests to register baptisms, marriages and burials. Although not many records of this

---

[1] Mathorez, J., *Les étrangers en France sous l'Ancien Régime*, Paris, Librairie ancienne Edouard Champion, 1919, 2 vols., 437 and 446 pp. The remarks quoted are from Vol. 1, p. 53.
[2] Duplessis-Leguelinel, G., *Les Marriages en France*, Paris, Armand Colin, 1954, ix + 198 pp.

period have survived, there is no doubt at all that these regulations familiarized the population with the registration of marriages and the religious equivalents of births and deaths, thereby making things easier for the Crown, whose first act in this domain was in 1539 (Edict of Villers-Cotterets). It is a fact that the regions in which the records go back the farthest and are the most generally preserved are those where the bishops took such action (Haute-Bretagne, Anjou, Maine, Normandy, Ile-de-France, Franche-Comté, Comtat-Venaissin, Provence). In the departments of Ille-et-Vilaine and Loire-Atlantique (as early as the beginning of the fifteenth century the Bishop of Nantes decreed that records should be kept), there is a very high proportion of rural parishes which still have sixteenth-century records: in Loire-Atlantique the figure is as high as 58·5 per cent, and in Ille-et-Vilaine 62·7 per cent. Out of 580 villages in these two departments, there are 21 with records going back to the fifteenth century.[3]

The royal edict of 1539 applied only to baptisms and some deaths (those of holders of ecclesiastical benefices), and the edict of Blois (1579) extended this to the compulsory registration of marriages. For deaths, royal legislation remained very vague until 1667; but it must be noted that meanwhile, in 1614, the *Rituale Romanum* decreed by Pope Paul V laid down the registration of deaths and confirmations, as well as baptisms and marriages, the registration of which had been made compulsory in 1563 by the Council of Trent.[4]

The question is dealt with again as a whole by the act of 1667, which stipulates registration in duplicate, a signed original and an authenticated copy. The main details of this act were reaffirmed in 1736, but from that date both copies have to be signed. An act of 1787 extended registration to non-Catholics, and finally, under a decree of September 1792, registration was secularized. It remains to be seen how far this legislation was put into practice.

For the whole of France, during the period extending from the act of 1667 to the secularization, the sample analysis carried out in 1959 yielded the following results:

TABLE I

Years covered by the registers for baptisms, marriages and burials

	1668–99 %	1700–36 %	1737–92 %
Rural parishes	62·0	76·4	91·3
Small towns	89·7	96·2	99·1
Medium-sized towns	87·9	94·6	97·8
Large towns	92·2	98·1	99·4
All parishes	62·9	77·0	91·5
Hospitals (burials only)	17·8	35·1	79·3

To this table must be added monasteries and convents (burial records); the situation concerning them is confused, for they did not all keep records, but it

[3] Biraben, J. N., Fleury, M., Henry, L., 'Inventaire par sondage des registres paroissiaux de France', *Population*, 15, 1960, pp. 25–58.
[4] According to these regulations, the age at death had to appear in the burial entry, and nearly always, in fact, it is to be found there; but since civil legislation did not require this, we owe the mention of the age at death to the Church. Note that the age at marriage, required by the Crown, is very often missing. No doubt we have to thank the *Rituale Romanum* for the Confirmation lists which are sometimes to be found in parish registers.

is very probable that the proportion of registers which have survived is small.

With this exception, the situation is very satisfactory from 1737 onwards; before that date it is less so, particularly for hospitals. However, sufficient records remain in all parts of France for valuable studies to be made, provided that there is little or no connexion between the demographic characteristics of a place and the survival of records. There is no reason to suppose that this is not the case; but there is another and more limiting condition to consider, namely whether the registration was itself sufficiently complete.

It is difficult to reach a conclusion on this point before having available overall evaluations obtained from the surveys currently being carried out. However, a number of village monographs and the analysis of numerous registers give the following impression.

The registration of baptisms and marriages was sufficiently complete; registration of deaths must also have been satisfactory, at least from 1737 onwards, in large areas, particularly in Northern France; in other areas, registration of deaths, especially of children, remained inadequate until a somewhat later date—1770 in the south-west according to some evidence.

The situation during the Revolution is not known very precisely. Taken as a whole, the proportion of years covered certainly remains very considerable, although registration may have become defective locally during the most troubled years. The quality of registration was perhaps more seriously affected, especially in small parishes, by the ignorance of the official replacing the priest as responsible for registration.

Censuses have not been the subject of such systematic research. Lists of the names of inhabitants of Grenoble and Aix-en-Provence have recently come to light, and we may hope for other discoveries of the same kind; if these were in sufficient number, they would enable us to judge more effectively the accuracy of the censuses before 1800, and possibly to understand more clearly the evolution of the population during the eighteenth century. In any case, J. N. Biraben is preparing a synthesis of all that is known, both source material and evaluations. For the Revolution, M. Reinhard has undertaken a complete inventory of the various censuses.

Finally, mention must be made of the great possibilities offered for the study of particular groups by genealogies. Unfortunately, good genealogies are rare, and France is not very well off in this respect. It has for instance been very difficult, working from genealogies, to collect the data concerning the French Peerage (*les Ducs et Pairs*).

Evaluations

In the present state of research, we have as yet few evaluations; there are none, or next to none, covering the whole of the country.

These evaluations come from various sources:

(*a*) Eighteenth-century authors, principally Deparcieux, Expilly, Messance, and Moheau.

(*b*) Studies of privileged groups, based on genealogies. If we confined ourselves strictly to France, we should have only the one on the Peerage. I think, however, that we can also take into account the study of the ruling class in

Geneva, which has been extremely fruitful and offers a good example of the possible demographic transition in a middle class group.

(c) Village monographs. The first and the most complete of these is the one on Crulai, a village in Normandy; but this is concerned mainly with the end of the seventeenth century and the first half of the eighteenth. There have been other studies, less complete, but on the same model and using the same methods, based on a parish near Rouen, Sotteville-lès-Rouen; a suburb of Le Havre, nowadays part of the town, Ingouville; a parish in Morvan, St. Agnan; a parish in Lot, Ganic (unpublished); and a parish in Haute-Garonne, Lévignac-sur-Save (unpublished).[5] Further information is provided by other studies, often carried out by students for a degree or for a thesis.

(d) Sample analysis of the population of France before 1800. The main lines of this investigation were described in *Population* at the end of 1958.[6] At the time of writing (end of May 1961), more than 450,000 register entries from rural parishes of the sample have been noted, 120,000 of them by name with a view to the reconstruction of families. There has so far been no examination of records for towns.

At first, the non-nominal examination of records was exhaustive: note was taken of all entries in the registers of the sample rural parishes between 1670 and 1829.

This procedure has been continued for the nominal survey (about 1 in 10 of the sample of 1 in 100); for the non-nominal survey, it has been replaced by a selection, normally of one sheet in five, or occasionally of one entry in five.

The exhaustive examination of records was carried out in the Paris area; analysis of the results has been begun and is providing some information about the rural population of the following 9 departments, taken as a whole, between 1740 and 1789: Aisne, Aube, Eure-et-Loir, Loiret, Oise, Seine, Seine-et-Marne, Seine-et-Oise, and Yonne.

Rather than present separately the results of these four main types of study, I prefer to give them jointly, as elements of solutions or provisional solutions to the problems of eighteenth-century demography already mentioned. Analogies

---

[5] The studies on Sotteville and Ingouville were carried out by Prof. Reinhard's students, and the one on Lévignac-sur-Save partly by me and partly by Mlle Labarthie, a pupil of Prof. Godechot The latter has had other parishes studied, but the results are not available. In addition, Prof. Valmary has undertaken a monograph on two parishes in Lot, St. Sernin and Thézels, which will be as considerable as the Crulai one; but these results are not yet available either.

[6] Fleury, M. and Henry, L., 'Pour connaître la population de la France depuis Louis XIV', *Population*, 1958, 13, pp. 663-86.

The way in which the sample has been selected has given rise to a long criticism by Prof. Baehrel (*Annales*, 1960 (15), pp. 702-41). The author of this criticism has forgotten two things:
(a) that our aim is to produce evaluations for France as a whole, and if possible for large areas of, say, about ten departments;
(b) that considerations of convenience affect the choice of the method of sampling: there is no need for stratification if the objective can be attained more conveniently without it; a stratification which may be less effective than another, and thus apparently unsatisfactory, will be quite acceptable if it enables us to achieve our object more cheaply or more quickly. Now a stratification by departments has two advantages: (1) it has a certain effectiveness since there are differences from department to department; (2) it is convenient because parishes are classified by department in the census returns of the early nineteenth century, and evaluations based on the data provided by the sample cannot be made without reference to these returns. To make the same evaluations by geographical regions, we should have to reclassify on this basis the returns of at least one of these censuses. This would mean losing a great deal of time for an uncertain advantage; for it is by no means sure that within a department, the geographical region plays a much more important part in the differentiation of villages demographically than any other factor, and in particular the proximity of main roads.

and differences, agreements and disagreements, which are significant only for each chapter of demography, will thus become more apparent.

Evolution of the population during the eighteenth century

This evolution has been the subject of arguments, sometimes very heated, for two centuries. In the eighteenth century, many writers, the most famous of whom was Montesquieu, maintained that the population of France was declining; Voltaire held the opposite opinion, and, about two hundred years ago, the abbé Expilly attempted to show that the population had considerably increased since the beginning of the eighteenth century. During the last century, the influence of the Revolution on the population of France was the most debated point[7]; but as this question cannot be discussed without some evaluation of the population at the end of the *Ancien Régime*, the debate soon passes beyond its original subject on to the wider problem of the evolution of the population of France during the eighteenth century. Here now is an overall picture of the data available, with some suggested conclusions.

At the beginning of the century, we have the figures given by Vauban, or his figures as more recently corrected by various writers[8]: for the present-day territory of France, Vauban gives 21 million inhabitants, while the corrected figure is 22 million. Vauban added up figures of widely differing nature, obtained in different ways and spread out over some 20 years; these figures do not then indicate the population at a given date, but rather during a given period. It is simplest to take them as an assessment of the population of France in 1700.

At the end of the century, we have the retrospective evaluations of Bourgeois-Pichat. The 1806 figures, for the total population and age-distribution, and the 1801 figures, for the total population, are the earliest which are factually established; the others, from 1776 to 1796 or 1801, introduce hypotheses concerning the changes in mortality before 1806, and this brings up again the controversy over the influence of the Revolution.[9]

The following figures, giving in millions the population of the present territory at various dates, are based on Bourgeois-Pichat's evaluations:

	1770	1776	1781	1785	1791	1801	1806
Bourgeois-Pichat's figures		26·0	26·5		27·6	28·8	29·5
Complementary figures	25·2		26·8	27·0			

The complementary figures are deduced from the 1776 figure and the excess of births over deaths, as calculated from the statistics for the period 1770-84.[10] In 1781, there is a difference of 300,000 between the complementary figures and Bourgeois-Pichat's; this is a result of the irregularities in the excess of births over deaths.

If we compare these figures with those for the beginning of the eighteenth

[7] Levasseur, E., *La Population française*, Arthur Rousseau 1892, 3 vols. *Cf.* particularly Vol. 3, pp. 500-37.　　　　[8] Levasseur, E., *op. cit.* Vol. I, p. 201-6.
[9] Bourgeois-Pichat assumed a regular decline in mortality during the period 1770-1806. This hypothesis is open to criticism, particularly for the Revolutionary period. In any case little is known of mortality about 1770; the value of Duvillard's table, which is supposed to give it, is very dubious. See below, pp. 480.
[10] Vincent, P., 'French demography in the eighteenth century', *Population Studies*, 1947, I, pp. 44-71. *Cf.* Table on pp. 69 and 70.

century, it would appear that in about 70 years, the increase was between 3·2 and 4·2 millions, i.e. between 14·5 per cent and 20 per cent of the initial population; the corresponding rate of natural increase is between 2 and 2·6 per 1,000.

On the other hand, during the eighteenth century itself, the abbé Expilly had had enumerated the marriages, births and deaths for 1690-1701 and for 1752-63 in a large number of parishes, with a view to proving that the population had increased. Here, presented in a slightly modified form, is Expilly's summary[11]:

TABLE 2

Generality, Administrative Area or Province	Number of parishes examined	Period 1690-1701			Period 1752-63		
		Marriages	Births	Deaths	Marriages	Births	Deaths
Châlons-sur-Marne	1,906	71,438	335,813	237,109	70,661	332,388	243,650
Caen	717	32,045	129,457	92,029	34,639	140,596	113,083
Alençon	717	30,066	125,707	97,231	32,987	140,146	112,002
Tours	1,350	130,355	553,361	420,113	119,486	539,974	416,747
Bourgogne	1,212	60,760	269,446	219,694	73,064	347,474	267,196
Moulins	616	29,137	120,677	96,567	44,951	198,596	145,431
Dauphiné	1,149	61,322	266,373	214,077	61,135	299,098	233,087
Provence	627	66,144	297,470	205,810	59,991	315,754	250,968
Montauban	1,027	44,372	164,233	145,734	50,293	217,908	166,875
Auch and Pau	1,098	50,817	203,892	162,740	58,754	261,123	197,000
TOTAL	10,419	576,456	2,466,429	1,891,104	605,961	2,793,057	2,146,039

From this table we obtain the following one, giving a calculation for each period of the apparent rate of natural increase[12] and the proportion of births to marriages, and showing at the same time the index of marriages, births and deaths for 1752-63, taking the corresponding figure for 1690-1701 as 100:

TABLE 3

Generality Administrative Area or Province	Natural increase per 1,000		Proportion of births to marriages		Index number of marriages, births and deaths, 1752-63 (1690-1701 = 100)		
	1690-1701	1752-63	1690-1701	1752-63	Marriages	Births	Deaths
Châlons	11·8	10·7	4·70	4·70	99	99	102·5
Caen	11·6	7·8	4·04	4·06	108	108·5	123
Alençon	9·1	8·0	4·18	4·25	109·5	111·5	115
Tours	9·6	9·1	4·24	4·52	91·5	97·5	99
Bourgogne	7·4	9·3	4·44	4·76	120	129	122
Moulins	8·0	10·7	4·14	4·44	154	165	151
Dauphiné	7·8	8·8	4·34	4·89	100	112·5	109
Provence	12·3	8·2	4·50	5·26	90·5	106	122
Montauban	4·5	9·4	3·70	4·33	113·5	132·5	114·5
Auch and Pau	8·1	9·8	4·01	4·45	115·5	128	121
Total for 10 areas	9·3	9·3	4·28	4·61	105	113·2	113·5

[11] Expilly, *De la population de la France*, Amsterdam, 1765. Expilly omitted to eliminate those parishes which had no records for the period 1690-1701. The results would not however be greatly modified if they were eliminated.

[12] For this calculation, the crude birth rate has been taken as 40 per 1,000.

The apparent rate of natural increase is the same during the two periods, although the first includes at least two very bad years, 1693 and 1694, due to a very serious famine, with no equivalent in the second period. Expilly's opinion of the registration of deaths about the end of the seventeenth century is thus confirmed: it was manifestly incomplete. Since registration improved considerably, especially after 1736, the 1752-63 figures for deaths are much more accurate. This will explain the fact that deaths apparently increased rather more than births, when they ought to have increased less, as the period 1752-63 does not seem to have contained any disaster comparable to the one of 1693-4.

This decline in mortality may also explain the fact that marriages increased distinctly less than births: a famine like the one in 1693-4 causes a temporary drop in the birth rate, either directly (the effect of starvation on fertility), or by the premature ending of marriages; on the other hand, it tends to increase the number of marriages, by the numerous remarriages following the famine.

Over a period of 12 years, however, the direct influence of the famine on the birth rate remains slight[13]; so that the increase in the number of births from 1690-1701 to 1752-63 is not due solely to the direct influence of the famine of 1693-4. It must then be the result either of an increase in the population, or of a rise in the birth rate. A rise in the birth rate might be permanent, as a result of a considerable change in nuptiality for instance, or it might be due to an increase, necessarily temporary, in the proportion of young adults; this increase could only result from a bulge in the birth rate some 30 years previously, and the existence of such a bulge about 1720-30 is a pure hypothesis which we shall ignore. The only other possibilities are an increase in p opulation or a rise in the birth rate; but as a rise in the birth rate without a rise in mortality leads to an increase in the population, Expilly's observations on births alone lead to the conclusion either that the population increased between 1690-1701 and 1752-63, or that it was increasing when these observations were made. This latter conclusion is confirmed by the observation of deaths: they are clearly less than births, and the difference is not, in this case, merely an apparent one due to under-registration.

In any case, the increase in the population between 1690-1701 and 1752-63 would only be more than 13 per cent in the areas observed if the birth rate had declined during the same period, which seems out of the question; 5 of this 13 per cent must be reckoned as the population increase during the years 1752-7 (0·87 per cent a year for 6 years); so that the increase from 1690-1701 to 1752 was no more than 8 per cent. If we assume that the increase from 1700 to 1752 was approximately of the same size, then the increase from 1700 to the end of 1763 would be something like 19 per cent, and from 1700 to the beginning of 1770 about 25 per cent, provided that the population increase during the period 1764-9 followed more or less the same pattern as in 1752-63. To sum up, for the 10 areas in which these observations were made, one of the possible conclusions, with the reservations indicated, is a population increase of 8 per cent from 1700 to 1752, and of between 19 per cent and 25 per cent from 1700 to 1770, in other

[13] At Crulai, the decline in the birth rate directly attributable to the famines of 1693-4 and 1709-10 was about 5 per cent.

words a greater increase than that revealed by a comparison of Bourgeois-Pichat's figures with Vauban's, whether corrected or not.

Unfortunately, this difference means very little: the presumed population increases vary a great deal from province to province; so that the average of a sample of 10 provinces may well still be very different from the average of all the provinces. So, disregarding all reservations about the quality of the observations or about their interpretation, Expilly's enormous work fails to achieve its object, the evolution of the population of France, because, in spite of the abundance of the data he amassed, it is based on a very inadequate sample. A much better result could have been obtained with, say, ten times less data provided that the selection had been drawn from all areas.

On the other hand, Expilly's investigation gives us fairly precise information about the rate of increase for the period 1752-63, since the variation from province to province was relatively slight.[14] The rate of increase would not have been less than 0·8 per cent for the whole of France; such a rate, however, seems very high, for during the period 1770-84, which would seem to have quite a high rate of increase, this rate reaches or exceeds 0·8 per cent in only 4 years out of 15.

So here too Expilly's data turn out to be disappointing. We need not, however, be confined to this negative conclusion; taken as a whole, all the data and the figures we have available at least give us grounds for presuming that, if the population of France did increase from 1700 to 1750, the increase was a modest one, and that during the *Ancien Régime* the main increase was from 1750 to 1790.

The sample analysis of the population of France before 1800 is intended to throw light on these points which are still obscure. So far as it has gone up to the present time, the investigation gives us some information only about the rural population of 9 departments of the Paris basin.[15] As, in addition, we know the vital statistics for Paris in the eighteenth century,[16] we can obtain rough figures for the whole of the 9 departments.

The average rate of natural increase in each of the 5 cohorts 1740-9 to 1780-9 is as follows for the rural population of the 9 departments (children of town families out to nurse in the country are not of course included).[17]

1740-9	*1750-9*	*1760-9*	*1770-9*	*1780-9*
		rate per 1,000		
− 0·3	8·7	6·5	11·0	7·0

[14] Of the 4 other Generalities in which the data obtained refer to a slightly different period, one, Rouen, has a considerably smaller rate of increase, 0·33 per cent. But Lyonnais has 0·77 per cent, Franche-Comté 0·78 per cent, and the Generality of Poitiers 0·92 per cent; so that the figures for the whole of France are scarcely affected.

[15] Aisne, Aube, Eure-et-Loir, Loiret, Oise, Seine, Seine-et-Marne, Seine-et-Oise, Yonne; the figures have been obtained from the registers of 41 rural parishes for the whole of the 9 departments.

[16] The Paris registers were burnt in 1871; the statistics in question were published in 1823 in *Recherches statistiques sur la ville de Paris et le département de la Seine*. A complementary study on seasonal variations in the figures was published in 1826.

[17] For each department, the number of births (and deaths) in each cohort has been calculated by the quotient method, multiplying the number of births (and deaths) observed in the sample by the ratio of the rural population of the department to that of the sample in 1821.

For the towns, the Paris results have been multiplied by 1·42, still following the census of 1821. The natural rate of increase has been calculated on the assumption that the birth rate was 40 per cent in the country and 33 per cent in Paris. These are the figures accepted in the eighteenth century as a result of contemporary observations based on partial censuses.

For Paris, the apparent rates, i.e. not counting children who died while out to nurse away from Paris, are as follows:

$-2 \cdot 6$	$0 \cdot 6$	$-0 \cdot 8$	$1 \cdot 9$	$0 \cdot 0$

The two sets of figures show a very marked correlation, which is particularly interesting since they were obtained from independent observations.

The second set of figures is valid for the whole urban population of the 9 departments, if we accept that this had the same characteristics as the population of Paris. If the children who died while out to nurse are added, we arrive at the following rates of increase, all negative:

$-8 \cdot 7$	$-5 \cdot 7$	$-7 \cdot 7$	$-4 \cdot 2$	$-6 \cdot 0$

As Parisian children who died in departments other than those studied are not included in these figures, the actual rates were in fact still lower.

In other words, the population of Paris only maintained its level by means of a considerable contribution from outside.

Taking the population of 1740 as 100, the index of the rural population of the 9 departments, discounting migrations, is as follows:

1740	1750	1760	1770	1780	1790
100	99·7	108·7	115·9	129·4	138·1

So that, not counting migrations, the rural population would appear to have increased by nearly 40 per cent from 1750 to 1790, after dropping very slightly from 1740 to 1750.

For the whole of the 9 departments, towns included, the decline from 1740 to 1750 can be assessed roughly at 3 or 4 per cent, and the subsequent increase at about 15 per cent.

Let us now consider the differences between Paris and the rural areas. From 1750 to 1790, the apparent excess of births over deaths in Paris was almost nil, even though the number of births was increased by foundlings born in the provinces, and the number of deaths decreased by all the deaths of children put out to nurse outside Paris. At first sight, this difference between Paris and the country could be the result of a difference in birth rate: according to Expilly, it was in the region of 33 per 1,000 in Paris and 40 per 1,000 in the country. In fact, there was certainly a difference in mortality as well. It is relevant to quote Deparcieux's estimate of 23·5 years as the expectation of life for children born in Paris at the beginning of the eighteenth century.[18] The rural population certainly had a lower death rate, since, with a birth rate which was scarcely more than 40 per 1,000, it did not decrease; therefore its death rate did not on the average reach this figure; the rural expectation of life was consequently greater than 25 years.

It is not enough merely to observe that the population was increasing more rapidly in the country than in the town; the various urban classes ought also to be compared. Unfortunately, we have little information about them. The example of the ruling class in Geneva,[19] in which the size of generations in 1575

[18] Deparcieux, A., *Essai sur les probabilités de la vie humaine*, Paris 1746.
[19] Henry, L., *Anciennes familles genevoises*, Paris, P.U.F., 1956, 232 pp.

had approximately doubled by 1675, whereas the population of Geneva increased by only 23 per cent, shows that the smaller rate of growth of the privileged classes, which is so common in the transition period, is nothing like a general law.

In fact, it is very likely, judging from the study of the Peerage, that the Parisian upper classes were declining numerically, chiefly because of their very low fertility[20]; but there is no reason to suppose that it was the same for the intermediate classes or even for the provincial upper classes. The examples of very large families which some people like quoting are taken from these classes; in the absence of birth-control, this may have been a natural consequence of the very widespread practice of putting children out to nurse, and of the fact that marriages tended perhaps to be earlier than among country people.

Age distribution

According to Bourgeois-Pichat's figures, the distribution by broad age-groups was as follows in 1776 and in 1801:

Age	1776	1801
0–19	43	42
20–59	50	49
60 and over	7	9
Total	100	100

In 25 years, then, the average age of the population rose slightly, as a result of the drop in fertility noted by Bourgeois-Pichat. Previously, there was probably no sustained decline in fertility. In the absence of fluctuations, the age distribution would have kept close to what it was in 1776; for, contrary to popular belief, a decline in mortality does not produce a rise in the average age so long as it affects mainly children, adolescents, and young adults. And this has been the case until very recently.

In fact, there were fluctuations, particularly at the beginning of the century; so that there must have been some age-groups relatively deficient. Were they sufficiently so to affect seriously the age-pyramid? I do not think we have enough data to answer this question. Besides, there has been less theoretical study of populations characterized by an alternation of calm periods and severe crises than of stable populations with constant characteristics, even though long periods in history without fluctuations are the exception rather than the rule.

Mortality

Duvillard's table (infant mortality 233 per 1,000, expectation of life at birth, 28·8 years) is supposed to show mortality in France towards the end of the Ancien Régime. Duvillard was not unaware of the disadvantages of Halley's method for working out the mortality rate; yet it is difficult to see how else he could have proceeded. As the population of France was increasing at the period

---

[20] Levy, C. and Henry, L., 'Ducs et Pairs sous l'Ancien Régime', *Population*, 1960, 15, pp. 807–30. (*Editor's note*: we have used the terms 'peers' and 'peerage' in this translation, although this is not quite a correct rendering of 'Ducs et pairs', a more restricted group.)

to which these figures refer, the view they give of the situation is no doubt too pessimistic; in other words, infant mortality would be less than 230 per 1,000, and the expectation of life more than 29 years.

In the absence of any overall figures, various monographs have yielded the following data; they relate chiefly to child mortality, which is much easier to evaluate than adult mortality as soon as there is appropriate registration:

TABLE 4

Place	Region	Period	Mortality quotients			Expectation of life at birth
			q_0	$_4q_1$ per 1,000	$_5q_5$	e_0 years
Crulai[21]	Normandy	1690–1750	210 to 230	122	77	32 to 33
Sotteville-lès-Rouen[22]	Normandy	1760–90	244	192	64	
Ingouville[23]	Normandy	1730–90	286	213	119	
St. Agnan[24]	Morvan	1730–93	240			
Ganic[25]	Quercy	1770–92	230	227		
Lévignac-s.-Save[26]	Languedoc	1720–90	210	212	61	33

Some of the child mortality rates of this table are higher than those given by Duvillard, and others lower; the highest ones apply to as recent a period as the one covered by Duvillard's table, but they are for populations with special characteristics, particularly in the case of Ingouville, a suburb of Le Havre in which the mortality situation was made even worse by poverty and the proximity of the town. The rate for Crulai, on the other hand, which is rather lower, refers to an earlier period.

In addition, we have some data on the mortality of children in the rural population of the Paris region, provided by the analysis of the first observations made as part of the investigation into the population of France before 1800. The following are the infant mortality rate and mortality quotients $_4q_1$ (from the 1st to the 5th birthday) and $_5q_5$ (from the 5th to the 10th birthday) for the cohorts 1740–9, 1750–9, 1760–9, 1770–9, and 1780–9:

TABLE 5

Cohorts	Mortality quotients per 1,000		
	q_0	$_4q_1$	$_5q_5$
1740–9	278	230	86
1750–9	220	190	78
1760–9	240	186	61
1770–9	220	174	76
1780–9	241	187	

[21] Gautier, E. and Henry, L., La Population de Crulai, paroisse normande, Paris, P.U.F., 1958, 270 pp.
[22] Girard, P., 'Aperçus de la démographie de Sotteville-lès-Rouen vers la fin du XVIIIème siècle', Population, 1959, 14, pp. 485-508.
[23] Terrisse, M., 'Un faubourg du Havre: Ingouville', Population, 1961, 16, pp. 285-300.
[24] Houdaille, J., 'Un village du Morvan: St. Agnan', Population, 1961, 16, pp. 301-12.
[25] Unpublished.
[26] Unpublished.

Not counting the first period, the quotients do not show any definite tendency to decrease; the average infant mortality rate for the period 1750-1789 is 230 per 1,000, the average quotient 4^q1 is 184 per 1,000, and the average quotient 5^q5 68 per 1,000. The difference between these figures and Duvillard's table is particularly marked for age 1-4 (184 per 1,000 instead of 240 per 1,000).

For Crulai, we have another series of quotients by cohorts; but they are mortality quotients from birth to the 10th birthday, as follows:

1720-9	362 to 392 per 1,000
1730-9	384 to 397 per 1,000
1740-9	454 to 463 per 1,000
1750-9	298 to 304 per 1,000
1760-9	422 per 1,000
1770-9	297 per 1,000
1780-9	336 per 1,000
1790-9	307 per 1,000

N.B. Before 1760, the age at death is sometimes omitted; hence the two possible outside limits given in the above figures.

The overall impression is of a considerable decrease during the eighteenth century; but the fluctuations are such that it cannot be counted as significant. Furthermore, the peak in 1760-9 is mainly the result of a local epidemic in 1761; if we discount this, we arrive at an evolution which is fairly similar to that of the Paris region: a considerable decrease from 1740-9 to the following cohort, and subsequently relative stability.

Thus, for the rural population, such evidence as is available scarcely suggests a continuous decline in mortality during the second half of the eighteenth century. It seems rather that mortality in this period remained fairly stable, apart from the considerable fluctuations which characterized past centuries, but at a definitely lower level than during the previous half-century.

About the urban population, we have still less information. For the Peerage, it has only been possible to study adult mortality, in which there is no observable improvement during the eighteenth century. In the ruling class in Geneva, to which it is very useful to refer even though it is outside France, the improvement for adults is at the end of the seventeenth century or at the beginning of the eighteenth; there is little change after that until towards the end of the nineteenth century; but for young people, the improvement appears to be continuous. In fact, however, the figures are averages over 50-year periods, so that here too the improvement may well have been by stages separated by periods of stability.

It would be prudent to stop there. Nevertheless, let us risk a provisional conclusion, if only to try to sort out a somewhat heterogeneous collection of data.

In the first half of the eighteenth century, we find:

The last great famine, in 1709-10: this is followed by bad years up to the end of the reign of Louis XIV.

A bad year in 1719.

The plague of 1720; admittedly it was limited to Provence, but its effects were disastrous.

Bad years during the decade 1740-9.

From 1750 to 1789, there certainly continue to be bad years, epidemics and famines, but they reach neither the extent nor the intensity of the earlier crises; so that it is natural that mortality should have been less during this period than during the previous half-century. Besides, progress in medical practice was still too slight for there to be a steady improvement in national health. It is consequently perfectly understandable that the last 40 years of the *Ancien Régime* should have been much better on the whole than the previous 50, without this indicating any continuous improvement from 1750 to 1790. In other words, it seems that the first drop in mortality was due to the absence of those major catastrophes which until the beginning, or even the middle, of the eighteenth century, destroyed in a few years, if not months, the surplus accumulated during a few decades free from such calamities. We still do not know whether this reduction in disasters was produced by man, the result for instance of economic progress, or whether it was just a piece of good luck, the continuation of which was made possible by the undeniable progress of a later period.

This reduction in the level of mortality in the period 1750–90 is enough to explain why the increase in the population during this period was much more pronounced than it had been previously.

In short, the sum total of all the fragmentary information we possess about the population and about births and deaths leads to one coherent conclusion about mortality: that it was lower during the second half of the eighteenth century than during the first.

Fertility and birth-control

Rates of legitimate fertility for the past can only be determined after the reconstitution of families, so that here we have only a few sets of figures. To begin with, here are the rates for some villages by age-groups, taking together all ages at marriage:

TABLE 6

	Age specific legitimate fertility rates Wife's Age						
	15–19	20–24	25–29	30–34	35–39	40–44	45–49
Crulai (marriages 1674-1742)	0·320	0·419	0·429	0·355	0·292	0·142	0·010
Sotteville-lès-Rouen (1760-90)	no figures available	0·491	0·440	0·429	0·297	0·125	0·010
Ingouville (marriages 1730-70)	no figures available	0·428	0·436	0·409	0·292	0·091	0·005
St. Agnan (1730-92)	0·245	0·403	0·429	0·378	0·242	0·246	0·032
Ganic (1747-92)	0·333	0·380	0·336	0·335	0·315	0·163	0·020
Lévignac-s.-Save (2nd half of 18th century)	no figures available	0·396	0·424	0·308	0·253	0·096	0·000

N.B. The figures for Sotteville-lès-Rouen have been corrected to eliminate the disturbing effect of premarital conceptions. In the 45-49 age-group, the rates for Crulai and St. Agnan are only for those women whose exact age is known.

These results are imperfect for various reasons. The number of observations is often very small, particularly in the lower age-groups. In the higher age-groups, where this fault is less significant, there is another source of error, namely the lack of precision in the women's ages. This can of course be avoided by taking into account only those women whose date of birth is known, but this would be at the expense of a loss of information. Finally, all these rates are probably somewhat lower than they were in reality, as a result of failure to register baptisms, probably very rare, and of temporary absences; in both these cases, births which ought to be included are not. In actual fact, the error resulting from these omissions is small, certainly less than 5 per cent.

On the whole, these various sets of figures follow the same pattern. Fertility begins by increasing from the age-group 15-19 to the age-group 20-24; from this group to the next there are slight variations, sometimes up and sometimes down.[27] After this, fertility declines more and more quickly; although it is still quite high at age 40-44, it is pretty well negligible at age 45-49. This decline with age is due on the one hand to the progressive increase in the proportion of sterile couples; when the wife is 20, this proportion is very low, less than 5 per cent, whereas it is close to 100 per cent when she is 50. On the other hand, even the fertility of couples who are still fecund tends to diminish as the woman grows older.

At about age 25, the rates of legitimate fertility range from slightly less than 0·400 to more than 0·450; I do not think that it often goes below the lower limit, although on the other hand one can expect the upper limit to be quite frequently exceeded. At Ingouville, for instance, 0·500 is reached in the farm-labourer-gardener group; this may be just chance, but rates of 0·500 at about age 25 have also been observed in Canada in the eighteenth century, and in the Genevan middle class in the seventeenth. We may wonder whether the differences between villages of different regions are significant or merely due to chance. The general impression from all the information available about fertility in the absence of birth-control is that populations differ considerably from one another; what we know at present about the eighteenth century seems to suggest that fertility was higher in the North of France than in the South, even before birth-control. Research being carried out at the moment will no doubt show whether or not this hypothesis is correct.

To give a more concrete picture of fertility in the past, let us take the example of Crulai; this village, which has been studied more thoroughly than the others, offers the advantage of a fertility which appears to be average for the period. Let us first of all consider complete families, in which the marriage is not broken before the woman reaches the latest age for having children, i.e. 50, or at the very least 45. Depending on whether the woman marries at 20 (exact age), 25 or 30, the distribution of 100 families according to the number of children is as Table 7 overleaf.[28]

Primary sterility is very rare when the woman marries young, which is a common situation, occurring in most populations; if some writers have given a

[27] With a sufficiently large number of observations, we should no doubt see a drop in fertility from age 20-24 to age 25-29.

[28] This is an estimated distribution, since an insufficient number of complete families have been observed for these results to be used on their own.

different impression, it is because, fearing the possibility of sterility, they treat it as more important than, from the strictly statistical point of view, it really is.

The mean number of children per complete family is approximately 8, 6, and 4 for women who marry at 20, 25 and 30 respectively.

TABLE 7

Number of children	Woman's age at marriage		
	20	25	30
0	2	5	10
1-3	6	12	27
4-6	17	39	57
7-9	43	40	6
10 and more	32	4	0
TOTAL	100	100	100

The modal number, i.e. the number to be found most frequently, is higher : it is 8, 9 or 10 (about 15 per cent of cases for each number, 45 per cent for the three together) for women married at 20, 6 or 7 or women married at 25 (36 per cent for the two, 18 per cent for each), and 4 or 5 for women married at 30 (44 per cent for the two, 22 per cent for each). These figures are certainly high compared with today. But we are still a long way from the figures which some people are fond of quoting, figures based on observations to which more attention has been paid than their frequency permits. This is all the more significant as marriages were not generally early; since about 25 was the most frequent marriage age for women, complete families of 6 to 8 children must have been the most common.

At Crulai, premarital conceptions were rare, less than 3 per cent of first children. But this was not so everywhere, since 30 per cent was reached at Sotteville-lès-Rouen, 15 per cent at Ingouville and 9 per cent at St. Agnan, even though there were not many illegitimate births in any of these places. In any case, the first child was usually born soon after marriage: about half the first children conceived in wedlock by women married between 20 and 30 were born before the first wedding anniversary.[29] At Crulai, for the same group of women, the average interval between marriage and birth of the first child is about 16 months.

Children continue to be born at generally regular intervals, except for the last ones. The overall picture presented by the information available is as follows: the average intervals lengthen slightly from the first to the last but two; the last but one shows a more noticeable increase; and from this to the last there is generally a very marked increase.

At the birth of the last child, still in complete families, the average age of the mother is about 40. At Crulai, at the birth of the last child, 60 per cent of women are aged between 38 and 41, the average age being 40; in this village, 40 is also the median age. Half the married women of 40 have no more children; almost all the others have their last child between 40 and 45, since the proportion of women of 45 who have no more children is more than 95 per cent.

[29] For women married before 20, and especially before 18, the proportion is lower, because of the phenomenon known as 'adolescent sterility'.

Those are the outlines of the situation in complete families. But many marriages were ended prematurely by the death of husband or wife; so that the average number of births per marriage was 4 at Crulai, whereas the average number of children per complete family was 6 for women married at 25, the average age at marriage.

In rural areas, illegitimate births were negligible; they formed only a tiny proportion of the total births (less than 1 per cent for the whole of the 9 departments of the Paris region).[30] It is of course possible that some of the country girls who became pregnant went to the town to have their babies; but this behaviour is further evidence that rural society disapproved of illegitimacy. It may well be that at certain periods and in certain circles illegitimacy was very easily accepted, as some authors seem fond of saying.[31] At any rate, this is not true of country people in the eighteenth century.

We have far less information about urban society. One of its most striking characteristics in the eighteenth century is the huge proportion of foundlings (31 per cent of baptisms in Paris between 1770 and 1789). We know that most were illegitimate. Some of them came from elsewhere, but it seems likely that the majority were the children of the very large number of serving women to be found in towns at this time.

The last subject that remains to be discussed in this connexion is that of birth-control in marriage. Writers of the second half of the eighteenth century have spoken much of this, and often as if the practice had spread to all sections of the population—including the rural population.[32]

The study of the ruling class in Geneva has shown that, in this case, birth-control in marriage began to be practised at about the end of the seventeenth century or the beginning of the eighteenth, and that subsequently it gained ground rapidly. It would consequently not be in the least surprising if it were the same in the French upper classes at the same period, if not before; in such matters, however, we must beware of *a priori* conclusions, however obvious they may seem.[33] That is why a special study has been made of the Peerage, a small section of the upper classes about which it was possible to obtain enough information.

The following are the rates of legitimate fertility of the wifes of Peers, married before 30 during the eighteenth century; they are compared with the arithmetic average of the sets of rural figures quoted above:

		Wife's age					
		20-24	*25-29*	*30-34*	*35-39*	*40-44*	*45-49*
Peers (marriages 1700-95)	rate	0·226	0·167	0·063	0·018	0·006	0·000
	index (rural figures taken as 100)	54	40	17	6	4	0
Arithmetic average of 6 sets of rural figures		0·420	0·412	0·369	0·282	0·144	0·013

[30] In all the investigations now in progress, the rarity of illegitimate births is apparent.

[31] Cf. for instance *Duplessis-Leguelinel, op. cit.*

[32] The I.N.E.D. has devoted a study to this question: Bergues, H. and others, *La Prévention des naissances dans la famille*, Paris, P.U.F., 1960, 400 pp.

[33] The fertility of the English Ducal families studied by Hollingsworth seems scarcely to have been affected by birth-control before the middle of the nineteenth century. See above, p. 366 f.

The level of fertility is much lower for the Peers. In addition, the difference between the two sets of figures increases with the age, so that the variation in fertility with the woman's age is very different in the two cases; amongst the Peers it is comparable to the state of affairs in modern populations, in which birth-control is a common practice.

Other characteristics of the fertility of the Peers point to this deliberate reduction of fertility. For instance, the relationship between fertility rates and marriage age: fertility at a given age decreases as the marriage age is lowered, this kind of relationship is non-existent, or at most very doubtful, in rural populations of the past, whereas it is general in modern populations. Finally, for women married before 20, the age at the birth of the last child is in the region of 27, as against about 40 at Crulai.

To conclude, birth-control in marriage was certainly practised in the French upper classes during the eighteenth century; the above-mentioned study even leads us to suspect that it was already practised at the end of the seventeenth. But there is scarcely any evidence enabling us to verify the assertions of authors of the second half of the eighteenth century, who maintained that birth-control was also practised by the peasantry. The studies referring to the end of the eighteenth century, those on Ingouville, Sotteville, Ganic and St. Agnan, scarcely give the impression of a deliberate reduction in fertility. For Crulai, fertility does not seem to have diminished before the Revolution. Nevertheless, the observations made at Lévignac-sur-Save tend to indicate the existence of a beginning of birth-control during the second half of the eighteenth century. It is not then too much to hope that future research will bring to light conclusive examples of the practice of birth-control being already established in the rural population before the Revolution.

Marriage and celibacy

As we have pointed out, writers of the period were convinced that celibacy, both ecclesiastic and secular, was abnormally high and was thus a threat to the future of the population. Contemporary witnesses tend to take notice of the upper classes, and we must ask two questions about their testimony:

(1) Is it correct for the upper classes?

(2) Can it be applied to the rest of the population?

The only indisputable observation concerns the sons of Peers; among those born between 1700 and 1749 who passed the age of 50, from 17 to 27 per cent died without having married. There is a large margin of uncertainty, but even the lowest proportion, 17 per cent is already high, since the corresponding figures for French males born towards the end of the nineteenth century is not more than 10 per cent. So that celibacy was relatively common at the top of the social scale, at least among men. It is likely that the same was true for women. A lack of data makes it impossible to verify whether this was a recent situation, or whether it had already existed for a long time.

Admittedly, we have one piece of evidence that fully bears out the opinion of contemporary writers, that of the ruling class in Geneva; but we should have to accept that the nuptiality crisis apparent in this case reflects an evolution common to the whole of the upper classes of the period and is not merely the result of special local conditions. Among persons who died aged 50 or more, the proportion unmarried is as follows:

	Persons born in				
	1600–49	1650–99	1700–49	1750–99	1800–49
Men	13 to 17%	12 to 18%	26 to 31%	18 to 20%	22%
Women	7%	26%	29%	32%	25%

N.B. The figures for men include a considerable proportion of undetermined cases; hence the limits indicated.

In any case, these examples refer only to the upper classes; in the population as a whole, the position seems rather different.

To begin with, we know the number of marriages from 1770 to 1784; the corresponding crude marriage rate is 8·5 per 1,000 higher than today.

Furthermore, Moheau gives the proportion of unmarried persons in certain regions (Provence, Touraine, Lyonnais, Auvergne, Normandy and Saintonge).[34] Cross checks confirm that the age-composition of the populations of these regions was the same as the approximately known age-composition of the population of the Kingdom. If we apply to this population the proportions of unmarried persons at successive ages, as observed in 1851 and 1936, we obtain aggregate proportions which can be compared with those given by Moheau. The following table gives these proportions, together with Moheau's figures.

TABLE 8

Number of unmarried persons per 1000 inhabitants aged more than . . .

	Males			Females		
	Moheau	1851	1936	Moheau	1851	1936
12 years (a)	154	217	201	150	219	183
14 years (b)	147	200	185	167	188	164
16 years (c)	170	182	168	165	184	143
18 years (d)	154	231	148	138	164	121

(a) Provence and the generality of Tours.
(b) 192 parishes from the generalities of Lyons, Riom, and Rouen.
(c) 24 parishes from the generality of La Rochelle and Ile de Ré.
(d) 11 scattered parishes.

All the proportions obtained from Moheau are lower than those based on the proportions of unmarried persons at successive ages in 1851. For males, they are less than or near enough the same as the figures based on the 1936 census; they are again lower than these 1936 figures for females in the Provence and generality of Tours group, the largest of Moheau's samples (1 million inhabitants).

In short, for the regions to which they apply, Moheau's data do not indicate a very high rate of celibacy: in 1851 the proportion of unmarried persons aged about 50 was in the region of 10 per cent for men and 13 per cent for women; the 1936 figures are 9 per cent and 11 per cent respectively.

As further evidence, the following are some percentages of women aged 50 or more at death (or 45 or more in some cases) who had never married:

[34] Moheau. *Recherches et considérations sur la population de la France*, 1778, H. L., 'La nuptialité à la fin de l'Ancien Régime', *Population*, 1954, 9, pp. 542–6.

Table 9

Percentage of women dying unmarried at 50 (or 45)

	Lower limit %	Upper limit %
Crulai (1750–1800)	2	11·6
Sotteville-lès-Rouen (1760–90)	2·6	7·8
St. Agnan (1730–93)	not computed	6·3
Ganic (1747–92)	3·2	7·3
Lévignac-sur-Save (1757–91)	16·4	18·7
Eure-et-Loir* (1740–89)	2·8	7·5
Oise* (1740–89)	4·3	6·7
Seine-et-Marne* (1740–89)	2·6	9·4

* Parishes in the sample. Results for the other departments were not available at the time of writing.

Apart from Lévignac-sur-Save, the proportion of old women who were spinsters is low, if not very low. It would seem then either that nuptiality was high at least in the country, or that country women who did not marry left their villages. The investigation of town records will show whether the latter hypothesis is right or wrong. At any rate, it does not seem that unmarried women stayed in their villages to help their married brothers or sisters.

We know little about celibacy in men, as the marital status of men at death is too often undetermined. But if it is confirmed that the proportion of women never married was low, there will be reason to think that the same applied also to men.

Age at first marriage

On this point, as on the others, the data available are few and far between; some relate to the Peerage, and others to the rural population. Let us confine ourselves to the average age at first marriage, for both males and females, in years to one decimal place.

Table 10

	Average age at first marriage	
	Males	Females
Peers		
Marriages 1650–99	25·5	20·0
1700–49	23·6	19·4
1750–99	21·3	18·4
Crulai		
Marriages 1674–1742	28·0	25·5
Sotteville-lès-Rouen		
1760–90	27·4	26·2
St. Agnan		
1730–93	26·0	24·7
Ingouville		
1730–90	28·0	26·0
Lévignac-sur-Save		
1750–91	29·7	25·6

Marriage was obviously not early in the 5 villages in the above table. These observations can, without much danger, be generalized; the numerous investigations of records already carried out show in fact that few males, and even few females, married very young. But this situation is not peculiar to the eighteenth century: for the whole of France, the average age of males at first marriage remained slightly higher than 28 from the middle of the nineteenth century up to the first World War; during the same period, the corresponding age for females was just about 24.

It is mainly when compared with the upper classes that the peasants seem to have married late; the average age at marriage of the sons of Peers drops to about 21 in the second half of the eighteenth century, and of the daughters to about 18. On this point, there is as much difference between the top of the social scale and the mass of the population as between two populations of different cultures, such as Mohammedans and Europeans.[35]

Resumé and conclusion

The study of the population of France in the eighteenth century is based mainly on parish registers. From 1668 onwards, these were kept in duplicate, and a great number have survived. They cover more than 90 per cent of the years between 1736 and 1792, and under-registration, which was confined to deaths, was no doubt slight, at least in the north of the country. A systematic sample analysis of these records is in progress.

Evolution of the population

Little is known about this, particularly at the beginning of the century; the population of what is now France seems to have risen from 21-22 million inhabitants in about 1700 to 25 millions in 1770 and nearly 29 millions in 1800. Taken as a whole, the data available suggest that the increase was slight in the first half of the eighteenth century, but rather rapid in the second half. The age-distribution probably remained more or less constant until 1770-80, as fertility and the birth rate probably did not change.

Mortality

Apart from Duvillard's table, and we know neither how this was arrived at nor exactly to what period it applies, we have only fragmentary data. For the rural population after 1750, infant mortality must have been roughly 200 to 250 per 1,000, and the expectation of life at birth about 30 to 35 years. The situation in other sections of the population is much less well known; but it is most probable that mortality was higher in the towns than in the country, and that, in the towns, it was lower in the upper classes than in the others. Mortality was very irregular, and might double or treble in periods of famine or during epidemics. One of the characteristics of the eighteenth century in France was that it had few real famines, especially in the second half, and no general plague epidemic, for the 1720 one did not spread beyond Marseilles and part of Provence. This is no doubt why mortality was lower in the second half of the century than in the first, without there having been any noticeable progress in medical practice.

Fertility and birth-control

The eighteenth century is usually considered to be a period of loose morals.

[35] See J. Hajnal, above, p. 101 f. (Ed.)

This opinion is the result of observations based too exclusively on the aristocratic society of Versailles and Paris. Although it is still very incomplete, observation of the rural population reveals a very different situation: illegitimate births, for instance, were very rare, even though marriage was generally rather late. Even premarital conceptions were infrequent in some districts, although this characteristic is much less general than the previous one.

Although of course it is not necessarily a sign or a consequence of a deterioration in morals, birth-control was practised among the upper classes throughout the eighteenth century. The fertility of the Peers shows the same characteristics as that of present-day European populations.

In the rural population, the practice of birth-control began probably before the Revolution in some areas, although we have so far little proof of this. The majority of studies reveal a fertility as yet unaffected by birth-control, corresponding to 4 to 5 children per marriage for a woman married at 25, the average age at marriage in the rural population, and 6 to 7 children in complete families; in complete families, the average age of the woman at the birth of the last child was 40.

Celibacy and age at marriage

All the available data suggest that celibacy was much less widespread than many writers have maintained. Here again, it seems that unwarranted conclusions have been drawn from observations confined to the upper classes. Among the masses, the proportion of men and women never married may have been no greater than towards the end of the nineteenth century.

Marriage was very early in certain privileged sections of the population, such as the Peers. Among the rural masses, on the other hand, it was slightly later than it is today; on an average, it seems that women married at about 25, and men about 28.

All these results come from limited studies, and are as yet merely tentative. Research in progress will enable us to draw more certain conclusions, but these conclusions will not necessarily be very different.

19

RECENT THEORIES AND RESEARCH IN FRENCH POPULATION BETWEEN
1500 and 1700

PIERRE GOUBERT
Translated by Margaret Hilton

Editor's Note: The reader is referred to Professor Goubert's study, *Beauvais et le Beauvaisis de 1600 à 1730*, 2 vols, 1960 (published by S.E.V.P.E.N. for the École Pratique des Hautes Études—VIe section) in which he gives the full data and statistical tables to which he refers in the course of his chapter, e.g. the village of Auneuil.

A SUBJECT such as this must be approached in a spirit of profound humility. We can claim to have to some degree elucidated the problems of French population from 1750 onwards, but it is more questionable whether we have any sure knowledge of the earlier period. There are two indispensable conditions for future progress in the field of the history of population: a recognition of our ignorance and a determination to understand what accounts for it.

However, most respectable general historical treatises discourse on the history of population with the greatest assurance. For the layman, this branch of historical discipline seems as clear and reliable as the clauses of the Treaty of Münster or the articles of the *Ordonnance du Commerce*. Even the bland assertions of Emile Levasseur[1] who believed an increase in the numbers of men to be bound up with the excellence of their government, and *vice versa*, are still to be found in many a history book. We read that the good administration of a Sully or a Colbert led the population to increase, whilst maladministration reduced it. More widely-accepted still is the belief that the minor wars of the *Ancien Régime* had an adverse effect from the demographic point of view. A few years ago a geographer, who shall be nameless, attributed the exceptionally high mortality in a village in the centre of France between 1693 and 1694 to the War of the League of Augsburg. Wars, however, which made use of little man-power as soldiery, could only kill on the battle-field itself, and the wars fought by France after 1660 were almost always pursued outside her own territory. Georges Livet has shown that even in Alsace in the course of the Thirty Years War the devastation was much less extensive than has generally been supposed, and furthermore that the presence of the military led rather to an increase in fertility, for Benfeld had never seen so many baptisms as in the years between 1633 and 1648![2]

---

[1] *La Population française*, Vol. 1, 1889.
[2] G. Livet, *L'Intendance d'Alsace sous Louis XIV*, 1956, p. 285, note 4 and graph 5.

457

Though these shibboleths die hard they are however less frequently invoked today than they have been. But others that appear on the surface to have a more scientific character are taking their place. In some recent works for instance— often valuable studies from some points of view—one can find the most surprising 'rates' of demographic movement cited. Thus in one author we read that in the age of Louis XIV a certain village in Touraine enjoyed a birth rate above 70 per 1,000[3]; a remarkable feat, even for wine-growers. In another work it is maintained that in the seventeenth century 'half the children died in the first year of life'.[4] If this rate were accurate and if it had been steady, the French Revolution would never have occurred for there would have been no men to make it!

A single explanation can account for the persistence of all these traditions, gratuitous ideas, rash approximations and sheer errors of fact. We have too often omitted to go back to our sources for the history of population and to examine them in a sharp critical spirit; or to put the point in another way, we have neglected the recent work of professional demographers, who are statisticians rather than historians, and whose researches adhere to a rigorous method.

The sources

If we set aside literary sources, which are discursive, vague and contradictory and which have a place only in rather elementary demographic thought, there remain, in France as in other countries, two types of sources for the history of population: censuses, which are few and far between and give the state of a population at a given date; and parish registers, of which there is an abundance and which supply more or less continuous lists of baptisms, marriages and burials.

For France in the seventeenth century we have only one general census. The Duc de Beauvillier called for it in 1697 from the Intendants of the provinces in order to instruct his pupil the Duc de Bourgogne; Vauban then tried to interpret the replies of the Intendants in his *Dîme Royale*, drawn up between 1700 and 1704.[5] This means that all the figures which have been put forward in various works on the population of France in 1500, 1600 or 1660, are pure inventions or at best bold extrapolations; not one of them merits acceptance, and we must similarly reject any calculations made on the basis of these conjectural figures, and in particular the estimation of any 'rate of demographic growth' for the country between 1500 and 1700.

The census of 1697-1700 itself presents considerable weaknesses, as A. des Cilleuls pointed out some hundred years ago. Vauban's figure of a little more than 19 million inhabitants refers to France within her frontiers of 1700. (The frontiers were altered at least six times in the course of the seventeenth century, and three times in the eighteenth.) This figure is the result of one of those mistakes in addition which were so common in the period. Vauban forgot one

---

[3] Aries, *Histoire des populations françaises et de leurs attitudes devant la vie*, 1948, p. 170.
[4] *Histoire générale des civilisations, Les XVIe et XVIIe siècles*, 1954, p. 147.
[5] The *Dîme Royale* of Vauban is easily accessible in the Coornaert edition (Paris 1933), p. 157. The criticism is summed up in detail by Vincent 'French Demography in the 18th Century' (*Population Studies*, Vols. 1-2, 1947-49, Part I).

province altogether—the Generality of Bourges; he grossly overestimated Paris by alloting that city 720,000 inhabitants in 1694; he interpreted the data which eight intendants supplied concerning hearths multiplying the figure by an arbitrary and variable coefficient (4 or 4·5); the intendants themselves obtained the information from their subordinates, either clerks or officers; no one knows how these latter went about their work, and it is likely that each one followed his own whim, and either made use of partial censuses twenty years old, or else made a rough estimate; some intendants forgot to count the towns, and others no doubt made mistakes in addition or left some items out. In short after subjecting this work to detailed criticisms, it seems that one can take the figure of 19,300,000 as a probable one for the population of France in 1700 but *with a margin of error of not less than 10 per cent either way*. Moreover, most of the data for this census refer to a very unfavourable period following the large mortality of the years 1691-4, which recurred in many areas in 1699.

Some partial censuses were carried out in France between 1660 and 1700, particularly in newly-conquered towns and territories such as Flanders and the Franche-Comté. They have been very little studied. All of them present serious problems of interpretation. Furthermore some administrative authorities, mainly those with fiscal, military or religious responsibilities, were in a position to carry out at any point in the course of the century what one might call 'counts', and these have sometimes come down to us: they pose even more difficult problems of interpretation. As for the vague estimates of the sixteenth century, they are valuable above all as evidence for the mentality of the times: did not the serious-minded Froumenteau in his book *Le Secret des finances de France* (1581) reckon that there were 132,000 parishes or church towers in Henry III's kingdom! These partial censuses, in fact, raise more questions than they solve, as the following examples will show.

Parish priests sometimes made lists of the names of persons confirmed. These can be an indication of some demographic value (e.g. of the presence of such and such individuals in the parish) and can also provide information on religious practices. Priests also sometimes gave the number of Easter communicants in the parish, all non-communicants being children. Unfortunately there are three factors which limit the usefulness of these figures. In the first place, the age of communion varied in France from one diocese to another and from one period to another, though usually it was between twelve and fifteen years. Secondly, the priest often forgot to enter this figure, or noted it occasionally. And finally they cited the figure in very round numbers, such as 200 or 250 or 300. At the very best therefore such indications can only help us to form an approximate idea of the population of a parish.

In the case of censuses made for fiscal purposes we must first know who was subject to the tax. Those exempt through privilege and those exempt on account of indigence are more often than not omitted from the list. Even the reliable *Dénombrement des Gabellans* of 1724-6 leaves out the many privileged persons and all children under eight years of age as not subject to the salt-tax, and it was possible to cheat on the question of age.[6] Any fiscal census is by its

[6] For this census, referred to and used by Esmonin, cf. Goubert, *Beauvais et le Beauvaisis . . .* p. 252 and note 26.

nature partial, and subject to fraud, *Un feu* or 'a hearth' is often a family, especially in the north of France, but there are also incomplete hearths, half-hearths and hearths with subsidiary off-shoots. Above all there were fiscal hearths or *feux de compoix* of a purely artificial nature, especially in the south of France. One example will suffice to illustrate the bewildering nature of the data supplied by fiscal censuses: the town of Foix counted 142 *feux de compoix* under Louis XIV, but there were 538 *feux allumants*.

It has sometimes been proposed to use seigneurial documents to elicit demographic information, for *censiers* and *terriers* give lists of the *censitaires* of a domain. Usually these are lists of heads of families. But unfortunately the *seigneuries* and the parishes rarely coincide, so that these documents too raise more questions than they solve, and they can only be used to support the evidence of other documents which are usually more widespread and more reliable—that is to say the parish registers. Before turning to these, it is necessary to reiterate the warning against any over hasty use of censuses. The census attributed to Orry, dated 1745,[7] has lately been assigned a role lamentably in excess of its capacities, by a usually serious author in a generally respectable review. In spite of the criticism to which it has been subjected (by Mols, by the present author, by Henry, who omits it from mention in his article in this volume)[8] this document is currently presented in manuals produced for the instruction of young Frenchmen of fifteen as embodying Gospel truth. I need not discuss other eighteenth-century censuses, which M. Reinhard has dealt with in a recent work[9] and which L. Henry analyses in his contribution to the present volume.

Though France is very poor in good censuses, she is rich in her store of parish registers. The listing of these is now well advanced[10] but their methodical study has barely been begun. L. Henry has drawn attention to their fine state of preservation, particularly in the west and south-east of the country. They were very accurately kept from 1737 onwards, with passable accuracy but very unevenly between 1670 and 1736, and usually with great laxity before 1670 although there are some happy exceptions to the general rule. All of them however have one grave defect: the deaths of children and even young people are hardly ever entered in the registers before the end of the seventeenth century. This applies particularly to the south; even in the eighteenth century, the deaths are frequently incomplete.[11] This gap has led even good historians into committing serious errors of judgment. Then there is the fact that registers in France as in all other countries can only concern themselves with persons resident in the parish at the time the entry is made; they cannot therefore take account of migration, except in cases such as that occasioned by marriage, when a record is left. As they scarcely ever refer to a closed population, all the rates which have been calculated on the bases of these registers bear the stigma of a defect which

---

[7] *Population*, 1952, p. 49.

[8] See p. 440 f.

[9] Reinhard and Armengaud, *Histoire générale de la population mondiale* (Paris, Montchrestien, 1961).

[10] Biraben, Henry and Fleury, 'Inventaire par sondage des registres paroissiaux de France', *Population*, 1960, no. 1.

[11] Ch. Pinède, *La Population du Quercy à la fin du 18e siècle* (Actes du 82e Congrès des Sociétés Savantes, 1958) quotes examples taken from the parish of Issepts of priests who in 1787 purposely refrained from entering the deaths of children in their register.

If there were many who acted likewise, we are forced to ask ourselves what an entry is worth.

cannot be remedied, which varies in extent, and which defies evaluation. In spite of these disturbing weaknesses however, the parish registers of eighteenth and seventeenth century France, in view of the almost complete absence of censuses, constitute the first and often the only source available to historians of population.

They have been used for a very long time. Well before the surveys of the population of Paris ordered by Colbert, Rabelais himself had undertaken an inquiry into the seasonal variation of births, and used the parish registers of Thouars as his source.[12] Setting aside this forerunner, however, there are three main motives which have led historians of population to consult the parish registers, and we will do well to look at these three motives in succession in order to gain a better understanding of the relevance and the aims of the many works which are based on an examination of these registers.

In the first place, researchers of varied qualifications for the task have gone to these old registers in order to find evidence on the history of their native village. The least competent concentrated above all on picking out accounts of the extraordinary events which the priests had obligingly recorded: hail-storms, tempests, floods and the visits of soldiers or important personages, the marriage of the *seigneur*, the deaths of reputed centenarians, the birth of triplets, and so on. We need not linger over these. Others have tried to calculate the population of the village and to trace its variations, and they used methods which were more or less well-chosen. For the seventeenth century, for example, they have some-times subtracted the number of adult deaths (which are the only recorded deaths) from the total number of baptisms, and reached the conclusion that in those happy days the population was increasing at a noble rate, thus proving the ex-cellence of the absolute monarchy. On the other hand, as the priests recorded the deaths of infants in the eighteenth century, the answer to the sum looked less rosy at a later date, and they concluded that the eighteenth century was indeed less prosperous, Louis XV, alas, a bad king and the Revolution just what one would expect after so many misfortunes. We need to look back to these childish conclusions because traces of them are still to be found in our history-books; but researchers of the old type—these priests, notaries and schoolmasters who were so devoted to the history of their locality, and whose race is not yet extinct, often published lists of figures extracted from the old registers of their parishes in a very competent way, and provided they are checked over these can often serve as secondary sources of great usefulness.[13] Unfortunately they are to a large extent scattered in small provincial reviews or in old monographs that are difficult to unearth. Works of this type represent the stage in the amateur examination of parish registers.

Secondly, we reach the stage of the economic historian, deeply influenced by the work of Simiand and Ernest Labrousse's first books. Graphs of prices, incomes, and wages were drawn up, and these revealed seasonal, short-term and cyclical movements and long-term trends, and it was thought that it should

[12] Quoted by Helin in *La Prévention des naissances dans la famille* (Cahier no. 35 de l'I.N.E.D., P.U.F., 1960), p. 248.

[13] For example: Segondy, *Une Châtellenie du Saint-Ponais, Cessenon-sur-Orb* (Montpellier 1949); Canard, *Les Mouvements de la population à Saint-Romain d'Urfé* (Bulletin de la Diana, t. 29, no. 4); Clement, *Routot des origines à la Révolution* (Fécamp 1950); etc.

be possible to study demographic movements in the same way with the help of
lists of births, deaths and marriages, and to obtain considerable results fairly
rapidly. Indeed the speed with which counts could be made was considered the
great advantage of the method. The drawbacks were soon apparent: some of
these lay in the fundamental weaknesses of the registers mentioned above; others
were due to unforeseen gaps (it is rather difficult to interpolate deaths), or to the
very uneven quality of those who had drawn up the documents; finally a
difficulty which cannot be too much emphasized was created by the high degree
of variation in practice as between one region and another and even as between
one village and the next. In spite of these considerations much work of this
nature has been undertaken in France in the last twenty years, particularly since
the example set by J. Meuvret in his memorable article in *Population* in 1946.

Finally we reach the typically 'demographic' stage. The rules of the method
have been defined by Henry and Fleury in a manual which has enjoyed a great
success.[14] The first time the method was employed was in a truly exemplary
study of the parish of Crulai.[15] The essential idea governing the procedure is as
follows: the researcher, by slowly amassing a body of personal and family index-
cards, builds up parish population groups of a closed and if possible stable nature;
these are then subjected to demographic and statistical analysis so that he can calculate the classic 'rates', particularly the fertility rates, and finally deduce those
features which are traditional and which have prevailed with minor variations
for hundreds if not thousands of years.[16] There are certain disadvantages in this
method as it entails very lengthy labour, and can usually only be applied to
periods subsequent to 1670; its great advantage however is its unrivalled
reliability and the almost scientific accuracy of the information it provides on
the 'reconstituted family groups'. The half-avowed hope of Louis Henry, to
whom we owe this method, is that, by using strictly determined samples and
treating them with the rigour of laboratory methods, we may be able to infer
true 'laws of population', valid over a whole period or even perhaps over entire
centuries in the history of humanity. I cannot myself however entirely share in
this splendid optimism, particularly when it is envisaged that the results drawn
from the 'reconstitutions' which are feasible from the second third of the seventeenth century onwards might be extrapolated into the past. We may remember
that R. Baehrel has recently, in the midst of other controversies, launched an
attack upon the bare possibility of applying sampling methods to demographic
problems[17]; it may indeed well be that there are some difficulties in this direction.
When we possess some twenty-odd studies such as that on Crulai, we shall certainly be able to see more clearly than we do at present the nature of the problems involved.

The sixteenth century

The historians of the sixteenth century, at any rate those concerned with
southern Europe, seem to be characterized by a highly sensational approach to

[14] Fleury and Henry, *Des registres paroissiaux à l'histoire de la population, Manuel de dépouillement et d'exploitation de l'état civil ancien*, Paris, I.N.E.D. 1956.
[15] Gautier and Henry, *La Population de Crulai*, Paris, P.U.F. 1958.
[16] Henry, *The Population of France in the 18th Century*. (See p. 434.)
[17] *Annales E.S.C.*, 1960, no. 4, p. 702.

their subject. This was a century of expansion in every field, of great adventures, of enormous wealth, and so could not fail to have been the scene also of a great demographic advance! But it was also the century in which great dramas were played out, shameful wars were waged, and plague and famine rife, and so, from time to time, in certain regions, pitiful disasters befell. . . . How do these highly coloured and indeed contradictory images fare when the facts of demography are set beside them?

Except in Savoy and in the *Midi* we have no census with which to counter the bold hypotheses of these enthusiasts—only a handful of parish registers, which seem after the 1 in 50 sampling test carried out by L. Henry and his team to exist mainly in Provence and the north-west, above all in Upper Brittany. They are, frankly, old, torn and dirty registers, scribbled over in all directions and very irregularly kept. It is only by great good luck that one finds any entry of burials. Marriages are noted off and on, but more frequently towards the end of the century. Baptisms are the main item. Even so it is unusual for the registration of baptisms to be continuous and to present no gaps throughout the whole of the century. It should be possible, in fact, with a little goodwill and a little money, to accomplish fairly rapidly a complete investigation of all the registers covering France in the sixteenth century, and once that task has been finished we shall have to formulate hypotheses on what the lost registers can have contained. Needless to say, there is no possibility whatsoever of proceeding to a 'reconstitution' of families.

These ancient registers, then (I am mainly acquainted with those of the west), although they consist more often than not of lists of baptisms, can assist us in answering three questions:

(i) Was there a marked increase in population during the sixteenth century, as is generally believed?—in other words, does the number of baptisms increase significantly, and in what way?

(ii) Did the Wars of Religion (1562-98) leave France as a 'corpse bled white'?—in other words, does the number of baptisms decrease during the last third of the century?

(iii) Are 'demographic crises' violent and prolonged, and do they correspond to the periods of high grain prices which have been clearly dated in works on the history of prices?—in other words, are there sharp drops in the number of births which would allow us to identify these crises, since we have very little data on deaths caused by them?

Some research in this field is in progress but not yet complete, and I shall confine myself to giving a few examples in advance of publication (by the VIth Section of the *École Pratique des Hautes Études*).

The number of baptisms often increases perceptibly in the course of the sixteenth century. In the depths of Sologne, at Souvigny (Loir et Cher), there were on an average 23 baptisms a year between 1502 and 1504, whereas the average exceeded 35 between 1583 and 1587. In Montreuil-sur-Ille (Ille et Vilaine), where there is a continuous series of registers, there were about 15 births between 1500 and 1515, more than 20 round about 1550, and after a sudden drop in the sixties they rose steeply to about 35 for the years between

1575 and 1585. During the last ten years of the century they dropped to about 24. If France as a whole developed on the model of the small parish of Montreuil, the population underwent surprising vicissitudes in the sixteenth century, and must have doubled within the period. Of course we shall never know whether France did in fact develop on the same lines as Montreuil-sur-Ille; all we shall know is what happened in Upper Brittany and in Anjou. Meanwhile, here are one or two other examples:

In La Chapelle-des-Fougerets (Ille-et-Vilaine) baptisms are noted without serious interruption from 1521 onwards. They number between 30 and 40 a year from that date until 1535, and then, after a pronounced fall for 10 years (during which time they number less than 30) a sharp increase is discernible which proceeds by three stages and stretches over the years 1545 to 1610. By this latter date the figure reaches and often surpasses 50. It would seem that the population increased by 50 per cent between 1520 and 1610. I may say that most of the results from registers in Brittany which I have seen give roughly the same picture, but the parishes in Anjou, where in any case the registers were less scrupulously kept, do not lend themselves readily to clear interpretation. Three parishes situated between Baugé and Angers for example allow of only one definite conclusion: in spite of considerable fluctuations the number of baptisms was maintained throughout the sixteenth century and perhaps rose slightly. As work in this field progresses we shall be able to add one example to another, although we shall never have reliable conclusions for the whole country but only for some regions, and these regions are probably precisely the ones which were spared the horrors of the wars, particularly of the wars of religion.

The question of the effect of the wars of religion on population growth is therefore very problematical. It is clear that it will not be possible to estimate the effects in an equally rigorous fashion for all the French provinces, but it will nevertheless be possible to cite some examples of localities where massacres and fires took their toll. Usually such places are fortified towns or boroughs. This was the case at Toucy (Yonne) at the end of the reign of Henry III. There were on an average 140 baptisms there between 1549 and 1584. Then the soldiers came through, burning, slaying, putting the inhabitants to flight. But they did not all flee, for one finds an average of 92 baptisms between 1585 and 1599. And when peace returned the town slowly built up its population again, without however attaining its pre-1585 level; 110 to 115 infants a year were baptized there in about 1625.

From almost all the examples we have the following pattern emerges: baptisms, and marriages when these are recorded, definitely increased during wars, except for those of the decade 1590-9, when they declined almost everywhere though in varying proportions. In spite of the unfavourable conditions of the last ten years of the century, the net result is clearly positive, and Father Mols seems to have been inspired by a happy intuition when he wrote, 'From the demographic point of view, one can say of the wars of religion that their bark was worse than their bite.' Let us run over a few examples. In Souvigny (Loir-et-Cher) there were 23 baptisms at the beginning of the century, 37 in the eighties, and round about 30 in the nineties. In Saint-Lambert des Levées (Maine-et-Loire) there were 124 baptisms in the period before the wars, 127 between 1564 and 1589, still 120 between 1590 and 1599, and thereafter a slow progression. In Saint-Erblon (Ille-et-Vilaine) we find 34 baptisms before the wars and 41 during hostilities. We also know the marriages in this parish from 1571 onwards: in the first ten years there were 93, in the second (1581-90) there were 125, and in the last decade only 70; but at the opening of the seventeenth century a prodigious outburst of matrimony brought the annual average to 16 after 1625. In short, the available documents show that the wars of religion in no way seriously hindered the general upward movement of the number of baptisms (or of marriages in so far as these latter are known), provided we disregard the ten years 1590-9.

A closer examination of these last ten years leads us to the conclusion that the relative decline observable during this period is mainly due to the influence of two or three bad years—1591, 1597 and above all 1598. Often in these years the number of births is halved, as at Souvigny, for example, where it was 14 as against the usual average of 30. Marriages almost cease to take place: there was only one solemnized in Saint-Erblon in 1598. A rapid glance at prices known for the time is enough to afford confirmation of the first hypothesis that springs to mind: i.e. that there was a great crisis in subsistence, felt over a large part of Europe in the year 1597. A crisis of this nature was also experienced in places in 1591, though it was less severe and less general in its incidence. Two crises within a decade amply suffice to account for a modification of the demographic trend, and the upward movement re-asserts itself almost everywhere in the first years of the new century.

A straightforward list of baptisms is sufficient to enable us to pick out the great crises of subsistence in the sixteenth century. On five occasions after 1537 the births in Saint-Lambert des Levées fell beneath 100, and each of these occasions corresponds to a subsistence crisis: 1545, 1566, 1586-7 and 1597. (The crisis of 1573-4 does not stand out clearly, but they were nevertheless 164 deaths as against 110 conceptions followed by births. On the other hand the regional crisis of 1583-4 accounts for the considerable figure of 857 deaths, infants included, in a year, as against 100 conceptions.) One can amuse oneself by observing, here and there, close correspondences between the great crises of subsistence and sudden reductions in the number of baptisms. At Toucy (Yonne) in 1573-4 and in 1583-4; at Saint-Erblon, as already mentioned, in 1574, 1587, 1592 and 1597. But this being said, certain things remain unexplained, such as the deficient year of 1538 in one place, and that of 1551 or 1559 in another, and it seems that local crises and local epidemics doubtless contributed their effects to complicate the main outline.

With the documents we have at our disposal today (few in number and richer for the west than for other regions), we are in a position to put forward the following conclusions: neither the subsistence crises, although they are clearly discernible and were very severe, nor indeed the effects of the Wars of Religion except in so far as a few towns are concerned, were sufficient to act as a break on the probable population growth of the sixteenth century; this growth varied in extent from one place to another, but appears often to have been considerable and in some places was such that the population nearly doubled. The increase never occurred steadily however; it proceeded in waves, or as a tide interrupted by an abrupt back-flow of the waters. And it would seem, indeed, that this type of progress is to be found also throughout part of the seventeenth century in many areas.

Before turning to the next century, it is important to realize that changes in conditions provided the framework for this probable demographic increase of the sixteenth century. If the numbers of men rose, then the conditions of existence must have changed too. The additional men must have been fed from the produce of new lands—which raises the question of clearing virgin soil—or else they lived on newly introduced crops or by virtue of increased productivity of the soil—which leads us to the question of maize, of buckwheat in Brittany, and of methods of cultivation, of which we are completely ignorant. As for those who did not produce their own food (and we know them to have been very numerous in France, probably the majority of the population) they force us to face questions concerning manufactures, as these alone can have provided them with the means of buying their bread. It is interesting to note that the regions in the west where one observes a great upsurge in the number of births, and indeed of marriages too, are precisely those where the production of hempen and linen cloth was concentrated and organized by the merchants of Vitré, Laval and Nantes, and recent works of research such as those by Lapeyre on the Ruiz,[18] show that there was intense activity in this sphere in the second half of the sixteenth century. The clearing of fresh land, the introduction of a few new plant species, and above all the general prosperity that resulted from the export of canvas mainly to Spain, the mistress of the Indies: these are the factors which laid the basis for the increase of the rural population in the sixteenth century, as revealed to us in the humble parish registers of the west of the kingdom.

The seventeenth century

Throughout this century the sources become progressively more plentiful. Parish registers exist almost everywhere and they supply information fairly regularly on marriages while beginning to supply information on deaths, or at least on deaths of adult persons. Simultaneously documents concerning sickness, epidemics, prices and crises of subsistence increase in number and reliability. The years round about 1670 mark a real turning-point.

Up till 1670 we are still dealing with the 'dark' seventeenth century, which yields too few documents on deaths, in which the plague prowls sporadically and bursts suddenly but briefly into dreadful ferocity; the age of the Thirty Years War with its thieving and pillaging armies, and of large-scale and tragic disasters. An age too where in many places we find indeed a vigorous upsurge of births produced by fertile and undepleted generations. In short, an age which conserves many of the characteristics of the preceding century.

Towards 1670 and sometimes earlier, as I believe I have shown in my work on the Beauvais region, demographic documents suddenly become more abundant and more reliable, and it has been possible for L. Henry to begin to recommend to others, and indeed to carry out himself, family reconstitutions

---

[18] Lapeyre, *Une Famille de marchands, les Ruiz* (École Pratique des Hautes Études, Affaires et Gens d'Affaires, Vol. 8, 1955).

of the type that he has made for Crulai, where 1674 is used as the starting date. Strangely enough, the plague recedes at this time, either spontaneously or because the population managed to hem it around, to hedge it in, to prevent it from spreading. Such limiting action can be clearly observed in 1720 when the plague launched a return offensive on Marseilles. On the other hand, and as if to compensate for the departure of this scourge, one then sees the appearance of demographic crises of subsistence (from 1661 onwards, to be precise) and then at a slightly later date demographic crises provoked by epidemics whose nature is still ill-defined. Finally there clearly begins, in the economic sphere, a phase of difficulty and maladjustment which we call a recession or a period of stagnation, or at the very least a slowing-down in the rate of growth, and concerning which we have to ask ourselves: what is its relationship with demographic phenomena?

One cannot say that two contradictory methods have been used in the study of the demography of seventeenth-century France: rather that there are two tendencies, or two ways of thinking and going to work. The first carries over the method used for the sixteenth century: counts taken from parish registers are translated into graphs in such a way as to reveal demographic development and a demographic situation. For the period prior to 1650-70 no other procedure is possible. The other approach favours systematic research based on the 'reconstitution' of families into the demographic characteristics of the period, on the hypothesis that the period had a real unity and that its characteristics were stable: in the main the method of L. Henry. I may perhaps be allowed to say that I have used a method which is comparable to this though less rigorous in my study of reconstituted families of the large village of Auneuil in the Beauvais region from 1653 onwards, and of a few other villages outside this area. It is not impermissible to think, with Henry, that the results obtained by the second method apply to all 'pre-Malthusian' times, but prudence suggests that we should consider their relevance as confined to the period studied—that is to say, roughly the personal reign of Louis XIV and the first twenty-five years of the reign of Louis XV.

(1) *The demographic characteristics of the period 1660-1704*

The brief summary of conclusions I shall now give is drawn from the work of M. Henry (above all his work on Crulai) and from work of my own (either published in my book on the Beauvais region or to be published shortly), and is based on 'reconstituted families' although some results are also used which can be obtained without complete reconstitution of families, as for example masculinity, illegitimacy, celibacy at age 45 and infantile mortality.

In general, there is at present agreement on the following points:

(*a*) The gross birth rate is nearly 40 per 1,000 in the countryside.

(*b*) The proportion of male births is close to the present day rates provided one looks at large groups (i.e. of at least 1,500), but it undergoes disturbing fluctuations both in space and time (perhaps under the influence of demographic crises?) and no systematic study of this phenomenon has yet been made.

(*c*) The rate for the birth of twins is pretty much the same as in the twentieth century.

(*d*) Illegitimacy is extremely low in the countryside (being often below 1 per cent); is higher in the towns (4 or 5 per cent, except in Paris), but never reaches the high rate for Paris in the eighteenth century. Illegitimate children are often born to servants. (This is shown by recent unpublished findings of work done on Rennes.) The general impression is indisputably one of a certain strictness of morals, particularly in the countryside. Further confirmation of the same point is afforded by the examination of pre-marital conceptions, which M. Henry and myself find, in rural parishes, to show rates which lie between 1 and 4 per cent; these rates too seem much higher in towns, particularly in workers' districts, but the study on which these findings is based is concerned with Normandy in the eighteenth century.

(*e*) Almost a quarter of the children die in the first year of life though great variations exist from place to place; M. Henry has found on the whole rates below 25 per cent, whereas I have found rates somewhat higher (Auneuil in the Beauvais region, 28·8 per cent; Saint-Laurent des Eaux, which is an extreme case of an insalubrious parish in Sologne, 32·6 per cent); infantile mortality in the wretched workers' quarters of Beauvais, or in Mouy, the large borough of weavers, sometimes approaches 40 per cent; many rural parishes however (in Crulai in Normandy or in Picardy or the Beauce) have a rate a little below 25 per cent. Further studies of mortality will almost certainly reveal many factors making for variation.

(*f*) We have less knowledge of mortality for ages 1-20, and scarcely any for adults. It is generally believed that, on an average, 50 per cent of the children failed to reach the age of 20: in other words, that two births were necessary to produce an adult, and the term 'demographic wastage' has been used in this connexion.

(*g*) The marriage rate is not very well known for this period. On at least three occasions it has been possible to calculate it strictly thanks to 'reconstitutions' or to ingenious calculations (Henry), or else by using the rare and valuable censuses by heads (Villers-Saint Barthélemy in the Beauvais region, Montreuil sur Ille in Brittany). The results are in the region of 180 newly-married persons per 10,000 inhabitants. This rate is a very high one—higher than that found in the nineteenth century. A study of female celibacy at age 45 (the accepted age of female sterility) leads to the same conclusions, though these are naturally of a provisional nature: the marriage rate is very high and celibacy very rare except in the towns—indeed rarer than in the nineteenth century.

(*h*) Researches into age at first marriage are making rapid progress. It is relatively late, for girls 24 or 25 years and sometimes more, and for men 27 years at least. On this point it seems however that we soon come up against regional differences. Evidence from Poitou (to be published by me shortly in the study already mentioned) points in the same direction, and to even later marriages. There is one point clearly worthy of note, and that is that the traditional beliefs that marriage took place very early or very late must be discarded. The only clear fact is that women did not begin to bear children until a late age.

(*i*) Having been rigorously studied for the first time by L. Henry, the birth rate is beginning to reveal its secrets. It is found to be about the same figure everywhere, except in certain exceptional classes such as the patriciate of Geneva, and it seems likely that the 'laws' of fertility are far more general and constant than the 'laws' of mortality. Whatever the reasons may be, women find themselves in childbed, on an average, every 25 or 30 months (excepting the first child, which arrives much more quickly). I have found no exceptions to this rule, which destroys the myth of 'a child a year'.

(*j*) From this fact, and also from the fact that many marriages were interrupted before the normal onset of female sterility, it follows that family size is much smaller than had been believed from observation of a few exceptional cases. In Crulai, 7 families out of about 300 had more than 10 children, and one family alone had 14. Even in Canada, a country of high fertility, M. Henripin[19] only found one family where there were 18 births. The average of births per family, according to the findings of both M. Henry and of myself, almost always falls between 4 and 5, and rather nearer 4 than 5 (Crulai 4·06; Caunes between 4·1 and 4·3).

(*k*) One can deduce from these few results which are often however very reliable, that between 1660 and 1740 the rate of replacement of the generations oscillated around unity; that is to say, the population grew very little, or did not grow, or fell slightly, as may be. In Auneuil and all the more so at Crulai growth is indisputable; elsewhere, particularly in Sologne, and perhaps in Upper Brittany, there was probably a decrease. Any consideration of migration is obviously omitted from these calculations.

Two general points emerge from this type of research. In the first place, no profound changes seem to have occurred between 1660 and 1740 or perhaps even 1750. M. Henry and I have both sufficiently emphasized this point in dealing with the villages or regions we have studied. Secondly, as demographic research advances, individual cases and fresh problems are brought to light. Slowly we come to see once again the profound truth of the dictum of Lucien Febvre, '*France, c'est diversité*'. A diversity, it would seem, that is above all manifest in the death rates.

(2) *Research into demographic fluctuations over the seventeenth century as a whole*

Although it is more rapid and of a less rigorously scientific nature, the other type of research can be highly revealing on certain topics and is well worth pursuing. Series of figures are drawn from parish registers, after these have been critically examined. Various graphs are then constructed which permit the study of seasonal movements, and then of movements in the short run and in the long run or trend. Let us glance at the results obtained.

Seasonal movements are the ones most easily identified. The seasonal movement of marriages can be explained by the religious rules barring certain activities in Advent and in Lent, by certain local customs—in the south-west for instance it is believed that the month of May brings ill-luck—and by the heavy work, mainly harvesting work, of the summer. There is nothing here of thrilling interest. The movement scarcely changes between 1600 and 1740, but there are a few regional differences.

The seasonal movement of births almost always confirms the notion of the predominant influence of spring, the classic season of love, which brings natural

---

[19] Henripin, *La population canadienne au début du XVIIIe siècle*, I.N.E.D. Paris 1954.

consequences. It is even possible to amuse oneself by tracing the progress of spring from the south to the north, from Languedoc to the Beauvais region. Likewise a minimum is reached in autumn: conceptions are often at their lowest in September and October, as if the second equinox had to compensate for the excess of the first. Can the explanation lie in the dietary régime? Some historians have maintained that sexual 'abstinence' in Lent was reflected in the seasonal movement of births, but the recorded facts do not always confirm this theory. In any case, it should be realized that the church has not always advised 40 days restraint with equal firmness. Further, the statistical measurement of this influence is very difficult for the dates of Lent change each year and the interval between conception and birth, roughly accepted as 9 months, can easily vary between 8 and 10 months. In view of these difficulties the problem of Lent does not permit of an easy solution.

The seasonal movement of deaths is less well known and more difficult to define. One has first to pick out the years of shortage or of epidemics from the rest. Deaths of infants, adolescents and old persons must be distinguished from one another. And one knows that parish registers of the seventeenth century cannot be relied on to include burials. It is however possible to state that young children died above all in summer and at the beginning of autumn, and old people in the winter, and this enables us to risk a retrospective diagnosis of some credibility: children died from digestive disorders and old men from infections of the chest. Epidemics, even the plague, struck mainly between May and October. One might say that winter put them in cold storage. As for famine, it had no favourite month, and its effects were often confused with those of the epidemics it had caused or favoured.

More attention has been given to short run than to seasonal movements. The demographic crises or crises of mortality which stand out so obviously and tragically, have been the subject of an enormous literature. Their characteristics, causes, dates and consequences of all kinds, immediate or remote, are continually discussed. Jean Meuvret treats this subject in another chapter,[20] and so it is not for me to discuss it here. However I wish to revise somewhat what I have written on these crises in previous articles of mine or in my book on the Beauvais region, and one example will suffice to illustrate this.

A very recent piece of work[21] carried out on the town of Rennes and on five parishes situated to the west (Chantepie, Cesson, Domloup, Noyal sur Vilaine, Saint-Jacques de la Lande) has revealed in this corner of Brittany the existence of a sort of 'maritime constitution', and these findings had been partly fore-shadowed by a study published earlier by M. Reinhard on a group of Norman parishes.[22] On the one hand, the demographic crises connected with bad harvests are relatively mild, even in 1693-4, and sometimes fail to assert themselves. Thus the crisis during the Fronde (1648-53) and that of 1661-3 are observable but not severe, and bear no resemblance to what has been found in other regions.

[20] See p. 507.

[21] *Epidémies et famines dans l'évêché de Rennes au XVIIe siècle*, Diplôme d'Études Supérieures (manuscript), by Mlle J. Galpin, Rennes 1961.

[22] M. Reinhard, 'Les répercussions démographiques des crises de subsistances', in *Actes du 81e Congrès des Sociétés Savantes*, 1956, pp. 67-86. A recent book by P. Gouhier, *Port-en-Bessin 1597-1792 étude d'histoire démographique* (Cahiers des Annales de Normandie, No. 1, 1962) presents very original views on this 'maritime constitution' (demographic crises weak, low rate of infant mortality).

The great peaks in mortality, sometimes of tremendous proportions, are often due to epidemics—to the 'plague' before 1660, to 'dysentery' in 1676, 1701 and 1719 (the two terms '*peste*' and '*dysenteries*' figure in the parish registers). Almost always the peak reached by mortality due to dysentery in 1701 dominates the whole period of a century running from 1630 to 1730. These devastating diseases struck down young people above all, raged mainly at the end of the summer, and had very little effect on conceptions. The general explanation of this 'original constitution' of Upper Brittany involves the climate, the peculiar features of the diet in which 'black wheat' or buckwheat was an important item, and the sanitary conditions which for a very long time were among the worst in France. This example lends support to the view that demographic crises were of a diverse nature. It also lends weight to a theory recently defended by P. de Saint Jacob,[23] viz. that financial exhaustion due to excessive taxation and the shortage of work were in part responsible for certain great crises such as that of 1709-10. Indeed, in Brittany in 1709 the *grand hiver* was not very severe and the harvests often good, in spite of which mortality was serious although it did not reach the level experienced elsewhere.

This diversity in the factors involved does not however alter the general interpretation of demographic crises. In the seventeenth century, especially between 1640 and 1740, they are usually connected with the high price of grain. They periodically interrupted the natural expansion of the population. By killing the youngest and reducing conceptions they created several depleted generations, *classes creuses*, which are apparent for a long time on the age pyramid as notches cut out of its sides. The recovery of the marriage and birth rates which habitually followed the termination of these crises give rise to a new burst of life which produced well-stocked generations, and these in turn carry over and thirty years later, at the fertile age, stand out as a well-manned age-group. Whatever their nature or their cause, demographic crises rarely disappear before 1740; the years 1738-43 were often very bad ones; in some regions crises continue to recur till a very late date. M. Valmary and myself have found them persisting till the end of the eighteenth century in the as yet unpublished study we have made on the Quercy, and M. Cobb has analysed them in Rouen in the year III and the year IV.[24]

The study of long-term movements or trends is very difficult. The defects of the parish registers which we have already mentioned limit their scope, particularly in the seventeenth century. A thorough knowledge of the detailed history of each parish studied is essential for the researcher if he is to avoid committing gross errors of interpretation. An example will illustrate this danger. In all the parishes of Rennes one finds a considerable drop in baptisms, marriages and burials between 1675 and 1690. The explanation for this is not to be sought in the economic situation, but in strictly political events, for in 1675 a district of the town was destroyed, the *Parlement* exiled, and many inhabitants expelled. This history is well-known perhaps, but other incidents which are much less so may catch us unawares, and should lead us to exercise extreme caution. How-

[23] Pierre de Saint Jacob, *Les Paysans de la Bourgogne du Nord au dernier siècle de l'Ancien Régime*, Paris 1960.
[24] Cobb, 'Disette et mortalité, la crise de l'an III et de l'an IV à Rouen', in *Annales de Normandie*, 1956, p. 267.

ever, with all the fervour of our researchers and whatever their ingenuity in interpretation, incomplete series of local results, themselves liable to legitimate criticism, are the best we can ever hope to obtain. It is also probable that we shall find great divergencies not only from one region to another but from one type of locality to another. There will doubtless be found a distinct demographic 'behaviour-pattern' for small isolated villages, for big market towns, for small administrative centres, military and commercial centres, and regional capitals.

Elementary analysis of figures obtained from parish registers in the Beauvais region and a few villages in Anjou allow me to put forward the following as the probable development of seventeenth century population: there was a marked increase in population which lasted from 1600 to 1630 or from 1600 to 1647, and which was suddenly interrupted in some places in 1630 but more usually towards 1650; between 1660 and 1690 the population oscillated to a varying degree, and between 1690 and 1720 or 1730 we encounter a sharp decline. Other research, some published and some awaiting publication, offers solid confirmation of two other points in this outline, that is to say, of the high number of baptisms and marriages in the first third or the first half of the seventeenth century, for their level is often higher than in the eighteenth, and also of the decline in the years between 1690 and 1720. Some exceptions have been found and are easily accounted for. For instance, the outskirts of large towns such as Paris or Rennes were continually growing by immigration, and workers followed to the weaving villages in Picardy after 1700 as a result of a considerable increase in orders from Spain. The villages in the neighbourhood of Rennes in Upper Brittany studied by Mlle Galpin also confirm the general outline that I have put forward for the Beauvais area. All these studies however are so far mere pilot-studies, too few in number and perhaps deficient in their quality too.

In my book on the Beauvais region I also advanced the hypothesis of the 'ebb and flow' of population spreading over thirty-odd years under the influence of the great crises. On the population graphs of baptisms, marriages, and sometimes of deaths, an alternation of full generations and depleted generations produces 'bumps' and 'hollows' which succeed one another every thirty years or thereabouts. But the uneven length and imperfect regularity of the demographic crises forces us to modify considerably this pattern of 'waves', particularly in the middle and at the end of the century. Often the crises of the Fronde (1648-53) were prolonged, and crises came one upon another at the end of the reign of Louis XIV (1692 to 1694; 1698 and 1699; epidemics in 1701; crisis in 1709-10 in some places recurring in 1714). These may well be responsible for the two great downward fluctuations, and the second of these may have had effects carried over well into the eighteenth century, possibly even up till 1750. This would mean that in a more or less constant demographic structure the long run is determined by the short run, and reproduces, after a time lag, both its rhythm and the anomalies of this rhythm. For once in a recent article of his[25] M. Baehrel seems to promise some confirmation of views of my own of tidal waves of population and their thirty-year cycle of consequences.

Whatever these partial results and provisional hypotheses may be worth, it cannot be said that they entail any major modification of the broader general

[25] In *Annales, E.S.C.* 1961, no. 5, p. 922.

picture. Let us look again at this in outline. The population of the French king-dom within its frontiers of 1700, whether we look at it as a whole, or in its age groups, or as one generation succeeding another, oscillates vigorously from minimum to maximum around a sort of equilibrium position representing possibly 19 million Frenchmen. In 1700 it probably stood nearer the minimum than the maximum point. The oscillations depend at one and the same time on all the following factors: the conditions of the food-supply (its quantity, and composition); on economic, monetary and financial conditions which deter-mined the capacity of the immense majority of the populace not producing its own basic nourishment to buy subsistence; on sanitary and physiological con-ditions and on general and local hygiene; on whether the great epidemic diseases and epidemics were active or dormant and whether the battle against infection was effective or not; on sociological factors such as the religious atti-tude which might demand respect for certain commandments of the Lord; on ancient traditional customs concerning marriage, fertility, the upbringing of children and the care of the sick. It was enough for one of these conditions to be substantially altered to produce changes in the general demographic situation.

We are coming more and more to the belief, and on good grounds, that decisive changes did not occur in France before the second half, and maybe not before the end, of the eighteenth century. There was one change however: after 1665 or 1670 the plague receded. It seems however that other epidemics of a less terrifying nature, but which killed as surely, took its place. In any case, the plague attacked Provence again in 1720, and time was needed for men to adjust themselves to the absence of this terror-breeding disease ('Le mal qui répaud la terreur', wrote La Fontaine).

One should not be surprised by the extremely cautious tone of many passages in this chapter. The more one progresses with the investigation of French population problems, the more they appear complex and dissimilar. Each new piece of research, each new article, opens up more questions than it answers. It is true that historians and demographers are gradually becoming aware of how modest their knowledge is and how fragile their hypotheses. This common feeling, painful as it is, was required. But they are also convinced that it will be possible, step by step, to throw some light on the areas of darkness. The task of the historical demographer is considerable. Towards the end of the twentieth century (if there is still such a century) our pupils' pupils will no doubt have some clear ideas (and this is comparatively easy) but also some proven ideas and that will be more difficult.

20

THE GENERAL DEVELOPMENT OF THE POPULATION OF FRANCE SINCE THE EIGHTEENTH CENTURY

J. BOURGEOIS-PICHAT

Editor's Note: This article originally appeared in *Population*, Vol. VI, 1951, pp. 635-62.
The tables in Appendix II were printed in the same journal, Vol. VII, 1952, pp. 319-29.
The author has not revised this article. The reader should compare the material taken from Duvillard with M. Louis Henry's remarks on this writer, above.
Certain tables which appear in both the articles and the appendix have been reprinted only once.

Translated by Peter Jimack

THE demographic evolution of European nations during the last two centuries has followed a classic pattern. Let us recapitulate briefly the successive stages in this evolution. The fundamental characteristics of these populations before the beginning of their 'demographic revolutions' were very high fertility and mortality, which on the average more or less balanced each other.[1] During the first stage, mortality declined without any alteration in fertility. Births constantly outnumbered deaths and the population increased rapidly. Then fertility diminished in its turn, this marking the beginning of the second stage. But this decline was at first without any apparent effect on the number of births, which continued to increase because of the favourable age-structure acquired during the previous stage, and also because mortality continued to decrease.

Finally, as the decline in fertility became more pronounced, the excess of births over deaths grew progressively less, and in some cases there was even an excess of deaths. This is the last stage in the phenomenon. If the trend had continued, there would have been a regular decrease in the population. In fact, no country has yet reached this stage of evolution. The revival in the birth rate in recent years opens up less pessimistic perspectives, suggesting the possibility of a new balance between births and deaths, on a very different basis from the natural balance which existed formerly.

Only the last stage can be studied accurately. It is in fact recent in date, and detailed statistics are available. A considerable amount is, however, known about the second stage, which begins with the decline in fertility. For countries

---

[1] A. Landry has used the phrase 'demographic revolution', indicating as its first stage a reduction in nuptiality. This reduction seems very much less important than various contemporaries and later writers have thought, basing their opinion on fragmentary observations.

other than France, this decline occurs about 1880, a date at which we begin to have satisfactory demographic statistics. For France, however, this second stage cannot be precisely dated. The first French statistics enabling fertility to be measured accurately date from 1891, and estimates have been possible for as far back as 1800. All these data show that fertility in France had begun to decline before the end of the eighteenth century.

As for the first stage, which starts with the fall in mortality, only a few Scandinavian statistics enable us to observe it from its beginning, which for such countries can be fixed at about 1750.

To sum up, if qualitatively the outline just described appropriately represents the demographic history of European populations, it is difficult, at least for the first stage, to pick out the details of their evolution, and quantitatively, to assess the magnitude of the variations in mortality and fertility. The difficulty is particularly great for France, where the 'demographic revolution', considerably earlier than in other countries, began at a period when statistics were few and very incomplete. Nevertheless, in spite of their scarcity, by no means all the data have been utilized.

Let us now make some factual contribution towards answering these problems, making the best use we can of the documents available, however imperfect they may be.

The choice of indices of measurement

To measure mortality, we shall use rates for the following age-groups: under 1 year, 1 to 4, 5 to 14, 15 to 24, and so on in groups of 10 years. To compute these rates, we need to know both the population and the deaths for the different age-groups: all that is then necessary is a simple division. Using these rates, it is very easy to draw up mortality tables giving all the standard parameters: life tables, expectations of life, etc.

For fertility, the ratio of births per year to the number of women aged from 15 to 45 is quite sufficient for the problem we are concerned with: this is the general fertility rate. As we are in fact interested in long-term variations, in other words variations of considerable magnitude, more detailed measurements are not necessary. For this rate, as for the others, we need to know the age-structure of the population. For France, the general fertility rate, when divided by 0·0695, differs very little from the gross reproduction rate.[2] Let us now see how we can calculate these indices of mortality and fertility.

[2] The gross reproduction rate represents the mean number of girls born to women, without taking account of mortality, and exposed to the conditions of fertility which are specified for the given period.

Gross reproduction rate in France

	(a)	(b)		(a)	(b)
1851–5	1·65	1·69	1881–5	1·65	1·62
1856–60	1·68	1·70	1886–90	1·53	1·51
1861–5	1·71	1·71	1891–5	1·45	1·46
1866–70	1·71	1·70	1896–1900	1·41	1·42
1871–5	1·68	1·64	1901–5	1·37	1·36
1876–80	1·69	1·65	1906–10	1·27	1·27

(a) computed by the usual method from age-specific fertility rates (exact calculations after 1891, estimates from 1851 to 1891).

(b) computed by dividing the general fertility rate (average number of births to women aged from 15 to 45) by 0·0695.

As I have already pointed out, from 1851 onwards all the necessary statistics are available. Before this date, two periods should be distinguished:

(1) from 1806 to 1850, a period when demographic statistics are fairly numerous and cover the whole country, although certain data are lacking;

(2) before 1806, when the information available is only fragmentary.

Demographic statistics from 1806 to 1850

From 1801 to 1850, there were seven general censuses of the population,[3] giving the total figures, by sex and marital status. No details on age were recorded before 1851.

In addition, for every year from 1801 onwards, we know the number of births and deaths, classified by sex. From 1806 onwards, we also have the distribution of deaths by sex for the following age-groups: under 1 year, 1 to 4, 5 to 9, 10 to 14, and so on in groups of 5 years. These figures admittedly contain some errors, as the age at death was not always very certain for persons born at a time when registration of births was rather rudimentary. As in all statistics of this kind, the attraction of round numbers introduces distortions. The error must, however, be smaller than in a census, as the death of a person is a more important event than the filling in of a census form. On the assumption that this error is not great, we shall not allow for it. The coherence of the results obtained will enable us to judge the validity of this basic assumption. The only element now lacking for us to compute our indices is thus the age-composition of the population. Let us attempt to reconstruct it.

Reconstruction of the age-composition of the population

The distribution of deaths by age-groups enables us to distribute at least approximately, the deaths each year by cohorts, i.e. according to the year of birth of the deceased. We shall then be able to compute the survivors of each cohort at 1 January every year by subtracting from the initial size of the cohort the total deaths which have occurred in it up to that date. This assumes that the population is a closed one, i.e. that migrations to and from outside are negligible. We shall provisionally take this second assumption as having been more or less correct for France before 1900. If we allow both our assumptions, we can then reconstruct the age-distribution, at 1 January of any given year, of *persons born after 1806*.

For persons born before 1806, we shall use the same method, but the other way round, as it were. Let us take as an example persons born in 1790. We may suppose that by 1890 they were all dead, and by means of the distribution of annual deaths according to year of birth, we can determine the number who died in 1806, 1807, 1808, etc. to 1890. By cumulating the deaths from 1890 backwards, we shall obtain the total number of survivors, at 1 January every year, of the cohort in question.

The above method, used in the two ways described, makes it finally possible to reconstruct the age-distribution of the population at 1 January of each year. Since, however, its full application would take too long, I have modified it to

---

[3] In 1801, 1806, 1821, 1831, 1836, 1841, and 1846.

obtain quicker results, using age-groups of 5 years, and periods of 5 calendar years. This modified method of computation is less precise than the full method, but, considering our initial assumptions, the approximation seems adequate.

As the age-distribution of the population is only lacking before 1851, we could have confined the application of our method to the first half of the nineteenth century; but by applying it to the period 1851-1901, we can test its validity by comparing our computed results with those obtained from the censuses. Graph I illustrates this comparison for the census year 1881. If we leave aside the first two age-groups, and the 20-24 group, our calculations never differ by more than 3 per cent from the census figures,[4] and are often much closer. On the other hand, we get considerably more young children and considerably fewer young adults aged 20 to 24. It is, however, well known that in censuses children are often forgotten, and that the number of people in the 20-24 age-group is always exaggerated, as adolescents tend to exaggerate their ages and adults to understate them. In these age-groups then, our calculations yield better results than the census. The excess of men aged 25 to 64 is probably due to the fact that we have not allowed in our calculations for foreign immigration. In the 20-24 group, the difference between the two sets of figures is greater for women than for men, because of the number of soldiers serving outside France.

GRAPH I

Population of France in 1881

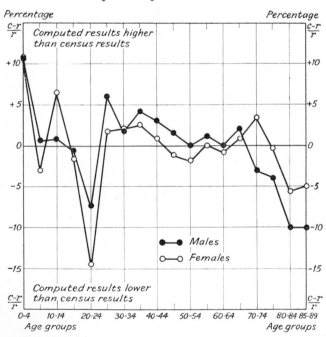

Differences between the computed figures and the 1881 census figures, calculated as percentages of the census figures; with c representing the computed figures and r the census figures, the ordinate for each age-group is $\frac{c-r}{r}$.

[4] Except for very advanced ages. But in this case the calculations are based on very small numbers.

The results of the comparison for 1881 are completely typical. For every census from 1851 to 1901, there are differences of similar magnitude between the computed figures and those obtained from the census, for both males and females. We can thus be sure of knowing the figures for the population of France from 1806 to 1901, in 5-year age-groups, with an error of less than 3 per cent.

Corrections for losses due to war

Every war produces modifications in the sex-ratio of the age-groups. Let us take 1816 as an example: for those who had taken part in the wars of the Revolution and of the Empire, the proportion of males must be abnormally low. Graph 2 shows that this is indeed the case. The shaded area represents the difference between normal and actual sex ratios. By reconstructing this normal sex ratio, we can estimate the losses due to the wars of the Revolution and the Empire. The results of this calculation are given in Table 1.

GRAPH 2

Sex ratio of the population of France by age-groups in 1806 and 1816

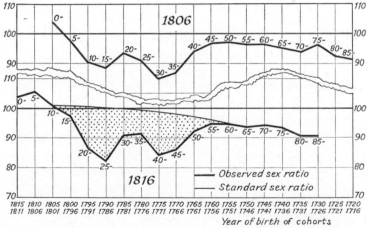

For a given age-group, the sex ratio is defined as the number of men per 100 women. The figures on the curves show the age-groups.

TABLE 1

Losses in France from 1790 to 1815[5]

Male cohorts born	aged 20 in	Losses (in thousands)
1791–5	1811–15	200
1786–90	1806–10	230
1781–5	1801–5	100
1776–80	1796–1800	90
1771–5	1791–5	140
1766–70	1786–90	100
	Total losses:	860

[5] Not necessarily men killed, but including those who, for various reasons, did not return to France.

If war deaths were included in ordinary registration statistics, the sex ratio ought to be abnormally low only in those age-groups affected by the war, i.e. over age 20. Let us take, for example, the group consisting of persons born from 1786 to 1790. Its sex ratio should only be abnormally low when the oldest in the group are beginning to take part in the war, i.e. after 1806. In 1806, the sex ratio of this group should be normal. Graph 2 shows that this is not so. There must therefore be many war deaths or cases of people leaving France not included in the registration statistics. I have corrected these errors of registration by restoring normal sex ratios in the age-groups below 20.

Having reconstructed in 5-year periods the age-composition of the population of France from 1806 onwards, and having the official statistics for the distribution of deaths by age-groups, it is easy to compute mortality rates by age, and gross reproduction rates. These rates are given in the Appendixes. Before commenting on the results obtained, however, we shall study the second period, prior to 1806.

Demographic statistics before 1800

For the period before 1806, we have only incomplete data, varying greatly in value. For the total population, there are only estimates. At the beginning of the eighteenth century, working from the returns of the provincial administrators, Vauban estimated the population of France at slightly over 19 million. On the eve of the Revolution, 80 years later, other estimates gave it as 25 or 26 million, which represents a mean annual rate of increase of 4 per 1000.[6] Partial enumerations enable us to form a fairly good idea of the age-composition around 1775. Table 2 gives the figures arrived at by Paul Vincent, who has examined all the relevant available data.[7]

Let us now consider the analysis of population movements: for the period 1770-84, we know the annual figures for marriages, births and deaths for the whole of France. I agree, however, with writers of the period who considered that these figures were slightly lower than they should have been.

TABLE 2

Age-composition of the population of France around 1775,
based on partial enumerations

Age-groups	Males	Females	Both sexes	
0-9	119	119	238 ⎫	426
10-19	92	96	188 ⎭	
20-29	83	87	170 ⎫	
30-39	68	71	139 ⎪	
40-49	54	57	111 ⎬	503
50-59	40	43	83 ⎭	
60-69	23	26	49 ⎫	
70-79	8	11	19 ⎬	71
80 and over	1	2	3 ⎭	
All ages	488	512	1000	1000

[6] For further details, see E. Levasseur, *La Population française*, Paris, A. Rousseau, 1891.
[7] Paul E. Vincent, 'French demography in the eighteenth century', *Population Studies*, Vol. 1, no. 1, June 1947, p. 44 ff.

In addition, there are a few life tables for the eighteenth century (calculated solely on the basis of death statistics), which assumed the population to be stationary. In a stationary population, the distribution of deaths by age immediately enables us to calculate a life table. If we cumulate the distribution, working from the higher ages backwards, we can calculate the survivors from which we can easily work out mortality rates. In fact, however, the population of France during the eighteenth century was not stationary but increasing, so that the particular method exaggerates the level of mortality.[8] The only table to which this criticism does not seem to apply is Duvillard's, published in 1806, and based on observations relating to 2,290,672 persons and 101,542 deaths registered in France before 1789. Duvillard described his method in a work which was never published, and the manuscript of which has not been found. In his other works, however, he gives indications which enable us to understand the principle of his method.

He relates deaths at a certain age *a* to the number of births *a* years before, and takes the figures thus obtained as giving the curve of mortality for the life table which he is trying to construct. This method is correct for a fairly long period of constant mortality, as was probably the case during the first half of the eighteenth century. The period to which Duvillard's table refers remains to be determined: as we know only that the source data were obtained before 1789, we have taken them as referring to about 1770, a date which has been confirmed by subsequent findings.

The mortality rates by age-groups corresponding to Duvillard's table fit well enough into the pattern of mortality rates during the nineteenth century, giving further confirmation of the validity of the table in question, which is given in Appendix I (see Graphs 3 and 4).

Knowing mortality in 1770 and having already computed mortality in 1806, I have determined mortality for the intervening years by assuming a regular development during this period. There is one exception, for mortality in age-group 1-4; as we shall see in a moment, this mortality is in a considerable measure attributable to smallpox. I have taken the improvement in this respect as occurring especially after 1770. Now, starting from the population in 1806 distributed by age, we can work backwards by means of the mortality rates computed as described, so as to reconstruct the age-distribution of the population from 1770 to 1806. We can only obtain results in this way for those age-groups which still have survivors in 1806, and these groups become fewer and

[8] We have the following three life tables for France: Dupré de Saint-Maur's table, published in Buffon's *Histoire naturelle*, and partially reproduced by Moheau. This table was computed by the deaths method, using registers of deaths before 1749 for 3 parishes in Paris and 12 from the surrounding area. Moheau computed similar tables for some other French parishes.

The Abbé Expilly's table. Expilly had observed that the populations of France and Sweden must have a very similar age-composition. Assuming that the age-composition is exactly the same as the survivorship table, which implies the assumption that the population is stationary, Expilly takes as the life tables for France the age-composition given by Swedish census returns, having slightly modified this age-composition to allow for errors in the enumeration of young children. This method is based on the same hypotheses as the deaths method, and it exaggerates mortality in just the same way when the population is increasing.

Duvillard's table, which seems to have been computed correctly.

Finally, there are various other tables based on particular population groups and which cannot therefore be treated as characteristic of the mortality of the whole country. This is the case with Deparcieux's table (1746).

fewer the farther back we go. Let us consider as an example the year 1775, for which we have a direct estimate of this age-distribution: Table 3 compares this estimate with the results obtained in the above manner.

GRAPH 3

Mortality rate per 10,000 persons,
for age-groups from 11-24

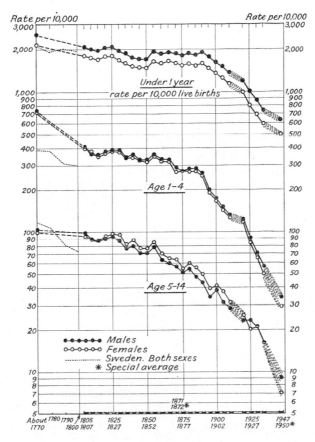

TABLE 3

Age-distribution of the population of France in 1775

Age-groups (a)	Direct estimate	Computed estimate
0–9	281	278
10–19	222	229
20–29	201	199
30–39	164	159
40–49	132	135
0–49	1000	1000

(a) Persons aged over 49 had only very few survivors in 1806: their number cannot therefore be assessed by working back from the population in 1806.

The agreement is very close. Next, I have used the distribution given by the direct estimate (Table 2) to complete the 1775 figures for ages over 49, and, by means of this complementary fraction for 1775 taken in conjunction with mortality rates, I have computed figures for the age-groups missing from our estimates (i.e. age-groups having no survivors in 1806).

To sum up, the adoption of Duvillard's table as indicative of mortality in around 1770 enables us to work out from the population of 1806 the age-composition in 1775, which we also know from direct observations. The agreement of the two results, obtained independently of each other, confirms the value both of Duvillard's table and of the age-composition given for 1775.

The method used also gives us an estimate of births from 1771 to 1806, which it is interesting to compare with the registration figures (Table 4). As might be expected, the estimates are slightly higher than the registration figures. The gross reproduction rates corresponding to these estimated births are given in the last line of the table.

TABLE 4

Mean annual births from 1771 to 1806
(in thousands)

Period	1771–5	1776–80	1781–5	1786–90	1791–5	1796–1800	1801–5
Births registered	919	963	964 (a)				912
Estimated	984	980	988	975	980	973	916
Women aged 15 to 45 in the middle of the period	5921	6012	6121	6251	6373	6464	6564
Estimated gross reproduction rate (b)	2·39	2·30	2·32	2·24	2·21	2·16	2·01

(a) The figure for 1785 is not known, so the average is over 4 years only.

(b) Estimate obtained by dividing by 0·0695 the average number of births per woman aged 15 to 45.

Fertility and mortality before 1771

Knowing the age-composition of the population in 1775, we are now in a position to determine the levels of fertility and mortality before that date. As I have already pointed out, Duvillard's method assumes a rather long period of stable mortality. If fertility also varies little during the same period, we know that the population at the end of the period will have the age-composition of a stable population, i.e. with the numbers in each age-group varying in geometric progression. We can see from Table 5 that this is in fact the case. The age-composition of a stable population computed from Duvillard's table and an annual rate of increase of 4 per 1000 is almost exactly identical with the age-composition of the actual population. This figure of 4 per 1000 is precisely the rate we have accepted for the growth of the population during the first half of the eighteenth century. The corresponding gross reproduction rate is 2·50, 6·4 per cent higher than the rate for the period 1771-5.

Let us now sum up. We start from the following hypotheses:

(a) Mortality remained unchanged from 1700 to 1770 at the level of Duvillard's table.

TABLE 5

Age-distribution of the population of France in 1775, compared with the age-distribution of a 'stable' population corresponding to Duvillard's mortality table and an annual rate of increase of 4 per 1000

Age-groups	Actual population		'Stable' population	
0	130		132	
5	106		107	
10	98		100	
15	95		94	
20	89	518	87	520
25	78		79	
30	69		72	
35	64		65	
40	60		58	
45	54		51	
50	46		44	
55	38		36	
60	28		29	
65	21	458	21	455
70	13		14	
75	7		7	
80	3		3	
85	1		1	
90	0	24	0	25
	1000	1000	1000	1000

(*b*) The mean rate of annual increase remained at about 4 per 1000 during the same period. This would mean that fertility also remained constant at a level corresponding to a gross reproduction rate of 2·50.

The age-distribution of the population about 1775 can then be computed mathematically. The results of this computation coincide with the age-distribution as determined by direct observation from partial enumerations, and this agreement retrospectively justifies our hypotheses. It was therefore about 1770 that fertility and mortality in France began to decline. This is of course merely an approximate date, which could only be established more accurately by research into actual records of vital statistics. Our computations do, however, indicate that we should concentrate on 1770 as the period in respect of which research of this kind should be undertaken.

Nuptiality around 1770

Let us take 100 women, assuming them not to be subject to mortality, but exposed to the risk of dissolution of their marriages by divorce or by the death of their husbands. M_0, the average number of marriages (or remarriages) per woman is a useful index of nuptiality. In addition, the mean age at marriage, *m*, tells us how these M_0 marriages occur.

At the present moment in France, $M_0 = 1$ and $m = 25$. In other words, if women were not exposed to mortality, there would be on the average one marriage (or remarriage) per woman, and these marriages (or remarriages) would occur at the average age of 25.

Now, in a stable population, there is a very simple relationship between the gross reproduction rate R_0, the proportion M_0,[9] and the ratio f of marriages to births of the same period; this can be shown as:

$$\frac{k \times 2 \cdot 04 \, R_0}{M_0} = f$$

k is a coefficient which depends on the mean age at marriage, the mean age of mothers at the birth of their children, and the life table. For a given life table, it is affected only slightly by these two mean ages, and with Duvillard's table, we can take k as 0·94. As for f, we can obtain this from official registration statistics: around 1770 there were 4780 births for every 1000 marriages. Given these values, we find $M_0 = 1 \cdot 004$, which is much the same as its present-day value. This mean number of marriages includes remarriages, which today amount to about 10 per cent. In the eighteenth century, mortality was higher than today, and remarriages of widows must have been more frequent; but there were no remarriages of divorcees, so that the two cancel each other out. If then we keep this proportion of 10 per cent, the mean number of first marriages per woman must have been 0·9 in the eighteenth century, almost exactly the same as it is today.

What was the mean age of these marriages? In a stable population, if $C(m)$ represents the number of people in the middle of a given year aged between m and $m + 1$ years, and if M represents the number of marriages registered during the year in question, we may say that

$$M_0 \, C(m) = M.$$

The application of this equation to the years around 1770 gives $m = 27$ years. This mean age is higher than today; but it includes remarriages, the mean age of which was higher then, as the only women remarrying were widows, whereas today they include young divorcees. The mean ages at first marriage around 1770 and today would thus be closer.[10] To conclude, marriage two centuries ago was slightly later than today, but just as frequent. The picture presented by some writers, of a population vowed to celibacy to avoid having too many children, is not therefore a realistic one.[11]

Mortality since 1771

As we now know mortality rates by age-groups from 1771 to the present day, we can see how they evolved during this period. A brief look at Graphs 3

[9] Theoretically, the hypothesis of a stable population does not necessarily mean that nuptiality is also unchanging. But if it were to change, every fall in nuptiality, for example, would have to be accompanied by a corresponding increase in the fertility of couples. There is no chance of concomitant variations of this kind occurring in an actual stable population, and M_0 can be taken as constant, as also can the average age m.

[10] It is relevant to point out that direct research into registration records in Paris has yielded a figure of 24 years 9 months as the mean age of women at first marriage during the eighteenth century. Cf. *Recherches statistiques sur la ville de Paris et le département de la Seine*. Paris, Imprimerie royale, 1829.

[11] Notice similarly that the number of people taking religious vows has been greatly exaggerated; the figures given by Moheau and confirmed by the vital statistics for 1770 to 1784 indicate that out of 100 persons at age 20, only one took vows.

and 4 will show that we must distinguish between mortality before and after age 24, the point at which the mortality of men begins to develop differently from that of women. Most of all, however, one must emphasize the marked decline in mortality throughout the later part of the eighteenth century. This decline is confirmed by the rates for Sweden, which can be computed with precision, and which I have included up to 1800 on the graphs.

A. *Mortality before age 24*

We shall use 4 age-groups under 24: under 1 year, 1-4 years, 5-14, and 15-24. Let us take first the last 3 groups, which are those principally affected by deaths from epidemic diseases. In the first year of its life, the child in fact benefits from the mother's immunity, and over 24 he has himself become immunized by previous attacks of illness.

GRAPH 3a

*Mortality rate per 10,000 persons,
for age-groups from 15-24*

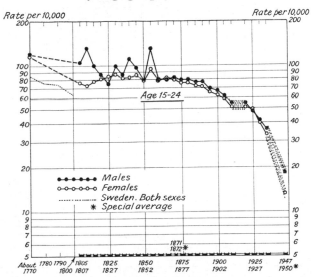

Since the beginning of the nineteenth century, the mortality rates for each of the 3 age-groups 1-4, 5-14 and 15-24, have followed a very similar pattern: a slow decline until 1890, after which it became more rapid as the discoveries of Pasteur began to have their effect. Table 6 shows, for the age-group 1-4, how the decline was distributed among the various epidemic diseases.

The reader will note the progressive disappearance of diphtheria, as a result of the perfecting of anti-diphtheria serum in 1895.

While mortality for age-groups 5-14 and 15-24 remained almost unchanged before 1800, for age 1-4 it declined considerably, as a result of the almost complete disappearance of smallpox. Before 1789, this disease was responsible for nearly 30 per cent of all deaths at this age (Table 7). But it had been noticed that it was serious only in people with weak constitutions, so that the inoculation of people who were suitably prepared amounted to employing vaccination.

GRAPH 4

*Mortality rates per 10,000 persons,
for age-groups over 24*

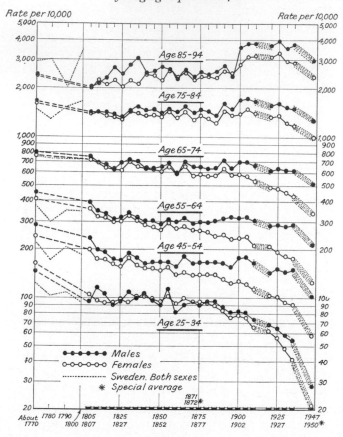

GRAPH 4a

*Mortality rates per 10,000 persons,
for age-groups 35-44*

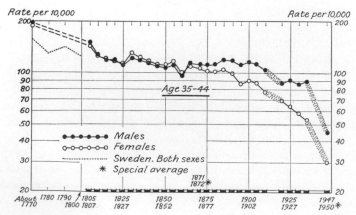

TABLE 6

Rates of mortality due to various causes for age-group 1-4 in Paris
(per 10,000 persons)

	1886-90	1891-5	1896-1900	1901-5
Diphtheria	109	65	17	22
Measles	76	48	43	27
Scarlet fever	10	6	5	3
Whooping cough	20	17	13	15
Meningitis (non-tubercular)	74	54	37	26
Respiratory diseases	120	108	88	71
Diarrhoea	38	36	28	18
Tuberculosis	56	67	61	52
Other causes	23	25	28	23
All causes	526	426	320	257

The method was applied as early as 1750, and then generalized after 1795, when Jenner had discovered that the inoculation of a related but far less virulent disease, namely cowpox, produced the same effects. There was violent opposition to this revolutionary method. Table 7 shows the improvement brought about in some 30 years.

TABLE 7

The number of smallpox deaths per 100 deaths in each age-group

Age-groups	Before 1789 in Geneva	From 1817 to 1821 in Paris
1 year	5	1
1-4	26	7
5-14	15	11
15-24	2	2

Infant mortality, however, developed differently. As I have already pointed out, the baby benefited from its mother's immunity with respect to epidemic diseases, so that infant mortality was little affected by the discovery of sera and vaccines. Apart from a brief improvement from 1831 to 1836, the incidence of sickness and mortality in infancy varied little before the end of the nineteenth century. On the other hand, after 1900, the spread of hygiene produced a swift and steady improvement.

B. *Mortality after age 24*

We distinguish here the following age-groups: 25-34, 35-44, 45-54, and so on in groups of 10 years up to age 85-94. Mortality rates for these various age-groups have evolved similarly. Up to about 1860, there is a gradual decrease in both female and male rates, with the latter slightly higher. From 1860 onwards, female mortality drops more sharply, while male mortality remains unchanged. This situation continues until 1945, so that the difference between male and female mortality grows larger and larger (Graph 5). This emergence of excess male mortality over age 24 is to be found in all countries having a European type of civilization, and so seems to be a consequence of this civilization.

GRAPH 5

Excess male mortality in France from age 35 to 54

(Female mortality rate taken as 100)

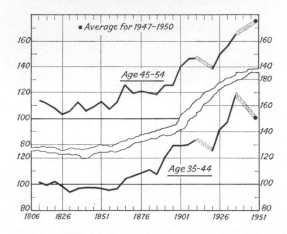

Tuberculosis and respiratory diseases account for the major part of this excess male mortality. Genetically, man is more frail than woman, but this does not seem a sufficient explanation for the difference in mortality between adult males and females, and it would in any case be as valid before 1860 as after. The effect of differences in male and female ways of life seems a more likely cause. In France, the high consumption of alcohol among men further increases this phenomenon.

This stability of the mortality of men over 35 throughout the nineteenth century and the beginning of the twentieth is one of the most curious facts of demography. The expectation of life for men beyond this age has altered little for two centuries. What is more, since 1900 there has actually been an increase in mortality rates over age 75. For the period 1947-50, in spite of all the advances in medicine, mortality for the age-group 85-94 was higher than when Duvillard computed his table, and for the age-group 75-84 it was only very slightly lower.

Since 1945, a new factor has intervened, the use of anti-biotics. In two years, from 1945 to 1946, the rates underwent a sudden marked change, which is very apparent on a graph. The improvement applied particularly to men, and abruptly ended the stability in male mortality rates which we have been discussing. Excess male mortality has not, however, disappeared.

To sum up, mortality in France has fallen continuously since 1770. Up to 1890, the improvement was slow, except for mortality for the age-group 1-4, which declined sharply at the end of the eighteenth century, once protection from smallpox had been discovered. After 1890, the improvement became quicker at every age for women, and up to age 24 for men. Above this age, mortality for men remained stable until 1945, producing an increasing excess of male mortality. From 1945 onwards, there is a very sudden drop in mortality rates, produced by the appearance of anti-biotics.

Fertility since 1770

Graph 6 shows the evolution of the gross reproduction rate since 1770. It scarcely ceased to decline until 1935. This decline was particularly rapid in the last 10 years of the eighteenth century, but it had already begun 20 years earlier, around 1770. From 1851 to 1871, during the Second Empire, the decline became slower, as was pointed out earlier by M. Depoid in his study of reproduction in Europe.[12] The method of computation used by M. Depoid, however, exaggerated this deceleration. Our figures show that it was in fact very slight, and it is only apparent on the graph because of the abnormally low fertility of the period 1851-5, itself no doubt related to a fall in nuptiality.

Persons newly married per 1000 population

1841-5	16·3
1846-50	15·6
1851-5	15·6
1856-60	16·2

From 1881 onwards, the decline in the gross reproduction rate becomes faster. As I have already pointed out, fertility in other countries of Western Europe begins to fall at this date. The same happens in France, although its birth-rate had begun to decrease more than a hundred years earlier.

GRAPH 6

The gross reproduction rate since 1770
(Quinquennial averages)

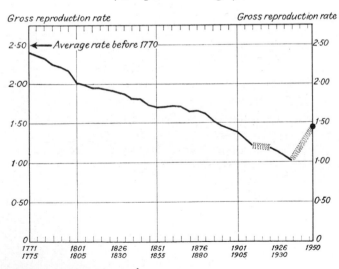

[12] Statistique générale de la France. Études démographiques no. 1. *Reproduction nette en Europe depuis l'origine des statistiques de l'état civil*, Paris, Imprimerie nationale, 1941.
M. Depoid estimated the gross reproduction rates before 1851 by multiplying the crude birth rates by a constant coefficient. But we have seen that in 1815, after the wars of the Revolution and the Empire, there were some 860,000 men missing in France. As a result of the progressive disappearance of the generations affected by these wars, this gap also disappeared gradually, so that the male population increased more rapidly from 1801 to 1861 than the female population. The birth rate therefore exaggerates variations in fertility.

I have interrupted the graph from 1938 to 1950, as during this period the war was too great a disturbing influence. In 1950, when these disturbances had practically disappeared, the existence of a gross reproduction rate much higher than before the war indicates a considerable rise in fertility in some 15 years. The known figures for 1951 confirm that this high level will not be maintained; but a return to something approaching the low levels reached about 1935 is very unlikely, at least as legislation now stands.

Some general points

The facts established in the preceding pages will enable us to determine rather more precisely what exactly is implied by the phrase used at the beginning, 'demographic revolution'. It will be remembered that the example of other countries had led us to consider this revolution in terms of three stages. The first began with the decline of mortality, the second with the decline of fertility, and the third with the decline, or at least the stabilization, of the population. In France, however, mortality and fertility fell at the same time. The drop in fertility was even at first more pronounced than the drop in mortality, and perhaps preceded it. Hence the first stage in the demographic revolution did not occur in France, which moved straight into the second stage, only begun by other countries a hundred years later. Now it is the first stage which was marked by a considerable increase in population, which is why, during the nineteenth century, the French population increased far less than the populations of surrounding countries: if France had maintained up to 1880 the fertility shown during the eighteenth century, it would have had by 1880 a population of 88 million, whereas it was in reality only 38 million.

Declines in mortality and fertility produce considerable modifications in the age-structure of populations. The consequences of a fall in fertility are simple: a diminution in the proportion of younger age-groups, and an increase in the proportion of older age-groups.[13] The effects of a fall in mortality are more complex. At the lower ages, it decreases the proportion of the younger age-groups without affecting the proportion of upper age-groups. At the higher ages, it increases the proportion of older age-groups without affecting that of the lower. Finally, a fall in the mortality of adults *increases* the proportion of the upper age-groups and *diminishes* that of the lower age-groups. But in addition to these direct effects, there are indirect results which are quite as important. A fall in mortality before age 45 increases the number of women of child-bearing age, thereby producing an increase in fertility, which tends to *increase* the proportion of lower age-groups and *diminish* that of upper age-groups. Thus the direct and indirect effects partly cancel each other out. For upper age-groups, computations indicate that this cancelling out was almost complete. For the lower age-groups, however, it was only partial, and the decline in mortality ultimately increased their proportion.

Graph 7 illustrates these points. The lower age-groups are taken as below age 10, and the upper age-groups as 65 and over. It will be seen that in 1776,

---

[13] Here, and in all that follows, it is the mean ratio of 'lower' and 'upper' age-groups to 'adults' that is referred to. We shall not for the moment specify the age limits of these three groups.

GRAPH 7

Distribution in broad age-groups of the population of France, assuming actual and hypothetical fertility

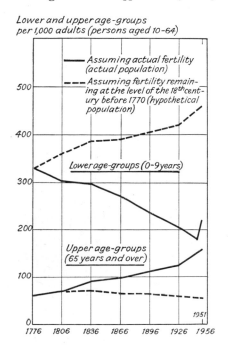

GRAPH 8

Variations in the proportion of dependent upper age-groups under the hypothesis of a constant proportion of young dependants

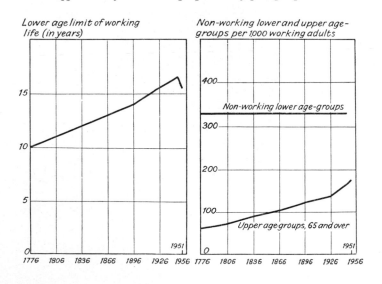

for 1000 adults, there were 330 members of the lower age-groups and 60 of the upper. If fertility had remained unchanged since then, with mortality evolving as it actually has done, for 1000 adults in 1951 we should have 460 in the lower age-groups, and 55 in the upper. In reality, fertility has fallen greatly, and we have instead 221 in the lower and 158 in the upper groups. The increase in the proportion of the upper age-groups is therefore due solely to variations in fertility. But it is quite certain that a decline in mortality inevitably produces an eventual drop in fertility. Fertility in France could have remained unchanged up to 1880, as it did in other nearby countries; but if this level of fertility had continued until the present day, the population of France in 1951 would have been 437 million. However optimistic a view we take of it, technical progress could not possibly have coped with such a rate of growth. The ageing of populations is thus inevitable, being finally brought about by the decline in fertility. This decline itself may in fact be sparked off by people taking precautions against old age, having fewer children so as to build themselves up an income for their later years. We are faced then with this paradox: it is the fear of growing old that increases the age of the population.

The age limits we have chosen for the lower and upper age-groups on Graph 7 correspond roughly to the beginning and end of the working life round about 1776. Thus the proportions quoted, 330 in the lower age-groups and 60 in the upper per 1000 adults, indicates the burden on the working population (the adults), constituted, two hundred years ago, by the non-working (children and old people).[14] If we now try to see how the lower age limit of the working life would have had to vary for the proportion of young dependants to have remained constant since 1770, we obtain Graph 8, which also shows how the proportion of the upper age-groups would have varied under this hypothesis. It will be seen that from 10 in 1776 the lower age limit would have risen steadily to $15\frac{1}{2}$ in 1946. In fact, this is just what has happened. As we have seen, the drop in fertility diminished the proportion of the lower and increased that of the upper age-groups. One might have thought that the decrease of the one would have offset the increase of the other, so that the total proportion of non-working dependants would have remained the same. But nothing of the kind occurred. All that has happened points to the proportion of dependent lower age-groups having remained constant, for the commencing age of working life has risen steadily. Everything in fact combined to produce this effect. Technical advances have made a longer period of training necessary for the worker. Furthermore, children have stayed within the family, whereas old people have for a long time been outside the family circle. It is only to be expected that the adult should have his children benefit from the lessening of his responsibilities brought about by having fewer children. This of course speeded up the ageing of the population.

We see then the extreme complexity of the problems raised by the ageing of populations. First of all, one is tempted to blame it on the decline of mortality. It then becomes apparent that if fertility remained unchanged, the ageing

---

[14] It is assumed here that the needs of the lower age-groups are the same as those of the upper age-groups. The adoption of different coefficients to correct this would not significantly alter our conclusions.

would not occur, even though mortality fell. The drop in fertility would thus seem to be the sole cause. But this drop in fertility is itself brought about in part by the drop in mortality, which thereby again becomes a significant factor. If we take the analysis a stage further, we see that every variation in the proportion of dependent old people is accompanied by an opposite variation in that of dependent children, and that the two variations almost exactly cancel each other out; thus changes in fertility and mortality would cease to appear relevant and the problem would seem to have vanished. But we immediately observe that this cancelling out, although possible in theory, did not in reality occur: technical advances, making necessary a longer period of training, as well as the social changes which drove the old out of the family circle, together delayed the age at which the working life began; so that the number of dependants in the family remained more or less the same, although there were fewer actual children. It can be seen that all these factors are very closely interlinked.

The ageing of the population is thus one of the consequences of our civilization, and there does not seem any possibility of the process which has led to it being reversed.

APPENDIX I

TABLE I

Duvillard's mortality table showing mortality for males and females combined in the eighteenth century (1700–1770)

Age n	Survivors at age n	Expectation of life at age n in years	Age n	Survivors at age n	Expectation of life at age n in years	Age n	Survivors at age n	Expectation of life at age n in years
0	1000	28·8	30	438	28·5	60	214	11·9
1	767	36·3	31	431		61	204	
2	672	40·4	32	425		62	195	
3	625	42·4	33	418		63	186	
4	599	43·2	34	411		64	176	
5	583	43·4	35	404	25·7	65	166	9·7
6	573	43·1	36	397		66	157	
7	566	42·7	37	390		67	147	
8	560	42·1	38	383		68	137	
9	555	41·5	39	376		69	127	
10	551	40·8	40	369	22·9	70	118	7·6
11	547		41	362		71	108	
12	543		42	355		72	99	
13	538		43	348		73	89	
14	534		44	341		74	84	
15	529	37·3	45	334	20·1	75	72	5·8
16	524		46	327		76	63	
17	519		47	319		77	55	
18	513		48	312		78	48	
19	508		49	305		79	41	
20	502	34·3	50	297	17·9	80	35	4·5
21	496		51	289		81	29	
22	490		52	281		82	24	
23	484		53	274		83	19	
24	478		54	265		84	15	
25	471	31·4	55	257	14·5	85	12	4·0
26	465		56	249		86	9	
27	458		57	240		87	7	
28	452		58	231		88	6	
29	445		59	223		89	5	
						90	4	3·2
						91	3	
						92	2	
						93	2	
						94	2	
						95 and over	2	

Mortality rates per 10,000 persons in successive age groups (males)

	Under 1 year (b)	1–4	5–14	15–24	25–34	35–44	45–54	55–64	65–74	75–84	85–94
About 1770 (a)	2500	724	103	118	145	194	282	447	794	1636	2394
1805–7	2070	401	97	103	94	148	233	388	745	1410	2020
1810–12	1990	260	88	130	115	125	197	345	688	1426	2120
1815–17	1960	356	85	98	105	118	190	332	664	1415	2300
1820–2	2000	374	89	85	90	118	172	307	620	1375	2660
1825–7	2030	384	92	74	94	111	170	315	690	1320	2430
1830–2	1940	385	86	98	108	122	187	334	716	1450	2780
1835–7	1850	341	76	85	99	118	177	315	698	1515	3060
1840–2	1720	353	79	109	105	115	162	299	636	1450	2450
1845–7	1680	326	70	95	96	109	165	300	631	1470	2520
1850–2	1670	323	78	78	90	107	166	286	648	1380	2690
1855–7	1900	358	78	130	112	111	166	307	680	1475	2610
1860–2	1820	326	62	80	80	96	156	296	587	1410	2280
1865–7	1870	324	59	80	90	113	181	314	695	1525	2580
1871–2	1830	283	56	82	94	112	163	287	645	1396	2330
1875–7	1780	268	51	78	90	111	166	295	644	1465	2520
1880–2	1840	279	54	79	94	112	166	292	631	1435	2410
1885–7	1780	281	48	76	94	119	165	300	636	1350	2510
1890–2	1870	261	43	76	87	118	163	312	710	1600	2730
1895–7	1740	198	34	69	81	111	154	318	636	1470	2360
1900–2	1590	171	38	66	82	116	176	316	698	1680	3570
1905–6	1480	149	31	61	80	113	178	318	692	1710	3750
1910–12	1340	129	28	54	73	103	165	301	662	1650	3780
1920–2	1180	122	23	54	68	87	143	281	615	1560	3660
1925–7	990	89	23	48	54	91	151	286	635	1610	3900
1930–2	860	70	21	41	58	86	145	278	618	1520	3520
1935–7	730	56	16	36	54	89	149	286	615	1496	3700
1947–50	620	34	9	18	28	45	102	215	511	1265	2957

(a) Rates for about 1770 have been computed by assuming that Duvillard's table gives mortality for both sexes combined and that the ratio of male to female mortality was the same as in 1806.

(b) Per 10,000 live births.

TABLE 3

Mortality rates per 10,000 persons in successive age groups (females)

	Under 1 year (b)	1–4	5–14	15–24	25–34	35–44	45–54	55–64	65–74	75–84	85–94
About 1770 (a)	2140	710	98	114	161	186	239	407	759	1597	2370
1805–7	1760	393	92	75	104	142	198	354	712	1376	2000
1810–12	1710	375	88	72	95	124	173	318	685	1415	2220
1815–17	1670	347	86	77	92	119	171	314	639	1350	2080
1820–2	1760	365	92	80	93	116	160	297	619	1325	2220
1825–7	1770	378	96	83	98	113	165	298	615	1290	2015
1830–2	1650	372	94	86	93	130	177	324	695	1435	2210
1835–7	1580	336	81	81	101	122	158	302	646	1390	2100
1840–2	1500	339	87	82	102	118	153	283	624	1340	2405
1845–7	1470	323	76	85	98	112	152	236	620	1350	2390
1850–2	1450	315	76	78	94	111	147	263	607	1330	2210
1855–7	1620	345	84	94	103	116	155	291	645	1438	2590
1860–2	1560	318	69	79	92	99	139	268	592	1305	2310
1865–7	1620	317	64	82	99	109	144	277	650	1420	2500
1871–2	1570	266	63	80	94	106	137	263	568	1267	2236
1875–7	1500	270	54	75	94	102	138	262	580	1350	2340
1880–2	1550	272	59	75	93	101	139	255	566	1290	2340
1885–7	1500	269	55	72	89	104	139	242	570	1210	2300
1890–2	1560	249	49	71	83	98	130	246	632	1440	2540
1895–7	1440	187	39	65	75	86	123	232	578	1350	2460
1900–2	1320	168	41	62	78	90	127	235	580	1385	2770
1905–6	1230	141	37	58	75	87	122	241	565	1485	3110
1910–12	1120	126	31	51	65	77	113	212	527	1395	3160
1920–2	970	116	25	51	62	69	103	208	482	1325	3100
1925–7	790	83	20	49	56	64	101	193	476	1350	3300
1930–2	680	64	21	40	48	58	93	182	451	1215	2940
1935–7	580	49	16	33	41	53	91	176	427	1174	2878
1947–50	490	29	7	13	21	30	58	125	333	955	2361

(a) Rates for about 1770 have been computed by assuming that Duvillard's table gives mortality for both sexes combined and that the ratio of male to female mortality was the same as in 1806.

496

Mortality rates (death per 10,000 population) by age groups (both sexes)

	Less than one year (a)	1-4	5-14	15-24	25-34	35-44	45-54	55-64	65-74	75-84	85-94
About 1770 (b)	2330	715	100	116	152	190	270	420	776	1620	2380
1805-7	1920	398	94	89	105	144	215	370	728	1390	2039
1810-12	1860	366	89	100	105	125	185	331	687	1420	2155
1815-17	1820	351	86	87	98	119	180	337	656	1380	2180
1820-2	1890	269	91	82	92	126	167	302	621	1325	2405
1825-7	1910	381	94	78	96	115	167	321	653	1295	2190
1830-2	1800	377	90	92	107	126	181	327	698	1450	2455
1835-7	1710	301	78	84	99	121	167	307	678	1445	2470
1840-2	1610	346	83	97	104	116	157	291	629	1395	2430
1845-7	1590	323	73	90	97	111	158	285	622	1405	2440
1850-2	1570	319	72	78	93	109	156	277	626	1350	2400
1855-7	1760	352	81	112	108	114	161	298	655	1445	2590
1860-2	1690	319	66	79	86	98	148	281	588	1355	2290
1865-7	1750	318	62	81	94	111	163	295	672	1480	2540
1871-2	1770	274	60	81	94	109	150	276	605	1324	2273
1875-7	1670	269	52	82	92	107	152	278	609	1405	2615
1880-2	1720	277	57	77	93	107	153	273	596	1354	2370
1885-7	1680	292	52	74	92	112	152	278	598	1270	2425
1890-2	1740	256	46	73	85	108	147	290	671	1505	2620
1895-7	1610	193	37	67	78	98	142	254	608	1395	2415
1900-2	1570	171	40	63	80	103	150	262	618	1440	2665
1905-6	1410	145	34	60	78	100	149	278	623	1580	3350 (c)
1910-12	1250	128	30	52	69	91	138	255	586	1505	3460
1920-2	1010	120	17	52	65	78	122	237	541	1420	3290
1925-7	890	86	22	49	60	77	125	236	535	1450	3520
1930-2	740	67	21	41	53	71	117	228	524	1388	3140
1935-7	670	53	16	35	48	70	117	227	510	1292	3175
1947-50	550	31	8	16	24	38	78	162	403	1069	2494

(a) Per 10,000 live births.
(b) Rates according to Duvillard's table.
(c) From 1806, the population figures which form the basis of the rates are taken from the census. Before 1906, reconstructed figures, as explained in the article, have been used. In the highest age groups, we are dealing with very small numbers and the transition from one method to another involves some discontinuity which is, however, insignificant.

APPENDIX II

TABLE I

The population of France by age-groups (in 1000's)

Age-groups	Present-day territory less Nice and Savoy																
	1776	1781	1786	1791	1796	1801	1806	1811	1816	1821	1826	1831	1836	1841	1846	1851	1856
0–4	3307	3304	3317	3406	3547	3619	3549	3603	3653	3771	3847	3864	3858	3910	4001	3876	3767
5–9	2716	2711	2716	2751	2848	2991	3095	3010	3085	3205	3331	3306	3326	3374	3438	3500	3397
10–14	2499	2584	2582	2587	2622	2713	2854	2947	2872	2952	3020	3116	3130	3192	3260	3303	3369
15–19	2436	2398	2485	2487	2495	2541	2634	2761	2785	2785	2860	2928	3011	3064	3097	3148	3205
20–24	2287	2308	2280	2296	2185	2267	2351	2355	2467	2675	2689	2744	2809	2892	2932	2957	3005
25–29	2002	2147	2175	2157	2085	2078	2165	2233	2200	2354	2572	2564	2593	2663	2746	2772	2791
30–34	1772	1866	2008	2043	2031	1971	1970	2062	2109	2098	2264	2457	2455	2454	2529	2597	2626
35–39	1649	1636	1729	1866	1903	1808	1850	1850	1950	2000	2003	2154	2322	2307	2347	2400	2468
40–44	1550	1510	1503	1594	1724	1765	1765	1727	1734	1832	1892	1887	2025	2192	2182	2211	2270
45–49	1395	1403	1372	1370	1459	1584	1627	1625	1598	1610	1720	1764	1782	1892	2054	2032	2029
50–54	1168	1235	1247	1225	1229	1314	1430	1472	1478	1457	1487	1580	1612	1619	1752	1890	1864
55–59	973	1004	1067	1083	1071	1080	1162	1263	1303	1317	1314	1335	1405	1445	1468	1575	1692
60–64	729	794	824	880	899	894	907	975	1064	1109	1139	1124	1134	1205	1257	1260	1352
65–69	541	550	603	630	677	700	697	707	769	849	902	907	889	912	982	1003	1002
70–74	321	358	365	404	427	464	485	488	499	554	657	642	644	637	672	707	707
75–79	172	187	209	215	238	253	277	290	290	305	358	382	390	390	397	405	415
80–84	71	76	84	95	100	113	125	135	137	133	157	171	183	187	190	187	187
85–89	19	21	23	26	30	33	42	46	48	46	54	51	58	65	66	63	60
90 and more	5	6	7	7	8	10	11	12	12	13	14	15	14	14	16	16	14
0–19	10958	10997	11100	11231	11512	11864	12132	12321	12395	12713	13058	13214	13325	13540	13796	13827	13738
20–64	13525	13903	14205	14414	14586	14851	15227	15562	15903	16452	17080	17609	18137	18669	19267	19694	20097
65 and more	1129	1198	1291	1377	1480	1573	1637	1678	1755	1900	2142	2168	2178	2205	2323	2381	2385
Total	25612	26098	26596	27022	27578	28288	28996	29561	30053	31065	32280	32991	33640	34414	35386	35902	36220

TABLE I (continued)

The Population of France by age-groups (in 1000's)

Age-groups	Present-day Territory (90 departments)		Present-day Territory less Alsace-Lorraine (87 departments)									Present-day Territory (90 departments)					
	1861	1866	1871	1876	1881	1886	1891	1896	1901	1906	1911	1921	1926	1931	1936	1946	1951
0-4	3910	4041	3841	3786	3822	3804	3585	3516	3532	3581	3471	2402	3660	3592	3302	2868	4036
5-9	3401	3491	3394	3344	3362	3422	3454	3278	3256	3310	3325	3006	2284	3535	3374	2732	2710
10-14	3347	3291	3223	3292	3254	3276	3323	3371	3213	3216	3298	3411	3096	2332	3502	3082	2745
15-19	3342	3244	3041	3140	3206	3183	3184	3257	3307	3191	3185	3451	3430	3056	2268	3200	3109
20-24	3139	3201	2952	2896	3004	3102	2066	3069	3145	3156	3101	3050	3367	3384	2956	3133	3293
25-29	2906	2996	2904	2790	2750	2886	2973	2946	2948	3082	3073	2789	3284	3493	3314	2094	3327
30-34	2717	2787	2765	2748	2657	2628	2756	2850	2832	2869	2977	2769	2813	3268	3370	2777	2143
35-39	2560	2593	2517	2570	2619	2534	2502	2638	2735	2703	2802	2774	2786	2790	3158	3105	2794
40-44	2400	2424	2336	2372	2438	2485	2398	2378	2417	2532	2568	2760	2699	2682	2645	3117	3088
45-49	2117	2189	2164	2177	2231	2291	2332	2245	2247	2346	2414	2605	2658	2582	2535	2816	3060
50-54	1906	1965	1896	2005	2025	2091	2156	2163	2116	2121	2165	2339	2444	2490	2408	2355	2744
55-59	1685	1720	1740	1782	1817	1842	1905	1970	1994	1848	1886	2119	2153	2255	2289	2185	2240
60-64	1467	1452	1474	1511	1570	1592	1621	1675	1740	1641	1648	1808	1875	1912	2001	1989	2018
65-69	1095	1185	1162	1184	1248	1291	1305	1319	1355	1352	1357	1414	1507	1575	1600	1722	1764
70-74	725	797	847	837	880	915	951	960	962	968	980	1068	1097	1143	1211	1299	1421
75-79	432	439	487	514	515	556	573	582	598	563	571	623	639	682	746	801	947
80-84	200	205	209	235	245	257	277	277	277	267	274	301	323	329	352	384	480
85-89	64	68	67	70	79	87	90	90	90	79	81	88	94	103	119	127	172
90 and more	14	15	15	16	16	19	20	21	20	16	17	20	21	22	25	26	41
0-19	14000	14067	13499	13562	13644	13685	13546	13422	13308	13298	13279	12270	12470	12518	12446	11882	12598
20-64	20897	21327	20838	20851	21111	21451	21709	21934	22174	22298	22634	23013	24079	24856	24676	23591	24707
65 and more	2530	2709	2787	2856	2983	3125	3216	3249	3302	3245	3280	3514	3681	3854	4058	4359	4825
Total	37427	38103	37124	37269	37738	38261	38471	38605	38784	38841	39193	38797	40230	41228	41180	39832	42130

Note: From 1906 the figures given are those of the census. Before 1906, the figures have been reconstructed as detailed in the text of the article.

TABLE Ia

French population by age-groups—males (in 1000's)

Age-groups (in years)	Present-day territory less Nice and Savoy																
	1776	1781	1786	1791	1796	1801	1806	1811	1816	1821	1826	1831	1836	1841	1846	1851	1856
0-4	1667	1660	1671	1720	1796	1835	1809	1836	1860	1906	1954	1949	1955	1977	2018	1950	1899
5-9	1375	1371	1373	1390	1437	1510	1570	1510	1583	1635	1664	1679	1682	1717	1748	1775	1717
10-14	1209	1302	1301	1303	1321	1364	1437	1490	1440	1510	1553	1582	1583	1618	1651	1680	1713
15-19	1198	1160	1252	1253	1257	1280	1324	1384	1373	1398	1466	1504	1531	1558	1570	1605	1637
20-24	1215	1135	1103	1020	1004	1079	1135	1090	1142	1318	1357	1409	1443	1468	1490	1498	1524
25-29	982	1056	1070	1044	969	955	1030	1068	990	1087	1272	1292	1322	1359	1385	1402	1408
30-34	868	915	988	1005	983	916	905	982	1002	943	1052	1220	1250	1250	1291	1312	1328
35-39	804	802	848	918	936	919	860	848	930	950	905	1007	1155	1167	1194	1226	1247
40-44	756	736	737	782	848	868	855	802	792	875	900	855	948	1092	1105	1130	1156
45-49	680	684	669	672	716	779	800	783	738	735	820	837	795	885	1022	1027	1023
50-54	571	602	608	597	603	645	705	720	708	670	677	750	762	732	817	938	937
55-59	474	491	520	528	522	530	570	618	633	627	602	605	665	678	658	730	835
60-64	355	387	403	429	438	436	445	475	517	537	542	512	512	565	585	560	625
65-69	266	268	294	308	330	339	340	345	372	412	437	430	402	410	460	463	442
70-74	156	176	178	197	209	226	235	238	242	267	307	310	302	285	302	332	322
75-79	84	91	103	105	116	124	135	140	140	148	173	185	185	180	175	180	190
80-84	34	37	41	47	49	55	60	65	65	61	75	81	83	87	85	80	82
85-89	9	10	11	13	15	16	20	23	23	21	25	22	23	32	30	25	25
90 and more	2	3	3	3	4	5	5	5	5	5	5	6	5	5	7	7	6
0-19	5449	5493	5597	5666	5811	5989	6140	6220	6256	6449	6637	6714	6751	6870	6987	7010	6966
20-64	6615	6808	6946	6995	7019	7127	7305	7386	7452	7742	8127	8487	8852	9196	9547	9823	10083
65 and more	551	585	630	673	723	765	795	816	847	914	1022	1034	1000	999	1059	1087	1067
Total	12615	12886	13173	13334	13553	13881	14240	14422	14555	15105	15786	16235	16603	17065	17593	17920	18116

TABLE 1a (continued)

Present-day Territory (90 departments)

Present-day Territory less Alsace-Lorraine (87 departments)

Present-day Territory (90 departments)

French population by age-groups—males (in 1000's)

Age-groups (in years)	Present-day Territory (90 departments)		Present-day Territory less Alsace-Lorraine (87 departments)									Present-day Territory (90 departments)					
	1861	1866	1871	1876	1881	1886	1891	1896	1901	1906	1911	1921	1926	1931	1936	1946	1951
0-4	1996	2039	1927	1931	1927	1903	1794	1765	1780	1797	1747	1214	1845	1818	1661	1458	2063
5-9	1707	1760	1712	1644	1725	1742	1732	1638	1633	1659	1670	1506	1156	1789	1696	1376	1374
10-14	1697	1659	1622	1664	1601	1687	1695	1693	1605	1616	1660	1713	1558	1185	1768	1553	1381
15-19	1697	1641	1533	1582	1621	1570	1639	1664	1664	1589	1591	1732	1729	1539	1146	1586	1576
20-24	1602	1629	1502	1450	1511	1569	1508	1575	1611	1558	1533	1408	1660	1719	1483	1494	1687
25-29	1473	1523	1482	1405	1373	1448	1499	1445	1517	1525	1521	1234	1629	1796	1673	1033	1693
30-34	1369	1412	1389	1398	1338	1307	1378	1439	1388	1434	1480	1254	1271	1622	1713	1367	1082
35-39	1295	1311	1276	1315	1334	1275	1243	1312	1375	1333	1398	1275	1275	1257	1553	1543	1393
40-44	1214	1229	1184	1211	1240	1261	1203	1172	1154	1261	1268	1318	1248	1224	1179	1555	1543
45-49	1048	1075	1092	1090	1124	1157	1172	1115	1102	1155	1190	1272	1264	1181	1140	1357	1526
50-54	945	965	996	1004	1009	1058	1088	1074	1039	1028	1056	1133	1185	1170	1085	1006	1305
55-59	845	850	891	887	901	908	952	985	987	886	911	1016	1025	1072	1053	937	945
60-64	722	725	744	759	783	785	793	824	860	775	763	847	880	887	926	840	844
65-69	505	580	570	578	618	635	628	645	651	641	631	645	683	712	719	732	722
70-74	318	365	407	405	415	427	447	467	450	443	440	461	472	495	531	539	577
75-79	195	187	220	242	240	258	262	271	275	250	249	261	267	281	303	313	372
80-84	90	90	87	103	110	115	122	122	122	112	111	117	125	122	131	135	173
85-89	27	30	27	27	33	37	37	40	40	30	30	31	33	35	38	39	54
90 and more	6	6	6	6	6	7	8	8	8	5	5	6	6	6	7	7	10
0-19	7097	7099	6794	6821	6874	6902	6860	6760	6682	6661	6668	6165	6288	6331	6271	5973	6394
20-64	10513	10719	10556	10519	10613	10768	10836	10941	11033	10955	11120	10757	11437	11928	11805	11132	12018
65 and more	1141	1258	1317	1361	1422	1479	1504	1553	1546	1481	1466	1251	1586	1651	1719	1765	1908
Total	18751	19076	18667	18701	18909	19149	19200	19254	19261	19097	19254	18173	19311	19910	19795	18870	20320

Note: From 1906 the figures given are those of the census. Before 1906, the figures have been reconstructed as detailed in the text of the article.

TABLE 1b

French population by age-groups—females (in 1000's)

Present-day territory less Nice and Savoy

Age-groups (in years)	1776	1781	1786	1791	1796	1801	1806	1811	1816	1821	1826	1831	1836	1841	1846	1851	1856
0-4	1640	1644	1646	1686	1751	1784	1740	1767	1793	1865	1893	1915	1903	1933	1933	1926	1868
5-9	1341	1340	1343	1361	1411	1481	1525	1500	1502	1570	1667	1627	1644	1657	1690	1725	1680
10-14	1200	1282	1281	1284	1301	1349	1417	1457	1432	1422	1467	1534	1547	1574	1609	1623	1656
15-19	1238	1238	1233	1234	1238	1261	1310	1377	1412	1387	1394	1424	1480	1506	1527	1543	1568
20-24	1162	1173	1177	1176	1181	1188	1215	1265	1325	1357	1332	1335	1366	1424	1442	1459	1481
25-29	1020	1091	1105	1113	1116	1123	1135	1165	1210	1267	1300	1272	1271	1304	1361	1370	1383
30-34	904	951	1020	1038	1048	1055	1065	1080	1107	1155	1212	1237	1205	1204	1238	1285	1298
35-39	845	834	881	948	967	979	990	1002	1020	1050	1098	1147	1167	1140	1153	1174	1212
40-44	794	774	766	812	876	897	910	925	942	957	992	1032	1077	1100	1077	1081	1114
45-49	715	719	703	698	743	805	827	842	860	875	900	927	987	1007	1032	1005	1006
50-54	597	633	639	628	626	669	725	752	770	787	810	830	850	887	935	952	927
55-59	499	513	547	555	549	550	592	645	670	690	712	730	740	767	810	845	857
60-64	374	407	421	451	461	458	462	500	547	572	597	612	622	640	672	700	727
65-69	275	282	309	322	347	361	357	362	397	437	465	477	487	502	522	540	560
70-74	165	182	187	207	218	238	250	250	257	287	350	332	342	352	370	375	385
75-79	88	96	106	110	122	129	142	150	150	157	185	197	205	210	222	225	225
80-84	37	39	43	48	51	58	65	70	72	72	82	90	100	100	105	107	105
85-89	10	11	12	13	15	17	22	23	25	25	29	29	35	33	36	38	35
90 and more	3	3	4	4	4	5	6	7	7	8	9	9	9	9	9	9	8
0-19	5509	5504	5503	5565	5701	5875	5992	6101	6139	6264	6421	6500	6574	6670	6809	6817	6772
20-64	6910	7095	7259	7419	7567	7724	7921	8176	8451	8710	8953	9122	9285	9473	9720	9871	10014
65 and more	578	613	661	704	757	808	842	862	908	986	1120	1134	1178	1206	1264	1294	1318
Total	12997	13212	13423	13688	14025	14407	14755	15139	15498	15960	16494	16756	17037	17349	17793	17982	18104
15-44	5963	6061	6182	6321	6426	6503	6625	6814	7016	7173	7328	7447	7566	7678	7798	7912	8056

TABLE 1b (continued)

French population by age-groups—females (in 1000's)

Age-groups (in years)	Present-day Territory (90 departments)		Present-day Territory less Alsace–Lorraine (87 departments)									Present-day Territory (90 departments)					
	1861	1866	1871	1876	1881	1886	1891	1896	1901	1906	1911	1921	1926	1931	1936	1946	1951
0–4	1914	2002	1914	1855	1895	1901	1791	1751	1752	1784	1724	1188	1815	1777	1641	1410	1973
5–9	1694	1731	1682	1700	1637	1680	1722	1640	1623	1651	1655	1500	1128	1746	1678	1356	1336
10–14	1650	1632	1601	1628	1653	1589	1628	1678	1608	1600	1638	1698	1538	1147	1734	1529	1362
15–19	1645	1603	1508	1558	1585	1613	1545	1593	1643	1602	1594	1719	1701	1517	1122	1614	1533
20–24	1537	1572	1450	1446	1493	1533	1558	1494	1534	1598	1568	1642	1707	1665	1473	1639	1606
25–29	1433	1468	1422	1385	1377	1438	1474	1501	1431	1557	1552	1555	1655	1697	1641	1061	1634
30–34	1348	1375	1336	1350	1319	1321	1378	1411	1444	1435	1497	1515	1542	1646	1657	1410	1061
35–39	1265	1282	1241	1255	1285	1259	1259	1326	1360	1370	1404	1499	1511	1533	1605	1562	1401
40–44	1186	1195	1152	1161	1198	1224	1195	1206	1263	1271	1300	1442	1451	1458	1466	1562	1545
45–49	1069	1114	1072	1087	1107	1134	1160	1130	1145	1191	1224	1333	1394	1401	1395	1479	1534
50–54	961	1000	990	1001	1016	1033	1068	1089	1077	1093	1109	1206	1259	1320	1323	1349	1439
55–59	840	870	849	895	916	934	953	985	1007	962	975	1103	1128	1183	1236	1248	1295
60–64	745	727	730	752	787	807	828	851	880	866	885	961	995	1025	1075	1149	1174
65–69	590	605	592	606	630	656	677	674	704	711	726	769	824	863	886	900	1042
70–74	407	432	440	432	465	488	504	493	512	525	540	607	623	648	690	760	844
75–79	237	252	267	272	275	298	311	311	323	313	322	362	372	401	443	488	575
80–84	110	115	122	132	135	142	155	155	155	155	163	184	198	207	221	249	307
85–89	37	38	40	43	46	50	53	50	50	49	51	57	61	68	81	88	118
90 and more	8	9	9	10	10	12	12	13	12	11	12	14	15	16	18	19	31
0–19	6903	6968	6705	6741	6770	6783	6686	6662	6626	6637	6611	6105	6182	6187	6175	5909	6204
20–54	10384	10602	10282	10332	10498	10683	10873	10993	11141	11343	11514	12256	12642	12928	12871	12459	12689
65 and more	1389	1451	1470	1495	1561	1646	1712	1696	1756	1764	1814	1993	2093	2203	2339	2594	2917
Total	18676	19021	18457	18568	18829	19112	19271	19351	19523	19744	19939	20354	20917	21318	21385	20962	21810
15–44	8414	8495	8109	8155	8257	8388	8409	8531	8675	8833	8915	9372	9567	9516	8964	8848	8780

Note: From 1906, the figures given are those of the census. Before 1906, the figures have been reconstructed as detailed in the text of the article.

503

TABLE 2

Mortality table

SURVIVORSHIP—MALES

Age in years	1947–1950	1935–1937	1930–1932	1925–1927	1920–1922	1910–1912	1905–1907	1900–1902	1895–1897	1890–1892	1885–1887	1880–1882	1875–1877	1871–1872	1865–1867	1860–1862	1855–1857	1850–1852	1845–1847	1840–1842	1835–1837	1830–1832	1825–1827	1820–1822	1815–1817	1810–1812	1805–1807
0	10000	10000	10000	10000	10000	10000	10000	10000	10000	10000	10000	10000	10000	10000	10000	10000	10000	10000	10000	10000	10000	10000	10000	10000	10000	10000	10000
1	9380	9270	9140	9010	8820	8660	8510	8410	8260	8130	8220	8160	8220	8170	8130	8180	8100	8330	8320	8280	8150	8060	7970	8000	8040	8010	7930
5	9224	9037	8866	8679	8390	8218	8028	7861	7639	7349	7379	7331	7409	7329	7170	7210	7055	7350	7334	7227	7139	6944	6869	6293	7010	6971	6798
10	9183	8964	8773	8564	8293	8103	7903	7712	7509	7191	7202	7133	7220	7124	6958	6986	6780	7093	7081	6941	6867	6645	6553	6615	6712	6614	6468
20	9065	8730	8510	8271	7970	7770	7547	7310	7134	6775	6770	6676	6771	6646	6491	6505	6110	6590	6522	6324	6340	6053	6030	6066	6129	5926	5858
30	8852	8345	8100	7863	7505	7316	7050	6800	6621	6241	6214	6120	6215	6084	5958	6069	5410	6058	5926	5679	5810	5467	5543	5550	5530	5245	5297
40	8530	7770	7774	7304	6960	6684	6370	6192	6009	5638	5580	5520	5630	5492	5392	5497	4854	5481	5345	5088	5234	4875	5006	5000	4945	4650	4701
50	7953	6900	6930	6474	6194	5850	5491	5345	5264	4897	4854	4800	4901	4786	4675	4850	4216	4787	4659	4429	4511	4171	4344	4325	4242	3961	3925
60	6769	5550	5600	5215	5000	4626	4282	4179	4160	3883	3839	3815	3890	3796	3654	3870	3329	3815	3696	3520	3530	3215	3414	3406	3268	3022	2870
70	4712	3540	3245	3280	3200	2860	2584	2521	2500	2330	2405	2410	2432	2400	2206	2486	2034	2376	2442	2200	2120	1906	2064	2143	1986	1805	1630
80	1938	1236	1115	1233	1078	948	782	771	909	762	893	856	845	862	724	915	692	865	857	711	701	638	760	787	705	628	556
90	239	90	83	86	83	65	47	54	135	86	130	128	115	135	90	114	88	78	113	111	69	80	111	106	107	106	57

EXPECTATION OF LIFE—MALES
(in years and tenths of years)

Age in years	1947–1950	1935–1937	1930–1932	1925–1927	1920–1922	1910–1912	1905–1907	1900–1902	1895–1897	1890–1892	1885–1887	1880–1882	1875–1877	1871–1872	1865–1867	1860–1862	1855–1857	1850–1852	1845–1847	1840–1842	1835–1837	1830–1832	1825–1827	1820–1822	1815–1817	1810–1812	1805–1807
0	61·8	55·7	54·7	52·8	50·7	48·6	46·3	45·1	44·5	41·8	41·9	41·5	42·1	41·4	40·1	41·1	37·7	41·8	40·7	39·1	39·2	37·0	37·8	38·0	37·6	35·9	35·3
1	64·9	59·1	58·6	57·5	56·4	55·0	53·3	52·5	52·7	50·3	49·9	49·7	50·1	49·5	48·2	49·2	45·5	49·0	47·8	46·2	47·0	44·8	46·2	46·3	45·3	43·7	43·4
5	61·9	56·5	56·5	55·7	55·2	53·8	52·4	52·1	52·8	51·5	51·4	51·1	51·4	51·0	50·5	51·5	47·9	51·3	50·0	48·6	49·4	47·6	49·3	49·2	48·1	45·9	46·3
10	57·3	52·0	52·1	51·4	50·8	49·6	48·2	48·0	48·7	47·6	46·6	47·5	47·7	47·4	46·9	48·1	44·4	47·4	46·7	45·5	46·2	44·7	46·6	46·4	45·1	43·3	43·5
20	48·0	43·3	43·6	43·0	42·6	41·5	40·3	40·4	41·0	40·2	40·3	40·4	40·5	40·4	41·3	41·3	38·8	40·6	40·3	39·5	39·7	38·6	40·2	40·1	38·9	37·8	37·6
30	39·0	35·1	35·6	35·0	35·0	33·6	32·8	33·0	33·8	33·2	33·5	33·6	33·6	33·7	34·3	34·3	33·1	33·7	33·9	33·4	39·7	32·2	33·3	33·4	32·6	32·0	31·0
40	30·3	27·3	26·9	27·3	27·4	26·5	25·8	25·8	26·7	26·2	26·7	26·8	26·6	26·8	26·1	27·1	26·4	26·8	27·0	26·7	24·9	25·5	26·3	26·5	25·9	25·9	24·3
50	22·2	20·1	19·5	20·2	20·1	19·5	19·0	19·1	19·8	19·4	20·0	20·0	19·9	20·0	19·3	20·0	19·6	19·9	20·2	19·9	19·3	19·0	19·6	19·9	19·3	19·0	18·1
60	15·2	13·8	12·9	13·8	13·7	13·4	13·4	13·0	13·7	13·2	13·2	13·9	13·7	13·9	13·3	13·8	13·5	13·7	14·2	13·8	13·2	13·2	13·6	13·9	13·6	13·4	13·0
70	9·6	8·7	8·7	9·0	8·6	8·5	8·2	8·3	9·0	8·6	9·3	9·1	8·9	9·2	8·7	8·7	8·8	9·0	8·9	9·0	8·6	8·8	9·2	9·2	9·1	9·1	9·0
80	6·2	5·7	5·8	5·7	5·8	5·7	5·6	5·6	6·5	6·1	6·5	6·5	6·4	6·6	6·1	5·2	6·3	5·9	6·2	6·4	6·0	6·3	6·5	6·3	6·5	6·7	6·7

504

TABLE 2 (continued)

Mortality table

SURVIVORSHIP—FEMALES

Age in years	1805–1807	1810–1812	1815–1817	1820–1822	1825–1827	1830–1832	1835–1837	1840–1842	1845–1847	1850–1852	1855–1857	1860–1862	1865–1867	1871–1872	1875–1877	1880–1882	1885–1887	1890–1892	1895–1897	1900–1902	1905–1907	1910–1912	1920–1922	1925–1927	1930–1932	1935–1937	1947–1950
0	10000	10000	10000	10000	10000	10000	10000	10000	10000	10000	10000	10000	10000	10000	10000	10000	10000	10000	10000	10000	10000	10000	10000	10000	10000	10000	10000
1	8240	8290	8330	8240	8230	8350	8420	8500	8530	8550	8380	8440	8380	8450	8500	8450	8510	8440	8560	8680	8770	8880	9030	9210	9320	9420	9510
5	7100	7183	7289	6926	7122	7245	7401	7280	7538	7580	7339	7474	7424	7605	7656	7605	7659	7664	7958	8132	8295	8446	8619	8898	9065	9213	9374
10	6447	6867	6975	6608	6780	6904	7101	6963	7251	7292	7031	7216	7186	7365	7445	7389	7448	7476	7803	7965	8140	8315	8512	8809	8970	9139	9343
20	6231	6338	6425	6066	6195	6310	6554	6396	6691	6753	6433	6704	6684	6614	6975	6900	6994	7040	7405	7566	7765	7984	8197	8510	8700	8910	9250
30	5697	5829	5910	5564	5660	5756	5978	5840	6105	6197	5828	6146	6108	6079	6416	6345	6450	6516	6905	7056	7270	7526	7739	8070	8315	8590	9090
40	5039	5224	5315	5009	5099	5141	5345	5234	5495	5592	5223	5591	5496	5500	5828	5755	5854	5958	6375	6485	6700	7016	7251	7602	7895	8210	8816
50	4246	4504	4596	4361	4427	4417	4650	4551	4814	4913	4535	4971	4841	4873	5159	5105	5184	5514	5726	5814	6030	6376	6655	7004	7310	7722	8491
60	3224	3522	3613	3469	3519	3430	3692	3655	3891	4002	3650	4046	3923	3975	4229	4190	4282	4403	4783	4730	5030	5421	5695	6051	6376	6671	7743
70	1890	2135	2210	2194	2224	2063	2300	2486	2317	2589	2285	2634	2471	2622	2769	2781	2851	2840	3191	3066	3361	3741	4035	4325	4645	4935	6145
80	670	748	823	826	861	711	831	870	928	962	808	1017	877	1048	1057	1100	1170	1001	1225	1147	1213	1430	1635	1735	2234	2220	3232
90	122	124	147	139	163	117	142	132	145	160	105	166	122	177	164	177	194	142	180	143	122	150	179	167	278	292	617

EXPECTATION OF LIFE—FEMALES
(in years and tenths of years)

Age in years	1805–1807	1810–1812	1815–1817	1820–1822	1825–1827	1830–1832	1835–1837	1840–1842	1845–1847	1850–1852	1855–1857	1860–1862	1865–1867	1871–1872	1875–1877	1880–1882	1885–1887	1890–1892	1895–1897	1900–1902	1905–1907	1910–1912	1920–1922	1925–1927	1930–1932	1935–1937	1947–1950
0	38·0	39·4	40·2	39·2	39·0	39·0	40·7	40·1	41·9	42·7	40·1	42·6	41·9	42·3	44·2	42·9	44·7	44·8	47·8	48·3	50·1	52·3	54·4	56·8	59·4	61·3	67·5
1	45·0	46·4	47·1	45·3	46·2	45·6	47·3	46·1	48·1	48·8	46·7	49·4	48·9	49·0	50·9	50·9	51·3	52·0	54·6	54·6	56·0	57·8	59·2	60·7	62·7	64·1	69·9
5	47·9	49·2	49·6	49·5	49·1	48·2	49·5	50·1	50·1	50·8	53·3	51·5	50·9	50·3	52·3	52·3	52·9	53·0	54·8	54·1	55·1	56·7	57·9	58·7	60·4	61·5	66·9
10	45·1	46·4	46·7	46·8	46·5	45·5	46·5	46·7	47·1	47·7	46·1	48·3	47·5	46·9	48·7	48·8	49·3	49·4	50·8	50·2	51·1	52·7	53·6	54·3	56·0	57·0	62·1
20	38·5	39·9	40·3	40·6	40·4	40·0	40·0	40·3	40·7	41·1	39·9	41·7	40·7	41·7	41·7	41·9	42·1	42·2	43·3	42·6	43·3	44·6	45·5	46·1	47·6	48·3	52·6
30	31·5	32·9	33·3	33·8	33·8	32·6	33·4	33·7	34·1	34·4	33·5	35·0	34·0	34·9	34·9	35·1	35·3	35·2	36·1	35·3	35·9	37·1	37·9	38·3	39·6	41·0	43·5
40	25·1	26·1	26·5	26·9	27·0	25·9	26·7	27·0	27·3	27·6	26·8	27·9	27·2	28·1	28·0	28·2	28·4	28·0	28·7	28·0	28·5	29·4	30·1	30·4	31·4	31·5	34·7
50	18·9	19·5	19·8	20·2	20·3	19·3	20·0	20·3	20·5	20·7	20·1	20·8	20·3	21·0	20·9	21·2	21·4	20·8	21·4	20·6	21·2	21·8	22·3	22·5	23·5	23·2	25·9
60	13·3	13·5	13·9	14·1	14·2	13·4	13·9	14·1	14·2	14·2	13·8	14·4	13·9	14·7	14·4	14·7	14·9	14·0	14·6	14·2	14·3	14·8	15·3	15·3	16·2	16·2	17·9
70	9·2	9·1	9·3	9·4	9·6	9·0	9·0	9·2	9·3	9·3	9·0	9·5	9·5	9·7	9·4	9·6	9·8	9·0	9·4	9·0	9·0	9·2	9·5	9·4	10·4	10·1	11·8
80	6·8	6·7	6·8	6·1	6·9	6·6	6·7	6·6	6·6	6·7	6·3	6·6	6·4	6·7	6·6	6·6	6·7	6·4	6·5	6·2	6·1	6·1	6·1	6·0	6·2	6·3	6·9

TABLE 3

Gross and net feminine reproduction rates in France (per 100 women) (a)

Period	1771–75	1776–80	1781–85	1786–90	1791–95	1796–1800	1801–05	1806–10	1811–15	1816–20	1821–25	1826–30	1831–35	1836–40	1841–45	1846–50
Gross rate	240	236	232	224	221	216	201	198	194	194	192	189	186	181	180	173
Net rate	108	110	112	112	114	115	110	112	112	110	107	107	108	105	105	105

Period	1851–55	1856–60	1861–65	1866–70	1871–75	1876–80	1881–85	1886–90	1891–95	1896–1900	1901–05	1906–10	1911–13	1921–25	1926–30	1931–35	1936–38	1950–
Gross rate	169	170	171	170	164	165	161	151	145	141	137	127	120	118	112	106	101	145
Net rate	100	99	103	102	101	104	102	97	96	90	97	93	90	92	91	89	87	132

(a) Before 1891, the gross rates have been derived from the general fertility rates. The net rates have been obtained by multiplying the gross rates by the probability of women surviving to age 28 years, calculated by interpolation from Table 3, Appendix I.

TABLE 4

Development of crude birth and death rates in France (per 10,000 population)

Period	1771–75	1776–80	1781–85	1786–90	1791–95	1796–1800	1801–05	1806–10	1811–15	1816–20	1821–25	1826–30	1831–35	1836–40	1841–45	1846–50
Crude birth rate	386	381	375	364	359	348	320	316	313	312	307	299	293	282	280	266
Crude death rate	344	344	338	328	322	298	298	264	240	266	230	256	254	236	224	237
Excess (positive or negative) of births over deaths	42	37	37	36	37	50	22	52	73	46	77	43	39	46	56	29

Period	1851–55	1856–60	1861–65	1866–70	1871–75	1876–80	1881–85	1886–90	1891–95	1896–1900	1901–05	1906–10	1911–13	1921–25	1926–30	1931–35	1936–38	1950
Crude birth rate	261	264	266	253	250	251	246	230	222	220	216	202	190	194	182	165	148	204
Crude death rate	243	239	230	233	239	226	218	219	209	216	196	191	181	172	168	157	152	125
Excess (positive or negative) of births over deaths	18	25	36	20	11	25	28	11	13	4	20	11	9	22	14	8	4	79

21

DEMOGRAPHIC CRISIS IN FRANCE FROM THE SIXTEENTH TO THE EIGHTEENTH CENTURY

J. MEUVRET

Translated by Margaret Hilton

EVEN in our own era and in countries which are in the forefront of economic, social and medical development, there still occur, in their demographic history, short phases of a few months' to a few years' duration in the course of which birth, death and marriage rates present striking anomalies. War is the obvious cause of these disturbances in our own day; the seriousness of epidemics is constantly diminishing, so that today they can be said to represent a factor of only secondary importance compared with the effects of wars. Furthermore, in countries of advanced civilization acute food-shortages have completely disappeared, and only the under-developed countries can offer us examples comparable to those of our own past.

If we consider this matter as far as France is concerned, it appears straight away that the respective roles played by the three factors of war, epidemics and famine have radically changed from what they were two and a half centuries ago; the change stands out even more clearly if we look back three or four centuries. Wars did indeed produce demographic disturbances in the past, but it is difficult to attribute to them the sole and clearly-defined responsibilities which can be imputed to them in our own times. It is true that long periods of conflict of an internal and civil as well as an international nature contributed to the depopulation of certain regions, and if these conflicts were prolonged and repeated there is no doubt that they took their toll. But by their duration as much as by their nature these occurrences differed profoundly from the catastrophes of the contemporary world. The sum of deaths on the battlefield was only impressive in comparison with the strength of the forces involved, and man-power strength was always extremely modest. Besides, armies consisted above all of a professional militia, and the effect of losses from their ranks on marriage or birth rates could not be very great. General mobilization of the able-bodied population was unknown, and indeed its introduction at the end of the eighteenth century constituted a new factor which profoundly modified conditions. On the other hand the disorders provoked by armed bands—either those in the pay of the sovereign or those in the pay of his adversaries—were almost always to be feared, and their ruinous destruction of agricultural produce and waste of food supplied aggravated shortages. The armies, themselves ill-nourished and uncared-for, often lost more men from disease than they did in combat. At the same time their movements tended to spread disease in the regions through which they passed. Indeed, populations sometimes fled in terror before their presence or even at their mere approach.

It can be seen that, although far from negligible, the events connected with war do not fall into categories which make it possible for the demographer to isolate them and to attribute to each a distinctive role. Consequently it is with acute crises arising from epidemics and from dearth that we shall alone concern ourselves.

1. *Epidemics*

The fear of contagion—or one might say an obsession with it—was in the past always and generally manifest among town-dwellers. The deliberations of municipal magistrates of which the texts have often come down to us from the sixteenth century, particularly from the south of France, bear ample witness to this fact. On the other hand, although the texts are many, there are a number of points on which they supply very little information.

We do not learn the nature of the diseases in question. Among the many possible infectious agents which have since been rigorously defined by microbiologists it is often difficult to determine which is meant. There are certainly some cases in which the descriptions given by the documents are sufficiently explicit to enable us to make a retrospective diagnosis, and it can happen that it is possible to affirm that a certain number of 'plagues' were in fact bubonic plague. But identification is often more difficult and sometimes even extremely doubtful. The expressions used are frequently vague or ambiguous. It is by no means the case that the terms 'plague' or 'dysentery' necessarily refer to the diseases at present designated by them in modern nomenclature.

When dealing with the period prior to the nineteenth century, one must constantly bear in mind that living-conditions were nothing like our own, and that almost complete ignorance reigned on questions of hygiene. We know today that extremely simple precautions of cleanliness almost completely eliminate the risk of typhus. We know likewise that the absence of contamination in water and foodstuffs destined for human consumption will bring about the elimination of cholera, typhoid and amoebic dysentery. But in the past when men had not even these elementary notions and took no specific precautions all forms of infection were lumped together, and the struggle against infection could only consist in the use of the most violent prophylaxis.

Prophylactic measures had been organized in the Middle Ages by the urban authorities. It was a major preoccupation of all who had responsibility for the administration of a city to see that suspected cases were isolated, that they were prevented from entering the bounds of the city, and that all relations between the city and places known to be infected were broken off. However, until the end of the seventeenth century, one finds few regulations or decisions taken in this sphere emanating from the central power. Under Louis XIV and Louis XV however the control of all frontiers—not only maritime frontiers —with the improved organization of quarantines and even the establishment of customs offices in greater numbers and with improved efficiency, led to a greater importance of the role of the State. And within the frontiers more regular means of administration increased the possibilities of making provision for certain contingencies and for taking over-all measures.

The great epidemics had not however disappeared in the eighteenth century or even by a later period. When they broke out they seem to have operated during their short striking period with the same deadly effects as before. The plague in Marseilles in 1720 and the cholera epidemic of 1832 are sufficient illustration of this. If there was any difference, it lay perhaps in the fact that they recurred for several years consecutively or at dates in close succession. The first two-thirds of the seventeenth century, with certain qualifications concerning the interweaving of dearth and epidemic which we shall discuss later, offer a striking picture in this respect. The narrative or administrative documents, which are difficult to use or even unhelpful if one is aiming at exact measurement of demographic consequences, do at least indicate those peaks of morbidity which had struck the imagination of contemporaries and had led them to attempt counter-measures.

The 'plague' is thus mentioned here and there in local monographs whose scientific worth is very uneven,[1] but which we would be wrong to disregard entirely as they can often make a contribution to our knowledge by virtue of the fact that they are based on documents which are widely scattered or even no longer extant. From this ill-assorted conglomerate of material we learn, for example, of the existence of some of the great crises, of which the most considerable in geographic extent in the seventeenth century seems to have been that of 1628-33, though in 1630 and 1631 it was most general and most intense. It will be noted that this crisis afflicted a large area of Europe, as we encounter it in Germany and in Italy too.

Another fact of great importance which emerges from the seventeenth-century accounts of epidemics, as from those of the sixteenth, is that they provoked panic amongst the well-to-do sections of the town populations, who frequently fled the cities, this being apparently the only protective measure possible. We do not notice the same behaviour when dearth of subsistence is the only, or the major, factor in a crisis. In time of epidemics the most solidly-established magistrates would often take refuge in their country houses. But many lesser personages tended to do likewise. Among them there might sometimes be members of the clergy whose duty it was to keep the registers —when such were kept. But even when these priests stuck to their posts the general turmoil was often such that they had neither the opportunity nor the courage to make their entries immediately, and many scholars have noticed the gaps which exist in these circumstances in the series of the parish registers, when the register is extant for preceding and subsequent years. It is also significant that when the documents do exist they have sometimes been made good with back-entries filled in at a later date, so that they are less trustworthy than immediate registrations made day by day.[2]

[1] For antiquarian works, see the summary bibliography in Fosseyeux, *Bulletin de la Société d'histoire de la médecine*, vol. 12, 1913, p. 115. There is a list—very incomplete however—of documentary publications in A. André, *Les sources de l'histoire de France au XVIIᵉ siècle*, Vol. 7, Paris 1934, pp. 420-40.

[2] Dr L. Couyba, *Le Régistre paroissial de Casseneuil*, Agen 1901, pp. 23-24, and by the same author, *La Peste en Agenais au XVIIᵉ siècle*, Villeneuve-sur-Lot 1905, p. 56. L. Bouchot, *La Dépopula-*

A year of virulent epidemic, such as engendered great fear of contagion, is not therefore a year for which an exact computation of the victims of disease is easy. If the register has indeed been kept up the abstracts which can be made from it are likely to suffer from sins of omission. On the other hand, if it has been made up retrospectively it will be of no more value to us than the estimates scattered throughout other sources. Now in general we can say that there are grounds for suspecting these other accounts of exaggerating the figures; but we must stress the following point: that it is difficult to check them against parish registers, even when these survive and were regularly kept, for the reasons explained above. It must be added that local antiquaries of the last century and even of our own day have often omitted to supply us with all the details we could wish, either out of a childish distaste for figures or from some other motive. For instance, it is only rarely that they give us the figures for the normal years preceding or following the crisis even when they cite them for the crisis years themselves; nor do they habitually attempt a serious estimation of the whole of the population for the period under consideration.

2. *Epidemics and dearth*

Another problem, and by no means the least of those which bedevil the study of the demographic effects of epidemics, arises from the fact that certain outbreaks of disease coincided with acute famines which were themselves killers.

A critical analysis of the research published on the epidemic crisis of 1630-1 would reveal that the two phenomena frequently coincided or succeeded so closely one another that the documents scarcely permit us to distinguish them. In any case, modern writers have concerned themselves very rarely with making this distinction. At all events it is clear that their coincidence was not always a matter of chance—and herein lies the major difficulty as well as the keen interest of the problem.

Contemporaries were aware of this problem themselves, but they had an over-simplified view of it which modern biology is tending to render untenable. '*First dearth and then plague.*' This often-repeated formula was based on often-repeated experience. Nevertheless, on seeing men die who were without doubt famished though they also carried the germs of disease, the observer in the past failed to distinguish between the two causes, and it is now even more difficult, through the medium of their clumsy terminology, to distinguish for ourselves between deaths caused by epidemics and those which famine brought in its train of consequences. Contemporaries were even less capable of sorting out clearly the question of cause and effect. The general view, which was long shared by the doctors themselves and which lasted even until recent years, so that *a fortiori* lay historians took it over and fell in with popular prejudice, was that under-nourishment created through exhaustion a field of lowered resistance to disease—i.e. to all or any disease without distinction. Current scientific theory may be driving us too far in the other direction.[3] However

tion dans le pays lorrain, 1927, p. 151, Charles Bourgeat, *Famine et peste dans un coin du Lectourois (Saint-Mézard) au XVIIe siècle*, Auch 1929.
[3] Dr Joseph Rolland, *Contribution à l'étude des oedèmes de famine*, Paris 1945.

the fact that the most amply-nourished trembled before certain epidemic maladies would seem to indicate that over-feeding could be just as harmful for them as hunger was for the beggars!

It remains an undeniable fact however that the dates when beggars swarmed were frequently also the dates when epidemics were rife, and that the multiplication of beggars often heralded the outbreak of disease.

In my opinion the problem of the causes of mortality in the poorer classes of the population while under the influence of food shortage is not one question but an intricate complex of questions. And one of these is the problem of determining whether the poorer classes showed less resistance than the wealthier classes to diseases to which they were both subject. As far as the wealthier classes are concerned we must obviously examine causes of mortality excluding that of hunger, as hunger cannot be involved. But the connexion between disease and dearth seems to be mainly due to the spread of infection consequent upon movements undertaken to escape regions experiencing food-shortage. The towns had good cause to try to close their gates to the poor from the countryside. This unwillingness to accept extra mouths to feed is readily understandable, but on many occasions sanitary considerations seem also to have played a part. The poor beggar, though not the only carrier, was certainly one of the possible bearers of elements which, though not fully understood, clearly brought contamination to even the best-provided households. In the light of this working hypothesis, which, as I propose to show, can be supported by factual evidence, it will be necessary to re-open the study of epidemics and their demographic consequences.

From an examination of periods such as the years 1630-1, in which we have a good example of these interlocking causes at work, the observations are clear. The first is that there exists a remarkable coincidence between a fresh outbreak of plague and an exceptional rise in the price of grain. This fact contemporaries did not attribute to chance, and we should be unwise to do so ourselves. Nevertheless the two phenomena were in the first place independent of one another, as the epidemic was already raging and its agent, the microbe, owed nothing directly to the rise in grain-prices! The price-rise, which was short and sharp, can be explained, all other things being equal, by bad harvests.

There are therefore two possibilities: either two distinct crises are confused, or else they are to be seen linked together in their development if not in their origins. It does indeed seem that in considering the events of 1630 and 1631 we must sort out one from another the roles of these two factors. Historians who confine themselves to brief allusions or very general statements rarely observe the specific role of famine, and yet there are cases in which it acted independently of disease, or at least operated in a fairly autonomous manner. At Saint-Mézard in the Lectourois, between 26 November and 22 June 1631, opposite most of the entries of deaths though not beside all, the incumbent has inscribed the information: 'Died from hunger'. While we must concede that the meaning of this expression lends itself to discussion, at the same time there was no thought in this priest's mind of 'plague' or any other terrifying epidemic.[4]

At a date not far removed from this (August 1630 to September 1631), the

[4] Bourgeat, *op. cit.*

parish of Sainte Livrade d'Agen experienced a sharp rise in deaths. Now the scholar to whom we owe these figures, and who has undertaken a serious inquiry into the whole background of events, considers that they point to food-shortage as the cause. In another piece of research, however, he admits that in the Agen district as a whole there was dearth followed by plague.[5] Indeed, in the south of France as in the rest of the country the harvests of 1629 and particularly 1630 were mediocre or poor: the exceptional rise in the cost of grain is evidence of this. The two examples we have referred to, when seen placed against the background of the harvest of the year to which they belong, seem to be fairly typical examples of the effects of food-shortages. Yet plague was present in the Agen region, appearing after the dearth of food but also acting in conjunction with it. In other examples dearth is mentioned neither by contemporary witnesses nor in scholarly studies, and exceptional mortality is attributed to epidemics.

The poor left their homes when goaded by hunger and went in search of help far off. They usually liked to make for the towns. There has been some dispute as to the number of deaths which thus occurred away from the usual domicile of the victim.[6] The exact figure is impossible to assess, as it is likely that a certain proportion of these deaths among vagrants were not entered in any register, and in any event it is far from being the case that we can always distinguish among the deaths registered those that refer to strangers to the parish. The real figure being therefore higher than the recorded number, either to a greater or lesser degree but certainly to a degree that is unknown, one can at best affirm that the phenomenon was very general. 'A poor stranger believed to be of such and such a place. . . .' Entries such as this are met with too frequently to be ignored. It is true that they are found sometimes in years when normal prices ruled, but at times of great price increases they are much more numerous.

Moreover in the years of price-increases we find an influx into the towns of the poor from the countryside. It would seem likely that the wretches arriving in a town in this way did not all die, and therefore the movement was doubtless more considerable than the extra number of deaths registered in urban parishes and above all in hospital establishments would seem to indicate.

That being said, the poor wanderer was often accused, and probably with reason, of being the bearer of contagion. Of what disease? Plague, smallpox and other epidemics have no need to make use of this social mechanism in order to propagate themselves. Epidemic crises unaccompanied by famine did occur; there is every reason to think however that conditions of shortage favoured the spread of an epidemic. On the other hand there were few famine years which did not lead into epidemic phases. All the endemic maladies were liable to be generalized by these movements of beggars, who might cover fairly long distances during the incubation period.

Whatever may be its possible connexion with disease, a crisis of subsistence is relatively easy to define by the very clear correlation which exists between exceptional increases in the price of grain and the two-sided demographic

[5] Couyba, *La Peste en Agenais*, p. 103.
[6] P. Goubert, *Beauvais et le Beauvaisis de 1600 à 1730*, Paris 1960, p. 67.

phenomenon of a sudden increase in deaths and a drop in births. This correlation becomes much less marked in the course of the eighteenth century, and in the nineteenth a sharp demographic crisis had always behind it an epidemic or military cause.

3. *Mortality in times of crisis*

As is well known, we possess in France a certain number of registers of births, deaths and marriages which, though they improve in quantity and quality in the seventeenth and eighteenth centuries, are by no means negligible before 1667, in spite of the fact that their preservation is sporadic—and certainly they are more plentiful and preserved in more continuous and valid series after that date. This fortunate circumstance, added to the fact that the end of the seventeenth and beginning of the eighteenth centuries knew great food short-ages, make this period a relatively suitable one for the demographic study of acute crises. Unfortunately it can by no means be said that the wealth of docu-ments has always been well used. Even when other data are lacking, a simple account of deaths per month in time of crisis can very often, provided it begins shortly before, and ends some time after the crisis, make it possible to define its duration, and to compare mortality in the crisis period with mortality figures that one can assume to be close to normal. Let us look at the records of two parishes, both from the south-west of France, during the crisis of 1630-1.

In Sainte-Livrade d'Agen,[7] during the 12 months between August 1630 and July 1631, we observe 713 deaths, whereas for the 7 months preceding this period and the 5 months following the total was 125. If we consider this last figure as approximately normal, and take it as base 100, we can speak of a mortality of an exceptional character shown by an index of 570. One can also try to make comparisons on the basis of months or groups or months. Along these lines, January and February 1631 with 207 deaths form a sharp contrast with January and February 1630, when 12 were recorded.

Similarly in Saint-Médard in the Lectourois,[8] the total number of deaths attributed, rightly or wrongly, to famine during 8 months was 118, and if we set this beside deaths from other causes, which numbered only 11, we have an index of more than 1000. More usefully perhaps we should take as the figure for the normal death rate the 12 deaths of the last 6 months of 1632, which would give us an index of 738 per cent. It must be added that the author of this inquiry suggests 700 as the total number of inhabitants of Saint-Médard. The general death rate in ordinary years would on this basis be 34·3 per thousand which is quite a convincing figure, and for the crisis period it would work out at 253 per thousand.

Gondreville,[9] in Lorraine, again for the years 1630-1, has also been studied by our author, but in this case he does not quote figures by months, although the information was available. However, he has given us the totals for the ten years preceding the crisis: 398 births, 189 deaths and 56 marriages. In view of the danger of under-registration, generally to be feared in periods so far back in history, we cannot have complete confidence in these figures. Maybe it is

---

[7] Dr L. Couyba, *op. cit.*   [8] Bourgeat, *op. cit.*   [9] L. Bouchot, *op. cit.*

for this reason that the ratio between marriages and births seems rather surprising. It would be a mistake, though, to judge these figures on the basis of rates worked out for the eighteenth century, still more so rates which refer to the end of that century. The figures for births and marriages in Crulai[10] in Normandy during the years from 1681 to 1690, were 358 and 102 respectively. During the years 1632 to 1641 the same village shows figures of 329 and 56. Certainly the ratio between the figures at the earlier period, i.e. 5·87, is still very different from that of 7·11 for Gondreville. In any case, the total number of deaths for the ten-year period, 189, seems low, and the figures we are given for Gondreville by calendar years of 118 deaths for 1630 and 240 for 1631 lend themselves less easily to interpretation than the monthly figures cited for the two other villages. Nevertheless, taking the ten-yearly average of 18·9 as base 100, one obtains for 1630 an index of 630 and for 1631 an index of 1311. These results might possibly be even more telling if we could use groups of months of high mortality and compare them with other months as we did before, but on the other hand they might appear less impressive if we were able to establish a firmer figure for normal mortality on a reliable basis. However that may be, there is no doubt that in Gondreville we can say that the deaths certainly had epidemic causes for we are considering the onslaughts of a virulent pestilence which was recognized as such.

This epidemic has indeed already been the object of a piece of research undertaken some time ago and covering the whole of Lorraine.[11] But as the many figures quoted by the author are unaccompanied by any data from which we might estimate the death rate in normal times, the material needs to be worked over again.

More positively however it can be said that on the basis of figures such as those we have just analysed, it is possible, although we have less data than we should like, to form an idea of the order of magnitude of the consequences of great crises of subsistence or great crises of an epidemic nature. And from there it is possible to go on to suggest a probable over-all figure, though this will necessarily be tentative. When, for example an historian estimates the losses undergone in 1631 in Riom in Auvergne during 7 months of pestilence as representing a third of Riom's total population,[12] we have no *a priori* right to reject an estimate of this nature, although it would certainly be preferable to know on what data he is basing his suggestion so that discussion might become possible.

In the second half of the seventeenth century the sources improve in both quantity and quality. We are still a long way however from completing the task of collecting and analysing them. For the time being we must make do with the sample-studies made to date. These are multiplying and becoming more reliable, though they have not yet reached a point which would justify any hope of large-scale information permitting clear conclusions within the near future.

As has been said elsewhere,[13] epidemics which came back in force in the

---

[10] E. Gautier and L. Henry, *La Population de Crulai, paroisse normande*, Paris 1958, p. 242-3.
[11] Deligny, *Des épidémies et en particulier de la Grande Peste du XVIIᵉ siècle en Lorraine*, Nancy 1891.
[12] Hippolyte Gomot, *Chronique de Riom. La peste noire de 1631*, Riom 1874.
[13] *Cf.* in the present work the chapter contributed by M. Goubert, p. 466.

years of the Fronde,[14] subsequently seemed less likely to recur at short intervals and were more rarely generalized. Plague raged again in Dunkerque in 1666, in Lille in 1667, in Beauvais, Laon and particularly in Amiens, in 1668, but it did not reach Paris, and except in the case of Amiens, had not the gravity of previous crises. It represented in these years the aftermath of the great plague of England of 1665-6 and was far from attaining the scope or intensity of the parent outbreak. Sporadically, as in the following centuries, we seem to come upon abrupt outbreaks of local morbidity. For instance, in Sury-le-Comtal in the Forez, almost a tenth of the population seem to have died in 1676,[15] and in Saint-Christophe-des-Bois (Maine-et-Loire) the terrible ravages of an epidemic are observable between 1 September and 13 November 1686.[16] Elsewhere some years, such as that of 1701 in Normandy, show peaks of mortality due to disease, and these are often all the more noteworthy in that they occur in parishes untouched by shortage of subsistence.

It is, however, shortage that accounts in the majority of cases for the high levels of deaths in the reign of Louis XIV. In an article of mine published some fifteen years ago, when our only data was taken from a few parish registers on the one hand and from plainly inadequate old publications on the other, I mapped out a provisional scheme of work and suggested certain practical precautions to be observed in pursuing these studies and presenting the material.[17] Sample-studies made since have confirmed some of the points I was then concerned to stress, but we now need to revise some of our hypotheses and modify our views on some questions. At that time it was the great shortages of 1693-4 and of 1709-10 which occupied our attention. It had always been known of these crises—particularly of the second, whose memory had never been erased —that they had led to an increase in deaths. Contemporary memoirs, and administrative correspondence too, such as the letters of the *Intendants* of the Provinces, which are well preserved from this period, bear effective and sometimes tragically eloquent witness to the psychological effects of these famines, though naturally documents of this nature can have no scientific value for the scholar attempting an actual estimate of their demographic results. Publications such as those of Oursel for Dijon or of Brossard for Bourg-en-Bresse were moreover open to criticism on the grounds that the calendar year from 1 January to 31 December was chosen as a basis for the figures for deaths, whereas the rise in deaths characteristic of conditions of food-shortage can best be observed within the framework of what the statisticians working on the history of grain-prices have called the 'harvest-year'. That the two phenomena should coincide is not, when we reflect upon it, a matter of chance. Each time the danger of a lack of grain was felt the mechanisms which made prices rise on the principal markets came rapidly into play, and the small local markets saw their goods dwindle or even disappear. If the preceding economic

[14] Audiat, 'L'Epidémie de 1652 en Saintonge', in *Bulletin de la Société des archives historiques de la Saintonge et de l'Aunis*, Vol. 4, 1883-4. *Cf.* also, for 1653 in the Lectoure region, Bourgeat, *op. cit.*, and for the Agen region, Couyba, *op. cit.*, pp. 136-62.

[15] Relave, 'Sury-le-Comtal. Mortalité et natalité au XVIIe et au XVIIIe siècle', in *Bulletin de la Diana*, 1902-3, Vol. 13.

[16] C. Arnault, 'Cholet aux XVIe et XVIIe siècles', in *Bulletin de la Société des sciences, lettres et beaux-arts de Cholet*, Vol. 24, 1940, p. 86.

[17] *Population*, October-December 1946.

situation was already unfavourable the numbers of the poor soon rose, and bit by bit, between the two harvests, the numbers of the hungry poor increased too. Conversely, even before harvest or threshing-time, the prospect of a good crop produced a drop in prices, usually in the course of the month of July, and this, taken together with the liquidation of stocks, produced an immediate improvement in the supplies of food.

Subsequent research into the history of prices and the phenomena specifically connected with crises of subsistence has enabled us to define precisely the relationships between preliminary economic instability, dearth, and finally famine. Simultaneously other sample-studies in parish registers in other regions of France and for different years have revealed analogous results as far as demographic data is concerned, but have also brought out divergencies and even inconsistencies. These we must now review and reconcile with one another.

First let us accept the principle that when discussing dearth one must keep one's eyes fixed on grain-prices, as they act as a barometer, though this is not to say that one can simply accept that the amount of suffering caused was proportional to the rise in prices. It would also be a great mistake to take as basic for a price index an average price for one calendar year. But even an average based on one 'harvest-year' is too rough and ready for our needs, for though it allows us to pick out the bad years it does not, as does a detailed study month by month, enable us to trace the parallelism between a rise in prices and an increase in deaths, and it is this which furnishes the final proof that we are confronted by an acute crisis of subsistence. Finally, the most palpable historical fact available to empirical observation is that a seasonal movement of prices took place within a typical year of this kind. They rose to a clearly-defined maximum between April and the beginning of July. If, moreover, deaths rise within the framework of the harvest-year as compared with the preceding months and the subsequent months, then we can confidently make a retrospective diagnosis. This was the case in the example of Gien-le-Vieil to which I drew attention in 1944,[18] and the inquiry was then extended to cover several neighbouring parishes at the time of the crisis of 1693-4. Other studies have produced results which corroborate these findings. To the north as to the south-west of Paris the one crisis manifested itself with analogous characteristics; it was the same in Sologne; the same again in the north of Berry, in Vatan, and in Belâbre to the south which was already suffering depletion. In all these cases the chronological unit which reveals the great mass of deaths is the harvest-year. As for grain-prices, I was shortly afterwards able to collect sufficient data concerning markets fairly close to the places which had been the object of the demographic studies, and the connexion between the two appears to be solidly established.

These findings can be summed up in a table. For reasons of convenience and because continuous data over a long period is so often lacking, I have adopted here a system of indices on base 100 in which I assign this conventional value both to deaths and to prices of wheat for the harvest-year immediately preceding the acute crisis. For the example taken this means the year from

[18] *Journal de la Société de statistique de Paris*, May 1944.

August 1692 to July 1693 inclusive. Only approximate value, of course, can be attached to these rough and ready calculations.

TABLE I

Place of demographic inquiry	Index of deaths from August 1693 to July 1694 on the basis of 1692–3 = 100	Location of market	Indices of wheat prices (3-monthly period April to June 1694 on the basis of 1692–3 = 100)
N.E. of Paris	270	Pontoise	237
S.W. of Paris	299	Houdan	247
Gien	272	Montargis	464
Villemurlin (Sologne)	433	Orléans	314
Vatan	330	Chateauroux	300
Belâbre	294	Brioude	260

Orléans is the only large market centre whose prices are considered here. In large markets, the rise in the price of grain is often already marked in 1692 and particularly in the autumn of 1693. The small markets reveal prices at these dates which are in comparison often much lower. This time-lag does not mean however that a shortage of food was not already causing suffering around these small markets. We must remember the extremely low purchasing-power of the mass of rural labourers and of the artisans of the small towns, which meant that in normal times wage-levels and price-levels were both very low. As concerns the last column, it was felt that the maximum prices reached during the tiding-over months of April to June 1694 would provide indices which would be most telling.

Since our first research other work has been done which seems to bear out the suggestions previously made. The work of Abbé Canard on Saint-Romain-d'Urfé[19] and particularly the demographic sections of M. Goubert's work on the Beauvais region are in accord, generally speaking, with the original hypotheses and the first conclusions drawn: i.e. that deaths tripled during the year of acute shortage, and in some places and in exceptional circumstances multiplied fourfold, as had already been observed.

Other findings may seem to be casting doubt on these results at the present time. At the *Congrès des Sociétés savantes* in 1956, M. Reinhard presented a résumé of several studies carried out under his direction, two of which concerned the late seventeenth century. In the village of Le Houlme (*arrondissement* of Rouen) the year 1693 contained no surprises. Deaths calculated over harvest-years rose in 1693-4 to 50 from 15 for normal years, showing on the graph as a sharp and isolated peak. But at Les Mesnil-Vigot (Manche) in the *arrondissement* of Saint-Lô, deaths were relatively low in 1693 and particularly low in 1694.[20]

Here again, however, price-movements can afford some illumination. The destruction of documents that previously existed for the Manche department makes it unlikely that we shall be able to refer to detailed and reliable series of

---

[19] Canard, *Les Mouvements de population à Saint-Romain-d'Urfé*, Macon 1946.
[20] M. Reinhard, 'Les Répercussions démographiques des crises de subsistances', in *Actes du 81e Congrès des Sociétés savantes*, 1956, pp. 67-86.

figures showing grain prices. But for the neighbouring department of Mayenne
we have such a series for Laval, and in addition there is some data, unfortunately
not very extensive as yet, on prices ruling on the markets of western Normandy
and of Brittany still further west. An examination of these prices has led to the
conclusion that the shortage of 1693-4 was not very severe in these regions. But
the fate of eastern Normandy was quite different. Figures for deaths in Rouen
taken from the parishes of Saint-Sever, Saint-Maclou, Saint-Patrice and Saint-
Godard reach maxima in 1693-4 comparable to the peaks we have observed
elsewhere, and this fits in with what we know of price-increases in this zone,
in fairly close proximity to the Paris and Beauvais regions.

It is very likely that there is an analogous explanation of the case of Les
Mesnil-Vigot, which would be valid also for Le Houlme on this occasion, in
so far as the crisis of 1709 and 1710 is concerned, for in the crisis phase following
the 'grand hiver' of 1709 neither of these villages reveal an exceptional number
of deaths. When more studies have been done on the Channel regions in these
tragic months this fact will probably seem less surprising. We may remark
straightway, however, that we possess a simple annual record of grain-prices
for Lannion, and that as it corresponds very closely to English prices in Exeter
its authenticity can be trusted. Here we read of a modest but appreciable rise
between 1661 and 1662, but there is no reaction whatever to the wheat-shortage
in 1693 and very little in 1709. This is confirmation of evidence presented to
us in the last century on the market of Coutances by Deschamps de Vadeville.[21]

We may go so far as to say that these anomalies confirm rather than contradict the correlation between great increases in the price of grain and demographic crises. When the geography of prices on the one hand and the geography
of exceptional mortality on the other have both made sufficient progress,
there is little doubt that this correlation will be even more clearly attested.

Another phenomenon which deserves mention and which M. Goubert
observed in his study of the Beauvais area, is that an increase in deaths which
can legitimately be attributed in the first place to food-shortage is carried over
and extends beyond the period of the harvest-year. This phenomenon is clearly
observable in Senonches and in Digny in the Thimerais region, to the north of
the Beauce and on the edge of the Perche district. It can be observed also in
Crulai, a Norman parish in the north-west of the Orne department. In both
these cases the rise in deaths is very clear in 1693-4, without reaching record
levels. The index for 1693-4 calculated in relation to 1692-3 works out at 278
for Digny and 238 for Crulai, and it should be noted that these places are in a
geographical zone which lies between the areas severely affected by the crisis
and the regions it seems to have spared. But the significant point here is that the
subsequent reduction of deaths was much less rapid in these places than in the
examples quoted above. The index as calculated remains at 200 for Crulai for
the year 1694-5, and for Digny it is 309—i.e. higher than for 1693-4.

These after-effects, forming an extension of the crisis and manifesting
themselves in continued heavy mortality, arise without any doubt from lack
of subsistence. M. Goubert considers their immediate cause to be disease

---

[21] Deschamps de Vadeville, 'Tableau des apprécies de différentes denrées vendues au marché de
Coutances', in Mémoires de la Société académique du Cotentin, Vol. 2, 1877.

propagated or even engendered by the preceding food-shortage but failing to disappear simultaneously with it.[22] One cannot but agree with this hypothesis.

Death from starvation pure and simple is obviously an extreme case. But hunger can lead to the same end by roundabout means. Bad food—even more dangerous than prolonged fasting—could kill. The many descriptions of poor men near to death have usually been collected on account of their dramatic effect. Useful work could be done by an historian and a biologist in collaboration if they would examine the physiological aspects of the cases which figure most frequently in these reports. In order to ease their hunger the most wretched consumed substitutes for food—mixtures in which there might be a few grains of corn but in which there were other elements such as tree-bark. We quite frequently read of cases of corpses being found in the fields with their mouths stuffed with grass. The decomposing flesh of dead beasts might also be consumed. Food-poisoning needs to be studied systematically in normal conditions. Furthermore, if we are tending today to relinquish the view that extreme simplicity of diet offers on the whole a field of lowered resistance to disease, it can still be maintained that intestinal disorders consequent on such abnormal diets were certainly no good preparation to enable the patient to withstand fevers such as scarlatina and measles—the 'fièvres pourpres' reported in 1693-4. At all events, the fatal diseases of the years of crisis seem to have struck principally among the popular classes, and in this they were unlike the great epidemics of plague or smallpox which spared no one.

This could very probably be proved by some research into hospital archives, which no one has yet undertaken. Here however is a single example from the records of the hospital in Provins, and it is sufficient to show the potential interest of such a study.[23]

For 1688 there is by great good fortune a total figure for admissions: 375 sick. In the same year deaths numbered 41. A death rate of 109 per thousand is about three times above the normal rate of the population known to us from the parish registers. Now 1688 was not a crisis year, as can be seen from the abstract of deaths for the other years, and indeed deaths were even somewhat lower than the average for the five-year period (by harvest-years) from 1687 to 1691, which works out at 46. However, the number of deaths in 1693-4 rose to 157, and this figure might just as well be explained by the overcrowding of the patients, who sometimes lay several to a bed, as by a leap in deaths. We must emphasize once again that these inmates were both of humble or poor social position and also, and almost always, strangers to the town.

Another piece of information of a rarer sort comes to us by chance from the parish registers of Saint-Godard in Rouen. There we find the number of burials broken down into burials 'on charity' which can then be compared with the number of fee-paying burials. We find that a normal year saw on an average, out of 121 deaths, 92 burials which were paid for as against 29 charity burials. The harvest-year 1693-4 includes 208 burials paid for: that is to say, double the usual number. 116 were performed on charity; four times the usual number.

[22] P. Goubert, op. cit., p. 53.
[23] Archives of the Hôpital de Provins, F 4.

4. The fall in births

Today it is generally accepted as a fact that a reduction in the number of births occurs in conjunction with acute crises of subsistence, and this holds good for the crises of 1661-2 and of 1693-4 just as much as for that of 1709-10. This phenomenon of a fall in births had been noticed in the past, but until the last few years it had been little discussed and even less studied. Research has so far concentrated on the drop in births following subsistence crises, and the question of the existence of an analogous reaction accompanying the passage of the great autonomous epidemics remains an open one.

We must first remind ourselves of a point which has been very commonly noted. When a shortage of food led to a sudden upward movement of deaths, births then fell, but only after an interval of a few months. The fact that this interval of time corresponded roughly to the gestation period led researchers to undertake two distinct operations which must not be confused with one another.[24] The first, which is of a purely technical nature, consisted in shifting the figures collected nine months back in date, in order to make this date coincide with the rise in deaths. This operation was justified on the hypothesis that the two series of phenomena were both caused by the food-shortage. Their collation with the price-increases was then much easier. This is simply a method of presenting the facts which facilitates the observation of correlations between them. At this juncture, however, the notion of 'conception' was introduced, and this raises debatable points. Its use might well pre-judge the issue by favouring the idea that the lack of births was due to the failure of pregnancies to occur, either for psychological or for physiological reasons.[25] There is another hypothesis which cannot be rejected out of hand: that pregnancies were interrupted by the illness or death of pregnant women. On the whole, however, it seems unlikely that deaths among women already pregnant or capable of bearing children played more than a minor role. An argument against such an explanation, or rather against over-reliance on it, is that usually the number of births rose again to a fairly high figure after the crisis. This is brought out by the following table, which also conveys a clear impression of the abruptness of this drop in births.

TABLE 2

Indices of births, calculated on base 100
representing the period May 1693-April 1694

Place	May 1694-April 1695	May 1695-April 1696
Crulai (Normandy)	42	129
Digny (Thimerais)	58	106
Gien	53	109
Villemurlin et Viglain (Sologne)	54	167

Births, which fall from one twelve-month period to another to almost half or less than half, rise again steeply during the next twelve months to reach

[24] See my article in *Population*, 1946.
[25] J. Ruwet, 'Crises démographiques: problèmes économiques ou crises morales?' in *Population*, 1954, p. 470.

a level higher than that of the first period examined. This second movement seems to preclude any considerable disappearance of women of child-bearing age. It stands out as all the more remarkable in Crulai and Digny where, as we have already observed, the high level of deaths was maintained. Of course if we shift the dates of the table backwards by nine months we find ourselves dealing in harvest-years again and may well suspect a diminution in the number of conceptions.

For periods earlier than the end of the seventeenth century the observation of this drop in births has an intense interest for us, as it often makes it possible, as we work backwards through history, to detect periods of crisis, births being recorded in the oldest registers when these are silent on the subject of deaths.

Thus the fall in the number of 'conceptions' in Crulai during the harvest-year 1661-2 to a level which represents a third of that of the preceding year constitutes, in the absence of any data on deaths, a fact of great significance. In Digny, where we have the figure for deaths, and where they rise during this same 1661-2 crisis to an index of 442 as compared with the previous year, the 'conceptions' drop to an index of 64 to mount again immediately afterwards to an index of 120.

As we have no series of prices in Normandy going back so far, it is at present very difficult to understand why the crisis of 1630, which stands out clearly on the price-lists for Paris, has only left a slight trace in the records of Crulai (30 conceptions as against 45) compared with the year 1626 when conceptions reached the low figure of 16. It is to be hoped that future research will throw some light on this point. Another line of inquiry open to us is the examination of extant baptismal registers in order to determine whether the effects of epidemics of plague during these years were analogous to the effects of the food-shortages. Figures drawn from Riom in Auvergne for 1631 and 1632, which are said to represent the results of a period afflicted by plague, give only 83 births between September 1631 and September 1632, that is to say 'rather less than a third of the usual number'.[26]

In any case, even when there exist gaps in the documents on the question of deaths, any detailed information on births is welcome. In a book which is scarcely the work of a demographer and which is imbued with much conventional optimism, it is stated that in Yerville (Seine-Maritime, *arrondissement* of Yvetot) births dropped to their lowest in 1694—again less than a third of the normal figure.[27] We can hazard a guess that 1693 was not an uneventful year.

These observations on crises in the seventeenth century, though based on data which are still very fragmentary, seem to lead to conclusions under three heads. The first is that the pursuit of evidence on births and deaths should be supported by parallel studies on grain-prices and on the severity of food-shortages in general. The second is that close collaboration is needed between historians and biologists, for all the factors apart from military events or naked starvation belong to the field of endemic or epidemic disease—that is to say, to medicine.

[26] Gomot, *op. cit.*
[27] Andrieu-Guittancourt, *Yerville*, Yvetot 1953-9.

One last point which is perhaps less obvious deserves our attention all the more on that account. Professional demographers rightly attempt to classify all data such as that we have just been passing under review according to age structure. Births, deaths and marriages and the coefficients that can be derived from them are particularly significant when one can divide the data in this way. I have no doubt that, with the help of specialists, our future research will be orientated along these lines. But this will not be enough. There is need also for social classification. The socio-professional descriptions used in the old parish registers are of course very incomplete and awkward to interpret even when they are supplemented from other local sources, supposing these to exist. And we must never forget that in times of crisis a proportion of the deaths escaped entry in the registers. The study of mortality amongst vagrant persons by the examination of hospital archives would from this point of view be a useful complement to the traditional inquiries being carried out today. Whatever importance one attaches to the question of vagrants, no realistic demography has a right to ignore them. In general we may surmise that if the poor died in great numbers, there were included among them many whose fertility was low, and therefore a decrease in the number of births refers to a narrower population-field than does an increase in deaths. In his search for the constants of demography, the historian must hope to be able to take into account the variations affecting the numerous elements of the population whose domicile and economic conditions were less fixed than was the case for the mass of the sedentary citizens. The numbers of these floating elements may well be very small in some areas and much more important in others. Again, their numbers swelled in times of acute crisis to a variable degree. In view of these considerations we may find that we have to modify our judgements on crises and their consequences.

22

TWO ESSAYS ON POPULATION IN EIGHTEENTH-CENTURY SCANDINAVIA

GUSTAF UTTERSTRÖM

1. A SURVEY OF SOME RECENT WORK AND CURRENT PROBLEMS

NO effort will be made in the following to give equal attention to each of the Scandinavian countries. There are several reasons for this. Conditions in Finland are dealt with more thoroughly in another paper in this collection. Further, researchers during recent decades seem to have been more attracted by demographic conditions in the eighteenth-century Sweden than those in Norway and Denmark. Moreover, the results and problems of the Swedish research are best known to the author.

The first half of the eighteenth century will be given deeper consideration than the period following 1750. The main reason for this is not that demographic or economic changes were greater during the first part of the century—probably quite the opposite is true—but simply that much less is known about the early decades. Perhaps that is also why they have recently given rise to keener debate. Moreover, information as to what was really new in the development after 1750 can be gained first through an investigation of the preceding period.

I

Previous investigations into eighteenth-century demographic conditions in the Scandinavian countries have been based mainly on old population statistics. It is quite natural that efforts were at first concentrated on establishing the main lines of the demographic situation and population development for large areas (usually the individual states) from the point in time made possible by available statistics. Interest focussed, therefore, on the period after about 1750. For it is from that date—and for the entire second half of the century actually for Sweden-Finland only—that there exists a detailed and fairly reliable statistical base concerning such fundamental data as population size and age distribution. The high degree of reliability of these figures is bound up with the fact that they are based not on census counts taken on particular dates, but rather on continuous church records; information on population size and age structure appear on catechetical lists which were kept without interruption in all the parishes of the kingdom, only the capital excepted. It is worth pointing out, however, that the Swedish catechetical lists were not set up in the parishes generally until after the introduction of population statistics about 1750, at which time they were also improved to better serve their new purpose.

Certain errors in these clerical statistics, especially in the older tables, are probably attributable to the fact that the catechetical lists were not originally intended to cover the entire population at the turn of each year. A new list was usually made up only when the old one became difficult to supplement or decipher due to additions and changes. Still other deficiencies (even smaller gaps) in the lists can be pointed out; for example the double entry of some persons who changed residence within the parish. Nonetheless, the statistics for Sweden-Finland, based on the catechetical lists, are undoubtedly far more reliable than those for Denmark-Norway, based on ordinary census returns; censuses were taken in 1769, 1787 (Denmark only), and 1801. Swedish statistics give an account of the population at short, regular intervals and with greater detail on very many factors such as age and sex distribution.

The difference in quality between the statistics of the countries also helps to explain, why Danish and Norwegian eighteenth century statistics are seldom analysed except in conjunction with the Swedish. This is true, at any rate, of the investigations by Adolph Jensen and Halvor Gille.[1]

The statistics of the latter half of the eighteenth century have also been used as the starting point for efforts to determine the demographic development in Sweden-Finland during the decades immediately preceding the middle of the century. The two pioneers were Eli F. Heckscher and Eino Jutikkala. Using census data of 1750 and statistics which they traced and supplemented relating to annual births and deaths in various districts between 1721 and 1749, they were able to calculate population size for both main parts of the Swedish State from the beginning of the 1720's. They also estimated annual births and deaths per 1,000 of mean population for the period 1721-49 in Sweden and Finland (for Sweden Heckscher could only give averages for 1721-35, together with separate series for Stockholm and nine countries; annual national figures first from 1736).[2]

The study of the early eighteenth-century population development in

---

[1] On demographic data for and differences between the Scandinavian countries see H. Gille, 'The Demographic History of the Northern European Countries in the Eighteenth Century', *Population Studies*, iii (1949-50), 3-65. Gille's treatise remains the most complete survey yet issued of the demographic conditions in all the countries of the North including Iceland. In the main Gille confined himself to analysing demographic data, i.e. he was not principally concerned with the clarification of the relation between demographic phenomena on the one hand and economic, sociological and other kinds of contingencies on the other. Apart from Gille's study the most important purely demographic historical contribution of the 1950's, based exclusively on the population statistics, is probably H. Hyrenius, 'Reproduction and Replacement. A Methodological Study of Swedish Population Changes during 200 years', *Population Studies*, iv (1951).—Detailed accounts of the Norwegian statistical material have been published by J. E. Backer and K. Ofstad (*Population Studies*, i (1947-8), 212-26; iii (1949-50), 66-75. *Cf.* also the recent official publication (by Backer) 'Dødeligheten og dens årsaker i Norge 1856-1955 (also English title: Trend of Mortality and Causes of Death in Norway 1856-1955), *Samfunnsøkonomiske Studier*, 10 (Oslo, 1961); this volume—containing also a few tables for the period 1736-1855—is to be followed by a second one dealing with marriage and fertility as well as migration. Of recent publications in which material for Sweden is presented the most important one is *Historisk statistik för Sverige*, i, *Befolkning 1720-1950* (also English title: *Historical Statistics of Sweden*, i, *Population 1720-1950*) (Stockholm, 1955) the introduction and also the tabular and diagram headings are rendered in English whereas the detailed source references and source discussions are in Swedish only. For the period *c.* 1750-1900 the publications of G. Sundbärg still remain indispensable.—The essay by A. Jensen referred to is 'Befolkningsforhold i de nordiske Lande i det 18. Aarhundrede' (Population conditions in the Scandinavian countries during the eighteenth century), (Danish) Nationaløkonomisk Tidsskrift, lxxiii (1935), 1-63. On the parish records see text below, p. 533 f.

[2] E. F. Heckscher, 'Sveriges befolkning från det stora nordiska krigets slut till tabellverket sbörjan (1720-1750) (The population of Sweden from the end of the Great Northern War to the beginnng of the official population statistics), *Ekonomisk-historiska studier* (1936), pp. 255-85.—*Re* Jutikkala's contributions see his own article in this volume.

Denmark and Norway has not made fully comparable progress. True, these countries also have available statistics on annual births and deaths after 1734. But as already mentioned, their population data are not nearly as reliable as those for Sweden-Finland. Nevertheless, data from the censuses of 1769, 1787 and 1801, and from the vital statistics covering the period 1735-1801, have been used in both countries to estimate population size between the census years and annual births and deaths *pro mille*. The results obtained are, however, less reliable than could be wished, due partly to the inadequacy of the source material, but also to another circumstance.

There are no statistics in the Scandinavian countries on eighteenth century migration, either internal or external. As regards Sweden-Finland, the main body of the ample population data from the second half of the century indicates only a trifling net emigration surplus. At any rate, researchers considered it unnecessary to take account of either immigration or emigration, since the quantities were small and probably cancelled out one another. In Denmark-Norway, the situation was somewhat different. It is probable that Norway had a larger emigration surplus than Sweden and that Denmark had a not altogether insignificant emigration from the countryside (Jutland), as well as immigration from abroad to the towns; it is impossible on the basis of the incomplete data to say if they cancelled out.[3]

Danish scholars seem to show scant interest nowadays in the censuses of the eighteenth century, especially the first one of 1769. They regard these data as of little value for studies demanding a high degree of precision and for regional investigations. However, the two later census counts and the vital statistics are far from valueless for throwing light on the general features of the demographic picture and the short-term fluctuations in fertility and mortality. In Heckscher's and Gille's diagrams of birth and death rates in all the Scandinavian countries a series of palpable similarities are apparent in the population trends, as well as in the direction and amplitude of the changes from year to year, especially between Norway and Sweden.[4]

The greatest gap in our knowledge of demographic conditions in the Scandinavian countries during the first half of the eighteenth century concerns the age structure of the populations. Nor would it seem to be possible to reconstruct this information even in broad outline except, inadequately—and with a great deal of work—for some small areas (parishes).[5] Furthermore, we do not have statistics on sex distribution, marriage rates, and migration. Without data on age distribution it is not only impossible to estimate net reproduction and net

---

[3] On the problem of immigration and emigration see A. Olsen, *Bybefolkningen i Danmark paa Merkantilismens Tid* (The population of Denmark in the Era of Mercantilism) (Aarhus, 1932); G. Olsen *De danske Købstaeder gennem Tiderne* (Danish towns through the centuries) (Copenhagen, 1943), and O. A. Johnsen, *Norwegische Wirtschaftsgeschichte* (1939), p. 316.

[4] Heckscher, *Sveriges ekonomiska historia från Gustav Vasa*, ii (1949), appendices (in separate cover); Gille, *op. cit.*

[5] N. Friberg has succeeded in reconstructing roughly the age structure of two parishes in the province of Dalarna (Mora 1666, Grangärde 1686) on the basis of fairly complete catechetical lists. On the possibilities of constructing similar age-sex pyramids for other parishes in Dalarna and the difficulties involved see Friberg, *Dalarnas befolkning på 1600-talet* (The population of Dalarna in the seventeenth century) (Stockholm, 1954), English summary p. 255 f. The age pyramid of Mora is to be found in the work quoted above, the pyramid of Grangärde in a smaller study 'The Growth of Population and its Economic-Geographical Background in a Mining District in Central Sweden 1650-1750', *Geografiska Annaler* (1956), p. 429.

replacement, specific birth and mortality rates, etc., but also very difficult to ascertain correctly the factors which lie underneath the fluctuations in the crude birth and death rates.

However, it may perhaps be not entirely impossible to gain a rough idea of fluctuations in age composition before the middle of the eighteenth century. Gustav Sundbärg pointed out that one could draw certain general conclusions about age distribution in earlier periods from the 1750 population pyramid for Sweden, and its deviation from a normal pyramid. His thesis was that age groups which at birth were larger or smaller than normal in relation to the total population retained this character throughout life. For 1750, the statistics show the number of survivals as divided into five-year age groups—0-4, 5-9, etc.—up to 85-89 years of age. The number of persons in the older five-year age groupings were unusually large at that time. From this Sundbärg drew the conclusion that the number born in the years 1661-89 must also have been unusually large. Furthermore, the age distribution for the latter part of the eighteenth century and during the nineteenth century indicate that the number of births had exceeded the normal figures also during the periods 1721-34, 1746-64, 1776-9, 1791-4 and 1816-34. The larger number of births during these periods should also show up in the age groups 20-34 being above normal size some decades later—that is, 1681-94, 1711-29, 1745-59, 1776-94, 1811-24 and 1846-59.[6]

Actually, it is only for the two earliest periods that Sundbärg's conclusions must be regarded as uncertain: from the middle of the eighteenth century we know both the age distribution and the crude and age-specific birth rates. That is to say, age particulars for those born between 1661-89, who reached the usual marriageable age 1681-94, could not be obtained from birth and christening records as in the case of the younger age groups, since such records were not generally kept in Sweden before the end of the 1680's. It is doubtful whether the age of elderly people could be correctly stated, either by the aged themselves or their relatives, in 1750. Nevertheless, the fact that all age groups from 60-64 years and over were unusually large in relation to the total population in that year speaks for the correctness of the conclusion that the crude birth rate was very high between 1661-89.

Other circumstances also support that conclusion. Both the 1660's and the 1680's were, by and large, periods of peace—unusually long for seventeenth century Sweden. These decades were also free from severe crop failures. The 1670's were not as propitious. Skåne was laid waste during the war between Sweden and Denmark 1675-9, and during the early years of the war there were several bad harvests. Last but not least birth figures (five-year averages) from the province of Närke in central Sweden from the late 1660's onward indicate a baby boom in the early 1670's followed by a decline with a marked minimum around 1675. The birth figures recovered, however, and in the 1680's their level was on the whole rather high especially when compared with the two subsequent decades.[7]

---

[6] G. Sundbärg, *Bevölkerungsstatistik Schwedens 1750-1900* (1923), pp. 10 ff.

[7] On harvests and economic conditions in Sweden see Heckscher, *Sveriges ekonomiska historia*, II:i (1936), 405 f. Cf. D. Hannerberg, *Närkes landsbygd 1600-1820. Folkmängd och befolkningsrörelse, åkerbruk och spannmålsproduktion* (The countryside of Närke 1600-1820. Population and population development, agriculture and grain production) (Göteborg, 1941), p. 54 f.

Quite naturally, there were troughs between the crests in the number born and the number of youths. The deepest trough was between the years 1705 and 1721. It has been related to the effects of the Great Northern War (1700-21), poor crops and the plague which harried the population about 1710.[8]

What has been said above concerning the quality of the national population figures and the age distribution estimated from them applies also to comparable data on sex distribution. In 1750, the sex imbalance in Sweden was very apparent: 1,000 men to 1,127 women. During the following century, the difference diminished.

TABLE I

Females per 1,000 males in Sweden 1750 in comparison with the average for the period 1750-1855

| Females | | Sex |
Born in	Aged	ratio
1745-50	0-4	1,009
1740-44	5-9	1,000
1735-39	10-14	1,008
1730-34	15-19	1,019
1725-29	20-24	1,032
1720-24	25-29	1,048
1715-19	30-34	1,047
1710-14	35-39	1,033
1705-09	40-44	1,040
1700-04	45-49	1,021
1695-99	50-54	1,065
1690-94	55-59	1,115
1685-89	60-64	1,133
1680-84	65-69	1,081
1675-79	70-74	1,057
1670-74	75-79	1,072
1665-69	80-84	1,000
1660-64	85-89	828
Previous to 1660	90—	756
Total population: females per 1,000 males		1,035

Source: G. Sundbärg, 'Rikets folkmängd 1750-1900', *Statistisk tidskrift* (1903), Table G, p. 159 f.

A closer analysis has shown (see Table 1) that the disproportion between the sexes in 1750 was especially marked for the age groups born between the years 1670 and 1700—that is to say, for those who at the close of the Great Northern War were between 20 and 50 years of age. For the age groups born after 1700, the disproportion was fairly moderate compared with the arithmetic mean for the century between 1750 and 1855. The disproportion was largest for the age groups born between 1715 and 1720. For the age groups born before 1670 the figures can hardly be right; they indicate a surplus of men.

The trough for men between 1670 and 1700 can be interpreted as a consequence of the war. But consideration must also be given the fact that age

[8] Heckscher, *ibid.*, pp. 408 ff.

details for this very period are more uncertain than for the following years because church registers were not yet common. More normal sex distribution appears in later periods for which more reliable data are available. Another reason for the especially great uncertainty regarding the oldest age groups is, of course, that the numbers involved are so small. However, even if one must be cautious about conclusions as to the size of the imbalance for particular five-year age groups, it can hardly be mere chance that six successive groups show such disproportions.

II

All the Scandinavian countries were markedly agrarian in the eighteenth century. The farming population made up between 70 and 80 per cent of the total population. Types of farming varied greatly, however; between Denmark and some of the Swedish plains on the one hand, and Finland, Norway, and large parts of Sweden on the other. There were also wide regional differences in the socio-economic structure. It is hardly surprising, therefore, that the rate of population growth varied considerably, both between the countries and between different areas in the same country. The causes of these variations have been only superficially investigated.[9]

In any case, the regional differences cannot be explained merely by divergencies in mortality rates. There were also marked differences in fertility, even when the marriage rates were nearly the same. The exceptionally rapid population increase in Finland must be ascribed in large part to unusually high fertility and, considering the high birth rate, to moderate mortality. The relatively insignificant rise in the population of Denmark and some of the Swedish plains should be viewed in the light of both low fertility and high mortality. In Finland, as in Sweden, the sex ratio was highly abnormal. The sex imbalance probably tended to lower both marriage and birth rates. No investigation has been made of the extent to which fertility variations were related to age differences in women at marriage and/or to voluntary birth control, but both factors obviously played a role. High marital fertility and birth rates evidently existed in areas where opportunities for internal colonization were good, such as Finland and some Swedish (and probably Norwegian) woodlands. Low fertility and birth rates occurred in old, cultivated plains areas where tenant farmers made up a relatively large part of the population; Denmark is the outstanding example.

The average crude death rates for Denmark, Norway and Sweden 1735-1800 are calculated at 28·1, 26·2 and 28·1 per thousand. However, Denmark probably had a more unfavourable death rate (infants excepted) than these figures would indicate, since the average birth rate in Denmark was only 30·8 per thousand, as compared with 33·0 for Norway and 33·6 for Sweden. In Sweden, infant deaths (under 1 year) per 1,000 live births were 203·5 for 1751-99. Infants ac-

    [9] Cf. Gille, op. cit., pp. 26 ff. On regional demographic differences in Norway see S. Steen, Det gamle samfunn (The old society) (Oslo, 1957), pp. 17 f; in Sweden G. Utterström, 'Some Population Problems in Pre-Industrial Sweden', Scand. Econ. Hist. Rev., ii (1954), 150 f, 155 ff. As for Denmark some notes on the regional variations of the women's age at marriage are interspersed in F. Skrubbeltrang, Husmand og Inderste (Crofters and farm hands living-in) 1660-1800 (Copenhagen, 1940), pp. 57 f, 67.

counted for almost 25 per cent of total deaths at that time, and children between the ages of 1 and 15 for about 23 per cent. In Denmark, mortality rates for infants and children were scarcely lower than in Sweden and probably higher, while their relation to total deaths was probably about the same.[10]

However, Denmark experienced a marked acceleration in population growth towards the end of the century. Her population increased by 8·9 per cent in the period 1787-1800, as compared with 8·3 per cent for Sweden. In the seventy-eight years between 1787 and 1865, Denmark's population doubled; it took ten years longer for Sweden to double her 1787 population. This reversal in rates of population growth in the two countries was clearly connected with their somewhat divergent economic development. A population increase similar to that in Denmark took place somewhat later in Sweden's most important agricultural area, Skåne.[11]

The economic factor underlying Denmark's (and Skåne's) rapid population increase after the late 1700's was a series of comprehensive agrarian reforms which chiefly benefited the peasantry. In conjunction with the steep rise in grain prices, especially during the French Revolution and Napoleonic Wars, the reforms led to a great deal of new cultivation and a large increase in agricultural employment.

Among the reforms was the abolition in 1788 of *Stavnsbåndet*, the Danish form of serfdom, and the initiation of *Udskiftningen*, most nearly comparable to the enclosures in England. By virtue of the reforms, a large number of tenant farmers became independent farmers. At the same time, the number of landless agricultural workers (husmän) increased, thus satisfying the need for labour power on the demesnes – after the tenant farmers' work-dues (*hoveri*, which included 'week-days', 'boon-days', carting) had been abolished. However, as Dr F. Skrubbeltrang has shown, the landless class was already sizeable before the late 1700's, and therefore was not primarily a product of the reorganization of agriculture. But he does not deny either that this element in the agrarian population increased much more rapidly from the end of the century.[12]

The special position of Finland during the eighteenth century was conditioned by a persistent decrease in population, owing first to crop failures in the 1690's, and later to the Great Northern War, in the last stage of which Finland was occupied by Russian troops. The plague also caused ravages there as it did in Sweden and Denmark (1710-12). Moreover, opportunities for internal colonization were for a long time better in Finland than in the other countries.

[10] On death and birth rates see Gille, *op. cit.*, pp. 30, 33.—The percentage figures are based on Sundbärg, *Bevölkerungsstatistik Schwedens*, Tables 51-52.

[11] Utterström, 'Population and Agriculture in Sweden, *circa* 1700-1830', *Scand. Econ. Hist. Rev.*, ix (1962), p. 194.—As Gille pointed out, the marriage rate in Denmark 1775-1800 averaged 8·8 per thousand compared with 8·5 for both Sweden and Finland, and in 1800 legitimate fertility in Denmark was higher than in the other two countries. My own explanation, differing somewhat from Gille's (*op. cit.*, p. 26), is based on the assumption that there was a rise in the Danish marriage rate during the last quarter of the eighteenth century, possibly also in fertility; this would explain both the relatively low average birth rate 1751-1800, and the relatively high legitimate fertility in 1800. However, one must not rely very much on Danish statistics until the late 1780's.

[12] On the Danish agrarian reforms see the old but still indispensable work by V. Falbe-Hansen, *Stavnsbaandsløsningen og Landboreformerne* . . . (The abolition of the Stavnsbånd (Serfdom) and the Agrarian Reforms), i (1888). A great many more or less important studies from the last decades are surveyed by G. Olsen in the journal *Fortid og Nutid*, xviii (1952), pp. 263 ff, and xx (1959), pp. 273 ff.—F. Skrubbeltrang, *op. cit.*, *passim*.

At this point it can be of value to note the demographic differences between various parts of Sweden. They show up clearly in the statistics even during the first part of the nineteenth century, and probably date from very early times.[13]

Eastern Sweden, with a high death rate, had a high marriage rate and a low marriage age. Western Sweden, with a fairly low death rate, had a lower marriage rate than Eastern Sweden and a higher marriage age. The higher death rate in Eastern Sweden probably resulted in a more rapid turnover of population and may thereby have led to a higher marriage rate and to earlier marriages. In view of this, one might expect high fertility and few illegitimate births, but the opposite was, in fact, true and to a greater extent than for Western Sweden. At least part of the explanation for this is probably to be found in the influence of the many towns in this region, closely connected with Stockholm, where the demographic characteristics of Eastern Sweden appear in more extreme form than anywhere in the countryside.

Variations in social structure also help to elucidate these regional differences. In the provinces to the north and to the south of Stockholm (Uppland, Söder-manland, Östergötland) the proportion of landless agricultural workers (labourers, crofters, squatters, etc.) and tenants in relation to farm owners (peasants) was much greater than in most other parts of the country. In fact, it was only on the plains of Skåne that a comparable situation was to be found. The main reason was that the higher social classes, nobility and gentlefolk, were relatively more numerous in the countryside around Stockholm than elsewhere. A large part of the land was in their hands as estates, employing tenants and landless farm labourers.

Thus, at least two factors, urbanization and a socio-economic structure which was marked by widespread poverty among the lower classes, combined to create unfavourable demographic conditions in this part of the country. Furthermore, it seems very probable that some form of birth control was practised in Eastern Sweden at least as early as the eighteenth century. To use Malthusian phraseology, Eastern Sweden supplemented epidemics and war with vice to keep down the population, while Western Sweden relied to a greater extent on moral restraint.

Demographic conditions were best in Northern Sweden. The marriage rate was midway between those for the Eastern and Western parts of the country, but fertility was extremely high and illegitimacy very low. Norrland's demographic profile was strongly suggestive of a sparsely settled colonial country.

Some figures from the decade 1841-9 may illustrate how great the differences in mortality were even then. The county of Jämtland, on the Norwegian border, had a crude death rate of 12·95 per thousand. Blekinge, a county east of Skåne in southernmost Sweden, had a rate of 22·84, the county of Stockholm 24·53, and the city of Stockholm 38·11. Thus, the death rate in Jämtland was slightly more than half that of the county of Stockholm, and a little more than a third of that of the capital. The low figure for Jämtland was probably due mainly to the sparse settlement, the absence of towns, and the healthy location and climate; until about 1870, it was the healthiest district in Sweden. Blekinge had the third largest town in Sweden until the middle of the century.

[13] Utterström, *Scand. Econ. Hist. Rev.*, ii (1954), pp. 145 ff, 155 ff.

III

When one looks through local studies to clarify the population picture of the early eighteenth century, one must, of course, consider the demographic peculiarities of different areas as they appear in the statistics after 1750. It might be argued, nowadays, that one should put the national averages aside, and concentrate instead on a closer analysis of the population data from 1750 and half a century forward for the smaller areas chosen for investigation. One could then follow the development backward in time from 1750 as far as the source material permitted.

In principle, it is to be desired that many studies of local scope should be made for various parts of the Scandinavian countries. However, it is not difficult to explain why the method is not very often used quite apart from the fact that the results reached only have a limited range. For Sweden, part of the explanation lies in the difficulties of mastering the source material; the unreliability of the existing statistics relating to small ecclesiastical units being only one of the obstacles to be overcome.

The official population statistics for the period 1750 to 1900 are in large part comprised not of the original figures, but of tables revised by Gustav Sundbärg. Only the national figures have been thoroughly revised; the provincial figures are still unpublished. Nothing at all has been done with the provincial tables or the tables relating to smaller units than provinces (i.e. parishes and rural deaneries); this material is only partly preserved. Since Sundbärg was unable to check and correct the national and provincial figures by comparing them with the tables for the smaller areas, he confined himself to the correction of statistical absurdities and obvious errors. This he often did by means of linear interpolation.

Professor C. E. Quensel's scrutiny of some of the oldest tables for small ecclesiastical units reveals that the population figures are frequently too low, in some cases because one parish or another failed to submit statistics. Deficiencies also appear in the vital statistics of the parish and rural deanery tables, although the errors in birth and death data are relatively smaller, both in frequency and magnitude, than in the population numbers. At present, until the tables for smaller areas have been checked and corrected, they must be used with the utmost caution for intensive analysis.[14]

Deficiencies of the same kind as in the vital statistics of the provincial tables from the later half of the century, but greater and more numerous, appear in the tables for 1721-48, especially for the years 1721-35. The figures relating to the latter period were not called for until 1736; only from that year were the statistics calculated and augmented year by year. Professor David Hannerberg has estimated the extent of errors for 1721-35 within a limited area—the province of Närke (Örebro county) in central Sweden—by comparing Heckscher's figures which were based on data from tables with his own results obtained by sifting data on births and deaths from still extant parish registers. He found that

---

[14] C. E. Quensel, 'Tillförlitligheten i de äldsta befintliga befolkningsdata' (The reliability of the oldest existing population data), Minnesskrift med anledning av den svenska befolkningsstatistikens 200-åriga bestånd, *Statistiska Meddelanden*, Ser. A vi:4 (1949), pp. 9-31. *Cf. Historical Statistics of Sweden*, i, *Population 1720-1950* (1955), p. 13.

Heckscher's figures were too low; for births by 10 per cent and for deaths by 12 to 13 per cent. This applies only to Närke, but it is fairly certain that the tables for other districts also fall somewhat short. In fact, it has already been established that this is the case for Stockholm and some parts of the province of Dalarna.[15]

If we assume that in respect of magnitude of errors Närke is representative of Sweden as a whole, then Heckscher's figure for births per thousand would have to be raised from 32·4 to 35·7 and for deaths from 21·2 to 23·9. This does not involve any radical change. Hardly anyone now doubts that Heckscher's main conclusions on the actual population changes and short-term fluctuations during the period 1721-49 still hold good. He has been borne out, first by Jutikkala's inquiry into the population trends in Finland, and further by various Swedish investigations of local scope by Hannerberg and other scholars, as well as by my own study of eighteenth century population changes and the causative factors explaining them.[16]

However, the difference between Heckscher's and Hannerberg's figures are of importance in trying to determine which demographic factors lie behind the low mortality in Sweden during the years 1721-35. An effort has been made earlier on the basis of Heckscher's figures to explain the low mortality, at least in part, by low birth rates. It seemed reasonable to assume that the age groups of men and women of marriageable age in 1721-35 had been decimated by the crop failures of the 1690's; hence the low birth rate. Because of the high death rate normally prevailing among infants and children at this time, a low birth rate might explain a low crude death rate.[17] The birth rate figure 32·4 is low even for Sweden of that time; the average for 1751-99 was 33·6. But if we accept the corrected figure 35·7 as an average for 1721-35, we put the birth rate as high as the highest figures recorded for any decade of the next hundred years (it again reached 35·7 for 1751-9, the next highest being 34·6 for 1821-9). Then, of course, we can no longer explain the low death rate prevailing in 1721-35 by a low birth rate. The death rate remains very low, even if raised to 23·9 per thousand. This figure was not surpassed in any subsequent decade until 1821-9 when it dropped to 23·6.

In evaluating the 1721 population figure for Sweden proper, calculated by Heckscher at about 1,440,000, one must consider the deficiencies in the vital statistics for the period 1721-48. To that must be added the errors consequent on the method used to compute population prior to 1750. These inaccuracies probably mean that Heckscher's figure for the population in 1721 is somewhat too high.

[15] Hannerberg's criticisms of Heckscher's figures were presented in his review of Sveriges ekonomiska historia, II:i-ii, in Rig, xxxiii (1950), pp. 70-83; cf. Hannerberg, op. cit., pp. 61 ff, 73 f.— On gaps in the material for Stockholm see Utterström, 'Stockholms folkmängd' (The population of Stockholm 1663-1763), Historiska studier tillägnade Nils Ahnlund (Stockholm, 1949), p. 250. Re Dalarna see the studies by N. Friberg referred to in footnote 5.

[16] Hannerberg, op. cit., p. 93; G. Kellgren, Gotland 1690-1720 (Södertälje, 1942, pp. 68-73, containing (in spite of the title), for 18 parishes of the island, annual population figures 1694-1751 as well as crude birth and death rates 1695-1751, Jutikkala, Die Bevölkerung Finnlands in den Jahren 1721-49 (Helsinki, 1945), passim; Utterström, Scand. Econ. Hist. Rev., ii (1954), pp. 112-32.

[17] H. E. Pipping, 'Befolkning och näringar i Sverige och Finland under 1700-talet' (Review article of Heckscher's Sveriges ekonomiska historia), Ekonomisk tidskrift, lii (1950), 155-74; Gille, op. cit., p. 50. Cf. Utterström, Scand. Econ. Hist. Rev., ix (1962), pp. 179 ff.

As for periods prior to 1750 the source material dictates that research must have rather narrow geographical limits. However, the inquiries must be based preferably on other sources than old statistics.

The other sources I have in view are especially parish records and the tax lists which were usually set up in connexion with national taxation. Generally speaking, the ecclesiastical registers are of greater value for demographic studies, since tax lists usually aim to include only part of the population and, moreover, people have always been eager to avoid taxation. This evaluation applies especially to countries where, as in Scandinavia, practically the whole nation belongs to the same Church. Only the church records can be used as a basis for vital statistics. Unfortunately, however, there was less interest in recording the members of the parishes, usually counted according to households, than in registering births (christenings), marriages, and deaths (burials). That is why, in almost all countries, one must also look to tax lists for information on the size and composition of the population.

The practice of keeping church registers came late to the Scandinavian countries. It was probably introduced mainly by clergymen who had received their education in Northern Germany and learned the practice there.[18] Registers of christenings, weddings and burials, and sometimes fairly complete population lists kept in connexion with instruction in the catechism, began to be kept in all the Scandinavian countries during the first half of the seventeenth century. The keeping of records was made obligatory for all parishes first in Denmark-Norway (Christian V's *Danske Lov* 1683 and *Kirkeritualet* 1685). In Sweden-Finland, comparable regulations were issued only a year later (*Kyrkolagen* 1686).[19]

If these instructions had been strictly followed from the very beginning, or if all the registers which were set up had at least been preserved, the ecclesiastical records would give a better basis for demographic studies than they now do. The church ordinances of 1686 for Sweden-Finland called for christening, marriage and burial books and registers of removals from and arrivals in the parishes, as well as catechetical lists. It is doubtful if registers of departures and arrivals were actually set up in most cases; they are usually lacking for the early period in the archives of the parishes. Complete catechetical lists are to be found there only occasionally (from the very beginning there also exists incomplete catechetical lists, mostly including only participants in the communion). Many early church archives have been almost completely destroyed, and in those which exist there are often gaps in one or another of the series of registers. Thorough studies of the extant body of various registers for various dioceses

---

[18] On church registers in Europe including Northern Germany see R. Mols, *Introduction à la Démographie Historiques des Villes d'Europe du xive au xviiie siècle*, 1 (Louvain, 1954), pp. 75-102. Scandinavia and Eastern Europe are not dealt with.

[19] Denmark: see S. Nygård, 'Danmarks Kirkebøger . . . indtil 1891 (Denmark's parish registers . . . up to 1891,) *Vejledende Arkivregistraturer*, v, ed. by Rigsarkivet (Copenhagen, 1933); A. Fabritius and H. Hatt, *Haandbog i Slaegtsforskning* (Introduction to genealogical research) (Copenhagen, 1943), pp. 214 ff. See also W. Jensen, 'Die Kirchenbücher Schleswig-Holsteins, des Landesteils Lübecks und der Hansestädte', *Quellen und Forschungen zur Familiengeschichte Schleswig-Holsteins*, ii (1936).—Norway: see O. Olafsen, 'Kirkebøgerne i den norske Kirke', *Norsk theologisk Tidskrift* (1905), pp. 226-52.—Sweden: A. Sandberg, *Linköpings stifts kyrkoarkivalier till och med år 1800* (Lund, 1948), with an important review by S. A. Nilsson in (Sw.) *Historisk tidskrift* (1949), pp. 84-93; idem (Sandberg), 'The Archives of the Church and the Religious Movements in Sweden', *Archivum*, iv (1954), Paris (1955); N. Friberg, *Dalarnas befolkning på 1600-talet* (1954), pp. 25 ff.

or districts are rare. Investigators of this material meet many difficulties also in trying to interpret this material and in judging the completeness of a particular register.[20]

For certain localities in Sweden—Västerås diocese, for example—there are numerous fairly complete catechetical lists from the seventeenth century (the oldest ones from the 1660's). For the province of Dalarna, which is part of this diocese, the seventeenth-century lists have been critically examined and revised by N. Friberg in his work *Dalarnas befolkning på 1600-talet* [Population in the seventeen-century Dalarna] (1954). The most important table in the book (pp. 230 ff.) gives an account of the total population by sex as well as by number of households for certain parishes according to the catechetical lists, together with the number of taxed persons on the poll-tax lists (discussed below), and the percentage of taxed persons in the total population. For the sake of comparison we also get the population numbers of the same parishes according to the oldest extant statistical parish tables. However, in this work Friberg has refrained from analysing the population structure, that is to say, the age, sex, and marriage distributions, except for one large parish, Mora (1666). In a smaller investigation of another parish in Dalarna, he has calculated the population of the parish for each year from 1650 to 1750, as well as the crude rates for births, deaths and marriages. These computations are based partly on population data from six catechetical lists (or six separate years 1663-1730) and the earliest statistical parish tables (1749, 1750), and partly on statistics of annual births and deaths based on other church records. He then related these demographic facts to such aspects of the economic development as pig-iron production and harvests.[21]

From a general point of view, the most interesting thing about these investigations is the method used. To be sure, it is not entirely new to Sweden, and one might wish that additional demographic questions had been dealt with. But in principle one cannot but agree with Friberg that it is only through a systematic examination of the extant catechetical lists and other clerical registers that one can gain a sure basis for further work in determining Sweden's demography prior to the origin of official national population statistics.

The value of the catechetical lists may be limited only to a certain degree by the fact that such lists exist only for a minority of the nation's parishes prior to 1750. That is to say, it should be possible to combine the results of spot investigations in the parishes with less reliable data for larger areas found in the tax lists.

The most important tax lists for Sweden-Finland are the poll-tax lists. They exist in almost unbroken series for most of the counties from as early as the 1630's. They list taxable population by parish, district (*härad*) and county. To use the lists for demographic purposes, one must know the principles of taxation. The legal prescriptions are fairly clear, but the important thing is what principles were actually followed in practice. On this point there is, as yet, no complete agreement. Certainly, investigators are now agreed that no definite conclusions can be drawn regarding the development of total population, even from the long-term changes in the population as given in these tax lists. But that

[20] *Cf.* Hannerberg, *op. cit.*, pp. 96 ff. and *passim*; Friberg, *op. cit.*, pp. 35 ff.
[21] See footnote 5.

is about the extent of accord. Heckscher, who revised the majority of the extant lists for the period 1634-1820, found it noteworthy that the population curves for various counties so often ran parallel. He interpreted this to indicate that a common factor, the ability to pay taxes, determined the fluctuations. The tax lists could not be used as a measure of total population. On the other hand, they were a 'gauge of the prosperity of the Swedish people'.[22]

Although it is now conceded that this viewpoint contains an important truth, there are probably few investigators who accept it as the whole explanation of either the long or the short-term movements. Nor are researchers agreed that the tax lists should be entirely rejected as source material for the study of total population. Of course, it is clear that one cannot use any one common coefficient to calculate total population from the taxable population. This implication is evident from many comparisons made of poll tax lists with catechetical lists; the poll tax population may vary from 40 to 80 per cent of the total population. On the other hand, one should be able to use the tax list data to show the relative size of different, geographically adjacent parishes with a socio-economic structure of the same kind. If the trend of the taxable population and its components of different social strata is, by and large, uniform over a number of years in the parishes in question, and if one knows the total population for one of them, it should be possible to calculate, with fair certainty, the population size of other parishes. It is in this connexion that spot investigations of the catechetical lists can become very important.[23]

Denmark also has extensive tax list material from the seventeenth and eighteenth centuries. A real contribution in ferreting out, evaluating and analysing these lists has been made by F. Skrubbeltrang.[24] However, his interest was directed primarily towards agrarian and social development. A Danish list for 1660 has recently served as the point of departure for Aksel Lassen's effort to outline the development of population in Denmark 1660-1769; the latter date is the year in which the first general census was taken in the country. He tries to connect the population figures for the two dates with the help of vital statistics from christening and death registers, supplemented by calculations and conceptions which are sometimes rather bold. Lassen credits the 1660 list with considerably greater value than has been usual. In using church records he proceeds from the investigations G. Bang made at the turn of the century, concerning mortality and births for the rural population on the island of Zeeland from the 1640's to the end of the 1770's. However, Lassen's interest in the clerical records, as Bang's, seems to be limited to the question of whether or not births exceeded deaths for the period under investigation and a number of shorter time intervals within that period.[25]

[22] Heckscher, 'En mätare på svenska folkets välståndsutveckling: Den mantalsskrivna befolkningen 1634-1820' (A gauge of the prosperity of the Swedish people: the population on the poll tax lists 1634-1820), *Ekonomisk-historiska studier* (1936), pp. 219-54.
[23] Hannerberg, 'Mantalsskriven befolkning och total folkmängd' (Poll tax and total population), *Gothia*, v (1940); E. Jutikkala, 'Can the Population of Finland in the seventeenth century be calculated?', *Scand. Econ. Hist. Rev.*, v (1957), 155-72; N. Friberg, 'Om mantalsskrivningen i Grangärde (On poll tax registration in the parish of Grangärde) 1650-1750', *Ymer* (1956).—Hannerberg and Jutikkala have a more optimistic view than Friberg of the possibilities of basing calculations of total population on poll tax lists.   [24] F. Skrubbeltrang, *Husmand og Inderste* (1941).
[25] A. Lassen, 'Befolkningsudviklingen i Danmark 1660-1769. Nogle iagttagelser og foreløbige resultater' (Population changes in Denmark 1660-1769. Some observations and preliminary results), *Jydske Samlinger*, New ser., v: 2 (1960), 173-97.

II. AN OUTLINE OF SOME POPULATION CHANGES IN SWEDEN *ca.* 1660-1750 AND A DISCUSSION OF SOME CURRENT ISSUES

I

The most peculiar aspect of population development during the eighteenth century, at least in Sweden and Finland, is the unusually large increase in population which took place 1721-35, the first period which can be illuminated with the help of more comprehensive statistics. H. Gille gives a good summary of the explanation generally accepted until a few years ago[1]:

> After the long and exhausting Great Northern War, the Scandinavian countries entered a period of peaceful reconstruction. The death rate in Sweden and Finland remained at a remarkably constant and very low level during a post-war period covering about 15 years. On the average, the death rate was 21·2 per 1,000 in Sweden and 20·8 in Finland in 1721-35, and in no year did the rate exceed 24 or fall below 18. For no subsequent period during the rest of the century did the death rate remain at so low a level and in spite of wide fluctuations in the death rate in later years it was very rare for the rate to fall again to the low level of 1721-35, and in no year did it fall below that earlier level. Not until the 1830's in Sweden and the 1870's in Finland did the death rate fall to a comparably low figure. More than one cause may have contributed to this extraordinary low death rate during 1721-35. There seems to be no doubt that the Great Northern War killed a large proportion of less resistant persons, resulting in many premature deaths. But while this may account for a low death rate during the immediate post-war years, it is doubtful if the continuance of a low rate for a 15-year period can be thus explained. The low birth rate in the same period may have been an additional influence. In the eighteenth century, infant mortality was a very important component of total mortality, and a low birth rate would result in a low death rate. Finally, it is likely that the long period of war had reduced the rate of population growth and thus relieved the pressure of population on food supplies.

No one denies that mortality was unusually low during the period even if it be raised somewhat because of deficiencies in the statistics. On the other hand, it is very uncertain if the crude birth rate was low, and consequently, if the low death rate can be explained at all by low nativity.[2] One can also question if the effects of the Great Northern War have not been exaggerated in certain respects with regard to areas not directly war-damaged, especially Finland but also Skåne. One wonders what is meant by 'less resistant persons' and 'premature deaths'. It would seem that the reference is to old persons and children. The age structure of the population in 1750 showed unusually large age categories for the five-year age groups born 1661-89. When the war ended in 1721,

[1] H. Gille, 'The Demographic History of the Northern European Countries in the Eighteenth Century', *Population Studies*, iii (1949-50), p. 50.
[2] G. Utterström, 'Population and Agriculture in Sweden, *circa* 1700-1830', *Scand. Econ. Hist. Rev.*, ix (1962), p. 180.

at least those born in the 1660's had passed middle age; in other words, if the statistics be reliable, the war had not caused a radical weeding-out of the aged. Further, the sex composition of the population in 1750 indicates that one must include among 'less resistant persons' even men born 1679-1700, that is to say in the prime of life during the war years. It is difficult to understand how their 'premature deaths' can be said to 'account for a low death rate' even during 'the immediate post-war years'.[3]

It is probable that the marriage rate was lowered by the war, due mainly to soldiers' absence from home. This should have led also to lower fertility than one would have anticipated under peaceful conditions. The age pyramid for 1750 shows a definite slump for age-groups born about 1690-1720. It is not easy to determine, however, how much of the decrease is to be explained by the war and how much by other factors. Nevertheless, it is 'likely that the long period of war had reduced the rate of population growth'.

However, if one would assign to the war and post-war adjustment decisive importance in the population growth 1721-35, it is not enough to point out that the increase was retarded by the war. It is not at all clear that such retardation 'relieved the pressure of population on food supplies'. The mobilization for war of a large proportion of the physically fit males naturally meant a decrease of labour power in agriculture. There may have been a subsequent decrease in production which, relatively seen, can have been as great or greater than the reduction in the annual increments to population. Argumentation along Malthusian lines, to be valid, requires at least that the increase in mortality applied principally to the non-productive members of the society, that is to say especially children and old people, or alternatively, that the surplus of deaths over births had been very high within almost all age groups so that an abundant supply of easily cultivated land became available.

The first alternative has already been touched upon. The burden of proof rests with those who hold that mortality had such a distribution; at present we can only say that available data do not support that hypothesis.

The same is true of the other alternative. No general picture of population development in Sweden during the Great Northern War arises out of the spot investigations which have been made; circumstances may have varied considerably in different parts of the kingdom. However, almost all the studies point in the same direction. They pertain to the province of Närke, in the heart of Central Sweden, and to a number of parishes in provinces bordering Närke on the north and east (Västmanland, Uppland, Dalarna) as well as some parishes on the island of Gotland and in the province of Halland on the west coast south of Gothenburg.[4] These investigations all show a continuous population growth even during the war, except for a couple of years around 1710. But the decrease in population during these few years was considerably less than during the end

---

[3] Above, p. 526-8.
[4] D. Hannerberg, *Närkes landsbygd 1600-1820* (1941); N. Friberg, 'The Growth of Population and its Economic-Geographical Background in a Mining District in Central Sweden 1650-1750', *Geografiska Annaler*, xxxviii (1956); S. Bonnesen, 'Om Hallands folkmängd under Karl XII:s regering', *Karolinska förbundets årsbok* (1911); G. Kellgren, *Gotland 1690-1720* (1942); A. T:son Björkroth and B. Sjöholm, 'Befolkningsutvecklingen i socknarna Medåker, Sevalla, Skerike, Västerfärnebo, Bälinge och Skepptuna 1695-1750', due to be published in *Västmanlands fornminnesförenings tidskrift*, vol. 45, 1963-4, pp. 5-54.

of the 1690's when peace reigned but harvests were very bad. However, the devastation then suffered by certain parts of Finland seems to have had no real counterpart in Sweden.

II

From the time population statistics are available for the whole country, the province of Närke, situated in the border area between Eastern and Western Sweden, shows marriage, birth and death rates which lie near the average for the entire nation. Thanks to Hannerberg's investigation, we know the approximate population size and crude rates for Närke from 1690. Population size has been calculated on the basis of catechetical lists, poll-tax lists and vital statistics. The figures for population size, births and deaths, have been complemented in various ways. They must therefore be regarded as less reliable than the statistics from the second half of the eighteenth century. However, there can hardly be any doubt but that the five-year averages give a correct picture of the main lines of the development. They tally well with the results of studies of smaller areas in provinces bordering on Närke: the studies referred to are based only on catechetical lists and church registers of marriages, births and deaths.[5]

TABLE I

Population and vital statistics (crude rates) in Närke, Central Sweden,
1691-95—1746-50

Period	Population (1000's)	Marriage rate	Birth rate	Death rate	Surplus of births (1000's)
1691-95	38·8	9·7	34·2	26·3	1·5
1696-1700	37·9	9·5	32·6	41·7	− 1·8
1701-05	38·0	8·2	33·5	21·9	2·2
1706-10	38·4	8·1	28·6	30·4	− 0·3
1711-15	36·0	12·5	35·4	17·1	3·3
1716-20	40·7	9·5	32·9	29·0	0·8
1721-25	40·9	10·0	38·1	24·0	2·9
1726-30	44·6	8·0	34·3	22·7	2·6
1731-35	46·6	8·2	31·5	23·4	1·9
1736-40	47·3	8·4	30·0	31·1	− 0·3
1741-45	47·0	9·5	30·7	28·6	0·5
1746-50	47·5	9·0	33·7	26·6	1·5

Source: D. Hannerberg, *Närkes landsbygd 1600–1820* (1941), Tables 34 and 16.

The lack of data on the age structure of the population makes it impossible to explain comprehensively the fluctuations in the different series. It is worth noting, however, that not only the marriage rate but also the birth rate was better maintained during the 1690's than the following decade. The crop failures in 1696-7 were very serious in Närke, though certainly much worse in some other provinces. Harvests in Närke were poor in 1702-3 also, and even worse 1706-10 but scarcely as miserable as the worst harvests during the 1690's. Fluctuations in the crude rates, in large part parallel and synchronous with

[5] Hannerberg, *op. cit.*, pp. 81 ff. As for areas bordering on Närke see Friberg, *op. cit.*, and Björkroth and Sjöholm, *op. cit.*

those for Närke, emerge also in the parishes investigated in the provinces bordering Närke to the north. That the phenomenon corresponds with reality can therefore hardly be doubted. It is possible that the marriage rate was maintained during the nineties partly by virtue of the high mortality, which should have stimulated not only new marriages but also remarriages of individuals who lost their spouses through death. It is the high level of the birth rate which is surprising. It is at least possible that the high figure for the nineties and the following decline can be explained in part by a corresponding decrease in the age-groups which are normally child-bearing. This is true also for the decline during the 1730's. Harvests during the 1740's, especially the first half of the decade, were much worse than during the 1730's, but despite this the crude marriage and birth rates went up. We know that during the forties the age categories 15-45 years grew, relatively seen, and were larger than normal in relation to the total population also during the 1750's.[6]

As the figures in Table 1 show, the population in Närke during the period 1690-1721 did, indeed, fluctuate but hardly declined. On the contrary, a considerable increase in population is indicated as having begun already during the five-year period after 1710; both plague and famine harassed the land in 1709 and 1710. The retardation during the five-year period 1716-20 was no doubt caused less by the war than by several poor harvests. The new peak 1721-25 for both marriage and birth rates probably is due mainly to the cessation of war and return of soldiers to their homes. The crops in Närke were fair in these years with the exception of 1723.[7]

Fluctuations in nuptiality and nativity were slight, of course, in comparison with those for mortality. The three years with the highest mortality in Närke during the period 1690-1721 were 1697, 1698 and 1709. For the worst year, 1698, the crude death rate has been calculated as 91 per thousand, that is to say, somewhat higher than the highest mortality known through population statistics: in 1773 it rose to 84 per thousand in Närke.[8]

In a number of parishes in Västmanland and Uppland, mortality for 1697-8 was about the same as in Närke or somewhat lower; in some districts the highest point was attained in 1697. The flat country in Central Sweden, with which the figures are primarily concerned, were usually considerably less affected by serious food crises than were the iron and charcoal producing regions or woodlands to the west and north—Dalarna and Värmland for example. It is not at all surprising, therefore, that the parish of Grangärde in Dalarna had a crude death rate of 104·9 per thousand in 1698. If one compares the two periods 1696-1700 and 1703-7, mortality in this parish averaged 58·5 per thousand during the first period and only 16·0 during the second.[9]

If population development is viewed in long terms, the period 1691-1710 in Närke stands out as a temporary slump in a population growth which probably began long before 1690.[10] The results of studies in other parts of the country indicate that Närke can be regarded as representative, at least for large parts of

[6] Cf. Hannerberg, op. cit., p. 78 f; Björkroth and Sjöholm, op. cit.
[7] Hannerberg, op. cit., Tables 16, 22-23, 26-27.   [8] Ibid., pp. 113 ff.
[9] Björkroth and Sjöholm, op. cit. The mortality rates for Grangärde published in the text have been calculated on the basis of figures in Friberg, op. cit.
[10] Cf. Hannerberg, op. cit., p. 78 f.

Central Sweden, as regards population changes during the period 1690-1720, even if the dip may have been deeper and of somewhat longer duration in certain provinces. To judge from these circumstances and from the age composition in Sweden in 1750, considerable population growth had been going on at least from the beginning of the 1660's. Sweden is not among those countries in Europe which experienced a population stagnation during the second half of the seventeenth century. It is probable that the development in Finland and Norway during the seventeenth century, as in the following century, was similar to that in Sweden.[11] The birth and death figures indicate that even Denmark experienced a considerable population increase after the 1650's when war and plague combined to decimate the population, perhaps by as much as a fourth or a fifth; however, stagnation seems to have set in during the first half of the eighteenth century when Denmark was harassed by a severe agrarian crisis.[12]

III

The incomplete demographic data at our disposal do not indicate any decrease in population or radical weeding out of physically less-fit elements in Sweden during the Great Northern War. It is therefore just as difficult to attribute the low mortality during 1721-35 to war as it is to relate it to changes in the crude birth rate. Apparently, one must explain the population growth during this period not as a reaction after an earlier, severe depletion but as an acceleration of a development which had long been under way.

The main economic factors behind the long-term population development were scarcely of the nature of technical or organizational progress, new markets or the like. No important changes of this sort are known to have occurred in the century 1650-1750. On the other hand, an internal colonization was going on in various parts of the kingdom—that is an expansion of the area under cultivation and new settlement. There was also some growth of rural textile and other industries.[13] It is probably land reclamation and rural industries which principally made the long-run development economically possible—which is far from saying that the economic factors determined the development.

The short- and medium-term fluctuations in population growth were often related to a high or low frequency of poor harvests and/or epidemics. These naturally checked the birth surplus and struck hardest at the poorest elements in the community. Poverty was widespread in a pre-industrial economy such as the Swedish one, because technique was primitive and productivity low; it is not axiomatic that a moderate population growth in such a society, even over a long period, led to an increasing population pressure on the means of subsistence.

Eli Heckscher believed he had explained population fluctuations in eighteenth century Sweden with the help of the hypothesis that changes in popula-

[11] Comparisons between Norway and Sweden have no reliable basis until the 1730's from which time we have vital statistics for both countries.

[12] A. Lassen, 'Befolkningsudviklingen i Danmark 1660-1769', *Jyske Samlinger*, New Ser., v (1960).

[13] The Swedish internal colonization is treated in a number of dissertations in human geography generally of a regionally limited scope; some short notes are given in E. Heckscher, *Sveriges ekonomiska historia från Gustav Vasa*, I:ii (1936), pp. 395 ff.

tion pressure occurred every time a period with relatively low mortality was followed by a period with considerably higher mortality. But in other connexions he made some observations which, though undoubtedly correct, are difficult to reconcile with his Malthusian views. He found that poor harvests seriously affected even those farmers who did not suffer any land scarcity; their distress arose not from lack of sufficient arable soil but from the violent annual fluctuations in yield. He found it probable, furthermore, that the Scandinavian countries had lower mortality and fertility rates than most countries on the Continent during the eighteenth century—Adolph Jensen had pointed out that the figures for Sweden 1751-1800 were lower than the corresponding figures pertaining to the latter half of the nineteenth century for almost all the non-Scandinavian countries of Europe for which fertility and mortality were known. Heckscher was inclined to attribute the low mortality in Sweden and the other Scandinavian countries to the small degree of urbanization. It is notorious that mortality was higher in the towns than in the countryside; in Sweden it was incomparably highest in Stockholm and lowest in the sparsely settled areas. 'It cannot be denied', he concluded, 'that this explanation presents certain difficulties from the viewpoint of Malthus' own model, but this does not preclude that the interpretation is correct'.[14]

Whatever may have been the causes of poor harvests and fluctuations in yield, it can be said, of course, that they constituted positive checks which held population within the limits of the means of subsistence. But the main question is whether or not the death rate following bad harvests would have been lower during the seventeenth and eighteenth centuries if the population had been stationary or had grown more slowly than it did. That question cannot be answered. We must content ourselves with the observation that the peaks in mortality gradually became lower during famines, probably due to the reduction of economic isolation between the various regions, the development of the grain trade and the break up of the individual households' subsistence economy. This development was slowly proceeding in Sweden during the eighteenth century and became pronounced during the first half of the nineteenth.

The peaks in mortality were followed consistently by troughs, but as long as the peaks did not constitute as much as a fifth or still more of the total population, as in parts of Denmark in 1659 and of Finland in 1697, it must be regarded as uncertain if they were of any great importance in the long run for population development or even for the crude death rate.[15] Among the Scandinavian countries, Denmark had the most even mortality rate from year to year during the eighteenth century, but despite this the relatively smallest population increase— at least up to the last quarter of the century. In Sweden, the provinces which experienced the strongest fluctuations in mortality (e.g. Värmland and Dalarna) had a larger population increase than did more typically agricultural regions (e.g. around Stockholm) where deaths fluctuated less but the general level was higher. In regions with a highly fluctuating mortality the levelling off of the peaks must for some time have accelerated the population increase; what mat-

[14] Heckscher, op. cit., II: i (1949), pp. 47, 56.
[15] Re Denmark see A. Lassen, op. cit.; idem, Skaebneåret 1659. Hungersnød og pest over Sydvestdanmark (Århus, 1958).—Re Finland see E. Jutikkala, 'The Great Finnish Famine in 1696-97', Scand. Econ. Hist. Rev., iii (1955) and below, p. 556.

tered was probably not so much the death (or marriage) pattern as the very change in a given pattern.[16]

IV

It should be stressed that the Scandinavian countries, with the exception of Denmark, lie in great part at the climatic margin for grain cultivation. The limiting climatic factors are first and foremost the temperature of the summer months and the length of the growing season. These factors were much more decisive in earlier centuries, primarily because of the primitiveness of agricultural technique. Drainage of the fields was very inadequate, which delayed sowing in the spring and increased the frost risks. Horses and oxen used as draught animals were usually half starved and weak in the spring, with obvious results for the end product. Rainfall during the summer season does not coincide very well with crop needs; spring and early summer are often too dry, especially after a long and severe winter, and autumn is too wet. If the crop was late in maturing, the threat from autumn rains and night frosts was even greater. Most exposed to risks were the spring grains, barley and oats, which were the dominating grains in Western and Northern Sweden as well as in large parts of Norway and Finland.[17]

The length of the winter also affected the supply and consumption of fodder. If the winter turned out to be long and severe cattle had to be fed in their sheds with more fodder and for a longer period than would otherwise be necessary. In many parts of the country farmers adjusted the numbers of their livestock as closely as possible to the available summer pasturage, which was usually in good supply: in other words, they concentrated on maximum production for this period rather than on even production all the year round. The supply of winter fodder was therefore generally extremely short, the minimum necessary to maintain life between two periods at pasture. The exceptionally cold and long-drawn winters that occurred from time to time during the eighteenth century (see Table 2) thus brought acute shortage of fodder, and death to much of the stock.

Further, as has already been said, a long winter was often followed not merely by a late, but also by a dry spring. This meant further delay before the pastures were fit for use, as well as less hay and straw. The beasts that pulled the farmer's plough were weaker, and the supply of manure, which was never adequate on the plains anyway, was further reduced. This in turn affected the grain harvest.

Probably poor people were not much less harassed by severe winters than were their animals. There is no doubt but that the dwellings and clothing of the poor did not give them adequate protection against the winter cold; in some plains areas they even suffered fuel scarcity. Rigorous winters may have curbed certain infectious diseases but also favoured others, for example typhus fever: a hard winter prolonged the time which had to be spent confined in cramped and unhygienic homes. Severe winters were extremely dangerous

---

[16] Regional variations in Swedish mortality: see Utterström, 'Some Population Problems in Pre-Industrial Sweden', *Scand. Econ. Hist. Rev.*, ii (1954), pp. 155 ff.
[17] *Ibid.*, pp. 115 ff; see also Utterström in *Scand. Econ. Hist. Rev.*, ix (1961), pp. 185 ff.

for infants and old people, for whom diseases of the respiratory organs always form a major cause of death. Resistance to infectious diseases was reduced not only by half-starvation but also by winter deficiencies of vitamins. Equally the importance of sunshine is not to be forgotten. Most important, perhaps, employment was much easier to find in summer and autumn than in winter. The poor, dependent on others for work, were most vulnerable of course, and in

TABLE 2

Summary of the dates of the break-up of ice on Lake Mälaren at Västerås, 1713-1869

Period	Mean date of break-up; decennial (and other) periods		Number of break-ups in each period in		
	Month	Date	March	April	May
1713-19	April	21	—	7	1
1720-9	„	14	2	8	—
1730-9	„	16	1	9	—
1721-35	„	14	3	12	—
1740-9	May	2	—	4	6
1745-9	„	8	—	—	5
1750-9	April	17	1	7	2
1760-9	„	27	—	6	4
1770-9	„	20	1	9	—
1780-9	May	6	—	3	7
1790-9	April	21	1	6	3
1800-9	May	2	—	3	7
1810-19	April	30	—	4	6
1799-1818	May	5	—	6	14
1820-9	April	23	1	6	3
1830-9	„	27	1	3	6
1840-9	„	24	—	7	3
1850-9	„	25	—	7	3
1860-9	„	24	1	6	3

Source of data: H. H. Hildebrandsson, 'Sur le prétendu changement du climat europeén en temps historiques', *Nova acta regiae societatis scientiarum Upsaliensis*, 4th Ser., iv: i (Uppsala, 1915), where particulars are given year by year.

late winter, when even hauling and threshing were finished, their situation was precarious. They often suffered severe distress when spring was late and the supplies laid up in the autumn began to run out even among the well to do; they had to tighten their belts, a literal truth which became a proverb—in Norway (and on the Shetlands) the saying was '*dagarne lengjast, magarne svengjast*', i.e. as the days grow longer the stomachs grow 'thronger'.[18]

An old investigation (1879) of the seasonal variations of mortality in Sweden 1749 to 1872 illustrates what has been said here above. The total number of deaths (almost 8 millions) was reduced to an index of 10,000 deaths per year and 30 days a month. With the months grouped in accordance with the usual temperature conditions, the distribution of the 10,000 is shown in Table 3.

The minimum number of deaths thus occurred in the summer months, the number rising through the autumn and winter to the maximum in the spring.

[18] Quotation from M. Macleod Banks, *British Calendar Customs: Orkney & Shetlands* (1946), p. 6.

The difference between the two extremes is more than 31 per cent. Winter and spring together had 1,136 more deaths than summer and autumn. From the autumnal to the vernal equinox, the number of deaths was 5,158; from the vernal to the autumnal equinox, 4,842. The relatively small difference shows that light was much less important than warmth.

TABLE 3

Seasonal distribution of deaths in Sweden 1749-1872

Seasons	Deaths
December-February (winter)	2,684
March-May (spring)	2,884
June-August (summer)	2,192
September-November (autumn)	2,240
January-December	10,000

There is also a definite regularity of distribution between the different months: the smallest number of deaths occurred in July; the number rose throughout the following months to the maximum in April, the difference between these two months being more than 43 per cent.[19]

While the seasonal variations in mortality were determined by climatic conditions, it did not follow that mortality was highest during the coldest months of the year. The increase in deaths was probably connected with the change from winter to spring. The changeability of the weather during spring-time, often with large and sudden variations of temperature, might easily break down a constitution which had been weakened by being cooped up all through a lengthy winter and nourished by food which was inadequate in many respects. In view of the fact that the seasonal decrease in mortality began several months before the new harvest, the latter can scarcely have had quite the great importance often attached to it. Changes in employment and increasing opportunities for the poor to find their outcome during the more clement seasons must not be overlooked. The difference between town and country is also significant. In the towns mortality did not decline during the milder half of the year by nearly as much as in the country. Everything suggests that the main reason for this was the condition of sanitation; typhoid fever caused great havoc every autumn, especially in Stockholm. An outdoor life allowed the peasants to escape many of the disadvantages of their dwellings.

V

In early times epidemic diseases accounted for a large proportion of total deaths. Some investigators, following a Malthusian model, have regarded epidemics by and large simply as the instrument which held population at the level determined by the means of subsistence. Of course it is quite clear that there were always certain contagious diseases in progress and that deaths from such epidemics usually rose when the food situation became critical. But this by no means precludes that diseases which were given a common name could appear in different forms and with varying degrees of fatality irrespective of the food

[19] Utterström, *op. cit.*, *Scand. Econ. Hist. Rev.*, ii (1954), pp. 118 ff.

supply. Furthermore, certain diseases were not endemic but broke out at irregular intervals—e.g. the plague, cholera and ague. Nor is there any reason to believe that epidemic diseases occurring irregularly in Europe in early times were limited to those now enumerated.[20]

There were times in Sweden during the eighteenth century when mortality rose only slightly despite serious crop failures (1726-8, 1781-3); there are also examples of good harvests being followed by a steep rise in mortality (1736-8, 1779). The highest death rates were attributable, as a rule, to a conjuncture of crop failures, epidemics and severe winters (1697-8, 1709-10, 1740-43, 1771-3, etc.). War was sometimes an added factor.

The troughs in mortality, which usually followed for several years after the peaks, are ordinarily said by Malthusians to have been due to the weeding-out of the physically weak. However, the ability to withstand serious epidemic illnesses is not just a question of physical strength but also of varying biological resistance and immunity. When a peak in deaths is followed by a period of low mortality, the explanation can just as well lie in a temporary increase in immunity among the broad masses as in the elimination of the physically weak, especially children and old people.

Infant and child mortality are of special interest in this connexion since children under fifteen constituted such a large share of total deaths—normally 45 to 50 per cent during the second half of the eighteenth century. In an earlier examination (1954) of the relation between the harvests and mortality in smallpox, the worst of the childhood diseases, I drew the following conclusions[21]:

> For the most part, smallpox followed its own cycles. Since these were short and since disappointing harvests were frequent, it is not surprising that years of famine and years of smallpox sometimes coincided. It is also likely that crop failures had a secondary influence on mortality from smallpox. When increased numbers of beggars were wandering the roads—especially when times were so acute that entire families left their homes—the risk of infection must have been increased. At the same time, the famine lowered the resistance of those attacked by the disease.
>
> It is possible that, on some occasions, famines may have influenced the smallpox cycle in such a way as to bring the peak forward by a year or so. That this influence was only secondary is shown by the years 1751-2, 1768 and 1779 and by the years of crop failures in the 1780's.

Vaccination was quickly accepted in Sweden after 1800. The ravages of smallpox were quite small in the 1790's and, after the severe epidemic of 1800-1, the number of deaths fell heavily as a result of vaccination to a minimum in 1810-15. If one compares the figures for expectation of life during the periods 1751-90 and 1791-1815, one finds that average life expectancy increased for children of both sexes up to 10 years of age in the second of the periods, while

---

[20] Among the epidemic diseases in nineteenth-century Sweden tuberculosis was by far the most devastating. Its ravages were especially severe in Stockholm, Eastern Sweden and the towns. Its effects on mortality seem to have been relatively less in the eighteenth century though even then very impressive, see G. Sundbärg, 'Dödligheten af lungtuberkulos i Sverige åren 1751-1830', *Statistisk tidskrift 1905*, pp. 163-209. The increasing prevalence of tuberculosis in many regions of the country must evidently be ascribed mainly to other causes than a deteriorating food consumption.

[21] *Scand. Econ. Hist. Rev.*, ii (1954), pp. 137 ff.

it decreased for adults 20 years of age and over. In other words, the improvement only concerned the age groups in which smallpox had earlier found most of its victims[22].

In considering the effects of climate and epidemics, the emphasis here is not on the short-term fluctuations of mortality, but rather on the circumstance that in earlier times one decade or some decades in succession might experience a relatively low or high frequency of severe winters or epidemics which influenced mortality. The best example regarding contagious diseases is the trough in mortality, especially for children between 1 and 10 years of age, which occurred about 1820-50, followed by a rather high mortality level about 1850-85. These changes cannot be explained simply by a reference to vaccination against smallpox. The death rate for the ages 1-2 years fell to as low as 24·71 per thousand in 1835, the lowest figure since the beginning of the Swedish vital statistics in 1749. The figure was a record which stood for over fifty years, until 1888 when it reached 24·37. For the ages 3-4 years, there was also a minimum in 1835 with a rate of 8·83, a figure which, still more remarkable, was not improved upon until the twentieth century.

Gustav Sundbärg was the first one to draw attention to the peculiar circumstance that, after smallpox had been almost eradicated, a curious reaction set in some decades later, in the 1850's:

> The germs of new children's diseases seem now to have assembled themselves in sufficient force for fresh attacks to be made. It is the task of medical statistics to state more accurately what these diseases were. The population statistics indicate that the new epidemic which then broke out lasted for about thirty years, coming to an end after the middle of the 1880's.

We now know, broadly speaking, the causes of this unfavourable reaction: a pandemic of diphtheria in Europe which seems to have come from the east and in the process to have scourged also Sweden. In addition, scarlet fever became more frequent after the middle of the nineteenth century and proved more dangerous than in earlier times.[23]

Economic factors, population pressure and the like cannot, alone, possibly account for the changes in mortality within the age groups referred to. Infant mortality, which is usually a fairly good indicator of economic conditions, decreased almost continuously from one five-year period to another beginning in 1806-10, as did the death rates for the older age groups especially those over 20 years of age.[24]

VI

Long, severe winters were more frequent from the 1560's to the latter part of the nineteenth century than has been the case during the last threequarters of a century.[25] However, there was a relatively long period of mild winters

[22] Scand. Econ. Hist. Rev., ii (1954), pp. 139 ff.   [23] Ibid., p. 142.
[24] Re the age specific mortality 1750-1900 see G. Sundbärg, 'Dödstalen efter ålder och kön', Statistiska tidskrift 1909, pp. 177-287.
[25] C. E. P. Brooks, Climate through the Ages, 2nd ed. (1949); H. H. Lamb, 'Climatic Change Within Historical Times', Annals of the New York Academy of Science (1961), pp. 124-61. Cf. Utterström, Scand. Econ. Hist. Rev., ii (1954), p. 132 f.

during the first half of the eighteenth century, as is shown in Table 2. The question is if there was a more or less simultaneous drop in epidemic diseases similar to that observed for the period 1820-50. The low crude death rate 1721-35 points in that direction, especially if that rate cannot be satisfactorily explained by a low crude birth rate or a harsh weeding-out of the aged previous to 1721. The hypothesis is to some extent supported by medical historians and contemporary doctors' reports. It should be emphasized, however, that further confirmation is needed from research in death and burial registers. At any rate, it appears indisputable that the upswing in mortality which began in 1736 was initiated by serious epidemics which entered the country from abroad; their effects were aggravated a few years later by the succession of rigorous winters and poor crops which began in 1740.[26]

It is also clear from what has been said above (p. 532) that the mild winters 1721-35 must have made it easier for the poor to survive. Small fluctuations in climate may not have had any great effect on population development in the countries south of Finno-Scandia. Statistics, relating to births and deaths in various parts of Denmark, suggest that neither in 1721-35 nor in 1751-60 was there any increase in Danish population of a magnitude comparable to that in Sweden. Denmark does not lie as near the 'climatic margin' for grain production as do the other three Scandinavia countries. The majority of farmers elsewhere in Scandinavia, even after a normal harvest, had little grain to spare, but many Danish farmers grew grain for sale and even after a bad harvest they seem to have had enough, at any rate on the islands. This may well be one of the main reasons why the death rate fluctuated less violently in Denmark than in the other Scandinavian countries, though even in Denmark the marriage, birth and death rates were markedly influenced by the yield of the harvest. These circumstances may explain why a series of clement seasons and good harvests in the northern Scandinavian countries were followed by prosperity and population increase while at the same time and partly for the same reasons Denmark experienced a severe agricultural crisis.[27]

The high figures for survival among age groups born in Sweden during the period 1721-35 had cumulative consequences. By the time they reached marriageable age, during the 1750's and early 1760's, the specific as well as the crude marriage and birth rates were high, in the case of the specific rates probably mainly because of good harvests and favourable economic conditions. For the following generation the situation was different. In spite of the fact that the child-bearing age groups in the 1780's were very large in relation to total population, marriage and birth rates were low during that decade. The cause is in large part undoubtedly to be found in a long series of harsh winters and poor crops (see Table 2), but probably also, in this instance, in a population pressure of a Malthusian type. However, the effects stand less clearly out in the death rates than in the marriage and birth rates, and in the changing social structure; especially during the two last decades of the century there emerged an agricultural proletariat consisting of married servants, squatters, etc.

[26] Utterström. loc. cit., pp. 114 ff.
[27] V. Falbe-Hansen, Stavnsbaandsløsningen og Landboreformerne (1888), pp. 1 ff; V. Falbe-Hansen and W. Scharling, Danmarks Statistik (1885), i, 417 ff.

As is apparent from the foregoing, factors other than agricultural development are now more than formerly thought to have affected population growth. When agriculture has been considered here in various contexts as a determinant, my concern has been not so much with its own development as with the fluctuations in its output determined by outside factors. It remains evident, however, that the great population increase of 1660–1750, and later, cannot solely or even principally be explained as the result of fluctuations of harvests or of epidemics; the opportunities for land reclamation and internal colonization have been mentioned but should once more be stressed. On the other hand, I do not believe that long-term developments in population (nor in agriculture) can be explained without reference to these fluctuations. They would not, broadly speaking, have been the same without them.

23

FINLAND'S POPULATION MOVEMENT IN THE EIGHTEENTH CENTURY

EINO JUTIKKALA

Editor's Note: This article has been compiled by Professor Jutikkala largely from his other published work, with substantial revisions and additions. The tables and graphs have been adapted from his treatise, 'Die Bevölkerung Finnlands in den Jahren 1721-49', *Ann. Acad. Scient. Fenn.,* B., LV 4, 1945.

I

FROM the source material available the student of Finland's demographic history must divide the eighteenth century into three periods; of these, only the middle period is discussed in detail in the present paper. In 1749, the clergy in Sweden and Finland were for the first time required to provide information about population for their parishes, and from 1751 onwards the clergy submitted annual figures for births, deaths and marriages to the Royal Chancery via the county governors. Every third—from 1775 every fifth—year, parish rectors reported on the total population of the parish, its distribution by sex, marital status and age, and even by occupation and social group, according to directives very peculiar by modern standards. No direct information exists on migration between parishes, but if the population figures given at three or five year intervals are assumed to be roughly correct the migration gain or loss in each parish may be calculated by comparing the differences in population totals with natural population increases in the intervals between reports. The information submitted by the rectors was assembled, totalled and published for the whole kingdom, and in this way there exists for the latter half of the century, the period of the '*Tabellverket*' (Central Statistical Office), fairly complete, moderately reliable, part printed and part unpublished material for research.

For the preceding period, 1721-48, there are no direct total population figures, but even in the seventeenth century bishops had required the clergy, for the better maintenance of congregational order, to enter in special files known in Finland as 'history books' all those baptized, buried and married in the parish. As the government in 1736 asked chapters to provide information on births and deaths in each parish 'since the date God granted the kingdom blessed peace', i.e. 1721, it must have had reason to assume that the clergy was able to provide the data from the 'history books'. Later, the parish rectors had to submit reports on population movement annually, and in 1737-8 even quarterly.[1]

---

[1] A. Hjelt, Det svenska tabellverkets uppkomst, organisation och tidigare verksamhet, *Fennia* 16, 1900, pp. 8-11, 37-61.—E. F. Heckscher, Sveriges befolkning 1720-50, *Ekonomisk-historiska studier,*

The reports submitted to the government by the parish priests are kept in the Swedish Statistical Central Office. Copies of congregational 'history books', from which the clergy must have drawn at least the data subsequently requested for 1721-35, and which doubtless also provided the material for their later annual reports, are kept at the Finnish State Archives. Theoretically, the information from each source should be compatible, and it should make no difference which of the sources the research worker might use. The material is not, however, always consistent, and the differences may run counter to each other so that now the one source, now the other gives a higher figure. Yet these slight differences are ironed out when periods covering several years, and districts comprising several parishes, are studied. They may, at least in 1736-48, have resulted from the fact that the 'history books' included outsiders whom the priest had baptized or buried but whom he had excluded from his report to the government, or they may have occurred if the priest entered births and deaths in his report according to the date of birth and the date of death, although the entries had been made in the 'history books' according to the date of christening and the date of burial, and hence, occasionally, in a different year. The reports, therefore, seem to be a more reliable source than the 'history books'; although the latter were seemingly the primary source and the reports the secondary source, it should be remembered that the 'history books' were not kept as vital statistical records. For this reason, the present study has in the first instance relied on the reports. It has, on the other hand, been essential to refer to the 'history books': first, to fill the frequent gaps in the reports; second, on rare occasions when the reports quoted suspiciously low figures while the 'history books' gave figures corresponding to 'normal' birth rates and death rates; third, for all data on marriages, because figures for married couples were not reported to the government. The total number of marriages, unlike the number of births and deaths, is not necessary for the calculation of population changes, and for this reason when the marriage rate has been studied only parishes for which the 'history books' supplied complete or fairly complete data have been taken into account.

Real difficulty is only encountered when a gap in the 'history books' coincides with a year for which the report is missing—a situation which, bearing in mind the interdependence of these sources, is readily understandable. In occasional cases it has been possible to bridge the gaps with information collected from parishes by the Central Statistical Office in Finland at the end of the nineteenth century. To supply this information, the parish clergy obviously used congregational 'history books' which were subsequently lost before this source series was copied for the State Archives. Usually, however, gaps occurring simultaneously in both sources have had to be bridged by interpolation or extrapolation. Various methods of interpolation have been necessary, especially because gaps in the 'history books' often extended not over a year but only over a part

1936, p. 263. St. Bolin suspected (in *Scandia* 1954, p. 228) that the increased mortality from the year 1736 onwards observed by Heckscher only depended on the annual reports which, he thought, were more reliable than the data requested subsequently. His theory is refuted by the Finnish congregational history books, from which the same change is apparent in the population movement about 1736. *Cf.* also Sv.-U. Palme, Befolkningsutvecklingen som bakgrund till partiomvälvningen 1738, *Scandia* 1960, p. 312.

of it. When full years have been interpolated, the calculation of the mean values for the two adjacent years has not been satisfactory, for a gap may occur in a year during which the local death rate or birth rate was exceptionally high or low. In such cases the interpolation has been based on figures for parishes in the same province with complete information. If either figure, for births or deaths, has been known, the other has been calculated on the assumption that the ratio of births and deaths in the parish concerned was the same as in those parishes of the province for which both figures were recorded.[2] There are so few cases of interpolation per year that even considerable mistakes in estimation, which may lead to incorrect results in the calculation of the population of an individual parish, do not appreciably affect the overall picture for the province. The year 1721, when on 30 August, the Uusikaupunki Peace was concluded, has been omitted, or rather, it has been referred to the preceding period, for the extremely low figures in many parish reports for this year, and the dates in the 'history books', combine to indicate that many rectors started the congregational book-keeping only after the Russian occupation had ended in the autumn. In addition, a considerable proportion of the Ostrobothnian, and the bulk of the Åland Islands population, were in exile and could not return instantly. The figures for the subsequent years, on the other hand, may be taken as relatively reliable, and the low birth and death rates were not, as certain eighteenth-century specialists believed, the result of the continued effect of the exceptional circumstances of the years on congregational bookkeeping.[3]

The first period of the century, the years 1700-21, was a time of uninterrupted war. There are no direct demographic sources available for this period other than the 'history books', and even in these there are more gaps than are to be found in the following decades. Besides, almost all persons of standing and a part of the west coast peasantry were in exile during 1713-21, and no records of their births and deaths were kept in the books of their Finnish parish. Nor were the soldiers killed entered in their parish registers of the buried, but their approximate total can be obtained since the approximate number of recruits is known and since the Finnish troops were practically annihilated by the end of the war. No satisfactory information is available on the total of civilians that were, willingly, or by force, deported to Russia by the enemy during the occupation.

As a result of the variation in the source material the task of a student of Finland's eighteenth century demography assumes a different character in all three periods. For 1700-21, hardly more than a rough estimate can be hazarded of the extent to which the population decreased (or possibly increased) during the period; a high death rate and its annual fluctuations need no special comment. The period 1722-49 is the most interesting. For this period the task is twofold: first, the annual fluctuations in population must be studied and, on their basis, the population calculated retrospectively from the 1749 figure, always review-

[2] After the publication of the present writer's paper mentioned in Editor's note, authentic figures have been discovered for a few of the interpolated figures. These authentic figures, not unnaturally, differ somewhat from the interpolated. Since the present paper does not quote any figures for individual parishes and since the effect of corrections on the figures for the whole province or the whole country is insignificant, the unaltered figures of the earlier papers will be used here.

[3] C. Fr. Mennander, Afhandling om Åbo stifts tilväxt i folkrikhet på 30 år, *Kongl. Vetenskapsakad. Handlingar* 1769, p. 198.

ing the sources critically. Second, the results are so reliable and the rises and falls in the demographic curves so steep, that the reasons for the temporal and local variations in the population movement demand to be analysed.[4] From 1749 onwards, fairly reliable, complete statistics are available to the student. Almost the only problem that remains is to account for the causes of fluctuation in population.

Before the 'history books' and the reports submitted to the government in 1722-48[5] are utilized as a source for statistics, the reliability of this material must be checked even in those cases when it has been preserved intact.

To start with, it must be recognized that stillbirths are unlikely to have been included among the births: it should be remembered that the reports either represent, or are based on, registers of baptisms. Stillbirths may, however, have been included in the mortality figures.[6] Some 'history books' expressly mention stillbirths among the buried; but even if these records were scrutinized entry by entry they would not reveal all stillbirths as distinct from other deaths, since information is often incomplete or ambiguous. This problem finds its solution with the next uncertain item, which concerns the possible incompleteness of registers of the baptized and the buried.

Christening could and often did take place in the child's home, and for this reason alone the priest may have forgotten to enter it in the 'history book'. But a burial always took place in the church or the churchyard, and the registers of burials may be considered practically complete, while those of the baptized are not.[7] One should also bear in mind the purpose of congregational book-keeping: the priest wanted his books to show what people he had in his congregation and he was not interested in the population movement. If a child died and was buried before it had been christened or before it had been entered in the register of baptisms, the parish rector may have considered it superfluous to record the name in the book which he consulted, if necessary, for information on the living members of his congregation. Efforts were made to have the child christened soon after birth, and not later than the third day,[8] but the interval from christening to recording the entry may have been long. When Rector Th. Pacchalenius, of Vanaja, was arrested for political reasons in the autumn of 1748, his deputy had to make the entries in the register of baptisms right from the beginning of the year on the basis of notes left by Pacchalenius; 'but whether one or another such note has gone astray is not known'.[9]

Our assumption of the incompleteness of the register of baptisms cannot be based on mere theoretical suspicion or on an exceptional instance from the congregation of Vanaja. Fortunately enough, it can be proved or disproved by an analysis of source material, and the number of births missing from the register

[4] An attempt to do both is included in the papers entitled 'Hämeen väestöolot Uudenkaupungin rauhasta taulustolaitoksen alkuun (1721-49)', *Tilastollisia Tiedonantoja* 36, 1939, and 'Die Bevölkerung Finnlands in den Jahren 1721-49', *Ann. Acad. Scient. Fenn.* B., LV 4, 1945.

[5] The data quoted below on 1749 births and deaths were taken from unpublished 'Tabellverket' reports.

[6] *Cf.* Heckscher, l.c., pp. 261-2, and A. Jensen, 'Befolkningsforhold i de nordiske Lande i det 18 Aarhundrede', *Nationaløkonomisk Tidskr.* 1935, p. 5.

[7] The same observation made in Denmark by G. Bang, *Kirkebogstudier*, 1906, pp. 107-9.

[8] M. Juva, *Varsinais-Suomen seurakuntaelämä puhdasoppisuuden hallitsemina vuosisatoina* (1600-1808), 1955, pp. 111-12.

[9] 'History books' of the parish of Vanaja 1748.

of baptisms may even be roughly estimated. In some congregations, the ages and other illustrative particulars of the deceased were entered in the burial registers. I have made investigations in four such congregations over a period of 4-6 years, during which time their baptismal registers listed a total of 1,131 children. When the burial registers for the same period are consulted for the number of children who died unchristened, it is found that on this basis alone the total of births has to be increased by 2 per cent. In this way, admittedly, stillbirths, contrary to the usual custom, come to be included in the total of births—at least such stillbirths as have been buried by the church—but this method is indispensable for the calculation of the total population since not all stillbirths can in any case be eliminated from the total of deaths (see above). The comparison of the registers of baptisms and burials reveals other features, too. The names of the small children who died include several which cannot be traced in the baptismal registers. Apart from the cases already mentioned, 9 per cent of the total number of children in the parishes described above that had died before they had reached the age of one year were not to be found in the relevant parish's list of baptisms. If the study had been extended to include older children, identification would have presented greater difficulties but the result would hardly have changed. Naturally, there was among the agrarian communities of that period some migration from one parish to another. Owing to the vast extent of Finnish parishes, however, local interchanges remained largely within the parish, but in spite of this it is possible that some children who died in their first year had come into the parish with their immigrating parents from another congregation where they had been christened. For this reason, not all the 9 per cent difference can be blamed on carelessness in the baptismal register, but it might, perhaps, be judiciously cut to 8 per cent. When one adds the cases mentioned above as definitely missing from the registers the round figure arrived at for the error is 10 per cent.

A third factor which may limit the usefulness of the registers of baptisms and burials for the illustration of population changes is migration movement. Since the annual population totals are not known, the migration gains or losses of the various districts in 1722-49 cannot be calculated simply by comparing the totals and the natural population increase. Contemporary estimates of migration gains and losses for the administrative counties in the 1750's and 1760's [10] are based on this very method even though the results are made even less reliable by a fourth factor of error which will be described in detail below (p. 554). When these contemporary calculations claim that in 1722-56 the county of Nyland (Uusimaa), and Tavastia (Häme) suffered an annual migration loss of 0·6 per cent, the figure can be taken as a proved minimum, below which the migration loss cannot have fallen but which it may have slightly exceeded in reality. The only established fact about migration movement is that people from Finland —as from other parts of the kingdom—continuously emigrated to Stockholm. The annual migration gain secured by the capital between 1721 and 1750 averaged 1,006 persons, and between 1751 and 1755 2,165 persons.[11] Migration

[10] P. Wargentin, Undersökning om Folk-utflyttningen — — i anledning af Tabellverket för åren 1750, til och med året 1773, Sv.Vetenskapsakad. Nya Handlingar I, 1780. — A. Hjelt, De första officiela relationerna om svenska tabellverket 1749-1757, Fennia 16, pp. 57-69.
[11] Statistisk Årsbok för Stockholm 1905, p. 71.

from the county of Nyland and Tavastia may be assumed to have increased to the same extent as that from other parts of the kingdom, and the migration loss of the county in 1722–49 thus averaged about 0·3 per cent per year. People from everywhere moved to Stockholm: in 1761 a civil servant from Savo requested that the burghers of the coastal towns be forbidden to transport in their ships people who 'ran away' from the eastern interior of Finland to the capital.[12] If the ratio of 0·3 per cent per year is applied to the whole of Finland, the two big factors of error eliminate each other: the total births were probably higher than those that will be quoted below for different years and in different provinces, but Finland lost annually an equal number of people through migration.

The migration between Finnish counties does not affect the population of Finland as a whole, but may upset the retrospective calculations of the population in the different counties and consequently their nativity and mortality rates. According to reports given by some local crown officials for a couple of years and a statement by one Ostrobothnian parish rector, it has been estimated, that some 120–50 persons annually migrated from Central Finland to Ostrobothnia.[13] However, this estimate is very unreliable, and if such a copious flow of migrants had moved to Ostrobothnia during the whole period, the earlier population of this county should have been correspondingly lower, with the result that the birth rates would have risen to phenomenal heights, especially in the 1720's.

In the static agrarian community of the Finland of that time, one may not reasonably assume that one province would make any appreciable migration gain at the expense of another. Without any major errors, the population totals of individual provinces can therefore be calculated back from 1749 to 1721 in the same way as those for the whole of Finland, i.e. by adding the dead and subtracting the children born. It must be assumed, it is true, that emigration to Sweden was greatest from the coast and smallest from the interior of the country, while at the same time, the baptismal registers were more complete in the small coastal than in the extensive inland parishes. As a result of the influence of these two factors the growth of population was slightly slower on the coast and slightly quicker in the interior than reported in my calculations. The only reasonable-sized city in Finland, Turku, with a population of some 6,000 at the end of the period, must be discussed separately from the surrounding province of Finland Proper. Its death rate, like that of other European cities at that time, was extremely high, and it already needed migration gains to maintain its population level. Immigrants were obviously provided by all the other parishes of the country, containing in all some 400,000 inhabitants.[14] Their migration loss in favour of Turku is divided among such a high number of inhabitants that it is without significance in the calculations.

A fourth error factor, already referred to above, is the possibility that incorrect figures were quoted by the clergy when they reported in 1749 for the

[12] K. Wirilander, *Savo kaskisavujen kautena*, 1960, p. 64.
[13] Y. S. Koskimies, Muuttoliikkeestä Suomessa 1700-luvun alkupuoliskolla, *Hist. Aikakauskirja* 1954, pp. 142–6.
[14] Migration from Tavastia to Turku shown by Y. S. Koskimies in *Lounais-Hämeen kotiseutu-ja museoyhd. vuosikirja* XXI, 1952.

first time on the total population of their parish.[15] The increase, far exceeding the natural increase, in the population totals of the subsequent reports (1751, 1754, 1757, etc.) suggests that the clergy, when working out the first report, did not have information about all parishioners, since the alternative explanation— a migration gain in Finland—can hardly be entertained. This assumption is supported in particular by the observation that the differences were greater for remote sparsely populated districts, where contact between the parish priest and the congregation was necessarily less close than in more central districts with a denser population. If the population totals reported 20 years after the establishment of the 'Tabellverket' were roughly correct, it may be estimated that the

TABLE I

Births, deaths and marriages in Finland, 1722-1749

	Births	Deaths	Natural increase	Birth rate	Death rate	Natural increase	Marriage rate
				per thousand of the mean annual population			
1722	8,764	6,664	2,100	30·2	23·0	7·2	12·2
1723	9,914	5,911	4,003	33·8	20·2	13·6	11·6
1724	10,347	5,695	4,652	34·7	19·1	15·6	9·6
1725	9,997	5,658	4,339	33·1	18·7	14·4	9·2
1726	10,327	5,733	4,594	33·7	18·7	15·0	9·1
1727	11,166	6,271	4,895	35·8	20·1	15·7	8·9
1728	12,100	6,142	5,958	38·2	19·4	18·8	10·7
1729	12,830	7,633	5,197	39·8	23·7	16·1	9·8
1730	12,642	7,214	5,428	38·6	22·0	16·6	9·3
1731	13,216	7,273	5,943	39·6	21·8	17·8	8·8
1732	12,099	7,137	4,962	35·7	21·1	14·6	7·4
1733	12,553	7,119	5,434	36·5	20·7	15·8	8·6
1734	13,842	7,291	6,551	39·5	20·8	18·7	9·0
1735	14,232	7,919	6,313	39·9	22·2	17·7	8·7
1736	15,127	9,242	5,885	41·7	25·5	16·2	8·5
1737	14,989	12,888	2,101	40·9	35·2	5·7	8·4
1738	15,404	10,525	4,879	41·6	28·4	13·2	8·1
1739	15,247	11,950	3,297	40·7	31·9	8·8	7·4
1740	14,153	19,408	− 5,255	37·9	52·0	− 14·1	7·3
1741	13,306	11,741	1,565	35·8	31·6	4·2	6·2
1742	10,011	16,806	− 6,795	27·2	45·6	− 18·4	6·0
1743	10,561	13,864	− 3,303	29·0	38·1	− 9·1	8·1
1744	13,135	9,108	4,027	36·1	25·0	11·1	11·2
1745	15,852	8,273	7,579	42·9	22·4	20·5	11·8
1746	15,619	7,753	7,866	41·4	20·5	20·9	9·8
1747	15,224	9,116	6,108	39·6	23·7	15·9	8·9
1748	15,238	11,967	3,271	39·1	30·7	8·4	9·1
1749	16,730	11,589	5,141	42·5	29·5	13·0	9·5

[15] Sundbärg, an expert on Swedish population statistics whose corrections have assumed a semi-official character, considers the 1749 figures correct and adds 1 per cent to the total population, only because information is missing for a few parishes. Hj. Gullberg-G. Sundbärg, 'Folkmängden och folkökningen i Skandinavien 1815-1880, Statistisk Tidskrift 1882, supplement p. 4. — C. E. Quensel, Tillförlitligheten i de äldsta befintliga befolkningsdata, Minneskrift med anledning av den svenska befolkningsstatistikens 200-åriga bestånd, 1949, pp. 12, 23.

The Greek-Orthodox population in Finland was evidently generally excluded, but within the then Kingdom of Sweden their numbers were very small. G. Fougstedt-A. Raivio, Suomen väestön sääty ja ammattiryhmitys 1751-1805, Tilastollisia Tiedonantoja 40, 1953, p. 9.

official population in 1749 was 3 per cent less than the actual population.[15a]

Fifth, it is not clear which turn of the year the reported population totals refer to—it might be the beginning or the end of the year or the rectors may have worked out their sums, as one of their contemporaries put it, 'whenever it was most convenient for them'. Some completed congregational forms show indisputably that the figures referred to the end of the year, and a contemporary demographer, Wargentin, states that a high death rate one year had a reducing effect on the population total for that very year.[16] The population tables of 1749, and those of the subsequent years, must therefore be considered as indicating the population total at the end of the year.

Finally, it must be pointed out that all calculations refer to the Finnish area that belonged to the kingdom of Sweden in 1749 (cf. p. 568).

II

Demographic fluctuations of the period 1722-49 are easier to grasp if the period is divided into four shorter periods. The first, that of post-war recovery, extends to 1728. At the outset, annual crops[17] were satisfactory but at the end of the period, especially in 1726, they were poor.[18] Birth rates (Table 1) were initially low, but rose without interruption (1722: 30·2 per thousand, 1728: 38·2 per thousand). The average marriage rate was as high as 10·2 per thousand, but was on a slow decline. This was a surprisingly low mortality rate for l'ancien régime; as can be seen from Table 2, it was even lower than in the ten counties of Sweden for which Heckscher has collected information. Excluding the first post-war year, when conditions had not yet been restored to normal, the mortality rate varied within narrow limits (18·7 per thousand to 20·2 per thousand).

The population movement of this period can be explained by the exceptional age structure which was the outcome of the serious famine of 1696-7[19] and of the Great Northern War. The dreadfully high mortality in the year of famine, possibly no less than 30 per cent, had made the greatest breach in the then youngest age groups born in the 1690's. In the 21-year war, nearly 20 per cent of Finland's population had been killed in action, and the longer the war lasted the fewer were the young men left at home. After peace had returned, men born in the 1670's, 1680's and 1690's obviously constituted very narrow strata in the population pyramid. This theoretical assumption is supported by the age and sex distribution of the 1749 population which showed such anomalies as, for instance, that among the 60-65 age group (those born 1685-9) there were

[15a] When birth rates for different years and different provinces are discussed below, the 10 per cent correction justified in the text has not been made to the figures for births. On the other hand, the total population figures in these calculations have not been raised by the 3 per cent justified deficiency (p. 12), which tends to make the birth and death rates slightly higher than they actually were.

[16] Wargentin, l.c., p. 249. Cf. the figures in Heckscher, l.c., Tables III and V.

[17] The criterion employed for the harvest results is a temporary rise or fall of grain prices. The best source for fluctuations in grain prices consisted of the so-called 'markegång' prices, fixed for each county at the end of the year after the harvest was generally known, and applied to money payment of taxes assessed in kind. As long as the value of money was stable (until 1745) they were at least sufficient as evidence of whether the harvest in the relevant county or the whole kingdom had been better or worse than that of the previous year. For 'markegång' prices of grain since 1731, see V. F. Johansson, Verohinnat Suomessa 1731-1870, Tilastokatsauksia 7-8, 1926; for earlier years information was obtained from Finnish State Record Office and Provincial Record Office at Turku.

[18] Cf. Heckscher, Sveriges ekonomiska historia II: 1, 1949, pp. 34-35.

[19] E. Jutikkala, 'The great Finnish famine 1696-97', Scand. Econ. Hist. Rev., 1955.

43 per cent more women than men. The assumption is similarly confirmed by the wartime 'history books' sporadically preserved; according to their records, marriages were exceedingly rare during the period of occupation, even if, in addition to the population structure, the abnormal and restless times naturally made the conclusion of marriage difficult.

When peace had returned, the population therefore contained exceptionally few young married couples, a large number of old people, especially widows, and many young persons aged 10-25 years. The marriage rate rose to a very high level in the immediate post-war years, because marriages postponed during the war were now concluded. The rate remained high, since the marriageable age was annually reached by age groups which were young enough to have avoided a thinning out of male members by war[20] but were, on the other hand, old enough to have escaped the reducing effect of war at birth and infancy. These conclusions are supported by the fact that the birth rate, in spite of the high marriage rate, at first remained relatively low but continued to increase. In the marriages of *l'ancien régime*, the actual reproductive period normally lasted a dozen to a score years after the wedding, and the low number of marriages concluded in the 1710's thus still exercised a minimizing effect on births in the 1720's. In these circumstances, the proportion of children in the population was, of necessity, exceptionally low, and bearing in mind the exceedingly high mortality of the youngest age group at that time[21] and the deviation of the age structure from the normal level in *l'ancien régime*, the low mortality rates of the 1720's can be satisfactorily accounted for. There is no need to appeal to popular and only semi-scientific assertions such as the claim that war had eliminated all the members of the population of insufficient stamina.[22] After the deep wounds inflicted first by the famine in the 1690's and then by prolonged war, there is no reason to assume that any population pressure existed in Finland. As soon as deserted farms could again be cultivated, enough food could be produced for the growing population. The poor crop of 1726[23] produced no reduction in births the following year and only a very slight increase in mortality. In some provinces the mortality even dropped, and if it rose heavily in Finland Proper, the cause was probably a local epidemic. The crop failure had not been caused by frost, as was usually the way in Finland, but by drought. Besides, the following winter was mild, and usually, a long cold winter, irrespective of whether the supply of food was adequate or not, increased the susceptibility to epidemics and so increased mortality.[24] There was, however, an obvious correlation between the good crop and the high marriage rate of 1728.[25]

[20] Apart from guerilla bands, the Swedish army could raise levies in Finland for the last time in 1713-14. Some 2000 men were levied for the Russian army in 1720, the majority of whom were soon executed for contumacy.

[21] From 'history books' in which the ages of the dead were recorded, it can be calculated that often more than half those buried were children under the age of 5.

[22] Some value is also attached to them by Utterström, 'Population problems in pre-industrial Sweden', *Scand. Econ. Hist. Rev.*, 1954, p. 114.

[23] Even in the Diet it was announced that crop failures had occurred e.g. in Finland, Utterström, l.c., p. 115.

[24] Utterström, l.c., p. 115.

[25] Since, according to a study of Nyland, two-thirds of all marriages (P. Tommila, Hääpäivän määrääminen vanhan talonpoikaisyhteiskunnan aikana, *Kalevalaseuran Vuosikirja* 1960, p. 244) were concluded in the autumn, the harvest of the year affected the marriage rate of the current year.

In 1729-36, the numerous marriages concluded in the preceding period raised the birth rate. The marriage rate still remained at a fairly high level (average, 8·8 per thousand) but was on the decrease, for the small age groups born during the worst years of the war or during the Russian occupation now began to reach marriageable age. Nevertheless, all prerequisites still remained for a continued rise in the birth rate, and rise it did, reaching a record figure, 41·7 per thousand, in the last year of the period. The proportion of children in the population increased, and with it the mortality rate, though it nevertheless remained below that of the ten Swedish counties (Table 2). Grain prices were exceptionally low and, judging by this, crops were obviously good, especially around 1730, but only occasionally in some province can any correlation be noted between crop fluctuations and population movement. The highest mortality rates of the period are for the year 1736 which, in the Aland Islands and Finland Proper, marked the transition to the next period unfavourable for population increase, and for the year 1729, when an influenza epidemic is known to have raged both in Russia and in Sweden,[26] whence it evidently spread to Finland.

Very different in character from the two preceding periods in Finland's demographic history is the period covering the years 1737-43; quite different factors determined its course. The influence of an abnormal age structure cannot, admittedly, be overlooked here either; the small age groups born during the years of occupation in 1713-21 reached marriageable age, and as a result of this, and the short new war, the marriage rate dropped to 7·3 per thousand. Yet the numerous marriages of the preceding period kept the birth rate at such a high level that in the first three years the 40 per thousand limit was passed. The bottom layer of the population pyramid was exceedingly broad, and mortality therefore tended to increase.[27] More visible than these remote-controlled phenomena, however, are the exceedingly strong effects of certain temporary factors on the most sensitive spot in population movement, mortality. During this period, more people died than were born in Finland and in the ten Swedish counties; in Finland both the birth rate and the mortality rate were higher than in Sweden.

One of the central and most interesting problems of Finland's population history in the eighteenth century is the cause of this rise in mortality which in 1737 reached the high level of 35·2 per thousand, while the year before, a sudden increase in deaths had been observed in Sweden and in the westernmost parts of Finland. It is true that grain prices rose slightly in 1736, but the following autumn the rise was arrested in one part of the country and turned into a fall in another. No available information suggests famine—on the contrary, county governors described the crops as very good[28]—but we learn from the comments, often colourful, attached by the clergy to the reports submitted to the government (at that particular time quarterly) that a severe epidemic had spread in 1736 to the Aland Islands, the Turku Archipelago, and the south-western and southern coast of the country, and that the year after it went on to spread throughout the country. The disease was characterized by recurrent feverish attacks, and contemporaries took it to be malaria (febris intermittens). Subse-

---

[26] Utterström, l.c., p. 113.   [27] Utterström, l.c., p. 132.   [28] *Historiallinen Arkisto* VIII, p. 368.

quent medical research, however, has shown that malaria has occurred in only a few districts in Finland where epidemics have recurred in the spring and autumn of several years, and that it was not accompanied by a high mortality rate. The 1737 epidemic came from the west, raged throughout every month of the year, spread throughout the country, produced a high mortality rate, then disappeared completely for a long time.[29] The descriptions by the clergy indicate, in fact, that the disease was no intermittent fever but either relapsing fever (typhus recurrens), in which up to two-thirds of the patients may die if their conditions are poor hygienically, or a severe influenza with widely varied symptoms.[30]

In Heckscher's opinion, the phase of high mortality that began in Sweden in 1736 could be accounted for by over-population and a drop in the standard of living, for undernourished people were more susceptible to epidemics and had less stamina than they had had in the period of wellbeing that had just ended. An epidemic may account for the steepness of the demographic swing, but not for the existence of a turn in population movement. 'Nature balanced accounts with a red pen.'[31] For Finland at least it seems doubtful whether there was any surplus to be deducted from the accounts; it is not certain that the growth in population had been so rapid that agricultural production was outstripped. It is also probable that in the previous years nature would not have had a red pen in her hand in case of need, since no dangerous epidemics had occurred in Northern Europe. That the fundamental causes of the turn in popu- lation movement were biological and not economic is suggested by the fact that morbidity and mortality rates in 1736-7 also rose dramatically along the southern and eastern coasts of the Baltic. Moreover, if resistance to disease had been lowered, unfavourable weather conditions may have been the direct cause even when they were not accompanied by a shortage of food.[32] Admittedly, neither relapsing fever nor the various influenzas—nor the dysentery nor the spotted fever that raged in subsequent years—leave a permanent immunity,[33] which explains why smallpox epidemics occur cyclically. But the sudden occur- rence of these diseases after a long interval may have been provoked by un- known biological factors, independent, to a considerable extent, of human nutritional condition.

In the years 1738 and 1739 the mortality rate in Finland was slightly lower than in 1737, about 30 per thousand. From the vague descriptions in reports made by the clergy, it can be gathered that, in addition to typhus diseases and dysentery which had been dormant for roughly 40 years,[34] smallpox, measles

[29] Medical-historical literature on malaria and relapsing fever: F. J. Rabbe, 'Några anteckningar om frossan i Finland samt botemedlen däremot', *Finska Läkaresällsk. handlingar* VI, 1856-7; O. Hjelt, 'Das Vorkommen des Wechselfiebers in Finnland', *Archiv. für pathologische Anatomie* 65, 1875; F. A. Bergman, *Om Sveriges folksjukdomar II*, 1875, pp. 141, 173; R. Sievers, 'Om frossan i Finland', *Finska Läkaresällsk. handlingar* XXXIII, 1891, pp. 568, 612-3, 728; O. T. Hult, 'Forschungen über das Auftreten des Typhus recurrens in Schweden', *Nordiskt medicinskt Arkiv* II: 12, 14, 1913, pp. 55, 64, 102-6, 109.

[30] The disease was considered to be influenza by Utterström, l.c., p. 124.

[31] Heckscher, *Ekonomisk-historiska studier*, p. 269; idem, *Sveriges ekonomiska historia* II:2, pp. 36, 38.

[32] Utterström, l.c., pp. 121-5.

[33] Utterström claims (p. 136) that no immunity existed because epidemics had not occurred for a long time.

[34] Utterström, l.c., p. 126.

and diphtheria had been common. The proportion of young people in the population was high, and they had not been through previous smallpox, measles or diphtheria epidemics, which would have rendered them immune. In Ostrobothnia, so many children died in 1739 that even if no one over the age of 5 had fallen victim, the mortality rate would still have exceeded 20 per thousand, while in the following year the child mortality alone raised the rate above the 30 per thousand limit. In 1740, the mortality rate of the entire country reached no less than 52 per thousand. The main causes were dysentery and spotted fever which spread among the civilian population from Swedish troops billeted in the south-western parts of Finland.

The 1740 crop was poor, and in the summer of 1741 war (the War of the Hats) broke out against Russia. Although both these factors might be expected to have increased civilian mortality in 1741,[35] the mortality rate in four south-Finnish provinces dropped to a lower level than in any one year since 1735,[36] even though, for the country as a whole, it remained at more than 30 per thousand because of the epidemics still raging in the northern provinces. In the following two years, as war rolled across the country spreading diseases, mortality rates rose to very high levels and birth rates were lower than they had ever been during the period 1722-49. The decline in the birth rate was due in part to the exceptionally low marriage rate in 1741-2 but, as has already been pointed out, changes in the marriage rate can explain only to a small extent the rise or fall in the number of births registered for the following year. The total number of men levied for military service was so small that it could not exert any appreciable effect on the birth rate, and once the Finnish army had surrendered the men were demobilized. Furthermore, the decrease in the marriage rate was roughly the same throughout Finland, and men had been levied evenly from all parts of the country, whereas the fall in the birth rate was clearly very uneven in different provinces. Over the whole country the drop from the 1741 to the 1742 level was 24 per cent, and to the 1743 level, 19 per cent, but in Nyland the figure for 1741-2 was 42 per cent, in Aland for 1741-3, 44 per cent. In these very provinces and in these same years, the mortality rates soared to terrifying heights. It seems, therefore, that an important, if not the most important, factor responsible for the reduction in the birth rate during the war was morbidity.

After the conclusion of peace, in the period 1744-9, the number of men and women reaching marriageable age could not, initially, be particularly high. Yet the average marriage rate was as high as 10·0 per thousand, a figure essentially affected by the wartime postponement of potential marriages to the post-war years 1744-5. Towards the end of the period, the influence of the large age groups born in the latter half of the 1720's and spared serious epidemics during childhood, began to be felt in the marriage markets. It can be no coincidence that the highest marriage rates are evident in North and East Finland where the

[35] War casualties are not shown in the burial registers but they were not numerous, because throughout this languidly-waged war there was, apart from slight skirmishing, only one major battle. Judging from the exceedingly high mortality rates of the parishes along the frontier of the northern wilderness in 1742, however, the peasants killed in local fighting were entered in the registers of the buried.

[36] The effect of undernourishment in Finland was hardly as important as Utterström (l.c., pp. 121, 127) estimated for Sweden.

birth rates for 1722-8 were higher than elsewhere. At no time after the War of Hats did the mortality rate sink to the level it had reached after the Great Northern War, although again it was lower in Finland than in Sweden. The gap in the age pyramid of the 25-40 year olds—whose mortality risk is relatively low—reduced the chances of lowering mortality. In the first four years mortality remained at the 1729-36 level, but it rose sharply in 1748. Since a particularly steep rise was evident in the city of Turku as early as 1747, it was obviously caused again by an epidemic arriving from the west. The type of epidemic is not known with any certainty, but it may have been smallpox. In any case, the 1749 mortality rate varied considerably from parish to parish, and where there were peak figures the majority of the deaths were, according to information provided by the clergy, from smallpox. Apart from some minor epidemics in 1738, smallpox had not occurred in the country for a long time, and as a result very few people had acquired immunity to it.[37] Increased grain prices in Finnish counties in the autumn of 1747 are no evidence of crop failure but were the result partly of a drop in the value of money and partly of the poor crop harvested in Sweden. The tone of reports issued by Finnish county governors was not complaining.[38] The negligible drop in the marriage rate and the birth rate is explicable as a reaction to the temporary rise that had followed the conclusion of peace, and there is no reason to see it as the result of harvest conditions.

III

During the 30 years following the Great Northern War, Finland's population history shows violent fluctuations both in the marriage rate and the birth rate, but particularly in the mortality rate. They can all be traced to the age structure of the population, highly abnormal even at the beginning of the period, or to its spontaneous changes, or to wars and epidemics. Variations in the harvest and the possible shortage of food they caused, do not seem to have affected population movement appreciably. Although it must be remembered that the climatic conditions in the second quarter of the eighteenth century were particularly favourable and no severe crop failures occurred, the *details* of Finnish demographic history in the period 1722-49 do not seem to confirm the Malthusian-Heckscherian theory of surplus population.

Even so, this theory cannot be overlooked. In the same way as the student of short-term business fluctuations will observe phenomena and factors different from those seen by the student of such secular trends as the 40-year waves noted between the Napoleonic wars and the Second World War, a study of the general features of population movements in Finland during *l'ancien régime* reveals that the growth of population depended ultimately on economic factors —on the expansion of agricultural production—and that excessive growth of population was always succeeded by a thinning arranged in one way or another by Nature.[39] Catastrophes recurred at roughly 30-year intervals and afflicted

---

[37] Utterström reports cases of smallpox in Sweden in 1736, 1741 and 1743 (l.c., pp. 125-6), but it is not known whether the disease spread to Finland.

[38] *Historiallinen Arkisto VIII*, p.370.—M. Kovero, 'Katovuosista Suomessa Ruotsin vallan aikana isonvihan jälkeen', *Kansantal. Aikakauskirja 1945*, pp. 409-10.

[39] In his study otherwise critical of Heckscher, Utterström also admits the ultimate importance of economic factors (l.c., p. 147).

the Finnish nation with a shocking inevitability, at least for the periods for which regular information about population exists. This frequently continued up to the 1860's when a slow industrialization began (Diagram 1). The 'lean' years, however, could not fully offset the growth of the 'fat' years, as they did in the Central European countries. The periodicity in the birth rate was doubtless a sequel of the age structure[40]; the total number of men and women reaching marriageable age varied from one decade to another, depending both on the birth rate 20-30 years earlier and on whether the age class concerned had been spared serious epidemics in childhood. Abnormalities in the age structure, however, are insufficient, if not inadmissible to account for the steeper fluctuations in mortality. It is only during the period 1722-49 that the typical 30-year cycle is not observed, for the 'lean' years had already come after 15 years of 'fat'.

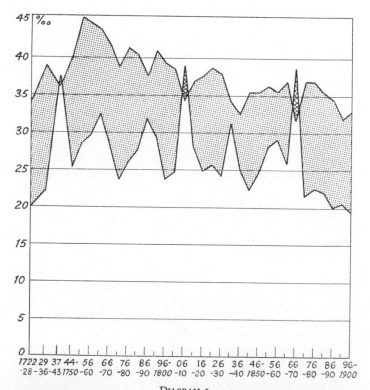

DIAGRAM I
Birth-rate (upper line), death-rate (lower line) and natural increase (or decrease) in five-year-periods in Finland 1722-1900.

The validity of the Malthusian-Heckscherian theory for the general features of Finland's population history in the eighteenth century can, however, be also verified in the period 1722-49 *by comparing geographical districts*. Table 2 shows how great the differences were between demographic conditions in the various districts. In the south-western mainland provinces, which had suffered comparatively little from the Great Northern War, and where the fertile Fin-

[40] *Cf.* H. E. Pipping, 'Befolkning och näringar i Sverige och Finland under 1700-talet', *Ekonomisk Tidskrift 1950*, pp. 158-62.

land Proper had pulled through the year of great famine with fairly low population losses,[41] the growth of population in the period 1722-49 was poorest: in Tavastland it was 28 per cent, in Nyland 29 per cent, in Finland Proper (excluding Turku) 33 per cent, and in Satakunta 37 per cent. For the eastern interior, i.e. Savo and Carelia, which had suffered most heavily from the war and, because of greater susceptibility to frosts, had evidently suffered also from the years of famine in the 1690's, the corresponding figures were 41 per cent; for Ostrobothnia, 51 per cent; and for Aland, which had been totally devastated by the war, 64 per cent. All these percentages have been calculated, as was seen from the critical review of source material, after excluding migration movements. Where the gaps inflicted by catastrophe were greatest, there the population could expand more, by bringing back into use the economic resources previously enjoyed, that is, by working the deserted farms. In no province did birth and mortality rates—studied according to the four periods for 1722-49 as outlined above, or year by year—remain as steady as in Satakunta, and although the birth rates of Satakunta remained lower than the average for the whole country, the growth of population in the province from 1721 to 1749, 37 per cent, exceeded that for the whole country, which was 33 per cent. This excellent result was due to the chances of clearing new land on the clay plains, chances that existing techniques were able to exploit.[42] It might also be mentioned that, after the War of Hats, the birth rate in Savo and Carelia, a district which had suffered particularly badly from the war, reached a peak and even passed the figures for Aland and Ostrobothnia where the birth rate usually was the highest in the country.

The demographic development of Ostrobothnia differs from that of all the other provinces of Finland, and even from that of Aland and the eastern interior, in that the birth rate immediately after the Great Northern War reached a high level, over 40 per thousand and there it remained.[43] The difference in the marriage rate was much smaller even though in 1722-8 it was slightly higher in Ostrobothnia than in the country as a whole (10·7 per thousand). The high birth rate in Ostrobothnia in the 1720's can be explained to a lesser degree by assuming that marriages were concluded between very young people as soon as the war ended, in order to get the exceptionally numerous deserted farms inhabited. The high birth rate, at that time and later, was mainly a result of the high number of children per marriage—higher than in the rest of Finland. In Ostrobothnia, the women were largely responsible for agricultural work and hardly ever lactated their children, with the result that infant mortality was exceptionally high.[44] The short duration of the lactation may have accelerated the birth

[41] Unpublished treatise by a student of mine, S. Muroma.

[42] Cf. H. Hassel-J. Velin, *Velmente tankar om landthushållningens förbettrande i Finland*, 1751, p. 5.

[43] In my work *Die Bevölkerung Finnlands* (pp. 22, 23, 55) I attributed this to the fact that Ostrobothnia had not lost so many men in the war as had other parts of Finland, and in the Ostrobothnian age pyramid the steps representing the 25-50 year old male population were not therefore so narrow as they were elsewhere in Finland. This assertion may not hold good. The military burden, it is true, was originally lighter in Ostrobothnia than in the southern provinces (A. J. Alanen, *Etelä-Pohjanmaan historia* IV: 1, 1948, p. 15) but some parishes lost as irregulars in the single battle of Isokyrö up to half their grown male population (l.c., p. 119).

[44] Mennander, l.c., p. 206.—H. Tegengren, *Kronoby sockens historia*, 1943, pp. 172-3.—E. W. Juvelius, 'Muutamia tietoja vastasyntyneitten lasten ruokkimisesta Suomessa 1750-luvulla', *Hist. Aikakauskirja* 1921, p. 249.

TABLE 2

Analysis by period and areas

	1722-28 Birth rate	1722-28 Death rate	1722-28 Natural increase	1729-36 Birth rate	1729-36 Death rate	1729-36 Natural increase	1737-43 Birth rate	1737-43 Death rate	1737-43 Natural increase	1744-49 Birth rate	1744-49 Death rate	1744-49 Natural increase
Finland Proper (SW)	31·0	22·5	8·5	38·4	22·7	15·7	37·7	33·1	4·6	37·0	25·7	11·3
Aland (SW)	33·5	13·0	20·5	49·4	25·3	24·1	44·9	44·8	0·1	44·0	20·4	23·6
Satakunta (W)	33·4	20·0	13·4	38·1	20·5	17·6	32·4	32·8	-0·4	35·1	21·3	13·8
Tavastland (Western interior)	30·9	20·5	10·4	37·6	23·0	14·6	36·2	39·9	-3·7	38·0	24·2	13·8
Nyland (S)	31·7	19·4	12·3	35·4	20·8	14·6	34·0	37·7	-3·7	36·2	23·8	12·4
Central Finland, Savo, and Carelia (Eastern interior)	34·8	17·0	17·8	35·3	18·9	16·4	34·6	41·0	-6·4	46·2	24·0	22·2
Ostrobothnia (N)	42·7	21·4	21·3	47·0	26·1	20·9	39·8	38·5	1·3	44·6	30·4	14·2
Whole country (Turku included)	34·2	19·9	14·3	38·9	22·2	16·7	36·2	37·5	-1·3	40·3	25·3	15·0
Sweden (10 provinces, in 1737-49, the whole country)	30·5	20·8	9·7	30·5	22·7	7·8	32·3	35·0	-2·7	33·8	26·1	7·7

of the next child, irrespective of whether it depended on high infant mortality or a local custom.[45] The Ostrobothnian birth rate, calculated according to the 'history books', exceeded the 50 per thousand limit in two years and if those omitted from the 'history books' (10 per cent, *cf.* p. 553) are included, in nine

DIAGRAM 2

Population movement in Nyland

——— Birth rate   - - - - - Death rate   ——— Marriage rate
—·—·— The tariff price for rye, fixed at the end of the previous year (copper *taler* per barrel)

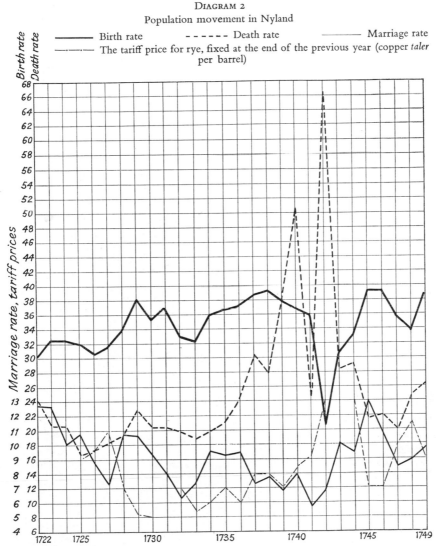

years (see Diagram 3). The average number of surviving children in an Ostrobothnian family, however, did not exceed the figure for the rest of Finland to the same extent as did the number of children born per marriage. Admittedly, there was a difference also in that the natural population increase was quicker in Ostrobothnia than elsewhere in Finland: in the period 1722–8 Ostrobothnia ranks first among the provinces, and during the whole period under review it was second only to Aland. According to the Malthusian-Heckscherian theory,

[45] *Cf.* P. Vincent, Recherches sur la fécondité biologique, *Population* 1961, p. 112, and L. Henry, La fécondité naturelle, *ibidem*, p. 633.

this is attributable to the exceptionally deep wounds inflicted on the civilian population of the province by the Great Northern War.

The Finnish birth rates and the figures for natural increase were higher than those for Sweden in three of the four periods into which the total period under review was divided, and when both countries in 1737-43 showed a natural decrease in population, the decrease was slighter in Finland than in Sweden. In the period 1751-1800 the average annual population increase in Finland was 13·2 per thousand, in Sweden 6·4 per thousand, in Norway 7·4 per thousand and in Denmark 2·8 per thousand. The average birth rates in these three Scandinavian countries were roughly the same (33·6, 32·4 and 31·0 per thousand), but in Finland the birth rate was 41·3 per thousand.[46] It may be asked whether the similarity of conditions prevailing in Sweden, Norway and Denmark and the persistent and obvious difference between these conditions and those of Finland, did not result from the fact that the populations of the former were closely related while the bulk of the Finnish population belonged to a different ethnic group. A geographical analysis of the demographic material for 1722-49 efficiently dismisses such a romantic assumption. A high birth rate, a rapid growth in population and steep fluctuations from one year to the next prove to be Finnish characteristics which are less strong in the Scandinavian countries, but in Finland they were most marked in Aland, which was inhabited exclusively by a Swedish-speaking population. The first two characteristics are found strongly marked in Ostrobothnia, where about a quarter of the population spoke Swedish. Inter-provincial demographic differences were smallest between Tavastia and Nyland. The former was purely Finnish-speaking, while two-thirds of the population of the latter spoke Swedish.[47]

Finland's more rapid population increase compared with that of the other Northern Countries cannot therefore be derived from mysterious racial characteristics, but it is satisfactorily accounted for by the Malthusian-Heckscherian theory. First, both the years of famine in the 1690's and the Great Northern War had cut more serious gaps in Finland's population than in that of Sweden. Second, Finland offered infinitely more opportunities for clearing new land, unutilized and cultivable even by primitive techniques, than did Sweden, not to mention Denmark. The rapid increase in population obviously did not, in the first half of the eighteenth century, produce in Finland a surplus population living at bare subsistence level, as was perhaps later the case, until the revolutionary development of forestry around 1870 began. This surplus population was one cause, maybe the most important, of the recurrent population catastrophes shown in Diagram 1.

[46] The figures are taken from Heckscher, *Sveriges ekonomiska historia* II: 1, p. 61. Heckscher has argued against the present writer's *Bevölkerung*, claiming that had the comparison between Finland and Sweden included the whole of Sweden, not merely the ten counties for which annual information exists, the difference between Finland and Sweden would diminish or even disappear, at least taking the period as a whole (*Sveriges ekonomiska historia* II:2, notes p. II). The first part of this assertion holds good only to a limited extent, and the latter part is invalid. The natural increase in population in Finland 1722-35 averaged 15·5 per thousand, in ten counties of Sweden 9·7 per thousand, and in the whole of Sweden 11·2 per thousand. Over the whole period 1722-49 (in Sweden, 1721-50), again, the respective figures were: 11·3 per thousand, 6·1 per thousand, and 7·2 per thousand.
[47] For the distribution of the population according to language see E. Gylling, *Statistiska bidrag till svenska folkstammens historia i Finland*, 1911, and H. Wallén, *Språkgränsen och minoriteterna i Finlands, svenskbygder omkr. 1600-1865*, 1932, pp. 145-7.

Since the birth rates in Finland were higher than those in Sweden, the bottom layer of the age pyramid in Finland was relatively broader than that in Sweden. This fact could not but raise the Finnish crude death rate; yet the death rate in Finland in the 17 years of the period 1722-49 was lower than that in Sweden, and higher in only 11 years.[48] Age-specific mortality rates, therefore, seem to have been lower in Finland than in Sweden. This fact, surprising as it may appear at first sight, was partly the result of the fact that there was no big city in Finland, while Stockholm, by contemporary standards, was a big city.

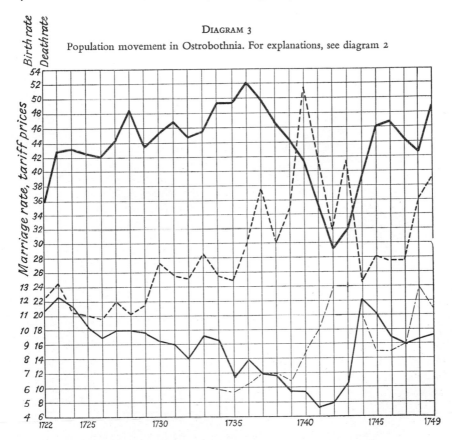

DIAGRAM 3

Population movement in Ostrobothnia. For explanations, see diagram 2

The capital of the country was a breeding ground for diseases, where regularly many more people died than were born. Yet Stockholm's population was only 2-3 per cent of the total population of Sweden, and the aggregate population of all Swedish towns (1760) amounted to only 9·4 per cent of the total; the corresponding figure for Finland was around 5 per cent.[49] Sweden was also an agricultural country, and the slight relative superiority of the urban population there, compared with Finland, does not suffice to account for the higher mortality.

[48] Up to 1735, the data for Sweden applied only to ten counties (Heckscher, *Ekonomisk-historiska studier*, p. 274).
[49] An exact figure cannot be calculated since the urban congregation and the subordinate rural congregation are often combined in one report. *Cf.* Heckscher, *Sveriges ekonomiska historia* II: 1, pp. 55-6.

IV

The sources for Finland's population history, and their reliability, may be of interest in international demographic research, as may also be the methods by which information of demographic history can be deduced from these sources. Above all, the demographic behaviour of a primitive agrarian community can be seen reflected in the calculated or estimated figures. Finland's actual population figures and their fluctuations in the eighteenth century are less likely to arouse interest, but if they are completely disregarded, we do less than justice to the title of this article.

By 1800, according to the already highly accurate data held by the 'Tabell-verket', the population of Finland totalled 833,000. In 1749, according to the earliest population tables, the total had been 405,000,[50] a figure that, on the basis of the argument put forward above (p. 556), should be raised by some 13,000. In half a century the population had doubled. If we calculate backwards from the year 1749, using the registers of burials and baptisms and assuming that migration losses and the incompleteness of the baptismal registers cancel out each other, we arrive at a population figure of 305,500 at the end of 1721. These people lived in the area which between 1743 and 1809 constituted Finland as a part of the Kingdom of Sweden. In the parishes ceded to Russia in the Peace of Turku, 1743, and the Peace of Uusikaupunki, 1721, there were, according to the Russian census of 1753, 105,000 inhabitants. If the percentage growth of population in this part of Finland (the western districts of which suffered from the War of Hats more heavily than any other part of Finland), is taken to be the same over the 32 years as it was over the 28 years in that part of Finland connected the whole time to Sweden, the population of these districts at the end of 1721 would have numbered 85,500, and that of all Finland, therefore, 391,000. This total would include the prisoners-of-war released by Russia only after the turn of the year, and the refugees who did not return from Sweden until 1722 or later.

The most reliable estimates suggest that approximately 60,000 men were levied from Finland for the Great Northern War. The Finnish army was practically annihilated: at the end of the war only a couple of thousand men were on the army rolls. To this number may be added the few thousand prisoners in Russia who lived to return home, a number of deserters, and those demobilized after heavy disablement. Total losses may be estimated at 50,000 men.[51] Did the increase among the civilian population offset these losses, or did the reduced birth rate, plague, famine and terrorism by the occupying forces bring about an inevitable reduction in the civilian population, too?

'History books' from the period of the Great Northern War are so sporadic that even partial calculations are not possible except for the south-western

---

[50] Contemporary and later calculations of Finland's population totals differ somewhat among themselves and from each other, obviously because it was not always known whether the population of a subordinate congregation was included in that of the mother congregation or whether it had to be added to it. In the present investigation, 405,000 was the figure from which retrospective calculation began.

[51] E. Hornborg, *Karolinen Armfelt och kampen om Finland under stora nordiska kriget*, 1953, pp. 317, 339.

provinces (Tavastia, Satakunta, Finland Proper, and Nyland),[52] and no other sources are available at all. For the 11 parishes of Tavastia, on which complete or almost complete data are preserved, the 1698 population—after the great famine—can be estimated at approximately three-quarters of the 1721 population, excluding war casualties. In spite of all negative factors, the number of births thus considerably exceeded the number of civilian deaths. The fundamental reason for this was the favourable age structure: the big age groups born in the 1680's had reached maturity at the beginning of the war and before enemy occupation, and many marriages had been concluded. A similar picture is gained from the other south-western mainland provinces, even though the depravations of bubonic plague in 1710 were greater in Nyland and Finland Proper than in Tavastia. Yet it must be remembered that in the districts for which no information is available the civilian population suffered much more from the war than did the above-mentioned provinces. It was precisely because the conditions were so chaotic that congregational bookkeeping was interrupted, while even earlier documents may have been destroyed. But since at least one half of Finland's population lived in the south-western mainland provinces, there is no doubt that the population may have increased during the war if war casualties are excluded. Yet the growth was by no means proportional to that of the 11 Tavastian parishes mentioned; if it had been, the increase in the civilian population would have been no less than 90,000. It is possible, however, that the increase did suffice to offset the sacrifices directly resulting from the war, and estimated above at 50,000 men.

[52] For Tavastia, Jutikkala, Tietoja ja arviointeja Hämeen väestöoloista vuosina 1690-1721, *Historiallinen Arkisto* L, 1944. For the other provinces, *cf.* unpublished study by a student of mine, R. Valpas.

24

FOUR CENTURIES OF ITALIAN DEMOGRAPHIC DEVELOPMENT

CARLO M. CIPOLLA

REASONABLY reliable figures for total Italian population begin in the sixteenth century. On the basis of a vast material carefully and patiently collected, K. J. Beloch could estimate the population of Italy to be 'at least 10 million and perhaps more' around 1500, about 11·6 million around 1550, about 11·5 million around 1650, about 13·4 million around 1700 and about 15·5 million around 1750.[1]

After Beloch's *Bevölkerungsgeschichte Italiens* numerous local studies on the demographic history of single regions or towns have brought new materials to light.[2] Although Beloch's results were left substantially unaltered, this more

---

* This chapter has been translated from the original Italian text by Mr David Rees to whom I would like to express my deep appreciation.

[1] K. J. Beloch, *Bevölkerungsgeschichte Italiens*, vol. 3, Berlin 1961, pp. 349-52.

[2] Among the numerous essays which have been published I will mention here only the most important ones.

For PIEDMONT:

G. Prato, 'Censimenti e popolazione in Piemonte nei secoli XVI, XVII e XVIII', in *Rivista Italiana di Sociologia*, 10 (1909); G. Melano, *La popolazione di Torino e del Piemonte nel secolo XIX*, Turin 1961; G. Muttini Conti, *La popolazione piemontese nel secolo XIX*, Turin 1962.

For LOMBARDY:

G. Mira, *Aspetti dell'economia comasca all'inizio dell'età moderna*, Como 1939; C. M. Cipolla, 'Per la storia della popolazione lombarda nel secolo XVI', in *Studi in onore di Gino Luzzatto*, Milano 1949; M. Romani, *Un secolo di vita economica lombarda*, Milano s.d.; M. Romani, 'Il movimento demografico in Lombardia dal 1750 al 1850', in *Economia e Storia*, 2 (1955); D. Sella, 'Premesse demografiche ai censimenti austriaci', in *Storia di Milano* (Fondaz. Treccani), t.12, Milano 1959; G. Aleati, *La popolazione di Pavia durante il dominio spagnolo*, Milano 1957.

For VENETO and FRIULI:

P. Fortunati, *Quattro secoli di vita del popolo friulano*, Padova 1932; D. Beltrami, *Storia della popolazione di Venezia dalla fine del secolo XVI alla caduta della Republica*, Padua 1954; D. Beltrami, *Saggio di storia dell'agricoltura della Republica di Venezia durante l'età moderna*, Vicenza 1955.

For LIGURIA:

G. Felloni, 'Per la storia della popolazione di Genova nei secoli XVI e XVII', in *Archivo Storico Italiano*, 110 (1952); G. Felloni, *Popolazione e sviluppo economico della Liguria nel secolo XIX*, Roma 1961.

For the EMILIA:

R. Zangheri, *Misure della popolazione e della produzione agricola nel dipartimento del Reno*, Bologna 1958; A. Bellettini, *La popolazione di Bologna dal secolo XV all'Unificazione Italiana*, Bologna 1961.

For TUSCANY:

G. Parenti, *La popolazione della Toscana sotto la Reggenza Lorense*, Florence 1937; P. F. Bandettini, *L'evoluzione demografica della Toscana dal 1810 al 1889*, Turin 1960.

For the PAPAL STATES:

F. Corridore, *La popolazione dello Stato Romano dal 1656 al 1901*, Rome 1904.

For the KINGDOM OF THE TWO SICILIES:

G. Coniglio, *Il Viceregno di Napoli nel secolo XVII*, Rome 1955; D. Demarco, *Il crollo del Regno delle Due Sicilie*, Naples 1960. C. Trasselli, 'Ricerche sulla popolazione della Sicilia nel XV secolo', *Atti Accad. Scienze, lettere ed arti di Palermo*, serie 4, vol. 15 (1954-5); L. Cassese, *La statistica del Regno di Napoli del 1811: relazione sulla Provincia di Salerno*, Salerno 1955; G. Galasso, 'Lineamenti di storia demografica dell' Italia meridionale dopo l'Unita (1861-1951)', *Atti Accad. Scienze Morali e Politiche*

TABLE I

Areas and populations of Italian regions 1550–1840
(Areas in thousands of sq. km., populations in millions)

Year	Piedmont		Lombardy		Veneto		Liguria		Tuscany		Papal States		Two Sicilies		Sardinia	
	a.	p.	a.	p.	a.	p.	a.	p.	a.	p.	a.	p.	a.	p.	a.	p.
1550	19	0·6	16	0·5	32	1·6	4	0·4		0·8	42	1·6	102	3·6		
1700	20	0·9	16	1·0	32	2·2	4	0·4	22	0·9	42	2·0	102	4·0	24	0·3
1770	29	2·1	8	1·1	32	1·9	5	0·5	22	1·0	42	2·2	102	5·6	24	0·4
1820	29	2·2	22	2·2	24	2·2	5	0·6	23	1·3	42	2·5	102	7·2	24	0·5
1840	29	2·5	22	2·5	24		5	0·7	23	1·7	42	2·8	102	8·1	24	0·5

Note: In the period 1550–1770, Piedmont does not include Nice, Oneglia, Sospello and the provinces beyond the Alps (Savoy, Genevieve and Chiablese), but includes Aosta and, after 1750, Lomellina, taken from Lombardy. For the period 1820–40 the area of 1950 has been used. The data concerning Tuscany and Liguria for the period 1820–40 refer to the area of these regions in 1950.

recent literature was duly taken into account in compiling Table 1. This Table gives the approximate estimated total population of the various Italian regions at selected dates. Up to 1861, the Italian Peninsula was divided into various states whose area varied with the political and military vicissitudes of the times. Only the Papal States and the Kingdom of the Two Sicilies remained practically unaltered in area in the course of the time. For these two cases therefore, population figures as given in Table 1 refer to the political entity. For the rest of the country it is impossible to do the same and it is more convenient to refer population totals to geographical regions. However, the areas of the geographical regions as considered by contemporaries also varied from time to time; therefore when regional population totals are given it is necessary to define the area to which these totals refer. Unfortunately, on this point also our knowledge is not always exact or complete. This is why in Table 1 the area of each territory, at the selected dates, is given in round figures to the nearest thousand square kilometres.

The political unification of the greatest part of the Peninsula was first accomplished in 1861. In that same year 31st December the first complete census was carried out. The area of the newly-formed state was not, however, destined to remain unaltered with the passing of time. As a result of political and military vicissitudes the area of modern Italy has varied in the following way[3]:

1861	259,320 sq. km.
1866	274,527 „ „
1871	286,610 „ „
1919	310,120 „ „
1947	301,181 „ „

Taking as a basis the figures in Table 1 for the period 1550-1850 and national censuses for the period beginning 1861, I have calculated the Italian population for the whole period 1550-1950 in relation to a standardized area of 301 thousand sq. km. (i.e. the area of the Republic of Italy since 1947). The results are given in Table 2.

The slight differences between the population totals given in Table 2 and those calculated by Beloch should not be taken too literally. The standardized area to which I refer does not coincide exactly with the area to which Beloch refers. Furthermore, the figures calculated for the pre-1800 period are subject to a margin of error which I put at ± 15 per cent and which is larger than the differences between my figures and those by Beloch. Data in Table 2 indicate that between 1500 and 1660 the population of Italy fluctuates considerably, but tends to beat against a ceiling of 12 million, which it does not succeed in surpassing. The population broke through this ceiling in the second half of the seventeenth century when there began a period of expansion which was destined to last down to present days. After 1660 in fact the Italian population continued

in Napoli, 69 (1958); G. Galasso, 'Lo sviluppo demografico', Napoli dopo un secolo 1860-1960, Napoli 1961; G. Galasso, 'Migrazioni e insediamenti nell' Italia Meridionale', Problemi demografici e questione meridionale, Napoli s.d.; G. De Meo, Saggi di statistica economica e demografica sull' Italia meridionale nei secoli XVII e XVIII, Roma 1962.
    For SARDINIA:
    F. Corridore, Storia documentata della popolazione di Sardegna, Turin 1902.
    [3] Istat, Sommario di Statistiche Storiche Italiane, Roma 1958, p. 1.

to increase, and between 1660 and 1951 it more than quadrupled, reaching in 1951 a total of almost 48 million.

TABLE 2

Population calculated for a standardized area of 301,000 sq. km.

Year	Total population (in millions)		Inhabitants per sq. km.
1500	more than	10	
1550	about	11	about	36
1600	,,	12	,,	37
1660	,,	11	,,	40
1700	,,	13	,,	37
1770	,,	17	,,	43
1820	,,	20·4	,,	57
1840		23·3		68
1861		26·1		77
1871		28·0		87
1881		29·8		93
1891		31·8		99
1901		34·0		106
1911		37·0		113
1921		37·9		123
1931		41·2		126
1941		44·5		137
1951		47·6		148
			158

II

Between 1550 and 1660 high birth rates and high mortality rates were the rule everywhere. The rate of 'normal' mortality remained generally below the birth rate, so that in 'normal' times there was a natural rate of increase in the region of 5-7 per thousand per year. The mortality rate, however, fluctuated violently because of the occurrence of frequent and recurrent peaks of 'extraordinary' mortality. These peaks were due to famines and various types of epidemics, but it was usually the plague which produced the highest peaks which could reach 200 or 300 per thousand. The plague of 1527-31 produced a drastic fall in population totals. The plague of 1576-7 slowed down the demographic rise of the second half of the sixteenth century. The pandemics of 1630 and 1657 cancelled the gains of the periods 1580-1629 and 1631-55 and brought back the Italian population to the level of about 11 million.

After 1657, however, the plague ceased to visit Italy. The fact was so striking that it did not fail to be noticed. In the second decade of the eighteenth century, when the plague spread through central Europe, the Abbé L. A. Muratori wrote[4]: 'The rumours of plague (from Central Europe) during the past year 1713 have caused us much anxiety and fear . . . since for a long time Italy has remained free of what some people call God's war; since it has been observed on the one hand that for many centuries now the plague has returned to countries after varying intervals, but has been almost never absent for as long as a hundred

[4] L. A. Muratori, *Del governo della peste*, Milan 1832, p. 1.

years, and on the other hand that between 1630 and 1713 Lombardy has enjoyed almost complete immunity,[5] it was to be feared that this disaster was to be sent us by God's gracious providence, especially in view of our faults which merit this and worse.' However, despite Abbé Muratori's worries and the Italians' 'faults' the plague did not spread to Italy.

The disappearance of the plague since the mid-seventeenth century was a fact not confined to Italy: it was a phenomenon experienced by the country in common with the whole of Western Europe. The causes of the change are not at all clear. One might feel tempted to connect it with improvements in the levels of living, in medical practice or in public sanitation. But medical knowledge and especially medical practice in the second half of the seventeenth century and in the eighteenth century were certainly not superior, as far as plague is concerned, to those prevailing before 1650. The same can be said about public sanitation. As to quarantine measures in particular, Italy had been indeed a pioneer and could boast quite a tradition.[6] There is no evidence however that noticeable improvements had occurred in this respect after 1660 until at least the end of the eighteenth century. As for the standard of living, the case of Italy is particularly instructive. Unlike England, France or Holland, Italy in the decade 1620-30 embarked on a long period of economic decline which lasted beyond the middle of the eighteenth century and during which levels of living progressively deteriorated.[7] A demographic index of this deterioration is provided by the progress of infant mortality. We do not possess data on the subject for the whole of the country, but particular surveys of the city of Pavia in the seventeenth century, the city of Venice in the seventeenth and eighteenth centuries, and the whole of Lombardy in the second half of the eighteenth century, all agree in pointing to a progressive increase in the infant mortality rate.[8]

Some authors suggested that the substitution of brick-houses for timber-houses, making life more difficult to rats, was possibly a factor in the mechanics of the disappearance of plague. But for Italy it can easily be shown that, apart from remote regions in the mountains, timber-houses had become very rare as early as the fourteenth and fifteenth centuries.

One is left with the hypothesis of the substitution of an outdoor rat (R. norvegicus) bearing an outdoor species of flea (N. fasciatus and L. segnis) for an indoor rat (R. rattus) bearing an indoor flea (X. cheopis).[9] But the evidence in support of this hypothesis is extremely weak and recent research tends to disregard the hypothesis altogether.[10]

While we are left in the dark, on the causes of the disappearance of plague our ideas are very much clearer on the consequences of the phenomenon. Traditionally, the plague had performed an essential role in keeping the popu-

[5] In 1656-7 the plague had again invaded various areas of Italy (especially Naples, Rome and Genoa), but Lombardy, which had been hit in 1630, was spared this new wave of epidemic.

[6] J. M. Eager, 'The early history of Quarantine', Bulletin of the Yellow Fever Institute, 12 (Washington, D.C. 1903).

[7] C. M. Cipolla, 'The Decline of Italy', in Economic History Review, 5 (1952).

[8] For Venice, D. Beltrami, Storia della popolazione di Venezia, op. cit., pp. 159-79; for Pavia, G. Aleati, La popolazione di Pavia durante il dominio spagnolo, op. cit., pp. 90-94; for Lombardy, M. Romani, Il movimento demografico in Lombardia, p. 431.

[9] For all the abundant bibliography on the subject see L. F. Hirst, The conquest of Plague, Oxford 1953, pp. 332-45.

[10] R. Pollitzer, Plague, Geneva 1954 and bibl. quoted in it.

lation in balance. When the plague disappeared, the recurrent high peaks of 'extraordinary' mortality due to famines or infectious diseases other than plague did not prove sufficient in the long run to check the gap between the birth rate and the rate of 'normal' mortality. Population began therefore to increase: from about 11 million in 1660, to about 13 million around 1700, to about 17 million around 1770, to about 20·4 million in 1820.

One might easily argue that if there had not been a simultaneous and well-documented increase in agricultural production, sooner or later severe famines would probably have taken the place of the plague as a check to demographic expansion. Among the various factors which made possible the population growth of the period 1660-1820 one has most certainly to include the improvements in agriculture that took place in Italy during the second half of the seventeenth and more especially during the eighteenth century. But we must, I think, agree with K. Helleiner that the first round in the 'vital revolution' was accomplished as a result of the mysterious decline of a microbic infection.[11]

III

After 1820, the annual rate of increase of total population which between 1660 and 1820 had been in the region of 3 per thousand, moved up to levels around 7 per thousand. After the end of the Napoleonic wars in Tuscany, as well as in other parts of the Peninsula, there seems to have been during at least a decade a slight but appreciable rise in the crude birth rate. Between 1820 and 1835 there was also a fall in the crude death rate relating to 'normal' mortality.[12] However, the Lombard series suggest that the most important factor was further gain in 'extraordinary' mortality. The plague had not been the only source of 'extraordinary' mortality, although certainly the most fearsome one. Hunger, smallpox, typhus, etc. had co-operated with the plague to check at intervals the effects of the gap between births and 'normal' deaths. After 1820 these checks became more and more rare, especially as a result of improvements in agricultural production, in transportation, and in the levels of living of some areas of the Peninsula. In Lombardy (Table 3), in the two decades 1770-89 there were six peaks of 'extraordinary' mortality which exceeded the annual rate of 40 per thousand whereas in the two decades 1820-39 the figure of 40 per thousand was exceeded only once (in 1836 when there was a cholera epidemic). Again in Lombardy, during the two decades 1770-89 deaths outnumbered births in five years, whereas during the two decades 1820-39 the prevalence of death occurred only in the cholera year of 1836.

[11] K. F. Helleiner, 'The Vital Revolution reconsidered', in *The Canadian Journal of Economic and Political Science*, 23 (1957). See above p. 79.
[12] P. F. Bandettini, *L'evoluzione demografica della Toscana*, op. cit.; M. Romani, *Il movimento demografico in Lombardia*, op. cit.; G. Felloni, *Popolazione e sviluppo economico in Liguria*, op. cit.

TABLE 3

Crude birth and death rates (per thousand) in selected Italian regions 1760–1860

Year	Piedmont		Lombardy		Veneto		Liguria		Tuscany	
	Births	Deaths	Births	Deaths	Births	Deaths	Births	Deaths	Births	Deaths
1768			38	37						
69			40	33						
1770			40	32						
71			41	35						
72			39	36						
73			38	34						
74			40	41						
75			37	38						
76			41	33						
77			41	36						
78			38	37						
79			39	40						
1770-9										
1780			41	36						
81			37	35						
82			43	43						
83			38	42						
84			40	37						
85			42	42						
86			42	35						
87			40	34						
88			45	42						
89			42	47						
1780-9										
1790			45	38						
91			40	33						
92			41	35						
93			42	38						
94			40	39						
95			40	37						
96										
97										
98			40	41						
99			45	43						
1790-9										
1810			42	36					36·9	32·3
11			43	40					36·4	29·4
12			42	41					35·5	33·2
13									34·7	30·2
14			39	36					35·2	27·7
15			37	36					34·0	30·2
16			39	41					31·7	36·2
17			38	50					28·9	51·9
18			39	36					35·8	29·6
19			43	33					41·8	27·9
1810-19									35·1	32·9

TABLE 3

Crude birth and death rates (per thousand) in selected Italian regions 1760–1860
(contd.)

Year	Piedmont Births	Deaths	Lombardy Births	Deaths	Veneto Births	Deaths	Liguria Births	Deaths	Tuscany Births	Deaths
1820			42	34					41·8	27·9
21			42	33					43·1	28·2
22			44	35					43·8	28·7
23			40	32					43·7	25·2
24			43	32					43·6	26·5
25			41	31					43·7	26·0
26			43	34					43·8	27·2
27			41	32					42·4	24·7
28	39·5	30·2	41	32			37·6	21·9	42·1	25·5
29	38·3	34·4	39	35			34·8	31·6	41·0	38·2
1820–9									42·9	27·8
1830	37·6	32·4	40	36			35·6	26·7	39·4	27·9
31	40·1	31·5	42	33			37·7	24·0	41·0	28·5
32	36·2	30·2	39	37			32·8	24·1	38·8	25·7
33	36·4	33·2	40	37			34·4	25·8	37·7	29·0
34	37·8	32·5	42	36			35·8	26·5	39·7	27·6
35	36·1	34·0	42	34			35·8	29·7	38·3	27·6
36	37·3	31·8	42	52			33·3	27·9	37·8	23·4
37	35·3	31·6	42	33			33·1	31·6	36·9	26·9
38			43	35					33·2	23·8
39			43	35	40·9	32·1			34·9	24·5
1830–9									37·8	26·5
1840			41	34	38·4	32·3			33·2	27·6
41			43	32	40·7	31·3			34·1	29·6
42			43	36	39·3	36·0			34·9	28·0
43			42	32	39·2	34·4			35·5	24·0
44			42	34	39·5	32·0			33·9	25·1
45			41	30	39·5	29·2			35·5	24·3
46			41	30	38·0	29·8			35·3	24·9
47			38	34	36·5	33·9			34·6	25·9
48									36·1	26·2
49			37	38					35·4	31·2
1840–9									34·9	26·7
1850			38	34					36·6	26·5
51			39	30	38·8	30·6			37·3	25·6
52			38	30	37·6	30·6			34·8	26·3
53			39	28	38·4	27·2			37·3	25·6
54			36	32					32·8	31·4
55									32·5	50·4
56									35·1	30·0
57									35·2	28·4
58									37·5	28·7
59									39·7	29·1
1850–9									35·9	30·2

IV

With the political unification of Italy, we have at our disposal more detailed and satisfactory statistics. For the decade 1871-80[13] the following figures are available for the whole country[14]:

Births	36·9	per thousand
Deaths	29·9	per thousand
Infant deaths	215·0	per thousand
Life expectancy at birth	35·0	years
Population aged { 14 and less (1871)	30·5	per cent of total population
66 and more (1871)	5·1	per cent of total population
Illiterates	69·0	per cent *ca.* of population aged 6 and over
Employed in agriculture	60·0	per cent *ca.* of total active population

These figures are indeed very similar to those that we find today in most of the so-called 'underdeveloped' countries. The fact is not at all surprising because by 1870 Italy as a whole had not industrialized. As to the birth rate, one might remark that a crude birth rate of about 37 per thousand per year is by any standards a 'high' one, but that many underdeveloped countries have been accustomed to rates in the region of 40 to 45 per thousand. Were there any factors that operated negatively on the birth rate in pre-industrial Italy?

F. Moryson, an English traveller contemporary to Shakespeare and a keen observer of various countries' customs and institutions, once said this about Italy: 'Never I did observe brothers to live in such unity as in Italy, so as the father being dead, many of them ordinarily live in one house together, not deviding their patrimony, but having all goods in common or as they call it brotherhood (vulgarly *fratellanza*) and persuading one to marry for procreation, the rest living unmarried and much respecting theire brothers wife and her honour as theire owne .... In Italy marryage is indeed a yoke, and that not easy one but so grievous as brethren no where better agreeing yet contend among themselves to be free from marryage and he that of free will or by persuasion will take a wife to continue their posterity, shall be sure to have his wife and her honour as much respected by the rest, besyde their liberall contribution to mantayne her, so as themselves may be free to take the pleasure of women at large. By which liberty they live more happily than other nations. For in those frugall commonwealths the unmaryed live at a small rate of expenses, and they make small conscience of fornication, esteemed a small sinne and easily remitted by Confessors.'[15]

If what Moryson wrote is correct, one is led to believe that in the sixteenth century the percentage of the adult population that remained unmarried must

---

[13] The decade 1871-80 has been chosen instead of the decade 1861-70 because during this latter decade (more precisely in 1866) the new Kingdom acquired the Veneto area. The figures relating to the first part of the 1860's are therefore not comparable to those of the second part.

[14] *Sommario di statistiche storiche italiane, op. cit.*, pp. 39-64, and *Annuario Statistico Italiano 1944-48*, Rome 1949, pp. 21-48.

[15] F. Moryson, *Itinerary*, ed. Ch. Hughes, London 1903, Vol. I, pp. 156 and 409.

have been rather high. This was certainly the case in the second half of the nine-teenth century. According to the census figures, in 1871 about 34 per cent of the women between 18 and 49 years of age had never been married.[16] In the decade 1871-81 the average age of girls at their first marriage was in the region of 24.[17] Whenever these habits started,[18] it seems abundantly clear that if around 1870 we find in Italy a crude birth rate somewhat inferior to those experienced by several underdeveloped countries of our own days, this was mainly due to the fact that a large section of the female population in childbearing age never got married, and that those who got married did it at a relatively late age.

Italian conditions around 1870 differed also in another respect from those of the 'pure' state of 'underdevelopment'. 'Extraordinary' mortality had been long since brought progressively under control. As has already been mentioned this fact was mainly responsible for the growth of the population since 1660.

Both because 'ordinary' mortality continued to remain at high levels and because there were social factors that acted negatively on the birth rate, the rise of population since 1660 was never too violent. There was an acceleration after 1820, as we have seen, but the average annual increase constantly remained below 1 per cent; a figure which clearly contrasts with the one that characterizes the 'demographic explosion' of the underdeveloped countries of our own days. However the example of Italy does illustrate how even a low rate of growth may in the course of time, because of the effects of compound cumulation, produce alarmingly large figures. It should be added that Italy had started out from a position of high population density. An average density of 35-40 per sq. km. in the sixteenth and seventeenth centuries (Table 2) was certainly amongst the highest in Europe. Starting from a density level which was already high, two centuries of uninterrupted increase, even at a moderate annual average rate, finally produced a difficult situation. A density of 87 persons per sq. km. around 1870 was enough to cause uncomfortable pressures in a country which continued to be essentially agricultural. The situation worsened dramatically after 1870.

V

After 1870 a new phase started typically characterized by those patterns that scholars describe as 'demographic transition'.[19] The death rate began to fall: from about 30 per thousand around 1875 mortality fell to about 15 per thousand around 1930. The fall which in Italy took place in about 55 years, had

[16] On 31 December, 1871 of a total of 6,035,361 women in the age group 18-49, 2,045,307 (=33·9 per cent) had never been married and 338,873 (=5·6 per cent) were widows.

[17] *Sommario di Statistiche Storiche Italiane*, pp. 45-48.

[18] Unfortunately enough we do not possess reliable data for sufficiently large groups of popula-tion for the centuries preceding 1860. G. Aleati, *La popolazione di Pavia, op. cit.*, found that in a num-ber of parishes of the town of Pavia around 1700, of the women in the age groups 19-49, about 22 per cent had never been married and about 13 per cent were widows. The sample of population analysed is however too small to allow any generalization. If similar figures could be obtained for other areas for the sixteenth and seventeenth centuries, Moryson's statements would be substantiated. Although I do not have any evidence, I have the feeling that Moryson's observations applied mainly to urban population.

[19] This is certainly true for the country considered as a whole. For particular areas some authors think that the movements of fertility and mortality did not always adhere to the patterns of the demo-graphic transition. See for instance P. F. Bandettini, *La popolazione della Toscana dal 1810 al 1959*, Florence 1961, p. xx, and G. Felloni, *Popolazione e sviluppo economico, op. cit.*, p. 191. It must be noticed, however, that these authors limited their observation only to the movements of the crude birth and death rate.

taken about 150 years in France and Sweden, about 125 years in England, about
40 years in Germany. The birth rate did not adapt itself immediately to the new
situation. It remained practically stable until about 1889 and only after that date
it began to follow the death rate in its downward movement. A time lag of
about fifteen years for this readjustment is not excessive. But given the speed
of the fall in the death rate, this lag was enough to cause the figures for the crude
rate of natural increase to rise rapidly—from 6·3 per thousand in 1872-5 to
10·7 per thousand in 1881-5. Once the birth rate did begin to fall, it went down
rapidly enough, but never more rapidly than the death rate. As a result, the
average annual crude rate of natural increase continued to fluctuate right down
to 1930 around 11 per thousand, with the highest values in the quinquennium
1911-15 and the quinquennium 1921-5 (Table 4).

TABLE 4

*Crude birth and death rates, rate of natural increase and infant mortality rate for
Italy 1872-1940*

	Births (per thousand)	Deaths (per thousand)	Excess of live births (per thousand)	Infant mortality (per thousand)
1872-75	36·8	30·5	6·3	219
76-80	36·9	29·4	7·5	209
81-85	38·0	27·3	10·7	195
86-90	37·5	27·2	10·3	195
91-95	36·0	25·5	10·5	185
96-1900	34·0	22·9	11·1	168
1901-05	32·7	22·0	10·7	167
06-10	32·7	21·2	11·5	155
11-15	31·5	19·7	11·7	140
16-20	23·0	24·4	− 1·4	152
21-25	29·8	17·4	12·4	127
26-30	26·8	16·0	10·9	119
31-35	23·8	14·1	9·8	105
36-40	23·3	13·9	9·4	103

More specific rates can give a more precise picture of the whole development. On the basis of the censuses of 1881, 1901, 1911, 1921, 1931 and 1951 life
tables have been calculated for the Italian population at the corresponding dates.
The reciprocal of life expectancy at birth $\left(=\dfrac{1}{\overset{\circ}{e}_o}\right)$ as calculated on the life
tables can be assumed as a synthetic index of mortality unaffected by changes
in the age composition of the population. The value of $=\dfrac{1}{\overset{\circ}{e}_o}$ at the selected
dates gives the following results[20]:

	M	F	MF		M	F	MF
1881	28·4	28·1	28·2	1921	20·3	19·7	20·0
1901	23·5	23·3	23·4	1931	18·6	17·9	18·2
1911	21·5	21·1	21·3	1951	15·7	14·9	15·3

[20] G. Chiassino, 'Sull'andamento della mortalità in Italia dal 1881 al 1951, in *Rivista Italiana di
economia, demografia e statistica*, 15 (1961), p. 55.

The life tables show furthermore that between 1881 and 1931:

(a) for x (age) $\leq$ 5 gains have been greater in male mortality than in female mortality while for $x >$ 5 the opposite is true;

(b) the greater gains in mortality have been made for people at the age around 5;

(c) on the whole, the gains in female mortality have been greater than in male mortality.[21]

One of the components of the fall of mortality has been the fall of infant mortality. In the period 1830-49 the prevailing rates of infant mortality were fluctuating between 200 and 300 per thousand: about 230 per thousand in Piedmont, 280 per thousand in Lombardy, 310 per thousand in the Veneto, 200 per thousand in Liguria, 210 per thousand in Tuscany, 210 per thousand in Puglia.[22] In 1871-80 for the whole kingdom of Italy the annual average infant mortality rate was still as high as 215 per thousand. By 1901-10 the rate was down to 160, by 1931-40 it was at 104 and by 1951-5 it was at 58 per thousand.[23] The series of yearly figures for the whole kingdom available from 1862 clearly indicates that the downward course of infant mortality began around 1870.[24]

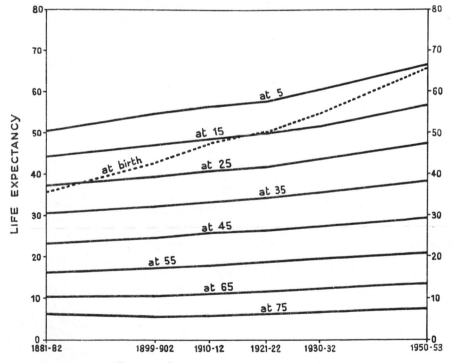

FIG. 1. Life expectancy in Italy at selected dates.

[21] G. Chiassino, *op. cit.*, p. 63 and S. Somogyi, *La misura della mortalità della popolazione italiana attraverso le tavole di eliminazione*, in *Atti del XX Congresso Nazionale di Igiene*, Roma 1958.

[22] For Piedmont, G. Melano, *La popolazione di Torino e del Piemonte, op. cit.*, p. 95; for Lombardy and Veneto, *Tafeln zur Statistik der Oesterreichichen Monarchie*; for Tuscany, P. F. Bandettini, *op. cit.*, pp. 34-41.

[23] *Sommario di Statistiche Storiche Italiane, op. cit.*, p. 44.

[24] *Ibid.*

The turning point seems therefore to coincide roughly with the turning point of the crude death rate. As will be noticed later on, with the seventies Italy entered a period of economic depression. Levels of living certainly did not improve after 1870: there are actually many reasons to believe that they worsened noticeably. The gains in infant mortality seem therefore to be imputable more to improved medical and hygienic practices than to changes in economic conditions. With the decrease of the probabilities of death at different ages, life expectancy increased. In 1881-2 life expectancy at birth was 35·4 years and at sixty-five 10·2 years. In 1950-3 it was 65·3 at birth and at sixty-five 13.[25] Following a worldwide experience, the gains were greater in the lower age groups. Table 5 and fig. 1 give further and detailed information in this respect.

TABLE 5

Life expectancy in Italy at selected dates

Age	1881-2	1899-1902	1910-12	1921-2	1930-2	1950-3
			Males and females			
0	35·42	42·78	46·94	49·99	54·88	65·34
5	50·02	54·42	56·22	57·73	60·54	65·79
15	44·11	46·95	48·32	49·54	51·85	56·29
25	37·19	39·50	40·73	41·85	43·60	46·94
35	30·22	32·09	33·18	34·05	35·39	37·91
45	23·08	24·53	25·44	26·07	27·19	28·72
55	16·19	17·06	17·82	18·31	19·31	20·39
65	10·21	10·46	10·99	11·35	12·30	13·00
75	6·27	5·57	5·89	6·07	6·89	7·20
85	3·93	2·89	3·00	3·21	3·66	3·67
			Males			
0	36·16	42·59	46·57	49·27	53·76	63·48
5	50·32	54·60	56·17	57·42	59·68	64·10
15	44·29	46·98	48·15	49·18	50·98	54·62
25	37·36	39·42	40·49	41·52	42·69	45·35
35	30·12	31·82	32·80	33·65	34·47	36·19
45	22·89	24·15	25·01	25·64	26·37	27·33
55	16·23	16·88	17·56	18·00	18·70	19·32
65	10·40	10·46	10·93	11·25	11·92	12·42
75	6·38	5·60	5·87	6·02	6·68	6·88
85	3·92	2·85	2·96	3·06	3·52	3·45
			Females			
0	35·65	43·00	47·33	50·75	56·00	66·55
5	49·63	54·24	56·28	58·04	61·37	67·30
15	43·92	46·92	48·49	49·90	52·67	57·74
25	37·04	39·57	40·98	42·18	44·47	48·29
35	30·32	32·37	33·56	34·45	36·27	38·99
45	23·26	24·91	25·86	26·50	28·00	29·93
55	16·14	17·24	18·06	18·59	19·91	21·28
65	10·01	10·45	11·04	11·44	12·66	14·22
75	6·14	5·54	5·91	6·13	7·09	7·52
85	3·91	2·93	3·04	3·33	3·78	3·92

Source: S. Somogyi, 'La misura della mortalità della popolazione italiana attraverso le tavole di eliminazione', *Atti del XX Congresso Nazionale d'Igiene*, Roma 1958.

[25] S. Somogyi, *La misura della mortalità op. cit.*, p. 30.

It has been said before that the birth rate showed a time lag in adjusting itself to the changes in the death rate. As a matter of fact, the crude birth rate does not show a definite downward trend till about 1890. A more specific index—the ratio of births to the number of women in the age group 15 to 50—confirms that fertility began its downward course only late in the eighties.[26] The contraction of fertility does not seem to have been caused by any substantial change in the marital status of the population. Considering the female population in the age group 18 to 49 one observes that the percentage of those who had never been married remained practically stable from 1871 to 1951.[27]

TABLE 6

*General fertility rate in Italy 1862 to 1950**

Year	Rate (per thousand)	Year	Rate (per thousand)	Year	Rate (per thousand)
1861	—	1891	151·2	1926	106·5
1862	145·6	1892	147·7	1927	105·2
1863	151·5	1893	149·1	1928	101·9
1864	146·8	1894	145·4	1929	97·5
1865	149·8	1895	143·4	1930	101·5
1866	152·1	1896	143·2	1931	94·3
1867	143·0	1897	143·4	1932	91·0
1868	138·4	1898	138·7	1933	91·3
1869	145·8	1899	140·5	1934	91·0
1870	143·6	1900	137·2	1935	91·2
1871	145·7	1901	135·4	1936	88·0
1872	149·6	1902	138·7	1937	89·7
1873	143·6	1903	131·1	1938	92·8
1874	137·9	1904	135·3	1939	92·1
1875	149·3	1905	134·1	1940	91·6
1876	155·4	1906	131·3		
1877	146·8	1907	129·1	1946	86·3
1878	143·6	1908	137·3	1947	83·6
1879	150·2	1909	133·4	1948	82·5
1880	134·5	1910	135·7	1949	76·3
1881	151·0	1911	128·7	1950	73·5
1882	147·5	1912	132·4		
1883	148·3	1913	130·0		
1884	155·7	1914	131·0		
1885	154·4	1915	126·4		
1886	148·4				
1887	156·7	1921	120·3		
1888	151·5	1922	120·1		
1889	154·8	1923	116·5		
1890	145·3	1924	120·1		
		1925	109·3		

* Number of births per 1,000 women in the age group 15-50. The rate has been calculated by L. Livi, 'La prolificità in rapporto alla produzione agricola in Italia dal 1861 al 1960', in *L'Economia Italiana dal 1861 al 1961*, Milano, 1961, pp. 68-69.

[26] See Table 6.
[27] The percentage of women who had never been married and of widows in the age groups 18 to 49 was as follows:

	never married	widows
1871	33·9	5·6
1901	31·8	4·6
1931	36·5	4·6
1951	37·3	3·2

Also the average age at marriage did not show remarkable changes between 1880 and 1950.[28] It seems indeed as if the decline of fertility was mainly due to more conscious family planning connected with the urbanization of the population and with other socio-cultural changes.

It has been already noticed that the time lag with which the birth rate adjusted itself to the movements of the death rate caused an acceleration of population growth. In the 1870's, the annual crude rate of natural increase which had been till then the region of 6 to 8 per thousand moved up to levels of about 11 per thousand per year. Unfortunately at that very moment the economic situation unexpectedly deteriorated.

VI

With the seventies, thanks to the enormous progress made in long-distance transport, American corn and maize began to invade the European market. The competition from across the Atlantic which had begun to make its effects felt in France and Britain around 1875, became noticeable in Italy with the beginning of the 1880's.

The prices of principal agricultural products collapsed. For corn and maize the course of prices in Italy was as follows[29]:

	Soft Wheat	Maize
	(Lire per quintale)	
1880	32·27	24·23
1881	26·36	19·01
1882	25·42	20·55
1883	23·11	17·38
1884	21·52	14·94
1885	21·24	14·10
1886	21·28	15·51
1887	21·48	13·41

In addition there took place a drastic cut in production. The annual production of wheat for instance fell from about 40 million quintals around 1870 to about 30 million in 1888-89.[30] A disastrous commercial war with France added new fuel to the depression from about 1888.[31] The price of fresh cocoons—a main item among exports to France—fell from about 6 lire per kilo in 1870 to about 2·6 lire in 1896.

It is not difficult to guess the consequences of an agricultural crisis of this magnitude for a country in which roughly 60 per cent of the population was employed in the primary sector. The years between 1885 and 1895 are rightly labelled in the Italian textbooks as 'the blackest years in the economic history of the new Kingdom'.[32] It was precisely in these years of economic collapse that—as it has been shown before—the population pressure became more acute,

[28] S. Somogyi, *L'attrazione matrimoniale dei nuovi sposi in Italia, op. cit.*, p. 7, and *Annuario Statistico Italiano 1944-48, op. cit.* p. 43.
[29] *Somario di statistiche storiche italiane, op. cit.*, pp. 173-74.
[30] *Ibid.*, p. 14.
[31] G. Luzzatto, *Storia economica.* Padua, 1952, vol. 2, pp. 410-22.
[32] G. Luzzatto, *ibidem.* See also G. Luzzatto, 'Gli anni più critici dell'economia italiana' in *L'Economia italiana dal 1861 al 1961, op. cit.*, pp. 424-33.

and the annual crude rate of natural increase rose from about 7 per thousand to about 11 per thousand.

Against such a background Italian emigration in the last decades of the nineteenth century has to be viewed—the fortuitous and unfortunate coincidence of a population explosion with a sudden and deep economic depression. Well-known American studies have accustomed us, in the investigation of migratory phenomena, to lay the principal stress on the forces operating on the 'pull' side.[33] This emphasis is certainly justified when one is dealing with short and medium-term fluctuations,[34] but late nineteenth century Italy is a good example for illustrating the decisive role played, at least in the long run, by the forces operating on the 'push' side.[35]

VII

In the 1890's Italy entered the phase of what present-day economists would call industrial 'take-off'. However the idea and the mirage of emigration were by now widely disseminated. Furthermore the rate of development in Italy was not such as to permit the rapid absorption of superfluous manpower.[36] The flood of emigrants thus continued to grow until it reached its maximum by the eve of the First World War. Table 7 gives the figures relating to Italian emigration from 1876 to 1915. These figures refer to gross emigration, for unfortunately no reliable data are available concerning repatriations.[37] In order to estimate the extent of the effective loss in population brought about by emigration, Italian demographers are therefore obliged to have recourse to ingenious but indirect methods like comparing the actual population increase with the hypothetical increase resulting from the application of life tables. By this method it has been calculated that net emigration must have fluctuated about an average of 100 thousand units a year in the period 1880-1900 and that this average must have risen to around 150 thousand units in the period 1901-11. In this latter period there was a net average annual loss of 4 persons in every thousand. The greatest losses were to be in the 25-30 age group.[38] Taking the period 1881-1936 as a whole, the actual population increased from 29 million to 42 million, whereas it may be supposed that without any migratory movements but all other things being equal, the population should have risen from 29 million to 48 million.[39]

[33] For example H. Jerome, *Migration and Business Cycles*, New York 1926.
[34] F. Coletti, *Dell'emigrazione italiana* in *Cinquant'anni di storia italiana*, t. 3, Milano 1911, p. 34, had noted that the Italian emigration curve for the period 1901-9 presented 'great peaks and great troughs. One feels the ever increasing influence exerted on emigration figures by the international labour market, especially the American market.' See also: M. Livi Bacci, *L'Immigrazione e l'assimilazione degli Italiani negli Stati Uniti*, Milan 1961, who emphasizes the relevance of the 'pull'.
[35] R. F. Foerster, *The Italian Emigration of our Time*, Cambridge, Mass. 1924, pp. 47-50 and 64-82. *Cf.* also the general observations in this sense made by F. Thistlethwaite, 'Migration from Europe in the nineteenth and twentieth centuries', in *Rapports du XI Congrès International des Sciences Historiques*, Stockholm 1960, vol. 5, pp. 32-60.
[36] On the relatively low rate of development of the Italian economy of the time *cf.* the remarks by A. Gerschenkron, 'Sul saggio di sviluppo industriale dell'Italia', in *Moneta e Credito*, 33-34 (1956), pp. 50-63.
[37] A good description of the statistical sources available for the study of Italian emigration is given in F. Coletti, *Dell'emigrazione italiana, op. cit.*, pp. 5-30.
[38] M. Boldrini, 'Un secolo di sviluppo della popolazione italiana', in *L'Economia italiana dal 1861 al 1961*, Milan 1961, p. 49.
[39] M. Boldrini, *Demografia*. Milan 1956, pp. 329-30. On various aspects of the Italian emigration during the period 1870-1950 see *L'emigrazione Italiana dal 1910 al 1923*, Roma 1926; R. F. Foerster,

To sum up, between 1880 and 1915 emigration removed every year from the population of Italy something like 3-4 persons in every thousand.[40] This proportion corresponded more or less to the rise in the rate of natural increase (that is to the widening of the demographic gap) for the period of 'demographic transition'. While the crude rate of natural increase was in the region of 11 per thousand, the population of Italy continued to grow after 1880 at a rate of about 6·5 per thousand every year, that is to say, at a rate practically not dissimilar from that at which it had expanded from 1820 onwards.

TABLE 7

Gross annual emigration from Italy 1876–1915

Years	Average annual number of emigrants (in thousands)	Number of emigrants per 1,000 inhabitants
1876–80	109	3·9
1881–5	154	5·4
1886–90	222	7·4
1891–5	257	8·3
1896–1900	310	9·7
1901–5	554	16·8
1906–10	651	19·1
1911–15	549	15·5

VIII

Up to now we have treated the Italian population as a single unit. In effect, from the middle of the sixteenth century up to about the middle of the nineteenth century there is, as far as we know, a considerable similarity of structures and tendencies in the populations of the various regions of the country. But from the middle of the nineteenth century appreciable differences become apparent. If one were to consider the matter in detail, one would have to make out a long list of particular cases and dissimilarities of varying significance. But by far the most striking and significant phenomenon is the difference which grew up between North and South.

The Italian industrial development definitely had the peculiarity of remaining concentrated almost exclusively in the north of the country. Classical economists in their optimism used to trust that automatic mechanisms would restore the balance between developed and underdeveloped areas. But the economic history of the world in the last hundred years has shown that, without drastic political corrective action, the unbalance between varying levels of development tends, in time, to become aggravated rather than cured. Italy provides a striking example of the formation and the increasing aggravation of a 'dual economy'. By the workings of 'vicious spirals', while the North, once set in motion, continued to progress, the South continued to stagnate in a

The Italian Emigration of our Time, Cambridge Mass. 1924; E. Antonucci and U. Trillo, 'Provenienze e destinazioni delle correnti dell'emigrazione italiana per l'estero dal 1876 al 1930', *Atti del congresso internazionale per gli studi sulla popolazione*, vol. 9, Roma 1933; G. Dore, *Bibliografia per la storia dell' emigrazione italiana in America*, Roma 1956; M. Livi Bacci, *L'immigrazione e l'assimilazione degli italiani, op. cit.*

[40] This estimate, now put forward by M. Boldrini, *Un secolo di sviluppo, op. cit.*, is not appreciably different from that put forward in its time by Coletti, *Dell'emigrazione italiana, op. cit.*, p. 73.

state of underdevelopment. In 1928, while the annual per capita income (in 1938 lire) in the North had risen to about 3,000 Lire, in the South it was about 1,800 Lire.[41]

The different rates of economic growth of the two areas did not fail to have demographic consequences.[42] Thanks above all to the jointly shared store of information and services in matters of public health and medicine, the fall in the death rate in the two areas was roughly proportional (between 1872-5 and 1951-2 the crude death rate fell by 65 per cent in the North and 69 per cent in the South) and the death rates in the two parts of the country arrived finally at more or less the same levels. The birth rate, however, fell drastically in the North (by 59 per cent between 1872-5 and 1951-2) but much more slowly in the South (by only 38 per cent between 1872-5 and 1951-2). The consequences of this phenomenon are clearly apparent in Table 8. At mid-twentieth century the North finds itself in the state of demographic equilibrium of a developed country, with a low birth rate (one of the lowest in Europe, 15·4 per thousand), a low death rate (9·9 per thousand), and therefore a low rate of natural increase (5·5 per thousand). The South on the other hand constitutes an area of high population pressure displaying all the explosive characteristics of present-day underdeveloped countries: the death rate is low (9·8 per thousand), but the birth rate has remained relatively high (25·5 per thousand): the gap between births and deaths has thus progressively widened and pushed up the rate of natural increase to a figure of 15·7 per thousand, which is much higher than any rate of increase which the population of Italy has ever experienced during the last four centuries. In terms of the theoretical concept of 'demographic transition' it can be said that whereas the North has now passed clearly beyond the phase of 'transition' itself, the South is still involved in it. Thus within the frontiers of Italy are to be found the essential features of that demographic unbalance which disturbs the history of the world today.

TABLE 8

Crude birth rates, death rates, and natural increase rates for the North (N), for the South (S) and for the whole of Italy (I), 1872-1951

	Birth rate			Death rate			Rate of natural growth		
	N	S	I	N	S	I	N	S	I
1872-5	35·6	38·6	36·7	29·5	32·0	30·5	6·1	6·6	6·2
1891-5	35·0	38·3	36·3	24·5	27·6	25·7	10·5	10·7	10·5
1936-40	20·2	29·1	23·4	12·8	15·6	13·8	7·4	13·5	9·5
1950-1	15·4	25·5	19·2	9·9	9·8	9·9	5·5	15·7	9·3

[41] Svimez, *Statistiche sul Mezzogiorno d'Italia 1861-1953*, Rome 1954, p. 683.
[42] For all that follows see G. Mortara, *Alcune caratteristiche demografiche differenziali del Nord e del Sud dell'Italia*, Rome 1960, pp. 4-6.

25

THE POPULATION OF BARMEN BEFORE AND DURING THE PERIOD OF INDUSTRIALIZATION

W. KOELLMANN

Translated by M. K. B. Beaton

THE town of Barmen, which was combined in 1929 with Elberfeld and some other formerly independent municipalities to form the city of Wuppertal, is particularly suited for research into social and economic history. Up till 1923, when two rural communities were incorporated into it, the town had not changed its boundaries, so that all available figures refer to the same district, 21·71 square kilometres in area. Besides there is from at least the eighteenth century an abundance of source material, which makes it possible to examine and survey many important problems. In particular the social and economic effects of industrialization in all its phases can be studied here. Barmen

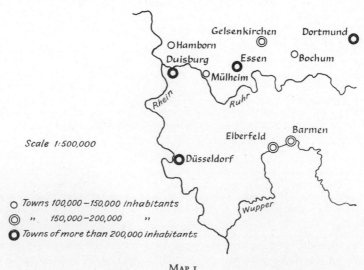

MAP 1

Gelsenkirchen and Barmen in relation to the Ruhr industrial towns, 1910

is one of the oldest areas of industrial activity in western Germany. It is a part of the Wuppertal textile area, to which Elberfeld and Ronsdorf as well as Schwelm in the Westphalian border country belong. The Barmen textile industry developed from a bleachery, which since 1527 was protected by a licence of the sovereign prince. In the nineteenth century braids and bindings, known throughout the world as Barmen articles, were the main products. Alongside the textile industry and in the beginning closely connected with it, there developed in the nineteenth century other branches of industry, the most important being the button industry, mechanical engineering and the chemical industry, so that at the end of the period of industrialization, the town had—as did the whole Wuppertal industrial area—a particularly varied production.[1] Whereas in the Ruhr to the north of Barmen (as a comparison we shall quote figures for Gelsenkirchen) the decisive impetus to industrialize was not felt until the fifties of the nineteenth century, the change from craft to industrial means of production occurred very early in Barmen. English competition, which was especially menacing for the textile trade, forced manufacturers after the Napoleonic Wars to overtake the English lead as soon as possible, if they wanted to survive. This made industrialization imperative, so that the forms of industrial life and work developed here relatively early for Germany; the typical manifestations of industrialization can be observed from the beginning. The history of the populating of the town is consequently an excellent example of the development of a city population under conditions of commercial and industrial expansion.

TABLE I

The population of Barmen 1698-1910*

Year	Population	Inhabitants per km²	Increase	Average annual rate of increase in per thousand	Gain by migration	
					absolute	as per cent of increase
1698	2,134	98				
1747	3,790	175	1,656	11·8	?	
1809	16,464	758	12,674	23·9	?	
1818	19,178	883	2,714	17·1	1,265	46·6
1843	32,984	1,519	13,806	21·9	5,419	39·3
1850	36,069	1,661	3,085	12·8	888	28·8
1858	44,698	2,059	8,629	27·2	4,972	57·6
1871	75,074	3,458	30,376	35·0	19,735	65·0
1885	103,068	4,747	27,994	24·7	4,841	17·3
1895	126,992	5,849	23,924	21·0	4,736	19·8
1905	156,080	7,189	29,088	20·8	5,523	19·0
1910	169,214	7,794	13,134	16·3	1,455	11·1

* 1698, 1747 and 1809 from: Heinrich Haake: 'Die Entwicklung der Besiedlung Barmens bis zum Beginn des 19 Jahrhunderts' (The development of the settlement of Barmen until the beginning of the nineteenth century), *Zeitschrift des Bergischen Geschichtsvereins*, vol. 52, 1920-21, p. 130.

In the 200 odd years, which the period under investigation comprises, the population of the area grew about seventy-five-fold; this growth was however, as the average annual rates of increase show, not regular but in the various periods very uneven. In the first half of the eighteenth century, the increase remained quite small but in the second half, a period of intensive commercial expansion, it was considerably larger. This period shows an even greater rate

[1] Cf. Wolfgang Köllmann, *Sozialgeschichte der Stadt Barmen im 19. Jahrhundert* (Social History of Barmen in the nineteenth century), Tübingen 1960, particularly the chapters 'Wirtschaft' and 'Bevölkerung'. All data in this paper for which no other source is given come from this thesis.

of increase than the first half of the nineteenth century, within which the years
of the war and post-war crises 1809-18 and the years of the agricultural depression 1843-9 show lower rates. This period, in which industrialization began,
was followed between 1850 and 1871 by years of stormy industrial expansion.
In these 21 years alone, the population of the town more than doubled. Then
followed a period of industrial consolidation, which is reflected in the population figures by still quite high, but gradually sinking rates of increase; nevertheless it took about 35 years for the population to double again.

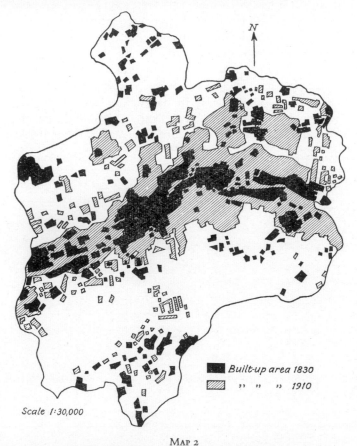

Scale 1:30,000

MAP 2
The evolution of settlement in Barmen, 1830-1910

The growth of the density of population (see second column of figures)
shows impressively the results of the increase in the nineteenth century. In the
eighteenth century the inhabitants were spread over the whole area in small
villages and hamlets. In 1702 the old common property was partitioned; a
square, which had been common property, was divided into 19 building blocks
and so became the centre of the settlement; from the beginning this part had
the character of a 'city' and soon expanded so that at the beginning of the nineteenth century a city centre had been formed. In the course of the nineteenth
century the older settlements grew together and joined up with this centre; the
centres of these villages with their churches and markets have however been

preserved. Towards the end of the nineteenth century a united settlement was formed, which covered the valley of the Wupper and the slopes on either side up to the summits.

TABLE II

Population of Gelsenkirchen from 1818-1910*

Year	Population	Inhabitants per km²	Increase	Average annual rate of increase in per thousand
1818	1,818	59		
1843	2,135	69	317	6·5
1858	3,578	116	1,443	34·8
1871	16,023	520	12,445	122·1
1885	54,696	1,776	38,673	91·6
1895	94,649	3,074	39,953	56·4
1905	147,005	4,774	52,356	44·9
1910	169,513	5,505	22,508	28·9

* The urban area of Gelsenkirchen was only formed in 1903 but the population before then can be calculated from the statistics of the municipalities then grouped together. Figures about the natural movement of population, from which the gain from migration could be calculated, are however not available. 1818-1905 from Stephanie Reekers, Johanna Schulz: *Die Bevölkerung in den Gemeinden Westphalens 1818-1950*; 1910 from: *Statistisches Jahrbuch für das deutsche Reich 1912*, p. 8.

As a comparison let us take the population development of the mining town of Gelsenkirchen, 30·79 sq. km. in area, which lies in the northern part of the Ruhr district. This city was formed in 1903 when 7 municipalities were combined; the largest of these was the older town of Gelsenkirchen.[2] In 1818 this area was still purely rural. The great upsurge began with the sinking of the mine 'Hibernia' by an Anglo-Belgian company in the fifties of the last century.[3] The next decades show an increase of population which is nothing short of explosive. In the thirteen years between 1858 and 1871 the population increased fivefold, a rate of increase which is more than three times as high as Barmen's. This is also true of the following decades. Although in 1910 Gelsenkirchen had not reached the same density of population as Barmen and although in the Ruhr cities the rate of increase continued to fall, the population of Gelsenkirchen had already passed that of the older industrial town. Here a process was completed in sixty-five years, which had taken two hundred and ten in Barmen.

The density of population in Barmen as early as 1698 suggests that it was no longer an area of purely agricultural settlement. A sign that even then industrial activity predominated was the small supply of corn, which the householders possessed. An enquiry showed this, which had been ordered by the ducal government principally to obtain, because of an imminent famine, an estimate of the supplies and needs until the next harvest. It revealed that in Barmen scarcely

[2] Stephanie Reekers and Johanna Schulz, *Die Bevölkerung in den Gemeinden Westphalens 1818-1950* (The Population of the Municipalities of Westphalia), Dortmund 1952, pp. 1, 334.
[3] Wilhelm Brepohl, *Der Aufbau des Ruhrvolkes im Zuge der Ost-West-Wanderung* (The Development of the Population of the Ruhr in the Course of the East-West Migration), Recklinghausen 1948, pp. 83 f.

a quarter of the demand was covered.[4] The farms were not able even in years with good harvests to supply all the requirements of the people in this area. The growth in population was determined solely by industrial development. The crafts created the necessary employment, the income from which supported the workers and their families. Even in the eighteenth century the number of newly created positions exceeded the natural increase of the population, so that the surplus ones had to be filled by people from outside. So the development of crafts sparked off the process of immigration, which from then on determined the development of the population of Barmen.

TABLE III

Development of the population excluding migration

| Year | Base Year | | | | | | Assumed increase in per thousand* |
	1698	1747	1818	1843	1858	1885	
1698	2,134						
1747	2,725	3,790					5
1818	4,150	5,800	19,178				6
1843	5,460	7,600	25,200	32,984			11
1858	5,970	8,300	27,600	36,100	44,698		6
1885	7,400	10,300	34,200	44,800	55,400	103,068	8
1910	10,200	14,200	47,200	61,900	76,500	142,400	13
As per cent of actual population							
1910	6·0	8·4	27·9	36·5	45·2	84·1	

* Based on the rates of increase for the German Empire; up to 1818 these are only rough estimates.

How great the effect of migration was, is shown by a calculation of the population, which takes as its starting point the population of the separate census years and excludes the effects of migration (both immigration and emigration). Between 1698 and 1910 the population would have increased fourfold but Barmen would still have been a small rural town; the population of 1818 with an increase of two and a half times would have produced a medium sized town and even the population of 1885 would have risen by 1910 only to five-sixths of the actual population.

The immigration of individuals had already begun by 1698 as the list of names from that year shows. In so far as surnames point to the origin of their bearers, we can assume that the earliest migrants came from the direct vicinity: Olpe in Westphalian Sauerland, Soest and Essen were the most distant places of origin. It is not ascertainable whether the father named in the list had come as a single man or with his family or whether one of his forebears had already migrated in the seventeenth century. Only a few details can be established about migration in the eighteenth century, considerable as it was particularly in the latter part of the century. Two causes for migration are however known even though their influence cannot be put down in figures: the first is the flight from conscription in the Prussian county of Mark to the west, and the second the

[4] Heinrich Haacke, *Barmens Bevölkerung im 17. und 18. Jahrhundert* (The Population of Barmen in the seventeenth and eighteenth centuries), Barmen 1911, pp. 3 ff.

development of new branches of production in the textile industry by migrant merchants. Both groups of migrants, the one seeking safety from the dreaded military service, the other attracted by the possibility of rapid economic advance, came from the immediate surroundings or from neighbouring regions.[5] It is probable that at least in the last decades of the century the first migrants came to Barmen from Hessen-Waldeck, an area of relative rural overpopulation. The Hessians and the Waldeckians formed the oldest group of distant migrants; their biological influence on the population of Wuppertal is greater than their proportion in the total population (which we shall ascertain below).

As early as the eighteenth century, in the second half of which there were, at a rough estimate, for every three inhabitants born in Barmen about two migrants, these did not form, in the developing area, a special group enjoying fewer rights and less respect but were assimilated without recognizable resistance into all classes of the population. Not only the landless poor migrated but also the well-to-do, who founded new firms. Even the refugees from conscription were not always completely without means but possessed training and skill in a craft or trade, which made their integration and social rise easier. How the economic upper class was broadened by migrants, is shown by the names of the members of the first town council, appointed on 14 January, 1808 by Joachim Murat, the Bergian Grand Duke by grace of Napoleon. The mayor and his two assistants were members of old established families; but of the 20 councillors 9 belonged to families which in 1698 had not even been resident in the district; 18 were traders and 1 a doctor. It is probably just as significant that the four presidents of the Barmen chamber of commerce, which existed between 1871 and 1917,[6] all came from families which had immigrated in the eighteenth century. This shows that the economic upper class of the nineteenth century was formed by the oldest migrants. If Barmen's economic advance attracted migrants, it was at the same time considerably influenced and accelerated by migrants. There existed therefore a reciprocal relationship which cannot be overlooked in explaining the growth of Barmen as an industrial area.

The material available from the beginning of the nineteenth century onwards gives more exact information about conditions because of the fortunate circumstance that in Berg the French introduced compulsory civil marriage according to Article 68 of the Code Napoléon. All the records of the Barmen registry office have been preserved. In the registry of marriages the occupation as well as the place of birth is given; these can therefore yield information about migration. However two reservations hold for the evaluation of this material: the proportion of migrants among those marrying does not correspond to their proportion within the population as a whole, because the age stratification of the migrants was different from that of the total population; and not all those contracting marriage remained domiciled in Barmen, though at this time perhaps nearly all did.

[5] Cf. Edmund Strutz, 'Wirtschaftsgeschichte' (Economic History), in Bergische Geschichte (History of Berg), Remscheid 1958, pp. 366 f; Walter Dietz: Die Wuppertaler Garnnahrung Neustadt an der Aisch 1957, pp. 98 f.

[6] The Chamber of Commerce in Barmen was formed in 1871 by separating from the Chamber of Commerce for Elberfeld and Barmen, which had been founded in 1831. In 1917, however, they joined together again.

TABLE IV

The places of origin of those contracting marriage

Place of origin	Men	As per cent	Women	As per cent	Together	As per cent
			1815			
Barmen	69	35·9	89	46·4	158	41·4
Rhineland	45	23·4	50	26·0	95	24·7
Westphalia	44	22·9	41	21·4	85	22·1
Hessen-Waldeck	22	11·5	11	5·7	33	8·6
Others	12	6·2	1	0·5	13	3·4
Total	192	100·0	192	100·0	384	100·0

Place of origin	Men	As per cent	Women	As per cent	Together	As per cent
			1855			
Barmen	158	50·3	161	51·3	319	50·8
Rhineland	79	25·2	78	24·8	157	25·0
Westphalia	60	19·1	62	19·7	122	19·4
Hessen-Waldeck	10	3·2	11	3·5	21	3·3
Others	7	2·2	2	0·6	9	1·4
Total	314	100·0	314	100·0	628	100·0

The table is to be interpreted with the above reservations: in 1815 far less than half and in 1855 just half the men and women marrying in Barmen were also born there. Local migration from the Rhineland and Westphalia together provided in 1815 the largest group and in 1855 the second largest. It should of course be remembered that marriage links beyond the city boundary played a certain part in this. It is striking that in this group there is a slight preponderance of women, whereas among the distant migrants the men were in the majority. The Hessen-Waldeckian group stands out among the distant migrants; it is at this period, even if proportionally smaller than in 1815, far larger than all the other distant migrants together.

Taking all requisite care, we can draw the following conclusions: those who migrated to Barmen came mainly from the surroundings or from the two West-German provinces of Prussia, near whose border the town lay. Barmen therefore took principally the excess rural population from the neighbouring areas. Among the distant migrants, the only important group, whose strength within the total population declined however in the first half of the nineteenth century, was the Hessen-Waldeckian. Among the Rhineland-Westphalian migrants, the proportion of women was perhaps higher than that of men; among the distant migrants the proportion of men was considerably higher than that of women.

The register of marriages also provides information about the intermixture of the total population: in 1815 in only 16 per cent of all marriages were both parties born in Barmen; in another 50 per cent of the marriages one of the parties was born there and in the remaining 34 per cent neither was born there. In 1855 the proportion of marriages contracted in which both parties were born in Barmen, had, it is true, risen to 30 per cent but the increase is mainly at the expense of the marriages in which both parties were migrants; the proportion of these sank to 25 per cent. This decline excludes the possibility of a tendency, though slight, for the natives to isolate themselves from the migrants; without

TABLE V

Marriages according to places of origin (per 100 marriages)

| | 1815 | | | | |
| | | The women came from | | | |
The men came from	Barmen	Rhineland	Westphalia	Hessen-Waldeck	Other areas
Barmen	16·1	9·4	7·8	2·6	—
Rhineland	12·5	7·8	3·1	—	—
Westphalia	9·9	3·6	7·8	1·0	0·5
Hessen-Waldeck	4·2	4·2	1·6	1·6	—
Other areas	3·6	1·0	1·0	0·5	—

| | 1855 | | | | |
| | | The women came from | | | |
The men came from	Barmen	Rhineland	Westphalia	Hessen-Waldeck	Other areas
Barmen	29·9	10·5	9·2	0·6	—
Rhineland	11·8	7·6	4·1	1·0	0·6
Westphalia	7·0	5·7	4·5	1·9	—
Hessen-Waldeck	1·3	0·6	1·3	—	—
Other areas	1·3	0·3	0·6	—	—

due care, the proportionately greater number of marriages in which both parties were born in Barmen might have suggested this possibility. If one considers that the forties of the nineteenth century were a decade of relatively low migration and that with the growth of population the possibilities of choice of partner increased, the higher proportion of marriages with two Barmen-born parties can be explained without difficulty. The choice of spouse then shows that hardly any social barriers can have existed between the old inhabitants and the migrants and that the biological intermixture proceeded without hindrance. It may therefore be claimed with sufficient probability that already by the middle of the nineteenth century scarcely one citizen of Barmen could show three generations of forefathers who all had been born there. This process of intermixture was facilitated by the fact that the bulk of the migrants—not only Rhinelanders and Westphalians but also Hessians and Waldeckians—did not differ greatly in their characteristics from the natives, while even strangers all spoke 'hochdeutsch' and could therefore make themselves understood, even though at first they might have had difficulties with the dialect, which was spoken by all classes of the population until the turn of the century but which is now no longer completely understood by most inhabitants of the town.

There was certainly opposition to the migrants particularly in the thirties and forties, decades shaken by economic crises. This did not spring from a general antipathy to them nor even from racial resentment but from the fear, that the already strained fund for poor relief would be further burdened by the migrants. This opposition was expressed in the repeated declarations of the town council against excessive immigration from 'abroad', i.e. from non-Prussian territories, because as things stood, nothing could be done about migration from provinces of the Prussian state. These 'foreigners'[7] who wished to settle in

[7] In the statistics presented here foreigner means not born in the German Empire (boundaries of 1871).

Barmen had to produce evidence that they possessed a certain amount of money or that they had secure employment. But in 1859 the council supported a petition of the Chamber of Commerce to the government that all such restrictions on immigration should be abolished; these restrictions became superfluous after the unification of Germany.[8]

The first figures available for the volume of migration, i.e. the total of immigrants and emigrants, are for the years 1871-5. In these five years, the last of the greatest wave of migration, a total of 13,979 came to the town and 7,709 left it, so that annually an average of 5·5 per cent of the total population was involved in some form of migration. The volume of migration was much higher between 1906 and 1910, years in which the population gained little by migration although 104,800 people arrived in the town, 103,350 left it, so that as an annual average 25 per cent of the total population was involved in migration. At this time there was therefore a relatively large section of mobile population in the town, whose economic volume was no longer expanding and whose population had reached its highest point. Presumably this consisted in the main of inland migrants, who could not settle down and who moved on after a short stay; they therefore appear twice in the volume of migration as immigrants and emigrants. Not until Barmen became a city do the censuses, which present this class of town separately, give more exact information about the process of migration by analysing the population at the time of the census. We shall now analyse the results of the three censuses of 1890, 1900 and 1907.

TABLE VI

*The population of Barmen according to place of origin**

Born in	1890					
	Male	As per cent	Female	As per cent	Together	As per cent
Barmen	34,740	61·7	36,498	61·0	71,238	61·3
Rhineland†	9,180	16·3	10,470	17·5	19,650	16·9
Westphalia	6,073	10·8	8,433	14·1	14,506	12·5
Local migrants	15,253	27·1	18,903	31·6	34,156	29·4
Hessen-Waldeck‡	2,793	5·0	2,068	3·5	4,861	4·2
North-East Germany§	804	1·4	658	1·1	1,462	1·3
Rest of Prussia	1,356	2·4	834	1·4	2,190	1·9
Rest of Germany	982	1·7	595	1·0	1,577	1·4
Abroad	391	0·7	269	0·4	660	0·6
Distant migrants	6,326	11·2	4,424	7·4	10,750	9·3
Total population	56,319	100·0	59,825	100·0	116,144	100·0

* *Sources:* 1890: *Statistik des deutschen Reiches*, New Series, Vol. 68, pp. 156 ff.
   1900: *ibid.*, New Series, Vol. 151, pp. 152 ff.
   1907: *ibid.*, New Series, Vol. 210, pp. 276 f.
† Excluding those born in Barmen; of those born in the Rhine province, 3,747 were born in Elberfeld in 1890 and 5,033 in 1900.
‡ Province Hessen-Nassau, Grand Duchy of Hessen and the Principality of Waldeck.
§ Provinces East-Prussia, West-Prussia and Posen.

[8] *Cf.* Wolfgang Köllmann, 'Industrialisierung, Binnenwanderung und "soziale Frage"—Zur Entstehungsgeschichte der deutschen Industriegroßstadt im 19. Jahrhundert' (Industrialization, Internal Migration and the social Question—the origin of the industrial cities in Germany in the nineteenth century), in *Vierteljahresschrift für Sozial- und Wirtschaftsgeschichte*, Vol. 46, 1959, Table, pp. 63 ff.

TABLE VI (*cont.*)

1900

Born in	Male	As per cent	Female	As per cent	Together	As per cent
Barmen	42,425	62·2	44,924	60·9	87,349	61·5
Rhineland†	10,759	15·8	12,912	17·5	23,671	16·7
Westphalia	6,413	9·4	9,405	12·8	15,818	11·1
Local migrants	17,172	25·2	22,317	30·3	39,489	27·8
Hessen-Waldeck‡	3,047	4·5	2,518	3·4	5,565	3·9
North-East Germany	1,233	1·8	1,168	1·6	2,401	1·7
Rest of Prussia	2,119	3·1	1,304	1·8	3,423	2·4
Rest of Germany	1,506	2·2	1,048	1·4	2,554	1·8
Abroad	724	1·1	434	0·6	1,158	0·8
Distant migrants	8,629	12·7	6,472	8·8	15,101	10·6
Total population	68,227‖	100·0	73,717¶	100·0	141,944	100·0

1907

Born in	Male	As per cent	Female	As per cent	Together	As per cent
Barmen	47,872	62·8	50,826	61·8	98,698	62·3
Rhineland†	11,910	15·6	14,575	17·7	26,485	16·7
Westphalia	6,595	8·7	9,790	11·9	16,385	10·3
Local migrants	18,505	24·3	24,365	29·6	42,870	27·0
Hessen-Waldeck	2,743	3·6	2,180	2·7	4,923	3·1
North-East Germany	1,533	2·0	1,435	1·7	2,968	1·9
Rest of Prussia	2,483	3·3	1,666	2·0	4,149	2·6
Rest of Germany	1,729	2·3	1,216	1·6	2,945	1·9
Abroad	1,361	1·8	548	0·7	1,909	1·2
Distant migrants	9,849	12·9	7,045	8·6	16,894	10·7
Total population	76,226	100·0	82,236	100·0	158,462	100·0

‖ Including 1 born at sea.
¶ Including 4 whose birth place is not given.

TABLE VII

As a comparison:

*The population of Gelsenkirchen according to origin**

Born in	Male	As per cent	Female	As per cent	Together	As per cent
Gelsenkirchen	29,472	36·3	30,140	41·0	59,612	38·6
Rhineland	6,360	7·8	6,229	8·5	12,589	8·1
Westphalia†	15,868	19·6	15,562	21·2	31,430	20·3
Local migrants	22,228	27·4	21,791	29·7	44,019	28·5
Hessen-Waldeck	2,322	2·9	1,174	1·6	3,496	2·3
North-East Germany	18,813	23·2	15,512	21·1	34,325	22·2
Rest of Prussia	4,961	6·1	3,210	4·4	8,171	5·3
Rest of Germany	1,538	1·9	723	1·0	2,261	1·5
Abroad	1,776	2·2	925	1·3	2,701	1·7
Distant migrants	29,410	36·3	21,544	29·4	50,954	32·9
Total population	81,110	100·0	73,475	100·0	154,585	100·0

* Source: *Statistik des deutschen Reiches*, New Series, Vol. 210, pp. 184 f.

† Excluding those born in Gelsenkirchen; all other groups correspond to those used for Barmen.

The Barmen-born are, as the table shows, relatively settled. Their proportion within the total population rose in the period under consideration, if only

to a minor extent. According to the census of 1907 Barmen had after Aachen
the highest proportion of locally born inhabitants of all German cities. This too
points to a gradual stabilization of population, as far as this is possible in such a
small area. Among the migrants the local ones predominated by far but their
proportion dropped: in 1885 it was three times, but in 1907 only two and a half
times as high as that of the distant migrants. Among the distant migrants the
Hessians and Waldeckians formed the biggest group, which however declined
relatively between 1890 and 1900 and absolutely between 1900 and 1907. In
contrast to the enumerations of 1890 and 1900 which were conducted on
1 December in these years as proper population censuses, that of 1907 was
merely an occupational census. This took place on 12 June, and though census
methods were adopted, the difference in dates and other factors lead to difficulties in making comparisons. Whether the drop in the numbers of those
originating in Hessen-Waldeck is due to such differences, or to a mistake in the
enumeration (as seems most likely), cannot be said with any finality at present.
The North-East Germans formed a second self-contained group of distant
migrants, a splinter group, which had been driven to Barmen as a result of the
large-scale German east-west inland migration, which reached its peak in these
years. The proportion of North-West Germans in the total population rose but
not as much as that of the other distant migrants. The changes in the proportions were not, however, large enough to indicate a change within the structure
of migration. It is therefore permissible, by connecting this with the results of
the analysis of the marriage registers to assume that migration in the nineteenth
century retained the same characteristics throughout: at the beginning of the
century about 85 per cent of all migrants, towards the end about 70 per cent
came to Barmen from the Rhineland and Westphalia. The Hessians and Waldeckians may have constituted about 10 per cent of all migrants at the beginning
of the century and about 8 per cent at the end, whereas all other distant
migrants comprised barely 5 per cent at the beginning and during the last
decades before the First World War perhaps a little more than 20 per cent. Of
these distant migrants a quarter were North-East Germans. Although distant
migration became more important in Barmen towards the end of the period of
migration, it weakened the influence of local migration less than it would seem
from the population statistics.[9]

Gelsenkirchen, which offers a comparison in 1907, has a completely different
migration structure. It has a much lower proportion of locally born inhabitants
than most other German cities and among the migrants the proportion of distant
migrants exceeded that of local migrants to a degree known only in such
agglomerations as Berlin and Kiel. That was the result solely of North-East
German migration, which determined the development of population in Gelsenkirchen even more than in the other Ruhr cities.[10] The influx of people from

[9] In 10 other German cities the proportion of locally born inhabitants is even lower: these are
mainly the large suburbs of Berlin, which have grown into cities as defined by the statistics (towns
with more than 100,000 inhabitants) and which today form part of Greater Berlin; also the ports of
Kiel and Stettin as well as Frankfurt am Main and Wiesbaden, the largest towns in the newest industrial area in Germany, the Rhine-Main area.

[10] Cf. Wolfgang Köllmann, 'Binnenwanderung und Bevölkerungsstrukturen der Ruhrgebiets-
großstädte im Jahre 1907' (Internal Migration and the population structure in the cities of the Ruhr),
in Soziale Welt, Vol. 9, 1958, pp. 219 ff.

the Rhineland and Westphalia was smaller than in Barmen though with 44 per
cent of migrants the proportions are about the same; likewise migrants from
Hessen and Waldeck comprised only 4 per cent of the total. On the other hand
the percentage of the North-East German group, at 36 per cent of all migrants
in Gelsenkirchen, exceeded the percentage of this group in Barmen sevenfold.

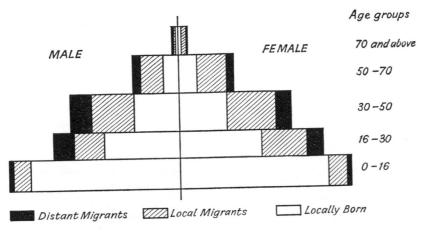

DIAGRAM I

Age structure and origins of the population of Barmen, 1900

The census of 1900 provides information about the influence of migration
on the structure of the population in Barmen, because it divides the population
into age and origin groups (see Diagram 1). Whereas of the total population in
that year about 63 per cent were locally born, about 24 per cent local migrants
and about 13 per cent distant migrants, there were

in the under 16 age group:
 86 per cent locally born, 11 per cent local migrants, and 3 per cent distant
migrants;

in the age group between 16 and 30:
 58 per cent locally born, 28 per cent local migrants, and 14 per cent
distant migrants;

in the age group between 30 and 50:
 42 per cent locally born, 41 per cent local migrants, and 17 per cent
distant migrants;

in the age group between 50 and 70:
 34 per cent locally born, 51 per cent local migrants, and 15 per cent
distant migrants;

and in the age group over 70:
 37 per cent locally born, 52 per cent local migrants, and 11 per cent
distant migrants.

In the differences in composition of the various groups three different circumstances are reflected: the high percentages in the groups over 30 are, with due allowance made for ageing, the result of the great wave of migration between 1850 and 1875. The relative increase in the percentage of distant migrants at the expense of that of local migrants in the age group 16 to 30, the overwhelming majority of whom must have moved after 1875, confirms the decline of the Rhineland and Westphalian element among the newcomers. The low proportion of migrants in the under 16 group suggests that to an overwhelming extent single people migrated, not families with children.

TABLE VIII

Proportion of men and women in the groups within the population
(women per 100 men)

| Group | Barmen | | | Gelsenkirchen |
	1890	1900	1907	1907
Locally born	105·1	105·9	106·2	102·3
Rhinelanders	113·9	120·0	122·4	97·9
Westphalians	139·0	146·7	148·4	98·1
Local migrants	123·9	130·0	131·7	98·0
Hessen–Waldeckians	74·0	82·6	79·5	50·6
North-East Germans	81·8	91·7	93·6	82·5
Other Prussians	61·5	61·5	67·1	64·7
Other Germans	60·6	69·6	70·3	47·0
Foreigners	68·8	59·9	40·3	52·1
Distant migrants	69·9	75·0	71·5	73·2
Total population	106·2	108·0	107·9	90·6

At first sight the proportions of the sexes seem to contradict this claim. While the situation remains almost the same among the locally born, the figures show an increasing surplus of women among the local migrants; the distant migration brought far more men than women into the town, the North-East German group being the only exception. The population of the town shows a considerable surplus of women. This however does not indicate family migration on a large scale but is a consequence of the special demand for women workers in the Barmen textile industry and for women servants (see below). Among the 70,258 employed there were in 1907 20,304 women (=28·9 per cent) and among the 23,352 employees of the textile industry as many as 8,294 (=35·5 per cent) were women. Moreover, marriages with women living outside the city probably increased the surplus of women among the local migrants.

The situation was completely different in the mining town of Gelsenkirchen, whose industries had no work for women. Here there was a considerable surplus of men; only among the locally born and the local migrants were the proportions approximately equal. Here too the North-East Germans have a special position among the distant migrants. If one excludes those born in Posen from this group, there were in it in Barmen as many as 101 women for every 100 men but in Gelsenkirchen only 88. This fact reveals a peculiarity of the North-East German migration to Western Germany. The North-East Germans formed a united and socially isolated group. It is true that usually unmarried workers

arrived first but as soon as they had gained a foothold they fetched a bride from
their old homes, if she had not come earlier and worked as a servant in a household. The North-East German family, founded in this way in Western Germany,
fulfilled a double function: the fact that they were settling down indicated that
they intended to make a home in the new surroundings but the marriage indicated a further close connexion with their native country which would be preserved in the family. However, the North-East German group remained, even
if one disregards the Polish minority in the town, a foreign body in the total
population, like the self-contained migrant groups in the USA , but this isolation
helped them considerably in settling down in their new home.[11]

The structure of the population reveals yet another effect of internal migration. A comparison of the population of Barmen and the German Empire
(Diagram 2) shows that the age group 16 to 30 in Barmen comprises 23·6 per
cent more women and 8 per cent more men than the corresponding group in
the population of the Empire. The age group 30 to 50 contains the same proportion in both populations; the older groups and the youngest have, however,
smaller proportions. Seen as a whole the population of Barmen in 1900 was
relatively younger than the population of the country.

As the young marriageable age groups in the Barmen population form a
particularly high proportion of the whole, one would expect a higher birth rate.
But as early as 1890 this was no longer so; it is, however, true for the earlier
decades as the birth figures show. Before 1880 proportionately more children
were born in the town than in Germany as a whole. Until then migrants increased the population in two ways: first by their presence in the town and

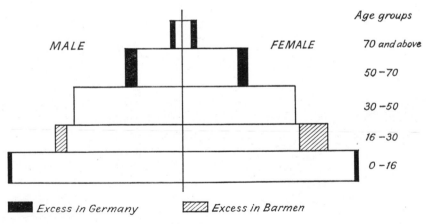

Age groups

MALE   FEMALE   70 and above

50 – 70

30 – 50

16 – 30

0 – 16

■ Excess in Germany   ▨ Excess in Barmen

DIAGRAM 2
Comparison of age and sex structure, Barmen and Germany, 1900

[11] *Cf.* the results of Wilhelm Brepohl's investigations. Apart from the one given above, the
most important is: *Industrievolk im Wandel von der agraren zur industriellen Daseinsform dargestellt am
Ruhrgebiet* (The Industrial nation in the process of change from an agricultural to an industrial way
of life, illustrated by the example of the Ruhr), Tübingen 1957. It is not possible to go into the question of the Poles here. In this paper all those born in the North-East provinces of Germany are denoted
as North-East Germans, irrespective of their nationality. The development of the Polish group in
the Ruhr area is newly investigated by Hans-Ulrich Wehlir: Die Polen in Ruhrgebiet bis 1918
(The Poles in the Ruhr area until 1918), Vierteljahresschrift für Sozial- und Wirtschaftsgeschichte,
vol. 48, 1961, pp. 203-35.

Table IX

Natural movement of population*

(per 1,000 inhabitants)

Period	Births		Deaths		Excess of Births	
	Barmen	Germany	Barmen	Germany	Barmen	Germany
1851–60	39·1	35·3	24·6	26·3	14·5	9·0
1861–70	42·4	37·2	28·0†	26·9	14·4	10·3
1871–80	45·7	39·1	26·9	27·2	18·8	11·9
1881–90	36·8	36·8	20·8	25·1	16·0	11·7
1891–1900	34·1	36·1	17·2	22·2	16·9	13·9
1901–10	29·1	32·9	13·7	18·6	15·4	14·3

* Figures for Germany from: *Statistisches Jahrbuch für das Deutsche Reich 1914*, p. 22.

† The death rate is abnormally high because of the cholera epidemic of 1867, as a result of which the death rate in that year rose to 42 per thousand. Without this year the death rate for the period would be 26·4 per thousand and the excess of births 16·0 per thousand.

then by an increase in births as a result of the large number of women of child-bearing age. In the last decades this does not seem to be the case any more but here too the figures are deceptive at first sight, because another factor, which determines the development of population in the industrial age, made itself felt earlier and more strongly in the industrial town than in the country as a whole: this factor is the decline in the birth rate. It is a question of a decline in fertility. Whereas in Barmen as late as 1880 186 children were born for every 1,000 women between 15 and 45, in 1910 only 90 were born. By contrast the general rate of fertility in Germany declined from about 165 to about 130.[12] It is not possible to go into the sociological reasons for this decline here[13] but it is permissible to conclude, that without immigration the decline in the birth rate in Barmen would have been even greater.

The relative youth of the population as a result of immigration affected not only the birth rate but also the mortality rate. If we presuppose the same conditions for both areas, the mortality figures must have been lower in Barmen than in Germany as a whole, because there were proportionately fewer people in the older age groups. This is the principal explanation of the lower mortality rate in the town before 1880. Further causes were the effects of better medical care available there and, at least since the turn of the century, of the better hygienic conditions, so that the death rate in the years when the birth rate first began to decline sank more rapidly than the birth rate. Although the decline in the birth rate overtook the decline in the death rate between 1900 and 1910, even then the mortality rate was a full quarter lower than for the population of the country as a whole. At the same time the excess of births over deaths re-

[12] Calculated from the numbers in the corresponding age groups as given in the censuses and the birth figures (these include stillborn children, who are however not taken into consideration in the table of natural population increase).

[13] *Cf.* Gerhard Mackenroth, *Bevölkerungslehre* (Theory of Population), Berlin-Göttingen-Heidelberg, 1953.

mained proportionately higher in the industrial town than in Germany as a whole.

The analysis of the marriage registers provides initial evidence about the assimilation of the immigrants into the economy of the town and about their importance for its economic development. According to these most of the men from Hessen-Waldeck were artisans; also among the local migrants there were more craftsmen than among the locally born. In 1815, of the 22 men born in Hessen-Waldeck 12 were craftsmen, of the 99 born in Rhineland-Westphalia 29 were craftsmen and of the 68 born in Barmen only 8 were craftsmen. In 1855 of the 158 Barmen citizens 30 were craftsmen and 108 were employed in industry; for the 139 local immigrants the figures were 48 and 63; and for the 10 from Hessen-Waldeck 4 and 2. The figures for the other migrant groups are too small to permit an assessment.

These statistics reveal a peculiarity of the development of Barmen: the old inhabitants worked mainly in industry while the new arrivals were mainly employed in supply services. Moreover of the 22 business men who married in Barmen in 1855 13 were not locally born. Although not all those who married in Barmen necessarily settled there, as the marriage was usually arranged by the parents of the bride, at least some of these men were probably resident in Barmen.

Only the census of occupations in 1907 can give further information. The results show—unfortunately both craftsmen and industrial workers are included under the one heading—that the locally born group is more numerous in industry and crafts, whereas the distant migrants have above-average numbers in commerce, transport and in the public services. As already mentioned, the number of North-East Germans who become servants in households was strikingly high. This applies too to the local immigrants. This helps to explain the high surplus of women in this group. The situation was different in Gelsenkirchen. Here the distant migrants, mainly the North-East Germans, were employed in industry, and more of the local migrants and those locally born in commerce and transport. The conditions in both towns, fundamentally different types of industrial town, explain the trend and economic importance of the German internal migration in the nineteenth century.

Barmen was a town with a varied, specialized and highly developed industry. Its main branch, the textile industry, needed mainly skilled workers; the natives found employment here; in the textile industry 68·8 per cent of all employees were born in Barmen, while their proportion in industry as a whole amounted to only 51·7 per cent. By contrast the population of Gelsenkirchen was influenced by mining, which according to the opinions then current required unskilled or only semi-skilled workers.

Only 11·7 per cent of all those employed in mining were locally born, in industry as a whole 13·4 per cent. In occupations connected with commerce and transport only 46·2 per cent of employees in Barmen were locally born and in Gelsenkirchen only 17·5 per cent. If one considers that because of the lower proportion of locally born inhabitants the percentages in Gelsenkirchen must be considerably lower than in Barmen, one can conclude that industry was more attractive for the citizens of Barmen than for those of Gelsenkirchen. When one

TABLE X

Employees according to occupation and origin, 1907

Of every 100 employees from the same area were employed in:	Locally born		Local migrants		Distant migrants	
	Barmen	Gelsen-kirchen	Barmen	Gelsen-kirchen	Barmen	Gelsen-kirchen
Agriculture	0·7	1·1	1·0	1·3	1·5	0·8
Industry and Crafts	80·5	72·6	63·4	67·0	61·5	86·0
Domestic Services†	1·9	2·3	2·9	1·4	3·0	0·9
Commerce and Transport	13·3	15·3	16·3	18·7	17·5	7·4
Servants in households	1·1	6·3	11·1	5·6	7·8	3·4
Public services	2·4	2·4	5·3	6·0	8·7	2·5

Of every 100 employees from the same area were employed in:	Hessen-Waldeck		North-East Germany		Other distant migrants	
	Barmen	Gelsen-kirchen	Barmen	Gelsen-kirchen	Barmen	Gelsen-kirchen
Agriculture	1·2	0·9	1·4	0·5	1·9	1·0
Industry and Crafts	61·6	77·3	55·8	88·7	57·8	78·1
Domestic Services†	3·6	0·9	5·3	0·9	1·8	0·8
Commerce and Transport	21·1	14·7	18·1	4·8	17·9	17·5
Servants in households	8·1	3·9	11·1	3·9	7·9	2·8
Public services	4·3	1·1	8·2	1·1	12·8	5·7

Total employees

Occupation	Barmen	As per cent	Gelsen-kirchen	As per cent
Agriculture	626	0·9	547	1·0
Industry and Crafts	47,994	72·0	40,822	77·1
Domestic services†	1,614	2·4	666	1·3
Commerce and Transport	9,979	15·0	6,587	12·4
Servants in households	3,599	5·4	2,433	4·6
Public services	2,907	4·4	1,943	3·7
Total	66,719	100·0	52,998	100·0

† Domestic services: This group comprises all servants not living in the household, for instance charwomen and washerwomen who may work for more than one household, also male servants not living in, casual and day labourers of all kinds other than those employed in agriculture.

considers the different industrial structure of the two towns, it means, however, that the locally born inhabitants strove mainly for skilled industrial work. Because of their better knowledge of conditions they could avail themselves of special opportunities in industry. The same held for the local migrants who had grown up fairly near industry. Although in both towns they occupied fewer industrial positions than their proportion in the population would lead one to suspect, there are proportionately more self-employed among them (in Barmen 16·7 per cent of all local migrants employed in industry and crafts were self-employed) than among the locally born (in Barmen 11·1 per cent). This was the effect of the migration of artisans, as the figures from the marriage registers suggest. There were also more local migrants in commercial positions than their proportion within the population would suggest; in Barmen 34·9 per cent of all local migrants in transport and commerce were independent. This shows that the local migrants saw their particular opportunity in providing the town population with necessary services. Another occupation frequently taken up by local migrants was serving in households, where their proportion, particularly in Barmen, was very high. As these servants were with few exceptions women (in Barmen there were 3,591 women servants and only 8 men), this explains the high proportion of women among the local migrants. Besides the greater chances of employment, the greater chances of marrying may have played a part in their decision to migrate.

Among the distant migrants there were greater variations. Whereas the occupational structure of the Hessian-Waldeck group resembles that of the local migrants but with a greater proportion of self-employed, there appears at first sight to be considerable differences between the North-East German groups in Barmen and Gelsenkirchen. In Gelsenkirchen the North-East Germans make up the majority of those employed in industry; in mining the North-East Germans account for 66·5 per cent of all employed. The bulk of this mass influx of North-East Germans, who did not possess any particular qualifications and were only driven to migrate by the poverty in their homes, had to make do with unskilled work. This was also true of Barmen; indicative of this was the fact that this group had a higher proportion of workers than all others. The differences between the North-East German groups in both towns are explained by the large number of North-East Germans working in the public services in Barmen. In Barmen every 12th North-East German employee worked for a public service, in Gelsenkirchen only every 90th. It is true that only 5·1 per cent of the employees in the Barmen public services were North-East Germans as compared with 9·7 per cent in Gelsenkirchen; this, however, is only of consequence in an investigation of the employees in this sector, not in an examination of the migrant group itself. With this exception, the North-East German group in both towns presents a unified picture: they took employment which no one else wanted. This explains their special position in the West-German industrial town, which led to the preservation of their group character and delayed their assimilation.

The migrants from the rest of Germany present a different picture. They were mostly qualified workers, who were consciously following up an opportunity. In the public services (under this heading the census lists besides civil servants (this includes all state and local government employees) the professions, doctors, lawyers, etc.) this group filled 12·8 per cent of all positions in Barmen and 20·4 per cent in Gelsenkirchen. This group brought the town for the most part especially qualified men. It also had great influence among the academically educated; it should be pointed out, that neither town offered facilities for training for academic professions. As far as the foreigners are concerned, it is important to remember, that in 1907 the seasonal workers employed in building trades were counted. Without these the structure of this group would probably resemble that of the group 'other Germans' though with a lower proportion employed in the public services.

TABLE XI

*Middle class employees**
(as per cent of total employees in each group)

Groups	Barmen	Gelsen-kirchen
Locally born	24·4	14·9
Local migrants	29·6	26·6
Hessen-Waldeckians	29·7	21·4
North-East Germans	20·1	4·5
Other Germans	37·5	20·9
Foreigners	16·1	11·1
Distant migrants	29·7	10·1
Total employees	26·9	16·4

* Self-employed and salaried employees of the occupational divisions industry and crafts and commerce and transport and all employees in the public services and professions.

The compilation of the proportions of the middle class employees within the separate groups confirms this finding. In both towns the local migrants, the other Germans and the Hessen-Waldeckians have the higher percentages. Both the upper and the lower middle classes therefore gained considerably from migration at this time. What holds for Barmen in the eighteenth century was true of both towns in the nineteenth, viz. that migration influenced economic development in two ways. The newcomers not only filled newly created positions but actively influenced industrial development by founding new firms and occupying positions of leadership and management. They brought the town not only working-power but also additional capital and so exercised a considerable influence on the process of industrialization. The industrial town was therefore not only a refuge for the surplus population growing up in small towns and rural areas but also the goal of active forces.[14]

More problematic than the economic integration and security of the new arrivals was their adaptation to the new surroundings. Did not moving mean for almost all internal migrants, even if the links with their old homes remained close, their uprooting from all family and social connexions and the necessity to adapt themselves to new and strange surroundings? Every internal migrant had the opportunity in a growing industrial town to train and prove his abilities, to improve his material position and to rise socially, but in a large town he was at first isolated and abandoned. He had to find his way in an unknown industrial world and was integrated into this world, which valued him merely according to his function in its productive process. The civil servants who were transferred to an industrial town fared better, for they still remained in a group which was not primarily determined by the town to which they had moved but even they found that their privileged position was not so readily accepted in an industrial town as it was in the country or in a small or medium-sized town. The leaders of industry and most of the academically trained found contact more easily.

[14] Only a few results are given. For a more thorough analysis of the census of 1907 for both towns, see the works mentioned in notes 1 and 10.

Certain factors helped the others: the local migrants had contact with others in their group and the North-East Germans formed at first a separate group but even they were eventually assimilated. The large industrial town was a melting-pot, in which local differences soon disappeared.[15]

This process of assimilation hardly affected the character of the people of Barmen. Even peculiarities of the various villages, from which the town had grown in the course of the centuries, were preserved. In the Ruhr area however there developed a new kind of people: the 'Ruhrvolk'. This is the most significant difference between the Ruhr cities and the other cities in Rhineland-Westphalia and the only lasting effect of the internal migration in the nineteenth century.

[15] *Cf.* the works of Brepohl given in notes 3 and 11.

26

THE DEMOGRAPHIC DEVELOPMENT OF FLANDERS IN THE EIGHTEENTH CENTURY

P. DEPREZ

Translated by Margaret Hilton

IN view of the somewhat unusual approach which has guided my work in this paper, it seems to me to be essential to deal at the outset with the question of the context and scope of the history of population or demographic history, as it is more usually called nowadays.

The first point to be made, and it is one on which there is no longer any disagreement, is that the history of population cannot be separated from economic and social history, and, conversely, economic and social history is inconceivable without a thorough knowledge of population developments and of the various demographic facts concerning births, deaths, marriages, fertility and also, as far as possible, migration. Such knowledge, however, cannot be achieved unless the methods hitherto employed by historians, and of which the inadequacy has become more and more apparent, are radically revised. The historians must turn to the demographers, for they alone by virtue of their training in the techniques and methods of contemporary demography are in a position to supply the theories and methods needed for a salutory overhaul. Research in historical demography will then be able to free itself from a certain tendency to mark time; it would be hard to deny that such a tendency has latterly been apparent.

This is however only one side of the problem, and other changes will also be necessary if valid comparisons are to be made between demographic development and economic and social developments. Such comparisons must not be undertaken in a superficial way; nor are they possible concerning regions which contain within their own boundaries a variety of economic structures and modes of growth. The study of population problems must always be made in connexion with, and at the same time refer to, a region with a specific economic structure and development; otherwise there is a grave danger that the picture one is attempting to reconstruct will be a distorted one. This caution may seem to some historians to be somewhat exaggerated, but studies which have been made of certain present-day situations have amply justified it.

It must also be said by way of conclusion to this brief introduction that I believe team-work to be essential. Historians, archivists, statisticians, demographers must all participate in joint research, and without a high degree of collaboration we shall be courting failure.[1]

---

[1] What is known as the 'Fleury-Henry method' provides a fine example of team-work in this

In this present paper I shall confine myself to a discussion of research dealing with various regions of Flanders, but particularly to the modern province of Eastern Flanders whose capital is Ghent. Some of the findings have already been published and other manuscripts are awaiting publication. In view of the increased interest shown lately in this line of research it is likely that they will be published in the near future.

I. *Literature and sources*

In the analysis which is to follow, I shall draw on the studies already carried out for the countryside surrounding Ghent, i.e. for the *Châtellenie du Vieuxbourg de Gand*,[2] and for the region of Schorisse (in French: le pays d'Escornaix) which is a seignorial domain to the east of Audenarde,[3] for a few villages in the neighbourhood of Alost,[4] and for a few others situated close to the Dutch frontier.[5] I shall also refer to two unpublished monographs prepared by the Henry-Fleury method, of which the first concerns the village of Adegem, situated on the boundary between Eastern and Western Flanders,[6] and the second the village of Elversele, which lies in the north-east of the province of Eastern Flanders, near to the small town of Saint-Nicolas-Waas.[7] I shall compare the results contained in these two works with those obtained for various Flemish towns—here I am using the term 'Flemish' in its wider sense, to include, as well as the two provinces of Flanders, the province of Antwerp and the western and northern section of the province of Brabant. The towns which have already been studied are as follows: Antwerp,[8] Audenarde,[9] Bruges,[10] Eeklo,[11] Ghent[12] and Malines.[13]

---

field of research. See M. Fleury and L. Henry, *Des registres paroissiaux à l'histoire de la population. Manuel de dépouillement et d'exploitation de l'état civil ancien*, Paris, 1956, 84 pp.

[2] For this region I have used in the first place a study which I made a few years ago but which has not yet been published. Two articles on this *châtellenie* have been published: A. De Vos, 'De Bevolkingsevolutie van Evergem, Lovendegem, Sleidinge, Waarschoot en Zomergem gedurende de XVIIe en XVIIIe eeuwen' (L'évolution de la population d'E., L., S., W. et Z. aux 17e et 18e siècles), *Appeltjes van het Meetjesland*, tome VIII, 1957, pp. 1-72. P. Deprez, 'Het Bevolkingscijfer in de Heerlijkheid Nevele gedurende de 16e, 17e en 18e Eeuwen' (L'évolution de la population dans la seigneurie de Nevele aux 16e, 17e et 18e siècles), *Handelingen der Maatschappij voor Geschiedenis en Oudheidkunde te Gent*, Nouvelle série, tome IX, Ghent 1955, pp. 50-119.

[3] C. De Rammelaere, 'De Bevolkingsevolutie in het Land van Schorisse (1569-1796)' (L'évolution de la population au Pays de Schorisse), *Handelingen der Maatschappij voor Geschiedenis en Oudheidkunde te Gent*, nouvelle série, tome XIII, Gand 1959, pp. 53-98.

[4] J. De Brouwer, 'De demografische evolutie in enkele dorpen in de omgeving van Aalst gedurende de 17e en 18e eeuw' (L'évolution démographique dans quelques villages dans les alentours d'Alost aux 17e et 18e siècles), *Land van Aalst*, tome XIII, 1961, no. 1, pp. 14-53. We may further cite, by the same author, an article which is to appear shortly concerning the villages of Erembodegem, Iddergem, Teralfene, Welle, Oordegem and Smetlede. All these villages are also in the *Pays d'Alost*.

[5] G. Vanlaere 'De demografische evolutie in Assenede, Bassevelde, Boekhoute, Ertvelde, Oosteeklo en Watervliet gedurende de 17e en 18e eeuwen' (L'évolution démographique dans A. . . . aux 17e et 18e siècles), *Handelingen der Maatschappij voor Geschiedenis en Oudheidkunde te Gent*, nouvelle série, tome XV, 1961, pp. 49-105.

[6] This study, carried out with the assistance of the *Institut national belge de Statistique*, will be published shortly.

[7] The inquiry into Elversele was made by F. Verhoeyen. It is greatly to be hoped that he will one day publish the entire findings of his research.

[8] F. Blockmans, *De Bevolkingscijfers te Antwerpen in de XVIIIe eeuw* (Les chiffres de population à Anvers au 18e siècle), dans Antwerpen in de XVIIIe eeuw, Anvers, 1952, pp. 395-412.

[9] C. De Rammelaere, 'De Bevolking van de Onze-Lieve-Vrouwparochie te Pamele (Oudenaarde) gedurende de XVIIIe eeuw' (La population de la paroisse de Notre-Dame à Pamele (Audenarde) au 18e siècle), *Cultureel Jaarboek voor de Provincie Oostvlaanderen 1954*, Gand 1960, pp. 273-88.

[10] A. Wyffels, 'De Omvang en de Evolutie van het Brugse bevolkingscijfer in de 17e en de 18e eeuw' (L'importance et l'évolution de la population brugeoise au 17e et 18e siècle), *Revue belge de philologie et d'histoire*, Bruxelles 1958, tome XXXVI, pp. 1243-74. [notes continued overleaf

In addition to these studies I must also mention: the work of D. Dalle on *le Métier de Furnes*, a group of villages lying close to the French frontiers in Western Flanders[14]; the study carried out by L. Van Speybroeck on the region between Ghent and Antwerp,[15] which Sir Richard Weston described in his 'Discourse of Husbandry in Flanders and Brabant'[16]; and two unpublished papers concerning the neighbourhood of Termonde[17] and the countryside around Antwerp.[18] I have also drawn on articles by A. Ryserhove which contain much useful data.[19] Two other studies have dealt in a rather general way, but mainly for the towns, with the correlation between demographic development and economic problems: the first is that of J. Verbeemen who points to a certain number of correlations[20]; the second is by H. Van Werveke and this latter gives an account of the present state of studies in this field.[21]

The sources used in these inquiries were parish registers, censuses, and figures for communicants. The parish registers come first, as they are in general very well preserved and very complete, and they supplied the greater part of the data used in the studies which have already been published. It must be observed, however, that for the period prior to 1740 stillbirths were not always recorded, and hence the data on mortality are imprecise.

[14] D. Dalle, 'Volkstelling van 1697 in Veurne-Ambacht en de evolutie van het Veurnse bevolkingscijfer in de XVIIe eeuw' (Le recensement de 1697 dans le Métier de Furnes et l'évolution du chiffre de la population de Furnes au 17e siècle), *Handelingen van het Genootschap voor Geschiedenis 'Société d'émulation' te Brugge*, Bruges, tome 90 (1953), pp. 97-130, et tome 91 (1954), pp. 18-54. D. Dalle, 'De Volkstellingen te Veurne en in Veurne-Ambacht op het einde van de Zeventiende Eeuw' (Les dénombrements à Furnes et au Métier de Furnes à la fin du 17e siècle), *Bulletin de la Commission Royale d'Histoire*, tome 120, 1955, pp. 1-34. I have also drawn on the unpublished doctorate thesis of Dalle, and wish to extend to him my sincerest thanks.

[15] L. Van Speybroeck, 'De wijziging van het landschapsbeeld en van het leven van den mensch in het Land van Waas in de 18e eeuw' (Le changement de l'image rural et de la vie de l'homme au Pays de Waes au 18e siècle), *Annalen van den Oudheidkundigen Kring van het Land van Waas*, tome 55, 1947-8, pp. 5-56, 93-129.

[16] R. Weston, *A discours of Husbandrie used in Brabant and Flanders: shewing the wonderful improvement of land there; and serving as a pattern for our practice in this common-wealth*, published in 1644 in London by Samuel Hartlieb.

[17] Unpublished paper by H. Verelst, which, however, I have not been able to examine at first hand.

[18] J. Dyck, *Evolutie van de bevolking, de bewoning en de landontginning in het landelijk district ten Zuid-Oosten van Antwerpen* (Evolution de la population, de l'habitat et du défrichement dans le district rural au sud-est d'Anvers), unpublished monograph, Ghent 1943.

[19] *De Familie Ryserhove* in *Appeltjes van het meetjesland*, vol. 5, pp. 91-171, and vol. 7, pp. 127-208. I wish also to thank MM. Buntinx, De Vriendt, Winnepenninckx and Wyffels, who have been kind enough to allow me to use the data in their unpublished genealogical tables.

[20] J. Verbeemen, 'De Werking van economische factoren op de stedelijke demografie der XVIIe en der XVIIIe eeuw in de Zuidelijke Nederlanden' (L'influence des facteurs économiques sur la démographie urbaine aux Pays-Bas méridionaux, XVIIe et XVIIIe siècles), *Revue belge de Philologie et d'Histoire*, tome XXXIV, 1956, pp. 680-700, 1021-55.

[21] H. Van Werveke, Demografische problemen in de Zuidelijke Nederlanden (17e en 18e eeuw) (Problèmes de démographie historique relatifs aux Pays-Bas méridionaux (XVIIe et XVIIIe siècles), *Mededelingen van de Koninklijke Vlaamse Academie voor Wetenschappen, Letteren en Schone Kunsten van België, Klasse der Letteren*, XVIIe année, 1955, no. 1, 19 pp. + graphs.

---

[11] A. De Vos, *De Omvang en de Evolutie van het Eeklose bevolkingscijfer tijdens de 17e en de 18e eeuw* (L'importance et l'évolution de la population d'Eeklo au 17e et 18e siècle), to be published.

[12] H. Van Werveke, 'De Curve van het Gentse bevolkingscijfer in de 17e en de 18e eeuw' (La courbe de la population gantoise au 17e et 18e siècle), *Verhandelingen van de Koninklijke Vlaamse Academie voor Wetenschappen, Letteren en Schone Kunsten van België*, 10e année, no. 8. P. Deprez, 'Het Gentse Bevolkingscijfer in de 2e helft van de achttiende eeuw' (Le chiffre de la population gantoise durant la seconde moitié du 18e siècle), *Handelingen der Maatschappij voor Geschiedenis en Oudheidkunde te Gent*, nouvelle serie, tome XI, 1957, pp. 177-95.

[13] J. Verbeemen, 'De demografische evolutie van Mechelen (1370-1800)' (The demographic evolution of Mechelen), *Handelingen van de Koninklijke Kring voor Oudheidkunde, Letteren en Kunst van Mechelen*, tome LVII, 1953, pp. 63-97.

Censuses and *status animarum* are very plentiful, and we have here a considerable advantage over some other countries—for example, France—for which
documents of this nature are almost entirely absent. This statement is equally
valid for the censuses demanded for the whole of the southern Low Countries
as for the *status animarum* carried out in individual parishes, and as a result of
this it is possible to obtain a very clear idea, relatively quickly and without
much difficulty, both of number of inhabitants and of demographic structure
and evolution.

Finally the figures of communicants are important in their own way. They
give us the number of persons who, having reached the age of 12, were admitted
to communion or took part in Catholic religious services during Easter week.[22]
But as Catholicism was the state religion and was practised, with the exception
of a few places, over the whole of what is today Belgium by the totality of the
population, these figures have for us the value of a census. In spite of this, however, it is wise to mention that many of the figures for communicants are only
rough estimates, so that they must be treated with caution. Their importance
remains great, however, for they can give us an idea of the development of a
particular part of the population.

II. *General development of the population*

The main outline of the development of the population of Flanders, both
rural and urban, is already known, and this fact affords us an initial advantage as
it enables us to direct all our attention to other problems and to inquire into
the causes of demographic development.

Let us remind ourselves briefly of the major demographic developments.
After the economic and demographic crisis of 1580-6, which, following the
revolt of the Netherlands, had resulted from the disasters of the war fought by
the Spanish for the reconquest of Flanders, under the command of Alexander
Farnese, the rural population increased considerably, but in an uneven fashion,
until 1640 or 1650. A period of stagnation then ensued in some parts of Flanders
whilst other areas showed a certain retrogression, though in fact this latter
movement never reached the dimensions of a pronounced decline. This was
the situation until the two years of acute crisis which afflicted all Europe in
1708-9; thereafter the population of Flanders was on the increase again until
1794, when another acute and lethal crisis provoked by dysentery had serious
repercussions on the population figures. These general lines of development in
the seventeenth and eighteenth centuries have been borne out by the work of
all the historians who have worked on rural demographic development: by
Vanlaere and De Vos for the villages of the north and north-east of Ghent and
for the *châtellenie du Vieuxbourg*; by De Rammelaere for the *Pays de Schorisse*;
by Dalle for *le Métier de Furnes*, for the region between Ghent and Antwerp,
and for the district of Termonde and for the countryside surrounding Antwerp.

But within this general development two important differences can be observed. In the first place we cannot consider the growth of the population after
1709 as being a steady growth, for in point of fact it took place in three distinct

[22] On this topic, *cf. inter alia* R. Mols, *Introduction à la démographie historique des villes d'Europe du
XIVe au XVIIIe siècle*, Vol. I, *Les problèmes*, Louvain 1954, p. 232 et seq.

612   DEPREZ

phases. In the first phase, which lasted till about 1740, growth was very slow, but in the second phase the population grew rapidly until 1775 when it entered a period of markedly slower growth lasting until 1794.

The second difference, or rather the second series of differences, concerns particularly the question of regional variations which are observable in the second half of the seventeenth century, and in the second phase of growth in the eighteenth, that is to say in the period for which we have established a large increase in the rural population. We can locate these regional differences as follows: in the least fertile part of Flanders, and particularly in the sandy area of the *châtellenie du Vieuxbourg*, the decline in population which manifests itself from 1650-60 onwards (though we are not yet in a position to pin down more narrowly the onset of this period) was on a larger scale and lasted longer than it did in more fertile regions. In these latter the stagnation period lasted only for about a decade. The same distinction between sandy regions and fertile regions is valid for the period 1740-75: in the former the increase in population begins in 1740 and exceeds the growth observable for fertile regions although the increase in the latter had begun twenty years earlier, i.e. in about 1725. Research projects which are at present in hand seem to suggest that the increase was greater in certain villages in the Alost region in the 1709-40 period than it was to be in the second half of the century. (For location of areas, see Map 1.)

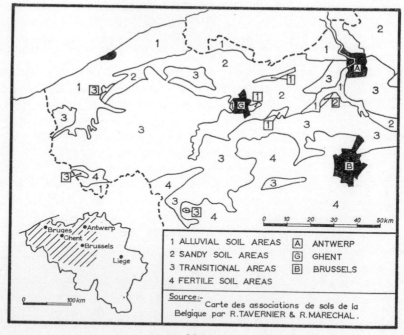

MAP 1

The demographic development of the four great Flemish towns, Antwerp, Bruges, Ghent and Malines, was quite different. One very important point stands out at once: throughout the seventeenth and eighteenth centuries the demographic development of the four towns was completely identical. They show a considerable and uninterrupted increase during the whole of the seventeenth century, followed by a decline which lasted till 1755. After this there was a revival of growth which lasted until the end of the century. The increase in the population in the towns was not however as great as the increase in the countryside between 1745 and 1794; it merely made up the losses incurred in the preceding period, and the maximum figures reached in the seventeenth century were never surpassed.

This short summary of the present state of knowledge on the general development of the population must suffice not only for Flanders and the Flemish towns but for the whole of the present territory of Belgium, as we are obliged to admit that except in some rare instances we are still almost completely ignorant of the demographic history of the other Belgian provinces. This imbalance in favour of Flanders needs to be quickly remedied by other regional studies, even if these must be of a superficial nature, confining themselves to the adding-up of annual totals of births, deaths and marriages or to statements of the situation at a given moment of time, or to the estimating of gross annual rates. I shall return to this question at the end of my article.

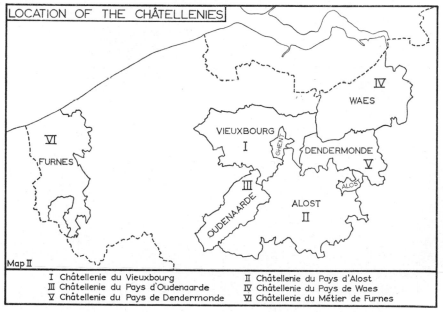

LOCATION OF THE CHÂTELLENIES

I Châtellenie du Vieuxbourg	II Châtellenie du Pays d'Alost
III Châtellenie du Pays d'Oudenaarde	IV Châtellenie du Pays de Waes
V Châtellenie du Pays de Dendermonde	VI Châtellenie du Métier de Furnes

MAP 2

III. *Crude rates for births and marriages*

As most studies in demographic history have confined themselves, apart from a discussion of the general evolution of a population, to calculations of the different crude rates as being indispensable for estimating the total figure for the population, it seems to me reasonable that we should in our turn look first at these crude rates, and particularly at the crude rates for births and marriages. The neglect of death rates is due to the fact that historians have always, and in many cases justifiably, mistrusted the data on deaths contained in the parish registers.

Although the rates at present available to us are few and far between, it is possible to put forward certain conclusions of a tentative nature. Both marriage and birth rates fell quite clearly in the course of the eighteenth century, and this drop is specially perceptible for the last twenty years of the century. It would appear also that marriage rates dropped more sharply than birth rates. In 1709 the gross birth rates stood between 43 and 38 per thousand, in 1786 between 42 and 36, and in 1792 between 37 and 33. For 1709 the crude marriage rates show wide divergences and may vary between 21 and 4 per thousand; in 1786 and between 9 and 6·5 in 1792. These rates vary not only in time but also in space. One finds the highest rates for both marriages and births in the villages examined by Vanlaere, situated in the north of the present-day province of Eastern Flanders. The same high rates are encountered again in the villages of *le Métier de Furnes* to which Dalle has devoted his two articles. Generally speaking, this region can be said to present the same characteristics as the region studied by Vanlaere; that is to say, fertile soil and sandy soil alternate in both areas. The crude birth rates calculated by Dalle for the whole of the seven villages he has studied for the years 1655, 1688, 1693, 1696 and 1697 range between 47 and 63 per thousand (48, 47, 57, 63 and 62 respectively). Crude marriage rates are also very high, being between 12 and 17 per thousand (13, 12, 15, 16 and 17 respectively).

These rates are of the same order of magnitude as those for the villages in the north of the province of Eastern Flanders: 58 per thousand in 1709 and 49 per thousand in 1786 for the birth rates and 20 per thousand in 1709 and 11 per thousand in 1786 for crude marriage rates.

For the large Flemish cities such as Ghent, Bruges, Antwerp and Malines the birth rates are distinctly lower and scarcely ever exceed the 36 per thousand mark. The marriage rates on the other hand vary between 10 and 8 per thousand at the end of the eighteenth century: they present therefore no contrast with the countryside. One aspect of these urban rates is however very revealing. It is that at the end of the eighteenth century the birth rates in the peripheral parishes forming a transitional zone between town and country are higher than in the central parishes of specifically urban character. Ghent and Antwerp both present this phenomenon, and the difference is one of between 7 and 8 per thousand. We can say, in general, that rates were high in the countryside, and indeed very high in the intermediate zones—in *le Métier de Furnes* for example—whereas in the towns the crude birth rates were lower but the marriage rates show no variation.

The crude rates reveal important differences therefore, which serve to accentuate further the differentials already noted in the course of our analysis of the general population developments. Although the rates do not in themselves offer any explanation of the observed trends they must be taken into consideration in any future research, as they are, and will remain, valuable indications which can serve as bases for comparisons in both time and space.

IV. *Age at marriage and average age of women at last confinement*

In this section and in those that follow I shall attempt to study as far as is possible a group of demographic facts which may throw light on the underlying factors and causes of the various demographic movements we encounter within a strictly limited area.

I shall discuss successively: the age of women at first marriage, their age at their last confinement, the spacing of births, and the rates of legitimate births by age groups, the ratio of births to marriages, and various aspects of mortality.

The data on age at first marriage I have drawn from genealogical studies which fulfil the standards required by demographers as defined by L. Henry in his book on Geneva.[23] I have also used data from the villages of Adegem and Elversele, which were studied in accordance with the Henry-Fleury method.[24] This means that the average ages have been calculated from ages of marriage recorded in a 'reconstituted' family. Let us examine firstly the data derived from the two above-named monographs.

Average age at first marriage—Adegem and Elversele (in years)

Period considered, according to year of birth	Adegem Men	Women	Elversele Men	Women
1608–49			27·2	24·8
1650–99			29·6	26·9
1680–99	24·9	23·3		
1700–49			29·4	28·0
1700–19	25·8	24·4		
1720–39	26·0	25·3		
1740–59	26·5	26·4		
1750–96			29·6	28·5
1760–79	23·5	23·4		
1780–96		25·8		

(For sources *cf.* studies mentioned in notes 6 and 7.)

In the case of the data drawn from the genealogical studies, I have divided these into two groups, the first concerning families of the *châtellenie du Vieuxbourg* and the other the families living in villages situated to the west of it, and comprising Beernem, Maldegem, Oedelem and Saint-Joris in Western Flanders.

Average age at first marriage in le Vieuxbourg and in some villages of Western Flanders (in years)

	Group I Men	Women	Group II Men	Women
		(divided according to their year of birth)		
1680–99	26·0	24·5	26·1	25·5
1700–19	27·3	25·2	24·5	22·4
1720–39	27·9	26·3	26·0	22·8
1740–59	26·3	24·2	26·7	22·5
1760–79	24·2	22·0	27·1	22·5

Sources: For le Vieuxbourg: unpublished studies by Buntinx, C. Wyffels and Winnepenninckx (see note 19). For the villages in Western Flanders: A. Ryserhove, *De Familie Ryserhove* in *Appeltjes van het Meetjesland*, Vol. 7, pp. 127-208. Number of cases in each period:
Group I: Men: 23, 24, 23, 9, 9. Women: 20, 30, 20, 14, 10.
Group II: Men: 26, 19, 14, 10, 9. Women: 22, 24, 16, 14, 9.

[23] L. Henry, *Anciennes familles genevoises. Étude démographique XVIe-XXe siècle*, Institut national d'études démographiques, Travaux et Documents, cahier no. 26, Paris 1956, p. 15 et seq. (see also note 9).
[24] See notes 6 and 7. Number of cases in different periods: Adegem: Men: 73, 54, 55, 49, 34; Women: 75, 63, 85, 75, 49; Elversele: Men: 21, 95, 86, 84; Women: 41, 173, 128, 141.

Except perhaps for the men in Group II (in which we may notice a slight increase or even just a tendency to slight increase), no general increase or decrease is observable. There are only fluctuations. Finally it should be noted that the ages cited here are generally lower than others at present known to us: in particular they may be compared with the ages obtained for Crulai,[25] Sotteville-lès-Rouen,[26] Ingouville,[27] and Canada.[28]

The average age of women at the time of the birth of their last child also constitutes useful information for the study of legitimate fertility. Here are the figures for Adegem and Elversele and those drawn from the genealogies concerning le Vieuxbourg.

Average age of women at last confinement, in Adegem, Elversele and in the châtellenie du Vieuxbourg (in years)

	Adegem	Elversele	Vieuxbourg
1608–49		40·8	
1650–99		41·7	
1680–1719	39·5		41·5
1700–49		40·3	
1720–59	41·0		41·6
1750–96	(insufficient data)		
1760–96	40·0		41·8

Number of cases used for the three periods:
Adegem   86, 92, and 60
Elversele   8, 38 and 18
Vieuxbourg   17, 18 and 24

Sources: For Adegem and Elversele: unpublished studies, see notes 6 and 7.
For Vieuxbourg: the unpublished studies of Buntinx, Wyffels and Winnepenninckx, see note 19.

In Crulai the age of women at the time of their last confinement lies between 38 and 41 years.[29] In Geneva the average age of mothers of whose families we have complete records is, at their last confinement, round about 38 or 39 between 1600 and 1649, for women who married between 20 and 24 years of age. In the eighteenth century the age was lower still.[30] It would seem that we may draw the conclusion that, in the case of marriages which were not interrupted by the premature death of one or other of the partners, the effective reproductive period of women who married between 20 and 24 could be as long as twenty years, and that the period of legitimate fertility generally covered sixteen or seventeen years, having regard to age at marriage. This means that the effective reproductive period was usually longer in Flanders than elsewhere. The extreme limits within which legitimate fertility was, or might be, operative having been established in this way, let us now turn our attention to the characteristics marking this fertility itself.

[25] E. Gautier and L. Henry, *La population de Crulai: paroisse normande, Institut national d'études démographiques, Travaux et Documents, cahier no 33,* Paris 1958, p. 84.
[26] P. Girard, Aperçus de la démographie de Sotteville-lès-Rouen vers la fin du XVIIIe siècle, *Population,* 1959, 14e année, no. 3, p. 489.
[27] M. Terrisse, 'Un faubourg du Havre: Ingouville', *Population,* 1961, 16e année, no. 2, p. 286.
[28] J. Henripin, *La population canadienne au début du XVIIIe siècle,* Institut national d'études démographiques, Travaux et Documents, cahier no. 22, Paris 1954, p. 96.
[29] E. Gautier and L. Henry, *La population de Crulai,* pp. 134-5.
[30] L. Henry, *Anciennes familles genevoises,* p. 88.

V. *The spacing of births*

In the development of legitimate fertility we find again the four periods into which we had been able to divide the general demographic development of Flanders; that is to say: a rapid growth in the first half of the seventeenth century, a period of stagnation or even a decline during the second half of the same century, followed by a revival which was slow at first but which after 1740 gained momentum. I have been able to establish the fact that there is a certain fluctuation in the spacing of births on the one hand and in the rates of legitimate fertility as calculated by age groups on the other.

Let us consider first the spacing of births, which I have calculated for all women grouped according to age at marriage and dating from age at marriage. Pre-marital conceptions are left out of account.

The reason for this is that there are no prenuptial conceptions in the sample of the Vieuxbourg. So it would not have been possible to make a comparison between the three groups if we had included prenuptial conceptions in the intervals for Adegem and Elversele.

Nevertheless we should like to give here, without further comments, the percentage of prenuptial conceptions (births less than 8 months after marriage) compared to the total number of births.

	Adegem	Elversele
1608–49		12·5
before 1660	13·7	
1650–99		14·8
1660–99	4·8	
1700–39	5·1	
1700–49		21·5
1740–96	6·4	
1750–96		23·4

Intervals between marriage and first birth and between first and second births (Adegem, Elversele, Le Vieuxbourg) (in months)

	Intervals, marriage—1st birth				Intervals, 1st—2nd birth		
	Adegem	Vieuxbourg	Elversele		Adegem	Vieuxbourg	Elversele
1608–49	—	14·3	16·3		—	22·7	28·8
Before 1660	15·3	—	—		24·4	—	—
1650–99	—	16·2	17·8		—	22·5	24·7
1660–99	16·4	—	—		25·3	—	—
1700–39	15·2	—	—		23·3	—	—
1700–49	—	14·1	15·2		—	24·7	24·4
1740–96	14·4	—	—		22·2	—	—
1750–96	—	11·5	14·2		—	19·0	23·1
Average interval	15·3	13·8	16·4		23·6	22·1	25·4

Number of cases used for the four periods:

Intervals between marriage and first birth:

Adegem	107, 411, 369 and 492
Vieuxbourg	19, 37, 51 and 51
Elversele	54, 88, 66 and 26

Intervals between first and second births:

Adegem	71, 312, 289 and 385
Vieuxbourg	31, 46, 53 and 53
Elversele	54, 88, 66 and 26

Sources: See preceding table.

The only data we have at present for Ghent in the eighteenth century yield similar results: 13·8 months between marriage and the first birth disregarding pre-marital conceptions, and 12·5 months if these are taken into consideration. However, these intervals have been calculated for the parish of Saint-Jacques only and cover marriages solemnized during the period 1700–9.[31]

If we disregard the shorter intervals between first and second births at Elversele and the steady length of the intervals in Le Vieuxbourg, the above table brings out a tendency for a slight increase of the intervals between marriage and the first birth and between the first and second births in the course of the second half of the seventeenth century. In the following century on the other hand they become increasingly shorter. These data are consistent with our notion of a stagnation or decline in the rural population between 1650 and 1700 and the continuous growth which took place in the eighteenth. It may be appropriate to mention that in Flanders in the eighteenth century the intervals between marriage and first confinement are shorter than those observed by P. Goubert in the *Beauvaisis*, where they were slightly longer than 16 months,[32] or by L. Henry for Crulai (16·2 months),[33] or by J. Houdaille for Saint-Agnan (18·5 months).[34] The intervals between first and second confinements are shorter than those of Crulai (26·0 months)[35] but longer than those that have been worked out for Sotteville-lès-Rouen.[36] In this last instance, however, the intervals were only calculated for families where there had been more than five births, and it has been shown that in these cases the intervals between births are shorter than the average for all families.

VI. *Rates of legitimate fertility by age groups*

Another element in the establishment of legitimate fertility is the calculation of rates of legitimate fertility by age groups. To date we possess only the unpublished results of research undertaken by F. Verhoeyen on Elversele. Although it would be preferable to await other findings before drawing any final conclusions, I think it may serve a useful purpose to give these rates for legitimate fertility in advance of publication.

Rates of legitimate fertility by age groups in Elversele

Women married in	Observed age of the woman 15–19	20–24	25–29	30–34	35–39	40–44	45–49
1608–49	—	0·571	0·406	0·310	0·343	0·232	0·023
1650–99	0·444	0·430	0·432	0·407	0·386	0·202	0·037
1700–49	0·666	0·542	0·492	0·396	0·348	0·166	0·018
1750–96	0·666	0·661	0·572	0·452	0·272	0·171	—
Averages	0·518	0·485	0·459	0·400	0·358	0·190	0·027

Source: Unpublished paper by M. F. Verhoeyen (see note 7).

[31] Data taken from the results of an inquiry at present uncompleted.
   Number of cases including pre-marital conceptions: 164.
   Number of cases excluding pre-marital conceptions: 136.
[32] P. Goubert, *Beauvais et le Beauvaisis de 1600 à 1730*, Ecole pratique des Hautes Études—VIe section, Centre de Recherches historiques. Démographie et Sociétés, III, Paris 1960, p. 33.
[33] E. Gautier and L. Henry, *La population de Crulai*, p. 138.
[34] J. Houdaille, 'Un village du Morvan: Saint-Agnan', *Population*, 1961, 16e année, no. 2, p. 304.
[35] E. Gautier and L. Henry, *La population de Crulai*, p. 140.
[36] P. Girard, 'Aperçus de la démographie de Sotteville-lès-Rouen', p. 495.

The cautious attitude adopted earlier in this article turns out to be justified by certain surprising features shown in this table of rates for legitimate fertility by age groups. The rates at ages 15-19 are abnormally high, whilst the general trend of the curve of the rates does not correspond with what has been observed elsewhere, except in the case of the rates for women married in 1650-99. The fact remains, however, that in spite of these reservations the rates seem to confirm our views of the general development of the spacing of births. If we limit our analysis to the two periods of the eighteenth century we find a well-marked difference between them. Fertility seems to rise in the age-groups of from 20-34 years. The rates for the period 1750-95 are definitely higher than those for the preceding period, and they are also higher if we compare them with those for Crulai,[37] Sotteville-lès-Rouen,[38] Ingouville[39] and Saint-Agnan.[40]

VII. *The relationship between births and marriages*

The development of legitimate fertility is reflected up to a point in the development of the number of persons per household and also in the development of the births-marriages ratios. In this connexion we have been able to show that in the *châtellenie du Vieuxbourg* of Ghent the number of persons per household increased considerably: it was 5·01 in 1708, 5·17 in 1745 and 5·48 in 1767. Such a movement is by no means unique, and we find the same thing wherever there was an increase in legitimate fertility, as for example in the *Pays de Schorisse* and in the small town of Eeklo, twenty kilometres from Ghent.[41] In the villages in the north of the province of Eastern Flanders (i.e. those studied by Vanlaere) we find however that the contrary is the case and that the number of persons per household steadily declines.[42]

The same can be said of the ratios between births and marriages. I have worked out these ratios on the following basis: the number of births occurring within one ten-year period is taken as the result of marriages contracted within that same period, within the preceding ten-year period and even of marriages solemnized twenty years earlier, in the proportion of about 50, 35 and 15 per cent respectively. What justification is there for such a method of calculation? We have seen that the period of legitimate fertility can be, when it is not prematurely interrupted, of about twenty years duration, and that this period might be even longer in the case of women who married very young. Obviously in the latter case the intervals between births grew increasingly longer. And so in this way I have calculated the movement of a series of births-marriages ratios with reference to the *châtellenie du Vieuxbourg*, the villages of the *Pays d'Alost*, the *Pays de Schorisse*, the villages studied by Vanlaere, and the city of Ghent. As the basic figures are lacking for the seventeenth century for some villages I have confined my attention to the figures for the eighteenth century.

[37] E. Gautier and L. Henry, *La population de Crulai*, p. 97 et seq.
[38] P. Girard, 'Aperçus de la démographie de Sotteville-lès-Rouen', p. 492.
[39] M. Terrisse, 'Un faubourg du Havre: Ingouville', p. 287.
[40] J. Houdaille, 'Un village du Morvan: Saint-Agnan', p. 304.
[41] Here is the data derived from the unpublished study of A. de Vos, *cf.* note 11: 4·40 in 1748, 4·72 in 1770 and 5·01 in 1794. C. De Rammelaere, 'De Bevolkingsevolutie . . .', pp. 3-6.
[42] G. Vanlaere, *De demografische evolutie . . .* , p. 85.

Ratios of births to marriages

Column 1.   Le Vieuxbourg of Ghent.
Column 2.   The villages of the *Pays d'Alost*.
Column 3.   The *Pays de Schorisse*.
Columns 4-6.   These three columns refer to the villages studied by Vanlaere.
Column 4.   The villages in the fertile sector.   ⎫ For explanations of
Column 5.   The villages in the sandy sector.   ⎬ these areas see
Column 6.   The villages in the intermediate zone   ⎭ Map 2.
Column 7.   Ghent.[43]

	Col. 1	Col. 2	Col. 3	Col. 4	Col. 5	Col. 6	Col. 7
1706-15	4·18	4·2	4·3	3·0	3·3	3·3	3·7
1716-25	4·32	4·3	4·7	4·2	3·3	3·9	3·4
1726-35	4·47	4·4	4·4	3·5	3·2	3·4	3·4
1736-45	4·66	4·8	4·5	3·6	3·7	3·7	3·6
1746-55	4·76	4·7	4·8	3·8	4·0	3·5	3·8
1756-65	4·96	4·7	4·7	3·3	4·2	3·7	3·9
1766-75	5·27	4·7	4·5	3·5	4·0	4·5	4·0
1776-85	5·02	4·4	4·6	3·5	3·9	3·8	4·1
1786-95	5·06	4·3	4·6	3·9	4·8	4·3	4·2

Sources:

For Vieuxbourg:

(1) Unpublished study, see note 2.
(2) A. De Vos, 'De Bevolkingsevolutie van Evergem, Lovendegem, Sleidinge, Waarschoot en Zomergem gedurende de XVIIe en XVIIIe eeuwen', in *Appeltjes van het Meetjesland*, Vol. 7, pp. 63-66, 68-71.
(3) P. Deprez, 'Het Bevolkingscijfer in de Heerlijkheid Nevele gedurende de 16e, 17e en 18e eeuwen', *Handelingen der Maatschappij voor Geschiedenis en Oudheidkunde te Gent*, New series, Vol. IX, 1955, pp. 98-105 and 108-15.

For the villages of the Pays d'Alost:

(1) J. De Brouwer, 'De demografische evolutie in enkele dorpen in de omgeving van Aalst gedurende de 17e en 18e eeuw', *Land van Aalst*, Vol. XIII, no. 1, pp. 39-41 and 44-47.
(2) See also note 4 concerning an unpublished study by the same author, from which we have drawn some basic data.

For Le Pays de Schorisse:

(1) C. De Rammelaere, 'De Bevolkingsevolutie in het Land van Schorisse (1569-1796)' *Handelingen der Maatschappij voor Geschiedenis en Oudheidkunde te Gent*, New series, Vol. XIII, 1959, pp. 90-92 and 95-97.

For the villages studied by Vanlaere:

(1) G. Vanlaere, 'De demografische Evolutie in Assenede, Bassevelde, Boekhoute, Ertvelde, Oosteeklo en Watervliet gedurende de 17e en 18e Eeuwen', *Handelingen der Maatschappij voor Geschiedenis en Oudheidkunde te Gent*, New Series, Vol. XV, 1961, pp. 97-100 and 102-5.

For Ghent:

(1) H. Van Werveke, 'De Curve van het Gentse Bevolkingscijfer in de 17e en 18e Eeuw', *Verhandelingen van de Koninklijke Vlaamse Academie voor Wetenschappen, Letteren en Schone Kunsten van België*, 10th year, no. 8, pp. 21-26 and 32-37.

Although these calculations are rather rough and ready and have no definitive value, they do reveal some remarkable contrasts, and can serve as one of our few elements of comparison for use within a wider context. Research now in progress is tending to confirm some of the points which emerge from them.

From the preceding table we can deduce a number of differences which we can compare with the known facts on the general lines of the development of the population. But before going any further it will be necessary to review the economic structure of Flanders and the regional variations within the general

---

[43] The births-marriages ratios for Ghent reflect an overall and complex situation which will be broken down later.

framework of its development, so that we may perceive the relevance of the studies we have mentioned and which have furnished the data for the table above.

The *châtellenie du Vieuxbourg* in Ghent which comprised 47 villages with a population of about 85,000 inhabitants at the end of the eighteenth century, lies mainly in the sandy area of Flanders where the soil is far from being highly fertile (see Map 2). Twelve villages, however, are in an exceptional situation, being in a transitional zone on the approaches to an area of clay soil, and are in consequence more fertile. These differences are reflected in the economic structure and development of the *châtellenie* as a whole. Whereas throughout the seventeenth and eighteenth centuries agriculture was steadily giving way to the linen industry in the sandy regions, the opposite tendency prevailed in the twelve villages whose economic situation was more favourable to the development of agriculture. This contrasting development on the part of the two sections of the *châtellenie* was not without its effects on the social conditions of the inhabitants, and as might be expected the standard of living fell considerably in the industrialized region, whereas it remained steady or even improved somewhat in the sector which had retained a more agrarian character.

The other studies are concerned with villages situated in the transitional zone or in the fertile areas, where the linen industry was either in decline or else, as was the case for the fertile regions generally, was of merely secondary importance throughout the seventeenth and eighteenth centuries. Both these types of region remained predominantly agricultural and the effect of this on the social life of the inhabitants was beneficial. The villages of the *Pays de Schorisse*, those close to the Netherlands frontier, and also Adegem and Elversele, are in the transitional zone and are consequently half-industrial and half-agrarian in character. The villages around Alost belong to the same category, but their linen industry was nevertheless declining. These economic differences will be revealed as being of major importance when we come to compare purely demographic conclusions, for we shall then see clearly that demographic and economic and social development are closely linked.

We can now sum up the differences which are brought out by the first table of this section:

(1) In the *châtellenie du Vieuxbourg* and the sandy parts of the north of Flanders which have a highly developed linen industry it is apparent that the ratios of births to marriages are very high and that they increase in the course of the eighteenth century. This increase in births-marriages ratios corresponds to a considerable increase in the population from 1740 onwards. The slight drop in the ratios for *Le Vieuxbourg* after 1775 coincides with the slowing-down in the rate of growth of the population of the *châtellenie* which occurred during the last quarter of the eighteenth century.

(2) As regards the *Pays de Schorisse* and the intermediate villages studied by Vanlaere—that is to say the industrialized areas in a state of transition, with mixed soil which is however mainly sandy—it appears that the ratios are not so high and remain almost stable throughout the second half of the eighteenth century. The increase in population is less considerable although it began twenty years earlier than in *Le Vieuxbourg*.

(3) In the *Pays d'Alost*, which is a region in transition and where rural industry is in decline and in which the soil is mixed though for the most part clayey,
the demographic development is in its main outline the same as that of the *Pays
de Schorisse*. The births-marriages ratios are also in the same order as those of
the preceding category, though they reveal a perceptible decrease in the course
of the second half of the century.

(4) Of the fertile region belonging to the villages of the north of Eastern
Flanders, which is both fertile and non-industrialized, it can be said that the total
population was diminishing after 1740, and the births-marriages ratios are very
low.

(5) The births-marriages ratios for the whole of the city of Ghent are not
very high and are in any case definitely lower than those which figure in the
first three columns of the table.

When analysing the crude rates for births and marriages I drew a distinction
between the central and peripheral parishes. The differences observed between
these two groups are evident again in the births-marriages ratios.

Ratios of births to marriages in Ghent

	Peripheral parishes[44]	Central parishes[45]
1706-15	4·15	3·48
1716-25	3·67	3·17
1726-35	3·61	3·09
1736-45	3·88	3·32
1746-55	4·41	3·40
1756-65	4·46	3·49
1766-75	4·68	3·51
1776-85	4·87	3·50
1786-95	4·88	3·82

Source: see previous table of figures for Ghent.

There is a remarkable difference between the births-marriages ratios of the
central parishes and those of the periphery of the city. In the former the ratio is
definitely lower than in the peripheral parishes where it rose further during the
eighteenth century, so that the difference was one of 1·06 children per marriage
at the eve of the Revolution. This difference in births-marriages ratios reflects
the peculiar economic and social features presented by the two series of parishes
in exactly the same way as we have seen was the case with the rural communities:
whilst the central parishes are usually richer and more typically urban, the peripheral parishes have to a large extent retained their rural character and support
a working population poorer than the true city-dwellers.

It is obvious that this explanation is not an exclusive one: the fluctuations in
births-marriages ratios can of course be partly due to the effects of migration.
This is especially true for the village of Watervliet studied by Vanlaere (col. 4
of the births-marriages ratios table): the low births-marriages ratios may be
the result of an emigration of just married couples having their children outside
the village.

[44] The peripheral parishes are: Saint-Sauveur, Saint-Martin and Saint-Pierre.
[45] The central parishes are: Saint-Michel, Saint-Nicolas and Saint-Jacques.

VIII. *Infantile mortality and mortality among children between
two and fourteen years of age*

Changes in mortality also affected the growth of the population. We have
been able to establish the fact that infantile mortality scarcely fell at all during
the first half of the eighteenth century. In the course of the second half of the
century however it shows a considerable rise. This can be seen clearly from an
examination of the number of deaths in the first year of life per thousand births.
I have made this calculation for the village of Lovendegem (to the west of Ghent)
whose population numbered about 4,000 inhabitants in 1786.[46] Here are the
figures in twenty-year periods.

1700-19: 206·7	1740-59: 204·2	1780-96: 220·9
1720-39: 193·9	1760-79: 228·1	

We also know the infantile mortality rate per 1,000 births over fifty-year
periods for the village of Elversele. 151 per thousand for the years 1650-99; 152
per thousand for 1700-49 and 215 per thousand for 1750-96.

In both villages the rates remain almost unchanged until the middle of the
eighteenth century. They rise during the following years although they do not
reach the levels of comparable rates so far known to us, as for example Sotteville-
lès Rouen 244 per thousand,[47] Ingouville 286,[48] Saint-Agnan 240,[49] Auneuil
288, Saint-Laurent-des-Eaux 326 and almost all quarters of Beauvais[50]—and I
am only quoting the data obtained by most recent research. Crulai is the only
exception to this general pattern, for there the rate was 205 per thousand births.[51]
The work of R. Mols on European towns also contains valuable indications on
this aspect.[52]

In his article on Ingouville, Terrisse gives a table of differential infantile mortality rates which brings out clearly the fact that the rates are higher in the lowest
social strata of the population and that they drop progressively as one rises in
the social scale.[53] Considering the difference between the rates for Lovendegem
and Elversele, a similar phenomenon is perhaps not to be ruled out in the case
of Flanders, for Lovendegem is a highly industrialized village containing in consequence among its numbers a strong element of a proletariat whose social conditions were very poor. Elversele on the other hand has less rural industry for
this had largely given way in the course of the eighteenth century to agricultural
activity which was constantly gaining ground. Social conditions in Elversele
will in general have been superior to those obtaining in Lovendegem.

The case of Lovendegem indicates moreover that mortality between 2 and
14 years of age decreased during the second half of the eighteenth century, and
this confirms the findings in Crulai, where mortality between birth and 10 years
of age shows a decline after 1750.[54] The results for Elversele are not in accordance with those obtained for Lovendegem, for there mortality from birth to

[46] *Cf.* A. De Vos, 'De Bevolkingsevolutie van Evergem . . .', p. 14.
[47] P. Girard, 'Aperçus de la démographie de Sotteville-lès-Rouen', p. 498.
[48] M. Terrisse, 'Un faubourg du Havre: Ingouville', p. 295.
[49] J. Houdaille, 'Un village du Morvan: Saint-Agnan', pp. 291-2.
[50] P. Goubert, *Beauvais et le Beauvaisis*, p. 40.
[51] E. Gautier and L. Henry, *La population de Crulai*, p. 163.
[52] R. Mols, *Introduction*, II, p. 315, III, p. 147 et seq.
[53] M. Terrisse, 'Un faubourg du Havre: Ingouville', p. 291.
[54] E. Gautier and L. Henry, *La population de Crulai*, p. 175.

10 years stands at 274 per thousand in the years 1650-99, at 332 in 1700-49, and at 346 in the period 1750-96.

The lowering of mortality rates as compared with those of the surrounding regions and the fall in mortality rates for those under 14 years of age led to a considerable reduction in the age of the rural population. This movement was further accentuated by the favourable evolution of mortality for ages under 50 years, so that the reduction in the age of the population was as it were consolidated. Let us therefore now turn to consider this second aspect—the lowering of the average age of the rural population—more thoroughly.

IX. *Adult mortality*

I must first advance a justification of the method I shall employ. In the present state of our researches in Belgium it is not possible to adopt the method that was used for the study of Crulai, and we have to make do for the moment with a division into age groups at death of both men and women, and with average ages at death from a given age onwards (15 years in this case) and at different points in time. I have had recourse to this index—often a deceptive one, though much used by historians—because the observations already made justify this method of calculation. Indeed it has emerged from our foregoing analysis that the age-structure of the rural population was developing in the direction of a rejuvenation. From this it follows also that if mortality rates had remained stable the proportion of the deaths accounted for by adults of less than 45 or 50 years of age would have increased. The figures I am about to give indicate the opposite however, and we are consequently entitled to affirm that there was a decline in mortality.

From calculations I have made for the *châtellenie de Vieuxbourg*, and from those made by F. Verhoeyen for Elversele it appears that the average age of death of persons of more than 15 years rose appreciably in the course of the eighteenth century. Here is a table for *Le Vieuxbourg* giving the average age at death of persons aged 15 years and over.

Vieuxbourg: Average age at death of persons of 15 years and over (in years)

	1700-19	1720-39	1740-59	1760-79	1780-96
Men	46·1	48·0	48·4	51·0	52·2
Women	47·4	48·4	49·2	50·7	51·9

Number of instances obtainable for the five periods:
Men: 1,594, 1,841, 1,924, 1,997 and 1,958.   Women: 1,599, 2,101, 1,970, 2,165 and 2,024.
Source: An unpublished study, see note 2.

Elversele: Average age at death of persons aged 15 years and over (in years)

	Men	Women
1650-99	53·6	51·3
1700-49	50·2	51·1
1750-96	56·3	56·4

Number of instances obtainable for the three periods:
Men: 225, 337 and 272.   Women: 167, 320 and 359.
Source: The unpublished study of F. Verhoeyen, see note 2.

The average age can be said therefore to have risen during the second half of the eighteenth century. Compared with the first half of the eighteenth century it is above all the average age of the men which rose between 1750 and 1796. We may remark also that the average ages are higher in Elversele than they are in *Le Vieuxbourg*.

In the case of *Le Vieuxbourg* this increase in the average age of death resulted from a fall in deaths occurring between the ages of 25 and 54 for men and between 20 and 64 for women. In Elversele the drop is above all apparent between 20 and 39 years for men and between 20 and 49 years for women. The fall among women is mainly apparent during the effective reproduction period, i.e. 20-44 years of age, and this should have repercussions on the duration of marriages, as more women were left alive and capable of conceiving and bearing children.

The progress of these diminutions in deaths clearly shows that they took place mainly after 1759, thus confirming and explaining the movement of the average ages at death.

Le Vieuxbourg

	Deaths of males between 25 and 54 years per thousand male deaths of ages over 15 years	Deaths of females between 20 and 44 years per thousand female deaths of ages over 15 years
1700–19	516·1	402·0
1720–39	461·9	397·6
1740–59	451·4	394·6
1760–79	385·8	352·8
1780–96	346·0	327·8

Source: as above, see note 2.

Elversele

	Deaths of males between 20 and 39 years per thousand male deaths of ages over 15 years	Deaths of females between 20 and 49 years per thousand female deaths of ages over 15 years
1650–99	271·1	407·1
1700–49	258·1	409·3
1750–96	165·4	309·1

Source: as above, see note 7.

Parallel to this diminution in mortality in age groups of under 50 years we observe an increase in the percentage of persons of over 65 years of age at the time of their death. In *Le Vieuxbourg* this percentage (out of 100 deaths of those over 15 years) was 19·5 per cent for men between 1700 and 1719, and 34·9 per cent between 1780 and 1796, and this development takes place over the two periods without a sudden break.[55] The same is observable for women; here the figures are respectively 21·8 per cent and 34·1 per cent.

The same developments are observable in Elversele but here the percentages

[55] The percentages for the intermediate periods are:
24·8 for 1720–39,
25·4 for 1740–59,
32·4 for 1760–79.

are high: for men 31·7 per cent for the period 1700-49 and 41·1 per cent for 1750-96; for women the figures are 32·1 per cent and 42·3 per cent respectively. The causes of this evolution in Elversele may be found in the explanation given for *Le Vieuxbourg*. Migration may also have been of a certain importance; emigration of men and women to Flemish towns could have been partly responsible for the higher percentages.

This increase in the proportion of the population who died at more than 65 years of age justifies us in thinking that the reduction in the average age of the population which we discussed earlier was to a certain extent offset by ageing at the summit of the pyramid. From the small amount of information we have at our disposal at present this ageing seems to have been greater in the non-industrialized villages than in the villages of *Le Vieuxbourg* with their well-established linen industry.

X. *General conclusions*

What general conclusions—though it must of course be emphasized that these will be of a provisional nature—can we draw from the preceding analysis of various demographic phenomena? The development of the population from 1740 onwards is the most interesting aspect, for that was the year which marked the great turning-point in the demographic history of Europe.[56]

With the aid of the data we now have at our disposal we can put forward the following as a possible explanation of the population growth in rural Flanders. We can attribute it to two main factors: an improvement in legitimate fertility and a decline in mortality among adults.

The changes in legitimate fertility resulted from a combination of factors some of which remained stable while others fluctuated. Among the stable factors must be included the relatively low age of women at the time of their first marriage, and, at the other end of the effective legitimate reproduction period, the relatively advanced age of women at the time of their last confinement. The effect of these two phenomena taken together was that the effective reproductive period in Flanders lasted in general longer than it did elsewhere. The factors which underwent change are of course even more important; the closer spacing of successive births and the higher rates of legitimate births calculated on the basis of age groups under 50 years, as one of the immediate results of the fall was a lengthening of the duration of marriages. Another aspect of the general improvement was the considerable decline in mortality amongst women of child-bearing age.

The only negative element in the picture is the rise in infantile mortality, which was, however, offset by a fall in the mortality rate for children between the ages of 2 and 14.

These remarks are valid for the whole of Flanders and particularly for the Flemish rural areas.

Certain variations are, however, discernible as between regions which differ in their economic and social structure. The variations we have observed point to the fact that legitimate fertility may have been higher, if it was not unduly influenced by migration, in the villages where industrial activity was on a smaller

[56] *Cf.* in this connexion the work of P. Goubert, p. 59 et. seq.

scale. But in the first category of villages infantile mortality was higher than it was in the second. In the less industrialized villages the average age at death of persons over 15 and the ageing at the top of the age-pyramid are both more marked.

In addition we can observe a striking disparity between urban and rural demographic developments, and this raises many problems which are unlikely to be solved in the near future. Several historians, among them H. Van Werveke,[57] J. Verbeemen,[58] D. Dalle,[59] and the present author[60] have already contributed to a discussion of this topic. They have all tried, each in his own way, to advance an explanation of this divergence, but it has to be admitted that so far the discussion has not been very fruitful, owing to the fact that the data on which the discussion was based were of very limited scope—and little attempt has been made to enrich the basic material.[61]

However this may be, this present inquiry seems to confirm the view that economic and social conditions have influenced demographic phenomena. There is nothing new in this statement of course, but it is of its nature so important that I feel impelled to pursue my analysis of this correlation a little further.

In this context a brief summary of the social and economic development of Flanders giving particular attention to *Le Vieuxbourg*, the *Pays d'Alost* and *Pays de Schorisse* seems called for, and will throw the purely demographic points into sharper relief.

Firstly, the case of *Le Vieuxbourg*. The considerable increase in the rural population after 1740 and the consequent increase in the working population led to an increased demand for employment. But as the density of the population was very high—between 220 and 250 inhabitants per square kilometre—agriculture could offer no solution for this acute problem. The nearby city of Ghent was itself passing through a period of economic stagnation and could not therefore syphon off this excess labour-force. The only solution to the problem was found to be in rural industry, and particularly the linen industry, and this solution was a very natural one as flax was one of the great Flemish crops. Until this time the weaving of linen had been an additional occupation practised by a large proportion of the population, particularly in winter—the off-season for agricultural work. After 1740 the linen industry came to occupy an ever-increasing number of countryfolk on a full-time basis. This change fostered the creation of a rural

[57] H. Van Werveke, 'Demografische Problemen . . . ', p. 9 et seq.
[58] J. Verbeemen, 'De Werking . . . ', p. 1041 et seq.
[59] D. Dalle, doctorate thesis, Vol. I, p. 134.
[60] P. Deprez, 'Het Gentse Bevolkingscijfer . . . ', p. 185 et seq.
[61] M. Van Werveke's explanation is that in general the development of urban population has been determined by the changes which occurred in the fertility of marriages and the general economic situation. The part played by migration was merely subordinate. M. Dalle concurs with this opinion. On the other hand M. Verbeemen's explanation stresses the role of migration: this alone, he believes, according to the economic situation in the towns, is responsible for the development of urban populations, especially during periods of growth and therefore immigration. According to Verbeemen changed marital fertility has been of no significance.

At an earlier stage we shared M. Verbeemen's opinion. (See note 60.) Meanwhile we have had occasion to correct our view in a communication presented to the Conference of the International Union for the Scientific Study of Population, held at New York in September 1961. Since then M. Dalle has attacked our original point of view in a doctoral thesis which has not yet been published.

It is now quite clear that neither migration (about which information is rare and fragmentary) nor changes in legitimate fertility alone can provide a satisfactory and convincing explanation of the demographic evolution of the Flemish towns.

proletariat composed for the most part of unskilled workers who were consequently ill-paid and lived in deplorable conditions. Most of them were without
work in winter and worked only in summer and in the autumn. The standard
of living of these workpeople was extremely low. As they were ill-paid and
permanently under-nourished they preferred to work at harvest-time for the
farmers from whom they earned more although they were paid as day-labourers.
These tendencies became even more general in the course of the second half of
the eighteenth century—so much so that one can say that by the end of the
eighteenth century at least 75 per cent of the working population in the *châtellenie du Vieuxbourg* earned their bread in the linen industry. In this region the
proletarianization and pauperization which characterized the second half of the
century assumed proportions which can be justly termed alarming, and it is
precisely here that we have found the heaviest population increase, the highest
legitimate fertility and also, not very surprisingly, the highest infantile mortality.

This black picture of the situation in *Le Vieuxbourg* forms a contrast to the
generally favourable conditions prevailing in the *Pays de Schorisse* and the *Pays
d'Alost*. In these regions the population increase was smaller. The division of
land-holdings, and the reduction in the size of properties which had hitherto
been economically viable characterized the development of *Le Vieuxbourg*; in
the other two regions however the same thing occurred on a considerable scale
yet without assuming such alarming proportions.

Equally the process of industrialization proceeded at a steadier pace. As a
consequence the rural character of these two regions was better preserved from
the purely structural point of view. In the course of the second half of the eighteenth century a movement towards the intensification of agriculture added its
effects, and this intensification was to underlie the high reputation enjoyed by
Flemish agriculture at the end of the century when harvests were obtained such
as had not been known before.

On the fertile soils of these regions intensification achieved fine results, and
thus the prospects were improved even for relatively small holdings.

The preceding points taken in conjunction explain how it came about that
in the *Pays d'Alost* and the *Pays de Schorisse* the agricultural sector gained in
importance during the second half of the eighteenth century. A decline in rural
industry and a return to agriculture on the part of a considerable proportion of
the population had a beneficial effect on the social conditions of the great masses
of the country people.

This relative prosperity was not without its consequences on the purely
demographic front: legitimate fertility fell, as did infantile mortality, and the
adult expectation of life very probably increased.

The contrast between industrialized areas and those more typically agrarian
can also be observed in other places than Belgium. In Overysel in the Netherlands we find the same situation: in the industrialized region of Twente where
the linen industry expanded considerably in the course of the eighteenth century
there was a greater increase of population than is found in Salland and Friesland,
regions still dominated by agriculture.[62]

[62] B. H. Slicher van Bath, *Een Samenleving onder Spanning* (A society under tension), Assen 1957,
pp. 59 and 125. H. K. Roessingh, *Historisch-demografisch onderzoek* (Historical-demographic research),
The Hague 1959, pp. 13-14.

I cannot conclude this article without expressing my point of view on the way in which research into historical demography should be tackled in the future, and in order to do so I must necessarily overstep the narrow bounds set by the subject of the present paper.

In the first place I should like to return to the question of the 'imbalance' I mentioned at the beginning of this article, and which has the effect of according to Flanders, and particularly to Eastern Flanders, a privileged position—in my view an excessively privileged position. I believe that this imbalance needs to be remedied, and that this is one of the most urgent tasks before Belgian scholars. For apart from a few isolated research-workers in other universities—I might mention Ruwet at Louvain, Hélin in Liège, Arnould in Brussels and Verbeemen and Cosemans in the *Archives Générales du Royaume*—the great majority of the studies in this field have been conducted in the University of Ghent and more especially in the seminar of Professor C. Verlinden. It is therefore incumbent on other universities to make a real effort in their turn and to publish their results. Three separate aspects to be distinguished in the work which needs to be done in the course of the future progress of our research in historical demography: the geographical framework, the periods to be considered, and the methods to be employed.

The geographical framework will, I believe, need to be considered, as it is important to concentrate less attention on regions where different economic and social structures overlap one another, as they did in Eastern Flanders. We should turn all our attention to the great regions whose structure and economic and social development were more homogeneous—such as: the Campine which is consistently infertile; the clayey areas of Central Belgium with their big landed estates; the Condroz to the south of the Sambre-Meuse line which was also a country of big landed estates though here they were founded on stock-breeding; the wooded region of the Ardennes; or the valley of the Sambre and Meuse where rural industry was very extensive.

Three periods would seem to be of prime importance and should consequently receive priority treatment in future studies. They are the second half of the seventeenth century; the second half of the eighteenth century, and the first half of the nineteenth century. Each of these three periods is of capital importance. The first affords us the opportunity of studying the possible consequences of the last great epidemics. The second period constitutes the transition between the old demographic structure and the modern régime, whilst the third represents the period of rapid industrialization in the towns accompanied by many possible repercussions on the economic and social structures which doubtless affected movements of the population.

I have mentioned our conception of our subject and the methods it should use as the third aspect of our work to be considered. It seems to me that we need to proceed simultaneously along two parallel lines. On the one hand studies of an elementary nature are required and on the other there must be more detailed inquiries. By 'elementary studies' I mean those which give merely the results of censuses, annual totals of births, deaths and marriages, the various crude rates and data on infantile mortality. More detailed studies should be conducted according to the Fleury-Henry method. In both cases demographic research must be accompanied by companion studies in economic and social history. The first type of study should inform us rapidly of the number of inhabitants, its development and certain of its characteristics; the second type should provide explanations, and give an account of the causes and factors contributing to the demographic development.

In concluding this article it is necessary to utter a warning against exaggerating its implications. I have attempted to bring out the permanent correlation which existed, and always exists, between demographic movements and social and economic phenomena, but more than this I have not aimed to do. Anything further would be premature, as the research we have at our disposal is not yet sufficient in quantity to permit of it. It is for this reason that I have presumed to indicate—or rather, to suggest—the possible lines along which our future work should be directed.

I trust historians will bear in mind the plea that has been made in the present article for employing certain new tools and new approaches in our research for a just appraisal of our material.

27

THE GROWTH OF POPULATION IN AMERICA, 1700-1860

J. POTTER

IN sharp contrast with the vigour of the debate over the causes of the increase of the English population during the eighteenth and early nineteenth centuries, the amount of attention devoted to demographic problems in American historical writing is small. Either from excessive confidence in the soundness of accepted views or from despair at the enormity of the task of re-appraisal, the general historian has tended to treat American population statistics as known, uncontroversial and not requiring explanation. Most economic history textbooks, for example, merely give the decennial population figures starting with the Census of 1790 with little or no discussion of their implications.[1]

Yet the subject is of great interest in itself and is essential to the interpretation of American social and economic history. For non-Americans, to whom this chapter is primarily addressed, it can have important bearing on their own attempts to interpret the European, and especially the English, data. Above all perhaps America offers a yardstick against which the significance of the English figures may be measured. Between 1700 and 1860 the rate of population growth in America is usually supposed to have been about 34 per cent per decade, i.e. about twice the English rate. There is surely a danger in analysing the English data of explaining too much. Is it not important to ask occasionally not why the English population grew so fast during this period, but why it did not grow faster, why it grew at a particular rate, why its rate of growth did not approximate more closely to the American rate?

It is worth while to start with a reminder of the weight Malthus himself attached to the American evidence. He frequently referred to the greater speed of American population growth, 'a rapidity of increase, probably without parallel in history'.[2] Indeed, it was directly from America that he deduced his demographic law, in the second chapter of the first edition of his *Essay on Population*:

'In the United States of America, where the means of subsistence have been more ample, the manners of the people more pure, and consequently the checks to early marriage fewer, than in any of the modern states of Europe, the population has been found to double itself in twenty-five years.

---

[1] It might be noted that this is not true of two recent works. Seymour E. Harris's *American Economic History* (1961) contains a chapter on 'Population and Immigration', by Elizabeth W. Gilboy and Edgar M. Hoover. Another textbook of 1961, *American Economic History*, by L. E. Davis, J. R. Hughes, and D. M. McDougall, also contains a short section (chapter 6) devoted to population. As will become evident in the course of this chapter, this neglect of demographic history by general historians does not extend to the professional demographers who usually, however, are not primarily historians.

[2] T. R. Malthus, *An Essay on the Principle of Population*, 1798, p. 105 (the page references given here are to the Royal Economic Society Reprint of 1926).

This ratio of increase, though short of the utmost power of population, yet as the result of actual experience, we will take as our rule; and say,

That population, when unchecked, goes on doubling itself every twenty-five years, or increases in a geometrical ratio.'[3]

Malthus had no doubts about the reasons for this unique American experience. It arose from a combination of favourable circumstances, but above all from the abundance of land and the absence of political, social or institutional obstacles to its alienation and cultivation. The further west one looked, the greater the speed of population growth. In the back settlements, where the settlers devoted themselves solely to agriculture, the population had been known to double itself in as little as fifteen years. And to this observation, Malthus added a footnote containing the second part of his law:

> In instances of this kind, the powers of the earth appear to be fully equal to answer all the demands for food that can be made upon it by man. But we should be led into an error, if we were thence to suppose that population and food ever really increase in the same ratio. The one is still a geometrical and the other an arithmetical ratio, that is, one increases by multiplication, and the other by addition. . . .[4]

The time would nevertheless come, Malthus went on, when all the fertile land would be occupied, even in America. Then any further increase in food production would depend 'upon the amelioration of the land already in possession'.[5]

Malthus went on to ask why a given number of emigrants, living in the American environment, produced a greater number of descendants than a simi-

[3] Ibid., pp. 20-21. The first known mention of this rate of increase is found in Benjamin Franklin's Observations Concerning the Increase of Mankind and the Peopling of Countries (clause 22) written as early as 1751, where it appears as a supposition:

'Thus there are supposed to be now upwards of one million English souls in North America (though it is thought scarce eighty thousand has been brought over sea). . . . This million doubling, suppose but once in twenty-five years, will in another century be more than the people of England, and the greatest number of Englishmen will be on this side the water.' (B. Franklin, Works, ed. J. Bigelow, 1887, ii, 225 ff, my italics.) Malthus's opponent of 1820, William Godwin, took the view that Malthus accepted Franklin's hypothetical phrase as a statement of proven fact, and attempted to demolish Malthus by first demolishing Franklin.

The figure of twenty-five years apparently carried no particular significance for Franklin. Earlier in the same Observations (clause 7) he wrote of a doubling every twenty years. One year earlier, in Poor Richard Improved, Franklin had written of a computation in England, according to which the 'Colonies . . . double the Number of their Inhabitants every Thirty Years'. (The Papers of Benjamin Franklin, ed. L. W. Labaree, Yale 1961, iii, 440.) For further discussion of Franklin's views, see below, pp. 643-4.

A later statement, similar to Franklin's, is also found in a 24-page tract, by a Harvard Professor of Divinity, Edward Wigglesworth, M.A. (the Younger), Calculations on American Population (Boston 1775): 'From a comparison of the most authentic estimates of the inhabitants of the several British colonies in America, taken at different times, it appears that the British Americans have doubled their numbers, in every period of twenty-five years from their first plantation. A rapidity of population not to be parallaled [sic] in the annals of Europe! . . . This rapid population of the Americans arises, partly from the great accession of foreigners, but principally from the natural increase of the inhabitants.' (p. 1.) Wigglesworth then uses this assumed doubling every twenty-five years as the basis for his Calculation which attempts to predict the American population as far as the year A.D. 2000.

About the same time, the mid-1770's, two French philosophes Count Buffon and Abbé Raynal also refer to a doubling of the American population every twenty-five years (see below, footnote 23).

[4] Ibid., pp. 106-7, footnote.

[5] He returned to this argument later: at present a famine appeared to be almost impossible in America; but 'it may be expected, that in the progress of the population of America, the labourers will in time be much less liberally rewarded' (p. 131).

lar number remaining behind in Great Britain. Why did not 'an equal number produce an equal increase, in the same time'? His answer remained the same as before: the 'great and obvious cause' of the slower growth in Britain was 'the want of room and food, or, in other words, misery'.[6] The same could also be said of parts of Europe.[7] Certainly in America free institutions had done much to promote industry, happiness, and population growth. But 'even civil liberty, all powerful as it is, will not create fresh land'.[8] The worst effects of land hunger would be alleviated in America through the absence of primogeniture[9] and through the relatively equal spread of property, the possession of land being in itself a source of happiness; but these circumstances, 'though they may alleviate, can never remove the pressure of want'.[10]

Malthus repeated these views in the subsequent versions of the *Essay*, adding fresh documentation. In the edition of 1826, the sixth and the last to appear during his lifetime, he made use of the American Fourth Census of 1820.[11] The USA had 'millions and millions of acres of fine land'; in England the only land remaining to cultivation was comparatively barren. The argument was thus unchanged. The American population was growing by the postulated geometrical progression; this represented the rate of increase to be expected under conditions of land abundance, until such time as all the good land would have been occupied and only marginal soils would remain.

Despite the confidence of Malthus's assertions about the size and the rate of growth of the American population in the eighteenth century, and the subsequent general acceptance of those assertions, the facts are by no means certain. For decades after 1790, when the decennial Censuses begin, the information available is far from complete. Until well into the nineteenth century, the difficulties of deriving and interpreting historical demographic statistics for America are immense.

The first problem arises simply from deficiencies in the data. These shortcomings are due at least in part to the fact that the population was widely dispersed over a vast area; as late as 1870 the highest population density in any single state was that of Rhode Island with 200 persons per square mile (compared with 389 persons per square mile in England and Wales in 1871); only four states out of 38 in that Census had a density of over 100 (*cf.* Scotland in 1851 with a density of 96). Correspondingly, the urban population remained small; in 1870 roughly 10 million out of a total population of 40 million lived

---

[6] *Ibid.*, p. 109. But later, in his discussion of William Godwin's *Enquiry concerning political justice*, he stated, rather paradoxically: 'England is certainly a more healthy country than the back settlements of America' (p. 185).

[7] *Ibid.*, pp. 116-18.   [8] *Ibid.*, p. 342.

[9] At the time of the *Essay*, however, the general abolition of primogeniture (and entail) in America had only recently become effective.

[10] *Ibid.*, p. 345. The reasons given by Malthus to explain the rapidity of growth in America are very close to those given by Wigglesworth, who wrote: 'The reasons, why the Americans are more prolific than the Europeans, are, that they are less luxurious in their manner of living, and the means of supporting a family can be more easily obtained. For the last reason the Americans are induced to marry earlier in life, and consequently their families of children are more numerous. And their temperance in diet renders them more healthy. The ease of procuring subsistence for a family is occasioned by the boundless tracts of uncultivated forests, bordering on their plantations. For every new-married couple can, at small expence, purchase a freehold; which by their industry, will afford them and their children a comfortable support.' (*op. cit.*, pp. 1-2.)

[11] Malthus, *Principle of Population*, 6th ed., 1826, Book II, ch. xiii, pp. 516 ff.

in places of over 2,500 inhabitants. The second problem is that all aggregate figures contain an important component of immigrants; in each Census between 1860 and 1920, foreign-born residents amounted fairly consistently to around 14 per cent of the recorded population; the Census of 1850, however, was the first to distinguish the foreign-born, and the further back in time one goes before that date, the more difficult becomes the task of separating the natural increase of population from the increase due to immigration. Thirdly, America was a geographically expanding society, with very high internal migration; again it is not until the Census of 1850 that the state of birth is given for the native-born inhabitants; hence, although the total population is known for each state in each of the preceding Census years, it is not possible to divide that population into foreign-born, native Americans born out of state, and those born within the state. Fourthly, the presence both of Indians and more particularly of Negroes adds a further area of uncertainty. And finally, in all these respects, great regional differences are found, associated with the heterogeneous nature of topography, climate, social behaviour and economic conditions.

One therefore needs to know, for each colony or state at any point of time, not merely the aggregate population, but also the figures of native-born and foreign-born; migrant and non-migrant native-born; white and coloured; rural and urban. Such complete information would be essential for an accurate interpretation of the growth of the American population in the eighteenth and nineteenth centuries. Until the middle of the nineteenth century, however, much of the detail is lacking and one has to be content with much less than these basic requirements. It is not until 1850 that the Census data are adequate to permit an analysis of the components of the American population in the desired detail, and even then, though the material in the 1850 and 1860 Censuses appears very comprehensive, considerable deficiencies and inaccuracies still remain.[12]

The nature and size of the regional variations may be seen in Tables 11 and 12 presented at the end of this chapter, showing the data for 1850 and 1860, and it is appropriate at this point to draw attention to some of their features. Above all it must be emphasized that aggregates and averages for America as a whole are liable to be highly misleading. The great diversity of conditions between state and state, region and region, in all the particulars outlined above is obvious from the Tables. A few examples will suffice to illustrate the point.

Despite the fact that in 1850 85 per cent of the total population is shown as 'rural', two states, Massachusetts and Rhode Island, have an 'urban' population of over 50 per cent (a ratio not reached by the nation as a whole until 1920); on the other hand only five states in all show an urban population of over 25 per cent while sixteen are below 10 per cent (cols. 24 and 25). These figures use the low American definition of 'urban' (2,500 inhabitants), but a much more intensive analysis by size of towns would be possible. It may be noted that, at the other extreme, the USA had a number of towns which, for the date, were large; in 1860 America had eight towns with populations of over 150,000, three of which were west of the Appalachians; England at that date had only

---

[12] The problem is discussed at length in Yasukichi Yasuba, *Birth Rates of the White Population in the United States, 1800-1860* (LXXXIX, No. 2, in the Johns Hopkins University *Studies in Historical and Political Science*, Baltimore 1962), *passim* (v. Index, 'Underenumeration').

seven towns over 150,000.[13] Such large towns add great weight to the urban figure in some states; in Louisiana in 1850, for example, 116,000 of the total urban population of 134,000 lived in New Orleans.

The uneven distribution of immigrants in the USA is well known and is amply demonstrated in the Tables (cols. 6, 22 and 26). In 1850 and 1860 over half the foreign-born were in three states: New York, Pennsylvania and Ohio. Immigrants rarely settled in the South, there being in 1850 only just over 300,000 (out of 2¼ million) foreign-born in all the slave states together; not one of the four states of the Old South, Virginia, the Carolinas and Georgia, had a foreign-born element of over 2 per cent of the total population. At the other extreme Wisconsin had 35 per cent, California 23 per cent and New York 20 per cent, foreign-born populations. The pattern of distribution of the 4·1 million foreign-born in 1860 was very similar.

Internal migration (cols. 8, 13 and 30) shows similar regional differences. Just under one-quarter of all free native-born are found outside their state of birth in both 1850 and 1860. The general movement was from the eastern sea-board to the western states, but the detail is complicated. Roughly one person out of three born in Vermont, Connecticut, Delaware, Virginia, the Carolinas and Georgia had by 1850 left his state of birth and was living elsewhere. At the same time over half a million native-born residents in the three mid-Atlantic states, and a third of a million in New England, were immigrants into those states. New York gained over a quarter of a million natives through immigration but lost over half a million through emigration. The westward movement was a continuing process, however, and even westerly states lost population through internal migration; Ohio, Indiana, Illinois, for example, all lost substantial numbers of their state-born (almost 1 million in 1860) and in 1860 Ohio records a net loss through internal migration. In 1850 over half the native-born population of nine states were migrants. At the other extreme the South Atlantic states in the nineteenth century were little more attractive to native-born immigrants than to foreign-born immigrants, the population of the Carolinas, for example, including only about 2 per cent of both foreign and native immigrants.

The Censuses do not record the birth-place of slaves. The free coloured population was less mobile than the white population. 75,000 out of 440,000 (or about 17 per cent) are recorded in states other than their state of birth. Free coloured are to be found in all states, including the slave states: the leading states in 1850 were Maryland 75,000 free coloured, Virginia 54,000, Pennsylvania 53,000, New York 49,000, North Carolina 27,000 and Ohio 25,000; one-half of the free coloured in Ohio and one-third of those in Pennsylvania were born outside the state—evidence of the northward movement of the coloured population in the years before the Civil War.

Throughout the nineteenth century the Negro population was more rural

---

[13] USA: New York, Philadelphia, Brooklyn, Baltimore, Boston, New Orleans, Cincinnati, St. Louis; total population 2½ millions. England: London, Liverpool, Manchester, Birmingham, Leeds, Sheffield, Bristol; total population, 4½ millions. If New York and London are excluded, the total populations in such towns become: USA, 1·7 millions; England, 1·6 millions. Even in the late colonial period, Philadelphia was unusually large; with 40,000 inhabitants in 1775, its population exceeded that of any English town except London.

than the white population, reflected in the low urban percentage in the states with a high proportion of Negroes. Compared with the national average of 15 per cent urban in 1850, the percentage of Negroes in towns was less than 8 per cent. It was only after the Civil War that there was much acceleration in the process of Negro urbanization.

The sex composition of the white population shows a preponderance of males in every American Census (until that of 1950): the ratio was 103·8 in 1790, 105·2 in 1850. The sex ratio varied between states and between groups. In 1850 Massachusetts, Rhode Island and New Hampshire had a female surplus among their native-born, whether born in or out of state; Connecticut had a female surplus among state-born only.[14] The first two of these, together with New Jersey in 1850 and New Hampshire and New York in 1860, had a small female surplus even among their foreign-born. The foreign-born otherwise always show an excess of males (though this proportion in 1850 is only 12:10). With the exception of the three New England states mentioned above and Washington D.C., native-born migrants in 1850 show an excess of males (in the ratio 11:10); the male surplus in the total white population in 1860 is particularly evident in the West. The states which show a net loss through internal migration also tend to show an excess of females (minuses in column 13 corresponding to minuses in column 18 in Tables 11 and 12) in the population born, and left behind, in the state. The Negro sex ratio differs significantly from the white sex ratio, with a female surplus in every Census since 1840, the 1850 ratio being 99·1.

These Tables could obviously be subjected to a very much more thorough analysis, but the above examples illustrate some of the variables with which one has to contend. There is no reason whatever to assume that either 1850 or 1860 was in any sense a typical year. On the contrary, this was clearly not true of 1850, if only because of the cholera epidemic of 1849. There is evidence in the Tables themselves of considerable change between 1850 and 1860. What one can deduce from the 1850 figures, e.g. concerning the number and distribution of immigrants, would be demonstrably untrue of earlier and later years. One is in fact dealing throughout with a highly dynamic society in which change and interchange, fluidity and flexibility are generally characteristic; even so, not all regions shared all the dynamic characteristics and the features of change are themselves not universal enough to be accepted as typical of all parts of the nation.

With these reservations and warnings in mind, the remainder of this chapter will be devoted to an exploratory consideration of the evidence relating to American population growth in the eighteenth and early nineteenth centuries.

THE COLONIAL PERIOD

The Malthusian postulate, that the American population doubled every twenty-five years, would have required an average decennial increase of 32 per cent. The first question then is whether the evidence for the colonial period provides support for the assumption of such a rate of growth.

[14] The 1860 Census does not distinguish sex according to place of birth. Accordingly, column 18 in the 1860 Table refers to Total White.

The statistical records for the seventeenth and eighteenth centuries are very limited. Some colonial governors, especially in the North, conducted enumerations of the population, usually at the behest of the British government. These are too sporadic in occurrence, restricted in scope, and unreliable in content, however, to provide anything like a complete picture of the demographic history of the colonial period. Consequently much weight has often been placed on the observations of contemporary Americans like Judge Samuel Sewell and Benjamin Franklin, or the impressions of European travellers like Peter Kalm or Jean de Crèvecoeur. While such literary evidence can clearly not be ignored, it is no substitute for detailed quantitative information.

Various estimates have, however, been made of the colonial population. The first 'official' estimates were contained in the 1850 Census (pp. xxx-xxxi). The statistics most usually quoted in more recent writings are those which appeared in 1909 in a publication of the Bureau of the Census, *A Century of Population Growth*, written by the Chief Clerk of the Bureau, W. S. Rossiter.[15]

Rossiter gives estimates of total colonial population and of the total population of the separate colonies by decades from 1620 to 1780. Valuable though these figures are, they leave large areas of uncertainty.[16] Above all, the absence of reliable immigration figures makes it impossible to distinguish natural increase from growth due to immigration.[17] Similarly it is not until the First Census of 1790 that separate figures are available for white and coloured. Rossiter's figures are aggregate and do not distinguish between these two very different groups. Finally, information about internal migration in the colonial period is slight, and not at all comparable with that available from the Censuses from 1850 on.[18] Without much more knowledge of these aspects of colonial population it is very difficult to put Malthus to the test.

Rossiter's estimates, and calculations based upon them, are presented in Table 1. It is seen from Table 1(d) that the total American population increased

[15] Since Rossiter there have been two other major works on colonial population: E. V. Greene and V. D. Harrington, *American Population before the Federal Census of 1790* (New York 1932) and Stella H. Sutherland, *Population Distribution in Colonial America* (New York 1936). Neither work reconstructs a complete series of population statistics for the whole of the eighteenth century, however, and it is therefore necessary to continue to use Rossiter's tables as the basic material. If these are checked as often as possible against the revisions of Greene and Harrington, and Sutherland, the total impression is of broad agreement in the long run, but considerable discrepancy in detail. Compare also estimates in Timothy Pitkin, *A Statistical View of the Commerce of the USA* (New York 1817).

[16] Rossiter gives a useful, brief description of the sources for the colonial period and these are discussed further in Greene and Harrington (pp. 3 ff). There were various obstacles to census-taking in eighteenth-century America, besides the physical difficulties. Rossiter quotes a communication of 1712 to the Board of Trade from Governor Hunter of New York: 'The people were deterred by a simple superstition and observation that sickness followed upon the last numbering of the people'. Still more poignantly, Governor Burnett of New Jersey wrote in 1726: 'I would have then ordered the like accounts to be taken in New Jersey, but I was advised that it might make the people uneasy, they being generally of a New England extraction, and thereby enthusiasts; and that they would take it for a repetition of the same sin that David committed in numbering the people, and might bring the same judgments.' See also footnotes 31 and 62.

[17] It is acknowledged that the use of the word 'immigrant' in this context is probably anachronistic. Colonial Americans still thought and spoke of themselves as 'emigrants' from the old country, not 'immigrants' into the new. The word 'immigrant' appears to have been an Americanism first used about 1790, but not in general use until the fourth decade of independence, i.e. towards 1820.

[18] The main attempt to examine internal migration in colonial America is in Stella H. Sutherland, *op. cit.* This work contains calculations of the size of population for the 'Revolutionary Period', i.e. about 1775-6, and these have been inserted in the appropriate column in Table 1, to pro vide a comparison with Rossiter's figures.

TABLE 1

American population in the eighteenth century

(a)

Estimated total population (000)

		1700	1710	1720	1730	1740	1750	1760	1770	(1775-6)	1780	1790
New	New Hampshire	6	7·5	9·5	12	22	31	38	60	(81)	85	142
England	Massachusetts	70	80	92	125	158	180	235	299	(339)	363	476
	Rhode Island	6	8	11	17	24	35	44	55	(58)	52★	69
	Connecticut	24	31	40	55	70	100	142	175	(198)	203	238
	TOTAL	106	127	152	209	274	346	459	589	(676)	703	925
Mid-	New York	19	26	36	49	63	80	113	185	(193)	240	425
Atlantic	New Jersey	14	20	26	37	52	66	91	110	(122)	137	184
	Pennsylvania	20	35	48	65	100	150	220	275	(308)	372	493
	TOTAL	53	81	110	151	215	296	424	570	(623)	749	1,102
South	Maryland	31	43	62	82	105	137	162	200	(255)	250	320
Atlantic	Virginia	72	87	116	153	200	275	346	450	(504)	565	822
	North Carolina	5	7	13	30	50	80	115	230	(247)	300	395
	South Carolina	8	13	21	30	45	68	95	140	(170)	160	249
	Georgia						5	9	26	(33)	55	83
	TOTAL	116	150	212	295	400	565	727	1,046	(1,209)	1,330	1,869
TOTAL		275	358	474	655	889	1,207	1,610	2,205	(2,507)	2,781	3,930†

(b)

Distribution of population (per cent)

		1700	1710	1720	1730	1740	1750	1760	1770	(1775-6)	1780	1790
New	New Hampshire	2	2	2	2	2	3	2	3	(3)	3	4
England	Massachusetts	25	22	19	19	18	15	15	14	(14)	13	12
	Rhode Island	2	2	2	3	3	3	3	3	(2)	2	2
	Connecticut	9	9	8	8	8	8	9	8	(8)	7	6
	TOTAL	39	35	32	32	31	29	29	28	(27)	25	24
Mid-	New York	7	7	8	7	7	7	7	8	(8)	9	10
Atlantic	New Jersey	5	6	5	6	6	5	6	5	(5)	5	5
	Pennsylvania	7	10	10	10	11	12	14	12	(12)	13	13
	TOTAL	19	23	23	23	24	24	26	25	(25)	27	28
South	Maryland	11	12	13	13	12	11	10	9	(10)	9	8
Atlantic	Virginia	26	24	24	23	22	23	21	20	(20)	20	21
	North Carolina	2	2	3	4·5	6	7	7	10	(10)	11	10
	South Carolina	3	4	4	4·5	5	6	6	6	(7)	6	6
	Georgia								1	(1)	1	2
	TOTAL	42	42	45	45	45	47	45	46	(48)	47	47
TOTAL		100	100	100	100	100	100	100	100	(100)	100	100

★ In parts (c) and (d) the population of Rhode Island in 1780 is taken as 60,000, in view of Sutherland's figure of 58,228 from a Rhode Island census of 1774.

† In part (a) the grand total population for 1790 of 3,929,625 includes 35,691 persons in Tennessee not listed in the sectional figures.

TABLE I (cont.)

(c)
Decennial increase (000)

		1700-10	10-20	20-30	30-40	40-50	50-60	60-70	70-80	80-90
New England	New Hampshire	1·5	2	2·5	10	9	7	22	25	57
	Massachusetts	10	12	33	33	22	55	64	64	113
	Rhode Island	2	3	6	7	11	9	11	(5)	9
	Connecticut	7	9	15	15	30	42	33	28	35
	TOTAL	21	25	57	65	72	113	130	(122)	214
Mid-Atlantic	New York	7	10	13	14	17	33	72	55	185
	New Jersey	6	6	11	15	14	25	19	27	47
	Pennsylvania	15	13	17	35	50	70	55	97	121
	TOTAL	28	29	41	64	81	128	146	179	353
South Atlantic	Maryland	12	19	20	23	32	25	38	50	70
	Virginia	15	29	37	47	75	71	104	115	257
	North Carolina	2	6	17	20	30	35	115	70	95
	South Carolina	5	8	9	15	23	27	45	20	89
	Georgia					5	4	17	29	28
	TOTAL	34	62	83	105	165	162	319	284	539
TOTAL		83	116	181	234	318	403	595	576	1,149

(d)
Percentage decennial increase

		1700-10	10-20	20-30	30-40	40-50	50-60	60-70	70-80	80-90	Average
New England	New Hampshire	25	27	26	83	41	23	58	41	68	44
	Massachusetts	14	15	36	26	14	31	27	21	31	24
	Rhode Island	33	38	54	42	46	26	25	9	17	32
	Connecticut	29	29	38	27	43	42	23	16	17	29
	TOTAL	20	20	38	31	26	33	28	21	30	27·5
Mid-Atlantic	New York	37	39	36	29	27	41	64	29	77	42
	New Jersey	43	30	42	41	27	38	21	25	34	34
	Pennsylvania	75	37	35	54	50	47	25	35	32	43
	TOTAL	53	36	37	42	38	43	34	31	47	40·1
South Atlantic	Maryland	39	44	32	28	31	18	24	25	28	30
	Virginia	21	33	32	31	38	26	30	26	45	31
	North Carolina	40	87	130	67	60	44	100	30	32	66
	South Carolina	63	60	44	50	51	40	47	14	56	47
	Georgia						80	189	112	50	108
	TOTAL	29	41	39	36	41	29	44	27	41	35·3
TOTAL		30·0	32·7	38·1	35·7	35·8	33·4	37·0	26·1	41·3	34·5

Notes to Table 1

(i) The above data are transcribed or calculated from W. S. Rossiter, *A Century of Population Growth* (US Bureau of the Census), pp. 9-10. The column headed '(1775-6)' is from S. H. Sutherland, *Population Distribution in Colonial America*, p. xii.

(ii) For the years 1770-90, separate figures are available for Maine, Vermont, Delaware, Kentucky (1780-90) and Tennessee (1790). For the earlier years Maine is included with Massachusetts, Vermont with New York, Delaware with Pennsylvania, and Kentucky with Virginia. This grouping is used throughout in the table above, for simplicity of presentation. This has introduced, however, a small inaccuracy, especially in the sectional totals, for the years 1770–90, as the following revision of the percentage distribution table will show (cf. (b) above):

	Maine	Ver-mont	Mass.	Total New Eng-land	New York	Penn-syl-vania	Total Mid-Atlan-tic	Vir-ginia	Total South Atlan-tic	Ken-tucky	Tenn-essee	Total East-South-Central
1770	2	1	12	28	7	11	24	20	48			
1780	2	2	11	27	7	12	24	19	48	1		1
1790	2	2	10	26	8	11	24	19	47	2	1	3

between 1700 and 1790 at an average rate of 34·5 per cent per decade.[19] This rate of growth conforms closely with that of the first half of the nineteenth century down to 1860. Population increase in the eighteenth century was apparently uneven; particularly rapid growth is found in the 1720's, 1760's and 1780's (the last of these being the decade with the fastest rate of growth in America's history); particularly slow growth is found in the 1700's, 1710's, 1750's and 1770's.

Similarly, there is an unevenness of growth between region and region. It appears from Table 1(b) that New England as a whole failed to maintain its share of the population, declining from 39 per cent of the total in 1700 to 26 per cent (note ii) in 1790; the decline was most pronounced in Massachusetts, whose share fell from 25 per cent to 10 per cent (note ii), but Connecticut also shows a decline which is especially sharp after 1760. Both the middle and the southern colonies increased their share, from 19 to 24 per cent, and from 42 to 47 per cent respectively. The rise in the share of the South mainly depended on the rapidity of the growth of the Carolinas, which offset the fall in the Virginian percentage.

It may be noted that, of the colonies which appear in part (d) of the Table to have particularly high growth rates,[20] Georgia and the Carolinas included an important slave element, and also, in this period, a significant group of white immigrants; Pennsylvania and New York were also immigrant-receiving areas in the eighteenth century. At the other end of the scale the New England colonies were relatively unattractive to white immigrants in the eighteenth century; but even if immigration is assumed to have been negligible, the indicated rates are probably below the natural rate of growth as a result of net emigration from the area (suggested for example in the statement by Governor Burnett quoted in footnote 16).

Before these first approximations could be made any more accurate it would be necessary to know the respective contributions made to colonial population growth by (i) the importation of slaves, (ii) white immigration, (iii) natural increase of white population and (iv) internal migration.

On the first problem, a starting point may be found in the Census of 1790 which distinguishes white and non-white population, as shown in Table 2.

[19] The decennial average of 34·5 per cent is of course dependent on the arbitrary choice of 1700 as the starting date for the calculation. Still using Rossiter's estimates, but with different starting dates, the decennial averages become: 1660–1790, 34·0; 1670–1790, 34·3; 1680–1790, 34·1; 1690–1790, 33·8; 1700–90, 34·5; 1710–90, 35·0; 1720–90, 35·3; 1730–90, 34·9. The difference created by the use of different starting dates is thus not more than one per cent.
[20] The appearance may be in part deceptive, of course, because of the different starting-points.

TABLE 2

Structure of the American population in 1790

		White (000)	Free non-white (000)	Slave (000)	White %	Non-White %	Distribution of white population %	Distribution of non-white population %
New England	Maine	96	0·5	none	99	1	3	
	New Hampshire	141	0·6	—	99	1	4	
	Vermont	85	0·3	—	99	1	3	
	Massachusetts	373	5	none	99	1	12	
	Rhode Island	65	3	1	94	6	2	
	Connecticut	232	3	3	97	3	7	1
	TOTAL	992	12	4	98	2	31	2
Mid-Atlantic	New York	314	5	21	92	8	10	3
	New Jersey	170	3	11	92	8	5	2
	Pennsylvania	424	7	4	97	3	13	2
	TOTAL	908	15	36	95	5	29	7
South Atlantic	Delaware	46	4	9	78	22	1	3
	Maryland	209	8	103	65	35	7	14
	Virginia	442	13	293	59	41	14	40
	North Carolina	288	5	101	73	27	9	14
	South Carolina	140	2	107	56	44	4	14
	Georgia	53	0·4	29	64	36	2	4
	TOTAL	1,178	32	642	64	36	37	89
East-South-Central	Kentucky	61	0·1	12	84	16	2	1·5
	Southwest Territory	31	0·4	3	91	9	1	0·5
	TOTAL	92	1·0	15	86	14	3	2
USA		3,171	60	697	81	19	100	100

Thus in 1790 there were just over 750,000 Negroes in the newly created USA, either imported as slaves themselves or descendants of imported slaves. The number of slaves in America in 1700 is not known; it is generally assumed to have been small, in the range 5,000 to 20,000. Importations between 1700 and 1790, however, probably amounted to between 250,000 and 300,000. The inflow was uneven, the biggest decennial importation being in the 1760's when about 75,000 were imported. It may be assumed that practically all these went to the South Atlantic colonies; in other words the increase of 319,000, or 44 per cent, shown by the southern colonies in that decade contains an importation of perhaps 70,000 slaves, the increase otherwise being about 35 per cent (Table 3, columns 16 and 17).[21]

An attempt is made in Table 3 to estimate the population growth rates when allowance is made for the increase caused by slave imports. The calculations are obviously very crude and the findings can be no more than a rough approximation. Two rather arbitrary assumptions are made: the figure used of total slaves imported (just over 250,000) is a low one, but it is 'allocated' to the different decades roughly according to the estimates quoted by Rossiter. Secondly, it is assumed that throughout the eighteenth century the geographical distribu-

---

[21] These assumptions are based on figures cited in Rossiter, *op. cit.*, p. 36.

POTTER

tion of the imported slaves was the same as the distribution of the non-white population in the Census of 1790.[22]

TABLE 3

American population growth in the eighteenth century with allowance for imported slaves

	Total						Maryland	
	1 Total Population in base year (000)	2 Total increase (000)	3 Assumed total importation of slaves (000)	4 Increase without slave import (000)	5 Col. 2 as % of Col. 1 %	6 Col. 4 as % of Col. 1 %	7 Assumed slave import (000)	8 Percentage increase without slave import
1700-10	275	83	10	73	30·0	26·8	1·5	34
1710-20	358	116	20	96	32·7	24·0	3	38
1720-30	474	181	25	156	38·1	32·8	3·8	29
1730-40	655	234	25	209	35·7	31·9	3·8	23
1740-50	889	318	25	293	35·8	32·9	3·8	27
1750-60	1,207	403	35	368	33·4	30·5	5·3	14
1760-70	1,610	595	75	520	37·0	32·3	11·4	16
1770-80	2,205	576	20	556	26·1	25·2	3	23
1780-90	2,781	1,149	20	1,129	41·3	40·6	3	27
1700-90			255		34·5	30·8		25

Virginia		North Carolina		South Carolina		Total South Atlantic		
9 Assumed Slave import (000)	10 Percentage Increase without slave import	11 Assumed Slave import (000)	12 Percentage Increase without slave import	13 Assumed Slave import (000)	14 Percentage increase without slave import	15 Assumed slave import (000)	16 Total Percentage increase	17 Percentage increase without slave import
4	15	1·5	10	1·5	44	9	29	22
8	24	3	43	3	39	18	41	29
10	23	3·8	102	3·8	25	22·5	39	29
10	24	3·8	54	3·8	37	22·5	36	28
10	32·5	3·8	53	3·8	42	22·5	41	36
14	21	5·3	37	5·3	32	31·5	29	23
30	21	11·4	90	11·4	35	67·5	44	35
8	24	3	29	3	12	18	27	25
8	44	3	31	3	54	18	41	39
	25		50		35			29

With this adjustment made for slave importation, the average decennial increase of the total population falls from 34·5 to 30·8 per cent. If the first two decades are excluded as being the most conjectural, the fall is from 35·3 to 32·5 per cent. The greatest effect is naturally seen in the figures for the southern colonies whose calculated rate falls from 35·2 to 29·4 per cent. Revised in this way, the southern rate of growth more closely resembles the New England average of 27·5 per cent. Within the south, North Carolina, where just under

[22] The 'allocation' by decades is based on Rossiter, *op. cit.*, p. 36, the figures assumed for the first two decades being the most doubtful. The geographical allocation used is: Virginia, 40 per cent, Maryland, 15 per cent, the Carolinas, 15 per cent each, total South Atlantic, 90 per cent.

three-quarters of the population was white in 1790, still shows a particularly high rate of growth.

The growth rate derived by this calculation includes the natural increase of the slave population. An estimate of the rate of growth of the white population only may be made via a different route. If it is assumed that there were 25,000 non-whites in America in 1700—probably a high figure—then the increase in the white population in 90 years was from 250,000 to 3,171,000, which would require an average decennial growth of 32·5 per cent; an assumption of 5,000 non-whites in America in 1700 gives a decennial growth for the white population in the same 90 years of 31·5 per cent.

In view of the irregularities from decade to decade, such century-long averages are of course only of very limited value. But with due reservations, the findings to this point are as follows: average decennial growth of whole population from all causes, between 34 and 35 per cent; average decennial rate of growth of whole population, with allowance for importation of slaves, between 30·8 and 32·5 per cent; average decennial rate of growth of white population, in the range 31·5 to 32·5 per cent. This suggests that during the eighteenth century the total white population in America did increase at roughly the Malthusian rate.

Viewed regionally, there are considerable variations. Of those provinces with a white population of over 90 per cent, New Hampshire, New York and Pennsylvania are still significantly above the 32 per cent level, Rhode Island and New Jersey are very close to 32 per cent while Massachusetts and Connecticut are significantly below 32 per cent. There are three possible explanations of these disparities: immigration, internal migration and differences in natural increase. It is tempting to suppose that these regional differences may be quite simply explained: that Massachusetts and Connecticut are low because of emigration from these regions to other parts of America; that New Hampshire, New York and Pennsylvania are high because of immigration from Europe and from other parts of America; and that Rhode Island and New Jersey represent something like the norm at the Malthusian 32 per cent.

One would like to be able to substantiate, or refute, this conclusion with data on colonial immigration. Benjamin Franklin, at any rate at mid-century, seems to have attributed a major role in American population growth to immigration, but without any statistical basis for his assumption. 'This quick Increase', he wrote in *Poor Richard Improved*, 'is owing not so much to natural Generation, as to the Accession of Strangers. . . .' Nevertheless, Franklin went on to argue, natural increase is greater in America than in Europe.

> 'I believe People increase faster by Generation in these Colonies, where all can have full Employ. . . . For in old settled Countries, as England for instance, as soon as the Number of People is as great as can be supported by all the Tillage, Manufactures, Trade and Offices of the Country, the Over-plus must quit the Country, or they will perish by Poverty, Diseases, and want of Necessaries. Marriage, too, is discouraged, many declining it, till they can see how they shall be able to maintain a Family.'[23]

[23] *The Papers of Benjamin Franklin*, iii, 440. *Poor Richard Improved* (1750). Franklin was then 44 years of age. (continued on next page)

Thus Franklin linked the lower rate of natural growth in Europe directly with migration to America. In his *Observations* of 1751 he carried this further. In America there were more marriages, younger marriages (he suggested that a marriage age of 20 was average), and more children per marriage.

> 'Hence, marriages in America are more general, and more generally early, than in Europe. And . . . if in Europe they have but four births to a marriage (many of their marriages being late) we may here reckon eight, of which, if one half grow up, and our marriages are made, reckoning one with another, at twenty years of age, our people must at least be doubled every twenty years. . . . The great increase . . . is . . . not always owing to greater fecundity of nature, but sometimes to examples of industry in the heads, and industrious education; by which the children are enabled to provide better for themselves, and their marrying early is encouraged from the prospect of good subsistence.'[24]

Regrettably, it seems impossible to assess with any degree of reliability or accuracy the number of immigrants in the eighteenth century. The sources of information are few and the estimates made by students of the period vary widely. The usual assumptions are that, while the absolute numbers entering America from Europe in the eighteenth century were far greater than in the seventeenth century, immigrants nevertheless constituted a smaller proportion of total population than in the later seventeenth century; and that the flow varied greatly over time, being small in years of war in Europe and encouraged by the return of peace. But beyond these generalities most of the leading writers both on migration and on colonial history refrain from committing themselves to quantitative assessments.

One of the highest estimates of colonial immigration is that cited by the eminent historian of the colonial period, C. P. Nettels. This writer asserts that

It may be noted here that the French *philosophes*, Count Buffon (G. L. Le Clerc) and the Abbé Raynal, though arguing that in North America 'la nature vivante est beaucoup moins agissante, beaucoup moins forte', that animals were smaller and the aboriginal humans less fertile, appear nevertheless to have accepted Franklin's view: '. . . il est prouvé . . . que le nombre des citoyens double tous les quinze ou seize ans dans quelques-unes de ces provinces, & tous les dix-huit ou vingt ans dans les autres. Une multiplication si rapide doit avoir deux sources. La premiere, est cette foule d'Irlandois, de Juifs, de François, de Vaudois, de Palatins, de Moraves, de Saltzbourgeois. . . . La seconde source de cette étonnante multiplication, est dans le climat même des colonies, où l'expérience a démontré que la population doubloit naturellement tous les vingt-cinq ans. Les réflexions de M. Franklin, rendront cette vérité sensible.

'Le peuple, dit ce philosophe, s'accroît partout, en raison du nombre des mariages; & ce nombre augmente à proportion des facilités qu'on trouve à soutenir une famille. . . .

'Le terrein, vaste & inculte, s'y donne, ou pour rien, ou à si bon marché, que l'homme le moins laborieux trouve, en peu de tems, un espace, qui, pouvant suffire à l'entretien d'une nombreuse famille, y nourrira long tems sa postérité. Ainsi les habitans du nouveau-monde, sollicités d'ailleurs par le climat, se marient en plus grand nombre, & beaucoup plus jeunes que les habitans de l'Europe.' (continuing with an almost literal translation of the words of Franklin quoted in the text above.) G. T. F. Raynal, *Histoire Philosophique et Politique* (1774), vol. vii, pp. 134-7. See also Thomas Jefferson's discussion of Buffon's views in his *Notes on the State of Virginia* (written 1781-2, published 1787), pp. 71 ff.

I am grateful to Professor H. S. Commager for drawing my attention to the writings of Buffon and Raynal.

[24] B. Franklin, *Observations Concerning the Increase of Mankind* . . . (1751), clauses 7 and 19. On the age of marriage, see discussion below of Connecticut evidence. Franklin's guesses both about the age of marriage and about the average number of children per marriage have some support in calculations by F. S. Crum based on the selective evidence of genealogical records (Frederick S. Crum, 'The Decadence of the Native American Stock. A Statistical Study of Genealogical Records', *American Statistical Association*, vol. xiv, Sept. 1914. See also note 50).

'the eighteenth century was pre-eminently the century of the foreigner: in 1760 the foreign-born represented a third of the colonial population'.[25] This would imply the presence of over half a million immigrants and in the context of the quotation Nettels does not appear to include Negro slaves in this figure. Even if one 'spread' these arrivals over as much as fifty years and made no allowance for deaths, this would require an average annual immigration of over 10,000 (or 100,000 per decade) between 1710 and 1760; it would also account for almost half the total population increase, of 1·2 millions, in that same period. If such immigration figures could be definitively established, they would play havoc with the usual assumptions about the natural growth of population in colonial America.[26]

At the other extreme, one finds the view that immigration was insignificant, with a suggested figure of about 10 per cent foreign born in 1790. This is, however, a mathematical solution unsupported by historical evidence, reached by applying an assumed birth rate of 55 to the total population of 1·2 millions in 1750, giving about 66,000 annual births; from this it is deduced that the immigrant contribution was slight.[27]

Such is the width of the gulf in possible interpretations created by the lack of reliable data of immigration. Can one go any further than to point out the apparent coincidence between the decades of most rapid population growth (1720's, 1760's and 1780's) and the decades of high immigration?[28]

The balance of probability, on the evidence known to the author, seems to suggest a total immigration, additional to imported slaves, of about 350,000 between 1700 and 1790 (though it must be emphasized that this is little more than a shot in the dark).[29] If we use this figure as a hypothesis, a calculation similar

[25] C. P. Nettels, *The Roots of American Civilization* (New York 1938), p. 383. The history of this notion is itself interesting. In making his assertion Nettels gives a footnote reference to a group of articles by Max Farrand in *The New Republic*, 1916, especially 'A Nation of Immigrants', 9 Dec. 1916, p. 148. If we trace it back still further, Farrand in this passage is seen to be quoting directly from Edward Channing's *History of the United States*, where Channing stated, 'About one-third of the colonists in 1760 were born outside of America.' Farrand does not give the reference but this passage is found to be an isolated sentence in vol. ii of Channing's *History* (New York 1908), p. 492. Channing explains his statement in a footnote on the same page, citing as his sources Benjamin Franklin, *Works*, iv, 24, and the work by Edward Wigglesworth referred to in footnote 3 of this chapter. Neither source gives a satisfactory statistical foundation for Channing's statement.

Farrand supports his own view with the well-known passage from Crèvecoeur's *Letters from an American Farmer* (1782): 'What is an American? They are a mixture of English, Scotch, Irish, French, Dutch, Germans and Swedes. From this promiscuous breed that race, now called Americans have arisen . . .'

[26] If the half million foreign born are assumed to have arrived within the 30 years prior to 1760, this 'spread' would account for well over half the probable total population increase in those three decades.

[27] W. H. Grabill and others, *The Fertility of American Women* (New York 1958), pp. 8-9. Grabill contrasts these assumed births of 66,000 with an assumed annual net immigration of about 4,000. If a much lower birth rate of 35 is assumed, however, this would have produced about 42,000 births, a figure which might be reconcilable with 10,000 annual arrivals in the middle of the century. It is possible that immigration tended to lower the birth rate, owing to the later age of marriage of immigrants; see J. P. Monahan, *The Pattern of Age at Marriage in the United States* (Philadelphia 1951), pp. 73-5. It should be noted however that the evidence for this view is taken largely from the second half of the nineteenth century.

[28] Marcus Hansen, the pioneer historian of migration, speaks of the migration of the 1760's, especially after the final defeat of France, as 'the greatest of all colonial migrations', M. L. Hansen, *The Atlantic Migration* (Harvard 1945), p. 51. This inflow came after the date mentioned by Nettels.

[29] This figure is based on the sporadic glimpses, based especially on ships' lists, to be found in such works as Abbot E. Smith, *Colonists in Bondage* (1947), Warren B. Smith, *White Servitude in Colonial South Carolina* (1961), and from Marcus Hansen. It implies a somewhat lower immigration than that suggested by the Beards who estimate an influx of 750,000 Europeans between 1660 and 1770. C. A. and Mary R. Beard, *The Beards' Basic History of the United States* (1944), p. 17.

to that used in Table 3 reveals a rate of natural increase for the white population of slightly over 28 per cent per decade.[30] Assuming a concentration of the immigrants in certain known areas, especially Pennsylvania, North Carolina, Georgia and to some extent New York, some of the disparities in the rates of growth between colony and colony disappear (but of course this procedure involves to some extent assuming what one seeks to prove). If about 100,000 of these immigrants, for example, settled in Pennsylvania, then the rate of growth for that colony was not 43 but under 30.

An extremely approximate calculation may be made to assess the birth rates and death rates required to satisfy the assumptions made earlier about the size of the white population, at different assumed levels of immigration. The possible combinations which emerge from such a calculation are as follows:

Assumed white immigration 1700–90	Assumed white birth rate	Resultant white death rate (approx.)
350,000	35	11
	45	21
	55	31
600,000	35	13
	45	23
	55	33

If the lower immigration figure is accepted as the more likely, then three combinations of birth rates and death rates would produce the given population growth. The balance of probability seems to suggest the second combination, or a mid-point between the second and the third, with a birth rate of 45–50 (see discussion below, p. 672, of the birth rate in 1800) and a moderate death rate of 20–25 per thousand. The death rate of 30–31 required by the assumption of as high a birth rate as 55 seems rather implausible.

In the absence of further evidence, the findings of this section have to remain hypothetical. Let it simply be repeated at this point that there can be no definitive picture of American demographic history in the eighteenth century until the problem of immigration has been satisfactorily solved.

SURVEY BY REGIONS

It has been emphasized in the foregoing sections that all attempts to discover the characteristics of American population growth must be subject to serious reservations unless adequate consideration is given to regional differences. It would be inappropriate to leave the subject without a brief summary of the main characteristics of each colony. In particular, the materials so far discussed are supplemented in the following survey by evidence which has come to light in a collection of Governors' Reports dated 1773.[31]

[30] Of course if a higher immigration figure is assumed the calculated natural increase falls. An immigration of 600,000 between 1700 and 1790 gives a natural increase figure of just over 25 per cent per decade.

[31] The collection, *Present state of the British colonies in America*, is contained in the *Downshire Papers*, in the Berkshire Record Office, Reading, England. The author expresses his thanks to the owner of the documents, the Marquess of Downshire, for permission to cite them in this chapter. The reports are hand-written returns from colonial governors in reply to questions from the British government requesting information on the following subjects: 1. situation of province; 2. boundaries; 3. size;

New England

A stereotype picture exists of New England society in the colonial period derived largely from diaries, sermons and other literary sources.[32] Its assumed main features are clearly defined.

1. The dictates of Puritanism were stern and unremitting. Family life was the corner-stone of New England society.
2. Marriage occurred at a young age.[33] Bachelors were distrusted, almost classified with suspected criminals. Old maids, i.e. women unmarried at twenty-five, were objects of ridicule.
3. The rapid remarriage of widows was common.[34]
4. Marriages were extremely fertile; maternity was an annual event.[35] The children in turn married early and were similarly prolific.[36] Deaths in childbirth were common and many women died between the ages of 20 and 30 from a combination of overwork and child-bearing.[37]
5. The severity of the climate in New England resulted in high infant mortality.[38] The resultant family size consisted, on the average, of between six and eight children.[39]

This picture makes little, if any, differentiation between the various sub-regions within New England. It also assumes fairly static conditions, quotations from seventeenth century documents being set in immediate juxtaposition with others from a century later.[40] It is based on generalizations made from particular,

4. rivers; 5. harbours; 6. constitution; 7. trade; 8. imports from and exports to Britain; 9. trade with foreign parts; 10. prevention of illegal trade; 11. produce, manufactures, etc.; 12. mines; 13. inhabitants; 14. population growth; 15. militia; 16. defence; 17. Indians; 18. revenue; 19. government expenses and 20. civil and military establishment. Question 13 asked, 'What is the Number of Inhabitants Whites and Blacks?' Question 14 asked, 'Are they increased or decreased within the last Ten Years? How much and for what Reasons?' The collection comprises returns from Massachusetts, New Hampshire, Connecticut, New York, New Jersey, Pennsylvania, Virginia and Georgia. The most informative are those from Connecticut and New Jersey. Two Governors (New Hampshire and New Jersey) note that they had no funds with which to pay the costs of making their inquiries, and no means of compelling the County Assessors to submit returns. Although there are many gaps (and some colonies not represented), this collection of reports gives many very revealing glimpses of the structure of American population in the last colonial decade.

[32] These traditional views are summarized in, and perhaps largely derived from, *A Social History of the American Family*, vol. i, Colonial Period, by Arthur W. Calhoun (New York 1917; page references given here are to the 1945 reprint).

[33] By this Calhoun appeared to mean sixteen or under for women, twenty or under for men; child marriage, however, was not permitted (p. 67).

[34] Judge Sewell's diary reveals him to have paid court, after the death of his first wife, to at least five widows, two of whom he married (the first of these dying within a year). *The Diary of Samuel Sewell, 1624-1729*. The famous Puritan preacher, Cotton Mather, married a widow eight months after the death of his first wife.

[35] Neatly expressed by one contemporary: 'Uxor praegnans est; sic semper uxoribus'. According to Calhoun (p. 87), families of 10 to 12 children were common; those of 20 to 25 not rare.

[36] There are various claimants for outstanding productivity in the literary records. One Maria Hagard, for example, who lived to be 100 years old in Rhode Island, claimed 500 descendants; at her own death, 205 of these were still alive and a grand-daughter of hers had herself been a grand-mother for fifteen years. (Henry W. Lawrence, *The Not-Quite Puritans*, Boston 1928, p. 83). See also footnote 54, citing a similar example from the Downshire Papers.

[37] This could in part at least explain why widows were in such great demand.

[38] 'In the bareness and cold of Massachusetts', wrote Calhoun, 'the mortality of infants was frightful'. He cites a Plymouth grave-stone: 'Here lies —— with twenty small children.' Only two of Cotton Mather's fifteen children survived him, only three of Judge Sewell's fourteen.

[39] A manuscript of 1675 stated the average size of New England households to be 9·02 persons (cited in Lawrence, *op. cit.*, p. 86).

[40] This would imply that economic differences between regions, and economic development in the eighteenth century, had no influence on population change.

known cases. The task now is to inquire whether the available statistical evidence seems to corroborate these generalizations.

In the most northerly parts of New England settlement was slow in the first half of the eighteenth century. Apart from local boundary disputes and the difficulties of the terrain, the Indians were persistently hostile and there was a constant possibility of war with the French further north.[41] Both Maine and New Hampshire had a troubled history for most of the century and at the end of the colonial period had population densities (1·5 and 8·7 per square mile respectively[42]) which were so low that most counties were 'frontier'. Here then there should have been the backwoods environment for rapid natural increase. *New Hampshire* was one of the areas with a growth rate above average. On the other hand, it appears from Tables 1(c) and 1(d) that there are great irregularities in this growth, being high in the 1730's, low in the 1750's and about 50 per cent per decade after 1760. The main explanation for these irregularities is probably to be found in internal migration. It is unlikely that many foreign-born settled immediately in these northern areas, but some may have moved there after living elsewhere for a period of time.[43] Immigration occurred in periods of relative peace and calm, and particularly after the fall of Quebec. Between 1760 and 1790 settlers moved in from all the other parts of New England. Governor Wentworth reported in 1773: 'The Inhabitants are increased the last seven years (the only period I can judge of as there were no numbers taken before my Administration) owing to the natural increase of the people, and to the rapid influx from other Colonies, to obtain and settle Crown Lands.'[44] No firm conclusion can be drawn about the rate of natural growth in view of the indeterminate contribution to total growth made by this immigration. Unless there was a considerable emigration in certain decades, however, the figures for the first half of the century hardly suggest an abnormally high rate of natural increase. Tentatively one might suggest a natural increase of 25-30 per cent per decade in the first half of the century and of 30-35 per cent in the second half.

Massachusetts shows a consistently low rate of population growth despite the existence of Boston as port of arrival of foreign immigrants.[45] From being the second largest colony in 1700, with 25 per cent of total population, its share fell to 10 per cent in 1790. Only in the 1730's was the rate of growth above the Malthusian 32 per cent. Massachusetts was a colony of religious and racial intolerance (Jews were not permitted to live there until after the Revolution). Few non-English immigrants were attracted there. There was certainly a net movement out of Massachusetts in the course of the century. In the middle of the century the Massachusetts growth rate moved in the opposite direction to that of New Hampshire: Massachusetts, 14, 31, 27; New Hampshire, 41, 23, 58. The Governor wrote in 1773:

'The number of whites according to a List taken in 1765 with some allow-

[41] Sutherland, *op. cit.*, pp. 33-5.
[42] *Ibid.*, p. 37.
[43] One thousand Irish were reported in New Hampshire in 1731 (out of a total population of about 12,000).
[44] *Downshire Papers*, Report on New Hampshire.
[45] Yet it is on examples from Massachusetts that much of the stereotype picture depends.

ance for such places as made no return amounted to 250,000 Souls. It is the general opinion that in eight years they have increased to at least 300,000 allowance being made for the emigration of many Families to the frontier Towns in New York and New Hampshire. . . .'[46]

Nevertheless the Governor's general impression was of the rapidity of increase: 'I do not believe that the increase of Sheep has been greater in Proportion than the Increase of Inhabitants.' Figures for 1776-7 shown by Greene and Harrington, and the Census of 1790, however, both confirm the impression of considerable migration from Massachusetts.[47] Further the 1790 Census shows a female surplus in Massachusetts, compared with a male surplus in America as a whole, also suggesting emigration. The figures are:

	Massachusetts				USA (free white)			
	Males		Females		Males		Females	
	No.	%	No.	%	No.	%	No.	%
Total	182,742	48·9	190,582	51·1	1,615,625	51·0	1,556,839	49·0
Under 16	87,289	23·4			813,298	25·6		
Over 16	95,453	25·6			802,327	25·3		

As with New Hampshire, the rate of natural increase was perhaps greater in the later decades of the century than in the earlier, probably being around 28 per cent per decade after 1750. Nevertheless, in the figures shown above Massachusetts has a smaller percentage of males under 16 than the national average.

The movements in the rate of growth were very similar in *Connecticut* (except for the two decades of exceptionally rapid growth in Connecticut, the 1740's and 1750's). In the 1790 Census, Connecticut, like Massachusetts, has a slight female surplus:

Percentages	Total	Over 16	Under 16
Males	49·5	26·1	23·4
Females	50·5		

The percentage of males under 16 is almost exactly the same in Connecticut and in Massachusetts.

The Governor's Report of 1773 for Connecticut contains some highly useful information. The total population is reported to be 'on an exact census Whites 191,392, Blacks 6,664' (totalling 198,000, the figure which also emerged from the 1775 Census[48]). This, it is said, represents an increase of 52,266 since 1762, although 'also within this Time, there have been frequent and numerous emigrations from hence to settle on New Lands, in His Majesty's other Colonies'. The Governor attributes the increase to 'Industrious, temperate Life, and early Marriage'.

[46] *Downshire Papers*, Report on Massachusetts Bay. The population figures given here appear to confirm very broadly the Rossiter (and Sutherland) figures for Massachusetts shown in Table 1(a). Greene and Harrington, however (*op. cit.*, p. 10), citing the *Zee Papers* in the *New York Historical Society Collections*, give the much higher figure of 420,000 in 1774, with New England as a whole having 746,000. Other evidence in Greene and Harrington (p. 17) seems to support the lower figures.
[47] Greene and Harrington, *op. cit.*, pp. 31-46.
[48] Sutherland, *op. cit.*, p. xii.

The most informative part of this Report is an Appendix which gives 'An Account of the Number of Inhabitants in the several Counties in the Colony of Connecticut, taken on the 1st January, 1774'. Table 4 shows the aggregate figures for the white population derived from this Account and presents percentages calculated from these.

TABLE 4

The population of Connecticut on 1 January, 1774

	Age years	Single	Number Married	Total (000)	Percentage Single	Married	In age group
Males	Under 10	31,114		31·1	100		32·3
	10–20	24,049	222	24·3	99·1	0·9	25·3
	20–70	9,941	28,866	38·8	25·7	74·3	40·3
	Above 70	554	1,436	2·0	27·9	72·1	2·1
	TOTAL	65,658	30,524	96·2			100
Females	Under 10	30,050		30·1	100		32·0
	10–20	21,860	697	22·5	96·9	3·1	23·8
	20–70	10,486	29,026	39·5	26·5	73·5	41·9
	Above 70	1,264	922	2·2	57·9	42·1	2·3
	TOTAL	63,660	30,645	94·3			100
Both sexes	TOTAL	129,318	61,169	190·5			

This Table shows the usual American excess of males over females (and is thus in contrast with the situation in Connecticut evident, as noted above, in the Census of 1790 and strongly marked in those of 1850 and 1860). The detailed figures show this excess of males in 1774 to be common to all counties and occurring in roughly the same ratio in all parts of the colony. The male excess is not common to all age groups, however; above 20 there are 41,698 females to 40,797 males, only the counties of Fairfield and Litchfield having a surplus of males over 20 (Litchfield, in north-western Connecticut, having 5,668 males to 5,154 females). This would be consistent with emigration from the older settled counties of Connecticut.

The age structure shown by these figures combines youthfulness with evidence of longevity: 57·6 per cent of males and 55·8 per cent of females are under the age of 20; at the other extreme, over 2 per cent are over 70. This shows remarkable similarity with the age structure in the nineteenth century; in 1830 56 per cent, and in 1850 52 per cent, of the total population were under 20; the over 70 percentage was 1·5 in each year (see Table 9).

The most interesting material in the Report is that relating to marriage. The Connecticut figures can hardly be held to support the view that 'early' marriage was the norm in colonial New England. Of males aged 15–19 years, under 2 per cent were married; of females aged 15–19 years, under 6 per cent were married; the highest proportion married was in Litchfield county where about 9 per cent of females aged 15–19 were married.[49] It is not too much to suggest from this

[49] It was assumed for this calculation that the ratios over and under 15 years were the same as in the USA in 1830, and that all the married were over 15. *Cf.* Great Britain 1851 when 0·4 per cent of males and 2·5 per cent of females aged 15–19 years were married.

evidence that, in Connecticut at least, marriage before the age of 20 was for both males and females the exception rather than the rule in the 1770's.[50] This evidence, together with that of Crum, seems to indicate an average age of marriage for females of 21 or 22 years in the eighteenth century, and of just over 22 years in the first half of the nineteenth century, at least so far as Connecticut is concerned.[51]

The age range 20-70 years is unfortunately too large to permit any detailed analysis of the incidence of marriage. It has to be assumed that the category 'single' includes widowed. The rate of almost 75 per cent married for persons of both sexes is high; the highest incidence was in Litchfield county, with its male surplus, where 81 per cent of all women were married.[52]

It is impossible to know whether this marriage pattern was characteristic of the whole of the eighteenth century in Connecticut, or of other parts of America. The rate of population growth in Connecticut at this time appears to have been very low by American standards, 16 and 17 per cent in the 1770's and 1780's. It is of course not impossible to reconcile an age of marriage for females of over 20 with a Malthusian rate of growth, especially if the incidence of marriage was high and one assumes high fertility after marriage[53] and a favourable infantile survival rate.[54]

One would like to have more information about the remaining New England colony, *Rhode Island*. Its broad pattern corresponds with Connecticut rather than with New Hampshire; i.e. the rate of growth is distinctly slower in the late colonial period than in the early decades of the eighteenth century; the decline in the rate of growth starts earlier, however, in the 1750's. By the 1770's Rhode Island had the greatest population density, 45 per square mile. The

[50] This conclusion about Connecticut was also noted by J. P. Monahan (*op. cit.*, p. 103), citing Dr S. N. D. North. It also accords well with Franklin's remarks noted earlier and with Crum's estimates, based on his study of the genealogical records of 22 pioneer families 'originally settled in New England or the middle Atlantic states'. Crum calculated the following average marriage ages (the number of brides is shown in brackets): before 1700 (30), 21·4 years; 1700-49 (147), 21·7; 1750-99 (284), 22·0; 1800-49 (969), 22·3 years. (Crum, *op. cit.*, pp. 215 ff. See note 24.)

[51] Since many of the observers who commented on the habit of 'early' marriage were European, and especially English, it is possible that this evidence tells us more about European marriage habits than about American. The European observer reporting 'early' marriage presumably means 'earlier than in Europe'. If marriage in America was exceptional before the age of 20, occurring on the average at 21-22 years, but was nevertheless considered 'early', this could reflect a normal age of marriage in Europe of perhaps 25 years.

[52] British figures for the mid-nineteenth century were: 1851, 59·2 per cent of all females aged 20-69 were married, 62·6 per cent of males. On French Canada in the eighteenth century, see J. T. Krause, 'Some Implications of Recent Research in Demographic History' (*Comparative Studies in Society and History*, i, 167-8).

[53] This view is supported by a recent study by Michael Drake: 'Marriage and Population Growth in Ireland, 1750-1845' (*Economic History Review*, xvi, 2, December 1963, pp. 301 ff.). Drake compares Ireland and Norway in the mid-nineteenth century, concluding that 'in Norway . . . women married later than in Ireland, the proportion of married women in the younger age-group was smaller, and yet . . . there was little difference in fertility' (pp. 307-9).

[54] A postscript to the 1773 Report is worth reproducing here:
Posterity of Mary Loomis born at Windsor 1680.
Married to John Buell[?] of Lebanon Janry 1696
Died at Litchfield 4th November 1768.

	Children	Grand Children	Gt Gd Children	Gt Gt Gd Children	Total
Living at her Death	10	75	232	19	336
Died before her	3	26	42	3	74
	13	101	274	22	410

trend would be quite consistent with the gradual movement of population away from the settled area along the coast into the interior, but the full economic implications of this cannot be investigated in this context.[55] In the Census of 1790 there was a slight female surplus, 32,652 females against 31,818 males.

Mid-Atlantic

One of the outstanding demographic (and economic) features of eighteenth-century America was the rise to prominence of the Middle Colonies. In 1700 the population of the Middle Colonies was about half that of New England but by the time of the Revolutionary War the two were almost equal (Table 1, note ii). By 1780 Pennsylvania had become the second most populous colony (though still far behind Virginia). The middle colonies, especially Pennsylvania, attracted immigrants both from Europe and from other parts of America, especially New England. A considerable number of Negroes was to be found, especially in New York. It was therefore assumed earlier in this chapter that the decennial rates of growth shown in Table 1(d) were higher than the natural rate of growth.

The traditional picture of social life in these colonies is somewhat less clear-cut than that of New England. The population was much more heterogeneous and generally, though not universally, more tolerant; the climate and terrain were less rigorous. But for the most part it is usually assumed that what was true of New England was also true, with only slight modification, of the middle colonies.

Throughout the eighteenth century, *Pennsylvania* was the most populous of the middle colonies. It was also the most cosmopolitan, a fact which may have influenced Benjamin Franklin's observations. It is therefore particularly regrettable that the demographic information available for Pennsylvania is even sparser than that for other colonies. The only colonial census in Pennsylvania was taken in 1783–4 and lacks detail. The Governor's Report in the *Downshire Papers* is uninformative. It gives a total population of 302,000 (300,000 white, and 2,000 black). The numerous grants of land in the past 10 years are cited as evidence of a 'great increase of Inhabitants' which the Governor attributes to

> 'the annual importation of German and Irish servants and passengers and the natural increase of the Inhabitants who marry early, and more generally here than is usual in Europe'.

Benjamin Franklin's estimate that one-third of the population was foreign-born, while untrue of the colonies as a whole, may very well have been true of Pennsylvania. William Penn's promise of complete religious freedom, the humane criminal code and the economic prosperity of the colony attracted and retained large numbers of Europeans, especially Germans and Scotch-Irish. Many came as indentured servants. Despite attempts at restriction after Penn's death, the influx continued throughout the century. The immigrants, especially the Scotch-Irish, did not settle in clearly defined areas, but were highly mobile, moving readily to the expanding frontier. While Pennsylvania had immense tracts of frontier land for settlement, the growth of its towns, especially Philadelphia, should not escape notice.

[55] See Sutherland, *op. cit.*, pp. 52, 86.

All estimates of the foreign-born element confirm this picture of a very mixed society. Greene and Harrington cite a Board of Trade Report of 1755 which gives a total population of 220,000, 'of whom 100,000 are Germans and other foreign Protestants', while in 1766 Franklin spoke of 'third Quakers and perhaps another third Germans'.[56]

The Census of 1790 shows Pennsylvania to have the following age and sex structure:

	Total	Over 16	Under 16
Males	51·3	26·1	25·2
Females	48·7		

The *New York* materials are much more copious. A series of Censuses during the course of the century all provide some sort of classification into age and sex, and the data are summarized in Table 5.

TABLE 5

Age structure of the population of New York in the eighteenth century

	Percentages of total, white and negro							
	1703	1723	1746	1749	1756	1771	1786	1790
White								
Males under 16	25·8	24·8	24·7	24·6	24·8	23·5	24·9	24·9
Females under 16	26·9	23·4	24·4	23·3	22·8	22·6	23·5	(b)
Total under 16	52·7	48·2	49·1	47·9	47·6	46·1	48·4	
Males above 16	24·5	26·4	26·5	26·9	27·2	28·1	26·3	26·6
Females above 16	22·8	25·4	24·4	25·2	25·2	25·8	25·3	(b)
Total above 16	47·3	51·8	50·9	52·1	52·4	53·9	51·6	
Males above 60	(a)	(b)	2·6	2·5	3·3	2·9	2·2	(b)
Total males	50·3	51·1	51·1	51·5	51·9	51·6	51·1	51·5
Negro								
Males under 16	20·7	19·1	21·6	22·5	24·3	22·2	(b)	(b)
Females under 16	16·9	16·2	24·3	21·1	20·5	20·4	(b)	(b)
Total under 16	37·6	35·3	45·9	43·6	44·8	42·6		
Males above 16	31·3	35·3	31·8	31·3	31·6	31·3	(b)	(b)
Females above 16	31·1	29·4	22·3	25·1	23·6	26·1	(b)	(b)
Total above 16	62·4	64·7	54·1	56·4	55·2	57·4		
Males above 60	(a)	(b)	4·0	3·3	3·6	4·3	(b)	(b)
Total Males	52·0	54·3	53·3	53·7	55·8	53·1	50·4	(b)

(a) 125 persons (out of 20,000) are shown as 'Over 60', sex and colour not being distinguished.

(b) Not shown.

This Table has been constructed from data given in Greene and Harrington, *op. cit.*, pp. 95-105. As the figures are also given by counties, further detailed analysis would be possible; for example, the over-16 group is always high in New York city itself, where adult immigrants were likely to be found.

[56] Greene and Harrington, *op. cit.*, pp. 115-16. Franklin's estimate of the total population of Pennsylvania was lower than other contemporary estimates. Greene and Harrington contribute little fresh information for this very important colony. Sutherland suggests that 'the proportion of the German element to the whole population between the years 1730 and 1790 was probably about one-third of the total' (*op. cit.*, p. 148). This estimate presumably includes second and subsequent generations.

The percentages shown in Table 5 are remarkably consistent, especially for the white population. Apart from 1703, the percentage under 16 years kept within 2 per cent of an average of 47·5 per cent, with a male surplus, about 51 per cent, in all years. The Negro figures show greater variation, but the percentage under 16 is always lower than that of whites, below 40 in the first two Censuses and averaging 44 per cent from 1746 to 1771. Also the male surplus was more marked among Negroes, reaching 55·8 per cent in 1756.[57]

Comparing the New York age structure for 1771 with later figures for the USA, one might suggest that this distribution suggests the presence in the population of recently arrived immigrants, most of whom would be over 16 years of age; such a group of adult immigrants raises the percentage over 16 to above 50 per cent, the national percentage in 1800.

New York, like Pennsylvania, offered ample room for expansion. In his Report of 1773, Governor Tryon suggested that only one-fifth of the province was occupied. The Census of 1771 listed twelve counties, two of which in 1791 formed Vermont; the ten counties of New York proper were all on the Hudson River, or situated on the islands at the mouth.[58] Settlement was still largely confined to the Hudson valley, hemmed in by the hills on either side. North and west of Albany the population was extremely sparse. In addition to the difficulties of the terrain, these frontier settlements had encountered the same dangers from both Indians and the French as did the more remote parts of New England. After 1763 there was some expansion around Lake Champlain and further west along the Mohawk; because of the nearness to Canada, this movement was checked by the outbreak of the Revolutionary War.

Because of its land system, New York was not an attractive colony to the voluntary migrant in the eighteenth century.[59] There was, however, almost complete religious tolerance. In these circumstances, it is probable that New York received more European than American migrants, including a significant proportion of indentured servants (some involuntary).[60] The colony's cosmopolitan character increased in the course of the eighteenth century, with arrivals of Dutch, French, Scotch-Irish, Scots, Palatine Germans (though far fewer than in Pennsylvania) and especially English. New York City itself was already expanding as a major port, attracting foreign merchants, especially in the years just before 1790.

The problem of quantifying the contribution made by foreign immigrants to the growth of the population of New York is insuperable. With the assumption of about 60,000 immigrants over a 90-year period the rate of population growth in New York falls to a level very close to the Malthusian 32 per cent.

Governor Tryon's summary of the situation in 1773 followed the usual lines:

---

[57] Both these features also appear in two other Censuses, for 1731 and 1737, not included in Table 5 because of differences in classification.

[58] See Sutherland, op. cit., pp. 74-75.

[59] The Dutch patroonships of the seventeenth century were still the basis of land-holding. About three-quarters of the best land was owned by a very small number of individuals; in 1764 three owners possessed over a million acres. Taxes also fell heavily on the small owner.

[60] Abbot E. Smith comments, 'Fewer [indentured servants] came to New York [than to other colonies], but those who did were speedily purchased, and the inhabitants of that colony expressed several times a desire for more'. Colonists in Bondage, p. 35.

'The high price of labour, and the plenty and cheapness of new land fit for cultivation, as they increase the means of subsistence, are strong additional incitements to marriage; and the People entering into that state more generally at an earlier period of Life than in Europe, the proportion of marriages and births so far exceeds that of populous Countries, that it has been computed the Colonies double their Inhabitants by natural increase only in Twenty years.

The increase in this Colony has been nearly in the same proportion, but it cannot be denied that the addition to our numbers by emigrations from the neighbouring Colonies and from Europe, has been considerable, tho' comparatively small to the numbers thus acquired by some of the Southern Colonies'.

New Jersey maintained a fairly constant share of between 5 and 6 per cent of the total American population throughout the eighteenth century. Its rate of growth was thus very close to the average for the total population, though differing from decade to decade. As with New York, a number of colonial censuses make it possible to assess the age and sex structure.[61] The figures are shown in detail in Table 6 and are commented on below.

In addition the reports of Governor Franklin, dated 28 March 1774, contained in the *Downshire Papers*, is an extremely informative analysis of the population structure of New Jersey. The report begins with an estimate of a total population of 120,000 for 1772, with an increase of 20,000 in the previousdecade; both these figures accord well with those presented in Table 1. During that decade, the Governor noted, 'Great Numbers have quitted the Colony and have migrated to Virginia, North Carolina, the Ohio, Mississippi, etc.' This comment may explain the slowness of growth in the 1760's and 1770's, apparent in Table 2(*d*), and perhaps also something of the rapid growth of North Carolina in the 1760's.

Regrettably the information covers only eight counties, Sussex, Hunterdon, Burlington, Gloucester, Salem, Cumberland, Cape May and Morris, accounting for about 60 per cent of the total population.[62] It refers to the one-year period, 1 July 1771, to 1 July 1772. Table 6 includes the age and sex structure of these eight counties, and Table 7 gives the aggregate figures of all the data found in the Report.

A slight upward movement is seen in Table 6 of the total percentage under 16 years until 1771 when in the eight counties 50 per cent of all whites (and 45 per cent of Negroes) were under 16. A median age of 16 years is close to the national average in 1800, but lower than the New York figures shown earlier. The county figures in Table 6 (themselves to be regarded cautiously because of occasional boundary changes) show the range of variation in different parts of the colony. The 1771 figures show the usual preponderance of males, the sex

[61] Greene and Harrington, *op. cit.*, pp. 109-12. *Downshire Papers*, Report on New Jersey.
[62] 'I endeavoured in the year 1772 to get the exact Number of Inhabitants together with an Account of the Births, Burials, etc., for which purpose I had printed blanks (of the form sent herewith) sent to the several County Assessors but as it would occasion them some additional Trouble for which there was no Allowance, and as it was no part of the duty as enjoined them by Law many of them refused . . . ' (Governor Franklin's Report). Returns are lacking for Waterford Township and the counties of Bergen, Essex, Somerset, Middlesex and Monmouth. Maps showing colonial counties are to be found in Rossiter, *op. cit.*

TABLE 6

Age structure of the population of New Jersey, by counties, in 1726, 1737-8 1745 and 1771-2

Whites	Total	Middlesex	Essex	Monmouth	Somerset	Bergen	Burlington	Hunterdon	Gloucester	Salem	Cape May	Morris	Sussex	Cumberland
1726														
Males under 16	7,558	1,016	983	1,095	403	556	965	851	526	1,015	148			
Females „	6,948	859	926	1,056	405	547	844	750	529	891	141			
Total „	14,506	1,875	1,909	2,151	808	1,103	1,809	1,601	1,055	1,906	289			
Males above 16	8,179	953	992	1,234	582	569	1,080	892	608	1,060	209			
Females „	7,176	878	1,021	1,061	502	509	983	743	462	861	156			
Total „	15,355	1,831	2,013	2,295	1,084	1,078	2,063	1,635	1,070	1,921	365			
Total whites	29,861	3,706	3,922	4,446	1,892	2,181	3,872	3,236	2,125	3,827	654			
1737-8														
Males under 16	10,639	1,086	1,619	1,289	999	820	1,190	1,270	782	1,313	271			
Females „	9,700	956	1,494	1,295	867	708	996	1,170	676	1,327	211			
Total „	20,339	2,042	3,113	2,584	1,866	1,528	2,186	2,440	1,458	2,640	482			
Males above 16	(11,631)	1,134	1,118	1,508	967	939	1,487	1,618	930	1,669	261			
Females „	10,725	1,085	1,720	1,339	940	822	1,222	1,230	757	1,391	219			
Total „	22,356	2,219	2,838	2,847	1,907	1,761	2,709	2,848	1,687	3,060	480			
Total whites	(42,695)	4,261	(5,951)	5,431	3,773	3,289	4,895	5,288	3,145	5,700	962			
1745														
Males under 16	14,253	1,651	1,652	1,975	765	494	1,528	2,182	786	1,746	284	1,190		
Females „	13,754	1,695	1,548	1,899	719	585	1,454	2,090	808	1,595	274	1,087		
Total „	28,007	3,346	3,200	3,874	1,484	1,079	2,982	4,272	1,594	3,341	558	2,277		
Males above 16	15,086	1,728	1,694	2,071	740	721	1,786	2,302	913	1,716	306	1,109		
Females „	13,704	1,659	1,649	1,783	672	590	1,605	2,117	797	1,603	272	957		
Total „	28,790	3,387	3,343	3,854	1,412	1,311	3,391	4,419	1,710	3,319	578	2,066		
Total whites	56,797	6,733	6,543	7,728	2,896	2,390	6,373	8,691	3,304	6,660	1,136	4,343		

1771-2

	Total	(no returns)	(no returns)	(no returns)	(no returns)	(no returns)								
Males under 16	17,568						3,012	3,690	2,092	1,532	468	3,015	2,440	1,319
Females ,,	16,179						2,817	3,588	1,961	1,431	384	2,738	2,144	1,116
Total ,,	33,747						5,829	7,278	4,053	2,963	852	5,753	4,584	2,435
Males 16–50	15,170						2,947	2,987	1,995	1,243	374	2,505	2,003	1,116
,, 50–80	2,416						470	656	231	130	42	414	299	174
,, 80 and over	102						23	36	12	4	2	10	9	6
Females 16–50	13,821						2,663	2,952	1,724	1,196	339	2,142	1,749	1,056
,, 50–80	2,149						447	570	215	117	37	335	288	140
,, 80 and over	91						14	31	8	9	2	9	12	6
Total above 16	33,749						6,564	7,232	4,185	2,699	796	5,415	4,360	2,498
Total whites	67,496						12,393	14,510	8,238	5,662	1,648	11,168	8,944	4,933

Percentages

Data column	Under 16 1726	1737-8	1745	1771-2	Total Males 1726	1737-8	1745	1771-2	Negroes Under 16 1726	1737-8	1771-2
Total	48·5	47·6	49·3	50·0	52·7	52·2	51·7	52·2	41·8	40·8	44·5
(no returns)	50·6	47·9	49·7		53·1	52·1	50·2				
(no returns)	48·7	52·3	48·9		50·4	46·0	51·1				
(no returns)	48·4	47·6	50·1		52·4	51·5	52·4				
(no returns)	42·7	49·5	51·2		52·1	52·1	52·0				
(no returns)	50·6	46·5	45·1		51·6	53·5	50·8				
3,012	46·7	44·7	46·8	47·0	52·8	54·7	52·0	52·1			
3,690	49·5	46·1	49·2	50·2	53·9	54·6	51·6	50·8			
2,092	49·6	46·4	48·2	49·2	53·4	54·4	51·4	52·6			
1,532	49·8	46·3	50·2	52·3	54·2	52·3	52·0	51·4			
468	44·2	50·1	49·1	51·7	54·6	55·3	51·9	53·8			
3,015			52·4	51·5			52·9	53·2			53·1
2,440				49·4				51·3			53·0
1,319											

ratio being 109·3 (110·1 among the over 16's, and 116·4 among the migrants).

Table 7 shows 2,061 births to a white population of 67,496 in which there were 13,821 women between 16 and 50 years. This is equivalent to 30·5 births per thousand, and 150 births per thousand women between 16 and 50 years.

When the birth figures are analysed by counties, the following result is obtained:

	Births per 1,000 population	Births per 1,000 women aged 16–50 years
Burlington	26·4	125
Hunterdon	30·3	149
Gloucester	32·6	159
Salem	30·4	144
Cape May	21·9	107
Morris	31·9	166
Sussex	33·5	171
Cumberland	31·3	147
All counties	30·5	150

These figures give support to the general assumption of higher fertility in the frontier regions. The highest rates are found in Sussex and Morris counties, in the north-western part of New Jersey, along the Delaware River; the lowest (apart from Cape May where the total population was only 1,648) is in central Burlington County.

The Negro figures show 118 births to a coloured population of 3,313 in which there were 787 women of '16 and upwards'. This is equivalent to 35·6 births per thousand, and 130 births per thousand women over 16. Among the small Negro population in Sussex County the birth rate was as high as 49·1 per thousand (13 births in a population of 285 with only 69 women over 16).

Obviously no great reliance can be placed on these findings. The figures are for twelve months only. Above all, it would be extremely surprising if the births were not under-estimated. One can probably say that the birth rates and fertility rates were *no less* than those indicated above; the correct allowance to be made for under-enumeration of births is unknown.

For similar reasons it would be equally unwise to regard the reported total burials with finality. The death rate they show is as low as 10 per thousand for the white population. The variations by counties range from 7 and 8 in Sussex and Morris to 17 per thousand in Salem. The ratio of recorded burials to total population is over 50 per cent higher for Negroes than for whites.

At first sight it might appear from the burials data that an extremely high proportion was of under 16's: 47 per cent of white male deaths and 54 per cent of female. This was largely the result, however, of the youthful age structure; when the burials are related to the total population under 16, the death rate for that age group is 10 per thousand. At an extremely crude estimate, this evidence suggests a very low infant mortality rate: if one assumed that all 340 under-16 burials were in fact of under-5's, and assumed 10,000 births in the previous five years (2,000 in 1771-2, multiplied by 5) with allowance for deaths, then the

TABLE 7

'An Account of the Dwelling Houses and Inhabitants of Part of the Province of New Jersey and of the Marriages Births and Burials in the said Province for one year from the 1st of July 1771 to the 1st of July 1772'

| | Dwelling houses | Males | | | | | Females | | | | | M & F |
		Under 16	16-50	50-80	80 and over	Total	Under 16	16-50	50-80	80 and over	Total	Total
White totals	10,930	17,568	15,170	2,416	102	35,256	16,179	13,821	2,149	91	32,240	67,496
Percentages		49·8	43·0	6·9	0·3	100	50·2	42·9	6·6	0·3	100	
			16 and over					16 and over				
Negro totals		785	1,049			1,834	692	787			1,479	3,313
Percentages		42·8	57·2			100	46·7	53·3			100	

| Marriages | Births | Burials | | | | | | | | M & F | Migration | | | |
| | | Males | | | | Females | | | | | Families moved out of the province within the said year | | Families moved into the province within the said year | |
		Under 16	16-50	50 and over	Total	Under 16	16-50	50 and over	Total	Total	Families	Persons	Families	Persons
404	2,061	179	119	85	383	161	86	51	298	681	86	498	45	255
		46·7	31·1	22·2	100	54·0	28·9	17·1	100					
			16 and over				16 and over							
	118	18	15		33	7	12		19	52				
		55	45		100	37	63		100					

infant mortality rate was about 40 per thousand; if it is assumed that all 340 deaths were of infants in the first year of life, the death rate of infants under one was only 17 per 100 births.[63]

These calculations, let it be repeated, are highly tenuous, based on a small, incomplete and fortuitous set of data. Nevertheless, one could make an ex-

[63] One may perhaps find some support for this calculation in a rather vague statement by William Currie, Fellow of the College of Physicians of Philadelphia, in his remarkable work *An Historical Account of the Climates and Diseases of the United States of America* (Philadelphia, 1792). Writing of Philadelphia, he says: 'From the best information which I have been able to obtain, more than one-fifth of all the children born in this city, die under two years of age. A considerable portion of these, fall victims to the contagious diseases which never cease to prevail; but the greatest part die of Cholera, Diarrhoea, and Remitting Fever.' (pp. 112-13.) The strength of Dr Currie's 'more than' cannot be ascertained, but he does appear, in the context, to regard this Philadelphia infant mortality rate as unusually high, and continually draws attention to the 'disparity between the healthiness of a large town and the Country which surrounds it . . .' (p. 202-3.) Observations and occasional statistical information elsewhere in Currie's book suggest a low infant mortality rate; he observes for example 'an utter extinction of this scourge of infants [rickets].' (p. 24.)

tremely generous allowance for error and still be left with the conclusion that the infant mortality rate was very much lower than in contemporary England. The suggestion is therefore here put forward, based though it may be on slender evidence, that, if these New Jersey data are at all representative, at any rate of the middle colonies, the low infant mortality rate may well have been far more important than has usually been thought in accounting for the high rate of natural growth of population in eighteenth century America.

The migration figures show that, in this year, New Jersey suffered a net loss through internal migration of 243 persons. This would amount to about 2,500 per decade, or roughly 10 per cent of the actual increase. This would give New Jersey a decennial rate of natural growth in the 1770's of about 26 per cent, slightly lower than that suggested earlier for New York.

The South

The analytical problems created by the presence in the South of the coloured population, and in particular by the importation of slaves throughout the eighteenth century, have been discussed earlier in this chapter. Moreover only in the national period was the South avoided by white immigrants; in the colonial period certain parts of the South, notably Georgia and South Carolina, received an important contribution from different sorts of white immigrants, especially indentured servants.[64] The statistics available for the South, however, are very limited and fall far short of the minimum requirements for separating the different causes of growth.

Social conditions in the South are assumed to have had certain clear features. Settlement was widely scattered, penetrating far inland across the broad plain to the Piedmont; correspondingly there was little urbanization. Especially in the eighteenth century a quasi-aristocracy developed among the white population, with primogeniture in many colonies. The age of marriage was low—usually thought to be below that of the North. In contrast with the Puritanism of the North, sexual behaviour in the South is often supposed to have been lax, partly because of the presence of large numbers of indentured servants and slaves; illegitimacy at times seems to have been a serious problem. But, as with New England, these assumptions cannot be verified with detailed statistical evidence.

It is particularly to be regretted that little can be said about *Virginia*, the most populous colony. Like Massachusetts her share of the total fell in the eighteenth century but only from about one-quarter to about one-fifth. The early estimates may be unreliable, based as they are on such sources as militia numbers and lists of tithables[65]; at best, they only give estimates of total numbers, with occasional indications of the division into white and coloured. A combination of an incomplete census and a calculation from tax lists between 1782 and 1787 gives a picture of the distribution of the white and coloured population by counties,[66] but the published material provides no details other than the crude totals.

[64] See for example W. B. Smith, *White Servitude in Colonial South Carolina* (1961).
[65] See Greene and Harrington, *op. cit.*, pp. 139-43.
[66] Sutherland, *op. cit.*, pp. 174-6. Jefferson referred to the 1782 assessment in his *Notes on Virginia*, estimating '296,852 free inhabitants, 270,762 slaves'. In making his calculation, he makes an incidental remark about the age of marriage: 'Knowing how early marriage takes place here, we shall not be far wrong in supposing that the unmarried part of our militia are those between 16 and

The Governor's Report of 1773 contained only two careless sentences on population:

'Whites about three Hundred Thousand, Blacks about Two hundred Thousand, this is a very rough guess as there has been no Enumeration made for a great while'.

'The Inhabitants are increased at least one third within these ten years reckoning Births and Emigrants'.[67]

Colonial Virginia of course was dominated by the cultivation of tobacco, which involved a constant search for new soil (and hence mobility of population) and a high demand for labour. The unhealthy climate of the eastern plain meant that the main imported labour there was Negro slave labour, white immigrants moving west to the Piedmont regions. In view of the very considerable economic development of Virginia in the eighteenth century, it is most unfortunate that further quantitative evidence is not available. The population composition shown by the 1790 Census is:

Percentages	Total	Over 16	Under 16
White male	51·4	25·1	26·3
White female	48·6		
Total free	60·9		
Total slaves	39·1		

The two *Carolinas* both show an extremely high rate of population growth in the eighteenth century, but despite this still had a low density of population at the end of the period. North Carolina had poor rivers, a dangerous coastline with virtually no good harbours and no staple product to compare with Virginia's tobacco. The swamp lands were conducive to disease and it is likely that the death rate was high. There were serious outbreaks of smallpox and yellow fever in 1698-9, 1703 and 1732.[68] These general impressions, however, cannot be demonstrated in full statistical detail.

There was a continuing movement west throughout the colonial period, especially after the middle of the eighteenth century. Scotch-Irish, Swiss and German immigrants participated in the settlement of the frontier, especially in the Piedmont in both North and South Carolina. The more rapid rate of growth in North Carolina is particularly noticeable in view of the lower percentage of slaves in that colony.

The Census of 1790 shows the following percentages:

North Carolina

Percentages	Total	Over 16	Under 16
White male	51·2	24·6	26·6
White female	48·8		
Total free	74·5		
Total slave	25·5		

South Carolina

Percentages	Total	Over 16	Under 16
White male	52·2	25·4	26·8
White female	47·8		
Total free	57·0		
Total slave	43·0		

21. If there be young men who do not marry till after 21, there are as many who marry before that age.' (pp. 144-5.) This observation, if accurate, would confirm the impression that the age of marriage was lower in the South than in the North.

[67] *Downshire Papers*, Report on Virginia.

[68] Sutherland, *op. cit.*, p. 243.

Georgia, founded only in 1732 with philanthropic motivations, was settled
in the first instance by European migrants. Slavery was prohibited until 1750.
The 'headright' system of land settlement is usually assumed to have attracted
immigrants throughout the century from other colonies, as well as from Europe.
The Governor's Report of 1773 emphasized the economic attractiveness of
Georgia to the immigrant:

> 'The Reasons of their Increase are principally the great Inducement People
> have had to settle in a Province, where they could get fresh and good Lands
> at a moderate Price, and plenty of good rough for Cattle, Horses and Hogs,
> and where they will not be so much pent up and confined as in thick Settled
> Countries'.[69]

Georgia's small population of 83,000 in 1790 was made up as follows:

Percentages	Total	Over 16	Under 16
White male	51·3	24·7	26·6
White female	48·7		
Total free	64·4		
Total slave	35·6		

Thus the whole of the South affords us very little statistical evidence and,
despite all the detailed work on Southern history, including for example the
indenture system, one cannot go far beyond vague generalizations.

Conclusions

1. Population growth in colonial America was determined by the rate of
natural increase, the importation of slaves, and immigration.

2. With certain assumptions about slave importation and immigration, the
natural rate of growth seems to have been in the range 26–30 per cent per decade.
This is somewhat below the Malthusian formula of a doubling every 25 years
through reproduction. It is nevertheless a rate of natural growth considerably
higher than that to be found in England at any time in the eighteenth and
nineteenth centuries.

3. The growth was uneven in different parts of the colonies. There is no
reason to suppose that the same explanations of population growth hold good
for all regions. On the contrary generalizations are suspect, not merely because
of the broad differences between North and South, but also because of local
differences within each separate colony and particularly between town and
country. Internal migration was an important disturbing factor, immigration
areas having a higher rate of growth than emigration areas. But in addition
it appears probable that both fertility and mortality differed considerably from
area to area.

4. Growth was also uneven over time. These variations cannot be conclusively analysed without more reliable and more abundant statistics than are at
present available. There does, however, appear to have been fairly general

[69] *Downshire Papers,* Report on Georgia.

increase in the rate of growth, for one reason or another, in the second half of the century.

5. Contemporary opinion held strongly to the view that the rapid growth of population was due to 'early' marriage.[70] The views expressed, however, were rarely supported by statistical evidence; no general marriage data are available before the nineteenth century. Many writers have argued that a wife was an asset at the frontier, playing an essential part in pioneer life. Also the excess of males placed females, including perhaps widows, in great demand. Bachelors and spinsters were often held in opprobrium and some colonies imposed bachelor taxes. What evidence there is, however, does not suggest a normal marriage age below 20, at least in the North (though the age may have been somewhat lower in the South); certainly child marriage was everywhere a rarity. The Connecticut data, and other evidence, noted in this chapter indicated that marriage before 20 was unusual, especially for males. 'Early' marriage meant, to Thomas Jefferson, half below and half above the age of 21 years. Nevertheless there is a great deal of testimony that the age of marriage was lower in colonial America than in eighteenth-century England (and Europe).

6. The statistics are inadequate to permit the calculation of a firm birth rate figure. The fragmentary material from New Jersey gave a figure of 30 per thousand, but this is almost certainly too low.

7. The New Jersey evidence also suggested an astonishingly low infant mortality rate. If this has any reliability and general validity (at least for the North), then the good chances of infant survival could well have been a major factor in promoting the rapid rate of growth of the American population. A combination of a moderately high, rather than extremely high, fertility rate with low infant mortality might offer a satisfactory explanation for the rapidity of growth.

8. When allowance is made for immigration and slave importation the natural rate of increase seems to have been slightly below Malthus's suppositions. Nevertheless, the above interpretation is otherwise wholly consistent with Malthus's theory of population growth. The high productivity of American agriculture indeed appears as the key to American population growth. The food supply was generally adequate and became increasingly abundant, allowing population to grow despite all the rigours of the climate and of pioneer life.[71] Above all perhaps it sustained the health of women of child-bearing age and thus kept low the infant mortality rate.

[70] See above, and the examination of these opinions in T. P. Monahan, *op. cit.*, pp. 9-11, 31, 47, 51, 99, 329.

[71] It is worth noting, especially in view of Dr Utterström's work on Swedish population, that there are claims, based on human memory, of improvements in climate in colonial America. Thus William Currie, *op. cit.*, pp. 79-80, cites Peter Kalm's *Travels* to the effect that, when the English first settled in Pennsylvania, the river Delaware used to freeze in mid-November, while Kalm found that it did not freeze, in 1748-51, until mid-December. And of Virginia, Jefferson wrote in 1782: 'Both heats and colds are become much more moderate within the memory even of the middle-aged. Snows are less frequent and lie less deep. . . . The elderly inform me that the earth used to be covered with snow about three months in every year. . . . The accumulated snows of the winter in the spring produced those overflowings of our rivers, so frequent then and so rare now.' (*Notes on Virginia*, pp. 134-5.)

TABLE 8

The population of the USA, 1790–1860

State		Population (000)								Decennial increase (000)						
		1790	1800	1810	1820	1830	1840	1850	1860	1790–1800	1800–1810	1810–1820	1820–1830	1830–1840	1840–1850	1850–1860
New England	Maine	97	152	229	298	399	502	583	628	55	77	69	101	103	81	45
	New Hampshire	142	184	214	244	269	285	318	326	42	30	30	25	16	33	8
	Vermont	85	154	218	236	281	292	314	315	69	64	18	45	11	22	1
	Massachusetts	379	423	472	523	610	738	995	1,231	44	49	51	87	128	257	236
	Rhode Island	69	69	77	83	97	109	148	175	—	8	6	14	12	39	27
	Connecticut	238	251	262	275	298	310	371	460	13	11	13	23	12	61	89
	Total	1,009	1,233	1,472	1,659	1,954	2,235	2,728	3,135	224	239	187	295	281	493	407
Middle States	New York	340	589	959	1,373	1,919	2,429	3,097	3,881	249	370	414	546	510	668	784
	New Jersey	184	211	246	278	321	373	490	672	27	35	32	43	52	117	182
	Pennsylvania	434	602	810	1,049	1,348	1,724	2,312	2,906	168	208	239	299	376	588	594
	Total	958	1,402	2,014	2,700	3,588	4,526	5,899	7,459	444	612	686	888	938	1,373	1,560
South Atlantic	Delaware	59	64	73	73	77	78	92	112	5	9	—	4	1	14	20
	Maryland*	320	357	405	440	487	514	635	762	37	48	35	47	27	121	127
	Virginia†	748	880	975	1,065	1,211	1,240	1,422	1,596	132	95	90	146	29	182	174
	North Carolina	395	478	556	639	738	753	869	993	83	78	83	99	15	116	124
	South Carolina	249	346	415	503	581	594	669	704	97	69	88	78	13	75	35
	Georgia‡	83	161	202	227	234	232	272	299	78	41	25	7	-2	40	27
	Total	1,854	2,286	2,625	2,947	3,328	3,411	3,959	4,466	432	339	322	381	83	548	507
East-South-Central	Kentucky	74	221	407	564	688	780	982	1,156	147	186	157	124	92	202	174
	Tennessee	36	106	262	423	682	829	1,003	1,110	70	156	161	259	147	174	107
	Total	110	327	668	987	1,370	1,609	1,985	2,266	217	341	319	383	239	376	281
Total in area of 1790		3,930	5,247	6,779	8,294	10,240	11,781	14,570	17,326	1,317	1,532	1,515	1,946	1,541	2,789	2,756
Total in added area			61	461	1,344	2,626	5,288	8,622	14,117	61	400	883	1,282	2,662	3,334	5,495
Total USA		3,930	5,308	7,240	9,638	12,866	17,069	23,192	31,443	1,378	1,932	2,398	3,228	4,203	6,123	8,251

Table with two sections: *(b)* Distribution of population per cent, and *(d)* Percentage decennial increase.

	State	(b) Distribution of population per cent								(d) Percentage decennial increase							
		1790	1800	1810	1820	1830	1840	1850	1860	1790–1800	1800–1810	1810–1820	1820–1830	1830–1840	1840–1850	1850–1860	average
New England	Maine	2	3	3	3	3	3	3	2	57	51	30	34	26	16	8	32
	New Hampshire	4	3	3	3	2	2	1	1	30	16	14	10	6	12	3	13
	Vermont	2	3	3	2	2	2	1	1	81	42	8	19	4	8	—	23
	Massachusetts	10	8	7	5	5	4	4	4	12	12	11	17	21	35	24	17
	Rhode Island	2	1	1	1	1	1	1	—	—	12	8	17	12	36	18	15
	Connecticut	7	5	4	3	2	1	2	1	5	4	5	8	4	20	24	10
	Total	27	23	20	17	15	13	12	10	22	19	13	18	14	22	15	17·6
Middle States	New York	9	11	13	14	15	14	13	12	73	63	43	40	26	28	25	43
	New Jersey	5	4	3	3	2	2	2	2	15	17	13	15	16	31	37	21
	Pennsylvania	11	11	11	11	10	10	10	9	39	35	30	29	28	34	26	32
	Total	24	26	28	28	28	27	25	24	46	44	34	33	26	30	26	34·1
South Atlantic	Delaware	1	1	1	1	1	—	—	—	8	14	—	5	1	18	22	10
	Maryland*	8	7	6	5	4	3	3	2	12	13	9	11	6	24	20	14
	Virginia†	19	17	13	11	9	7	6	5	18	11	9	14	2	15	12	11
	North Carolina	10	9	8	7	6	4	4	3	21	16	15	15	2	15	14	14
	South Carolina	6	7	6	5	5	3	3	3	39	20	21	16	2	13	5	17
	Georgia‡	2	3	3	2	2	1	1	1	94	25	12	3	-1	17	10	23
	Total	47	43	36	31	26	20	17	14	23	15	12	13	2	16	13	13·4
East-South-Central	Kentucky	2	4	6	6	5	5	4	4	199	84	39	22	13	26	18	57
	Tennessee	1	2	4	4	5	5	4	4	194	147	61	61	22	21	11	74
	Total	3	6	9	9	11	9	9	7	197	104	48	39	17	23	14	63·1
Total in area of 1790		100	99	94	86	80	69	63	55	33·5	29·2	22·3	23·5	15·0	23·7	18·9	23·7
Total in added area		—	1	6	14	20	31	37	45	—	655·7	191·5	95·4	101·4	63·0	63·7	167·2
Total USA		100	100	100	100	100	100	100	100	35·1	36·4	33·3	33·5	32·7	35·9	35·6	34·6

* including Washington D.C.   † including West Virginia.   ‡ includes only population within the 1790 boundary of Georgia.

THE NATIONAL PERIOD

It is no mere coincidence that the first American Census of 1790 occurred at the very beginning of the national period. The first Census covering the whole of the USA was in fact taken some ten years before the first regular national Census in any European country except Sweden. The reason for this was political rather than statistical. The Constitution of 1787 required the apportionment of representatives according to the population of the separate states, and provision was made accordingly for the collection of population statistics for this purely political purpose. It is not until 1850 that the data necessary for complete demographic analysis begin to be available, although the earlier Censuses do contain much useful information.

It is not possible to deal exhaustively in this chapter with all the data afforded by the early Censuses. There are numerous demographic studies of the national period[72] and only main features will be considered here.

The first seventy years of the national period saw a maintenance of the same rapid rate of population growth as in the colonial period; the decennial increase between 1790 and 1860 ranged between the highest figure of 36·4, in the 1800's, and the lowest figure of 32·7 per cent, in the 1830's, with an average decennial growth of 34·6 per cent (a figure almost identical with that produced by the estimates for the period 1700-90). This is a rate of growth about twice the British rate during the same years. After 1860, the growth rate fell sharply and continuously, from 26·6 per cent in the 1860's to 20·7 per cent in the 1900's.

One of the analytical problems of the colonial period disappears soon after the turn of the century. The slave trade was made illegal in 1808, although slavery had been abolished in many states long before that date. It is unlikely that illegal trade was large enough to make a significant difference to the figures. Nevertheless two other great difficulties still remain, and indeed become more serious: the westward movement of population and immigration.

By 1860 the settled area of the USA was five times that of 1790, although more than 50 per cent of the population still lived within the territory of the original thirteen states. It is only by using the accumulation of evidence available in the Censuses after 1850, however, that a clear picture of the processes of internal migration can be ascertained.

Immigration statistics become increasingly reliable and detailed from 1820 on, when records of immigration first began to be collected. The immigration data compiled during the rest of the period under consideration counted all aliens arriving as ship passengers, including temporary visitors. They did not include arrivals over land and therefore omitted those who came by one important route of immigration during this period, i.e. via Canada.[73] Hence the official figures probably underestimate immigration at least until the 1840's. Also it has been suggested that, with the sudden upsurge of immigration in the

[72] The most recent is the book by Yasukichi Yasuba (see note 12).

[73] Until the early 1840's when there began a gradual reduction of the British timber duties which gave a protected market in Britain to Canadian timber, the timber ships returning empty to Quebec offered the cheapest means of transatlantic migration. See J. Potter, 'The British Timber Duties, 1815-60', *Economica*, May 1955, p. 132. It is not known how many emigrants, mainly Irish, went to Quebec by this means, or how many ultimately moved on into the USA.

late 1840's, the ports were unable to record numbers accurately, at least in the early years.

Table 8 gives the figures of American population growth to 1860, and is constructed on similar lines to Table 1. It will be seen from the total figures in 8(b) that by 1860 45 per cent of the population lived outside the land area of 1790; the greatest relative shift occurred in the 1830's when the share of the new lands increased by 11 per cent, from 20 to 31 per cent of total population (reflecting the rapid expansion which preceded the crash of 1837). In absolute numbers, however, seen in 8(c), every decade shows a greater increase in the population of the new lands than its predecessor, reaching $5\frac{1}{2}$ millions in the 1850's. By contrast the numerical increase in the population of the 1790 territory is irregular, rising and falling in alternating decades.[74]

If one assumes that unrecorded entrants from Canada were insignificant before 1820, it appears likely that the contribution of immigration to population growth was less in the first decades of the national period than in the eighteenth century. The exact number of immigrants between 1790 and 1820 is, however, uncertain: the 1860 Census gives the following figures, suggesting a deduction of 14·5 per cent to determine the number of settlers:

	Arrivals	Transients	Immigrants
1790-1800	50,000	7,250	42,750
1800-10	70,000	10,150	59,850
1810-20	114,000	16,530	97,470

By applying these immigrant totals to the data shown in Table 8 one may obtain a rough estimate of the natural increase:

	Total increase (000)	Percentage total increase	Increase due to immigration (000)	Natural increase (000)	Percentage natural increase
1790-1800	1,378	35·1	43	1,335	34·0
1800-10	1,932	36·4	60	1,872	35·2
1810-20	2,398	33·1	97	2,301	31·7

The immigrant contribution during the first thirty years of American nationhood, years of war in Europe, was thus relatively slight, raising the rate of increase by only one or two per cent.[75] By the 1840's, however, immigration accounted for over one-quarter of the total increase.[76]

The following figures attempt a similar calculation for the decades 1820-60[77]:

[74] This feature of alternating decades of growth and consolidation—a kind of 20-year cycle measured by the Census years—has counterparts in many different sectors of the American economy throughout the nineteenth century and into the twentieth. Suffice it to note here that the decades 1810-20, 1830-40 and 1850-60 saw a decline in the numerical increase in the old states and a correspondingly rapid growth of population in the new territories.

[75] A recent calculation shows a decline in the foreign-born element in the population until 1840: 1790, 12·8 per cent; 1800, 11·3 per cent; 1810, 11·1 per cent; 1820, 10·4 per cent; 1830, 9·3 per cent; 1840, 8·2 per cent. Ernest Rubin, 'Immigration and the Economic Growth of the United States, 1790-1914' (Conference on Research in Income and Wealth, Sept. 1957).

[76] Thompson and Whelpton attributed 26·5 per cent of the increase to immigration in the 1840's, 34·7 per cent in the 1850's. Warren S. Thompson and P. K. Whelpton, Population Trends in the United States (New York 1933), p. 132.

[77] No deduction has been made for transients between 1820 and 1860 in order to offset, to some extent at least, the unrecorded entrants from Canada.

	Total increase (000)	Percentage total increase	Increase due to immigration (000)	Natural increase (000)	Percentage natural increase
1820–30	3,228	33·5	152	3,076	31·9
1830–40	4,203	32·7	599	3,604	28·0
1840–50	6,123	35·9	1,713	4,410	25·8
1850–60	8,251	34·6	2,598	5,653	24·4

If the 14·5 per cent allowance is made, then the final column reads: 1820–30' 32·1; 1830–40, 28·6; 1840–50, 27·3; 1850–60, 26·1. In both these calculations there is to be found a continuous fall in the decennial natural increase.[78]

The Censuses give a fairly clear picture of the age structure of the American population, with increasing detail in the later years. Table 9 has been constructed to show the population structure in each Census year for the white and coloured (free and slave) populations; the Table also incorporates certain data indicative of the age structure of the immigrants, and finally makes some comparisons with selected European countries.

It seems clear that the American population was younger than the European. At mid-century, 70 per cent of the American population is under 30 (compared with 63 per cent in England, 60 per cent in Sweden and 52 per cent in France); in every Census to 1860, over 50 per cent of the white population is under 20 (the age groups for the coloured population are different, and presumably less reliable). Of the immigrants, also, 70 per cent were under 30. But, as is well known, the immigrant population contained an especially large group of people aged between 20 and 30 years. The following figures show the different composition of the under-30 groups:

	Total white population 1850	1860	Immigrants 1850	1860
Under 20	51·8	50·6	36·0	36·3
20–30	18·5	18·3	36·5	36·9
Total under 30	70·3	68·9	72·5	73·2

Despite the male surplus among the immigrants, a particularly high proportion, over 25 per cent, were women between 15 and 40 years of age. Although the proportion of women between 15 and 50 years increased steadily in the total white population from 19 per cent at the beginning of the century, it remains below 25 per cent.[79]

It may also be noted that the structure of the American population in 1850, with 24·2 per cent women of child-bearing age, was slightly less favourable than that of England in 1851, with 26 per cent. Hence the faster rate of popu-

[78] These calculations are, of course, extremely unsophisticated. They do *not* indicate what the population increase would have been without immigration. In order to make such an estimate, for what it would be worth, one would need to take account of the age and sex composition of immigrants (see text, below) influencing their fertility and mortality, and of the assumption that used to be made that immigration reduced native fertility. See Yasuba, *op. cit.*, pp. 93–96, 177–84.

[79] The number of immigrants in the age group 40–50 years is not recorded; the number of immigrant women between 15 and 50 must have been about 30 per cent of all immigrants.

TABLE 9

Age structure of the American population, 1800–1860

(a) Numbers

Age	Total white							Coloured Free				Coloured Slave				Total immigrants		European countries			
	1800	1810	1820	1830	1840	1850	1860	1830	1840	1850	1860	1830	1840	1850	1860	1850[e]	1820–60[f]	England 1821	England 1851	France 1851	Sweden 1850
Under 1						537	807				12				113						
1-4	(818)	(1,115)	(1,452)	1,895	2,474	2,359	3,310			61	53			540	540	59	419		2,348	3,322	438
5-9	1,479	2,016	2,626	1,533	2,011	2,704	3,528	96	111		62	701	844		576	58	380		2,092	3,295	372
10-14	677	916	1,218	1,309	1,716	2,403	3,114			110	60			915	541	56	361		1,913	3,146	336
15-19				1,169	1,548	2,129	2,855				53				448	99	754		1,757	3,148	340
20-24	795	1,110	1,557					91[a]	110[a]			621[a]	781[a]			160	1,099				
25-29				1,874	2,575	3,627	4,933			121	85			930	698	116	846		3,137	5,815	616
30-39				1,148	1,645	2,417	3,515	60[b]	77[b]		62	371[b]	475[b]		439	120	870		2,365	5,274	472
40-44	843	1,116	1,503													76	542				
45-49	510	703	958	724	1,039	1,589	2,286			93	45			572	280				1,768	4,457	348
50-59				453	620	958	1,401	47[c]	58[c]		28	231[c]	384[c]		156				1,235	3,637	289
60-69				266	347	521	781	25[d]	30[d]	39	16	84[d]	102[d]	202	90				809	2,307	179
70-79				116	161	223	311			10	7			35	31				396	1,078	78
80 and over				39	53	84	92				3				14				7	43	16
Total	4,304	5,862	7,862	10,526	14,189	19,553	26,933	320	386	434	486	2,009	2,586	3,194	3,926	744	5,272		17,827	35,522	3,484
Women 15-50	813[g]	1,106[g]	1,517[g]	2,325	3,326	4,723	6,568				130				931	215[h]	1,327[h]		4,641	9,355	906
Children under 5 per women 15-50	1,006	1,008	957	815	744	613	627				500				701	274	316		505	355	483

For footnotes see p. 671

669

TABLE 9 (cont.)

(b) Percentage in each age group

	Total white							Coloured								Total immigrants		European countries			
								Free				Slave						England	England	France	Sweden
	1800	1810	1820	1830	1840	1850	1860	1830	1840	1850	1860	1830	1840	1850	1860	1850[e]	1820 -60[f]	1821	1851	1851	1850
Under 1						2·7	3·0				2				3						
1-4	34·4	34·4	33·4	18·0	17·4	12·0	12·3	30	29	14	11	35	34	17	13	7·9	7·9	14·9	13·2	9·4	12·6
5-9	15·7	15·6	15·5	14·6	14·2	13·8	13·1				13				15	7·7	7·2	13·0	11·7	9·3	10·7
10-14				12·4	12·1	12·3	11·6			25	12			29	14	7·4	6·8	11·1	10·7	8·9	9·6
15-19				11·1	10·9	10·9	10·6				11				11	13·1	14·3	9·9	9·9	8·9	9·8
20-24	18·5	18·9	19·8					28[a]	28[a]			31[a]	31[a]			21·5	20·8				
25-29				17·8	18·1	18·5	18·3			28	17			29	18	15·6	16·1	15·8	17·6	16·4	17·7
30-39				10·9	11·6	12·4	13·0	19[b]	20[b]		13	19[b]	19[b]		11	16·1	16·5	11·8	13·3	14·8	13·5
40-44	19·6	19·0	19·1													10·2	10·3				
45-49	11·8	12·0	12·2	6·9	7·3	8·1	8·5			21	9			18	7			9·4	9·9	12·5	10·0
50-59				4·3	4·4	5·0	5·2	15[c]	15[c]		6	12[c]	11[c]		4			6·6	6·9	10·2	8·3
60-69				2·5	2·4	2·7	2·9	8	8	9	3	4	4	6	2			4·5	4·5	6·5	5·1
70-79				1·1	1·1	1·2	1·2			2				1				2·2	2·2	3·0	2·2
80 and over				0·4	0·4	0·3	0·3											0·8	0·1	0·1	0·5
Women 15-50	18·9	18·9	19·3	22·1	23·4	24·2	24·4				27				24	28·9[h]	25·2[h]	26·0	26·0	26·0	26·0

(c) Cumulative percentages

Age	1								2				3								
Under 1													2·7	3·0								
1–4	34·4	34·4	33·4	16	13	17	14		18·0	17·4	14·8	15·3			7·9	7·9	14·9	13·2	9·4	12·6		
5–9	50·1	50·0	48·9	31	26	30	29		32·6	31·6	28·6	28·4			15·7	15·2	27·9	24·9	18·6	23·2		
10–14				45	38	46	39		45·0	43·7	40·9	40·0			23·3	22·0	39·0	35·6	27·5	32·9		
15–19				56	49				56·1	54·6	51·8	50·5			36·6	36·3	48·9	45·5	36·3	42·7		
20–24	68·6	69·0	68·7	58ᵃ	57ᵃ	66ᵃ	65ᵃ	35							57·1	57·2						
25–29				74	67	75	67		73·9	72·8	70·4	68·9					64·7	63·1	57·7	60·3		
30–39				85	80	77ᵇ	77ᵇ	84ᵇ	84·8	84·4	82·7	81·9	85ᵇ		89·8	89·7	76·5	76·4	67·6	73·9		
40–44	88·2	88·0	87·8												98·5	100						
45–49	100	100	100	92	89	93	88		91·7	91·7	90·9	90·4					85·9	86·3	80·1	83·9		
50–59				96	94	92ᶜ	92ᶜ	97ᶜ	96·0	96·0	95·8	95·6	96ᶜ				92·5	93·2	90·3	92·2		
60–69				98	98	99	98		98·5	98·5	98·4	98·5	100ᵈ	100ᵈ	100ᵈ	100ᵈ	97·0	97·7	96·8	97·3		
70–79									99·6	99·6	99·6	99·7					99·2	99·9	99·9	99·5		
80 and over				100	100	100	100		100	100	100	100					100	100	100	100		

ᵃ 10–23
ᵇ 24–35
ᶜ 36–54
ᵈ 55 and over

ᵉ Immigrants in three one-year periods around 1850; years ending 30 Sept. 1845, 30 Sept. 1847 and 31 Dec. 1852 (1850 Census, p. xc).
ᶠ Estimates (1860 Census, p. xx).
ᵍ Women 15–45
ʰ Women 15–40

671

lation growth in America has to be explained despite this less favourable sex
and age structure.

The generally accepted explanation for the rapid American population
growth in this period is that there was an extremely high birth rate, with the
repeatedly quoted figure of 55·0 per 1,000 as the estimated birth rate in 1800.
This figure originated in an ingenious calculation by W. S. Thompson and
P. K. Whelpton in a work published in 1933.[80] Their estimates show a slowly
declining birth rate as follows:

1800:	55·0	1840:	48·3
1810:	54·3	1850:	43·3
1820:	52·8	1860:	41·4
1830:	51·4	1870:	38·3

These estimates were made on the basis of the scanty data shown in Table 9,
with the help of a number of supplementary assumptions.[81]

The recent study by Yasuba led to the conclusion that the Thompson-
Whelpton estimates were high and suggests that the rate lay somewhere between
the following[82]:

	Estimate A	Estimate B		Estimate A	Estimate B
1800	52·9	47·6	1840	47·9	43·0
1810	52·7	47·3	1850	42·9	38·4
1820	51·7	45·9	1860	42·1	37·7
1830	49·8	44·7			

All three estimates indicate a declining birth rate between 1800 and 1860[83];
this was in spite of the increasing percentage of women aged 15-50 years seen
in Table 9. The questions which now emerge are: whether this decline in the
birth rate was common to all states and how it is to be explained.

The Census data between 1830 and 1860 suggest that, while the number of

[80] Thompson and Whelpton, op. cit., pp. 263 ff.

[81] The method of calculation is explained in footnotes on pp. 263-4. The main assumptions were:
that the age distribution of children under 10 was the same in 1800-20 as in 1830; that a calculation
of specific death rates made in 1857 (E. B. Elliott, Proceedings of the American Association for the
Advancement of Science, 1857) based on Massachusetts data for 1855 could then be applied to this
assumed age distribution in order to obtain the exact number of births.

[82] Yasuba, op. cit., p. 99. The method of calculation is explained on pp. 97-98. Both estimates
used the United States life table for 1830 put forward by Paul H. Jacobson in 'An Estimate of the
Expectation of Life in the United States in 1850' (The Milbank Memorial Fund Quarterly, April 1957,
p. 198); the second estimate incorporated a modification to that table. Yasuba's Estimate B appears
to correspond the most closely to the tentative conclusions reached earlier in this chapter from the
eighteenth-century material; a birth rate of between 45 and 50 per thousand in 1800 would not be
incompatible with the Census data for that year, nor with the rate of population increase, or the age
structure, recorded in the following decades.

ADDITIONAL NOTE: Since this chapter was written a further work has appeared on this subject:
A. J. Coale and M. Zelnik, New Estimates of Fertility and Population in the United States, 1855-1960
(Princeton University Press, December 1963). These authors estimate a birth rate of 42·8 in 1855
and 41·8 in 1860 (p. 21); i.e. their estimates are slightly below Yasuba's Estimate A.

[83] The 1850 and 1860 Censuses both report by states the number of children under 1 year (similar
to the 1772 New Jersey data examined earlier). These figures are highly suspect because of under-
enumeration. The 1860 Census (i, xxxviii) suggests a factor of 12·5 per cent as the addition to be made
to allow for infant deaths and under-enumeration (based on a comparison between births registered
in the local or state registry in Massachusetts and Connecticut in the same 12-month period, and
those shown in the Census). If this factor is assumed to be applicable to all states, the result is a birth
rate of 30·9 in 1850 and 33·5 in 1860 (the former being lower because of the prevalence of cholera in
1849). The resultant birth rates for Massachusetts and Connecticut, presumably much more accurate
than the general figure, are Massachusetts: 1850, 26·2; 1860, 28·9; Connecticut, 1850, 23·2; 1860,
27·3.

children aged 0-14 years per 1,000 women aged 15-50 was generally declining, the regional variations were very great. These figures are presented in Table 10. It will be seen that the ratio to be found in most New England states is little more than half that to be found elsewhere, especially in the divisions East-South-Central, West-North-Central, West-South-Central, and Pacific. The second part of Table 10 gives a break-down of certain of the state data by counties or by districts; the cities of New York and Philadelphia, and the counties or districts which include Boston, Cincinatti and New Orleans, are shown separately. Whether one looks at the cities named, or at the more urbanized counties within Massachusetts (Essex, Hampden, Middlesex, Suffolk) or Connecticut (Hartford, Tolland), or at the more urbanized districts in other states, all show a distinctly lower proportion of children than the average for the state.[84]

These ratios do not in themselves prove a lower fertility rate. They might indicate a higher rate of infant mortality in urbanized areas (as suggested by Dr Currie in the extract quoted in footnote 63). But if, as many writers have assumed, there was a decline in the birth rate, it seems to have been heavily concentrated in the urbanized counties and above all in the industrializing areas of the North-East; the decline elsewhere may have been so slight as to be negligible.

Despite the high percentage of foreign-born in New England and the Mid-Atlantic states (see Tables 11 and 12, col. 26) and the somewhat higher sex ratio of immigrants compared with natives (see above, p. 636), both these divisions, in contrast to all other parts of the USA, had more females than males in 1860 (Table 12, col. 18).[85] The low sex ratio was particularly marked in New Hampshire, Massachusetts, Rhode Island, Connecticut and, in 1860, New York. These are precisely the same states as those seen in Table 10 to have the lowest number of children aged 0-4 years per 1,000 women aged 15-50 years. H. Yuan T'ien has suggested, and Yasuba denied, that this sex ratio directly explains the falling trend in fertility in those Northern states.[86] But as these were also states which were losing population heavily through internal migration (Tables 11 and 12, col. 13), the whole problem of mobility, and also the particular form of industrial organization, the Waltham system, found in parts of New England, seriously affect this argument.

The high proportion of immigrants in the North-East (Tables 11 and 12, cols. 6, 22 and 26) is another distinguishing feature of that region. Both contemporary observers and subsequent writers have been tempted to suggest a causal relationship between the presence of foreigners and the declining fertility (on the grounds that immigrants restricted economic opportunities for the natives). Recent research into the economic effects of immigration, however,

[84] This analysis could be carried very much further; one could, for example, isolate industrial towns from commercial towns; or, by careful comparison of dates, consider the effects of the growth of industry in particular counties. The conclusion suggested in the text is preliminary and superficial; no firm opinion could be expressed without a thorough survey at least by counties.
[85] This was also true of New England and the state of New Jersey in 1850. See also Yasuba, op. cit., p. 127.
[86] H. Yuan T'ien, 'A Demographic Aspect of Interstate Variations in American Fertility, 1800-1860' (The Milbank Memorial Fund Quarterly, Jan. 1959). Yasuba, op. cit., pp. 125-8. T'ien's argument is that in states of low sex ratio, not all females could be married.

TABLE 10

Number of children under 5 years of age per 1,000 women 15-50 years of age

State	County City or district	Number of children aged 0-4 years (000)				Number of women aged 15-50 years (000)				Number of children 0-4 per 1,000 women 15-50			
		1830	1840	1850	1860	1830	1840	1850	1860	1830	1840	1850	1860
New England	Maine	67	79	76	78	94	119	141	156	705	661	539	500
	New Hampshire	38	36	33	35	68	73	80	86	559	501	412	406
	Vermont	43	42	38	38	68	71	77	77	631	594	493	493
	Massachusetts	80	93	113	150	160	197	282	348	502	470	400	432
	Rhode Island	13	14	17	20	25	29	40	48	544	472	425	416
	Connecticut	37	37	40	54	74	79	96	123	506	474	408	442
	Total	278	301	317	375	489	567	716	838	570	530	442	447
Mid-Atlantic	New York	310	369	397	524	443	599	806	1,033	700	616	492	507
	New Jersey	49	56	64	94	70	86	118	169	698	657	542	556
	Pennsylvania	230	291	338	435	306	404	553	710	750	721	611	613
	Total	589	716	799	1,053	819	1,089	1,477	1,912	718	657	540	550
South-Atlantic	Delaware	9	10	10	14	14	15	17	22	666	660	588	636
	Maryland	46	53	60	75	73	81	104	133	638	648	576	563
	Virginia	128	135	136	164	163	175	213	250	788	768	638	656
	North Carolina	91	90	86	96	110	114	135	154	823	789	637	623
	South Carolina	49	49	41	43	59	60	66	71	829	812	621	605
	Georgia	64	84	89	96	63	86	117	137	1,017	981	760	700
	Florida	4	5	8	13	4	6	9	17	1,010	859	888	764
	Washington D.C.	5	5	5	9	7	9	11	17	608	549	454	529
	Total	395	427	435	510	492	545	672	801	800	783	647	636
East-North-Central	Ohio	186	282	307	359	200	337	457	557	933	838	671	644
	Indiana	77	137	166	226	70	149	217	308	1,112	945	764	733
	Illinois	36	93	141	292	31	98	190	396	1,165	948	742	737
	Michigan	6	38	60	111	6	48	91	177	945	798	659	627
	Wisconsin		5	51	138		6	69	175		867	740	788
	Total	306	555	725	1,126	306	634	1,024	1,613	1,000	875	708	698
East-South-Central	Kentucky	105	115	126	152	111	128	172	212	950	897	732	716
	Tennessee	115	130	127	134	112	138	174	193	1,023	943	729	694
	Alabama	44	71	71	86	38	68	96	121	1,171	1,040	739	710
	Mississippi	15	38	52	56	13	36	63	78	1,111	1,064	825	717
	Total	279	353	376	428	274	369	505	604	1,018	953	744	708

West-North-Central	Iowa	822	809	973	1,165	152	42	9	22	125	34	9	26
	Missouri	753	763	1,007		243	131	67		183	100	67	
	Minnesota	894				38				34			
	Kansas	791				24				19			
	Total	788	755	1,003	1,165	464	174	75	22	366	135	76	26
West-South-Central	Arkansas	814	882	1,128	1,196	70	34	15	5	57	30	17	6
	Louisiana	633	616	821	869	86	60	34	18	54	37	28	16
	Texas	850	838			87	31			74	26		
	Total	814	744	915	935	243	125	48	23	198	93	44	22
Mountain	Total	275	555			29	18			8	10		
Pacific	California	618	500			55	4			34	2		
	Oregon	1,111				9				10			
	Washington	1,000				1				1			
	Total	800	750			65	6			52	4		
USA	Total	626	613	743	781	6,568	4,723	3,327	2,426	4,117	2,896	2,474	1,895
Massachusetts	Barnstable	420	453	585	598	9·3	8·8	7·7	6·9	3·9	4·0	4·5	4·1
	Berkshire	475	449	528	559	14·4	12·9	10·2	9·3	6·8	5·8	5·4	5·2
	Bristol	426	460	494	438	25·5	20·0	15·6	12·9	10·9	9·2	7·7	5·6
	Dukes	327	399	491	501	1·1	1·1	1·0	·9	·3	·4	·5	·4
	Essex	428	385	504	474	47·2	37·2	24·6	21·9	20·2	14·3	12·4	10·4
	Franklin	462	443	503	573	7·8	7·8	7·2	7·1	3·6	3·5	3·6	4·1
	Hampden	393	373	428	502	16·9	14·8	10·3	8·3	6·6	5·5	4·4	4·1
	Hampshire	409	369	481	547	10·2	9·8	7·9	7·5	4·2	3·6	3·8	4·1
	Middlesex	410	363	396	475	65·0	50·0	32·6	21·2	26·6	18·1	13·0	10·0
	Nantucket	321	444	479	471	1·6	1·9	2·1	1·8	·5	·8	1·0	·9
	Norfolk	476	437	492	574	31·0	22·4	14·3	11·2	14·8	9·8	7·0	5·3
	Plymouth	480	435	493	519	16·4	14·2	11·8	10·7	7·9	6·2	5·8	5·6
	Suffolk*	407	381	435	416	59·3	45·1	26·8	19·0	24·1	17·2	11·6	7·9
	Worcester	467	409	475	538	42·4	35·4	25·0	21·3	19·8	14·4	11·9	11·4
	Total	432	401	470	502	348·1	281·5	197·0	159·8	150·3	113·0	92·6	80·1

* largely Boston

TABLE 10 (cont.)

State	County City or district	Number of children aged 0–4 years (000)				Number of women aged 15–50 years (000)				Number of children 0–4 per 1,000 women 15–50			
		1830	1840	1850	1860	1830	1840	1850	1860	1830	1840	1850	1860
Connecticut	Fairfield	6·1	6·4	6·4	9·5	11·3	12·5	15·8	20·7	534	512	404	458
	Hartford	6·3	6·5	7·2	10·7	13·0	14·6	19·0	24·5	480	447	382	436
	Litchfield	5·3	4·7	5·0	5·4	10·5	10·0	11·3	11·5	502	469	441	462
	Middlesex	3·4	3·1	2·8	3·7	6·2	6·3	7·1	8·0	556	493	403	458
	New Haven	5·2	5·8	7·3	12·2	11·0	12·5	17·7	26·8	474	464	411	454
	New London	5·1	5·3	5·6	6·9	10·3	10·8	13·0	16·3	498	494	433	426
	Tolland	2·4	2·1	2·1	2·1	4·6	4·6	5·2	5·4	521	456	393	390
	Windham	3·5	3·3	3·2	3·7	6·8	7·2	8·0	9·1	512	455	419	411
	Total	37·3	37·3	39·6	54·2	73·7	78·6	97·0	122·5	506	474	408	442
New York	Northern District	232·4	260·1	257·5	289·9	310·1	405·3	501·2	564·0	749	642	514	514
	Southern District	77·6	108·4	140·2	234·9	132·8	193·3	304·7	469·2	584	561	460	501
	Total	309·9	368·5	397·7	524·8	442·9	598·6	805·9	1033·2	700	616	494	508
	New York City	27·0	46·0	64·8	117·4	53·9	90·5	153·6	240·6	502	508	422	488
Pennsylvania	Eastern District	119·0	143·6	171·2	225·6	178·1	220·8	304·9	394·9	668	650	562	571
	Western District	110·8	147·7	167·0	209·5	128·2	183·4	248·9	315·3	865	805	671	664
	Total	229·8	291·3	338·2	435·1	306·3	404·2	553·8	710·2	750	721	611	613
	Philadelphia	9·1	36·7	51·6	76·7	21·8	70·7	113·2	158·1	417	520	456	485
Virginia	Eastern District	64·5	62·3	54·1	63·1	93·3	92·2	100·0	110·5	692	675	541	571
	Western District	63·7	72·3	69·1	77·5	69·5	83·1	96·1	109·9	916	870	720	706
	Total	128·2	134·6	123·3	140·6	162·7	175·3	196·1	220·4	788	768	628	638
Ohio	Hamilton★	8·9	12·4	22·5	35·0	11·8	19·6	39·7	55·3	754	632	567	633
	Total	186·3	282·3	306·6	359·1	199·6	337·0	456·7	557·2	933	838	671	644
Louisiana	Eastern District†	10·0	18·1	24·0	36·3	12·4	24·4	43·6	63·2	809	748	552	574
	Western District	5·8	9·4	9·8	13·4	5·8	9·2	12·0	16·9	997	1,023	815	796
	Total	15·8	27·6	33·8	49·7	18·2	33·6	55·6	80·1	869	821	609	620

★ includes Cincinatti   † includes New Orleans

does not support this thesis, at least for the period covered in this survey.[87] Tables 11 and 12 also show that both the East-North-Central and West-North-Central divisions had a substantial foreign element, but these regions maintain a higher fertility than the North-East.

Yasuba's conclusion was to attach more weight to the decrease in the availability of 'easily accessible land' in explaining the decline in fertility than to urbanization and industrialization; he sees particular significance in the correlation between low fertility and high density of population.[88] The argument is not very convincing: in the first place, high density is itself correlated with high urbanization (Tables 11 and 12, cols. 3 and 24 compared); secondly the terms 'availability' and 'ease of access' are ill-defined.[89] Once again, the westward movement of the population, and above all the economic and social pattern left behind in the areas from which emigration occurred, are crucial considerations.

Not much attention has been paid to the possible spread of the knowledge and practice of contraception in the North-East in the second quarter of the nineteenth century. The evidence is, almost in the very nature of the subject, circumstantial and inconclusive. One of the most interesting aspects of the Atlantic community of this period is the rapidity with which ideas passed between Great Britain and the USA. Francis Place's *Illustrations and Proofs of the Principle of Population* (London 1822) and his *Contraceptive Handbills* of 1823 were known in America at least by 1828.[90] *Every Woman's Book*, printed and published by (and authorship ascribed to) Richard Carlile (London 1828), was soon to become known there. One of the first persons to write on the subject in the USA was Robert Dale Owen (son of Robert Owen) whose *Moral Physiology* was first published in New York in 1830.[91] Above all, it was in January 1832 that Charles Knowlton's *Fruits of Philosophy* first appeared (anonymously) in New York.[92]

The extent of circulation of these works cannot be ascertained. Both Owen and Knowlton refer to a large circulation of *sub rosa* literature, alleged to be inaccurate and misleading, on the subject of contraception. In his Introduction to the 1839 edition of *Fruits of Philosophy*, Knowlton wrote:

'During these eight years I have permitted this work to pass through three editions, comprising in all only seven thousand copies. I have thus limited

[87] See esp. Oscar Handlin, *Boston's Immigrants, 1790-1865* (Harvard 1941). Much work still remains to be done on this problem.

[88] Yasuba, *op. cit.*, pp. 158-69. 'The coefficients between population density and fertility were much higher than those between urbanization and fertility during the first few decades of the nineteenth century' (p. 65).

[89] It is not self-evident that, with the building of the Erie Canal and the beginnings of railroad construction and with the liberalization of federal land policy, land was becoming less available and accessible, at least before the middle of the century. This is a complicated historical problem, going to the root of the frontier theory of F. J. Turner, and one would hesitate to generalise—in one direction or the other—without a great deal of research.

[90] See N. E. Himes, *Place on Population* (London 1930), Editor's Introduction. Forty years earlier, Jefferson had written that the North American Indians 'have learnt the practice of procuring abortion by the use of some vegetable; and that it even extends to prevent conception for a considerable time after' (*Notes on Virginia*, p. 101).

[91] Within eighteen months, this work was published in England, the eighth edition being dated London, September 1832.

[92] This was the book, for reprinting which in London in 1877, Charles Bradlaugh and Mrs Annie Besant were prosecuted, unsuccessfully, in the famous trial before Lord Chief Justice Cockburn.

the circulation of the work with a view of becoming entirely sure, from my own immediate observation and experience, that my method is infallible, before I gave the work free circulation. I can now say, that I have not a shadow of doubt but that the method of preventing conception, under free and entire intercourse, to which I allude, will invariably prove effectual. . . .'[93]

One can do no more than suggest the possibility that, from about the 1820's, the deliberate limitation of family size through contraception was beginning in certain parts of the northern states. If this were indeed a significant factor, then both the growth of towns and the improvement of communications must be granted an important role in facilitating the spread of knowledge.

The findings have to remain inconclusive. But the evidence still seems to support the view that industrialization and urbanization, with the accompaniment of higher living standards and greater social expectations (but possibly also higher infant mortality), were the main reasons for the declining rate of population growth, either through the postponement of marriage[94] or the restriction of family size.

The 1850 and 1860 Censuses contain mortality statistics, showing the number of deaths reported in the calendar years ending 1 June 1850 and 1 June 1860 respectively.[95] The Census acknowledges the figures to be 'not sufficiently complete to allow the actual rate of mortality to be determined; . . . no general and trustworthy estimate can be formed of the actual number of deaths which these returns represent'. Mortality appears to have been greatest in the lower Mississippi valley and the lowlands of the South Atlantic coast, and lowest in the Alleghany region, the Pacific coast and in Wisconsin, Iowa and Minnesota.

The data are the most useful in the light they throw on the causes of death, especially as these are compared with figures from England, Scotland, Ireland and some European cities.[96] In both 1850 and 1860, zymotic diseases were the leading cause of death, with cholera in 1850 and scarlatina in 1860 as the main disease. This group accounted for 34 per cent of all deaths in the USA in 1860 (compared with 21 per cent in England). Respiratory diseases were the next in importance: consumption accounted for 14 per cent of deaths (compared with 12 per cent in England). Among the causes of death shown to be much less common in USA than in England were convulsions, heart disease, paralysis, apoplexy and 'debility'.

Owing to the deficiencies of reporting, the data cannot be used to establish infant mortality rates with any degree of reliability. According to the figures reported, the lowest death rate of under-1's and under-5's was found in New England and New York, with New Jersey and Pennsylvania not far behind. The highest infant death rates were in South Carolina, Georgia, Florida and

[93] Knowlton was himself a physician, practising in Western Massachusetts. It is interesting to note that among Knowlton's arguments for the desirability of contraception were his claims that it would encourage early marriage and reduce illegitimacy and abortion.

[94] Yasuba found both a rise in the age of marriage and a fall in the incidence of marriage and concluded that 'the contribution of the change in marriage customs towards reducing the refined birth rate seems to have been considerable' (*op. cit.*, p. 135).

[95] There is a long section in Vol. IV of the 1860 Census (pp. 1-287) in which these mortality statistics are presented in very great detail, showing by states the number of deaths and the causes of death by age groups and in each month of the year.

[96] *Ibid.*, pp. 236-8.

Alabama. The states of the middle and far West fell between these two extremes. Thus this evidence from mid-century, for what it is worth, argues against increased infant mortality as a cause of the falling rate of population growth in the more urbanized regions.

It is unlikely that any weight can be attached to medical improvement as a cause of population increase in the USA in the first half of the nineteenth century. The work in American medical history of Professor Shryock has led him to the conclusion that, as in Britain, medicine made no significant contribution to life expectation until long after the period under discussion here.[97] Throughout the colonial period, from the ineffective attempts of Benjamin Rush to deal wth the yellow fever epidemics in Philadelphia in the 1790's, to the cholera outbreaks in the middle of the nineteenth century, medicine made little or no contribution to lowering mortality.

Conclusion

In so far as generalizations can be made for America as a whole, the rate of natural increase seems to have been at its height in the closing decades of the eighteenth century. One may tentatively suggest that fertility was constant in the eighteenth century in many areas, though increasing as the frontier pushed into new lands; if this is so then it is arguable that the main influence on demographic development in the eighteenth century was the improvement of health due to better nutrition, especially in the mid-Atlantic colonies. The decline in the rate of natural increase in the nineteenth century certainly seems to have been due to an early decline in fertility, especially in the areas of old settlement, New England and to some extent the Middle States.

The final Tables to this chapter, Tables 11 and 12, have been referred to earlier. They summarize the structure of the American population in 1850 and 1860. Above all, they demonstrate the considerable regional diversity and the tremendous internal mobility. The search for the typical or average American demographic pattern is as difficult as the search for the typical or average American.[98]

[97] R. H. Shryock, *Medicine and Society in America, 1660-1860* (New York 1960). Shryock considers American medicine to have lagged behind British and improvements to have been brought about even later in the USA than here. See McKeown and Brown, above, ch. 12.

[98] At the time this chapter was written, the author was not aware of the revised estimates of aggregate colonial population contained in the latest edition of the *Historical Statistics of the United States* (US Bureau of the Census, Table Z 1-19, p. 756, 'Estimated Population of American Colonies: 1610-1780', data compiled by Stella H. Sutherland). While differing in some detail from the figures presented in Table 1 (pp. 638-39), these revised estimates do not conflict with, and in some respects strengthen, the arguments presented in the first part of this chapter.

Division	State	Total Population 000 [1]	Density[b] Area 000 sq. miles [2]	Density[b] Population Density No. per sq. mile [3]	Residence[c] Urban Population 000 [4]	Residence[c] Rural Population 000 [5]	Nativity[d] Foreign Born Total 000 [6]	Nativity[d] Native-born Total 000 [7]	Native-born Free Born outside State of Residence 000 [8]	Native-born Free Born within State of Residence 000 [9]	Slave Total 000 [10]
New	Maine	583	35	17	79	504	32	550	35	515	—
England	New Hampshire	318	8	40	54	264	14	303	45	258	—
	Vermont	314	8	39	6	308	34	280	51	229	—
	Massachusetts	995	7	137	504	491	164	830	142	685	—
	Rhode Island	148	1	123	82	65	24	123	22	101	—
	Connecticut	371	5	78	59	311	38	333	42	290	—
	TOTAL	2,729	64	42	785	1,943	306	2,423	337	2,079	—
Mid-	New York	3,097	46	67	873	2,224	656	2,439	307	2,130	—
Atlantic	New Jersey	489	7	72	86	403	60	428	45	382	—
	Pennsylvania	2,312	47	49	545	1,767	303	2,007	181	1,825	—
	TOTAL	5,898	100	59	1,504	4,394	1,018	4,875	533	4,337	—
South	Delaware	92	2	43	14	78	5	86	11	73	2
Atlantic	Maryland	583	11	53	188	395	51	531	42	399	90
	Virginia	1,422	61	23	101	1,321	23	1,399	58	868	473
	North Carolina	869	46	19	21	848	3	866	21	556	289
	South Carolina	668	28	24	49	619	9	660	13	262	385
	Georgia	906	58	16	39	867	6	900	120	398	382
	Florida	87	59	2	—	87	3	84	25	20	39
	Washington DC	52	—	1,034	49	3	5	47	19	24	4
	TOTAL	4,679	265	18	460	4,220	105	4,573	309	2,600	1,664
East-	Ohio	1,980	40	50	242	1,738	218	1,758	542	1,216	—
North-	Indiana	988	34	29	45	944	56	931	405	526	—
Central	Illinois	851	55	15	64	787	112	736	402	334	—
	Michigan	398	56	7	29	369	55	341	203	138	—
	Wisconsin	305	54	6	29	277	110	194	140	54	—
	TOTAL	4,522	239	19	409	4,114	551	3,960	1,692	2,268	—
East-	Kentucky	982	38	26	74	909	31	950	151	588	211
South-	Tennessee	1,003	44	23	22	981	6	995	170	586	239
Central	Alabama	772	51	15	35	736	8	763	184	236	343
	Mississippi	607	47	13	11	596	5	601	155	136	310
	TOTAL	3,364	180	19	142	3,222	50	3,309	660	1,546	1,103
West-	Iowa	192	51	4	10	182	21	171	130	41	
North-	Missouri	682	65	11	81	601	77	604	250	267	87
Central	TOTAL[a]	880	923	10	90	790	100	780	383	310	87
West-	Arkansas	210	52	4	—	210	2	207	99	61	47
South-	Louisiana	518	41	13	134	383	68	450	62	142	245
Central	Texas	212	326	7	8	205	18	194	93	43	58
	TOTAL	940	419	2	142	798	88	851	254	246	350
Moun-tain	TOTAL[a]	73	399	2	5	68	4	68	9	59	—
Pacific	California	93	189	·5	7	86	22	71	63	8	—
	TOTAL[a]	106	531	·2	7	99	23	83	73	10	—
USA	TOTAL	23,192	3,307	7	3,544	19,648	2,245	20,912	4,251	13,457	3,204

Notes on p. 688

11

Population in 1850

Mobility: Total Born in State (000, 11)	Mobility: Emigrants: Born in State, Resident elsewhere (000, 12)	Net Gain (+) or Loss (−) through Internal Migration (Col. 8 −Col. 12) (13)	Net Gain (+) or Loss (−) Through Migration, Internal and External (Col. 6 −Col. 13) (14)	Colour: Total White (000, 15)	Colour: Total Negro Free and Slave (000, 16)	Sex White +=Surplus Male −=Surplus Female: Foreign-born (000, 17)	Born Outside State (000, 18)	Born Inside State (000, 19)	Distribution: Total Population (%, 20)	Urban Population (%, 21)	Foreign-Born (%, 22)	Total Coloured (%, 23)
584	69	−34	−2	582	1	+3	+3	+5	2·5	2·2	1·4	—
371	112	−67	−53	317	1	+2	−4	−4	1·4	1·5	·6	—
378	149	−98	−64	313	1	+5	—	+1	1·4	·2	1·5	—
895	210	−68	+96	985	9	−1	−4	−13	4·3	14·2	7·3	·3
146	45	−23	+1	144	4	−1	−1	−2	·6	2·3	1·1	·1
448	158	−116	−77	363	8	+2	+3	−7	1·6	1·7	1·7	·2
2,822	743	−406	−99	2,705	23	+10	−3	−20	11·8	22·1	13·6	·6
2,698	568	−261	+395	3,048	49	+33	+16	−9	13·4	24·6	29·2	1·3
519	137	−92	−32	466	24	−4	—	−3	2·1	2·4	2·7	·7
2,266	441	−260	+43	2,258	54	+28	+6	−7	10·0	15·4	13·5	1·5
5,483	1,146	−613	+406	5,770	127	+57	+22	−19	25·4	42·4	45·3	3·5
104	31	−20	−15	71	20	—	—	—	·4	·4	·2	·5
528	129	−87	−36	418	165	+5	+5	−5	2·5	5·3	2·3	4·5
1,261	393	−335	−312	895	527	+8	+5	−5	6·1	2·8	1·1	14·5
839	283	−262	−259	553	316	+1	+1	−8	3·7	·6	·1	8·7
449	187	−174	−165	275	394	+2	+2	−2	2·9	1·4	·4	10·8
526	128	−8	−2	522	384	+2	+7	+2	3·9	1·1	·3	10·6
25	5	+20	+23	47	40	+1	+3	—	·4	—	·1	1·1
32	8	+11	+16	38	14	—	−1	−1	·2	1·4	·2	·4
3,764	1,164	−855	−750	2,822	1,858	+19	+22	−19	20·2	13·0	4·7	51·1
1,515	299	+243	+461	1,955	25	+27	+17	+7	8·5	6·8	9·7	·7
633	107	+298	+354	977	11	+10	+16	+8	4·3	1·3	2·5	·3
390	56	+346	+458	846	5	+15	+20	+8	3·7	1·8	5·0	·1
153	15	+188	+243	395	3	+7	+11	+2	1·7	·8	2·4	·1
67	13	+127	+237	305	1	+14	+11	−1	1·3	·8	4·9	—
2,758	490	+1,202	+1,753	4,478	45	+73	+75	+24	19·5	11·5	24·5	1·2
859	271	−120	−89	761	221	+7	+10	+8	4·2	2·1	1·4	6·1
827	241	−71	−65	757	246	+2	+6	—	4·3	·6	·3	6·8
321	85	+99	+107	427	345	+2	+9	+2	3·3	1·0	·4	9·5
172	36	+119	+124	296	311	+2	+12	+3	2·6	·3	·2	8·5
2,179	633	+27	+77	2,241	1,123	+13	+37	+13	14·5	4·0	2·2	30·9
57	16	+114	+135	192	—	+3	+5	+2	·8	·2	·9	—
315	48	+202	+279	592	90	+13	+5	+5	2·9	2·3	3·4	2·5
374	64	+319	+419	790	90	+19	+19	+7	3·8	2·5	4·5	2·5
74	13	+86	+87	162	48	—	+7	+1	·9	—	·1	1·3
160	18	+44	+112	255	263	+14	+12	—	2·2	3·8	3·0	7·2
52	9	+84	+102	154	58	+4	+10	+2	·9	·2	·8	1·6
286	40	+214	+301	571	369	+18	+29	+3	4·0	4·0	3·9	10·1
60	1	+8	+12	73	—	+2	+1	—	·3	·1	·2	—
8	—	+63	+85	92	1	+19	+57	+1	·4	·2	1·0	—
·8	—	+73	+96	105	1	+19	+60	+1	·5	·2	1·0	—
				19,553	3,639	+238	+262	−11	100	100	100	100

TABLE 11

		Residence		Nativity				Mobility	
		Urban Population	Rural Population	Foreign-Born	Free Native: Born Outside State of Residence	Free Native: Born Within State of Residence	Slave	Gain (+) or Loss (−) Through Internal Migration Col. 13 as % of Col. 11	Gain (+) or Loss (−) Through Total Migration Col. 14 as % of Col. 11
		% 24	% 25	% 26	% 27	% 28	% 29	% 30	% 31
New England	Maine	13	87	5	6	89	—	−6	—
	New Hampshire	17	83	4	14	82	—	−18	−14
	Vermont	2	98	11	16	73	—	−26	−17
	Massachusetts	51	49	16	14	69	—	−8	+11
	Rhode Island	56	44	16	15	68	—	−16	—
	Connecticut	16	84	11	11	78	—	−26	−17
	TOTAL	29	71	11	12	77	—	−14	−4
Mid-Atlantic	New York	28	72	21	10	69	—	−10	+15
	New Jersey	18	82	12	9	78	—	−18	−6
	Pennsylvania	24	76	13	8	79	—	−11	+2
	TOTAL	25	75	17	9	74	—	−11	+7
South Atlantic	Delaware	15	85	5	12	79	3	−19	−14
	Maryland	32	68	9	7	68	15	−16	−7
	Virginia	7	93	2	4	61	33	−26	−25
	North Carolina	2	98	4	2	64	33	−31	−30
	South Carolina	7	93	1	2	39	58	−39	−37
	Georgia	4	96	6	13	44	42	+1	—
	Florida	—	100	3	29	26	45	+80	+92
	Washington DC	94	6	10	37	46	7	+34	+50
	TOTAL	10	90	2	7	56	36	−23	−20
East-North-Central	Ohio	12	88	11	27	62	—	+16	+30
	Indiana	4	96	5	40	55	—	+47	+56
	Illinois	8	92	13	46	41	—	+89	+117
	Michigan	7	93	14	51	35	—	+123	+159
	Wisconsin	9	91	35	44	21	—	+190	+354
	TOTAL	9	91	12	34	51	—	+44	+64
East-South-Central	Kentucky	7	93	3	14	61	22	−14	−10
	Tennessee	2	98	1	17	58	24	−9	−8
	Alabama	5	95	1	24	31	44	+31	+33
	Mississippi	2	98	1	25	23	51	+69	+72
	TOTAL	4	96	1	19	47	33	+1	+4
West-North-Central	Iowa	5	95	11	63	26	—	+200	+237
	Missouri	12	88	10	36	41	13	+64	+89
	TOTAL	10	90	11	42	37	10	+85	+112
West-South-Central	Arkansas	—	100	1	46	30	22	+116	+237
	Louisiana	26	74	13	12	28	47	+28	+70
	Texas	4	96	8	41	23	27	+162	+196
	TOTAL	15	85	9	26	27	37	+75	+105
Mountains	TOTAL	7	93	6	93	1	—	+13	+20
Pacific	California	7	93	24	68	8	—	+788	+1,063
	TOTAL	6	94	22	71	7	—	+913	+1,200
USA	TOTAL	15	85	10	18	58	14		

Notes on p. 688

(cont.)

Colour		Age											
		White							Negro : Slave				
Total White	Total Negro Free and Slave	Ages 0–4	Ages 5–14	Ages 15–29	Ages 30–49	Ages 50 and over	Total 0–29	Females Aged 15–49	Ages 0–4	Ages 5–14	Ages 15–29	Ages 30–49	Ages 50 and over
% 32	% 33	% 34	% 35	% 36	% 37	% 38	% 39	% 40	% 41	% 42	% 43	% 44	% 45
99	1	12	23	29	21	15	64	25					
99	1	11	20	28	23	15	59	26					
99	1	11	22	27	22	17	62	24					
99	1	12	20	30	25	12	62	28					
99	1	12	21	30	25	13	62	28					
99	1	12	20	29	25	15	60	27					
99	1	12	21	29	24	15	62	27					
98	2	13	22	29	24	11	65	27					
95	5	14	23	29	23	11	66	26					
98	2	15	25	28	21	10	68	25					
98	2	14	23	29	23	11	66	26					
77	23	15	24	30	21	10	69	24					
72	28	14	25	29	22	9	68	25	16	30	30	16	8
63	37	15	28	28	19	10	71	24	16	29	27	18	10
64	36	16	28	29	19	9	73	24	18	30	27	16	9
41	59	15	28	28	19	10	71	24	17	27	28	18	9
58	42	17	30	28	17	7	75	22	17	29	30	17	7
54	46	17	28	28	19	8	73	19	18	28	31	15	5
73	27	13	24	31	24	10	68	29					
60	40	15	28	28	19	9	71	24					
99	1	16	28	29	19	8	73	23					
99	1	17	29	28	18	7	74	22					
99	1	17	29	29	19	7	75	22					
99	1	15	27	27	22	9	69	23					
99	1	17	25	29	23	7	71	23					
99	1	16	28	29	19	8	73	23					
77	23	17	29	29	18	8	75	23	17	30	29	16	7
75	25	17	30	29	17	7	76	23	18	31	30	15	6
55	45	17	30	29	18	7	76	22	17	28	30	18	7
49	51	18	30	28	18	7	76	21	17	28	30	19	6
67	33	17	29	29	18	7	75	23	17	29	30	17	6
100	—	18	29	28	20	6	75	22					
87	13	17	29	29	19	6	75	22	18	31	31	15	5
90	10	17	29	29	19	6	75	22	18	31	31	15	5
77	23	19	30	28	17	5	77	21	17	30	32	17	4
49	51	15	24	31	25	6	70	24	14	23	30	25	8
73	27	17	27	29	20	6	73	20	17	29	31	17	3
61	39	16	27	30	22	6	73	22	15	25	30	23	7
100	—	14	25	31	20	9	70	25					
99	1	2	4	57	33	4	63	4					
99	—	4	8	53	30	5	65	6					
84	16	15	26	29	20	10	70	24	17	29	29	18	7

Division	State	Total Population	Density No. per sq. Mile	Residence[c] Urban Population	Rural Population	Nativity[d] Foreign Born Total	Native-Born Total	Free Born Outside State of Residence	Born within State of Residence	Slave Total
		000 1	000 3	000 4	000 5	000 6	000 7	000 8	000 9	000 10
New England	Maine	628	21	104	524	37	591	31	560	—
	New Hampshire	326	36	72	254	21	305	48	257	—
	Vermont	315	35	6	309	33	282	43	239	—
	Massachusetts	1,231	153	733	498	260	971	164	806	—
	Rhode Island	175	164	111	64	37	137	27	110	—
	Connecticut	460	96	122	338	81	379	55	324	—
	TOTAL	3,135	51	1,148	1,987	469	2,665	368	2,296	—
Mid-Atlantic	New York	3,881	81	1,524	2,356	999	2,882	275	2,602	—
	New Jersey	672	89	220	452	123	549	79	469	—
	Pennsylvania	2,906	65	895	2,012	431	2,476	193	2,280	—
	TOTAL	7,459	75	2,639	4,820	1,552	5,907	548	5,351	—
South Atlantic	Delaware	112	57	21	91	9	101	16	85	—
	Maryland	687	69	233	454	78	609	41	481	87
	Virginia	1,596	25	136	1,460	35	1,561	68	1,002	491
	North Carolina	993	20	25	968	3	989	24	634	331
	South Carolina	704	23	49	655	10	694	14	277	402
	Georgia	1,057	18	75	982	12	1,045	108	475	462
	Florida	140	3	6	135	3	137	39	36	62
	Washington DC	75	1,294	70	5	12	62	25	34	3
	TOTAL	5,365	20	615	4,750	162	5,198	335	3,024	1,838
East-North-Central	Ohio	2,340	57	400	1,939	328	2,011	477	1,530	—
	Indiana	1,350	38	116	1,235	118	1,232	456	775	—
	Illinois	1,712	31	246	1,466	325	1,387	676	707	—
	Michigan	749	13	100	649	149	600	304	295	—
	Wisconsin	776	14	112	664	277	499	250	247	—
	TOTAL	6,927	28	973	5,953	1,197	5,730	2,163	3,554	—
East-South-Central	Kentucky	1,156	29	121	1,035	60	1,095	148	722	225
	Tennessee	1,110	27	47	1,063	21	1,089	151	661	276
	Alabama	964	19	49	915	12	952	196	320	435
	Mississippi	791	17	21	771	9	783	145	196	437
	TOTAL	4,021	22	237	3,784	102	3,919	640	1,899	1,373
West-North-Central	Iowa	675	12	60	615	106	567	376	191	—
	Missouri	1,182	17	203	979	161	1,022	428	475	115
	Minnesota	172	2	16	156	59	113	79	34	—
	Kansas	107	1	10	97	13	95	83	11	—
	TOTAL[a]	2,170	3	290	1,880	346	1,824	986	716	115
West-South-Central	Arkansas	435	8	4	432	4	431	196	124	111
	Louisiana	708	16	185	523	81	626	74	214	332
	Texas	604	2	27	578	43	561	224	153	183
	TOTAL	1,748	5	215	1,532	128	1,619	494	491	626
Mountain	TOTAL[a]	175	·3	18	157	27	148	48	100	—
Pacific	California	380	2	79	301	147	233	154	78	—
	Oregon	52	·5	3	50	5	47	30	17	—
	Washington	12	·1	—	12	3	8	6	2	—
	TOTAL	444	1	82	363	155	289	190	97	—
USA	TOTAL	31,443	11	6,217	25,227	4,136	27,307	5,772	17,528	3,952

Notes on p. 688

12

Population in 1860

Total Born in State (000) [11]	Emigrants: Born in State, Resident Elsewhere (000) [12]	Net Gain (+) or Loss (−) through Internal Migration — Col. 8 −Col. 12 [13]	Net Gain (+) or Loss (−) Through Migration, Internal and External — Col. 6 −Col. 13 [14]	Total White (000) [15]	Total Negro Free and Slave (000) [16]	Foreign-born (000) [17]	Total White (000) [18]	Total Negro (000) [19]	Total Population % [20]	Urban Population % [21]	Foreign-Born % [22]	Total Coloured % [23]
676	116	−85	−48	627	1	+1	+6	—	2·0	1·7	·9	—
383	126	−78	−57	325	1	−1	−7	—	1·0	1·2	·5	—
414	175	−132	−99	314	1	+2	+3	—	1·0	·1	·8	—
1,041	235	−71	+189	1,221	10	−17	−37	−1	3·9	11·8	6·3	·2
155	45	−18	+19	171	4	−3	−6	—	·6	1·8	·9	·1
476	153	−97	−16	452	9	−2	−8	—	1·5	2·0	2·0	·2
3,145	850	−482	−13	3,110	26	−20	−49	−1	10·0	18·5	11·3	·6
3,469	867	−592	+407	3,832	49	−6	−11	−3	12·3	24·5	24·2	1·0
612	143	−64	+59	647	25	+2	−1	−1	2·1	3·5	3·0	·6
2,863	583	−390	+41	2,849	57	+19	+6	−4	9·2	14·4	10·4	1·3
6,944	1,593	−1,045	+507	7,328	131	+15	−6	−8	23·7	42·4	37·6	2·9
117	32	−16	−7	91	22	+1	+1	—	·4	·3	·2	·5
618	137	−97	−19	516	171	+3	−3	−2	2·2	3·7	1·9	3·8
1,401	400	−331	−296	1,047	549	+6	+10	+5	5·1	2·2	·8	12·4
907	273	−249	−246	630	362	+1	−3	+1	3·2	·3	·1	8·1
470	193	−179	−169	291	412	+2	+1	−10	2·2	·8	·2	9·3
666	190	−83	−71	592	466	+3	+11	−4	3·4	1·2	·3	10·5
42	7	+32	+35	78	63	+1	+4	+1	·4	·1	·1	1·4
42	8	+17	+29	61	14	—	−2	−2	·2	1·1	·3	·3
4,263	1,240	−905	−743	3,306	2,059	+17	+19	−11	17·1	9·9	3·9	46·4
2,123	593	−116	+212	2,303	37	+26	+40	—	7·4	6·4	7·9	·8
990	216	+240	+358	1,339	11	+15	+48	—	4·3	1·9	2·9	·2
842	135	+542	+867	1,704	8	+39	+93	—	5·4	4·0	7·9	·2
330	35	+268	+417	742	7	+18	+40	—	2·4	1·6	3·6	·3
278	31	+219	+496	775	1	+21	+39	—	2·5	1·8	6·7	—
4,563	1,010	+1,153	+2,350	6,863	64	+119	+260	—	22·0	15·7	28·9	1·4
1,053	332	−184	−124	919	236	+9	+29	+1	3·7	1·9	1·5	5·3
1,005	345	−193	−172	827	283	+7	+19	−3	3·5	·7	·5	6·4
458	138	+58	+70	526	438	+4	+14	—	3·1	·8	·3	9·9
265	69	+76	+85	354	437	+3	+19	+2	2·5	·3	·2	9·9
2,781	884	−244	−142	2,626	1,394	+23	+81	—	12·8	3·8	2·5	31·4
229	38	+339	+445	674	1	+11	+34	—	2·1	1·0	2·6	—
564	89	+339	+500	1,064	118	+25	+63	—	3·8	3·3	3·9	2·7
38	3	+76	+135	172	—	+7	+14	—	·5	·3	1·4	—
13	2	+81	+94	106	1	+3	+11	—	·3	·2	·3	—
844	132	+854	+1,200	2,050	120	+49	+126	—	6·9	4·7	8·4	2·7
148	24	+172	+176	324	111	+2	+8	+2	1·4	—	·1	2·5
241	27	+47	+128	357	350	+10	+22	+10	2·3	3·0	2·0	7·9
160	7	+217	+260	421	183	+8	+36	—	1·9	·4	1·0	4·1
549	58	+436	+564	1,102	644	+20	+66	+12	5·6	3·4	3·1	14·5
—	—	—	—	175	—	+3	+43	—	·6	·3	·7	—
82	4	+150	+297	376	4	+1	+161	+1	1·2	1·3	3·6	·1
18	1	+29	+34	52	—	+3	+11	—	·2	—	·1	—
—	—	—	—	11	—	+2	+5	—	—	—	—	—
—	—	—	—	439	4	+6	+179	+1	1·4	1·3	3·7	·1
				27,000	4,442	+319	+719	−7	100	100	100	100

TABLE 12

		Residence		Nativity				Mobility	
		Urban Population	Rural Population	Foreign-Born	Free Native: Born Outside State of Residence	Free Native: Born Within State of Residence	Slave	Gain (+) or Loss (−) Through Internal Migration Col. 13 as % of Col. 11	Gain (+) or Loss (−) Through Total Migration Col. 14 as % of Col. 11
		% 24	% 25	% 26	% 27	% 28	% 29	% 30	% 31
New England	Maine	17	83	6	5	89	—	−13	−7
	New Hampshire	22	78	7	15	79	—	−20	−15
	Vermont	2	98	10	14	76	—	−32	−24
	Massachusetts	60	40	21	13	66	—	−7	+18
	Rhode Island	63	37	21	15	63	—	−12	+12
	Connecticut	26	74	18	12	70	—	−20	−3
	TOTAL	36	64	15	11	74	—	−15	
Mid-Atlantic	New York	39	61	26	7	67	—	−17	+12
	New Jersey	33	67	18	12	70	—	−10	+10
	Pennsylvania	31	69	15	7	78	—	−14	+1
	TOTAL	35	65	21	8	71	—	−15	−7
South Atlantic	Delaware	19	81	8	14	76	2	−14	−6
	Maryland	34	66	11	6	70	13	−17	−3
	Virginia	9	91	2	4	63	31	−24	−21
	North Carolina	3	97	—	2	64	33	−27	−27
	South Carolina	7	93	1	2	39	57	−38	−36
	Georgia	7	93	1	10	45	44	−12	−11
	Florida	4	96	2	28	26	44	+76	+83
	Washington DC	93	7	16	33	45	5	+40	+69
	TOTAL	12	88	4	6	56	33	−21	−17
East-North-Central	Ohio	17	83	14	20	65	—	−5	+10
	Indiana	9	91	9	34	57	—	+24	+36
	Illinois	14	86	19	40	41	—	+64	+103
	Michigan	13	87	20	41	39	—	+81	+126
	Wisconsin	14	86	36	32	32	—	+79	+178
	TOTAL	14	86	17	31	52	—	+25	+52
East-South-Central	Kentucky	10	90	5	13	62	20	−17	−11
	Tennessee	4	96	2	14	60	25	−19	−17
	Alabama	5	95	1	20	33	45	+13	+15
	Mississippi	3	97	1	18	25	34	+29	+32
	TOTAL	6	94	3	15	47	35	−9	−5
West-North-Central	Iowa	9	91	16	56	28	—	+148	+194
	Missouri	17	83	14	36	40	10	+60	+89
	Minnesota	9	91	34	46	20	—	+200	+355
	Kansas	9	91	12	78	10	—	+623	+723
	TOTAL[a]	13	87	16	45	33	5	+101	+142
West-South-Central	Arkansas	1	99	1	45	29	25	+116	+119
	Louisiana	26	74	12	10	30	47	+20	+53
	Texas	4	96	7	37	25	30	+136	+163
	TOTAL	12	88	6	29	30	35	+79	+103
Mountains	TOTAL[a]	10	90	15	28	57	—	—	—
Pacific	California	21	79	39	41	20	—	+183	+362
	Oregon	5	95	10	58	32	—	+161	+189
	Washington	—	100	25	30	45	—	—	—
	TOTAL	18	82	35	43	22		—	—
USA	TOTAL	20	80	13	19	56	12		

Notes on p. 688

(cont.)

Colour		Age											
		White							Negro : Slave				
Total White	Total Negro Free and Slave	Ages 0–4	Ages 5–14	Ages 15–29	Ages 30–49	Ages 50 and over	Total 0–29	Females Aged 15–49	Ages 0–4	Ages 5–14	Ages 15–29	Ages 30–49	Ages 50 and over
% 32	% 33	% 34	% 35	% 36	% 37	% 38	% 39	% 40	% 41	% 42	% 43	% 44	% 45
100	—	12	23	29	21	15	64	25					
100	—	11	20	28	23	15	59	26					
100	—	11	22	27	22	17	62	24					
99	1	12	20	30	25	12	62	28					
98	2	12	21	30	25	13	62	28					
98	2	12	20	29	25	15	60	27					
99	1	12	21	29	24	15	62	27					
99	1	13	22	29	24	11	65	27					
96	4	14	23	29	23	11	66	26					
98	2	15	25	28	21	10	68	25					
97	3	14	23	29	23	11	66	26					
81	19	15	24	30	21	10	69	24					
75	25	14	25	29	22	10	68	25	16	29	30	16	8
66	34	16	27	28	20	10	70	24	16	29	27	18	10
64	36	15	27	28	20	10	71	24	17	31	27	16	9
41	59	15	27	29	20	10	71	27	17	28	28	18	9
56	44	16	28	29	18	8	73	23	17	29	29	18	7
56	44	17	28	28	18	7	73	22	18	27	29	19	8
81	19	15	21	30	25	9	66	28					
61	39	15	27	29	20	9	72	24	17	29	28	17	9
98	2	16	26	29	20	10	70	24					
99	1	17	27	29	19	8	74	21					
99	1	17	25	30	21	7	72	21					
99	1	15	24	30	22	13	67	24					
100	—	18	26	25	23	8	69	22					
99	1	17	25	28	21	9	68	23					
79	21	17	27	29	19	8	73	23	17	29	29	17	7
75	25	16	28	29	18	8	73	23	19	30	29	16	7
55	45	16	29	29	18	8	75	23	17	28	30	19	7
45	55	18	29	29	18	7	76	22	16	26	30	18	6
65	35	17	28	29	22	8	74	23	17	28	29	18	7
100	—	19	26	28	21	7	72	22					
90	10	17	26	30	20	7	74	23	18	31	30	16	5
100	—	20	22	27	24	6	70	22					
100	—	18	25	33	21	5	76	23					
95	5	18	26	29	21	6	73	23	18	31	30	16	5
75	25	18	30	29	18	5	77	21	16	27	33	18	5
50	50	15	25	29	24	6	69	24	14	26	30	24	9
70	30	18	28	29	19	6	74	20	18	28	31	17	5
65	35	18	27	29	20	6	74	22	15	25	31	21	7
100	—	10	11	40	30	6	62	13					
99	1	11	11	36	37	4	59	15					
100	—	19	25	29	23	6	73	17					
100	—	12	18	36	27	4	66	9					
99	1	12	13	35	35	5	61	15					
86	14	15	25	29	21	10	69	25	17	28	29	18	7

Notes to Tables 11 and 12

^a Includes Territories.

^b Density. The areas and densities shown in Table 11 are taken directly from the Census of 1850. Except for West-North-Central, Mountain and Pacific, the areas given correspond very closely with the land areas given in the 1950 Census; the differences are so slight as to make correction of the density figures unnecessary. The errors in the 1850 estimates of the area of the three exceptions, are however, considerable; the land areas given in the 1950 Census are: West-North-Central, 510·6; Mountain, 857·3; Pacific, 319·8. The total land area, according to the 1950 Census, is 2,975 sq. miles.

^c Residence. Urban = places of 2,500 inhabitants and over, as defined and recalculated in the 1940 Census (vol. i, pp. 20-24).

^d Nativity. The 1850 Census gives two slightly different figures for foreign-born. The figures used in Table 11 are the higher ones (total 2,245,000 rather than 2,211,000) shown in the separate state returns; these are probably the more accurate. Small discrepancies will be found in all totals, arising partly from the rounding of the figures, partly from the presence of 35 thousand of unknown birthplace.

^e Colour. Asiatics are included with White.

^f Sex. Owing to differences of reporting in the two Censuses, columns 18 and 19 in Tables 11 and 12 do not correspond.

Note to all Tables

As most figures have been shown to the nearest thousand, some slight discrepancies appear in the totals. All totals, and all percentages and other derived figures, have been calculated from the non-rounded figures.

NOTES ON CONTRIBUTORS

The contributors: their present (or former) appointments and their main book and monograph publications.

BOURGEOIS-PICHAT, J. L. E. Director, Institut National d'Études Démographiques, Paris.

Publications: *Mesure de la fécondité des populations*, Paris 1950, and numerous papers in demographic and statistical journals.

BROWN, R. G. Senior lecturer, Department of Social Studies, University of Adelaide, Australia.

CHAMBERS, J. D. Emeritus Professor of Economic History, University of Nottingham.

Publications: *Nottingham in the Eighteenth Century*, London 1932; *Dictators*, London 1941; *The Vale of Trent*, Supplement 3 to the *Economic History Review*, 1957; *The workshop of the world*, London 1961.

CHEVALIER, L. Professor at the Collège de France and at the Institut d'Études Politiques, Paris.

Publications: *Le problème démographique nord-africain*, Paris 1947; *La formation de la région parisienne au XIXe siècle*, Paris 1950; *Démographie générale*, Paris 1951; *Madagascar: populations et ressources*, Paris 1952; (ed.) *Le choléra: la première épidémie du XIXe siècle*, Paris 1958; *Classes laborieuses et classes dangéreuses à Paris pendant la première moitié du XIXe siècle*, Paris 1958.

CIPOLLA, C. M. Professor of Economic History, University of Turin (Italy) and University of California (Berkeley).

Publications: *Mouvements monétaires dans l'état de Milan, 1580–1700*, Paris 1952; *Money, prices and civilisations in the Mediterranean world: 5th to 17th century*, Princeton 1957; *The economic history of world population*, Harmondsworth 1962; *Guns and sails in the early phase of European expansion*, London 1965.

CONNELL, K. H. Senior lecturer in economic history, the Queen's University of Belfast (Northern Ireland).

Publications: *The population of Ireland, 1750–1845*, Oxford 1950; *Irish peasant society* (Oxford, forthcoming).

DEPREZ, P. *Chargé de cours* at the Belgian Institute for Cultural Development, University of Ghent.

EVERSLEY, D. E. C.   Reader in Social History, University of Birmingham.
            Publications: *Social theories of fertility and the Malthusian debate*,
                          Oxford 1959; editor (with E. A. Underwood and L.
                          Ovenall), of C. Creighton, *A history of epidemics in
                          Britain*, 2 vols. London 1965; (with P. Laslett and
                          E. A. Wrigley), *An introduction to English historical
                          demography* (forthcoming).

GLASS, D. V.   Professor of Sociology, University of London (London
                             School of Economics).
            Publications: *The Town*, London 1935; *The struggle for population*,
                          London 1936; *Population policies and movements in
                          Europe*, Oxford 1940; (editor and contributor) *Intro-
                          duction to Malthus*, London 1953; (editor and contributor)
                          Social mobility in Britain, London 1954; (with E. Greb-
                          enik) *The trend and pattern of fertility in Britain*, London
                          1954 (H.M.S.O., Papers of the Royal Commission on
                          Population, Vol. 6.)

GOUBERT, P.   Professor of Economic History, University of Rennes;
                             Director of Studies, École Pratique des Hautes Études,
                             VIe Section, (Paris).
            Publications: *Familles marchandes sous l'Ancien Régime*, Paris 1959;
                          Beauvais et le Beauvaisis de 1600 à 1730, Paris 1960; *Les
                          Français ont la parole (doléances de 1789)*, Paris 1964.

HABAKKUK, J. H.   Chichele Professor of Economic History, University
                             of Oxford.
            Publications: *American and British technology in the nineteenth century*,
                          Cambridge 1962.

HAJNAL, J.   Reader in Demography, University of London (London
                             School of Economics).
            Publications: 'Births, marriages and reproductivity, England and
                          Wales, 1938-47', in *Reports and Selected papers of the
                          Statistics Committee*, London 1950 (H.M.S.O., Papers of
                          the Royal Commission on Population, Vol. 2); and
                          numerous papers in demographic and statistical journals.

HELLEINER, K. F.   Professor of Economic History, University of Toronto.
            Publications: *Readings in economic history*, Toronto 1946; *The imperial
                          loans: a study in financial and diplomatic history*, Oxford
                          1965; 'The population of Europe from the Black Death
                          to the eve of the vital revolution', in *The Cambridge
                          Economic History*, Vol. 4, Cambridge 1965.

HENRY, Louis G. A.   *Chef de service* at the Institut National d'Études Démo-
                             graphiques, Paris; Professor at the Institut de Démo-
                             graphie, University of Paris; *Chargé de Conférences* at
                             the École Pratique des Hautes Etudes, Paris.
            Publications: *Fécondité des mariages—nouvelle méthode de mesure*, Paris
                          1953; *Anciennes familles genevoises*, Paris 1956; (with M.
                          Fleury) *Des registres paroissiaux à l'histoire de la population*,
                          Paris 1956; (with E. Gautier) *La population de Crulai,
                          paroisse Normande*, Paris 1958; (with A. Girard and R.
                          Nistri), *Facteurs sociaux et culturels de la mortalité infantile*,
                          Paris 1960; *Leçons d'analyse démographique*, Paris 1960
                          and 1964; *Perspectives démographiques*, Paris 1960.

HOLLINGSWORTH, T. H. Carnegie Research Fellow in Demography, University of Glasgow.

Publications: *The demography of the British peerage*, Supplement to *Population Studies*, November 1964.

JUTIKKALA, E. K. I. Professor of Finnish History, University of Helsinki.

Publications: *Die Bevölkerung Finnlands in den Jahren 1721-49* (Academia Scientarum Fennica, Annales, Series B., Vol. 55-4), Helsinki 1946; *Suomen historian Kartasto*, Helsinki 1949; *Turun Kaupungin historia, 1856-1917*, Turku 1957; *Suomen talonpojan historia*, Helsinki 1958; (with K. Pirinen) *A history of Finland*, London 1962.

KOELLMANN, W. Professor of Social and Economic History, Ruhr University, Bochum.

Publications: *Sozialgeschichte der Stadt Barmen im 19. Jahrhundert*, Tübingen 1960; *Friedrich Harkort*, Vol. I, 1793-1838, Düsseldorf 1964.

KRAUSE, J. T. Associate Professor of History, Rutgers University (Newark, U.S.A.)

Publications: Papers on historical demography in *Economic History Review*, 1958 and in International Union for the Scientific Study of Population, *International Population Conference, New York 1961* (London 1963), vol. 1.

McKEOWN, T. C. Professor of Social Medicine, University of Birmingham.

Publications: *Medicine in modern society*, London 1965.

MARSHALL, T. H. Formerly Professor of Sociology, University of London; formerly Director, Social Sciences Department, UNESCO.

Publications: *James Watt*, London 1925; *Citizenship and social class*, Cambridge 1950; *Sociology at the crossroads*, London 1963; *Social policy in the twentieth century*, London 1965.

MEUVRET, J. *Directeur d'Études*, École des Hautes Études, Paris.

Publications: *Le territoire de Memel et la politique européenne*, Paris 1936; (with M. Baulant), *Prix des céréales extraits de la mercuriale de Paris, 1520-1698*, 2 vols., Paris 1960-62.

PELLER, S. In private medical practice, New York City, since 1945. Formerly teaching and research in medicine and medical statistics at the Graduate School, New York University; Johns Hopkins School of Hygiene, Baltimore; Hebrew University, Jerusalem; and other medical appointments.

Publications: *Fehlgeburt und Bevölkerungsfrage*, Stuttgart-Leipzig 1930; *Der Geburtstod*, Leipzig & Vienna 1936; *Cancer in Man*, New York 1952; *Cancer in childhood and youth*, Bristol and Baltimore, 1960.

POTTER, J.   Reader in Economic History with special reference to the U.S.A., University of London (London School of Economics).

    Publications: Papers in *Scandinavian Economic History Review* (1962 and 1963) and other journals, and contributions to symposia.
An economic history of the U.S.A. (forthcoming).

UTTERSTRÖM, G. O.   Research Docent, The Council of the Social Sciences, Stockholm, and acting Professor of Economic History, Stockholm University.

    Publications: *Jordbrukets arbetare, Levnadsvillkor och arbetsliv på landsbyden från frihetstiden till mitten av 1800-talet*, 2 vols., Stockholm 1957.